PARKER'S WINE BUYER'S GUIDE Sixth Edition

The Complete, Easy-to-Use
Reference on Recent Vintages,
Prices, and Ratings for
More Than 8,000 Wines
from All the Major Wine Regions

ROBERT M. PARKER, JR., WITH PIERRE-ANTOINE ROVANI

VOLUME 2
REST OF THE WORLD

A Dorling Kindersley Book

Dorling Kindersley
LONDON, NEW YORK, MUNICH, MELBOURNE, and DELHI

Sixth edition published in Great Britain in 2002 by
Dorling Kindersley Limited
80 Strand, London WC2R 0RL

A Penguin Company

A complete CIP catalogue record for this book
is available from the British Library.

ISBN 0-7513-4979-8

Printed and bound by
Mondadori printing S.p.A.–Verona-Italy

ACKNOWLEDGMENTS

To the following people, thanks for your support: Hanna, Johanna, and Eric Agostini; the late
Jean-Michel Arcaute; Jim Arseneault; Ruth and the late Bruce Bassin; Jean-Claude
Berrouet; Bill Blatch; Jean-Marc Blum; Thomas B. Böhrer; Monique and the late Jean-
Eugène Borie; Christopher Cannan; Dick Carretta; Corinne Cesano; Bob Cline; Jean Delmas;
Dr. Albert H. Dudley III; Alain Dutournier; Barbara Edelman; Jonathan Edelman; Michael
Etzel; Paul Evans; Terry Faughey; Joel Fleischman; Han Cheng Fong; Maryse Fragnaud;
Laurence and Bernard Godec; Dan Green; Philippe Guyonnet-Duperat; Josué Harari;
Alexandra Harding; Kenichi Hori; Dr. David Hutcheon; Barbara G. and Steve R. R. Jacoby;
Jean-Paul Jauffret; Nathaniel, Archie, and Denis Johnston; Ed Jonna; Allen Krasner;
Françoise Laboute; Susan and Bob Lescher; Dr. Jay Miller; Christian, Jean-François, and
Jean-Pierre Moueix; Jerry Murphy; Bernard Nicolas; Jill Norman; Les Oenarchs (Bordeaux);
Les Oenarchs (Baltimore); Daniel Oliveros; Bob Orenstein; Frank Polk; Bruno Prats;
Dr. Alain Raynaud; Martha Reddington; Dominique Renard; Huey Robertson; Helga and
Hardy Rodenstock; Dany and Michel Rolland; Yves Rovani; Carlo Russo; Ed Sands; Erik
Samazeuilh; Bob Schindler; Ernie Singer; Park B. Smith; Betsy Sobolewski; Jeff Sokolin;
Elliott Staren; Daniel Tastet-Lawton; Steven "Ho" Verlin; Peter Vezan; Robert Vifian; Larry
Wiggins; Jeanyee Wong; Dominique and Gérard Yvernault; Murray Zeligman.

A very special thanks is in order for the people who have done a splendid job in bringing
this mass of information to book form: Amanda Murray, my editor at Simon & Schuster, and
her assistant, Nancy Fann; my copy editors, Lynn Anderson, Anne Cherry, Virginia Clark,
and Kate Lapin; Hanna Agostini, my assistant and translator in France; and Joan Passman
and Annette Piatek, my assistants stateside. All were immensely helpful, and I am indebted
to them. I also wish to acknowledge the superb contributions of my assistant and colleague,
Pierre-Antoine Rovani.

CONTENTS

In memory of a great woman and terrific mother,
Ruth "Siddy" Parker
May 14, 1924–April 8, 2002

and

In memory of a dear friend and wine lover,
Carol "Ma" Smith
September 9, 1950–May 16, 2002

2. ITALY

PIEDMONT

The Basics

TYPES OF WINE

The glories of Piedmont (aside from the scenery and white truffles) are the robust, rich, multidimensional red wines made from the Nebbiolo grape. The top wines made from the Nebbiolo—Barbaresco and Barolo and, to a much lesser extent, Gattinara and Spanna—are at their best between 6 and 15 years of age but can last up to 25 years. At the opposite extreme are the wines called Dolcetto, which are wonderfully supple, rich, and fruity but are meant to be drunk within their first 4–5 years of life. Then there is Barbera. It has historically been too acidic for non-Italian palates, but a new generation of wine-makers has begun to turn out delicious examples that are splendidly ripe, opulent, and frequently barrel-fermented and expensive. Lastly, there are Cabernet Sauvignon and a host of insipid, usually inferior red wines that are less likely to be seen in the international marketplace. I am referring to Freisa, Grignolino, and Brachetto. Piedmont's white wine production is growing, and while most of the wines remain over-priced and bland, some potential is evident with the indigenous Arneis grape and Cortese di Gavi. Chardonnay is making its ubiquitous presence felt; Erbaluce di Caluso is underrated; and Moscato, the low-alcohol, fizzy, slightly sweet wine, is perhaps Piedmont's finest value in white wine. Lastly, there is the ocean of sweet, industrially produced Asti Spumante.

GRAPE VARIETIES

Nebbiolo, Barbera, and Dolcetto are the top red wine grapes in Piedmont, producing the finest wines. For the white wines, the Muscat, Arneis, Cortese di Gavi, and Erbaluce di Caluso are the most successful. Of course, there are many other grapes, but the wines made from these varietals are generally of little interest.

Flavors

RED WINES

Barolo Barolo is one of the world's most stern, tannic, austere, yet full-flavored wines; the aromas of road tar, leather, cherries, tobacco, and dried herbs dominate. It is a massive yet intensely fragrant wine with 10–30 years of aging potential.

Northern Italy

0   100 KILOMETERS
0   60 MILES

WINE REGIONS

1 Valle d'Aosta
2 Piedmont
3 Liguria
4 Lombardy
5 Veneto
6 Trentino-Alto Adige
7 Friuli-Venezia Giulia
8 Emilia-Romagna

Bolzano • 6
Sondrio • Trento • Udine • Gorizia • Treviso • Trieste
Aosta • 5 Udine
1 Gattinara • Como • Bergamo • 4 Venezia
Vercelli • Milano • Brescia • Verona • Vicenza
Torino • Piacenza • Cremona • Soave
Asti • Parma • Mantua
2 Alessandria • Reggio • Ferrara
• Alba nell'Emilia • Modena • 8
Cuneo • 3 Genova • Bologna • Ravenna
Savona • La Spezia • Forli
SAN MARINO

N

Southern Italy

WINE REGIONS

1 Campania
2 Puglia
3 Basilicata
4 Calabria
5 Sicily

San Severo • Manfredonia
Benevento • Foggia • Bari
Napoli • 2 • Matera • Ostuni
Salerno • Rionero • Brindisi
1 • Potenza • Taranto
Metaponto • Gallipoli
3
TYRRHENIAN
SEA
Cetraro • Ciro
Paola • Cosenza
4
Catanzaro
Caraffa
N
Palermo • Messina • Reggio di
Trapani • Taormina • Calabria
Marsala • W E
5 Catania
Agrigento • S
Siracusa
Ragusa
0   60 MILES
0   100 KILOMETERS

Central Italy

MILES
0 — 60

KILOMETERS
0 — 50 — 100

ADRIATIC SEA

LIGURIAN SEA

•Lucca
•Pisa
•Livorno
•Firenze
Arrezo•
Siena•
Grosseto•

•Pesaro
•Ancona
•Macerata

3
Perugia•
•Spoleto
Terni•
Ascoli Piceno

1

•Pesaro

2

Viterbo•
5
Roma•
•Latina

L'Aquila•
•Pescara
•Chieti

4
Isernia•
6

CORSICA

TYRRHENIAN SEA

Olbia•
•Sassari
•Alghero
Nuoro•
•Bosa 7
Tortoli•
•Oristano

Cagliari•

N
W—E
S

WINE REGIONS

1 Tuscany	5 Lazio
2 Marche	6 Molise
3 Umbria	7 Sardinia
4 Abruzzo	8 San Marino

Barbaresco   Often better balanced as well as lighter than Barolo (less tannin, more fruit), with the same aromas and flavors, Barbaresco frequently has more intense jammy fruit, and sometimes more cedar and chocolate; like Barolo, it can be sublime.

Dolcetto   Purple in color and not at all sweet, as the name incorrectly implies, this dry, exuberant, effusively fruity and grapy wine tastes of blackberries, almonds, chocolate, and spices, and is very soft and supple. It is a joyful wine, which, in top vintages such as 1999 and 2000, is a hedonist's delight.

Barbera   In the old days it was too acidic, harsh, and oxidized—and was dirt cheap. The new-style Barberas, often aged in 100% new French oak, exhibit saturated purple color, great fruit, and superrichness that serve to balance out their naturally high acidity. The best Barberas will set consumers back $25–75, so their potential market is microscopic. But a taste of the finest 1998s, 1999s, and 2000s will make a lasting impression. But be forewarned, for the most part, these wines need to be consumed within 4–8 years of the vintage, regardless of how rich they taste.

Gattinara/Spanna   These wines come from Nebbiolo grown in the hills north of Barolo and Barbaresco. Intense tar and earthy aromas dominate, and there is a pronounced Asian spice box character to the bouquet. Frightfully irregular in quality, with no "superstars" to be found, these wines tend to be softer and fruitier than Barolo but also distressingly mediocre.

Carema   The lightest of the Nebbiolo-based wines, Carema, made in a marginal mountainous climate near Valle d'Aosta, can be quite smooth, fruity, and elegant, but significant ripeness is often a problem.

A CLOSER LOOK AT THE BAROLO AND BARBARESCO REGIONS

The Barolo region consists of more than 3,000 acres of vineyards, most of them situated on the hillsides surrounding five villages—La Morra, Serralunga d'Alba, Monforte d'Alba, Barolo, and Castiglione Falletto.

Barolo   This old village is located south of La Morra. Barolo is said to combine the velvety, supple, easygoing, more feminine side of Nebbiolo with considerable structure and concentration. The word "classic" is frequently used to describe the wines of Barolo by the local cognoscenti. Barolo ranks fourth in importance among the five most significant winemaking communes of Barolo. Barolo has 375 acres of vineyards shared by 139 growers. By analogy to Bordeaux, Barolo might be considered the Margaux or St.-Julien of this viticultural zone.

Highly Regarded Barolo Vineyards: Bricco delle Viole, Brunate (this vineyard is shared with La Morra), Cannubi (often considered the most historic and among the finest of the Barolo vineyards), Cannubi Boschis, Castellero, Cerequio (also shared with La Morra), Coste delle Rose, Sarmassa, and La Villa.

Castiglione Falletto   The smallest of the five principal Barolo communes in terms of acreage and growers, Castiglione Falletto is a picture-postcard-perfect hilltop village situated between Barolo and Serralunga d'Alba. The vineyards are all on steep hillsides ringing the village. Allowing for different styles of wines, Castiglione Falletto's reputation is for wines of boldness, richness, full body, power, and concentration—in brief, it is the Pauillac of Barolo. There are 255 acres of vines owned by 93 growers.

Highly Regarded Castiglione Falletto Vineyards: Bricco Boschis, Fiasc, Monprivato, Montanello, Rocche, and Villero.

Monforte d'Alba   The hilltop town of Monforte d'Alba is the third largest vineyard area in Barolo, consisting of 486 acres farmed by 185 growers. In this most southern of the Barolo zones, all the vineyards are situated on steep hillsides. Monforte d'Alba appears to be the St.-Estèphe of Barolo. The locals claim that Barolo's longest-lived, most concentrated, firmest wines are produced from the hillsides of this small town.

Highly Regarded Monforte d'Alba Vineyards: Bussia (there is a bevy of subvineyards within Bussia, such as Bricco Colonello, Bricotto, Cicala, Dardi, Gran Bussia, and Soprana) and Ginestra (another vineyard noted for its numerous subplots, such as Casa Maté, Ciabot, Le Coste, Mentin, Pernot, Pian della Polvere, Sorì Ginestra, and Vigne del Gris).

La Morra   La Morra, another picture-postcard-pretty hilltop village, is believed to produce the most supple, seductive Barolos. Keeping in mind that individual winemaking styles can easily transcend the historic generalities attributed to a particular area, La Morra's Barolos are believed to be the most velvety-textured and easiest to drink when young. La Morra is to Barolo what the appellation of Pomerol is to Bordeaux. Of the five winemaking zones, La Morra is the largest, with 955 acres under vine and 372 registered producers.

Highly Regarded La Morra Vineyards: Arborina, Brunate, Cerequio, Fossati, Giachini, Marcenasco, Monfalletto, Rocche, Rocchette, La Serra, and Tettimorra.

Serralunga d'Alba   With just under 500 acres, this is the second largest zone in the Barolo area. There is more limestone to be found in Serralunga d'Alba's hillside vineyards than elsewhere. Interestingly, it was in this zone that Angelo Gaja purchased a 70-acre parcel to launch his Barolo estate, and it is in this commune that Bruno Giacosa makes his famed Rionda vineyard Barolo, considered among Barolo's most classic wines. The wines of Serralunga d'Alba are among the richest and fullest-bodied, with great staying power. Continuing the comparison with appellations of Bordeaux, these wines might well be considered a synthesis in style of Pauillac/St.-Estèphe, but of course with a Nebbiolo personality.

Highly Regarded Serralunga d'Alba Vineyards: Arione, Brea, Cerreta, Delizia, Falletto, Francia, Gabutti, Lazzarito, Ornato, Parafada, Rionda, and Sperss.

Barbaresco   There are only three major production zones in the Barbaresco region— Neive (around the village of the same name), Barbaresco (around the picturesque old village), and Treiso (around the town of the same name). All of Barbaresco's vineyards are on hillsides.

Highly Regarded Barbaresco Vineyards: Barbaresco—Asili, Costa Russi, Montefico, Montestefano, Porra, Rabajà, Rio Sordo, Sorì San Lorenzo, and Sorì Tildin; Neive—Albesani, Basarin, and Gallina; Treiso—Marcarini and Pajoré.

SOME THOUGHTS ON THE MODERN VERSUS TRADITIONAL STYLES OF
BAROLO AND BARBARESCO

Today it is fashionable among wine journalists to argue about whether Barbaresco and Barolo are made in the so-called modern style or by "traditionalists" with a healthy respect for the customs of the past. The modernists are said to believe in producing supple wines from riper fruit and aging the wines in small new-oak casks. Since they are produced from riper fruit, the wines tend to be lower in acidity and possess a more creamy-textured personality with sweeter tannin. Many of these wines are stunning and have deservedly won plaudits from wine critics throughout the world. The old- or traditional-style wine-makers of Barolo (Giovanni Conterno, Aldo Conterno, and Bruno Giacosa being the most revered) usually eschew aging in new-oak casks, preferring to age the wines in large, old *foudres*. They make little concession to modern-day taste, which demands up-front, forward wines. These wines can also be profound. The traditionally made Barolos and Barbarescos often taste more tannic. But when they are rich and concentrated (as many are), wines made by the modern style are compelling, since they rely entirely on the intensity of their fruit to express the personality of the vineyard. It is irrefutable that great wines emerge from both schools. In fact, the finest Barolos or Barbarescos, whether made by a modernist or a traditionalist, share more common characteristics than differences. Both schools of thought believe in harvesting physiologically mature fruit. Both schools adhere to the belief that low yields and nonmanipulative winemaking result in wines that best express their *terroirs*. Both schools avoid the excessive use of clarification techniques such as fining and filtration. Barolo and Barbaresco are produced in what must be one of the most pure, unspoiled, virgin countrysides of Europe. All of the finest vineyards are situated on steep hillsides. The locals all possess firmly held opinions as to the quality that emerges from the vineyards throughout these two zones.

WHITE WINES

Arneis   The ancient wine of Piedmont, Arneis is a rich, gloriously fruity, mouth-filling wine that is soft and sexy. This may seem to imply a certain heaviness, but the best examples are light and a joy to drink.

Gavi or Cortese di Gavi   Often outrageously overpriced and frightfully bland, this supposedly prestigious wine is high in acidity, has a lemony, flinty, stony character, and, in the best examples, has good body.

Moscato d'Alba   One of the world's most seductive wines to smell and drink, Moscato d'Alba, when well made and drunk within 12 months of the vintage, is a gorgeously fragrant, apricot- and floral-scented, slightly sweet, crisp, vibrant wine that is ideal as an aperitif. It should not be confused with the cloyingly sweet Asti Spumanti.

AGING POTENTIAL

Barbera: 5–15 years	Gattinara/Spanna: 8–20 years
Barbaresco: 8–25 years	Arneis: 2–3 years
Barolo: 8–25 years	Gavi: 2–4 years
Carema: 6–12 years	Moscato: 12–18 months
Dolcetto: 3–5 years	

OVERALL QUALITY LEVEL

The best Piedmont wines are impeccably made, brilliant wines. Producers such as Bruno Giacosa, Angelo Gaja, Elio Altare, and Luciano Sandrone, to name just a few, fashion wines of great individuality and uncompromising quality. But despite the number of compelling Barolos, Barbarescos, and some *barrique*-aged Barberas, a considerable quantity of wine made in Piedmont is still technically defective, with shrill levels of acidity and a flawed, musty taste. Some of this is the result of inferior grapes still being utilized, but most of it is due to indifferent, as well as careless and primitive, winemaking methods. In short, Piedmont offers both the best and the worst in wine quality. To shop with confidence, you must know who are the finest producers.

MOST IMPORTANT INFORMATION TO KNOW

Learning the top producers of Barbaresco, Barolo, Nebbiolo, Barbera, and Dolcetto is of utmost importance. However, since the early 1980s, more and more of the best producers have begun to make single-vineyard wines, so some understanding of the finest vineyards and who is successfully exploiting them is essential to maximize your purchasing dollars. Below is a list of the major Piedmontese vineyards that consistently stand out in my tastings, and the producers making the finest wine from these vineyards.

PIEDMONT'S BEST RED WINES

VINEYARD	*WINE*	*BEST PRODUCER(S)*
Alfiera	Barbera d'Asti	Marchesi Alfieri
Annunziata	Barolo	Lorenzo Accomasso, Silvio Grasso, the late Renato Ratti

VINEYARD	WINE	BEST PRODUCER(S)
Arborina	Barolo, Nebbiolo	Elio Altare
Arionda or Rionda	Barolo	Bruno Giacosa
Asili	Barbaresco	Ceretto, Produttori del Barbaresco, Bruno Giacosa
Baroco	Barbaresco	Roagna
Basarin	Barbaresco	Castello di Neive, Moccagatta
Batasiolo	Barolo	F.lli Dogliani
Bernadotti	Barbaresco	Giuseppe Mascarello & Figlio
Bianca	Barolo	Fontanafredda
Big	Barolo	Podere Rocche dei Manzoni
Bofani	Barolo	Batasiolo
Boscareto	Barolo	F.lli Dogliani, Scarpa, Batasiolo
Briacca	Barolo	Vietti
Bric Balin	Barbaresco	Moccagatta
Bric del Fiasc	Barolo	Paolo Scavino, Azelia
Bric in Pugnane	Barolo	Giuseppe Mascarello & Figlio
Bricco Asili	Barbaresco	Ceretto
Bricco Asili Faset	Barbaresco	Ceretto
Bricco Boschis	Barolo	Cavallotto
Bricco Cicala	Barolo	Aldo Conterno
Bricco Colonello	Barolo	Aldo Conterno
Bricco del Drago Vigna Le Mace	Dolcetto	Cascina Drago
Bricco Faset	Barbaresco	La Spinona
Bricco Fiasco	Barolo	Azelia
Bricco della Figotta	Barbera d'Asti	Giacomo Bologna
Bricco Marun	Barbera d'Alba	Matteo Correggia
Bricco Punta	Barolo	Azelia
Bricco Rocche	Barolo	Ceretto
Bricco dell'Uccellone	Barbera	Giacomo Bologna
Bricco delle Viole	Barolo, Barbera d'Alba	G. D. Vajra
Bricco Visette	Barolo	Altilio Ghisolfi
Briccolina	Barolo	Batasiolo
Brich Ronchi	Barbaresco	Albino Rocca
Brunate	Barolo	Giuseppe Rinaldi, Elvio Cogno, Ceretto, Luigi Coppo & Figli, Roberto Voerzio, Vietti, Mauro Sebaste, Michele Chiarlo, Marcarini, Enzo Boglietti
Bussia	Barolo	Bruno Giacosa, Domenico Clerico, Giacomo Fenocchio, Giuseppe Mascarello & Figlio, Michele Chiarlo, Mauro Sebaste, Prunotto, Armando Parusso
Camp Gros	Barbaresco	Marchesi di Gresy
Campo Quadro	Barbaresco	Punset
Cannubi	Barolo	Luciano Sandrone, Francesco Rinaldi, Bartolo Mascarello, Marchesi di Barolo, Paolo Scavino, Enrico Scavino, E. Pira,

VINEYARD	*WINE*	*BEST PRODUCER(S)*
		Carretta, Giacomo Brezza & Figli, Prunotto
Cannubi Boschis	Barolo	Luciano Sandrone, Francesco Rinaldi
Casa Maté	Barolo	Elio Grasso
Cascina Alberta	Barbaresco	Contratto
Cascina Francia	Barolo, Dolcetto, Barbera	Giacomo Conterno
Cascina Nuova	Barolo	Elio Altare
Cascina Palazzo	Barolo	Francesco Rinaldi
Cascina Rocca	Barbaresco	Riccardo Cortese
Castelle	Gattinara	Antoniolo
Cerequio	Barolo	Michele Chiarlo, Marcarini, F.lli Oddero, Roberto Voerzio, Mario Marengo
Ciabot Berton	Barolo	Luigi Oberto
Ciabot Mentin Ginestra	Barolo	Domenico Clerico
Clara	Barbera d'Alba	Eraldo Viberti
Codana	Barolo	Paolo Scavino, Vietti
Cole	Barbaresco	Moccagatta
Collina della Vedova	Barbera d'Asti	Alfiero Boffa
Conca	Barolo	Renato Ratti
Conca Tre Pile	Barbera d'Alba	Aldo Conterno
Costa Russi	Barbaresco	Angelo Gaja
Crichet Pajé	Barbaresco	Roagna
Il Crottino	Barbera d'Asti	Giorgio Carnevale
Cua Longa	Barbera d'Asti	Alfiero Boffa
Darmagi	Cabernet Sauvignon	Angelo Gaja
Delizia	Barolo	Fontanafredda
D'la Roul	Barolo	Podere Rocche dei Manzoni
Il Falé	Barbera d'Asti	Viarengo & Figlio
Falletto	Barolo	Bruno Giacosa
Faset	Barbaresco	F.lli Oddero, Luigi Bianco, Ceretto
Francia	Barolo	Giacomo Conterno
Gaiun	Barbaresco	Marchesi di Gresy
Gallina	Barbaresco	Bruno Giacosa, La Spinetta di Giuseppe Rivetti
La Ghiga	Barbaresco	La Spinona
Giachini	Barolo	Corino
Giada	Barbera d'Alba	Andrea Oberto
Sorì Ginestra	Barolo	Domenico Clerico, Prunotto, F.lli Seghesio, Conterno Fantino
Gramolere	Barolo	Giovanni Manzone
Gran Bussia	Barolo	Aldo Conterno
Gris	Barolo	Conterno Fantino
Larigi	Barbera	Elio Altare
Lazzarito	Barolo	Fontanafredda, Vietti
Marcenasco	Barolo	Renato Ratti
Margaria	Barolo	Michele Chiarlo
Margheria	Barolo	Vigna Rionda di Massolino, Luigi Pira

VINEYARD	WINE	BEST PRODUCER(S)
Maria di Brun	Barbaresco	Ca' Romè
Mariondino	Barolo	Armando Parusso
Martinenga	Barbaresco	Marchesi di Gresy
Masseria	Barbaresco	Vietti
Messoirano	Barbaresco, Barbera, Dolcetto	Castello di Neive
Moccagatta	Barbaresco	Produttori del Barbaresco
Monfalletto	Barolo	Cordero di Montezemolo
Monfortino	Barolo	Giacomo Conterno
Monprivato	Barolo	Giuseppe Mascarello & Figlio, F.lli Brovia
Montanello	Barolo	Montanello
Montefico	Barbaresco	Produttori del Barbaresco
Montestefano	Barbaresco	Produttori del Barbaresco, Prunotto
Montetusa	Barbera	Bertelli
La Mora	Barolo	Corino
Mugiot	Barbera d'Alba	Piazzo
Ornato	Nebbiolo, Barbera, Barolo	Pio Cesare
Osso San Grato	Gattinara	Antoniolo
Otinasso	Barolo	F.lli Brovia
Otin Fiorin Collina Gabutti	Barolo	Giuseppe Cappellano
Ovello	Barbaresco	Produttori del Barbaresco
Pajana	Barolo	Domenico Clerico
Panirole	Barbera d'Alba	Giuseppe Mascarello & Figlio
Pian della Polvere	Barolo	Giacomo Fenocchio
Pian Romualdo	Barbera d'Alba	Prunotto
Pomorosso	Barbera d'Asti	Luigi Coppo & Figli
Pora	Barbaresco	Produttori del Barbaresco
Pozzo	Barbera	Corino
Prapò	Barolo	Ceretto
Rabajà	Barbaresco	Produttori del Barbaresco, Giuseppe Cortese, Bruno Rocca
Rapet	Barolo	Ca' Romè
Ravera	Barolo	G. D. Vajra, Giuseppe Rinaldi
Rio Sordo	Barbaresco	F.lli Brovia, Produttori del Barbaresco
Rionda (same as Arionda)	Barolo	Bruno Giacosa, Michele Chiarlo, Giuseppe Mascarello, Vigna Rionda di Massolino, Luigi Pira
Rocche	Barolo	F.lli Brovia, Corino, Andrea Oberto, Armando Parusso, Aurelio Settimo, Vietti
Rocche di Bussia	Barolo	F.lli Oddero, Armando Parusso
Rocche di Castiglione	Barolo	Vietti
Rocche di Castiglione Falletto	Barolo	Bruno Giacosa, Vietti, Armando Parusso
Rocche di La Morra	Barolo, Barbera	Rocche Costamagna
La Rosa	Barolo	Fontanafredda
Rosignolo	Barbera d'Alba	Cantine Sant'Evasio

VINEYARD	WINE	BEST PRODUCER(S)
San Pietro	Barolo	Fontanafredda
San Rocco	Barolo	Virginia Ferrero, Azelia
Santo Stefano	Barbaresco	Bruno Giacosa, Castello di Neive
La Serra	Barolo	Marcarini, Roberto Voerzio
Serraboella	Barbaresco	F.lli Cigliuti
Sorì Paitin	Barbaresco	Elia Pasquero
Sorì San Lorenzo	Barbaresco	Angelo Gaja
Sorì Tildin	Barbaresco	Angelo Gaja
Sorì Valgrande	Barbaresco	F.lli Grasso Cascina Valgrande
Sperss	Barolo	Angelo Gaja
Terlo Ravera	Barolo	Marziano & Enrico Abbona
La Val dei Preti	Nebbiolo	Matteo Correggia
Vecchie Vigne	Barbera d'Asti	Cantina Sociale di Serra, Vinchio e Vaglio
Vignabajla	Dolcetto d'Alba	Angelo Gaja
Vignarey	Barbera d'Alba	Angelo Gaja
Vignasse	Barbera d'Alba	Roberto Voerzio
Le Vigne	Barolo	Luciano Sandrone
La Villa	Nebbiolo d'Alba, Barbera d'Alba	Elio Altare, F.lli Seghesio
Villero	Barolo	Giuseppe Mascarello & Figlio, Bruno Giacosa, Cordero di Montezemolo
La Volta	Barolo	Bartolomeo di Cabutto
Zonchera	Barolo	Ceretto

PIEDMONT'S BEST WHITE WINES

Americans have always had a fondness for the slightly sweet, sparkling Asti Spumantis of Italy. While "serious" wine enthusiasts have an attitude problem with Asti drinkers, the fact is that there is Asti Spumante in the market, even from such industrial-sized producers as Cinzano, Martini e Rossi, and on a smaller scale, Fontanafredda, that is fresh, clean, and— yes—delicious!

However, the real jewel among these slightly sweet, sparkling wines from northern Italy is not Asti Spumante, but rather Moscato d'Asti. While most Asti Spumantis possess an alcohol level similar to most of the world's dry wines (around 12%), Moscato d'Asti rarely has an alcohol level in excess of 5.5%. Although these sparkling wines are usually bottled with a regular cork rather than a champagne-style cork, they are effervescent, bubbly wines. Their low alcohol content, combined with their extraordinary fragrant, perfumed character, makes them the most underrated delicious aperitif or dessert wines produced in Europe. Most Moscato d'Asti is vintage-dated, and readers should be purchasing nothing older than 2001 in late 2002. These wines are meant to be drunk within 7–8 months of release. They are among the most thrillingly light, exuberant, fresh, perfumed wines in the world. Their lack of aggressive bubbles, in addition to their low alcohol level, accentuates the freshness and liveliness of these wines. They are the perfect summer wine!

The following Moscato d'Asti producers make wines that have consistently stood out for their freshness, elegance, and wonderfully perfumed peach, apricot, and floral bouquets. Most Moscato d'Asti is attractively priced between $12 and $18 a bottle.

MOSCATO D'ASTI'S BEST PRODUCERS

Note: Buy only the freshest vintage.

Giuseppe Barbero Bricco Riella	Icardi La Rosa Selvatica
Gianni Luigi Bera	La Morandina
Giorgio Carnevale	Elio Perrone Clarté
Cascina Fonda	Elio Perrone Sourgal
La Caudrina	La Spinetta di Giuseppe Rivetti (various
La Caudrina La Galeisa	cuvées)
Tenuta del Fant Il Falchetto	Paolo Saracco
Marchesi di Gresy La Serra	Paolo Saracco Moscato d'Autunno
Sergio Grimaldi	Gianni Voerzio Vigna Sergente

OTHER FINE WHITE WINES FROM PIEDMONT

For what one gets in the bottle, the top white wines of Piedmont are vastly overpriced (Gavi prices have fallen, but this neutral-tasting wine continues to be a rip-off). The exceptions are the aforementioned lovely flower blossom and apricot-scented Moscato and the dry version of Erbaluce. Arneis, a perfumed dry white wine with loads of character, is my favorite white from Piedmont. However, at prices of $18–30, it is expensive. Chardonnay and Sauvignon have arrived in Piedmont; Angelo Gaja produces the finest, but also the most expensive.

The best Piedmont white wines are listed below. Anything older than 1999 should be approached with considerable caution.

WINE	PRODUCER(S)
Arneis	Bruno Giacosa, Ceretto
Brut Spumante	Bruno Giacosa
Chardonnay Gaia & Rey	Angelo Gaja
Chardonnay Giarone	Bertelli
Cortese di Gavi	Pio Cesare, Albino Rocca
Erbaluce di Caluso	Carretta, Boratto, Luigi Ferrando & Figlio
Gavi	La Scolca, La Chiara
Sauvignon	Angelo Gaja
Traminer	Bertelli

BUYING STRATEGY

The marketplace is awash in top vintages of Piedmontese wines. Starting in 1996 and running through 2000, there has been an unprecedented succession of remarkable years for Piedmont. While most of the top 1996s and 1997s have been sold and are squirreled away in the cellars of Italian wine enthusiasts, the 1998s are present in abundant quantities. All things considered, with the relatively strong dollar, there is an embarrassment of riches from Piedmont.

RECENT VINTAGES

2000—This is an exceptional vintage that has produced ripe, concentrated wines with dense colors, sweet fruit, ripe tannin, and sumptuous aromatics—a synthesis in style between the exotic, eccentric, overripe 1997s and the classically styled, fragrant, supple 1998s.

1999—Slightly below the quality (at least for Nebbiolo) of the 2000, 1998, 1997, and 1996, the 1999 is an excellent year, but overall less impressive than the aforementioned vintages. However, it is an undeniably spectacular year for Dolcetto and Barbera.

1998—While the 1998s can appear less concentrated and exotic than the 1997s, less powerful and tannic than the 1996s, and less showy than the 2000s, they are remarkably elegant, symmetrically balanced wines with more depth than the 1995s. They have gained opulence and voluptuousness as they have aged in the cellar as well as bottle. For readers who love Nebbiolo's aromatic fireworks, this vintage may be the most strikingly perfumed year since 1996. With sweet tannin and impeccable balance, this is a classy, highly regarded vintage that can be drunk in its youth, yet has the overall harmony in the finest wines, to be cellared for 15–20 years. In terms of production, 1998 was a slightly more abundant vintage than 1997.

1997—A relatively small crop of overripe, low-acid, high-alcohol, unctuously textured Nebbiolos and Barberas that are off the charts in terms of the hedonistic pleasures they deliver. There is nothing "classic" or "typical" about the vintage, but the wines, while often over the top, are among the most extraordinary Barolos, Barbarescos, and Barberas I have ever tasted. This is the type of vintage that comes along only every 30–40 years. The only comparisons that could be made are with 1947, a year when the alcohol was also extremely high and the acidity very low. Skeptics claim that in the Barolo villages of Barolo and Monforte d'Alba a number of growers harvested too soon, fearing a complete loss of grape acidity. However, this was not borne out in my tastings, although these are low-acid wines. Undoubtedly villages such as La Morra and to a lesser extent Castiglione Falletto hit the bull's-eye. These wines are superexpensive. Contrary to my belief that the Barolos and Barbarescos would be magnificent young, from bottle tastings, these wines have consistently exhibited more definition and firmness than expected. In fact, most of the big wines require 3–5 years of cellaring. Ironically, it is the 1998s that frequently reveal more charm and precociousness than their more exotic siblings.

1996—A great classic vintage made in a style similar to 1978 and 1971, the 1996s are tannic, concentrated, structured, muscular wines that require time in the bottle. It was a cool year with little sunshine, but the saving grace for this fabulous vintage was nearly two months of abnormally dry and warm weather in September and October. The finest wines were made by the producers who waited to harvest until mid-October. All of the big wines require considerable patience—8–10 years.

1995—Called by everybody a very good to excellent vintage, the reality is that it is an irregular vintage with some highlights, as well as a bevy of uninspiring wines. The wines are evolved, forward, and not always well concentrated. Quality varies, so select with care.

OLDER VINTAGES

The early 1990s were a disastrous time for Piedmont, with 1991 and 1992 poor years and 1993 and 1994 average years—despite hype to the contrary. The last great Piedmontese vintages were 1989 and 1990, with 1998 a close third. Prior to that, 1985 and 1982 have turned out to be good rather than exceptional years. 1978 is a fabulous year with very long lived wines that are just reaching their peak of maturity. Before that, the great classics are 1971 and 1964.

RATING PIEDMONT'S BEST PRODUCERS

Where a producer has been assigned a range of stars (***/****), the lower rating has been used for placement in this hierarchy.

*****(OUTSTANDING)*

Gianfranco Alessandria Barolo San Giovanni

Elio Altare Barolo Brunate

Elio Altare Barolo Vigneto Arborina

Azelia Barolo Bricco Fiasco

Azelia Barolo San Rocco

Braida Barbera d'Asti Ai Suma

Braida Barbera d'Asti Bricco dell'Uccellone

Cavallotto Barolo Bricco Boschis Vigna
San Giuseppe

Ceretto Barbaresco Bricco Asili

Ceretto Barolo Bricco Rocche
Domenico Clerico Barolo Ciabot Mentin
  Ginestra
Domenico Clerico Barolo Mosconi
  Percristina Riserva
Domenico Clerico Barolo Pajana
Aldo Conterno Barolo Bussia Soprana
Aldo Conterno Barolo Gran Bussia Riserva
Aldo Conterno Barolo Cicala
Aldo Conterno Barolo Colonnello
Giacomo Conterno Barolo Cascina Francia
  Riserva
Giacomo Conterno Barolo Monfortino
Angelo Gaja Barbaresco
Angelo Gaja Conteisa
Angelo Gaja Costa Russi
Angelo Gaja Sorì San Lorenzo
Angelo Gaja Sorì Tildin
Angelo Gaja Sperss
Bruno Giacosa Barbaresco Asili
Bruno Giacosa Barbaresco Rabajà
Bruno Giacosa Barbaresco Santo Stefano
Bruno Giacosa Barolo Falletto dei
  Serralunga
Bruno Giacosa Barolo Collina Rionda
Bruno Giacosa Barolo Rocche di Falletto
Icardi Barbera d'Alba Surì di Mù
Icardi Barolo Parej
Insieme (seven different proprietary wines
  produced by such top producers as
  Alessandria, Altare, Corino, Grasso,
  Molino, Revello, and Veglio)
Bartolo Mascarello Barolo
Giuseppe Mascarello & Figlio Barolo
  Monprivato

Armando Parusso Barolo Bussia Vigna
  Rocche
E. Pira Barolo Cannubi
Luigi Pira Barolo Marenca
Luigi Pira Barolo Margheria
Luigi Pira Barolo Vigna Rionda
Prunotto Barbaresco Bric Turot
Prunotto Barolo Bussia
F.lli Revello Barolo Vigna Rocche
  dell'Annunziata
La Spinetta di Giuseppe Rivetti Barbaresco
  Valeirano
La Spinetta di Giuseppe Rivetti Barbaresco
  Vigneto Gallina
La Spinetta di Giuseppe Rivetti Barbaresco
  Vigneto Starderi
Albino Rocca Barbaresco Vigneto Brich
  Ronchi
Albino Rocca Barbaresco Vigneto Loreto
Sandrone Barolo Cannubi Boschis
Sandrone Barolo Le Vigne
Paolo Scavino Barolo Bric del Fiasc
Paolo Scavino Barolo Cannubi
Paolo Scavino Barolo Rocche
  dell'Annunziata
F.lli Seghesio Barolo Vigneto La Villa
G. D. Vajra Barolo Bricco delle Viole
Vietti Barolo Brunate
Vietti Barolo Rocche
Roberto Voerzio Barbera d'Alba Vigneto
  Pozzo dell'Annunziata
Roberto Voerzio Barolo Brunate
Roberto Voerzio Barolo Capalot delle
  Brunate Riserva
Roberto Voerzio Barolo Cerequio

* * * * *(EXCELLENT)*

Marziano & Enrico Abbona Barbaresco
Marziano & Enrico Abbona Barbera d'Alba
Marziano & Enrico Abbona Barolo
Giovanni Abrigo Barbera d'Alba
  Marminela
Marchesi Alfieri Barbera d'Asti
Elio Altare Barbera Vigna Larigi
Elio Altare Barolo
Elio Altare Dolcetto d'Alba
Elio Altare Langhe La Villa
Azelia Dolcetto d'Alba Bricco Oriolo
Azelia Dolcetto d'Alba Vigneto Azelia
Batasiolo Barolo Bofani
Enzo Boglietti Barolo Brunate

Enzo Boglietti Barolo Case Nere
Enzo Boglietti Barolo Fossati
Alessandro Brero Barolo Poderi Roset
F.lli Brovia Barolo Ca' Mia
F.lli Brovia Barolo Monprivato
F.lli Brovia Barolo Rocche dei Brovia
F.lli Brovia Barolo Villero
Bussia Soprano Barolo Mosconi
Cantina Sociale di Vinchio e Vaglio Serra
  Barbera d'Asti Superiore Vigne Vecchie
Carretta Barolo Vigneta Cannubi
Cascina Drago Bricco del Drago
Cascina Drago Dolcetto d'Alba
Cascina Drago Nebbiolo

Cascina Luisin Barbera d'Alba Asili
Cascina Luisin Barbera d'Alba Maggiur
Cavallotto Barolo Vignolo
Ceretto Barolo Brunate
Ceretto Barolo Prapò
Ceretto Barolo Zonchera
Sergio Cerutti Barbera d'Alba Ca' du
  Ciuvin
Pio Cesare Barbaresco
Pio Cesare Barolo Ornato
Quinto Chionetti & Figlio Dolcetto di
  Dogliani Briccolero
Quinto Chionetti & Figlio Dolcetto di
  Dogliani San Luigi
F.lli Cigliuti Barbaresco Serraboella
Domenico Clerico Langhe Arte
Domenico Clerico Barolo Bricotto Bussia
Domenico Clerico Dolcetto d'Alba
Elvio Cogno Barbera d'Alba Bricco dei
  Merli
Elvio Cogno Dolcetto d'Alba
Elvio Cogno Langhe Rosso Montegrilli
Aldo Conterno Barbera d'Alba Conca Tre
  Pile
Paolo Conterno Barbera d'Alba Ginestra
Conterno Fantino Barolo Sorì Ginestra
Conterno Fantino Barolo Vigna del Gris
Luigi Coppo & Figli Barbera d'Asti Camp
  du Rouss
Luigi Coppo & Figli Barbera d'Asti
  Pomorosso
Codero di Montezemolo Barolo Bricco
  Gattera
Codero di Montezemolo Barolo Monfalletto
Codero di Montezemolo Barolo Vigna
  Enrico VI
Corino Barbera Vigna Pozzo
Corino Barolo
Corino Barolo Arborina
Corino Barolo Vigna Giachini
Corino Barolo La Morra
Corino Barolo Vigneto Rocche
Corino Dolcetto d'Alba
Matteo Correggia Barbera d'Alba Bricco
  Marun
Matteo Correggia Nebbiolo d'Alba La Val
  dei Preti
Giuseppe Cortese Barbaresco Rabajà
Gianpaolo Destefanis Dolcetto d'Alba
Gianpaolo Destefanis Dolcetto d'Alba
  Vigna Monia Bassa

Luigi Einaudi Barolo
Luigi Einaudi Barolo Cannubi
Luigi Einaudi Barolo Costa Grimaldi
Luigi Einaudi Dolcetto d'Alba Vigna
  Tecc
Luigi Einaudi Dolcetto d'Alba I Filari
Stefano Farina Barbaresco
Stefano Farina Barolo
Giacomo Fenocchio Barolo Bussia
Giacomo Fenocchio Barolo Villero
F.lli Ferrero Barolo Annunziata
Fontanafredda Barolo Coste Rubin
Fontanafredda Barolo La Delizia
Fontanafredda Barolo Vigna Lazzarito
Fontanafredda Barolo Vigna La Rosa
Fontanafredda Barolo di Serralunga
Gianni Gagliardo Barolo Preve
Angelo Gaja Barbaresco
Angelo Gaja Barbera d'Alba Vignarey
Angelo Gaja Cabernet Sauvignon
  Darmagi
Attilio Ghisolfi Barolo Bricco Visette
Bruno Giacosa Barbaresco Gallina
Bruno Giacosa Barolo Villero
Silvio Grasso Barolo Bricco Luciani
Silvio Grasso Barolo Ciabot Manzoni
Marchesi di Gresy Barbaresco Martinenga
Marchesi di Gresy Barbaresco Camp Gros
  Martinenga
Marchesi di Gresy Barbaresco Gaiun
  Martinenga
Marchesi di Gresy Dolcetto Monte
  Aribaldo
Giovanni Manzone Barbera d'Alba
Marcarini Barolo Brunate
Marcarini Barolo La Serra
Mario Marengo Barolo Bricco delle Viole
Mario Marengo Barolo Brunate
Giuseppe Mascarello & Figli Barbera
  d'Alba Panirole
Mauro Molino Barolo Vigna Conca
Mauro Molino Barolo Vigna Gancia
F.lli Mossio Dolcetto d'Alba Bricco
  Caramelli
Andrea Oberto Barbera d'Alba Giada
Andrea Oberto Barolo Vigneto Rocche
Luigi Oberto Barolo Ciabot Berton
Palladino Barolo Serralunga
Palladino Barolo Vigna Broglio
Palladino Barolo Vigna San Bernardo
Armando Parusso Barolo

Armando Parusso Dolcetto d'Alba
Mariondino
Elia Pasquero Barbaresco Sorì Paitin
F.lli Pecchenino Langhe La Castella
F.lli Pecchenino Dolcetto di Dogliani
Bricco Botti
F.lli Pecchenino Dolcetto di Dogliani Sirì
d'Jermu
Luigi Pelissero Barbaresco Vanotu
Vignaioli Elvio Pertinace Barbaresco
Castellizzano
Vignaioli Elvio Pertinace Barbaresco
Marcarini
Vignaioli Elvio Pertinace Barbaresco
Nervo
Luigi Pira Barolo
Produttori del Barbaresco Barbaresco Asili
Produttori del Barbaresco Barbaresco
Moccagatta
Produttori del Barbaresco Barbaresco
Montestefano
Produttori del Barbaresco Barbaresco
Ovello
Produttori del Barbaresco Barbaresco
Rabajà
Prunotto Barbaresco Montestefano
Prunotto Barbera d'Alba Pian Romualdo
Prunotto Barolo Cannubi
Quorum Barbera d'Asti
Renato Ratti Barolo Marcenasco
Renato Ratti Barolo Marcenasco Conca
Renato Ratti Barolo Marcenasco Rocche
F.lli Revello Barolo
F.lli Revello Barolo Vigna Conca
F.lli Revello Barolo Vigna Giachini
Francesco Rinaldi Barolo
Giuseppe Rinaldi Barolo
Giuseppe Rinaldi Barolo Brunate Riserva
La Spinetta di Giuseppe Rivetti Monferrato
Rosso Pin
Roagna Barbaresco
Roagna Barbaresco Baroco
Bruno Rocca Barbaresco Coparossa
Bruno Rocca Barbaresco Rabajà
Rocche Costamagna Barolo Rocche di La
Morra
Rocche Costamagna Barolo Rocche Vigna
Francesco
Podere Rocche dei Manzoni Barolo Riserva
Podere Rocche dei Manzoni Barolo Riserva
Vigna D'la Roul

Podere Rocche dei Manzoni Barolo Riserva
Vigna Big
Luciano Sandrone Dolcetto d'Alba
Giancarlo Scaglione Le Grive
Paolo Scavino Barbera d'Alba Affinato in
Carati
Paolo Scavino Barolo
Mauro Sebaste Barolo Monvigliero
Mauro Sebaste Barolo Prapò
Mauro Sebaste Barolo La Serra
Aurelio Settimo Barolo Rocche
Sottimano Barbaresco Cottà Vigna Brichet
****/*****
Sottimano Barbaresco Currà Vigna
Masué ****/*****
Sottimano Barbaresco Gaia Principe Vigna
del Salto ****/*****
Sottimano Barbaresco Pajoré Vigna
Lunetta ****/*****
Tenuta La Tenaglia Emozioni Vino da
Tavola
Tenuta La Tenaglia Giorgio Tenaglia Vino
da Tavola
Terra da Vino Barbera d'Asti La Luna e I
Falò
Giuseppe Traversa Barbaresco Sorì
Ciabot
Giuseppe Traversa Barbaresco Sorì
Starderi
G. D. Vajra Barbera d'Alba Riserva Bricco
delle Viole
Mauro Veglio Barolo Arborina
Mauro Veglio Barolo Castelletto
Mauro Veglio Barolo Gattera
Mauro Veglio Barolo Rocche
Viarengo & Figlio Barbera d'Asti Il Falé
Superiore
Eraldo Viberti Barbera d'Alba Vigna
Clara
Eraldo Viberti Barolo
Vietti Barbaresco Masseria
Vietti Barolo Castiglione
Vietti Barolo Lazzarito
Vietti Barolo Villero
Gianni Voerzio Barolo La Serra
Roberto Voerzio Barbera d'Alba Vignasse
Roberto Voerzio Barolo La Serra
Roberto Voerzio Dolcetto d'Alba Privino
Roberto Voerzio Vignaserra Vino da
Tavola
Attilio Zunino Barolo Sorì di Baudana

*** *(GOOD)*

Renato Anselma Barolo
Antoniolo Gattinara
Antoniolo Gattinara Osso San Grato
Antoniolo Gattinara San Francesco
Antoniolo Gattinara Vigneto Castelle
Azelia Barolo Bricco Punta ***/****
F.lli Barale Barbaresco Rabajà
F.lli Barale Barolo Castellero
Marchesi di Barolo Barbaresco
Marchesi di Barolo Barolo di Barolo
Marchesi di Barolo Barolo Cannubi
Marchesi di Barolo Barolo Sarmassa
Batasiolo Barbaresco
Batasiolo Barolo
Batasiolo Barolo Cru Boscareto
Batasiolo Barolo Cru Briccolina
Batasiolo Dolcetto d'Alba
Batasiolo Moscato d'Asti
Pietro Berruti Barbaresco La Spinona
Bersano Barbera d'Asti Cascina Cremosina
Bertelli Barbera d'Asti Giarone
Bertelli Barbera d'Asti Montetusa
Bertelli Cabernet Sauvignon I Fossaretti
Boasso Barolo Gabutti
Alfiero Boffa Barbera d'Asti Collina della
    Vedova
Alfiero Boffa Barbera d'Asti Vigna Cua
    Longa
Alfiero Boffa Barbera d'Asti Vigna More
F.lli Serio & Battista Borgogno Barolo
    Cannubi
Giacomo Brezza & Figli Barbera d'Alba
    Cannubi
Giacomo Brezza & Figli Barolo Bricco
    Sarmassa
Giacomo Brezza & Figli Barolo Cannubi
Ca' del Baio Barbaresco Asili
Ca' dei Gancia Barolo Cannubi
Ca' Romè Barbaresco
Ca' Romè Barbaresco Maria di Brun
Ca' Romè Barolo Vigneto Carpegna
Ca' Romè Barolo Rapet
Ca' Romè Barolo Vigna Rionda
Bartolomeo Di Cabutto Barbera d'Alba
    Bricco delle Viole
Bartolomeo Di Cabutto Barolo Vigna La
    Volta
Giuseppe Cappellano Barolo
Giuseppe Cappellano Barolo Otin Fiorin
    Collina Gabutti

Giorgio Carnevale Barbera d'Asti Il
    Crottino
Carretta Barbaresco
Carretta Barbera Bric Quercia
Carretta Nebbiolo d'Alba Bric Paradiso
Carretta Nebbiolo d'Alba Bric Tavoleto
Casa Vinicola Conte Vaselli Santa Giulia
    Rosso
F.lli Casetta Barbaresco Vigna Ausario
F.lli Casetta Barbera d'Alba Vigna
    Lazaretto
Cascina Castlèt Barbera d'Asti
Cascina Castlèt Barbera d'Asti Superiore
Castello di Neive Barbaresco Santo Stefano
Castello di Neive Dolcetto d'Alba Basarin
Castello di Neive Dolcetto d'Alba
    Messoriano
Cavallotto Barolo Bricco Boschis
Ceretto Barbaresco Asij
Ceretto Barbaresco Bricco Asili Faset
Ceretto Barbera d'Alba Piana
Ceretto Dolcetto d'Alba Rossana
Ceretto Nebbiolo d'Alba Lantasco
Pio Cesare Barbera d'Alba
Pio Cesare Barolo
Pio Cesare Dolcetto d'Alba
Michele Chiarlo Barbera d'Asti
Michele Chiarlo Barbera d'Asti Valle del
    Sole
Michele Chiarlo Barilot
Michele Chiarlo Barolo Brunate
Michele Chiarlo Barolo Vigna Rionda
Michele Chiarlo Countacc!
F.lli Cigliuti Barbera d'Alba Serraboella
Aldo Conterno Il Favot
Giacomo Conterno Barbera d'Alba Cascina
    Francia
Conterno-Fantino Barbera d'Alba Vignato
Cordero di Montezemolo Barbera d'Alba
Cordero di Montezemolo Barolo Enrico VI
Cordero di Montezemolo Dolcetto d'Alba
    Monfalletto
Giuseppe Cortese Dolcetto d'Alba
Luigi Dessilani & Figlio Gattinara
Luigi Dessilani & Figlio Ghemme
Luigi Dessilani & Figlio Spanna
Dosio Barolo Vigna Fossati
Cascina Drago Bricco del Drago Vigna Le
    Mace
Poderi Luigi Einaudi Dolcetto di Dogliani

F.lli Ferrero Barolo Manzoni

Fontanafredda Barbera d'Alba Vigna
Raimondo

Fontanafredda Barolo

Gianni Gagliardo Barolo La Serra

Angelo Gaja Dolcetto d'Alba Vignaveja

Angelo Gaja Nebbiolo d'Alba Vignaveja

Attilio Ghisolfi Barolo Bricco Visette

F.lli Giacosa Barbaresco Rio Sordo

F.lli Giacosa Barolo Pira

F.lli Grasso Barbaresco Bricco Spessa

F.lli Grasso Barbaresco Riserva

Silvio Grasso Barbera d'Alba Fontanile

Icardi Barbera d'Alba Vigna dei Gelsi

Icardi Nebbiolo delle Langhe

Eredi Lodali Barbaresco Rocche dei Sette
Fratelli

Giovanni Manzone Barolo Le Gramolere

Giovanni Manzone Barolo Le Gramolere
Bricat

Giovanni Manzone Barolo Santo Stefano di
Perno

Giovanni Manzone Dolcetto d'Alba

Giovanni Manzone Nebbiolo

Mario Marengo Barbaresco Le Terre Forti

Mario Marengo Barbera Le Terre Forti

Bartolo Mascarello Dolcetto d'Alba

Giuseppe Mascarello & Figlio Barbera
d'Alba Fasana

Giuseppe Mascarello & Figlio Barolo Dardi

Giuseppe Mascarello & Figlio Dolcetto
d'Alba Gagliassi

Il Milin di Michelino Rovero Barbera
d'Asti

Il Milin di Michelino Rovero Barbera
d'Asti Vigneto Gustin

Luigi Minuto Barbaresco Cascina Luisin
Rabajà

Luigi Minuto Barbaresco Sorì Paolin

Moccagatta Barbaresco Basarin

Moccagatta Barbaresco Cole

Moccagatta Barbera Basarin

Mauro Molino Barolo

Luigi Oberto Barbera d'Alba Ciabot Berton

Ochetti Barbera d'Asti Superiore

F.lli Oddero Barbaresco

F.lli Oddero Barolo Mondoca di Bussia
Soprana

F.lli Oddero Barolo Rocche di Rivera di
Castiglione

F.lli Oddero Barolo Vigna Rionda

Armando Parusso Barbera Pugnane

Agostino Pavia e Figli Barbera d'Asti
Bricco Blina

Elio Perrone Barbera delle Langhe Vigna
Grivò

Piazzo Barbaresco Riserva

Piazzo Barbaresco Sorì Fratin

Piazzo Barbera d'Alba Mugiot

Piazzo Barolo Poderi di Mugiot

Produttori del Barbaresco Barbaresco

Produttori del Barbaresco Barbaresco
Pora

Prunotto Barbaresco

Prunotto Barbera d'Alba

Prunotto Barbera d'Alba Fiulot

Punset Barbaresco Campo Quadro

Bruno Rocca Nebbiolo d'Alba

Rocche Costamagna Barbera d'Alba
Rocche di La Morra

Rocche Costamagna Rocche della Rocche

Gigi Rosso Barbaresco Viglino

Gigi Rosso Barolo Arione

Scarpa Barbaresco

Scarpa Barbaresco Payore Barberis di
Treiso

Scarpa Barolo Boscaretti di Serralunga
d'Alba

Scarpa Barolo I Tetti di Neive

Scarpa Rouchet Vino da Tavola

Enrico Scavino Dolcetto d'Alba

Mauro Sebaste Barolo Le Coste

F.lli Seghesio Barbera

F.lli Seghesio Dolcetto d'Alba

Sigilla dell'Abate Barolo Riserva

Tenuta dei Fiori Barbera d'Asti

Renato Trinchero Barbera d'Asti La
Barslina

Mauro Veglio Barolo Arborina

Mauro Veglio Barolo Castillero

Mauro Veglio Barolo Gattera

Mauro Veglio Barolo Rocche

Viarengo & Figlio Barbera d'Asti Il Falé

Viarengo & Figlio Barbera d'Asti Bricco
Morra

Eraldo Viberti Barolo

Vietti Barbera d'Alba Pian Romualdo

Vietti Barbera d'Alba Scarrone

Vigna Rionda di Massolino Barolo
Parafada

Vigna Rionda di Massolino Barolo Sorì
Vigna Rionda

Vigna Rionda di Massolino Barolo Sorì
  Vigneto Margheria

Vigna Rionda di Massolino Barolo Vigna
  Rionda

GIOVANNI ABRIGO

1999 Barbera d'Alba Marminela	C	89
1998 Barbera d'Alba Marminela	C	88
2000 Dolcetto Diano d'Alba Garabei	C	88
1999 Dolcetto Diano d'Alba Garabei	C	90
2000 Dolcetto Diano d'Alba Söri Crava	C	89
1999 Dolcetto Diano d'Alba Söri Crava	C	88
1998 Nebbiolo d'Alba	C	89

All of Abrigo's unfined/unfiltered red offerings represent attractive values, particularly in today's wine marketplace. They are tank-fermented and -aged, and production is 300–500 cases annually.

The 2000 Dolcetto d'Alba Garabei displays surprising structure for this varietal, as well as abundant notions of chocolate and violet-tinged berry fruit, medium body, and a soft personality. Consume it over the next 2–3 years. An explosively fruity, smoky, ripe, black cherry/chocolate-styled Dolcetto that saw no *barrique* aging, this luscious, opulent 2000 Dolcetto Diano d'Alba Söri Crava offers gobs of fruit as well as a fleshy, pure finish. Drink it over the next 3 years. Two top-notch Dolcettos, the 1999 Dolcetto Diano d'Alba Söri Crava exhibits explosive fruit aromas of black cherries, blackberries, and violets. The flavors are pure cherry and blackberry jam. This excellent effort will drink well for 2–3 years. Even better is the 1999 Dolcetto Diano d'Alba Garabei. This opaque purple-colored Dolcetto boasts intense aromas and flavors of black cherry/blackberry liqueur, chocolate, and flowers. There is enough acidity to provide vibrancy and delineation. Drink this hedonistic fruit bomb over the next 2 years.

The 1999 Barbera emerges from an old-vine vineyard called Marminela. It is tank-fermented and aged in French barrels, of which one-third are new. Ruby/purple in color, it is sweet and fat on the palate, medium-bodied, and fruit-driven, and should be enjoyed before 2003. Readers seeking more complexity and an intensely fragrant style should check out the 1998 Nebbiolo d'Alba. Exhibiting classic characteristics of rose petals, melted road tar, tobacco, and sweet cherry fruit, it could easily pass for a Barolo in a blind tasting. However, the price is about one-third the going rate for most entry-level Barolos. Drink it over the next 5–6 years.

ORLANDO ABRIGO

1997 Barbaresco Vigna Montersino	E	87
1997 Barbaresco Vigna Rongallo	E	88

This producer from the village of Treiso has fashioned a very good, dark ruby-colored 1997 Barbaresco Vigna Montersino. Its aromatic profile consists of new saddle leather, berry fruit, and spice box presented in a medium- to full-bodied, graceful style. With abundant sweetness from its glycerin and alcohol, this 1997 is best drunk over the next 2 years. Deeper and longer, the 1997 Barbaresco Vigna Rongallo exhibits telltale aromas of plums, cherries, prunes, spice box, licorice, and smoke. Medium- to full-bodied and richer than its sibling, it should be consumed over the next 2–3 years.

CLAUDIO ALARIO

1998 Barolo Vigneto Riva	E	89
1997 Barolo Vigneto Riva	E	88

1996 Barolo Vigneto Riva	E	91
1995 Barolo Vigneto Riva	E	87

A new estate from the village of Verduno, Claudio Alario produces small quantities of hedonistic, sumptuous Barolos that are fermented in open-top fermenters and aged in 60–80% new French oak casks.

Alario's 1998 Barolo Vigneta Riva has turned out slightly better than his 1997. It offers a classic concoction of balsam wood, coffee, tar, cherries, and spice box, a sweet entry, medium body, and soft but noticeable tannin in the finish. Drink it over the next 8 years.

Not quite as good from bottle as it was from barrel, the dark ruby-colored, elegant 1997 Barolo Vigneto Riva exhibits restrained, subtle black cherry aromas and flavors mixed with road tar, tobacco, smoke, and earth. It is of an atypical medium weight for a 1997, without the vintage's flamboyant side in evidence. Anticipated maturity: 2003–2015. The saturated ruby/purple 1996 Barolo Vigneto Riva reveals an intense cherry, coffee, cedar, and smoky-scented nose. There are great richness, full body, terrific purity, surprisingly low acidity for a 1996, and a lush, multidimensional personality. While tannin is present in the finish, this is a large-scaled, gorgeously made Barolo that should be at its best before 2015. The 1995 Barolo Vigneto Riva exhibits copious quantities of cedar, smoke, and cherry fruit in its evolved aromatics. With good fat and medium to full body, it is a hedonistic, evolved, lush Barolo to enjoy over the next 2–3 years.

PODERI ALASIA

1999 Barbera d'Asti Rive	C	89
1998 Barbera d'Asti Rive	C	92

The dense, opaque purple-colored 1999 Barbera d'Asti Rive offers a big, sweet nose of black fruits, underbrush, tar, and spice. Medium- to full-bodied, with excellent concentration, admirable purity, and a long finish, this fleshy, mouth-filling Barbera can be enjoyed over the next 2–3 years. The exquisite, opaque ruby/purple-colored 1998 Barbera d'Asti Rive possesses huge body, massive fruit concentration, and copious quantities of toasty new oak. A blockbuster Barbera made in a modern, international style, it offers seductive fruit, glycerin, and new wood. Enjoy it over the next 4–5 years.

GIANFRANCO ALESSANDRIA

1997 Barolo	E	89
1996 Barolo	E	88
1995 Barolo	E	87
1998 Barolo San Giovanni	E	90+
1997 Barolo San Giovanni	E	92+
1996 Barolo San Giovanni	E	90
1995 Barolo San Giovanni	E	88

From Monforte d'Alba, this producer believes in using small open-top fermenters and punching down as opposed to many of his colleagues, who use rotary fermenters. The generic Barolo is aged in *foudres* (large wooden vessels), and the single-vineyard San Giovanni, which emerges from a vineyard facing Bussia, stays in *foudres* and *barriques* (approximately 30% new). These classic Barolos exhibit rose petal, tobacco leaf, and tar-like fragrances with additional nuances. They are generally less seductive and plush, but more powerful and dense, than their counterparts from La Morra.

I did not taste the regular 1998 Barolo. However, I did enjoy the special *cuvée*. Just a notch below the brilliant 1997, Alessandria's 1998 Barolo San Giovanni boasts an opaque ruby/garnet color in addition to an intriguing nose of melted chocolate, cedar and balsam wood, rose petals, and cherry liqueur. The opulent fatness on the attack is followed by plenty of power, structure, and tannin in the long finish. Anticipated maturity: 2005–2020.

The 1997 Barolo is a structured, garnet-colored effort with pink/amber at the edge. Aromas of melted caramel, Chinese black tea, kirsch, tobacco, and licorice emerge from this dense, full-bodied, fleshy, powerful 1997. It is a moderately tannic wine, to be consumed before 2012. The impressively endowed, dark plum-colored 1997 Barolo San Giovanni is a blockbuster. It boasts terrific concentration as well as a sweet bouquet of chocolate, blackberries, cherries, tobacco, asphalt, and smoke. Structured and powerful, with muscle to spare, this massive wine needs 1–2 years of cellaring (despite its low acidity). Anticipated maturity: 2004–2020.

The 1996s are richer and possess more formidable personalities than the 1995s. For example, the 1996 Barolo exhibits Nebbiolo's telltale tobacco, damp earth, black cherry, and melted road tar aromas and flavors. The wine is dense, rich, and full-bodied, with considerable muscle, outstanding purity, and a deep, concentrated, moderately tannic finish. Anticipated maturity: now–2014. The textbook 1996 Barolo San Giovanni offers a classic tar and rose petal–scented bouquet with hints of cherry liqueur, smoke, and dried herbs. This dark ruby-colored wine is full-bodied, dense, and layered, with outstanding concentration and purity. There is moderate tannin plus superb depth and muscle. Anticipated maturity: now–2015.

The traditionally styled 1995 Barolo possesses structure, tannin, and a masculine, austere personality. Although not as fruit-driven as some offerings, it is well made and enjoyable. Drink it over the next 8 years. The dark ruby-colored 1995 Barolo San Giovanni offers a big, sweet nose of soy, seaweed, black cherry liqueur, and pepper. This wine is exotic, medium- to full-bodied, and moderately tannic. It will be at its finest until 2012.

GIOVANNI ALMONDO

1998 Barbera d'Alba Bianchera	C	85?
1998 Roero Bric Valdiana	C	88

The charming 1998 Roero Bric Valdiana reveals a classic Nebbiolo bouquet of floral rose water, sweet cherries, tobacco, and tar. Round and supple with a sweet attack, this delicious 1998 will drink well for 2–3 years. Denser and less charming, but more concentrated as well as structured, with chalky roughness in the finish, is the 1998 Barbera d'Alba Bianchera. There is more size to this 1998 Barbera but less character and sexiness. It, too, should be drunk over the next 2–3 years.

ELIO ALTARE

1996 Barolo	E	89+
1995 Barolo	E	89
1998 Barolo Brunate	E	(92–94)
1996 Barolo Brunate	E	90?
1995 Barolo Brunate	E	90
1998 Barolo Vigneto Arborina	E	(91–93)
1996 Barolo Vigneto Arborina	E	92
1995 Barolo Vigneto Arborina	E	91

Elio Altare, a brilliant La Morra producer, uses rotary fermenters, large oak *foudres* for his regular Barolo, and small *barriques* for his two single-vineyard wines (50% new oak for the Arborina and 75% for the Brunate). Malolactic is done in barrel, and there is no filtration at bottling. These are among the most feminine, gloriously perfumed offerings from Piedmont. They represent beautiful examples of symmetry, complexity, and rich, ripe fruit.

Elio Altare has fashioned two elegant, perfumed, concentrated, immensely satisfying 1998s. The 1998 Barolo Vigneto Arborina boasts a glorious perfume of overripe black cherries intertwined with Asian spices, new oak, and flowers. Layered, gorgeously concentrated, superbly balanced, and seamless, with fabulous fruit, good underlying tannin, and a long, 40+-second finish, it can be drunk now and over the next 15 years. The dark ruby/plum-colored 1998 Barolo Brunate exhibits a smoky, mineral, jammy strawberry, and black cherry–scented nose with notions of leather, toast, and spice box. The wine has fabulously well integrated wood, tannin, and acidity in addition to a complex, layered mid-palate and finish. The outstanding balance, purity, and seamlessness are immensely admirable. Enjoy this 1998 Barolo over the next 12–15 years. The story of Altare's 1997s is worth mentioning. These wines looked spectacular when they were tasted prior to bottling, but they were re-called in a qualitative move that is largely unprecedented in the wine world. In fact, Elio Altare discovered that 40% or more of his 1997s were corked with a batch of tainted corks. Most producers who realize that they have a problem with contaminated corks let the con-sumer assume the risk. But Altare, because of his extraordinary morality and honesty, could not stomach the thought of having his fans have a 40% or better chance of tasting one of his wines tainted to some degree by a moldy cork. Hence, all of his 1997 Barolos were recalled and will not be available in the market. Obviously this is a huge financial loss, but even more so, a spiritual one. Altare deserves admiration by all consumers for making this decision, for being a man of great morality, and for putting the interests of the consumer ahead of his own. Readers should note that the wines that will never be released include all his 1997 Barolos, including the single-vineyard Arborina (rated 93–96), Brunate (92–94), and generic Barolo (90–91), as well as his 1999 Vigneto Arborina and Vigna Langhe Larigi.

The 1996s are superb. The 1996 Barolo exhibits a saturated, evolved dark ruby color. It reveals notes of *sur-maturité* in its ripe, fruity style. Not as sexy and forward as the 1995, the 1996 is less evolved, spicy, rich, and highly extracted. Anticipated maturity: now–2010. Altare's 1996 Barolo Vigneto Arborina is reminiscent of a terrific grand cru from Burgundy's Côte d'Or. Intensely aromatic, with copious quantities of black cherry jam, earth, toast, and floral scents, this saturated dark ruby-colored offering reveals superb ripeness, substantial richness, a full-bodied, layered personality, adequate acidity, and sweet tannin in the finish. It is a stunning Barolo to drink now and over the next 12 years. The 1996 Barolo Brunate is the proverbial "iron fist in a velvet glove." It possesses a dark ruby color, closed personality, powerful, muscular flavors of cherries, incense, smoke, and dried herbs, and a tannic finish. Enjoy it over the following 15–18 years.

Altare has turned out a gorgeous 1995 Barolo with a medium ruby color and a sweet nose of high-quality tobacco intermixed with jammy cherry fruit. It is lush, with spice and oak in the background, a nicely layered, exotic mouth-feel, and no hard edges. This evolved Barolo requires consumption over the next 2 years. The two crus are also stunning efforts. The lush, voluptuously textured 1995 Barolo Vigneto Arborina exhibits one of the most saturated dark ruby/garnet colors of this vintage. Full-bodied, with great purity, the layered complexity that comes from low yields and ripe fruit, and a bouquet of Asian spices, tobacco, smoke, and black cherries, this is a sweet, rich, forward, but hedonistically styled Barolo. Anticipated maturity: now–2008. In contrast, the outstanding 1995 Barolo Brunate is more muscular and backward, although it possesses good density, superb ripeness, and more tannin and body. Consume it over the next 8 years.

ANSELMA

1998 Barolo Adasi	D	87
1997 Barolo Adasi	D	86

An evolved, forward Barolo despite the presence of moderate tannin levels, the medium garnet-colored 1998 Barolo Adasi possesses aromas of fudge, damp earth, cedar, cigar box, and dried red fruits. Although medium-bodied and complex, it lacks the necessary substance as well as length to be considered superb. Anticipated maturity: 2003–2013.

The traditionally made, dark ruby/garnet-colored 1997 Barolo Adasi exhibits notes of soy, dried herbs, earth, and leather. Good density on the attack is followed by abundant tannin, giving the wine a compressed, astringent finish. Drink it over the next 10 years.

GIACOMO ASCHERI

1997 Barolo Sorano	D	(76–78?)
1996 Barolo Sorano	D	87+
1995 Barolo Sorano	D	88

This small producer has turned out a 1995 and 1996 that are much more impressive than the herbaceous, slightly diluted, unusual 1997.

The 1997 Barolo Sorano is unimpressive, with hard, dry tannin, an element of dilution, and a vegetal character to the meager fruitiness. It did reveal such classic Nebbiolo characteristics as melted tar and a floral component, but it was compressed and lean.

The tannic, well-structured, muscular 1996 Barolo Sorano offers an intriguing nose as well as flavors of melted asphalt, tomato skin, and jammy strawberry and cherry fruit. It exhibits some tannin, more muscle than the 1995, an understated, restrained style, and a longer finish than its older sibling. Drink it over the next 8–10 years.

Less structured and less tannic than the 1996, the 1995 Barolo Sorano exhibits a rose petal–scented fragrance. This medium-bodied, elegant, finesse-styled, racy wine offers a graceful combination of cherry fruit intermixed with cedar, leather, and dried herbs. This lovely, forward Barolo can be drunk now and over the next 8 years.

AZELIA

1997 Barolo	D	90
1998 Barolo Bricco Fiasco	E	(92–93)
1997 Barolo Bricco Fiasco	E	93
1996 Barolo Bricco Fiasco	E	(91–93+?)
1995 Barolo Bricco Fiasco	E	90+
1998 Barolo San Rocco	E	(91–93)
1997 Barolo San Rocco	E	94
1996 Barolo San Rocco	E	(91–93)
1995 Barolo San Rocco	E	90

A believer in the use of rotary fermenters, short maceration periods, and 40% new French oak for aging his single-vineyard Barolos, Azelia has been on fire over recent vintages. He produced great 1996s and excellent 1995s, as well as stunning 1997s and 1998s. All the wines emerge from his Castiglione Falletto vineyards except for the San Rocco, which comes from the adjacent commune of Serralunga. They are all topflight.

Two superb efforts, the 1998s are virtually equivalent (although more classic) to Azelia's brilliant 1997s. The 1998 Barolo San Rocco's dark plum/garnet color is followed by a gorgeously fragrant perfume of dried Provençal herbs, smoke, tar, black cherry liqueur, cedar, and soy. Ripe, opulently textured, full-bodied flavors caress the palate with no hard edges. This hedonistic Nebbiolo fruit bomb possesses plenty of complexity. The 1998 Barolo Bricco Fiasco exhibits additional notes of Asian spices, new saddle leather, earth, soy, and nori (the seaweed wrap for sushi). It displays phenomenal sweetness on the attack and mid-palate, full body, no hard edges, and a plush, generously rich finish revealing copious quantities of fruit as well as glycerin. Drink both 1998s over the next 12–15 years.

The generic 1997 Barolo is a delicious, forward, round, supple, approachable effort to consume over the next 5–6 years. Revealing amber and pink at the edge of its color, it is an expansive, sweet, sexy example with overripe cherry, cedar wood, licorice, smoke, and tar characteristics. Dark garnet-colored with an amber edge, the 1997 Barolo San Rocco possesses a phenomenal perfume of tobacco, leather, cedar, fruitcake, and cherry liqueur. Tar and rose petals (classic scents of ripe Nebbiolo) also emerge. Once past the terrific aromatics, the wine is full-bodied, rich, and supple, with an expansive texture, sweet tannin, low acidity, and gobs of fat as well as extract. This alluring Barolo is best drunk over the next 10–12 years. More structured yet also opulent, the dark ruby/garnet-colored, unctuous 1997 Barolo Bricco Fiasco reveals abundant quantities of smoke, tobacco, leather, licorice, and kirsch aromas and flavors. Full-bodied, lusty, and intense, it can be drunk now and should keep for nearly two decades.

Azelia produced two compelling 1996s. The 1996 Barolo San Rocco possesses a spicy, cedar box, fruitcake, and cherry liqueur–scented nose, a sweet, full-bodied personality with loads of glycerin, evidence of charred wood, oak, and a rich, multilayered, low-acid, structured/delineated finish. It is a big, mouth-filling Barolo with considerable complexity. Anticipated maturity: now–2020. The 1996 Barolo Bricco Fiasco explodes with tobacco, balsam wood, cedar, tar, and the telltale cherry fruit. In the mouth, toasty oak makes an appearance. Full-bodied, tannic, deep, and powerful, with a huge impact and density, this modern-styled wine has the body and force of a more traditionally made Barolo. Anticipated maturity: 2004–2020.

The 1995 Barolo San Rocco displays classic rose petal/melted tar aromas combined with exotic scents of soy and roasted meat–like smells. Intense, with full body, toasty oak, and black cherry fruit, this large-scaled, concentrated wine is on a fast evolutionary track, already exhibiting compelling complexity and richness. Anticipated maturity: now–2008. The 1995 Barolo Bricco Fiasco offers a pronounced bouquet of tobacco smoke intermixed with melted asphalt/tar, truffles, and kirsch/cherry liqueur. This fragrant, dense, concentrated, full-bodied Barolo is powerful and long, but more backward than the San Rocco. Anticipated maturity: now–2016.

F.LLI BARALE

1998 Barolo Castellero	D	85

Aromas of apple skins, cherry fruit, earth, and pepper are reminiscent of a straightforward Pommard from Burgundy. While medium-bodied and ripe, this soft 1998 Barolo Castellero lacks depth. Drink it over the next 2 years.

MARCHESI DI BAROLO

1998 Barolo Vigna Cannubi	E	(90–92)
1997 Barolo Vigna Cannubi	E	90
1998 Barolo Vigna Sarmassa	E	(90–92)
1997 Barolo Vigna Sarmassa	E	92

The two 1998s are impressive. The 1998 Barolo Vigna Cannubi exhibits a dark plum/purple color as well as a soft, modern style displaying notes of lavender, rose petals, ripe black fruits, and a touch of toasty oak. A sweet attack is followed by a rich, medium- to full-bodied, long Barolo with tannin as well as outstanding balance. Anticipated maturity: 2005–2015. Even fleshier and more opulent, the 1998 Barolo Vigna Sarmassa is made in a voluptuous, contemporary style with full body, abundant glycerin, and copious amounts of black cherry fruit infused with licorice, espresso, and melted road tar. Layered, pure, and impressive, it will be at its finest between 2004–2016.

The dark ruby-colored, internationally styled 1997 Barolo Vigna Cannubi shows plenty of new oak, but it does not overwhelm the wine's rich black raspberry, currant, and cherry fruit. Sweet, dense, and full-bodied, with low acidity and firm tannin, this pure, clean Barolo will drink well young, yet age for 15–20 years. More extracted, fleshy, powerful, and tannic is the 1997 Barolo Vigna Sarmassa. A dark ruby/purple color is accompanied by copious quantities of ripe, concentrated, black raspberry fruit, licorice, smoke, and mineral aromas and flavors. Dense and powerful, this 1997 is best cellared for 2–3 years and drunk over the following 15+.

A. S. BIAGIO

1997 Barolo	D	(88–90)
1996 Barolo	D	(87–89)

The 1997 Barolo exhibits that overripe fruit characteristic that the French refer to positively as *sur-maturité*. Its dark ruby color is followed by aromas of cherry and blackberry fruit and *garrigue* (that Provençal mélange of earth and herbs). Full-bodied, fat, succulent flavors, low acidity, and a chewy, high-alcohol finish further characterize this wine. This full-throttle Barolo, while not complex, is impressive in a hedonistic sense. Anticipated maturity: now–2015. The 1996 Barolo is an opulent, dark ruby-colored effort with gobs of cherry fruit, earth, olive, Provençal herbs, and cedar. Rich, with good ripeness, and a medium-bodied, firm, but fleshy finish, it should be at its finest before 2014.

FRANCO BOASSO

1998 Barolo Gabutti	D	87
1997 Barolo Gabutti	D	89
1996 Barolo Gabutti	D	(88–91+?)
1995 Barolo Gabutti	D	90

This producer from Serralunga d'Alba uses open-top fermenters with no new oak, preferring to age the wines in small *foudres*. His Barolos emerge from a vineyard with a southern exposure. This light-styled, forward, medium ruby/garnet-colored 1998 Barolo Gabutti offers plump cherry fruit, a velvety texture, and good roundness. Enjoy it over the next 4 years. The 1997 Barolo Gabutti is dark garnet-colored with an amber edge. Aromas of smoke, tobacco, Provençal herbs, kirsch, and dried cherries are followed by a medium- to full-bodied, dense, concentrated, powerful wine with excellent ripeness, a lush texture, and firm tannin in the finish. It gives conflicting indications of whether it will evolve quickly or become more structured and enjoy 18 or more years of longevity. In any event, it is an excellent wine that falls just short of being outstanding. Anticipated maturity: 2003–2016. The dark plum/ruby-colored 1996 Barolo Gabutti offers a nose of overripe black cherries, incense, licorice, smoke, and earth. It is monolithic, dense, and concentrated but slightly disjointed. Hence the question mark. There is huge potential, but this wine has not yet pulled itself together. Anticipated maturity: 2005–2015. The 1995 Barolo Gabutti reveals a Châteauneuf-du-Pape-like, kirschy, peppery nose with licorice and dried herbs. I had expected a more muscular, old style Barolo, but this is a fruit bomb with extraordinary ripeness and glycerin and a sexy, lush style. Anticipated maturity: now–2012.

ENZO BOGLIETTI

1998 Barbera d'Alba Vigna dei Romani	C	90
1998 Barolo Vigna delle Brunate	E	(88–89)
1997 Barolo Vigna delle Brunate	E	90+
1996 Barolo Vigna delle Brunate	E	(87–89)
1998 Barolo Vigna Case Nere	E	(90–91)
1997 Barolo Vigna Case Nere	E	91
1996 Barolo Vigna Case Nere	E	(87–88)
1995 Barolo Vigna Case Nere	E	85
1998 Barolo Vigna dei Fossati	E	(89–91)
1997 Barolo Vigna dei Fossati	E	91
1996 Barolo Vigna dei Fossati	E	(87–90)
1999 Dolcetto d'Alba Tigli Neri	C	90
1998 Langhe Rosso Buio	C	87

This up-and-coming La Morra producer, who fashions attractive wines, deserves significant attention. Based on recent vintages, Boglietti, who produces new-wave, *barrique*-aged Barolos, appears to be racheting up his performance level. His 1998s are fine successes. The superb 1997s all possess saturated purple colors and display copious levels of glycerin and extract. Each appears to have more of the black fruit, cassis/black raspberry character than the more red fruit–dominated 1996s and 1995. These wines are also lower in acidity and more open-knit than their older siblings.

Readers looking for an amazing Dolcetto should check out the 1999 Dolcetto d'Alba Tigli Neri. This astonishing, black/purple-colored, opulent, full-bodied, exquisitely fruited effort displays copious black fruits intermixed with notes of violets and chocolate. Unctuously textured yet not heavy, this beauty should be drunk within 2 years.

Also outstanding, the 1998 Barbera d'Alba Vigna dei Romani reveals plenty of spicy toast characteristics from its *barrique* aging. It is a full-bodied, modern-styled, deep ruby/purple-colored Barbera boasting an explosive bouquet of jammy tomato confit intertwined with black cherries and plums. Dense, chewy, yet soft, it can be drunk now and over the next 2–3 years. The more elegant, earthy, slightly acidic 1998 Langhe Rosso Buio is a blend of declassified young-vine Nebbiolo and Barbera. Exhibiting smoky, cherry notes, plenty of spice, medium body, and some tartness, it should drink well for 2 years. The 1998 Barolo Case Nere is a full-bodied, opaque purple-colored, modern-styled effort. A heady perfume of black fruits intermixed with new oak is followed by a wine with sweet tannin, a layered texture, outstanding richness, and a long finish. The dark plum/purple-colored 1998 Barolo Brunate is a medium-bodied, more elegantly styled effort displaying less obvious new oak influence in its round, sweet flavors but a less impressive finish than the Case Nere. Consume it during its first decade of life. The plum/purple-colored, spicy, smoky, opulent, full-bodied 1998 Barolo Fossati exhibits abundant quantities of black cherry and berry fruit, new oak, sweet tannin, and a long, chewy, lush finish. There are no hard edges to this 1998 Barolo. While it currently reveals the least typicity of these three offerings, it is impossible to hide a good *terroir* no matter how the wine is treated as long as the yields are low and the fruit is ripe. I suspect its Barolo/Nebbiolo character will emerge with another 1–2 years of cellaring. Anticipated maturity: 2003–2016.

The 1997 Barolo Case Nere displays an intriguing perfume of hickory/barbecue smoke intermixed with tar, rose water, black cherries, toffee, and maple syrup. Full-bodied, with large volume, a plush, multilayered texture, low acidity, and a boatload of glycerin, it is a thick, succulent Barolo to consume now and over the next 12+ years. The dark plum/garnet-colored 1997 Barolo Brunate exhibits a strikingly pure nose of melted licorice, kirsch, tobacco, spice box, and toasty oak. Deep, massive, full-bodied, and layered, with huge extract, this is a structured, powerful effort without the charm of its siblings. Nevertheless, it is an immensely impressive 1997 and may be the longest-lived of this trio. Anticipated maturity: 2003–2020. The saturated ruby/garnet-colored 1997 Barolo Fossati possesses thick, blackberry, raspberry, and cherry flavors intermixed with new oak, licorice, and smoke. Pure, opulent, and succulent, this intense, low-acid wine displays the vintage's exoticism as well as copious alcohol and glycerin. Anticipated maturity: now–2015.

The dark ruby-colored 1996 Barolo Case Nere is dense (denser than the 1995, in fact), with licorice, fennel, cedar, and black cherry aromas. Medium- to full-bodied, with moderate tannin and excellent purity, this traditionally made Barolo will be at its finest before 2012. The 1996 Barolo Brunate offers a classic nose of melted tar, cherry and black raspberry fruit, weedy tobacco, herb, and leather scents. Rich, with medium body, moderate tannin, and a dusty, rustic finish, it will keep for 8–10 years. The 1996 Barolo Fossati's bouquet reveals the influence of new oak, along with cherry liqueur, spice, and licorice. Broad and expansive in the mouth, with full body and moderate tannin, it should prove to be Boglietti's longest-lived 1996. Anticipated maturity: now–2018.

The only 1995 I tasted was the Barolo Case Nere, a medium ruby-colored, elegant wine with a smoked herb, cedar, tar, and cherry-scented nose. Spicy, with good ripeness, medium body, and an open-knit, evolved character, it can be drunk now and over the next 1–2 years.

BONGIOVANNI

1998 Barolo	D	(85–86)
1997 Barolo	D	87
1996 Barolo	D	87
1998 Barolo Pernanno	D	(86–87)
1997 Barolo Pernanno	D	87
1996 Barolo Pernanno	E	90
1999 Dolcetto d'Alba	C	89
1998 Langhe Rosso Falletto	D	87
1997 Langhe Rosso Falletto	D	91+

This Castiglione Falletto producer is not one that I know well. However, these are impressive offerings. The 1999 Dolcetto d'Alba is a dense ruby/purple-colored fruit bomb, with a supple texture, thick, juicy flavors, little complexity, but impressive mouth-filling levels of fruit and extract. Drink it over the next 2 years. The 1998 Langhe Rosso Falletto (a 50% Barbera, 25% Cabernet Sauvignon, and 25% Nebbiolo blend aged in *barrique*) is too internationally styled for me, but the wine's quality is unquestionably good. Elegant black currant and cherry notes are combined with abundant quantities of toasty new oak, resulting in a medium-bodied, well-made wine to drink over the next decade.

The following two 1998s are good but uninspiring. Bongiovanni's 1998 Barolo displays a soft, spicy perfume of cola, coffee, chocolate, and red fruits. This easygoing, quaffable (unusual for Barolo), supple 1998 has a moderate finish. Drink it over the next 3–4 years. The darker plum-colored 1998 Barolo Pernanno exhibits more toasty new oak in the aromatics along with notions of caramel, black cherries, and vanilla. Round, generous, and ripe, but not complex, it will drink well for 5–6 years.

As for the 1997s, they are modern, forward-styled Barolos exhibiting evidence of *barrique* aging. Neither will make old bones, but for drinking over the next 5–6 years, they represent an attractive, commercial style with some character. The 1997 Barolo offers a deep ruby color and a fat, low-acid, plush style with low acidity as well as copious cherry fruit. While similarly styled, the 1997 Barolo Pernanno reveals more chocolate in its open-knit, fleshy, medium-weight personality. It, too, should be drunk over the next 5–6 years. The 1997 Langhe Rosso Falletto is an awesome wine! This black/purple-colored blend of 50% Barbera, 25% Cabernet Sauvignon, and 25% Nebbiolo, all aged in new French oak, is hugely extracted and extremely full-bodied. It boasts layer upon layer of jammy, concentrated cassis-dominated fruit with notes of cherry liqueur, spice box, licorice, and cedar. As the wine sits in the glass, some of Nebbiolo's telltale melted asphalt and rose petal perfume emerges. Exceptionally rich, pure and velvet-textured, with a tannic finish, this is another sumptuous wine from the extraordinary, albeit atypical 1997 vintage. Anticipated maturity: now–2015.

The fairly light, medium-weight, round 1996 Barolo exhibits coffee, tobacco, cherry, and herb aromas and flavors, good concentration, fine ripeness, and sweet tannin. It is meant to be drunk over the next 7–8 years. The 1996 Barolo Pernanno reveals spicy new oak (from *barrique* aging), melted tar, rose petal, and black cherry fruit aromas and flavors. Ripe, medium- to full-bodied, concentrated, and supple, it can be drunk over the next 8 years.

BRAIDA

1998 Barbera d'Asti Ai Suma	E	96
1997 Barbera d'Asti Ai Suma	E	95
1998 Barbera d'Asti Bricco dell'Uccellone	E	94
1997 Barbera d'Asti Bricco dell'Uccellone	E	90
1999 Monferrato Rosso Il Bacialé	D	90

One of the original producers of super, "Whopper"-sized, *barrique*-aged Barbera, Braida continues to set the standard, although there are increasing numbers of challengers to these over-the-top, amazingly concentrated, prodigious wines that are nearly impossible to believe are made from Barbera. Braida's top two *cuvées*, which are aged 15 months in French oak prior to bottling, represent the essence of Barbera in a modern but thrillingly concentrated, layered style. Although these wines do not improve significantly in the bottle, they provide sumptuous drinking during their first 5–7 years of life. Their acidity and extract level ensure that they will hold up for two decades or more, but will they taste any better at age 10 than they did at age 5? I don't think so. However, for hedonistic levels of fruit, extract, glycerin, and complex aromatics, in their youth these wines are amazing.

The less expensive 1999 Monferrato Rosso Il Bacialé (a blend of 80% Barbera and 20% Pinot Noir) offers sexy, complex aromas of herb-tinged red and black fruits intermixed with earth and spicy oak. Ripe, round, and succulent, with a supple finish, it can be enjoyed over the next 2 years.

The opaque purple-colored 1998 Barbera d'Asti Bricco dell'Uccellone offers a seductive nose of spicy toast characteristics infused with espresso, roasted meats, black cherries, and raspberries. Dense and full-bodied, with a luxurious texture, this is a superintense, plush Barbera to enjoy over the next 5–6 years, although it will last longer. Even more remarkable is the 1998 Barbera d'Asti Ai Suma. This is the quintessential expression of super-concentrated, *barrique*-aged Barbera that other producers attempt to emulate (successfully so in the case of Roberto Voerzio). Braida's inky black/purple-colored 1998 boasts an explosive bouquet of blackberry and cherry jam mixed with graphite, vanilla, roasted meats, and spice. A sensual, full-bodied, voluptuously textured offering with extraordinary purity, this is a monumental Barbera. Whether it will improve beyond 5–7 years is open to conjecture, but who can resist its provocative charms?

Unquestionably one of the most massive Barberas ever made, the blockbuster 1997 Barbera d'Asti Ai Suma (800 cases) reveals off-the-chart density as well as a terrific bouquet of smoke, blackberries, cherry liqueur, licorice, and violets. With exquisite richness and amazing harmony for such a gargantuan wine, this full-bodied giant should drink well for 10–12 years. However, its low acidity and almost over-the-top richness, so typical of many 1997s, give it immediate appeal. It is a very sexy effort! The dense ruby/purple-colored, explosive 1997 Barbera d'Asti Bricco dell'Uccellone is overwhelmed by its sibling. It boasts aromas of concentrated strawberry jam intermixed with cherries, blackberries, smoky toasty oak, and glycerin. Minimal acidity and a lusty personality result in an already delicious wine, but it should last for 8 years. These are two very impressive Barberas!

ALESSANDRO BRERO

1998 Barbera d'Alba Poderi Roset	C	92
1998 Barolo Poderi Roset	E	88
1997 Barolo Poderi Roset	E	90
1996 Barolo Poderi Roset	E	92+
1995 Barolo Poderi Roset	E	89
2000 Dolcetto d'Alba Poderi Roset	C	88
1999 Dolcetto d'Alba Poderi Roset	C	90

With extremely low yields, ripe fruit, and no filtration at bottling, it is not surprising that Brero's wines are loaded. The 600-case, dense purple *cuvée* of fat, chewy, fruit-driven 2000 Dolcetto d'Alba Poderi Roset possesses loads of berry fruit, a notion of coffee and chocolate, and a full-bodied, compact finish. Although not complex, it has excellent purity as well as a mouth-filling style. Enjoy it over the next 3 years.

Brero's 1999 Dolcetto d'Alba Poderi Roset was fermented and aged in tank. Its saturated ruby/purple color is accompanied by a huge, blackberry, cherry, and chocolate-scented nose, exuberant fruit, and low acidity. This soft, ripe Dolcetto is captivating and delicious. It should drink well for 2 years. Another dazzling effort is the 1998 Barbera d'Alba Poderi

Roset. Aged in both small barrels and larger Slavonian oak *foudres*, it exhibits a dark ruby/ purple color, a superb herbaceous, smoky, toasty, and black cherry liqueur–scented nose, terrific texture, full body, and layers of Barbera fruit. The acidity is low, the purity superb, and the wine chewy and intense. Drink it over the next 5 years.

The soft, supple, Burgundy-styled 1998 Barolo Poderi Roset exhibits a dark ruby color in addition to scents of smoke, chocolate, and black cherries. Medium-bodied and seductive, it can be drunk now as well as over the next decade. While not as exotic or concentrated as the 1997, it is beautifully balanced, pure, and harmonious.

The highly extracted, flavorful, quasi-modern-styled 1997 Barolo Poderi Roset possesses the power, tannin, and force of old-style Barolos but the color, sweet fruit, and ripe tannin of the modernists. Dense chocolate, blackberry, and cherry flavors are thick, heady, and persistent. Surprisingly youthful and unevolved, it is nicely textured as well as extremely long. Anticipated maturity: 2003–2016. The impressive 1996 Barolo Poderi Roset requires some additional bottle aging. Aged entirely in large Slavonian oak *foudres* and bottled unfiltered, it boasts a deep ruby color with an amber edge. Spectacular aromatics of sweet black Chinese tea, rose petals, tar, and gobs of strawberry and black cherry fruit explode from the glass. Although still an infant, this wine is rich and full-bodied, with loads of flavor, abundant glycerin, and enough concentration and extract to cover the framework and tannin. Anticipated maturity: now–2020. The traditionally styled 1995 Barolo Poderi Roset exhibits an evolved deep garnet color with amber at the edge. It offers a spicy, dried herb, earthy, foresty nose with hints of cherry cough syrup, smoke, and leather. Medium- to full-bodied and expansive, it is soft enough to be drunk now and over the next 4–5 years.

GIACOMO BREZZA & FIGLI

1998 Barolo Sarmassa	D	88
1997 Barolo Sarmassa	D	89

While I was disappointed with Brezza's 1999, I enjoyed his 1998 and 1997. This excellent, fat, juicy, silky-textured 1998 Barolo Sarmassa is unusually evolved and forward. It exhibits a dark garnet color as well as copious quantities of smoky, weedy, cherry fruit intermixed with tobacco and damp earth. Chewy, plump, and surprisingly opulent, it will drink well over the next 8 years. The 1997 Barolo Sarmassa is a big, full-bodied, thick, unctuously textured effort with considerable amber at the edge. Notes of dried red fruits, flowers, toffee, chocolate, plums, and cherries are found in this concentrated wine, best consumed over the next 10 years.

F.LLI BROVIA

1997 Barbaresco Riosordo	E	(83–85)
1996 Barbaresco Riosordo	E	86
1995 Barbaresco Riosordo	E	86+
1998 Barolo Ca' Mia	E	(85–87)
1997 Barolo Ca' Mia	E	90+
1996 Barolo Ca' Mia	E	(86–87+?)
1995 Barolo Ca' Mia	E	88
1998 Barolo Rocche dei Brovia	E	(87–89+?)
1997 Barolo Rocche dei Brovia	E	91
1996 Barolo Rocche dei Brovia	E	(88–90)
1995 Barolo Rocche dei Brovia	E	86
1998 Barolo Villero	E	(88–89+)
1997 Barolo Villero	E	(86–88)
1996 Barolo Villero	E	(90–91+)
1995 Barolo Villero	E	89

Brovia, whose cellars are in Castiglione Falletto, produced sound 1995s, very good 1996s, and less impressive 1997s, which nevertheless performed better than their 1998 counterparts. It must be remembered, however, that Nebbiolo, much like Pinot Noir, is an extremely challenging grape to taste and assess at a young age. The 1997s reveal less color saturation and concentration than the 1996s, which adds to the minority school of thought that 1997 was not as consistently superb a vintage as believed. And Brovia's 1996s are far denser, more complete wines, as well as more tannic than the 1995s.

The 1998 Barolo Ca' Mia's dark plum/garnet color is followed by sweet aromas of chocolate, cherries, smoke, and dried herbs. It is a medium- to full-bodied, monolithic effort displaying tough tannin in the finish. If it sweetens and expands in texture, it will merit a higher score. Anticipated maturity: 2005–2015. The dark garnet-colored 1998 Barolo Villero reveals more softness as well as complexity in its spice box, molasses, and cherry-scented nose. There are excellent concentration, sweeter tannin, a more layered personality, and a seamless finish with excellent concentration of fruit (primarily cherries dosed with earth and spice). Anticipated maturity: 2004–2014. Lastly, the plum/garnet-colored 1998 Barolo Rocche dei Brovia is superficially appealing. Its smooth texture is accompanied by complex notes of caramel, cedar, cherry jam, smoke, and flowers. However, in the mouth, the wine shuts down, revealing little texture or depth. It may have been going through an awkward stage when I tasted it. There is plenty up front, but there is a lack of follow-through, depth, and what appears to be concentration in the finish. It will need to be retasted in order to pinpoint its potential quality. Anticipated maturity: 2005–2016.

The complex, supple 1997s do not compromise the power and muscle Brovia's wines routinely achieve. The dark garnet-colored 1997 Barolo Ca' Mia displays a complex bouquet of soy, tobacco, cedar, licorice, and smoke. Expansive, full-bodied, and intensely concentrated, this is an atypically backward 1997 with tightly packed flavors. Anticipated maturity: 2005–2018. The dark plum/garnet-colored 1997 Barolo Rocche dei Brovia begins slowly but grows incrementally until it totally coats the palate. Thick and powerful, it exhibits sexy aromatics of prunes, cherries, and plums. In the mouth, dried fig notes also make an appearance in this intensely flavored, concentrated, muscular wine. Despite its precociousness, there is plenty of tannin lurking beneath the viscosity. Anticipated maturity: now–2018. The 1997 Barbaresco Riosordo tastes similar to a light- to medium-bodied Pinot Noir. Its framboise and cherry flavors are alluring, but the wine is smoky and light. Drink it over the next 3 years. The 1997 Barolo Villero offers spice, cinnamon, and cherry fruit in its moderately endowed nose. Elegant, medium- to full-bodied and lush, it does not reveal any of the vintage's hallmark glycerin, high alcohol, and sweet fruit. Anticipated maturity: now–2012.

The 1996 Barbaresco Riosordo is the most forward. Displaying a ruby color with purple nuances, it offers fresh, tangy black currant flavors with dried herbs in the background. It possesses good concentration but a compressed, narrowly constructed finish. Anticipated maturity: now–2007. The 1996 Barolo Rocche dei Brovia's opaque ruby color with purple nuances is followed by dense black cherry fruit intermixed with raspberry liqueur, spice, and earth. This is a fuller-bodied, rich, potentially outstanding wine with moderate tannin and 15 years' longevity. Anticipated maturity: 2005–2018. The dark ruby-colored 1996 Barolo Ca' Mia is severe and austere, with high levels of tannin and sweet fruit that tastes like cherry cough syrup mixed with cedar and spice box notes. The tannin level is worrisome, thus the question mark. Anticipated maturity: 2004–2015. The outstanding, ruby/purple-colored 1996 Barolo Villero displays a nose of melted road tar, chocolate, earth, black cherries, dried herbs, and coffee. Rich, full-bodied, and nearly massive, this is a classic Barolo that will last for 20–22 years. Anticipated maturity: 2007–2030.

The 1995 Barbaresco Riosordo is a light- to medium-bodied effort for drinking over the next 1–2 years. Forward and evolved, with a medium garnet color already exhibiting considerable amber at the edge, it offers weedy tobacco, smoke, earth, and dried fruit aromas and flavors. Although soft, elegant, and medium-bodied, it lacks depth. Anticipated maturity: now–2005. The 1995 Barolo Rocche dei Brovia is a darker plum-colored wine with cherries, cranberries, and red currants in its slightly spicy nose. Made in a light- to medium-bodied, elegant style, it is soft and easy to drink. Anticipated maturity: now–2007. The more serious 1995 Barolo Ca' Mia exhibits a darker garnet color in addition to more black raspberry and currant fruit in the nose along with new saddle leather and cigar smoke. It possesses good purity, medium to full body, excellent richness, and a moderately long finish. Anticipated maturity: now–2009. The dark ruby/garnet-colored 1995 Barolo Villero is the most backward, youthful, concentrated, and complete of the 1995s. While closed, it does offer aromas of roasted herbs, minerals, tobacco, and leather. In the mouth, sweet black cherry fruit makes an appearance. Anticipated maturity: now–2012.

COMMENDATOR G. B. BURLOTTO

1998 Barolo Vigneto Cannubi	D	(87–88)
1997 Barolo Vigneto Cannubi	D	86

This Verduno producer has fashioned a flavorful, medium-weight, elegantly styled 1998 Barolo Vigneto Cannubi with good softness, finesse, and no hard edges. There is not a great deal of concentration, but the wine is well balanced and ideal for drinking over the next 4–5 years. The medium-bodied, earthy, powerful, tannic, rustic 1997 Barolo exhibits a dark ruby color, good licorice and cherry fruit notes, but a certain toughness as well as compression to its texture. Anticipated maturity: 2003–2012.

BUSSIA SOPRANA

1998 Barolo Mosconi	D	(90–92)
1997 Barolo Mosconi	D	89
1997 Barolo Vigna Colonnello	D	90

A sleeper producer from Monforte d'Alba that I discovered through his 1997s, Bussia Soprana turns out a Barolo Mosconi and a Barolo Vigna Colonnello that are nearly outstanding. Both wines are traditionally made but are bottled early to preserve their rich, concentrated fruit. There is little evidence of new oak, although subtle smoke and vanilla notes are present. I enjoyed the two 1997s immensely, but I tasted only one 1998 *cuvée* from this producer. The full-bodied, traditionally made 1998 Barolo Mosconi is a sleeper of the vintage. A dark plum/garnet color is accompanied by aromas of espresso, smoke, kirsch, dried herbs, and tobacco. Dense and chewy, with sweet tannin as well as ripe fruit, its harmony and overall balance suggest 10–12 years of longevity.

The creamy-textured, fat (because of the vintage's high glycerin) 1997 Barolo Mosconi reveals excellent concentration as well as a complex bouquet of rose water, licorice, smoke, minerals, and black cherries. In the mouth, the wine is full, rich, and ready to drink. Anticipated maturity: now–2014. The dark plum/garnet-colored 1997 Barolo Vigna Colonnello offers a fragrant, intense perfume of wood smoke, licorice, kirsch, Provençal herbs, and tobacco. Full-bodied, powerful, and dense, it reveals no hard edges, a seamless texture, and a 30-second finish. Drink it now and over the next 12 years.

PIERO BUSSO

1996 Barbaresco	D	86
1998 Barbera d'Alba Vigna Majano	C	91

The 1998 Barbera d'Alba Vigna Majano exhibits spicy new oak, concentrated, opulently-textured flavors redolent with cherry and strawberry jam as well as new oak. Ripe, full-bodied, and super-concentrated, this is another surprisingly voluptuous Barbera to drink over the next 5–6 years. It is a very good value given the wine's quality. Less impressive but competently made is the dark plum/ruby-colored 1996 Barbaresco, which offers an attractive bouquet of leather, wood smoke, sweet and sour cherries, medium body, moderate tannin, and an elegant, restrained style. It should be drunk over the next 4–5 years.

CA' DEL BAIO

1998	Barbaresco Asili	D	(84–85)
1998	Barbaresco Valgrande	D	(83–86)

Both 1998s are light to medium-bodied, pleasant, fruity, superficial Barbarescos meant to be consumed during their first 4–5 years of life. Although cleanly made, they lack substance.

CA' ROMÈ

1997	Barbaresco	D	87
1997	Barbaresco Maria di Brun	E	85
1997	Barolo Rapet	E	90
1996	Barolo Rapet	E	88
1997	Barolo Vigna Cerretta	E	89
1996	Barolo Vigna Cerretta	E	87

This is the producer that I have the most trouble understanding. Many of Ca' Romè's wines seem to lack intensity and are too angular and astringent for my taste (1998 Barbera d'Alba La Gamberaja; 1997 Da Pruvé, a Barbera/Nebbiolo blend; 1997 Barbaresco; and 1997 Barbaresco Maria di Brun). However, I enjoyed the upcoming Barolo releases.

The generic 1997 Barbaresco exhibits a dark plum color in addition to a moderately intense bouquet of sweet cherries, cedar, spice box, licorice, and herbs. With excellent richness and purity as well as a supple texture, it should be consumed over the next 4–5 years. The 1997 Barbaresco Maria di Brun displays an evolved garnet color with considerable amber at the edge. Offering Chinese black tea, cedar, and cherry characteristics, this soft wine appears to be drying out. Drink it over the next 2–3 years.

The opulent 1997 Barolo Rapet exhibits a deep ruby color, sweet, concentrated fruit (cherries, smoke, cedar, and licorice), layers of texture, and a spicy, intense finish. Drink it over the next 12+ years. The 1996 Barolo Rapet reveals an excellent dark ruby color in addition to abundant aromas of cedar wood, spice box, rose petals, and cherries in its medium-bodied, moderately tannic personality. It should drink well for 5–6 years. The 1996 and 1997 Barolo Vigna Cerretta differ only in that the 1997 has less tannin, more sweetness of fruit and glycerin, and the vintage's telltale opulence. The 1997 possesses more volume, ripeness, richness, and intensity. Both wines are best drunk during their first 10–12 years of life. The 1996 exhibits notes of soy and tobacco in its medium- to full-bodied, tannic, cedary, spicy, black cherry–dominated personality.

GIUSEPPE CAPPELLANO

1998	Barolo Franco	E	90
1997	Barolo Franco	E	90
1998	Barolo Gabutti	E	88
1997	Barolo Gabutti	E	83

Both of these offerings are produced from the Gabutti vineyard, but the Franco *cuvée* comes from ancient, ungrafted Nebbiolo vines that are believed to be more than 100 years of age. The 1998 Barolo Franco's medium garnet color is accompanied by a sweet, attractive bouquet of jammy strawberry and cherry fruit, rose petals, licorice, and autumn leaves. There are good fatness, an opulent texture, a fleshy mid-palate, and a lush finish with well-concealed tannin and acidity. Anticipated maturity: 2004–2015. The dark ruby-colored, similarly styled 1998 Barolo Gabutti's aromatics are not as complex, but it offers scents of cherry cough syrup, licorice, tobacco, leather, and spice. Sweet, ripe, medium- to full-bodied, and seductive, it will drink well until 2015.

The finer of the two 1997s, the dark garnet-colored 1997 Barolo Franco reveals an explosive, decadent aroma of mushrooms, jammy red and black fruits, coffee, caramel, smoke, and dried herbs. Thick, fat, plush, and chewy, it tastes like candy. Consume it over the next 8 years. On the other hand, the 1997 Barolo Gabutti is a lighter, straightforward, medium-bodied effort displaying cherry fruit but not a great deal of complexity, texture, or length. Drink it over the next 3 years.

CARRETTA

1997	Barbaresco Cascina Bordino	E	88
1996	Barbaresco Cascina Bordino	E	87
1995	Barbaresco Cascina Bordino	E	86
1998	Barolo Vigneta Cannubi	E	(90–91)
1997	Barolo Vigneta Cannubi	E	90
1996	Barolo Vigneta Cannubi	E	(87–88)
1995	Barolo Vigneta Cannubi	E	86
1997	Bric Quercia	E	88

Carretta's offerings tend to be firmly structured, masculine wines with considerable body and tannin.

A powerful old-style Barolo, Carretta's 1998 Vigneta Cannubi offers up scents of new saddle leather, underbrush, earth, truffles, vitamins, black cherry fruit, rose petals, and tar. Abundant tannin, serious concentration, high extract, and a structured, formidable personality suggest an atypical style in 1998, but one that will repay cellaring. Anticipated maturity: 2008–2020. Contrary to the general style of the estate, the 1997 Barolo Vigneta Cannubi is approachable, although it ideally needs 1–2 more years of cellaring. Notes of camphor intermingle with ripe berry fruit, earth, soy, tobacco, and leather in this full-bodied, powerful, traditionally made Barolo. Anticipated maturity: 2004–2020. In contrast to the tannic, powerful Barolo, the sexy, lush, open-knit 1997 Barbaresco Cascina Bordino is more charming as well as accessible. Offering aromas and flavors of red/black fruits, spice box, and fruitcake, this soft, round wine is best drunk over the next 6–7 years.

The opulently textured and flamboyant 1997 Barbaresco Cascina Bordino is dark ruby/purple-colored. It offers copious quantities of sweet black raspberry and cherry fruit meshed with earth, loamy soil scents, weedy tobacco, and spice. A medium-bodied example, with more glycerin, alcohol, and lower acidity than its siblings, it should drink well young and last for 6 years. The outstanding, powerful 1997 Barolo Vigneta Cannubi exhibits a dense ruby/purple color, in addition to intense aromas of jammy black fruits, spice, cedar, and dried herbs. Powerful and rich, with outstanding ripeness, it will drink well between 2005–2020. The 1997 Bric Quercia *vino da tavola* (a blend of Barbera and Bonarda) was aged in barrel and bottled unfiltered. It is an exotic, opaque purple wine with a beautiful nose of sweet cherry jam and kirsch intertwined with toasty, smoky oak and floral scents. Opulently textured, fat, and chewy (a characteristic of this vintage), this low-acid, hedonistic wine should drink well for 4–5 years.

The 1996 Barbaresco Cascina Bordino exhibits a dark ruby color, as well as attractive scents and flavors of jammy strawberries and cherries, roasted nuts, cedar, and spice box scents. Long, rich, and medium-bodied with moderate tannin, it will be at its finest before 2012. The 1996 Barolo Vigneta Cannubi is a powerful, masculine wine with good tannin and dusty, earthy aromas intertwined with sour cherries. Tobacco and asphalt scents also make an appearance. This structured, muscular wine will be at its finest before 2012.

The 1995 Barbaresco Cascina Bordino is surprisingly soft for a wine from this estate. Exhibiting a plum/garnet color, smoky, soy, gamey, spicy, earthy, fruit flavors, and damp foresty scents, it is medium-bodied and round, and will provide ideal drinking over the next 2 years. The 1995 Barolo Vigneta Cannubi is totally different from its younger sibling, the 1996.

More open-knit, with good power for the vintage, it is destined to be drunk over the next 3 years. It possesses attractive licorice and tar scents, medium body, and some tannin, but not enough depth to encourage further aging.

CAVALIER BARTOLOMEO DI BORGOGNO DARIO

1998 Barolo Vigneti Solanotto	D	(88–90)
1997 Barolo Vigneti Solanotto	D	88

This Castiglione Falletto producer has turned out an excellent, medium ruby/garnet-colored 1998 Barolo Vigneti Solanotto with a big, spicy, sweet, black cherry–scented nose with hints of soy and balsam wood. There are fine fruit density, medium to full body, and moderate tannin in the admirable finish. Consume it over the next 10 years. An old-style, nicely textured, rich, spicy offering, the 1997 Barolo Vigneti Solanotto reveals aromas of black fruits, ripe cherries, cedar, earth, and seaweed. Medium- to full-bodied, pure, and nicely textured, it can be drunk now and over the next 8–10 years.

CAVALLOTTO

1997 Barolo	D	90
1998 Barolo Bricco Boschis Vigna San Giuseppe	E	(92–93+)
1997 Barolo Bricco Boschis Vigna San Giuseppe	E	93
1998 Barolo Vignolo	E	(91–93)
1997 Barolo Vignolo	E	91

Cavallotto's well-situated vineyards are on the hillsides surrounding the village of Castiglione Falletto. He owns one of the region's great monopole sites, the Bricco Boschis. Older vintages of these wines have tended to be good but never inspiring. However, after tasting through the 1997s, 1998s, and 1999s, it is apparent that something has changed as they are stunning Barolos. They represent a synthesis in style between the old-guard traditionalists and the new wave of rotary fermented, *barrique*-aged wines. The estate produces one standard *cuvée* and two special *cuvées*, the Bricco Boschis and the Vignolo, the latter emerging from a Castiglione Falletto vineyard situated just west of Bricco Boschis and northwest of the famed Monprivato vineyard. The deep ruby/purple-colored 1998 Barolo Vignolo exhibits a gorgeously sweet, textbook bouquet of rose petals, melted road tar, cherry liqueur, spice box, and minerals. Full-bodied, concentrated, seamless, and harmonious, it is reminiscent of a grand cru red Burgundy from Musigny or Flagey-Echèzeaux. Anticipated maturity: 2003–2018. Cavallotto's monopole vineyard, the famed Bricco Boschis Vigna San Giuseppe, produces a singularly styled Barolo with incredible fruit, a layered texture, moderately high tannin, and an enormous follow-through on the palate. It brilliantly marries finesse/elegance with unbridled power and concentration. Although it requires 2–3 years of cellaring to drop some tannin and develop more fully, it should be a spectacular 1998 that will rival the more ostentatious 1997. Anticipated maturity: 2006–2020.

The 1997 Barolo is an impressive generic effort whose fruit all came from the Bricco Boschis. A dense dark ruby/purple color is accompanied by a surprisingly high-toned, well-delineated wine without the over-the-top style evident in many 1997s. Notes of black cherries and blackberries are intertwined with minerals, wet stones, rose petals, and spice. Rich and full-bodied, with fine acidity, this classic, potentially long-lived Barolo should be at its finest between 2003–2018. The 1997 Barolo Vignolo is an elegant old-style offering. The color is a dark plum/ruby. The bouquet offers sweet aromas of melted asphalt, kirsch, leather, dried herbs, truffles, and smoke. It is a pure, full-bodied, moderately tannic effort with classic breeding, terrific purity as well as balance, and a long finish. Anticipated maturity: 2004–2017. The outrageously delicious 1997 Barolo Bricco Boschis Vigna San Giuseppe offers a spectacularly gorgeous nose of ripe fruits, herbs, leather, scorched earth, coffee, and cherry liqueur. A singular style of wine with wonderful spice, full body, and tremendous delineation as well as class, this large-scaled Barolo offers a classic rose petal fragrance as it sits in the glass. It is a quintessential Barolo. Anticipated maturity: 2003–2025.

CEREQUIO

1997 Barolo	D	84

This is an internationally styled, monolithic, straightforward 1997 Barolo without much typicity or depth. It possesses new oak and ripe fruit but little character or soul. Drink it over the next 3–4 years.

CERETTO

1998 Barbaresco Asij	EE	92
1997 Barbaresco Asij	EE	89
1998 Barbaresco Bricco Asili Bernadotte	EE	88
1997 Barbaresco Bricco Asili Bernadotte	EE	90
1998 Barbaresco Bricco Asili Bricco Asili	EE	89+
1997 Barbaresco Bricco Asili Bricco Asili	EE	91
1996 Barbaresco Bricco Asili Bricco Asili	EE	(91–93)
1995 Barbaresco Bricco Asili Bricco Asili	EE	89
1998 Barbaresco Bricco Asili Faset	EE	89+
1997 Barbaresco Bricco Asili Faset	EE	89+
1996 Barbaresco Bricco Asili Faset	EE	(89–91)
1995 Barbaresco Bricco Asili Faset	E	87
1998 Barolo Bricco Rocche	EEE	92
1997 Barolo Bricco Rocche	EEE	96
1996 Barolo Bricco Rocche	EEE	(92–96)
1995 Barolo Bricco Rocche	EE	90
1998 Barolo Brunate	EE	87
1997 Barolo Brunate	EE	94
1996 Barolo Brunate	EE	(91–93)
1995 Barolo Brunate	E	88+
1998 Barolo Prapò	EE	91
1997 Barolo Prapò	EE	95
1996 Barolo Prapò	EE	(92–94)
1995 Barolo Prapò	EE	89
1998 Barolo Zonchera	EE	90
1997 Barolo Zonchera	EE	91

The Ceretto brothers have long produced some of Piedmont's most elegantly styled, complex, flavorful wines from their vineyards in and around the village of Castiglione Falletto. They offer an impressive portfolio of 1995s, 1996s, 1997s and 1998s. Their 1998s are nearly as sensational as their 1997s. While these wines are all relatively well developed, they admirably display the vintage's intense perfume along with wonderful balance as well as harmony. True to the vintage, the 1997s possess more glycerin and lower acidity than the 1996s as well as a forward, unreal, atypical lushness and opulence. The 1996s, which exhibit a more saturated ruby color than the 1995s, are also richer, with more extract, tannin, and body. Of all four vintages, the 1995s are the most evolved, with garnet colors revealing amber at their edges. They are delicious wines that should drink well for another 6–7 years.

The glorious, dark plum/garnet-colored 1998 Barbaresco Asij offers a complex nose of earth, truffles, cherry liqueur, licorice, spice, and tobacco. Sweet and supple with nearly perfect symmetry as well as abundant glycerin and length, it will drink well for 5–6 years. The softer, lighter 1998 Barbaresco Bricco Asili Bernadotte offers notes of leather, balsam wood, underbrush, and cherries. Supple-textured, extremely fragrant, elegant, and light- to medium-bodied, it will drink well for 5–6 years. Similarly styled, but with a harder finish, the 1998 Barbaresco Bricco Asili Faset exhibits a plum/garnet color in addition to intense aromas of cherry liqueur, licorice, and leather. It is medium-bodied, with more concentration than the Bernadotte, but hard tannin in the finish suggests that a few supplementary months of cellaring are required. This wine may become slightly austere. The aromatically complex, medium- to full-bodied, dark garnet-colored 1998 Barbaresco Bricco Asili Bricco Asili offers intense aromas of soy, black cherries, tobacco, spice box, licorice, and incense. With ripe but noticeable tannin and excellent length, this potentially outstanding Barolo needs several more years of cellaring. Anticipated maturity: now–2014.

The dark plum/garnet-colored 1998 Barolo Zonchera is an elegant, spicy, medium-bodied effort revealing the vintage's telltale perfume as well as excellent concentration and purity. Drink it over the next 10–12 years. The concentrated, dark plum/garnet-colored, rich 1998 Barolo Prapò displays a smoky, earthy, black cherry, and new saddle leather–scented bouquet infused with licorice and espresso. Although tight, it is crammed with extract. Dense, full-bodied and long, with moderate tannin, it will be at its best until 2016. Notes of dried herbs, soy, underbrush, tobacco, and red cherries characterize the narrowly constructed, leaner, more austere 1998 Barolo Brunate. This is one example where the 1998 is clearly overshadowed by its spectacular, exotic, compelling 1997 counterpart. Anticipated maturity: now–2016. Ceretto's finest Barolo of the vintage appears to be the 1998 Barolo Bricco Rocche. An incredibly complex perfume of creosote, minerals, smoke, soy, black cherries, and incense is accompanied by a full-bodied, sweet, layered, powerful wine with outstanding balance. Long as well as elegant, this beauty will be at its finest before 2017.

I tasted four 1997 Barbaresco offerings. The most evolved, the 1997 Barbaresco Asij reveals a garnet color with considerable amber already apparent. It exhibits aromas of soy, cedar, ripe fruit, dried herbs, licorice, and rose water as well as a fleshy, open-knit, expansive personality and a medium- to full-bodied, soft finish. It will provide delicious drinking over the next 4–5 years. More tannic, with a firm edge and additional structure, is the dark ruby/purple-colored, amber-edged 1997 Barbaresco Bricco Asili Bernadotte. This medium- to full-bodied, backward, ripe effort possesses aromas of new saddle leather, dried herbs, brandied cherries, and licorice. Consume it over the next 10–12 years. The 1997 Barbaresco Bricco Asili Faset's exquisite perfume offers aromas of ginger, cedar, cigar box, and cherry liqueur. Excellent concentration, medium to full body, undeniable elegance, soft tannin, and copious glycerin result in a seductive wine to enjoy over the next 12 years. The superlative 1997 Barbaresco Bricco Asili Bricco Asili boasts a dark garnet color with amber at the edge as well as smoke, vanilla, leather, cherry liqueur, licorice, dried herb, and subtle oak aromas and flavors. The most complex of Ceretto's Barbarescos, this rich, medium- to full-bodied, suave, seductive 1997 can be drunk now and over the next 12 years.

The evolved, mature ruby/amber color of the 1997 Barolo Zonchera is perplexing since the wine tastes young and vigorous. An exotic offering, it exhibits aromas of smoke, coffee, vanilla, maple syrup, brown sugar, and overripe cherries. This is a full-bodied, luxuriously rich, decadent, young Barolo that should be drunk now and over the next 8 years. Reminiscent of a right bank Pomerol from the late 1940s, the dark garnet/amber-edged 1997 Barolo Prapò possesses aromas and flavors of singed leather, espresso, melted caramel, black cherries, smoke, and fruitcake. Atypical for a young Nebbiolo, it is succulent, fleshy, and undeniably compelling, rich, seamless, and concentrated. Drink it over the next 12 years. The 1997 Barolo Brunate displays a similar evolved dark garnet color with an amber edge. However, in the mouth, it is dense, full-bodied, moderately tannic, structured, and backward with plenty of power, concentration, and youthfulness. Despite the evolved color, this wine should age well for 15+ years. The ostentatious, staggering 1997 Barolo Bricco Rocche also possesses a dark garnet color with amber at the edge. The explosive bouquet of coffee liqueur, licorice, spice box, black cherries, kirsch, raspberries, and cedar is to die for. The wine reveals numerous dimensions and nuances as well as a boatload of glycerin. Full-bodied, massively concentrated, and exceptionally thick and juicy, with a sweetness due to the high glycerin and ripeness, this is Barolo on steroids. Anticipated maturity: now–2018.

The seductive, dark ruby-colored 1996 Barbaresco Bricco Asili offers a classic bouquet of road tar, cherry liqueur, tobacco, and dried herbs. Medium- to full-bodied and surprisingly supple for the vintage, it exhibits firm tannin in the finish. Anticipated maturity: now–2014. The 1996 Barbaresco Faset is not as aromatically complex as the Bricco Asili. It reveals more oak, in addition to a raspberry/black cherry fruit component. Rich, medium-bodied, and potentially outstanding, it will be at its finest before 2014.

The opaque ruby/purple-colored 1996 Barolo Prapò offers a moderately intense nose of scorched earth, dried herbs, and sweet black fruits. It is medium- to full-bodied, with an exciting level of fruit extract, superb purity, and a multidimensional, layered personality. This terrific Barolo will be best before 2018. The 1996 Barolo Brunate's dark ruby color is followed by aromas of Chinese black tea, pepper, earth, and cherries. Ripe, full-bodied, and structured, with excellent depth, a sweet mid-palate and a firm finish, this wine should be consumed before 2016. Ceretto's opaque ruby/purple-colored 1996 Barolo Bricco Rocche is sensational stuff. The richest of these offerings, it combines explosive levels of fruit, glycerin, and extract with an uncanny sense of elegance and finesse. There are copious quantities of black cherry fruit intermixed with raspberries, cedar, spicy oak, licorice, and tar. This terrific, complex, multidimensional Barolo should be at its finest before 2018.

The 1995 Barbaresco Bricco Asili exhibits a beautifully etched nose of cherry jam, vanilla, and dried herbs. Elegantly styled, with medium body, sweet, smoke-tinged fruit, and soft tannin, this is a sexy, complex, easygoing Barbaresco to enjoy over the next 5–7 years. The 1995 Barbaresco Faset is less complex, with a dark ruby/garnet color, lushness, medium body, a spicy, cedary, cigar box–scented nose, ripe fruit, and a supple finish. Drink it over the next 2–3 years. The 1995 Barolo Prapò offers a dried herb, cedar, tomato, and red currant–scented nose. Cherries as well as plums make an appearance along with smoked herb and toasty oak. Medium-bodied, graceful, and layered, it can be drunk over the next 4–5 years. The 1995 Barolo Brunate is more of a fruit-driven wine, with gobs of cherry liqueur as well as sandalwood, cedar, and flowers. Firmer, with more tannin, and an earthier personality than the more open-knit Prapò, it is drinkable but may improve with a few years of bottle age. Anticipated maturity: now–2010. The most concentrated and massive of the Ceretto Barolos is the 1995 Barolo Bricco Rocche. It offers a classic nose of melted tar, Asian spice, incense, and cedar, as well as gobs of black fruits, a whiff of high-quality tobacco, full body, and a layered, moderately tannic finish. Anticipated maturity: now–2015.

PIO CESARE

1998	Barbaresco	E	87
1996	Barbaresco	E	(90–91)
1995	Barbaresco	E	88
1998	Barbaresco Bricco	E	(88–90)
1997	Barbaresco Bricco	E	90+
1998	Barolo	E	(86–87+)
1997	Barolo	E	(90–92)
1996	Barolo	E	(89–92)
1995	Barolo	E	(88–89)
1998	Barolo Ornato	E	(90–92)
1997	Barolo Ornato	E	(91–93)

One of the oldest firms in Piedmont (founded in 1881) and one of the few to operate out of the village of Alba, Pio Cesare is the most recent in an unending string of traditional Piedmontese wine-makers. The house is going through a transitional stage, trying to fashion a middle ground between the traditionally styled wines of the past and the new-wave modernists. It continues to make subtle winemaking refinements that enhance the wines' fruit character without compromising their full-bodied, ageworthy style. I still have bottles of 1969 and 1970 Pio Cesare Barolos that are drinking beautifully at nearly 30 years of age. Proprietor Pio Boffa feels that 1998 is qualitatively behind 1996, 1997, and 1999, but, as the following tasting notes demonstrate, there is plenty to admire. Interestingly, he also claims that his 1996s are clearly more successful than his 1997s. He believes that 1996, not 1997, will be considered the great classic vintage for the villages of Barolo and Monforte d'Alba. The 1995s are soundly made.

The elegant, medium ruby-colored 1998 Barbaresco (from the vineyards in Treiso) is a more austere version of the 1997. Aromas of dried herbs, balsam wood, flowers, and cherries are followed by a medium-bodied Barbaresco with good density but a slightly angular, austere finish. Anticipated maturity: 2004–2012. The single-vineyard 1998 Barbaresco Bricco (750 cases produced) boasts a deep ruby color as well as a tight but promising nose of spicy new oak, black cherries, and blackberries. It is powerful, full-bodied, and high in tannin. Anticipated maturity: 2006–2015.

The dark ruby-colored 1998 Barolo is a tough-textured, backward effort showing a certain austerity along with notes of minerals, earth, pepper, and truffles. Red fruit notes emerge as the wine sits in the glass, but this is a decidedly stern, backward, atypical 1998. Anticipated maturity: 2006–2018. Cesare's single-vineyard 1998 Barolo Ornato (from a Serralunga vineyard) offers a more explosive perfume of sweet black cherries intermixed with blackberries, new saddle leather, smoke, and vanilla. It possesses outstanding purity, full body, fine density, and a boatload of tannin. However, the glycerin, extract, and concentration are more than adequate to balance out the wine's muscle. Anticipated maturity: 2007–2025.

Pio Cesare's 1997 Barbaresco Bricco is a dense, rich, full-bodied, powerful effort with evidence of *barrique* but wonderfully sweet black cherry and raspberry fruit with notes of spice box, fruitcake, soy, and licorice. Give it 1–2 years of cellaring and drink it over the following 12–15 years. The 1997 Barolo was performing well prior to bottling. Broad, sweet, fat flavors with considerable glycerin and alcohol are present in this full-bodied, structured, powerful, muscular Barolo. Anticipated maturity: 2003–2020. The spectacular 1997 Barolo Ornato (1,000 cases, produced only in the finest vintages), from a Serralunga vineyard planted next to Bruno Giacosa's famous parcel of Falletto di Serralunga, offers a terrific fragrance of raspberries, cherries, smoke, leather, and toasty oak. There are huge quantities of glycerin, a stupendous finish, and gorgeous purity as well as overall symmetry. This 1997 will require 1–2 years of cellaring but will keep for 2–3 decades.

The 1996 Barbaresco is more tannic, with a firmer, more muscular style, but not the charm of the 1995. The wine is concentrated, with dense fruit, and plenty of black cherries, leather, smoke, and tobacco nuances. Anticipated maturity: now–2016. The classic 1996 Barolo is potentially outstanding. Its dark ruby color is accompanied by a smoky, black cherry–scented nose with roasted herb, nuts, and mineral nuances. Full-bodied, spicy, long, and needing 1–2 years of cellaring, this should prove uncommonly long-lived. Anticipated maturity: 2004–2022. The excellent 1995 Barbaresco is one of the vintage's most delicious wines. A smoky, black cherry, and leathery-scented nose is followed by excellent ripeness, medium to full body, moderate tannin, an excellent texture, and a long, spicy finish. Anticipated maturity: now–2011. The dark ruby/garnet-colored 1995 Barolo exhibits a spicy, aromatic nose with scents of earth, dried herbs, leather, and sweet black fruits. In the mouth, it is powerful, with excellent richness, moderate tannin, and a rustic but impressively endowed finish.

MICHELE CHIARLO

1997 Barolo Cannubi   **E 87**

This internationally styled, dark ruby/purple-colored Barolo displays noticeable new oak along with an elegant, stylish, medium-bodied personality without a great deal of regional typicity. However, it is well made, with sweet tannin, excellent concentration, and plenty of black fruits intermixed with wood, smoke, and spice. The wine's tannin as well as firmness suggest that 1–2 years of cellaring will be beneficial. Anticipated maturity: 2004–2015.

QUINTO CHIONETTI & FIGLIO

1999 Dolcetto di Dogliani Briccolero	C	90
1999 Dolcetto di Dogliani San Luigi	C	89

This Dolcetto specialist never disappoints, as evidenced by these beautifully made 1999s. Chionetti's 1999 Dolcetto di Dogliani San Luigi's dark ruby/purple color is accompanied by a sexy, sweet perfume of espresso, chocolate, almonds, and copious quantities of berry fruit. Lush, layered, fat, and voluptuous, it is all that a Dolcetto should be. Savor it over the next 2–3 years as these wines do not improve in the bottle. Even better, the 1999 Dolcetto di Dogliani Briccolero is a 4,000-case *cuvée* offering a saturated ruby/purple color, medium to full body, and compelling levels of chocolate-tinged black cherry fruit. It is a big, chewy, fleshy, pure effort with admirable vibrancy. When are American consumers going to discover Dolcetto's appeal, particularly when drunk in its first 2–3 years of life?

F.LLI CIGLIUTI

1998 Barbaresco Serraboella	D	90
1997 Barbaresco Serraboella	D	89
1996 Barbaresco Serraboella	D	?
1998 Barbera d'Alba Serraboella	C	88

A complex bouquet of mushrooms, balsa wood, dried red and black fruits, cedar, and black cherries jumps from the glass of the medium to dark plum-colored 1998 Barbaresco Serraboella. Sexy, aromatic, and rich, with a lush, concentrated, tannic finish, it should be drunk over the next 5–6 years. It represents a classic example of the fragrant, harmonious, silky-textured 1998 vintage. The 1998 Barbera d'Alba Serraboella exhibits a dark ruby/purple color as well as a sweet nose of blackberry, raspberry, and toasty oak aromas. Medium-bodied, plump, and fleshy, with enough tangy acidity to provide definition and vibrancy, it can be drunk over the next 2–3 years. Cigliuti's 1997 Barbaresco Serraboella reveals a lighter, medium ruby color, excellent rose petal, cedar, black cherry, and raspberry-scented aromatics, opulent, medium-bodied flavors, moderate tannin, and good acidity. Still young, it is capable of 8 years of evolution.

I had trouble with the only sample I tasted of the 1996 Barbaresco Serraboella, which seemed to possess vegetal tannin and a hard, tough texture. The color is a healthy dark ruby/purple. While the wine exhibits sweet fruit on the attack, it becomes narrow, with greenness and astringency dominating its personality. Given the high quality of this producer, I look forward to tasting another bottle.

DOMENICO CLERICO

1998 Barbera d'Alba Trevigne	C	90
1998 Barolo Ciabot Mentin Ginestra	E	93+
1997 Barolo Ciabot Mentin Ginestra	E	94
1996 Barolo Ciabot Mentin Ginestra	E	90
1995 Barolo Ciabot Mentin Ginestra	E	91
1998 Barolo Mosconi Percristina Riserva	E	(92–93+)
1997 Barolo Mosconi Percristina Riserva	E	93+
1996 Barolo Mosconi Percristina Riserva	E	95
1995 Barolo Mosconi Percristina Riserva	E	92

1998 Barolo Pajana	E	92+
1997 Barolo Pajana	E	93
1996 Barolo Pajana	E	94
1995 Barolo Pajana	E	90+
1998 Langhe Arte	E	89

For almost two decades, Domenico Clerico has been turning out some of Piedmont's most compelling wines. Another modernist who utilizes rotary fermenters, short macerations, and various percentages of new oak, ranging from a minimum of 20% for his Ginestra to 100% for his Mosconi Percristina Riserva (a *cuvée* named after his daughter, who, tragically, died at the age of seven), Clerico's wines could be called the Pauillac premier crus of Monforte d'Alba. They are structured, large-scaled, concentrated Barolos with plenty of muscle and tannin. Moreover, they will handsomely repay two decades of cellaring. I am just finishing my still beautiful 1982s, a very good but less concentrated and lighter vintage than any of Piedmont's recent vintages (1996, 1997, 1998, and 1999). Clerico's wines possess enough character to be accessible young but still require cellaring. These are wines of extraordinary richness, amazing aromatics, and sensual personalities that satiate both the hedonistic and intellectual senses. In general, the 1995s are the most forward and evolved, the 1996s the most muscular and structured, and the 1997s off the chart in terms of their thickness, exoticism, and sumptuousness. While less fragrant than some of their peers, Clerico's 1998s are classic, backward, well-structured wines with superb depth, purity, and overall balance.

Clerico's proprietary offering, the 1998 Langhe Arte, is a blend of 90% Nebbiolo, 5% Barbera, and 5% Cabernet Sauvignon aged for 20 months in 100% new French oak. Internationally styled, it reveals abundant aromas of toasty new oak, red currant as well as cherry fruit, leather, cedar, and spice box. Medium-bodied and elegant, it is best drunk during its first 5–7 years of life. More sumptuous, the dazzling 1998 Barbera d'Alba Trevigne boasts explosive fruit, full body, power, and super-concentration, as well as finesse, elegance, and overall balance. This is a gorgeously rendered Barbera to enjoy over the next 3–4 years. The dense ruby/purple-colored 1998 Barolo Pajana reveals copious new oak along with lead pencil, black cherry, blackberry, licorice, and earth aromas. This structured, powerful, full-bodied, chewy wine requires 1–2 years of cellaring. Anticipated maturity: 2003–2016. The super-extracted, blockbuster 1998 Barolo Ciabot Mentin Ginestra assaults the palate with a blast of broodingly tannic, super-concentrated black cherry and raspberry fruit infused with minerals, new oak, licorice, and truffles. With a huge mid-palate as well as an astonishingly long finish, it is not yet ready to drink. Anticipated maturity: 2006–2020. The 1998 Barolo Mosconi Percristina Riserva reveals aromas of sweet black fruit intermixed with new oak, blueberry, flowers, and an underlying minerality. Full-bodied, powerful, deep, and chewy, this youthful, backward 1998 rivals the spectacular efforts produced in 1996 and 1997. Anticipated maturity: 2003–2018.

Clerico's saturated purple-colored 1997 Barolo Pajana offers a classic bouquet (reminiscent of a cross between Mouton and Lafite Rothschild) of cedar wood, cassis, licorice, lead pencil, and mineral scents. The wine possesses abundant quantities of black fruit, tar, truffle, and cigar box flavors. A huge, monstrous Barolo, it is not one of the most forward 1997s, so 1–2 years of cellaring are recommended. Anticipated maturity: 2004–2020. The 1997 Barolo Ciabot Mentin Ginestra is a fearsomely powerful, tannic, ultraconcentrated, explosively rich wine with a mid-palate in which one could get lost. A saturated ruby/purple color is accompanied by scents of lead pencil, cedar, black fruits, smoke, earth, and vanilla. Massive richness, monster extract, sweet tannin, and a blockbuster finish characterize this dazzling, 20–25-year wine. Anticipated maturity: 2005–2025. Clerico's 1997 Barolo Mosconi Percristina Riserva is the most tannic and backward of this group of unevolved, massive 1997s. A dense ruby/purple color is followed by aromas of new saddle leather, licorice, black cherries, and the telltale rose petals. More closed aromatically than its siblings, with huge flavors, copious glycerin, as well as abundant tannin, this full-bodied, loaded 1997 requires an additional 3–4 years of cellaring . . . unusual for the exotic, over-the-top style of many 1997s. Anticipated maturity: 2007–2030.

The 1996s are spectacularly powerful, rich, concentrated wines. The 1996 Barolo Ciabot Mentin Ginestra possesses a deep, dark purple color, and a nose of overripe plums, cherries, and cassis. Rich and full-bodied, with admirable glycerin, subtle oak, and licorice/floral nuances, it is a large-scaled yet beautifully balanced Barolo to drink between 2004–2018. The striking resemblance of the 1996 Barolo Pajana to a top-class Pomerol is unmistakable. This massive wine possesses fabulous purity of fruit and toast that complements the wine's highly concentrated black cherry/chocolaty personality. Dense and layered, with considerable viscosity, low acidity, and moderate tannin in the impressive, long finish, it will be at its best between 2006–2020. The profound 1996 Barolo Mosconi Percristina Riserva exhibits a black raspberry liqueur–like nose. As it sits in the glass, notes of cherries, cassis, toast, and smoke emerge. Massive, powerful, chewy, unctuously textured, and long, with subtle oak and immense fruit concentration, this spectacular Barolo should age effortlessly for 15–16 years.

The 1995 Barolo Ciabot Mentin Ginestra offers a knockout nose of tobacco, mint, dried red fruits, balsa wood, and cherry liqueur. There are tons of glycerin, low acidity, medium to full body, and striking richness and lushness. It is about as sexy a 1995 Barolo as readers will find. I would opt for drinking it over the next 4–5 years as it is already irresistible. The 1995 Barolo Pajana is a synthesis in style between a grand cru Burgundy and a first growth Bordeaux. It is slightly less aromatic than the 1995 Ciabot Mentin Ginestra, with a saturated ruby/purple color, lush black raspberry and cherry fruit, and a touch of black currants. The medium- to full-bodied, fruit-driven, low-acid 1995 Pajana should be consumed over the next 8 years. The amazing 1995 Barolo Mosconi Percristina Riserva is the richest, most complete of these offerings. This debut vintage offers up kirsch, Chinese black tea, flowers, licorice, and subtle spicy new oak. Amazingly rich and full-bodied, with terrific purity, symmetry, and length, it can be drunk now but should be even better with 1–2 years of cellaring; it will keep for 10 years.

ELVIO COGNO

1999	Barbera d'Alba Bricco dei Merli	C	89
1998	Barbera d'Alba Bricco dei Merli	C	90
1996	Barolo Ravera	E	90
2000	Dolcetto d'Alba	B	89
1999	Dolcetto d'Alba	B	90
1999	Langhe Rosso Montegrilli	D	90
1998	Langhe Rosso Montegrilli	D	86

A topflight Barolo producer, Cogno also makes excellent Dolcetto and Barbera, as well as a superb proprietary *barrique*-aged blend of Barbera and Nebbiolo called Langhe Rosso Montegrilli. The black/purple-colored 2000 Dolcetto d'Alba possesses extremely powerful, concentrated, monolithic, chunky, dense, full-blast flavors. If a few additional nuances emerge from behind the mass of fruit and body, this wine will merit an outstanding score. However, readers need to keep in mind that these wines rarely improve, so even this offering requires consumption during its first 3–5 years of life. Cogno's 1999 Dolcetto d'Alba is an excellent example of this tasty varietal. An opaque purple color is accompanied by chewy, berry flavors, excellent purity, not much complexity, but mouth-staining levels of richness and intensity. It is a fruit-dominated blockbuster to drink over the next 3–4 years. The spicy, fragrant, medium-bodied 1999 Barbera d'Alba Bricco dei Merli exhibits black cherry fruit mixed with strawberry jam, earth, and spicy oak. Pure and fleshy, with a ripe, opulent finish, it will be at its finest before 2007. The most serious, sexiest, and complex of the 1999s is the Langhe

Rosso Montegrilli. This smoky, medium- to full-bodied wine offers scents and flavors of toast, plums, cherry jam, and tobacco. Round, velvety-textured, and seamless, it is a hedonistic turn-on. Enjoy it over the next 3–4 years.

The dark ruby/purple-colored 1998 Barbera d'Alba Bricco dei Merli is made in a sexy, opulent, forward style, with sweet, jammy strawberry and blackberry flavors, good underlying acidity, fat, and density, and a chunky, spicy finish. It should drink well for 4–5 years. Readers seeking a more internationally styled wine will enjoy the 1998 Langhe Rosso Montegrilli. It offers abundant quantities of spicy new oak, sweet, currant/cherry flavors, and toast. Medium-bodied, with good density and purity, it does not reveal the Piedmontese soul of Cogno's other offerings, but it is a well-made effort. Serious connoisseurs will be turned on by the complexity, austerity, and nobility of the 1996 Barolo Ravera. Its dark plum color is accompanied by a sweet nose of smoked herbs, black cherries, minerals, spice, and tobacco. Complex and full-bodied, with outstanding richness and moderately high tannin, this 1996 is approachable but promises to be even better with an additional 1–2 years of cellaring. Anticipated maturity: 2004–2020.

PODERI COLLA

1997 Barbaresco Tenuta Roncaglia	D	89
1996 Barolo Bussia	D	88

This winery has produced forward efforts in both 1996 and 1997. The 1997 Barbaresco Tenuta Roncaglia exhibits a medium ruby color with garnet at the edge. A classic nose of rose petals, strawberry jam, tobacco, and spice emerges gracefully from the glass. Rich, savory, and fleshy, with sweet tannin, well-integrated acidity, and a moderately long finish, this 1997 should drink well for 10 years. The 1996 Barolo Bussia reveals telltale aromas of cedar wood, tobacco, and dried herbs, along with earthy black cherry fruit notes. A supple texture, admirable concentration, medium body, and noticeable tannin in the finish result in an overall impression of a sweet, precocious, up-front Barolo to enjoy over the next 10 years.

ALDO CONTERNO

1998 Barolo Bussia Soprana	E	(90–92)
1997 Barolo Bussia Soprana	E	91+
1996 Barolo Bussia Soprana	E	92
1995 Barolo Bussia Soprana	E	88
1998 Barolo Cicala	EE	(87–89)
1997 Barolo Cicala	EE	91+
1996 Barolo Cicala	EE	94+
1995 Barolo Cicala	EE	87
1998 Barolo Vigna Colonnello	EE	(90–92)
1997 Barolo Vigna Colonnello	EE	91+
1996 Barolo Vigna Colonnello	EE	92+
1995 Barolo Gran Bussia Riserva	EEE	93
1999 Dolcetto d'Alba	B	88
1998 Langhe Rosso Quartetto	D	89

The quintessential gentleman, 70+-year-old Aldo Conterno, the brother of Giovanni Conterno, is one of Piedmont's unapologetic traditionalists. His portfolio includes three single-vineyard Barolos as well as a proprietary red, Langhe Rosso Quartetto, that is a blend of Nebbiolo, Merlot, Cabernet Sauvignon, and Barbera. In great vintages, a limited-production Barolo Gran Bussia Riserva is also produced. The classic and long-lived Barolos represent an enlightened traditional style, often needing 5–6 years to reveal their full character. Conterno, although successful in 1995, produced brilliant wines in 1996, 1997, and 1998. I feel that all of Conterno's 1996s possess greater density, concentration, and overall potential compared to his 1997s, which are nonetheless superb. Moreover, his 1998s appear to be great classics.

Conterno's glorious red wine offerings include the 1999 Dolcetto d'Alba. Aromas of black fruits and violets jump from the glass of this deep, richly fruity yet elegant, round wine. It will provide delicious drinking over the next several years.

The dark ruby/purple-colored 1998 Langhe Rosso Quartetto offers an intense bouquet of black cherry jam, currants, oak, earth, and spice. Dense, medium- to full-bodied, round, and richly fruity, it is meant to be consumed over the next 5–6 years. The dark ruby/garnet color 1998 Barolo Cicala possesses the highest acidity, least weight, and most elegance of the three Barolos. Notes of soy, Asian spices, red cherries, minerals, and herbs are found in this spicy, medium-bodied, stylish, moderately tannic 1998. Anticipated maturity: 2003–2014. The most textured, powerful, and concentrated of this trio is the 1998 Barolo Vigna Colonnello. Offering aromas and flavors of roasted coffee, new saddle leather, black cherry jam, underbrush, earth, and spice box, this tightly structured, full-bodied, dense, impressively extracted wine needs cellaring. Anticipated maturity: 2006–2020. Similarly styled, the 1998 Barolo Bussia Soprana exhibits moderately intense aromas of cedar, spice box, licorice, tar, and cherry jam. This full-bodied, powerful, concentrated 1998 possesses good acidity, excellent cleanliness, and a moderately tannic finish. Anticipated maturity: 2005–2020.

The dense ruby/garnet-colored, tightly knit 1997 Barolo Bussia Soprana offers notions of earth, cherries, and balsa wood. Full-bodied, with good acidity (particularly for the vintage), moderately high tannin, and a firm finish, it possesses plenty of power, although not as much as 1996. Consume this outstanding effort between 2006–2020. The full-bodied, dark garnet-colored 1997 Barolo Vigna Colonnello displays licorice, spice box, and kirsch characteristics as well as more noticeable acidity. As the wine sits in the glass, aromas of soy, herbs, and incense emerge. It is a tightly framed, full-bodied, powerful yet close-to-the-vest offering. Anticipated maturity: 2006–2018. The 1997 Barolo Cicala (from a parcel of vines further up the slope from Colonnello) offers a distinctive bouquet of soy, fresh sardines, earth, cedar, and tar. In the mouth, leather notes are added to this mix. It was my least favorite of the trio, perhaps because the tannin dominates the wine's back end, giving it a more compressed character. Aldo Conterno explained that this wine always takes longer to come around than his other crus and frequently possesses a mineral/steely framework compared to the Colonnello or the Barolo from Bussia Soprana. Anticipated maturity: 2005–2020.

I tasted the three single-vineyard Barolos in 1996. The 1996 Barolo Vigna Colonnello is very aromatic, offering scents of melted asphalt, cedar, tobacco, spice box, and assorted red and black fruits. Following a soft entry, the immense richness and fleshy, full-bodied power of this wine became apparent. The finish offers considerable tannic clout and power. Anticipated maturity: 2005–2022. The dense ruby/plum-colored 1996 Barolo Bussia Soprana exhibits a promising, classic Nebbiolo/Barolo bouquet of tobacco, cigar box, rose petals, melted tar, and copious quantities of sweet black cherry fruit. Although impressively full-bodied, powerful, tannic, and dense, it is oh, so young and backward. Patience . . . please! Anticipated maturity: 2010–2025. The stunning aromatics of the 1996 Barolo Cicala offer everything found in the Bussia Soprana, but even more intensity and fireworks. Full-bodied and muscular, it possesses high tannin as well as extract and a mouth-searing acidity that gives the wine both great precision as well as a frightfully backward character. A superdense, extracted, and rich Barolo, it will not be ready to drink for a decade. Discipline in the form of cellaring is definitely required for this fabulous Barolo. Anticipated maturity: 2012–2030.

The dark ruby-colored 1995 Barolo Cicala possesses a muted but promising nose of spice box, cedar, tobacco, and cherry fruit. It exhibits good ripeness, medium body, high tannin, and noticeable yet subtle oak. This very good 1995 can be drunk now as well as over the next 4–5 years. The denser 1995 Barolo Bussia Soprana displays a more saturated ruby color. The rich, cedary, smoky, tobacco, and tar-scented nose is classic Nebbiolo. Excellent, with a layered texture, and a rich, spicy, austere, moderately tannic finish, it is accessible enough to be drunk now but should evolve nicely for 3–4 years.

The limited-production Gran Bussia was made only in 1970, 1971, 1974, 1978, 1982, 1985, 1988, 1989, 1990, and 1995. In all likelihood, it will be made in 1996, 1997, 1998, and 1999. Seventy percent of this wine comes from the Romirasco vineyard and the rest from Cicala and Colonnello. It is aged for three years in *foudres* and two years in bottle prior to being released. The dense garnet/ruby-colored 1995 Barolo Gran Bussia offers classic scents of rose petals, melted asphalt, kirsch, and dried herbs. Sweet, full-bodied, and rich, it is a terrific effort for the vintage, ranking alongside the fabulous 1995 Monfortino produced by Giacomo Conterno. The Gran Bussia possesses ripe tannin as well as a huge finish. Anticipated maturity: now–2020.

GIACOMO CONTERNO

1996 Barolo Cascina Francia	EE	88+?
1995 Barolo Cascina Francia	EE	92
1994 Barolo Cascina Francia	EE	90
1993 Barolo Cascina Francia	EE	91
1998 Barolo Monfortino	EEE	(93–95+)
1997 Barolo Monfortino	EEE	(91–94)
1996 Barolo Monfortino	EEE	(89–91)
1995 Barolo Monfortino	EEE	(94–95)
1993 Barolo Monfortino	EEE	92
1998 Dolcetto d'Alba Cascina Francia	B	87

Visiting Giovanni Conterno, a stern, initially humorless man who warms up the longer one spends in the cellars, and his son Roberto offers a fascinating view of the traditional school of Piedmontese winemaking. Seventy-three-year-old Giovanni has five children, and it is his youngest, Roberto, who now does most of the work in the cellars. His two Barolo *cuvées*, Cascina Francia and Monfortino, come from hillside vineyards in Serralunga d'Alba. The regular Barolo *cuvée*, the Cascina Francia, is actually the same wine as the Monfortino, at least in theory. However, there are differences in the way in which they are vinified, and they are segregated in the cellars at an early age. As a general rule, Monfortino spends more time on the skins and appears to be a selection of particular lots. It is also bottled much later than the Cascina Francia, which tends to be bottled within four years of the vintage, the Monfortino being bottled between 7–10 years of the vintage. For example, the 1993 Barolo Monfortino was bottled in 2000. These wines are often hard to understand in their youth since they do not have the color saturation of most modern-day reds and seem unyielding, austere, tannic, and hard. Take it from someone who knows better. I have been buying these wines since the late sixties and still have a few bottles of the majestic 1964 and 1967 that are just beginning to tire. The 1970 and 1971 remain relatively young wines, with the 1971 Monfortino one of the most prodigious Barolos anyone could pour over the palate. Surprisingly, this estate does not always produce the finest wines in what are considered to be Barolo's top vintages. In my tastings, the 1995 Barolo Monfortino appeared to be one of their great efforts and significantly richer and more complex than the 1996 or 1997. The 1998, which will not be released for 8–10 years, is another profound vintage for Conterno, but both Roberto and Giovanni think 2000 is their finest vintage in ten years.

The 1998 Dolcetto d'Alba Cascina Francia, a rustic, full-bodied, powerful example with a deep ruby color as well as considerable berry fruit intermixed with minerals, smoke, dried herbs, and fresh almonds. Drink it over the next 2–3 years.

Probably because of its recent bottling, the 1996 Barolo Cascina Francia was subdued, but it does not appear to have the depth of a great vintage for this estate. The color is medium ruby with pink at the edge. Notes of balsa wood, spice box, tar, and rosewood reluctantly emerge from the aromatics. In the mouth, flavors of spice and leather compete with dusty cherry fruit in a tannic, austere, closed, steely style. I do not find enough sweetness, glycerin, or extract to make this profound, but it is very good to excellent. Anticipated maturity: 2008–2025. The youngest and densest of the current Barolo releases is the 1995 Barolo Cascina Francia. It possesses classic Nebbiolo traits of melted asphalt, cedar wood, sweet cherries, rose petals, and truffles. Full-bodied, deep, and chewy, with an intriguing earthy smokiness, this tannic, impressively concentrated, and well-endowed Barolo can be drunk now but will be even better with an additional 2–4 years of cellaring; it will last for 15+ years. The 1994 Barolo Cascina Francia reveals more amber in its ruby/garnet color. Scents of Chinese black tea, cedar wood, smoked duck, soy, licorice, and tobacco jump from the glass of this aromatic Barolo. It is more forward than the 1993, with sweet, round, old-style flavors, dusty tannin, and wonderful glycerin and concentration. It should drink well for 12–15 years.

The 1993 Barolo Cascina Francia exhibits a dark ruby color with purple nuances, in addition to aromas of roasted herbs, tobacco, tar, kirsch, and dried cherries as well as some volatile acidity. In the mouth, it is dense, medium- to full-bodied, with good concentration and dusty tannin in the finish. This 1993 Barolo can be drunk now but promises to evolve for another 15–20 years. The light garnet/ruby-colored 1993 Barolo Monfortino is undoubtedly the wine of the vintage for this challenging year. Like all Conterno wines, it was bottled without fining or filtration, thus preserving its full *terroir* and varietal characteristics. It boasts a knockout aromatic profile of rose petals, tar, new saddle leather, sweet, jammy black cherries, licorice, and raspberries, decent acidity, sweet tannin, copious alcohol, wonderful density, a fleshy texture, and beautiful harmony as well as elegance. It can be drunk now and over the next 15 years. Look for this effort to be one of the great sleeper wines of Piedmont given the fact that most 1993 Barolos are austere and hard-edged.

One of the great Barolo Monfortinos is the 1995, which I hope will be bottled and released before 2005. This was the finest wine I tasted in Conterno's cellars (everything between current releases and 2000). Significantly more concentrated than their 1996 Monfortino, it represents a tiny crop because of hail damage. The wine reveals the essence of licorice, kirsch, smoke, red currant, and cherries, as well as the telltale rose petal and licorice notes. It is ripe and full-bodied, with sweet fruit, copious glycerin, and a seamless finish that lasts for nearly 45 seconds. As the wine sat in the glass, it became even more floral and concentrated. There is abundant tannin, and the wine will undoubtedly taste more structured when it is released. Anticipated maturity: 2010–2040. To reiterate, the 1996 Barolo Monfortino is not as concentrated as the 1995, nor as rich or complex as the 1993. Nevertheless, it is an elegant, stylish, medium-weight effort with less flesh and more austerity than the other offerings. I know that does not make sense given the vintage conditions, but it is what has been produced by Giovanni and Roberto Conterno. The 1997 Barolo Monfortino appears to be a sexy, atypically forward wine for this estate. Dense and sexy, with abundant glycerin, and lush, seamless, black cherry, kirsch, smoke, tar, and meat-like flavors presented in a full-bodied, concentrated style. While much denser than the 1996, it is not as complex and concentrated as the 1995. Anticipated maturity: 2007–2022.

I also tasted the 1998 and 1999 Monfortinos, but they are at least 7–10 years away from release. Both look to be fabulous efforts that should easily surpass the 1997 as well as the lighter 1996. Tasted from a gigantic *foudre* (where the entire Monfortino *cuvée* is sitting), the 1998 Barolo Monfortino is a ruby-colored wine with a forward, evolved style (typical of the vintage) and a sweet bouquet of rose water, tar, truffles, minerals, and cherry fruit. Full-bodied but beautifully balanced, it is delicious enough to drink now, although that would be considered heresy in these cellars.

Let's hope the style at this winery never changes as it produces the quintessential traditional Barolo (along with those of Bruno Giacosa and a handful of other Piedmontese producers). In a world where immediate gratification is often the holy grail, the reality is that most consumers will not wait ten years for the wine to be released and another 10 years for it to hit its peak of maturity. For the few who do, the rewards are immeasurable. The wines produced by Giovanni Conterno are monuments to Nebbiolo as well as to the glory of Piedmont.

PAOLO CONTERNO

1998 Barolo Ginestra	E	(88–90)
1997 Barolo Ginestra	E	88+

Another Conterno from Monforte d'Alba (although less renowned than Giovanni and Aldo), Paolo's dark ruby/purple-colored 1998 Barolo Ginestra exhibits aromas and flavors of soy, balsa wood, dried cherries, tobacco, and herbs. Subtle notions of new oak in the aromatics suggest that at least a portion of this *cuvée* saw some *barrique* treatment. Deep, full-bodied, and opulent, with sweet tannin, it should drink well young (atypical for this producer and region). Anticipated maturity: 2003–2015. The dark ruby/purple-colored 1997 Barolo Ginestra is a traditionally made wine with considerable tannin as well as subtle evidence of new oak. Dense, ripe, and surprisingly tannic, it should be drunk between 2005–2015.

CONTERNO FANTINO

1999 Barbera d'Alba Vignota	C	87
1998 Barbera d'Alba Vignota	C	90
1998 Barolo Sorì Ginestra	E	92
1997 Barolo Sorì Ginestra	E	92+
1996 Barolo Sorì Ginestra	E	92
1995 Barolo Sorì Ginestra	E	85?
1998 Barolo Vigna del Gris	E	90
1997 Barolo Vigna del Gris	E	93
1996 Barolo Vigna del Gris	E	90
1995 Barolo Vigna del Gris	E	87?
2000 Dolcetto d'Alba Bricco Bastia	C	87
1999 Dolcetto d'Alba Bricco Bastia	C	89
1998 Monprà	D	90
1997 Monprà	D	90
1996 Monprà	D	89

Usually a reliable producer, Conterno Fantino, located in the village of Monforte d'Alba, has a mixed portfolio in 1995, 1996, 1997, and 1998. While the 1996s and 1998s are successful, both 1995 Barolos are tannic, with austere personalities, and the 1997s are noticeably oaky and made in an international style that submerged some of the Nebbiolo character behind a veneer of heavy toasty wood.

Conterno Fantino's 2000 Dolcetto d'Alba Bricco Bastia is a lovely, fruity, soft wine offering berries, cherries, cola, and earth in its uncomplicated but pleasing aromatics as well as flavors. Medium-bodied, with fine purity, it is best consumed over the next several years. Tangier and lighter-weight, with notes of tomato skins, strawberries, cherries, and a touch of oak, is the well-made 1999 Barbera d'Alba Vignota. Neither a blockbuster nor a big, oaky Piedmontese Barbera, it is a stylish, restrained effort to enjoy over the next 3–4 years. The 1999 Dolcetto Bricco Bastia may deserve an outstanding rating. The charge against Dolcetti, particularly from a top vintage such as 1999, is that they do not possess a great deal of complexity, even though they deliver a boatload of hedonistic fireworks. This opaque purple-colored, dense, chewy, full-bodied Dolcetto cuts a gloriously robust swath across the palate. Powerful and super-concentrated, it is as hedonistic a Dolcetto d'Alba as readers will find. Drink it over the next 3–4 years. A blend of equal parts *barrique*-aged Nebbiolo and Barbera, the outstanding 1998 Monprà exhibits a dark ruby color with purple hues. A sweet perfume of red and black fruits, smoke, licorice, and flowers jumps from the glass. On the palate, it is Burgundy-like in its medium-bodied, plush, round, beautifully pure style with excellent texture. Not a long-distance runner, it should be consumed over the next 3–4 years.

Two outstanding efforts from Conterno Fantino, the 1998 Barolos combine the best of the traditional school with the modern, enlightened approach to making young Barolo somewhat accessible. The 1998 Barolo Vigna del Gris offers a deep ruby/garnet color, medium to full body, and a sweet nose of lead pencil, new oak, black cherries, and rose petals. Elegant, powerful, beautifully harmonious, and well delineated, with a moderately tannic finish, it will be at its finest between 2003–2016. Even better is the compelling 1998 Barolo Sorì Ginestra. A dense, full-bodied, super-extracted, complex, multilayered Barolo, it exhibits aromas and flavors of tar, camphor, black cherry liqueur, smoke, minerals, and subtle new oak. Full and velvety-textured, with a 40-second finish, this large-scaled yet immensely elegant wine will drink beautifully between 2004–2018.

Another fine effort is the complex, medium- to full-bodied 1998 Barbera d'Alba Vignota, which offers superb black cherry fruit tinged with hints of tomato skins, fresh almonds, and chocolate. With extravagant ripeness as well as a complex, Médoc-like scent of lead pencil shavings, this spicy, dense, fruity Barbera can be drunk over the next 5–6 years. An outstanding blend of equal parts Barbera and Nebbiolo, the 1997 Monprà reveals the vintage's opulent personality. Opaque ruby/purple-colored, with a big, smoky, internationally styled bouquet of black fruits and new oak, it possesses admirable intensity, loads of glycerin, low acidity, and a spicy, chewy finish. Drink it over the next decade.

Conterno Fantino's 1997 Barolo Vigna del Gris displays beautifully sweet black fruits in its aromatic profile and huge, concentrated, full-bodied flavors with enormous muscle, amazing glycerin levels, and exceptional purity. This super-concentrated effort is just beginning to reveal the telltale Nebbiolo/Barolo traits of tar, rose petals, and sweet black cherry fruit. It should easily last for two decades, although I doubt it will ever close down. The 1997 Barolo Sorì Ginestra exhibits a deep ruby/purple color in addition to complex aromas of tobacco smoke and gloriously sweet, jammy cherry liqueur. Ripe, opulent, and full-bodied, with huge amounts of glycerin and extract, yet high tannin in the finish, this 1997 needs 2–3 years of cellaring and should keep for 20+ years. These are superimpressive Barolos.

The 1996 vintage is very successful. The ruby/purple-colored, mineral-dominated 1996 Barolo Sorì Ginestra offers spicy oak in the nose, as well as attractive black cherry fruit intertwined with prunes and toasty oak. With moderate levels of glycerin, full body, high tannin, excellent purity as well as superb richness and extract, this layered wine requires cellaring. Anticipated maturity: 2005–2020. The opaque purple-colored 1996 Barolo Vigna del Gris is dense, with considerable evidence of new oak, powerful, muscular, black currant/cherry flavors, as well as less minerality and earth than in the Sorì Ginestra. It is a huge wine of great intensity. Anticipated maturity: 2004–2020. Although the 1996 Monprà *vino da tavola* (equal parts Barbera and Nebbiolo) is tannic, it is an impressively endowed effort with notes of toasty vanilla, cherries, dried herbs, leather, and spice. Dense, huge, and full-bodied but closed, it should drink well for a decade or more.

The 1995 Barolo Sorì Ginestra reveals cedar and plumlike fruit in the nose but is intensely vegetal and hard and lacks length. The darker ruby-colored 1995 Barolo Vigna del Gris is astringently tannic, extremely compressed, and exceptionally earthy. With airing, cedar, dried herbs, spicy oak, and cherries emerge, but this wine is difficult to evaluate. Anticipated maturity: now–2012.

LUIGI COPPO & FIGLI

1997 Alter Ego	D	87
1999 Barbera d'Asti Camp du Rouss	D	88
1998 Barbera d'Asti Camp du Rouss	D	88

1998 Barbera d'Asti Pomorosso	D	92
1997 Barbera d'Asti Pomorosso	D	90

It is unusual for a Piedmontese winery to accept advice from someone outside the region. The renowned Umbrian oenologist Riccardo Cotarella has been a consultant at Coppo & Figli for several years. As a result, the wines are taking on more ripeness, texture, and complexity. The 1999 Barbera d'Asti Camp du Rouss sees 20% new oak and is bottled unfiltered. Sweet black jammy cherry and earthy aromas emerge from this supple, medium- to full-bodied, lush, sexy Barbera. Enjoy it during its first 3–5 years of life.

1998 was a fine vintage in Piedmont, although it does not appear to have the opulence and flamboyant richness found in the 1997s or the classic structure and long-lived potential of the 1996s. Nevertheless, there is a lot to like, as evidenced by Coppo's 1998 Barbera d'Asti Camp du Rouss. A very good value, this deep ruby-colored wine exhibits toasty new oak, sweet, jammy, strawberry and cherry scents, good spice, medium body, and a round, lush texture. Enjoy it over the next 3–4 years. The stunningly complex 1998 Barbera d'Asti Pomorosso (2,500 cases) was aged in French barrels, of which 80% were new, and also bottled unfiltered. This full-bodied, thick, awesomely concentrated Barbera boasts abundant quantities of black fruit, licorice, tomato skin, and spice box scents. Powerful, rich, and concentrated, it has completely soaked up its exposure to new oak, something the better Barberas seem to do with surprising ease. Drink it over the next 4–5 years. The more ambitiously styled 1997 Barbera d'Asti Pomorosso (13,500 bottles produced) is aged in French oak, of which 80% is new. It exhibits more density and oak in addition to gorgeous, full-bodied, concentrated flavors offering up notes of smoked herbs, ripe cherry jam, plums, and spice. This rich, nicely textured, super-concentrated, moderately acidic Barbera should drink well for a decade. Coppo's proprietary red, Alter Ego, is a blend of 65% Cabernet Sauvignon, 30% Barbera, and 5% Freisa. The 1997 Alter Ego possesses red currant and cherry fruit, toasty new oak, medium body, fine ripeness, and a moderately concentrated finish. Although very good, it is not up to the quality of the two Barberas.

CORDERO DI MONTEZEMOLO

1996 Barolo	D	(90–92)
1995 Barolo	D	86
1998 Barolo Bricco Gattera	E	(87–88)
1997 Barolo Bricco Gattera	E	90+?
1998 Barolo Monfalletto	E	(87–88)
1997 Barolo Monfalletto	E	90
1996 Barolo Monfalletto	E	(91–93)
1995 Barolo Monfalletto	E	88
1998 Barolo Vigna Enrico VI	E	?
1997 Barolo Vigna Enrico VI	E	91+

I had a slight preference for this La Morra producer's 1997s over its 1998s. While the latter are attractive wines, at the prices fetched these days by top Barolos, there are more reasonably priced alternatives. The 1996s and 1995s are also fine successes. The wines of this estate are aged in oak. The Barolo Vigna Enrico VI sees 50% new *barriques* rather than the 100% for the Bricco Gattera and 33% for the Monfalletto.

The medium- to full-bodied 1998 Barolo Monfalletto exhibits scents of earth, leather, cherries, and licorice in a nicely textured, expansive style. With elegance as well as harmony, it can be drunk now and over the next 12–15 years. The dark ruby/garnet-colored 1998 Barolo Bricco Gattera is a midweight, soft, finesse-styled effort displaying some influence of *barriques*. It offers good richness on the attack but narrows in the mouth. I would not be surprised to see it close down to reveal more tannin and less early appeal than the Monfalletto (which may be due to the percentage of *barriques* utilized). Anticipated maturity: 2003–2015. I was perplexed by the closed, lean, austere 1998 Barolo Vigna Enrico VI. This *cuvée* can be a blockbuster, but the 1998 was leathery, compressed, and spartan. Judgment reserved until this wine can be retasted. Anticipated maturity: 2005–2015?

Cordero's 1997 Barolo Monfalletto is a soft, structured offering with muscular, earthy, licorice, and black cherry aromas as well as flavors. With airing, notes of chocolate, truffles, meat, and pepper emerge. Muscular and rustic but substantial and rich on the palate, it requires 1–2 years of cellaring. Anticipated maturity: 2004–2016. The dark ruby/purple-colored 1997 Barolo Bricco Gattera possesses good structure, huge tannin, and a long, powerful, rustic, intense finish. It is a difficult wine to evaluate being huge in the mouth, and the rustic, dry, astringent tannin could be troublesome with aging. It has the potential depth to be outstanding, but is the necessary balance present? Anticipated maturity: 2006–2020. The 1997 Barolo Vigna Enrico VI is the most complex and intense of this trio. The wine's dense ruby/purple color is followed by classic aromas of road tar, rose petals, leather, cedar, and black fruits. Full-bodied, dense, chewy, and powerful, with good underlying acidity as well as sweeter tannin than the Bricco Gattera, this classic should age well for two decades. Anticipated maturity: 2006–2020.

The greatness of the 1996 vintage is obvious in the saturated ruby/purple colors of Codero's wines. The knockout 1996 Barolo will require patience. It possesses a black/ruby/purple color as well as superrich blackberry and cherry flavors combined with licorice, fennel, and subtle new-*barrique* aromas. Long and dense, with mouth-searing tannin, it will be at its finest between 2007–2020. The 1996 Barolo Monfalletto reveals more mineral and new saddle leather scents in addition to black raspberries, cherries, tar, and rose petals. Extremely full-bodied, with new oak coming through in the flavors, this powerful, multidimensional, sensational Barolo should offer thrilling drinking after 4–5 years of cellaring. Anticipated maturity: 2008–2025.

The dark ruby-colored, evolved 1995 Barolo exhibits the telltale rose petal and melted road tar fragrance, along with sweet black fruit notes. Round, medium-bodied, and delicious, it can be enjoyed over the next 3–4 years. The classic 1995 Barolo Monfalletto is an old-style *vin de garde*. It reveals a dark ruby/garnet color, and an earthy nose of truffles, black cherries, tar, and dried herbs. Rich and full-bodied, with excellent concentration, it should keep for 12 years. It will be uncommonly long-lived for a 1995.

CORINO

1997 Barolo	D	89
1996 Barolo	D	87
1995 Barolo	D	88
1998 Barolo Arborina	E	92
1997 Barolo Arborina	E	90
1996 Barolo Arborina	E	(88–92)
1995 Barolo Arborina	E	90
1998 Barolo Vigna Giachini	E	91
1997 Barolo Vigna Giachini	E	94
1996 Barolo Vigna Giachini	E	90
1995 Barolo Vigna Giachini	E	89
1998 Barolo Giachini Vecchie Vigne	E	95+
1997 Barolo Giachini Vecchie Vigne	E	95
1998 Barolo Vigneto Rocche	E	90
1997 Barolo Vigneto Rocche	E	91
1996 Barolo Vigneto Rocche	E	(89–92)
1995 Barolo Vigneto Rocche	E	90

Corino is one of the increasing number of Piedmontese producers utilizing rotary fermenters. With respect to wood cooperage, no new oak is utilized for the generic Barolo, and approximately 40% new-oak casks are employed for the single-vineyard wines. 1997 marks the debut vintage for a limited-production, old-vine (40–65-year-old Nebbiolo) *cuvée* from the Giachini vineyard, the Vecchie Vigne, which emerges from a tiny parcel that sits adjacent and to the east of the famed Rocche cru. The estate also produces a Barolo Vigneto Rocche that comes from a larger cru west of Giachini. Corino's offerings tend to be velvety and forward, even in the classic vintages, so readers can imagine the decadent level of richness they reach in the exotic years. Those looking for up-front, sexy Barolos made with a Pomerol-like lushness should check out those from this La Morra producer. Little cellaring is necessary before purchasers can enjoy the immense pleasures provided by Corino's wines.

The 1998 Barolo Arborina is a sexy, in-your-face, dark ruby/garnet-colored offering with a big, sweet perfume of soy, nori (the seaweed wrapped around sushi), ripe black cherry fruit, and smoky oak. Rich, full, fat, opulent, and decadent, it is meant to be drunk now and over the next 8 years. The more structured and delineated 1998 Barolo Vigna Giachini exhibits a dark ruby color in addition to aromas of earth, coffee, black cherries, and smoke. Full-bodied, ripe, moderately tannic, and long, it will drink well for 12–15 years. The beautifully balanced, seamless, dark ruby/garnet-colored 1998 Barolo Vigneto Rocche possesses fine elegance, a terrific texture, superb purity, light to moderate tannin, low acidity, and total integration of acidity, tannin, and wood. Drink it over the next 10 years. The blockbuster 1998 Barolo Giachini Vecchie Vigne is an awesome follow-up to the spectacular 1997. This dark ruby/garnet-colored, expressive 1998 boasts a provocative bouquet of roasted espresso, chocolate, black cherry liqueur, soy, earth, herbs, leather, and cherry cough syrup. Powerful, unctuously textured flavors cascade over the palate, revealing no hard edges. It is a wine of great purity and intensity, as well as an awesome finish. This is truly spectacular Barolo. Anticipated maturity: now–2012.

The 1997 Barolo exhibits a plum/garnet color with a pink rim. Scents of black tea, cherry liqueur, and sandalwood are followed by an opulent, lush, fleshy wine with copious spice, glycerin, and alcohol as well as low acidity. It is a voluptuous, disarming Barolo to enjoy over the next 6–7 years.

As for the 1997 single-vineyard crus, the dark plum/garnet-colored 1997 Barolo Vigne Giachini offers a luxurious bouquet of black fruits, espresso, roasted herbs, and cherry liqueur. Full-bodied and lush, with layers of glycerin, multidimensional flavors, and great persistence on the palate, this is a fabulously concentrated, compelling offering to drink now and over the next 15 years. The explosive 1997 Barolo Giachini Vecchie Vigne is similarly styled, with additional levels of glycerin and flavor. The plum/garnet color is accompanied by an awesomely layered texture, great purity, abundant quantities of fruit, and complex aromatics as well as flavors. It should drink well over the next 12–15 years. Corino's 1997 Barolo Vigneto Rocche exhibits a deep garnet color in addition to a hedonistic, explosive nose of soy, resin, black cherry liqueur, balsa wood, leather, olives, and roasted meats. Stunningly concentrated, fleshy, and flamboyant, with huge glycerin levels in its low-acid, full-bodied personality, it is impossible to resist yet promises to age for 12–15 years. From a tiny yet renowned hillside vineyard, the 1997 Barolo Arborina displays the most evolved garnet color with considerable amber at the edge. Spice box, licorice, cedar wood, cherries, currants, rose petals, and framboise aromas jump from the glass of this textured, full-bodied, fat, lush wine. This is a sexy, hedonistic, seamless, herb-tinged Barolo for drinking over the next decade.

The 1996s, true to the vintage character, possess more color saturation, tannin, structure, and depth than the 1995s, but they are less evolved. The 1996 Barolo is supple and velvety but not very complex aromatically. Perhaps additional nuances will emerge with further bottle age. Spicy, ripe, and attractive, it can be consumed now and over the next 5–6 years. The dark ruby-colored 1996 Barolo Vigna Giachini offers a big, smoky, Asian spice, seaweed, and cherry liqueur–scented nose. Medium- to full-bodied, lush, and sexy, with some tannin, this delicious wine should be at its finest before 2012. The 1996 Barolo Arborina is a dense, severe, muscular effort with intriguing peppery, seaweedlike scents (or is it *garrigue?*) in the bouquet as well as rich, concentrated, black cherry fruit with subtle oak in the background. This powerful, structured, macho-styled Barolo should be drunk before 2015. The 1996 Barolo Vigneto Rocche also reveals a dried Provençal herb, peppery, smoky character reminiscent of some wines from southern France. The wine has plenty of tannin and sweet black cherry fruit intermixed with charcoal scents. Medium- to full-bodied, moderately tannic, and complex, it will be at its best before 2012.

The surprisingly evolved 1995 Barolo displays a ruby/garnet color with amber at the edge. It offers abundant black cherries in the perfumed, woodsy aromatics. Succulent, round, and gentle, this is a delicious Barolo to enjoy over the next 1–2 years. Corino's 1995 single-vineyard offerings are complex, aromatic, developed, and forward wines. The medium ruby-colored 1995 Barolo Vigna Giachini exhibits a knockout nose of sweet cinnamon, allspice, coffee, black fruits, and toast. An expansive, ripe, medium- to full-bodied, seductive effort, it is not huge but complex and disarming. Consume it over the next 2–3 years. The 1995 Barolo Arborina reveals a more deeply saturated ruby color in addition to an attractive nose of sweet black cherry liqueur, dried herbs, tobacco, and cedar scents. Lush and sexy, with medium to full body, an alluring texture, low acidity, and an evolved, complex style, it can be savored over the next 3–4 years. The 1995 Barolo Vigneto Rocche possesses a dark ruby color, medium to full body, and spicy roasted herb, tobacco, and cherry fruit aromas. As the wine sits in the glass, more of Nebbiolo's road tar and rose petal nuances emerge. Deep and rich, this outstanding 1995 can be drunk over the next 5–6 years.

MATTEO CORREGGIA

1998 Barbera d'Alba Bricco Marun	C	90
1998 Nebbiolo d'Alba La Val dei Preti	C	88
1998 Roero Ròche d'Ampsej	C	90
1997 Roero Ròche d'Ampsej	C	91

Correggia, who died in late 2001, was undoubtedly a star of Piedmont's up-and-coming Roero area. Hillside vineyards, low yields, and meticulous attention to detail resulted in outstanding wines. The 1998 Nebbiolo d'Alba La Val dei Preti offers gorgeous aromas of cherries, tobacco, and spice box, a sweet entry on the palate, abundant glycerin, medium to full body, and a silky finish. It should drink well for 2–3 years. Readers looking for a blockbuster, thick, juicy, fruit-dominated red should check out Correggia's 1998 Barbera d'Alba Bricco Marun. Its black/purple color is followed by aromas of sweet fruit (cherries and blackberries), smoke, new oak, and a lush, succulent finish. Drink it over the next 4–5 years for its exuberance and intensity. Both the 1997 and 1998 Roero Ròche d'Ampsej are outstanding examples of 100% old-vine (50–60 years) Nebbiolo. The 1997 exhibits more succulence, glycerin, and fat, but both are deeply concentrated, dense efforts revealing oodles of black cherry fruit, perfumed personalities, sweet tannin, and medium to full body. The 1998 is more elegant and symmetrical, whereas the 1997 is more exotic and thick. While they are impossible to resist, both should drink well for a decade.

GIUSEPPE CORTESE

1998 Barbaresco Rabajà	D	89
1997 Barbaresco Rabajà	D	92
1996 Barbaresco Rabajà	D	86
1995 Barbaresco Rabajà	D	76

These traditionally made Piedmontese Barbarescos are aged completely in old *foudres*. This delicious, sexy, open-knit 1998 Barbaresco Rabajà reveals a medium ruby color with amber already appearing at the edge. Stunning aromatics of melted licorice, cherry jam, spice box, balsam wood, and herbs leap from the glass of this fleshy, medium- to full-bodied, ripe offering. Drink this seductive 1998 over the next 4–5 years. The 1997 Rabajà is the finest Cortese Barbaresco I have tasted in more than a decade. This wine, which exhibits notes of root vegetables, raspberry and cherry jam, cedar and balsa wood, smoke, and minerals, is full-bodied, powerful yet elegant, supple-textured, and surprisingly deep as well as delineated. Drink this hedonistic as well as intellectually satisfying Barbaresco over the next 10 years. The 1996 Barbaresco Rabajà displays a saturated ruby color and a spicy, tobacco, licorice, and cherry-scented nose. A traditionally styled Barbaresco, with dry tannin, medium body, and very good extract, it should keep for 10 years. Cortese's 1995 Barbaresco Rabajà is disappointing, even in this irregular vintage. Spicy tobacco and dried tomato scents dominate the nose. The wine is medium-bodied, compressed, austere, and lean, with hard tannin in the finish. It will become increasingly attenuated as it ages. Drink it up.

GIANPAOLO DESTEFANIS

2000 Dolcetto d'Alba	C	86
1999 Dolcetto d'Alba	C	87
2000 Dolcetto d'Alba Vigna Monia Bassa	C	89
1999 Dolcetto d'Alba Vigna Monia Bassa	C	90
1998 Dolcetto d'Alba Vigna Monia Bassa	C	90

A new discovery for me, this estate produces only Dolcetto and Barbera, never filters, and, based on these five efforts, makes extremely ripe, explosively fruity wines. Both 1999s possess denser, riper fruit than their 2000 counterparts, with gobs of berries, a touch of chocolate, and medium- to full-bodied personalities. The 1999 Dolcetto d'Alba Vigna Monia Bassa in particular fills the mouth with gorgeous fruit. Just a step behind are the 2000s, which are tangier but loaded with purity, ripeness, and character. Dolcetto remains a great bargain in the wine world, but it must be consumed during its first 2–4 years of life, before the fruit fades. A huge fruit bomb, the tank-fermented and -aged 1998 Dolcetto is produced from 50–60-year-old vines. It offers explosive blackberry and cherry fruit with a hint of violets in the background. As the wine sat in the glass, aromas of roasted coffee also emerged. While it may not get any better, it will drink well for 2–3 years.

LUIGI EINAUDI

1999 Barbera d'Alba	C	89
1998 Barbera d'Alba	C	87
1998 Barolo	D	(90–92)
1997 Barolo	D	90
1996 Barolo	D	90
1995 Barolo	D	86
1998 Barolo Cannubi	E	(91–94)
1997 Barolo Cannubi	E	90+
1996 Barolo Cannubi	E	92+
1995 Barolo Cannubi	E	89+?
1998 Barolo Costa Grimaldi	E	(92–93)
1997 Barolo Costa Grimaldi	E	92
1996 Barolo Costa Grimaldi	E	90+
1995 Barolo Costa Grimaldi	E	87+
1999 Dolcetto d'Alba I Filari	C	90
1998 Dolcetto d'Alba I Filari	C	90
1999 Dolcetto d'Alba Vigna Tecc	C	89
1998 Langhe Rosso	D	90

1997 Langhe Rosso	D	88
1996 Langhe Rosso	D	90

This traditional producer has an excellent portfolio and, at the top level, some undeniably exciting wines. It produces three *cuvées* of Barolo and a proprietary blend composed of equal parts Cabernet Sauvignon, Merlot, Barbera, and Nebbiolo, aged 18 months in French oak. The 1998s appear to be just as impressive as the stunning 1997s. Even in this latter vintage, characterized by low acidity, overripe fruit, and an over-the-top style, Einaudi produced classic, backward, chewy, blockbuster Barolos that will require nearly as much cellaring as its 1996s. Though good, the 1995s are less successful than the other vintages reviewed here. The early-released 1999s are delicious wines, to be drunk within the next several years.

The impressive 1999 Dolcetto d'Alba Vigna Tecc exhibits a saturated dense purple color as well as an uncomplicated yet explosive bouquet of black fruits, excellent texture, big, chewy, thick flavors, abundant glycerin, and good intensity. Tasters should not expect a great deal of nuance now or in the future, but for a robust, large-scaled, well-balanced wine to gulp down with antipasto or steak, this hits all the sweet spots. Drink it over the next 3 years. Sadly, there are only 100 cases of the amazing, super-concentrated, old-vine *cuvée* of 1999 Dolcetto d'Alba I Filari. It boasts dazzling levels of berry fruit, full body, incredible length, and astonishing concentration, extract, and overall balance. There is not a hard edge to be found in this succulent, prodigious Dolcetto. Although it will last for a decade, it will not get any better, so enjoy its blast of fruit and uncomplicated joys over the next 4 years. New oak makes an appearance in the 1999 Barbera d'Alba, a dense, chewy, modern-styled offering with plenty of smoky toasty scents intermixed with strawberry and cherry jam. Medium- to full-bodied and lush, it is best consumed during its exuberant youth . . . over the next 4 years.

At 14.5% alcohol, the sensational 1998 Dolcetto I Filari is no shy wine. A huge, massive, opaque purple Dolcetto, it boasts super-concentrated, raisiny fruit, a massive mid-section, and no hard edges. Drink this mouth-filling, teeth-staining effort over the next 5 years, although I suspect it will last much longer. The 1998 Barbera d'Alba reveals a surprisingly soft personality for this traditional producer. The deep ruby color is accompanied by round, sweet cherry/strawberry fruit flavors, good fat in the mid-section, and a clean, pure finish. Drink it over the next 3–4 years. More complex but equally supple is the 1998 Langhe Rosso. This full-bodied 1998 offers complex notes of tobacco, black currants, and toast. Glycerin and extract coat the palate in this deep, chewy offering that borders on being internationally styled yet retains plenty of Piedmontese typicity. Drink it over the next 4–5 years, although I suspect it will last longer. The 1998 Barolo exhibits a saturated plum/ruby color as well as a classic Nebbiolo perfume of melted road tar, rose petals, tobacco, and sweet cherry jam. Dense, moderately tannic, and balanced, it possesses great fruit on the attack, mid-palate, and finish. Compared to the 1997, the 1998 appears less powerful but just as concentrated, with sweeter tannin and more fragrance. Anticipated maturity: 2004–2018. The dark-colored, well-structured, elegant 1998 Barolo Costa Grimaldi offers purity and harmony allied with power, density, and extract. While relatively seamless for such a young Einaudi Barolo, there is plenty of tannin underneath the glycerin and fruit. I suspect it is only a matter of time before the tannin asserts itself and closes the wine down. Rich and impressive, with no hard edges, it is built for the long haul. Anticipated maturity: 2004–2022. The enormously concentrated, dense ruby-colored 1998 Barolo Cannubi possesses stunningly concentrated black cherry fruit intermixed with truffles, graphite, asphalt, and smoke. Extremely full-bodied, superpowerful, and palate-staining in its richness and dense flavors, it is the most obviously tannic offering of this trio, as well as the most concentrated. It is only for those with patience. Anticipated maturity: 2006–2025.

All three of Einaudi's 1997 Barolos are stunning efforts from this freakish but compelling vintage. The dense ruby-colored 1997 Barolo exhibits a complex bouquet of rose petals, melted tar, cherry liqueur, and Parmesan cheese. Full-bodied, ripe, dense, and chewy, with adequate acidity, ripe, mature tannin, and a 30–40-second finish, this big, old-style, robust Barolo will continue to develop for 10–12 years. The 1997 Barolo Costa Grimaldi exhibits a more saturated dense ruby/purple color as well as aromas of sweet black cherries and plums, licorice, smoke, and minerals. Full-bodied, with impressive fruit, richness, extract, mouth-filling levels of ripe, chewy tannin, and a huge, sweet, concentrated, explosive finish, this 1997 is just beginning to develop secondary nuances. It should age effortlessly for two decades. The most controversial of this trio, the gigantic, austere, tannic 1997 Barolo Cannubi is more raisiny, tasting like brandy-macerated juice from Amarone-styled Nebbiolo grapes. Extremely full-bodied, with high tannin, deep, chewy, formidable flavors, and a backward, chunky personality, this wine could develop spectacularly—if everything goes right. Anticipated maturity: 2004–2025. The 1997 Langhe Rosso is a full-bodied effort with huge levels of fruit and extract, but not much complexity. The new oak is largely hidden by the wine's wealth of jammy red and black fruits. If more complexity emerges, look for the score to rise a few points, but for now, it is a big, thick, monolithic fruit bomb made in an international style. It should drink well for 10 years.

I am not generally a fan of Piedmontese proprietary reds, but the terrific raw materials available in the 1996 vintage have given the 1996 Langhe Rosso a multidimensional, slightly international style with exhilarating levels of black cherry and cassis fruit, spicy new oak, dried herbs, and a long, dense, velvety-textured finish. Luscious and complex, it is ideal for drinking now and over the next 10 years. The backward 1996 Barolo offers a classic bouquet of licorice, tar, and black cherries. It is extremely powerful, large-scaled and full-bodied yet austere, seriously endowed, and aggressively tannic. Cellaring should smooth it out, but it is an old-style powerhouse. Anticipated maturity: 2004–2015. I have no reservation about the outstanding scores given both the 1996 Barolo Costa Grimaldi and 1996 Barolo Cannubi. Both are terrific, old-style, impressively endowed efforts. The saturated ruby-colored 1996 Barolo Costa Grimaldi is a full-bodied, husky, hefty wine with gorgeous aromas of roasted nuts, cherries, dried herbs, licorice, and flowers. This ripe, rich, huge Barolo will require 4–5 years of cellaring. Anticipated maturity: 2008–2020. The opaque ruby/purple-colored 1996 Barolo Cannubi is a powerfully built, uncompromising wine with huge extract, brawny earthy, cherry, licorice, and tobacco flavors, and high levels of tannin. It is a traditionally made Barolo that requires 5–6 years of cellaring. Everything is present for future brilliance, but patience will be essential. Anticipated maturity: 2010–2025.

The medium garnet/ruby-colored 1995 Barolo exhibits a soft, elegant style, as well as herb-tinged berry fruit meshed with foresty, truffle, and dried herb/smoky notes. Round and moderately endowed, it should be consumed over the next 4–5 years. The complex 1995 Barolo Costa Grimaldi is a stylish, graceful, easy to understand and drink wine from this open-knit vintage. Medium-bodied, with smoked herb, cherry, earth, and cedar aromas, it possesses sweet fruit, and a spicy, moderately tannic, lovely finish. Anticipated maturity: now–2012. The dark ruby/garnet-colored 1995 Barolo Cannubi offers aromas of cedar, tobacco, new saddle leather, cherries, and melted road tar. In the mouth, the tannin is astringent and the wine austere. With airing, hints of sweet cherry jam, fennel, and earth emerge. Impressive, but does it possess the fat and concentration to support its structure? Anticipated maturity: now–2014.

ALESSANDRO E GIAN NATALE FANTINO

1998	Barolo Vigna dei Dardi	D	(88–90)
1997	Barolo Vigna dei Dardi	D	88

Fantino appears to be doing a fine job making wines in the modern style. It produces elegant, flavorful, midweight wines that reveal a judicious use of *barriques*.

The 1998 Barolo Vigna dei Dardi is a soft, sexy, dark ruby/purple-colored, well-textured, impressively rich effort offering copious quantities of sweet black cherry fruit mixed with toasty new oak. Clean, ripe, and concentrated, with both depth and personality, it will drink well for a decade. The internationally styled 1997 Barolo Vigna dei Dardi possesses aromas and flavors of ripe cherries and spicy new oak, a creamy texture, and enough Nebbiolo character to provide spice, licorice, leather, and cherry fruit. Drink it over the next 5–6 years.

STEFANO FARINA

1997 Barbaresco	D	89
1996 Barbaresco	D	89
1995 Barbaresco	D	87
1997 Barolo	D	91
1996 Barolo	D	90
1995 Barolo	D	89

While unfamiliar with this La Morra producer, I was impressed by what he has achieved with these six wines. They are well balanced, with nicely integrated acidity, alcohol, and tannin. As a general rule, the Barolos offer more complex aromas and intense, rich, chewy flavors. If new oak was utilized, it has been better integrated than with the Barbarescos.

The 1997 Barbaresco exhibits an opaque purple color, and overripe, cherry, blackberry, smoky, oaky aromas. The wine is fleshy, with excellent richness and a low-acid, succulently textured finish. Anticipated maturity: now–2010. The most gigantic wine of this series is the 1997 Barolo. It displays telltale aromas of roasted herbs, jammy cherries and blackberries, spice, and tar. Thick and viscous, with outstanding ripeness, the vintage's low acid, fleshy/accessible personality, and a heady, high alcohol finish, it will become more civilized as it ages. Anticipated maturity: now–2016.

The opaque purple 1996 Barbaresco would have merited an outstanding score were it not for its slight lack of complexity. There is spicy new oak intertwined with black fruits in this modern-styled effort, as well as good flesh, texture, and purity. The acidity provides vibrancy, and buttresses the wine's weightiness. Drink it over the next 8 years. The superb 1996 Barolo exhibits purple nuances in its plum/ruby color. It possesses an opulent texture, superrichness, copious sweet red fruits and glycerin in the mid-palate, and a long, nicely nuanced, layered finish. Still youthful but impressively endowed, it will be at its peak before 2014.

The saturated ruby/purple 1995 Barbaresco offers a sweet, jammy nose of herb-tinged cherry liqueur intermixed with a touch of toasty new oak. The wine is evolved, fleshy, round, and made with a hedonist's mentality. Drink it over the next 3 years. The evolved plum/ruby-colored 1995 Barolo offers a sweet, fragrant bouquet of roses, black and red fruits, spice, and tar. It is a classic Barolo with medium to full body, fine depth, and an intriguing earthiness in the smooth finish. Anticipated maturity: now–2012.

GIACOMO FENOCCHIO

1997 Barolo Bussia	D	86
1996 Barolo Bussia	D	(85–87)
1995 Barolo Bussia	D	84
1997 Barolo Villero	D	83
1996 Barolo Villero	D	(85–87)
1995 Barolo Villero	D	85

These traditionally made, old-style Barolos are aged in big old Slovenian oak casks. Fenocchio, whose cellars are in Monforte d'Alba, has turned out a competent but largely uninspiring group of wines from 1995 and 1996. His 1997s are relatively light for the vintage.

Fenocchio's 1997 Barolo Bussia exhibits a dark ruby color with amber at the edge. Aromas of minerals, smoke, coffee, raspberries, and earth are present in this medium-bodied, slightly acidic offering. Anticipated maturity: 2003–2016. Even lighter as well as more austere, the 1997 Barolo Villero is a surprisingly mediocre effort for the vintage. It displays plenty of earthiness as well as excessive tannin. Avoid it.

The 1996 Barolo Bussia displays a more saturated color with amber at the edge. It is an elegant, lighter-styled effort with attractive floral/berry fruit combined with herbs, leather, and spice. It should be consumed during the next 2–3 years.

The 1996 Barolo Villero reveals textbook rose petal, melted tar, and cherry fruit flavors, but not much depth or length. I was surprised by its softness as well as by its lack of intensity, although the wine is good to very good. It should be drunk over the next 2 years.

The evolved 1995 Barolo Bussia exhibits an earthy, dried herb, smoky, *garrigue*-scented nose. Drink this soft Barolo over the next 1–2 years. The 1995 Barolo Villero is reminiscent of its 1996 counterpart with its classic aromas of rose petal, melted tar, and cherry fruit flavors. Just as its older sibling, it lacks depth and length but is more structured and intense than the 1996. Drink it over the next 2–3 years.

F.LLI FERRERO

1998	Barolo Manzoni	D	(88–90)
1997	Barolo Manzoni	D	90
1996	Barolo Manzoni	D	(88–90)
1995	Barolo Manzoni	D	86

All four wines from this sleeper La Morra producer are at least very good, with the 1996, 1997, and 1998 potentially outstanding.

Ferrero's excellent dark ruby-colored 1998 Barolo Manzoni reveals sweet, plum, cherry, licorice, espresso, and cedary aromas as well as flavors, supple tannin, medium to full body, and a velvety, layered finish. The overall impression is of sweet fruit presented in a well-endowed format with no hard edges. It should drink well for 10 years although it could prove to be even longer-lived given its impeccable balance. The dark plum/purple-colored 1997 Barolo Manzoni offers a rich, complex perfume of cedar, espresso, licorice, raspberry, and cherry fruit. This full-bodied, concentrated, outstanding Barolo is long, purely made, and impeccably balanced. Anticipated maturity: now–2016. The 1996 Barolo Manzoni is powerful, full-bodied, tannic, and intense. This traditionally made offering reveals earthy, leather, and dried herb–scented cherry fruit in both its bouquet and flavors, as well as dusty, astringent tannin in the finish, suggesting that a couple more years of cellaring is recommended. Anticipated maturity: 2004–2013. Lighter-bodied and less intense than the 1996, the dark ruby-colored 1995 Barolo Manzoni offers up a textbook nose of tar, roses, cherry fruit, and spice. The attack is sweet and the wine medium-bodied, cleanly made, and soft. It lacks concentration and length but will provide attractive drinking over the next 1–2 years.

VIRGINIA FERRERO

1998	Barolo San Rocco	D	(86–87)
1997	Barolo San Rocco	D	86

I have fond memories of Ferrero's Barolos from the 1960s, but recent vintages have possessed less stuffing as well as limited longevity.

A supple, elegantly styled effort without the stuffing of the vintage's most prominent wines, the evolved, medium ruby/garnet-colored 1998 Barolo San Rocco offers notes of balsa wood, smoke, dried herbs, tobacco, and cherries. Soft and moderately endowed, it is best drunk during its first decade of life. Although the 1997 Barolo San Rocco exhibits an evolved medium garnet color with amber at the edge, it has excellent aromatics of caramel, toffee, cherries, licorice, and tobacco. Soft and supple on the entry, with medium body, it does not display the finish expected from a top producer. Drink it over the next 5–6 years.

FRANCO FIORINA

1997 Barbaresco	D	(87–88)
1997 Barolo	D	(88–91)

These 1997s from *négociant* Franco Fiorina are the most impressive I have tasted. The dense ruby-colored 1997 Barbaresco exhibits copious quantities of licorice, cedar, and spice box aromas, medium to full body, a silky texture, and a long finish. It should drink well for 4–5 years. The powerful, super-concentrated, rich, chocolaty, dense, massive 1997 Barolo offers notes of charcoal, hickory smoke, licorice, leather, and cedar. What a blockbuster!

FONTANABIANCA

1998 Barbaresco Sorì Burdin	D	(88–89)
1997 Barbaresco Sorì Burdin	D	89

A sleeper selection from this Neive producer, Fontanabianca's dark garnet-colored 1998 Barbaresco Sorì Burdin reveals classic Nebbiolo aromas of cherry cough syrup mixed with licorice, asphalt, and dried Provençal herbs. Medium- to full-bodied, dense, supple-textured, and loaded with fruit as well as glycerin, it will drink well for 5–6 years. The well-made 1997 Barbaresco Sorì Burdin exhibits an evolved garnet color as well as spicy, dried herb, licorice, tobacco, and red berry aromas. Drink this medium-bodied effort over the next 3–4 years.

FONTANAFREDDA

1998 Barbaresco Coste Rubin	E	(88–90)
1997 Barbaresco Coste Rubin	E	88
1998 Barolo Vigna Lazzarito	E	(89–91+?)
1997 Barolo Vigna Lazzarito	E	91
1998 Barolo Vigna La Rosa	E	(91–93)
1997 Barolo Vigna La Rosa	E	93+
1998 Barolo di Serralunga	E	(90–93)
1997 Barolo di Serralunga	E	92+

One of the great names of Piedmontese winemaking, this estate has had a history of mixed performances. I began purchasing Fontanafredda's wines in the late 1960s, and have enjoyed several stunning bottles of its 1971 Barolo. In the late 1970s and early 1980s, the wines began an irregular period that continued into the 1990s. However, this magnificent estate appears to have rebounded brilliantly with its 1997s, 1998s, and 1999s . . . super news for aficionados of Piedmontese wines.

The dark ruby/purple-colored, impressively extracted, full-bodied, yet monolithic 1998 Barbaresco Coste Rubin should be outstanding after another 1–2 years of cellaring. Anticipated maturity: 2003–2015. The exquisite, well-balanced, sweet 1998 Barolo di Serralunga displays a Graves-like character in its full-bodied, concentrated style. With abundant tannin in the finish, it will require additional cellaring. Anticipated maturity: 2005–2018. Even more powerful and backward, with a hugely sweet, dense mid-palate, is the fat, voluptuous, yet broodingly backward, superextracted 1998 Barolo Vigna La Rosa. It is one of the vintage's most concentrated as well as longest-lived efforts. Anticipated maturity: 2005–2020. More monolithic and muted is the saturated deep purple 1998 Barolo Vigna Lazzarito. Dense, chewy, full-bodied, and tannic, it does not reveal the complexity, sweetness, or overall style of Fontanafredda's other Barolo offerings. Although impressively endowed, this ruggedly muscular 1998 needs 4–5 years of cellaring. Anticipated maturity: 2006–2018.

The dark ruby-colored 1997 Barbaresco Coste Rubin offers an intriguing perfume of roasted peanuts, vanilla, cherries, tar, and spice box. The most internationally styled of Fontanafredda's 1997s, it possesses excellent fruit and a medium- to full-bodied personality. It should drink well for 10 years. The 1997 Barolo di Serralunga exhibits a saturated purple/ garnet color in addition to a stunning bouquet of underbrush, kirsch, lead pencil, licorice, and toasty new oak. Full-bodied and exotic (but not over the top), this is a structured, muscular, concentrated Barolo that will benefit from 2–3 years of cellaring and keep for 2–3 decades. It is an impressive, classic effort that threads the needle between the traditional and modern styles. The opaque plum-colored 1997 Barolo Vigna La Rosa reveals the influence of toasty new oak in its fabulously pure, concentrated nose, which represents the essence of melted licorice, blackberries, and assorted black fruits. As the wine sits in the glass, scents of toast, smoke, leather, tar, and fennel emerge. Full-bodied, massively concentrated, powerful, and dense, it requires 3–5 years of cellaring. Anticipated maturity: 2005–2022. Lastly, the opaque plum/garnet 1997 Barolo Vigna Lazzarito possesses full-bodied notes of dried herbs, leather, tar, black fruits, and truffles presented in a powerful, monolithic style. There is a lot going on in this marvelously endowed, moderately tannic Barolo, but it is not as potentially complex or nuanced as the Serralunga or La Rosa. Nevertheless, it is an outstanding effort and may just have been more muted the day I tasted it. Anticipated maturity: 2003–2016.

GIANNI GAGLIARDO

1997	Barolo Preve	D	(87–89)
1996	Barolo Preve	D	(88–89)

These are two excellent offerings from Gagliardo. The 1996 Barolo Preve is a full-bodied, classically textured and flavored wine with savory cedar, cigar box, and black cherries intertwined with melted road tar. Rich, fleshy, and purely made, it should drink well for 10–12 years. The 1997 Barolo Preve is a fatter, more layered wine with low acidity and powerful cherry liqueur, spice box, fruitcake as well as dried herb aromas and flavors. There is good purity in addition to a rich, fleshy mouth feel. Anticipated maturity: now–2018.

ANGELO GAJA

1998	Barbaresco	EEE	91
1997	Barbaresco	EEE	94
1996	Barbaresco	EE	91
1995	Barbaresco	EE	90
1995	Barbaresco Costa Russi	EEE	90
1995	Barbaresco Sorì San Lorenzo	EEE	91+
1995	Barbaresco Sorì Tildin	EEE	91+
1997	Cabernet Sauvignon Darmagi	EEE	90+
1996	Cabernet Sauvignon Darmagi	EEE	90
1995	Cabernet Sauvignon Darmagi	EEE	88
1998	Conteisa	EEE	92
1997	Conteisa	EEE	98
1996	Conteisa	EEE	95+
1998	Costa Russi	EEE	92
1997	Costa Russi	EEE	96
1996	Costa Russi	EEE	93
1998	Sorì San Lorenzo	EEE	96
1997	Sorì San Lorenzo	EEE	98
1996	Sorì San Lorenzo	EEE	96
1998	Sorì Tildin	EEE	95
1997	Sorì Tildin	EEE	99+
1996	Sorì Tildin	EEE	96+
1998	Langhe Sperss	EEE	94
1997	Langhe Sperss	EEE	99
1996	Langhe Sperss	EEE	(94–96)

It may seem cavalier if not ridiculous to suggest that Angelo Gaja may have produced some of the finest wines in his renowned career over the last vintages, but certainly the 1995s, 1996s, 1997s, and 1998s are astonishing efforts. Readers should note that beginning in 1996, Gaja dropped the appellation names of Barbaresco and Barolo from his single-vineyard wines. At this stage, the 1997s look to be the finest wines he has ever made. My enthusiasm is obviously due in part to the stylistic preference I have for more opulently textured wines with lower acidity and thus a broader window of drinkability. However, the 1998s nearly rival the superexotic, concentrated 1997s and monumental 1996s. Stylistically, the latter vintages are more classic and elegant than the exaggerated but compelling 1997s, but they do not lack intensity. Gaja's wines generally see 40–45% new oak (50% French and 50% from Austria as well as Poland) and spend 24 months in wood, half of that time in small barrels and half in larger wood uprights.

A persuasive argument can be made that Angelo Gaja has long been Piedmont's spiritual and qualitative leader. His recent controversial move to drop the Barbaresco and Barolo appellations from his three Barbaresco crus and two Barolo crus has had an unsettling impact on the local cognoscenti. His rationale for this move is that he wants to pick his Nebbiolo superripe (to obtain what the French call *sur-maturité*) and then blend in some higher-acid Barbera (in 1997, 1998, and 1999, approximately 5% Barbera was used in the Barbaresco crus, 6% in Sperss, and 8% in Conteisa). Gaja believes this gives the wines more freshness as well as focus. Whatever his rationalizations, it seems to me that he would not make this decision unless it improved the wines. And in any case, the results are spectacular.

The dark ruby/purple-colored, supple-textured 1998 Costa Russi possesses sweet, jammy raspberry and cherry fruit, medium to full body, gorgeous glycerin, low acidity, and a lightly tannic finish. Although large-sized, it has good finesse as well as beautifully pure fruit. Anticipated maturity: 2003–2020. More chocolate, coffee, smoke, licorice, and tobacco characteristics are found in the complex, deep purple 1998 Sorì Tildin. Surprisingly seductive for such a young wine, it exhibits abundant aromatic fireworks, fabulous fruit concentration, a layered opulence, more intensity, glycerin, and depth than the Costa Russi, and a spectacularly long finish. Anticipated maturity: now–2025. The multifaceted 1998 Sorì San Lorenzo offers up notes of lead pencil, smoke, tobacco, tar, rose petals, black fruits, and espresso. Already incredibly expressive, soft, sexy, and voluptuous, jammy fruits infused with toasty oak cascade over the palate. This easily understood, seamless, pure, classic 1998 should drink well for 20–25 years.

From the Barolo appellation, the 1998 Conteisa displays a distinctive bouquet of black cherry jam mixed with vitamins, smoke, iron, minerals, and spicy oak. In the mouth, earth, truffle, lead pencil, and espresso-infused cherry flavors make an appearance. Deep, rich, and full-bodied, with moderate tannin and power, this impressive offering requires 2–3 years of cellaring and should age well for two decades. More perfumed, with additional richness, the 1998 Sperss reveals a perfume of black fruits, truffles, earth, and spice box. Dense, massive, yet seamless, this beautifully integrated wine possesses low acidity as well as a terrific finish. Although well evolved and delicious for such a youthful Barolo, it will age well for 20–25 years. While the 1998 Barbaresco may not equal the extraordinary 1997, it is a beautiful effort displaying fleshy, oaky, deep black cherry, raspberry, tar, and truffle scents with subtle new oak in the background. Dense, voluptuously textured, and full-bodied, with gorgeous overall symmetry and beautifully integrated tannin, acidity, alcohol, and wood, it will drink well for 15 or more years.

Gaja's 1997 Barbaresco is undoubtedly the finest he has made. An exquisite effort, it boasts a dense ruby/purple color in addition to an extraordinary nose of black cherry liqueur, smoke, licorice, mineral, and floral aromas. The wine is full-bodied, opulent, and loaded with fruit. Despite its precocious nature, there is abundant tannin, and thus 3–4 years of cellaring is required. It should age effortlessly for 25 years. The opaque ruby/purple-colored 1997

Costa Russi displays a striking bouquet of blackberry and cherry fruit intermixed with espresso and wood scents. Typically the most internationally styled Gaja offering, the 1997 comes across as a Nebbiolo on steroids. Full-bodied, gorgeously pure and symmetrical, it should be at its best between now–2025. The awesome 1997 Sorì Tildin is a candidate for perfection. The saturated purple color is followed by a dense, full-bodied wine possessing extraordinary vibrancy for such a heavyweight, muscular Nebbiolo. It offers a supersweet entry, a boatload of glycerin, notes of earth, licorice, cedar, blackberry and cherry liqueur, and a touch of blueberries. Extremely full, gorgeously pure, with a seamless texture, this spectacular 1997 will enjoy three decades of cellaring. Equally profound, the 1997 Sorì San Lorenzo is, as usual, the most elegant, nuanced, and complex Gaja offering. It exhibits a striking perfume of lead pencil, roasted nuts, black fruits, spice box, leather, cedar, and Chinese black tea. Forward yet enormously well constituted and rich, with an ethereal elegance underpinning its personality, the Sorì San Lorenzo displays a classic combination of power and finesse. As this wine sat in the glass, notes of Japanese soy sauce made an appearance. Anticipated maturity: now–2030.

The 1997 Conteisa offers classic aromas of licorice, melted tar, black cherries, wet stones, and tobacco. It is a full-bodied, unctuously textured wine of remarkable density and thickness. The tannin is high but sweet. This brawny offering cuts an immense swath across the palate, but there are hard edges and all the component parts are pure as well as well integrated. There are 15,000 bottles of this spectacular wine. Anticipated maturity: 2003–2030. Another virtually perfect effort is the 1997 Sperss, which represents the essence of truffles, earth, and black cherries in its striking aromatics and multidimensional, opulent, full-bodied palate. The acidity seems low because of the huge glycerin levels and prodigious concentration of fruit, but I suspect it is normal in the scheme of oenological measurement. This profound wine requires 2–3 years of cellaring and should age well for 30–35 years.

The exceptional black/purple 1997 Cabernet Sauvignon Darmagi (3–4% Cabernet Franc was added to the blend) is redolent with abundant quantities of smoky, concentrated fruit as well as tannin. It exhibits the vintage's low-acid, thick, glycerin-imbued character and a layered, full-bodied finish. It should develop nicely for two decades.

One of the great wines of the vintage, the spectacular 1996 Barolo Sperss boasts an opaque ruby/purple color plus enormously ripe black cherries, tar, flowers, and white truffles. Extremely full-bodied, with compelling intensity and purity, this is a large-scaled, massive Barolo with plenty of tannin and 2–3 decades of ageability. Anticipated maturity: 2005–2030.

Angelo Gaja likes his 1996 Barbarescos every bit as much as his 1995s. I tend to think the 1996s are more powerful and concentrated. Perhaps it is just a question of Gaja preferring the finesse and elegance of the 1995s to the structure, muscle, and potential of the more massive 1996s. The 1996 Barbaresco exhibits a dense ruby color as well as a forward nose of cherry liqueur, earth, truffle, mineral, and spicy scents. Rich, full-bodied, and seductive, with its moderate tannin largely concealed by the wine's wealth of fruit and extract, this gorgeously pure offering gets my nod as the finest Barbaresco produced by Gaja since 1990. Anticipated maturity: now–2016.

The dense opaque purple 1996 Sorì San Lorenzo possesses the most complex aromatics, consisting of classic Nebbiolo scents of rose petals, dried herbs, spice box, cedar, and abundant jammy black cherry and berry fruit. It is impressively powerful and muscular, with moderate tannin, a sweet, unctuous texture, and a 40+-second finish. Although the aromatics are stunning, this 1996 remains youthful and backward. Anticipated maturity: 2005–2025. It is hard to argue with those who claim that the finest of these single-vineyard offerings is always the Sorì Tildin. The 1996 Sorì Tildin reveals a more pigmented/saturated ruby/purple color in addition to a tighter nose, with aromas of blackberries, cherry liqueur, smoke, licorice, incense, and spice box. Enormous on the palate, with multiple layers of fruit, soft tannin, huge body, and a knockout finish, this is the most backward and brawniest of the single-vineyard 1996s. Anticipated maturity: 2005–2030. Lastly, the 1996 Costa Russi reminds me of how a great Zinfandel or a great red Burgundy would taste if made by Angelo Gaja. A seductive nose of black raspberries, violets, licorice, and toast is followed by a rich wine with pure black fruit flavors intertwined with sweet, smoky oak. Full-bodied, with ripe tannin, this internationally styled, stunningly proportioned, big, compelling 1996 will be at its peak between 2003–2023. The opaque purple 1996 Barolo Conteisa reveals a sweeter, riper nose with an element of *sur-maturité* given its overripe cassis, melted road tar, licorice, and spice-scented bouquet. More accessible than the Sperss, it exhibits a voluptuous texture, layers of concentrated fruit, and full body. Its tannin is largely concealed by the wine's glycerin, alcohol, and extract. Anticipated maturity: now–2020.

The outstanding 1996 Cabernet Sauvignon Darmagi is a structured, dense, black/purple-colored wine with excellent cassis fruit and an unevolved but promising personality. There are copious quantities of tannin, a massive mid-palate, and a sweet, long finish. However, it will require considerable patience. Anticipated maturity: 2008–2025.

1995 tends to be a good rather than great vintage in Piedmont, but Gaja's sensational 1995s are among the stars of the vintage. All of the following wines possess extremely saturated dark ruby/purple colors, almost atypical for Nebbiolo. The 1995 Barbaresco offers a superb nose of licorice, cherry fruit, strawberries, flowers, and toasty scents. Ripe, dense, and lush, with an alluring, sexy personality, it is one of the more forward, generic Barbarescos Gaja has produced. Anticipated maturity: now–2011. The three single-vineyard wines are qualitatively similar but represent different expressions of Nebbiolo. The 1995 Barbaresco Sorì San Lorenzo offers telltale cigar tobacco, spice box, and cedar with black currant and cherry fruit in the background. The new oak plays a subtle role. Structured and more noticeably tannic than the regular *cuvée*, this is a dense wine with surprising levels of glycerin, a saturated plum color, and intriguing flavors of black fruits, soy, and cedar. Although accessible, it needs more bottle age. Anticipated maturity: now–2016. The 1995 Barbaresco Costa Russi reveals the most saturated purple color of any of Gaja's 1995 Barbarescos. A full-bodied, more fruit-driven, and powerful wine, it possesses copious quantities of black raspberry and cherry fruit, as well as toasty new oak. There is even an element of *sur-maturité* in this large-scaled, expansively flavored effort. I would not be surprised to see it age for 20 years. Anticipated maturity: 2004–2020+. The 1995 Barbaresco Sorì Tildin reveals a liqueurlike viscosity to its richness. It offers spicy, black raspberry fruit in addition to melted asphalt, smoke, truffle, and toast. This complex, expansive Barbaresco does not possess the saturated purple/plum color of the Costa Russi, but it is deeply colored for the vintage, with superb richness, full body, and beautifully integrated acidity, tannin, and alcohol. Anticipated maturity: 2004–2020+. The 1995 Cabernet Sauvignon Darmagi is an elegant wine with medium body, classic weedy tobacco and cassis flavors, sweet, supple tannin, and excellent equilibrium. Anticipated maturity: 2003–2018.

GASTALDI

1995 Barbaresco	D	87

It is hard to define these wines as from either the new *barrique*-aged winemaking school or the classical/traditional persuasion, but they may demonstrate a bit more allegiance to the latter. The 1995 Barbaresco's dark garnet color is followed by a classic bouquet of cherry cough syrup, coffee, rose petals, tar, and cedar. Spicy and medium-bodied, with fine density, a supple texture, and light tannin in the finish, it should drink well for 4–5 years.

ATTILIO GHISOLFI

1998 Barolo Bricco Visette	D	(87–88)
1997 Barolo Bricco Visette	D	85

1996 Barolo Bricco Visette	D	(86–87)
1995 Barolo Bricco Visette	D	86

This small producer in Monforte d'Alba has fashioned a fine 1998 Barolo Bricco Visette. This wine is made in a moderately endowed, forward style with sweet black cherry fruit, medium to full body, and ripe tannin. Admirable extract and richness as well as an atypically precocious, up-front personality suggest drinking this 1998 between 2003–2012.

Not nearly as dense and rich as it was from the barrel, the light, commercially styled 1997 Barolo Bricco Visette possesses pleasant fruit but little stuffing or intensity. This medium-weight wine is best drunk over the next 3–4 years. The dense, saturated ruby-colored 1996 Barolo Bricco Visette is full-bodied and extracted, with weedy tobacco intermixed with dried herbs, cherry liqueur, and copious new saddle leather. The wine starts off impressively, but it becomes more compressed and shorter in the finish, which kept my score low. Anticipated maturity: now–2012. The 1995 Barolo Bricco Visette is soft, evolved and mature. The color is already revealing amber and orange at the edge. This Barolo offers the hallmark tar, rose petal, and spicy nose. Medium-bodied and not terribly concentrated, it is ideal for drinking over the next 4 years.

BRUNO GIACOSA

1998 Barbaresco Asili	EE	93
1997 Barbaresco Asili	EE	94
1996 Barbaresco Asili (Red Label Riserva)	EE	98+
1995 Barbaresco Asili	E	90
1998 Barbaresco Rabajà	EE	95
1997 Barbaresco Rabajà	EE	96
1996 Barbaresco Rabajà	EE	93
1998 Barbaresco Santo Stefano	E	92
1997 Barbaresco Santo Stefano	C	93
1996 Barbaresco Santo Stefano	E	94+
1995 Barbaresco Santo Stefano	E	91
1998 Barolo Falletto di Serralunga	EEE	(94–96)
1997 Barolo Falletto di Serralunga	EEE	93
1996 Barolo Falletto di Serralunga (Red Label Riserva)	EEE	98+
1995 Barolo Falletto di Serralunga	EE	90+
1998 Barolo Rocche di Falletto	EEE	(96–98)
1997 Barolo Rocche di Falletto	EEE	96+
1996 Barolo Villero	EE	93
1998 Nebbiolo d'Alba Valmaggiore	C	89
1997 Nebbiolo d'Alba Valmaggiore	C	88

It is always thrilling to visit Bruno Giacosa, Piedmont's undeniable guardian of the traditional school of winemaking. His Barolos and Barbarescos (i.e., memories of his 1978s, 1971s, and 1964s) are among the most exhilarating wines of the world.

This producer acquired some choice vineyard parcels several years ago, from which he is producing the finest wines ever to emerge from these sites. He now owns Barbaresco vineyards in the crus of Rabajà (where the début vintage was 1996) and Asili (first wine produced in 1995), as well as Barolo vineyards in Falletto, from which he makes two *cuvées*. Since 1997, four blocks of the Falletto vineyard have been used for the virtually perfect Rocche di Falletto. These plots possess a southeastern exposure, which accounts for the better maturity of the grapes that emerge from them. None of Giacosa's wines sees any *barrique* treatment, and they are bottled "when they are ready." His humility, unassuming character, dignity, extraordinary pride, and remarkable integrity are reflected in his wines, which, for me, are the benchmarks for great Nebbiolo. Much as I get turned on by some of the modernists' wines, the Giacosa treasures that exist in my cellar are unprecedented in their complexity and rich-ness. I rarely open a bottle of his Barbarescos or Barolos before their tenth birthday and find that most of them do not hit their stride until age 15–18. However, impatient readers should be warned: these wines are frequently uninspiring immediately after bottling and arrival to these shores, but after 10 years of cellaring, their magic always emerges. I have seen this happen in Giacosa's greatest vintages (1964, 1971, 1978, 1982, 1985, and 1988) as well as in lesser years (1980 and 1986). Given my twenty-five years of glorious experience with Bruno Giacosa's wines, I know that cellaring them is not a leap of faith. They have never dis-appointed, assuming I wait the 8–10 years they require in great vintages (his 1978s are still emerging from a long period of dormancy). To put it another way, Giacosa's Barolos and Bar-barescos are among the few wines I will purchase without having tasted first. Bruno Giacosa considers that both 1996 and 1998 are far better vintages than 1997 (according to him, a dif-ficult year—too hot and dry, with raisined grapes, low acidity, and excessive sugars and alco-hol). He was not the only producer to express such an opinion (shared by Pio Boffa of Pio Cesare). However, as critical as Bruno Giacosa was of his 1997s, I thought the wines were all potentially outstanding, but I still think that the 1996s are even more spectacular (because of a disastrous flowering in 1996, the crop size was 50% smaller than normal!) and the 1998s are practically on a par with them. That being said, readers should not forget what this pro-ducer achieved in 1995, though this vintage does not offer any red label Riserva. The estate's standard *cuvées* bear white labels.

The spice box, tobacco, cherry liqueur, and smoke-scented 1998 Nebbiolo d'Alba Valmag-giore is reminiscent of Giacosa's bigger-styled Barbarescos. It is extremely complex, intense, spicy, and long in the mouth. Consume it over the next 4–5 years. Giacosa's 1998 Barbaresco Asili needs 4–5 years of cellaring. It exhibits a dark ruby color along with a big, sweet nose of dried herbs, cedar, tobacco, tar, and red fruits. Opulent on the attack, with moderately high tannin as well as good underlying acidity, this is a fragrant effort for Giacosa, without the flamboyant size of the 1997 or the massive structure and density of the 1996. Anticipated maturity: 2006–2020. In 1998, the renowned Barbaresco Santo Stefano is the most forward offering, with its medium ruby color already displaying amber at the edge. Aromas of new saddle leather, fennel, smoke, tobacco, kirsch, and licorice soar from the glass of this ripe, opulent, medium- to full-bodied Barbaresco. I hesitate to say it can be drunk young, given the tendency of these wines to shut down, but readers who purchase it (that includes me) should let it settle down for a year or two and drink it over the following 15+ years. An-other terrific Barbaresco is the 1998 Rabajà. Complex notes of soy, earth, candied cherry fruit, and cigar box emerge from this concentrated yet intellectually challenging effort. Full-bodied, with a soft attack as well as a tannic finish, it will be drinkable between 2007–2020.

The fabulous 1998 Barolo Falletto di Serralunga appears to be superior to the 1997. When the two are tasted side by side, the 1998 reveals more intensity and volume, although that's splitting hairs. A dark plum color is accompanied by a classic Nebbiolo perfume of rose water, melted tar, truffles, and cherry jam. As the wine sits in the glass, aromas of spice box and cigar smoke also emerge. Full-bodied, dense, and powerfully tannic yet extremely har-monious, it will be at its finest between 2008–2030. Lastly, the limited *cuvée* made from four blocks of the Falletto vineyard called Rocche, the 1998 Barolo Rocche di Falletto borders on perfection. I thought it performed better than the 1997, but in the lofty point scores above 95, that's a matter of personal taste. In any event, this wine is spectacular. A dark plum color re-veals lightening at the edge. Stunning aromatics offer up scents of crushed stones intermixed with cherry jam and sweet tobacco. There are loads of glycerin, moderately high tannin, and an amazingly long finish of nearly 50 seconds. As staggering as it is now, I am sure it will close down and require 5–6 years of cellaring. Anticipated maturity: 2008–2035.

The 1997 Nebbiolo d'Alba Valmaggiore is a robust, big-styled Nebbiolo with aggressive tannin, copious quantities of tar, black cherry, cigar box, and spice notes, medium to full body, excellent concentration, and a fine finish. It should drink well for 5–6 years.

The 1997 Barbaresco Asili has developed stunningly since it was first tasted from barrel, a typical characteristic of Giacosa's wines. Surprisingly precocious and well evolved for a wine from this estate, it possesses a dark ruby color with an amber edge, and abundant quantities of tobacco, cherry liqueur, incense, spice box, and licorice in its flamboyant nose. It is like candy, fleshy, full-bodied, unctuous, and silky. This seamless classic should drink well young and last for 10–12 years. The classic 1997 Barbaresco Santo Stefano is more evolved and flamboyant than its more backward 1996 counterpart. A medium ruby/garnet color with an amber edge is followed by a sweet perfume of black cherries, tobacco, leather, spice box, licorice, and tar. Full-bodied, with a creamy texture, superb concentration, and an exquisite finish, it can be drunk now or cellared for 15+ years. Giacosa's second release from the Rabajà vineyard, the 1997 Barbaresco Rabajà, may be better than his debut vintage, the 1996. The 1997 boasts a fabulous nose of caramel, soy, herbs, black cherries, plums, and kirsch. Dense and full-bodied, with a spectacular, silky texture, gobs of glycerin, and a layered, multidimensional palate, it is immensely satisfying from both hedonistic and intellectual perspectives. Anticipated maturity: now–2020.

Giacosa's 1997 Barolo Falletto di Serralunga is an exquisite Barolo offering superb notes of tar, earth, truffles, licorice, minerals, and cherry/raspberry fruit. There is plenty of acidity as well as high tannin, but concentrated, chewy flavors. The wine is tight, dense, impressive, and surprisingly well structured for a 1997. However, it is going to be more accessible than most young Giacosa Barolos. Anticipated maturity: 2003–2025. As mentioned above, the debut vintage of Bruno Giacosa's Barolo Rocche di Falletto, the 1997, emerges from four blocks of his Falletto vineyard with a southeastern exposure; thus the fruit is slightly riper. The amazing, deep plum/garnet-colored 1997 possesses huge body as well as a sweet, sexy, fleshy mid-palate and finish. Classic aromas of rose petals, melted tar, and cherry liqueur not only soar aromatically but saturate the palate and coat the taster's teeth. Profoundly complex and multilayered, with an exquisite texture and overall harmony, for a Giacosa Barolo it is uncommonly precocious, making me think it will provide profound drinking in 1–2 years and last for three decades.

The stunning series of 1996 includes a 1996 Barbaresco Santo Stefano red label that is simply spectacular. Giacosa continues to believe this is the greatest wine he has produced since his legendary 1971 (which is still a prodigious Barbaresco, although clearly near the end of its life). The tight, youthful 1996 requires 3–4 more years of bottle age. The color is a dark ruby/garnet. The bouquet is just beginning to open, revealing scents of dried Provençal herbs, cherry liqueur, tobacco, spice box, and white truffles. In the mouth, the wine is stunningly concentrated, extremely full-bodied, with high tannin, and fabulously pure, sweet, cherry cough syrup–like, licorice, smoke, and dried herb flavors. The finish lasts for more than 45 seconds, although this 1996 is still young and tight. It should enjoy a glorious evolution. Anticipated maturity: 2006–2030. The 1996 Barbaresco Rabajà (Giacosa's debut vintage from this noted vineyard) displays an intriguing nose of soy, dried Provençal herbs, new saddle leather, and red/black fruits. Tannic and full-bodied, with an enormous impact on the palate, it is extremely concentrated, yet the fruit, alcohol, tannin, and acidity are all marvelously well integrated. Anticipated maturity: 2006–2025. The utterly perfect, dense ruby/purple-colored 1996 Barbaresco Bricco Asili (Red Label Riserva) is a heroic offering brilliantly displaying both power and elegance. The bouquet develops incrementally, offering up aromas of black raspberries, cherries, cigar box, licorice, and leather. The wine impresses with its nuances as well as its extraordinarily rich, dense mid-palate and a finish that lasts nearly a minute. There is huge tannin but equally massive concentration, extract, and overall harmony. This is the finest Giacosa Barbaresco since his two greatest classics, the 1990 and 1971 Barbaresco Santo Stefano (Red Label). Anticipated maturity: 2006–2025.

There are two Red Label Riserva Barolos in 1996. The 1996 Barolo Villero should be used to teach a course in what great Barolo smells like. It possesses a classic, rose petal, melted tar, and cherry liqueur–scented nose that soars from the glass. In the mouth, it exhibits licorice, black cherry fruit, fruitcake, spice box, and other assorted nuances in its profoundly complex personality. Full-bodied and marvelously concentrated, with exquisite harmony, this appears to be a fabulously young Barolo that will age effortlessly for three decades. Anticipated maturity: 2010–2035. The 1996 Barolo Falletto di Serralunga (Red Label Riserva) possesses extraordinary presence and stature. Dark garnet/ruby-colored, it offers a tight but promising nose of road tar, scorched earth, truffles, blackberries, cherries, and espresso. This muscular, massive wine gave me chills. It is an exquisite, virtually perfect Barolo that requires a decade of cellaring and should last for 30–40 years. I remember wishing I were twenty years younger when I tasted it prior to bottling . . . I still feel the same way. Awesome! Anticipated maturity: 2010–2040.

The gorgeously elegant 1995 Barbaresco Bricco Asili emerges from a renowned Asili vineyard in Barbaresco. The color is a deceptively light ruby with some amber at the edge. The nose offers aromas redolent of kirsch, dried Provençal herbs, new saddle leather, and smoke. In the mouth, Asian spice and soy make an appearance in the rich, jammy cherry flavors that also offer an intriguing tomato-like characteristic. This lush, open-knit, full-bodied Barbaresco will drink well before 2014. The 1995 Barbaresco Santo Stefano reveals an intensely fragrant nose of coffee, soy, tobacco, dried herbs, and cherry cough syrup. Full-bodied, with moderate tannin in the finish, this is an expressive, rich, expansively flavored Barbaresco that can be drunk now as well as over the next 10–12 years. I also enjoyed the outstanding 1995 Barolo Falletto. It possesses a medium dark ruby color with some lightening at the edge. The intense nose of cedar, spice box, soy, tar, rose petals, and black fruits is followed by a wine with a sweet attack, full body, and dense, layered, concentrated, spicy flavors. As this muscular, tannic wine sat in the glass, allspice and dried herbs became increasingly apparent. Cellar it for 2–3 years, and consume over the following 12 years.

F.LLI GRASSO

1998	Barbaresco	D	87
1997	Barbaresco	D	89
1998	Barbaresco Bricco Spessa	D	90
1997	Barbaresco Bricco Spessa	D	88
1998	Barbaresco Sorì Valgrande	D	89+
1997	Barbaresco Sorì Valgrande	D	88+

This producer, based in the village of Treiso, completely renovated his cellars in 2000, and thus it is believed the quality will rise to an even more admirable level. He performed slightly better in 1998 than in 1997.

One of the 1998 vintage's hallmarks, gorgeous aromatics, appears in all three *cuvées*. The 1998 Barbaresco exhibits an unimpressive, medium ruby color, but it offers sweet, tobacco and herb-tinged cherry fruit presented in an elegant, slender yet beautifully balanced, restrained format. Enjoy it over the next 5–6 years. The gorgeous, exceptionally fragrant 1998 Barbaresco Bricco Spessa possesses an evolved nose of cigar tobacco, cedar wood, cherry jam, petroleum, and rose petals. A wine of finesse as well as lush, rich, concentrated fruit, this medium-bodied 1998 is a classic Barbaresco to drink now and over the next decade. Similarly styled, with more structure, the dark garnet-colored 1998 Barbaresco Sorì Valgrande offers intense, complex aromas of tobacco, cedar, spicy tomato skins, cherry liqueur, and coffee. The finish is more structured and leaner than the more expressive Bricco Spessa, hence the slightly lower score. Nevertheless, it is a flavorful Barbaresco that admirably displays Nebbiolo's extraordinarily complex perfume. Consume it over the next 10 years.

Grasso's 1997 Barbaresco reveals an evolved color with amber at the edge as well as a rich, exotic bouquet of superripe cherries, coffee, herbs, and spice box. Fleshy and seductive, with low acidity, medium body, and a sexy, up-front style, it should be consumed over the next 4–5 years. The dark garnet-colored, medium- to full-bodied 1997 Barbaresco Bricco Spessa is more tightly knit than its generic sibling but offers similar aromas of dried herbs, black cherries, tobacco, and leather, as well as more noticeable tannin. Drink it over the next 8 years. The most structured and tannic of this trio, the 1997 Barbaresco Sorì Valgrande, exhibits a dark garnet color, aromas and flavors of earth, tar, cherries, smoke, and spice, and good density, structure, and depth. Although it is the least appealing at present, it will ultimately be the longest-lived. Anticipated maturity: now–2014.

SILVIO GRASSO

1998 Barolo	D	88
1997 Barolo	D	89
1996 Barolo	D	88
1995 Barolo	D	87
1998 Barolo Bricco Luciani	E	(90–92)
1997 Barolo Bricco Luciani	E	92
1996 Barolo Bricco Luciani	E	92
1995 Barolo Bricco Luciani	E	88
1998 Barolo Ciabot Manzoni	E	(90–91)
1997 Barolo Ciabot Manzoni	E	90
1996 Barolo Ciabot Manzoni	E	91
1995 Barolo Ciabot Manzoni	E	87

Silvio Grasso does not employ any new oak for his standard Barolo and about 20% for his single-vineyard wines from the La Morra hillsides. Grasso has produced a bevy of sensational efforts in recent vintages.

This La Morra producer's 1998 Barolo exhibits abundant quantities of licorice and cherry fruit in a medium-bodied, elegant style with plenty of glycerin but not a great deal of weight. This soft, finesse-styled effort is meant to be drunk over the next 3–4 years. The dark ruby-colored 1998 Barolo Ciabot Manzoni offers a beautiful bouquet of sweet black cherry fruit intermixed with rose petals, tar, and new oak. It possesses fine ripeness, a fresh, lively, high-toned style, and lovely flavors. With sweet tannin, decent acidity, and a seamless style, it can be consumed now and over the next 10–12 years. More earthy and chewy, with cedary, spice box, and black cherry scents and flavors, the full-bodied, moderately tannic 1998 Barolo Bricco Luciani displays the vintage's notable fragrance, outstanding purity, and beautiful symmetry among its component parts. Anticipated maturity: 2003–2015.

The excellent 1997 Barolo is a forward, silky-textured effort exhibiting sweet jammy fruit, a roasted herb/spice box character, medium to full body, excellent weight, fat, and plushness, low acidity, and a chewy, expansive palate. Drink it over the next 8 years. Grasso's 1997 Barolo Ciabot Manzoni's dark ruby color reveals some amber at the edge. It possesses a forward, medium- to full-bodied character with plenty of leather and brandied cherry notes, high glycerin levels, and a velvety texture. The finish is tannic. Anticipated maturity: now–2016. The superintense, powerful, weighty, multidimensional, full-bodied, sweet, sexy 1997 Barolo Bricco Luciani exhibits a more forward character than it did prior to bottling. There are layers of fruit, glycerin, and extract, and the wine reveals abundant quantities of black cherry and berry fruit intermixed with spice box, leather, licorice, and Chinese black tea notes. As it sits in the glass, scents of melted asphalt, rose petals, and tobacco emerge. This is a superb, hedonistic, yet powerful, concentrated Barolo to drink between 2003–2020.

The classic character of the 1996 vintage is well displayed in Silvio Grasso's two single-vineyard crus. The fuller-bodied, lush 1996 Barolo offers a sexy display of glycerin and intense cherry and spice aromatics. It will drink well over the next 8 years. The 1996 Barolo Ciabot Manzoni offers a saturated ruby/purple color in addition to a sumptuous bouquet of truffles, saddle leather, black cherries, and floral scents. This expansive, full-bodied, chewy blockbuster is soft enough to be drunk early but should age nicely for 15 years. Even better is the 1996 Barolo Bricco Luciani. The classic Nebbiolo aromas of rose petals and melted road tar are intermixed with toast, cherry liqueur, tobacco, and spice. With explosive richness, high levels of glycerin, and a powerful, muscular, concentrated finish, this superb example possesses high levels of tannin and extract. Anticipated maturity: now–2016.

The 1995 Barolo exhibits a medium ruby/garnet color, in addition to a textbook nose of cherries, spice, balsa wood, and a touch of tar. Elegant, soft, and medium-bodied, it will provide ideal drinking over the next 4–5 years. The dark ruby-colored 1995 Barolo Ciabot Manzoni exhibits a big, toasty nose with scents of ripe cherries, saddle leather, cedar, and tobacco. This medium-bodied, evolved Barolo requires consumption over the next 4–5 years. The 1995 Barolo Bricco Luciani displays a more saturated ruby/garnet color with no amber at the edge. It possesses spicy oak, a fresh, medium- to full-bodied feel, moderate tannin, and an excellent cherry-dominated nose as well as flavors with hints of Asian spices, leather, and tar. Anticipated maturity: now–2010.

MARCHESI DI GRESY

1998	Barbaresco Martinenga	E	87
1997	Barbaresco Martinenga	E	86
1996	Barbaresco Martinenga	E	87
1995	Barbaresco Martinenga	E	87
1996	Barbaresco Camp Gros Martinenga	E	89
1995	Barbaresco Camp Gros Martinenga	E	87
1996	Barbaresco Gaiun Martinenga	E	90
1995	Barbaresco Gaiun Martinenga	E	86

One of my favorite producers of high-class Barbaresco, Marchesi di Gresy's style is one of exceptional refinement and gracious elegance, without the weight of the region's biggest wines but with considerable flavor authority. The 1995s are very good, and the 1996s are at least excellent. Unfortunately, I was able to taste only one *cuvée* in each of 1997 and 1998 that were sound.

The 1998 Barbaresco Martinenga's evolved dark plum/garnet color reveals considerable amber at the edge. The bouquet offers up spicy new oak, dried fruits (particularly cherries), and floral/rose petal aromas. The finish is slightly tannic as well as short. Drink it over the next 5–6 years. The 1997 Barbaresco Martinenga exhibits a garnet color with pink/amber at the edge. It is a soft wine with notes of lead pencil, cherry, strawberry, and espresso. While it reveals little mid-palate, extract, or length, it is charming and elegant in a spicy, medium-bodied, fruity manner. Consume it over the next 8 years. The 1996 Barbaresco Camp Gros Martinenga offers more black cherry and black raspberry notes with strawberry jam in the mouth. A fuller wine, with more fruit, extract, and structure, this potentially outstanding Barbaresco can be drunk now and before 2012. The superb 1996 Barbaresco Gaiun Martinenga boasts a dark ruby/purple color as well as a gorgeous, Musigny-like nose of flowers, minerals, and black fruits. It is impeccably made, with great elegance, medium body, terrific fruit intensity, and no sense of heaviness. Drink this stylish, harmonious Barbaresco over the next 10 years. For whatever reason, the 1996 Barbaresco Martinenga was backward, lean, austere, and impossible to evaluate. I am sure it has the same level of potential as the other single-vineyard offerings, but it was impossible to penetrate. I will wait until it has had another year of evolution to retaste it.

The 1995 Barbaresco Camp Gros Martinenga reveals a Burgundian nose of black cherries, flowers, spice, and subtle toasty oak. In the mouth, notes of tobacco emerge in this graceful, medium-bodied, refined, supple-textured, lush wine. Drink it over the next 5–6 years. Similarly styled, the 1995 Barbaresco Gaiun Martinenga displays more tannin as well as a more structured personality. The 1995 Barbaresco Martinenga possesses the finest delineation, undeniable finesse, and copious quantities of beautifully etched black cherry fruit interspersed with scents of new oak, minerals, flowers, and spice. It is an attractively rendered, medium-bodied Barbaresco to consume over the next 5–6 years.

GIACOMO GRIMALDI

1998 Barolo Le Coste	E	90+
1997 Barolo Le Coste	E	92
1996 Barolo Le Coste	E	87

This producer, a former policeman from the village of Barolo, whose debut vintage was 1996, produced impressive efforts in both 1996, 1997, and 1998.

Potentially as good as if not better than the 1997, the 1998 Barolo Le Coste exhibits a dark garnet color as well as a classic Barolo bouquet of melted road tar, rose petals, cherry syrup, tobacco, and spice box. Deep-textured and full-bodied, with sweet kirschlike flavors infused with creosote/tar and a moderately tannic finish, this old-style, intense effort will drink well between 2003–2018. A muscular, dark plum-colored Barolo, Grimaldi's 1997 Le Coste offers classic aromatics of melted road tar, rose petals, new saddle leather, beef blood, and kirsch. Impressively endowed, with moderately high tannin, this powerful, thick, juicy effort is a definitive Barolo that needs 2–3 years of cellaring and should keep for two decades. His 1996 Barolo Le Coste revealed a reduced character, and I did not have the opportunity to taste a second sample. Certainly there is a lot to like. This classic old-style Barolo exhibits aromas of melted road tar, rose petals, and petroleum. Although hard to evaluate, it is full-bodied and at least excellent. I look forward to tasting it again. It appears to be a wine that will last for 10–12 years.

ICARDI

1999 Barbera d'Alba Surì di Mù	D	92
1998 Barbera d'Alba Surì di Mù	D	89
1999 Barbera d'Asti Tabarin	D	89
1996 Barolo	D	87
1995 Barolo	D	86
1998 Barolo Parej	E	(90–92)
1997 Barolo Parej	E	92
1998 Langhe Nebbiolo Suris Jvan	D	88
1999 Monferrato Rosso Bricco del Sole	D	88

An impressive, modern-styled producer, Icardi has been doing some top-notch work, as evidenced by these offerings.

Readers looking for a dazzling value should check out the 1999 Barbera d'Alba Surì di Mù. Aged one year in *barrique*, this 3,000-case *cuvée* is dynamite. Opaque purple-colored and full-bodied, with a gorgeous perfume of strawberry, cherry, and blackberry jam aromas mixed with charcoal, graphite, and new oak, this is a succulent, hedonistic, Barbera fruit bomb to drink over the next 3–4 years. The 1999 Barbera d'Asti Tabarin is also a terrific value. Explosive aromas of smoke, cherry fruit, and strawberries jump from the glass of this medium ruby-colored wine. Rich and fleshy, with abundant fruit, it is a seductive Barbera for drinking over the next 5–6 years. More restrained and revealing a more international style, largely because the oak is more noticeable, is the 1999 Monferrato Rosso Bricco del Sole, a blend of Barbera, Nebbiolo, and Cabernet Sauvignon aged 15 months in new French oak. A fine effort, it reveals less typicity and character than the less expensive Barbera d'Alba Surì di Mù. It should mature for easily 10 years. The more classic 1998 Langhe Nebbiolo Suris Jvan displays that varietal's black tea, tobacco, rose petal, and asphalt aromas in its moderately intense perfume. There is lovely ripeness, a supple texture, and a rich, round finish. Tasted blind, it could easily be mistaken for a Barolo if not a Barbaresco. Drink it over the next 5–6 years. The 1998 Barbera d'Alba Surì di Mù is better balanced, with a dark ruby color, a luscious, black cherry and strawberry jam–scented nose, ripe, supple flavors, medium to full body, and enough acidity for delineation and balance. It should drink well for 4–5 years.

These modern-styled Barolos are forward and fruit-driven. Another sleeper of the vintage, Icardi's 1998 Barolo Parej, boasts an opaque purple color as well as a sweet nose of blackberry and cherry liqueur intertwined with aromas of *barriques*, smoke, and graphite. Dense, muscular, and rich, with terrific ripeness and opulence in addition to a layered, moderately tannic finish, it will be at its finest between 2006–2018. One of the sleeper Barolos of the vintage, Icardi's explosive, full-bodied, exotic, dense purple-colored 1997 Barolo Parej boasts a jammy blackberry/cherry bouquet with notions of toasty new oak (clearly from the modern school of Piedmontese winemaking). There are terrific density, purity, and symmetry, as well as an unctuous, long finish with copious quantities of sweet tannin and glycerin. Drink this Nebbiolo fruit bomb over the next 15 years. The 1996 Barolo Parej exhibits a more briery, raspberry, Zinfandel-like personality, with pepper and dried herbs in the background. There are excellent extract, medium to full body, and moderate tannin. The slightly austere, astringent finish suggests that 1–2 years of cellaring will be beneficial. It should keep for 10 years. The 1995 Barolo Parej possesses a dark plum color, plenty of glycerin, a rich, precocious, fleshy appeal, low acidity, and a mélange of tobacco, spice, dried herbs, and jammy cherry fruit. Drink this medium-bodied offering over the next 2–3 years.

INSIEME

1998	Alessandria	E	92
1997	Alessandria	E	92
1998	Altare	E	94
1997	Altare	E	96
1997	Corino	E	92
1997	Grasso	E	90
1997	Molino	E	89
1998	Revello	E	93
1997	Revello	E	91
1998	Veglio	E	92
1997	Veglio	E	94

Originated by Elio Altare to raise charitable contributions to help repair historical Piedmontese buildings, this association was formed by the above-mentioned La Morra producers. Fifteen percent of the proceeds go to charity. All of the wines are aged in *barrique*, ranging from 10% new oak for Revello to 100% new oak for Grasso and Veglio. Altare and Corino utilize 80% new oak and Molino 60%. The blends are as follows: Grasso: 44% Nebbiolo, 16% Barbera, 20% Cabernet Sauvignon, and 20% Merlot; Molino: 40% Nebbiolo, 20% Barbera, 20% Cabernet Sauvignon, and 20% Merlot; Corino: 50% Nebbiolo and 50% Barbera, with a touch of Cabernet Sauvignon and Merlot; Alessandria: 40% Nebbiolo, 20% Barbera, and 40% Cabernet Sauvignon; Revello: 40% Nebbiolo, 30% Barbera, and 30% Cabernet Sauvignon; Veglio: 40% Nebbiolo, 30% Barbera, and 30% Cabernet Sauvignon; Altare: 50% Cabernet Sauvignon, 20% Nebbiolo, and 20% Barbera (only 90%). The wines are all bottled unfiltered, and there are approximately 3,000 bottles of each producer's Insieme. As the scores suggest, they are all gorgeous wines, with terrific levels of perfume and intensity. Given the tiny quantities available, I have provided brief tasting notes only for the 1998s, but readers lucky enough to find either vintage should not hesitate to purchase them. At about $58, they are realistically priced for such high quality.

Veglio's 1998 Insieme is a spectacular effort offering notes of red and black fruits, vanilla, smoke, and tobacco. Made in a full-bodied, opulent style, it should be drunk over the next 7–8 years, although I suspect it will last longer. Revello's 1998 Insieme is a fragrant, lavishly rich, exotic, concentrated wine also best drunk during its first 7–8 years of life. The complex Altare 1998 Insieme is great stuff. It is a Piedmontese wine made in a modern style with the influence of *barrique*. Notes of tobacco, licorice, black cherries, currants, spice box, and cedar are present as well as blackberry jam and cassis. The wine possesses an unctuous texture, huge body, and gorgeous fruit, sweetness, and length. It should drink well for a decade, although who will have the self-discipline to wait? Alessandria's 1998 Insieme is a fabulous, extremely full-bodied effort offering aromas and flavors of blackberries, cassis, cedar, leather, and vanilla. This thick, viscous, chewy, seamless, gorgeously harmonious wine will drink well for 7–8 years.

LA LICENZIANA DI SILVIO GIAMELLO

1998 Barbaresco	D	85
1998 Barbaresco Licenziana	D	87

These are straightforward efforts, with the plum/garnet-colored 1998 Barbaresco revealing moderate levels of cherry, tobacco, and herb-tinged fruit, good spice, Chinese tea, and light to moderate tannin. Consume this easy to understand Barbaresco over the next 2–3 years. More concentrated and deeper is the 1998 Barbaresco Licenziana. It exhibits excellent tobacco, berry, cherry, spice box, and licorice aromas as well as flavors, medium body, good fruit, sweet tannin, and admirable structure. It should evolve nicely for 3–4 years.

GIOVANNI MANZONE

1998 Barolo Le Gramolere	D	86
1997 Barolo Le Gramolere	D	87
1996 Barolo Le Gramolere	D	88
1995 Barolo Le Gramolere	D	91
1998 Barolo Bricat Gramolere	D	86
1997 Barolo Bricat Gramolere	D	87
1996 Barolo Bricat Gramolere	D	86
1995 Barolo Bricat Gramolere	D	89+
1997 Barolo Santo Stefano di Perno	D	88
1996 Barolo Santo Stefano di Perno	D	87
1995 Barolo Santo Stefano di Perno	D	90
1997 Langhe Rosso Tris	D	88

Manzone, whose cellars are located in the village of Monforte d'Alba, owns some of the highest elevated vineyards of this area, and hence the wines he produces tend to have cool-climate characteristics. They are made in a rather herbaceous style, with red rather than black fruit characteristics, fairly high acidity, and a certain leanness. Readers who prefer such a style to more fleshy, opulent, powerful wines will rate these offerings higher. This producer follows a quasi-modern school of winemaking. He utilizes open-top fermenters and believes in pumping over, and uses 20% new-oak casks for the *élevage*, with the rest of the wine being aged in *foudre* prior to bottling, accomplished without filtration. The 1995s are successful and may be as good as what Manzone produced in 1996 and 1997. However, the 1998s leave me asking for more as they tend to be lean, herbaceous, and short.

The austerity and high tannin of the dry, attenuated 1998 Barolo Le Gramolere is a perfect example of this default, even though it possesses attractive underlying cherry, strawberry, and mineral notes. The same can be said for the 1998 Barolo Bricat Gramolere, a delicate Burgundy-style wine with sweet cherry fruit intermixed with earth, wet stones, and flowers. Both of these wines require consumption over the next 5–6 years.

Manzone produced potentially outstanding 1997s. They display the vintage's equilibrium, velvety texture, and an expansive, open-knit richness that conceals moderately high tannin. The 1997 Barolo Le Gramolere possesses a medium ruby color with pink at the edge. An elegant, lighter-styled 1997 with spicy tobacco/herbaceous notes intermixed with cranberries, cherries, and red currants, this vibrant wine, with better acidity than most 1997s, should be drunk over its first 10 years of life. The more sinewy, intellectual 1997 Barolo Bricat Gramolere is less hedonistic than many of its peers. Medium-bodied and tasty, with notions of cherries, coffee, and herbs, it is made in an austere, subdued style. Drink it over the next 8 years. Cut from the same mold but slightly richer, the 1997 Barolo Santo Stefano di Perno emerges from a vineyard on the lower slopes, where more sun exposure results in riper fruit. It offers aromas and flavors of road tar, rose water, minerals, and cherry liqueur. Medium-bodied, pure, stylish, and elegant, it will be drinkable between 2002–2015. Manzone has also turned out an interesting blend of equal parts Dolcetto, Barbera, and Nebbiolo called Langhe Rosso Iris. The 1997 is a sexy, round, dark ruby-colored wine with abundant fruit but not the volume or explosiveness of his Dolcetto. It is a more elegant, restrained offering to consume over the next 2–3 years.

Manzone's 1996s were tannic, austere examples that may have been going through a stubborn phase of their evolution. The ruby/purple-colored 1996 Barolo Santo Stefano di Perno displays an intriguing nose of licorice, cherry liqueur, oak, and earth. There is sweet fruit on the attack, but the tannin and structure take over, compressing the mid-palate and finish. This Barolo has the potential for an outstanding rating . . . if the tannin becomes more integrated. I will be anxious to retaste it after bottling. Anticipated maturity: 2004–2015. The 1996 Barolo Le Gramolere is a dark ruby-colored, earthy, structured, medium- to full-bodied wine with a great deal of muscle and intensity. It displays an herbaceous, tobacco, smoky, dried fruit–scented nose and an old-style, traditional, astringent finish. This wine could turn out to be a classic, but it could also be slightly rustic and tannic. Time will tell. Anticipated maturity: 2005–2016. Even more tannic is the 1996 Barolo Bricat Gramolere. An impressive, powerful example, with cherry cough syrup notes meshed with dried herbs, roasted scents, a touch of tar and earth, this backward Barolo requires 5–6 years of cellaring. Anticipated maturity: 2006–2015.

The 1995 Barolo Santo Stefano di Perno exhibits a deceptively light medium ruby color, as well as knockout aromas of sweet berry fruit intermixed with spice box, floral scents, and subtle toast. Sweet, rich, and fruit driven, with a supple, lush texture, medium to full body, and gorgeous balance, this wine can be drunk now or over the next 10 years. The 1995 Barolo Le Gramolere reveals a candied cassis character, as well as black raspberry and cherry fruit on the palate. The sumptuous aromas and silky texture are reminiscent of a top-class, opulently styled grand cru red Burgundy. Delicious and forward, it will provide ideal drinking over the next decade. The 1995 Barolo Bricat Gramolere, from his parcel of Nebbiolo planted at the top of this hillside vineyard, is more structured and backward, without the expressive characteristics of the other *cuvées*. Anticipated maturity: now–2014.

MARCARINI

1997 **Barolo Brunate**	E	89
1996 **Barolo Brunate**	E	89+
1998 **Barbera Ciabot**	D	86
1997 **Barolo La Serra**	E	88
1996 **Barolo La Serra**	E	90
1999 **Dolcetto d'Alba Boschi di Berri**	C	89

Made from 150-year-old prephylloxera vines (believed to be Italy's oldest Dolcetto plantings in existence), Marcarini's renowned 1999 Dolcetto d'Alba Boschi di Berri boasts an opaque purple color as well as thick, juicy berry fruit, almond extract, and underbrush aromas. Rich but not complex, this mouth-filling, palate-staining Dolcetto can be drunk now or cellared for 5+ years. The dark ruby/purple-colored 1998 Barbera Ciabot exhibits a rougher edge as well as an excellent attack, jagged acidity, and good, ripe fruit. Made in a more rustic style, it will drink well for 4–5 years.

The 1997 Barolo La Serra and 1997 Barolo Brunate are both closed at present, so they may ultimately merit an even higher rating. The 1997 Barolo La Serra exhibits a dark ruby color in addition to Barolo's telltale bouquet of rose petals, black cherries, and balsam wood with hints of underbrush/tobacco. There is good ripeness, medium to full body, moderately high tannin, and a firm but traditionally styled finish with no evidence of new oak. Anticipated maturity: 2004–2014. Sweeter and more elegant, as well as potentially more complex, the dark ruby-colored 1997 Barolo Brunate reveals aromas of cigar box and cherry jam as well as a sweet attack with notes of minerals, subtle spicy wood, firm tannin, and medium to full body. Anticipated maturity: 2004–2015. The first thing that came to mind when I smelled the 1996 Barolo La Serra was brandy-macerated cherries. The wine's medium ruby color is deceptive in view of its concentration. This showy 1996 Barolo offers abundant quantities of sweet black cherry fruit intermixed with high-octane, concentrated, spice box characteristics, medium to full body, fine opulence, and a long, lush, powerful finish that undoubtedly conceals more tannin than exhibited. It should drink well for 10–12 years. In contrast, the 1996 Barolo Brunate reveals a more saturated dark ruby color in addition to a complex bouquet of dried herbs, smoke, minerals, and black fruits. Dense, chewy, and powerful, this big yet backward 1996 requires discipline. Anticipated maturity: 2004–2018.

ALDO MARENCO

1999	Barbera Pirona	D	85
1999	Barbera Pirona Barrique	D	87
1999	Dolcetto di Dogliani Bric	C	86
1999	Dolcetto di Dogliani Parlapà	C	89
1999	Dolcetto di Dogliani Surì	C	88

The straightforward, non–wood-aged 1999 Barbera Pirona offers a medium dark ruby color and good spiciness, but it is essentially foursquare and monolithic. It will provide uncritical quaffing over the next 1–2 years. New oak works well with Barbera, and Marenco's 1999 Pirona Barrique reveals more character in its sweet black cherry, earthy, licorice, and toasty-scented nose. There is also a deeper, more saturated ruby/purple color, medium body, and a soft finish. Enjoy it over the next 1–2 years. Marenco's straightforward, medium-bodied 1999 Dolcetto di Dogliani Bric exhibits soft, mocha, chocolate, and berry fruit flavors along with good ripeness and purity. Consume it over the next 12–18 months. Riper, sweeter, and obviously produced from lower yields and/or older vines, the 1999 Dolcetto di Dogliani Surì possesses Dolcetto's rich, jammy berry fruit mixed with mocha and coffee. Well made, with sweet fruit, excellent length, and a succulent, hedonistic personality, it should be drunk over the next 1–2 years. Lastly, made from the estate's oldest vines, the 1999 Dolcetto di Dogliani Parlapà tips the scales at a lofty 14% alcohol, which is well hidden by the glycerin, fruit, and smoky, berry, fleshy character. Drink it over the next 2 years.

MARIO MARENGO

1998	Barolo Brunate	E	(87–89)
1997	Barolo Bricco delle Viole	E	88
1997	Barolo Brunate	E	89
1996	Barolo Brunate	E	91
1995	Barolo Brunate	E	91

This La Morra producer utilizes open-top vats as opposed to the rotary fermenters so popular with many of the newer-styled Piedmontese wine-makers, and uses approximately 25% new oak casks for aging his Barolos.

An intriguing nose of allspice, cinnamon, and cloves intertwined with cherry cough syrup and smoke is followed by a medium-bodied, complex, yet understated 1998 Barolo Brunate. Drink it over the next 10 years. In 1997, Marengo produced two Barolos. The excellent, soft, lush, exotic 1997 Barolo Bricco delle Viole displays distinctive strawberry liqueur intermixed with smoky oak, leafy tobacco, and dried herbs. Open, lush, and medium- to full-bodied, without much structure, this wine should drink well young and last for 10 years. An elegant, Burgundy-styled effort, Marengo's 1997 Barolo Brunate is a spicy, black cherry, and floral-scented, medium- to full-bodied wine with beautiful purity, moderate tannin and structure, and a midweight character that is less ostentatious than many of its peers. The subtle finish reveals well-integrated tannin, acidity, and alcohol. It can be enjoyed now or cellared for 15+ years. It is slightly less impressive from bottle than it was from *barrique*. The velvety-textured 1996 Barolo Brunate offers up a textbook bouquet of rose petals, cherry liqueur, and tobacco leaf scents. Melted tar also emerges with swirling. On the palate, there are gorgeous levels of black cherry and truffle flavors. Dense and full-bodied, with lofty but not excessive alcohol (14%), this sensational Barolo has moderate tannin underlying the layers of glycerin-imbued, rich, chewy fruit. Anticipated maturity: now–2016. The 1995 Barolo Brunate is a beauty for the vintage. It is a wine of tenderness, voluptuous, silky fruit, medium body, and lovely cherry, strawberry, and tobacco flavors with toasty, smoky notes in the subtle finish. Rich, fleshy, and medium- to full-bodied, this offering will drink well for a decade.

GIAN PIERO MARRONE

1997 Barolo	D	87

A modern, internationally styled 1997, Marrone's deep ruby-colored Barolo lacks typicity but is a full-bodied, powerful, mouth-filling, delicious red. Anticipated maturity: now–2010.

FRANCO M. MARTINETTI

1997 Montruc	D	91
1997 Sul Bric	D	89

A terrific example of Barbera is the 1997 Montruc (775 cases). Aging in new French oak gives this wine an international style initially, but with airing, sweet cherry liqueur and spicy notes emerge from this dark plum-colored offering. Voluptuously textured for a Barbera, this fat, ripe, full-bodied 1997 demonstrates how sexy wines from this vintage can be. Loaded with fruit and explosive on the palate, it offers a hedonistic wine-drinking experience. Enjoy it over the next 4–5 years. The elegant 1997 Sul Bric (a blend of equal parts Barbera and Cabernet Sauvignon, aged for one year in French oak) does not possess the power and explosiveness of the Montruc. The Sul Bric exhibits black currant fruit intertwined with toasty new oak, lead pencil, and dried herbs. In the mouth, there are excellent density, purity, and overall balance. While there is noticeable tannin in the finish, the wine is fat and sweet. Drink it over the next 8 years.

BARTOLO MASCARELLO

1998 Barolo	E	(90–93)
1997 Barolo	E	94
1996 Barolo	E	(87–88+)
1995 Barolo	E	86

One of my favorite traditional producers and a quintessential traditionalist, Bartolo Mascarello appears to have been less successful than some of his peers in 1995 and 1996, but his 1997 and 1998 are topflight.

The 1998 Barolo reveals a deceivingly unimpressive plum/garnet/ruby color. However, the aromatics explode from the glass offering scents of Chinese black tea, licorice, black cherries, tar, and truffles. In the mouth, it is sweet, fleshy, powerful, and heady, with exquisite purity as well as symmetry. This wine's aromas and flavors will convince readers that Nebbiolo is the Pinot Noir of Italy. It will undoubtedly tighten after bottling, reemerge in 2–3 years and age well for nearly two decades.

I underestimated the 1997 Barolo from barrel, but now that it is in bottle, it is an impressive, old-style, heavyweight effort that will age for three decades. A dark plum/garnet color is accompanied by a striking bouquet of cinnamon, balsa wood, roses, tar, minerals, and cherry liqueur. There is good acidity for a 1997, a broad, full-bodied, super-concentrated palate, and telltale truffle, leather, and dried herb notes. Powerful and long, but not as exotic as many 1997s, this well-delineated, gorgeously pure, structured Barolo is a classic from the old school of Piedmontese winemaking. Anticipated maturity: 2005–2030.

The 1996 Barolo reveals surprisingly high acidity in its relatively backward, tannic profile. It was closed and tough-textured when I saw it, with sour cherry, dried nut, and kirsch notes. The wine did not develop in the glass, remaining austere and compressed. Anticipated maturity: 2003–2014. The 1995 Barolo displays a moderate cranberry color with a pink edge leading to amber. It is light- to medium-bodied, with intriguing spice box aromas intermixed with strawberry and cherry fruit. Moderate tannin in the finish suggests this wine will have a limited longevity of 7–10 years. It is a light effort, even considering the vintage.

GIUSEPPE MASCARELLO & FIGLIO

1998	Barolo Monprivato	E	(89–91)
1997	Barolo Monprivato	E	92
1996	Barolo Monprivato	E	(87–89)
1995	Barolo Monprivato	E	87

Mascarello's Barolos rank among Piedmont's perennial stars, particularly in top vintages. A silky, full-bodied, opulent effort, the 1998 Barolo Monprivato reveals good intensity as well as a fleshy, up-front bouquet of licorice, tobacco, sweet cherries, melted asphalt, and rose petals. A classic Nebbiolo, this surprisingly soft, silky-textured Barolo can be drunk now as well as cellared for 15 years. While not as exotic or explosive as the 1997, the 1998 is still top-class. The 1997 Barolo Monprivato exhibits a dense ruby/garnet color as well as a sweet nose of cedar, black fruits, earth, tar, and rose petals. The explosive perfume is followed by a rich, seamless, full-bodied, unctuously textured wine. One of the most precocious and accessible Monprivatos I have ever tasted, the 1997 is the finest since the glorious 1990. Anticipated maturity: now–2015. The 1996 Barolo Monprivato is more structured and muscular, but not as concentrated or powerful as I expected given this producer's track record. It exhibits a dark plum color with amber at the edge. The smoky, dried herb, cedary, tobacco leaf elements compete with cherries, leather, and licorice. Medium- to full-bodied, with a soft attack and moderate tannin in the finish, this is a very good to excellent Barolo that falls short of being outstanding. Anticipated maturity: 2003–2012. This traditional producer has turned out a 1995 Barolo Monprivato with earthy, truffle, licorice, and dusty black cherry fruit. Medium- to full-bodied, with good ripeness, excellent purity, and a nicely extracted, rustic, generous style, it is already accessible, yet promises to last for 10 years.

CASCINA LUISIN DI LUIGI MINUTO

1997	Barbaresco Cascina Luisin Rabajà	D	90
1996	Barbaresco Cascina Luisin Rabajà	D	88
1995	Barbaresco Cascina Luisin Rabajà	D	87
1997	Barbaresco Sorì Paolin	D	86
1996	Barbaresco Sorì Paolin	D	81?
1995	Barbaresco Sorì Paolin	D	86

The standard *cuvées* are very good efforts, but Minuto's Barbarescos from the Cascina Luisin Rabajà vineyard are distinctly superior to his offerings from the Sorì Paolin vineyard. The velvety, supple, impressively extracted 1997 Barbaresco Sorì Paolin's opaque ruby/purple color is followed by gobs of blackberry and cherry fruit aromas, a sweet mid-palate, the vintage's telltale high glycerin and low acidity, and a thick, juicy finish. Drink it over the next 10 years. The outstanding dark ruby/purple-colored 1997 Barbaresco Cascina Luisin Rabajà offers an intense nose of licorice, black cherry fruit, dried herbs, and wood. In addition, it displays a velvety texture, full body, and an opulent, lush, low-acid finish. Already accessible, it should be delicious when released next year. Anticipated maturity: now–2010.

The more closed 1996 Barbaresco Sorì Paolin possesses medium body, high acidity, more tannin, and a colder feel in the mouth than the more generous 1995. It is a bigger, more muscular wine with plenty of structure and excellent fruit and purity, but it is closed, firmly knit and austere. Anticipated maturity: now–2010. The 1996 Barbaresco Cascina Luisin Rabajà is nearly outstanding. It possesses a distinctive cigar tobacco–scented nose with aromas of kirsch, spice, and earth. Medium- to full-bodied, with excellent richness and good spice and length, it displays more tannin than the 1995 but should be drunk over the next 5–6 years. The 1995 Barbaresco Sorì Paolin reveals a dark ruby color, as well as sweet, attractive cherry fruit blended with cedar, cigar box, and leather. Medium-bodied and supple, with decent acidity, this is a stylish, delicious Barbaresco to enjoy over the next 4–5 years. The 1995 Barbaresco Cascina Luisin Rabajà reveals an open-knit, intensely spicy, cedar box and black fruit–scented nose. It is fleshy, expansive, fully mature, and ideal for drinking over the next 3–4 years.

MOCCAGATTA

1998	Barbaresco Bric Balin	D	89
1997	Barbaresco Bric Balin	D	90
1996	Barbaresco Bric Balin	D	90
1998	Barbaresco Vigneto Basarin	D	84?
1997	Barbaresco Vigneto Basarin	D	90
1996	Barbaresco Vigneto Basarin	D	89
1998	Barbaresco Vigneto Cole	D	90+
1997	Barbaresco Vigneto Cole	D	90
1996	Barbaresco Vigneto Cole	D	90+
1998	Barbera d'Alba Vigneto Basarin	C	90

The opaque purple, thick, juicy 1998 Barbera d'Alba Vigneto Basarin oozes with black cherry fruit intermixed with cedar, strawberries, and toasty wood. It exhibits a supple texture, a tremendous palate impression, and a long, lush finish. Enjoy it over the next 2–3 years.

The 1998 Barbaresco Vigneto Basarin is an elegant, lighter-styled effort with an amber edge already noticeable in its medium ruby color. Scents of tobacco as well as ripe strawberry and cherry fruit are present, but the finish is attenuated and lean, without the depth or body expected in a top Barbaresco cru. The aromatically compelling 1998 Barbaresco Bric Balin exhibits aromas of new saddle leather intermixed with tobacco, cedar wood, black cherry liqueur, and smoke. Its dark ruby color also reveals some amber at the rim. Medium-bodied, soft, and well balanced, it is meant to be consumed over the next 4–5 years. The most massive, backward, concentrated, and complex of the 1998s is the 1998 Barbaresco Vigneto Cole. A dense dark garnet color is followed by high-toned, fragrant aromas of menthol, leather, spice box, cherries, and wood. Deep, rich, and medium- to full-bodied, with moderate tannin in the long finish, it will keep for a decade or more.

The 1997s are simply outstanding. While they all merit a 90-point rating, they represent different styles, with the Basarin the most evolved, the Balin the most subtle, and the Cole the most massive, backward, and exotic. They all possess 8–10 years of aging potential. The delicious 1997 Barbaresco Vigneto Basarin is the most forward of this trio, with a deep garnet color and a sweet nose of black cherry fruit, spice box, licorice, smoke, and earth. Full-bodied, silky-textured, seductive, and lush, it is hard to resist. Less aromatic as well as more tannic and firmer-structured is the 1997 Barbaresco Bric Balin. It exhibits a deep ruby color, copious quantities of glycerin, black fruits, herbs, cedar, tar, and spicy oak, medium to full body, admirable delineation, and firm tannin in the finish. Anticipated maturity: now–2013. The 1997 Barbaresco Vigneto Cole's dark plum/garnet color reveals some amber at the edge. The bouquet offers scents of mushrooms, soy, smoked meats, jammy black fruits, root vegetables, and more oak than the other *cuvées*. Complex, juicy, succulent, and full-bodied, with serious tannin in the finish, it should last for 10–12 years.

The terrific 1996s, while not huge, are beautifully knit with fruit-driven personalities and considerable complexity. The dark ruby-colored 1996 Barbaresco Vigneto Basarin offers a sexy bouquet of black cherry jam intermixed with spice and wood. The wine is dense and fat, with abundant glycerin and a hedonistic, up-front appeal. Drink it over the next 10 years. The sensational 1996 Barbaresco Bric Balin displays a saturated ruby color, and a provocative nose of black cherry liqueur, melted road tar, vanilla, and floral scents. Full-bodied, with layers of glycerin and fruit, this is a mouthcoating, rich, surprisingly silky-textured Barbaresco to drink over the next 10–12 years. The 1996 Barbaresco Vigneto Cole reveals more evidence of new oak in its smoky, toasty nose. There are also more extract, concentration, and tannin, as well as good purity and a 40-second finish. Full-bodied and in need of 1–2 years of cellaring, it should keep for 12–15 years.

MAURO MOLINO

1998	Barolo	D	88
1997	Barolo	D	88
1996	Barolo	D	(84–86)
1998	Barolo Vigna Conca	E	(90–92+)
1997	Barolo Vigna Conca	E	91+
1996	Barolo Vigna Conca	E	92+
1995	Barolo Vigna Conca	E	90
1998	Barolo Vigna Gancia	E	(88–90)
1997	Barolo Vigna Gancia	E	89
1996	Barolo Vigna Gancia	E	92
1995	Barolo Vigna Gancia	E	87

Molino continues to raise the quality level of his Barolos, with his 1998s performing as well as his 1997s. The 1998s are elegant and harmonious, with even more enticing aromatics, and the 1997s are very fine indeed.

The dark ruby-colored 1998 Barolo exhibits a classic bouquet of licorice, rose petals, tar, and sweet black cherry fruit. Medium- to full-bodied, delicate, and flavorful in a layered, harmonious style, it will drink well for 5–6 years. The opaque garnet-colored 1998 Barolo Vigna Gancia is made in a firmer style, with abundant nuances as well as muscle but not the expressive personality displayed by its two siblings. It offers excellent to outstanding depth, medium to full body, and moderate tannin in the finish. Give it 1–2 years of cellaring, and enjoy it over the following 10–12 years. The superb, saturated ruby/purple-colored 1998 Barolo Vigna Conca may not possess the opulence of its 1997 counterpart, but it exhibits impressive balance, terrific purity, and fragrant black fruit notes intermixed with smoke, new wood, licorice, and spice box. Given the moderate tannin in the finish, I would cellar it for 1–2 years and consume it over the following 10–15 years.

The generic 1997 Barolo reveals pink at the rim of its ruby/garnet color. A perfume of roasted peanuts, dried Provençal herbs, sweet currants, and cherries is more reminiscent of a classy St.-Emilion than Nebbiolo. However, in the mouth, the wine's opulence, fleshiness, and soft, forward character reflect this vintage's Piedmont style. Enjoy it over the next 4–5 years. Offering a more complex bouquet, the dark garnet-colored 1997 Barolo Vigna Gancia reveals scents of balsam wood, herbs, licorice, cherry liqueur, and soy. Additionally, it possesses firm tannin, good density and ripeness, and a rich, medium- to full-bodied, plush, yet delineated personality. Give it 1–2 more years of cellaring, and consume it over the following 10–12 years. The superb 1997 Barolo Vigna Conca is the most backward, powerful, and concentrated of these offerings. The color is a dark garnet, and the nose offers up aromas of smoke, meat, dried herbs, black fruits, earth, and spices. Dense, full-bodied, concentrated, powerful, and structured, it will be at its best between 2003–2016.

In 1996, Molino produced a generic Barolo in addition to his two single-vineyard cuvées. The 1996 Barolo is a pleasant, straightforward, soft, medium ruby-colored wine that needs to be drunk over the next 4–5 years. In contrast, the superb, saturated ruby/purple-colored 1996 Barolo Vigna Conca is a massive effort with oodles of black cherry fruit intertwined with licorice, smoke, and spicy elements. Full-bodied and super-concentrated, with copious quantities of glycerin, it is soft and voluptuous. Enjoy it now and over the next 10 years. The opaque dark ruby/purple-colored 1996 Barolo Vigna Gancia offers a nose of *surmaturité*. This unevolved, backward wine possesses chewy plum/cherry fruit, terrific extraction, fine purity, and a full-bodied, moderately tannic, youthful finish. Anticipated maturity: now–2016.

The 1995 Barolo Vigna Gancia is attractive, evolved, open-knit, and medium-bodied, with fine ripeness and a spice box/cherry-dominated personality. Although not a blockbuster, it is elegant, soft, and ideal for drinking over the next 3–4 years. The richer 1995 Barolo Vigna Conca possesses more depth than its medium ruby color suggests. Additionally, it is pure, well delineated, and made in an elegant, suave, savory style with abundant sweet red fruits, cigar box spices, and a touch of new saddle leather. It should drink well for 7–8 years.

MONTI

1998 Barbera d'Alba	C	89
1997 Barbera d'Alba	C	90+

These two Barberas are produced from exceptionally ripe fruit and low yields and are aged in new French oak. Sadly, there are only 100 cases of the dark ruby/purple-colored, flamboyant 1998 Barbera d'Alba. This wine offers aromas of exotic sweet new oak intermixed with jammy black fruits, coconuts, and dried herbs. Full-bodied and loaded with concentrated fruit, it lacks complexity but delivers plenty of hedonism in its plush personality. Drink it over the next 3–4 years. The internationally styled, blockbuster 1997 Barbera d'Alba is a monster-sized wine that boasts an opaque black/purple color, as well as sumptuous aromas of overripe cherries, strawberries, licorice, and toast. Thick, huge, massive, and layered, with a finish that lasts more than 30 seconds, this low-acid, impressive wine can be drunk now or aged for a decade.

F.LLI MOSSIO

1999 Dolcetto d'Alba	B	87
1999 Dolcetto d'Alba Bricco Caramelli	B	90
1999 Dolcetto d'Alba Piano delli Perdoni	B	86

These wines are evidence that 1999 is a strong vintage for Dolcetto and Barbera. The 1999 Dolcetto d'Alba and 1999 Dolcetto d'Alba Piano delli Perdoni are dark ruby/purple-colored, medium-bodied, sweet wines with plenty of chocolaty, cherry fruit. The Perdoni is tangier, with slightly higher acidity. The blockbuster of this trio is the 1999 Dolcetto d'Alba Bricco Caramelli. It possesses an opaque ruby/purple color as well as a knockout nose of chocolate, espresso, and berries. With copious glycerin, a fleshy, fat texture, and wonderful ripeness and purity, it will drink well for 2–3 years, as these wines rarely improve.

ANDREA OBERTO

1996	Barolo Vigneto Albarella	E	88+
1997	Barolo Vigneto Rocche	E	92
1996	Barolo Vigneto Rocche	E	91+
1995	Barolo Vigneto Rocche	E	86

From a consistently fine producer, the following examples are all fine for their respective vintages. These wines, that merit interest, are quasi-modern-styled wines that combine the best of the traditional and modern schools of winemaking.

The 1997 Barolo Vigneto Rocche boasts huge quantities of glycerin, which, combined with high alcohol, low acidity, and jammy black cherry and blackberry fruit, makes for an opulent texture and viscous mouth-feel. It is a freak as far as classic Barolo goes, but a delicious one. Layered, thick, and almost over the top, it is a knockout, dramatic effort that will be immensely popular. Anticipated maturity: 2003–2020.

The 1996 Barolo Vigneto Albarella's dark plum/ruby color is followed by sweet aromatics consisting of cedar wood, cherries, black raspberries, coffee, chocolate, and spice box. Dry tannin in the finish is typical of the 1996 vintage. Rich and full-bodied, it requires cellaring. Anticipated maturity: 2005–2020. The opaque plum/ruby/purple-colored 1996 Barolo Vigneto Rocche is a full-bodied, powerful, tannic effort with notes of rose petals, asphalt, cedar, black fruits, minerals, licorice, and fruitcake. Complex, layered, thick, and rich, it is best cellared for 3–4 years and drunk over the following 20–25 years.

The dark ruby-colored 1995 Barolo Vigneto Rocche exhibits a rich, modern style, as well as a textbook nose of roses, tar, spicy black cherry fruit, and a touch of *barrique* and foresty aromas. Rich and medium-bodied, with a short finish but excellent ripeness, this moderately sized Barolo can be drunk now as well as over the next 10 years.

F.LLI ODDERO

1997	Barbaresco	D	(85–87)
1996	Barbaresco	D	85
1997	Barolo Mondoca di Bussia Soprana	D	87
1996	Barolo Mondoca di Bussia Soprana	D	87?
1995	Barolo Mondoca di Bussia Soprana	D	88
1997	Barolo Vigna Rionda	D	86
1995	Barolo Vigna Rionda	D	87
1997	Barolo Rocche dei Rivera di Castiglione	D	88
1996	Barolo Rocche dei Rivera di Castiglione	D	87
1997	Furesté	D	89

Another producer from the village of La Morra, Oddero's 1997s exhibit the vintage's attractive levels of glycerin, fat, low acidity, and overripe style. All of them possess Nebbiolo's textbook aromas of cherry jam, dried herbs, tar, and spice. The 1997 Barbaresco displays a dark ruby color as well as chewy, exuberant, cherry liqueur fruit flavors intertwined with dried herb and spice. It is a luscious Barbaresco to enjoy over the next decade. The 1997 Barolo Vigna Rionda (a great vineyard in Serralunga) exhibits a dark garnet color as well as a sweet nose of cedar, spice box, licorice, toffee, and tobacco. In the mouth, it is creamy, round, medium-bodied, and easy to drink. Consume within 4–5 years. The dark ruby/purple-colored 1997 Barolo Rocche dei Rivera di Castiglione is full-bodied, fat, monolithic, and lacking complexity, but chewy and weighty. It is a husky Barolo to drink between now–2015. Even sweeter and riper is the medium- to full-bodied 1997 Barolo Mondoca di Bussia Soprana. It offers an excellent smoke, herb, licorice, and kirsch-scented bouquet. Soy and incense also make an appearance in the flavors. The wine is spicy, with low acidity and noticeable glycerin. Drink over the next 4–5 years. The dense 1997 Furesté (100% Cabernet Sauvignon) possesses cassis fruit, toasty new oak, and an opulent texture, but it is not yet totally formed or delineated. Given its concentration levels and intensity, it should merit an outstanding score after some more bottle age. Anticipated maturity: 2003–2012. Oddero's medium-bodied, garnet-colored 1996 Barolo Rocche dei Rivera di Castiglione exhibits aromas of leather, sour cherries, and ripe fruit. Well made, spicy, open-knit, and attractive, it can be consumed over the next decade.

The 1996 Barbaresco is a good, elegant offering with spicy tobacco-tinged cherry fruit, medium body, and a lightly tannic finish. It is ideal for drinking over the next 7–8 years. Oddero's 1996 Barolo Mondoca di Bussia Soprana possesses a dark color, considerable concentration, huge body, and brutal tannin levels (thus the question mark). The wine is leathery, chunky, and rustic. If the tannin melts away without a proportional loss of fruit, this could be close to outstanding, but the astringency of the tannin is cause for concern. Anticipated maturity: 2003–2015.

Oddero's two 1995s are similar in quality, although the Vigna Rionda is more tannic. The 1995 Barolo Mondoca di Bussia Soprana exhibits a smoky ashtray-like nose with notes of cedar, leather, and dried herbs and fruits. As the wine sat in the glass, the classic tar and rose petal concoction emerged. This is an old-style, rustic Barolo with an evolved plum/garnet color, hard tannin, and a lot of character and spice. It should drink well for 10 years. The herb- and smoke-infused 1995 Barolo Vigna Rionda possesses more rustic tannin, as well as good concentration, and an old-style, tough, chewy character that may not appeal to readers who enjoy modern, supple-styled wines. Nevertheless, it is a fine wine that can be drunk now or cellared for 10–12 years.

PALLADINO

1998	Barolo Serralunga	D	89
1997	Barolo Serralunga	D	89+
1998	Barolo Vigna Broglio	D	88
1997	Barolo Vigna Broglio	D	90
1998	Barolo Vigna San Bernardo	D	89
1997	Barolo Vigna San Bernardo	D	92

A sleeper Serralunga producer whom I discovered a couple of years ago, Palladino has vineyards in the village of Serralunga d'Alba. Its 1997s as well as its 1998s performed extremely well in my Piedmont tastings. These wines appear to be traditionally made with no evidence of *barrique* aging, although they do not display the backwardness or tannin found in most traditionalists' Barbarescos and Barolos.

The 1998s are stylish, elegant, evolved wines that should all drink well during their first 10 years of life. The 1998 Barolo Vigna Broglio exhibits a dark garnet color along with a sweet nose of spice, coffee, black cherry jam, medium to full body, adequate acidity, and a plush style. More evolved, the 1998 Barolo Serralunga displays a dark garnet color with amber hues. Moderately intense aromas of brown sugar, molasses, ripe cherries, soy, and earth are followed by a ripe, sweet, expansive, medium-bodied wine. It's a marginal call, but the garnet-colored 1998 Barolo Vigna San Bernardo may possess slightly more expansiveness and volume than its two siblings. Medium-bodied, long, and purely made, it displays a compelling sweetness in its ripe notes of tobacco, cherry fruit, and earth.

The generic 1997 Barolo Serralunga is a strong effort. Revealing notes of melted caramel, brown sugar, smoke, kirsch, and dried herbs, it tastes like a right bank Pomerol from an extremely ripe vintage. Unctuous, thick, and juicy but without the complexity of its two siblings, this delicious 1997 would merit an even higher score if numbers were given for pure hedonism. Anticipated maturity: now–2015. The outstanding, opaque garnet-colored 1997

Barolo Vigna Broglio is a powerful, impressively endowed effort with copious aromas of black cherry fruit, cedar, fruitcake, dried herbs, licorice, and hints of new oak. Impressive purity, symmetry, and overall winemaking make this an exceptional effort. Tannin in the finish suggests that several years of cellaring is warranted. Anticipated maturity: now–2016. Lastly, Palladino's opaque ruby/purple-colored 1997 Barolo Vigna San Bernardo exhibits a moderate style with new oak in the nose, fabulously concentrated black raspberry and cherry fruit, and subtle notions of minerals, maple syrup, and vanilla in the background. Full-bodied and exceptionally concentrated, with beautiful purity and well-integrated acidity as well as tannin, this terrific Barolo is a sleeper of the vintage. Anticipated maturity: now–2020.

ARMANDO PARUSSO

1999	Barbera d'Alba Ornati	D	91
1997	Barolo	D	(89–91)
1996	Barolo	D	88
1996	Barolo Bussia Vigna Fiurin	E	91
1998	Barolo Bussia Vigna Munie	E	(91–93)
1997	Barolo Bussia Vigna Munie	E	91+
1996	Barolo Bussia Vigna Munie	E	92
1995	Barolo Bussia Vigna Munie	E	90
1998	Barolo Bussia Vigna Rocche	E	(90–92)
1997	Barolo Bussia Vigna Rocche	E	92
1996	Barolo Bussia Vigna Rocche	E	92
1995	Barolo Bussia Vigna Rocche	E	90
1998	Barolo Mariondino	E	(87–88)
1997	Barolo Mariondino	E	90
1996	Barolo Mariondino	E	(90–92)
1995	Barolo Mariondino	E	87
1998	Barolo Piccole Vigne	E	(88–89)
1997	Barolo Piccole Vigne	E	90
1998	Langhe Rosso Bricco Rovella	D	89

Young Marco Parusso, who has completely modernized his cellars on the slopes of Monforte d'Alba, has come of age with his 1995s, 1996s, and 1997s. Moreover, those three vintages have been followed by impressive wines in both 1998 and 1999. As expected from such a youthful producer, Parusso is from the modernist school of winemaking. He believes in the use of rotary fermenters, short macerations, and 25–75% new oak for his finest crus.

The 1999 Barbera d'Alba Ornati is a *barrique*-aged Barbera revealing abundant quantities of strawberry jam intermixed with blackberries, cherries, and toasty, smoky oak. Deep, opulent, and voluptuous, with great purity and presence, it is a fabulous buy, but consume it over the next 3–4 years. The 500+ cases of the 1998 Langhe Rosso Bricco Rovella, a blend of 60% Nebbiolo, 30% Barbera, and 10% Cabernet Sauvignon aged 18 months in new French oak, offer plenty of smoky, toasty oak intertwined with black fruits, smoke, cedar, and cigar box notes. It is medium-bodied and surprisingly elegant for a wine of this modern, international style. Drink it over the next 3–4 years.

Parusso has turned out a deep ruby-colored 1998 Barolo Piccole Vigne with a spicy nose of balsam wood and black cherries. In the mouth, there is plenty of glycerin as well as an attractive open-knit style. Drink this 1998 over the next 5–6 years. More minty, peppery, and oaky, the medium-weight 1998 Barolo Mariondino exhibits plenty of wood and black cherry characteristics in its distinctive personality. It will age well for a decade.

The most powerful wine of this quartet is the 1998 Barolo Bussia Vigna Rocche. Structured, tannic, super-concentrated, well delineated, dense, full-bodied, and broodingly backward, this impressive effort reveals the 1998 vintage's telltale fragrance as well as the power and glycerin of 1997. Anticipated maturity: 2003–2015. The more graceful, delicate, smoky, leathery, earthy, dark ruby/garnet-colored 1998 Barolo Bussia Vigna Munie possesses medium to full body, terrific purity and ripeness, and a more delicate, lacelike style. It can be drunk over the next 10–12 years.

The 1997s reveal this terrific vintage's jammy, low-acid, exotic, flamboyant character. They all possess considerable tannin, but their ostentatious personalities are overwhelming. For example, sipping the dark ruby-colored, low-acid 1997 Barolo is akin to drinking strawberry jam. Ripe, fat, exotic, and hedonistic, this fruit bomb will be drinkable upon release and last until 2010.

Parusso's softest, most forward 1997 is the 1997 Barolo Piccole Vigne. Dark plum-colored with a hint of amber at the edge, it exhibits sexy, herbaceous, kirsch-scented aromas, a fleshy, full-bodied palate, and an evolved personality. Consume it over the next 10 years. The 1997 Barolo Mariondino, from a vineyard in Castiglione Falletto, possesses a dense ruby/purple color, more tannin and structure than Parusso's other offerings, notes of earth, black cherry jam, smoke, coffee, licorice, and soy, outstanding concentration, and a spicy, long finish. The fat and glycerin found in many 1997s are present but are buttressed by obvious tannin. Anticipated maturity: 2003–2020. The explosive, dense ruby/purple-colored 1997 Barolo Bussia Vigna Rocche possesses a dramatic, concentrated personality as well as an exceptional bouquet of minerals, black fruits, tar, tobacco, and subtle new oak. This massive, concentrated Barolo exhibits terrific glycerin and fruit, in addition to a fleshy, nicely structured, well-delineated finish. Anticipated maturity: 2003–2020. Similar in size, the dark ruby-colored 1997 Barolo Bussia Vigna Munie displays a Châteauneuf-du-Pape–like character in its combination of kirsch and roasted Provençal herbs. While not as powerful as the Bussia Vigna Rocche, it is an expansive, chewy, structured effort with wonderful intensity as well as the vintage's telltale overripeness and excessive exoticism. Anticipated maturity: now–2017.

The 1996 Barolo exhibits the most new oak. Sexy, forward, and made in a lush, medium- to full-bodied style with gobs of red and black fruits, lavish wood, sweet tannin, and a concentrated, fleshy mouth-feel, it will be drinkable between now–2012. The dark ruby-colored 1996 Barolo Mariondino displays a distinctive almond, cherry liqueur, licorice, and smoky oak–scented nose. Medium- to full-bodied, expansive, and pure, this classic, nicely structured, layered Barolo should be accessible young, yet keep for 10–12 years. The terrific 1996 Barolo Bussia Vigna Munie is more exotic, with sweet scents of melted road tar, cherries, tobacco, and cigar box. Medium- to full-bodied, dense, and full of fruit, this intense wine will also be accessible young but will keep for 12 or more years. Even better is the 1996 Barolo Bussia Vigna Rocche. In addition to the tar, smoke, dried herbs, leather, and cherry fruit aromas, it reveals a distinctive mineral/powdered rock character. A full-bodied, powerful Barolo that possesses superb richness, a multidimensional personality, and a boatload of tannin, this is Parusso's biggest, most concentrated 1996. There is moderate tannin in the finish, but the fruit and *terroir* characteristics dominate. Anticipated maturity: 2003–2020. While the full-bodied 1996 Barolo Bussia Vigna Fiurin is backward, tannic, and closed, it exhibits impressive potential. There are good spice, smoke, and intense fruit concentration in addition to high levels of tannin. This 1996 will require patience. Anticipated maturity: 2005–2020.

The 1995 Barolo Mariondino's medium ruby color is followed by a fragrant nose of dried herbs, tobacco, spice box, and cherry cola. Ripe, with subtle oak, medium to full body, and an expansive, fleshy, open-knit personality, this Barolo can be enjoyed over the next 5–6 years. The 1995 Barolo Bussia Vigna Munie is more opulent but just as evolved and tasty. It offers intriguing floral elements intertwined with melted tar and berry fruit. Exhibiting toasty oak and light tannin in the long finish, this lush, expansive wine can be drunk over the next decade. The 1995 Barolo Bussia Vigna Rocche is the fullest bodied, most powerful and tannic of the 1995s. In addition to the telltale dried herbs, cherry liqueur, leather, and floral scents, it offers layered, concentrated flavors, outstanding purity, admirable muscle and glycerin, and moderate tannin in the impressively endowed finish. Anticipated maturity: now–2012.

ELIA PASQUERO

1998 Barbaresco Sorì Paitin	D	90
1997 Barbaresco Sorì Paitin	D	89
1996 Barbaresco Sorì Paitin	D	92

A classic Barbaresco as well as a textbook expression of Nebbiolo, this exceptionally complex, dark ruby/garnet-colored 1998 Barbaresco Sorì Paitin offers gorgeous aromatics of cedarwood, Chinese black tea, cherries, smoke, and a whiff of creosote. Dense, fleshy, and voluptuous, yet structured and brilliantly well delineated, it will drink beautifully over the next 4–5 years. Pasquero's structured 1997 Barbaresco Sorì Paitin reveals more tannin and austerity than expected for this vintage. When tasted side by side, his 1998 and 1999 both seemed significantly richer and fleshier. Nevertheless, the 1997 is an excellent effort. It offers notes of tobacco, spice box, licorice, and cherries as well as a touch of herbaceousness. Medium-bodied and firmly structured, it should age for a decade or more. The 1996 Barbaresco Sorì Paitin exhibits terrific fruit intensity, along with toast in the flamboyant aromatics. In addition to oak, there are plenty of tobacco leaf, jammy cherries, and dried herbs. Full-bodied, round, luscious, and accessible, this Barbaresco should drink well for a decade.

F.LLI PECCHENINO

1998 Dolcetto di Dogliani Bricco Botti	C	92
1997 Dolcetto di Dogliani Bricco Botti	C	91
1999 Dolcetto di Dogliani Sirì d'Jermu	C	91
1998 Langhe La Castella	C	90
1997 Langhe La Castella	C	92

These wines' richness and concentration blew me away. All are aged in large wood *foudres* prior to being bottled with minimal intervention. The Bricco Botti is among the finest Dolcetti I have ever tasted. The fabulous 1999 Dolcetto di Dogliani Sirì d'Jermu exhibits an opaque inky/purple color as well as a striking bouquet of blackberry and cherry fruit intermixed with almond extract and chocolate. Full-bodied, with layers of fruit, glycerin, and intensity, it will not become any more complex, but it is a mouth-staining, palate-pleasing, sumptuous Dolcetto to enjoy over the next 3–4 years. As hard as it is to believe, the 1998 Dolcetto di Dogliani Bricco Botti is even more powerful, concentrated, and explosive. It also possesses surprising structure, a characteristic not found in most Dolcettos. This opaque purple-colored, massive (but not heavy) effort is vibrant, opulent, and chewy because of its intense fruit and glycerin. It represents Dolcetto at its most extreme and intense. If the famed Veneto producer of Valpolicella and Amarone, Dal Forno, made Dolcetto, it might taste like this!

The outstanding 1998 Langhe La Castella is a blend of 45% Nebbiolo, 50% Barbera, and 5% Cabernet Sauvignon. Opaque ruby/purple-colored, with a structured personality, it reveals less charm and massive fruit than the Dolcetti, but more perfume and nuances. It is medium-bodied and ripe, with a sweet attack offering notes of strawberries, cherries, tobacco, rose petals, and licorice. The finish reveals some tannin as well as acidity, but it is well integrated. Anticipated maturity: now–2012.

The explosive 1997 Dolcetto di Dogliani Bricco Botti is one of the greatest Dolcettos I have ever tasted. It boasts a black/purple color, awesome extract levels, a massive, chewy, full-bodied palate, with gorgeous sweetness and ripeness, as well as a 30+-second finish. These wines rarely develop much complexity, being fruit- and texture-driven, but this 1997 delivers the goods. Enjoy it over the next 4–5 years. It is an immensely impressive effort. Lastly, the blend of Barbera and Nebbiolo, with a touch of Cabernet Sauvignon, the 1997 Langhe La Castella reveals an opaque black/inky color, super high extraction, full body, high tannin, abundant toasty oak, amazing density and length, and a tightly knit yet opulent/voluptuous personality. Enjoy it over the next 10–12 years.

LUIGI PELISSERO

1998	Barbaresco	D	87
1998	Barbaresco Vanotu	D	91
1997	Barbaresco Vanotu	D	(86–88)
1996	Barbaresco Vanotu	D	86?
1995	Barbaresco Vanotu	D	85

These mainstream Barbarescos are competent, well-made efforts, with the 1998s faring much better than the three previous vintages. The estate produces a standard *cuvée*, as well as a special Barbaresco Vanotu, aged in French oak for two years, the annual production of which averages 575 cases.

The delicious, open-knit, spicy, cedary, herb, tobacco, and red fruit–scented and –flavored, medium-bodied 1998 Barbaresco can be enjoyed now and over the next 3–4 years. The dazzling 1998 Barbaresco Vanotu is sensational. A dark plum color is accompanied by sumptuous aromas of soy, tobacco smoke, Chinese black tea, kirsch, and spice box. Full-bodied and layered, with a multidimensional personality, sweet tannin, and adequate acidity, this exquisite Barbaresco will drink well for 10 years. The finest of this trio is the 1997 Barbaresco Vanotu, a deep ruby-colored wine with ripe black cherry and cassis fruit, a cedary, spicy component, very good ripeness, and a moderately long finish. It should be drunk during its first 5–6 years of life. The 1996 Barbaresco Vanotu reveals a more stemmy, vegetal character, in addition to a lean, tannic, hard finish. I have reservations about its ever achieving full harmony. In both its aromas and its flavors, the elegant 1995 Barbaresco Vanotu exhibits dusty cherry fruit, spice, earth, and medium body. Drink it over the next 2–3 years.

VIGNAIOLI ELVIO PERTINACE

1998	Barbaresco	E	89
1997	Barbaresco	E	87
1998	Barbaresco Castellizzano	E	91
1998	Barbaresco Marcarini	E	90
1997	Barbaresco Marcarini	E	90
1998	Barbaresco Nervo	E	88
1997	Barbaresco Nervo	E	92
1996	Pertinace	D	89

This cooperative (twelve wineries that pool their resources) produces fairly priced wines of impeccably high quality. The 1998s are the finest wines I have tasted from Vignaioli Elvio Pertinace, which seem to be ratcheting up its quality level. They reveal the vintage's open, forward characteristic but are balanced and concentrated enough to last for 12–15 years, particularly the three single-vineyard offerings. The 1997s are also of high quality.

The medium ruby-colored 1998 Barbaresco's sweet nose of cedar, black cherries, and spice box is followed by medium-bodied, ripe, concentrated, pure flavors. Drink it over the next 5–7 years. All three crus possess similar colors, ranging from medium ruby to saturated ruby. Production is moderate, with approximately 750 cases of each. The 1998 Barbaresco Marcarini exhibits a big, juicy, complex perfume of tobacco, cherry cough syrup, balsa wood, herbs, and rose petals. Deep, with a terrific texture, real elegance, an opulent, fleshy midpalate, and sweet tannin in the finish, it should drink well for 10–12 years. The more angular but similarly styled, attractive 1998 Barbaresco Nervo reveals more licorice in its aromatics and flavors. It, too, will drink well for 10–12 years. The most concentrated and dense offering is the 1998 Barbaresco Castellizzano. It boasts a deep plum/ruby color in addition to intense aromas consisting of cherry jam infused with smoky tobacco, Provençal herbs, licorice, and truffles. Full-bodied, opulent, dense, and accessible, it will drink well for 12 years.

The medium ruby/garnet-colored 1997 Barbaresco offers a fragrant bouquet of cedar, tobacco, plums, raspberries, and cherries, medium to full body, a sweet mid-palate, and a spicy, lightly tannic finish. Consume it over the next 3–4 years. The 1997 Barbaresco Marcarini reveals a classic Nebbiolo bouquet of tar and rose petals intermixed with sour cherries, leather, and earth. It possesses exceptional complexity, full body, exquisite density, and a long, impressive finish. Already approachable, it should continue to drink well for 12 years. Even better is the spectacular 1997 Barbaresco Nervo. An explosive nose of cigar tobacco, cherry liqueur, rose petals, and tar is followed by a full-bodied, gorgeously fruit-driven, dark ruby-colored wine with an expansive, chewy texture, as well as excellent purity and depth. As with its sibling, the Barbaresco Marcarini, the finish lasts for more than 30 seconds. It, too, will drink well for 12 years. Lastly, there are 700 cases of the 1996 Pertinace, a blend of 70% Nebbiolo and 30% Cabernet Sauvignon. This internationally styled, well-made effort possesses an opaque ruby/purple color in addition to a chocolaty, black cherry, tobacco, and spice box–scented nose, a full-bodied, rich, concentrated mid-palate, and a deep structured finish. Anticipated maturity: now–2012.

E. PIRA

1998	Barolo Cannubi	E	(90–91)
1997	Barolo Cannubi	E	91
1996	Barolo Cannubi	E	95

This estate has undergone a complete transformation under the inspired proprietress, Chiara Boschis. The wines' vinification and upbringing were changed beginning with the 1994 vintage, but the first truly great vintage was 1996.

The elegant, sweet, pure, medium ruby-colored 1998 Barolo Cannubi exhibits aromas of tar, rose petals, and cherry jam. These are followed by a medium-bodied offering with a firm tannic underpinning, excellent purity, and spicy, subtle new oak. This wine is a candidate for an outstanding rating after another 1–2 years of cellaring. Anticipated maturity: 2003–2016.

The 1997 Barolo Cannubi is another gorgeous wine, but unfortunately very little was produced. Aged in 100% new *barriques* and bottled with neither fining nor filtration, it is a full-bodied, rich, structured, garnet/ruby-colored effort offering an emerging bouquet of rose petals, cherries, leather, spice box, and tobacco. Powerful, concentrated, pure, dense, and moderately tannic, it is not as flashy and precocious as many of its peers, but is unquestionably a classic. Anticipated maturity: 2005–2020.

A compelling Barolo, as well as a classic example of the more traditional school of winemaking, the 1996 Barolo Cannubi exhibits an unimpressive medium ruby color. However, that is followed by an explosive nose of cherry jam infused with smoke, rose water, tobacco, and spice. With an amazing texture, evidenced by a fabulous concentration of fruit, full body, a boatload of glycerin, and moderately high tannin, this huge, complex, profound Barolo can be drunk now but promises to age effortlessly for two decades.

LUIGI PIRA

1997	Barolo	D	91
1996	Barolo	D	91
1995	Barolo	D	86
1998	Barolo Marenca	E	(94–96)
1997	Barolo Marenca	E	95
1996	Barolo Marenca	E	92
1995	Barolo Marenca	E	91+
1998	Barolo Margheria	E	(91–94+)

1997 Barolo Margheria	E	92+
1996 Barolo Margheria	E	90
1995 Barolo Margheria	E	91
1998 Barolo Vigna Rionda	E	(93–96)
1997 Barolo Vigna Rionda	E	97

Pira has quickly emerged as a fabulous talent, producing wines from vineyards surrounding his hometown village of Serralunga d'Alba. There are so many exceptional wine-makers in Barolo and Barbaresco that it is unfair to single out Luigi Pira as a star, but certainly his performances in 1995, 1996, 1997, and 1998 are remarkable. These wines, which qualify this estate as one of the leaders in Piedmont, are of extraordinary complexity and breathtaking richness. Each *cuvée* is given a different *élevage*, although malolactic is done in either *foudre* or *barrique*. This cellar also employs rotary fermenters. While the regular Barolo is aged completely in large wood *foudres*, the crus are aged in a combination of *foudre* and small casks, ranging from 20% new oak for Margheria to 100% for Rionda. Luigi Pira should not be confused with E. Pira from the village of Barolo, who has also been making spectacular wines, particularly since the 1996 vintage.

The 1998s are nearly as provocative and spectacular as the otherworldly 1997s. The great 1998 Barolo Marenca offers the essence of Nebbiolo in its sweet bouquet of roasted espresso, cedar, Chinese black tea, soy, and black cherry/plum-like fruit. Dense, full-bodied, and viscous, this exceptional Barolo's purity and essence of Nebbiolo-like character make it a compelling wine to drink now and over the next 12–15 years. The dark plum-colored 1998 Barolo Margheria exhibits more structure as well as a more backward character. While not as expressive as the Marenca, it is full-bodied with outstanding concentration, offering notes of chocolate, black cherry liqueur, spice box, and earth. There are plenty of glycerin, moderate tannin, and a long, 40-second finish in this tightly knit effort. It will drink well for 10–14 years. The dense, opulent, flamboyant 1998 Barolo Vigna Rionda possesses soaring aromas of plum and kirsch, smoke, balsa wood, black tea, licorice, and tobacco. Opulent, full-bodied, and gorgeously pure, it has enough glycerin, fruit, and tannin to fill and stain the mouth. This blockbuster Barolo requires 1–2 years of cellaring; it will drink beautifully between 2004–2018.

Luigi Pira's 1997 Barolo is a decadent, luxuriously rich effort offering an opulent texture and gorgeous jammy currant, cherry, licorice, smoke, and cured olive characteristics. It possesses a superb texture, a sexy, forward, low-acid style, and copious quantities of glycerin, fruit, and extract. It is a terrific wine to drink now and over the next 10 years. The profound, dense garnet/ruby-colored 1997 Barolo Marenca displays a spectacular bouquet of roasted espresso, kirsch, blackberries, tobacco, sardines, cedar, and leather. Sumptuous in the mouth, full-bodied, with an exotic overripe character, this dense, thick Barolo tastes sweet because of the high glycerin levels. As it was in cask, this 1997 Barolo remains dominated by its baby fat. Anticipated maturity: now–2015. Luigi Pira, who has the most massive hands I have ever encountered on a vigneron, has fashioned a more structured effort with his 1997 Barolo Margheria. This wine has become more delineated and civilized after spending time in cask and *foudre*. Telltale notes of kirsch, dried flowers, rose petals, licorice, soy, leather, and tobacco combine with scents of seaweed, chocolate, and red/black fruits. The Margheria possesses firmer tannin and more muscle, and is less open-knit and expansive than the Marenca. Nevertheless, it is a sensationally concentrated, full-bodied, powerful Barolo in need of 1–2 years of cellaring. It should drink well between 2004–2020. One of the greatest young Barolos I have ever tasted is Pira's 1997 Barolo Vigna Rionda. The total, minuscule production was aged in a new 600-liter *foudre*. A dense ruby/garnet color is followed by an explosive yet restrained bouquet of tobacco, black cherries, truffles, dried herbs, and new saddle leather, which intensifies as it sits in the glass. On the palate, it offers extraordinary opulence, luxurious richness, a viscous texture, exceptional purity, beautifully integrated acidity, tannin, alcohol, and wood, and a finish that lasts for nearly a minute. Like so many 1997s, it possesses unreal levels of glycerin, resulting in a texture comparable to a fine sauce as opposed to a beverage, yet it is impeccably well balanced. This is a sensational Barolo that magically combines both exoticism and classicism. Anticipated maturity: 2004–2020.

In 1996, Pira appears to have hit all the sweet spots. His 1996 Barolo should prove to be an uncommon value for a sensational generic Barolo. It offers road tar, rose petal, tobacco, woodsy spices, and cherry fruit aromas that jump from the glass of this evolved, gorgeously proportioned, full-bodied effort. The dark ruby color is followed by a sweet, expansive, hedonistic wine that offers a lot of pleasure. Complex and mouth-filling, it is ready to drink. Anticipated maturity: now–2012. The 1996 Barolo Margheria combines the best of the traditional style of Barolo with the more progressive modern winemaking style. The color is a saturated plum. Overripe aromas of black fruits are accompanied by scents of soy, coffee, smoke, licorice, and dried herbs. Dense and full-bodied, with terrific fruit intensity, this multidimensional, layered wine is exceptionally rich, yet sweet and forward. Anticipated maturity: now–2015. The 1996 Barolo Marenca is even more profound, with a dark ruby color and a sumptuous nose of jammy plum liqueur and black cherries. It is a sensual, full-bodied wine with an opulent texture, fabulous extract, and an explosive, 50-second finish. It coats the palate, is unbelievably rich in fruit, glycerin, and extract and should prove to be a modern-day classic. Anticipated maturity: 2005–2020.

The classic 1995s are among the superstars of that good vintage. The 1995 Barolo exhibits an evolved ruby color with some amber at the edge. It offers tobacco, licorice, and cherry fruit aromas, but the wine dries out a bit in the mouth. Fully mature, with a lean finish, it is ideal for drinking over the next 3–4 years. The 1995 Barolo Margheria reveals stunning aromas of smoky wood, truffles, cherry liqueur, cedar, and dried herbs. Evolved, with a soft, opulently textured mouth-feel, full body, and outstanding ripeness as well as purity, its forward, accessible style suggests that it should be drunk over the next 10 years. The 1995 Barolo Marenca displays classic rose petal scents in addition to melted asphalt, truffles, new saddle leather, and cherries. It is a layered wine with tea/coffee flavors that add nuances to the copious glycerin, rich black cherry fruit, and full-bodied, velvety texture. Anticipated maturity: now–2014.

GUIDO PORRO

1998	Barolo Vigna Santa Caterina	D	(88–89)
1997	Barolo Vigna Santa Caterina	D	88
1998	Barolo Vigna Lazzairasco	D	(87–88)
1997	Barolo Vigna Lazzairasco	D	88

This producer from the village of Serralunga has fashioned two excellent, elegant, forward 1998 Barolos. His 1997s performed much better from bottle than they did during their *élevage*.

The 1998 Barolo Vigna Lazzairasco is a soft, supple effort displaying copious quantities of smoky cherry fruit mixed with licorice, tobacco, and weedy notes. It is rich on the attack, medium- to full-bodied, and supple. The saturated ruby-colored 1998 Barolo Vigna Santa Caterina possesses more intensity and depth as well as high levels of volatile acidity (which should not be a problem if it does not become any more elevated). Its complex nose offers aromas of sweet black fruits, smoke, licorice, and incense. Medium- to full-bodied, with low acidity and ripe tannin, it will drink well for 5–6 years.

Both 1997s are evolved and meant to be drunk during their first 5–6 years of life. Offering considerable appeal, the fat, round, low-acid 1997 Barolo Vigna Lazzairasco exhibits a smoky, layered personality with notes of coffee, cherries, herbs, and tobacco. The medium- to full-bodied 1997 Barolo Vigna Santa Caterina reveals an evolved color with amber at the edge. It possesses dusty tannin, plump cherry fruit, and notes of dried roses, melted asphalt, camphor, and licorice.

FERDINANDO PRINCIPIANO

1998 Barbera d'Alba La Romualda	D	90
1997 Barbera d'Alba La Romualda	D	90

Isn't it amazing how many top-notch Barberas are emerging from Piedmont? An outstanding performance for this producer, Principiano's 1998 Barbera d'Alba La Romualda is a deep ruby/purple-colored, layered effort revealing aromas of spicy new oak, copious quantities of red and black fruits, and underlying notes of smoke, underbrush, and licorice. Consume it over the next 4–5 years. Readers looking for sweet, jammy strawberry and cherry flavors with toasty oak, plenty of glycerin, and a forceful, fleshy, full-bodied palate will love this enticing, disarming, thick, juicy 1997 Barbera d'Alba La Romualda. Enjoy it over the next 5–7 years.

PRODUTTORI DEL BARBARESCO

1996 Barbaresco Asili	E	91
1996 Barbaresco Moccagatta Riserva	E	90
1996 Barbaresco Montestefano Riserva	E	88
1996 Barbaresco Ovello Riserva	E	88+
1996 Barbaresco Pora	E	89
1996 Barbaresco Rabajà	E	90+
1996 Barbaresco Rio Sordo Riserva	E	90

The Produttori del Barbaresco, one of Piedmont's top cooperatives, offers these late-released 1996 Barbarescos. I began purchasing these single-vineyard Riservas in 1978 and have continued to do so in most of the top vintages. They are incredibly popular, as well as fairly priced, and hence they disappear rapidly from the marketplace. All of these 1996s had just been bottled and were about to be shipped to the United States when I saw them in 2001, so I suspect that with additional bottle age and rest, they will be even better. From the traditional school of winemaking, they are aged 3–4 years in old wood prior to bottling. While each reflects its vineyard, they are all full-bodied efforts offering complex tobacco, sweet cherry, licorice, smoke, and herb notes. The Ovello and Rio Sordo are the most evolved and elegant. The sweetest, most seductive include the Pora, Montestefano, and Moccagatta. The most profound are the Asili and Rabajà. Production ranges from a minimum of 10,000 bottles for the Asili to a maximum of just under 19,000 bottles for the other single vineyards. All are purely made and merit considerable attention. They all require an additional two years of cellaring, even the more forward Ovello and Rio Sordo. The aging potential of the Ovello, Rio Sordo, Moccagatta, and Pora is approximately 15 years, and 15–20 years for the Montestefano, Asili, and Rabajà.

PRUNOTTO

1998 Barbaresco	D	87
1996 Barbaresco	D	87
1995 Barbaresco	D	78
1998 Barbaresco Bric Turot	E	91
1998 Barbera d'Alba Pian Romualdo	C	90
1998 Barbera d'Asti Costamiole	D	91
1998 Barolo	D	90
1997 Barolo	D	87
1996 Barolo	D	89+
1995 Barolo	D	88

1998 Barolo Bussia	E	(91–93)
1997 Barolo Bussia	E	94

This famous estate was acquired by the Marchesi Antinori firm, which continues to upgrade the winery, vineyards, and quality of the wines. Given how well Prunotto's wines performed in difficult vintages such as 1993 and 1994, I expected more from the following years, but some of its Barbarescos (1995 and 1996) have been foursquare, monolithic, and lacking the character I have come to expect from Prunotto's wines, while the Barolos of the same year were sound. The 1997s show a clear improvement, confirmed by excellent 1998s.

From a strong vintage for Prunotto, the 1998 Barbaresco is the lightest offering, but it possesses stylish, attractive, sweet raspberry and cherry fruit mixed with dried herb and spice box characteristics. Although neither concentrated nor deep, it is round, luscious, well balanced, richly fruity, and harmonious. Enjoy it over the next 4–5 years. The *barrique*-aged, blockbuster 1998 Barbera d'Alba Pian Romualdo exhibits a saturated plum/purple color as well as a gorgeously explosive bouquet of sweet toasty new oak intermixed with chocolate, spice box, black fruits, and licorice. Superrich, medium-bodied, and crammed with fruit, it will drink well for 3–4 years, as these wines rarely improve. The complex 1998 Barbera d'Asti Costamiole reveals earthy, toasty notes intermixed with plums, cola, flowers, and roasted herbs. A boatload of fruit and glycerin hit the palate in this full-bodied, fat, fleshy Barbera. Fermented and aged in new oak for 12 months prior to being bottled unfiltered, it will drink well for 5–6 years. The stunning, dark plum/ruby-colored, deep, full-bodied 1998 Barbaresco Bric Turot is layered with smoky black fruit, graphite, new saddle leather, and vanilla aromas. Rich and concentrated, with sweet tannin, it will be at its finest between 2003–2015.

The 1998 Barolo is a full-bodied, fleshy effort revealing telltale notes of licorice, rose petals, melted asphalt, and dried red and black fruits. It is sweet and opulently textured, with surprising harmony for such a young Barolo. Both the tannin and acidity are well integrated in this fleshy, upfront offering. Consume it during its first 10–12 years of life. The dense ruby-colored 1998 Barolo Bussia displays a heady, intoxicating perfume of maple syrup mixed with kirsch, cigar smoke, dried herbs, and cedar. Voluptuously textured, beautifully concentrated, pure, rich, and long (the finish lasts for 35 seconds), it is soft enough to be drunk, but I suspect the tannin will soon reemerge and the wine will shut down. Anticipated maturity: 2005–2018.

Prunotto's generic 1997 Barolo offers an attractive dark ruby/garnet color, low acidity, and soft, fat flavors of smoke-infused cherry fruit, cedar, and toast. Ripe and medium-bodied, it is best drunk over the next 4–5 years. The profound 1997 Barolo Bussia boasts intense aromas of molasses, cherry liqueur, melted tar, licorice, and toast. Dense and full-bodied, with enormous quantities of glycerin and fat, this hedonistic, thick, viscous Barolo can be drunk now and over the next 12–15 years.

The dark ruby-colored 1996 Barbaresco exhibits attractive cherry fruit in the nose along with cedar, roasted almonds, and herbs. Well made, pure, and medium-bodied, with moderate tannin in the angular finish, it should be at its finest before 2008. The 1996 Barolo exhibits more minerality, along with black cherries and melted road tar. Medium- to full-bodied, spicy, rich, and potentially very good, it is foursquare and simple. Perhaps more complexity will emerge with bottle age. Anticipated maturity: 2003–2014.

The 1995 Barbaresco reveals soft, tobacco-tinged cherry fruit, moderate concentration, and a lean, compressed, diluted, austere finish. Drink it over the next 2–3 years. The 1995 Barolo is an elegant, lighter-styled example with attractive smoke-tinged, herbaceous cherry fruit, medium body, and an earth-driven personality. Moderate tannin in the finish suggests that aging is necessary, but this wine does not have the stuffing for extended cellaring. Drink it over the next 3–4 years.

QUORUM

1999 Barbera d'Asti	E	95
1998 Barbera d'Asti	E	96

This cooperative effort from a group of Piedmontese producers displays the spectacular quality that can be achieved with Barbera. The brilliant oenologist Riccardo Cotarella is the magic behind these wines, which are made from modest yields of 35 hectoliters per hectare, experience malolactic in barrel, with pump-overs and punch-downs, and are bottled without filtration after spending 10 months in 100% new French oak.

A spectacular achievement for this varietal, the 1999 Barbera d'Asti may not have the nobility to age longer than 6–8 years, but for drinking over the next 5–6 years, there is no doubting its explosive qualities as well as its extraordinary ripeness and richness. Its opaque purple color is followed by a sumptuous bouquet of black fruits, coffee, vanilla, chocolate, and licorice. This super-endowed, full-bodied, rich, intensely concentrated, opulent Barbera is prodigious. Anticipated maturity: now–2010.

The 1998 Barbera d'Asti has a whopping 13.7% alcohol as well as a reasonably high (for Barbera) pH of 3.6. In short . . . it's a dazzling Barbera. An intense, deep opaque plum/purple color is followed by super-concentrated blackberry, strawberry, and cherry aromas, an opulent, fat, luscious texture, and explosive fruit, purity, and richness. The wine's heady, luxuriously rich finish lasts 30+ seconds. It would be hard to make better Barbera than this! Drink it over the next 4–5 years.

RENATO RATTI

1998 Barolo Marcenasco	E	89
1997 Barolo Marcenasco	E	91
1998 Barolo Conca Marcenasco	E	87+?
1998 Barolo Rocche Marcenasco	E	87
1997 Barolo Rocche Marcenasco	E	92+
1996 Barolo Rocche Marcenasco	E	90
1995 Barolo Rocche Marcenasco	E	88

Ratti's wines tend to be made in a modern style, although they taste as if one foot were still firmly planted in the past—not a bad combination. All of the 1998 Barolos are midweight, fragrant, earthy efforts that are best drunk during their first decade of life. I tasted two 1997s, both of which outperformed the 1998s, and the excellent 1996 surpasses the soundly made 1995. The medium-bodied 1998 Barolo Marcenasco displays the most sweetness and fragrance in its aromas and flavors (leather, cherries, spice box, and tobacco). Although it does not possess much depth, it is charming and well made. Slightly lighter, with less concentration, is the 1998 Barolo Rocche Marcenasco. I may have caught it during a less expressive stage, but it appeared straightforward, with less volume and depth than its siblings. Consumption during its first 8–10 years of life is recommended. The most tannic of this trio is the 1998 Barolo Conca Marcenasco. While it reveals leanness, austerity, and tannin, it also possesses abundant spice in its backward, reserved personality. Ideally, I would wait 1–2 years before pulling the cork. This effort falls midway between the archconservative traditionalists (represented by Giacomo Conterno and Bruno Giacosa) and the vanguard of modernists (i.e., Elio Altare). Anticipated maturity: 2005–2015.

The fragrant, open-knit, sexy 1997 Barolo Marcenasco exhibits glorious sweetness, an expansive, full-bodied palate, a creamy texture, and overripe notes of black cherries, raspberries, currants, and a touch of maple syrup. Fleshy, powerful, and well delineated, it can be drunk now and over the next 12 years. The terrific 1997 Barolo Rocche Marcenasco offers complex aromatics of soy, earth, root vegetables, sardines, and smoky black cherry/berry fruit. This full-bodied Barolo displays more structure and tannin than its sibling as well as a denser, longer finish. Anticipated maturity: 2003–2018.

The 1996 Barolo Rocche Marcenasco exhibits a more impressively endowed ruby/purple color and an aggressive nose of roasted herbs, spices, and black cherry and berry fruit. Full-bodied, with subtle oak in the background, this dense, concentrated, highly extracted wine is a classic. Anticipated maturity: 2004–2018. The 1995 Barolo Rocche Marcenasco is a very good wine for the vintage, offering aromas of tobacco smoke, cedar, spice, and lively, sweet jammy cherries. There are excellent richness, an open-knit, round personality, a sweet mid-palate, and ripe tannin in the moderately long, medium- to full-bodied finish. Drinkable already, this Barolo promises to evolve for 8 years.

F.LLI REVELLO

1998	Barbera d'Alba Ciabot du Re	C	92
1997	Barolo	D	89
1996	Barolo	D	88
1995	Barolo	D	90
1998	Barolo Vigna Conca	E	(92–94)
1997	Barolo Vigna Conca	E	93
1998	Barolo Vigna Giachini	E	(90–91)
1997	Barolo Vigna Giachini	E	93
1996	Barolo Vigna Giachini	E	90
1995	Barolo Vigna Giachini	E	89+
1998	Barolo Vigna Rocche dell'Annunziata	E	(88–90)
1997	Barolo Vigna Rocche dell'Annunziata	E	91
1996	Barolo Vigna Rocche dell'Annunziata	E	91+

Another high-quality La Morra producer who has been making better and better wines, Revello makes 1998s that are all elegant, aromatic, beautifully flavored offerings. Its single-vineyard crus in both 1996 and 1997 are exceptional. Readers who prefer more structure, muscle, and tannin will like the 1996s better; those who are fond of flamboyant, spectacularly rich, nearly overripe, jammy wines with huge quantities of glycerin and extract will enjoy the 1997s.

Readers looking for a *barrique*-aged Barbera with spectacular concentration, density, and perfume should check out Revello's 1998 Barbera d'Alba Ciabot du Re. It possesses a dark ruby/purple color, great intensity, phenomenal aromas of smoke, chocolate, strawberries, cherries, and blackberries, a thick, fat, chewy texture, and a lush, smoky finish. Enjoy it over the next 2–3 years. The 1998 Barolo Vigna Giachini exhibits a dark ruby/garnet color as well as an intensely fragrant perfume of rose petals, herbs, new oak, plums, and black cherries. It reveals a classic structure, moderate tannin, good firmness and purity, and a long, well-delineated, medium- to full-bodied finish. Anticipated maturity: 2003–2015. The dark ruby/garnet-colored 1998 Barolo Vigna Conca offers up an explosive nose of creosote, cherry liqueur, cedar, new saddle leather, soy, and Provençal herbs. Dense, full-bodied, and super-rich, with a 45-second finish, this layered, multidimensional, well-balanced, stunning 1998 will drink well between now–2016. The symmetrical, restrained, delicately styled, dark ruby-colored 1998 Barolo Vigna Rocche dell'Annunziata possesses fine overall balance but not the depth, weight, or palate texture/volume of its two siblings. Nevertheless, there is a lot to like in this wine. Anticipated maturity: now–2012.

Revello's 1997 Barolo exhibits an earthy, root vegetable, herbaceous, black fruit–scented nose, medium to full body, plenty of glycerin, and the texture, fat, and succulence typical of this vintage in Piedmont. Already delicious, it will be best consumed over the next 5 years. The stunning perfume (meat, sausage, and spice) of the dark plum/garnet-colored 1997 Barolo Vigna Giachini is reminiscent of a French charcuterie. Full-bodied, opulent, fat, and rich, with notes of sausage, herbs, pepper, spice box, soy, and new oak, this lush, creamy-textured offering can be drunk now and over the next 15 years. The 1997 Barolo Vigna Conca

(100 cases produced) reveals a maple syrup/brown sugar–like aroma intermixed with scents of cherry liqueur, rose petals, tobacco, and spice. A corpulent, highly extracted, low-acid, plummy wine with a boatload of glycerin as well as flavors, it is one of the most hedonistic Barolos from this luxurious, decadently styled vintage. Drink it over the next 12 years. Based on cask tastings, I had higher hopes for the 1997 Barolo Vigna Rocche dell'Annunziata. While outstanding, my barrel-tasting notes suggested it might turn out to be profound. It possesses an evolved dark plum/garnet color, more structure than its siblings, copious tobacco, herb, pepper, and kirsch aromas, superrichness, and a sweet, full-bodied palate, but not the mass and overall structure I anticipated. Nevertheless, it is a stunning Barolo for drinking during its first 12–15 years of life.

The 1996 Barolo offers a tangy, black cherry–scented nose with hints of smoke, earth, and leather. Spicy, medium-bodied, and moderately tannic, it is more structured and muscular than its more evolved 1995 sibling. Anticipated maturity: now–2008. The 1996 Barolo Vigna Giachini reveals a deep ruby color as well as a muscular, powerfully scented nose of cherry fruit, cedar, fruitcake, dried herbs, and licorice. In the mouth, tobacco flavors make an appearance. This wine is layered, full-bodied, opulent, and dense, with most of the tannin concealed by high extraction and concentration. It is a wine of strength and symmetry with a superb inner core of fruit. Anticipated maturity: now–2020. The 1996 Barolo Vigna Rocche dell'Annunziata is extremely fragrant, offering dried herb, jammy cherry fruit, smoke, Asian spices, and new saddle leather aromas. In the mouth, there are superb purity, full body, and huge amounts of tannin. This backward, dense, monster-sized Barolo will be at its finest between 2005–2020.

Like the other generic Barolos from Revello, the 1995 Barolo was aged in 2–3-year-old oak casks. A successful wine for the vintage, it exhibits a sexy, explosive, Bing cherry–scented nose with chocolate, black tea, and spicy oak. Lush and round, it is not dissimilar from some of the idiosyncratic, opulent 1997s. This evolved 1995 should be consumed over the next 3–4 years. The medium-bodied 1995 Barolo Vigna Giachini is a more tannic, restrained example, with a moderate ruby color revealing amber at the edge. The moderately scented bouquet reveals tobacco, dried herbs, and cherry fruit. This closed Barolo needs another 1–2 years of bottle age. It should drink well for 10 years.

FRANCESCO RINALDI

1998 Barolo Cannubio	D	87
1997 Barolo Cannubio	D	88

The dark plum/garnet-colored, lighter-styled 1998 Barolo Cannubio displays classic Nebbiolo aromas of melted road tar, rose petals, and cherry fruit. Soft, ripe, and medium-bodied, this traditionally made 1998 reveals no evidence of new oak. Enjoy it over the next 4–5 years. The dark plum-colored 1997 Barolo Cannubio is revealing pink hues at the edge. Medium-weight, with rosewater, cherry, leather, and tar notes, this soft, round, gentle, yet flavorful Barolo can be enjoyed now and over the next 10 years.

GIUSEPPE RINALDI

1998 Barolo Brunate Le Coste	D	86?
1997 Barolo Brunate Le Coste	D	90+

Extremely high acidity and astringent tannin make the 1998 Barolo Brunate Le Coste hard to evaluate. The color is a dark plum with amber at the edge. The closed nose reveals hints of tar, rose petal, cherries, and tobacco. The attack is elegant, but the high acidity and tannin combine to compress the mid-palate and finish. There may be more behind the acidity and tannin than I was able to determine, but this closed 1998 needs 2–3 years of cellaring to display its full potential. An austere style for sure, I am not sure the fruit will ever be able to overcome the wine's structural components. An old-style Barolo, Rinaldi's 1997 Brunate Le

Coste exhibits a dense, saturated plum/garnet color in addition to aromas of flowers, cinnamon, allspice, dried herbs, earth, licorice, and mineral-infused black cherries. Layered and powerful, with astringent tannin as well as a huge concentration of fruit, this classic, tough-textured Barolo will be admired by traditionalists. The magic will emerge after 2–3 years of cellaring, although do not expect this wine to have the suppleness or sexy, new-oak style of a modernist's Barolo. Anticipated maturity: 2005–2018.

VIGNA RIONDA DI MASSOLINO

1999	Barbera d'Alba Gisep	C	91
1998	Barolo	D	(82–85)
1997	Barolo	D	82
1998	Barolo Vigna Margheria	D	(83–87)
1997	Barolo Vigna Margheria	E	87
1996	Barolo Vigna Margheria	E	89+
1998	Barolo Vigna Parafada	E	(88–89)
1997	Barolo Vigna Parafada	E	90
1996	Barolo Vigna Parafada	E	90
1998	Barolo Vigna Rionda	E	(87–88)
1997	Barolo Vigna Rionda	E	90
2000	Dolcetto d'Alba Vigna Barilot	B	87
1999	Langhe Rosso Piria	D	88
1997	Langhe Rosso Piria	D	89

Massolino, an important landholder in Serralunga d'Alba, owns some superb vineyards. This traditional wine-maker ages all his *cuvées* in *foudre* except for his Parafada, which sees about 50% *barrique*. His proprietary blend, Piria, is composed of equal parts Nebbiolo and Barbera fermented and aged in French oak casks. He has been fashioning better and better wines over recent vintages. That being said, I did not think the 1998s fared as consistently well as the superb 1997s, but the early-released 1999s and 2000 represent fine values.

The 2000 Dolcetto d'Alba Vigna Barilot is a modern-styled, ripe, richly fruity offering revealing good depth, a supple texture, and fine purity. It is an uncomplicated, quaffable wine to enjoy over the next 2–3 years.

The spectacular, modern-styled 1999 Barbera d'Alba Gisep is aged in 100% new French oak, and its fruit has totally absorbed the wood's toast and vanilla notes. A black/purple color is accompanied by a glorious perfume of licorice, blackberries, cherries, cola, and mocha. The finish is long, textured, full-bodied, and supple. Superripe Barbera seems to love new oak and absorbs it as well as any wine in the world. Drink this beauty over the next 4–5 years. These wines, while super-concentrated and youthful, rarely age well past a half-dozen years. Massolino's proprietary red, the 1999 Langhe Rosso Piria, exhibits a complex bouquet of tobacco, strawberries, and cherries with licorice and spice box in the background. While rich, medium-bodied, and complex, it lacks the exuberance, mass, and thickness of the astonishing Barbera. Readers looking for more subtlety and nuances should check out the 1999 Piria.

The straightforward, light, elegant, medium-bodied 1998 Barolo possesses good roundness and softness, but lacks depth and substance. Moreover, its evolved color is revealing considerable amber at the edge. This Barolo is best consumed over the next 4–5 years. The 1998 Barolo Vigna Parafada exhibits a complex aromatic profile of dried herbs and that autumnal, leafy character often found in traditionally styled Barolos. In the mouth, it is spicy and ripe, with excellent concentration, and a touch of vanilla from *barriques*. Good sweetness, abundant black cherry fruit, and ripe tannin suggest it will be drinkable between 2004–2015. Another soft, light, marginal effort is Massolino's 1998 Barolo Vigna Margheria, which reveals medium body, suppleness, and a short finish lacking depth and length. It requires consumption over the next 4–5 years. Lastly, the medium garnet-colored, silky-textured 1998 Barolo Vigna Rionda offers complex aromatics of cherry cough syrup mixed with Provençal herbs, spice box, and tar. Dense, with excellent fruit concentration, good sweetness on the attack and mid-palate, and ripe tannin, it will be at its peak between 2004–2014.

Exhibiting a dark ruby/garnet color with amber at the edge, the 1997 Langhe Rosso Piria reveals complex cedar, dried herb, cherry, and wood smoke in its fragrant bouquet. Round, ripe, spicy, medium-bodied, and supple-textured, it can be drunk over the next 5–6 years. Revealing surprisingly good acidity for the vintage as well as an evolved garnet color with an amber edge, the medium-bodied 1997 Barolo is a pleasant, traditionally made effort to consume over the next 4–5 years. The outstanding 1997 Barolo Vigna Parafada is a full-bodied, dense ruby/garnet-colored wine with a layered tactile impression and copious quantities of licorice, rose petal, tar, and kirsch aromatics as well as flavors. Deep, with moderate tannin and the vintage's unctuosity and sweetness, it will be at its best between now–2016. Also displaying an evolved appearance with considerable amber at the edge, the 1997 Barolo Vigna Margheria exhibits notes of dried flowers, figs, tobacco, old oak, mushrooms, and cherries in its aromatics as well as flavors. Medium-bodied and spicy, it should drink well for 10 years. The sexy, layered, evolved 1997 Barolo Vigna Rionda was obviously produced from extremely ripe fruit, as evidenced by the dark garnet/amber color and the sweet perfume of smoke, caramel, toffee, and espresso infused with black cherries, plums, and prunes. This multilayered, full-bodied offering exhibits a seamless personality with no hard edges. It should drink well for 15 years.

The outstanding dark ruby/garnet-colored 1996 Barolo Vigna Parafada offers aromas of cigar box, cherry liqueur, licorice, and spice, dense, intense, old-style, concentrated, sour cherry flavors with glycerin and extract. Rich and approachable, it will evolve nicely for 12 years. In contrast, the dark ruby/garnet-colored 1996 Barolo Vigna Margheria is more backward, with spicy, licorice, truffle, strawberry, and black cherry fruit notes, full body, moderately high tannin, sweetness, glycerin, and a dusty, concentrated, layered finish. Anticipated maturity: 2004–2018.

ROAGNA

1998 Barbaresco Pajé	E	(91–94)
1997 Barbaresco Pajé	E	90
1998 Barolo Rocche La Pira	E	(86–87)
1997 Barolo Rocche La Pira	E	87

As with Roagna's 1997s, the 1998s reveal a huge difference in richness and density. The more tannic and backward 1998 Barolo Rocche La Pira offers only hints of tobacco, cherry cough syrup, and dried herbs. With airing, tar and additional fruit notes emerge. However, the overall impression is one of austerity, leanness, and high tannin, atypical for this vintage. Anticipated maturity: 2006–2014? In total contrast, the saturated opaque purple-colored 1998 Barbaresco Pajé combines awesome extract levels with extraordinary precision. Medium- to full-bodied, it offers aromas and flavors of liquid minerals infused with black cherry and raspberry jam. As the wine sat in the glass, blackberry scents also emerged. Aging in small *barriques* has been totally absorbed by the wine's concentration and density. This terrific Barbaresco has an uncanny resemblance to a great grand cru Burgundy (Comtes de Vogüé's Musigny Vieilles Vignes?). Anticipated maturity: 2004–2016.

Although somewhat closed, Roagna's ruby/garnet-colored 1997 Barolo Rocche La Pira offers notes of tobacco, spice box, cherries, and dried herbs. Made in a medium-bodied, elegant style, it is not as complete or concentrated as the Barbaresco Pajé. The 1997 Barbaresco Pajé's evolved garnet color with an amber edge is followed by notes of sweet caramel, coffee, jammy cherry fruit, licorice, and smoke. Elegant, medium- to full-bodied, with wonderful lushness and an expansive, low-acid finish, this 1997 Barbaresco is meant to be drunk now and over the next 5–7 years. Readers should keep an eye out for Roagna's spectacular 1998 Pajé, which was the best of the three most recent vintages I tasted.

ALBINO ROCCA

1998	Barbaresco Vigneto Brich Ronchi	E	90+
1997	Barbaresco Vigneto Brich Ronchi	E	97
1996	Barbaresco Vigneto Brich Ronchi	E	93
1995	Barbaresco Vigneto Brich Ronchi	E	87
1998	Barbaresco Vigneto Loreto	E	91
1997	Barbaresco Vigneto Loreto	E	95
1996	Barbaresco Vigneto Loreto	E	91
1995	Barbaresco Vigneto Loreto	E	89

Albino Rocca, one of my favorite Piedmontese producers, produced very good 1995s and thrilling 1996s, but he hit the bull's-eye in 1997, as well as in 1998. His 1997s rank among the most spectacular Barbarescos I have ever tasted. They are awesomely thick, rich, and textured, with unreal opulence as well as glycerin levels that define the vintage, and while I thought it would be hard to improve on those spectacular, astonishing Barbarescos, this producer has come close to them in 1998.

Made in a more restrained, elegant style, the 1998 Barbaresco Vigneto Loreto exhibits a dark ruby color as well as an elegant, smoky, cherry, oak-scented bouquet. This quintessentially elegant, medium-bodied, supple, delicious Barbaresco will drink well for 6–7 years. The dark ruby/garnet-colored 1998 Barbaresco Vigneto Brich Ronchi reveals abundant aromas of new saddle leather mixed with spice box, kirsch, beetroot, and oak. In the mouth, it is richer as well as more tannic than its sibling. This pure, ripe, long Barbaresco is best cellared for another year and consumed over the following decade.

The 1997 Barbaresco Vigneto Loreto is a luxuriously fruited, nearly over-the-top effort. Extremely full-bodied and loaded with exotic, overripe glycerin, smoke, cedar, and cherry flavors, it is a thick, unctuously textured slut of a Barbaresco. It may not make old bones, but who cares given the extraordinary hedonistic pleasures to be found now and over the next 5 years. Even more awesome, the 1997 Barbaresco Vigneto Brich Ronchi is a tour de force in winemaking. Its dark plum/ruby color is accompanied by explosive blackberry/cherry fruit aromas. In the mouth, its viscous texture, low acidity, and overripe Nebbiolo characteristics provide remarkable intensity, and extraordinary flavor richness with notes of blackberries, cherries, coffee, smoke, licorice, and earth. The finish lasts for nearly 45 seconds. Drink this spectacular Barbaresco over the next 5–6 years.

In contrast to the 100% *barrique*-aged Brich Ronchi, the 1996 Barbaresco Vigneto Loreto is aged in moderately large *foudres*. This dazzling, sexy offering possesses an opaque ruby/purple color, terrific fruit and purity, and enough glycerin and concentrated flavors to conceal moderate levels of tannin. The black cherry characteristic combined with smoke, cedar, and fruitcake aromas is to die for. This full-bodied, intense Barbaresco will get even better over the next several years and will age for 12 years. The large-scaled as well as compelling 1996 Barbaresco Vigneto Brich Ronchi reveals spectacular aromas of intense chocolate-covered cherry candy intermixed with smoky new wood. It is dense and full-bodied, with layers of concentration and glycerin. This superb, mouth-filling Barbaresco can be drunk now or cellared for 10–12 years.

The 1995 Barbaresco Vigneto Loreto is a dark ruby/purple-colored offering with a sweet nose of cedar, Provençal herbs, chocolate, smoky, jammy black cherry fruit, and new oak. The wine is full-bodied, rich, round, and ideal for drinking now and over the next 7–8 years. The 1995 Barbaresco Vigneto Brich Ronchi is a more structured and noticeably tannic wine with a moderately intense nose of cedar, black cherries, and dried herbs. It has a long after-taste but seems closed and is less seductive than the Vigneto Loreto. This is one 1995 that should keep for a dozen years.

BRUNO ROCCA

1998 Barbaresco Coparossa	E	(90–92)
1997 Barbaresco Coparossa	E	90+
1996 Barbaresco Coparossa	E	90
1995 Barbaresco Coparossa	E	89
1998 Barbaresco Rabajà	E	(89–91)
1997 Barbaresco Rabajà	E	92+
1996 Barbaresco Rabajà	E	87
1995 Barbaresco Rabajà	E	88

Barrique aging clearly puts Bruno Rocca in the modern school of Piedmontese winemaking. This outstanding producer has followed his superb 1997s with two impressive 1998s. The 1996s were also excellent, although more tannic, structured, and less exotic than the 1997s.

The 1998 Barbaresco Rabajà exhibits an exotic perfume of overripe black cherry fruit mixed with blackberries, smoky espresso, and a touch of balsam wood as well as chocolate. Full-bodied, powerful, deep, and super-concentrated, this impressive wine should age nicely for 10 years. Although less complex, the saturated ruby/purple-colored 1998 Barbaresco Coparossa possesses sweet, concentrated aromas of new oak, black currants, and berries, abundant glycerin, and excellent concentration. However, it is more straightforward and less nuanced/layered than the Rabajà. Nevertheless, it will provide outstanding drinking over the next decade.

The large-scaled 1997 Barbaresco Rabajà requires some cellaring, unusual for the vintage. An opaque ruby/purple color is accompanied by aromas of chocolate, coffee, blackberry and cherry fruit, as well as noticeable new oak. This immense, powerful, rich, moderately tannic Barbaresco will be at its finest between 2003–2016. More opulent and accessible, the 1997 Barbaresco Coparossa exhibits abundant quantities of cedary black cherry fruit, a viscous texture, fine power, and a dense finish with sweeter tannin than the Rabajà. This full-bodied, gorgeous, ripe offering can be drunk now and over the next 12+ years.

The 1996 Barbaresco Coparossa is slightly higher in alcohol and more muscular, and, while not as sexy or forward as the 1995, is potentially a better wine. Full-bodied, with cherry cough syrup, tobacco, earth, and hints of white truffle aromas, this nicely layered wine possesses a muscular mouth-feel, no hard edges, and moderately sweet tannin in the long finish. Anticipated maturity: now–2012. The 1996 Barbaresco Rabajà exhibits toasty new oak, jammy cherries, dried herbs, and spice scents. Ripe and tightly structured, with medium body and a muscular, astringent, well-delineated finish, it should drink well between now–2012. The 1995 Barbaresco Coparossa is a sexy, opulently styled wine with elements of *garrigue* (an earthy/herb mélange), cedar, coffee, smoke, and jammy fruit. Round and opulently styled, with a lush texture, a forward, evolved personality, and fine glycerin and depth, this alluring Barbaresco can be drunk now and over the next 3–4 years. Because the oak was more obvious and the wine less exotic and accessible than its sibling, the 1995 Coparossa, the 1995 Barbaresco Rabajà was more subdued. It offered interesting balsam wood, cherry, toast, and spice notes, as well as medium body, attractive sweet fruit, good purity, and a well-endowed but tightly knit finish. Anticipated maturity: now–2009.

PODERE ROCCHE DEI MANZONI

1997 Barolo Vigna Big	E	91
1997 Barolo Cappella di Santo Stefano	E	90
1997 Barolo Vigna d'la Roul	E	90

This Monforte d'Alba producer, a modernist, believes in *barrique* aging for these fragrant, full-bodied, elegant, single-vineyard Barolos. Despite their 100% *barrique* aging, they are not particularly oaky. The dark plum-colored 1997 Barolo Cappella di Santo Stefano offers a gorgeous bouquet of cedar, spice box, maple syrup/brown sugar, and cherries. Sweet, sexy, and seductive, this medium- to full-bodied, low-acid, glycerin-imbued wine will be accessible upon release and should drink well for 12 years. The 1997 Barolo Vigna d'la Roul reveals more espresso characteristics, intermixed with chocolate, caramel, leather, and black cherry/berry fruit. Full-bodied and smoky, with a supple texture as well as hedonistic, luxuriously fat, fleshy appeal, it can be consumed now and over the next 12 years. Displaying the most color saturation, the dark plum/purple 1997 Barolo Vigna Big is a flavorful, dense effort with plenty of spice box, kirsch, pepper, chocolate, and coffee aromas and flavors. The wine possesses decent acidity, firm tannin, an expansive, concentrated, full-bodied palate, and more noticeable tannin as well as structure. Anticipated maturity: now–2018.

GIGI ROSSO

1997 Barolo Arione	D	90+

The 1997 Barolo Arione is significantly better in bottle than when tasted prior to bottling. An explosive, large-scaled effort with high levels of tannin and extract, this dark garnet-colored Barolo offers sweet licorice intermixed with leather, roasted herbs, black cherries, and sardines (I know that does not sound appealing, but believe me, it is). Rich and layered, it requires 1–2 years of cellaring to resolve the high tannin in the finish. There is a boatload of extract, so don't worry about the overall balance. Anticipated maturity: 2004–2020.

LUCIANO SANDRONE

1999 Barbera d'Alba	C	90
1998 Barbera d'Alba	C	90
1998 Barolo Cannubi Boschis	EE	(94–96)
1997 Barolo Cannubi Boschis	EE	96
1996 Barolo Cannubi Boschis	EE	96
1995 Barolo Cannubi Boschis	EE	89
1998 Barolo Le Vigne	EE	95
1997 Barolo Le Vigne	EE	94
1996 Barolo Le Vigne	EE	92
1995 Barolo Le Vigne	EE	90
1998 Nebbiolo d'Alba Valmaggiore	C	87

Brothers Luca and Luciano Sandrone have just finished constructing a fabulous new winery just outside the village of Monforte d'Alba. While everyone raves about their Barolos, they also produce spectacular Nebbiolo d'Alba and Dolcetto d'Alba. Readers who come across any of these wines should grab them, as they are terrific. The Dolcetti should be consumed within their first 2–3 years of life and the Nebbiolos within the first 5–6. I have been purchasing these wines since the 1982 vintage, and while it is tempting to say that Sandrone is part of Piedmont's modernist generation, the wines are really a synthesis in style between the traditional and *barrique*-aged, new school of winemaking. *Barriques* are used, but restraint is exercised when it comes to the aromas and flavors of toasty oak. For the wines' upbringing, the estate utilizes about 10% new oak, with the balance aged in *foudres*. It is not a member of the group that uses rotary fermenters, preferring open-top vats and doing considerable pumping over as well as punching down to extract flavor and color (the Burgundian method). More new barrels are utilized for the Barolos than the other offerings. To my surprise, in two of the three vintages (1995 and 1997) I enjoyed the Barolo Le Vigne as much as the renowned Cannubi Boschis.

One of Sandrone's least heralded yet consistently gorgeous efforts is his Barbera d'Alba.

Both the 1999 and 1998 were aged in old *foudres,* and are beautiful, supple, soft, fruit-driven offerings with fine elegance, loads of strawberry and cherry fruit, earth, and spice. The 1998 is more elegant and the 1999 fatter and deeper-colored. Both are best drunk during their first 4–5 years of life. As for the other 1998s, they are just as extraordinary as the 1997s as well as 1996s. The medium dark garnet-colored 1998 Nebbiolo d'Alba Valmaggiore (a 200-case lot of 100% Nebbiolo) offers complex aromas of tobacco, dried herbs, jammy cherries, and smoke. Round and generous, as well as graceful and well balanced, it will drink well for 3–4 years. The magnificent Barolos exhibit both power and elegance. The multidimensional 1998 Barolo Le Vigne may be even better than its 1997 counterpart. It possesses huge layers of black cherry fruit infused with rose petals, tar, balsa wood, mineral, and subtle new oak notes. Full-bodied, awesomely concentrated, and extraordinarily pure, this exquisite, youthful Barolo will be at its prime between 2004–2020. The deep ruby/purple-colored 1998 Barolo Cannubi Boschis boasts a spectacular bouquet of mineral-infused black cherry liqueur, new saddle leather, and toast. This powerful, ripe 1998 offers full-bodied flavors, silky tannin, low acidity, gorgeous levels of glycerin, and a creamy mouthful of complex, layered, superbly pure Nebbiolo fruit. While it will undoubtedly firm up and reveal more tannin, it is presently more approachable than the Barolo Le Vigne. Can I be accurate? Anticipated maturity: 2006–2020.

The dark ruby-colored 1997 Barolo Le Vigne reveals amber at the edge. It offers stunning aromatics consisting of flowers, black fruits, lead pencil, spice box, and minerals. As is typical of Sandrone's offerings, there are extraordinary purity as well as intensity to the blackberry and cherry fruit flavors. As the wine sits in the glass, mineral and tar notes become more apparent. This is a stunning, gorgeously pure, Château Margaux–like Barolo to consume between now–2018. The prodigious 1997 Barolo Cannubi Boschis, which was on an equal footing with Le Vigne from cask, has moved ahead. The color is a dark, saturated garnet. The sweet nose of black fruits, minerals, scorched earth, smoke, dried herbs, and wet stones is stunning. Amazingly concentrated, with tremendous unctuosity yet superb delineation, this large-scaled as well as elegant Barolo possesses fabulous extract as well as a multidimensional mid-palate and finish. More forward than the 1996 or 1990 were at a similar period, the 1997 will last for 20 years. It is an amazing effort! Anticipated maturity: 2003–2020.

The dark ruby/purple-colored 1996 Barolo Le Vigne is an elegant, large-scaled Barolo with everything in balance. There are sweet tannin and a measured yet powerful, rich style with copious amounts of black fruits intermixed with minerals, spice, and dried herbs. The wine is tight and in need of 3–4 years of cellaring. Anticipated maturity: 2004–2018. The spectacular 1996 Barolo Cannubi Boschis offers aromas of cassis, cherry liqueur, and flowers. It is dense, superb, and full-bodied, with fabulous intensity as well as layers of extract. Muscular, concentrated, broad, and powerful, it demands 3–4 years of cellaring. Anticipated maturity: 2006–2020.

In 1995, I actually had a slight preference for the Barolo Le Vigne. The classic 1995 Barolo Le Vigne offers telltale aromas of tar, rose petals, and cherry liqueur. It provides medium to full body, a silky, open, accessible style, sweet, expansive flavors, a gorgeous texture, and a classic finish with no hard edges. This beautifully made Barolo can be drunk now or cellared for 10–12 years. The 1995 Barolo Cannubi Boschis is more backward but may turn out to be just as exciting, if not more so. Although full-bodied, it was extremely closed and difficult to penetrate. It possesses a dark ruby color in addition to plenty of dried herb, balsa wood, and black cherry aromas and flavors. While it is unquestionably excellent, possibly outstanding, it needs 2–3 years of cellaring; it should keep for 15 or more years.

PAOLO SCAVINO

1997 Barolo	E	92
1996 Barolo	E	89

1995	Barolo	E	90
1998	Barolo Bric del Fiasc	E	(92–94)
1997	Barolo Bric del Fiasc	E	95
1996	Barolo Bric del Fiasc	E	93
1995	Barolo Bric del Fiasc	E	91+
1998	Barolo Cannubi	E	(91–93)
1997	Barolo Cannubi	E	95+
1996	Barolo Cannubi	E	92
1995	Barolo Cannubi	E	91
1998	Barolo Caro Bric	E	(88–90)
1997	Barolo Caro Bric	E	93
1998	Barolo Rocche dell'Annunziata	E	(92–95)
1997	Barolo Rocche dell'Annunziata	E	97
1996	Barolo Rocche dell'Annunziata	E	95
1995	Barolo Rocche dell'Annunziata	E	92
1997	Langhe Rosso Corale	E	91

Paolo Scavino, his wife, and his two daughters run this 8-hectare (20-acre) estate, situated in the commune of Castiglione Falletto. They have been producing extraordinary Barolos throughout the decade of the nineties. At this modern-styled domaine, Scavino employs rotary fermenters with paddles, temperature-controlled fermentation, and malolactic in *barrique*. All the top Barolos are aged with approximately 30% new oak and are bottled without filtration. If readers have not yet discovered Scavino's Barolos, they should, as they are fabulous wines. Their otherworldly 1997s have been followed by slightly lighter but more perfumed and accessible 1998s. The 1996s and 1995s are also excellent.

The 1998 Barolo Caro Bric is an elegant, stylish offering without the flamboyance of its 1997 counterpart. Aromas of black cherry liqueur, smoke, minerals, and new saddle leather are followed by a medium-bodied wine with a distinctive, restrained style. The full-bodied, seamless 1998 Barolo Cannubi offers the essence of black cherry jam/liqueur along with earth, mineral, new saddle leather, coffee, licorice, tobacco, and new wood. It saturates the mouth without any sense of heaviness. Drink this full-throttle, elegant, pure, classic Barolo over the next 12 years. Another dramatic, provocative effort is the 1998 Barolo Bric del Fiasc. It possesses awesome levels of concentration, considerable power, immense body, and a fabulously pure, concentrated style. With impressive quantities of black fruits, licorice, minerals, asphalt, earth, and truffles, this Barolo is notable for its purity, high extract levels, and seamlessness. Anticipated maturity: 2004–2016. The 1998 Barolo Rocche dell'Annunziata will be an undeniable showstopper. An exquisite combination of black fruits, coffee, smoke, new oak, licorice, and incense is found in this medium- to full-bodied, ripe, elegant, pure Barolo. Explosive aromatics are followed by equally riveting flavors as well as a 50-second finish. The tannin is sweet and beautifully integrated. Anticipated maturity: 2005–2018.

Scavino calls his 1997 Barolos "big and fat." He is one of many Piedmontese producers who has had a hard time understanding these wines, which are aberrations in terms of their sumptuous richness, viscous personalities, and high-alcohol, low-acid styles. Readers looking for an amazing generic Barolo should check out Scavino's saturated garnet-colored 1997 Barolo. It offers a marvelous bouquet of Chinese black tea, vanilla, kirsch, and jammy currants. Full-bodied, powerful, unctuously textured, and admirably concentrated, it is a remarkable achievement for a generic Barolo. Do not overlook it in your rush to purchase Scavino's single-vineyard wines. Anticipated maturity: now–2012. A new offering, the 1997 Barolo Caro Bric, is an elegant, stylish example when compared to the other Scavino wines. It reveals the telltale saturated garnet color with amber at the edge, in addition to intense aromas of coffee, smoke, kirsch, herbs, leather, and fruitcake. While full-bodied, with expansive, saturated layers of fruit and abundant stuffing as well as richness, it does not reveal the nuances of Scavino's greatest crus. Nevertheless, it is an exceptional Barolo to enjoy between now–2016. The surreal 1997 Barolo Cannubi boasts a saturated ruby/purple color and an exquisite bouquet of black fruits, lead pencil, minerals, smoke, and licorice. Full-bodied and opulent, with more obvious tannin than many 1997s, this structured, muscular, viscous, formidably concentrated effort will be at its best between 2004–2020. From a well-known Castiglione Falletto vineyard, the 1997 Barolo Bric del Fiasc reveals the essence of cherry jam in its massive constitution. It is a powerful, full-bodied effort displaying pronounced black cherry liqueur–like aromas and flavors, huge extract and glycerin, and 14.5–15% alcohol. Remarkably pure, delineated, and balanced for a wine of such massiveness, it is more forward than the Cannubi but still needs another 1–2 years of cellaring. Anticipated maturity: 2003–2020. The virtually perfect 1997 Barolo Rocche dell'Annunziata offers an amazing perfume of roasted nuts, cedar, Provençal herbs, black cherry jam, rose petals, vanilla, and meat. Fabulously concentrated, with multiple flavor dimensions and a texture that swells in the mouth, this full-bodied, seamless, compelling Barolo is destined to be a legend. Approachable now, it promises to age for two decades. The 1997 Langhe Rosso Corale is a *barrique*-aged (50% new oak) blend of 35% Nebbiolo, 35% Barbera, 20% Cabernet Sauvignon, and 10% Merlot. There are 250 cases of this wine, which should not go unnoticed by fans of Piedmontese winemaking. An opaque ruby/purple color is accompanied by a full-bodied, deep, chewy, Bordeaux-like offering. It reveals cassis, black cherry, leather, cedar, and spice box aromas, medium to full body, superb definition and intensity, and a long, ripe, opulent finish. It should drink well for 7–8 years.

Scavino produced one of the great wines of the classic year of 1996, the Barolo Rocche dell'Annunziata. The color is a healthy dark ruby. The nose offers scents of smoky charcoal, licorice, toast, black cherries, incense, tobacco, and leather. Full-bodied and massive, with superb balance, nicely integrated acidity and tannin, and a finish that goes on for nearly a minute, it is a profound Barolo to drink now and over the next two decades. Nearly as spectacular is the 1996 Barolo Bric del Fiasc. It displays a saturated plum color, a smoky, black cherry–scented nose, explosive, fleshy flavors with plenty of glycerin, a more evolved and seductive character than the larger-scaled Annunziata, extraordinary intensity, and impeccable balance. Exotic Asian spice and fruitcake aromas add to its complexity. Anticipated maturity: now–2018. The dark plum/ruby-colored 1996 Barolo Cannubi reveals cherries galore intermixed with smoke, tobacco, and new saddle leather scents. This full-bodied, suppletextured, glorious Barolo possesses exceptional extract and can be drunk now or cellared for 15–16 years. With more of a fruit-driven personality, the generic 1996 Barolo is also outstanding. Sexy and forward, it does not possess the complexity and stature of the three singlevineyard offerings, but it is a wonderful introduction to the Scavino style. It should age nicely for 10 years.

The medium ruby-colored 1995 Barolo is an expansive, evolved, aromatic offering with cedar and balsam wood, sweet cherry jam, and rose petals. The light color is deceptive given its intense bouquet and expansive, lush, concentrated style. It will not be long-lived, but for drinking over the next 5–6 years, this is a seductive, hedonistically styled Barolo. The 1995 Barolo Cannubi is very sexy. The dark ruby color is accompanied by a sumptuous nose of tobacco smoke, coffee, black fruits, and toast. The wine is dense, velvety-textured, full-bodied, and silky, with no hard edges. This is a voluptuous wine to enjoy over the next decade. The 1995 Barolo Bric del Fiasc is backward, with scents of smoke, tar, soy, jammy black cherry and blackberry fruit, and toast. Full-bodied, concentrated, expansive, soft, and seductive, with 13.5% alcohol and moderate tannin in the finish, it should be drunk over the next 10 years. The intensely fragrant (wood smoke, allspice, black fruits, and tobacco) 1995 Barolo Rocche dell'Annunziata boasts a dark ruby color, as well as terrific extract, full body, and copious quantities of glycerin. While it possesses the velvety, evolved personality of the other 1995s, there are more stuffing and richness but fewer nuances. Drink it over the next 12–14 years. Already complex and approachable, the 1995 Scavino Barolos are all sensual, fragrant, Burgundy-like, forward wines with fine balance.

MAURO SEBASTE

1998 Barbera d'Alba Santa Rosalia	D	88
1997 Barbera d'Alba Santa Rosalia	D	91
1997 Barolo Monvigliero	E	89
1996 Barolo Monvigliero	D	89+
1995 Barolo Monvigliero	D	87
1997 Barolo Prapò	E	90
1996 Barolo Prapò	D	89+
1995 Barolo Prapò	D	89
1997 Barolo La Serra	E	(88–91)
1998 Centobricchi	C	86
1997 Centobricchi	D	91

Sebaste tends to produce wines that reflect the finest aspects of both the traditional and more modern school of winemaking. The estate's total production is about 1,200 cases. Sebaste's Barolos from the Prapò vineyard are fuller-bodied, bigger-structured, and more muscular offerings. The 1998 Barbera d'Alba Santa Rosalia is less expansive and flamboyant than the 1997 but altogether an excellent wine with many of the same characteristics. It should drink well for 3–4 years. The 1998 Centobricchi, a blend of 90% Barbera and 10% Nebbiolo aged in 1- and 2-year-old French barrels, displays attractive strawberry, cherry, and currant aromas and flavors, medium body, good purity, spicy new oak, and a supple, fleshy finish. Drink it over the next 5–6 years.

An outstanding effort, the 1997 Centobricchi reveals an explosive bouquet of cedary, spice box, tobacco, blackberry and cherry aromas, a long, lush, multilayered, concentrated palate, with gorgeous spice and jammy fruit. Rich, unctuously textured, and thick, it is ideal for drinking now and over the next decade. The vintage's opulence is well displayed in the perfumed 1997 Barolo Monvigliero. The color is a dark ruby, and the wine is exotically rich, ripe, and obviously a creation of its vintage's conditions more than its *terroir*. The creamy, fat, succulent texture, gorgeously ripe fruit, and long, glycerin-imbued finish are admirable. It is a candidate for an outstanding rating after bottling. Anticipated maturity: now–2012. The licorice, smoky cassis, overripe style of the 1997 Barolo Prapò defines this exotic, flamboyant vintage. Dark ruby/purple-colored, it possesses abundant levels of glycerin, high alcohol, and low acidity. It should be delicious young yet keep for 15 years. The 1997 Barolo La Serra is the debut vintage of this sexy, lush, ostentatiously styled wine. The color is a dark ruby, and the wine is viscous and open-knit with gobs of fruit, glycerin, alcohol, and extract. This heady, chewy Barolo needs more delineation, but it displays considerable promise. Readers will undoubtedly enjoy the classic fragrance of jammy cherries, smoke, tar, and spice. Anticipated maturity: now–2016.

The two 1996 Barolos are backward. The medium dark ruby-colored 1996 Barolo Monvigliero exhibits a spicy, tobacco, strawberry, and kirsch-scented nose with dried herbs in the background. Dense, rich, and medium- to full-bodied, with high tannin, this wine is still an infant. Give it 1–2 years of cellaring and drink it through 2015. Even more dense, tannic, and muscular is the 1996 Barolo Prapò. A dark ruby color is followed by aromas of spice box, cherry liqueur, cedarwood, rose petals, and tar. This full-bodied, dry, muscular effort needs at least two years of cellaring. It is impressively built and dense and may merit an outstanding rating with additional bottle age. Anticipated maturity: 2005–2018.

The 1995 Barolo Monvigliero reveals an evolved garnet color with a pink/amber edge, in addition to expansive aromas of meats, dried herbs, spice, cedar, and cherries. There are excellent fruit in the mouth, medium to full body, a supple texture, and a fine finish. Drink this accessible Barolo over the next 4–5 years. The 1995 Barolo Prapò offers Nebbiolo's classic bouquet of melted road tar, rose petal, and cherry liqueur–like scents. Medium- to full-bodied, with a distinctive licorice/cherry fruitiness as well as excellent richness and purity, it is an open-knit Barolo to enjoy over the next 12 years.

F.LLI SEGHESIO

1998 Barolo Vigneto La Villa	E	94
1997 Barolo Vigneto La Villa	E	93
1996 Barolo Vigneto La Villa	E	91
1995 Barolo Vigneto La Villa	E	90

This Monforte d'Alba producer utilizes open-top fermenters and about 20% new oak, which is blended with the balance of the wine, which has been aged in *foudres.*

The fabulous 1998 Barolo Vigneta La Villa is even better than the 1997. Its saturated dense plum/garnet color is accompanied by a stunningly ostentatious, brilliantly aromatic nose of smoky tobacco, cedar wood, plums, cherry liqueur, coffee, and dried herbs. A rich, full-bodied, opulent wine, it possesses fabulous spice and fruit as well as a fresh, high-toned character. Powerful, full, and beautifully delineated, it can be consumed over the next 10–12 years. A dense plum/garnet color and exquisite bouquet of cigar box, smoke, licorice, black cherry/berry fruit, and subtle oak are found in the exotic, flamboyant 1997 Barolo Vigneto La Villa. Full-bodied, with a viscous texture and plenty of power, yet impeccable balance as well as harmony between the alcohol, acidity, tannin, and wood, this fleshy, super-concentrated, seamless effort can be drunk now and over the next 15 years. The explosive 1996 Barolo Vigneto La Villa offers redolent aromatics of kirsch, blackberries, soy, toasty new oak, licorice, and dried herbs. The wine is full-bodied, with huge quantities of glycerin, and fabulous concentration as well as richness. There are plenty of tannin and muscle in the finish, so it will benefit from 3–4 years of cellaring. Anticipated maturity: 2004–2018. The deep ruby 1995 Barolo Vigneto La Villa is a Burgundy-styled wine with a nose of cherry liqueur, dried herbs, smoke, toasty oak, and seaweed scents. There are low acidity and a medium- to full-bodied, plush texture. I would opt for drinking it over the next 4–5 years.

ENRICO SERAFINO

1998 Barolo	D	(87–88)
1997 Barolo	D	89

This producer from the village of Canale d'Alba has fashioned an attractive, well-made, smoky, black cherry–scented 1998 Barolo with considerable complexity in the evolved aromatics. It exhibits good density, medium body, moderate tannin, charming sweetness, and clean winemaking. Consume it over the next 12 years. The supple-textured, dark garnet-colored 1997 Barolo possesses full body, a fleshy, plush texture, low acidity, excellent concentration, and admirable length. It should drink well for a decade. I also liked Serafino's lighter, more elegant, fresher, less opulent 1999. A sleeper choice?

AURELIO SETTIMO

1997 Barolo Rocche	E	90
1996 Barolo Rocche	E	90
1995 Barolo Rocche	E	87

These are fine efforts from this small producer in La Morra. The vintage's sweet glycerin, low acidity, and lofty alcohol are well displayed in the 1997 Barolo Rocche. It possesses a boat-load of black cherry and berry fruit, as well as a voluptuous texture and a powerful, long, concentrated finish. This impressive old-style Barolo will be ready to drink upon release and should keep for 12 years. The traditionally made, impressively endowed 1996 Barolo Rocche exhibits a fragrant bouquet of chocolate, melted asphalt, soy, smoke, and white truffles. It is powerful, massive, moderately tannic, dense, and chewy, with considerable intensity. There are a few hard edges, and fans of the more modern-style Barolos will feel it is rustic, but it is loaded with flavor and personality. I adored it. Anticipated maturity: now–2015. Settimo's 1995 Barolo Rocche is a complex, evolved effort with scents of soy, roasted meats, dried herbs, and earthy fruits. The color is dark garnet with amber/orange at the edge. Complex, savory, fleshy, and ready to drink, this medium- to full-bodied Barolo should be at its best now and over the next 8 years.

SOTTIMANO

1996 Barbaresco Gaia Principe Vigna del Salto	D	89
1998 Barbaresco Cottà Vigna Brichet	D	90+
1997 Barbaresco Cottà Vigna Brichet	D	92
1996 Barbaresco Cottà Vigna Brichet	D	89+
1998 Barbaresco Pajoré Vigna Lunetta	D	90
1997 Barbaresco Pajoré Vigna Lunetta	D	89
1998 Barbaresco Currà Vigna Masué	D	90
1997 Barbaresco Currà Vigna Masué	D	91
1996 Barbaresco Currà Vigna Masué	D	(91–92)
1998 Barbaresco Fausoni Vigna del Salto	D	90
1997 Barbaresco Fausoni Vigna del Salto	D	90+
1997 Barbera d'Alba Pairolero	C	90
1998 Dolcetto d'Alba Cottà	B	89

Sottimano is based in Neive, where the Barbarescos tend to be larger-framed, deeper-colored, and more tannic and structured than the more elegant offerings from vineyards surrounding the village of Barbaresco or the cooler sites surrounding Treiso. All of the 1998 Barbarescos are complex, expressive offerings with dramatic bouquets as well as gorgeously ripe, multilayered flavors. The only difference is that some are more precocious than their siblings. The 1997s are freaks of Mother Nature, with opulence and levels of glycerin, alcohol, and fruit that are largely unprecedented in Piedmont. The 1996s look classic in the style of 1989 and 1971. I would not be surprised if all the 1996 Sottimano Barbarescos easily achieved 14% alcohol, and I am sure the 1997s are even higher, although it is completely hidden by the wines' wealth of fruit, glycerin, and concentration.

Sottimano's dense purple-colored 1998 Dolcetto d'Alba Cottà is not the soft style of Dolcetto usually produced. This example possesses more structure than most (unusual for Dolcetto), but it is crammed with fruit, extract, and richness. Massive for a Dolcetto, with excellent purity, it will last for 4–5 years. An earthy concoction of herbs, leather, cedar, spice box, and black cherry/plum-like fruit offers an enticing introduction to the 1998 Barbaresco Pajoré Vigna Lunetta. Supple-textured and seemingly low in acidity, with admirable density, excellent purity, and a fleshy finish, it will drink well for a decade. A similar earthiness, with the addition of vegetable root, plum, and cherry characteristics, is found in the 1998 Barbaresco Currà Vigna Masué. Its soft, velvety-textured, black fruit flavors reveal a distinctive spicy earthiness along with notes of leather. Drink this outstanding effort over the next 8 years. A leather component accompanies notes of cigar tobacco, spice box, cedar, herbs, and cherry cough syrup in the deep, full-bodied, richly fruity, dense, layered 1998 Barbaresco Fausoni Vigna del Salto. Again, this wine is delicious to drink, but it displays more tannin in the finish than its two predecessors. Unquestionably, the most backward of Sottimano's Barbarescos is the 1998 Barbaresco Cottà Vigna Brichet. Its dark ruby color is followed by tightly knit but promising aromatics of cherry liqueur, rose petals, melted asphalt, oak, and earth. Structured, powerful, broodingly backward, and extremely well made, with moderate tannin, this impressive effort requires 1–2 years of cellaring. Anticipated maturity: 2004–2020.

The superb 1997 Barbera d'Alba Pairolero offers a saturated black/ruby/purple color, glorious levels of blackberry and cherry liqueur–like fruit, low acidity, a voluptuous, thick, viscous texture, and an intense finish. Drink this superb, pure Barbera over the next 4–5 years. The dark garnet-colored 1997 Barbaresco Pajoré Vigna Lunetta offers sweet, ripe, exotic notes presented in an open-knit style. Fleshy and spicy, with aromas and flavors of tar, dried herbs, and cherry liqueur, it is medium- to full-bodied, lush, and best drunk over the next 4–5 years. For whatever reason, as good as it is (and I would be happy to drink it anytime) it is the least profound of this quartet. The dark garnet-colored 1997 Barbaresco Currà Vigna Masué exhibits aromas of soy, smoke, asphalt, black cherries, and incense, unreal opulence, huge levels of glycerin, plenty of power, a sweet, expansive palate impression, gorgeous purity, and loads of fruit, glycerin, and alcohol. Buried beneath all that is some serious tannin, but it is not causing the wine to shut down or taste astringent. It should firm up in the bottle and drink well for 12 years. The complex 1997 Barbaresco Fausoni Vigna del Salto displays an Asian spice profile to its explosive aromatics. A dark plum color is followed by elegant, full-bodied notes of coffee, cherries, soy, and star anise, in addition to a sweet, fleshy, low acid palate impression. Not as massive as the Currà Vigna Masué, it is a fleshy effort to enjoy over the next 12 years. Sottimano's garnet/plum-colored 1997 Barbaresco Cottà Vigna Brichet is the most structured of this quartet, yet it possesses extraordinary density, concentration, and intensity. The bouquet offers aromas of Asian spices, soy, dried cherries, tobacco, incense, and smoke. Full-bodied, thick, chewy, highly concentrated, and moderately tannic, this 1997 needs another 1–2 years of cellaring; it should drink well for 12 years.

The 1996 Barbaresco Gaia Principe Vigna del Salto is a wine of both richness and structure. Its dark ruby color is accompanied by an intriguing nose of spice box, tobacco smoke, cedar, and cherry liqueur. The wine is dense, medium- to full-bodied, and structured, with moderate tannin. It requires several years of bottle age. Anticipated maturity: now–2015. The 1996 Barbaresco Cottà Vigna Brichet is similarly styled, with more smoke and cherry liqueur components intermixed with attractive scents of new saddle leather and spice. The wine is ripe and full-bodied, with moderate tannin and outstanding purity. Anticipated maturity: now–2015. The 1996 Barbaresco Currà Vigne Masué is the most expansive, full-bodied, and concentrated of the three 1996s. The wine displays a dark ruby color, as well as an explosive nose of cherry liqueur, incense, dried herbs, smoke, cedar, and soy. Dense and powerful, with fabulous concentration and a sweet, layered mid-palate and finish, this large-scaled, mouthcoating Barbaresco will be at its finest between now–2016.

LA SPINETTA DI GIUSEPPE RIVETTI

1995	Barbaresco La Spinetta	E	87
1998	Barbaresco Vigneto Valeirano	E	92
1997	Barbaresco Vigneto Valeirano	E	91
1998	Barbaresco Vigneto Gallina	E	92
1997	Barbaresco Vigneto Gallina	E	96
1996	Barbaresco Vigneto Gallina	E	90
1998	Barbaresco Vigneto Starderi	E	90+
1997	Barbaresco Vigneto Starderi	E	92+
1996	Barbaresco Vigneto Starderi	E	90
1999	Barbera d'Alba Vigneto Gallina	E	96
1998	Barbera d'Alba Vigneto Gallina	E	95
1997	Barbera d'Alba Vigneto Gallina	E	95
1996	Barbera d'Alba Vigneto Gallina	E	92
1999	Barbera d'Asti	E	94
1998	Barbera d'Asti	E	93
1999	Monferrato Rosso Pin	E	95

1998 Monferrato Rosso Pin	E	91
1997 Monferrato Rosso Pin	E	90
1996 Monferrato Rosso Pin	E	89+

Giorgio Rivetti, who has received immensely favorable publicity in the Italian press, appears to have everything going his way. He displays a masterful touch whether he is making Barbera, Barbaresco, or his proprietary red wine, Pin. His most renowned offerings are his extraordinary, slightly sweet, sparkling Moscatos, which are not reviewed here since they must be drunk within a year of their release. His beautiful 1998 Barbarescos are just a notch below his flamboyant, superexotic, almost over-the-top 1997s, which all performed significantly better from bottle than they did from cask. All his vineyards are planted on hillsides surrounding the village of Treiso. Rivetti has recently purchased a vineyard in Barolo, from which small quantities will emerge beginning with the 2000 vintage. The Barbarescos are aged in an assortment of wood, with about 18% being new French oak.

Rivetti's blend of Cabernet Sauvignon and Nebbiolo, the 1999 Monferrato Rosso Pin, is an exotic, ripe, luxuriously intense effort displaying extravagant flavors that border on excess. It is voluptuously textured with terrific aromas of red and black fruits, smoke, and new oak. While there is a tendency to think of this as an internationally styled offering, Nebbiolo gives the wine a finesse and complexity not found in most new-breed wines. Its texture, richness, and thickness are a total turn-on. Who knows how it will age, but certainly it is impossible to resist at present. My instincts suggest drinking it over the next 5–6 years, but it may be uncommonly long-lived.

The 1999 Barbera d'Alba Vigneta Gallina is awesome! I am not sure it will get any better since Barbera is not one of the most noble varietals in terms of complexity and intensity. It does, however, offer glorious levels of concentration as well as a huge nose of smoked meats, blackberry, cherry, and strawberry jam intertwined with licorice, new oak, and barbecue spice. Viscous, remarkably dense, and sexy, it is impossible to resist. For drinking now and over the next 4–5 years, this is as profound a dry red wine as readers will find. More restrained (although that's hardly the appropriate word), the black/purple-colored 1999 Barbera d'Asti offers wonderful sweetness, jammy plum and currant characteristics, and toasty new oak from its new-*barrique* aging. It is viscous, thick, and jammy with oodles of fruit, glycerin, and extract. Extraordinarily pure, mouthcoating, and fascinating, this 1999 should be consumed over the next 3–4 years to take advantage of its exuberance and extraordinary fruit.

The complex, elegant 1998 Barbaresco Vigneto Gallina exhibits aromas and flavors of pepper, cedar, black cherries, plums, soy, earth, and new oak. Full-bodied, pure, seamless, and well balanced, with low acidity, this expressive, beautifully made wine should drink well for 10 years. The ravishingly complex 1998 Barbaresco Vigneto Valeirano possesses a distinctive bouquet of licorice, root beer, earth, cherry liqueur, rose petals, and truffles. Drink this complex, dense, opulently textured, hedonistic offering over the next decade. The 1998 Barbaresco Vigneto Starderi is less expressive than its two siblings, revealing more tannin and structure, as well as a restrained, backward bouquet. Dark ruby-colored, round, and full-bodied, with notes of licorice, new oak, and black cherries, it should drink well over the following 10–12 years.

The opaque purple-colored 1998 Barbera d'Alba Vigneto Gallina (a terrific Barbaresco vineyard outside Neive) was aged in 100% new oak. It offers a glorious perfume of chocolate, cedar, blackberries, cherry liqueur, and smoke. This massive yet well-balanced, layered wine is explosive. Drink it over the next 4–5 years. Of equal size, explosiveness, power, and richness is the 1998 Barbera d'Asti. Even more fruit-driven, with less spice and complexity but equal weight, mass, and intensity, it offers a dynamic mouthful of Barbera.

The 1998 Monferrato Rosso Pin, is a blend of 50% Nebbiolo, 30% Barbera, and 20% Cabernet Sauvignon that spent 20 months in 100% new French oak. The 1998 is terrific. It boasts a dense ruby/purple color as well as complex, Bordeaux-like aromas of cedar and black currants, full body, moderate tannin, and excellent overall balance. It will evolve nicely for a decade.

The magnificent 1997 Barbaresco Vigneto Gallina comes from a steep hillside vineyard just outside the village of Neive, even though it is part of the Treiso commune. A deep plum color is accompanied by a huge, complex, leather, soy, allspice, cherry liqueur, and smoky-scented bouquet. This full-bodied, impressively endowed, layered, ravishing Barbaresco can be drunk now or cellared for 15 years. Equally sensational but more structured is the 1997 Barbaresco Vigneto Valeirano. This wine exhibits more·licorice, glycerin, and berry fruit, along with exotic spices, leather, smoke, and herbs. Spicy and full-bodied, with more obvious tannin, structure, and muscle than the more seductive Gallina, it should keep for 15–20 years. The 1997 Barbaresco Vigneto Starderi is the least penetrable and ostentatious of this trio. It boasts a dark plum/purple color in addition to full body, great fruit concentration, and power, but it is firm and closed compared to its siblings. There is plenty of potential, but this wine needs 2–3 years of cellaring. It should keep for two decades.

The 1997 Barbera d'Alba Gallina may be one of the finest Barberas ever produced in Italy. Opaque purple-colored, with soaring aromatics, huge density and richness, a voluptuous texture and a finish that lasts for nearly a minute, this mind-boggling effort should age gloriously for a decade or more. A proprietary red wine made from a blend of equal parts Nebbiolo, Cabernet Sauvignon, and Barbera, the 1997 Monferrato Rosso Pin *vino da tavola* presents an outstanding combination of concentrated red and black fruits, spicy vanilla, and huge, thick, juicy flavors. Since the new oak is more apparent, the wine should be cellared for 1–2 years and drunk over the following decade.

The classic structure and power of the vintage is well displayed in both of Rivetti's 1996 Barbarescos. The 1996 Barbaresco Vigneto Starderi's deep ruby color is followed by an explosive nose of sweet cherry liqueur, vanilla, and wood smoke. This full-bodied, highly extracted, intense, sexy, moderately tannic wine is powerful yet well balanced. Despite its ability to improve for 10–12 years, it is easy to drink at present. The terrifically fruity, more flattering 1996 Barbaresco Vigneto Gallina is full-bodied, with outstanding concentration, plenty of earthy, plum/cherry, smoky, spice scents, low acidity, and moderate tannin in the layered finish. It should drink well for a dozen or more years. The terrific, formidably endowed, gorgeously pure, full-bodied 1996 Barbera d'Alba Vigneto Gallina has soaked up its new oak beautifully. It possesses such phenomenal layers of concentrated black fruits, full body, and amazing glycerin and depth that it must be tasted to be believed.

Another Rivetti wine that is worth seeking is the 1996 Monferrato Rosso Pin, a proprietary red wine blend of 50% Nebbiolo, 25% Cabernet Sauvignon, and 25% Barbera. The color is a saturated black/purple and the wine tannic and backward, made in a Médoc-like style. Although rich, it was closed and revealed too much oak to merit an outstanding score (it was brought up in 100% new oak casks).

Rivetti's medium garnet/ruby-colored 1995 Barbaresco La Spinetta exhibits a sweet, evolved nose of spicy oak, cherry liqueur, tobacco, and vanilla. Expansive (13.5% alcohol), ripe, and long, with copious quantities of fruit, this medium- to full-bodied Barbaresco should drink well now and over the next 8 years.

LA SPINONA

1997　Barbaresco	D	87
1996　Barbaresco	D	82
1997　Barolo	D	(87–90)

The more interesting 1997 Barbaresco exhibits a layered texture, riper, sweeter black cherry fruit with dried herbs and spice in the background, and medium to full body. It is ideal for drinking over the next decade. The dark ruby-colored 1997 Barolo reveals the vintage's jammy overripeness in its aromatics. Full-bodied, low in acidity, and thick but not complex, it will merit the higher score if more complexity emerges. Anticipated maturity: now–2014. The lean, straightforward, medium-bodied 1996 Barbaresco offers attractive fruit, but it falls away in the mouth. Consume it over the next 3–4 years.

STROPPIANA

1997 Barolo	D	89

Recent vintages of this La Morra producer's wines have all performed well. While made in a solid, muscular, tannic, monolithic style, they possess excellent depth, exuberance, and rustic tannin in the finish. More finesse would be beneficial, but there is a lot to like in this traditionally made Barolo. The dark plum/purple-colored 1997 Barolo reveals a boatload of tannin as well as big, thick flavors with abundant muscle, depth, and breadth. Give it 1–2 years of cellaring and consume it over the following 12–15.

GIANOLIO TOMASO

1998 Barbaresco	D	85
2000 Barbera d'Alba	C	87
1997 Barolo	D	90
1999 Nebbiolo d'Alba	C	88
1998 Nebbiolo d'Alba	C	85
1997 Nebbiolo d'Alba	C	89

The 2000 Barbera d'Alba exhibits more strawberry and cherry fruit as well as acidity, in addition to admirable ripeness, medium body, excellent texture, and a fine finish. Drink it over the next 2–3 years.

The three Nebbiolos d'Alba admirably reflect their vintages. The 1999 Nebbiolo d'Alba appears to be a blend of the exotic 1997 and elegant, streamlined 1998. It offers sweet aromas of strawberries, cherries, leather, and tobacco. It is best consumed over the next 4–5 years. The most elegant, the 1998 Nebbiolo d'Alba, is more measured and restrained and less exotic than the sweeter, voluptuous, deep, chewy 1997 Nebbiolo d'Alba. Both wines are meant to be drunk over the next 2–3 years.

Tomaso's 1998 Barbaresco reveals notes of spice box, leather, soy, tobacco, and cherry fruit, medium body, and a short finish. Far superior is the 1997 Barolo, a sweet, exotic, concentrated offering exhibiting aromas and flavors of espresso, cherry liqueur, soy, and wood in the background. Medium- to full-bodied, with excellent purity, it is best drunk now and over the next 7–8 years.

GIUSEPPE TRAVERSA

1998 Barbaresco Sorì Ciabot	E	90+
1997 Barbaresco Sorì Ciabot	E	89
1996 Barbaresco Sorì Ciabot	E	91
1995 Barbaresco Sorì Ciabot	E	90
1997 Barbaresco Sorì Starderi	E	87
1996 Barbaresco Sorì Starderi	E	(90–91)
1999 Barbera d'Alba La Burdinota del Ciabot	D	88
1997 Barbera d'Alba La Burdinota del Ciabot	D	90

This producer's outstanding, modern-styled Barbarescos are *barrique*-aged and bottled in heavy, thick antique bottles. Traversa also fashions superb Barberas.

The medium-bodied 1999 Barbera d'Alba La Burdinota del Ciabot offers tangy, sweet strawberry and cherry fruit infused with toasty French oak. Plump and fleshy as well as elegant and pure, it will drink well for 2 years.

The *barrique*-aged, dark plum/purple-colored 1998 Barbaresco Sorì Ciabot reveals ripe cherry and blackberry fruit intertwined with toast, smoke, and espresso characteristics. Rich, full-bodied, and powerful, with moderately high tannin, it is one of the few 1998 Barbarescos that requires cellaring. Anticipated maturity: 2003–2014.

As the spicy, complex 1997 Barbaresco Sorì Starderi sat in the glass, tobacco, new saddle leather, fennel, and sweet and sour cherry aromas emerged. Medium- to full-bodied, complex, and already drinkable, it should keep for a decade or more. The medium ruby-colored 1997 Barbaresco Sorì Ciabot already reveals amber at the edge. Notes of rose petals, tar, cedar, spice box, and copious quantities of red and black fruits are classic characteristics of ripe Nebbiolo. Medium- to full-bodied, with enough acidity for delineation and freshness, good spice and richness, and a long finish, it should be drunk over the next 10 years. The serious 1997 Barbera d'Alba La Burdinota del Ciabot boasts a dense ruby/purple color, and terrific fat, jammy blackberry and cherry fruit intermixed with licorice and spice. Medium- to full-bodied and intense, with good underlying acidity, this is a gorgeously pure, nicely textured Barbera to drink over the next 5–6 years.

The 1996 Barbaresco Sorì Ciabot is even richer and fuller-bodied, with huge extract and a terrific black cherry and raspberry fruitiness intermixed with toast, smoke, new saddle leather, and jam. Massive yet impeccably well balanced, this superb Barbaresco can be drunk now as well as over the next 10 years. The 1996 Barbaresco Sorì Starderi is an impressively endowed, modern-styled effort with copious quantities of black cherry and cassis fruit intermixed with new oak, weedy tobacco, and cigar box notes. All are presented in a silky-textured format. Anticipated maturity: now–2012. The 1995 Barbaresco Sorì Ciabot possesses a deep ruby/plum color as well as stunning aromatics consisting of dried herbs, smoke, tobacco, red and black fruits, cedar, and soy sauce. The wine is fleshy, rich, and full-bodied, with subtle new oak, terrific extract, and a succulent texture. It will not be long-lived but should drink well for 4–5 years.

G. D. VAJRA

1998 Barolo	E	(88–90)
1997 Barolo	E	91

Vajra's wines are well made, full-bodied, and powerful. The dense plum-colored 1998 Barolo exhibits a sexy, sweet, open-knit perfume offering aromas of melted licorice, smoke, plums, and cherries. While it does not possess the thickness or exotic, over-the-top character of his blockbuster 1997, the 1998 is supple, full-bodied, layered, forward, concentrated, and impressively rich. It is surprisingly fragrant for such a young Barolo (a consistent characteristic of most 1998 Barolos and Barbarescos). Harmony is the operative word for this young but promising effort. Anticipated maturity: 2005–2016. The dark plum-colored 1997 Barolo exhibits a big, thick, chocolaty, licorice, cherry liqueur, smoke, camphor, and truffle-scented bouquet. This complex, opulently textured wine possesses low acidity, superb ripeness, and a soft, unevolved personality. However, most tasters will not be able to resist its viscous style. Anticipated maturity: now–2016.

MAURO VEGLIO

1998 Barolo Arborina	E	(91–93)
1997 Barolo Arborina	E	90
1996 Barolo Arborina	E	90
1995 Barolo Arborina	E	89
1998 Barolo Castelletto	E	(90–93)
1997 Barolo Castelletto	E	91
1996 Barolo Castelletto	E	91
1998 Barolo Gattera	E	(90–92)
1997 Barolo Gattera	E	89

1996 Barolo Gattera	E	87
1995 Barolo Gattera	E	?
1998 Barolo Rocche	E	(89–91)
1997 Barolo Rocche	E	91
1996 Barolo Rocche	E	91
1995 Barolo Rocche	E	86

This producer has come of age after mixed performances in the mid-1990s. One of Marc de Grazia's "Barolo Boys," Veglio practices modern winemaking techniques. His first great vintage was 1996. He has turned out successful 1998s that are, qualitatively, as interesting as his brilliant 1997s. All of these wines share the vintage's characteristics: intense perfumes as well as harmonious, forward, softly tannic, approachable personalities.

The 1998 Barolo Gattera exhibits a dark plum color in addition to a sweet bouquet of black cherry and plum fruit, spice box, roasted meats, and smoked herbs, a beautiful texture, good softness, and a long (30+-second) finish. With exposure to air, this classic Barolo appears to grow in the glass. Drink it over the next 15 years. More layered as well as fuller-bodied, the 1998 Barolo Arborina boasts a sweet attack and an intense perfume of licorice, tobacco, black fruits, smoked herbs, and toasty oak. This dark garnet-colored, pure, seductive, rich Barolo is nearly exotic in a 1997 sense. Anticipated maturity: 2003–2015.

Although Veglio is from La Morra, his 1998 Barolo Castelletto comes from a vineyard in Monforte d'Alba. The least evolved of these single-vineyard offerings, it displays an opaque ruby/purple color and notes of cinnamon, minerals, earth, meat, and black fruits. In the mouth, the wine is medium-bodied and austere with more tannin and less seductiveness. However, it is loaded with glycerin and extract. Anticipated maturity: 2005–2017. The feminine, delicate 1998 Barolo Rocche is filled with finesse and elegance, without the weight, richness, or concentration of the other three crus. A moderately intense perfume of black cherries, damp earth, truffles, and Provençal herbs is followed by a measured, restrained, sweet, well-balanced wine with ripe tannin and a long finish. Anticipated maturity: now–2012.

The 1997 Barolo Gattera offers an intriguing bouquet of peat moss, licorice, fennel, dried herbs, root vegetables, and black cherry fruit. It possesses a luscious texture, medium to full body, and an up-front, forward ripeness. Look for this wine to drink well during its first decade of life. More tightly knit, with additional structure, the 1997 Barolo Arborina displays a dense plum color with pink/amber at the edge. Full-bodied and tannic, it is a reserved but concentrated effort exhibiting aromas and flavors of strawberry and cherry liqueur intertwined with smoke, earth, and spice. Anticipated maturity: now–2015.

Veglio's 1997 Barolo Castelletto has stunning aromatics of spice box, tobacco, kirsch, licorice, rose petals, and cedar. Corpulent, full-bodied, exotic, and richly layered, with the vintage's telltale glycerin and low-acid, fleshy, higher-than-normal alcohol levels well displayed, it is a nearly over-the-top, exotic Barolo to drink over the next decade. The dark garnet/amber-edged 1997 Barolo Rocche reveals notions of melted caramel, black cherry jam, licorice, fennel, and road tar in its evolved bouquet. Medium- to full-bodied with high glycerin levels, it provides a hedonistic, fat, chewy mouthful of wine that is performing far better from bottle than it did from *foudre/barrique*. Consume this exceptional Barolo over its first 12–14 years of life.

Three of the four Veglio 1996s appear to have outstanding potential. The 1996 Barolo Gattera is a more interesting example than the 1995. Medium-bodied and soft, with an elegant, kirsch-scented and -flavored personality, it is ideal for consuming over the next 5–6 years. Full-bodied and powerful, the 1996 Barolo Rocche possesses copious quantities of cherry liqueur intermixed with leafy tobacco, roasted nuts, smoke, and spice. This moderately tannic, classic Barolo should be at its finest between now–2014. The 1996 Barolo Arborina reveals the telltale rose petal, melted road tar, and jammy cherry–scented nose with tobacco in the background. Made in a soft, forward style, it is medium- to full-bodied, with dazzling fruit intensity, outstanding purity, sweet tannin, and a soft, lush finish. Anticipated maturity: now–2015. The 1996 Barolo Castelletto smells like an herb garden planted next to a roaring charcoal fire. There are copious amounts of cherry fruit, new saddle leather, and animal-like aromas. This is a more *sauvage* Barolo, with impeccable density, medium to full body, and gobs of spicy, cherry fruit flavors. It should drink well for 10–12 years.

I did not understand the lemony, grassy, vegetal 1995 Barolo Gattera. It tastes more like a white wine than a red and is completely at odds with the other Veglio offerings. The 1995 Barolo Rocche is a middleweight, elegant, finesse-styled Barolo with good spice, some tannin, medium body, and attractive cherry fruit. Drink it over the next 5–6 years. The epitome of finesse, the medium ruby-colored 1995 Barolo Arborina is already revealing amber at the edge. Evolved and stylish, with sweet cherry fruit, medium body, and a heady finish, it will drink well for 3–4 years.

ERALDO VIBERTI

1998	Barolo	E	88
1997	Barolo	E	90
1996	Barolo	E	(86–88)
1995	Barolo	E	87

These four attractive Barolos represent a synthesis in style between modern techniques and respect for tradition. A big, smoky, spicy perfume of licorice, truffles, cedar, tobacco, and black fruits jumps from the glass of this forward, dark plum/ruby-colored 1998 Barolo. The complex aromatics are followed by a medium-bodied, elegant, soft, succulent Barolo to enjoy over the next decade. The 1997 Barolo's complex bouquet of soy, earth, truffles, black fruits, iron, and a touch of vitamins is followed by a medium- to full-bodied, beautifully textured, spicy, lush, layered wine. Low acidity and high glycerin levels, in addition to fruit and alcohol, provide a hedonistic yet intellectually satisfying Barolo. Anticipated maturity: now–2015. The saturated ruby/garnet-colored 1996 Barolo possesses a classic, structured, broodingly backward personality with plenty of dried herbs, leather, and cherrylike fruit. The wine is medium- to full-bodied and compressed in the finish, but if the tannin melts away without significant loss of fruit, it will merit a score in the upper 80s. Anticipated maturity: 2003–2015. The 1995 Barolo reveals a healthy, modern dark ruby/purple color, toast notes in the nose, sweet fruit, medium to full body, moderate tannin, and a lush, accessible style. Drink it over the next 5–6 years.

VIETTI

1997	Barbaresco	E	89
1996	Barbaresco	E	85
1995	Barbaresco	E	86
1997	Barbaresco Masseria	E	93
1995	Barbaresco Masseria	E	88
1996	Barolo	E	85
1995	Barolo	E	83
1998	Barolo Brunate	E	(88–90+)
1996	Barolo Brunate	E	89+
1997	Barolo Brunate	E	92
1995	Barolo Brunate	E	86+
1998	Barolo Lazzarito	E	(88–89+)
1997	Barolo Lazzarito	E	93
1995	Barolo Lazzarito	E	85

1998 Barolo Rocche	**E**	**(90–91+)**
1997 Barolo Rocche	**E**	**90**
1996 Barolo Rocche	**E**	**90**
1995 Barolo Rocche	**E**	**85?**
1996 Barolo Villero Riserva	**E**	**91**

In spite of the modern-style labels that have been used for nearly three decades by the Vietti firm, these wines remain entrenched in a traditional school of winemaking. I have been purchasing Vietti wines since the 1971 vintage, and they have never disappointed in terms of their ability to age well. In top vintages, these big-styled Barolos easily last three decades or more. They often show significantly better after cellaring than they do early in life (much like those of Giacomo Conterno, Aldo Conterno, and Bruno Giacosa).

The saturated ruby-colored 1998 Barolo Lazzarito exhibits an elegant, sweet style with surprising suppleness for a young Vietti offering. Earthy black cherry fruit, dried herbs, and licorice are found in this medium-bodied 1998. It should be drinkable between 2003–2015. The 1998 Barolo Rocche reveals more muscle, volume, and power in its full-bodied, backward, yet well-balanced personality. Deep and chewy, with a saturated ruby color and broad flavors with mouthcoating tannin, it will be at its best between 2006–2020. Lastly, the 1998 Barolo Brunate is soft and forward for a Vietti wine. That could be due to the vintage's elegant, harmonious style, which tends to be less extroverted and more classical than 1997, and more evolved and accessible than either 1997 or 1996. This 1998's plum/ruby/purple color is followed by sweet black cherry fruit and balsa wood characteristics. Full-bodied and muscular, with sweet tannin and a supple style, it should drink well between 2004–2020.

The 1997s are the finest Vietti offerings in twenty years. For starters, the 1997 Barbaresco Masseria is a fabulous example from this appellation. A saturated dark plum/garnet color is followed by a broad, luxurious, sweet nose of cedar, plums, cherries, leather, herbs, earth, and spice. Deep, expansive, and full-bodied, with no hard edges, this mouthcoating, well-balanced effort will drink well now and over the next 15 years. The dark ruby/garnet-colored 1997 Barolo Lazzarito reveals a certain forwardness, no doubt because of the vintage's exotic, opulent, low-acid character. There are plenty of stuffing, full body, and notes of balsam wood, spice box, fruitcake, and cherries. Viscous, chewy, and deep, this precocious wine can be drunk upon release or cellared for 15–20 years. A classic licorice, dried tobacco, rose petal, cherry, and tar-scented bouquet is found in the dark plum-colored 1997 Barolo Rocche. Although broad and rich with noticeable tannin, it is also expansive and chewy. With more length than the Lazzarito, the Rocche will be approachable young and keep for 15–20 years. The exquisite 1997 Barolo Brunate is the most backward of these offerings. Dark ruby-colored with a purple hue, it offers a compelling nose of barbecued pork, cherry syrup, roasted coffee, rose water, and licorice. Full-bodied, muscular, and powerful, with a load of tannin as well as huge richness and thickness, it requires cellaring for 1–2 years and should drink well for 20–25 years.

In 1996 I tasted four Barolos, all significantly better than Vietti's 1995s. The 1996 Barolo exhibits good sweetness, in addition to a distinctive cedary, herb, and spice box aromatic profile. It is medium-bodied, with good concentration and moderate levels of astringent tannin. Anticipated maturity: now–2012. The 1996 Barolo Villero Riserva reveals spicy oak intermixed with copious quantities of jammy cherries, *garrigue*, smoke, and earth. Sweet, deep, and full-bodied, with classic rose petal and tar-like flavors, this bold, masculine, powerful Barolo possesses plenty of tannin. It should age easily for two decades. Anticipated maturity: 2006–2020. Exhibiting a more saturated color, the 1996 Barolo Brunate came across as more closed, but powerful, rich, and potentially outstanding. The wine has good depth but is broodingly backward and unevolved. Anticipated maturity: 2007–2020. The most saturated color and the sweetest, richest red/black fruits are found in the 1996 Barolo Rocche. It is extremely full-bodied and tannic, a bit hard, but impressively endowed. If the tannin becomes better meshed, it will be an outstanding wine, but it will require patience from prospective purchasers. Anticipated maturity: 2007–2015.

The 1995 Barbaresco exhibits an evolved garnet color in addition to a spicy, tobacco-tinged nose with scents of cherry jam and cigar smoke. It is an easygoing, round, fruit/spice-driven wine to drink over the next 3–4 years. More substantial is the 1995 Barbaresco Masseria. The nose offers dried Provençal herbs intermixed with seaweed, smoke, earth, and kirsch. Weighty, expansive, and lush, this medium- to full-bodied offering reveals some of the Nebbiolo's telltale tar characteristics with airing. Drink this beauty over the next 8 years. The dark ruby-colored 1996 Barbaresco reveals a spicy, cedary, sweet nose, excellent fruit, smoky oak, grilled herbs, and meat elements. The finish is short, but it should open with time. This will not be a blockbuster Barbaresco, but it is elegant and well made. Anticipated maturity: now–2010. The dark ruby-colored, fat, soft 1997 Barbaresco exhibits the vintage's succulence as well as gobs of tannin and black cherry fruit intertwined with smoke and damp foresty smells. With high glycerin and low acidity, it is an ideal candidate for consuming over the next 10 years.

I tasted four 1995 Barolos from Vietti. The regular 1995 Barolo's evolved garnet color is followed by a round, soft, fruity nose of dried herbs, red fruits, cedar, and spice box. The finish is slightly pinched, compressed, and austere. This fully mature Barolo is best consumed over the next 3 years. Frankly, I expected more. I was not impressed by the three single-vineyard Barolos, although they are all good wines. The 1995 Barolo Lazzarito exhibits a moderately intense nose of cranberries, cherries, dried herbs, smoke, and earth. It is compressed in the mouth, displaying high levels of astringent tannin. Although it will drink well for 5–6 years, the wine lacks the concentration to stand up to its structure. The well-made 1995 Barolo Brunate offers a low-key, weedy, cedary, herb, and smoky personality with moderate levels of sweet cherry fruit and a short, tannic finish. Anticipated maturity: now–2007. The 1995 Barolo Rocche possesses the most saturated color of all the Vietti 1995s, but it is evolved, with high levels of tannin that scorch the back of the palate. This gives the wine an attenuated, compressed, tough-textured finish. I am not sure it has the proper balance to age gracefully.

VILLA GIADA

1998 Barbera d'Asti La Quercia	D	90
1998 Barbera d'Asti Riserva Bricco Dani	D	90
2000 Barbera d'Asti Vigna d'Arturo	D	89

These are *barrique*-aged, modern-styled Barberas, which, despite their marvelous intensity and richness, require consumption during their first 4–5 years of life. The 2000 Barbera d'Asti Vigna d'Arturo reveals evidence of *barrique* aging. Medium- to full-bodied, with notes of toast, black cherry jam, tomato skin, and spice, gorgeous levels of fruit, and a long, uncomplicated, but delicious finish, it should drink well for 3–4 years. The dense purple-colored 1998 Barbera d'Asti La Quercia exhibits an intense nose of black cherry liqueur intertwined with new wood smells. As it is creamy-textured, intense, ripe, and loaded, with no hard edges, early consumption is mandatory. Even more opaque-colored (it resembles ink), the 1998 Barbera d'Asti Riserva Bricco Dani reveals a thicker, more unctuous personality, as well as additional amounts of toasty new oak in its aromas. Another year of bottle age may result in more nuances. This 1998 should be drunk over the next 3–4 years.

VILLA LANATRA

1998 Barolo	D	90
1997 Barolo	D	88

Even better than the excellent 1997, Villa Lanatra's 1998 Barolo is a well-textured, deep, full-bodied, opaque ruby/purple-colored effort revealing loads of black currant and blackberry fruit as well as evidence of *barrique* aging. Chewy and fleshy, with considerable substance, it is a product of the modern school of Piedmontese winemaking, but there is no shortage of Nebbiolo/Barolo typicity. Anticipated maturity: 2004–2018.

A modern-styled effort with good harmony, finesse, and graceful red currant/cherry flavors backed by subtle toasty oak, the full-bodied, deep, long 1997 Barolo is made in an international style. Anticipated maturity: now–2012.

GIANNI VOERZIO

1999	Barbera d'Alba Ciabot della Luna	C	87
1998	Barbera d'Alba Ciabot della Luna	C	88
1998	Barolo La Serra	E	89
1997	Barolo La Serra	E	88
1996	Barolo La Serra	E	(90–92)
1995	Barolo La Serra	E	90
2000	Dolcetto d'Alba Rocchettevino	C	90
1998	Langhe Rosso Serrapiù	C	88

Gianni Voerzio (Roberto's brother) follows the new school of winemaking, utilizing a high percentage of *barriques* for aging his wine. However, these are not internationally styled Nebbiolos as they all display the varietal's textbook characteristics. This small La Morra producer also fashions excellent Barbera, Dolcetto, and Nebbiolo from the Ciabot della Luna vineyard.

Voerzio's 2000 Dolcetto d'Alba Rocchettevino is an explosive offering loaded with chocolaty black cherry fruit. There are adequate acidity for balance, superb purity, and a plump, fleshy style that invites consumption over the next 2 years. Also very good, the 1999 Barbera d'Alba Ciabot della Luna reveals less color saturation but more complex berry, licorice, and herbal characteristics, a fleshy palate with noticeable new oak, and a smoky, spicy finish. It should drink well for 3 years. Not too exuberant but intense, with a spicy, strawberry, black cherry, licorice, and chocolate-scented bouquet, is the 1998 Barbera d'Alba Ciabot della Luna. There is evidence of toasty oak, but the fruit characteristics dominate. Drink it over the next 3–4 years. The 1998 Langhe Rosso Serrapiù (a blend of equal parts Nebbiolo and Barbera, aged in *barrique*) is an earthy, leathery offering with dried herbs, plums, cherry liqueur, and spice box aromas and flavors. Complex in the nose and rich, medium-bodied in the mouth, with good underlying acidity in addition to a nicely layered structure, it should be consumed over the next 4–5 years.

The elegant, medium-bodied, soft 1998 Barolo La Serra possesses aromas of cherry liqueur, tobacco, and smoke and an autumnal leafy characteristic. It is dense and rich, with its structure and tannin nicely concealed by the fruit and overall harmony. This well-balanced, elegant, stylish 1998 is best consumed over the next 12 years. The 1997 Barolo La Serra does not appear to possess the intensity of either the superb 1998 or the 1999. It is a medium-bodied, low-acid, spicy, round, soft, seductive effort with plenty of caramel, tobacco, cherry, and tar aromas as well as flavors. Drink it over the next 8 years. The 1996 Barolo La Serra exhibits a deeper, more saturated ruby color, as well as dried herb, tobacco, spice box, cherry liqueur and coffee aromas, superb density, huge extract, and a long, full-bodied, moderately tannic finish. This classic Barolo possesses super purity and considerable glycerin. Anticipated maturity: 2004–2024. The 1995 Barolo La Serra is unquestionably one of the vintage's most successful wines. Initially appealing spicy oak gets lost in a blast of black cherry fruit, tar, rose petals, dried herbs, and spices. Rich, full-bodied, open-knit, and chewy, with a noteworthy succulence and lushness, this beautifully knit, evolved, precociously styled, mouth-filling Barolo is ideal for drinking over the next 8 years.

ROBERTO VOERZIO

1999 Barbera d'Alba Vigneto Pozzo dell'Annunziata Riserva	E	(92–94)
1998 Barbera d'Alba Vigneto Pozzo dell'Annunziata Riserva	E	96
1997 Barbera Vigneto Pozzo dell'Annunciata Riserva	E	97
1998 Barolo Brunate	E	(91–92)
1997 Barolo Brunate	E	92+
1996 Barolo Brunate	E	93
1998 Barolo Capalot delle Brunate Riserva	EEE	(93–95)
1997 Barolo Capalot delle Brunate Riserva	EEE	98+
1996 Barolo Capalot Riserva	EEE	93
1995 Barolo Capalot Riserva	EEE	91
1998 Barolo Cerequio	E	(90–91+)
1997 Barolo Cerequio	E	92+
1996 Barolo Cerequio	E	90
1995 Barolo Cerequio	E	86
1998 Barolo Sarmassa di Barolo	E	(91–93+)
1998 Barolo La Serra	E	(90–91)
1997 Barolo La Serra	E	92
1996 Barolo La Serra	E	92
1995 Barolo La Serra	E	87
1999 Dolcetto d'Alba Priavino	C	89
1998 Langhe Rosso Vignaserra	E	87
1997 Langhe Rosso Vignaserra	E	90

While Roberto Voerzio's estate is just under 30 acres, he has quickly emerged as one of Piedmont's superstars. Qualitatively, he is on fire, producing one of the region's most profound Barberas as well as some of the most majestic, complex Barolos. He is a fanatical crop thinner, believes in organic growing, and often thins his vineyard by as much as 50% prior to the harvest. This results in 4–5 bunches of grapes per vine (compared with 30–50 bunches per vine in many Napa vineyards). Voerzio is a modernist, fermenting his wines with indigenous yeasts and putting them into a combination of Taransaud and Vicard French new oak. After a light fining, they are bottled without filtration. The Barolos spend 28 months in oak, with malolactic done in barrel. The SO$_2$ levels, not surprisingly for such a minimalist, are among the lowest in Piedmont. Over the last decade, Voerzio has produced some of Italy's most stunningly complete, complex wines. In fact, an argument can be made that no one makes better Barbera than his fabulous effort from the Vigneto Pozzo dell'Annunziata. In addition to a tiny parcel of Sarmassa di Barolo he purchased in 1998, he owns three vineyards from which emerge the Cerequio (350–400 cases), the Serra (400 cases), and the Brunate (300 cases) *cuvées*. The single-vineyard Capalot Riserva is made from a plot of the oldest vines in the Brunate vineyard. This wine, bottled only in magnums (approximately 1,000), is produced in only the top vintages. In 2000 Voerzio added an additional cru, the famed Pozzo dell'Annunziata, to his portfolio. Consequently, beginning in 2000, there will be six crus, as compared to four in 1997 and former vintages.

The dark ruby/purple-colored 1999 Dolcetto d'Alba Priavino exhibits toasty new oak along with mocha, blackberry, cherry, and herb-like aromas. Enjoy this fruit-driven Dolcetto over the next 3 years. I generally do not like *barrique*-aged Dolcetto, but the subtle influence of oak works well with this *cuvée*. The 1999 Barbera d'Alba Vigneto Pozzo dell'Annunziata Riserva may not hit the lofty peaks of the 1997 and 1998, but it is still a remarkable effort. An opaque blue/purple color is followed by thick, juicy aromas and flavors of chocolate, espresso, cherry and strawberry liqueur, smoke, and toast. Made from extremely low yields of 25–28 hectoliters per hectare, this unctuous 1999 offers an amazing mouthful of wine.

Voerzio does not believe 1998 is up to the level of 1997. Although the grapes were loaded with raw material, he felt that overall the wines were more elegant, without the high levels of extract found in the 1997s. The 1998 Langhe Rosso Vignaserra (a blend of Cabernet Sauvignon, Barbera, and Nebbiolo from La Serra vineyard) offers classic Piedmontese characteristics of licorice, tobacco, black cherry liqueur, and dried herbs, as well as a medium-bodied, elegant, stylish, moderately weighty palate impression. It is meant to be drunk during its first 5–7 years of life. The 1998 Barolo La Serra is the most finesse-styled of these offerings, exhibiting a deep ruby color in addition to a sexy nose of sweet black cherries, fennel, vanilla, and spice. Velvety texture, full body, and overall harmony suggest it will drink well young as well as over the next 10–12 years. Slightly denser, more masculine, and muscular, the 1998 Barolo Brunate displays abundant quantities of blackberry and cherry liqueur aromas intertwined with vanilla, licorice, tobacco, and rose petals. The new oak is brilliantly absorbed by this medium- to full-bodied, sweet, expansively flavored Barolo. Anticipated maturity: 2003–2016. The dark ruby/purple-colored 1998 Barolo Cerequio is the most structured and backward of this quintet. It emerges from a south-facing vineyard from which Angelo Gaja produces his Conteisa. This tannic, structured, rigidly styled Barolo is loaded with black cherry fruit, rose petal, and tar notes. It will be the least pleasing to drink initially but will emerge from its tannic cloak in 4 years and will evolve for two decades. Anticipated maturity: 2006–2020.

The debut vintage of Voerzio's Barolo Sarmassa di Barolo, the 1998, emerges from a vineyard parcel with a full southern exposure. It boasts an opaque black/purple color as well as a gorgeous bouquet of blackberry liqueur, blueberry, and flower aromas. As the wine sits in the glass, a liquid mineral quality develops. This wine could be mistaken for a 1990 grand cru from Burgundy's Côte de Nuits. Backward, dense, and potentially complex and concentrated, it may be even better than my notes suggest. It is an impressive first offering from this vineyard. Anticipated maturity: 2008–2025. From Voerzio's oldest vines (50 years), 1,200 magnums were produced of the 1998 Barolo Capalot delle Brunate Riserva. This effort ratchets up the intensity level, offering more volume, power, density, and flavor extraction. It is his biggest wine of the vintage and potentially the longest-lived. While the 1998 may not equal the nearly perfect 1997, it is an incredible achievement. Its dense ruby/purple color is accompanied by a big, thick nose of black cherries, cherry syrup, espresso, toast, and roasted meats. This massive, huge, tannic 1998 requires 6–7 years of cellaring; it should last for three decades.

The dense opaque purple-colored 1998 Barbera d'Alba Vigneto Pozzo dell'Annunziata Riserva resembles vintage port in its color, texture, and flavor saturation. Opulent, with extreme richness, this full-bodied, superintense, compelling, flamboyant Barbera (less than 1,400 magnums produced) possesses more freshness than the 1997, yet nearly as much exoticism. It boasts unctuous black cherry, chocolate, espresso, licorice, and strawberry liqueur aromas as well as flavors, immense body, major levels of glycerin, and gorgeously integrated sweet new oak (from 100% malolactic in new wood). While it is impossible to predict how such a wine will age, given its size and strength it will certainly drink well for a decade. I recommend consuming it at a young age to take advantage of its exuberance.

The 1997 Barolo La Serra is a sexy, dense ruby/purple-colored effort offering notes of currants, black cherries, and licorice, a huge, chewy texture, plenty of glycerin, and a creamy, supple, velvety finish. Although impossible to resist, it will develop even more nuances over the next 4–5 years and should last for two decades. Anticipated maturity: 2004–2023. The biggest wine of this trio, the dense opaque ruby/purple-colored, tannic 1997 Barolo Brunate, exhibits copious aromas of cassis, black cherry, kirsch, licorice, smoke, truffles, and new oak. Notes of coffee and chocolate emerge as the wine sits in the glass. It possesses amazing density, a lot of muscle, and a roasted character to its fruity personality. This back-strapping, full-bodied Barolo requires 2–3 years of cellaring and should keep for 25. The paradoxical 1997 Barolo Cerequio possesses exquisite purity as well as an open-knit bouquet, but restrained, tannic, forceful, backward flavors. Dense and rich, with the vintage's thickness well displayed but more tannin than its siblings, it will be at its best between 2005–2020. The formidable 1997 Barolo Capalot della Brunate Riserva is a candidate for Barolo of the vintage. A massive wine, it exhibits aromas and flavors of vitamins, coffee, chocolate, black cherry liqueur, licorice, and toast, a terrific palate entry with oodles of glycerin as well as extract, multiple flavor layers, and sweet tannin in the 60-second finish. There is plenty of tannin lurking beneath the surface, so ideally it needs to be aged for 4–5 years. It will age for three decades. This is a tour de force in winemaking!

The compelling 1997 Barbera Vigneto Pozzo dell'Annunciata Riserva (only 1,350 magnums produced) may be the greatest Barbera I have ever tasted. A prodigious effort, it displays the flamboyant opulence of the 1997 vintage in addition to extraordinary unctuosity, unbelievable layers of fruit, and an amazing finish that lasts for nearly 45 seconds. With gobs of black cherry fruit intermixed with chocolate, cedar wood, strawberries, licorice, and a touch of mint in the background, this spectacular wine—a prodigious effort—will age for at least a decade. Lastly, the 1997 Langhe Rosso Vignaserra (a blend of Nebbiolo, Barbera, and Cabernet Sauvignon, aged in 100% new oak and bottled unfiltered) exhibits a bouquet of wildflowers (particularly lavender) and blackberry and cherry fruit. There are fine suppleness, density, and spiciness, as well as a complex, elegant, rich, nicely layered palate and finish. It should drink well for 6 years.

The superb 1996 Barolo La Serra's opaque ruby/purple color is followed by aromas of black fruits (blackberry, cherry, and a hint of raspberry), superb purity, highly extracted, powerful, monster-sized flavors, mouth-searing levels of tannin, and an impressively endowed, 40+-second finish. This backward, pure, intensely concentrated Barolo will require patience. Anticipated maturity: 2008–2025. The opaque ruby/purple-colored 1996 Barolo Cerequio possesses extremely high tannin and extract, but it is very backward and even more closed and firm than the Barolo La Serra. Full-bodied, powerful, and rich but broodingly backward and stubborn, it possesses all the correct component parts, but patience will be required by potential purchasers. Anticipated maturity: 2010–2025. The black/purple-colored 1996 Barolo Brunate is the most gigantic of all the Voerzio Barolos I tasted. Monstrously sized, with huge alcohol content, high tannin, and spectacular extract, this layered, chewy wine is sensationally promising. Although stubbornly backward, it possesses wonderful ripeness, but it is so huge it needs 3–4 years to evolve. Anticipated maturity: 2006–2030. The profound 1996 Barolo Capalot Riserva boasts a dense, ruby/purple color and a pure nose of black cherries, raspberries, and blackberries. Layered and multidimensional, with a sweet mid-palate and a blockbuster finish, this is an immense, full-throttle Barolo that should age effortlessly for 15–20 years. Impressive!

The 1995 Barolo La Serra exhibits a textbook nose of melted road tar, rose petals, and cigar box aromas, moderate tannin, ripe fruit, medium body, and a dry, austere finish. It is a very good, classic Barolo, but the slight austerity kept my score more conservative. Drink it over the next decade. I was surprised that Voerzio's 1995 Barolo Cerequio displayed such an evolved color. The amber, rusty edge suggested a wine that was far older than four years. The nose of tea, dried herbs, and cedar aromas makes this a spice- rather than fruit-driven wine. It is medium-bodied, evolved, and fully mature. The finish is slightly compressed, but the wine possesses the textbook spice, melted road tar, and dried cherry–like flavors of an old-style Barolo. Drink it over the next 3–4 years. The 1995 Barolo Capalot Riserva is a thick, chewy offering with a stunning display of aromatics (cigar smoke, Chinese black tea, new oak, cherry liqueur, and dried Provençal herbs). Extremely full-bodied and rich, and surprisingly huge for a 1995, this Barolo possesses amazing extract as well as a finish that lasts for nearly a minute. Extremely rich and powerful, but accessible, it can be drunk now as well as over the next 12 years.

ATTILIO ZUNINO

1997 Barolo Sorì di Baudana	D	(88–89)
1996 Barolo Sorì di Baudana	D	(88–90)
1995 Barolo Sorì di Baudana	D	88

This small producer from the village of Serralunga has fashioned three very fine wines. The potentially outstanding 1997 Barolo Sorì di Baudana is the sweetest of these offerings, with the most viscosity and fullest body. It reveals low acidity as well as impressively chewy red and black fruit flavors intertwined with earth, soy, asphalt, and spice box characteristics. There is moderate tannin in the luscious, jammy finish. Anticipated maturity: now–2018. Although very close in style to the 1995, the backward 1996 Barolo Sorì di Baudana is fuller-bodied, with more muscle and chewy tannin. Anticipated maturity: 2003–2017. The excellent 1995 Barolo Sorì di Baudana offers up textbook Barolo aromas and flavors of tar, rose petals, cedar, and sour cherries. There are admirable concentration, a powerful structure, good sweetness in the mid-palate, and a fine finish. It is made in a dense, traditional style. Anticipated maturity: now–2012.

TUSCANY

The Basics

TYPES OF WINE

Beautiful Tuscany is the home of Italy's most famous wine, Chianti, and one of Italy's most celebrated wines, Brunello di Montalcino. Both wines can be either horrendous or splendid. Quality is shockingly irregular. Yet it was in Tuscany where Italy's qualitative wine revolution began, with adventurous and innovative producers cavalierly turning their backs on the archaic regulations that govern wine production. They are making wines, often based on Cabernet Sauvignon, Merlot, and Sangiovese, aged in small French oak casks, filled with flavor and personality, and put in designer bottles. I disagree completely with those critics who have called them French look-alikes, and, though not entitled to "appellation status," they represent some of the most exciting red wines made in the world. The same cannot be said for Tuscany's white wines. Except for the light, tasty whites called Vernaccia from the medieval hill fortress of San Gimignano, Tuscan whites are ultraneutral, boring wines. Shame on those producers who package these wines in lavish-looking bottles that are appallingly overpriced.

GRAPE VARIETIES

The principal and greatest red wine grape of Tuscany is Sangiovese. The highest-yielding, most insipid wine from Sangiovese comes from the most widely planted clone, called Sangiovese Romano. The better producers are using Sangiovese with local names such as Sangioveto, Prugnolo, and Brunello. These all produce a richer, deeper, more complex wine. Of course, Cabernet Sauvignon, Merlot, Cabernet Franc, and even Pinot Noir and Syrah are making their presence felt in Tuscany.

As for the white wines, there is the sharp, uninteresting Trebbiano, produced in ocean-sized quantities. Trebbiano is an inferior grape, and the results are distressingly innocuous wines. Vernaccia has potential, and of course there are such international bluebloods as Chardonnay and Sauvignon Blanc. Tuscany, in my mind, means red, not white, wine, but if you are inclined to try a white wine, then take a look at my list of recommended producers of Vernaccia di San Gimignano.

FLAVORS

Chianti Classico It is virtually impossible to provide specific information given the extraordinary range in quality—from musty, poorly vinified, washed-out wines to ones with soft, supple raspberry, chestnut, and tobacco flavors, crisp acidity, medium body, and a fine finish. Stick to only the recommended producers listed below. Remember, at least 50% of wines called Chianti, despite tighter regulations governing quality, are thin, acidic, and unpleasant.

Brunello di Montalcino This should be rich, powerful, tannic, superbly concentrated, and heady, with a huge, spicy bouquet of smoky tobacco, meat, and dried red fruits. Only a few are. Most close encounters offer an alarming degree of tannin and musty old oak, to the detriment of fruit. Selection is critical. Rosso di Montalcino is red wine made from the Brunello clone of Sangiovese that is not aged long enough to qualify as Brunello di Montalcino. It is often much less expensive and considerably fresher.

Carmignano This is an underrated viticultural area wherein the wines show good fruit, balance, and character. The best of them behave like Chiantis with more character and structure. Not surprisingly, Carmignano is made from Sangiovese with 10–15% Cabernet added.

Vernaccia di San Gimignano Tuscany's best dry white table wine, this nutty, zesty, dry, fruity white is meant to be drunk within 2–3 years of the vintage. It is a satisfying rather than thrilling wine.

Vino Nobile di Montepulciano A neighbor of Chianti with identical characteristics (the grape is the same), Vino Nobile di Montepulciano costs more but rarely provides more flavor or pleasure.

Morellino di Scansano This is an emerging viticultural region south of Siena. I have tasted the wines from only a few estates, but it appears that this is an area that requires more attention. Made from Sangiovese, Morellino di Scansano may be the frugal consumer's alternative to Brunello di Montalcino. The wines are rich, expansive, and, for now, undervalued!

Other Tuscan Whites The names Bianco di Pitigliano, Bianco Vergine della Valdichiana, Galestro, Montecarlo, Pomino, and any Tuscan producer's name plus the word "bianco" translate into wines that taste wretchedly neutral and bland and provide no more flavor than a glass of water. Sadly, most of them cost $20–35, so the operative words are *caveat emptor!*

Vini da Tavola The most thrilling red wines of Tuscany are the designer show wines that are being made by Tuscany's most innovative growers. They can be 100% Cabernet Sauvignon, 100% Sangiovese, or a blend of these two grapes plus Cabernet Franc. Even some Merlot, Syrah, and Pinot Noir can now be found. They are usually aged in mostly new French oak casks. Top Tuscan vintages, such as 1997, 1999, and 2000, can have sensational aromatic dimension and remarkable flavor breadth.

ITALY'S GREATEST IGTS (INDICAZIONI GEOGRAFICHE TIPICHE) *AND VDTS* (VINI DA TAVOLA)

PRODUCER	*WINE*	*GRAPE(S)*	*REGION*
L. Antinori	Ornellaia Masseto	Merlot	Tuscany
Argiano	Solengo	Cabernet Sauvignon, Merlot, Syrah, Sangiovese	Tuscany

PRODUCER	WINE	GRAPE(S)	REGION
Il Borro		Merlot, Cabernet Sauvignon	Tuscany
Casa Emma	Soloio	Merlot	Tuscany
Castello di Ambra	L'Apparita	Merlot	Tuscany
Castello di Farnetella	Poggio Granoni	Sangiovese, Merlot, Cabernet Sauvignon	Tuscany
Castello dei Rampolla	Sammarco	Cabernet Sauvignon, Sangiovese	Tuscany
Castello dei Rampolla	Vigna d'Alceo	Cabernet Sauvignon, Sangiovese, Syrah, Petit Verdot	Tuscany
Ciacci Piccolomini d'Aragona	Alteo	Sangiovese, Cabernet Sauvignon	Tuscany
Ciacci Piccolomini d'Aragona	Sant'Antimo Favus	Syrah	Tuscany
Collosorbo	Laurus	Sangiovese, Cabernet Sauvignon	Tuscany
Andrea Costanti	Culbello Ardingo	Merlot, Cabernet Sauvignon	Tuscany
Dei	Santa Catharina	Cabernet Sauvignon, Syrah, Sangiovese	Tuscany
Del Cerro	Manero	Sangiovese	Tuscany
Del Cerro	Poggio Golo	Merlot	Tuscany
Falesco	Montiano	Merlot	Umbria/Lazio
Fattoria di Felsina	Fontalloro	Sangioveto	Tuscany
La Fiorita– Lamborghini	Campoleone	Merlot, Cabernet Sauvignon, Sangiovese	Umbria
Fattoria Le Fonti	Vito Arturo	Sangiovese	Tuscany
Fontodi	Flaccianello	Sangiovese	Tuscany
Gagliole	Pecchia	Sangiovese	Tuscany
Galardi	Terra di Lavoro	Aglianico, Piedirosso	Campania
I Giusti & Zanza	Belcore	Sangiovese, Merlot	Tuscany
I Giusti & Zanza	Dulcamara	Cabernet Sauvignon, Cabernet Franc	Tuscany
Guado Al Tasso		Cabernet Sauvignon, Merlot, Syrah	Tuscany
Le Macchiole	Messorio	Merlot	Tuscany
Le Macchiole	Paleo Rosso	Sangiovese, Cabernet Sauvignon	Tuscany
Le Macchiole	Rosso	Sangiovese, Merlot	Tuscany
Le Macchiole	Scrio	Syrah	Tuscany
Marchesi Antinori	Solaia	Cabernet Sauvignon, Sangiovese, Cabernet Franc	Tuscany
Marchesi Antinori	Tignanello	Sangiovese	Tuscany
Monte Bernardi	Saetta	Sangiovese	Tuscany
Montepeloso	Gabbro	Cabernet Sauvignon	Tuscany

PRODUCER	WINE	GRAPE(S)	REGION
Montepeloso	Nardo	Sangiovese, Cabernet Sauvignon	Tuscany
Montevetrano		Cabernet Sauvignon, Merlot, Aglianico	Campania
Nozzole	Il Pareto	Cabernet Sauvignon	Tuscany
Fattoria Paradiso	Saxa Calida	Merlot, Cabernet Sauvignon	Tuscany
Fattoria Petrolo	Galatrona	Sangiovese, Merlot	Tuscany
Fattoria Petrolo	Il Torrione	Sangiovese	Tuscany
Poggiopiano	Rosso di Sera	Sangiovese, Colorino	Tuscany
Querciabella	Camartina	Sangiovese, Cabernet Sauvignon	Tuscany
Riseccoli	Saeculum	Sangiovese, Cabernet Sauvignon, Merlot	Tuscany
San Giusto a Rentennano	Percarlo	Sangiovese	Tuscany
San Giusto a Rentennano	Ricolma	Merlot	Tuscany
San Guido	Sassicaia	Cabernet Sauvignon, Cabernet Franc, Merlot	Tuscany
Sportoletti	Villa Fidelia	Merlot, Cabernet Sauvignon, Cabernet Franc	Umbria
Fattoria Terrabianca	Ceppate	Cabernet Sauvignon, Merlot	Tuscany
Terriccio	Lupicaia	Cabernet Sauvignon, Merlot	Tuscany
Terriccio	Tassinaia	Cabernet Sauvignon, Sangiovese, Merlot	Tuscany
Tenuta di Trinoro	Trinoro	Cabernet Franc, Merlot, Petit Verdot	Tuscany
Tenuta di Trinoro	Palazzi	Cabernet Franc, Merlot	Tuscany
Tua Rita	Giusto dei Notri	Cabernet Sauvignon, Merlot	Tuscany
Tua Rita	Redigaffi	Merlot	Tuscany
Fattoria Valtellina	Il Duca	Merlot	Tuscany
Villa Cafaggio	Cortaccio	Cabernet Sauvignon	Tuscany
Villa Cafaggio	San Martino	Sangiovese	Tuscany
Villa La Selva	Selvamaggio	Cabernet Sauvignon, Sangiovese	Tuscany

AGING POTENTIAL

Brunello di Montalcino: 8–25 years
Carmignano: 5–8 years
Chianti Classico: 3–15 years*
Rosso di Montalcino: 5–8 years

Tuscan whites: 1–2 years
Vino Nobile di Montepulciano: 5–10 years
VDTs and IGTs (red wine blends): 5–20 years
* Only a handful of Chianti producers make wines that age and last this long.

OVERALL QUALITY LEVEL
For one of the world's most famous wine regions, the quality, while on the upswing, is depressingly variable. Some famous estates in Brunello continue to live off their historic reputations while making poor wine, and there is an ocean of mediocre Chianti producers. The exciting new-breed Sangiovese/Cabernet, Cabernet Franc, and Merlot wines can be superb, but they are produced in limited quantities and are expensive. As for the white wines, the situation is intolerable, and the Tuscans need to wake up to the fact that high-tech, computerized, stainless-steel tanks, centrifuges, sterile bottling, and obsessive reliance on micropore filter machines (that result in denuded, characterless wine) are a fail-safe policy for making an insipid beverage.

MOST IMPORTANT INFORMATION TO KNOW
Forget the Italian wine regulations that are supposed to promote a better product. There are many disgustingly poor wines that carry the government's highest guarantee of quality, the DOCG, or Denominazione di Origine Controllata e Garantita. Many of the *vini da tavola* are vastly superior wines, and this title is supposedly left for Italy's lowest level, the generic wines. The operative rule is, who are the top producers? Then and only then will you be able to make your way through the perilous selection process for Italian wines.

BUYING STRATEGY
A fundamental rule with respect to Tuscan wines is to buy all the 1997s and 1999s you can afford. Both are extraordinary vintages of ripeness and richness that should surpass the finest wines produced in such great years as 1990 and 1985. Both are consistently superb throughout Tuscany's viticultural regions.

RECENT VINTAGES

2000—An exceptionally hot, dry year created exciting potential, but also problems from drought and vineyard stress. There will be more irregularity than the wine trade has suggested, but the producers who were able to avoid dehydrated vineyards and handle the ripe fruit impeccably should produce spectacularly ripe, voluptuous, concentrated wines with high tannin as well as intense flavors. This vintage will be more irregular than 1999, but the wines are potentially as great, if somewhat more roasted.

1999—A year that rivals 1997 as one of Tuscany's greatest vintages. Consistency is the operative word, from the humble Chiantis to the majestic proprietary red wine blends and Brunello di Montalcinos. The wines are extremely ripe, with low acidity as well as a freshness and delineation atypical for wines of such size and richness. Readers who love Italian wines, particularly those from Tuscany, should be stockpiling the 1999s.

1998—An irregular vintage of austere, dry, tannic wines with the exception of the wines from Tuscany's coastal regions of Bolgheri, Suvereto, and Val di Cornia. It is a vintage to approach with caution as many wines lack ripeness, fruit, and intensity.

1997—A spectacular vintage of exceptionally high quality, especially for Brunello di Montalcino and central Tuscany. The coastal regions are more irregular, mixing great successes with some uninspiring efforts (particularly Sassicaia).

1996—An average year that produced austere, dry, hard wines that will dry out before they ever provide much pleasure.

1995—A very good vintage that has not lived up to expectations and is now dwarfed by the potential of 1997, 1999, and 2000.

1994—A below-average quality vintage of diluted fruit lacking ripeness because of heavy rains before and during the harvest. There are some fine wines, but this inconsistent vintage needs to be approached with considerable caution.

1993—A below-average year.

1992—A horrendous vintage with few successful wines.

1991—A bad vintage with few interesting wines.

1990—This is the best year for Tuscany since the fabulous 1985 vintage, but not up to the level of 1985 and surpassed by what was achieved in 1997, 1999, and probably 2000. It is very good, but not the great vintage it was felt to be a decade ago.

RATING TUSCANY'S BEST PRODUCERS

Note: Most producers make both a Chianti Classico and a Chianti Classico Riserva. In the following chart, for purposes of simplification, the star rating shown for each producer's Chianti Classico also pertains to its Chianti Classico Riserva, unless otherwise noted. I have treated Brunello di Montalcino and Brunello di Montalcino Riserva in the same manner. Single-vineyard Chiantis are treated as a separate qualitative item, as are the vast number of *vini da tavola*. Production of the single vineyards, VDTs *(vini da tavola)*, and IGTs *(indicazioni geografiche tipiche)* is generally extremely small, often not more than 500–1,000 cases. Thus, as with so many great wines of the world, availability is poor outside a handful of the top Italian wine specialist shops.

* * * * * *(OUTSTANDING)*

Altesino Brunello di Montalcino Montosoli
Fattoria Ambra l'Apparita
Fattoria Ambra Carmignano Riserva Vigna Alta
L. Antinori Ornellaia
L. Antinori Ornellaia Masseto
Marchesi Antinori Solaia
Marchesi Antinori Tignanello
Argiano Solengo
Il Borro
Casa Emma Soloio
Castello di Farnetella Poggio Granoni
Castello dei Rampolla Sammarco
Castello dei Rampolla Vigna d'Alceo
Ciacci Piccolomini d'Aragona Alteo
Ciacci Piccolomini d'Aragona Brunello di Montalcino
Ciacci Piccolomini d'Aragona Sant'Antimo Favus
Collosorbo Laurus
Andrea Costanti Calbello Ardingo
Dei Santa Catharina
Del Cerro Manero
Del Cerro Poggio Golo
Falesco Montiano

Fattoria di Felsina Chianti Classico Riserva Rancia Berardenga
Fattoria di Felsina Fontalloro
La Fiorita–Lamborghini Campoleone
Fattoria Le Fonti Vito Arturo
Fontodi Flaccianello
Gagliole Pecchia
Galardi Terra di Lavoro
I Giusti & Zanza Belçore
I Giusti & Zanza Dulcamara
Guado Al Tasso
Le Macchiole Messorio
Le Macchiole Paleo Rosso
Le Macchiole Rosso
Le Macchiole Scrio
Monte Bernardi Saetta
Montepeloso Gabbro
Montepeloso Nardo
Montevetrano
Nozzole Il Pareto
Fattoria Paradiso Saxa Calida
Fattoria Petrolo Galatrona
Fattoria Petrolo Il Torrione
Poggiopiano Rosso di Sera
Querciabella Camartina
Riseccoli Saeculum

San Giusto a Rentennano Percarlo
San Giusto a Rentennano Ricolma
San Guido Sassicaia
Livio Sassetti & Figli Brunello di
   Montalcino
Soldera Case Basse Brunello di Montalcino
Soldera Intistieti Brunello di
   Montalcino
Sportoletti Villa Fidelia
Fattoria Terrabianca Ceppate

Terriccio Lupicaia
Terriccio Tassinaia
Trinoro
Trinoro Palazzi
Tua Rita Giusto di Notri
Tua Rita Redigaffi
Fattoria Valtellina Il Duca
Villa Cafaggio Cortaccio
Villa Cafaggio San Martino
Villa La Selva Selvamaggio

* * * * (EXCELLENT)

Altesino Alte d'Altesi
Altesino Brunello di Montalcino
Altesino Palazzo Altesi
Fattoria Ambra Carmignano
Marchesi Antinori Chianti Classico Il
   Pèppoli
Marchesi Antinori Chianti Classico Riserva
   Badia a Passignano
Marchesi Antinori Chianti Classico Riserva
   Marchese
Marchesi Antinori Secentenario
Avignonesi Vino Nobile di Montepulciano
Fattoria Baggiolino Poggio Brandi
Fattoria dei Barbi Brunello di Montalcino
   Vigna del Fiore
Poderi Boscarelli Boscarelli
Poderi Boscarelli Vino Nobile di
   Montepulciano
La Braccesca Vino Nobile di Montepulciano
Caparzo Brunello di Montalcino La Casa
Caparzo Ca' del Pazzo
Federico Carletti Vino Nobile di
   Montepulciano
Castelgiocondo Brunello di Montalcino
   Riserva
Castell'in Villa Chianti Classico
Castell'in Villa Chianti Classico Riserva
Castell'in Villa Santacroce
Castello di Lilliano Anagallis
Castello della Paneretta Chianti Classico
   Vigneto Torre a Destra
Castello della Paneretta Quattrocentenario
Castello di Gabbiano R & R
Castello di Querceto Chianti Classico
Castello di Querceto Chianti Classico
   Riserva
Castello di Querceto Cignale
Castello di Querceto La Corte
Castello di Querceto Il Querciolaia

Castello dei Rampolla Chianti Classico
   Riserva
Castello di Volpaia Balifico
Castello di Volpaia Chianti Classico
   Riserva
Castello di Volpaia Coltassala
Cerbaiona Brunello di Montalcino
Ciacci Piccolomini d'Aragona Rosso di
   Montalcino
Corelli Brunello di Montalcino
Corrina I Cipressi
Andrea Costanti Brunello di Montalcino
Andrea Costanti Rosso di Montalcino
Dei Vino Nobile di Montepulciano
Dei Vino Nobile di Montepulciano Riserva
Farneta Bentivoglio
Fattoria di Felsina Chianti Classico
   Berardenga
Fattoria di Felsina Fontalloro Berardenga
Fontodi Syrah Case Via
Fontodi Chianti Classico
Fontodi Chianti Classico Riserva
Fontodi Chianti Classico Vigna del Sorbo
   Riserva
Geografico Agricoltori del Geografico
Gracciano Vino Nobile di Montepulciano
Isole e Olena Collezione di Marchi l'Ermo
Lisini Brunello di Montalcino
Luce Luce
Monsanto Chianti Classico Il Poggio
Monsanto Nemo
Monsanto Sangioveto Grosso
Monsanto Tinscvil
Monte Antico Rosso
Fattoria di Montevertine Le Pergole Torte
Fattoria di Montevertine Montevertine
   Riserva
Moris Farms Morellino di Scansano
Nozzole Chianti Classico Riserva

Podere Il Palazzino Chianti Classico
Podere Il Palazzino Chianti Classico
  Riserva
Podere Il Palazzino Grosso Sanese
Pieve di Santa Restituta Brunello di
  Montalcino Rennina
Pieve di Santa Restituta Brunello di
  Montalcino Sugarille
Poggio Antico Altero
Podere Poggio Scalette
Il Poggione Brunello di Montalcino
Le Pupille Saffredi
Ricasoli-Firidolfi Chianti Classico
Ricasoli-Firidolfi Chianti Classico Riserva
Ricasoli-Firidolfi Chianti Classico Riserva
  Rocca di Montegrossi
Ricasoli-Firidolfi Rocca di Montegrossi
  Geremia
Ruffino Chianti Classico Riserva Ducale
  (gold label)

Ruffino Chianti Classico Riserva Ducale
  (tan label)
San Felice Brunello di Montalcino
  Campogiovanni
San Giusto a Rentennano Chianti
  Classico
Sant'Anna Vigna Il Vallone
Livio Sassetti & Figlio Rosso di
  Montalcino
Guicciardini Strozzi Sodole
Fattoria Terrabianca Campaccio
Fattoria Terrabianca Campaccio Riserva
Fattoria Terrabianca Chianti Riserva Croce
Fattoria Terrabianca Chianti Scassino
Fattoria Terrabianca Cipresso
La Torre (Luigi Anania) Brunello di
  Montalcino
Villa Cafaggio Chianti Classico
Villa Cafaggio San Martino
Villa Cafaggio Solatio Basilica

* * * *(GOOD)*

Altesino Rosso di Altesino
Altesino Rosso di Montalcino
Avignonesi Cabernet Sauvignon
Avignonesi Grifi
Badia a Coltibuono Chianti Cetamura
Badia a Coltibuono Chianti Classico
Badia a Coltibuono Coltibuono Rosso
Badia a Coltibuono Sangioveto di
  Coltibuono
Erik Banti Morellino di Scansano
Fattoria dei Barbi Brunello di Montalcino
Fattoria dei Barbi Brunello di Montalcino
  Riserva
Poderi Boscarelli Chianti Colli Senesi
Caparzo Brunello di Montalcino
Carpineto Chianti Classico Riserva
Castelgiocondo Merlot
Castellare di Castellina Chianti Classico
Castellare di Castellina I Sodi di San
  Niccolò
Castello di Ama Chianti Classico
Castello di Ama Chianti Classico single-
  vineyard *cuvées*
Castello di Brolio Chianti Classico
  Riserva
Castello di Farnetella Chianti Colli Senesi
Castello di Fonterutoli Brancaia
Castello di Fonterutoli Chianti Classico
Castello di Fonterutoli Chianti Ser Lapo

Castello di Fonterutoli Concerto
Castello di Gabbiano Ania
Castello di Gabbiano Chianti Classico
  Riserva
Castello La Leccia Chianti Classico
Castello di Lilliano Chianti Classico
Castello di Lilliano Chianti Classico
  Riserva Eleanora
Castello della Paneretta Chianti Classico
Castello di Volpaia Chianti Classico
Castruccio
Cennatoio Chianti Classico
Cennatoio Etrusco
Cennatoio Mammolo
Colognole Chianti Ruffina
Fattoria di Dievole Chianti Classico
  Novecento
Fattoria di Dievole Chianti Classico
  Riserva
Fattoria di Dievole Chianti Classico Vigna
  Dieulele
Fattoria di Dievole Chianti Classico Vigna
  Sessina
Fossi Chianti
Marchesi de' Frescobaldi Montesodi Chanti
  Ruffina
Marchesi de' Frescobaldi Mormoreto
Cantina Gattavecchi Chianti Colli
  Senesi

Cantina Gattavecchi Vino Nobile di
  Montepulciano
Geografico Brunello di Montalcino
Geografico Chianti Classico
Geografico Chianti Classico Castello di
  Fagnano
Geografico Chianti Classico Contessa di
  Radda
Geografico Sorbaiano Montescudaio
Isole e Olena Boro Cepparello
Isole e Olena Chianti Classico
Podere Lanciola II Chianti Colli Fiorentini
Podere Lanciola II Chianti Le Masse di
  Greve
Le Masse di San Leolino Chianti Classico
Le Masse di San Leolino Chianti Classico
  Riserva
Monsanto Chianti Classico Riserva
Fattoria di Montevertine Il Sodaccio
Fattoria di Petroio Chianti Classico
  Montetondo
Poggio Antico Brunello di Montalcino
Poggio Antico Rosso di Montalcino

Poggio Bonelli Chianti Classico Riserva
Poggio Galiga Chianti Rufina
Roccadoro Chianti Classico
Rodano Chianti Classico
Ruffino Cabreo Il Borgo
Ruffino Chianti Classico
Ruffino Chianti Classico Aziano
Ruffino Chianti Classico Nozzole
San Felice Vigorello
San Quirico Chianti
Sant'Anna Rosso di Santa Anna
Talosa Chianti
Talosa Rosso di Montalcino
Talosa Vino Nobile di Montepulciano
La Torre Rosso di Montalcino
Toscolo Chianti Classico
Toscolo Chianti Classico Riserva
Trerose Vino Nobile di Montepulciano
  Riserva
Val di Suga Brunello di Montalcino
Val di Suga Brunello di Montalcino Vigna
  Spuntali
Villa di Geggiano Chianti Classico Riserva

RATING THE BEST OF THE REST OF ITALY

Following are wines and/or producers not to be missed from other viticultural regions of Italy.

* * * * * (OUTSTANDING)

Tommaso Bussola Amarone TB (Veneto)
Tommaso Bussola Valpolicella TB (Veneto)
Dal Forno Romano Amarone della
  Valpolicella (Veneto)
Dal Forno Romano Recioto (Veneto)
Dal Forno Romano Valpolicella (Veneto)
Damijan (Friuli–Venezia Giulia)
Falesco Montiano (Lazio)

Maculan Acininobili (sweet) (Veneto)
Maculan Breganze Torcolato (sweet)
  (Veneto)
Montevetrano (Campania)
La Palazzola Rubino (Umbria)
Quintarelli Alzero Cabernet Franc (Veneto)
Schiopetto (Friulia–Venezia Giulia)
Terra di Lavoro (Campania)

* * * * (EXCELLENT)

Abbazia di Novacella—white wine cuvées
  (Trentino–Alto Adige)
Abbazia di Rosazzo—white wine cuvées
  (Friuli–Venezia Giulia)
Allegrini La Poja (Veneto)
Allegrini Valpolicella La Grola (Veneto)
Allegrini Valpolicella Palazzo della Torre
  (Veneto)
Roberto Anselmi Capitel Croce (Veneto)
Roberto Anselmi Capitel Foscarino
  (Veneto)
Arano Amarone (Veneto)

Antonio Argiolas Costera (Sardinia)
Antonio Agriolas Turriga (Sardinia)
Bellavista sparkling wine cuvées
  (Lombardy)
Boccadigabbia Akronte (Marche)
Boccadigabbia Saltapicchio (Marche)
La Cadalora—white wine cuvées (Trentino)
La Carraia Fobiano (Umbria)
Cataldi Madonna Montepulciano di
  Abruzzo (Abruzzo)
Ceuso (Sicily)
Coffele—Soave cuvées (Veneto)

Cooperativa San Patrignano Sangiovese
(Emilia-Romagna)
Di Majo Norante Don Luigi (Molise)
Diesel Farm (Friuli–Venezia Giulia)
Girolamo Dorigo (Friuli–Venezia Giulia)
Feudi di San Gregorio (Campania)
Walter Filiputti (Friuli–Venezia Giulia)
Foradori Pinot Bianco Sgarzon
(Trentino–Alto Adige)
Foradori Teroldego Sgarzon (Trentino–Alto
Adige)
Gini—Soave cuvées (Veneto)
Giorgio Grai—white wine cuvées
(Trentino–Alto Adige)
Francesco Gravner—white wine cuvées
(Friuli–Venezia Giulia)
Il Carpino (Friuli-Venezia Giulia)
Librandi Cirò Rosso Duca Sanfelice
Riserva (Calabria)
Librandi Gravello (Calabria)
Roberto Mazzi Amarone (Veneto)
Roberto Mazzi Valpolicella (Veneto)
Salvatore Molettieri Aglianico (Campania)
Monti Montepulciano d'Abruzzo (Abruzzo)

Morgante Don Antonio (Sicily)
Murgo Cabernet Sauvignon (Sicily)
Cantina del Notaio Aglianico del Vulture
(Basilicata)
La Palazza—red wine cuvées (Emilia-
Romagna)
La Palazza Massa di Vecchiazzano (Emilia-
Romagna)
Planeta—red wine cuvées (Sicily)
F.lli Pra Soave (Veneto)
Regaleali Cabernet Sauvignon (Sicily)
Ronchi di Manzano—red and white cuvées
(Friuli–Venezia Giulia)
Sant'Elena (Friuli–Venezia Giulia)
Santa Lucia (Puglia)
Schiopetto—white wine cuvées (Collio)
Fattoria Le Terrazze (Marche)
Tormaresca (Puglia)
Valori Montepulciano d'Abruzzo
(Abruzzo)
Vie di Romans—white wine cuvées
(Friuli–Venezia Giulia)
Zenato Amarone (Veneto)
Zenato Valpolicella (Veneto)

*** (GOOD)

Bellavista Solesine (Lombardy)
Bellavista Chardonnay Annunciata
(Lombardy)
Bellavista Chardonnay Storica (Lombardy)

Bellavista Chardonnay Uccellanda
(Lombardy)
Regaleali Chardonnay (Sicily)

PROSECCO (ITALY'S GREAT VALUE IN SPARKLING WINE)
Readers in search of terrific values in light-bodied, crisp, refreshing sparkling wines should check out the delectable Proseccos from a viticultural region less than fifty miles north of Venice. Some of my favorite producers include the following (all of which sell for less than $16 a bottle): Cartizze, La Cincie, Nino Franco, Zardetto. One caveat: these wines must be consumed within 12–18 months of their release, as freshness and youth are essential.

ALTESINO

1998	Alte d'Altesi	D	89
1997	Borgo d'Altesi	D	91
1998	Palazzo Altesi	D	90
1998	Quarto d'Altesi IGT	D	88
1997	Quarto d'Altesi IGT	D	88
1999	Rosso di Altesino IGT	B	88

One of the leading estates in Brunello di Montalcino, Altesino has been owned by the same proprietor, Giulio Consonno, since 1970. The wines have always been of high quality, but the last decade has consistently revealed a superlative level of performance. A 100% Sangiovese cuvée aged in one-third new French oak (it's all raised in cask), the 1998 Palazzo Altesi reveals terrific aromatics, including violets, cigar box, smoke, black currants, and kirsch. It is dense, rich, and ripe, with moderate tannin as well as a long, full-bodied finish that offers hints of mocha and chocolate. This is a complex wine to drink over the next 7–8 years, although it may last longer. The 1998 Alte d'Altesi, a *barrique*-aged blend of 70% Sangiovese and 30% Cabernet Sauvignon, boasts a deep ruby color along with a big, sweet nose of chocolate, espresso, and berry fruit. It also reveals some of Cabernet's weedy tobacco character, excellent ripeness, and a medium- to full-bodied, long, textured finish. Drink it over the next 5–7 years.

Altesino has fashioned a high-quality, tank-fermented and -aged blend of 95% Sangiovese and 5% Cabernet Sauvignon. The 1999 Rosso di Altesino IGT offers a wonderful concoction of espresso beans, smoky black currant and cherry fruit, excellent texture, medium body, and a lush, heady finish. It is meant to be enjoyed in its exuberant youth—over the next 3–4 years.

The 1998 Quarto d'Altesi IGT, a Merlot-dominated blend with Sangiovese and Cabernet Sauvignon included, spends 15 months in new French oak prior to bottling. While it is not as complex aromatically as Altesino's other wines, it possesses good depth, flesh, and succulence, with abundant quantities of roasted herbs and chocolaty black fruits. If it develops more aromatic nuances, it may merit a higher score. It should drink well for 7–8 years.

The 1997 Borgo d'Altesi (100% Cabernet Sauvignon, just under 1,000 cases produced, aged in French barrels) is California-like with its thick, jammy, black currant fruit, low acidity, opulent texture, and succulent, fat, round finish. Given its up-front appeal, it should be consumed over the next decade. Slightly less successful but still attractive is the 1997 Quarto d'Altesi IGT (a blend of Merlot and Sangiovese aged in French oak). It offers notes of roasted mocha, coffee, and berry fruit, a monolithic attack, but a fine finish. Drink it over the next 6–7 years.

FATTORIA AMBRA

1998	Carmignano Elzana Riserva	D	88
1997	Carmignano Elzana Riserva	D	92
1998	Carmignano Le Vigne Alte Riserva	D	88
1997	Carmignano Le Vigne Alte Riserva	D	90+
2000	Carmignano Vigna di Santa Cristina in Pilli	B	89

One of my favorite Tuscan wineries (the prices are usually fair as well), Ambra's 2000 Carmignano Vigna di Santa Cristina in Pilli is a knockout bargain. A dark ruby/garnet color is accompanied by sweet aromas of smoke, leather, cherry jam, and roasted nuts. Spicy, medium-bodied, long, and generous, it will drink well for 5 years.

The two single-vineyard 1998 Riservas reveal some of the vintage's austerity and dusty tannin. Displaying more new oak as well as excellent berry fruit, Provençal herbs, black fruits, and spice, the 1998 Carmignano Le Vigne Alte Riserva's earthy complexity will be enjoyed by many. Readers who prefer their wines slightly austere will enjoy it even more than I did. The well-made, similarly styled 1998 Carmignano Elzana Riserva exhibits plenty of tannin, a restrained, leaner personality, a more compressed palate, and attractive red and black fruits mixed with smoke, earth, spice, and peppery herbs. Both of these 1998s should evolve nicely for 5–7 years.

These are two terrific 1997s from Carmignano, an undervalued region of Tuscany. The flamboyant, gorgeously rich, dark ruby/purple-colored 1997 Carmignano Elzana Riserva offers exotic aromas of smoke, nuts, new saddle leather, and blackberry/cherry fruit, medium to full body, and a succulent texture and finish. This fully mature, ostentatious Carmignano will age for 5–6 years. In contrast, the 1997 Carmignano Le Vigne Alte Riserva is a less sexy, opulently textured effort that emphasizes structure, tannin, and ageability. Dense, with an impressively saturated ruby/garnet/purple color as well as notes of smoke, roasted herbs, and leather in the aromatics, it is tight and muscular, with broodingly backward, concentrated flavors. Give it 2–3 years of cellaring and drink it over the following decade.

MARCHESI ANTINORI

1996 Brunello di Montalcino	E	90
1999 Chianti Classico Il Pèppoli	C	(87–88)
1998 Chianti Classico Il Pèppoli	C	89
1998 Chianti Classico Riserva Badia a Passignano	D	91
1997 Chianti Classico Riserva Badia a Passignano	D	92
1998 Merlot IGT	E	90
1997 Merlot IGT	E	93
1998 Solaia IGT	EEE	93+
1997 Solaia IGT	E	96
1997 Tenute Marchese Antinori Chianti Classico Riserva	D	92
1998 Tignanello IGT	E	91
1997 Tignanello IGT	D	93
1998 Villa Antinori Chianti Classico Riserva	D	90
1997 Villa Antinori Chianti Classico Riserva	C	90
1997 Vino Nobile del Montepulciano	C	89

Consistently two of Italy's finest *vini da tavola*, Piero Antinori's Tignanello and Solaia have been reference point wines for Tuscany. Both have been produced for more than 20 years, but it would be hard to find a past vintage that surpasses what was achieved in 1997. The 1997 Tignanello is a blend of 80% Sangiovese, 15% Cabernet Sauvignon, and 5% Cabernet Franc, aged in small French oak casks for 12 months and bottled with no filtration. It possesses a dense, ruby/purple color and an expansive nose of black currants, cherry compote, vanilla, and earth. Sweet, jammy, and opulently textured, this expansive, concentrated, low-acid wine is flashy and gorgeously proportioned. It should drink well for 10–15 years, although who can ignore it now? There are 30,000 cases of the 1998 Tignanello, a blend of 80% Sangiovese, 15% Cabernet Sauvignon, and 5% Cabernet Franc. It offers a classic bouquet of berry fruit, new saddle leather, underbrush, earth, and toast from its new-*barrique* aging. Medium- to full-bodied, with more tannin than the plusher, more opulent 1997, good delineation, and a firm, classic style, it requires 2–3 years of cellaring and should drink well for 15–16.

Solaia has been one of Italy's most brilliant wines since the early 1980s. Made in a Bordeaux-like style, it will age for two decades or more. The 1998, a blend of 75% Cabernet Sauvignon, 20% Sangiovese, and 5% Cabernet Franc (8,000 cases), was aged for 14 months in new and one-year-old French oak casks prior to being bottled without filtration. Yields were a low 30 hectoliters per hectare. While less flamboyant, exotic, and voluptuous than the 1997, the 1998 is a classically structured, youthful, well-balanced wine designed for cellaring. Its opaque ruby/purple color is accompanied by a classic bouquet of black currants, vanilla, earth, tobacco, and a touch of mint. Full-bodied, moderately tannic, dense, and concentrated, this backward 1998 needs 3–4 years of cellaring. Anticipated maturity: 2005–2020. The unfiltered 1997 Solaia (75% Cabernet Sauvignon, 20% Sangiovese, and 5% Cabernet Franc from a single 25-acre vineyard) is aged slightly longer than the Tignanello in 100% new French oak. There are 8,000 cases of the 1997. Perhaps the greatest Solaia yet made, it rivals the outstanding 1985. The sensational, opaque blue/purple-colored 1997 exhibits a complex nose of cedar, spice box, cassis, and subtle oak. With yields of only 30 h/h and malolactic fermentation in barrel (à la Tignanello), this wine reveals extraordinary concentration and a thick, viscous texture, yet no sense of heaviness or ponderousness. It is a thrilling Solaia to consume over the next two decades. If a first growth Pauillac were made in Tuscany, this would be it!

The 1998 Villa Antinori Chianti Classico Riserva, a superb blend of 90% Sangiovese and 10% Canaiolo, was aged 14 months in *barrique* and 12 months in bottle prior to release. Its dense plum/garnet color is followed by a sweet nose of black fruits, underbrush, earth, leather, and spice. Sweet on the attack, with medium to full body, good underlying acidity, and a rich, authoritative, concentrated finish, it should age well for a decade or longer. The 1997 Villa Antinori Chianti Classico Riserva (90% Sangiovese and 10% Canaiolo, aged in large French oak casks) reveals the vintage's superripeness as well as abundant quantities of black currant fruit mixed with cherry liqueur, tobacco, saddle leather, and spice aromas. Sweet because of high glycerin and low acidity, this dark ruby-colored, beautifully made, plump, lush Chianti should be drunk over the next 5–7 years. Even better is the 1997 Tenute Marchese Antinori Chianti Classico Riserva. Aged 14 months in small oak *barriques* and one year in bottle, it reveals *sur-maturité* (overripeness) in its strawberry/cassis-scented nose. Full-bodied, with low acidity, superb concentration of black fruit, spice box, cedar, earth, and smoke, it is a wine of exceptional extract and marvelous balance that reflects the vintage's low-acid, opulent/voluptuous personality. It should drink well for 10–15 years. Bravo!

This 123-acre Badia Chianti estate, planted with 100% Sangiovese, is one of the treasures of the Marchesi di Antinori empire. Made from 100% Sangiovese aged 14 months in both barrels and *foudres*, the outstanding 1998 is a smoky, earthy, Tuscan-styled offering with notes of underbrush, black cherries, strawberries, licorice, and herbs. Notes of tobacco and minerals also make an appearance. The wine possesses a supple texture, medium to full body, and excellent length as well as concentration. It will benefit from 1–2 more years of cellaring and should last for 15–16. The dense ruby/purple-colored 1997 Badia Chianti Classico Riserva is the finest wine I have tasted from this relatively new estate (the average age of the vines is a lowly 12 years). The bouquet offers sweet black cherry, strawberry, and plum aromas. Medium- to full-bodied and concentrated, with low acidity and ripe tannin, it is a voluptuous, pure, super-concentrated yet accessible wine. Enjoy it over the next 7–8 years.

The 1997 Vino Nobile del Montepulciano is a lovely, rich, fruity effort revealing excellent ripeness, admirable purity, and a medium-bodied, attractive texture. It should age nicely for 5–6 years.

In 1996, a 100% Merlot *cuvée* was added to the portfolio. The 1,000-case *cuvée* of 1997 Merlot *vino da tavola* is a real blockbuster. Aged 14 months in 100% new French oak, it offers overripe aromas of black cherries, Asian spices, cedar, chocolate, and mocha. Full-bodied, with rustic tannin, it comes across like a huge California Merlot with its thick, unctuous texture, and powerful, concentrated finish. I was surprised to learn that the alcohol is only 13.4%, given the wine's size and intensity. It should drink well for 10–12 years. The intriguing 1998 Merlot was also aged 14 months in new French oak. It offers textbook Merlot aromas of earth, mocha, coffee, chocolate, and black cherry/berry fruit with dried herbs in the background. Full-bodied and thick, with low acidity, it is best drunk over the next 7–8 years. It is an impressive Merlot from Tuscany's Montepulciano area.

Il Pèppoli's vineyards (136 acres) are planted primarily with Sangiovese in addition to tiny quantities of Merlot and Canaiolo. The east/northeast-facing vineyards are unusual for Tuscany. There are approximately 30,000 cases of this Chianti Classico made from a blend of 90% Sangiovese and 10% Merlot. The dark ruby-colored 1998 exhibits a smoky, cherry, earthy, leather-scented nose, excellent fruit purity, and fine elegance as well as focus. It is best drunk over the next 5–6 years. In contrast, once past the sweet cherry fruit, the 1999 is medium-bodied, shorter, and less complex.

The Antinori firm purchased a Brunello estate in July 1995, and although 1995 is generally a superior vintage for Brunello than 1996, they feel their work in the vineyard and stricter selection in 1996 produced a better wine. Most 1996 Brunellos I have tasted are austere and tannic, although there are some gorgeous exceptions. This is certainly one of them. Pian delle Vigne's 1996 Brunello di Montalcino offers a complex bouquet of new saddle leather, spice box, soy, and earthy/plum/cherry fruit. Its deep ruby/garnet color is accompanied by a sweet attack as well as a ripe, medium-bodied, slightly austere finish. It should drink well for 10 years.

ARGIANO

1999 Rosso di Montalcino	C	88
1998 Rosso di Montalcino	C	91
1999 Solengo IGT	E	94
1998 Solengo IGT	E	91
1997 Solengo IGT	E	94+

An impressive producer, Argiano continues to turn out some of Tuscany's finest red wines. This 100-acre estate is owned by the Countess Cinzano and managed by Sebastiano Rosa, who spent six years at the University of California at Davis and also worked at both Lafite-Rothschild and Sassicaia—not a bad résumé.

The soft, fragrant, medium ruby-colored 1999 Rosso di Montalcino exhibits a sexy aromatic profile offering scents of herbs, leather, cherries, and underbrush. Round and richly fruity, with good glycerin as well as a lush follow through, it will drink well for 5–6 years. Not surprisingly, one of Argiano's finest offerings is the 1999 Solengo, a blend of equal parts Cabernet Sauvignon, Merlot, Sangiovese, and Syrah. This opaque purple-colored offering exhibits gorgeously ripe blackberry and cassis fruit mixed with scents of leather, charcoal, earth, and wood. Dense, opulent, and full-bodied, with sweet tannin in the finish, it is still youthful and unevolved but promises to drink splendidly between 2004–2015.

The profound 1997 Solengo *vino da tavola* (a blend of Sangiovese and Cabernet Sauvignon with a tiny dosage of Syrah) is spectacular. Opaque purple-colored, it displays a fabulously sweet nose of crème de cassis, new saddle leather, toasty new oak, licorice, and flowers. This wine boasts amazing richness, a huge, full-bodied impact on the palate (yet no sense of heaviness), low acidity, gorgeous ripeness, and a finish that lasts for 35+ seconds. I predict a brilliant future for this compelling proprietary red wine.

While not as sumptuous as the 1997, the 1998 Solengo is a terrific offering. An intriguing blend aged in 100% new French oak for 16 months prior to bottling, it boasts an opaque ruby/purple color, as well as a classic black currant and blackberry-scented bouquet infused with high quality, toasty oak, and elements of roasted espresso. Intense, medium- to full-bodied, chewy, and rich, with a multilayered mid-palate and sweet tannin, this mouth-filling, dry red can be drunk now as well as over the next 10–15 years. Impressive!

A terrific value, the 1998 Rosso di Montalcino possesses supersweet, smoke-infused, black cherry fruit, and spice. Round, medium- to full-bodied, velvety-textured, hedonistic, and seductive, it can be consumed over the next 6–7 years.

BADIA A COLTIBUONO

1998 Chianti Classico	C	89
1997 Chianti Classico Riserva	D	91
1997 Coltibuono Chianti Classico Roberto Stucchi	C	90
1997 Sangioveto	E	93

One of Tuscany's historic estates (its origins can be traced back to the third century B.C.), this property, owned by the Stucchi Prinettis, produces a range of wines that offer consumers terrific values at the lower end and world-class wines at the upper end.

A serious wine, the 1998 Chianti Classico was produced from a blend of 90% Sangiovese and 10% Canaiolo. It offers distinctive strawberry jam scents intermixed with dried herbs and earth. Sexy, with a round, voluptuous texture, an elegant, sweet, richly fruity mid-palate, and a medium-bodied, supple finish, it will drink well for 3–4 years. I was knocked out by the exceptional quality of the 1997 Chianti Classico Riserva. Also made from 90% Sangiovese and 10% Canaiolo, it spends part of its 24-month cask aging in once-used French oak casks. The wine reminded me of what Chianti might taste like if it were made in Pomerol. The vintage has a lot to do with the fruit's opulent, succulent character, but this wine shows plenty of complex vanilla, herb, and black cherry fruit, with a noteworthy suggestion of roasted meat juices. Dense and full-bodied, with terrific fruit, high glycerin levels, and a chewy, plush texture, this is about as hedonistic and sumptuous a Chianti as one is likely to find. Drink it over the next 7–10 years.

Coltibuono's 1997 Chianti Classico Roberto Stucchi is an outstanding, remarkably silky-textured wine with the velvety tannin and voluptuous texture that most great vintages in Italy, France, or elsewhere tend to possess. Jammy black cherry and berry notes soar from the glass of this medium-bodied, thick, juicy, succulently styled Chianti. Tannin and acidity lurk just beneath the surface of this hedonistic, full-flavored wine. It should drink well for 7–10 years.

Another thrilling wine is the 1997 Sangioveto. Aged in 25% new French casks, it boasts a splendid bouquet of overripe blackberry/strawberry fruit, smoke, licorice, and spice box aromas. Dark plum-colored, with an explosive mid-palate and finish, this full-bodied, dense, concentrated wine (made from a highly regarded clone of Sangiovese) should continue to drink well (because of its low acidity and superripe fruit) for a decade or more. Impressive!

FATTORIA DI BASCIANO

1999 Il Corto	C	89+

A modern-styled effort from Fattoria di Basciano, the 1999 Il Corto is a blend of 90% Sangiovese and 10% Cabernet Sauvignon. This wine reveals complex aromas of leather, dried herbs, black cherries, charcoal, and earth. Ripe, with a subtle notion of toasty new oak, excellent sweet red and black fruits, and a nicely textured, medium-bodied finish, it should drink well for 7–12 years.

TENUTA DI BIBBIANO

1997 Chianti Classico Montornello	C	88

It could be said that Bibbiano is making Pomerol-styled Chianti. Silky-textured, hedonistic efforts have emerged from both the good 1996 vintage and the splendid 1997. Sultry, sexy, and lush, with gobs of fruit and low acidity, the plump, heady 1997 Chianti Classico Montornello will have huge crowd appeal. Drink it over the next 2 years.

BORGO SALCETINO

1998 Chianti Classico	B	88
1998 Chianti Classico Riserva Lucarello	D	88
1997 Chianti Classico Riserva Lucarello	D	90
1999 Rossole IGT	D	90
1998 Rossole IGT	D	90

The exceptional 1999 Rossole (a proprietary blend of 70% Cabernet Sauvignon and 30% Merlot aged in French oak for 12 months) is a fat, jammy, seductive, deep ruby/purple-colored wine with plenty of sweet oak as well as copious fruit, considerable glycerin, and a low-acid, thick, juicy finish. It should develop more definition in the bottle and age nicely for 12–15 years. The dark ruby-colored 1998 Chianti Classico Riserva Lucarello (aged 24 months in French oak) is an impressive, stylish, but restrained offering. It exhibits aromas of sweet jammy cherries intertwined with licorice, herbs, tobacco, and earth. Medium-bodied, with excellent texture and fine ripeness as well as lushness (atypical for the austerely styled 1998 Chiantis), it will drink well for 5–7 years.

The 1998 Chianti Classico is one of the finest examples I have tasted from this vintage, which appears to be superior to 1996 but less flamboyant and opulent than 1997 or 1999. This 1998 exhibits a dark ruby/purple color as well as beautifully pure, nicely textured, ripe, smoky, black cherry and currant aromas and flavors intermixed with high-class new leather and Provençal herbs. It is medium- to full-bodied, with excellent depth in addition to impressive balance and length. Like all of the wines from proprietor Tonino Livon, it was bottled without filtration. The deep ruby/purple-colored 1997 Chianti Classico Riserva

Lucarello reveals a more international personality, with copious quantities of spicy new oak, black currants, strawberries, and cherries, dense, ripe, medium- to full-bodied flavors, adequate acidity, and a plush, nicely layered, sweetly tannic finish. It should drink well for 7–8 years. The 1998 Rossole, a *barrique*-aged blend of 65% Sangiovese and 35% Merlot, combines power with elegance and finesse with considerable flavor authority. A dark ruby/purple color is accompanied by sweet, jammy, black fruit with the oak better meshed and more subtle than in the 1997 Lucarello. Lovely ripe berry fruit is present in the medium- to full-bodied palate, which shows considerable harmony and refinement. This wine is soft enough to be drunk now or cellared for another decade.

IL BORRO

1999 Il Borro	E	92

A Bordeaux-inspired blend of 50% Merlot, 40% Cabernet Sauvignon, and small quantities of Syrah, Petit Verdot, and Sangiovese, this *barrique*-aged 1999 produced from 5-year-old vines is an impressive debut release. A dead ringer for a top-class Médoc, it offers a deep purple color in addition to a complex bouquet of chocolate, earth, black currants, and toast. It possesses a full-bodied, concentrated, layered, harmonious personality, sweet fruit, abundant glycerin, and exceptional purity. The finish lasts for 25–30 seconds. Consume it now and over the next 12–15 years.

PODERI BOSCARELLI

1997 Boscarelli IGT	D	88
1998 Vino Nobile di Montepulciano	D	90
1997 Vino Nobile di Montepulciano	D	89
1997 Vino Nobile di Montepulciano Riserva del Nocio	D	91

The stars of proprietor Paola De Ferrari's estate are the Vini Nobili di Montepulciano. A sensational effort, the 1998 Vino Nobile di Montepulciano is a blend of 90% Sangiovese, 7% Merlot, and 3% Cabernet Sauvignon aged in various-sized wood *barriques*. A dark plum/purple color is accompanied by an exotic, ripe, earthy, spicy, flowery, sweet perfume, gorgeous fruit on the attack, excellent texture, medium body, and an elegant, pure, balanced finish. With all its component parts in perfect harmony, this 1998 can be enjoyed now, or cellared for a decade. The 1997 Vino Nobile di Montepulciano's dark ruby/purple color is accompanied by aromas of singed dried herbs, saddle leather, and sweet and sour cherry fruit. It possesses an attractive lushness as well as a seductive, sexy style with admirable finesse and flavor. Drink it over the next 7–8 years. A blend of 85% Sangiovese, 7% Mammolo, and 8% Merlot, aged in small oak casks, the terrific 1997 Vino Nobile di Montepulciano Riserva del Nocio exhibits a saturated ruby/purple color in addition to aromas of lead pencil, jammy blackberry and cherry fruit intermixed with smoke and high-quality new oak. There is remarkable sweetness on the palate, a lush, concentrated, fleshy texture, low acidity, and a long, spicy finish with a note of roasted nuts. Dense, ripe, and intense, it can be drunk now or cellared for 10–15 years. Lastly, the 1997 Boscarelli (a *barrique*-aged blend of 93% Sangiovese and 7% Cabernet Sauvignon) offers up aromas of tobacco as well as spicy cherry, strawberry, and red currant fruit. Long, elegant, and sweet, with firm tannin and an overall sense of restraint and balance, it should be consumed over the next 7–8 years.

CA' DEL VISPO

2000 Rovai IGT	C	89

The internationally styled yet seriously concentrated, ambitious 2000 Rovai exhibits an opaque ruby color as well as a sweet nose of black currants, blackberries, licorice, and spice. A fleshy, opulently textured, medium-bodied wine with excellent extract in addition to impeccable balance and purity, it is a sexy, up-front effort to enjoy over the next 5–6 years.

LE CALCINAIE

2000	Chianti Colli Senesi Gimignano	B	88
1999	Teodoro	D	90
1998	Teodoro	D	92

This trio includes an excellent bargain from proprietor Simone Santini. The 2000 Chianti Colli Senesi Gimignano (a 90% Sangiovese and 10% Merlot blend) is a fine value. An excellent, fat, chewy Chianti, it provides further evidence that this will be an exciting vintage for Tuscany. A deeply colored effort, it possesses plenty of glycerin as well as a heady, medium-bodied finish. Enjoy it over the next 3–4 years.

Undoubtedly the finest red wine I have tasted from Tuscany's San Gimignano region, the super-concentrated 1998 Teodoro (a blend of *barrique*-aged Cabernet Sauvignon, Sangiovese, and Merlot) boasts a deep, thick, black/purple color, chewy, full-bodied, opulently textured flavors, admirable purity, and a long, velvety, seamless finish. Drink this loaded 1998 over the next 7–8 years to take advantage of its exuberant youth. The 1999 Teodoro is a *barrique*-aged blend of Sangiovese and Merlot. This dense, chewy, internationally styled 1999 reveals plenty of espresso, toast, chocolate, and black cherry fruit aromas as well as flavors. Drink it over the next 10–12 years.

LE CALVANE

1997	Borro del Boscone	D	92+
1997	Chianti Classico Riserva Il Trecione	B	89

My first experience with the wines of Le Calvane was promising. Its superb 100% Cabernet Sauvignon, the 1997 Borro del Boscone, boasts an opaque purple color, super-concentrated cassis aromas and flavors, moderate tannin, and a full, thick, unctuous style. Dense and chewy, with superb ripeness, it needs 2–3 years of cellaring and should age well for 15–16 years. The 1997 Chianti Classico Riserva Il Trecione (an 800-case blend dominated by Sangiovese) exhibits a dark ruby/garnet color and a classic bouquet of earth, cedar, tobacco, black cherries, and dried herb aromas. Medium- to full-bodied, sweet, concentrated, supple, and fleshy, it is a hedonistic turn-on. Enjoy it over the next 4–5 years.

LA CAMPANA

1999	Rosso di Montalcino	D	89

The seductive, sexy, soft, plum/cherry fruit characteristics of the 1999 Rosso di Montalcino will make it a big hit with consumers. It exhibits abundant fruit and glycerin, as well as a succulent texture. It will provide considerable pleasure over the next 4–5 years.

CAPANNELLE

NV	Capannelle 2000 IGT	EEE (1.5 liters)	91+
1997	Capannelle & Avignonesi 50 & 50	EE	90+
1997	Chianti Classico Riserva	D	91

It has been almost a decade since I tasted these wines, which at that time were imported into the Washington, D.C., market by the now-defunct Mayflower Wine & Spirits. While they have always been impressive, they were made in extremely limited quantities and were outrageously expensive. The company's ownership has changed, but there does not appear to have been any philosophical shift in pricing. The proprietor, American James Sherwood, owns many famous luxury commodities (the Hotel Splendido in Portofino, Cipriano in Venice, and the world-renowned Orient Express). Only minute quantities of Capannelle's new releases are available, but there is no doubting that this state-of-the-art winery spares no expense in turning out world-class wines, all aged in French oak prior to bottling.

Available only in magnums, the sensationally packaged nonvintage Capannelle 2000 is an intriguing 80% Sangiovese/20% Cabernet Sauvignon blend of six vintages, 1990, 1991,

1992, 1993, 1994, and 1995 (obviously the year 2000 relates to the release date, not the vintage). It is a serious, concentrated, medium- to full-bodied, dark plum/ruby-colored effort with an excellent perfume of balsam wood, black fruits, tobacco, spice box, and smoke. It is rich, youthful, exuberant, and full-bodied. Although it may be expensive, it is an exceptional, rare offering. Anticipated maturity: now–2012.

The least expensive effort (and to my palate the finest) is the 1997 Chianti Classico Riserva, a *barrique*-aged blend of 90% Sangiovese and 10% Cabernet Franc and Malvasia Nero. It is beautifully textured, dense, chewy, rich wine, with a glorious bouquet of spring flowers, red and black fruits, tobacco, spice box, leather, and earth. The sweet tannin, acidity, and oak are all well integrated in this medium- to full-bodied, beautifully harmonious 1997. It will be at its apogee between 2003–2018. Bravo!

Lastly, the joint effort between Capannelle and Avignonesi, 1997 50 & 50, is a blend of equal parts Sangiovese from Capannelle and Merlot from Avignonesi's vineyard. It is sold only as a future, but I was told by the importer that there are about 25 cases available for the United States. A seriously endowed, dense ruby/purple-colored effort with plenty of new oak, it is somewhat internationally styled, with loads of extract, tannin, and richness. Wines such as this can be found at lower prices, but they will not have the names Capannelle and Avignonesi on them. Anticipated maturity: 2003–2016.

PODERE LA CAPPELLA

1997 Corbezzolo IGT	D	91

A gorgeous, sweet perfume of black cherry liqueur, high-quality French oak, and black raspberries soars from the glass of this dark ruby/purple-colored, supple-textured, rich, layered, and multidimensional wine. Despite its size and richness, it is extremely elegant and well balanced. Drink it now and over the next 10–15 years. Very impressive!

CASA EMMA

1997 Chianti Classico	C	88
1998 Soloio IGT	D	90+
1997 Soloio IGT	D	90

Casa Emma's 1997 Chianti Classico displays all the hallmarks of this fascinating vintage. The dark ruby color, silky texture, round, opulent, fruit flavors, and easy accessibility make it a reasonably good value that should drink well for 5–6 years. The outstanding, dark ruby/purple-colored, dense, rich 1997 Soloio reveals intense aromas of roasted herbs intermixed with chocolate, mocha, and black fruits. Long, chewy, and fleshy, with outstanding richness and purity, this impressive Merlot was aged for 15 months in 100% new French oak. Production was 500 cases. Drink it over the next 10–12 years.

One 1998 that has developed beautifully is Casa Emma's 1998 Soloio (a 500-case *cuvée* of 100% Merlot aged in French oak for 15 months). Its opaque ruby/purple color is accompanied by a sweet perfume of berry jam mixed with smoke, espresso, and chocolate. There are superb concentration, terrific purity, and a layered, opulent, nearly exotic character. The vintage's structure is noticeable, but it does not overwhelm the wine's personality. Anticipated maturity: 2003–2016.

FATTORIA CASALOSTE

1997 Chianti Classico Riserva	D	90
1997 Chianti Classico Riserva Don Vincenzo	EE	91

The ambitious, complex, full-bodied, *barrique*-aged 1997 Chianti Classico Riserva Don Vincenzo exhibits a dense ruby color as well as a superb nose of black fruits, tobacco, spice box, and vanilla. Chewy, layered, and intense, it can be drunk now and over the next 8–9 years. Nearly as good, the 1997 Chianti Classico Riserva (100% Sangiovese) is a seriously endowed effort revealing evidence of *barrique* aging as well as copious quantities of strawberry and black cherry fruit, new saddle leather, tobacco, and spice box. Rich and full-bodied, it is best drunk over the next decade.

CASANOVA DI NERI

1999 Rosso di Montalcino	C	88

A big, sweet Rosso di Montalcino offering up aromas of overripe cherries, new saddle leather, incense, and spice, this medium-bodied, plush 1999 is meant to be drunk now and over the next 3–4 years.

FATTORIA I CASCIANI

2000 Chianti di Montespertoli	B	88
1999 Villa Gaia	C	91

A 50–50 blend of Merlot and Cabernet Sauvignon aged 12 months in French oak, the 1999 Villa Gaia is an impressive, unfiltered offering from a vineyard farmed biodynamically. It boasts a dense dark ruby/purple color in addition to a sweet bouquet of blackberry and cassis fruit intertwined with toasty new oak. Initially I thought it was too international, but with airing, Tuscany's earthy, underbrush, leather, truffle, spice box, and dried red/black fruit characteristics emerged. Impressive purity, texture, and length suggest it will age well for 10–15 years. The boldly styled, tank-fermented and -aged 2000 Chianti (primarily Sangiovese) boasts a youthful dark ruby color, excellent texture, fine flesh, and loads of black cherry and currant fruit intertwined with subtle herb and cedar components. Enjoy this robust, exuberant Chianti over the next 2–3 years.

CASTELLO DI AMA

1998 L'Apparita IGT	EEE	(91–93)
1997 L'Apparita IGT	EEE	92+
1997 Chianti Classico	D	89
1997 Chianti Classico Bellavista	EEE	91
1997 Chianti Classico La Casuccia	EEE	92

With 500 acres, 200 of which are in vine, Castello di Ama is one of Tuscany's most significant high-altitude vineyards. My first experience with a Castello di Ama offering was the 1985 L'Apparita tasted in Brussels more than a decade ago. After a period of experimentation, when multiple single-vineyard offerings were produced, Ama has focused on producing a Chardonnay, rosé, Merlot, a terrific regular Chianti, and, in top vintages, two single-vineyard Chiantis. Recent releases are all impressive.

Readers seeking fine Chianti Classico should check out Castello di Ama's 1997 Chianti Classico. Made from a blend of 80% Sangiovese, 12% Merlot, and 8% Caniolo whose yields were 2.4 tons of fruit per acre, this dark ruby-colored Chianti possesses a pure style, outstanding ripeness, and spicy, cedary aromas and flavors intertwined with black raspberries, cigar box, and vanilla. Dense, medium-bodied, soft, and opulent, it will drink well for 7–8 years. The dark ruby-colored 1997 Chianti Classico Bellavista (8,000 bottles produced) is filled with finesse and elegance. Intense black cherry aromas intertwined with berry fruit, tobacco, and spice box are followed by good denseness and richness, medium to full body, sweet tannin, and impeccable symmetry and balance. This youthful Chianti is approachable and should drink well for a decade. The dense purple-colored 1997 Chianti Classico La Casuccia (another microproduction of 8,000 bottles) is fuller-bodied, more powerful and opulent, with the most flamboyant personality of Castello di Ama's Chiantis. Long, with more tannin as well as richness and structure, it will benefit from 1–3 years of cellaring and will keep for 15+ years.

The impressive L'Apparita (a 100% Merlot *cuvée* of approximately 8,000 bottles) is aged completely in French oak casks. At a recent mini–vertical tasting, it was hard to find an unimpressive effort, with the 1993 rated at 87 points, the 1992 at 90 points, and the 1990 at 88 points. The stunning 1997 L'Apparita may be the finest L'Apparita since the 1985. It exhibits a deep ruby/purple color in addition to a distinctive nose of mocha, espresso bean, cherry liqueur, and blackberries. Full-bodied, dry, and rich, with good sweetness and fatness on the mid-palate, this long, dense, still youthful wine requires an additional 3–5 years of cellaring; it should keep for two decades. New oak (about 70% new French wood is utilized) plays a secondary role in the wine's aromatic and flavor profiles. Also impressive, although less flamboyant, the opaque purple-colored 1998 L'Apparita reveals aromas and flavors of new saddle leather, spicy oak, and blackberry/cherry fruit. Powerful, muscular, and tannic, without the sweet, silky, sumptuousness of the 1997, it needs 4–5 years of cellaring and should keep for 15+ years.

CASTELLO DI BROLIO

1998 Chianti Classico Castello di Brolio	D	88

This opaque purple-colored, tannic effort is somewhat internationally styled but chewy, well made, and reminiscent of a midlevel Bordeaux. Aged in *barrique*, of which 65% was new French oak, it easily carries its 13.7% alcohol but requires another year or two of cellaring given its big, backward style. It should age well for 12–15 years.

CASTELLO DI CACCHIANO

1997 Chianti Classico Millennio Riserva	D	90
1999 Rosso Toscano IGT	B	89

A terrific buy, the 1999 Rosso Toscano IGT is a delicious, opulently textured blend of 85% Sangiovese and 15% Merlot. It boasts a dark ruby color as well as sweet, jammy aromas of strawberries, cherries, and currants backed up with earth, old wood, and leather. Medium- to full-bodied, lush, and fleshy, it provides a balanced, chewy mouth-feel. Drink it over the next 3–4 years. The outstanding, saturated ruby/garnet-colored 1997 Chianti Classico Millennio Riserva boasts an opulent nose of ripe plums, black cherries, licorice, earth, and cedar. Fleshy and full-bodied, this exotic, rich, concentrated, low-acid Chianti possesses this vintage's flamboyant personality. Enjoy it over the next 10–12 years.

CASTELLO DI FARNETELLA

1999 Chianti Colli Sensi	B	90
1999 Lucilla IGT	C	91
1998 Lucilla IGT	C	90

Wow! Castello di Farnetella's explosive 1999 Chianti Colli Sensi boasts a deep saturated ruby color as well as superripe black cherry jam characteristics intermixed with blackberries, graphite, and spice. Succulent, medium- to full-bodied, opulent, fleshy, and rich, it exhibits considerable depth in addition to burgeoning complexity. For the amount of richness and complexity, it is about as fine a Chianti as money can buy. Moreover, it can be drunk now or cellared for 7–8 years.

Farnetella's 1999 Lucilla is a stunning value. A blend of 90% Sangiovese and 10% Merlot aged for 10 months in French *barriques*, it boasts an explosive nose of smoke, blackberry, plum, and cassis fruit, leather, and pencil shavings. Dense, full-bodied, and voluptuously textured, it is a hedonistic turn-on that also satisfies the taster's intellectual cravings. Drink it over the next 5–7 years. Yummy! The 1998 Lucilla, which spent 12 months in French oak, is also a reasonably good value. Its opulent, dark ruby color, Pomerol-like lushness, and emphasis on black cherry liqueur infused with coffee and smoky notes are impressive. The wine exhibits gorgeous ripeness, admirable richness, and a long, low-acid, fleshy finish. It should drink well for 5–7 years.

CASTELLO DI FONTERUTOLI

1999 Brancaia IGT	E	88
1999 Chianti Classico	C	89
1998 Chianti Classico Riserva	D	88
1997 Poggio alla Badiola IGT	B	88
1999 Siepi IGT	EE	90

Another splendidly ripe, sweet, layered, exuberantly fruity Chianti Classico from the 1999 vintage, Fonterutoli has turned out a dark ruby/purple-colored effort with plenty of density, abundant mineral-infused black cherry fruit, and good spice as well as earthy overtones. It is supple, yet dense and structured enough to last for a decade. From a more austere vintage, the 1998 Chianti Classico Riserva exhibits a deep ruby/purple color as well as copious extract, more muscle and tannin, but neither the charm nor seductiveness of its younger sibling. It should age well for 12–15 years.

The 1999 Siepi, an outstanding blend of equal parts Sangiovese and Merlot aged for 16 months in French oak, boasts a dense ruby/purple color along with sumptuous aromas of new oak, black currants, blackberries, and new saddle leather. It is dense, powerful yet harmonious, with sweet tannin and plenty of structure. Give it 1–2 years of cellaring and enjoy it over the following decade. Along with a less saturated dark ruby color, the 1999 Brancaia reveals an interesting perfume of licorice, dried herbs, black fruits, and a hint of animal scents. On the palate, it is leaner and more compressed than the Siepi, with more noticeable tannin as well as more structure. Anticipated maturity: 2003–2012.

Another excellent value is the 1997 Poggio alla Badiola, a super Tuscan Sangiovese with a touch of Merlot and Cabernet Sauvignon in the blend. This dark ruby/purple-colored, fruit-dominated wine exhibits a sweet midsection, excellent purity, and a long, ripe, luscious finish. It can be drunk now and over the next 4–5 years.

CASTELLO DI MELETO

1998 Fiore IGT	D	89
1997 Fiore IGT	D	89

Castello di Meleto's 1998 Fiore (95% Sangiovese and 5% Merlot) is a sweet, oaky, ripe, opulent effort with sweet tannin, plenty of berry fruit, and notes of coffee. It is a round, generous red to consume over the next 5–6 years. For a 1998, it possesses an atypical forward, plump personality. Also primarily Sangiovese with a tiny dollop of Merlot added, the dark ruby-colored, medium- to full-bodied 1997 Fiore exhibits sweet jammy black cherry and currant fruit, smoke, and espresso aromas and flavors. Fleshy and soft, it is ideal for drinking over the next decade.

CASTELLO DELLA PANERETTA

1999 Chianti Classico	C	88
1998 Chianti Classico	C	88
1997 Chianti Classico Riserva	C	91
1997 Chianti Classico Vigneto Torre a Destra Riserva	D	90
1998 Quattrocentenario 1596–1996 IGT	E	90
1997 Quattrocentenario IGT	E	91
1998 Le Terrine IGT	D	88
1997 Le Terrine IGT	D	89

These are purely made efforts from an estate located in the Monsanto region of Tuscany. This small, 2,000-case winery has a 404-year winemaking history. The Castello della Paneretta's offerings are all bottled unfiltered and represent classic, pure expressions of Tuscany. The best buy is the deliciously fat, fruity, dark ruby-colored 1999 Chianti Classico. Revealing a vibrant nose of black cherries and subtle earth, as well as low acidity (for a Tuscan wine), this fleshy, ripe Chianti should drink well for 3–4 years.

The dark ruby-colored 1998 Le Terrine, an unusual blend of equal parts Sangiovese and Canaiolo, spent 12 months in French oak prior to bottling. The complex bouquet reveals scents of black fruits, flowers, and subtle minerals. Complex, supple-textured, and lush, this intriguing, character-filled, mid-weight Italian red will drink well for 5–6 years. Made from 100% old-vine Sangiovese, the 1998 Quattrocentenario 1596–1996 (celebrating the winery's 400th anniversary) boasts a dark ruby color in addition to a stunning nose of blackberries, cherries, spice, and earth. Sweet, rich, fleshy, and complex, it can be drunk now as well as over the next 7–8 years.

It is hard to find a better 1998 Chianti Classico than Paneretta's. It possesses a deep ruby color in addition to smoky, herb-infused, meaty aromas with abundant berry fruit, and excellent flavor concentration. A sense of finesse, elegance, and intensity, with medium body, sweet tannin, and fine acidity further characterize this wine. It should drink well for 4–5 years. Given the fact there is no oak influence, it should be remarkably flexible with an assortment of cuisines. The dark plum/ruby-colored 1997 Chianti Classico Riserva offers an opulent, sweet, jammy nose of black fruits, earth, and spice. Supple-textured, dense, and chewy, it reveals the vintage's gorgeous ripeness in addition to an exquisite balance between alcohol, acidity, and tannin. Ripe, rich, youthful, and exuberant, it should age effortlessly for 7–10 years. The 100% Sangiovese, single-vineyard, dark ruby-colored 1997 Chianti Classico Vigneto Torre a Destra Riserva exhibits melted tar and asphalt notes along with charcoal, cherry jam, and spice. It possesses more acidity and tannin than the 1997 Riserva, but the vintage's creamy texture and opulence are well displayed. Ripe, dense, and impressive, it should be consumed over the next decade. More monolithic, and, as the French would say, *sauvage* (wild or uncivilized, but not in a pejorative sense), the 1997 Le Terrine, a blend of equal parts Sangiovese and old-vine Canaiolo, exhibits more black fruits and foresty, earthy notes, as well as a foursquare personality. It possesses abundant concentration, body, and density but does not display the charm, complexity, or soul of the other offerings. It may improve with another year or so of bottle age.

In the finest vintages, a *cuvée* called Quattrocentenario is produced. The 1997 (celebrating the winery's first 400 years) was made from 100% Sangiovese aged in French *barriques*. Approximately 200 cases were produced. Not surprisingly, it is the most concentrated of these offerings, but only marginally more than the Chianti Classico Riserva and the Torre a Destra Riserva. It exhibits a dense ruby/purple color as well as abundant aromas of sweet black cherry fruit intermixed with minerals, smoke, iron, and meat. Chewy and full-bodied, with new saddle leather and black cherry–flavored fruit, it is powerful yet elegant, rich yet balanced. Sweet tannin and well-integrated acidity give it immediate accessibility, but the wine is capable of lasting for 10–15 years.

CASTELLO DI QUERCETO

| 1997 Cignale IGT | E | 91+ |

An impressive, French *barrique*–aged blend of 90% Cabernet Sauvignon and 10% Merlot from the Greve region of Tuscany, this deep ruby/purple-colored 1997 boasts a provocative perfume of black currants, cherries, balsa wood, cedar, tobacco, and smoke. Although backward, it possesses powerful, concentrated flavors, moderately high tannin levels, good acidity, and a style built for the long haul. Readers seeking immediate gratification should pass it by. Those with patience and cool cellars will be rewarded with a splendid wine in 4–6 years. Anticipated maturity: 2004–2025.

CASTELLO DEI RAMPOLLA

| 1997 Chianti Classico Riserva | D | 89 |
| 1998 Sammarco IGT | EE | 90 |

1999 Vigna d'Alceo IGT	EEE	99
1998 Vigna d'Alceo IGT	EEE	92

For 25 years this has been one of my favorite Tuscan producers. Amazingly, this 90-acre estate has been in the Di Napoli family for 300 years. Elegance, balance, and restraint are the operative words when it comes to understanding the wines of Castello dei Rampolla.

For more than two decades one of the greatest Tuscan proprietary red wines has been Castello dei Rampolla's Cabernet Sauvignon/Sangiovese blend called Sammarco. What has always made this wine exceptional, especially in the top vintages, is its complexity and elegance. It is closer to a great Graves than any other wine I have ever tasted outside France. The 1998 Sammarco, a blend of 85% Cabernet Sauvignon and 15% Sangiovese, reveals more structure and tannin than is present in the 1997 or, I suspect, the 1999. Additionally, it possesses formidable underlying concentration and depth, along with that multilayered mid-palate that always seems to separate exceptional wines from good ones. The 1998 Sammarco's deep, saturated ruby color is followed by a complex bouquet of charcoal, roasted herbs, smoke, hot gravel, black currants, and cherries. It is medium-bodied and deep, with high but sweet tannin and extraordinary purity as well as delineation. Anticipated maturity: 2003–2016. The monumental 1999 Vigna d'Alceo is a 20,000-bottle *cuvée* of 85% Cabernet Sauvignon and 15% Sangiovese aged in oak. It tastes like the Sammarco on steroids. The essence of both varietals, it boasts an exceptionally provocative nose of liquid minerals, graphite, plums, crème de cassis, and cherry liqueur. It is fabulously concentrated yet remarkably light on its feet, with medium to full body, sweet tannin, and layer upon layer of flavor nuances. There is plenty of glycerin in this rich but neither heavy nor overbearing effort. This is a thrilling tour de force! However, it requires cellaring. Anticipated maturity: 2005–2025. Bravo!

The dark ruby-colored 1997 Chianti Classico Riserva (90% Sangiovese and 10% Cabernet Sauvignon) offers aromas of toasty oak, tobacco, wood smoke, cherries, herbs, and new saddle leather. Medium- to full-bodied, concentrated, dense, and ripe, with moderate tannin, this fleshy, youthful Chianti is just reaching full maturity, where it should remain for 10–12 years. An even finer offering is the 1998 Vigna d'Alceo. An opaque purple-colored blend of Cabernet Sauvignon, Sangiovese, and small quantities of Syrah and Petit Verdot, it is a large-scale wine with exceptional elegance and complexity as well as more power and richness than the Sammarco. A sweet entry on the palate is followed by abundant quantities of smoky, complex, black currant fruit intermixed with lead pencil and vanilla flavors. Medium-bodied, beautifully knit, and suave, it possesses sweeter tannin than the Chianti Classico Riserva. Anticipated maturity: now–2017.

CASTIGLION DEL BOSCO

1997 Bernaia IGT	EE	90
1998 Rosso di Montalcino	C	89

Value seekers should search out the delicious, supple-textured, complex 1998 Rosso di Montalcino. A dark ruby color is accompanied by abundant aromas of spice box, sweet berry fruit, and grilled meat. With an accessible personality as well as fine concentration, it is close to full maturity, although it will keep for 4–5 years. The luxury-priced 1997 Bernaia (70% Sangiovese and 30% Cabernet Sauvignon) exhibits a Pomerol-like style. It offers notes of coffee, mocha, and chocolate in addition to black cherry and currant fruit. Toasty oak also makes an appearance as the wine sits in the glass. It is a medium- to full-bodied, perfumed effort with outstanding richness and purity. Sadly, only 500 cases were produced.

CENSIO

1999 Erte	B	89

The 1999 Erte, a proprietary blend of equal parts Sangiovese and Cabernet Sauvignon, sees no new oak but is *barrique*-aged. A fine value, it boasts a deep ruby/purple color as well as intense aromatics consisting of saddle leather, cherry jam, black currants, licorice, and cigar box. Medium-bodied with light tannin, this polished, elegant effort possesses power, richness, and finesse. Enjoy this classy Italian red over the next 2–3 years.

CERBAIONA

1997 Cerbaiona IGT	D	88

Cerbaiona's proprietary red wine, the 1997 Cerbaiona, is a blend of 60% Sangiovese and 40% Cabernet Sauvignon, Merlot, and Syrah. Its dark ruby/purple color is followed by a sweet nose of new saddle leather, soy, cherries, damp earth, and toasty oak. Round and ripe, this 1997 is ideal for consuming over the next 7–8 years.

FATTORIA DEL CERRO

1999 Manero	D	92
1998 Merlot Poggio Golo	D	91
1998 Vino Nobile di Montepulciano Vigneto Antica Chiusina	E	89+
1997 Vino Nobile di Montepulciano Vigneto Antica Chiusina	D	90

The 1998 Vino Nobile di Montepulciano Antica Chiusina could turn out to be an outstanding wine with another 1–2 years of cellaring. Concentrated and powerful (particularly for this vintage), it exhibits a dense plum/garnet color, and sweet, earthy, leathery, berry aromas mixed with underbrush, licorice, and cherry jam. Full-bodied and highly extracted, with noteworthy structure as well as moderately high tannin, it should be at its best between 2003–2016. The brilliant 100% Sangiovese *cuvée* aged in *barrique*, the 1999 Manero is internationally styled, but it is hard to resist its compelling cherry liqueur, espresso, toast, and spice box aromas and flavors. Dense, opulent, full-bodied, and thick, this brilliantly made, flamboyant, succulent 1999 will drink well for 7–8 years.

In a previous tasting, Cerro's stars were the 1998 Merlot Poggio Golo and 1997 Vino Nobile di Montepulciano Vigneto Antica Chiusina. The latter wine boasts an opaque ruby/purple color as well as a big, smoky, sweet nose of black cherries, blueberries, and cedar. Ripe and full-bodied with an opulent texture, and luscious, fat, concentrated flavors, it is a blend of 90% Prugnolo and 10% Colorino aged 18 months in French oak casks. It will drink well for a decade or more. Even more flashy/flamboyant is the opaque purple-colored 1998 Merlot Poggio Golo. This dense, chewy, voluptuously textured 100% Merlot is huge in the mouth, exhibiting gobs of chocolate/mocha-infused jammy black cherry fruit, a boatload of glycerin, low acidity, and sweet tannin. Thick and fleshy, it will have enormous appeal if drunk over the next 7–8 years.

VINCENZO CESANI

1997 Rosso di Pancole Luenzo	C	90

A terrific wine made from Sangiovese grown near the historic village of San Gimignano, this special *cuvée* made for American importer Eric Solomon of European Cellars is full-bodied, with a knockout nose of roasted hazelnuts, cappuccino, black currants, and toasty new oak. The wine is huge, with impressive structure, great purity, and a 30+-second finish. It can be drunk now or cellared for a decade.

CIACCI PICCOLOMINI D'ARAGONA

1998 Ateo IGT	D	93
1997 Brunello di Montalcino	EE	96

1999	Rosso di Montalcino Vigna della Fonte	C	89
1998	Rosso di Montalcino Vigna della Fonte	C	88
1999	Sant'Antimo Rosso Favius	D	94
1998	Sant'Antimo Rosso Favius	D	92

From one of my favorite Tuscan producers, Ciacci Piccolomini d'Aragona's 1999 Rosso di Montalcino Vigna della Fonte is another fine example from this vintage. Burgundy-like in its sweet strawberry, cherry, and mineral-infused flavors, this medium- to full-bodied, plump, complex, soft, lush *rosso* is best consumed over the next 3–4 years. Ciacci's 1998 Rosso di Montalcino Vigna della Fonte is a charming, seductive, ripe effort with sweet fruit but not a great deal of complexity. Richly fruity and sexy, it will provide enjoyment over the next 4–5 years. The terrific 1997 Brunello di Montalcino boasts a staggering aromatic profile of soy sauce, roasted meats, dried herbs, jammy black and red fruits, and Asian spices. This full-bodied, superbly concentrated, layered, multidimensional Brunello is the kind of wine one expects from such a renowned region but so rarely receives. This beauty should drink well young yet evolve effortlessly for 15+ years.

The 1998 Ateo (a blend of 60% Sangiovese and 40% Cabernet Sauvignon) is a gloriously ripe, full-bodied, velvety-textured effort with a dark ruby/purple color, plenty of smoky, earthy, blackberry, cherry, and currant fruit, a touch of graphite, decent acidity, and a seamless, opulent, voluptuous finish. This compelling wine is meant to be drunk over the next 10–12 years. There are only 15 barrels (approximately 375 cases) of the 100% Syrah 1998 Sant'Antimo Rosso Favius, which may be the finest Italian Syrah I have tasted. An opaque purple color is followed by a classic bouquet of bacon fat, blackberry liqueur, and cassis. This monstrous fruit bomb is unctuous, thick, and unbelievably concentrated. The wine's new-oak aging has been absorbed by its formidable concentration of fruit. Drink this exuberant, in-your-face offering over the next 5–7 years. Even more fabulous is the 1999 Sant'Antimo Rosso Favius (500 cases). A huge black/purple-colored effort, it boasts notes of roasted espresso, blackberries, asphalt, truffles, and pepper. Explosive, rich, unctuously textured, and full-bodied, with low acidity, it is stunning at present, yet unformed and primary. Anticipated maturity: 2003–2015. Bravo!

LE CINCIOLE

| 1997 | Chianti Classico Riserva Petresco | D | 90 |

The superb, deep ruby-colored 1997 Chianti Classico Riserva Petresco boasts a sweet bouquet of raspberries, strawberries, leather, dried herbs, and cedar. An elegant wine, it combines power and flesh with a stylish, graceful entry on the palate. Medium- to full-bodied and pure, it will provide delicious drinking over the next decade.

CISPIANO

| 1997 | Chianti Classico | B 88 |

What a sexy, opulently textured, delicious wine! Its dark purple color is followed by gorgeously rich blackberry, raspberry, and cherry fruit aromas intermixed with a touch of earth and wood. Low in acidity, fat, and juicy, with a succulent finish, this is a mouth-filling, dazzling Chianti to enjoy over the next 5–7 years. An excellent value.

COLLE SANTA MUSTIOLA

| 1997 | Poggio ai Chiari IGT | D | 90 |

This complex, dark ruby/purple-colored, 100% Sangiovese reveals the vintage's telltale opulence, low acidity, and ripe, jammy fruit. Aromas of wood smoke, new saddle leather, black cherry and strawberry jam, intermixed with toast emerge from this deep, concentrated, dense, medium- to full-bodied, velvety-textured 1997. Drink it over the next 10–12 years.

COLLELUNGO

1999 Chianti Classico	C	89
1998 Chianti Classico Riserva	E	89
1997 Chianti Classico Riserva	D	93
1999 Chianti Classico Roveto	E	91
1997 Chianti Classico Roveto	D	91

This impressive new estate (its first vintage was 1997) is turning out expensive but brilliant offerings (bottled without fining or filtration) from the Castellina region of Chianti. The 1999 Chianti Classico and its sibling, the 1999 Chianti Classico Roveto, are dense ruby/purple-colored efforts possessing loads of blackberry and cherry fruit, subtle dosages of wood, and multitextured personalities displaying considerable flesh and ripeness. The only difference is that the regular bottling is soft and best consumed over the next 3–4 years; the Roveto exhibits more structure although it is dominated by its fruit, glycerin, and concentration. Both represent modern, sumptuously styled Chiantis that are meant to be accessible in their youth. No Roveto was produced in 1998, but the modern-styled 1998 Chianti Classico Riserva is a 500-case *cuvée* exhibiting toasty new oak as well as copious quantities of black currant and cherry fruit intermixed with new saddle leather and tea notes. Tannin is present, but this 1998 is much sweeter than many of its peers, with good texture and length. It is an excellent Chianti to drink over the next 10–12 years.

The outstanding 1997 Chianti Classico Roveto exhibits superb ripeness, richness, and density, low acidity, and glorious levels of black cherry/raspberry fruit as well as spice box and toast characteristics. It should drink well for 7–8 years. It is unusual to compare a Chianti Classico with Burgundy, but there is no question that Collelungo's 1997 Chianti Classico Riserva could easily pass for a fine premier cru Volnay. Bottled unfined and unfiltered and made from 100% Sangiovese aged in new French oak, it boasts a glorious ruby/purple color in addition to fabulous aromatics, including flowers, black raspberries, and kirsch. As the wine sits in the glass, mineral and spicy new-oak scents emerge. Extraordinarily well delineated, full-bodied, and layered, with a sensationally deep mid-palate and a gorgeously proportioned finish, this dazzling Chianti can be drunk now or cellared for 10–12 years. Impressive!

COLLOSORBO

1997 Brunello di Montalcino	EE	90
1999 Laurus IGT	D	92
1999 Rosso di Montalcino	C	90
1998 Rosso di Montalcino	C	90

This impressive portfolio includes an outstanding 1999 Rosso di Montalcino. A deep ruby/purple color is accompanied by powerful, full-bodied, deep, chewy flavors, wonderful sweetness, good purity, and a whopping finish crammed with glycerin, black cherries, spice box, and currants. Enjoy this superb Rosso over the next 5–7 years. The 1999 Laurus, an intriguing, explosively scented and flavored blend of equal parts Sangiovese and Cabernet Sauvignon aged in new oak, is a Tuscan fruit bomb. It possesses a deep purple color, dazzling levels of plum, black cherry, and currant fruit, and a voluptuous, opulent, thick, rich personality. Drink it during its first 6–7 years to take advantage of its exuberance and lavishly fruited qualities.

Collosorbo's 1998 Rosso di Montalcino could easily be mistaken for a serious Brunello di Montalcino. There are sweet tannin and plenty of softness, as well as big, rustic, powerful, earthy, meaty, herb aromas and flavors. Complex, spicy, and medium- to full-bodied, it is ideal for drinking over the next 4–5 years. The dark ruby/garnet-colored 1997 Brunello di Montalcino boasts an intoxicating perfume of new saddle leather, cherry jam, dried

Provençal herbs, and spice box. This complex, medium- to full-bodied, supple-textured 1997 can be drunk early because of its fat and glycerin, but it promises to age well for 10–12 years.

COLOGNOLE

1997 Chianti Rufina Riserva del Don	C	88

I know it sounds unappealing, but occasionally (more frequently in Nebbiolo than in Sangiovese) an unmistakable scent of fresh sardines emerges along with aromas of cherries, earth, leather, underbrush, etc. I found that characteristic in this lean but impressively constituted, dark plum-colored 1997 Chianti Rufina Riserva del Don. It possesses complex aromatics, excellent texture, and a medium-bodied, ruggedly constructed finish. I am not sure it will ever resolve its rusticity, but it will provide a big mouthful of Chianti over the next 7–10 years.

COLOMBAIO DI CENCIO

1997 Chianti Classico Riserva	D	89
1997 Il Futuro IGT	D	90

Two impressive, modern-styled Italian reds, the dense ruby/purple-colored 1997 Chianti Classico Riserva exhibits aromas of black fruits, licorice, spice, and a touch of wood. Medium- to full-bodied and pure, with layers of flavor, this is a superb example of the renowned 1997 vintage. Consume it over the next decade. The 1997 Il Futuro is a well-endowed, *barrique*-aged effort with plenty of color, oak, and flavor. Revealing a saturated ruby/purple color, it boasts a superripe nose of blackberry liqueur mixed with crème de cassis and subtle oak. This layered, rich, concentrated offering should drink well for 10–12 years.

CONSTANTIA

1999 Morellino di Scansano Malfatti	D	90

A limited-production *cuvée* of Morellino di Scansano (a promising, up-and-coming subregion of Tuscany), this 1999 is a seriously endowed, opaque ruby/purple-colored offering boasting a dazzling aromatic display of violets, blueberries, black currants, minerals, and new oak. Rich, round, medium- to full-bodied, exceptionally pure, and beautifully textured, this stylish, classic red should drink well during its first decade of life.

CORRINA

1997 Chianti Rufina	B	89
1997 I Cipressi IGT	C	89
1997 Vigna Spartigalla IGT	C	90

This excellent winery practices a fair pricing policy that makes these offerings essentially steals, given today's inflated wine prices. The dark ruby/purple-colored 1997 Chianti Rufina (93% Sangiovese) offers a sweet nose of strawberries and cherries. Lovely glycerin gives the wine a creamy texture, and the finish is pure, ripe, and authoritative, with no hard edges or bumps. Drink this dense Chianti over the next 5–6 years. It is a terrific value. A steal in today's surreal wine market is the 1997 Vigna Spartigalla *vino da tavola*. A blend of 90% Sangiovese and 10% Cabernet Sauvignon aged in 75% new French oak, it borders on an international style, and mineral and lead pencil notes kick in to add complexity to the toasty wood. There are copious quantities of black currants and cherries, tangy acidity, and outstanding purity as well as harmony in this full-bodied wine. Delicious now, it will improve for 7–8 years and last for 12–15. Another excellent value is the dense ruby/purple-colored 1997 I Cipressi, a blend of equal parts Sangiovese and Cabernet Sauvignon. Medium-bodied and structured, with elegant, smoky, blackberry and cassis fruit intertwined with toast and leather, it will benefit from another 6–12 months of bottle age and last for a decade. These are all excellent values.

ANDREA COSTANTI

1999 Calbello Ardingo IGT	D	90
1998 Calbello Ardingo IGT	D	93

Costanti is a traditional winery consistently turning out classic offerings. Serious, stern, austere wines that age brilliantly are produced by Andrea Costanti. Bottled by Costanti under the Calbello label and produced from a vineyard in Montosoli, the terrific 1998 Calbello Ardingo (a *barrique*-aged blend of 75% Merlot and 25% Cabernet Sauvignon) is another example of the stunning quality Merlot can achieve in Tuscany (in my view, unequaled anywhere in the world except Pomerol). This opaque purple-colored 1998 boasts a knockout nose of espresso-infused cherry jam as well as dense, full-bodied, unctuously textured flavors that ooze across the palate. The new-oak characteristics from *barrique* aging are completely concealed by the wine's wealth of fruit and extract. This intense, chewy, internationally styled effort is in total contrast to the austere Brunellos di Montalcino produced by Costanti. It should drink well for a decade or more. The closest thing to a modern-styled red is the 1999 Calbello Ardingo, a dark plum/purple-colored, sexy effort revealing aromas of espresso, chocolate, and sweet, plum/black cherry fruit. Full-bodied and succulent, with sweet tannin as well as exceptional ripeness, it will drink well for 5–6 years.

DEI

1997 Santa Catharina IGT	D	92
1997 Vino Nobile di Montepulciano	C	90
1997 Vino Nobile di Montepulciano Riserva	D	90

The opulence of the 1997 vintage is well displayed in the dark ruby/garnet-colored 1997 Vino Nobile di Montepulciano Riserva. It exhibits jammy black fruits intermixed with underbrush, leather, tobacco, and caramel, plump, fleshy fruit, medium- to full-bodied, low-acid but impressively textured flavors. Drink it over the next 5–7 years. The spectacular, opaque purple-colored 1997 Santa Catharina (equal parts Cabernet Sauvignon, Syrah, and Sangiovese) boasts a rich, full-bodied, chewy personality with copious quantities of blackberry and cassis fruit intermixed with smoky wood. Thick, corpulent, dense, and moderately tannic, this enormously endowed yet harmonious wine can be drunk now and over the next 12+ years. Another gorgeously delicious 1997 from Tuscany, the dark ruby-colored 1997 Vino Nobile di Montepulciano offers up sweet, jammy, black cherry fruit intertwined with scents of new saddle leather. Aged in large *foudres* prior to bottling, it exhibits notes of overripeness, explosive fruit, and a boatload of glycerin. This medium-bodied, seductive wine should be drunk over the next 5–6 years.

ELISABETTA

1998 Le Marze	C	89

Elisabetta's 1998 Le Marze, a blend of 45% Merlot, 45% Cabernet Sauvignon, and 10% Cabernet Franc, is reminiscent of a midlevel St.-Emilion. It offers up scents of cedar, tobacco, licorice, dried herbs, red and black currants, but no evidence of new oak. Ripe, medium-bodied, complex, and supple, it should be consumed over the next 5–6 years.

FANTI

1999 Rosso di Montalcino	C	90
2000 Sant'Antimo	C	89

One of Italy's most brilliant winemaking consultants, Stefano Chioccioli, has been assisting this estate over the last several years. The 2000 Sant'Antimo (from a vineyard close to the appellation of Montalcino) is a 3,000-case *cuvée* of 100% Sangiovese aged in barrel. It is a full-bodied offering with an opulent, fleshy texture and copious quantities of red and black fruits intermixed with licorice and smoke. It is best drunk during its first 4–6 years of life. The superb 1999 Rosso di Montalcino flaunts sumptuous aromas of strawberry liqueur, cherries, grilled herbs, and meaty notes. Dense, rich, full-bodied, and succulent, with soft tannin, low acidity, and admirable plushness, this fruit bomb should be consumed over the next 3–5 years. Don't miss it!

FATTORIA DI FELSINA

1999 Chianti Classico	C	91
1997 Chianti Classico Riserva	D	90+
1998 Chianti Classico Rancia Riserva	D	90
1997 Chianti Classico Rancia Riserva	D	92+
1997 Fontalloro	E	92
1997 Maestro Raro	E	88

One of my favorite Tuscan producers, Felsina's estate vineyards are situated in a cooler microclimate not far from Siena. Felsina offers two Chianti Classico Riservas, its top-notch regular *cuvée* and its spectacular single-vineyard Rancia Riserva. The serious 1997 Chianti Classico Riserva (4,000 cases of 100% Sangiovese) is structured, dense, concentrated, and ageworthy. It is one of the few 1997s that requires 1–2 years of cellaring. A deep ruby/garnet color is followed by aromas of dried herbs, roasted beef, black cherries, plums, cedar, and leather. On the palate, blackberry fruit makes an appearance. Sweet, pure, long, ripe, and moderately tannic, it will be at its finest between now–2015. The dark ruby-colored 1997 Chianti Classico Rancia Riserva (3,000 cases) is aged two years in large wood as well as small *barriques*. With its chewy, powerful, meaty aromas, this wine begs to be drunk with steak. Notes of licorice, smoke, spice box, cedar, and black cherry jam can be found in this ripe, concentrated, muscular wine. Lay this one away for 2–3 years, and consume it over the following 17–18 years.

The 1998 Chianti Classico Rancia Riserva exhibits plenty of promise for a less highly regarded vintage. A deep ruby/purple color is accompanied by a sumptuous bouquet of sweet licorice intertwined with soy, herbs, leather, spice, black cherries, and plums. Ripe and medium-bodied, with good muscle and structure, it will be drinkable early but will not have the aging potential, volume, or concentration of the 1997.

A dazzling example of a fabulous vintage for Chianti, the full-throttle, opulently textured, explosively ripe, fruity 1999 Chianti Classico possesses a deep ruby color as well as glorious levels of black cherry and berry fruit mixed with tobacco and new saddle leather. It reveals superb purity, a generous mouth-feel with no heaviness, and enough acidity to provide delineation. This ripe, mouth-filling, impeccably balanced Chianti will drink well for 7–8 years, but who can resist its current charms?

Felsina produces two proprietary red wines, one made from 100% Sangioveto, called Fontalloro, and a Cabernet Sauvignon called Maestro Raro. The 1997 Fontalloro may be the finest made from this single vineyard (and I have tasted them back through the early 1980s). There are 3,000 cases of this spectacular wine, aged two years in French oak. Dense ruby/purple-colored, with a chocolate espresso–scented nose infused with cherry liqueur, it is a full-bodied, sweet wine with wonderful fatness, terrific ripeness, plenty of glycerin, and a chewy, long, spicy finish. There is some tannin in this youthful offering, but its appealing flamboyance is attention-getting. It should last for 12–15+ years. Last, the 1997 Maestro Raro (400 cases of 100% Cabernet Sauvignon) is still unformed. A ripe, plum/purple color is accompanied by straightforward cassis fruit, toasty oak, and a rich, chewy, but monolithic personality. It needs more time to firm up and reveal its complexity and delineation. Anticipated maturity: now–2014.

FATTORIA LA FIORITA

1997 Brunello di Montalcino	EE	90

Complex characteristics of leather, plums, prunes, Asian spices, licorice, and dried herbs jump from the glass of this full-bodied, rich, well-endowed Brunello. Its deep garnet/ruby color is accompanied by impressive sweetness, moderate levels of ripe tannin, and a long finish. Based on this effort, among the finest Brunellos I have tasted from this vintage, 1997 promises reasonably forward and accessible wines. Anticipated maturity: 2003–2016.

FONTALEONI

1999 Rosso di San Gimignano	B	88

The 1999 Rosso di San Gimignano represents a superb wine bargain. Its dark ruby/purple color is accompanied by a gorgeous perfume of berry fruit, spice, pepper, and minerals, a sweet entry, good fatness, and a lush, hedonistic finish. It is a wine to purchase by the case and consume over the next 2–3 years.

FATTORIA LE FONTI

1997 Chianti Classico Riserva	D	90
1998 Vito Arturo IGT	D	88
1997 Vito Arturo IGT	D	92

Readers seeking Chiantis with distinctive lushness as well as sweet, espresso-infused, black chocolate, and in-your-face black cherry and berry fruit should check out these offerings from Le Fonti. They reveal a sexy, Pomerol-like seamlessness as well as considerable fat and ripeness. The 1997 Chianti Classico Riserva (100% Sangiovese) reveals smoky notes, great concentration, a voluptuous personality, and gobs of sweet, jammy black fruits intermixed with smoke, chocolate, and espresso. With tremendous purity and ripeness, it is a total turn-on. Drink it over the next 5–7 years. Made in the same style, with more fat as well as additional layers of lush, plump fruit, is the 1997 Vito Arturo (100% Sangiovese Grosso, primarily aged in new French oak). This seamless effort tastes like a chocolate mocha/black cherry infusion. A dense ruby/purple color is accompanied by a creamy-textured, dense, concentrated, medium- to full-bodied, seductive wine. It should drink well for 7–10 years. Made from 100% Sangiovese Grosso, the 1998 Vito Arturo reveals an international style (it was obviously aged in French oak), as well as abundant character in its earthy, black currant, licorice, leathery nose and flavors. Medium-bodied, with ripe tannin and a lot of class, this modern-styled Sangiovese can be consumed now and over the next 7–8 years.

FONTODI

1999 Chianti Classico	D	91
1998 Chianti Classico	C	88
1998 Chianti Classico Vigna del Sorbo Riserva	D	89
1997 Chianti Classico Vigna del Sorbo Riserva	D	90
1998 Flaccianello della Pieve IGT	E	89
1997 Flaccianello della Pieve IGT	E	93
1998 Syrah Case Via IGT	D	90?
1997 Syrah Case Via IGT	D	90

One of Tuscany's finest producers, Fontodi is a name readers can rely on for high-quality wines, particularly in the finest vintages. In particular, its single-vineyard Chianti Classico

Vigna del Sorbo and proprietary Sangiovese, Flaccianello della Pieve, are among the best of their types. The knockout 1999 Chianti Classico (100% Sangiovese) provides more evidence of just how terrific this vintage is in Tuscany, particularly for Chianti. Complex aromas of new saddle leather, jammy black cherry liqueur, and other black fruits jump from the glass of this dense ruby-colored wine. There are layers of fruit and extraction, full body, no hard edges, and an explosive, long finish that lasts for nearly 30 seconds. Enjoy it now and over the next decade. The quality of the 1999 vintage is even more apparent when one tastes the 1998 Chianti Classico Vigna del Sorbo Riserva. This can be a stunning *cuvée*, but in the more austere, tannic 1998 vintage, the Riserva is not as good as the less expensive 1999 regular bottling. However, it is still a fine effort. The 1998's dark ruby/purple color is followed by a big nose of licorice, liquefied minerals, tar, underbrush, and plum/berry fruit. Spicy, dense, medium-bodied, and moderately tannic, 1–2 years of cellaring is recommended, although the tannin will never completely melt away. Anticipated maturity: 2003–2012.

The dark ruby-colored, soft, earthy, smoky, berry fruit–laden 1998 Chianti Classico possesses beautiful purity, sweet fruit, and adequate acidity. It is meant to be drunk over the next several years. The outstanding 1997 Chianti Classico Vigna del Sorbo Riserva (a 2,000-case blend of 85% Sangiovese and 15% Cabernet Sauvignon) exhibits a dense ruby color, as well as Chianti's quintessential blend of elegance and power. Deep, rich, and concentrated, with notes of sweet new saddle leather, black cherries, balsa wood, spice box, and smoke, it has terrific fruit intensity and purity, together with balance and finesse. This compelling Chianti should drink well for a decade.

The proprietary 100% Sangiovese *cuvée*, the 1998 Flaccianello della Pieve, was aged 12 months in French oak. Unlike the more opulent 1997 Flaccianello, the 1998 reveals dry, hard tannin in the finish. A deep ruby/purple color is followed by abundant scents of toasty new oak, black cherries, minerals, and spice box. Dry, long, and well made for the vintage, it will be at its finest between 2003–2012. The 1998 Syrah Case Via (100% Syrah aged one year in French oak) exhibits a classic bacon fat, blackberry, crème de cassis character, full-bodied, smoky flavors, rustic tannin, and gorgeous levels of fruit, extract, and ripeness. The only flaw in this impressive, somewhat internationally styled offering is the slightly elevated tannin. Drink it over the next 10–12 years.

There are 3,500 cases of the 1997 Flaccianello della Pieve, a 100% Sangiovese aged in new French oak for 18 months. The 1997 is one of the finest Flaccianellos yet produced. A dark ruby/purple color is followed by a strikingly fragrant nose of saddle leather, cedar, licorice, vanilla, and black cherry/blackberry fruit. The wine possesses medium to full body, gorgeous delineation, fine ripeness, and a sweet, glycerin-imbued, long finish. Given the vintage's glycerin level and opulence, it can be drunk now, but it promises to last for 15 or more years. One of Tuscany's breakthrough Syrah efforts is Fontodi's 1997 Syrah Case Via (1,000 cases). It offers textbook peppery, blackberry notes, low acidity (particularly for an Italian wine), deep, chewy, unctuously textured fruit, full body, and a chunky, husky finish. It should drink well for 8–10 years.

FRIGGIALI

1999 Rosso di Montalcino	C	90

Another gorgeous 1999 Rosso di Montalcino, Friggiali's offering exhibits a dark plum color along with a gorgeous bouquet of currants, cherry jam, underbrush, spice, and balsa wood. Extremely spicy, with tremendous fruit, a supple, fleshy texture, and medium to full body, it is meant to be consumed over the next 5–6 years.

LA FUGA

1999 Rosso di Montalcino	D	89

The delicious, sweet, fleshy, freakishly ripe, deep ruby-colored 1999 Rosso di Montalcino reveals copious quantities of glycerin as well as strawberry and black cherry fruit. This fruity Rosso should be enjoyed over the next 3–4 years for its exuberance and fruit.

EREDI FULIGNI

1997 Rosso di Montalcino Sanjacopo	D	90

The 1997 Rosso di Montalcino Sanjacopo is a gorgeously rich, ripe, low-acid offering made of 80% Sangiovese Grosso and 20% Merlot. It exhibits sweet strawberry jam–like notes intermixed with Asian spices, underbrush, and incense. Dense and rich, with a voluptuous texture, low acidity, and outstanding ripeness and fruit, it should be consumed over the next 3–4 years.

GAGLIOLE

1999 Pecchia IGT	E	92
1999 Rosso IGT	E	89
1998 Rosso IGT	E	90
1997 Rosso IGT	E	92

There are 1,200 cases of the 1999 Rosso and 250 cases of the 1999 Pecchia. More important, Gagliole's consulting oenologist is the brilliant Luca d'Attoma, the man responsible for some of the most exciting wines emerging from Tuscany. The 1999 Rosso is a blend of 90% Sangiovese and 10% Cabernet Sauvignon, aged 18 months in French oak prior to being bottled unfiltered. Its dense ruby/purple color is followed by smoky, ripe scents of black currants, cherries, and vanilla. Layered, with a plush midsection, an enticing texture, and a firm, elegant, pure finish, this stylized wine can be drunk now or cellared for a decade. The sensational, opaque ruby/purple-colored 1999 Pecchia (100% Sangiovese) displays how unusually ripe and concentrated the 1999 vintage was in Tuscany. It boasts an opaque purple color as well as a glorious bouquet of black fruits, lead pencil, vanilla, smoke, and flowers. Dense and full-bodied, with abundant structure, outstanding purity, harmony, and overall depth, this is a powerful (14.5% alcohol) effort with extraordinary finesse. Anticipated maturity: 2003–2020.

This relatively young (the debut vintage was 1994) operation fashioned two beautiful blends of 90% Sangiovese and 10% Cabernet Sauvignon in 1997 and 1998. Yields are kept extremely low (less than 30 hectoliters per hectare), and production prior to 1999 was approximately 1,300 cases of each vintage. The impressive 1997 Rosso boasts a dense purple color as well as a ripe nose of blackberries, smoke, tobacco, chocolate, and toast. Complex aromatics lead to a medium- to full-bodied wine with a gorgeously sweet, opulently textured attack and mid-palate. With beautiful purity, freshness, and overall harmony, it will drink well for a decade. Although less opulent, the 1998 Rosso is a medium- to full-bodied, ripe, evolved, tobacco-tinged, cedary, spice box, and red cherry/black currant–scented and –flavored wine with mature tannin, a fat, chewy mid-palate, and good acidity for freshness and delineation. It should drink well for 7–8 years.

LA GERLA

1997 Birba IGT	D	88

The deep ruby-colored 1997 Birba reveals a big, spicy, internationally styled nose of new oak, red and black currants, and smoke. Medium-bodied, clean, and supple, this 1997 red is best drunk over the next 3–4 years.

I GIUSTI E ZANZA

1999 Belcore	D	91
1998 Belcore	C	90

1998 Dulcamara	E	91+
1997 Dulcamara	E	93

A new limited-production winery (1996 was its first vintage), I Giusti e Zanza produces a 90% Sangiovese/10% Merlot blend called Belcore and an 80% Cabernet Sauvignon/20% Cabernet Franc and Merlot blend called Dulcamara. Both of these wines are aged in French oak and bottled following a light filtration. From one of Tuscany's warmest microclimates, these wines are fashioned by one of Italy's up-and-coming brilliant consultants, Stefano Chioccioli. The 1999 Belcore is a 3,000-plus-case *cuvée* of 90% Sangiovese and 10% Merlot aged in large, 300-liter barrels. Its dense purple color is followed by a sexy, open-knit nose offering explosive aromas of toast, blackberry, and cherry liqueur intermixed with currants. Spicy, fleshy, full-bodied, ripe, and seductive, it will drink well for 5–6 years. A blend of 80% Cabernet Sauvignon and 20% Cabernet Franc/Merlot, the 1998 Dulcamara was produced in only 580 cases. Opaque purple-colored, with a heavy overlay of graphite and smoky oak mixed with jammy cassis, it comes across like a top-quality Bordeaux with its cedar, mineral, and black fruit characteristics. Dense, full-bodied, long, ripe, and concentrated, with impressive delineation as well as extract, sweet tannin, and low acidity, it will be at its finest between 2003–2017.

The 1998 Belcore (17,000 bottles) is typical of the newer-styled, high-quality Italian reds, being low in acidity, dense, and opulent, with explosive ripeness (some might say overripeness) and rich black cherry and blackberry fruit infused with toasty oak, spice box, and cedar notes. There are gorgeous layers of concentration. Since there is no history on this wine, it is probably best consumed during its first 7–8 years of life. The opaque ruby/purple-colored 1997 Dulcamara (500 cases) exhibits a knockout nose of cigar tobacco, cedar wood, blackberry liqueur, cassis, and vanilla. Exciting on the palate, it offers a combination of power and glycerin in addition to a multilayered texture. The finish of this full-throttle, concentrated wine is equally impressive. It should drink well for a decade.

GORELLI

1997 Brunello di Montalcino Le Potazzine	E	96
1999 Rosso di Montalcino Le Potazzine	C	89

Another tasty Rosso di Montalcino from the superb 1999 vintage, the high-altitude vineyard of Le Potazzine produced a deep ruby/purple-colored effort with a sweet nose of black raspberry and cherry fruit, medium body, no hard edges, and excellent purity as well as liveliness. Drink it over the next 3–5 years. Gorelli's 1997 Brunello di Montalcino Le Potazzine is reminiscent of the famed Spanish wine called Pingus from Ribera del Duero. Its opaque garnet color is followed by an extraordinarily provocative perfume of black fruits, espresso, roasted meats, and plum/prune elements. New saddle leather and Asian spice aromas also make an appearance. Viscous, huge, and oozing with concentration, this remarkable effort is pure, thick, and surprisingly approachable for such a young, massive Brunello. Anticipated maturity: now–2016. This is a tour de force in winemaking!

PODERE LANCIOLA II

1997 Terricci IGT	D	89

One of Italy's young, talented wine consultants, Stefano Chioccioli, is behind Lanciola's rise in quality. The proprietary red wine offering, the 1997 Terricci, is a blend of 80% Sangiovese, 10% Cabernet Sauvignon, and equal parts Cabernet Franc and Merlot. It is a compressed, complex, plum/purple-colored effort with plenty of chewy currant/cherry fruit, saddle leather, animal fur, earth, and graphite. Although approximately 70% new French *barriques* were utilized, the oak characteristic is subdued in the wine's aromas and flavors. The finish is moderately tannic. Cellar this 1997 for another 1–2 years, and enjoy it over the following 12–14 years.

LISINI

1999 Rosso di Montalcino	C	90

With the consultation of Franco Bernabei, Lisini has been producing fine wines after a slump in quality during the late 1970s and early 1980s. Lisini has produced a stunning 1999 Rosso di Montalcino. Its deep ruby color is accompanied by terrific sweet black cherry and strawberry fruit notes intermixed with new saddle leather, balsa wood, spice box, and cedar. Sweet, with loads of glycerin, medium body, ripe tannin, and abundant spice, this wine will provide provocative, compelling drinking over the next 8–10 years.

FATTORIA DI LUCIGNANO

1999 Chianti Classico Colli Fiorentini	A	88

There are 8,000 cases of Lucignano's 1999 Chianti Classico Colli Fiorentini, consistently one of the finest values from Chianti. It is a richly fruity, delicious, strawberry and cherry fruit bomb with supple texture, abundant spice, medium body, and good glycerin. Enjoy it over the next 2–3 years.

LE MACCHIOLE

1999 Macchiole Rosso	D	90
1998 Macchiole Rosso	C	91
1998 Messorio	EEE	96+
1997 Messorio	EE	98
1997 Paleo Rosso	E	92
1999 Scrio	EEE	95
1997 Scrio	E	90

This 42-acre estate situated along the Tuscan coast is owned by Eugenio Campolmi, who had the foresight to bring in one of the region's most brilliant wine-makers, Luca d'Attoma. Production ranges from 2,000+ cases of the Macchiole Rosso to 2,500 cases of the Paleo Rosso and a minuscule 250 cases or less each of the Messorio (100% Merlot) and Scrio (100% Syrah). Among the most compelling wines being produced in Italy, they are extraordinary examples of an owner's uncompromising commitment to producing world-class wines.

The 1999 Macchiole Rosso is a blend of 95% Sangiovese and 5% Cabernet Sauvignon aged in French *barriques* before being bottled without fining or filtration. Its complex bouquet offers scents of cedar, new saddle leather, dried herbs, espresso beans, chocolate, and black fruits (plums and currants). Supple, complete, concentrated, and lush, it will drink well for 7–8 years. Even more promising is the 1997 Paleo Rosso, an unfined, unfiltered, *barrique*-aged blend of 80% Cabernet Sauvignon, 10% Sangiovese, and 10% Cabernet Franc. Its opaque ruby/purple color is followed by a sweet nose of licorice, smoke, graphite, blackberries, and cassis. Full-bodied, with a roasted meat character to its flavors, extraordinary purity and concentration, and beautifully integrated acidity as well as tannin, this blockbuster is a candidate for drinking now or cellaring for 15–17 years.

There are only microscopic quantities available of the following two wines, so I will keep my tasting notes somewhat streamlined, even though both wines merit near-perfect scores. Le Macchiole's Scrio is the most profound Syrah being made in Italy. Unfined, unfiltered, and produced from incredibly tiny yields, the black/purple-colored 1999 offers scents of licorice, melted tar, truffles, and blackberry liqueur. Full-bodied and opulent, with high tannin but compelling sweetness and a multilayered palate, it requires 3–4 years of cellaring but should age for two decades. It could easily compete with some of the Rhône Valley's great Hermitages. The 1998 Messorio (100% Merlot) rivals some of the finest Merlots being produced anywhere in the world. Mind-blowing in its richness and intensity, it can compete with the finest wines being made on the Pomerol plateau. Representing the essence of Merlot in its concentrated jammy blackberry and cherry notes, it is a well-defined, beautifully poised effort revealing both power and elegance. Full-bodied, dense, and super-concentrated, with an incredibly long 50-second finish, it is a tour de force in winemaking that must be tasted to be believed. Anticipated maturity: 2004–2016. These are prodigious wines. It's a shame that the quantities are so limited.

There are approximately 2,000 cases of the 1998 Macchiole Rosso, a wine aged in barrel prior to being bottled with neither fining nor filtering. Aromas of blackberry/cassis fruit intertwined with smoke and licorice jump from the glass of this fragrant wine. Intense and opulently styled, with low acidity, medium to full body, and nicely integrated toasty oak, this blend of 95% Sangiovese and 5% Cabernet Sauvignon will offer compelling drinking over the next 7–8 years.

Quantities of the Merlot from the Messorio vineyard are limited (approximately 40–50 cases in 1997), but production is expected to increase slightly in future vintages. The purpose of writing about a wine of such limited availability is that *Wine Advocate* subscribers can get a head start, as this will certainly become one of the great new wines of Italy. The awesome 1997 Merlot Messorio is truly prodigious. Black/purple-colored, it boasts an astonishingly rich nose of black raspberries, smoky new oak, dried herbs, and cedar. Chocolate, new saddle leather, and exhilarating levels of black fruits give this wine a luxurious, voluptuous texture. The finish lasts for nearly a minute! A winemaking tour de force that is already accessible given its expansive, open-knit texture, it should last for 12–15+ years.

The rustic 1997 Syrah Scrio is a dense, chewy, muscular wine with rough tannin, yet impressive concentration and purity. It should become more civilized with another 1–2 years of bottle age and will last for 10–12 years. Bravo!

LE MACIOCHE

1997 Brunello di Montalcino	E	88+

An attractive coconut-like aroma (reminiscent of American oak) rises from the glass of this medium-bodied, elegant, stylish, plum/garnet-colored 1997 Brunello di Montalcino. The coconut scents are accompanied by abundant quantities of currant fruit, smoke, and toast. While not the most flamboyant or concentrated of the soon-to-be-released 1997 Brunellos, it is exotic and distinctive. Drink it over the next 8 years.

FATTORIA LA MAGIA

1999 Rosso di Montalcino	C	89

1999 Rossos di Montalcino are high on my list of realistically priced wines to purchase in 2002. They offer loads of sweet fruit, plenty of glycerin, and a rich, concentrated, velvety style. Fattoria La Magia's 1999 (3,000 cases) is a chewy effort displaying gorgeous levels of sweet cherry fruit intermixed with a kirschlike note. Fresh, ripe, medium-bodied, and supple, it will drink well for 3–5 years. It was bottled unfiltered by the estate's oenologist, Roberto Cipresso.

LA MASSA

1999 Chianti Classico	D	88
1998 Chianti Classico Giorgio Primo	E	89+?
1997 Chianti Classico Giorgio Primo	E	90

Of these three attractive offerings, the less expensive 1999 Chianti Classico is further proof of how wonderful this vintage was throughout Tuscany. For a low-level wine, it delivers plenty of pleasure in its dark ruby color and a bouquet of sweet currant and black cherries intermixed with oak and spice. Fleshy and succulent, it should be consumed over the next 2–3 years to take advantage of its youthful charm. The single-vineyard Giorgio Primo *cuvée* is successful in both the more austere 1998 and more exotic, ripe 1997 vintages. The dark ruby-colored 1998 Chianti Classico Giorgio Primo offers dense currant and cherry aromas mixed with scents of new French oak. Structured, rich, and concentrated, it possesses abundant tannin but adequate sweetness for balance. Drink it over the next 12–14 years. The fleshier, more open-knit 1997 Chianti Classico Giorgio Primo exhibits that vintage's higher glycerin and more expansive nature. Beautiful notes of black cherries, currants, new oak, and spice are found in this dark ruby/purple-colored offering. Long, dense, youthful, and vibrant, it is best consumed during its first 10–15 years of life.

MONTE BERNARDI

1997	Chianti Classico	C	90
1999	Chianti Classico Paris	D	90
1999	Sa'etta IGT	E	91+
1997	Sa'etta IGT	E	90+
1999	Tzingana IGT	EE	90
1997	Tzingana IGT	E	92

These artisanal wines come at a high price, but they are interestingly packaged and, most important, impressive. The dazzling, dark ruby/purple-colored 1999 Chianti Classico Paris offers a fabulous aromatic profile of sweet black raspberry and currant fruit, new oak, and saddle leather. Ripe, textured, and intense, with super purity and a long, medium- to full-bodied, symmetrical finish, it is accessible but promises to be even better with another 1–2 years of cellaring. It will last for 12–15 years. The *barrique*-aged *cuvée* of 100% Sangiovese, the 1999 Sa'etta, boasts an opaque purple color in addition to a sweet nose of black currants, blackberries, smoke, and vanilla. The wine is full-bodied and ripe, with melted tannin, exceptional concentration, and a long finish. Initially, I thought it was internationally styled, but Sangiovese's distinctive character emerges as the wine sits in the glass. Anticipated maturity: now–2014. The superexpensive, internationally styled 1999 Tzingana (a Bordeaux-like blend of Merlot, Cabernet Franc, Cabernet Sauvignon, and Petit Verdot) is impeccably well made. There are copious quantities of new oak in its blackberry, currant, licorice, and smoke-scented bouquet, medium- to full-bodied flavors, and moderate tannin in the long finish. No trace of Tuscan typicity can be found in this exceptional offering. Drink it over the next 10–14 years.

It will be hard, even in the top-notch vintage of 1997, to find a better Chianti than Monte Bernardi's 1997 Chianti Classico. Dense ruby-colored, with fabulous fruit, it unwinds on the palate to reveal expansive, sweet black cherry and berry flavors intertwined with tobacco, spice box, and dried herbs. With abundant glycerin and an opulent texture, this *barrique*-aged Chianti is terrific. Drink it over the next 5–6 years. The proprietary red, the 1997 Sa'etta *vino da tavola*, is a *barrique*-aged 100% Sangiovese. The dense ruby/purple color is followed by a voluptuously textured, medium- to full-bodied, low-acid wine with stunning quantities of red and black fruits. It should drink well for 7–8 years. The Cabernet Sauvignon, Merlot, and Cabernet Franc *vino da tavola* from Monte Bernardi is called Tzingana. The 1997 Tzingana is undeniably sexy, revealing a dense purple color in addition to a gorgeous display of blackberries, plums, licorice, and toasty new oak. Sweet (because of high glycerin and alcohol), with low acidity and layers of concentrated fruit, this terrific proprietary red should drink well for a decade.

FATTORIA DI MONTELLORI

1997	Salamartano	D	89

Montellori's proprietary red wine, the 1997 Salamartano (equal parts Cabernet Sauvignon and Merlot), is noticeably tannic and backward, as well as internationally styled. The dark ruby/purple color is followed by moderately intense aromas of black currants, sweet cherries, and spicy new oak. Structured and tannic, it requires 1–2 years of cellaring and should age well for 10–12 years.

MONTEPELOSO

1999	Gabbro IGT	EE	94
1998	Gabbro IGT	EE	93
1999	Nardo IGT	EE	94
1998	Nardo IGT	E	90
1997	Nardo IGT	E	89
1999	Rosso Val di Cornia	D	92

This estate is located in Suvereto, a subregion of Tuscany that is becoming famous for the extraordinary quality of its wines. (The impressive estate of Tua Rita is nearby.) Montepeloso's wines are made by the highly esteemed consultant Luca d'Attoma. All three of the 1999s were produced from incredibly low yields (24 hectoliters per hectare for the Rosso and 8 hectoliters per hectare for the Gabbro and Nardo), aged in *barrique* (1–2 years old for the Rosso and 100% new for the Gabbro and Nardo), and bottled without filtration. The dazzling 1999 Rosso Val di Cornia combines power, luxurious fruit, and elegance. Its dense saturated ruby/purple color is followed by a sweet nose of ripe black fruits, licorice, smoke, and graphite. Opulent, rich, and full-bodied, with layers of fruit, no hard edges, amazing delineation, and admirable concentration, this pure, symmetrical effort should drink well for 8–10 years. The limited-production 1999 Nardo, a blend of 90% Sangiovese and 10% Cabernet Sauvignon, takes concentration to its limits. It exhibits toasty new oak and the essence of black cherry liqueur in its perfumed bouquet. A full-bodied as well as layered palate impression, combined with fabulous purity and depth, are hallmarks of this wine. The 14.5% alcohol content is high by Tuscan standards, but it is beautifully integrated and not the least bit hot. This tour de force in winemaking should age for 12–15 years.

Produced from 100% Cabernet Sauvignon and aged in 100% new French oak, the 1999 Gabbro boasts an inky, opaque purple color as well as a backward but promising bouquet of lead pencil, crème de cassis, toast, and melted licorice. Full-bodied, powerful, and profoundly concentrated, this dramatic wine could easily be inserted into a blind tasting with barrel samples of the 2000 Médocs. The finish lasts for 30–35 seconds. The evolution of this wine should be fascinating to follow.

The debut vintage of the 100% Cabernet Sauvignon *cuvée*, the 1998 Gabbro, is a terrific example of what can be produced in this area adjacent to the Mediterranean. Keep in mind that the famous Sassicaia is close by, as are the hillside vineyards of the cult wine Tua Rita. The saturated black/purple-colored 1998 Gabbro boasts sumptuous aromatics of cherry liqueur, cassis, toasty new oak, minerals, spice box, and tobacco. There are extravagant intensity, an opulent texture, and a large-scaled, rich, concentrated finish. It should be cellared for 2–3 years and drunk over the following 12–15.

The 1997 Nardo has an elegant, dark ruby/purple color followed by abundant quantities of sweet blackberry and currant fruit and a rich, spicy, concentrated, medium- to full-bodied palate with good underlying acidity. Gritty tannin kept my score low. This wine should age nicely for a decade. Better balanced is the 1998 Nardo. In this area of Tuscany, known as Bolgheri, many growers consider 1998 an even better vintage than 1997. That is certainly borne out by the 1998 Montepeloso Nardo. It exhibits a deeper, more saturated ruby/purple color in addition to gorgeously jammy blackberry and cassis flavors infused with smoke, minerals, licorice, and toast. There are terrific intensity as well as a long, medium- to full-bodied finish with well-integrated acidity, tannin, and wood. It should drink well for 10–15 years.

GIACOMO MORI

2000	Chianti	B	90
1999	Chianti Castelrotto	C	91
1998	Chianti Castelrotto	C	88

Since Marc De Grazia began working with this estate, quality has risen. For $13.50 it will be hard to find a better Tuscan offering than Mori's 2000 Chianti. An opaque purple color is accompanied by powerful aromas of black cherry jam, blackberries, licorice, minerals, and earth, considerable stuffing, a succulent, full-bodied, supple style, and loads of fruit as well as extract. A layered finish adds to the overall appeal of this dynamite Chianti. Drink it over the next 4–5 years, although I suspect it will last longer. Aged 100% in *barrique*, the single-vineyard 1999 Chianti Castelrotto is a full-bodied, dense purple-colored effort with extraordinary opulence, a more complex perfume than its less expensive sibling, and more volume/length. With higher tannin as well as extract, it will benefit from another 1–2 years of cellaring. It will age for 10–12 years. Giacomo Mori's 1998 Chianti Castelrotto reveals spicy oak along with leather, mineral, licorice, and cherry flavors. With medium body, some tannin, but unobtrusive structure, it is best consumed over the next 3–5 years.

I MORI

1999 Chianti Colli Fiorentini	B	88
1998 Moresco IGT	C	92

The 1998 Moresco, a *barrique*-aged blend of 70% Sangiovese and 30% Cabernet Sauvignon, boasts an opaque purple color as well as a bouquet of earth, vanilla, black currants, and espresso. Full-bodied, powerful, concentrated, and moderately tannic, with a long, intense, pure finish, this youthful, unevolved IGT requires 2–3 years of cellaring. It should evolve for 12–15 years. Bravo! The 1999 Chianti Colli Fiorentini (100% Sangiovese) is a serious effort, revealing cherries, strawberries, and new saddle leather joined by earth, dried herb, and tobacco characteristics. The wine is long and structured, with excellent fruit as well as depth. Drink it over the next 4–5 years.

MORIS FARMS

1999 Avvoltore IGT	D	90
1998 Avvoltore IGT	D	88+
1997 Avvoltore IGT	D	92
1999 Morellino di Scansano	B	88
1997 Morellino di Scansano Riserva	C	91

The two Morellinos di Scansano represent sensational bargains. They might be called the "poor person's Brunello di Montalcino," but they are qualitatively better than that suggests. The 1999 Morellino di Scansano smells like a chocolate espresso. Moreover, there are 2,500 cases exported to the United States. It exhibits lush, black cherry fruit, explosive ripeness, a supple texture, low acidity, and copious quantities of black fruit. Consume it now and over the next 4–5 years. The 1997 Morellino di Scansano Riserva boasts a dense ruby color as well as the telltale opulence of the 1997 vintage. Five hundred cases made it to U.S. shores. Creamy, coffee, blackberry, and cherry notes jump from the glass of this full-bodied, dense, supple-textured, voluptuous wine. A hedonist's dream, it is a fruit bomb with complexity, balance, and richness. Drink it over the next 6–7 years.

The 1999 Avvoltore from the single vineyard called Poggio alla Mozza is made from 75% Sangiovese, 20% Cabernet Sauvignon, and 5% Syrah aged for 18 months in French *barriques*. Yields were a lowly 24 hectoliters per hectare. The wine is deep, backward, medium-to full-bodied, powerful yet elegant, with sweet black currant and cherry fruit intermixed with lead pencil, vanilla, and spice. Displaying superb purity, a beautiful mid-palate, good fleshiness, and a long, pure finish, it is young and unevolved but accessible. Drink it over the next 10–15 years. Moris Farms' 1998 Avvoltore was closed the day I saw it, revealing a dense, dark ruby color, and notes of Provençal herbs mixed with black cherries, earth, and oak. Although medium- to full-bodied, with plenty of power, it was muted and not exhibiting nearly as much character, charm, or hedonistic appeal as its two less expensive siblings. Anticipated maturity: now–2014.

The 1997 Avvoltore, a blend of 20% Cabernet Sauvignon, 75% Sangiovese, and 5% Syrah, was aged for 12 months in French oak casks. Sadly, there were only 200 cases produced, but readers lucky enough to latch onto a bottle or two are in for a spectacular drinking experience. The wine's opaque purple color is followed by a sweet nose of minerals, white truffles, black raspberries, and cherry jam. Massively flavored, with full body, a silky texture, and a touch of spice and tar in the long, convincing finish, it should drink well for at least a decade.

LE MURELLE

1998 Niffo IGT	C	90

One hundred fifty cases of this opaque purple-colored blend of 90% Sangiovese and 10% Cabernet Sauvignon were produced. It exhibits aromas of blackberry and cassis fruit mixed with allspice, cinnamon, and vanilla. Deep and heady, with gorgeous fruit purity, full body, and low acidity, this superrich, lush, concentrated wine should drink well for 7–8 years.

NOTTOLA

1998 Vino Nobile di Montepulciano Vigna del Fattore	C	90
1997 Vino Nobile di Montepulciano Vigna del Fattore	C	92

The 1998 has a beautifully complex, elegant bouquet of cedar, spice box, tobacco, strawberries, and black cherry jam followed by medium body and supple texture, with luscious fruit, superb harmony, and ripe tannin. Nothing is out of balance in this seductive 1998. Drink it over the next 4–7 years. One of the finest Vini Nobili I have ever tasted, the dark ruby/plum-colored 1997 offers a sweet, explosive nose of melted chocolate, cedar, saddle leather, jammy blackberry/cherry fruit, and flowers. The wine offers tremendously dense, concentrated richness, a velvety texture, and low acidity, as well as this historic vintage's telltale high glycerin, opulence, and fruit. Drink this beauty over the next 12–15 years. Given the score vis à vis the cost, this is an exceptional value. Not surprisingly, Riccardo Cotarella is Nottola's oenologist.

OLIVETO

1999 Rosso di Montalcino Il Roccolo	C	90

An outstanding offering, Oliveto's 1999 Rosso di Montalcino Il Roccolo (100% Sangiovese Grosso aged 12 months in a combination of new and one-year-old French oak) exhibits a deep ruby color in addition to a provocative bouquet of sweet blueberry and black currant fruit, lovely ripeness, a balanced, medium-bodied personality, and a long, fruity, ripe, tannic finish. It should drink well for 5–7 years. Oliveto's oenologist is Roberto Cipresso.

PODERE IL PALAZZINO

1999 Chianti Classico Argenina	C	89
1998 Chianti Classico Grosso Sanese	D	91
1999 Chianti Classico La Pieve	C	91
1997 Grosso Sanese	D	88

The hallmark of these wines has always been concentrated intensity married to exceptional elegance in a delineated style. Il Palazzino's new offerings performed remarkably well, and the fact that I rated the 1998 Grosso Sanese higher than the 1997 makes me think that I seriously underrated the 1997 (a better vintage than 1998).

The two 1999 releases are both topflight. The deep ruby-colored 1999 Chianti Classico Argenina reveals an elegant style not dissimilar from that of a top-notch Burgundian Volnay from a producer such as d'Angerville. Sweet floral-infused black cherry/framboise-like aromas are accompanied by rich, medium-bodied flavors, a beautiful texture, considerable finesse, and stunning elegance as well as purity. It should drink well for a decade. The sensational 1999 Chianti Classico La Pieve represents a fabulous bargain for such a complex and multidimensional effort. It offers a gorgeous display of strawberry jam intermixed with nearly overripe cherries, subtle vanilla, and abundant mineral/floral notes. Extraordinary ripeness, tremendous fat and glycerin, and uncanny delineation/focus have resulted in a prodigious Chianti Classico to drink over the next decade. The opaque ruby/purple-colored 1998 Chianti Classico Grosso Sanese does not suffer from the excessively austere, tannic style revealed by many 1998 central Tuscan efforts. It is rich and multilayered, with copious quantities of blackberry and cassis fruit mixed with cherries, licorice, toast, and spice. This dense Chianti will benefit from 1–2 years of cellaring and last for 14–15 years. Bravo!

I expected the 1997 Grosso Sanese to possess more opulence and richness given the vintage, but it comes across like a mid-weight Burgundy with its raspberry and cherry fruit and floral character. Now, this makes an appearance in this dark ruby/purple-colored, stylish, graceful, subtle effort. It should drink well for 7–8 years.

FATTORIA PARADISO

1998 Eterno II IGT	D	90
1997 Paterno II IGT	D	91
1999 Saxa Calida IGT	D	92
1997 Saxa Calida IGT	D	93

An impressive quartet from proprietor Paolo Caciorgna, these gorgeous, heavy-duty fruit bombs are atypical for Tuscany. Produced from 100% Sangiovese, the 1998 Eterno II exhibits a striking nose of black fruits, cedar, and spice box aromas. Full-bodied, sexy, and silky-textured, this luscious Italian red deftly balances power and precision with a sense of freshness. Drink this hedonistic 1998 over the next 5–6 years. The inky/black/purple-colored 1999 Saxa Calida, a blend of Cabernet Sauvignon and Merlot, reveals a textbook bouquet of black currants, licorice, melted tar, and new-*barrique* aromas. Extremely full-bodied, low in acidity, and nearly viscous, this chewy, thick, modern-styled red is hard to resist. Importer David Hinkle claims that his clients refer to this wine as "hot sex." Ummm! Enjoy it over the next 7–8 years.

Made from 100% Sangiovese aged in French oak, the 1997 Paterno II exhibits a dense ruby/purple color, flamboyant, smoky, chocolate, espresso, and cherry-driven aromas and flavors, a voluptuous, beautifully rendered texture, fine purity, superb, jammy ripeness, and a dense, chewy, full-bodied finish that lasts for nearly 30 seconds. It is an outstanding wine that should drink well for 7–8 years. Even better is the single-vineyard 1997 Saxa Calida (Latin for "hot stones"). There are 300 cases of this Merlot/Cabernet Sauvignon blend aged in French oak. It boasts a dense ruby/purple color as well as big, thick, chewy, mocha, black currant, and kirschlike aromas and flavors, fabulous purity, well-integrated, smoky wood, an unctuous texture, low acidity, and an explosive finish. Already delicious, it promises to evolve for a decade. These are impressive offerings from the historic village of San Gimignano.

FATTORIA DI PETROIO

1999 Chianti Classico	C	90
1998 Chianti Classico Riserva	D	88?

I have enjoyed tasting the 1999 Tuscan wines, including the early-released, big, fruity Rossos di Montalcino and the first Chiantis to hit these shores. There are 4,000 cases of the 1999 Chianti Classico, an elegant, dark ruby/purple-colored Chianti with excellent sweet raspberry and cherry fruit presented in a pure style. Saddle leather, underbrush, and Provençal herb characteristics are present, but this wine is dominated by its fruit, purity, and symmetry. Medium-bodied and luscious, it will drink well for 2–3 years. The 1998 vintage produced more austere wines, except for the coastal areas, particularly Bolgheri. The densely-colored 1998 Chianti Classico Riserva possesses earthy, smoky, charcoal, meat, and truffle-like notes along with dark red fruits. Medium-bodied, well balanced, serious, tannic, and broodingly backward, this wine has tannins that will never fully melt away. Consume it over the next 7–10 years.

FATTORIA PETROLO

1999 Galatrona IGT	E	95
1997 Galatrona IGT	D	94
1999 Terre di Galatrona IGT	C	88
1998 Torrione IGT	D	89
1997 Torrione IGT	D	91

This 77-acre estate has turned out five interesting red wines. The 100% Sangiovese, *barrique*-aged 1998 Torrione avoids some of the vintage's austerity as well as its tough tannin. Unlike many 1998s, it is soft with sweet cherry, saddle leather, and damp soil aromas. Stylish, elegant, rich, and seamless, it will drink well for 6–7 years. The extremely concentrated, massive, full-bodied 1999 Galatrona takes Merlot to the limits of ripeness and intensity. This is "extreme" Merlot, but wow, what an impressive wine! Made from 100% Merlot aged in 100% new French oak, this opaque purple-colored 1999 exhibits phenomenally ripe notes of jammy blackberry and cherry fruit intermixed with roasted coffee and toast. Unctuously textured and thick, with moderate tannin, this huge, viscous wine needs to settle down, but there is unbelievable upside potential to the raw materials present in the bottle. Anticipated maturity: 2005–2020.

A blend of 70% Sangiovese and 30% Merlot, the dark ruby-colored 1999 Terre di Galatrona offers copious quantities of red and black fruits intermixed with spicy wood, new saddle leather, and earth. It possesses surprising complexity for its price, in addition to medium body, a harmonious palate, and nicely integrated acidity and tannin. It should drink well for 3–4 years. The stunning, opaque purple-colored 1997 Torrione (100% Sangiovese, aged 12–18 months in French barrels) offers a supersweet nose of cherry and strawberry jam intertwined with new saddle leather, spicy oak, tobacco, and cigar box aromas. Full-bodied, rich, and multilayered, with a sweet mid-palate and inner core of concentration, this sumptuous, low-acid, fat Sangiovese will provide opulent drinking for a decade. Absolutely awesome is the 100% Merlot *cuvée*, the 1997 Galatrona. Aged in 100% new oak, it offers additional evidence that outside Pomerol, the world's finest Merlot is produced in Tuscany. An opaque purple color is followed by an explosively rich bouquet of jammy blackberries, chocolate, mocha, and espresso. This full-bodied, thick, unctuously textured effort possesses superb purity, great concentration, and overall symmetry, as well as a finish that lasts for 35+ seconds. The acidity is low, with the wine's tannin largely concealed by the high extract level. Anticipated maturity: now–2015. Very impressive!

PIAGGIA

1997 Carmignano Riserva	D	93
1998 Piaggia Riserva	D	90+

A prodigious Carmignano, this 1997 is made primarily from Sangiovese, with 22% Cabernet Sauvignon and 10% Merlot. It offers spectacular aromatics consisting of cherry jam, chocolate, cedar, spice, and earth. The color is an opaque ruby/purple, and the wine possesses great purity, terrific texture, a rich, fleshy, medium- to full-bodied mouth-feel, and a seamless finish. Drink this opulent effort over the next 5–7 years.

A serious, slightly internationally styled offering, the 1998 Piaggia Riserva exhibits an opaque inky purple color in addition to a sweet blackberry/cassis-scented perfume with hints of new oak and espresso. Layered, massively rich, and full-bodied, with sweet tannin, it possesses considerable potential but needs another 2–3 years to settle down as it still tastes like a barrel sample. It is a very impressive effort from Tuscany's 1998 vintage! Anticipated maturity: 2003–2018.

FATTORIA DI PIAZZANO

1998 Chianti Classico Riserva Rio Camarata	B	89

The 1998 Chianti Classico Riserva Rio Camarata reveals more density along with smoky, leathery notes intermixed with black cherries, earth, and graphite. Medium- to full-bodied and harmonious, it is best consumed over the next 5–7 years.

SALADINI PILASTRI

1997 Rosso Piceno Vigna Monteprandone IGT	C	88+
1997 Rosso Piceno Vigna Piediprato IGT	B	89

The 1997 Rosso Piceno Vigna Piediprato *vino da tavola* (a 50–50 blend of Montepulciano and Sangiovese) exhibits an attractive dark purple color in addition to dense, rich, sweet, supple fruit flavors reminiscent of blackberries, cherry jam, and cassis. Low in acidity, with evidence of toasty oak, this is a fat, hedonistically styled wine to drink over the next 2–4 years. The 1997 Rosso Piceno Vigna Monteprandone *vino da tavola* (100% Montepulciano) sees more new oak, but I am not sure it is better for it. It gives the wine more serious ambitions, but it comes across as monolithic, with imposing tannin. It does have delicious fruit, so perhaps another 6 months or so of aging will give the wine as much character as its sibling. It should drink well for 4–5 years. The consultant for these wines is Roberto Cipresso.

PODERUCCIO

1997 Camigliano IGT	C	88

This unfiltered blend of 40% Cabernet Sauvignon, 50% Sangiovese, and 10% Merlot was aged in a combination of small French *barriques* and larger Slavonian *foudres*. The dark ruby/purple-colored 1997 Camigliano offers sweet chocolate, berry fruit, nicely integrated wood, and notes of underbrush. Soft, round, and velvety-textured, with excellent ripeness and overall balance, it should be drunk over the next 5–7 years.

POGGIO LUNGO

1998 Morellino Riserva	D	90

The debut vintage for a new producer from the up-and-coming appellation of Morellino di Scansano, this deep ruby/purple-colored 1998 exhibits abundant quantities of toasty new oak in addition to impressively ripe red and black currant fruit intermixed with cherry jam. Sweet, rich, and medium- to full-bodied, with a supple texture, it is a delicious offering with a hint of mineral and leather in the background. Drink it over the next 5–6 years.

PODERE POGGIO SCALETTE

1998 Il Carbonaione	E	91
1997 Il Carbonaione	D	91

One of my favorite new wines from Tuscany, this 30-acre estate, owned by Vittorio Fiore and Adriana Assjè, produces wines from a type of Sangiovese called Lamole. The wine is aged in small 350-liter *foudres* for 18 months prior to bottling. Yields are extremely low, averaging approximately 1.2 tons of fruit per acre (about 20 hectoliters per hectare). Every vintage to date has been impressive, and the 1997 Il Carbonaione is a spectacular effort. It may even improve further in the bottle. It is incredibly opulent and expansive, with copious quantities of fruit and glycerin as well as long, concentrated, blackberry and jammy cherry flavors. The tannin is beautifully integrated, the acidity is adequate but low, and the wine is fleshy and hedonistic. It should drink well for a decade.

A brilliant 100% Sangiovese *cuvée* aged in both French and American oak for six months, the 1998 Il Carbonaione (3,300 cases) boasts a deep ruby color in addition to a sweet nose of black cherries, vanilla, minerals, and tobacco. Medium-bodied, fleshy, and well balanced, with superb purity as well as overall harmony, this classy, concentrated red marries finesse with power. Drink it over the next 5–7 years.

FATTORIA DI POGGIOPIANO

1999	Rosso di Sera IGT	E	92
1998	Rosso di Sera IGT	E	89+
1997	Rosso di Sera IGT	D	93

Poggiopiano's Rosso di Sera (800 cases produced) spends 18 months in wood, of which 50% is new. It is made from extremely low yields of 20 hectoliters per hectare and is bottled unfiltered. Tuscany's well-known consultant Luca d'Attoma assists in the winemaking. The sumptuous 1997 Rosso di Sera is an explosive, full-bodied, magnificently concentrated wine with fabulous intensity. The saturated ruby/purple color is followed by aromas of jammy blackberries, currants, new saddle leather, chocolate, Provençal herbs, and smoky new oak. Ripe, voluptuously textured, and low in acidity, it should drink well for 10–15 years. The 1998 Rosso di Sera reveals leather, chocolate, and ripe berry fruit but possesses less opulence, more structure as well as a backward personality. Unlike the flamboyant 1997, the 1998 should be cellared for another year or two and drunk over the following decade.

The stunning 1999 Rosso di Sera is an unfiltered blend of 90% Sangiovese and 10% Colorino aged 12 months in French oak, of which 50% was new. A serious, opaque purple-colored, backward effort, it exhibits superb purity as well as copious quantities of black fruits intermixed with spice box, tobacco, and leather. Full-bodied, powerful, and structured, it is meant for serious cellaring. While promising, it is not yet ready for prime-time drinking. Anticipated maturity: 2003–2018.

POLIZIANO

1998	Vino Nobile di Montepulciano Vigna dell'Asinone	D	90

Poliziano's ambitious 1998 Vino Nobile di Montepulciano Vigna dell'Asinone is a medium-bodied, stylish effort revealing evidence of *barrique* aging, gorgeous coffee-infused black cherry and berry fruit, a lush, layered texture, sweet tannin (atypical for the vintage), and a spicy, ripe, succulent finish. Enjoy it over the next 7–8 years.

PRATESI

1999	Carmignano	D	92
1997	Carmignano Riserva	D	93
1999	Locorosso IGT	C	89
1998	Locorosso IGT	C	90

This small, 12-acre estate discovered by Italian wine importer Leonardo LoCascio has four impressive offerings, including one of the finest Carmignanos I have ever tasted. The 1998 Locorosso (100% Sangiovese) possesses a dense ruby color in addition to an explosive nose of roasted espresso beans, chocolate, cherry jam, and spice. In the mouth, it is rich, chewy, sexy, and opulently textured. It is a hedonistic mouthful of juicy red selling for a song. Enjoy it over the next 3–4 years. The profound, opaque purple-colored 1997 Carmignano Riserva is a multidimensional, opulently textured, voluptuously rich wine. A blend of 80% Sangiovese and 20% Cabernet Sauvignon, it possesses thrilling levels of extract, a seamless texture, extraordinary purity, and explosive aromatics and flavors. It can be drunk now and over the next decade. Wow!

This impressive quartet also includes the 1999 Locorosso, a 2,000-case *cuvée* of 100% Sangiovese aged in small oak *foudres*. Its dense ruby/purple color is accompanied by a sweet nose of black cherries, strawberry jam, leather, and tobacco. With excellent texture, fleshy, ripe, sweet, chewy flavors, fine purity, and a plump, precocious style, it will drink well for 5–6 years. The stunning, dense purple-colored 1999 Carmignano (a blend of 80% Sangiovese and 20% Cabernet Sauvignon, also aged in small *foudres*) exhibits fabulously ripe blackberry fruit intermixed with licorice, new saddle leather, and spice box. It possesses a layered, succulent texture, a full-bodied, multilayered mid-palate, and a finish that lasts for more than 30 seconds. Outstanding purity, ripeness, concentration, and overall harmony characterize this 1999 made by the brilliant winemaking consultant Stefano Chioccioli.

LE PUPILLE

1997 Morellino di Scansano Poggio Valente	D	90
1997 Saffredi IGT	E	96

One of the best-run estates of Tuscany, proprietor Elisabetta Geppetti, along with wine-maker/oenologist Riccardo Cotarella, has turned out two juicy, impressively concentrated, hedonistic wines. The single-vineyard 1997 Morellino di Scansano Poggio Valente spends time in barrel and is bottled without fining or filtration. This offering could be called a Tuscan Pomerol. Dense, opaque, and purple-colored, this 100% Sangiovese (made from extremely low yields of 2.3 tons of fruit per acre) is medium- to full-bodied with no hard edges. Succulent and velvety-textured, with copious amounts of fruit (black cherries, plums, and cassis), this gorgeously styled, hedonistic, plump wine will provide thrilling drinking. It should evolve nicely for 6–7 years.

Readers may remember the profound review given the 1990 Saffredi *vino da tavola* (it is still in terrific condition). The 1997 Saffredi appears to be equal, if not superior, to the 1990. Made from a blend of 70% Cabernet Sauvignon and the rest Merlot, with a touch of Alicante, it was aged for 18 months in 100% new French oak. It boasts an exquisite toasty, smoky, cassis, floral, and licorice-scented nose that is reminiscent of a hypothetical blend of Châteaux Mouton-Rothschild and Margaux. With fabulous richness, multiple dimensions, and outstanding symmetry, purity, and length, it is a compelling example of what can be achieved from tiny yields (2.2 tons of fruit per acre) as well as impeccable winemaking. Anticipated maturity: now–2020.

QUERCIABELLA

1997 Camartina IGT	E	92
1997 Chianti Classico Riserva	D	89

I have been pleased with this estate's wines in the past (particularly the 1995s), so I was not surprised to see how well these 1997s performed. The medium garnet-colored 1997 Chianti Classico Riserva exhibits a complex nose of smoke, dried berry fruit, truffles, cedar, and smoke. Sweet black cherry fruit intermixed with herb and spice notes are presented in a nicely layered, soft, well-structured format. There are some tannin, adequate acidity, and excellent delineation. Drink it over the next 6–7 years. A superb blend of Sangiovese and Cabernet Sauvignon, the stunning, *barrique*-aged 1997 Camartina offers toasty, smoky new-oak scents as well as a black cherry liqueur–infused aroma. Full-bodied, with low acidity, considerable glycerin, and a multilayered, concentrated, fat, opulent finish, this hedonistic, seductive effort is capable of lasting for a decade.

LA RAMPA DI FUGNANO

1999 Bombereto IGT	D	90
1998 Bombereto IGT	C	89

1997 **Bombereto IGT**	C	90+
1999 **Chianti Colli Senesi Via dei Franchi**	B	88
1999 **Gisèle IGT**	D	94
1998 **Gisèle IGT**	D	88
1997 **Gisèle IGT**	D	94

Run by a Swiss couple and situated a few kilometers west of the historic walled village of San Gimignano, La Rampa di Fugnano is quickly propelling itself into Tuscany's top echelon. The interesting red wines are fairly priced for their quality.

Two exceptional efforts from La Rampa di Fugnano include the 1999 Bombereto, a *barrique*-aged 100% Sangiovese, and the extraordinary 1999 Gisèle Merlot. The dense ruby/purple-colored 1999 Bombereto is a seriously endowed offering with abundant quantities of strawberry and black cherry fruit. Half of this *cuvée* is aged in French barrels, of which one-third are new, and the rest in larger *foudres*. This gives the wine good structure but no noticeable toasty notes. This ripe, layered, concentrated, impressive Italian red should drink well for 10–12 years. The blockbuster 1999 Gisèle is an exotic, over-the-top style of Merlot that is reminiscent of the provocative Pomerols produced by Le Pin and Clinet (especially those from the late 1980s). This opaque purple-colored, full-bodied, multilayered, unctuously textured, fabulous wine boasts a fascinating nose of espresso, blackberries, mocha, smoke, and minerals. New oak is noticeable, but this component will ultimately be absorbed by the luxurious wealth of fruit and glycerin. This wine offers profound evidence of my belief that the only place in the world other than Bordeaux where phenomenal Merlot can consistently be grown is Tuscany. Anticipated maturity: 2003–2015.

The 1999 Chianti Colli Senesi Via dei Franchi is a soft, tasty effort with aromas of cherry fruit, leather, and spice. This delicious, gorgeously ripe fruit bomb is the result of extremely ripe Sangiovese. It is 100% tank-aged and bottled early to preserve its freshness and lively fruit character. An outstanding value, it should be consumed over the next 1–2 years. The 1998 Bombereto may not be as spectacular as the 1997, but this single-vineyard, 100% Sangiovese aged in French *barriques* exhibits complex, earthy, strawberry, red currant, and leather characteristics. Elegant for a 1998, with good depth, spicy wood, and a moderately endowed, slightly tannic finish, it should evolve for 10–12 years. The 1998 Gisèle (100% Merlot) is a dark ruby/purple-colored offering made in an international style. While it possesses highly extracted fruit, toasty new oak, smoke, and coffee-tinged berry and cherry fruit, it does not display the personality of the Bombereto or, for that matter, the Chianti Colli Senesi Via dei Franchi. The 1998 Gisèles should drink well for a decade.

The outstanding 1997 Bombereto *vino da tavola* is a 100% Sangiovese that was picked ripe and bottled unfiltered. One-third of it spent time in new French oak. It is more structured and surprisingly tighter than the 1996, even though the vintage produced wines with more significant ripeness and lower acidity. The fruit, glycerin, and richness detonate on the palate. With undeniable promise and massive structure, it has the feel of a Cabernet-based wine. Cellar it for 2–3 years, and consume it over the following 10–12 years. Lastly, the fabulous 1997 Gisèle (100% Merlot aged in new French oak and bottled unfiltered) boasts an opaque purple color as well as a dense, jammy, enormous nose of blackberry liqueur, vanilla, and licorice. Its low acidity and almost over-the-top, hugely extracted, full-bodied style result in a behemoth impression in the mouth. Nevertheless, everything is in alignment, and the wine is exceptionally well balanced for its size and highly extracted style. This terrific Merlot should age effortlessly for 15+ years. Wow!

LA RASINA

1998 **Rosso di Montalcino**	C	89

A small, low-key estate run by farmers as opposed to aristocrats or millionaires, La Rasina has produced a delicious, dark ruby-colored, fruit-dominated 1998 Rosso di Montalcino. It possesses a jammy, sweet, black cherry and strawberry-scented bouquet. Seductive, round, and delicious, it should be consumed over the next 2–3 years.

E. REICHENBERG

1997 Villa Monte Rico IGT	C	89

Dark plum/ruby-colored, with an intriguing nose of brandy-macerated black cherries, earth, and dried herbs, this opulent, dense, heady, succulently textured wine is delicious. Made from 100% Sangiovese, it is best drunk over the next 5–6 years.

RIECINE

1997 Chianti Classico Riserva	D	88
1997 La Gioia IGT	E	90

I often find the wines from this estate austere and tannic, but the 1997 vintage's exceptional ripeness and sweet, jammy style have given these offerings more charm and early flesh. For example, the dark ruby-colored 1997 Chianti Classico Riserva exhibits abundant quantities of sweet berry and cherry fruit, cedar, balsa wood, and spice scents. Flavorful, with moderate tannin, medium to full body, and excellent to outstanding purity and length, this substantial Chianti can be drunk now or cellared for 10–12 years. The dark ruby/purple-hued 1997 La Gioia (100% Sangiovese) offers intriguing smoky, toasty aromas mixed with jammy red and black fruits. Plump and fat, with low acidity and exceptional richness and symmetry, this large wine offers plenty of muscle, glycerin, and concentration. Approachable already, it promises to evolve and improve for 4–5 years and last for 12–15 years.

RISECCOLI

1999 Saeculum IGT	D	93
1997 Saeculum IGT	D	92

Riseccoli's opaque, purple-colored 1999 Saeculum (a proprietary blend of 60% Sangiovese, 30% Cabernet Sauvignon, and 10% Merlot aged in 100% new French oak) offers spectacular aromas of jammy cherries, strawberry cream, and toasty oak. It is a full-bodied, layered, super-endowed offering with significant potential. There is plenty of glycerin, sweet tannin, and a 45-second finish in this terrific Tuscan red. Drink it over the next 10–15 years.

The 1997 Saeculum is superb. Opaque purple-colored, with a thick, viscous texture, this full-bodied, explosively rich, massive 1997 exhibits huge aromas of black fruits, smoke, charcoal, truffles, and toasty oak. It possesses sweet tannin, fabulous fruit extraction, an immense finish, and tremendous overall balance and purity. Give this spectacular effort 2–3 years to become more delineated, and drink it over the following two decades. Very impressive!

ROCCA DI MONTEGROSSI

1999 Chianti Classico	C	89
1997 Chianti Classico Riserva Vigneto San Marcellino	D	90
1998 Geremia IGT	D	88
1997 Geremia IGT	D	88+

The nearly outstanding, deep garnet/ruby-colored 1999 Chianti Classico boasts a fragrant perfume of leather, soy, strawberry jam, raspberries, and spice. Minerals make an appearance in this attractive, fresh, vibrant, medium-bodied wine. Drink this fruit bomb over the next 3–4 years. The proprietary red, the 1998 Geremia, exhibits a deep ruby/purple color in addition to a dry, medium-weight, tannic style with good texture but a certain toughness and rusticity. Although it reveals some new oak, it is primarily characterized by its black cherry and currant fruit intermixed with leather and earth. Anticipated maturity: 2003–2012.

The outstanding 1997 Chianti Classico Riserva Vigneto San Marcellino displays the vintage's superripe, glycerin-imbued, highly concentrated fruit flavors. Thick, candied, jammy, and hedonistic, it can be drunk over the next 5–7 years. Closed and tannic, yet promising is the 1997 Geremia (a blend of 95% Sangiovese and 5% Merlot). Not a blockbuster like the San Marcellino, it exhibits fine complexity in addition to an elegant mineral, dried herb, cherry, and toast-scented nose as well as flavors. Medium-bodied, moderately tannic, firmly structured, and backward, it requires 2–3 years of cellaring and should age for 10–12 years.

RUFFINO

1997 Cabreo Il Borgo IGT	D	90
1997 Romitorio di Santedame IGT	E	90
1997 Terzo Millennio	E (magnums only)	89

This historic Tuscan estate has fashioned some interesting wines. An outstanding effort, the 1997 Romitorio di Santedame is a blend of Prugnolo Gentile and Colorino aged in French *barriques*. It is a full-bodied, expansive, powerful wine with gorgeous levels of black cherry and cassis fruit, lead pencil, toast, and smoky scents. It reveals the vintage's telltale, lush, opulent texture, excellent purity, and oodles of fruit and glycerin. Drink it over the next 7–10 years. Another limited-production offering is the 1997 Terzo Millennio (20,000 magnums produced). It is a velvety-textured, deep ruby/purple-colored 1997 exhibiting flamboyant characteristics of flashy new oak, black fruits, dried herbs, smoke, and cedar. The wine's low acidity and plush, succulent texture suggest that it can be drunk now as well as over the next decade. The proprietary 1997 Cabreo Il Borgo (an 8,000-case blend of 70% Sangiovese and 30% Cabernet Sauvignon aged 16 months in new French oak) displays the vintage's voluptuous style. A single-vineyard offering first produced in 1982, the high-altitude vineyard results in an elegant personality. The vintage's richness is well displayed in this silky, low-acid, intense, medium- to full-bodied 1997 with copious quantities of red and black fruits infused with abundant quantities of smoky new oak. It can be drunk now, or cellared for a decade. I did a mini-vertical of this wine, and following are my scores: 1996 (78), 1995 (84), 1993 (87), 1988 (87), 1987 (86), 1985 (89).

PODERE SALICUTTI

1999 Rosso di Montalcino	D	88
1997 Rosso di Montalcino	C	91

A sweet cherry-scented effort with spice and tobacco notes in the background, the 1999 Rosso di Montalcino possesses medium body and good fruit as well as spice. Drink it over the next 3–4 years. Given the abundance of excellent, reasonably priced Rossos di Montalcino from the 1999 vintage, this offering appears pricy.

What an amazing 1997 Rosso di Montalcino! The 1997 vintage produced wines of exceptional ripeness and richness, both of which are hallmarks of this prodigious young wine. It is deep ruby/purple-colored, with a stunning nose of blackberries, tar, and truffles. An amazing glycerin content gives the wine a voluptuous texture to go along with its super purity and jammy, ripe flavors. Adequate acidity and tannin provide the framework. Drink it over the next decade.

SAN BIAGIO

1999 Bellaria IGT	C	88
1999 Cabernet Sauvignon Sant'Antimo IGT	C	89+

Two internationally styled offerings, the 1999 Cabernet Sauvignon Sant'Antimo (100% Cabernet Sauvignon) and 1999 Bellaria (a blend of Sangiovese and Cabernet Sauvignon) are muscular, concentrated, *barrique*-aged efforts revealing abundant quantities of new oak, deep ruby/purple colors, medium to full body, moderate tannin, excellent purity, and fine overall balance. The 1999 Bellaria is more muscular and rustic than the 1999 Cabernet Sauvignon, which exhibits that varietal's classic black currant/tobacco combination. Both wines are more sculptured and less Tuscan than San Biagio's other offerings. Nevertheless, they are well worth a look, particularly in view of their reasonable prices. Both wines should drink well for 12–14+ years.

FATTORIA SAN FABIANO

1997　Armaiolo IGT	D	89+

The 1997 Armaiolo, a proprietary blend of equal parts Sangiovese and Cabernet Sauvignon, exhibits an opaque ruby/purple color, as well as aromas of spice box, sweet leather, cigar smoke, and cherry jam. Ripe, full-bodied, moderately tannic, and powerful, this 1997 requires 2–0 more years of cellaring; it should keep for 15 years.

SAN GIUSTO A RENTENNANO

1999	Chianti Classico	C	90
1998	Chianti Classico Riserva	D	88
1997	Chianti Classico Riserva	D	92
1998	Percarlo IGT	D	91+?
1997	Percarlo IGT	E	98
1998	La Ricolma IGT	E	91+
1997	La Ricolma IGT	EE	96

This has been one of my favorite Tuscan producers since I first tasted its wines in the early eighties. In 1999 I had my last bottle of the 1985 Percarlo (100% Sangiovese aged in *barrique*), which remains one of the most sumptuous Tuscany offerings I have ever tasted, with years of life still left. One of Tuscany's blue-chip properties, this estate has an impressive track record of turning out top-notch wines for more than 20 years. In addition to its splendid Chiantis, its proprietary Percarlo (a luxury *cuvée* of 100% Sangiovese) and the new *bambino*, the 100% Merlot *cuvée* called La Ricolma, are cult wines. The newest releases include a sensational bargain, the 1999 Chianti Classico. This vintage has produced superripe, opulently textured, thick, juicy, sexy wines that will prove sensationally popular with consumers. A deep ruby color is followed by a sumptuous effort loaded with jammy black fruit, smoke, earth, and leather aromas as well as flavors. Enjoy this compelling Chianti over the next 4–5 years. I preferred it to the more expensive 1998 Chianti Classico Riserva. The vintage's austerity and high tannin are evident in this complex, herbaceous, medium-bodied Chianti. With notes of saddle leather, black cherry fruit, and asphalt, it reveals excellent texture and a slight austerity in the finish. Drink this well-made 1998 over the next 6–7 years.

The 1998 Percarlo IGT exhibits characteristics of overripe black cherry fruit, toasty new oak, and a touch of volatile acidity. Flamboyant, rich, chewy, and unctuously textured, it possesses abundant quantities of fruit as well as moderate tannin. Give it another 2 years of cellaring and enjoy it over the following 14–15. The limited production, superripe 1998 La Ricolma IGT (100% Merlot aged in 100% new French oak) exhibits huge tannin (not surprising given the vintage) along with equally massive concentration of fruit and extract. It is powerful, dense, and palate-staining. The sweet French oak is well displayed in the aromas of espresso, black cherries, caramel, and smoke. This 1998 needs 2–3 years of cellaring and should last for two decades. My only concern is that the tannin may never be fully absorbed, but only time will tell. Anticipated maturity: 2004–2020.

The spectacular, saturated ruby/purple-colored 1997 Chianti Classico Riserva reveals intense aromas of smoked meats as well as jammy black cherries, raspberries, and overripe plums. Opulent and full-bodied, with extraordinary power, richness, and concentration, this is a decadently intense, rich, voluptuous Chianti that must be tasted to be believed. Drink it over the next 10–15 years.

Is the dense ruby/purple-colored 1997 Percarlo as compelling as the 1985? It may be even more massive than I remember the 1985 tasting in the late 1980s. Enormous in aromas, flavors, and persistence on the palate, it exhibits profound levels of concentration as well as unbelievably dense black currant and blackberry liqueur notes infused with new saddle leather, licorice, truffles, and toasty oak. Enormously thick and viscous, with low acidity and mouthcoating levels of extract, this wine's tannin level is high but largely obscured by the wealth of fruit, glycerin, and extract. It is an amazing accomplishment! Anticipated maturity: now–2020. Another mammoth offering is the black/purple-colored 1997 La Ricolma (100% Merlot aged in 100% new French oak and bottled with virtually no clarification). It is unctuously textured, phenomenally concentrated, and extraordinarily intense, with surreal levels of extract, glycerin, and richness. Its olfactory bombardment begins with scents of melted chocolate, roasted espresso, and oodles of black cherry and blackberry fruit. It is reminiscent of La Mondotte, the ultraconcentrated St.-Emilion, in its thickness and phenomenal richness. However, despite its monstrous size, weight, and constitution, this wine is well delineated and remarkably refreshing to drink, although knocking off a bottle between two people might prove challenging. This sensational effort is a tour de force in winemaking. Anticipated maturity: 2003–2025.

FATTORIA SANTA MARIA DI AMBRA

1997	Casamurli IGT	D	88
1998	Chianti Riserva La Bigattiera	C	88
1997	Gavignano IGT	D	89

A delicious offering, the deep plum/garnet-colored, nicely textured 1998 Chianti Riserva La Bigattiera reveals spicy new oak along with sweet cherry/berry/currant flavors. Dense, chewy, and dry, with well-integrated tannin, wood, and acidity, it will drink well for 5–7 years.

Both of the proprietary reds are excellent but tightly knit wines begging for a few more years of cellaring, particularly the 1997 Gavignano. This *barrique*-aged blend of 60% Sangiovese and 40% Cabernet Sauvignon exhibits a deep ruby/purple color as well as a sweet nose of lead pencil, new saddle leather, black currants, and cherry liqueur. Deep, rich, medium- to full-bodied, well structured, and moderately tannic, it will be at its finest between 2004–2012. The 1997 Casamurli (a blend of Sangiovese and Malavasia Nera with a touch of Merlot) is structured, rich, backward, pure, and in need of another 1–2 years of cellaring. It should evolve nicely for 12–15 years.

LIVIO SASSETTI & FIGLI

1997	Brunello di Montalcino	E	96
1998	Fili di Seta IGT	D	90
1997	Fili di Seta IGT	D	90
1999	Rosso di Montalcino	C	90
1998	Rosso di Montalcino	C	90

I have been purchasing better vintages of Livio Sassetti's wines since 1982, and it remains a favorite. The new efforts are impressive. The 1999 Rosso di Montalcino's incredible perfume soars from the glass, offering up scents of raspberry liqueur, sweet new leather, flowers, earth, and minerals. A glorious, hedonistic turn-on, the wine is elegant, supply textured, and complex. It is one of the finest *rossi* this small artisan producer has made. Enjoy it over the next 5–6 years.

Readers should note that with the 1997 Brunello di Montalcino, the label changed to emphasize the proprietor's name, Livio Sassetti, rather than the estate name, Pertimali. These Brunellos have always been top-notch, but the 1997 is staggering in its aromatic fireworks and concentrated, long, intense flavors. Sumptuous aromas of dried Provençal herbs, roasted meats, soy, spice box, asphalt, truffles, and black fruits linger in the air. Flavors of new saddle leather are added to jammy black fruit characteristics. Opulently textured, full-bodied, and gorgeously pure, this wine creates an olfactory overload. Its low acidity, high glycerin, and huge fruit reserves suggest drinking it now and over the next 12–18 years. *Mamma mia!*

The 1998 Fili di Seta (a *barrique*-aged blend of 60% Sangiovese and 40% Cabernet Sauvignon) is a dark ruby/purple-colored, full-bodied, sweet, luscious offering. Rich and dense, it boasts abundant quantities of spicy new oak as well as fruit, earth, leather, black currants, and tobacco. Despite the addition of Cabernet Sauvignon, it has not lost any of its Tuscan typicity. Consume it over the next 10–15 years.

A gorgeously opulent, sweet, sexy, low-acid Rosso di Montalcino, Sassetti's ripe, fruit-driven 1998 will have many converts. Drink this beauty over the next 4–6 years. The 1997 Fili di Seta *vino da tavola* (75% Sangiovese and 25% Cabernet Sauvignon) offers a flamboyant nose of cedar wood, melted chocolate, underbrush, smoke, and red/black fruits. Medium-bodied, with gorgeous levels of dense, concentrated fruit nicely complemented by subtle new oak, this long, rich, opulently textured wine should be drunk over the next 6–7 years.

SASSOTONDO

1999 San Lorenzo Rosso di Sovana	D	89

This stylish *cuvée* is produced from an indigenous varietal called Ciliegiolo. It offers sweet black cherries and berries in its moderately intense nose, fine purity, medium body, admirable finesse, a supple texture, and a hint of spicy new oak in the finish. Drink it over the next 7–8 years.

MICHELE SATTA

1998 Piastraia IGT	E	90
1997 Piastraia IGT	D	93
1998 Vigna al Cavaliere IGT	E	92
1997 Vigna al Cavaliere IGT	D	91

Satta's two impressive 1998 offerings emerge from Tuscany's coastal area, which enjoyed a greater 1998 vintage than did the interior. The 1998 Piastraia (a blend of equal parts Merlot, Cabernet Sauvignon, Syrah, and Sangiovese aged one year in French oak) exhibits a complex, internationally styled bouquet of black currants, vanilla, smoke, and graphite. Medium-to full-bodied and dense, with supple tannin and a nicely layered mouth-feel, it should drink well for 7–10 years. More complex and distinctive is the 1998 Vigna al Cavaliere, a 100% Sangiovese *cuvée* also aged one year in French oak. A deep ruby/purple color is accompanied by sumptuous aromas of espresso infused with blackberries, licorice, soy, and truffles. This long, layered, multidimensional Tuscan wine is extremely impressive. Why can't California come remotely close to producing Sangiovese of this quality? This beautiful 1998 can be drunk now or cellared for 10–12 years.

This is another up-and-coming Tuscan star, with vineyards planted on the coastline near Bolgheri. Concentrated and made in an opulent, Pomerol-like style is the 1997 Vigna al Cavaliere. About 1,150 cases were produced of this 100% Sangiovese. A dark ruby color is accompanied by a fragrant bouquet of black fruits, smoke, toasty oak, and spice box. The wine is fleshy, luscious, low in acidity, and fat. With tremendous reserves of fruit, and a full-bodied, voluptuous texture, this plump, succulent 1997 lingers on the palate for more than 30 seconds. Drink it over the next 7–10 years. Even better is the riveting 1997 Piastraia, a blend of equal parts Merlot, Sangiovese, Syrah, and Cabernet Sauvignon aged in French oak for 14 months. It possesses a thick, dark ruby color, in addition to an explosive nose of red and black fruits, pepper, vanilla, and smoke. Full-bodied and opulent, with even more concentration and flavor dimensions than the 1997 Cavaliere, this is a wine of fabulous fruit intensity, complexity, and overall symmetry. It should drink well for 10–12 years. Bravo!

SCOPETONE

1999 Rosso di Montalcino	C	89

Sign me up for these 1999 Rossos di Montalcino, a great value from Tuscany in what looks to be an extraordinary vintage for Brunello di Montalcino. Scopetone's 1999 Rosso di Montalcino exhibits a Bordeaux-like bouquet of sweet black currants, saddle leather, dried herbs, earth, and spice. Complex and ripe, with gorgeous fruit, elegance, and symmetry, it will drink well for 4–5 years.

FATTORIA SELVAPIANA

1997 Chianti Rufina Riserva	D	90

One of the finest wines I have ever tasted from this producer, this powerful, dark ruby/purple-colored Chianti exhibits copious quantities of smoky, toasty scents intermixed with a Pomerol-like, mocha-infused, black cherry liqueur character. Rich and full-bodied, with a layered texture, decent acidity, superb purity, and a finish that lasts for 30–35 seconds, it should provide handsome drinking for 10–12+ years.

SEMIFONTE

1998 Chianti Classico Riserva	D	88
1998 Di Semifonte IGT	D	90
1997 Di Semifonte IGT	D	90

Semifonte is the property of the same Latini family that owns one of Florence's most famous *trattorie*/steak houses, Il Latini. The impressive 1998 Chianti Classico Riserva (85% Sangiovese and 15% Cabernet Sauvignon) displays more sweetness and depth than some of its harder peers. Offering aromas and flavors of lead pencil, dried herbs, black fruits, new saddle leather, spice, berry fruit, and subtle oak, it is a medium-bodied, smoky, earthy, tannic effort that should drink well for 5–7 years. The supple, elegant 1998 Di Semifonte (a blend of equal parts Sangiovese, Merlot, and Cabernet Sauvignon aged 16 months in French *barriques*) possesses sweet black and red fruits as well as new oak, tobacco, and spice box aromas. Dense, rich, medium- to full-bodied, and long, with attractive levels of glycerin as well as sweet tannin, it will drink well for a decade. These are two well-made offerings.

The 1997 Di Semifonte, a *barrique*-aged blend of 30% Sangiovese, 30% Merlot, and 40% Cabernet Sauvignon aged 15 months in French oak, is outstanding. It possesses impressive intensity, fine opulence, and a fat, chewy, black currant and cherry-flavored mid-palate with admirable purity, a layered texture, and an explosive finish revealing copious quantities of glycerin, fruit, and extract. It is a beautifully made, flashy effort to enjoy over the next decade. It would undoubtedly drink well with one of Il Latini's Florentine steaks.

FATTORIA LE SORGENTI

1998 Scirus IGT	D	88

This *barrique*-aged blend of 70% Cabernet Sauvignon and 30% Merlot exhibits an opaque bluish/purple color, a sweet bouquet of black currants, cherry jam, cedar wood, dried herbs, spice box, and vanilla, medium to full body, excellent flavor density, good purity and harmony, and nicely integrated acidity and tannin. It should drink well for 10–12 years.

TENUTA DEL TERRICCIO

1998 Lupicaia	EE	90
1998 Tassinaia	E	88

The dark ruby-colored 1998 Tassinaia is a blend of Cabernet Sauvignon, Sangiovese, and Merlot aged in French oak for 12 months prior to bottling. Copious quantities of black currant and cherry fruit are followed by medium body, sweet tannin, and plenty of spicy oak. Drink it over the next decade. A blend of Cabernet Sauvignon and Merlot, the 1998 Lupicaia reveals a darker, more saturated ruby/purple color along with a sweet nose of black currants, espresso, and chocolate. Dense, rich, and muscular, it needs an additional 1–3 years of cellaring and should drink well for 12–15 years.

TENUTA DI TRINORO

1999	Palazzi IGT	EE	93
1998	Palazzi IGT	EE	93
1997	Palazzi IGT	E	90?
1998	Tenuta di Trinoro IGT	EE	92
1997	Tenuta di Trinoro IGT	E	91
1999	Trinoro IGT	EE	92+

I continue to be amazed by the high-quality wines produced by proprietor Andrea Franchetti. Self-trained but a good friend of Jean-Luc Thunevin (of Château Valandraud and others) and Peter Sissick (of Pingus), Franchetti has been producing Cabernet Franc–based, Cheval Blanc–like efforts. Prices are steep, but the quality is in the bottle. In 2000, there will be a number of changes as 1999 is the last vintage for his *cuvée* of Palazzi. As a side note, barrel samples of the 2000 Trinoro IGT and his less expensive 2000 Trinoro Cupole di Trinoro were astonishing and clearly the finest wines he has yet produced. If they continue to evolve, they will be mid-90-point efforts when released in July 2002. Readers should keep in mind that these are prodigious offerings that will sell out quickly.

The 1999 Palazzi (800 cases of a blend of 50% Cabernet Franc and 50% Merlot) boasts a dense ruby/purple color in addition to a complex nose of currants, cigar box, plums, and cherry liqueur with a hint of toasty oak in the background. Full-bodied, elegant, and complex, with a savory mid-palate and sweet tannin, it will drink beautifully for 12–14 years. Even better are the 1,300 cases of the 1999 Trinoro, a blend of 70% Cabernet Franc, 20% Merlot, 6% Cabernet Sauvignon, and 4% Petit Verdot. Cropped at yields of 26 hectoliters per hectare, this profound, dark purple-colored offering reveals noteworthy aromas of mocha, black fruits, spice box, and toast. It possesses multiple layers, astounding richness, gorgeous purity, definition, and elegance, medium to full body, and a beautiful texture. Anticipated maturity: now–2015. These wines, in the style of Franchetti's friends Sissick and Thunevin, were not fined, filtered, or stabilized and essentially represent the most honest/authentic essence of their vineyard. They are the wines of a genius.

No expense has been spared in the replanting of this ancient vineyard (dating from 1892) or on the lavish attention given to the wine. Made from extremely low yields of 20 hectoliters per hectare, aged 14 months in 100% new French oak, and bottled without fining or filtration, these wines benefit from a process known as *microbullage*, which aerates the lees without having to rack the wines, thus minimizing damage to the wine's freshness. To date, these have been spectacular efforts with fabulous potential. The Tenuta di Trinoro is a blend of 80% Cabernet Franc, 10% Merlot, and 10% Petit Verdot. The Palazzi is a blend of 50% Cabernet Franc and 50% Merlot (reminiscent of St.-Emilion's famed Cheval Blanc). The 1998 Palazzi (1,000 cases) exhibits an exotic, sweet nose of blackberries and spices, an opulently textured, jammy, ripe style with wonderful sweetness on the attack, copious quantities of glycerin, supple tannin, and a blockbuster, rich finish with tremendous complexity. It should age effortlessly for 10–15 years. Also remarkably complex, the 1998 Tenuta di Trinoro reveals notes of coconut, Asian spices, and generous quantities of black cherry, blackberry, and smoke-infused fruit flavors. The wine is jammy, full-bodied, viscous, and voluptuously textured with extraordinary purity and overall balance. In both wines, the tannin is obscured by the luxurious fruit and high glycerin. The 1998 Tenuta di Trinoro will also drink well for 10–15 years.

The question mark concerning the 1997 Palazzi is because the bottle I tasted, while possessing a saturated purple color and gobs of sweet black cherry and berry fruit backed up by toasty new oak, also had a level of volatile acidity that was at the limit of my tolerance. Volatile acidity can add complexity, and it is certainly one of the hallmarks of some of this century's greatest wines (i.e., the 1947 Pétrus and 1947 Cheval Blanc), but it is surprising to find this much volatile acidity in such a young wine. The 1997 Palazzi possesses loads of glycerin, a thick, chewy texture, and superb fruit. It should evolve nicely for 12–15 years. If the volatile acidity does not become any more exaggerated, this wine will be controversial and thought-provoking, yet undeniably delicious. Less concentrated, the purple-colored 1997 Tenuta di Trinoro *vino da tavola* is cleaner, with pure blackberry and cherry notes nicely complemented by spicy oak. Medium- to full-bodied, with attractive oak, this sweetheart wine should drink well for 10–12 years.

TENUTA DI VALGIANO

1997 Scasso dei Cesari	C	88

This is primarily a Sangiovese-based wine with some Syrah in the blend. It offers an impressively saturated opaque purple color, and attractive black currant, berry, and cherry fruit flavors. Medium- to full-bodied, with the fruit dominating, this excellent, hedonistic wine should be drunk over the next 2–3 years. The consultant for these wines is Roberto Cipresso.

FATTORIA TERRABIANCA

1997 Campaccio IGT	D	91
1997 Campaccio Riserva IGT	E	92
1998 Ceppate IGT	E	93
1997 Ceppate IGT	E	90
1997 Chianti Classico Vigna della Croce Riserva	C	88
1999 Chianti Classico Scassino	C	88
1997 Piano del Cipresso IGT	D	89
1997 Scassino IGT	B	88

This excellent producer has fashioned his finest wines since 1990. All of the above-mentioned offerings merit serious interest. The largest production is the 7,000-case *cuvée* of 1999 Chianti Classico Scassino. This excellent, reasonably priced Chianti was aged in Slovenian oak for 8–9 months prior to bottling. Its dark ruby color is accompanied by aromas of sweet cherry fruit, herbs, earth, and spice. There is a nicely layered mouth-feel, adequate acidity, and a fleshy, concentrated palate. Drink it over the next 5–7 years.

The 100% Sangiovese *cuvée*, the 1997 Piano del Cipresso (3,700 cases) was aged 12 months in French oak. Its dark ruby color is followed by a big, leafy, earthy, underbrush-scented nose with sweet cherry and currant fruit in the background. Medium-bodied, moderately tannic, open-knit, and supple, it is meant to be drunk over the next 4–7 years. One of Terrabianca's finest *cuvées* is Campaccio. The 1997 (a 6,000-case blend of 70% Sangiovese and 30% Cabernet Sauvignon aged one year in primarily French oak) is a complex, deep ruby-colored wine displaying scents of saddle leather, dried Provençal herbs, and subtle toasty oak. It is medium- to full-bodied, with excellent depth, superb purity, and an open-knit, complex, structured personality. Delicious now, it promises to evolve for 7–8 years. The 1997 Campaccio Riserva (a 1,000-case blend of 65% Sangiovese and 35% Cabernet Sauvignon aged 2 years in primarily French oak) ratchets up the concentration level a notch or two, revealing a more expansive, layered palate, a deep ruby/purple color, more noticeable new oak, thicker, juicier flavors, plenty of power, yet admirable elegance, purity, and overall harmony. The tannin is well integrated in this large-scale, concentrated, complex red. Anticipated maturity: now–2015.

The 1998 Ceppate (a blend of 50% Cabernet Sauvignon from the Chianti Classico region and equal parts Cabernet Sauvignon and Merlot from the coastal Maremma region) is terrific, no doubt because the Tuscan coastline enjoyed a far better vintage in 1998 than the inland viticultural regions. The color is a healthy dark ruby/purple, and the bouquet exhibits super fruit (primarily crème de cassis and new oak). Aged 12 months in 100% new oak, of which 70% was French, this youthful wine (1,800 six-packs produced) is full-bodied, ripe, textured, rich, and promising. It should drink well for 12–15 years.

The dark ruby-colored 1997 Chianti Classico Vigna della Croce Riserva is a fruit-driven offering with abundant quantities of sweet strawberry, cherry, and currant fruit mixed with floral, spice, mineral, and wood notes. Round, ripe, and medium- to full-bodied, this delicious Chianti should be consumed over the next 5–7 years. The fat, hedonistic, intense, lavishly wooded 1997 Ceppate (a blend of 75% Cabernet Sauvignon and 25% Merlot aged in both French and American oak) exhibits a dense ruby/purple color, an exotic, flamboyant personality, gorgeous ripeness and richness, and a layered, full-bodied palate impression. The oak is a bit intrusive, but it should become better meshed given the extraction of fruit. This wine will benefit from another year of cellaring and should age well for 10–15 years. The excellent dark ruby/purple-colored 1997 Scassino *vino da tavola* (100% Sangiovese) is less expensive than the previous wines. It should be sought out by readers looking for a very good value. The wine offers a spicy, open-knit aromatic profile with notes of new saddle leather, cherry jam, dried herbs, and smoke. Rich, deep, medium-bodied, and spicy, this is delicious, low-acid Sangiovese without hard tannins. Drink it over the next 7–8 years.

TUA RITA

1999	Giusto di Notri IGT	E	96
1998	Giusto di Notri IGT	E	93
1997	Giusto di Notri IGT	E	90
1999	Perlato del Bosco	D	91
1999	Redigaffi IGT	EE	99
1998	Redigaffi IGT	EE	96
1997	Redigaffi IGT	EE	94

Many of the greatest wines made in central Italy emerge from one of three winemaking consultants, Riccardo Cotarella, Luca d'Attoma, or Stefano Chioccioli, the wine-maker for Tua Rita, a superstar of the coastal Tuscan region known as Bolgheri. As longtime readers know, these wines have received lavish praise in the past, and that continues with the 1999 releases. A new star in Tua Rita's galaxy is the 1999 Perlato del Bosco (1,000+ cases produced), a 100% Sangiovese aged in *barrique* and bottled with neither fining nor filtration. A friend of mine described it best—as a "sex machine." Supercharged, complex notes of espresso, chocolate, and black fruits emerge from the aromatics. Full-bodied, opulent, and voluptuous, this hedonistic turn-on will not make old bones, but for drinking over the next 5–6 years, it will provide an undeniable blast of fun. It is among the most explosively complex, succulent Sangioveses I have ever tasted. Amazing! The more brawny, serious, opaque purple-colored 1999 Giusto di Notri is a *barrique*-aged, unfined, unfiltered blend of 65% Cabernet Sauvignon and 35% Merlot. Its opaque purple color is accompanied by awesome aromas of weedy tobacco, espresso, smoke, chocolate, black currants, and blackberries. Dense, full-bodied, thick, viscous, rich, and pure, it requires another 2–3 years of cellaring and should last for 15+. Sadly, production was a measly 800 cases. The 250-case *cuvée* of 100% Merlot, the 1999 Redigaffi, has an astonishing 36 grams per liter of dry extract, which exceeds most top Pomerols in a great vintage! Unfined and unfiltered, it is as close to perfection as a wine can get. The color is a deep saturated blue/purple. The powerful, pure nose offers smoke, licorice, black cherry, and blackberries. The most structured of this trio, it boasts awesome concentration, a fabulously dense, viscous mid-section, and a finish that lasts for nearly a minute. I'm tempted to say this is the Pétrus of Tuscany, but the only recent vintages of Pétrus that have scored this high have been 1989, 1990, and 1998! This is riveting juice. Anticipated maturity: now–2015.

The spectacular 1998 Giusto di Notri is a 60% Cabernet Sauvignon/40% Merlot blend aged in French oak, of which 50% was new, and bottled unfined and unfiltered. A dense, murky ruby/purple color is followed by aromas of melted Valrhona chocolate, blackberries, smoke, and toast. Rich and full-bodied, with superb concentration, a seamless texture, low acidity, and a 40+-second finish, this huge wine should drink well for a decade.

The 1998 Redigaffi (2,000+ bottles produced) is profound. I do not normally quote dry extract numbers, because taste is more important than numbers. However, I could not help but notice one of the highest measured dry extract numbers I have ever seen in a wine in the 1998 Redigaffi—39 grams per liter! Made from 100% Merlot, aged in 100% new Allier and Troncais French barrels, it is bottled without fining or filtration. An opaque purple-colored, powerful, enormously endowed effort, it offers gorgeous black currant, plum, and blackberry fruit characteristics infused with spice box, chocolate, and vanilla. This harmonious wine oozes with extract and glycerin. Extraordinarily pure and impressive, with copious tannin nearly hidden beneath the wine's superb richness, this beauty should be at its apogee between 2004–2020.

The outstanding 1997 Giusto di Notri (a 60% Cabernet Sauvignon and 40% Merlot blend aged in French oak and bottled with neither fining nor filtration) exhibits a dark ruby/purple color, and excellent aromatics consisting of toasty new oak, lead pencil, black currants, chocolate, and smoke. Layered and rich but backward and unevolved, with copious tannin in the finish, this wine should improve with further cellaring. The low acidity and sweet fruit give it immediate accessibility, but the wine has not yet developed its secondary aromatics. Anticipated maturity: now–2012. The spectacular black/purple-colored 1997 Redigaffi boasts huge, chocolaty, blackberry, smoky nose and flavors, a full-bodied personality oozing with extract and ripe, juicy fruit, sensational length (45+ seconds), and brilliant purity and symmetry. Anticipated maturity: now–2012.

FATTORIA DELL'UCCELLIERA

1997	Brunello di Montalcino	E	94
1998	Rapace IGT	D	90
1999	Rosso di Montalcino	C	88
1998	Rosso di Montalcino	C	88

Fattoria dell'Uccelliera's 1999 Rosso di Montalcino is a herbaceous, creamy-textured, powerful effort displaying user-friendly, soft, lush fruit flavors, low acidity, and surprising levels of glycerin as well as ripeness. It is an excellent, modern-styled *rosso* for drinking over the next 3–4 years. Readers seeking a fruity Rosso di Montalcino should check out Uccelliera's 1998. Although not complex, it is velvety-textured, fleshy, and loaded with ripe, herb-tinged, berry fruit. It should be consumed over the next 2–4 years.

The 1998 Rapace (a blend of 60% Sangiovese, 30% Merlot, and 10% Cabernet Sauvignon) offers an opaque dense ruby/purple color and a gorgeous nose of roasted herbs, black fruits, chocolate, licorice, and espresso. Deep and full-bodied, with power and grace, this is a super-concentrated, velvety-textured effort to consume during its first decade of life.

The spectacular 1997 Brunello di Montalcino is a thrilling, seamless example of Brunello that I hope is indicative of how special this vintage will be. A deep opaque ruby/purple color is atypical for Brunello, but the nose of dried herbs, spice box, fruitcake, red and black fruits, minerals, and earth is stunningly complex. It is full-bodied, with supple tannin, a velvety texture, and a tremendously long finish. It can be drunk now or cellared for 14–15+ years.

VALDICAVA

1999 Rosso di Montalcino	D	90

A strong argument can be made that Valdicava is among the top three or four Brunello di Montalcino producers. I can't wait to taste the 1997s. Certainly the 1999 Rosso di Montalcino is a splendid example of what can be expected from this vintage. Its dark ruby/purple color is accompanied by a black cherry, spicy, tobacco, mineral, earth, and underbrush-scented nose and glycerin-imbued, sweet, jammy, fleshy fruit. Drink this dense, fat, luscious wine over the next 5–8 years. Has anyone made less than a delicious 1999 Rosso di Montalcino?

FATTORIA VALTELLINA

1997 Chianti Classico	C	89
1997 Chianti Classico Riserva	D	90
1997 Convivio IGT	E	91
1997 Merlot Il Duca	EE	92

These impressive offerings from proprietor Christoph Schneider come at a lofty price, but readers looking for dense, powerful, concentrated, muscular reds with considerable upside will appreciate this quartet. The extremely concentrated, dark ruby/purple-colored 1997 Chianti Classico Riserva possesses huge body along with gobs of black cherry fruit infused with licorice, truffle, leather, and earth notes. Dense, mouth-filling, and powerful, this wine has a tannic finish suggesting that 1–2 years of cellaring would be beneficial. This formidable Chianti will age well for 10–15 years. The opaque purple-colored 1997 Convivio (a *barrique*-aged blend of 75% Sangiovese and 25% Cabernet Sauvignon) exhibits abundant quantities of black currant and cherry jam, bay leaf, and toasty new-oak scents in its aromatic fireworks. Layered and massive, with moderately high tannin, this full-bodied, chewy 1997 requires additional time in the cellar. Anticipated maturity: 2003–2016.

The dense purple-colored 1997 Merlot Il Duca (100% Merlot, *barrique*-aged) is succulent, opulent, and explosive, both aromatically and flavor-wise. The vintage's overripeness, high levels of glycerin and alcohol are present in this full-throttle, multidimensional 1997. It already provides considerable pleasure and promises to age well for 15 years. Admittedly, this offering is priced for the rich and famous, but it delivers a boatload of flavor.

The 100% Sangiovese 1997 Chianti Classico offers a dense ruby/purple color as well as a sweet nose of black fruits, licorice, dried herbs, and damp soil. There is superb concentration, terrific fruit purity, and admirable density and opulence, all characteristics of this marvelous vintage. Drink it over the next decade.

VARRAMISTA

1998 Varramista IGT	E	90
1997 Varramista IGT	E	88

I would have rated the 1998 Varramista even higher had it not been for the aggressive new oak. Otherwise, this is an exotic, smoky, blackberry, and bacon fat–scented effort with sweet tannin, complex, full-bodied flavors, and an unctuous style. A blend of 90% Syrah, 5% Sangiovese, and 5% Merlot, its forward, precocious style suggests that consumption over the next 5–6 years is warranted. Made from 95% Syrah and 5% Sangiovese, the supple, smoky, toasty, black currant–scented and –flavored 1997 lacks the profound concentration of France or California's greatest Syrahs, but it possesses a delicious, superficial sweetness, ripeness, and heady perfume. Although not offering the tremendous finish of a great Syrah, it does possess plenty of charm as well as an open-knit, up-front appeal. Drink it over the next 5–6 years.

CARLA BENINI VENTIMIGLIA

1997 Sassotondo San Lorenzo Riserva Sovana	C	90

The outstanding black/purple-colored 1997 Sassotondo San Lorenzo Riserva Sovana was produced from old-vine Ciliegiolo and aged in 100% new oak. It possesses layers of black cherry and blackberry jam–like fruit. Full-bodied and rich, with superb purity, this terrific wine is a result of low yields and old vines. Drink it over the next decade.

IL VESCOVINO

1997 Il Merlotto	D	90

This small estate (just under 10 acres) is located in one of Tuscany's coolest microclimates. Its nearby neighbors include Castello dei Rampolla and Villa Cafaggio. My favorite effort from Il Vescovino is the 1997 Il Merlotto, a blend of 90% Sangiovese and 10% Cabernet Sauvignon aged in two-year-old French barrels. Its opaque ruby/purple color is followed by a sumptuously ripe nose of blackberries, cherry liqueur, and toast. Deep, full-bodied, and rich, with a layered, low-acid, chewy texture and an intense, lightly tannic finish, it can be drunk over the next 10–12 years.

VILLA ARCENO

1998 Arguzzio IGT	D	88
1997 Chianti Classico Riserva	D	89

These wines emerge from the Tuscan estate owned by California's incomparable Jess Jackson. Not surprisingly, both are of high quality. The 1997 Chianti Classico Riserva offers a dark ruby/purple color in addition to a sweet nose of black cherry and *barrique* smells. Nicely textured, medium-bodied, with supple tannin and vibrant acidity, this well-focused, pure, delicious Chianti should drink well for 7–8 years. The luxury-priced 1998 Arguzzio's deep ruby/purple color is followed by sweet aromas of new oak, blackberries, and cherries. The wine is spicy, slightly austere, and complex, displaying notes of saddle leather and black fruits. Consume it over the next 7–8 years.

VILLA CAFAGGIO

1997 Cortaccio IGT	E	96
1997 San Martino IGT	E	90

I have always admired the elegance and sweet raspberry/cherry flavors this producer tends to obtain. I was underwhelmed by its 1997 Chianti Classico Riserva, but there are no problems with the performances of the 100% Sangiovese 1997 San Martino or the 100% Cabernet Sauvignon 1997 Cortaccio. Both are stunning proprietary red wine offerings from the spectacular 1997 vintage. The plum-colored 1997 San Martino exhibits gorgeously thick, juicy aromas of black fruits, cherries, earth, smoke, and dried Provençal herbs. High in glycerin and husky, with ripe fruit, low acidity, sweet tannin, and a long, 35–40-second finish, its precocious, opulent texture and up-front fruit suggest that it will evolve effortlessly for 10–12 years. Impressive! Even more powerful, concentrated, and well endowed is the dark ruby/ purple-colored 1997 Cortaccio. Aromas of *sur-maturité* (overripeness, but in a positive sense) emerge from this wine. It also offers notes of espresso beans, chocolate, and jammy cassis/blackberry fruit. It is extraordinarily fat and juicy, with oodles of glycerin and concentrated fruit, full body, silky tannin, and a finish that lasts for 40+ seconds. This is a terrific example of Cortaccio. Drink it over the next 10–15 years.

FATTORIA VILLA LA SELVA

1997 Felciaia IGT	C	89
1997 Selvamaggio IGT	C	91

Fattoria Villa La Selva's wines are fashioned under the guidance of the well-known consulting oenologist Stefano Chioccioli. The 1997 Felciaia (100% Sangiovese aged in an assortment of French and American oak) exhibits a smoky, oaky, earth-scented bouquet with a distinctive international style. Complex in the mouth, revealing elegant black currant and herbaceous flavors, it is a stylish, restrained, soft (no doubt because of the vintage's ripeness) effort to be drunk over the next 7–8 years. The Selvamaggio is a blend of 70% Cabernet Sauvignon and 30% Sangiovese made from extremely low yields and aged in five separate types of oak. The 1997 Selvamaggio boasts a deep ruby/purple color as well as a sweet, ostentatious bouquet of smoked herbs, burning wood fires, jammy black currant and cherry fruit, an opulent texture, terrific fruit purity, and admirable intensity. For its quality, complexity, richness, and aging potential of 10–15 years, it is also a reasonably fine value.

OTHER SIGNIFICANT
RED WINES OF ITALY

ABBAZIA DI ROSAZZO (FRIULI–VENEZIA GIULIA)

1995 Pignolo	E	89

This winery is best known for its expressive, light- to medium-bodied, fruit-driven whites that are meant to be drunk within 18 months of the vintage. However, it also produces a very fine red from Pignolo, one of Friuli's indigenous varietals.

The 1995 Pignolo is tannic, but it possesses a wonderful chocolate-covered cherry–scented bouquet, dense, spicy, black fruit characteristics, medium body, and a structured, concentrated personality. It should age nicely for 10 years.

ALLEGRINI (VENETO)

1997 Amarone Classico	E	95
1996 Amarone Classico	C	95
1998 La Grola	B	90
1997 La Grola	C	90
1998 Palazzo della Torre IGT	B	88
1997 Palazzo della Torre IGT	B	90
1996 Palazzo della Torre IGT	B	87
1997 La Poja IGT	E	90
1996 La Poja IGT	E	91
1995 La Poja IGT	E	89
2000 Valpolicella Classico	A	87
1999 Valpolicella Classico	A	86

This estate, which has been on a hot streak for several years, offers three excellent bargain-priced wines—the Valpolicella Classico, Palazzo della Torre, and La Grola—as well as two more expensive luxury *cuvées* (La Poja and the Amarone Classico), which still represent good values in view of their quality. Frustrated with the relaxation of quality controls in Veneto,

Allegrini is another wine-maker who has left the appellation system to redefine local standards. As a consequence, La Grola and La Poja no longer carry Valpolicella designations.

A delicious, fruity, exuberant, zesty Valpolicella Classico, the 2000 offers notes of black cherries intermixed with crushed almonds and dried herbs. It possesses an excellent texture as well as elegant, medium-bodied flavors crammed with fruit and character. No wood is noticeable, the tannin is sweet, and the acidity is unobtrusive. Drink it over the next 1–2 years.

A good value, the 1999 Valpolicella Classico exhibits good berry fruit, notes of almonds, medium body, and light tannin. A delicious lighter-styled red with good purity, it can be drunk with simple pasta dishes or as an apéritif over the next 1–2 years.

The name Valpolicella has been dropped from Allegrini's stunning 1998 La Grola. Made from 70% Corvina, 15% Rondinella, 10% Syrah, and 5% Sangiovese, this 12,000+-case *cuvée* is aged in large wood *foudres* and endures a light filtration prior to bottling. It exhibits a full-bodied, dense, layered character with gobs of berry fruit intertwined with almonds and flowers. Opulent, sexy, and seductive, with low acidity in addition to abundant fat and flesh, this ripe, ostentatiously styled red can be drunk now and over the next 5–7 years. The outstanding dark ruby/purple-colored 1997 La Grola is a fuller-bodied, serious effort. It combines concentration with elegance, a supple texture, impressive levels of black cherry and currant fruit, sweet, subtle wood, and an intriguing underlying mineral note. Supple and rich, it should drink well for 3–5 years.

The Palazzo della Torre is aged in large 2,000- and 8,000-liter Slavonian wood *foudres*. The excellent 1998 Palazzo della Torre is a straightforward, earthy, Pomerol-inspired effort. It displays copious cola and black cherry fruit notes, medium body, low acidity, good lushness, and a fleshy, straightforward finish. Consume it over the next 5–6 years. The outstanding 1997 Palazzo della Torre is a dark ruby/purple-colored wine that is full-bodied, dense, with Rhône-like beef blood and *garrigue* (that blend of earth and dried Provençal herbs) scents intertwined with copious quantities of black cherry and currant fruit. Rich, chewy, and impressive, it should be drunk over the next 8 years. The 1996 Palazzo della Torre displays plenty of cherry and tar flavors with notes of chocolate and grilled herbs in the background. A dark ruby-colored wine with a good texture, medium to full body, and excellent purity and length, this robust Valpolicella should drink well for 2–3 years.

Readers should keep in mind that the grapes for the Amarones are dried for four months prior to being crushed and fermented. The spectacular, opaque purple-colored 1997 Amarone Classico (15.4% alcohol) is from an exceptional vintage for this appellation. It possesses a gorgeous bouquet of graphite, blackberries, plums, cherries, and truffles. Although it reveals some of Amarone's pruny, raisiny, nearly over-the-top characteristics, it is full-bodied, superrich, and concentrated, with striking purity as well as a fabulous perfume. A touch of volatile acidity gives it even more complexity and aromatic uplift. Full, voluptuous, and deep, with huge extract hiding impressive tannin levels, this winemaking tour de force will drink well for 20+ years. The outstanding, dark purple-colored 1996 Amarone Classico offers a knockout nose of wood charcoal intermixed with black truffles, melted asphalt, blackberries, and roast beef. Amazingly rich and full-bodied but not heavy, this chewy, thick, exceptionally pure, harmonious offering should drink well for 10–12+ years. Its low acidity and gorgeously ripe fruit provide immediate accessibility.

La Poja *vino da tavola*, a wine that emerges from the tenderloin hilltop of Allegrini's finest vineyard, displays the winery's belief that great wines can be produced from the indigenous Corvina Veronese grape. Made entirely from this varietal and aged in 100% Taransaud French barrels, La Poja is generally outstanding. The brilliant, young, still undeveloped 1,000-case *cuvée* of 1997 La Poja is derived from a six-acre vineyard situated at a high elevation. Combining power and finesse in a rich, concentrated style, it offers aromas and flavors of minerals, graphite, black currants, cherries, and subtle wood. This dense ruby/purple-colored effort unfolds by increments on the palate, always remaining noble, measured, and stylish. It will benefit from another 1–2 years of cellaring and last for 14–15 years. Built along the lines of the 1990 and 1993 (two superb vintages), the 1996 La Poja is an admirable effort. This dense purple-colored wine is rich and complex, with strong mineral undertones to its blackberry and currant fruit, medium to full body, and plenty of spice. It should continue to evolve for 10–12 years. Very impressive, it is unquestionably one of the finest dry reds I have ever tasted from Veneto. The 1995 La Poja boasts an opaque purple color and full-bodied, concentrated flavors with black raspberry and cherry notes. Powerful and rich, with a velvety texture, good underlying acidity, and moderate tannin, this serious, concentrated, intriguing wine should drink well for 4–7 years.

DE ANGELIS (CAMPANIA)

2000 Lacryma Christi del Vesuvio	B	86

This is a delicious, simple, dry red to drink with prosciutto or salami. Spicy, herb, cherry, currant, and pepper flavors are found in this medium-bodied, easygoing 2000. Consume it over the next 1–2 years.

APOLLONIO (PUGLIA)

2000 Copertino	A	88
1997 Copertino Riserva Divoto	B	89
1998 Primitivo Terragnolo	B	90
1998 Salice Salentino	A	85
1998 Valle Cupa	A	87

Apollonio is typical of the higher-quality producers emerging from southern Italy. Whereas once the wines were thin, astringent, rustic, and fruitless, they are now revolutionary in the sense of their ripeness, purity, supple textures, and concentration. All of them are bottled without filtration. Moreover, they represent very fine values. Apollonio's offerings should definitely be checked out by shrewd consumers.

The 2000 Copertino is a big, robust, full-bodied (14% alcohol), deep ruby/purple-colored effort displaying sweet aromas of jammy black fruits, melted licorice, and asphalt. There is no hint of oak in this fruit-driven, glycerin-filled, fleshy red. Drink it over the next 1–2 years for its exuberance as well as purity. Impressive!

The 1998 Salice Salentino is a modern-styled Salice exhibiting excellent fruit (black raspberries and berries) as well as scorched earth and melted tar. Chewy, rustic, dense, and mouth-filling, with good purity, it should drink well over the next 12 months. The 1998 Valle Cupa, which spends six months in old oak, comes across as more internationally styled, with abundant quantities of blackberry and cherry fruit intermixed with smoke and fennel scents. Full-bodied, ripe, and chewy, this forthright but savory 1998 will drink well for 3–4 years. Apollonio's top effort is the 1998 Primitivo Terragnolo. This opaque purple-colored wine offers up abundant quantities of jammy black cherry and blackberry fruit, truffles, tar, and spice. A full-bodied, luxuriously fruity 1998 with good glycerin, purity, and overall balance, it cuts a broad, rich, concentrated swath across the palate, with no hard edges. Drink it over the next 4–5 years. Interestingly, this wine spent 4–6 months in new oak, which is not discernible because of the wealth of fruit and concentration. Bravo!

The 1997 Copertino Riserva Divoto reveals more finesse and elegance along with sweet black cherry fruit, cedar wood, and spice box characteristics. There are good lushness, a velvety-textured palate, and fine ripeness, purity, and length. Drink it over the next 6–7 years.

ARANO (VENETO)

1997 Amarone	E	91
1997 Valpolicella	C	87

My first taste of this producer's offerings revealed a delicious, expansive, sweet 1997 Valpo-licella with good fruit, medium body, and good depth presented in a round, elegant, supple format. Drink this wine over the next several years. The seriously endowed, full-throttle 1997 Amarone (15% alcohol) offers a dark plum/ruby color in addition to a big, earthy nose of as-phalt, chocolate, roasted herbs, and black fruits. It saturates the mouth and possesses sweet tannin, gorgeously pure fruit, and none of the raisiny, oxidized characteristics found in old-style Amarones. This 1997 should drink well for two decades.

ANTONIO ARGIOLAS (SARDINIA)

1999 Costera	B	90
1998 Costera	A	89
1999 Korem	D	88+?
1998 Korem	D	88
1997 Korem	C	90
1999 Perdera	A	89
1998 Perdera	A	87
1997 Turriga	D	90
1995 Turriga	D	87
1994 Turriga	D	91

This large winery (494 acres) is fashioning splendid wine values from the island of Sardinia. It did particularly well in 1999, producing a Perdera and a Costera that rank among its finest successes to date. Argiolas also produces two luxury *cuvées*, Turriga and Korem (the debut vintage of which was 1997). They struck me as slightly more internationally styled and pos-sibly not as character-filled as their less expensive siblings.

It is hard to find a better bargain than the Perdera, a blend dominated by the indigenous varietal called Monica. This wine is generally rustic and Rhône-styled. The 1999 Perdera reveals a dark plum color as well as a big, smoky nose of earth, barbecue spices, black cher-ries, and a touch of white chocolate. It possesses terrific fruit intensity, big, full-bodied flavors, and a supple texture. Drink it over the next 1–2 years. The 1998 Perdera exhibits a deep ruby color that is followed by peppery, kirsch, and berry scents and flavors. Supple, fleshy, and deep, with excellent purity and good spice, this gutsy, Côtes du Rhône–like red tastes of sunshine and ripe fruit. Enjoy it over the next 12 months.

The quality level increases with the Costera—also an excellent value—which is primarily made from the Cannonau grape (believed to be a kissing cousin of Grenache) and aged with a touch of new French oak. The 1999 Costera is dense, chewy, full-bodied, layered, and seamless with sweet kirsch notes intermixed with licorice and vanilla. Drink it over the next 1–2 years. Nearly outstanding, the 1998 Costera is deep ruby-colored, with medium to full body, robust, peppery, black cherry, and raspberry flavors, high glycerin, a sweet, chewy mid-palate, and a dense, dry, powerful finish. This substantial, mouth-filling red can be drunk over the next 2–3 years.

Korem is a proprietary blend of Merlot, Syrah, Carignan, and two local varietals, Cannonau and Bovale Sardo. Aged 12 months in both tank and *barrique* before being bottled unfiltered, it was first produced in 1997. The 1999 Korem is a full-bodied, rich, spicy, layered effort that impacts the palate with high levels of tannin. There are noticeable wood and earth notes in the long finish. It is ambitious, dense, and chewy, but whether it will ever develop the charm found in Argiolas's less expensive wines remains to be seen. The 1998 Korem exhibits earthy, black cherry fruit, roasted herbs, good spice, medium to full body, and fine density. To my taste, it reveals less individuality than the other 1998s of this excellent winery. Drink it over the next 2–3 years. The 1997 Korem is a knockout, opaque ruby/purple-colored wine which possesses a rich, chocolaty, blackberry-scented nose and flavors, fabulous intensity, smoky, hickory, barbecue-like spice notes, low acidity, and a plump, flashy, luscious, full-bodied finish. It should drink well for 4–5 years.

This estate's flagship wine, the Turriga, is a blend of 85% Cannonau and 15% Malvasia Nera, with tiny dollops of Carignano and Bovale Sardo. It is a *barrique*-aged, unfiltered, gorgeous red that is more generally evolved than the Korem, but complex and attractive. In fact, this wine can be outstanding. The 1997 Turriga is aged in 100% new French oak. A serious effort, it boasts a dense ruby/purple color followed by scents of blackberries, cherry liqueur, and toast in its internationally styled bouquet. There are notes of new saddle leather, full body, a concentrated, powerful style, and copious tannin, depth, and structure. Still an infant, it should drink well for 10–12 years. The 1995 Turriga, which does not quite attain the level of previous vintages, is nevertheless very good. It exhibits abundant quantities of toasty, new French oak in its lavishly wooded nose. Competing with the oak are black cherry and berry notes. In the mouth, the wine is medium to full bodied, ripe, and internationally styled, with a compressed, dry, tannic finish. Drink it over the next 2–3 years. The 1994 Turriga's dark ruby color is accompanied by a textbook, internationally styled nose of spicy new oak, cedar, chocolate, and black currants. Dense, long, and rich, it has pure fruit and attractive fat, cedary, grilled meat–like flavors. This is an outstanding wine with considerable complexity plus a nicely layered texture and finish. Close to full maturity, it will continue to age for 4–5 years.

BASILISCO (BASILICATA)

1999 Aglianico del Vulture	D	88
1998 Aglianico del Vulture	D	89
1997 Basilisco	D	89

The intriguing, opaque purple-colored 1997 Basilisco possesses a bouquet of lavender, spring flowers, blueberries, and melted asphalt. As it sits in the glass, cigar box aromas emerge. Rich, dense, and full-bodied, with 14.5% alcohol, it may be controversial given its eccentric yet intriguing aromatics.

The two modern-styled Italian reds are produced from Aglianico, a grape that should begin receiving more attention given the level of quality evident in my tastings over the last few years. A serious varietal, it may not provide the complexity of such great international grapes as Pinot Noir, Syrah, Cabernet Sauvignon, Merlot, Cabernet Franc, Tempranillo, and Nebbiolo, but it is comparable to the quality of Sangiovese, Mourvèdre, and Zinfandel. Basilisco's Aglianicos are aged for 12 months in new oak, resulting in serious, dense purple-colored efforts with telltale notes of melted asphalt intermixed with earthy black cherry and currant fruit. While both vintages are similar in style, the 1998 appears to have more texture and volume than the 1999. The aging potential of these two wines is unknown, but I would recommend drinking them during their exuberant youth, over the next 5–6 years.

BOCCADIGABBIA (MARCHE)

1998 Cabernet Sauvignon Akronte	D	88
1997 Cabernet Sauvignon Akronte	D	90
1998 Rosso Piceno Saltapicchio	C	87
1997 Rosso Piceno Saltapicchio	C	88

Among the finest wines I have tasted from this region, these modern-styled, proprietary reds are exceptionally well made.

What the internationally styled 1998 Akronte lacks in soul and regional typicity, it makes up for in its blast of black currant fruit intermixed with toasty new oak. Made in a pure, fleshy, concentrated style, it is meant to be consumed over the next 5–6 years. The opaque ruby/purple-colored 1997 Akronte reveals classic Cabernet Sauvignon aromas of cedar and black currants presented in a rich, full-bodied, Bordeaux-like style. It displays low acidity, excellent purity, and the influence of new oak. Drink it over the next decade.

The medium-bodied 1998 Saltapicchio exhibits elegant, smoky, oaky black cherry and currant flavors presented in a moderately endowed, supple style. Tannin as well as intriguing espresso notes are present in the finish. Drink it over the next 2 years. The 1997 Saltapicchio (100% Sangiovese) offers an elegant, cherry, strawberry, and leathery-scented nose, medium body, good spice and ripeness, and a round, open-knit texture. It is meant to be drunk over the next 2–3 years.

BRIGALDARA (VENETO)

1997 Amarone	E	90
1995 Amarone	D	91
1998 Valpolicella Classico	A	86

The light ruby-colored 1998 Valpolicella Classico exhibits scents of sweet strawberry and berry fruit intertwined with smoke and almond extract. Fruity and round, it is ideal for drinking over the next 12 months. A smoky, full-bodied, earthy effort, the dark ruby-colored 1997 Amarone offers up scents of animal fur, melted tar, and ripe plum, prune, and black cherries. Drink this dense, chewy, heady Amarone over the next 10–15 years. More serious is the big, bold, southern Rhône–like 1995 Amarone. Full-bodied, dense, and chewy, with notes of melted asphalt and earthy, animal-tinged blackberry and cherry fruit, this is a concentrated, lusty effort. There are no hard edges in this impressively built, smoky, earthy Amarone. Drink it over the next 10 years.

TOMMASO BUSSOLA (VENETO)

1997 Amarone TB	E	92
1997 Amarone Vigneto Alto TB	EE	96
1995 Amarone Vigneto Alto TB	E	92
1997 Recioto della Valpolicella TB	E	98
1997 Valpolicella Classico TB	C	91
1995 Valpolicella Classico TB	C	88

The young, self-taught Tommaso Bussola, unquestionably one of the region's up-and-coming superstars, continues to fashion some of the finest wines of Veneto, a region enjoying the same kind of renaissance that occurred in Tuscany and Piedmont a decade ago. This young producer is making an effort to compete with some of Veneto's most serious wine-makers (i.e., Giuseppe Quintarelli and Dal Forno Romano). Bussola's wines are beautifully intense, with gorgeous purity and powerful ripe fruit flavors, yet a freshness and harmony that make them stand out. Readers should note that Tommaso Bussolo has two quality levels of wine. His introductory-level offerings have the letters "BG" on the label. I did not taste any of those wines. His top selections all have the letters "TB."

Forgetting the remarkable wines from Dal Forno Romano, it would be hard to find a better Valpolicella than Bussola's 1997 Valpolicella Classico TB. It puts to shame most of the industrial swill that dominates the marketplace. Bussola's 1997 exhibits terrific concentration, a gorgeously voluptuous texture, and plenty of sweet berry fruits intermixed with a touch of marzipan and spice. This seductive, luscious, richly fruity Valpolicella is best consumed over the next 3–4 years. The 1995 Valpolicella Classico TB is in stark contrast to the vast quantities of wine that emerge from this appellation. This is a medium ruby-colored, deliciously ripe, fat offering with gobs of herb-tinged, spicy, black cherry fruit with a touch of balsa wood, tar, and roasted nuts. Drink this medium-bodied, fleshy Valpolicella over the next 1–2 years.

The 1997 Amarone TB is a broad, expansive, muscular, dense, full-bodied, pure effort offering aromas and flavors of melted asphalt, black plums, cherries, and earth. This concentrated Amarone cuts a large swath across the palate. Drink it over the next 10–15 years.

The prodigious 1997 Amarone Vigneto Alto TB is reminiscent of Henri Bonneau's 1990 Châteauneuf-du-Pape Réserve des Célestins. The lofty 16% alcohol level is barely noticeable. Yields were a minuscule 20 hectoliters per hectare. Sadly, there are only 300 cases of this extraordinary Amarone. It boasts notes of smoke, truffle oil, blackberries, plums, and earthy, concentrated black currant jam. Layered, thick, full-bodied, and dry, with extraordinary purity as well as definition, it is an amazing achievement. While not for everybody, this is a singular, impeccably balanced wine. Anticipated maturity: now–2020. The profound 1995 Amarone Vigneto Alto TB exhibits a dense plum color as well as superb aromatics of melted chocolate, asphalt, and cherry liqueur intermixed with grilled steak and Provençal herb notes. Powerful, thick, full-bodied, muscular, and dry, this intense, layered, superb Amarone is ideal for drinking over the next 10–12 years. It should be paired with appropriately rich dishes or a cheese course.

Lastly, the 1997 Recioto della Valpolicella TB is a fabulously layered, slightly sweet offering with huge levels of glycerin, extract, and fruit. I am not a big fan of Recioto della Valpolicella as it usually too sweet and heavy, but this example is riveting. Concentrated and pure yet neither overwhelmingly heavy nor cloyingly sweet, it is great stuff. Moreover, it will last for three decades or more.

CA' DEI FRATI (LOMBARDY)

1998 Ronchedone IGT	C	89

The 1998 Ronchedone is a blend of Cabernet Sauvignon, Merlot, Barbera, Sangiovese, Groppello, and Marzemino. Notes of spice, smoke, cedar, and red fruits are presented in an elegant, pure format. There are good density on the palate, a sweet attack, abundant spice and red fruits, and light tannin in the finish. Drink it over the next 3–4 years.

LA CADALORA (TRENTINO–ALTO ADIGE)

1998 Majere IGT	C	88
1997 Majere IGT	C	89
2000 San Valentino	B	85
1999 San Valentino	B	86
1998 San Valentino	B	87
1998 Vignalet Pinot Nero	C	87

This is a fine group of wines emerging from La Cadalora, whose vineyards are located in the lower section of Trentino known as Vallagarina.

The three San Valentinos, which are good bargains, are essentially made of an indigenous grape called Marzemino. These tank-fermented and -aged wines reminiscent of a Beaujolais are meant to be consumed over the near term, within the next 2–3 years. The 2000 San Valentino exhibits tangy cherry fruit, good acidity, and a simple, straightforward style. The 1999 San Valentino boasts an opaque purple color in addition to scents of herbs, earth, and black fruits. Although not complex, it is a fat, mouth-filling, cleanly made red. The 1998 San Valentino is a Beaujolais-styled Italian red with plenty of dried herb, spicy, round, berry/cherry fruit as well as roasted espresso notes. With good fat in addition to a chewy, nicely textured mid-palate and finish, it lacks complexity but offers good flavor density.

The smoky, herb, and cherry-scented 1998 Vignalet Pinot Nero is medium-bodied, pleasant, and best drunk over the next 2–3 years.

With good body, structure, and delineation as well as evidence of *barrique* aging, the 1998 Majere reveals copious quantities of spicy oak, blackberries, and cherry fruit. A blend of 70% Casetta (a local varietal) and 30% Cabernet Sauvignon, it should drink well for 4–5 years. The tightly knit, but impressively endowed, nearly outstanding, opaque ruby/purple-colored 1997 Majere (70% Casetta and 30% Cabernet Sauvignon) is a dense, medium- to full-bodied, concentrated effort with moderate tannin as well as a youthful vigor and exuberance. It does not reveal many secondary nuances, but it should age well for 7–8 years.

ANTONIO CAGGIANO (CAMPANIA)

1999	Salae Domini	D	89
1998	Salae Domini	D	90
1997	Salae Domini	D	90
2000	Taurì	D	88
1998	Taurasi	D	89
1997	Taurasi	D	87

The attractive, medium-weight 2000 Taurì (100% Aglianico) does not reveal the roasted, eccentric characteristics often found in wines from Campania. Its deep ruby color is followed by copious quantities of berry fruit, melted asphalt, spice, and meat. Drink it over the next 2–3 years.

The 100% Aglianico 1998 Taurasi exhibits that varietal's telltale melted asphalt/soil notes along with saddle leather and black fruits. This perfumed, medium-bodied 1998 possesses supple tannin as well as considerable complexity. It should drink well for 5–6 years. The 1997 Taurasi reveals notes of melted road tar, black cherries, chocolate, leather, and spice box. Medium-bodied and husky, with some rusticity, it will drink well for 3–4 years.

An outstanding wine produced from 100% Aglianico, aged in small French oak casks, the Salae Domini usually reveals an international style in its youth, but its southern Italian heritage emerges with some further aging. Notes of earth, leather, pepper, mushrooms, and wood emerge from the 1999 Salae Domini. Dense, medium- to full-bodied, and rustic, it is made in the modern school yet retains some of the region's uncivilized aspects. Drink it over the next 5–6 years. The striking 1998 Salae Domini is a *barrique*-aged 100% Aglianico. Kirsch intermixed with chocolate, pepper, leather, spice, and earth are all present in this multilayered, rich wine produced from extremely young vines. This terrific effort is a reasonably fine value in today's inflated wine market. Drink it over the next 7–8 years. Deep ruby/purple-colored, with medium to full body, the ripe, concentrated 1997 Salae Domini offers abundant quantities of sweet toasty oak intermixed with black fruits and licorice. Deep, ripe, and nicely layered, with low acidity and a fine mid-section and length, it can be drunk now and over the next 4–5 years.

CANTINA DELL'ABBAZIA DI NOVACELLA (TRENTINO–ALTO ADIGE)

1999	Lagrein	D	85
1997	Praepositus Rosso Riserva	D	89

This winery, founded in 1142, boasts that it is the oldest in the world. It produces both whites and reds, the former being meant for near-term consumption—they are best drunk within 12–18 months after the vintage. The soft, round, dark ruby-colored 1999 Lagrein offers copious quantities of berry fruit, earth, and spice. Acidity and tannin are present but unobtrusive. Fresh, lively, and spicy, it is meant to be drunk over the near term. The more serious 1997 Praepositus Rosso Riserva (100% Lagrein) spent time in new oak. It offers toasty vanilla scents intermixed with jammy, ripe blackberry and cherry fruit. Thick, rich, and full-bodied, with admirable depth, this surprising effort is capable of lasting 5–6 years.

CANTINE DEL NOTAIO (BASILICATA)

1999	Aglianico del Vulture La Firma	D	90
1998	Aglianico del Vulture La Firma	D	92
1999	Aglianico del Vulture Il Repertorio	C	86

The blockbuster, super-concentrated, dense ruby/purple-colored 1998 Aglianico del Vulture La Firma is one of the finest Aglianicos I have ever tasted. It admirably displays the potential of this area of southern Italy. Impressively dense and concentrated, with competing aromas of blackberries, cherries, roasted herbs, meats, licorice, and high-quality toasty French oak, this thick, juicy, well-balanced, mouthcoating wine should age nicely for a decade.

The 1999 Aglianico del Vulture Il Repertorio is a soft, fleshy, straightforward, chunky effort with robust, earthy, peppery characteristics, red and black fruits, and dusty tannin. Consume it over the next 3–4 years for its primitive charm. The superior 1999 Aglianico del Vulture La Firma was aged in 50% new oak. It is a modern-styled red that has not lost the typicity of this region of southern Italy. It offers flamboyant aromas of pepper, earth, black fruits, sausage, and vanilla. Ripe, chewy, forceful, and dense, it should drink well for 7–8 years.

IL CARPINO (FRIULI–VENEZIA GIULIA)

1999 Rubrum	C	91

This is the debut release from Il Carpino, which had the foresight to bring in renowned oenologist Roberto Cipresso. It is an immensely impressive effort made from extremely small yields of 12 hectoliters per hectare, which contribute significantly to its intense flavors. After undergoing malolactics and 18 months aging in 100% new French oak, it is bottled unfiltered. The 1999 Rubrum may be the finest Merlot I have tasted from Friuli. This explosive effort must be tasted to be believed. A black/purple color is accompanied by sweet, toasty, black cherry liqueur, mocha, cola, and currant fruit aromas. Full-bodied, moderately tannic, and youthful, it resembles a barrel sample as opposed to a finished wine. A revelation for the appellation, this fabulous Merlot should evolve for 10–15+ years. Bravo!

LA CARRAIA (UMBRIA)

1999 Fobiano IGT	D	90
1998 Fobiano IGT	C	90
1997 Fobiano IGT	C	92
2000 Sangiovese IGT	B	88
1999 Sangiovese IGT	B	87

One of Riccardo Cotarella's Umbrian estates, La Carraia is a source of value-priced Sangiovese. Moreover, the quantities produced ensure large availability as there are about 250,000 bottles of this unfiltered/unfined, 100% Sangiovese, which embarrasses virtually all California Sangioveses selling for two to four times the price. The estate also fashions a Merlot-based wine called Fobiano, which, although it is more expensive than the Sangiovese, is a very fine value.

The 2000 Sangiovese IGT is a richly fruity wine with excellent texture, fine purity, and lively, tart flavors. This deep ruby-colored, medium-bodied offering is meant to be drunk during its first 2–3 years of life. La Carraia's 1999 Sangiovese IGT is dark ruby-colored, with an enticing bouquet of smoke, blackberries, strawberries, and spice, this elegant, soft wine has an attractive, supple-textured mid-palate, and sweet tannin. This medium-bodied, fruit-driven effort possesses complexity, charm, and suppleness. Drink it over the next 1–2 years.

The Fobiano, a blend of Merlot and Cabernet Sauvignon (the proportions varying with each vintage), is aged in new French oak casks and bottled without fining or filtration. Unfortunately, the production is extremely small and rarely exceeds 2,500 cases annually. The exceptional 1999 Fobiano (70% Merlot and 30% Cabernet Sauvignon) exhibits a dense ruby/purple color as well as an intensely perfumed nose of black cherries, mocha, smoke, and earth, deep, medium- to full-bodied flavors, and a nicely layered personality. This beauty should drink well for 7–8 years. The outstanding 1998 Fobiano (70% Merlot and 30% Cabernet Sauvignon) exhibits dense opaque purple color that is accompanied by notes of new saddle leather, blackberry liqueur, smoke, and licorice. An opulently textured wine with medium to full body, a chewy, lush mid-palate, and outstanding purity and ripeness, it can be drunk now as well as over the next 7–8 years. The Fobiano 1997 (90% Merlot and 10% Cabernet Sauvignon) reflects the great ripeness and richness achieved in 1997. The wine's black/purple color is followed by a stunning nose of licorice, smoke, black fruits, and minerals. Amazingly rich, with no hard edges, this sumptuous, silky-textured, full-bodied offering coats the mouth but is neither heavy nor out of balance. Its 40+-second finish is dazzling. Anticipated maturity: now–2015.

CASALE DEL GIGLIO (LAZIO)

1998 Cabernet Sauvignon	D	89
1997 Mater Matuta	D	89
1996 Mater Matuta	D	90
1995 Mater Matuta	D	88
1999 Merlot	C	88
1997 Merlot	C	87
1999 Petit Verdot	C	87

These are all exceptionally well made offerings from a region in central Italy, not far from Rome's international airport. All are *barrique*-aged, 12 months in the case of the Merlot and Petit Verdot and 15–18 months for the Cabernet Sauvignon and Mater Matuta (a blend of 85% Syrah and 15% Petit Verdot). All the wines are technically impressive, possessing dense ruby/purple colors as well as plenty of toasty new oak and sweet tannin. That being said, there is a certain international style to them. Tasting them blind, I would not have the slightest idea whether they were from Italy, Australia, France, or America. Nevertheless, there is a lot to like.

The plum/purple-colored 1999 Petit Verdot offers aromas of cedar, tobacco, underbrush, and new oak. Forceful and concentrated, with moderate levels of tannin, it will undoubtedly become increasingly cedary and herbaceous with age. Consume it over the next 5–8 years.

Readers looking for reasonably good Merlot that won't break the bank should check out Casale del Giglio's Merlots. The 1999 Merlot exhibits a deep ruby color in addition to dense, sweet notes of mocha, berry fruit, and espresso in its soft, fleshy, forward, jammy style. Enjoy it over the next 5–6 years. Dried herbs, mocha, coffee, and berry notes emerge from the dark ruby-colored 1997 Merlot. Soft, with supple tannin, fine richness, and a compact, fruity personality, it should be consumed over the next 12 months.

The opaque purple-colored, smoky, oaky, crème de cassis–scented and –flavored, seriously endowed 1998 Cabernet Sauvignon offers good density, soft tannin, and plenty of appeal. It is a fairly priced Cabernet to enjoy over the next decade.

The intriguing Mater Matuta is a blend of 60% Syrah and 40% Petit Verdot aged 18 months in French oak prior to bottling. The noteworthy, dense purple-colored 1997 Mater Matuta offers blackberries mixed with smoke (from its Syrah component) along with new oak characteristics, which give it an international feel. Overall, it is an excellent red with abundant ripeness, authentic varietal character, and a nicely textured, long, supple finish. Drink this appealing effort over the next 7–8 years. The deep ruby/purple-colored 1996 Mater Matuta reveals more density and complexity as well as medium to full body, fine opulence, and rich, peppery blackberry and cassis fruit intermixed with smoky wood. Not a blockbuster, it is an elegant, complex effort that should drink well for 7–8 years. The dark plum/purple-colored 1995 Mater Matuta exhibits a surprisingly complex, Bordeaux-like nose of cedar wood, black currants, licorice, and tobacco. Rich, spicy, and medium-bodied, it is ideal for drinking over the next 5–6 years.

I CASTEI (VENETO)

1997	Amarone della Valpolicella Campo Casalin	D	(87–89)
1995	Amarone della Valpolicella Campo Casalin	D	91
1997	Rosso Veronese	D	(88–90)
1997	Valpolicella Classico	B	85
1995	Valpolicella Classico Ripassa	C	88

The fresh, lively fruit found in these offerings stood out in my tastings. The 1997 Valpolicella Classico is a straightforward, ruby/plum-colored effort with attractive nut-infused cherry and strawberry fruit. It should be consumed over the next 12 months. The 1997 Rosso Veronese appears to be excellent, possibly outstanding. A dark ruby color is accompanied by copious quantities of smoky blackberry and cherry fruit. This medium- to full-bodied wine reveals evidence of cask aging but is dominated by its earthy, foresty, animal components. That being said, the fruit is extremely fresh, lively, and pure.

The Amarone della Valpolicella Campo Casalin is a single-vineyard selection, aged in both *foudres* and small French casks. The 1997 Amarone della Valpolicella Campo Casalin reveals sweet, ripe, nearly overripe blackberry and cherry fruit with a kirsch characteristic. Notes of truffles, damp forest, asphalt, and rose petals also emerge. Full-bodied, layered, and rich, this example should come close to being outstanding. The 1995 Amarone della Valpolicella Campo Casalin is a powerful, concentrated example of these robust, high-alcohol, heavyweight wines. It possesses a dark ruby/purple color, tremendous intensity, and gorgeous levels of chocolate-infused, truffle-scented black cherry and plum fruit. Full-bodied, heavy, and thick, it is a wine to drink with robust cheese or winter-weight dishes. It should age well for 10–12 years. The 1995 Valpolicella Classico Ripassa (made with the Ripassa technique, where the wine is passed over the pressed grape skins that are used to make Valpolicella's Amarones and Reciotos) is a leathery, dense, complex wine with notes of melted chocolate, creosote, and dense, dried cherry, medium-bodied flavors. It is a robust Valpolicella to drink over the next 1–2 years.

CATALDI MADONNA (ABRUZZO)

1999	Montepulciano d'Abruzzo	B	87
1999	Malandrino	C	88
1998	Malandrino	C	88
1997	Malandrino	C	88
1998	Tonì IGT	D	90
1997	Tonì IGT	D	90
1995	Tonì IGT	D	89

From one of my favorite Montepulciano d'Abruzzo producers, these delicious wines are robust, exuberant, and concentrated, and many readers will find them even better than my ratings suggest. Although not complex, they are loaded with fun and fruit, extremely pure (because of clean, healthy vinification), and well balanced, with fruit-dominated personalities. I highly recommend them, even though my scoring system does not do justice to wines such as these that represent 100% pleasure, yet may not be that complex.

The dark ruby-colored 1999 Montepulciano d'Abruzzo offers telltale aromas of cocoa, red and black currants, with a touch of herbs and cinnamon for additional complexity. In the mouth, it is sexy, ripe, opulent, and fleshy with plenty of fruit as well as a hint of almonds. Consume this pure, fat effort over the next year.

The Malandrinos are blends of Cabernet Sauvignon and the indigenous grape, Montepulciano. The 1999 Malandrino offers luscious red and black currant fruit intermixed with Bing cherry characteristics, a sweet attack, plenty of succulence, medium body, no evidence of wood, and a ripe, luscious finish. Enjoy it over the next 4–5 years. The 1998 Malandrino offers the same delicious, exuberant, fruity characteristics of its peers but is denser, with more ripeness and some of the structure afforded by Cabernet Sauvignon. A deep ruby color is followed by knockout aromatics (particularly if you are a fruit fanatic), excellent purity, and a supple, medium-bodied, lusty finish. Drink it over the next 1–2 years. The opaque ruby/purple-colored 1997 Malandrino reveals thick, juicy, roasted herb, earth, blackberry, and cherry flavors. Dusty tannin is present, but this wine is mouth-filling as well as substantial in weight and size. It should drink well for 1–2 years, but do not expect a great deal of finesse from this concentrated, earthy, full-bodied spice bomb.

The exceptional 1998 Tonì boasts a ruby purple color as well as a gorgeously expressive nose of black fruits, balsa wood, dried herbs, and soil notes. With superb purity, ripe fruit, a lush, layered texture, and a long, seamless finish, it will drink well for 5–6 years. The opaque purple-colored 1997 Tonì is a serious wine. It boasts great fruit, terrific ripeness, a black cherry/blackberry jammy character, medium to full body, wonderful density, but no hardness, angular acidity, or rough tannin. A fruit bomb from central Italy, it can be enjoyed over the next 2–3 years. The 1995 Tonì is a full-bodied, super-concentrated, earthy, tarry, chocolaty, blackberry-scented and -flavored wine with considerable concentration and force. Dense, thick, and juicy, with plenty of personality and soul, it should drink well for 2–3 years.

CEUSO (SICILY)

1998 Vigna Custera	D	90

An impressive effort from Sicily, this blend of 50% Nero d'Avola, 20% Merlot, and 30% Cabernet Sauvignon boasts a dark ruby/purple color along with a knockout nose of black fruits intermixed with smoke, minerals, and graphite. Displaying only a hint of its 12 months of aging in new French oak, there are no hard edges to this textured, rich, ripe, distinctive 1998. Consume it over the next 7–8 years.

COCCI GRIFONI (MARCHE)

1997 Rosso Piceno Il Grifoni	D	89
1997 Rosso Piceno Vigna Messieri	B	86

An excellent value from one of Italy's backwater regions, Cocci Grifoni's 1997 Rosso Piceno Vigna Messieri (a blend of Montepulciano and Sangiovese) offers copious quantities of fruit presented in an elegant, round, medium-bodied, soft, cherry-dominated format. Drink it over the next 1–2 years. The 1997 Rosso Piceno Il Grifoni (a blend of Montepulciano, Sangiovese, and Cabernet Sauvignon) may be outstanding. It offers an opaque ruby/purple color as well as a gorgeously sweet bouquet of black currants, cherry liqueur, fresh almonds, and minerals. Medium- to full-bodied and well made, with sweet tannin, spicy, ripe, concentrated fruit, excellent purity, and a long finish, it should drink well for 5–6 years.

COLLE PICCHIONI (LAZIO)

1998 Vigna del Vassallo	D	90
1996 Villa del Vassallo	D	92

The wines of Colle Picchioni taste amazingly similar to topflight St.-Emilions. Produced from a vineyard situated ten miles from Rome, they are blends of Cabernet Franc, Cabernet Sauvignon, and Merlot—could they be the Cheval Blancs of the Adriatic coast?—aged in French oak. The 1998 Vigna del Vassallo boasts a complex bouquet of black currants, toast, licorice, spice box, and tobacco. Rich, full-bodied, and chewy, with superb concentration, great individuality, and undeniable complexity, this is a stunning effort. Drink it over the next 12–15 years. The 1996 Villa del Vassallo, an intriguing blend of 50% Cabernet Franc and the remainder Merlot and Cabernet Sauvignon, is a saturated purple-colored, gloriously fragrant wine with a complex nose of saddle leather, flowers, black currants, and coconuts. It boasts a rich, medium-bodied, superintense attack, as well as a glorious mid-palate and a finish loaded with copious quantities of sweet tannin. Notes of licorice emerge on the palate. This brilliant wine was aged for 24 months in French wood before being bottled following a light filtration. Drink it over the next 7–8 years. Bravo!

COLLI AMERINI (UMBRIA)

1999	Carbio IGT	C	89
1998	Carbio IGT	C	87
1997	Carbio IGT	C	89
1998	Torraccio	C	90
1997	Torraccio	C	90

Winemaking genius Riccardo Cotarella is the guiding force behind this estate's substantial, flavor-filled, reasonably priced reds. Carbio is generally a blend of Sangiovese, Barbera, Merlot, Montepulciano, Canaiolo, and Ciliegiolo that ages seven months in 100% new French oak before being bottled unfined and unfiltered. It is a good value given today's inflated wine pricing. The estate also produces a fine unfined/unfiltered 100% Sangiovese Torraccio, a top-notch choice for readers seeking a quality Sangiovese with complexity as well as depth of flavor.

The 1999 Carbio is a complex, black cherry and berry-scented offering with a style not dissimilar from that of a topflight California Zinfandel. It displays excellent purity, medium body, and a subtle dosage of oak. As the wine sits in the glass, it displays a Burgundy-like character. Drink this lush, serious, plump 1999 during its exuberant youth—over the next 3–4 years. The 1998 Carbio is a dark ruby-colored effort that exhibits a noteworthy bouquet of strawberry jam intermixed with cherries, dried herbs, leather, and toast. Spicy and medium-bodied, with a lush personality, this nicely concentrated, supple-textured wine should drink well for 3–4 years. The highly extracted, well-balanced, soft, leathery 1997 Carbio possesses a dark ruby color and sweet plum, cherry, and black currant notes intermixed with scents of cedar and new saddle leather. Velvety-textured, rich, and exuberant, this tasty wine should be drunk over the next 2–3 years.

The 1998 Torraccio tastes like a premier cru Côtes de Beaune with its emphasis on black cherry and strawberry fruit mixed with floral, new saddle leather, and spicy new-oak notes. Supple, medium- to full-bodied, ripe, and harmonious, this is a beautifully made wine to enjoy over the next 6–7 years. The outstanding 1997 Torraccio boasts a dark ruby color as well as a terrific floral-scented nose with aromas of new saddle leather, strawberry jam, cherries, and spice box. Rich and medium-bodied, with a silky mid-palate and fine length, this is a beautifully knit, elegant red to enjoy over the next 2–3 years.

COOPERATIVA SAN PATRIGNANO TERRE DEL CEDRO (EMILIA-ROMAGNA)

1999	Sangiovese Avi Riserva	D	91
1998	Sangiovese Avi Riserva	D	87
1997	Sangiovese Avi Riserva	D	88

The story behind Terre del Cedro is a touching one. The proprietor, Vincenzo Muccioli, has dedicated this estate to trying to salvage the lives of drug addicts. There is a 100% Sangiovese vineyard of 112 acres worked by the young men and women who enter this program. They are required to give up drugs and work exclusively for the production of high-quality wine. While Chardonnay, Merlot, and Cabernet Sauvignon have been planted, the wines made under the guidance of consulting oenologist Riccardo Cotarella (who also feels a strong sense of commitment to this operation) are currently made from 100% Sangiovese, aged for 12 months in French oak casks and bottled without fining or filtration. Within this community, Vincenzo Muccioli has established a private vineyard known as San Patrignano, from which he produces a luxury *cuvée* Avi. Unfortunately, availability does not exceed 200 cases, with yields being as low as 15 hectoliters per hectare (i.e., one bottle per three vines).

The 1999 Avi is the finest yet produced. Its dry extract number of 38.5 grams per liter is one of the highest I have seen. My tasting notes said, "the Bryant Family Vineyard of Sangiovese." That probably says it all for anyone who has tasted Bryant Family's marvelous Napa Valley Cabernet Sauvignon. This large-scaled, superdense, concentrated Sangiovese should be tasted by California producers so they can understand just what heights this grape can achieve and how far they are from producing remotely legitimate Sangioveses. Long, concentrated, and filled with notes of grilled herbs intermixed with blackberry and kirschy fruit and a touch of spicy new oak, this opulent, voluptuous offering is a thrill to drink. Anticipated maturity: now–2010. I also enjoyed the 1998 and 1997 Avis. The deep ruby-colored 1998 Avi reveals aromas of black cherry fruit, dried herbs, earth, and spice. Medium-bodied, chewy, and spicy, with a Mediterranean-like personality, it should be consumed over the next 1–2 years. The smoky, meaty, low-acid, dark ruby/purple-colored 1997 Avi possesses more opulence in addition to a heady, ripe, rich, black cherry/plum fruitiness. Like its younger sibling, it is fruit-driven and ideal for near-term consumption—over the next 1–2 years.

COPPO-JULI (PIEDMONT)

1999	Barbera di Monferrato	D	90

Roberto Cipresso is the oenologist responsible for this offering. This big, thick, full-bodied Barbera from Coppo-Juli was produced from extremely low yields of 20 hectoliters per hectare, aged 18 months in new French oak, and bottled unfiltered. It exhibits hints of oak as well as vibrant mineral, strawberry, and cherry aromas in its explosive, ostentatious aromatics and high levels of glycerin and concentration. The wine hits the palate with a dense, concentrated, muscular feel, but the acidity gives uplift as well as delineation. Drink this impressive Barbera over the next 4–5 years.

DAL FORNO ROMANO (VENETO)

1996	Amarone della Valpolicella	EEE	99
1995	Amarone della Valpolicella	EEE	98
1994	Amarone della Valpolicella	EEE	97
1997	Valpolicella	D	93
1996	Valpolicella	EE	94
1995	Valpolicella	EE	91

The Dal Forno family is unquestionably the leading Veneto producer of Valpolicella and Amarone. It is remarkable what proprietors Luigi and Romano Dal Forno have accomplished, given the fact that they took over this estate in 1983 and built a new winery in 1990. In terms of European winemaking experience, they have a short résumé. Their wines, which go from strength to strength, have established new benchmarks for Valpolicella and Amarone, redefining this category—in both price and quality. Regrettably, they are both hard to find and priced in the stratosphere. However, anyone who has tasted a Dal Forno Romano offering realizes that this is the reference point for prodigious Valpolicella and Amarone. They possess off-the-chart levels of complexity, richness, and aging potential, and reveal a style totally unlike anything else produced in the region. If California's famed winemaking/viticultural husband-and-wife team of Helen Turley and John Wetlaufer were to make Valpolicella or Amarone, it would taste like Dal Forno Romano's. Sadly, there are only about 18,000 bottles of the Valpolicella and even less Amarone. Decent quantities are exported, although most stays in Italy to be drunk by the local cognoscenti and in the country's finest restaurants.

For example, the 1997 Valpolicella is the greatest Valpolicella I have ever tasted. An opaque purple color is accompanied by a thick, glycerin-imbued texture with immense concentration, fabulous purity, and copious quantities of smoky, earth-infused blackberry and cherry fruit. This awesome effort must be tasted to be believed. It should drink well for 10 years. The 1996 Valpolicella is amazing. Readers will have to redefine their definition of Valpolicella to understand this blockbuster. The color is a dense purple. The bouquet offers glorious levels of blackberry and cherry fruit intertwined with vanilla, minerals, lead pencil shavings, and spice. The wine is full-bodied and voluptuously textured, with sweet tannin and a seamless finish. It is an enormous yet incredibly symmetrical Valpolicella to drink over the next 2–5 years; it will last for 15–18 years. Though slightly less rich than the 1997, the 1995 Valpolicella is an amazing effort, with an opaque dark ruby color as well as an explosive nose of smoke, earth, jammy berry and blackberry fruit, great richness and purity, full body, and abundant glycerin and intensity. Remarkably, there is little evidence of new oak, even though the wine spent 36 months in barrel before being bottled without filtration. It tips the scales at a whopping 14.5% alcohol, high for Valpolicella. It should drink well for 10 years.

Amarone is an acquired taste, given its size as well as its earthy, tarry characteristics. Certainly Dal Forno Romano's Amarones reach new levels of extract and richness yet are dry, well balanced, and, because of their extravagant richness, able to hide the whopping 16–17% alcohol they routinely possess. The three following wines are the products of a true genius. The virtually perfect 1996 is undoubtedly the finest Amarone della Valpolicella I have ever tasted. Its inky black/purple color is accompanied by extraordinarily pure, graphite-infused, blackberry, plum, mineral, licorice, and espresso flavors. Despite its monumental intensity and richness, this wine is not heavy, somehow managing to conceal its 17.5% alcohol! As compelling an Italian wine as I have ever tasted, it should prove to be unbelievably long-lived. Anticipated maturity: 2004–2030. The opaque purple-colored 1995 Amarone della Valpolicella is nearly perfect. It is reminiscent of super-concentrated blackberry liqueur infused with incense, smoke, and minerals. Full-bodied, dense, and chewy, this huge offering possesses remarkable purity and liveliness for its size and intensity. The spectacular 1994 Amarone della Valpolicella exhibits amazing freshness for a wine of such mass, size, and concentration. It oozes across the palate but never comes close to being heavy. There are amazing quantities of truffles, smoke, black fruits, and licorice present in this exquisite wine. These two last wines should drink well for a minimum of 15–18 years.

DI MAJO NORANTE (MOLISE)

1997 Aglianico Vigneto Contato	A	87
1999 Don Luigi	B	91
1998 Ramitello Rosso	A	86
1997 Ramitello Rosso	A	87
1996 Ramitello Rosso	C	87
2000 San Giorgio	A	88
1999 San Giorgio	A	86

All of these offerings from Di Majo Norante are excellent values, especially since oenologist Riccardo Cotarella has been brought in as a consultant. He has changed the trellising system and lowered vineyard yields, in addition to modifying vinification techniques.

Di Majo Norante's San Giorgio (100% Sangiovese) may be the finest value in pure Sangiovese in the marketplace. There are 15,000 cases of this offering. A great buy, it is an embarrassment to 90% of the California Sangioveses that sell for three to five times the price—and are inferior wines. The deep ruby-colored 2000 San Giorgio offers an expressive perfume of sweet black cherries, new saddle leather, and spice. This fleshy, fruit-driven Sangiovese is a total treat to drink. It will not make old bones, but for consuming over the next 12–18 months, it delivers the goods. The 1999 San Giorgio exhibits a medium ruby color followed by a sweet nose of berry and currant fruit, earth, and dried herbs. This soft, tasty, richly fruity wine can be consumed over the next 12–18 months.

A superb breakthrough for Di Majo Norante, the 1999 Don Luigi is a barrel-fermented and -aged blend of 80% Montepulciano and 20% Tintiua. A monster, opaque purple-colored effort, it reveals a sexy, seductive nose of jammy black fruits combined with smoke, graphite, licorice, and new wood. It is voluptuous, full-bodied, chewy, and loaded with concentrated black fruits. Possessing adequate acidity, ripe tannin, and a multidimensional personality, it represents an amazing achievement for these two varietals. Drink it over the next 7–8 years.

The three following vintages of Ramitello Rosso are blends of Aglianico and Prugnolo, a type of Sangiovese, and are aged in large oak *foudres*. The 1998 Ramitello Rosso reveals some of the rusticity these wines possessed prior to the hiring of Riccardo Cotarella. It possesses chunky, dusty, berry fruit, medium body, and notions of leather and old wood. Drink it over the next year. The dark ruby-colored 1997 Ramitello Rosso offers notes of dried cherries and ripe plums in addition to a fat, lush, concentrated palate. Although not complicated, it displays quantities of fennel and black fruit characteristics, low acidity, and a fleshy texture. Drink this hedonistic effort over the next 12 months, preferably with meat dishes. The medium-bodied 1996 Ramitello Rosso reveals aromas and flavors of cedar, smoked almonds, chocolate, and cherries, a touch of fennel/anise, and a fine finish.

The dark ruby-colored, elegant 1997 Aglianico Vigneto Contato exhibits a supple texture in addition to smoke-infused black cherry and currant fruit intermixed with herb and earth notes. Round and concentrated, with a smooth finish, it should drink well for 1–2 years.

DIESEL FARM (VENETO)

1999 Rosso di Rosso IGT	D	89+

An oddly named Italian winery, Diesel Farm has turned out a fine 1999 Rosso di Rosso (a blend of 70% Merlot and 30% Cabernet Sauvignon). This is a backward, dense, powerful red exhibiting blackberry, cherry, and currant fruit with a touch of new oak. This chewy effort requires 3–4 years of cellaring and should last for 12–15. The highly talented Tuscan oenologist Roberto Cipresso is responsible for this wine.

GIROLAMO DORIGO (FRIULI–VENEZIA GIULIA)

1999 Montsclapade	EE	87
1999 Pignolo di Buttrio	EE	87?
1999 Refosco	E	92+

Not surprisingly, Dorigo's oenologist is the renowned Roberto Cipresso. The undisputed superstar in this trio is among the finest Refoscos I have ever tasted. Dorigo's opaque purple-colored 1999 Refosco smells like 1998 Lafite Rothschild but tastes like a barrel sample of 2000 Mouton-Rothschild—and that's no bull. It offers a gorgeous bouquet of graphite, black currants, plums, smoke, and licorice. This full-bodied effort exhibits more rusticity than a Bordeaux, as well as remarkable palate presence, huge flavors, and a massive, long finish. Everything is present for a splendid evolution—if you can resist its current exuberant, robust charms. There are 500 cases of this superb wine. It was produced from extremely small yields of 15 hectoliters per hectare, enjoyed malolactic in new French oak, and spent 18 months in new barrels before being bottled unfiltered.

Produced from an indigenous grape, the 1999 Pignolo di Buttrio (125 cases) may be Italy's answer to southwest France's brawny, muscular, oversized, excessively tannic Madirans. It boasts an opaque black/purple color as well as enormous concentration (yields were 15 hectoliters per hectare), but the wine is ferociously tannic, backward, and intimidating on the palate. Optimists and those with youth on their side might gamble on this 1999 as it is pure, intense, concentrated, and impressive. However, much of my fondness for it is due to its purity and size as opposed to its ultimate balance and/or drinkability. Nevertheless, it is a terrific effort for this varietal. Lastly, the internationally styled, dense ruby/purple-colored 1999 Montsclapade is a blend of Cabernet Sauvignon, Cabernet Franc, and Merlot aged 18 months in new French oak and bottled unfiltered. This rustic, monolithic offering is too international in style to merit a higher score. Nevertheless, it is well made and better balanced than the Pignolo. Drink it over the next decade.

LE DUE TERRE (FRIULI–VENEZIA GIULIA)

1997 Sacrisassi Rosso IGT	D	90
1996 Sacrisassi Rosso IGT	D	87

These two red wines are blends of Schioppettino and Refosco. Both are highly extracted, *barrique*-aged wines revealing the influence of toasty vanilla/spicy wood from new Taransaud barrels. The dark ruby/purple colored 1996 Sacrisassi Rosso offers a distinctive nose of chocolate, new oak, and black cherry fruit. The wine possesses good underlying acidity, but the smoky, chocolaty flavors dominate. Drink it over the next 1–2 years. The opaque purple 1997 Sacrisassi Rosso exhibits the vintage's greater ripeness and richness. It saturates the mouth with juicy, nearly unctuously textured black cherry flavors intertwined with smoke and toast. Drink this fat, opulently textured wine over the next 3–4 years. The consultant for these wines is Roberto Cipresso.

FALESCO (UMBRIA/LAZIO)

2000 Merlot	B	90
1999 Merlot	B	92
1998 Merlot	A	90
1999 Montiano	E	95
1998 Montiano	E	94
1997 Montiano	E	95
2000 Vitiano	A	91

Located only fifty miles from Rome is the 360-acre home vineyard of Riccardo Cotarella. His vineyards, which straddle the Umbria/Lazio border, produce some of Italy's finest wines, particularly his spectacular Montiano and his fabulous value-priced wines, Vitiano and Merlot dell'Umbria. No one makes better Merlot (not even France's Michel Rolland) in Italy than Riccardo Cotarella and his Vitiano, which is generally a blend of equal parts of Merlot, Cabernet Sauvignon, and Sangiovese and consistently qualifies as one of the greatest dry red wine bargains in the world. It is aged four months in new French oak and bottled with neither fining nor filtration. Production averages 45,000 cases annually, which ensures a fairly large availability. Also, there is only one bottling, so it is not a situation where various lots appear at different times. Vitiano is really a wine to buy by the case. Drink it before the end of 2003.

The spectacular 2000 Vitiano offers up a sweet nose of blackberries, cassis, licorice, and subtle toast scents. Amazingly concentrated, full-bodied, seamless, and beautifully pure, this spectacular wine will drink well for 3–4 years. Mouth-filling and harmonious, it is a fabulous achievement that must be tasted to be believed. Bravo!

Another remarkable achievement, and also one of the world's greatest red wine values, is the estate's 100% Merlot. This unfined/unfiltered effort aged in barrel is, unfortunately, less widely available than the Vitiano, production being 15,000–25,000 cases annually. The opaque purple-colored 2000 Merlot possesses an opaque purple color as well as a big, thick perfume of chocolate, mocha, blackberries, and cherry liqueur. Medium- to full-bodied and ripe, with low acidity and sweet tannin, this unfined, unfiltered, classy, concentrated red will drink beautifully over the next 4–5 years. The 1999 Merlot boasts an opaque purple color as well as a sumptuous nose redolent of blackberry liqueur, espresso beans, mocha, and smoke. Dense, full-bodied, chewy, and low in acidity, it provides a sumptuous drinking experience.

This remarkably intense, concentrated wine can be drunk now or cellared for 5–6 years. It is one of the greatest wine values I have ever tasted! The 1998 Merlot exhibits an impressively saturated ruby/purple color in addition to rich blackberry/cherry notes interspersed with vanilla, tobacco, and spice. It is medium- to full-bodied and dense, with great fruit purity and a layered texture. Most New World Merlots of this quality level sell for $50 or more a bottle. Drink it over the next 2–3 years.

Lastly, Cotarella's flagship wine, his 100% Merlot called Montiano, is aged in 100% new-oak casks for 12 months and bottled with neither fining nor filtration. In most vintages, this wine could be inserted into a blind tasting with the finest California Merlots and French Pomerols/St.-Emilions without suffering. Annual production averages 2,000 cases. The 1997 was spectacular and probably more opulent and voluptuous than the brilliant 1998 (but that is splitting hairs), while the 1999 is close to perfection. The profound, dense ruby/purple-colored 1999 Montiano offers a smorgasbord of aromas, including melted chocolate, espresso, blackberries, cherries, currants, and smoke. Full-bodied, with terrific purity, a multilayered texture, and surprising freshness for a wine of such depth, it can be drunk young or cellared for 10–15 years. For technicians who care about such things, it has a whopping 37 grams per liter of dry extract! The terrific opaque purple-colored 1998 Montiano exhibits a spectacular bouquet of black cherry liqueur, licorice, and toasty vanilla. The wine explodes on the palate, offering copious quantities of glycerin, cassis, black cherries, and blackberries. As it sits in the glass, aromas and flavors of melted chocolate and toasty oak emerge. The finish lasts for 40+ seconds. This 1998 should drink well for 10–12 years. Bravo! The 1997 Montiano is fabulous. It displays multiple layers that build in the mouth, exploding at the back of the palate. From its opaque purple color, the huge sweet notes of chocolate, smoke, black fruits, and toast satiate the olfactory senses, yet please the mind's intellectual yearnings. Pure and powerful, yet brilliantly knit together with no hard edges and no sense of high alcohol level or heaviness, this sensational wine is one of the finest Merlots made in Italy. Anticipated maturity: now–2014.

FEUDI DI SAN GREGORIO (CAMPANIA)

1999 Pàtrimo	D	90
1998 Rubrato	B	87
1997 Rubrato	B	87
1999 Serpico IGT	D	91
1996 Serpico IGT	D	89
1996 Taurasi	D	85
1995 Taurasi	D	86
1995 Taurasi Montevergine	D	89

This winery has made considerable qualitative progress, and these offerings are the finest I have yet tasted from Feudi di San Gregorio.

Readers should keep an eye out for the 1999 Pàtrimo (1,100 cases). Made from 100% Merlot and cropped at a low 22 hectoliters per hectare, this spectacular wine had not been bottled when I tasted it, but I was assured there would be no filtration prior to bottling. It did not surprise me to learn that the famed Umbrian oenologist Riccardo Cotarella had been brought in as a consultant for this wine. It reveals his signature in its opaque purple color, stunning notes of ripe blackberries, cherries, and full-bodied personality with super extract, high glycerin, sweet tannin, and beautifully integrated, toasty new French oak. This looks to be a terrific example of Merlot from southern Italy. It should drink well for 7–8 years.

The spectacular 1999 Serpico (a blend of 70% Aglianico and 30% Merlot, with a touch of Syrah and Piedirosso) is aged in French oak prior to being bottled without filtration. It is a blockbuster, opaque purple-colored effort offering a sumptuous bouquet of blackberry liqueur intermixed with truffle, licorice, and smoke. Full-bodied, with fabulous concentration, sweet tannin, a sumptuous mid-palate, and a knockout finish, this dazzling 1999 has an unbelievable statistic supporting its level of concentration. Numbers can sometimes add up to nothing, but this wine's level of dry extract measures 40 grams per liter, among the highest I have ever seen in a dry red. Give it another 1–2 years of bottle age, and enjoy it over the following 15–16 years. Bravo! The 1996 Serpico (a blend of 60% Aglianico, 30% Piedirosso, and 10% Sangiovese) displays an opaque ruby color with purple nuances. It is full-bodied and rich, with copious quantities of pepper, chocolate, and cherry jam. If not for the presence of gritty tannin in the finish, this wine may have merited an outstanding score. Perhaps that will dissipate with age as this offering is capable of evolving for 6–7 more years.

Among the red wines, the Rubrato (100% Aglianico) is aged in both steel tanks and large wood *foudres*. The 1998 Rubrato possesses black cherry/blackberry fruit with earth, licorice, and smoke in the background. Rich, medium- to full-bodied, and pure, with a nicely textured mid palate and finish, it should drink well for 2–3 years. The dark ruby-colored Rubrato 1997 reveals a moderately intense nose of chocolate, black cherries, and spice. It possesses good stuffing, a robust, richly fruity personality, medium body as well as a peppery, spicy finish.

I was not much impressed by the rustic, peppery, raspberry, and tar-scented and -flavored, medium-bodied 1996 Taurasi. While good, it is angular and lacks concentration and harmony. The competent 1995 Taurasi, which was aged in French oak, possesses a dark ruby color, a monolithic personality, medium to full body, and plenty of pepper, spice, berries, and new oak. It should drink well for 1–2 years. One of my favorite reds from Feudi di San Gregorio is the 1995 Taurasi Montevergine. This deep, flavorful wine boasts a dense ruby/purple color as well as a noteworthy bouquet of wood, new saddle leather, vanilla, and blackberry fruit. Peppery, spicy components emerge in the mouth. This full-bodied, dense, rich, forward yet concentrated wine can be drunk over the next 4–5 years, although it will last longer.

LA FIORITA–LAMBORGHINI (UMBRIA)

1999	Campoleone	E	96
1998	Campoleone	E	91
1997	Campoleone	E	97
1999	Trescone	B	87
1998	Trescone	B	84

As you may have guessed, this 79-acre estate is owned by a member of the luxury car manufacturer, and the two *cuvées* it offers are made with the assistance of the famed Umbrian oenologist Riccardo Cotarella. The flagship wine, the Campoleone, is emerging as one of the finest wines of central Italy. It is a blend of Merlot, Cabernet Sauvignon, and Sangiovese produced from a 20-acre plot. Picked at high sugars, vinified dry, and aged 12 months in new French oak, it is bottled with neither fining nor filtration. Production is just under 1,500 cases. Lately, the Lamborghini family has also added a lower-priced offering, Trescone, to its portfolio. This wine is a blend of Sangiovese, Merlot, and Ciliegiolo, and is bottled without filtration. Lamborghini's 1999 Trescone is a richly fruity, soft, seductive red meant to be consumed during its first 3–4 years of life. It exhibits abundant quantities of berry fruit, medium to full body, and an uncomplicated, disarming style. A straightforward blend of Sangiovese, Merlot, and Ciliegiolo, the 1998 Trescone is light-bodied and round, with pleasant raspberry and cherry fruit. Enjoy it over the next several years.

The compelling 1999 Campoleone may be as complex and majestic as the phenomenal 1997. A dense opaque purple color is accompanied by scents of new saddle leather, blackberry and cassis fruit, licorice, roasted meats, and graphite. Full-bodied and sweet, with a fabulous texture, ripe tannin, adequate acidity, and brilliant definition, this is a tour de force in winemaking. It should drink well for 10–15 years. While the 1998 Campoleone (50% Merlot, 30% Cabernet Sauvignon, 20% Sangiovese) is not as perfect as the 1997 (that is due to the vintage more than to a change in winemaking or commitment to quality), it is an impressive, exceptional effort. An opaque purple color is accompanied by knockout aromas of new saddle leather, roasted espresso, chocolate, blackberries, and grilled steak. This rich, multi-layered, full-bodied, moderately tannic wine is deep and serious. Cellar it for 1–2 years and consume it over the following 12–15. The 1997 Campoleone (a blend of roughly equal portions of Merlot, Cabernet Sauvignon, and Sangiovese) shows unbelievable concentration combined with uncanny balance and symmetry, as well as a staggering bouquet, flavor depth, and length, making for one of the most extraordinary wine-tasting experiences. The color is a saturated purple. Bursting with black fruits, spice, minerals, and character, this is a prodigious, fabulously intense wine that must be tasted to be believed. Anticipated maturity: now–2020.

FORADORI (TRENTINO)

1999 Granato	E	90+
1998 Granato	E	87
1997 Granato	E	90+
2000 Teroldego Rotaliano	C	87

One of the finest productions of Trentino, Foradori's dense ruby/purple-colored 2000 Teroldego Rotaliano is not complex, but it reveals sweet, earthy, black cherry and currant fruit, a rustic texture, generous roundness, and a chunky, muscular mouth-feel. It is a good country wine to enjoy over the next 5–6 years.

There are 2,500 cases of Granato, which spends 18 months in French oak. This wine possesses more polish and finesse as well as additional concentration and intensity than the Teroldego. The 1999 Granato's opaque purple color is followed by a chewy, black currant, cherry, saddle leather, earth, pepper, and underbrush-scented perfume. This full-bodied, complex, rich, highly extracted Bordeaux-style wine possesses abundant quantities of sweet tannin. Anticipated maturity: 2005–2016. Though it does not have the power, impact, or volume of its older sibling, the 1998 Granato is an intense wine, with a dark ruby/purple color, chocolaty, earthy, black cherry, and herb-tinged aromas and flavors, medium to full body, excellent ripeness, and plenty of guts. It should drink well for 10–12 years. The spectacular 1997 Granato is an enormously concentrated, massive, full-bodied, rustic, huge, chewy offering with abundant quantities of tarry black fruits drenched in toasty oak. Although far from drinkable, it is a highly promising blockbuster. Give it 1–2 years of cellaring; it should keep for 15–18 years.

GALARDI (CAMPANIA)

1999 Terra di Lavoro	E	96
1998 Terra di Lavoro	E	96
1997 Terra di Lavoro	D	95

Sadly, there are only 200+ cases of wine produced from the 5-acre Terra di Lavoro vineyard. Some past vintages have been too rustic (no doubt due to the indigenous grapes used in the blend), but recent vintages show sweet tannin as well as an extraordinary earthy, graphite character that undoubtedly is due to the vineyard's decomposed volcanic soils. If the Aglianico grape is to achieve world fame, it will be with a wine such as this. A blend of 80% Aglianico and 20% Piedirosso, it is aged for 12 months in new French oak and bottled with neither fining nor filtering. Not surprisingly, the winemaking genius behind this operation is Riccardo Cotarella.

The color of the 1999 Terra di Lavoro is an opaque black/purple. The bouquet offers up scents of concentrated black cherries and blackberries intermixed with leather, licorice, lead pencil shavings, and new oak. An unfined, unfiltered effort aged for 12 months in new French oak, this spectacular 1999 is the most harmonious and complete Terra di Lavoro to date. This is compelling juice! Anticipated maturity: now–2018. The profoundly complex, black/purple-colored 1998 Terra di Lavoro boasts wild blackberry/blueberry and mineral scents intertwined with smoke, tobacco, and licorice aromas. The flavors mirror the bouquet. Displaying a wealth of fruit, glycerin, concentration, and body, it is a massive, huge effort with sweet tannin, low acidity, and a spectacular 45+-second finish. This amazing offering is more civilized and less funky than some previous vintages, which have been stunning but clearly individualistic and rustic. Look for the 1998 to drink well for 15+ years. The 1997 Terra di Lavoro is a monster, with extraordinary intensity and richness. It is black/purple in color, and its knockout aromas of tar, jammy black raspberries, licorice, truffles, and smoke are simply intoxicating. It is fabulously concentrated, with terrific glycerin, multiple layers of flavor, and a blockbuster, pure finish that lasts more than 40 seconds. For the lucky few who are able to find a bottle, it will be absolutely amazing! Anticipated maturity: 2003–2020.

MACULAN (VENETO)

1998	Acininobili	EE	95
1997	Acininobili	EE	92
1998	Brentino	A	87
2000	Dindarello	B	87
1999	Dindarello	B	91
1999	Fratta	E	90
1998	Fratta	EE	88
1997	Fratta	EE	89
1999	Torcolato	C	90
1998	Torcolato	C	90

This producer consistently fashions some of Italy's most refreshing, light, zinging, dry whites in addition to that country's most profound sweet wines. The whites are not reviewed here as they must be consumed within a year or so of the vintage. The reds have historically tasted too herbaceous and vegetal, but that problem appears to have been rectified in recent vintages. A blend of 66% Cabernet Sauvignon and 34% Merlot, Maculan's outstanding 1999 Fratta is a dead ringer for a top-class Bordeaux. Made from extremely low yields of 1.5 tons of fruit per acre, it offers copious new oak notes, superb concentration, and high alcohol (14.5%). This boldly styled, full-bodied, concentrated, tannic blockbuster requires 3–5 years of cellaring and should age nicely for 15–16 years. Neither the 1997 nor 1998 Fratta (69% Cabernet Sauvignon and 31% Merlot, aged in new French oak) reveal any of the herbaceous, vegetal characteristics that plagued efforts in the past. Both vintages are similar in quality, although I suspect the 1997 has more opulence. The 1998 has more structure, depth, and complexity. Both are dense ruby/purple-colored, with ripe berry fruit drenched in chocolate and toasty new oak, in addition to fine balance, density, and weight. They are capable of drinking well for 5–6 years.

The 1998 Brentino (a blend of 85% Merlot, 10% Cabernet Sauvignon, and 5% Cabernet Franc, aged in small barrels) offers a spice box, cedar, and tobacco-scented bouquet, a soft, juicy, black and red currant–flavored palate, medium body, light, sweet tannin, and a clean finish. Drink it over the next 2–3 years.

Maculan's real glories remain its splendid sweet wines. At the introductory level, the Dindarellos are made from Moscato grapes that are dried until the January following the harvest and then vinified. The 2000 Dindarello is a richly fruity, straightforward, somewhat simple but delicious offering with moderate sweetness. It should be consumed during its first 1–2 years of life. Readers with a sweet tooth will get a blast from the hedonistic 1999 Dindarello. It is full-bodied, with gorgeous aromas of orange marmalade and tangerine blossoms, superb fruit purity, notes of honey and flowers, glorious levels of fruit, and a long, chewy, moderately sweet finish. This is unquestionably a dessert wine.

The Torcolatos are blends of Vespaiola, Tocai, and Garganega that are aged in one-third new French oak. The 1999 Torcolato is at once complex, intense, and complete. Its light gold color is accompanied by a sweet nose of honeysuckle, orange marmalade, caramel, and new oak. Full-bodied and rich, revealing evidence of botrytis, it should drink well for 7–8 years. The 1998 Torcolato exhibits crème brûlée, honeyed caramel, and apricots in both its aromatics and flavors. Medium- to full-bodied, with admirable zesty acidity, and a moderately sweet, rich finish, it will drink well for 5–8 years.

The top *cuvée* of botrytis-infected sweet wine is Acininobili. One of the greatest sweet wines made in Italy, it can compete with the finest Barsacs and Sauternes. The compelling 1998 Acininobili (made from 85% Vespaiola, 10% Tocai, and 5% Garganega) is an opulent, unctuously textured wine with notes of honeyed grapefruit, Mandarin oranges, overripe pears, and crème caramel presented in a full-bodied, concentrated style. The new oak has been totally absorbed by the wine's concentration and extract. It should drink well for 12–15 years. The 1997 Acininobili boasts enormous honeyed notes as well as underlying mineral characteristics in the sweet, rich, buttery pineapple and caramel aromas and flavors. Acininobili's intensity, richness, and overall refreshing personality make it one of the finest dessert wines produced in Italy. It will drink well for 10–12 years—at the minimum.

MARTILDE (LOMBARDY)

1997 Oltrepò Pavese Barbera La Strega, la Gazza e il Pioppo	D	92
1997 Oltrepò Pavese Bonarda Ghiro Rosso d'Inverno	D	87+
1996 Oltrepò Pavese Bonarda Ghiro Rosso d'Inverno	D	88+
1993 Oltrepò Pavese Pindaro Riserva	C	87

This winery is a source of very good to excellent values in today's overheated wine marketplace. A sensational wine, the black/purple-colored 1997 Oltrepò Pavese Barbera La Strega, la Gazza e il Pioppo is aged for six months in French oak. It is an explosive, huge, amazingly concentrated Barbera that may be over the top for some tasters. The natural alcohol level is 15%, and the wine is extraordinarily thick, unctuously textured, and dense. It is impressive, but most people will require assistance to finish a bottle. Nevertheless, it is a showstopping conversational work of vinous art. Drink it over the next 10–12 years, although it may last even longer.

The Oltrepò Pavese Bonarda Ghiro Rosso d'Inverno is made from extremely old, low-yielding vines. It is generally the best of this estate's portfolio, and certain vintages rank among the biggest and most massive efforts I have tasted from this varietal. The opaque purple 1997 Oltrepò Pavese Rosso d'Inverno Bonarda Ghiro is unevolved and rustic but immense, full-bodied, and chewy, with massive fruit and extract as well as huge levels of tannin and power. It requires 1–2 years of cellaring but should keep for a decade or more. It is probably the finest red wine I tasted from Martilde. The 1996 Oltrepò Pavese Bonarda Ghiro Rosso d'Inverno is the biggest, most massive, powerful wine I have ever tasted from this varietal. The wine has noticeable acidity, high tannin, an opaque purple color, and huge quantities of extract and richness. How complex it will turn out to be is uncertain, but it is a mouth-filling, rustic, gutsy, full-blast country red from Italy that is very distinctive and no doubt capable of lasting for another 6–7 years.

A field blend of 45% Bonarda, 45% Barbera, and 10% Uva Rara, the ruby-colored 1993 Oltrepò Pavese Pindaro Riserva exhibits concentrated, sweet/sour cherry fruit intertwined with almonds, spice, earth, and wood. The wine is round and tasty, but underneath the fruit and extract is sound acidity. Drink it over the next 1–2 years.

ROBERTO MAZZI (VENETO)

| 1997 Amarone Punta di Villa | D | 90 |
| 1996 Amarone Punta di Villa | D | 92 |

1998 Valpolicella Classico Vigneto Poiega	C	88
1997 Valpolicella Classico Vigneto Poiega	B	89

This brilliant Veneto producer has fashioned a delicious, slightly herbaceous sweet cherry, strawberry, and currant-flavored, medium-bodied, zesty 1998 Valpolicella Classico Vigneto Poiega. Reminiscent of a midweight Burgundy, it is ideal for drinking over the next 3–4 years. The terrific 1997 Valpolicella Classico Vigneto Poiega is an excellent value. Dark ruby-colored, with an intense, sweet, strawberry liqueur, new saddle leather, and tobacco-scented bouquet, this medium-bodied, fruit-driven, velvety-textured red possesses enough acidity to provide delineation. Drink it over the next 12–18 months.

The dry, chocolaty, dense, leathery 1997 Amarone Vigneto Punta di Villa is a full-bodied, powerful effort displaying notes of tar, prunes, raisins, and black fruits in its big, earthy aromas and robust, exuberant flavors. This mouth-filling Amarone should age well for 10–15 years. Readers seeking a robust, muscular, powerful wine should check out the dry 1996 Amarone Punta di Villa. A dense plum/garnet color is followed by oversized aromatics offering intense smells of licorice, tar, plums, tobacco, damp earth, and herb-lathered grilled steak notes. Rich, dense, and muscular, with abundant quantities of ripe fruit and a crushed seashell character, this dry, full-bodied wine should be served with intensely flavored dishes or sipped at the end of a meal. It is not sweet, but it has at least 15% alcohol. Drink it over the next 10–12 years.

MIANI (FRIULI–VENEZIA GIULIA)

1997 Merlot	E	92
1997 Ronco Calvari	E	94
1996 Ronco Calvari	D	91
1995 Ronco Calvari	D	87

Kudos to both Miani and consulting oenologist Roberto Cipresso for these extraordinary offerings. The wines of this estate are produced from unbelievably low yields.

The blockbuster 1997 Merlot (aged in 100% new oak) is an astonishing example, but coming from Friuli, it is even more noteworthy. The color is a saturated dark purple. The nose offers an amazing array of jammy black cherry fruit, smoke, berries, and sweet toast. Thick and full-bodied, with a long, nuanced finish, this exuberant, youthful Merlot should be at its peak in 1–2 years and last until 2010.

Miani's 100% Rufosco is called Ronco Calvari. All three following vintages were macerated for nearly a month, and in 1996 and 1997, the wines achieved natural alcohol levels of 14.5%. In essence, they taste more like Syrah than Rufosco. The unctuously thick, black/purple-colored 1997 Ronco Calvari is the most astonishing wine of the trio. It displays the most Syrah-like characteristics (crème de cassis, blackberries, and melted road tar), as well as a thick, unctuous texture and a blockbuster finish. This remarkable effort will be at its finest between now–2020. The spectacular 1996 Ronco Calvari is a massive, thick, full-bodied effort with great symmetry and balance. Sumptuous aromas of blackberries, creosote, and flowers jump from the glass. Although still unevolved, it exhibits considerable potential. Anticipated maturity: now–2012. The 1995 Ronco Calvari, a poor vintage for this area, is a very good wine, with more noticeable tannin than its two siblings but with ripe blackberry fruit intermixed with cherries, dusty earth, and spicy wood aromas. It should be drunk over the next 1–2 years.

SALVATORE MOLETTIERI (CAMPANIA)

1999 Aglianico Irpinia	B	90
1998 Taurasi Vigna Cinque Querce	C	86
1997 Taurasi Vigna Cinque Querce	D	90

The dense ruby/purple-colored 1999 Aglianico Irpinia reveals a distinctive licorice, floral, and black fruit–scented nose with truffles, earth, and spice in the background. Medium- to full-bodied and loaded with character, it is one of a new wave of wines from Campania that showcase how special the Aglianico grape can be. Drink it over the next 5–7 years.

The 1998 Taurasi Vigna Cinque Querce is stern, structured, and foursquare. It reveals an earthy/peppery note in addition to its lovely red and black fruit character. Consume it over the next 2–3 years. The finest Taurasi I have tasted since the 1968 Mastroberardino, the stunning 1997 Taurasi Vigna Cinque Querce offers a dense ruby/purple color in addition to aromas of cherry liqueur intermixed with melted asphalt, truffles, and spice. A touch of earthiness is dominated by the wine's high glycerin level, ripe, concentrated fruit, and full-bodied, unctuous texture. Drink this serious Taurasi over the next 8 years.

MONTEVETRANO (CAMPANIA)

1999 Montevetrano	E	94
1998 Montevetrano	E	92
1997 Montevetrano	E	96

Proprietor Silvia Imparato and her oenologist, Riccardo Cotarella, continue to fashion one of southern Italy's most distinctive wines. Since the debut vintage in 1994, this offering has been a testament to the conservative viticulture of the proprietor as well as the extraordinary winemaking skills of Cotarella. Sadly, this small vineyard of 10 acres produces only 500 cases of a blend of 60% Cabernet Sauvignon, 30% Merlot, and 10% Aglianico. The wines are bottled unfined and unfiltered after spending 12 months in 100% new French oak, and amazingly, the new oak is completely absorbed by the fruit. I love these wines' individualistic style. Each year, regardless of vintage conditions, they offer up compelling amounts of blueberry, blackberry, and black raspberry fruit presented in a distinctive medium- to full-bodied, fruit-driven, complex personality. They also exhibit a touch of minerals and marvelous purity and symmetry, as well as the potential for 10–20 years of evolution. Stylistically, they are reminiscent of an Italian version of the Colgin or Bryant Family Vineyard Cabernet Sauvignon and are generally staggering in their complexity and richness.

The elegant yet singular 1999 Montevetrano boasts a deep ruby/purple color as well as a sweet nose of blueberry pie, cassis, minerals, and violets. Dense, medium- to full-bodied, and harmonious, with a fabulous underlying liquid minerality, it is a distinctive, pure wine to drink now and over the next 15 years. The 1998 Montevetrano is another outstanding success, with elegance allied to power and intensity. Montevetrano's hallmark blackberry and black raspberry component is present, as well as beautiful purity/symmetry and a long, medium- to full-bodied, highly concentrated finish. The 1998 should drink well for 10–12 years. The mild blackberry/vivid blueberry, fabulously fragrant, floral-scented nose of the 1997 Montevetrano jumps from the glass. Opaque purple-colored, with a layered, naturally textured feel, this full-bodied, spectacularly concentrated, multidimensional wine must be tasted to be believed. A prodigious effort, it may be the finest Montevetrano yet made—which is saying something, given how spectacular other vintages have been. Anticipated maturity: 2004–2020.

MONTI (ABRUZZO)

2000 Montepulciano d'Abruzzo Pignotto	C	94

Undeniably the greatest Montepulciano d'Abruzzo I have ever tasted, this spectacular 15,000-bottle *cuvée* made by famed Umbrian oenologist Riccardo Cotarella must be tasted to be believed. It is a superb value and a revelation for the region. Cotarella's magic touch has produced a wine from extremely low yields with amazingly high concentration levels (37 grams per liter of dry extract!). It was bottled unfiltered after aging in barrel. The wine hides its 15.1% alcohol level with grace as there is no hotness given its super wealth of fruit and extract. Full-bodied and explosive, with terrific richness as well as a knockout nose of licorice, flowers, blackberries, and cassis, this pure, beautifully textured 2000 is a tour de force in winemaking. Don't miss it! This wine is best drunk during its exuberant youth, so early consumption (7–8 years) is recommended.

MORGANTE (SICILY)

1999 Don Antonio	C	92
1998 Don Antonio	C	89
1999 Nero d'Avola	A	88
1998 Nero d'Avola	C	86

This winery is making a breakthrough with Sicily's indigenous Nero d'Avola grape. Not surprisingly, their consultant for recent vintages has been the renowned Umbrian oenologist Riccardo Cotarella. His Midas touch has introduced more texture, fat, and flesh into the wines, as well as sweeter tannin.

The 1999 Nero d'Avola's deep purple color is accompanied by a sweet nose of blackberry and licorice-infused fruit, with plenty of fat and supple tannin in the lush, concentrated finish. It represents a super value in big, mouth-filling, robust dry reds. Drink it over the next 1–2 years. The 1998 Nero d'Avola reveals a Burgundy-like softness in addition to plenty of spicy, sour cherry notes in its elegant bouquet, medium body, and round, attractive, subtle flavors. It should be drunk over the next 12–18 months.

The Don Antonio *cuvées* are entirely made from Nero d'Avola. They undergo malolactics and age in 100% new French oak, and are bottled without filtration. They are more expensive than the standard *cuvées*. The finest wine I have ever tasted from the Nero d'Avola grape is Morgante's 1999 Don Antonio. This exquisite effort boasts an opaque purple/blue color as well as an extraordinary bouquet of creamy new oak intertwined with blackberry liqueur, flowers, and cassis. This ripe, full-bodied beauty possesses great intensity, explosive richness, and a finish that lasts for more than 35 seconds. This is a revolutionary example of a varietal indigenous to Sicily. Moreover, it should drink well for a decade or more. The more expensive opaque purple-colored 1998 Don Antonio boasts a gorgeous nose of blueberry and raspberry jam intermixed with smoke, licorice, and minerals. There is impressive fruit intensity as well as an undeniable elegance and overall symmetry/balance. The wine was aged in various sized wood vessels, and bottled unfiltered. It should drink well for 4–5 years.

ALESSANDRO MORODER (MARCHE)

1997 Rosso Conero Dorico IGT	C	88

Made from Sangiovese grapes aged in French barrels for two months, the dark ruby/purple-colored 1997 Rosso Conero Dorico displays abundant quantities of ripe, earthy, black cherry, and currant fruit, impressive density, rustic tannin, noticeable new oak, and a spicy, muscular finish. It should drink well for 4–5 years.

DAVIDE MOSCHIONI (FRIULI–VENEZIA GIULIA)

1999 Celtico Rosso	E	94
1999 Pignolo	EE	95
1999 Refosco	D	89+?
1999 Schioppettino	EE	90

I have never before tasted Refosco or Pignolo of this quality. These limited-production *cuvées* (200 cases) are obviously made from extraordinarily low yields and ripe fruit. All are aged in French oak for 12–15 months and bottled without filtration. These are compelling examples of dry reds from Friuli, and they set new standards in terms of what can be achieved in this region—at a high price. Nevertheless, readers with deep pockets should check out these astonishing efforts.

The 1999 Refosco offers a compelling bouquet of English walnuts (reminiscent of that of Château Latour), flowers, blackberries, licorice, and graphite. Highly extracted and full-bodied, with sweet tannin and well-integrated wood and acidity, this blockbuster will drink well for 10–15 years. Produced from 100% Ribolla Nera, the 1999 Schioppettino displays a distinctive character of blueberries, blackberries, liquid minerals, and licorice. Full-bodied, spicy, ripe, and extremely concentrated, with sweet tannin as well as adequate acidity, it should drink well for a decade or more (although I have no prior experience with this varietal's ageability).

The most prodigious offerings of the series include the 1999 Celtico Rosso (a blend of 60% Cabernet Sauvignon and 40% Merlot) and the 1999 Pignolo (100% Pignolo). They may be expensive, but they are blockbuster efforts of extraordinary richness and intensity. The 1999 Celtico Rosso, which spent 15 months in French oak before being bottled unfiltered, came in at an amazing 15% alcohol level, all of which is hidden by layers of concentrated blackberry and crème de cassis fruit. Smoky graphite, floral, and toasty notes emerge from the bouquet. The wine possesses a terrific entry, a multidimensional mid-palate, and a finish that lasts for nearly 40 seconds. This corpulent, concentrated, yet incredibly well balanced heavyweight should drink well for 15+ years. It is a tour de force. Lastly, the otherworldly 1999 Pignolo (also aged 15 months in new French oak and bottled without filtration) boasts an explosive nose of black fruits, violets, minerals, and tar. Full-bodied, super-extracted, immense, yet remarkably symmetrical as well as vibrant, it possesses amazing delineation for a wine of such mass and concentration. It is unquestionably the most astonishing Pignolo I have ever tasted. Since nothing like this has ever been produced from this grape (as far as I know), its aging potential is unknown. These are the wines of an eccentric genius who is pushing the envelope of quality to the maximum. Kudos to Moschioni!

LA PALAZZOLA (UMBRIA)

1999	Merlot	D	92
1998	Merlot	D	90
1997	Merlot	D	88
1999	Rubino	D	93
1998	Rubino	D	90
1997	Rubino	D	93

This 52-acre estate has fashioned a number of stunning wines in recent vintages. Proprietor Stefano Grilli works with Umbrian oenologist Riccardo Cotarella to produce two impressive reds, a Merlot and a Rubino. The average production of the Merlot, which emerges from a tiny 6.17-acre vineyard, is around 1,000 cases. The Rubino, a proprietary blend of 80% Cabernet Sauvignon and 20% Merlot, is more widely available (2,000 cases annually). The wines spend 12 months in 100% new French oak, and are bottled unfined and unfiltered.

The 1999 Merlot is stunning. It boasts a dense purple color along with a sweet perfume of espresso, blackberry and cherry fruit, licorice, cigar box, and vanilla. A fabulous texture, beautiful harmony, and admirable purity combine in this full-bodied, dense, concentrated offering. With adequate acidity, sweet tannin, and a long finish, it should drink well for 10–15 years. The 1998 Merlot exhibits an opaque purple color in addition to dense, chewy, full-bodied, succulent, fat flavors loaded with black cherry and blackberry fruit intertwined with mocha and chocolate notes. Full, concentrated, and thick, this effort is simply amazing. Drink it over the next 7–8 years. The 1997 Merlot is medium- to full-bodied, dense, monolithic, with an opaque purple color, as well as gobs of fruit, glycerin, and texture. As yet, it does not reveal the necessary complexity to merit an outstanding score. It can be drunk now or cellared for 10–12 years.

The prodigious 1999 Rubino is seductive. It exhibits a smoky, chocolaty bouquet with hints of cassis, tobacco, and toasty new oak. With superb definition, moderate tannin, excellent structure, and exceptional concentration as well as overall purity, this full-bodied, blockbuster effort can be drunk now or cellared for 10–12 years. The black/ruby-colored 1998 Rubino offers a complex bouquet of cedarwood, cigar box, black currants, and vanilla. While more linear and less fat than the Merlot, it is full-bodied, powerful, structured, and intense. It should last for 10–12 years. The staggeringly rich, complex 1997 Rubino exhibits a dense ruby/purple color in addition to a sumptuous nose of blackberries, raspberries, and cassis intertwined with toasty new oak, minerals, and licorice. Full-bodied, ostentatious, and flashy, with loads of glycerin and a 35+-second finish, it can be drunk now and over the next 12 years. Bravo!

PIEVE DEL VESCOVO (UMBRIA)

1998 Lucciaio IGT	C	87
1997 Lucciaio IGT	C	91
1998 Piovano	C	87

Riccardo Cotarella oversees the winemaking at this Umbrian estate, which offers two outstanding blends of Sangiovese, Gamay, Cannaiolo, and other miscellaneous indigenous varietals. The medium dark ruby-colored, fruit-dominated 1998 Piovano offers a sweet, fragrant nose of jammy blackberries and cherries. Round, with low acidity and a plump, fleshy, corpulent personality, this chunky wine makes an ideal trattoria red to consume over the next 12–18 months.

The 1998 Lucciaio reveals the influence of French *barrique* aging in its spicy, vanilla, toasty-scented nose, complemented nicely by currant and berry fruit. This offering is more structured and international in style, with medium body. Drink it over the next 2–3 years. A beauty, the 1997 Lucciaio boasts an opaque purple color, and dense, blackberry and currant flavors intermixed with subtle oak. The wine displays a natural texture (it was bottled unfiltered), outstanding purity, multiple dimensions, and an explosive finish. This terrific offering should age well for 10 years.

PLANETA (SICILY)

1999 Burdese	D	90
1998 Cabernet Sauvignon	D	90
1997 Cabernet Sauvignon	D	87
1999 Merlot	D	90
1998 Merlot	D	89
1997 Merlot	D	88
2000 Rosso La Segreta	B	87
1999 Rosso La Segreta	B	86
1999 Santa Cecilia IGT	D	89
1998 Santa Cecilia IGT	D	89
1997 Santa Cecilia IGT	D	86
1999 Syrah	D	88

This winery—now one of the most fashionable in Sicily—has won numerous accolades from the Italian wine press. It is encouraging to see wines of such quality emerging from this region. Except for Rosso La Segreta, which generally qualifies as a good value, Planeta's red wines are relatively expensive (in particular the Syrah/Nero d'Avola blend called Santa Cecilia as well as the Merlot and the Cabernet Sauvignon) but interesting. These three *cuvées* present an international style, no doubt due to their 12 months' aging in 100% new oak. These modern-styled, concentrated, complex wines merit significant attention. Prices are high but not out of control—yet.

The inexpensive, internationally styled 2000 Rosso La Segreta (a blend of 45% Nero d'Avola, 45% Merlot, and 10% Cabernet Sauvignon) offers sweet black cherry, mocha, and spice characteristics. Fat, fleshy, pure, and chewy, with 14% alcohol providing plenty of glycerin and texture, it will provide pleasure for 1–2 years. The 1999 Rosso La Segreta is also produced from Nero d'Avola, Merlot, and Cabernet Sauvignon. A dark ruby color is followed by loads of cherry and currant fruit. This fresh, crisp, tangy red is an ideal bistro/trattoria offering that will be flexible with an assortment of culinary dishes. Drink it over the next 12–18 months.

The supple, soft, California-style 1999 Syrah lacks the complexity of the finest Rhône Valley Syrahs and the old-vine Shiraz *cuvées* from Australia's Barossa and McLaren Vale regions. Nevertheless, it exhibits a good, creamy vanilla oakiness to its blackberry fruit characteristics, soft, fleshy flavors, medium body, and plenty of mainstream appeal. Drink it over the next 5–7 years.

The indigenous Nero d'Avola grape makes a brilliant appearance in the 1999 Santa Cecilia. It reveals a deep ruby/purple color along with a dense, chocolaty, black fruit–scented nose with telltale toasty new oak. Although not as complex as its siblings, it possesses plenty of suppleness and richness as well as a layered mouth-feel presented in a quasi-international style. Drink it over the next 6–7 years. The impressive, dark ruby/purple-colored 1998 Santa Cecilia (85% Nero d'Avola and 15% Syrah) offers abundant quantities of peppery blackberry fruit intermixed with cassis. Supple, with low acidity, fine density, and a chewy constitution, it can be drunk over the next 4–5 years. The dark ruby/purple-colored 1997 Santa Cecilia displays aromas of roasted nuts, black cherries, cassis, and licorice, medium body, sweet tannin, and excellent ripeness. While not complex, it is well made and mouth-filling. Drink it over the next 2–3 years.

I was knocked out by the remarkable 1999 Merlot, a multilayered, explosively ripe effort exhibiting aromas and flavors of espresso, black cherry jam, chocolate, and mocha. It is rich, full-bodied, and seamless with obvious toasty oak as well as admirable length and individuality. Consume it over the next 10–12 years. The sexy 1998 Merlot offers sweet, mocha-tinged, coffee, and black cherry notes with plenty of chocolate and toast. Medium-bodied, with good density and ripeness as well as a long finish, it will drink well for 4–5 years. The dark purple-colored 1997 Merlot, made in an international style, exhibits excellent purity, good fatness, and copious quantities of blackberry and cherry fruit intermixed with toasty oak and spice. A low acid, plump Merlot, it will offer pleasant drinking over the next 2–3 years.

Another exceptional effort, the 1999 Burdese (Cabernet Sauvignon) reveals Cabernet's complexity in its tobacco, cedar, herb-tinged, black currant, and toasty new oak–scented bouquet. There is more structure in the mouth, along with moderately high tannin, medium to full body, and sweet fatness in the mid-palate. This complex Cabernet Sauvignon will benefit from 2–3 years of cellaring and keep for 12–15 years. The Cabernet Sauvignon is the most complex of the three 1998s of the portfolio. It boasts textbook cedarwood, tobacco-tinged soy, and black currant flavors, an opulent texture, low acidity, full body, and outstanding ripeness, purity, and richness. It should drink well for 7–8 years. The dark purple-colored 1997 Cabernet Sauvignon exhibits a classic bouquet of cigar box, cedar, and black currant aromas nicely supported by subtle toasty oak. Made in an international style, without any characteristics that speak specifically of Italy or Sicily, it is chewy and rich, with good jammy fruit, decent acidity, and low tannin. It should drink well for 6–7 years.

PROMESSA (PUGLIA)

2000 A-Mano Primitivo	A	87
1999 A-Mano Primitivo	A	87
1999 Negroamaro	A	85
1999 Prima-Mano Primitivo	B	90

2000 Rosso Salento	A	87
1999 Sangiovese	A	86

These offerings are produced by a young American, Mark Shannon, who has decided that the isolated, rural lifestyle of southern Italy suits him fine. All the wines of his portfolio are excellent values. They share ripe fruit, little winemaking intervention, aging in stainless steel, and early bottling to protect their fruit and charm. Shrewd readers seeking bargains, as well as restaurants looking for wines to sell by the glass, would be well served to check out these fruity, cleanly made, value-priced Italian reds.

The 2000 Rosso Salento (a blend of 85% Negroamaro and 15% Primitivo aged three months in oak) is deep and complex. A deep ruby color is followed by a medium- to full-bodied red with a sweet nose of briery fruit intermixed with cherries, tar, and earth. Possessing excellent texture as well as purity, it is best consumed in its exuberant youth—over the next several years.

The 1999 Negroamaro exhibits a medium ruby color and a sweet bouquet of berries and melted asphalt that is reminiscent of a medium-weight Zinfandel. It reveals good ripeness, straightforward fruit, and a smooth personality. Drink it now. Slightly better is the dark ruby-colored 1999 Sangiovese. Earthy, peppery, herb notes as well as ripe fruit suggest plenty of sunshine. Exhibiting a Côtes du Rhône–like character, this 1999 possesses good ripeness, an attractive, round texture, fine purity, and a jammy berry character. Like the Negroamaro, it should be consumed now.

A notch up the ladder of concentration and seriousness is A-Mano Primitivo. This well-made 100% Primitivo *cuvée* is a noteworthy value. It is aged five months in a combination of French, American, and Slovenian oak. However, the wood is barely noticeable, given the wine's fruity character and fat. The 2000 A-Mano Primitivo offers a deep ruby color as well as a sweet, candied nose of berry fruit, earth, oak, and tar. There are loads of glycerin, sweet, succulent fruit on the attack and mid-palate, and a velvety-textured, seamless finish. Although not complex, it will provide delicious, uncomplicated drinking over the next year. The 1999 A-Mano Primitivo exhales a big, sweet, juicy, fruity nose with smoky, dried herbs, saddle leather, and soil overtones. A fruit-driven, fat, ripe, chewy effort with admirable density as well as appeal, it should drink well for 12–18 months.

Mark Shannon has decided that in great Puglia vintages he will offer a limited-production (1,000+ cases) *cuvée* from a single vineyard of old-vine Primitivo. The Prima-Mano Primitivo 1999 is aged in 100% new American oak, and bottled with neither fining nor filtration. It is an outstanding, modern-styled wine. A saturated deep ruby color is accompanied by aromas of sweet blackberry and cherry liqueur, vanilla, and smoke. Full-bodied, opulently textured, chewy, pure, and loaded with fruit, it will drink beautifully over the next 3–4 years.

RONCHI DI MANZANO (FRIULI–VENEZIA GIULIA)

1999 Merlot Ronc di Subule	C	89
1998 Merlot Ronc di Subule	C	87
1997 Merlot Ronc di Subule	C	90
1998 Refosco	B	86
1999 Rosazzo Rosso Ronc di Rosazzo	C	88
1998 Rosazzo Rosso Ronc di Rosazzo	C	88
1997 Rosazzo Rosso Ronc di Rosazzo	C	89
1998 Le Zuccole	C	87
1997 Le Zuccole	C	88+
1996 Le Zuccole	C	88

From one of Friuli's finest wineries, these offerings go from strength to strength with each new vintage. The proprietors continue to reduce yields, resulting in wines with distinctive personalities, exceptional purity, and vibrant freshness allied with considerable richness.

Readers should definitely take a look at these serious efforts being produced by Ronchi di Manzano.

The dense ruby-colored 1999 Merlot Ronc di Subule offers up scents of roasted coffee, dried herbs, and black cherries. Medium-bodied, with a restrained, elegant style, it should drink well for 7–8 years. The 1998 Merlot Ronc di Subule offers delicious black cherry fruit with a mocha fudge–like characteristic as well as subtle wood in the background and medium body, as well as an attractive texture and finish. It should drink well for 2–3 years. One of a handful of Friuli Merlots I have given an outstanding rating, Manzano's 1997 Merlot Ronc di Subule possesses sumptuous aromas of roasted coffee, blackberry, and cherry fruit. Dense, chewy, and lush, with decent acidity, this gloriously fruit-driven Merlot can be consumed over the next 3–4 years.

The Rosazzo Rosso Ronc di Rosazzo is a blend of equal parts Refosco, Merlot, and Cabernet Sauvignon aged in 100% new French oak. Although the 1999 Rosazzo Rosso Ronc di Rosazzo was closed the day I tasted it, what I could see was impressive. Notes of smoke, melted asphalt, graphite, and black currants/cherries were present. The wine was tight but spicy and pure, with a certain leanness. Give it 1–2 years of cellaring, and enjoy it over the following 10–12 years. It is a noteworthy choice for readers seeking subtlety and delicacy. The 1998 Rosazzo Rosso Ronc di Rosazzo offers a noteworthy berry fruitiness in addition to a melted chocolate flavor in its medium-bodied, lush, concentrated personality. Very close in style to the 1998, the 1997 Rosazzo Rosso Ronc di Rosazzo possesses a deep ruby/purple color and smoked ham–like aromas along with chocolate, berry flavors. It is medium-bodied, richly fruity, and ideal for drinking over the next 3–4 years.

I enjoyed the robust, gutsy, blackberry, and cherry-scented and -flavored 1998 Refosco. Displaying good ripeness, sweetness, and medium body, it can be drunk over the next 1–2 years.

Le Zuccole is a blend of equal parts Merlot and Cabernet Sauvignon from Manzano's finest vineyards. While 75% new oak is utilized in this wine's aging (the same as for the Merlot Ronc di Subule), the wood is kept in check. Like all reds from this estate, it is bottled without filtration. A stylish, measured effort, the evolved 1998 Le Zuccole reveals notes of cedar, spice box, herbs, red and black currants, and a touch of vanilla. Drink this medium-weight Italian red over the next 4–5 years. In a blind tasting, it could easily be mistaken for a mid-level Médoc. The 1997 Le Zuccole offers spicy, toasty new oak, an unevolved, ripe, black currant, and dense cherry style with notes of cedar and chocolate, moderate tannin, and plenty of depth and richness. It should improve over the next 1–2 years and last for a decade or more. The 1996 Le Zuccole reveals elements of overripeness, along with good acidity (particularly when compared to the low-acid 1997s), a complex, cedary, spice box, tobacco, and currant-scented nose, medium body, and light to moderate tannin. It should continue to drink well for 3–5 years.

F.LLI SPERI (VENETO)

1997	Recioto della Valpolicella	B	91
1998	Valpolicella La Roverina	A	86
1997	Valpolicella Sant'Urbano	C	90

It is amazing how much progress has taken place in Veneto. Speri is one of the estates of this region where the wines have greatly improved, and it now offers tasty and reasonably priced Valpolicellas. The elegant, dark ruby-colored 1998 Valpolicella La Roverina offers aromas of fresh almonds and sour cherries as well as a tangy, medium-bodied personality. It is soft and light enough to be drunk slightly chilled, if readers so desire. It is an excellent value. Consume it over the next 12–18 months.

The outstanding dark ruby/purple-colored 1997 Valpolicella Sant'Urbano exhibits tremendous density and richness, medium to full body, and notes of black truffles intermixed with cherry jam, spice, and minerals. It boasts super purity, wonderful, refreshing, lively, vivacious fruit, and a rich, concentrated, textured finish. Drink this beautiful Valpolicella over the next 3–4 years. Readers looking for robust, mouth-filling, earthy, meaty, full-throttle, sweeter reds should check out the 1997 Recioto della Valpolicella. Dense and full-bodied, with chewy, unctuously textured flavors of roasted meats, dried herbs, melted asphalt, and black fruits, it will provide a wonderful accompaniment to any hard cheese at the end of a meal. Drink it over the next 10 years.

F.LLI SPORTOLETTI (UMBRIA)

2000 Assisi Rosso	B	86
1999 Villa Fidelia Rosso	E	96
1998 Villa Fidelia Rosso	D	94

This 50-acre estate located between the towns of Assisi and Perugia produces 1,000 cases of Villa Fidelia each year. This is a prodigious 70% Merlot, 20% Cabernet Sauvignon, 10% Cabernet Franc blend made from modest yields of 35–38 hectoliters per hectare. The wine spends 12 months in French oak casks and is bottled with neither fining nor filtration. The estate also offers a *cuvée* called Assisi Rosso that is made of equal parts Sangiovese and Merlot and aged in large *foudres*. Both wines are made with the assistance of Riccardo Cotarella.

The 2000 Assisi Rosso is soft, ripe, stylish, and graceful. It displays Burgundy-like cherry and floral notes. Drink it over the next 1–2 years.

Sportoletti's compelling, unfiltered 1999 Villa Fidelia Rosso is undoubtedly the superstar of this area. Its dense ruby/purple color is accompanied by gorgeous aromas of blackberries, cassis, espresso, chocolate, and a touch of smoke. There are fabulous concentration, full body, great precision as well as purity, and a long, 45-second finish. Displaying an overall sense of elegance and gracefulness despite its depth and richness, this prodigious effort can be drunk now and over the next 14 years. The 1998 Villa Fidelia Rosso is an explosively rich, opulently textured, full-bodied red that offers aromas of chocolate, roasted espresso, blackberries, cherries, and currants. A smoky, thick, chewy wine with terrific flavor extraction, great harmony/symmetry, and a multilayered, sumptuous finish, it can be drunk now or cellared for 10–12 years. Wow!

TASCA D'ALMERITA (SICILY)

1998 Regaleali Cabernet Sauvignon	D	87
1997 Regaleali Cabernet Sauvignon	D	86+?
1999 Regaleali Rosso del Conte	D	88
1998 Regaleali Rosso del Conte	D	86
1999 Regaleali Rosso IGT	A	87

Perhaps the most important winery on the island of Sicily (in terms of quality), Tasca d'Almerita owns 600 acres of vineyards, produces more than 200,000 cases of wine, and has one of the most modern winemaking facilities in Italy. The estate fashions an array of wines, many of which are realistically priced. Moreover, the quality level appears to be increasing. Interestingly, the current releases seem less powerful than previous vintages (no doubt a result of vintage conditions).

The Regaleali Rosso is a blend dominated by a local varietal called Nero d'Avola that sees some aging in old wood. Although this wine spends time in oak, there is no evidence of wood in the aromas or flavors. The 1999 Regaleali Rosso exhibits notes of cherries, balsam, and pepper, which are followed by a soft, medium-bodied, flavorful wine to enjoy over the next 1–2 years.

Tasca d'Almerita has turned out some blockbuster Cabernet Sauvignons, but the 1998 Regaleali Cabernet Sauvignon is a more elegant, less weighty effort than previous vintages. A deep ruby/purple color is followed by sweet black currant/cassis fruit, and licorice aromas and flavors. This elegant, tasty, well-made Cabernet can be enjoyed young because of its low acidity, yet it possesses the capacity to age well for 7–8 years. While the 1997 Regaleali Cabernet Sauvignon is good, it is not equal to its older siblings. It displays more herbaceousness in addition to a distinctive note of briny olives intermixed with black currants. A sweet, heavy-handed, full-bodied wine with plenty of fat and fruit, its herbaceousness and cumbersome feel in the mouth kept my score down, particularly when compared to vintages where the wine had more concentration without as much heaviness. The 1997 should drink well for 6–7 years.

Lastly, the 1999 Regaleali Rosso del Conte is a *barrique*-aged offering made primarily from Nero d'Avola. The influence of new French oak is apparent in the toast, spicy bouquet, but the fruit comes through strongly on the palate. This medium- to full-bodied, rustic yet concentrated red is loaded with blackberries and cherries intertwined with tar, earth, and pepper and has plenty of depth and a mouth-filling finish. It should drink well for 4–8 years. The 1998 Rosso del Conte (90% Nero d'Avola and 10% Perricone) exhibits a complex, spicy, berry, cigar box, and smoke-scented nose with excellent fruit. Medium-bodied, soft, and round, it is ideal for grilled meats or barbecued dishes. Enjoy it over the next 1–2 years.

COSIMO TAURINO (PUGLIA)

1995	Notarpanaro	B	89
1994	Notarpanaro	B	87
1994	Patriglione	D	87?
1998	Salice Salentino	A	86
1997	Salice Salentino Riserva	A	84

Sadly, Cosimo Taurino, someone who has done much for this area of Italy, has passed away, but his son Francesco continues in his father's footsteps. He has built a state-of-the-art winery that was first used for the 2001 harvest. Under his auspices, this estate remains a perennial source of rustic, earthy southern Italian reds. It has made many friends in the international marketplace for its combination of quality and value.

The 1998 Salice Salentino's complex bouquet of damp earth, spice box, sausage, and dried herbs is followed by medium-bodied, flavorful, rustic flavors. It should drink well for 2–3 years. The amber/ruby/garnet-colored 1997 Salice Salentino Riserva, an old-style Italian red, offers scents of roasted herbs, sweaty saddle leather, dried cherries, medium body, and a slightly astringent finish. There is plenty of personality in this 1997, but it is not representative of the new, fruit-driven style of modern-day Italian reds. Drink it with spicy cuisine over the next 12–18 months.

The two following vintages of Notarpanaro are blends of Negroamaro and Malvasia Nera. These wines have spent some time in oak barrels, of which one-third were new. The 1995 Notarpanaro is a dense, rich, full-bodied wine displaying licorice, dried fruit, pepper, truffle, and spice characteristics. Filled with personality, it possesses rustic tannin but plenty of depth as well as a chewy, muscular, robust finish. It should drink well for 3–4 years. The dark garnet color of the 1994 Notarpanaro is followed by an earthy concoction of dried herbs, black cherry fruit, underbrush, truffles, and smoke. Ripe, chewy, and full-bodied, with abundant quantities of concentrated fruit, this gamey, robust, southern Italian red is the perfect foil for a cheese course or with grilled meats. Drink it over the next 2–3 years.

Made in a late-harvest, Amarone-like style, Taurino's 1994 Patriglione offers scents and flavors of melted asphalt, old saddle leather, licorice, and earth with sweet cherry fruit in the background. Although broad and dense, it is not as interesting, fresh, or lively as the Notarpanaro. It takes a cultivated palate to fully appreciate this 1994; hence, readers weaned on modern-styled wines should take heed. It should drink well for 3–4 years.

VIE DI ROMANS (FRIULI–VENEZIA GIULIA)

1997 Voos dai Ciamps	D	92

This 100% new-oak-aged luxury *cuvée*—a blend of 95% Merlot and 5% Cabernet Sauvignon—is fashioned only in the finest vintages, such as 1987, 1990, 1991, and 1997. Production averages 600 cases. An explosively rich and powerful as well as impressive effort, the 1997 Voos dai Ciamps ranks among the most astonishing red wines I have tasted from Friuli. It reveals copious quantities of toasty, smoky notes complemented by sweet, unctuously textured, full-bodied, black cherry, blackberry, caramel, and licorice aromas and flavors with terrific fruit intensity and purity. This superb, opulent wine can be drunk over the next 10 years. Impressive!

VILLA MATILDE (CAMPANIA)

1999 Falerno del Massico Rosso	B	87
1998 Vigna Camarato	D	90+?

Villa Matilde is an estate where the dominant red grape utilized is Aglianico. The potentially superb 1998 Vigna Camarato (100% Aglianico aged in 100% new French barrels and bottled without filtration) reveals a complex, blackberry and floral-scented perfume with a hint of licorice and new oak. Dense and full-bodied, as well as brutally tannic, it appears to possess the constitution, robustness, and depth of fruit to support such high tannin, but this is not certain, hence the question mark. Nevertheless, there is a lot going on in this individualistic, intense 1998. Anticipated maturity: 2004–2018. The attractively priced 1999 Falerno del Massico Rosso exhibits a deep ruby color as well as a big, sweet nose of chocolate-covered black cherries, plums, spice, and dried herbs. Drink this medium-bodied red over the next 1–2 years.

ZENATO (VENETO)

1997 Amarone	E	88
1995 Amarone	E	91
1997 Merlot delle Venezie	A	86
1998 Valpolicella Classico	A	86
1997 Valpolicella Classico	A	88
1998 Valpolicella Classico Ripassa	B	88
1997 Valpolicella Classico Ripassa	B	90

These wines are all super bargains.

The 1998 Valpolicella Classico offers light berry/cherry fruit in a lush, unstructured, round, tasty style. Drink it over the next year.

Readers seeking a fruit-driven, delicious Merlot that won't cost a fortune should check out Zenato's 1997 Merlot delle Venezie. Made from 90% Merlot and 10% Cabernet Sauvignon, it exhibits a dark ruby color, abundant fruit, low acidity, and a round finish. It will not make old bones, but for drinking over the next 12–18 months, it is a fine value.

The Valpolicellas Ripassa exhibit more substance and richness than most wines from this area in Veneto. The word "Ripassa" on the label indicates that it is made like Amarone, by passing the wine over the dry pomace during vinification, resulting in more complexity, body, and depth. The dense 1998 Valpolicella Classico Ripassa exhibits a Rhône-like, earthy, robust, peppery, spicy personality. Passing the grape must over the pomace left over from the Amarone adds concentration, complexity, and earthiness to Valpolicella's typically light style. This excellent, medium- to full-bodied, stuffed 1998 reveals notes of asphalt, black cherries, and berries. Drink it over the next 5–6 years. The 1997 Valpolicella Classico Ripassa is a full-bodied, plum/garnet-colored effort with dense, earthy, tar, and black fruit characteristics. Heady, ripe, pure, and well balanced, it should drink well for 2–3 years.

The standard Valpolicellas are made in steel tanks and aged in large Slavonian wood *foudres.* They make a joke of the industrial swill parading under the Valpolicella label. The medium dark ruby-colored 1997 Valpolicella Classico, which is lighter-bodied than the 1997 Ripassa, offers a gorgeous nose of chocolate-covered cherries, berries, and almonds, excellent suppleness, delicious fruit, and a medium-bodied, fruit-driven finish with considerable character. Drink it over the next 12–18 months.

The 1997 Amarone, a great vintage for this small appellation, possesses a deep plum/garnet color in addition to a sweet perfume of roasted herbs, melted road tar, dried black fruits, smoke, and truffles. Dense and chewy, this wine has pruny/raisiny characteristics. It will drink well for 10–15 years. Lastly, the outstanding 1995 Amarone reveals abundant charcoal wood notes in its melted asphalt, blackberry, meaty, roasted bouquet. Full-bodied, muscular, big, chewy, and thick, this pure wine cuts a heavy swath across the palate and offers a long, impressive finish. Drink it over the next 10–12 years.

FATTORIA ZERBINA (EMILIA-ROMAGNA)

1997	Marzieno Ravenna Rosso	D	89
1997	Sangiovese di Romagna Torre di Ceparano	B	86
1998	Sangiovese di Romagna Ceregio	B	87
1997	Sangiovese di Romagna Ceregio Vigna Querce	B	87
1997	Sangiovese di Romagna Pietramora	D	88

This well-run winery offers an attractive portfolio of wines. The 1998 Sangiovese di Romagna Ceregio and the 1997 Sangiovese di Romagna Ceregio Vigna Querce both exhibit dark ruby colors as well as attractive ripe strawberry and cherry jam aromas intertwined with new saddle leather and spice. Soft, medium-bodied, round Sangioveses, they possess excellent fruit and textures. The 1998 reveals a smokier character. Drink over the next several years.

Although not as seductive as the 1998 Sangiovese Ceregio and 1997 Sangiovese Ceregio Vigna Querce, the dense, chewy, mouth-filling, gutsy, rustic 1997 Sangiovese di Romagna Torre di Ceparano is ideal for drinking over the next several years.

Zerbina's two finest offerings are the 1997 Marzieno Ravenna Rosso and the 1997 Sangiovese di Romagna Pietramora. The dark ruby/purple-colored 1997 Marzieno Ravenna Rosso (a 62% Sangiovese/38% Cabernet Sauvignon blend) is a ripe, wonderfully textured effort with low acidity, a plush, Pomerol-like texture, toasty new oak in the nose, and abundant black fruits. This dense, medium- to full-bodied blend can be drunk now as well as over the next 7–8 years. The 1997 Sangiovese di Romagna Pietramora's (100% Sangiovese) dark ruby color is accompanied by abundant quantities of sweet black cherry, strawberry, earth, toast, and creosote aromas and flavors. With excellent richness, medium to full body, and a supple texture, it should drink well for 5–6 years.

3. GERMANY AND AUSTRIA

GERMANY

The Basics

TYPES OF WINE

Germany's wine kingdom is controlled by the 1971 law that divided German wines into seven grades, based on ascending levels of ripeness and sweetness, as well as price. These seven levels are:

1. Tafelwein
2. Qualitätswein (QbA)
3. Kabinett
4. Spätlese
5. Auslese
6. Beerenauslese
7. Trockenbeerenauslese

In addition to these there are other categories of German wines. The Trocken and Halbtrocken wines are the two generic types of dry German wine. The Trockens tend to be drier, but also boring, thin wines with little body or flavor. Halbtrockens also taste dry but are permitted to have slightly more residual sugar and are marginally more interesting. I rarely recommend either because they are not very good; they are commercial creations made to take advantage of the public's demand for "dry" wine. A third type of wine is called Eiswein, Germany's rarest and most expensive wine. It is made from frozen grapes, generally picked in December or January, or even February. It is quite rare and a very, very sweet wine, but has remarkably high acidity and can last and improve in the bottle for decades. It does have great character, but one must usually pay unbelievably steep prices to experience it.

There are also the sparkling wines of Germany called Deutscher Sekt, which should be drunk only by certified masochists, as they are a ghastly lot of overly sulfured wines. Lastly, there is the German wine that everyone knows about, the ubiquitous Liebfraumilch. This sugary, grapy drink is to quality German wine what California wine coolers are to that state's serious wines.

GRAPE VARIETIES

Müller-Thurgau   Representing 25% of Germany's vineyards, Müller-Thurgau has become the most widely planted grape because it can give prolific yields of juice (90–100 hectoliters per hectare is not uncommon). Ignore all of the self-serving promotion from German wine importers about Müller-Thurgau, because it is not a great wine grape and the Germans have planted it for quantity, not quality.

Riesling   Riesling accounts for only 20% of the vineyards in Germany, but it produces about 95% of that country's finest wines. If the bottle does not say Riesling on it, then chances are you are not getting Germany's best wine. Riesling produces some of the world's most complex whites, and it achieves its greatest pinnacles of success in Germany, whether it be a dry, crisp, tangy Kabinett or a decadently sweet, nectarlike Trockenbeerenauslese.

Sylvaner   This unimpressive grape accounts for 10% of Germany's vineyards and rarely results in anything interesting. Most Sylvaners either have a nasty vegetal streak to them or are simply dull and flat.

Other Grape Varieties   Much of Germany's problem today is that a large proportion of its vineyards are planted with mediocre grape varieties. The remaining 45% of the vineyards generally consist of grapes that have little personality and names such as Kerner, Gutedel, Morio-Muskat, Bacchus, Faberrebe, Huxelrebe, Optima, and Ebling. The only other grapes that can do something special are Gewürztraminer, Rulander (Pinot Gris), Scheurebe, and Germany's answer to Pinot Noir, Spätburgunder.

FLAVORS

Müller-Thurgau   At its best it resembles a can of fruit salad, obvious but pleasant in an open-knit, uncomplicated manner. At its worst, it tastes washed out, acidic, green, and reminiscent of a watered-down, mediocre Riesling.

Riesling   The most exciting flavors in German wines come from Riesling. In the drier and slightly sweet versions there is a lovely concoction of apple, lime, wet stone, and citric flavors and scents. As the Riesling becomes sweeter, the flavors move in the direction of tropical fruits such as mangoes and pineapples, as well as honeyed apples, peaches, and apricots. Behind all the flavor (in the top Rieslings) is a steely, zesty, vibrant natural fruit acidity that gives those wines an exceptional degree of clarity and focus.

Rulander   From some of the best vineyards in Baden and the Rheinpfalz, this grape produces oily, rich, honeyed, intense wines that are probably the most underrated great white wines of Germany.

Scheurebe   Discovered by Dr. G. Scheu, Scheurebe is a clone achieved by crossing Sylvaner and Riesling. Once scoffed at for its neutral character, this varietal has become increasingly popular with consumers. Top producers of Scheurebe, such as Müller-Catoir, H. & R. Lingenfelder, and Kruger-Rumpf, have performed wonders with this grape, producing deeply flavored wines that feature flowery, curranty fruit and rich, complex personalities.

Spätburgunder   This is the German Pinot Noir, a grotesque and ghastly wine that tastes akin to a defective, sweet, faded, diluted red Burgundy from an incompetent producer. Need I say more?

Sylvaner   On occasion, Sylvaner from selected vineyards in Franken and the Rheinhessen can be a rich, muscular, deep wine, but more often it is vegetal, thin, and dull.

AGING POTENTIAL

Auslese: 3–18 years   Qualitätswein (QbA): 2–4 years
Beerenauslese: 10–40+ years   Spätlese: 3–12 years
Kabinett: 3–6 years   Tafelwein: 8–16 months
Liebfraumilch: 8–16 months   Trockenbeerenauslese: 10–40+ years

OVERALL QUALITY LEVEL

The top level of quality is impeccably high, dominated by small estates that usually produce Riesling. However, the German government has been inexcusably remiss over recent decades in allowing too many high-yielding, low-quality grapes to be planted (the 1987 average yield per hectare was an incredible 97 hectoliters), and this has caused consumers to become increasingly skeptical about the seriousness of German wine quality. For example, in the me-

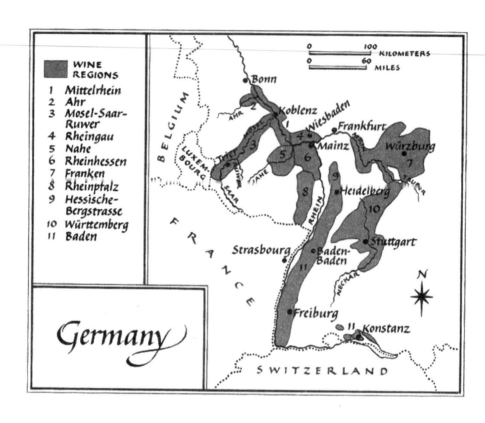

WINE
REGIONS

1 Mittelrhein
2 Ahr
3 Mosel-Saar-
   Ruwer
4 Rheingau
5 Nahe
6 Rheinhessen
7 Franken
8 Rheinpfalz
9 Hessische-
   Bergstrasse
10 Württemberg
11 Baden

Germany

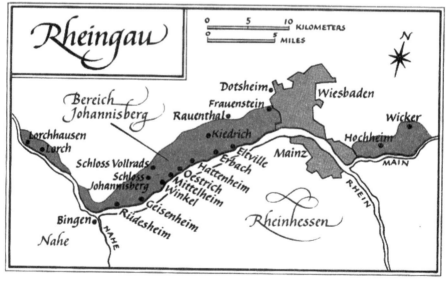

Rheingau

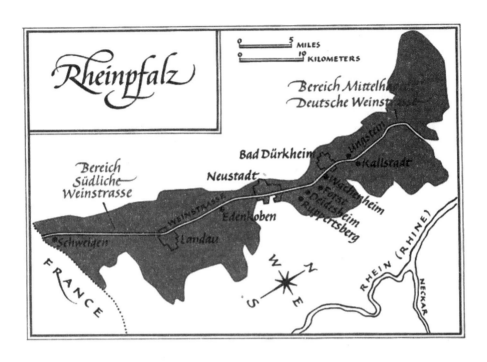

Rheinpfalz

0 — 5 MILES
0 — 10 KILOMETERS

Bereich Mittelhaardt
Deutsche Weinstrasse

Bad Dürkheim
Kallstadt
Neustadt
Haardt
Wachenheim
Forst
Deidesheim
Ruppertsberg

Bereich
Südliche
Weinstrasse

WEINSTRASSE

Edenkoben

Schweigen
Landau

FRANCE

RHEIN (RHINE)

NECKAR

W N E S

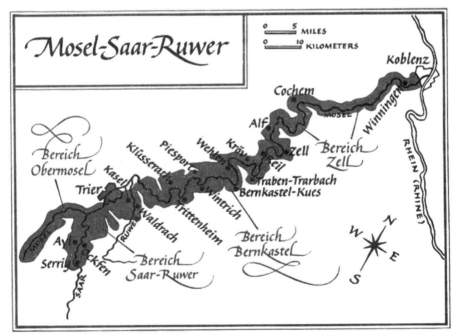

Mosel-Saar-Ruwer

0 — 5 MILES
0 — 10 KILOMETERS

Koblenz
Cochem
MOSEL
Winningen
Alf
Zell
Bereich
Zell
Bereich
Obermosel
Klüsserath
Piesport
Wehlen
Kröv
Zeil
Kasel
Traben-Trarbach
Trier
Wintrich
Bernkastel-Kues
Trittenheim
RUWER
Waldrach
Bereich
Bernkastel
MOSEL
Ayl
Serrig
Ockfen
Bereich
Saar-Ruwer
SAAR

RHEIN (RHINE)

W N E S

diocre year of 1987, 77% of the wine produced was allowed to be called QbA and only 2% was declassified as simple table wine (Tafelwein). That's ridiculous. A campaign to promote the top-quality German estates that are making the finest German wines is long overdue. Until the consumer begins to believe that Germany is serious about quality, sales of these wines will remain difficult.

MOST IMPORTANT INFORMATION TO KNOW

For Americans, though a number of importers have small portfolios of German wines, there are three major players who dominate the German wine business in America. From a consumer's perspective, the most important is Terry Theise Selections, whose wines are imported by Michael Skurnik Imports in New York City. By ignoring many of the overrated, more famous German wine names and by beating the back roads of less-renowned viticultural regions, Theise has put together a portfolio of producers who turn out individualistic wines of astonishing quality, often at modest prices. Theise keeps his profit margins low so the wines can be effectively represented in the marketplace. The result is a bevy of phenomenal wines and extraordinary wine bargains. If you are going to buy German wines seriously, look for *Terry Theise Selection* on the label. You are unlikely to be disappointed.

Between the other two major players in the German wine market, the most visible and promotion-conscious is Rudy Weist of ILNA Selections in Santa Barbara, California. Weist's portfolio is concentrated on the more renowned and prestigious domaines that are all members of an elite association of winemaking estates collectively referred to as the VDP. Each of these estates sports a neck or back label that identifies its more than 200 members. In theory, all of them are dedicated to producing the highest-quality wines, usually from Riesling. There are a number of fabulous producers in this group, as well as an appalling number of underachievers who charge exceptionally high prices because their wines are produced from renowned vineyards. The third major importer of German wines is Chapin Cellars/Billington Imports in Springfield, Virginia. Formerly owned by Romaine "Bob" Rice, this importer has numerous excellent wines that are reasonably priced.

In addition to becoming familiar with these German wine importers, there are other facts to keep in mind when buying German wines:

• There are 11 major wine-producing zones in Germany. Within these zones there are three subdistricts, the most general of which is called a Bereich. This is used to describe a wine from anywhere within the boundaries of that particular Bereich. An analogy that may help facilitate this distinction would be the closest French equivalent, a wine entitled to appellation Bordeaux Contrôlée or Appellation Bourgogne Contrôlée. Within the Bereich there are more specific boundaries called Grosslagen, to which the closest French equivalent would be the generic Appellation St.-Julien Contrôlée or Appellation Morey St.-Denis Contrôlée. These are wines that are not from a specific château or specific vineyard but from a specific region or collection of sites for vineyards. There are 152 different Grosslagen in Germany. The most specific zone in Germany is called an Einzellage, which is a specific site or vineyard. There are 2,600 of them in Germany, and again, by analogy, the closest French equivalent would be a specific St.-Julien château such as Ducru-Beaucaillou or a specific premier cru or grand cru Burgundy vineyard in Morey St.-Denis such as Clos des Lambrays. Perhaps this will help one to understand the breakdown of the German wine zones. However, few people have the patience to memorize the best Einzellagen or Grosslagen, so it is much more important to try to remember the names of some of the best producers.

• The majority of the best producers in Germany are located in the following nine wine zones.

OVERALL CHARACTERISTICS OF THE NINE MAJOR GERMAN WINE ZONES

Middle Mosel   For German wine lovers, as well as tourists to Germany's wine regions, the Middle Mosel is the most beloved and scenic. The frightfully steep, slate-based slopes are so forbidding it seems impossible that vineyards could be planted on them. With its plethora of high-profile producers, such as J. J. Prüm, Willi Haag, Ernest Loosen, and Dr. Thanisch, this region has no shortage of admirers and potential buyers. The fact is that while Riesling grown on these slopes has unlimited potential, this is also an area filled with overpriced, under-achieving producers who have long lived off their reputations. Nevertheless, anybody who has tasted a great Wehlener Sonnenuhr, Brauneberger Juffer, Erdener Treppchen, Zeltinger Sonnenuhr, or Graacher Himmelreich knows that this area's soils can produce magical Ries-lings. The Middle Mosel is to Germany what Puligny-Montrachet is to Burgundy. There are a number of great producers, but prices are high, and the quality is frightfully irregular.

Lower Mosel   This obscure vineyard area with supersteep slopes is located at the junction of the Mosel and the Rhine. The wines from the Lower Mosel are underestimated, a fact that consumers should put to good use. Try some recent vintages from two of this area's most spec-tacular producers, von Schleinitz and von Heddesdorff, and experience the high quality available at reasonable prices. Although the vineyard sites are not considered to be as ideal as those in the Middle Mosel, the best Lower Mosel producers can produce wines equal in quality to those from the Middle Mosel.

Saar   Also referred to as the Upper Mosel, this cool region is able to maintain the steely, razor blade sharpness of the Riesling grape. Many authorities consider the Saar vineyards among the greatest in Germany, but, as in the Middle Mosel, fame has its price. Some fabu-lous producers are located in this area. However, some well-known Saar producers have a tendency to overcrop, making relatively hollow, flabby wines that lack definition. Superlative producers include Egon Müller, Dr. Wagner, von Kesselstatt, and, from time to time, Zilliken.

Ruwer   Trier is the spiritual and commercial center for the Ruwer wines. Textbook, quin-tessential Rieslings emerge from this area from producers such as Friedrich-Wilhelm-Gymnasium, Geltz Zilliken, Karthäuserhof, von Kesselstatt, Karlsmuhle, and von Schubert's Maximin Grunhaus.

Rheingau   Many of the most famous producers of German wine are located in this highly renowned region. However, it is not unusual for many of the unknown overachievers to out-perform their more celebrated neighbors. Three of the most prominent underachievers are Schloss Groenesteyn, Schloss Vollrads, and Schloss Johannisberg. If you want to taste what many consider to be some of the finest Rieslings made in Germany, check out producers such as H. H. Eser, Freiherr zu Knyphausen, Deinhard's Konigin Victoria Berg, Dr. Heinrich Nagler, and the best *cuvées* of Schloss Schonborn.

Rheinhessen   All of the German wine zones offer considerable diversity in quality, but none more than the Rheinhessen, which has Nierstein as its commercial center. Müller-Thurgau and Sylvaner are the two most popular grape varieties of this region. In addition, odd grapes such as Scheurebe, Huxelrebe, and Kerner have found an enthusiastic reception among this region's producers. This is also the region where most of Germany's Liebfrau-milch is produced. Consumers often make major errors in buying wines from this region. Over recent years, some of the best producers have included Freiherr Heyl zu Herrnsheim, J.U.H.A. Strub, and Merz.

Rheinpfalz   The Rheinpfalz is the warmest of the major German wine zones. Although Müller-Thurgau is widely planted, it is Riesling, Rulander, and Scheurebe that produce the most stunning wines. If you think German wines are too understated, light, and wimpy, check out the powerful, meaty, fleshy, supergenerous wines from the Rheinpfalz. The quality level appears to be hitting new heights with every vintage. This is the home of the producer Müller-Catoir, who is making some of the most riveting wines of Germany. It is also the base for supertalented producers such as H. & R. Lingenfelder, Kurt Darting, Klaus Neckerauer, Koehler-Ruprecht, Kimich, Werleaa, and perhaps one of the best-known Rheinpfalz estates, Dr. Burklin-Wolf.

Nahe   This is another underrated source of high-class Riesling, as well as a wine zone with a competitive group of producers who, for now, lack the one superstar needed to draw world-wide attention to this region's virtues. A Nahe wine is considered to possess some of the character of a Saar wine and the spice, meatiness, and flesh of a Rheingau. The curranty, smoky aromas of a Nahe are reminiscent of those found in a red wine, making it among the most distinctive of all German wines. None of the Nahe producers is well known, so prices tend to be low, except for those producers who are members of the prestigious VDP group (e.g., Hans Crusius). Top producers include von Plettenberg, Hehner-Kiltz, Kruger-Rumpf, Adolph Lotzbeyer, and perhaps the finest, Helmuth Donnhoff and Prince zu Salm.

Franken With the wonderful city of Würzburg as its commercial center, the wines of Franken have developed a considerable cult following. Although these wines fetch high prices and are put in unattractive squat bottles that are impossible to bin, Franken wines can be bold, dramatic, and heady. Moreover, they enjoy remarkable loyalty from their admirers. This is one region where the Sylvaner grape hits heights that exist nowhere else on earth. The two best estates are Burgerspital and Hans Wirsching. I have also been increasingly impressed (especially by the 1990s) with wines from Schloss Sommerhausen. Once past the quality of these superlative producers, caveat emptor.

MOST IMPORTANT INFORMATION TO KNOW (CONTINUED)

• The best German wines are those produced at the Kabinett, Spätlese, Auslese, Beerenauslese, and Trockenbeerenauslese levels of ripeness and sweetness. Most consumers tasting a Kabinett would not find it particularly sweet, although there is residual sugar in the wine. Because of a high natural acidity found in German wines, a Kabinett generally tastes fresh, fruity, but not sweet to most palates. However, most tasters will detect a small amount of sweetness in a Spätlese, and even more in an Auslese. All three of these types of wines are ideal as an apéritif or with food, whereas the wines entitled to Beerenauslese and Trockenbeerenauslese designations are clearly dessert wines, very rich and quite sweet. One should keep in mind that the alcohol level in most German wines averages between 7–9%, so one can drink much more of this wine without feeling its effects. One of the naive criticisms of German wines is that they do not go well with food. However, anyone who has tried a fine Kabinett, Spätlese, or Auslese with Asian cuisine, with roast pork, or even with certain types of fowl such as pheasant or turkey can tell you that these wines work particularly well, especially Spätlese and Auslese.

• The best German wines age like fine Bordeaux. In great vintages, such as 1990 or 1971, one can expect a Kabinett, Spätlese, or Auslese from a top producer to evolve and improve in bottle for 3–20 years. Beerenauslese and Trockenbeerenauslese have the ability in a great vintage to improve for two to four decades. This is a fact, not a myth, to which those who have recently tasted some of the great Auslesens from 1959 can easily attest. German wines at the top levels, from the top producers, do indeed improve remarkably in the bottle, although the trend among consumers is to drink them when they are young, fresh, and crisp.

RECENT VINTAGES

2000—The 2000 vintage in Germany is the third in a row that suffered from late-season rains. A warm, humid, muggy year led to huge yields and major outbreaks of rot in the vineyards. A mediocre vintage at best, 2000 suffers from the debilitating effects of high yields and excessive rains. The mildew and rot that were rampant in the vineyards can be found in all too many of the 2000s.

1999—Stylistically, the 1999 vintage is reminiscent of 1997 in that the wines are soft, fruit-forward, and easily appreciated by those who do not usually like German wine. Those searching out the vibrancy and complexity that only Riesling can attain will not be enamored with this vintage. A warm growing season led to high yields throughout Germany. Rains in September and October were soaked up by the vines, resulting in many wines exhibiting signs of dilution. The finest 1999s, generally those at the Kabinett level from conscientious producers, should be consumed in the near term.

1998—The last excellent year of the millennium, 1998 succeeded despite nature. A scorching sun in August led to sunburn on a significant percentage of grapes, and constant rains began in mid-September and didn't stop until late October. The following three weeks were dry and windy, concentrating the grapes and preventing the onset of rot. The finest wines (mostly at the Auslese level and above) have appealing levels of acidity, loads of intensity, and vibrant personalities. This is a vintage that, unlike 1997, 1999, and 2000, reflects *terroir*. In addition, the finest 1998s will be excellent candidates for cellaring.

1997—After the tooth-shattering acidity of the 1996s, Mother Nature reversed gears for the 1997 vintage. As opposed to the 1996s, the 1997s are forward, lush, low-acid offerings for near-term drinking. In this vintage consumers should concentrate on wines from the Spätlese level and below; the Auslesen rarely have the complexity to match their higher prices, nor do they have the balance for extended cellaring. This is an excellent vintage for consumers who want to discover German wines, as there are multitudes of delicious Kabinetts at reasonable prices.

1996—This is an atypical vintage. High levels of maturity are combined with exceedingly high levels of acidity. In fact, the 1996 Germans may be the most acidic wines I have ever tasted. At the Spätlese level and above (Auslese and above for those fearing searing acidity) a multitude of incredibly pure wines were fashioned. These efforts will require patience for their richness to cover some of the acid. Below the Spätlese level the vast majority of wines are to be avoided; they simply don't have the stuffing to face the record acidity levels. Consumers searching for extraordinary wines at the Auslese level and above for extended cellaring are well advised to search out 1996s crafted by Germany's finest producers.

1995—The 1995 vintage is extremely uneven, with some concentrated, profound, and exceptionally balanced wines having been produced, as well as many that are plagued by the negative characteristics of rot (as opposed to the positive effects of botrytis). The Mosel fared best, and the Rheinpfalz suffered immensely (even outstanding producers such as Lingenfelder were unable to escape the vintage's rot in the Pfalz).

1994—Superb weather in October resulted in an abundant crop of sweeter-styled wines. Quality is uneven, but some outstanding wines were produced. In complete contrast to the stylish, elegant, high-acid 1993s, the 1994s are relatively powerful, rich, and made for near-term drinking.

1993—Delicate, crisp, light-bodied wines were produced in bountiful quantities. The vintage favors Kabinett, Spätlese, and Auslese producers.

1992—This is a good vintage with some superlative, drier-style wines coming from the Ruwer and Middle Mosel. Most estates reported it was very difficult to produce sweet wines in these areas. Therefore, this is a vintage of mostly Kabinetts and Spätleses—a good sign for consumers looking for wines from the drier end of the German wine spectrum. All things considered, 1992 is a good to very fine year throughout the Mosel, Saar, and Ruwer regions, with fewer superrich dessert wines than in years such as 1990 and 1989. In the Rheingau, Rheinpfalz, and Rheinhessen, the vintage looks to be very good to excellent, with plenty of rich wines as well as sweet late-harvest wines, particularly in the Rheinhessen.

1991—This has turned out to be a surprisingly good vintage, far better than many of the doom-and-gloom reports suggested. Although not of the level of 1990 or 1989 in terms of rich, intense, sweet Spätlese and Auslese wines, it is a very appealing vintage, particularly for the top estates in the drier Kabinett styles. The downside of the 1991 vintage is that some wines have shrill levels of acidity, raising questions as to whether their fruit will hold up. Most German-wine specialists suggest this was a year of the wine-maker rather than of Mother Nature, and those producers who were able to keep yields down and who picked physiologically ripe fruit made wines with crisp acidity and good depth and character. Those who didn't made hollow, high-acid wines that merit little attention.

1990—An outstanding, perhaps even great vintage. The wines have fabulous ripeness, surprisingly crisp acidity, and an intense perfume and mid-palate. In addition to many outstanding Kabinetts and Spätleses, this is another vintage, much like 1989, where there were spectacular sweet Ausleses and even more decadently rich Beerenauslese and Trockenbeerenauslese wines produced. If you are a German-wine enthusiast, this vintage is a must buy.

1989—This is another top-notch vintage that has been compared with 1976, 1971, and 1959. The late harvest and the extraordinary amount of sweet wine made at the Auslese, Beerenauslese, and Trockenbeerenauslese levels have garnered considerable enthusiasm. Unlike in 1990, where every wine zone enjoyed success, or 1991, where it was a question of the wine-maker's ability, in 1989 the Saar, Rheinpfalz, Ruwer, and Rheinhessen produced top wines. This was not a rain-free harvest, production yields were high, and acidity levels in many cases remain suspiciously low, suggesting that most consumers would be well advised to drink up the wines below the Auslese level. One area of good but somewhat disappointing wines in the context of the vintage is the Middle Mosel, where a number of the most famous domaines overcropped and produced somewhat fluid, loosely knit, fragile wines.

1988—The strength of this vintage is the Middle Mosel. Based on my tastings, the drier Kabinetts and Spätlese offerings look to be the best wines made. This vintage has now been largely forgotten in the hype over 1989 and 1990.

1987—A mediocre vintage followed an unusual growing season that was characterized by a poor, wet, cold summer but a glorious September and mixed-bag weather in October. The quality is expected to be better than in either 1980 or 1984, and many growers reported harvests close in size to those in 1986. The average production was a whopping 96 hectoliters per hectare, which is excessive. Interestingly, this appears to be a good year for the rare nectarlike Eisweins. All 1987s should have been drunk by 1998.

1986—A copious crop resulted in pleasant, agreeable, soft, fruity wines that had broad commercial appeal. Because of the crop size, prices dropped after the smaller-than-normal crop in 1985. This vintage will be regarded by the trade as a useful, practical year of good rather than great wines. Wines below the Auslese level should already be drunk up.

1985—The German wine trade has touted this year rather highly, but except for a handful of areas, it is not comparable to the outstanding 1983 vintage. Nevertheless, it is a very good year with a moderate production of wines with good acidity and more typical textures and characteristics than the opulent, richly fruity 1983s. As in 1983, the dryness during the summer and fall prevented the formation of *Botrytis cinerea*. The Rieslings in many cases can be very good but will be firmer and slower to evolve and less open than the more precocious, overt, fruity 1983s. Overall, the 1985s should be past their prime. The top successes are in the Middle Mosel, with potentially great wines from villages such as Urzig and Erden. Wines below the Auslese level should already have been drunk and the Auslesen are at their peak.

1984—Fresh, light, very pleasant, straightforward wines that are neither green nor too acidic were produced in this vintage of average quality and below-average quantity. The Mosel estate of Dr. F. Weins-Prüm Erben made excellent wines in 1984, as did Monchhof. All 1984s should have been drunk by 1998.

1983—This vintage received the most publicity between the 1976 and 1990 vintages. Most growers seemed to feel that it was certainly the best since the 1976. It was a very large crop throughout all viticultural areas of Germany, but it was especially large and exceptional in quality in the Mosel-Saar-Ruwer region. The wines have excellent concentration, very fine levels of tartaric rather than green malic acidity, and a degree of precocious ripeness and harmonious roundness that gives the wines wonderful appeal now. However, because of their depth and overall balance, Ausleses remain delicious but should be drunk by 2004. The vintage seemed strongest at the Spätlese level, as there were very little Auslese, Beerenauslese, and Trockenbeerenauslese wines produced. This was also a great year for Eiswein, where, as a result of an early freeze, above-normal quantities of this nectarlike, opulent wine were produced. However, despite larger quantities than normal, the prices are outrageously high for the Eisweins but very realistic and reasonable for the rest of the wines.

OLDER VINTAGES

The great sweet wine vintage that can sometimes still be found in the marketplace is 1976, a vintage that, by German standards, produced incredibly ripe, intense, opulent wines, with a significant amount of wine produced at the Auslese and Beerenauslese levels. The top wines should continue to last another 2–12 years. Some critics have disputed the greatness of this vintage, saying that the 1976s are low in acidity, but that is a minority point of view. The wines remain reasonably priced at the Auslese level, but the Beerenausleses and Trockenbeerenausleses from this vintage are absurdly expensive. The 1977 vintage should be avoided, and 1978, unlike in France, was not a particularly successful year in Germany. Well-kept 1975s can provide great enjoyment, as can the 1971s, another great vintage. I would avoid the wines from 1972, and the once good 1973s are now in serious decline.

RATING GERMANY'S BEST PRODUCERS

Where a producer has been assigned a range of stars (***/****), the lower rating has been used for placement in this hierarchy.

* * * * * (OUTSTANDING)

J. J. Christoffel (Mosel)

Kurt Darting (Rheinpfalz)

Hermann Dönnhoff (Nahe)

Fritz Haag (Mosel)

Heribert Kerpen (Mosel)

J. F. Kimich (Rheinpfalz)

H. & R. Lingenfelder (Rheinpfalz)

Egon Müller (Saar)

Müller-Catoir (Rheinpfalz)

Klaus Neckerauer (Rheinpfalz)

J. J. Prüm (Mosel)

Willi Schaefer (Mosel)

von Schubert-Maximin Grünhaus (Ruwer)

Selbach-Oster (Mosel)

* * * * (EXCELLENT)

Christian-Wilhelm Bernard (Rheinhessen)

Josef Biffar (Rheinpfalz)

von Bretano (Rheingau)

Burgerspital (Franken)

Dr. Burklin-Wolf (Rheinpfalz)

Schlossgut Diel (Nahe)

August Eser (Rheingau)

H. H. Eser-Johannishof (Rheingau)

F. W. Gymnasium (Mosel)

Willi Haag (Mosel)

Freiherr von Heddesdorff (Mosel)

Hehner-Kiltz (Nahe)

Weingut-Weinhaus Henninger (Rheinpfalz)

Freiherr Heyl zu Herrensheim
    (Rheinhessen)

von Hoauvel (Saar)

Immich-Batterieberg (Mosel)

E. Jakoby-Mathy (Mosel)

Weingut Karlsmühle (Mosel-Ruwer)

Christian Karp-Schreiber (Mosel)

Karthauserhof (Christophe Tyrell) (Ruwer)

von Kesselstatt (Mosel-Saar)

Freiherr zu Knyphausen (Rheingau)

Koehler-Ruprecht (Rheinpfalz)

Königin Victoria Berg-Deinhard
    (Rheingau)

Kruger-Rumpf (Nahe)

Kuhling-Gillot (Rheinhessen)

Franz (Günter) Künstler (Rheingau)

Dr. Loosen-St.-Johannishof (Mosel)

Alfred Merkelbach (Mosel)

Meulenhof/Erben Justen/Erlen (Mosel)

Monchhof (Mosel)

Nahe Staatsdomaine (Nahe)

Pfeffingen (Rheinpfalz)
von Plettenberg (Nahe)
Jochen Ratzenberger (Mittelrhein)
Jakob Schneider (Nahe)

von Simmern (Rheingau)****/*****
J.U.H.A. Strub (Rheinhessen)
Dr. Heinz Wagner (Saar)

* * * (GOOD)

Paul Anheuser (Nahe)
Basserman-Jordan (Rheinpfalz)
Erich Bender (Rheinpfalz)
Bischoflisch Weinguter (Mosel)
Bruder Dr. Becker (Rheinhessen)
Christoffel-Berres (Mosel)
Conrad Barta (Mosel)
Hans Crusius (Nahe)
Josef Deinhart (Mosel-Saar)
Epenschild (Rheinhessen)
Dr. Fischer (Saar)
Four Seasons Co-op (Rheinpfalz)
Hans Ganz (Nahe)
Gebrüder Grimm (Rheingau)
Gernot Gysler (Rheinhessen)
Grans-Fassian (Mosel)
Gunderloch-Usinger (Rheinhessen)
J. Hart (Mosel)
Dr. Heger (Baden)
von Hoauvel (Mosel)
Toni Jost (Mittelrhein)***/****
Klaus Klemmer (Mittelrhein)
Johann Koch (Mosel)
Gebrüder Kramp (Mosel)
Lehnert-Matteus (Mosel)
Josef Leitz (Rheingau)
Licht-Bergweiler (Mosel)
Lieschied-Rollauer (Mittelrhein)
Schloss Lieser (Mosel)
Weingut Benedict Loosen Erben (Mosel)
Adolf Lotzbeyer (Nahe)
Mathern (Nahe)***/****
Weingut Merz (Rheinhessen)
Herbert Messmer (Rheinpfalz)
Theo Minges (Rheinpfalz)
Eugen Müller (Rheinpfalz)

Dr. Heinrich Nagler (Rheingau)
Peter Nicolay (Mosel)
von Ohler'sches (Rheinhessen)
Dr. Pauly Bergweiler (Mosel)
Petri-Essling (Nahe)
Ökonomierat Piedmont (Mosel-Saar-
    Ruwer)
S. A. Prüm (Mosel)
S. A. Prüm-Erben (Mosel)
Erich Wilhelm Rapp (Nahe)
Reuscher-Haart (Mosel)
Max Ferdinand Richter (Mosel)
Salm (Nahe)
Prinz zu Salm (Nahe)
Peter Scherf (Ruwer)
von Schleinitz (Mosel)
Georg Albrecht Schneider (Rheinhessen)
Schloss Schönborn (Rheingau)
Schumann-Nagler (Rheingau)
Wolfgang Schwaab (Mosel)
Seidel-Dudenhofer (Rheinhessen)
Bert Simon (Saar)
Schloss Sommerhausen (Franken)
Sturm (Rheinhessen)
Dr. Thanisch (Mosel)
Unckrich (Rheinpfalz)
Christophe Vereinigte Hospitien (Mosel)
Wegeler-Deinhard (Mosel, Rheinpfalz,
    Rheingau)
Adolf Weingart (Mittelrhein)
Dr. F. Weins-Prüm (Mosel)
Domdechant Werner (Rheingau)
Winzer Vier Jahreszeiten (Pfalz)
Günter Wittman (Rheinhessen)
Wolff-Metternich (Rheinhessen)
G. Zilliken (Mosel)

* * (AVERAGE)

Baumann (Rheinhessen)
Bollig-Lehnert (Mosel)
von Buhl (Rheinpfalz)
Stephan Ehlen (Mosel)
Alexandre Freimuth (Rheingau)
Le Gallais (Mosel)
Siegfried Gerhard (Rheingau)

Martin Gobel (Franken)
Schloss Groenestegn (Rheingau)
Louis Guntrum (Rheinhessen)
Schloss Johannishoff (Rheingau)
Burgermeister Carl Koch (Rheinhessen)
Lucashof (Rheinpfalz)
Milz-Laurentiushof (Mosel)

Claus Odernheimer/Abteihof St.-Nicolaus (Rheingau)

Geh. Rat Aschrott'sche (Rheingau)

J. Peter Reinert (Mosel-Saar)

Schloss Reinhartshausen (Rheingau)

Schloss Saarstein (Saar)

Schmidt-Wagner (Mosel)

Henrich Seebrich (Rheinhessen)

Staatsweingüter Eltville (Rheingau)

Studert-Prüm/Maximinhof (Mosel)

Schloss Vollrads (Rheingau)

AUSTRIA

The Basics

Thanks to the enormous talents of some of its wine-makers as well as the dedication and hard work of two high-quality U.S. importers (Terry Theise and Vin Divino), Austria is bursting onto the American scene as a source of superb white wines. Since the 1985 scandal (when it was discovered that many Austrian wineries were adulterating their wines with diethylene glycol to give them the appearance of more body and sweetness), Austria has made great strides to improve the quality of its wines. Presently, Austria's average yields are less than half of Germany's (where industrial winemaking still dominates the market), and it has a number of super-high-quality producers that consistently fashion world-class white wines.

While many varietals can be found in Austria, Grüner Veltliner and Riesling dominate its fine dry wine production. Grüner vines make up more than one third of the nation's plantings. It is a pepper, spice, pear, and citrus-flavored white wine that sometimes reveals characteristics reminiscent of rhubarb and green beans. As cutting-edge sommeliers have discovered, it is extremely versatile when paired with food as well as delicious to drink immediately after bottling. While they are capable of aging, my inclination is to consume Grüner Veltliners young, generally within their first 3–6 years of life.

The finest Austrian Rieslings are as mind-boggling as any dry Rieslings produced in the world. They tend to have the expressive nature and harmony reminiscent of Alsatian wines, yet often have the focus and balance of Rieslings from Germany (but not as searing). They are less floral and candied (and generally drier) than their Alsatian counterparts but more fruit-driven than those from Germany. Like Alsatian Rieslings, those from Austria successfully complement a wide variety of foods. While ageworthy, they are generally best consumed within 10 years of the vintage (unlike a number of German and Alsatian Rieslings, which require aging).

Austria's most famous (and deservedly so) dry wine–producing region is the Wachau. As with all of this nation's top wine regions, it is located in eastern Austria. This small area (only 3,500 acres of vines), is situated to the west of Vienna (in fact, it is the westernmost of eastern Austria's wine-producing regions) on the Danube River. Its terraced vineyards are located on steep hillsides and enjoy the full benefit of the area's warm days and cool nights. The Wachau has instituted strict labeling rules to allow consumers to know the natural potential alcohol of the grapes at harvest (Steinfeders are from grapes with 9.5% to 10.7%

natural alcohol, Federspiels with 10.7% to 12%, and the finest, richest wines—over 12% natural potential alcohol—are Smaragds). Other high-quality, dry wine–producing regions include Kremstal, Kamptal, Styria, and Wien. Austria's finest sweet wines come from an area adjacent to the Neusiedlersee area of Burgenland. The Neusiedlersee is a large, shallow lake that separates Austria from Hungary. This humid area regularly benefits from outbreaks of *Botrytis cinerea* (noble rot), essential for the production of complex sweet wines.

Austria's red-wine producers have made efforts in recent years to improve the quality of their wines. However, with a few notable exceptions, they are generally lean, metallic, vegetal, and hard.

A MINI GLOSSARY

The following are a few words that readers will find in the accompanying notes as well as on the labels of other Austrian wines. Familiarizing yourself with these words should assist you in making your initial forays into the vinous treasures of Austria less intimidating.

-er: Words ending in "er" indicate what village or small area the wine comes from, and it is generally followed by the name of the actual vineyard. Thus, a label that reads "Dürnsteiner Freiheit" means it comes from the Freiheit vineyard in the town of Dürnstein.

Alte Reben: The Austrian term for old vines, or *vieilles vignes*.

Ausbruch: Sweet wines made near the town of Rust. To earn the right to include this term on a label, a wine had to have a must weight of at least 139° Oeschle (this German term relates to the must weight of a wine. 139° is extremely high and indicates that Ausbruchs are very sweet).

Beerenauslese: Sweet wine made from must with at least 127° Oeschle. The grapes may have been affected by noble rot (*Botrytis cinerea*).

Ried: Often found on labels preceding another word, this simply means vineyard or cru. For example, in California, Araujo's famous Cabernet Sauvignon would be referred to as Ried Eisele by Austrians. Not every single-vineyard wine has this term on its label.

Smaragd: This term is earned by Wachau's top dry wines. To merit this designation, the wine's grapes had to be harvested with more than 12% natural potential alcohol, and they cannot have been chaptalized or sweetened with *süssreserve* (unfermented grape juice).

Spätlese: Wines with this term on the label must have been harvested with more than 12% natural potential alcohol (94° Oeschle) and cannot be chaptalized or sweetened by using a *süssreserve* (this technique of adding unfermented grape juice is allowed and commonly employed in Germany).

Trockenbeerenauslese: Sweet wine made from must with at least 156° Oeschle. The grapes must have been affected by noble rot (*Botrytis cinerea*).

RATING AUSTRIA'S BEST PRODUCERS

Where a producer has been assigned a range of stars (***/****), the lower rating has been used for placement in this hierarchy.

* * * * * (OUTSTANDING)

Franz Hirtzberger   F. X. Pichler
Emmerich Knoll   Prager
Alois Kracher

* * * * (EXCELLENT)

Willi Bründlmayer****/*****   Hirsch
Feiler-Artinger****/*****   Nikolaihof
Hiedler   Nigl****/*****

Rudi Pichler
Erich & Walter Polz

Heidi Schröck
Tement

*** *(GOOD)*

Leo Alzinger
Gross***/****
Josef Jamek
Dinstlgut Loiben
Fred Loimer***/****

Erich Salomon
Ernst Triebaumer
Freie Weingärtner
Fritz Wieninger

WILLI BRUNDLMAYER (KAMPTAL)

1999 Grüner Veltliner Ried Lamm	D	88
1999 Riesling Zöbinger Heilingenstein	D	88

The 1999 Grüner Veltliner Ried Lamm offers intense mineral and spice aromatics. It is plump, medium- to full-bodied, velvety-textured, and deep. This large, expressive offering has butterscotch and spices intermingled with its mineral backbone. It reveals its high alcohol in the finish and lacks the balance necessary for aging (and for a better review), yet is an excellent, full-flavored Grüner for near-term drinking. Anticipated maturity: now–2003.

The 1999 Riesling Zöbinger Heilingenstein has a demure, mineral-scented nose. On the palate, this medium-bodied, silky-textured offering has powerful stone, gravel, flower, and citrus flavors. It is delineated, expressive, and reveals a long, precise finish. Anticipated maturity: now–2007.

FEILER-ARTINGER (NEUSIEDLERSEE)

1997 Weißburgunder Ruster Ausbruch Essenz "Kurt"	375ml/D	95
1997 Welschriesling Ruster Ausbruch Essenz "Sabine"	375ml/E	92+

The superb 1997 Weißburgunder Ruster Ausbruch Essenz "Kurt" is an apricot jam, honey, and papaya-scented wine. Its full-bodied, viscous, and tangy character is decadently unctuous. Loads of apricots and tropical fruits, as well as bananas, can be found in this intensely sweet, forward offering. While it obviously has good acidity, it is doubtful that it is high enough to face its monstrously powerful fruit, and therefore this wine should be drunk in the near term. Anticipated maturity: now–2005. The 1997 Welschriesling Ruster Ausbruch Essenz "Sabine" is a more civilized, oily-textured, medium- to full-bodied wine. Apricots and peaches can be discerned in its boisterous aromatics. On the palate, this wine has better balance than the "Kurt" yet remains a thick, sweet, plump wine. It is supple, pure, and immensely flavorful. Anticipated maturity: now–2010.

GROSS (STYRIA)

1999 Sauvignon Blanc Ratscher Nussberg	D	89
1999 Sauvignon Blanc Sulz	D	89

Lively gooseberries and white flowers can be discerned in the aromatics of the 1999 Sauvignon Blanc Sulz. This fresh, intense, juicy, silky-textured, medium-bodied wine is loaded with zesty white fruits and gravel-like notes. Well made and balanced, it also possesses an appealingly long, soft finish. The 1999 Sauvignon Blanc Ratscher Nussberg displays white berries, spices, and citrus fruits in its aromas. Medium-bodied, complex, and rich, it is a focused pear, apple, smoke, and spice-flavored wine. Interestingly, its favor profile would lead me to guess that it was aged in oak barrels for at least a few months, yet Seth Allen of Vin Divino (this estate's American importer) assures me that it is oak free. Drink both of these excellent Sauvignon Blancs over the next 2–3 years.

HIEDLER (KAMPTAL)

1999 Grüner Veltliner Thal-Novemberlese   D   88

The fresh white fruit and hazelnut purée–scented 1999 Grüner Veltliner Thal-Novemberlese is a rich, medium-bodied wine. Its red and white fruit–flavored character is plump, satin-textured, and powerful. This harmonious wine should be consumed over the next 4–5 years.

HIRSCH (KAMPTAL)

1999 Riesling Zöbinger Heilingenstein   D   88+

Hirsch's 1999 Riesling Zöbinger Heiligenstein displays delightful perfume, white fruit, and floral aromas. It is medium-bodied, rich, fat, and reveals layers of well-delineated pear, mineral, and gravel flavors. This excellent wine has the potential to improve with a year or two of cellaring. Anticipated maturity: now–2008.

FRANZ HIRTZBERGER (WACHAU)

1999 Grauburgunder Smaragd Pluris	D	88
1999 Grüner Veltliner Smaragd Axpoint	D	89
1999 Grüner Veltliner Smaragd Honivogl	E	92
1999 Grüner Veltliner Smaragd Rotes-Tor	D	90+
1999 Riesling Smaragd Hochrain	E	91
1999 Riesling Smaragd Singerriedel	EE	95+

The mineral-dominated nose of Franz Hirtzberger's 1999 Grauburgunder Smaragd Pluris leads to a medium-bodied and oily-textured character. Tangy citrus fruits and stones can be found in this well-balanced, appealingly intense, concentrated offering. Drink it over the next 4–5 years. The 1999 Grüner Veltliner Smaragd Axpoint displays spicy white fruit aromas. Medium-bodied, fat, and voluptuous, it offers a complex flavor profile made up of green beans, white pepper, and pears. This wine has excellent depth and concentration. It should be consumed over the next 7 years.

The 1999 Grüner Veltliner Smaragd Rotes-Tor exhibits white flower and mineral aromas. Medium-bodied and satin-textured, it offers gravelly white fruit, stone, and mineral flavors in its highly expressive, concentrated, admirably persistent personality. This outstanding wine can be drunk now or over the next 7–9 years. Honeysuckle, acacia blossoms, and stones can be discerned in the aromatics of the 1999 Grüner Veltliner Smaragd Honivogl. This tobacco, cedar, and mineral-flavored wine has gorgeous definition, precision, and focus. It is medium-bodied, silky-textured, and possesses a long, flavorful finish. Anticipated maturity: now–2008.

The Earl Grey tea–scented 1999 Riesling Smaragd Hochrain is medium-bodied, tangy, and silky-textured. Minerals, quinine, zesty citrus fruits, and candied white berries are found in this well-delineated and persistent wine. Anticipated maturity: now–2008.

The 1999 Riesling Smaragd Singerriedel is a legitimate candidate for Austria's dry white wine of the vintage. It displays candied lemon, mineral, honeysuckle, spice, and herb tea aromas. Medium-bodied, rich, and oily-textured, this is a highly concentrated and complex wine with exquisite balance. Minerals, tangy citrus fruits, gravel, pear, apples, and cherries can be found in its superbly rich and focused character. If that were not enough, it also possesses an exceptionally long, wild strawberry–laden finish. Readers taken aback by its high price should consider that its cost is approximately equivalent to that of premier cru white Burgundy or one-third the price of Haut-Brion blanc. Anticipated maturity: now–2015.

JOSEF JAMEK (WACHAU)

1999 Riesling Smaragd Ried Klaus   D   89

The 1999 Riesling Smaragd Ried Klaus reveals fresh mineral, chalk, and flower aromas. Medium-bodied and silky-textured, this is an expansive, complex, and elegant wine with spice-laden mineral and citrus flavors. Anticipated maturity: now–2008.

KNOLL (WACHAU)

1999	Grüner Veltliner Smaragd Ried Loibner Loibenberg	D	90
1999	Riesling Smaragd Loibner Loibenberg	D	89
1999	Riesling Smaragd Ried Dürnsteiner Schütt	D	93

While many of Knoll's colleagues in the Wachau produce wines that are excellent to drink in their youth, Knoll's tend to require patience. Readers who have never seen Knoll's labels should make a special effort to do so, as Knoll's wines sport some of the world's most distinctive labels within the small community of the world's finest producers.

The stone- and mineral-scented 1999 Grüner Veltliner Smaragd Ried Loibner Loibenberg is tightly wound, complex, and light- to medium-bodied. This deep gravel- and mineral-flavored wine is intense and powerful. Anticipated maturity: now–2010.

The 1999 Riesling Smaragd Loibner Loibenberg offers powerful petrol and herbal tea aromas. Medium-bodied, broad, expansive, and exquisitely balanced, this is a backward, mineral- and quinine-dominated wine. It is extremely well made and tangy and should, with cellaring, blossom into an outstanding wine. Anticipated maturity: 2003–2012.

The 1999 Riesling Smaragd Ried Dürnsteiner Schütt displays intense petrol aromas. This medium-bodied, muscular, oily-textured wine has extraordinary focus, depth, and strength. It is extremely backward, revealing only hints of its mineral and candied citrus fruit–dominated personality, yet its thick, dense, and deep flavor profile promises a long, outstanding future. Anticipated maturity: 2004–2012+.

ALOIS KRACHER (NEUSIEDLERSEE)

1997	Bouvier Beerenauslese Number 2 (ZDS)	375ml/E	91
1997	Chardonnay Beerenauslese Number 6 (NV)	375ml/E	91
1998	Chardonnay Trockenbeerenauslese Number 2 (NV)	E/375ml	93
1998	Chardonnay Trockenbeerenauslese Number 9 (NV)	E/375ml	96
1998	Chardonnay Trockenbeerenauslese Number 13 (NV)	EE/375ml	98
1998	Chardonnay/Welschriesling Trockenbeerenauslese Number 7 (NV)	E/375ml	94
1998	Grande Cuvée Trockenbeerenauslese Number 10 (NV)	E/375ml	94
1997	Muskat Ottonel Beerenauslese Number 1 (ZDS)	375ml/E	92
1997	Muskat Ottonel Beerenauslese Number 5 (ZDS)	375ml/E	94
1998	Muskat Ottonel Trockenbeerenauslese Number 5 (ZDS)	E/375ml	96
1997	Scheurebe Beerenauslese Number 3 (ZDS)	375ml/E	92+
1998	Scheurebe Trockenbeerenauslese Number 3 (ZDS)	E/375ml	95
1998	Scheurebe Trockenbeerenauslese Number 12 (ZDS)	EE/375ml	93
1998	Traminer Trockenbeerenauslese Number 8 (NV)	E/375ml	93
1998	Welschriesling Trockenbeerenauslese Number 4 (NV)	E/375ml	95
1998	Welschriesling Trockenbeerenauslese Number 6 (ZDS)	E/375ml	92
1997	Welschriesling Trockenbeerenauslese Number 7 (ZDS)	375ml/EE	94+
1998	Welschriesling Trockenbeerenauslese Number 11 (ZDS)	EE/375ml	96
1997	Zweigelt Rosé Beerenauslese Number 4 (NV)	375ml/E	91
1998	Zweigelt Rosé Trockenbeerenauslese Number 1 (NV)	E/375ml	92

As always with Alois Kracher, he has labeled his sweet wines either "Nouvelle Vague" or "Zwischen den Seen." The Nouvelle Vague (listed as NV above) were vinified and aged in new-oak barrels, whereas the Zwischen den Seen (ZDS) were produced using the area's traditional oakless methods. Nouvelle Vague means "new wave" in French, and Zwischen den Seen means "between the lakes" in German. Kracher also numbers his wines based on concentration, with the least concentrated receiving the lower numbers.

The 1997 Muskat Ottonel Beerenauslese Number 1 (ZDS) reveals sweet orange blossom aromas. On the palate, loads of candied kumquats can be found in this pungent, extroverted, satin-textured wine. Medium-bodied and well balanced, its forward flavors last at least a minute and a half in its seemingly unending finish. Drink this powerful, concentrated wine over the next 10 years. The 1997 Bouvier Beerenauslese Number 2 (ZDS) has a smoke- and apricot-laden nose. Medium- to full-bodied and thickly textured, this peach- and apricot-flavored, decadently strewn wine is plump, fat, and supple. Drink this extroverted beauty over the next 6–7 years.

The fresh orange- and apricot-scented 1997 Scheurebe Beerenauslese Number 3 (ZDS) offers a broad red berry, spice, citrus, and yellow fruit–packed character. This well-balanced, lush, thick-textured wine is concentrated, powerful, and exceptionally long. Drink this outstanding wine over the next 12 years. The dark sherry-colored 1997 Zweigelt Rosé Beerenauslese Number 4 (NV) displays nut, dark roasted berry, spice, and stone aromas. It is thick, oily-textured, medium- to full-bodied, and loaded with mulling spice flavors. This concentrated, flavorful wine should be consumed between now–2009.

The 1997 Muskat Ottonel Beerenauslese Number 5 (ZDS) displays superb orange blossom, candied kumquat, spice, and apricot aromas. This hugely complex, deep, and concentrated wine is crammed with red, yellow, and tropical fruits. Spices, flowers, and oranges are intermingled throughout this medium- to full-bodied, decadent effort. Anticipated maturity: now–2010. Oak spices and yellow fruits can be discerned in the aromatics of the 1997 Chardonnay Beerenauslese Number 6 (NV). Its medium- to full-bodied and satin-textured core of apricots, spiced pears, and tropical fruits also reveals Kracher's use of new oak barrels. It is plump, forward, and reminiscent of an over-the-top California Chardonnay. Because of its loads of sweet fruits and oak, drink it over the next 6–7 years. The thick, almost impenetrable nose of the 1997 Welschriesling Trockenbeerenauslese Number 7 (ZDS) offers spicy red and white fruit flavors. On the palate, this extraordinarily concentrated, thick, viscous, decadent, backward wine is densely packed with untold quantities of red, yellow, and white fruits. It coats the palate with layers of honey-dripping fruit flavors that linger for two minutes or more. Drink this gorgeous sweet wine over the next 12+ years.

According to Alois Kracher, 1998 is the first of a three-year string of outstanding vintages for sweet wines from Austria's Burgenland/Neusiedlersee region. "We have never before had three successive vintages of such high quality," he said. It is a vintage of massive ripeness and huge amounts of *Botrytis cinerea*, the noble rot that concentrates and provides additional complexity to the world's finest sweet wines. These are some of the finest sweet wines produced on earth, and they are less expensive than many of their qualitative equals from Germany and Sauternes/Barsac.

The 1998 Zweigelt Rosé Trockenbeerenauslese Nouvelle Vague Number 1 has a deep goldish amber color (in previous vintages this wine has had a redish pink color, but Kracher says that "botrytis steals color"). Aromatically, it reveals rich, spicy caramel scents. This is a medium- to full-bodied, velvety-textured wine with boisterous botrytis, spice, candied kumquat, caramel, and butterscotch flavors. It has excellent focus and freshness, yet is extremely concentrated (and this is the least concentrated of Kracher's thirteen 1998 Trockenbeerenausleses!). Its extensive finish reveals the drying effect of wines dominated by botrytis. Anticipated maturity: now–2012.

The pale yellow-colored 1998 Chardonnay Trockenbeerenauslese Number 2 (NV) displays aromas of jammy peaches and apricots dusted with botrytis. Medium- to full-bodied and thick, this is a sweet red raspberry, jellied apricot, candied peach, and spice-flavored wine. It is dense and oily-textured, yet pure and fresh. Anticipated maturity: now–2020. The orange/yellow 1998 Scheurebe Trockenbeerenauslese Number 3 (ZDS) explodes from the glass with spices, lychee nuts, roses, and candied white raisins. It is gorgeously focused, fresh, medium-bodied, and packed with smoky minerals as well as loads of jammy yellow fruits. This exceptionally long wine reveals a firm tannic backbone, a rarity for a white wine but typical of its varietal. It has an immensely impressive combination of power, concentration, balance, and elegance. Anticipated maturity: now–2020+.

The 1998 Welschriesling Trockenbeerenauslese (NV) Number 4's color reveals hints of gold. This medium- to full-bodied wine offers candied white raisin and caramel aromas. It is fat, thick, and dense on the palate. Loads of jellied fruits, spices, botrytis flavors, and over-ripe apricots conquer the palate (my notes say "Wow! Rolling thunder!") and refuse to relinquish their grip for what seems like minutes. Remarkably, given this wine's intensity and thickness, it appears fresh, well balanced, and precise. Drink it over the next 25+ years. The similarly colored 1998 Muskat Ottonel Trockenbeerenauslese Number 5 (ZDS) displays kumquat and candied apricot aromas. Fat jellied oranges explode on the palate and appear to transform themselves into elegant orange blossoms, red berries, and cherries. This is a refined wine with exemplary focus, precision, and purity to go along with its massive concentration as well as power. It is medium- to full-bodied, muscular, and graceful. Drink it over the next 20+ years.

The 1998 Welschriesling Trockenbeerenauslese Number 6 (ZDS) has a musty (it wasn't corked) nose (from its massive levels of botrytis) that also reveals loads of sweet white and yellow fruits. It is crammed with overripe fruit flavors, as well as the distinctive effects of spicy botrytis. This superbly focused wine has bountiful levels of acidity to cope with its lush, opulently thick character. Drink this refined liquid botrytis over the next 20+ years. The yellow/orange 1998 Chardonnay/Welschriesling Trockenbeerenauslese Number 7 (NV) exhibits aromas reminiscent of poached pears, flowers, and candied berries. It is medium- to full-bodied, ample, velvety-textured, and crammed with fresh pears, apples, oranges, white flowers, and jammy apricots. It is rich, broad, lively, and has exceptional acidity and an impressively long finish. Anticipated maturity: now–2025+.

The 1998 Traminer Trockenbeerenauslese Number 8 (NV) is a scrumptious gold-colored wine with an intensely spicy nose, packed with white peaches, freshly cracked pepper, apricots, herbs, and botrytis flavors. It is seamless, harmonious, and has the distinctive tannic mark of its varietal in its botrytis-laced finish. Anticipated maturity: now–2025. The oak, vanilla, toast, acacia blossom, and crème brûlée–scented 1998 Chardonnay Trockenbeerenauslese Number 9 (NV) is an intensely sweet, fat, and candied wine. Full-bodied and powerful, this is a dense (yet harmonious) offering jam-packed with sugarcoated oranges, candied apples, and honey. Its seemingly unending finish reveals additional layers of luxurious jellied fruits. Drink this exceptional wine over the next 25–30 years.

Produced from 50% Chardonnay and 50% Welschriesling, Kracher's 1998 Grande Cuvée Trockenbeerenauslese Number 10 (NV) reveals hints of sweet oak in its otherwise jammy yellow fruit–dominated aromatics. This medium- to full-bodied wine has abundant candied white grapes and apples intermingled with poached pears in its peppery character. It is thick, spicy, oily-textured, and possesses an amazingly long, apricot-flavored finish. Anticipated maturity: now–2030. The 1998 Welschriesling Trockenbeerenauslese Number 11 (ZDS) has a yellow color with golden hues. It exhibits white peach, apricot, smoke, botrytis, and freshly cracked white pepper aromas. Medium- to full-bodied and elegant, this wine is stuffed with candied kumquats, jellied peaches, spices, and fresh apricots. It has an exceptional combination of refinement, power, and concentration. This decadently textured wine is intense, pure, and immensely long. Anticipated maturity: now–2030+.

The gold-colored 1998 Scheurebe Trockenbeerenauslese Number 12 (ZDS) has a chemical-scented nose that also displays white pepper and graham cracker aromas. Medium- to full-bodied and lush, this wine offers copious layers of jellied yellow fruits in its fat, plump, yet wonderfully fresh personality. As its nose sheds its chemical notes with air, this wine offers a compotelike character that reveals caramel and butterscotch flavors. Readers who wish to drink this wine while it displays fruit should consume it over the next 5–8 years. Those who prefer aged, dark-colored, heavily botrytized wines dominated by burnt sugar flavors can drink it between 2007–2030+. The 1998 Chardonnay Trockenbeerenauslese Number 13 (NV) is Kracher's most concentrated wine from this vintage. Cedar, spices, apricots, and overripe peaches are displayed by this full-bodied, muscular offering. It is hugely dense, almost syrupy, with loads of jammy and jellied fruits in its round, sexy personality. This Rubenesque wine has untold quantities of fruit (mostly apricots), spices, and botrytis in its expressive, seamless flavor profile. This harmonious, muscular, and graceful wine will retain its fruit for at least 15 years and will potentially live longer than anyone reading this book.

DINSTLGUT LOIBEN (WACHAU)

1999 Riesling Loibner Loibenberg "L"	C	88

The herbal tea and sweet spice–scented 1999 Riesling Loibner Loibenberg "L" has a medium-bodied and satin-textured character. It is a brown honey wine, a forward Riesling loaded with potpourri, perfume, and white raisin flavors. This expressive wine should be consumed over the next 3–5 years.

LOIMER (KAMPTAL)

1999 Grüner Veltliner Spiegel Alte Reben	D	89

The sweet spring onion–scented 1999 Grüner Veltliner Spiegel Alte Reben is medium- to full-bodied, rich, and plump. Broad layers of minerals, white fruits, freshly cracked white pepper, and garbanzo beans can be discerned in this excellent wine's complex personality. Drink it over the next 4–5 years.

FAMILIE NIGL (KREMSTAL)

1999 Grüner Veltliner Alte Reben	D	88
1999 Riesling Senftenberg Piri Privat	E	89+
1999 Sauvignon Blanc	D	89

The 1999 Grüner Veltliner Alte Reben offers lovely mineral aromas. It displays excellent depth to its quinine, pear, and citrus fruit–flavored personality. This medium-bodied, well-made, seamless wine also possesses a long, tangy finish. Anticipated maturity: now–2006.

Nigl's 1999 Sauvignon Blanc is a strange yet compelling wine. Consumers who dislike Sauvignons with vegetal aromas and flavors are advised to steer clear of Nigl's 1999. However, readers searching for wines that are distinctively unusual will love this controversial wine. It offers bell pepper and roasted peanut scents as well as a complex, medium-bodied personality. Spices are intermingled with sautéed green beans in this detailed and silky-textured effort's character. Unlike the vast majority of wines with distinct vegetable aromas and flavors, this one is ripe and rich. Drink it over the next 2–3 years. Pears and apples can be discerned in the aromatics of the 1999 Riesling Senftenberg Piri Privat. Light to medium-bodied and satin-textured, it has a flavor profile composed of white fruits, red berries, flowers, minerals and lemons. Refined, this flavorful wine has impressive depth as well as a finish that appears to roar back to life after 30 seconds or so. Anticipated maturity: now–2008.

NIKOLAIHOF (WACHAU)

1999 Grüner Veltliner Smaragd im Weingebirge	D	88
1999 Riesling Jungfernweim im Weingebirge	E	89
1999 Riesling Spätlese Steiner Hund	E	91+

The white pepper and flower-scented 1999 Grüner Veltliner Smaragd im Weingebirge is a medium-bodied, satin-textured wine. This explosively rich, layered Grüner is filled with expressive pear, apple, and spice flavors that linger throughout its long finish. Anticipated maturity: now–2005. The Nikolaihof winery, a biodynamically farmed estate, produced a superb 1999 Riesling Spätlese Steiner Hund. Its gorgeous aromas of perfume, flowers, and spices lead to a highly expressive core of voluptuous red and white berries that nearly obscure this outstanding wine's underlying minerality. Well balanced and delineated, it is a rich, refined Riesling that can be drunk over the next 10–12 years. The 1999 Riesling Jungfernwein im Weingebirge is an excellent wine for near-term drinking. It displays creamed spice aromas and a plump, medium-bodied, velvety-textured character. This offering has impressive depth to its cherry, raspberry, and spice-flavored personality. Anticipated maturity: now–2005.

F. X. PICHLER (WACHAU)

1999 Grüner Veltliner Smaragd Dürnsteiner Kellerberg	E	91
1999 Grüner Veltliner Smaragd M	D	90
1999 Grüner Veltliner Smaragd von den Terrassen	D	90
1999 Riesling Smaragd Dürnsteiner Kellerberg	EE	93
1999 Riesling Smaragd Loibner Berg	EE	92

The 1999 Grüner Veltliner Smaragd von den Terrassen boasts an explosive nose of spices and deep white fruits. Medium-bodied and hugely expressive, this is a precise, satin-textured wine. Loads of pepper, pears, apples, and spices can be discerned in its boisterous flavor profile. Drink this wine over the next 7–8 years. The quinine- and mineral-scented 1999 Grüner Veltliner Smaragd Dürnsteiner Kellerberg is medium-bodied and silky-textured. Red and white berries as well as minerals can be found in this highly detailed, concentrated, complex wine. It is extremely well balanced and possesses a long, supple finish. Anticipated maturity: now–2008. The 1999 Grüner Veltliner Smaragd M has rather subdued aromas and a light- to medium-bodied character. Silky-textured, tight, and powerful, this is a bell pepper and freshly cracked white pepper–flavored wine, highly defined yet rich, with an admirably long, lush finish. Anticipated maturity: now–2007.

The extroverted nose of the 1999 Riesling Smaragd Loibner Berg offers red/white berries and flowers. This deep, hugely concentrated, medium-bodied, intricate wine is packed with a myriad of spices as well as pears, apples, white peaches, apricots, and minerals. This out-standing Riesling can be enjoyed over the next 12 years. The superb 1999 Riesling Smaragd Dürnsteiner Kellerberg offers searing mineral, candied lemon, flower, and spiced pear aromas. Medium-bodied, magnificently elegant, and complex, this is a cherry, wild strawberry, and tropical fruit–flavored wine whose flavors seamlessly last throughout its exceptionally long finish. Rich, deep, yet highly detailed and refined, it is a wine that is forward and drinkable young yet has all the requisites for a long, fruitful life. Drink this beauty over the next 15 years.

RUDI PICHLER (WACHAU)

1999 Grüner Veltliner Smaragd Wösendorfer Hochrain	D	89
1999 Grüner Veltliner Smaragd Wösendorfer Kollmutz	D	88
1999 Riesling Smaragd Weissenkirchner Achleiten	D	90
1999 Riesling Smaragd Wösendorfer Kirchweg	D	89

Pure, racy minerals can be found in the aromatics of the 1999 Grüner Veltliner Smaragd Wösendorfer Kollmutz. Medium-bodied, rich, and dense, it reveals minerals, white pepper, and pearlike flavors in its silky-textured character. Anticipated maturity: now–2006. The herbal tea and mineral-scented 1999 Grüner Veltliner Smaragd Wösendorfer Hochrain is light- to medium-bodied, broad, and plump. Grapefruit and assorted other citrus fruits are intermingled with spices and pepper in this complex, silky-textured wine. Anticipated maturity: now–2007.

The 1999 Riesling Smaragd Wösendorfer Kirchweg has tangy berry and freshly cracked black pepper aromas. Medium-bodied, zesty, and broad, it reveals pear, apple, mineral, and stone flavors in its long, focused character. Drink it over the next 7–8 years. Expressive lemon and white flower aromas are found in the nose of the 1999 Riesling Smaragd Weissenkirchner Achleiten. This medium-bodied, expansive, admirably focused wine is spicy and filled with minerals, quinine, and red/white berries. Satin-textured and intricate, it is full-flavored, elegant, and admirably persistent. Drink this wine over the next 8–10 years.

ERICH & WALTER POLZ (SUDSTEIERMARK)

1999 Sauvignon Blanc Hochgrassnitzberg	D	89

Lively lemons and gooseberries can be found in the aromatics of the 1999 Sauvignon Blanc Hochgrassnitzberg. This medium-bodied, rich, concentrated Sauvignon displays a wonderful velvety-textured character. Its powerful personality is filled with an assortment of white and citrus fruits, as well as a complex underlying minerality. Anticipated maturity: now–2003.

PRAGER (WACHAU)

1999 Riesling Smaragd Dürnstein Hollerin	D	89+
1999 Riesling Smaragd Dürnstein Kaiserberg	D	92
1999 Riesling Smaragd Weissenkirchen Achleiten	E	92
1999 Riesling Smaragd Weissenkirchen Klaus	E	92+
1999 Riesling Smaragd Weissenkirchen Steinriegl	C	90
1999 Riesling Smaragd Weissenkirchen Wachstum Bodenstein	E	94

The 1999 Riesling Smaragd Dürnstein Hollerin displays chalk, mineral, and herbal tea aromas. This vivacious, medium-bodied, highly focused (almost searingly so) wine is packed with stones, white fruits, and minerals. Anticipated maturity: now–2008. Pears, apples, and expressive mineral aromas are found in the nose of the 1999 Riesling Smaragd Dürnstein Kaiserberg. Medium- to full-bodied, rich, broad, and massively concentrated, this gravel-flavored beauty has extraordinary precision and an exceptionally long, flavorful, and delineated finish. Drink it over the next 8–10 years.

The 1999 Riesling Smaragd Weissenkirchen Steinriegl has a mineral-dominated nose. This medium-bodied, silky-textured, and tangy wine is redolent with lemony minerals, quinine, and flowers. This admirably balanced wine should be consumed over the next 7–9 years. The stone- and mineral-scented 1999 Riesling Smaragd Weissenkirchen Achleiten is medium-bodied, powerful, and tightly wound. This citrus, mineral, and white fruit–dominated wine has outstanding intensity and complexity to its persistent personality. Drink it over the next 8 years.

The 1999 Riesling Smaragd Weissenkirchen Klaus offers mineral, lemon, and pear aromas. Medium-bodied and silky-textured, it has outstanding depth, intensity, and focus. White flowers, gravel, minerals, and quinine (slightly reminiscent of a gin and tonic) can be found throughout its tangy flavor profile as well as in its impressively long finish. Drink it over the next 8–10 years. The superb 1999 Riesling Smaragd Weissenkirchen Wachstum Bodenstein has a nose of citrus fruits, flowers, white pepper, honeysuckle blossoms, and minerals. Medium-bodied and explosive, this powerful, gorgeously detailed, and intense wine coats the taster's palate with deep layers of liquid minerals and white fruits. It has exquisite balance, an expressive yet elegant personality, and a seemingly unending finish. Drink this wine over the next 10–12 years.

ERICH SALOMON (KREMSTAL)

1999 Riesling Kögl Reserve	D	89

The acacia blossom–scented 1999 Riesling Kögl Reserve is light- to medium-bodied and well delineated. It possesses a complex white fruit, gravel, spice, and mineral-filled character as well as an impressively long, flavorful finish. This extremely well made and highly detailed wine should be consumed over the next 6–8 years.

TEMENT (STYRIA)

1999 Sauvignon Blanc Zieregg	D	88

The 1999 Sauvignon Blanc Zieregg was aged four months in new-oak barrels. It displays sweet white fruits intermingled with spicy oak notes in its aromatics. On the palate, this buttery-textured, medium-bodied wine is redolent with ripe pears, gooseberries, and spices. Drink it between now–2003.

ERNST "ET" TRIEBAUMER (NEUSIEDLERSEE)

1997 Blaufrankisch Ried Mariental	EE	88

The medium to dark ruby-colored 1997 Blaufrankisch Ried Mariental displays a lovely nose of spices and deep red fruits. Medium-bodied, chewy-textured, and well structured, this is an intense, stony black fruit–flavored wine. Drink it over the next 4–5 years.

WEINGARTNER (WACHAU)

1999 Riesling Smaragd Loibner Loibenberg	C	89
1999 Riesling Smaragd Weissenkirchner Achleiten	D	88+

The 1999 Riesling Smaragd Weissenkirchner Achleiten displays a powerful, spice-laden nose. Medium-bodied, juicy, and fat, it is well balanced and offers a deep stone- and mineral-laden character. Anticipated maturity: now–2007. The 1999 Riesling Smaragd Loibner Loibenberg has aromas of bergamot (the zesty citrus fruit used to flavor Earl Grey tea) and stone. It is medium-bodied, rich, and loaded with white and red berries, as well as notes of spicy herbal teas. This detailed, flavorful, complex wine should be consumed over the next 6 years.

WIENINGER (VIENNA)

1999 Grüner Veltliner Nussberg	C	88
1999 Nussberg Alte Reben	C	88

The smoke, spice, and fresh earth–scented 1999 Grüner Veltliner Nussberg is medium-bodied and silky-textured. This juicy, rich, well-balanced wine reveals pear, spice, and white pepper flavors in its focused character. Anticipated maturity: now–2005. The 1999 Nussberg Alte Reben is the result of a field blend (when the different commingled grape varietals within a specific vineyard or *terroir* are harvested and vinified together). Its subdued aromatics are followed by a rich, complex, medium-bodied personality. Spices, pepper, apples, and pears can be found throughout its silky-textured character, as well as in its long, lush finish. Anticipated maturity: now–2005.

4. SPAIN AND PORTUGAL

SPAIN

The Basics

TYPES OF WINE

Aside from the glories of sherry, which is synonymous with Spain, this beautiful sun-drenched country is best known as a treasure trove for red wine values. The majority of white wines, which in the past tasted musty and oxidized, are now, thanks to high technology, usually innocuous, with sterile personalities and no real flavor. There are exceptions, such as the fragrant, crisp, tasty whites made from the Albarino grape. Other refreshing, inexpensive white wines have emerged, but they are in the minority. And while the booming Spanish sparkling wine business stays in the headlines, few makers of sparkling wine actually produce exceptional wine; most of it is reliably pleasant, relatively innocuous, and very cheap—under $15—hence the appeal.

Red wine is king in Spain, but regrettably this country is still one of largely unrealized potential. The best red wines all come from northern Spain. The two areas best known for quality are Rioja and Penedès. Yet these traditional bastions of Spanish wine are being rivaled and occasionally surpassed by upstart regions. The Ribera del Duero, Priorato, Navarra, and Toro are today's overachievers, and Jumilla is beginning to attract attention.

To understand Spanish red wines one must first realize that the Spanish want their red wines supple, with an aged taste of maturity, as well as a healthy (many would say excessive) dosage of oak, usually the blatant American variety. Once you realize this, you will understand why many Spanish wineries, called *bodegas*, age their wines in huge oak or concrete vats for seven or eight years before they are released. While tastes are changing, the Spanish are not fond of grapy, tannic, young wines, and historically have expected the wineries to mature the wines for the Spanish consumer. Consequently, traditionally styled Spanish wines have an advanced garnet color, and are smooth and supple with the sweet vanilla taste of strong oak well displayed. Many wineries actually hold back their best lots for a decade or more before releasing them, enabling the consumer to purchase a mature, fully drinkable wine. However, the international demand for big, dark wines with intense flavors is causing a revolution in winemaking, led by the aforementioned regions.

GRAPE VARIETIES

RED WINES

Cabernet Sauvignon   An important part of Vega Sicilia, Spain's most expensive and prestigious red wine, Cabernet Sauvignon has flourished in Spain.

Carinena This workhorse grape (Carignan in English) has muscles like Arnold Schwarzenegger. Big and brawny, the tannic, densely colored wine made from this grape varietal is frequently used as a blending agent, particularly with Grenache.

Garnacha Garnacha (Grenache) is widely planted in Spain. There are three types of Garnacha utilized. Garnacha Blanc, which produces white wines, is relatively limited, although it is especially noticeable in Tarragona. Garnacha Tinto, similar to the Grenache known in France, is one of the most widely planted red wine grapes in Spain. There is also the Garnacha Tintorera, which is actually Alicante, the grape that produces black-colored, tannic, dense wines, and is primarily used for blending.

Merlot This relatively new varietal for Spain has performed competently.

Monastrell This varietal (Mourvèdre) primarily produces surprisingly rich, alcoholic wines. Although widely planted, it is most frequently found in hotter microclimates. Some producers from the backwater viticultural region of Jumilla have done interesting work with Monastrell.

Tempranillo The finest indigenous red wine grape of Spain, and a noble one, Tempranillo travels under a number of names. In Penedès it is called Ull de Llebre and Tinto in the Ribera del Duero. It provides rich, well-structured wines with good acidity and plenty of tannin and color. The bouquet often exhibits an intense berry/black raspberry character with a floral note. It makes an ideal blending mate with Garnacha, but it is easily complex enough to stand on its own. Tempranillo is also called Tinta del Pais, Tinta del Toro, Tinto de la Rioja, and Tinto Madrid.

WHITE WINES

The white wine grapes parade under names such as Albarino, Chardonnay, Macallo, Malvasia, Palomina (utilized for sherry), Parellada (the principle component of most sparkling wines), Pedro-Ximenez, Riesling, Sauvignon, Torrontés, Verdejo, Xarello, and Moscatel. Few of these varietals have proven to be capable of making anything more than neutral-tasting wines, but several appear to have potential, as yields have been kept low and the wines have been impeccably vinified, not eviscerated by processing. The best is the Albarino, which, when produced by a top winery in Galicia, has a stunning perfume similar to that of a French Condrieu. However, in the mouth the wine is much lighter, with less body and intensity. At its finest, it is light, refreshing, fragrant, and an ideal apéritif or seafood wine.

Other white wines that have shown potential include some of the Chardonnays, and Torrontes, which, when made in Galicia, has a perfumed personality, lovely fruit salad–like flavors, and a pleasant finish.

FLAVORS

Penedès The dominant winery here is Torres, which produces a bevy of red wines from the typical Spanish varietals. But the top wine is the 100% Cabernet Sauvignon Black Label Gran Coronas, which has a rich, open-knit bouquet of plums, sweet oak, and often licorice and violets. Its chief rival is the Cabernet Sauvignon from Jean Leon, another concentrated, blackberry-scented and -flavored, full-throttle wine with a whopping influence from sweet, toasty oak. The best recent vintages are 1998, 1996, 1995, and 1994.

Ribera del Duero Three of Spain's greatest red wines are produced in this broad river valley: Pesquera, which comes primarily from the Tempranillo grape, Vega Sicilia, primarily a Cabernet Sauvignon/Merlot/Malbec blend, and Tempranillo-based Pingus. These are world-class wines of considerable majesty. What is noticeable about them is the remarkable purity of berry fruit that can be found in the top vintages. Take superripe fruit and combine it with a minimum of three years (in the case of Vega Sicilia, 8–12 years) in oak casks, and you have powerfully heady, supple, explosively rich wines that offer a great deal of spicy, sweet,

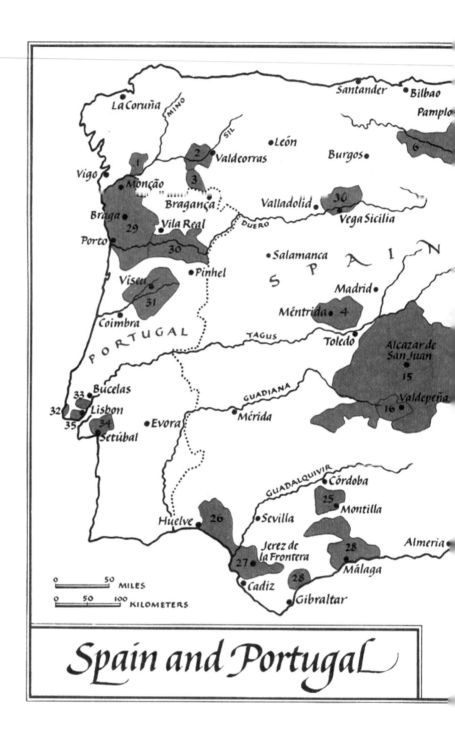

Spain and Portugal

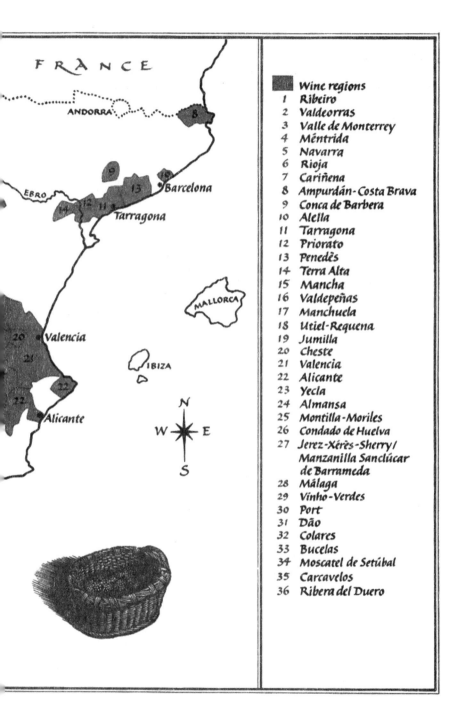

FRANCE

ANDORRA

EBRO

Barcelona

Tarragona

MALLORCA

Valencia

IBIZA

Alicante

N
W — E
S

Wine regions
1 Ribeiro
2 Valdeorras
3 Valle de Monterrey
4 Méntrida
5 Navarra
6 Rioja
7 Cariñena
8 Ampurdán - Costa Brava
9 Conca de Barbera
10 Alella
11 Tarragona
12 Priorato
13 Penedès
14 Terra Alta
15 Mancha
16 Valdepeñas
17 Manchuela
18 Utiel-Requena
19 Jumilla
20 Cheste
21 Valencia
22 Alicante
23 Yecla
24 Almansa
25 Montilla-Moriles
26 Condado de Huelva
27 Jerez-Xérès-Sherry/
    Manzanilla Sanclúcar
    de Barrameda
28 Málaga
29 Vinho-Verdes
30 Port
31 Dão
32 Colares
33 Bucelas
34 Moscatel de Setúbal
35 Carcavelos
36 Ribera del Duero

toasty, vanilla-scented oak. The best vintages have been 2001, 2000, 1999, 1996, 1995, 1994, 1991, 1990, 1989, 1986, 1983, 1982, 1976, 1975, 1968, and 1962.

Rioja When made by the finest traditional producers, Rioja is a mature wine having a medium-ruby color, often with a touch of orange or brown (normal for an older wine), and a huge, fragrant bouquet of tobacco, cedar, smoky oak, and sweet, ripe fruit. On the palate, there will be no coarseness or astringence because of the long aging of the wine in cask and/or tank prior to bottling. Despite its suppleness, the wine will keep for 5–10 years after its release. Even a young Rioja, released after just 3–4 years, will show a ripe, fat, rich, supple fruitiness, and a soft, sweet, oaky character. Increasingly, progressive antitraditional winemaking has taken over Rioja, producing wines with more color, riper fruit, and the influence of French rather than American oak. It is a different animal from the traditional Rioja. The best vintages include 2001, 1996, 1995, 1994, 1991, 1990, 1989, 1987, 1982, 1981, 1978, 1973, 1970, 1968, 1964, and 1958.

Toro Once known for overwhelmingly alcoholic, heavy wines, Toro has adopted modern technology, and the results have been some rich, full-bodied, deeply flavored, southern Rhône–like wines from wineries such as Farina. They taste similar to the big, lush, peppery wines of France's Châteauneuf-du-Pape and Gigondas, and they represent astonishing values. The luxury cuvée of Numanthia, created by cutting-edge Spanish wine importer Jorge Ordoñez, showcases the great potential this region possesses. The best vintages are 2001, 1999, and 1998.

AGING POTENTIAL
Albarino (whites): 1–2 years
Navarra: 5–7 years
Penedès: 6–15 years
Priorato: 6–25 years
Ribera del Duero: 6–30 years
Rioja: 6–25 years
Sparkling white wines: 1–4 years

OVERALL QUALITY LEVEL
While it may be fashionable to tout the quality and value of all Spanish wines, the only wines with serious merit are the red wines and a handful of the Albarinos. The finest Spanish reds can hold up to the best international competition. Most of the whites are still atrociously boring, and while the sparkling wines are inexpensive, only a few offer value. Despite the fabulous climate and high percentage of old vines, most of Spain's wine-makers have not yet realized their potential, which is formidable.

MOST IMPORTANT INFORMATION TO KNOW
Knowing the names of the best producers, and a few top recent vintages (1994, 1995, 1996, and 1999) will get you a long way if you avoid most of the white wines from this country, except for the Albarinos that require consumption within 1–2 years of the vintage.

BUYING STRATEGY
Spain has become fashionable for both high quality and excellent wine values. Thanks to the work of several innovative importers, particularly Jorge Ordoñez and Eric Solomon, this country is securing a bigger and bigger share of the fine-wine market, as well as continuing to provide many exceptional bargains. The slow transformation of the Spanish mentality from a cooperative-based, industrial winemaking philosophy to one based on quality, individuality, and *terroir* has resulted in better and better wines. There are some storm clouds on the

horizon due to the fact that much of Spain had less than stellar vintages in 1997 as well as 1998. Combine that with increasingly high prices for many wines with no established track record, and consumer resistance is inevitable. However, there are abundant quantities of high-quality 1994s, 1995s, and 1996s in the marketplace, as well as others scheduled to be released over the next several years. Given the terrific climate, multitude of fabulous *terroirs*, and the requisite financial incentive to produce world-class wine, look for more and more unknown names to become overnight stars, assuming prices do not get out of touch with the realities of the marketplace.

RECENT VINTAGES

2000—A huge harvest throughout Spain, especially in Rioja, Ribera del Duero, and Navarra, this will be an irregular year with some superb wines. Rioja will be more irregular than Ribera del Duero.

1999—It was a sensational harvest in Ribera del Duero, although rain was a problem in some areas. Rioja is at best average because of uneven ripening and a rainy harvest. Overall, it is a good vintage in Ribera del Duero, mediocre in Rioja, and average to above average in such regions as Navarra and Penedès.

1998—This is a relatively tannic vintage for most Spanish wine regions, with a good-sized crop. The Ribera del Dueros are less successful than in 1999, but the Riojas are better. Priorato enjoyed an excellent vintage, nearly as fine as the great 1994.

1997—A difficult vintage throughout Spain, the quality in 1997 is significantly below the levels achieved in 1994, 1995, and 1996, and in subsequent years such as 1999 and 2000.

1996—A spectacular vintage in Ribera del Duero, good to very good in Rioja, and mediocre in Priorato.

1995—In many areas of Spain, this vintage has turned out to be as stunning as 1994. Everyone from Rioja, Ribera del Duero, and Priorato was thrilled with the ripeness and richness. It appears to be a great vintage for Spain's top producers.

1994—Spanish wine producers have pronounced 1994 as Spain's vintage of the century. It was one of the hottest years on record and, unlike France, Spain was not troubled by September rain. From bottle, the top wines are indeed impressive, especially those from Priorato, Rioja, and Ribera del Duero.

RATING SPAIN'S BEST DRY RED TABLE WINES

* * * * * *(OUTSTANDING)*

Abadia Retuerta Cuvée El Campanario (Sardon del Duero)

Abadia Retuerta Pago Negralato (Sardon del Duero)

Abadia Retuerta Valdebon (Sardon del Duero)

Bodegas Ismael Arroyo Valsotillo Reserva (Ribera del Duero)

Artadi Rioja Grandes Anadas Reserva Especial (Rioja)

Artadi Rioja Viña El Pison Reserva (Rioja)

Cims de Porrera (Priorato)

Clos Erasmus (Priorato)

Clos Mogador (Priorato)

l'Ermita (Priorato)

Mauro Vendimia Seleccionada (Ribera del Duero)

Muga Prado Enea Reserva (Rioja)

Muga Torre Muga (Rioja)

Marqués de Murrieta Castillo Ygay Gran Reserva (Rioja)

Marqués de Murrieta Dalmau Reserva (Rioja)

Numanthia (Toro)

Pesquera Ribera del Duero (Castilla-León)

Pingus (Ribera del Duero)

Fernando Remirez de Ganuza Rioja Old Vines Unfiltered (Rioja)

Rotllan Torra Tirant (Priorato)

Sierra Cantabria Rioja Coleccion Privada (Rioja)

Vega Sicilia NV Gran Reserva Especial (Ribera del Duero)

Vega Sicilia Unico Reserva (Castilla-León)

* * * * (EXCELLENT)

Abadia Retuerta (Sardon del Duero)

Abadia Retuerta Cuvée El Palomar (Sardon del Duero)

Abadia Retuerta Rivola (Sardon del Duero)

Albet I Noya Sat (Penedès)

Finca Allondo (Rioja)

Bodegas Ismael Arroyo Valsotillo (Ribera del Duero)

Artadi Rioja Pagos Viejos Reserva (Rioja)

Artadi Rioja Viña de Gain Crianza (Rioja)

Bodegas Arzuaga Reserva (Ribera del Duero)

René Barbier (Cataluna)

Can Rafols dels Caus Penedès (Cataluna)

Capcanes (Tarragona)

Capcanes Garnacha Especial (Tarragona)

Casa Castillo (Jumilla)

Castano (Yecla)

Bodegas Julian Chivite 125 Anniversario Reserva (Navarra)

Clos Dofi (Priorato)

Oliver Conti (Costa Brava)

Costers del Siurdana—Clos de l'Obac (Priorato)

CVNE Contino (Rioja)

CVNE Imperial (Rioja)

CVNE Viña Real (Rioja)

J. M. Fuentes Gran Clos (Priorato)

Fra Fulco (Priorato)

Grandes Bodegas Marqués de Velilla Reserva (Ribera del Duero)

Marqués de Griñon (Ribera del Duero)

Marqués de Griñon (Rioja)

Iberus (Terra Alta)

Leda (Castilla-León)

Jean Léon Penedès (Cataluna)

Martinez Bujanda Conde de Valdemar (Rioja)

Martinez Bujanda Conde de Valdemar Gran Reserva (Rioja)

Mas Igneus (Priorato)

Bodegas Mauro (Ribera del Duero)

Bodegas Moro (Ribera del Duero)

Bodegas Muga (Rioja)

Marqués de Murrieta Coleccion 2100 (Rioja)

Olivares Monastrell (Tarragona)

Pago de Carraovejas (Ribera del Duero)

Remelluri (Rioja)

Castell de Remei (Costers del Segre)

Bodegas Reyes Teofilo Reyes (Ribera del Duero)

La Rioja Alta Reserva 890 (Rioja)

La Rioja Alta Reserva 904 (Rioja)

Bodegas Roda (Rioja)

Telmo Rodriguez (Ribera del Ducro)

San Vicente (Rioja)

Hermanos Sastre (Ribera del Duero)

Sierra Cantabria (Rioja)

Bodegas Valcona (Rioja)

Val Llach (Priorato)

Vega Sicilia Valbuena Ribera del Duero (Castilla-León)

Villa Creces (Ribera del Duero)

* * * (GOOD)

Agricola de Borja (Campo de Borja)

Señorío de Almansa (Castillo-La Mancha)

Amezola de la Mora (Rioja)

Arboles de Castillejo (La Mancha)

Palacio de Arganza Bierzo (Castilla-León)

Bodegas Ismael Arroyo (Ribera del Duero)

Pablo Barrigon Tovar (Castilla-León)

Pablo Barrigon Tovar San Pablo (Castilla-León)

Pablo Barrigon Tovar Viña Cigalena Reserva (Castilla-León)

Pablo Barrigon Tovar Viña Solona (Castilla-León)

Masia Barril Priorato (Cataluna)

Bilbainas Viña Pomal (Rioja)

Marqués de Cáceres (Rioja)

Marqués de Cáceres Reserva (Rioja)

Campo Viejo (Rioja)

Julian Chivite Gran Feudo (Navarra)

Martin Codax Albarino white wine
(Galicia)
CVNE Cune (Rioja)
Domecq-Marqués de Arienzo Reserva
(Rioja)
Enate Crianza (Somontano)
Estola (Castillo-La Mancha)
Farina Colegiata Toro (Castilla-León)
Farina Gran Colegiata Toro (Castilla-
León)
Faustino Martinez Faustino (Rioja)
Franco Españolas Bordon (Rioja)
Marqués de Griñon Cabernet Sauvignon
(Dominio de Valdepusa)
Inviosa Lar de Barros (Extremadura)
Baron de Ley El Coto (Rioja)
Lan Viña Lanciano Reserva (Rioja)
Los Llanos Valdepeñas (Castillo-La
Mancha)
Lopez de Heredia Bosconia Reserva
(Rioja)
Lopez de Heredia Tondonia Reserva
(Rioja)
Bodegas Magana (Navarra)
Martinez Bujanda Conde Valdemar Viño
Tinto (Rioja)
Mauro Ribera del Duero (Castilla-León)
Montecillo Viña Monty Reserva (Rioja)
Bodegas Hermanos Morales (La Mancha)
De Muller Tarragona (Cataluna)
Marqués de Murrieta Reserva (Rioja)
Bodegas Nekeas Vega Sindoa El Chaparral
Old Vine (Navarra)
Ochoa Reserva (Navarra)
Baron de Ona Rioja Reserva (Rioja)
Parxet Alella white wine (Cataluna)
Perez Pascuas Viña Pedrosa Ribera del
Duero (Castilla-León)
Pazo de Señorans Rias Baixas white wine
(Galicia)
Piqueras Castilla de Almansa (Castillo-La
Mancha)
Salvador Poveda (Alicante)

Raimat Costers del Segre (Cataluna)
La Rioja Alta Viña Alberdi (Rioja)
La Rioja Alta Arana (Rioja)
La Rioja Alta Ardanza (Rioja)
Rioja Santiago Gran Condal (Rioja)
Riojanas Monte Real Reserva (Rioja)
Marqués de Riscal Baron de Chirel
(Rioja)
Bodegas Rodero S.L. Val Ribeno Crianza
(Ribera del Duero)
Santiago Ruiz Rias Baixas Albarino white
wine (Galicia)
Bodegas de Sarria Gran Viño del Señorío
Reserva (Navarra)
Bodegas de Sarria Viña del Perdon
(Navarra)
Scala dei Priorato Cartoixa Priorat
(Cataluna)
Scala dei Priorato Clos Mogador (Cataluna)
Scala dei Priorato Negre (Cataluna)
Miguel Torres Coronas Penedès
(Cataluna)
Miguel Torres Gran Coronas Penedès
(Cataluna)
Miguel Torres Gran Coronas Black Label
Penedès (Cataluna); since 1981, for
vintages prior to and including
1981*****
Miguel Torres Gran Sangre de Toro
Penedès (Cataluna)
Miguel Torres Gran Viña Sol Green Label
Penedès (Cataluna)
Miguel Torres Viña Sol Penedès
(Cataluna)
Vega Sauco Reserva (Toro)
Bodegas de Vilarino-Cambados (Rias
Baixas)
Viñas del Vero Compania Somontano
(Aragon)
Castilla de Vinicole Grand Verdad
(Castillo-La Mancha)
Castilla de Vinicole Señorío de Duadianeja
(Castillo-La Mancha)

RATING SPAIN'S BEST SPARKLING WINES

*****(OUTSTANDING)

None

****(EXCELLENT)

None

*** *(GOOD)*

Albet I Noya Cava Brut	Juvé y Champs Gran Cru
Bilbainas	Juvé y Champs Gran Reserva
Cadiz	Juvé y Champs Reserva de la Familia
Cava Avinyo	Mont Marcal Brut
Cavas Ferret	Josep-Maria Raventos Blanc Brut
Chandon	Segura Viudas Aria
Gran Cordornieu Brut	Segura Viudas Brut Vintage
Freixenet Cuvée DS	Segura Viudas Reserva
Freixenet Reserva Real	

SPAIN'S GREATEST WINE BARGAINS

Abadia Retuerta Primicia (Sardon de
    Duero)
Abadia Retuerta Rivola (Sardon de Duero)
Agricola de Borja Viña Borgia (Campo de
    Borja)
Agricola de Borja Borsao (Campo de Borja)
Albet I Noya Cava Brut (Penedès)
Señorío de Almansa (Castillo-La Mancha)
Capcanes Mas Donis (Tarragona Zona
    Falset)
Casa Castillo (Jumilla)
Castano Hecula (Yecla)
Castano Solana (Yecla)
Martin Codax Albarino (Rias Baixas)
Dominico de Egueren (Manchuela)
El Cep Marquis de Gelida (Penedès)
Los Llanos Valdepeñas (Castillo-La
    Mancha)

Finca Luzon Merlot (Jumilla)
Castillo de Maluenda Viña Alarba
    (Calatayud)
Martinez Bujanda Conde Valdemar Viño
    Tinto (Rioja)
Montecillo Rioja (Rioja)
Bodegas Nekeas—various *cuvées*
    (Navarra)
Osborne Solaz (Spain)
Real Sitio de Ventosilla (Ribera del Duero)
Castell de Remei (Costers del Segre)
Thelmo Rodriguez Dehesa Gago (Ribera
    del Duero)
Bodegas Sierra Cantabria Rioja (Rioja)
Solar de Urbezo (Carinena)
Tresantos (Zamora)

ABADIA RETUERTA (SARDON DEL DUERO)

1999	Abadia Retuerta	C	92+
1998	Abadia Retuerta	C	90
1997	Cuvée El Campanario	D	90
1997	Cuvée Lapsus	EEE	92
1997	Cuvée El Palomar	D	89
2000	Primicia	A	88
1999	Rivola	B	90
1998	Rivola	B	89

This multimillion-dollar showcase winery is best known for its classic, potentially long-lived
reds that sell for moderately high prices. However, it is also a bargain hunter's dream, as
there are 10,000 cases of value-priced Primicia. The 2000 Primicia is a blend of 60% Tempranillo, 20% Cabernet Sauvignon, and 20% Merlot. This fruit bomb offers pure flavors of
black cherries and berries intermixed with spice box and minerals. It offers good sweetness,
exceptional purity, and a boatload of fruit. Enjoy it over the next 2–3 years.

The U.S. received 6,000 cases of the 1999 Rivola, a blend of 60% Tempranillo and 40%
Cabernet Sauvignon aged eight months in both French and American oak before being bottled unfiltered. Another fabulous value, it reveals all the characteristics of a great vintage—

superripeness, terrific purity, a multidimensional, textured feel on the palate, and copious quantities of black cherry and currant fruit nicely dosed with spicy, toasty oak. Drink it over the next 4–5 years. Kudos to wine-maker Angel Anociba for not only making great wines but also for providing consumers with needed relief at this level. The 1999 Abadia Retuerta also reveals an opaque purple color as well as a classy, complex bouquet of flowers, black currants, raspberries, cherries, and vanilla. Full-bodied and elegant yet concentrated and powerful, with impressive overall harmony, this nicely textured, rich 1999 can be drunk now or cellared for 10–15 years.

The 1998 Rivola is one of the finest that Abadia Retuerta has made. A blend of 60% Tempranillo and 40% Cabernet Sauvignon from their estate vineyards, many readers may award this wine an outstanding score. The opaque ruby/purple color is accompanied by a knockout nose of tobacco, cedar, spice box, black currants, and a Zinfandel-like briary fruitiness. The wine is medium- to full-bodied and opulently textured, with outstanding purity, extract, and balance. There are no hard edges, and the finish lasts over 20 seconds. This is a remarkable value! Moreover, it will drink well for 2–4 years, perhaps longer. The unfiltered, opaque purple-colored 1998 Abadia Retuerta (65% Tempranillo, 30% Cabernet Sauvignon, and 5% Merlot) was aged 16 months in both French and American oak (50% new). Although closed and tannic, it offers a promising nose of minerals, vanilla, and black currants. Powerful and full-bodied, with moderately high tannin as well as an austere finish, it requires 2–3 years of cellaring. Anticipated maturity: 2004–2020.

The 1997 Cuvée El Palomar (equal parts Cabernet Sauvignon and Tempranillo from a chalky, hillside vineyard) is Bordeaux-like with its notes of dried Provençal herbs intermixed with smoke, cedar, and red and black currants. After spending 16 months in French oak barrels, it was bottled unfiltered. The wine reveals good softness, plenty of spice, attractive red and black fruits, medium body, and excellent symmetry and harmony between all of its elements. Drink it over the next 5–8 years. The 1997 Cuvée El Campanario (100% Tempranillo) reveals greater intensity, ripeness, and richness. Made from some of this huge estate's finest Tempranillo parcels, its dark ruby color is followed by sweet, jammy, black raspberry fruit aromas with notes of licorice and toasty oak. Soft and voluptuously textured, with meaty notes in the mouth, this wine reveals good ripeness, well-integrated acidity and tannin, and a long, 20–25-second finish. Drink it over the next 10–15 years.

Abadia Retuerta introduced a new *cuvée* in 1997, the Cuvée Lapsus. Made from equal parts Merlot, Syrah, and Petit Verdot, this unfiltered wine was made from extremely low yields of 18 hectoliters per hectare. Only 150 cases were produced, approximately one-third of which will make it to America's shores. The grapes were vinified together, and the resulting wine is one of considerable intensity, concentration, and color. Notions of blackberries, chocolate, melted asphalt, and flowers jump from the glass of this medium- to full-bodied, opulently textured, gorgeously proportioned offering. The acidity is present but low, and the wine is concentrated, fleshy, and seamless. Interestingly, malolactic fermentation was done completely in new French oak. Enjoy this beauty over the next 10–15 years.

ALBET I NOYA (PENEDÈS)

1999 Tempranillo	C	90
1998 Tempranillo Col-Leccio	B	88

Albet I Noya produces a bevy of wines, many of them compact and austere. I immensely enjoyed the 1998 Tempranillo Col-Leccio, which was aged one year in French and American oak. It offers an opaque purple color as well as a gorgeous nose of black cherries, blackberries, smoke, and toasty oak. Mouth-filling, rich, and supple-textured, with abundant extract and richness, it will drink well for 5–7 years.

The 1999 Tempranillo represents a positive departure from Albet I Noya's typical austere style. It reveals less rugged tannin, a pleasing mid-palate and texture, and less aggressive notes of wood and herbs. This textured, long, full-bodied effort reveals beautiful sweet black cherry fruit mixed with smoke, spice, and lead pencil. Multilayered, rich, open-knit, and supple, it is a seductive, nicely concentrated offering to drink over the next 4–5 years.

FINCA ALLENDE (RIOJA)

1998	Aurus	EE	90
1997	Aurus	EE	88
1996	Aurus	EEE	91+
1999	Calvario	D	91
1997	Cuesta Dulce	C	90+
1996	Rioja	C	90

There is little value to be found from Allende, but the quality of the wines is impressive

The luxury-priced 1997 Aurus emerges from old vines planted at 1,200–1,500-foot elevations. Made from 85% Tempranillo (60 years old) and 15% Graciano, and low yields of 1.5 tons of fruit per acre, it is bottled unfiltered after undergoing malolactic fermentation as well as aging in new French oak. There are 125 cases of both the 1997 and 1998 imported to America. From a difficult vintage, the dense ruby/purple-colored 1997 Aurus offers an elegant, classy bouquet of red and black fruits, minerals, and smoke. Medium-bodied and deep for a 1997, with moderate tannin, and sweet, earthy black fruits, it will be at its prime between now–2012. The 1998 Aurus exhibits more toasty new oak in the nose, as well as more depth, fruit, glycerin, and body. This Bordeaux-like effort possesses good structure in addition to notes of black cherries, black currants, licorice, and tobacco/spice box. Full-bodied and backward, it requires 1–3 years of cellaring. Anticipated maturity: 2003–2014.

The 1997 Cuesta Dulce (216 cases), made from small-grained Tempranillo, is produced from microscopic yields of 0.8 tons of fruit per acre (or about a pound of fruit per vine). The wine was aged 14 months in new French oak before being bottled unfiltered. An opaque purple color is followed by licorice, blackberry, cherry, and currant fruit, a layered texture, superb extract, enormous weight and richness, and a huge, tannic, muscular finish. It represents a remarkable achievement for the vintage. While it has enormous potential, it requires 3–4 years of cellaring. Anticipated maturity: 2004–2020.

My favorite offering from Finca Allende is the 1999 Calvario, a single-vineyard Rioja produced from vines planted in 1945. Aged completely in new French oak, this wine is layered, rich, and concentrated, with soft tannin, better balance, and more up-front appeal than the two vintages of Aurus. A blend of 90% Tempranillo, 8% Grenache, and 2% Graciano, it is made from small yields of 1.8 tons of fruit per acre. Deep, layered, and impressive, it should drink well for 10–15 years.

The 1996 Aurus, an estate-bottled, unfiltered Rioja made from a blend of 85% Tempranillo and 15% Graciano, is the first release from what the Spanish refer to as a "super Rioja." This opaque purple-colored wine spent 18 months in 100% new French oak casks after a 28–day maceration. Its international style of new French oak combined with intensely concentrated, ripe, black fruits may be criticized, but with aging, this wine should reveal some of its typicity and Rioja character. Call it "traditional winemaking meets international inclinations." Full-bodied, with great purity of fruit, this impressive, limited production (about 450 cases) Rioja should meet with enthusiastic reviews, even if eyebrows are raised at the price. Anticipated maturity: 2003–2018. A modern-styled, exotic Rioja, the dark ruby/purple 1996 Rioja from Finca Allende reveals sumptuous aromas/flavors of roasted coffee and sweet jammy blackberries as well as cassis. Fruit-driven, with sweet French oak in the background, this medium- to full-bodied, intensely concentrated, luscious offering is truly exciting. It can be drunk now or aged for a decade.

JOAN D'ANGUERA (TARRAGONA)

1998 El Bugader	D	89+?

The 1998 El Bugader, a limited-production (333 cases) blend of 70% Syrah, 15% Grenache, and 15% Cabernet Sauvignon, enjoyed malolactic fermentation in wood and spent 18 months in new French oak before being bottled unfiltered. It offers a saturated opaque purple color along with a sweet nose of black fruits, earth, truffles, and chocolate. Full-bodied, rich, dense, and powerful, with moderate tannin, it requires 2–3 years to become more civilized. If it ages as gracefully as I suspect, it will last for 12–15 years.

ANIMA NEGRA (MAJORCA)

1997 Anima Negra	D	88

A rarity from the island of Majorca, this 55% Cabernet Sauvignon/45% Callet blend from a red clay soil vineyard enjoyed a long maceration, and was then aged in a combination of French and—get this—Virginian oak barrels. The nose offers up notes of smoked meats, red and black fruits, and toasty wood. Cassis as well as cherry liqueur make an appearance on the succulent palate. An internationally styled effort with dominant characteristics of new oak and jammy fruit, it is well made, pure, and ideal for enjoying over the next decade. I suspect more regional characteristics (whatever they might be) may emerge with cellaring.

BODEGAS ISMAEL ARROYO (RIBERA DEL DUERO)

1998 Valsotillo	C	89
1996 Valsotillo Reserva	D	91+

The wines from Arroyo tend to be enormously rich, muscular, rustic efforts filled with mouth-staining levels of extract, and sometimes tannin. I have laid away a few vintages hoping that everything will come into balance, but only time will tell. The new releases are all impressive, especially the 1996 and 1994.

The 100% Tinta del Pais (Tempranillo) 1998 Valsotillo emerges from this family's 38.4 acres of hillside vineyards. It is an earthy, tannic effort exhibiting notes of plums, black raspberries, mushrooms, and tree bark. Yields were only 1.25 tons of fruit per acre, and the wine was aged 14 months in American oak casks. Because Arroyo's cellars are extremely cold, these wines are often unevolved upon release. While the 1998 does not have the power, depth, and volume of previous vintages, it is an excellent effort offering earthy, ripe tobacco, cedar, and black cherry flavors, high tannin levels, and underbrush characteristics with toasty oak in the background. This chunky, nearly uncivilized, mouth-filling Spanish red will drink well for 10–12 years. The 1996 Valsotillo Reserva, a selection of the vineyard's finest fruit, is aged for two years in American oak, in a cellar where the temperature never exceeds 52°F. Sadly, only 300 cases of this behemoth have made it to America's shores. A young, muscular heavyweight, it boasts an opaque plum/purple color in addition to aromas and flavors of melted road tar, jammy black fruits, truffles, and roasted meats. Dense, powerful, and full-bodied, with sweeter tannin than the 1998 possesses, this monstrously sized wine is not for everybody, but it has abundant power, weight, richness, and extract. Anticipated maturity: 2005–2022.

ARTADI (RIOJA)

1997 Crianza Viñas de Gain	C	88
1998 Grandes Anadas	EE	96+
1998 Pagos Viejos	E	96
1996 Pagos Viejos	E	93
1998 Viña El Pison	E	95
1996 Viña El Pison	EE	97
1998 Viñas de Gain	B	92

This extraordinary Rioja producer is one of my personal favorites from that famed viticultural area. 1997 was a poor vintage in Rioja, yet Artadi has produced an elegant 1997 Crianza Viñas de Gain with notes of red cherries, peanut butter, and vanilla. It is a beautifully etched, finesse-styled Crianza with sweet fruit, medium body, and fine length. Drink it over the next 3–5 years.

The dark ruby/purple 1996 Pagos Viejos (400 sixpacks available for the U.S.) is a fabulous Rioja boasting a complex bouquet of lead pencil, red and black currants, spice box, cedar, and tobacco. Made from low yields, the wine displays a gorgeous mid-palate, great depth and purity, and a finish that lingers nearly 40 seconds. Drink this spectacular effort over the next 15–25 years. The superb 1998 Pagos Viejos is one of the greatest Riojas I have ever tasted. A dense ruby/purple color is accompanied by a sweet nose of violets, black fruits, minerals, toasty new oak, and smoke. The wine is full-bodied, with gorgeous purity, amazing symmetry for its exceptional size, and an incredibly well delineated finish. In short, it is great stuff! Anticipated maturity: 2005–2025.

At the top of the Artadi hierarchy are the limited-production *cuvées* of El Pison and Grandes Anadas. El Pison is Burgundian in its orientation, whereas Grandes Anadas is a majestic, ageworthy Rioja that may well be the single greatest wine made in that appellation. The 1998 El Pison is made from a Tempranillo vineyard planted in 1945, and aged 18–24 months in new French oak, from yields of only 22 h/h. It offers a deep ruby/purple color and a glorious nose of raspberry jam intermixed with cherries and smoky new oak. As the wine sits in the glass, more complex, floral aromas with a graphite-like character emerge. A sexy, elegant, medium- to full-bodied, beautifully made wine transcends the Rioja appellation with a singular style and character. Drink it over the next 12–15 years. The 1998 Grandes Anadas (100% Tempranillo from 70–100-year-old vines) has only been made twice in the last seven years, 1994 and 1998. It is more tannic and highly extracted, with more body and is a less sexy and seductive effort than either El Pison or Viñas de Gain. However, it is a broodingly backward, formidable wine with amazing concentration, purity, and overall balance. It is more of a Bordeaux style than the Burgundy-like El Pison. Long and concentrated, with a 40–50-second finish, it requires 3–4 years of cellaring and should evolve gracefully for 30 years. These are classic yet singular expressions of Rioja the likes of which can be found nowhere else in that viticultural area. Anticipated maturity: now–2027.

The 1996 Viña El Pison is outrageously rich, complex, and profound. A dense ruby/purple color is followed by aromas of sweet black fruits, vanilla, flowers, and minerals. There are layers of fruit, great flavor extraction, unbelievable finesse, complexity, and elegance. The finish lasts for nearly a minute. Full-bodied and super-concentrated, this compelling Rioja will be at its peak between now–2025. Sadly, only 300 sixpacks were exported to the U.S., but it is well worth seeking out.

Readers should check out the sensational 1998 Viñas de Gain (1,500 cases made it to the U.S.). A selection from three hillside parcels where the vines average 40 years, and bottled after 18 months in French oak (no filtration), it is an elegant, stylish effort with terrific fruit, a sweet, complex nose of black cherries, minerals, lead pencil, spice box, and vanilla. Made from 100% Tempranillo, it possesses an impressive texture, medium to full body, and beautiful balance as well as purity. It is a wine to drink now and over the next 10–12 years. For $18, it is a superb value.

BODEGAS BG (PRIORATO)

1998 Gueta Lupia	D	90

An intensely concentrated, fat, full-bodied Priorato, the 1998 Gueta Lupia exhibits notes of new oak, minerals, black raspberry, and cassis. While more fruit-driven than some of its peers, it has plenty of body, mass, and structure underneath all the glycerin and concentrated fruit. Give it 2–3 years to develop more complexity and fragrance, and drink by 2016.

AGRICOLA DE BORJA (CAMPO DE BORJA)

2000 Borsao	A	89
2000 Borsao 3 Picos	B	90

Year after year the wines from the Agricola de Borja have made the pages of *The Wine Advocate* as superb values. Based on the positive mail I have received, they are a huge hit with readers who are into pleasure rather than insufferable elitism or prestige labels. That being said, these are the finest wines Borja has yet produced. Even their new, more expensive selection qualifies as one of the greatest wine values in the marketplace. The 2000 Borsao is a tank-fermented and aged blend of 80% Grenache and 20% Tempranillo. This luxurious, seamless, voluptuous red reveals an array of sweet, jammy red and black fruits, excellent purity, fine texture as well as concentration, multiple dimensions, and a finish normally found in wines costing $20–30 a bottle. However, its low acidity and precocious character suggest it is best drunk during the next 2–3 years. Readers should not have any problem finding this wine as there are 15,000 cases of the Borsao.

There are 2,000 cases of the 100% old-vine *cuvée* called 2000 Borsao 3 Picos. It is an explosive, rich, concentrated, deep ruby-colored wine offering a gorgeous bouquet of black fruits, kirsch, licorice, and minerals. Full-bodied, spicy, and seamless, with low acidity as well as layers of fruit and glycerin, this amazing effort easily competes with good southern Rhônes and premier cru red Burgundies. Put this wine in a blind tasting with the finest red Burgundies and see what happens. Anticipated maturity: now–2003.

CAPCANES (TARRAGONA)

1999 Cabrida	D	90+
1998 Cabrida	D	94
1998 Capcanes Costers del Gravet Les Vinyasses	C	89
1999 Mas Donis Barrica	A	89
1997 Pansal del Calas	C (500 ml)	93
1998 Val del Calas	B	90

A special *cuvée* made for importer Eric Solomon, the 1999 Mas Donis Barrica is a blend of 80% Grenache and 20% Syrah that spent eight months in barrel. A super value, it is a big, rustic, concentrated, dense, dark ruby/purple effort with notes of earth, licorice, black fruits, meat, and spicy wood. Chewy and thick, it admirably displays Grenache's wonderful sweetness. Moreover, there are 5,000 cases. Enjoy it over the next 3–5 years.

Another impressive effort from this Tarragona winery, the 1998 Val del Calas, a blend of Grenache, Cabernet Sauvignon, and Syrah, is an exceptional value. Six hundred cases of this serious Côtes du Rhône look-alike offer up scents of chocolate, smoky, black cherry fruit, and a robust, concentrated, full-bodied palate impression. It is dominated by its purity as well as a wealth of black fruits. Buy this one by the case, and drink it over the next 4–5 years. A Grenache/Cabernet Sauvignon blend aged 14 months in small barrels, the 1998 Les Vinyasses is made in a lighter style. Although more serious and ambitious, it is not as hedonistic and visceral as the Val del Calas. Medium- to full-bodied, with moderate tannin, good purity, and a more international style, it should drink well for a decade.

The limited-production 1998 Cabrida is the product of 100% Grenache from a single nine-acre vineyard. Made only in the finest vintages, from 95–110-year-old vines, it is aged in 100% new French oak casks. A remarkable effort, it has copious quantities of black cherry, chocolate, and vanilla aromas. Full-bodied, concentrated, tight, and muscular, with moderate tannin, this wine will benefit from 1–3 years of cellaring, and will keep for 12–15 years. This is undoubtedly the most impressive offering I have ever tasted from Tarragona. Anticipated maturity: 2003–2016. The 1999 Cabrida is a serious, though closed offering for true connoisseurs. Made from small yields of 17 h/h, it exhibits a deep purple color as well as a muscular, powerful personality with notes of kirsch mixed with blackberries, currants, licorice, truffles, new saddle leather, and roasted meats. As the wine sat in the glass, the essence of cherry liqueur exploded with even more ferocity. Deep, robust, moderately tannic, and in need of several years of cellaring, it will age well for 12–15 years.

Readers should treat Capcanes's 1997 Pansal del Calas as they would a Banyuls from France, or even a young vintage port. Made from 90–110-year-old Grenache vines, it displays moderate sweetness, as well as Grenache's thick, chewy richness, and roasted nut, herb, and kirsch character. This is a full-bodied, high-alcohol, blockbuster effort that is meant to be served after a meal with cheese or by itself. It should last for a decade or more, but I would opt for drinking it in its exuberant, fiery youth.

CASTANO (YECLA)

1998 Coleccion	B	89
1999 Hecula	B	90
1999 Solana	B	92

The Hecula and Solana are strong candidates for the two best values in dry red wine that I have tasted this year. Both come from terraced vineyards at high elevations (for this area), not far from the emerging viticultural region of Jumilla. The 1999 Hecula is a blend of 70% Mourvèdre, 20% Tempranillo, and 10% Merlot aged six months in new American oak prior to being bottled with no filtration. It exhibits an opaque black color and a dense, chewy, muscular personality with copious quantities of licorice-infused blackberry fruit, saddle leather, and roasted meat aromas as well as flavors. This full-bodied, powerful effort should drink well for a decade. While it is not the most refined style of red winemaking, for $10–12, it is an excellent value. The U.S. will receive 2,000 cases of this *cuvée*. Some of the Mourvèdre (Monastrell) component is from 100-year-old vines. Drink it over the next 8–10 years. The 1999 Solana (2,500 cases for the U.S.), primarily old-vine Mourvèdre aged seven months in wood, is a special *cuvée* made for importer Eric Solomon. This spectacular, opaque black/purple, seamless, fabulously concentrated offering is deep and chewy, with glorious quantities of earthy black cherry/blackberry fruit, full body, velvety, sweet tannin, and a mouthcoating, long, concentrated finish with no hard edges. The oak has been totally absorbed by the wine's wealth of fruit. Like its sibling, it is an astonishing value. Consume it over the next decade.

The 1998 Coleccion (90% Mourvèdre and 10% Cabernet Sauvignon that receives a small amount of barrel aging) is elegant and complex, revealing notes of licorice, black raspberries, and plums. It possesses good density, firm tannin, excellent purity and ripeness, and the potential to last 7–8 years. It is a very good value.

CASA CASTILLO (JUMILLA)

1999 Las Gravas	B	90
1998 Las Gravas	B	90+
2000 Jumilla	A	89
1999 Monastrell	A	88

If we begin seeing more wines such as this from Jumilla, this region will take on the importance and prestige now accorded Priorato. The 1999 Monastrell is a blend of 85% Monastrell (Mourvèdre) and 15% Syrah from the estate's vineyards. Much of the Mourvèdre comes from 40-year-old, ungrafted vines. Yields were an absurdly low 1.0 to 1.25 tons of fruit per acre, all hand-harvested. The wine was aged completely in new American oak for four months prior to bottling. It exhibits a dense purple color with expressive aromatics of tree bark, mushrooms, blackberries, and earth. Boasting an elegant yet powerful mid-palate as well as a forceful personality, it reveals high tannin in the chalky finish. This impressively rich, full-bodied 1999 will benefit from several years of cellaring, and keep for a decade.

A remarkable value for $8.50, the 2000 Jumilla, a blend of 85% Mourvèdre and 15% Syrah, exhibits a saturated purple color in addition to a full-bodied, serious, *vin de garde* style, and dense cherry, blackberry, mineral-tinged fruit. Frankly, this impressive red is too big, rich, and structured for a wine in this price category. It enjoyed malolactic fermentation in new French and American oak where it was aged four months prior to bottling. Yields were a minuscule 1.0–1.25 tons of fruit per acre. For power, intensity, and richness, this wine must be tasted to be believed! Drink it over the next 5–6 years.

The 1999 Las Gravas is not as massive as the 1998, but many readers will consider it better balanced. The tannin is sweeter, and the wine reveals less volume but beautiful harmony as well as gorgeous notes of blackberries, cherries, underbrush, sweet oak, minerals, and earth. Luxuriously rich and supple-textured, it is best consumed over the next 12–15 years. For the quality, it is a super value. The 1998 Las Gravas (a blend of 40% Mourvèdre and 60% Cabernet Sauvignon) gets its name from the large stones that overlay the chalky soils of these hillside vineyards. Again, yields were preposterously low, 0.4 tons of fruit per acre for the Mourvèdre and 0.5 tons per acre for the Cabernet Sauvignon. Malolactic fermentation occurred in wood barrels, and the wine was fined, but not filtered. Fifty percent new French and 50% new American wood was utilized. There are 700 cases of this spectacular wine, which sets a new reference point for Jumilla. Opaque black/purple (it looks more like vintage port than wine), it reveals a fabulous nose of crushed stones and black cherry/blackberry liqueur intermixed with smoke and vanilla. Intensely concentrated, full-bodied, and muscular, with sweet tannin, low acidity, and a fabulous, concentrated finish that lasts 40+ seconds, this is an enormously endowed yet well-balanced offering that is not over the top. Because of the wealth of fruit, glycerin, and extract it is accessible, but give it another 2–3 years of cellaring, and drink it over the following 15+ years. Both of these wines are exceptional values, particularly the 1998 Las Gravas.

CERVOLS (COSTERS DEL SEGRE)

1998 Costers del Segre	C	89

This blend of 40% Tempranillo, 30% Cabernet Sauvignon, and 30% Grenache was aged 14 months in new French oak casks prior to being bottled unfiltered. It is made in an international style, with sweet black currant and berry fruit intertwined with toasty new oak. Ripe, dense, and medium- to full-bodied, with excellent purity, it will drink well for 6–7 years.

CIMS DE PORRERA (PRIORATO)

1998	E	91

This blend of 65% Carignan (from 80-year-old vines), 32% Grenache, and the rest Cabernet Sauvignon exhibits a saturated purple color as well as a gorgeous perfume of overripe grapes, blackberries, prunes, licorice, smoke, and earth. Full-bodied, with high alcohol (14.9%), huge unctuosity and density, it is extremely well balanced despite its weight and mass. Drink it over the next two decades.

CLOS ERASMUS (PRIORATO)

1998 Priorato	E	99
1997 Priorato	D	93
1996 Priorato	D	90

Along with l'Ermita, this is the most concentrated, powerful, and ageworthy of the promising wines of Priorato. I was disappointed with most of the 1996s I tasted from Priorato. However, Clos Erasmus made one of the finest wines I have tasted to date. Production of the 1996 Clos Erasmus was only 300 cases. This is a dark ruby/purple wine with a spicy, oak-driven nose intermixed with black cherry and raspberry fruit notes. Spicy and dominated by wood at present, it is full-bodied, rich, and promising. Yields were a mere 18 h/h. This wine requires 2–4 more years of cellaring and should drink well for 10–15 years. The 1997 exhibits a dense ruby/purple color as well as scents of minerals, toasty new oak, blueberry, black raspberry, and currant fruit, and a full-bodied, impressively endowed, highly extracted personality. Gorgeously pure, with adequate underlying acidity, and a well-delineated, structured, muscular, and concentrated finish, this unevolved 1997 is accessible because of its wealth of fruit and suppleness. It should age gracefully for 10–20 years.

The spectacular 1998 flirts with perfection. Its saturated opaque blue/purple color is not dissimilar to ink. Dazzling aromas of ripe, pure blackberries, violets, blueberries, wet stones, and smoky, toasty oak soar from the glass. Powerful, with an unctuous texture, and super-extracted, rich, concentrated flavors, this blockbuster effort boasts extravagant quantities of fruit, glycerin, extract, tannin, and personality. The wine displays a firm, structured edge, but a viscous texture from super-concentration gives it immediate accessibility. This 1998 should hit its plateau of maturity in 7–8 years, and is a strong candidate for 20–30 years of aging. It is a winemaking tour de force.

CLOS MARTINET (PRIORATO)

1997 Priorato	E	90

Far better than the lean, tough, high-acid 1996, Clos Martinet's 1997 reveals a dark ruby/purple/plum color, sweet black raspberry and blackberry fruit, full body, an expansive, rich, heady, alcoholic finish, and nicely integrated wood. It is a concentrated, lusty style of Priorato to consume over the next decade.

CLOS MOGADOR (PRIORATO)

1998 Priorato	D	94
1997 Priorato	D	91

It is a pleasure to see how much better the 1997 Priorato wines are performing than the lean, emaciated 1996s. Clos Mogador's 1997 boasts a saturated ruby/purple color, a fat, dense, concentrated, black currant, mineral-infused character, full body, layers of concentration, sweet tannin, and a 35-second finish. Impressive and pure, with nicely integrated toasty oak, it will drink well for 10–15 years. Perhaps the finest Clos Mogador to date, the inky purple-colored 1998 (40% Grenache, 35% Cabernet Sauvignon, 20% Syrah, and 5% Mourvèdre and Petit Verdot) boasts a huge nose of blueberries, blackberries, minerals, and vanilla. It is a wine of great purity, intensity, and mass, with extraordinary richness, a blockbuster mid-palate, and a whoppingly long finish. This decadent offering requires a few more years to fully develop. Anticipated maturity: 2003–2020.

OLIVER CONTI (AMPURDAN-COSTA BRAVA)

1998	C	90

This new winery, located four kilometers from the Mediterranean Sea, not far from the internationally renowned Spanish restaurant El Bulli, is making a Bordeaux-like blend of 70% Cabernet Sauvignon, 20% Merlot, and 10% Cabernet Franc aged in French oak for six months prior to being moved to large vats. This sleeper effort needs time in the bottle to reveal its full potential. Aromas of black currants, blackberries, olives, cedar, and spicy French oak are followed by a long, impressively built red with a fat midsection and supple tannin in the finish. Concentrated as well as elegant, it should drink well for 10–12 years.

COSTERS DEL SIURANA (PRIORATO)

1999 Clos de l'Obac	D	92
1998 Clos de l'Obac	D	90
1999 Miserere	D	88

Although I was disappointed with this winery's tough-textured, undernourished 1998 Miserere, their 1998 Clos de l'Obac, a blend of Cabernet Sauvignon, Grenache, Syrah, Merlot, and Carignan, is outstanding. While many Prioratos can be superrich, thick-textured efforts, Clos de l'Obac represents a more elegant, restrained effort from this highly promising, relatively new appellation. Bottled unfiltered, and made from meager yields of 0.5 tons of fruit per hectare, the opaque ruby/purple 1998 offers up notes of black raspberries intertwined with strawberry and cherry fruit. As it sits in the glass, mineral and subtle oak aromas emerge. Beautifully textured and pure, with high tannin, it is a wine of undeniable elegance, finesse, and concentration. It requires 3–4 years of cellaring and should keep for 15+ years. This is unquestionably the most stylish, restrained, high-quality wine emerging from Priorato. Anticipated maturity: 2005–2016.

The two 1999 offerings are the finest wines I have tasted from this estate in a number of years. The 1999 Miserere, a blend of Cabernet Sauvignon, Grenache, Tempranillo, Merlot, and Carignan, spent 12 months in French oak before being bottled unfiltered. It is an elegant, mineral-laced, medium-bodied effort with notes of raspberry and cherry fruit, good purity, and a soft, tangy finish. It should drink well for 4–6 years. The only problem is the price. The impressive 1999 Clos de l'Obac is produced from a similar blend, but the Grenache and Carignan vines range in age from 50–100 years, and yields were kept to a microscopic 14 h/h (about one ton of fruit per acre). The wine spent 14 months in new French oak. Sadly, there are only 200 cases for the U.S. Its opaque purple color is accompanied by a sweet nose of raspberry liqueur intermixed with black currants, minerals, and toasty oak. Medium- to full-bodied and rich, with moderate levels of tannin, decent acidity, excellent delineation, and a long, concentrated finish, it is still youthful and unformed. Anticipated maturity: 2005–2018.

DEHESA GAGO (TORO)

2000 Toro	B	89

Made from 100% Tinta de Toro, this wine, aged in temperature-controlled stainless steel tanks, offers a dense ruby/purple color in addition to a glorious nose of jammy black fruits intermixed with underbrush and pepper. Dense, chewy, and fleshy, it is best consumed over the next 3–4 years. Of all these best buys, this is the most limited *cuvée*, as only 700 cases are exported to America.

CASA DE LA ERMITA (JUMILLA)

2000 Tinto	B	90

Jumilla, one of Spain's up-and-coming backwater areas, is the origin of this estate-bottled blend of 75% Tempranillo, 15% Cabernet Sauvignon, and 10% Mourvèdre. The wine boasts a dense purple color as well as a big, smoky, volcanic ash–like, chocolate, graphite, and blackberry/cassis-scented nose. Layered, full-bodied, dense, and super-concentrated, it is an amazing offering for the price. Enjoy it over the next 5–6 years.

AGRICOLA FALSET MARCA (TARRAGONA)

1999 Etim	B	90
1998 Etim	B	88+?

A blend of 85% Grenache and 15% Cabernet Sauvignon, the sumptuous, thick, juicy 1999 Etim offers knockout aromas of black fruits and earth, outstanding ripeness, impressive purity, and a long, layered finish. Drink it over the next 3–4 years.

The 1998 Etim is a monster wine (a blend of 85% old vine Grenache and 15% Cabernet Sauvignon that was aged in French and American oak) possessing sensational concentration, power, and depth. However, the rustic tannin in the finish may be off-putting to readers looking for a more succulent, velvety-textured style. Nevertheless, there is amazing depth and richness in this clean, blockbuster-sized offering. If the tannin becomes better integrated, the score could increase. For now, think of it as a muscular, full-throttle powerhouse that should be consumed with robustly flavored foods. It should last 5–7 years.

J. M. FUENTES (PRIORATO)

1998 Gran Clos   **D   90**

This internationally styled effort from Priorato is a blend of 70% Grenache, 20% Carignan, and 10% Cabernet Sauvignon. It displays aggressive levels of toasty new oak as well as concentrated black currant and kirsch characteristics. While full-bodied, pure, and rich, the oak needs to become better integrated to justify my rating. Nevertheless, there is plenty of depth, and the fruit quality is impeccable. Cellar this 1998 for 3–4 more years, and enjoy it over the following 15+ years.

FRA FULCO (PRIORATO)

1999 Priorat   **D   91**

Made from 60–100-year-old Carignan vines, and aged in new oak, the exuberant, full-bodied, rustic, but mouth-staining as well as filling 1999 Priorat is loaded with concentrated black fruits intermixed with scents of earth, new saddle leather, and vanilla. Full-bodied, powerful, and rich yet seamless, this terrific wine is best drunk during its first 5–6 years of life to take advantage of its exuberance and purity. Carignan is not a noble varietal, and despite how impressive this wine is, I cannot imagine it developing more complexity. Consume it early for its intensity, richness, and freshness.

LO GIVOT (PRIORATO)

1998 Priorat   **D   90**

This oak-aged, attractive, sweet, concentrated, dense purple 1998 is a blend of 33% 90–100-year-old Grenache, 32% 100-year-old Carignan, and the rest young-vine Cabernet Sauvignon and Syrah. While still tightly knit, it is deep, pure, and rich, offering notes of black fruits, minerals, licorice, and barrique. Anticipated maturity: now–2012.

GRANDES BODEGAS (RIBERA DEL DUERO)

1996 Monte Villalobon   **D   88**

The 1996 Monte Villalobon, made from 90% Tinta del Pais and 10% Cabernet Sauvignon, exhibits a deep saturated purple color in addition to sweet blackberry and cherry fruit intertwined with earth and underbrush notes. Following an excellent entry on the palate, the wine reveals an internationally styled personality. Spicy, ripe, monolithic, the wine should develop over the next 3–4 years and evolve for 12–15.

IBERUS (TERRA ALTA)

1999   **D   91+**

Sadly, there are only 100 six-bottle cases of this wine, which emerges from an area near the Mediterranean coastal appellation of Penedès. A blend of Grenache, Tempranillo, Cabernet Sauvignon, Syrah, and two local varietals, Morenillo and Morselan, this is a powerhouse. Opaque purple-colored, with a thick, jammy bouquet of blackberries, licorice, prunes, and plums, its aroma is reminiscent of Turley Cellars's famed Petite Syrah. Full-bodied and highly extracted, with monstrous levels of flavor balanced by equally high tannin, this massive 1999 requires 5–6 years of cellaring and should keep 20 years. It is an impressive, monolithic wine of considerable power as well as richness.

LEDA (CASTILLA Y LEON)

1998	E	90+

This 20,000 bottle *cuvée*, made from old-vine Tempranillo fermented and aged in new oak, is essentially a *vin de pays*, even though it is just outside the appellation of Ribera del Duero. It reveals abundant spicy oak, full body, and layers of fruit and richness in its concentrated, powerful personality. Two to three years of cellaring will help it become more civilized, but there is a lot going on in this massive offering.

FINCA LUZON (JUMILLA)

2000 Merlot	A	89
1999 Merlot	A	89

A blend of 85% Merlot and 15% Monastrell (Mourvèdre), Finca Luzon's Merlot is produced from a family-owned estate vineyard located a mere 60 miles from the Mediterranean. The Mourvèdre vines are 45 years old, and the Merlot are 18. Unbelievably, yields for the Merlot were 1.6 tons per acre, and for the Mourvèdre, 1.25 tons per acre—lower than yields for most of the great châteaux on the Pomerol plateau (i.e., Pétrus, Lafleur, Vieux Château Certan). The wine boasts a saturated opaque purple color, an amazingly rich, chocolaty, blackberry, and mocha-scented nose of moderate intensity, and explosive, full-bodied, concentrated flavors with chewy extract. The 1999 Merlot may merit an outstanding rating given its purity, richness, and potential to evolve for a decade. The wine's low acidity provides immediate accessibility, but it will keep for 10 or more years. It is an amazing effort from what may be Spain's most promising undiscovered viticultural region.

A sensational value, the 2000 Merlot boasts an opaque ruby/purple color as well as big, thick, dense flavors of black fruits, earth, graphite, and minerals. It possesses soft tannin, outstanding palate richness, and impressive overall purity and balance. More good news— 7,000 cases were exported to the U.S. Buy this one by the case and drink it over the next 4–5 years to take advantage of its exuberant youth.

MAS IGNEUS (PRIORATO)

1998 Costers de Poboleda	D	90
1998 F.A. 112	C	90
1998 F.A. 206	B	88

A noteworthy producer from Priorato, Mas Igneus's 1998 F.A. 206 is a blend of 70% Carignan, 19% Grenache, and 11% Cabernet Sauvignon aged six months in French oak. Soft and round, with earthy, strawberry, and cherry flavors, an elegant personality, and fine purity as well as overall balance, it is meant to be consumed now and over the next 4–5 years. It is an excellent value. The more expensive as well as more compelling 1998 F.A. 112 is a blend of 65% Grenache, 25% Carignan, and 10% Syrah grown in primarily slate-based soils. Yields were a minuscule 0.6 tons of fruit per acre. A deep ruby/purple color is accompanied by sweet, jammy aromas of blackberries and cherries intermixed with minerals and toast. The wine is full-bodied, intense, and pure, with moderate tannin as well as low acidity. It can be drunk now or cellared for 7–8 years. Another outstanding effort is the 1998 Costers de Poboleda. A blend of 80–100-year-old Grenache (65%) and 80-year-old Carignan (35%), aged for one year in 100% new French oak, and bottled unfiltered, it is a full-bodied, powerful effort revealing notes of new saddle leather, kirsch, minerals, and spicy new wood. Intensely concentrated and spicy, with a tannic finish (although the tannin is both sweet and well integrated), it will drink well for 10–15 years.

MAS MARTINET (PRIORATO)

1998 Bru	C	88
1998 Clos Martinet	E	91

Mas Martinet's 1998 Bru (a blend of 45% Grenache, 20% Cabernet Sauvignon, 20% Merlot, and the rest Carignan and Syrah) possesses a deep ruby/purple color as well as thick, juicy notes of black cherries and currants intermixed with earth, minerals, and oak. This wine is dominated by its fruit and richness. Additional complexity should emerge after more time in the bottle. Impeccably made, pure, and medium- to full-bodied, with no hard edges, it should be consumed between now–2014. Its bigger sibling, the 1998 Clos Martinet, boasts a dense purple color and a huge nose of liquid minerals, blackberry liqueur, and cassis. Full-bodied and unctuously textured with terrific presence on the palate, this large-scaled effort is never heavy or overbearing. Sweet tannin in the finish suggests 2–3 years of cellaring will be beneficial, but readers can drink it now as well as over the next 12–18 years.

MAURO (RIBERA DEL DUERO)

1998 Terreus	EE	91+
1996 Terreus	EE	91+
1996 Vendimia Seleccionada	E	90

These offerings are produced just outside the appellation of Ribera del Duero from 100% Tempranillo, barrel-fermented, and bottled with minimal clarification. The dense purple-colored 1996 Vendimia Seleccionada exhibits a sweet bouquet of black cherries, toasty new oak, licorice, and smoke. Full-bodied, ripe, and moderately tannic, this internationally styled Tempranillo will be at its peak between now–2015.

The huge, full-bodied 1998 Terreus (a single-vineyard effort) demands 4–5 years of cellaring. Packed with concentrated blackberry and cassis fruit interspersed with notes of licorice, new wood, and melted asphalt, this potent effort possesses high tannin and extract as well as abundant glycerin. Anticipated maturity: 2005–2020. If everything comes together over the next 4–5 years, look for my rating to go even higher. The muscular, broodingly backward 1996 Terreus exhibits a saturated dark purple color, as well as a tight but promising nose of minerals, black raspberries, and blackberries. Spicy new oak makes an appearance in this dense, full-bodied, nearly impenetrable wine. It requires 4–6 years of cellaring, and should last two decades. Everything appears to be well balanced enough to present fascinating potential for the future.

ABEL MENDOZA (RIOJA)

1999 Rioja	D	92
1998 Rioja	D	90+

This micro-estate sold 200 cases of its stylish, individualistic 1998 Rioja to the U.S. Impressive depth but a closed, structured style make the 1998 a wine for connoisseurs rather than those seeking immediate gratification. The saturated plum/purple color is accompanied by aromas of cherry liqueur, black currants, spice box, vanilla, and underbrush. It is dense and rich, with sweet tannin, a notable, layered midsection, and a long, moderately tannic finish. Anticipated maturity: 2003–2016. Even better is the 1999 Rioja (100% Tempranillo aged in new French oak for 12 months). Sadly, there are less than 100 cases for the U.S. From a producer who strives to fashion one of the world's greatest wines, this Rioja is the result of a fanatical selection process. An opaque purple color is accompanied by a fabulous, sweet perfume of blackberry liqueur, licorice, vanilla, and mineral aromas. Thick and rich, with a beautiful texture, superb purity, and supple tannin, this compelling Rioja possesses more depth and overall complexity than the impressive 1998. Consume it over the next 10–15 years.

HACIENDA MONASTERIO (RIBERA DEL DUERO)

1996 Crianza	D	90

This project, from a large estate in Ribera del Duero, has the gifted Danish wine-maker Peter Sisseck (of Pingus fame). Produced from extremely low yields (15–20 hectoliters per hectare), the 1996 Crianza is a blend of Tempranillo, Cabernet Sauvignon, and Merlot. It is unquestionably an outstanding wine. It possesses 14.5% alcohol, and plenty of guts and richness. The color is a saturated plum/purple. The wine reveals copious quantities of sweet toasty new oak intermixed with nearly overripe scents of prunes, blackberries, and cassis. Full-bodied and spicy, with a lush texture and low acidity, this generous wine can be drunk now and over the next decade.

BODEGAS EMILIO MORO (RIBERA DEL DUERO)

1998	Malleolus	C	90+
1999	Moro	C	92
1998	Moro	C	90
1997	Ribera del Duero	C	89

The Moro family has been fashioning wines from Ribera del Duero for over 120 years. These impressive offerings emerge from relatively young vines (12–20 years of age), and modest yields of 1.6–2.1 tons of fruit per acre. The vinification and upbringing are classical, with 25 days of maceration and 12 months of aging in a combination of old and new French and American oak. One thousand cases of each vintage have been exported to the U.S. Given the quality, these are realistically priced wines that merit considerable attention. The difference between the 1999 and 1998 comes down to structure and accessibility. The 1999 Moro, which reveals the vintage's superripeness, is a sexy, full-bodied, opulently styled effort bursting with black fruits, licorice, smoky, toasty oak, and truffle notes. Lush and dense, it is an ideal candidate for drinking over the next 10–12 years. The 1998 Moro exhibits a saturated color, more tannin, structure, and muscle, but not the charm and forward fruit of the 1999. I would not be surprised to see the 1998 catch up in 5–6 years, but for now, they are both outstanding wines, with a slight edge going to the 1999.

The 1998 Malleolus is produced from 25–75-year-old vines and minuscule yields of 0.85–1.0 ton of fruit per acre. Aged completely in French oak, it is a tighter, more structured effort revealing some of the same characteristics of the 1998 Moro, but more underlying depth as well as aging potential. While dense, powerful, and concentrated, it requires 2–3 years of cellaring and should age gracefully for 12–15 years.

The opaque ruby/purple, 100% barrel-fermented 1997 Ribera del Duero (American oak) is an exuberant, exotic-styled offering with copious quantities of blackberry and cherry fruit, chocolate, smoked herbs, and barbecue spices. Delicious, with abundant oak in addition to the jammy fruit, it has not developed much complexity or delineation, but I suspect that will emerge with another 1–2 years of bottle age. It might even merit an outstanding rating. Anticipated maturity: now–2012.

BODEGAS MUGA (RIOJA)

1996	Rioja Reserva	B	91
1995	Rioja Reserva Seleccion Especial	C	88
1994	Rioja Reserva Seleccion Especial	C	92
1996	Torre Muga	D	92

As longtime readers know, this is one of my favorite Spanish producers. The late-released 1994 Rioja Reserva Seleccion Especial (a blend of 70% Tempranillo, 20% Grenache, and 10% Mazuelo and Graciano) is a selection of the finest vineyard sites. After spending six months in large oak vats, and 30 months in small French and American barrels, it was bottled without filtration. A dark garnet color is followed by aromas of roasted coffee, smoke, black as well as red currants, minerals, and scorched earth. Dense and sweet, with notions of lead pencil, plum, and black currant fruit, this spectacular, medium- to full-bodied Rioja possesses gorgeous purity. It is a harmonious effort with intense flavor concentration, a beautiful texture, and subtle wood. Enjoy it now as well as over the next 20 years.

The 1995 Rioja Reserva Seleccion Especial reveals leathery, earthy, leafy notes along with graphite, cherry jam, and minerals. The bouquet is reminiscent of a lighter-styled Lafite-Rothschild. The wine spent 30 months in a combination of both French and American oak before being bottled without filtration. Although elegant and stylish, it lacks the substance as well as depth necessary to merit an outstanding rating. Anticipated maturity: now–2012.

The 1996 Rioja Reserva (a blend of 70% Tempranillo, 20% Grenache, and 10% Mazuelo and Graciano) spent 24 months in French and American oak prior to being bottled without filtration. The color is a dense plum/purple. The wine displays an Haut-Brion–like note of asphalt, roasted earth, lead pencil, smoke, and black cherry jam. Medium- to full-bodied and complex, with moderate tannin, adequate acidity, and a spicy, classy, rich finish, it requires 2–3 more years of cellaring. Anticipated maturity: 2003–2017.

The luxury *cuvée* of 1996 Torre Muga is a blend of 75% Tempranillo, 15% Mazuelo, and 10% Graciano that spent 22 months in large American oak vats, followed by 16 months in French casks prior to being bottled without filtration. An amazing effort, it somehow benefits from such a long wood aging regime. The opaque dense purple color is accompanied by scents of black fruits, minerals, scorched earth, cedar, tobacco, and spice box. Full-bodied, with great concentration, as well as a tightly knit personality, this powerful, muscular wine demands 4–5 years of cellaring. Anticipated maturity: 2005–2025.

BODEGAS DE MURRIETA (RIOJA)

1970	Castillo Ygay Gran Reserva Especial	EE	89
1996	Dalmau Reserva	D	90
1995	Dalmau Reserva	D	90+?

Murrieta's finest wines include a surprisingly youthful, exuberant 1970 Castillo Ygay Gran Reserva Especial. It possesses a remarkably deep ruby color as well as a pronounced nose of fresh mushrooms and toasty new American oak. The wine narrows in the mouth, but it provides cherry, cedary, and leather-infused fruit. It is hard to believe this wine is over 30 years old, as it appears capable of lasting another decade.

The luxury *cuvée* of 1996 Dalmau Reserva offers a dense saturated plum/ruby color followed by aromas of ripe black fruits intermixed with smoked meats, new oak, and game. Full-bodied, moderately tannic, rich, and concentrated, this structured, accessible yet youthful Rioja will benefit from 4–5 years of cellaring. It will last for 15+ years. The dark plum/ruby 1995 Dalmau Reserva appears to be closing down, but it has promise. New oak dominates at present, but notions of lead pencil, black fruits, earth, and smoked game are all present. A creamy attack is followed by copious amounts of tannin. I would cellar this wine for another 3–4 years and drink it over the following 15.

BODEGAS NEKEAS (NAVARRA)

1998	Vega Sindoa El Chaparral	B	88
1999	Vega Sindoa Merlot	A	88
1998	Vega Sindoa Merlot	A	88
1995	Vega Sindoa Izar de Vega	C	88
2000	Vega Sindoa Tempranillo/Merlot	A	88

Readers looking for wine bargains should make Bodegas Nekeas and its wines called Vega Sindoa must purchases. Nekeas owns approximately 550 acres of nonirrigated hillside vineyards in an area that was far more famous in the 15th century under King Phillip II than today. Most of the vineyards were uprooted because yields were too low. Thankfully, this area is enjoying a resurgence, and the following wines (which are priced preposterously low) are amazingly good. They merit interest especially from those who do not believe an $8–10 wine can provide delicious, complex drinking. A new offering from this reliable producer, the

1995 Izar de Vega (a 3,000-case blend of 40% Cabernet Sauvignon, 30% Merlot, and 30% Tempranillo) is Spain's version of a mid-level Pauillac. Notes of cassis, plums, tobacco, and cedar emerge from this dark ruby/purple-colored wine. Rich and medium-bodied, with supple tannin as well as low acidity, it should be consumed over the next 2–3 years.

Consumers know how difficult it is to find good Merlot in the marketplace. There is an ocean of industrial/insipid swill parading under the name Merlot, most of it thin, acidic, vegetal, and uninteresting. The finest Merlot tends to come from Bordeaux or Tuscany, but Bodegas Nekeas's soft, ripe, chunky 1999 Merlot (3,000 cases made from 100% Merlot from 10-year-old vines) is a winner. Aged in both American and French oak, it offers scents of wood, coffee, and berry fruit presented in a medium-bodied, user-friendly format. Drink it over the next 1–2 years. Another serious effort, the 1998 Merlot is also available for a song. Aged in 60% American and 40% French oak, it exhibits a dark ruby/purple color in addition to a classic Merlot bouquet of mocha, coffee, and berry/cherry fruit. The wine possesses low acidity, well-integrated, soft tannin, medium to full body, a fat, plush texture, and a surprisingly long finish. An exceptional value, it should drink well for 2–3 years.

The 1998 El Chaparral, the second vintage of this sensational old-vine Grenache (60–100-year-old vines), is once again a hedonist's dream. This inexpensive, dark ruby-colored offering is loaded with kirsch, pepper, and spice as well as lusty levels of glycerin. Additionally, it has sufficient underlying acidity to give vibrancy and freshness. Think of this fleshy, meaty Grenache as Spain's answer to France's Gigondas. Two thousand cases were imported. Drink it over the next 2 years.

Ten thousand cases of the 2000 Vega Sindoa Tempranillo/Merlot, a Spanish fruit bomb, were exported to the United States. A blend of 80% Tempranillo and 20% Merlot, aged in tank prior to bottling, it exhibits wonderful sweetness, soft, explosive, berry and cherry aromatics as well as flavors, medium to full body, low acidity, and superb purity. It ranks alongside wines costing 2–3 times as much. Anticipated maturity: now–2003.

NUMANTHIA (TORO)

1999 Toro	D	95
1998 Toro	D	95

This sensational wine will prove to be a breakthrough effort for the Toro appellation. Made from old (70–100 years), ungrafted vines planted at an elevation of 2,300 feet, yields were a minuscule 1.5 tons of fruit per acre. The wine was aged 18 months in 100% new French oak, with malolactic in barrel, and was bottled without fining or filtration. This 100% Tinta de Toro (the local name for Tempranillo) comes from a vineyard with sandy, chalky-textured soils overlaying clay. The wine is named after a legendary Spanish city that was destroyed (after 20 years of resistance) by Roman legions in 133 B.C. It is to Spain what the hilltop village of Masada is to Israel, a monument to foreign and national aggression.

The 1998 Numanthia is an explosively rich, super-concentrated wine of riveting intensity. The color is a dense purple, and the wine has soaked up 18 months in new French oak. It offers a smoky, blackberry- and cherry-scented nose of extraordinary purity and precision. Full-bodied, enormously endowed, and unctuously textured, this monstrous wine displays tremendous potential. Because of its low acidity, it can be approached now, but it is best aged for another 2–3 years and drunk over the following two decades. This compelling new offering proves what can be achieved in the appellation of Toro. Bravo! The 1999 Numanthia confirms just how special these wines are. An amazing effort from Toro, it was made from yields of 1.5 tons of fruit per acre, aged 18 months in new French wood, and bottled with neither fining nor filtration. A black/ruby color is followed by an explosive perfume of sweet blackberries, cassis, licorice, minerals, and smoke. With great intensity, fabulously sweet tannin, and high glycerin levels, this wine, likes its sibling, establishes a new benchmark for the Toro appellation. There are 300 cases of the 1999 for the U.S. marketplace.

OLIVARES (TARRAGONA)

1998 Dulce Monastrell	C	91?
1996 Dulce Monastrell	D	88?

Both of these wines may be controversial. They are late-harvest offerings exhibiting notions of prunes, raisins, and moderate levels of residual sugar. They are clearly designed to be drunk with flavorful cheese, or served at the end of the meal as dessert. Neither is overly sweet, and both are thick, heavy, and overripe. They are produced from 128-year-old Mourvèdre vines! The 1996 is more uncertain as it possesses rustic animal-like notes, whereas the purer 1998's blackberry and raisiny fruit is more cleanly displayed. Nevertheless, both wines will be met with "love it or leave it" sentiments. Both should last for at least a decade.

PAGO DE CARRAOVEJAS (RIBERA DEL DUERO)

1998 Tinto	D	90
1998 Tinto Reserva	D	92

The noteworthy 1998 Tinto reveals a dark plum color in addition to sweet aromas of black cherries, earth, and spice. Round and velvety-textured, with ripe, chewy fruit, and a supple, round, generously constituted personality, this seamless, full-bodied offering should be enjoyed over the next 6–7 years. Although similarly styled, the 1998 Tinto Reserva has a deeper color saturation, the use of new American and French casks is more noticeable, and the wine is fleshier, with additional layers of flavor. It is an impressive effort to drink over the next 10–12 years. Both wines are approximately 75% Tempranillo and 25% Cabernet Sauvignon.

ALVARO PALACIOS (PRIORATO)

1998 l'Ermita	EEE	97
1998 Finca Dofi	D	92
1998 Les Terrasses	C	88

An increasingly well known and pricy superstar, Alvaro Palacios has fashioned three fine wines from what appears to be a top-notch Priorato vintage. The soft, opulently styled 1998 Les Terrasses offers a deep dense ruby color as well as abundant quantities of blackberry and cherry fruit, subtle wood, a lush, juicy texture, and low acidity. This is a *négociant* offering from Palacios made to satisfy the immense demand for his wines. Drink it over the next 2–5 years. From his estate-bottled production, the terrific 1998 Finca Dofi boasts an opaque ruby/purple color in addition to a gorgeous bouquet of minerals, black fruits, and vanilla. It offers a full-bodied, concentrated, intense style with great purity, symmetry, and length. Enjoy it over the next 10–12 years.

The blockbuster, opaque purple-colored 1998 l'Ermita (the finest since the 1995 and 1994) exhibits a full-bodied personality with copious quantities of sweet oak, a boatload of glycerin, and superb blackberry, cassis, and cherry fruit that explodes on the mid-palate and in the finish. The elevated quantities of new oak should become better integrated as the wine ages over the next 15–20 years. This is an exceptionally impressive and expressive wine.

PESQUERA (RIBERA DEL DUERO)

1995 Gran Reserva	E	91
1994 Gran Reserva	EE	92
1996 Reserva	D	90

Dense plum/ruby/purple, with a sweet perfume of earth, herbs, jammy black fruits, and oak in the background, the opulently textured, round, fleshy 1994 Gran Reserva possesses full body, moderate tannin, and an accessible yet structured personality. It should drink well for 12–15 years. The dense plum-colored 1996 Reserva exhibits an ostentatious bouquet of smoky oak, earth, tobacco, licorice, and jammy red and black fruits. Full-bodied, thick, rich, and mouth-filling, this opulent wine possesses structure as well as tannin. However, it is delicious already. Anticipated maturity: now–2014.

While the regular 1997 and 1998 Tintos were less inspiring than expected (scoring in the low 80s), the 1995 Gran Reserva possesses a deep ruby/garnet/plum color as well as a sweet nose of earth, licorice, black fruits, underbrush, and spicy new oak. In the mouth, it is medium- to full-bodied, with refreshing acidity, and outstanding depth, ripeness, and complexity. It should drink well for 10–15 years.

Past Glories: 1994 Crianza (95), 1994 Gran Reserva (91), 1990 Gran Reserva (90), 1989 Gran Reserva (92), 1986 Gran Reserva (94), 1994 Janus (97)

PINGUS (RIBERA DEL DUERO)

1999	EEE	98
1998	EEE	90
1997	EEE	89
1999 Flor de Pingus	D	90

This limited-production offering, first created by wine-maker/owner Peter Sisseck in 1995, is one of the most exciting wines emerging from Europe. The 1995 is virtually perfect, the 1996 is also spectacular, and the 1999 is brilliant. A barrel sample of the 2000 looks to be magnificent. There were approximately 2,000 cases of the Flor de Pingus in 1999, and 450 cases of Pingus.

The 1997 Pingus reveals a herbaceous note to its medium-bodied, austere character. Aromas and flavors of cedarwood, olives, spice box, black currants, leather, and smoke emerge from this medium-bodied, rich, concentrated wine. It is best consumed now and over the next decade. Though similarly styled, the 1998 Pingus exhibits more chocolate, espresso, and leather characteristics as well as a more expansive mid-palate, a denser, more opaque ruby/purple color, medium to full body, moderate tannin, and gorgeous purity and sweetness. Although outstanding, it is not one of Sisseck's most prodigious efforts. Anticipated maturity: now–2012.

Readers can look forward to a nearly perfect 1999 Pingus. It boasts an opaque ruby/purple color, sensational extract, gorgeous concentration, and spectacularly intense blackberry and cherry aromas and flavors infused with incense, coffee, chocolate, and toasty new oak. Enormous levels of extract and richness are accompanied by a full-bodied, glycerin-imbued, thick, viscous finish. The tannin is nearly hidden by the wine's wealth of fruit and concentration. Anticipated maturity: now–2025. Pingus's second wine, the outstanding 1999 Flor de Pingus, is as good as the 1998 grand vin and unquestionably better than the 1997 Pingus. Sweet, ripe blackberry and currant notes intermixed with licorice, smoke, coffee, and earth emerge from this full-bodied, opulently textured offering. Already evolved and delicious, it is best consumed during its first decade of life.

Past Glories: 1996 Pingus (96), 1995 Pingus (98)

FINCA LA PLANETA (PRIORATO)

1997 Pasanau	D	89+

Sweet black raspberry aromas intermingle with mineral and new oak in this impressively endowed, well-delineated effort from Priorato. The percentage of new oak is high, but there is plenty of concentration and extract for balance. Young, exuberant, and pure, it will last for a decade—at the minimum.

REAL SITIO DE VENTOSILLA (RIBERA DEL DUERO)

1996 Crianza Prado Rey	C	88

A delicious, soft fruit bomb, this Ribera del Duero can be bought for a reasonable price. A round, well-made 1996 Crianza, it possesses a dark ruby color with purple nuances as well as abundant chocolate, black cherry, and berry fruit flavors. The velvety texture in addition to hedonistic up-front aromas and flavors provide a luscious mouthful of wine. Drink it over the next 5–6 years.

CASTELL DEL REMEI (COSTERS DEL SEGRE)

1998	Cervoles	B	88
1998	Gotim Bru	A	90
1997	Gotim Bru	A	90
1996	Gotim Bru	A	89
1997	Oda	B	88
1998	"1780"	C	92
1996	"1780"	C	91

These are serious efforts produced from different proportions of Tempranillo, Merlot, Cabernet Sauvignon, and Grenache. The elegant, polished, refined 1998 Cervoles is a blend of 40% Tempranillo, 40% Cabernet Sauvignon, and 20% Grenache. Its deep ruby/purple color is accompanied by aromas of spicy new oak, creosote, kirsch, and pepper. Medium-bodied and stylish with a Burgundy-like personality, it will drink well for 6–8 years. Although more expensive, the 1998 "1780" (the year this company was founded) is still an excellent value. A blend of 40% Cabernet Sauvignon, 35% Tempranillo, and 25% Grenache, it boasts a deep purple color as well as a sweet nose of vanilla, toast, black cherries, currants, and leather. It is ripe, medium- to full-bodied, and elegant, with sweet glycerin on the attack, great follow-through, and wonderful purity, depth, and length. Moderate tannin in the finish suggests another 1–3 years of cellaring will be beneficial. It should last for two decades.

Readers seeking a sensational bargain should check out the 4,000 cases imported to the U.S. of the 1998 Gotim Bru, a blend of 50% Tempranillo, 25% Merlot, and 25% Cabernet Sauvignon aged 10 months in French oak. From a viticultural area not far from Priorato, it is a deep ruby/purple offering with a delicious, sweet perfume of black cherries, a smooth, velvety texture, medium to full body, light tannin, and nicely integrated new wood. Fleshy and pure, it is best consumed over the next 5–6 years. Consumers seeking a wine that resembles a dry vintage port for $10 a bottle should check out the 1997 Gotim Bru. There are 3,000 cases of this delicious Tempranillo/Cabernet Sauvignon/Merlot blend. Fat, with thrilling levels of jammy cherry and black currant fruit, chocolate, and spice, this dense, chewy effort is a great bargain. Drink it over the next 2–3 years.

The more expensive as well as monolithic 1997 Oda (a blend of Cabernet Sauvignon and Merlot) is pure, rich, and deep, with an overripe character to its fruit. It should age nicely for 5–7 years, and is undoubtedly a very good bargain. The 1996 Gotim Bru is a robust, earthy, spicy, fruity blend of 50% Cabernet Sauvignon and 50% Tempranillo. Aged 15 months in used American oak casks, the wine exhibits a saturated black/plum color, sweet, chewy fruit, full body, obvious glycerin, and a rich, nicely textured, plump finish. This is a mouth-filling, silky-smooth, robust Spanish red to drink over the next 3–4 years. It merits buying by the case.

Readers also do not want to miss Castell del Remei's 1996 "1780," a blend of 70% Cabernet Sauvignon, 20% Tempranillo, and 10% Grenache aged one year in new American casks. Even though it is twice the price of its less expensive sibling, it is an exotic, ostentatiously styled wine that could be called Spain's answer to California's Caymus Special Selection! It should drink well for a decade or more.

REMELLURI (RIOJA)

1999	Rioja	C	90
1996	Rioja	C	89

Remelluri's 1996 Rioja (80% Tempranillo with small quantities of Grenache, Graciano, and Mazuelo) may not be as compelling as the 1995, but it is a smoky, sweet, oaky, rich, complex,

Pomerol-like Rioja with copious quantities of black cherry fruit highly dosed with sweet vanilla. With a velvety texture, medium to full body, and excellent, possibly outstanding concentration, this soft wine can be drunk now as well as over the next 10–12 years.

The 1999 is significantly better than the disappointing 1998. It boasts sweet black cherry fruit infused with toast, smoke, herbs, and tobacco. Layered, rich, medium-bodied, and elegant yet concentrated, it should drink well for 7–10 years.

BODEGAS FERNANDO REMIREZ DE GANUZA (RIOJA)

1998 Rioja	D	95
1996 Rioja	D	94+

Importer Jorge Ordonez told me of the fanatical attention to detail at this estate, which consists of 72 acres of old vines. Crop yields are kept low, and the estate practices the relatively new technique of cutting not only bunches of grapes, but also the bottom of a bunch off, leaving the shoulder to mature. The wine is a blend of 85% Tempranillo, 10% Graciano, 3% Grenache, and 2% diverse varietals, and is bottled unfined and unfiltered after spending two years in a combination of French and American oak. These (the 1994 and 1995 were previously recommended) are spectacular Riojas, but require patience. The 1995 still needs an additional 4–5 years of cellaring, and the 1996, while capable of 25–30 years of evolution, also needs 4–5 years. There are 500 cases exported to the United States.

The 1996 could be called the Château Latour of Rioja. An opaque black/plum color is followed by aromas of minerals, cigar tobacco, cedar, lead pencil, and sweet black currant, plum, and cherry fruit. One of the greatest young Riojas I have ever tasted, it exhibits full body, a huge, concentrated palate feel, an immense, chewy texture, and high tannin in the finish. The proprietor, who started this bodega in 1989, was not satisfied with anything until 1994, when the first wine was released. This looks to be a prodigious Rioja that should age effortlessly for three decades. Anticipated maturity: 2005–2030. To the proprietor's credit, no 1997 was produced, but the 1998 exhibits a dark plum/purple color along with an extraordinary perfume of liquid minerals, cassis, black cherries, tobacco, spice box, and vanilla. There is fabulous density on the palate, high tannin, admirable concentration, and a structured finish reminiscent of a first or second growth Pauillac from a year such as 1996. This Rioja requires 3–5 years of cellaring, but appears to be the finest *cuvée* yet produced by this estate, eclipsing even the 1994. Anticipated maturity: 2004–2020.

HERENCIA REMONDO (RIOJA)

1996 La Montesa	E	88

The internationally styled 1996 La Montesa (30% Tempranillo, 40% Merlot, and 30% Graciano) is given a longer maceration on its skins, then aged for 8 months in new French oak followed by 5 months in American wood. A dense ruby/purple color is accompanied by notes of caramel, cherry liqueur, plums, and licorice. Although monolithic, it is impressively endowed, rich, supple, and long. The obvious wood should become better integrated as the wine ages. Anticipated maturity: now–2010.

BODEGAS REYES (RIBERA DEL DUERO)

1997 Teofilo Reyes	D	88

This is a sexy, open-knit, low-acid wine exhibiting lusty chocolate and black cherry flavors with foresty/herb scents in the background. Deep, rich, round, opulent, and easy to understand and consume, this forward, in-your-face offering can be drunk now as well as over the next 5–6 years.

LA RIOJA ALTA (RIOJA)

1990 Gran Reserva 904	D	90
1985 Gran Reserva 890	EE	92

La Rioja Alta's classics, the Gran Reserva 904 and Gran Reserva 890, are not released until they are 10 and 15 years of age, respectively. These offerings spend a minimum of 10 years in primarily old American oak (about 5% new). Traditionally styled Riojas, they are wines of great subtlety and complexity with slightly oxidized personalities. They are not for everybody, but readers who enjoy mature wines will be impressed.

The medium garnet-colored 1990 Gran Reserva 904 displays considerable amber at the edges. The fragrant, complex aromatics consist of scorched earth, smoke, lead pencil, spice box, and red and black fruits. In the mouth, the wine is round, with no hard edges, medium body, and graceful subtlety as well as delicacy. Though there is a lot going on, it is extraordinarily restrained, and does not bash the taster over the head as so many modern-day "smashmouth" wines do. Fully mature, it will remain at its peak for another decade. Even more aged, complex, and subtle is the 1985 Gran Reserva 890. A compelling nose of smoke, earth, plums, tobacco, cherries, and vanilla emerges from this light garnet-colored 1985 that also reveals considerable amber at the edges. If it were a Bordeaux, the color would suggest a wine of 30+ years of age. It offers complex, savory flavors of spice, faded flowers, and red fruits. There is suppleness yet vivacity to this medium-weight wine that is all finesse and restraint. Although not for everybody, it is a brilliant example of this style of Rioja. Look for the 1985 to continue to drink well for 7–8 years.

Past Glories: Gran Reserva 890 1978 (93), 1981 (92), 1982 (92)

BODEGAS RODA (RIOJA)

1998 Cirsion	EEE	90
1996 Roda I Reserva	D	88+

The striking 1996 Roda I Reserva is made from 100% Tempranillo. It reveals a saturated ruby color in addition to abundant new oak and smoky, earthy, red and black fruits in the nose. With admirable volume and flesh as well as elegance, this spicy, well-made Rioja should improve for 4–5 years and last for 12–15. The 1998 Cirsion is a bigger, richer effort offering a gorgeous bouquet of ripe black fruits, licorice, oak, and spice. Tobacco, herb, black cherry, and currant fruit intermingle with toast and truffle flavors. Medium- to full-bodied, sweet, and pure, this impressive 1998 is youthful but accessible. It promises to evolve for 15 years.

TELMO RODRIGUEZ (RIBERA DEL DUERO)

1999 Dehesa Gago	B	91
1999 Valderiz	C	90

Made from 100% Tinto de Toro (the local clone of Tempranillo), the 1999 Dehesa Gago was vinified and aged in stainless steel tanks. A majestic fruit bomb, it boasts a dense ruby/purple color as well as an intense nose of melted licorice, crème de cassis, and flowers. Extremely full-bodied and unctuously textured, with superb purity, this rich, gorgeously layered wine is almost too good to be true. The bad news is that only 700 cases were made; the good news is that all of it was shipped to the U.S. Enjoy this beauty over the next 5–8 years, although it may last even longer. Readers should run, not walk, to their favorite wine merchant to grab a few bottles of this nectar. The hedonistic, rich, lush, fat, fruity 1999 Valderiz displays notes of melted chocolate, cherries, and blackberries. Supple, with low acidity, ripe tannin, and jammy fruit, it should be consumed over the next 5–7 years for its unabashed display of joy.

SAN VICENTE (RIOJA)

1999 San Vicente	D	92
1998 San Vicente	D	90
1997 San Vicente	D	89
1996 San Vicente	D	91

This continues to be one of the sexiest, most voluptuously textured, exotic wines to emerge from Rioja. At times, it resembles a flashy Pomerol, and at other times, a hypothetical blend of the best of Spain with the finest of the New World. The dark ruby-colored 1996 (100% Tempranillo from a single vineyard called Peludo) displays a flamboyant nose of vanilla, jammy black cherries, Asian spices, licorice, and roasted meats and herbs. Big in the mouth, with medium to full body, outstanding richness, and plenty of sweet tannin, this opulently textured, hedonistically styled wine can be drunk now as well as over the next 10–12 years. The 1997, from a more difficult vintage than 1996 or 1995, is a sexy, dark ruby/purple-colored effort exhibiting notes of Provençal herbs, smoke, roasted tobacco, jammy black fruits, and cherry liqueur. Lush, with a multilayered, expansive texture, exceptional purity, and a touch of overripe prunes in the finish, this supple, voluptuous, compelling Rioja can be drunk now and over the next 5–6 years.

The dark ruby/purple-colored 1998 reveals a big, splashy nose of toasty oak intermixed with jammy black cherries, berries, vanilla, and espresso. Ripe, rich, medium-bodied, and more structured than the explosive 1999, the 1998 should drink well for 7–8 years. The denser, more hedonistic 1999 boasts loads of fruit and glycerin, as well as additional ripeness, volume, fat, and depth. Displaying the same black currant, jammy cherry fruit, and copious toasty new oak characteristics, it will provide enjoyment during its first decade of life.

HERMANOS SASTRE (RIBERA DEL DUERO)

1999 Pago de Santa Cruz	EEE	(92–94)
1996 Pago de Santa Cruz	EEE	90+
1999 Regina Vides	EEE	(92–94)
1998 Regina Vides	EEE	92

This estate's flagship wine, Pago de Santa Cruz, is made in limited quantities and very little will be exported to the U.S. It is made from 100% destemmed Tempranillo, aged 24 months in new American oak, moved to 100% new French oak for an additional 12 months, and bottled unfiltered. The four vintages tasted were all extremely concentrated, dense wines with a quality not dissimilar from the super-extracted, rich, full-bodied blockbusters of Peter Sisseck's Pingus. All three were seamless, opulent, and concentrated efforts offering notes of chocolate, coffee, blackberry liqueur, and sweet cassis fruit. These wines' smoky richness and broad, expansive thickness are sure to provoke excitement, assuming readers can find any of the 400+ cases produced. The narrowly focused 1996 will last 15+ years. The 1999 is spectacular. According to the importer, yields from 60-year-old Tempranillo vines average 20–25 hectoliters per hectare.

The other superb offering I tasted from Hermanos Sestre is the 1998 Regina Vides, a 100% Tempranillo produced from 80-year-old vines with yields of 20 h/h. It is an impressive, opaque purple, full-bodied, opulently textured effort with abundant quantities of sweet, toasty oak, blackberry and cassis fruit, and a long, concentrated, powerful finish. It will drink well for 10–15 years. The 1999 Regina Vides emerged from a far greater vintage for Ribera del Duero than 1998. Extremely full-bodied, unctuously textured, and supersweet, it boasts blackberry, coffee, chocolate, and cassis aromas as well as flavors. This outstanding Spanish red should age effortlessly for two decades.

BODEGAS SIERRA CANTABRIA (RIOJA)

1999 Rioja	A	88
1999 Rioja Coleccion Privada	C	90
1997 Rioja Crianza	B	89
1996 Rioja Crianza	B	89
1999 Rioja Cuvée Especial	B	89

Another name synonymous with excellent value and extremely well made Rioja, Sierra Cantabria has turned out five attractive offerings. The 1997 Rioja Crianza (100% Tempranillo bottled after 14 months aging in a combination of French and American oak) is an excellent, nearly outstanding effort, no small achievement in 1997. Its deep ruby/purple color is accompanied by a gorgeously sweet nose of strawberry and cherry jam intermixed with dried herbs, smoke, earth, and vanilla. Medium- to full-bodied and opulently textured, with a tannic finish, it requires 1–2 years of cellaring, and should age well for 10–12 years.

The dark ruby-colored 1999 Rioja exhibits a sweet, hedonistic style with plenty of fat, smoky, toasty, black cherry and berry flavors presented in a lush, user-friendly format. Drink it over the next 2–3 years. The 1996 Rioja Crianza is another exceptional wine value. The dark ruby color is followed by copious quantities of sweet, spicy oak along with candied black cherries and dried herbs. Noteworthy, complex lead pencil notes also make an appearance. This cuvée (6,000 cases imported) possesses good fruit, medium body, and an elegant yet mouth-filling style with no hard edges. It is a gorgeously proportioned, modern-styled Rioja to enjoy over the next 3–4 years.

The 1998 Rioja Cuvée Especial exhibits scents of lead pencil shavings intermixed with tobacco, black cherries, currants, minerals, roasted herbs, and toasty American oak. Layered, ripe, and impressive, it will drink well for 5–7 years. The 1999 Rioja Coleccion Privada (an unfiltered, 100% Tempranillo wine made from tiny yields of 1.3 tons of fruit per acre) was aged 19 months in both American and French oak. Sadly, there are only 250 cases available for the U.S. The wine grows by increments in the glass, improving dramatically with 15 minutes of airing. A deep ruby color is followed by a spicy, herb, berry, graphite, and licorice-scented bouquet. This rich, medium-bodied, elegant, well-balanced Rioja is not a blockbuster, but expands in flavor and nuances as it crosses the palate. Drink it over the next 7–8 years.

ROTLLAN TORRA (PRIORATO)

1997 Amadis	D	90
1998 Tirant	E	93
1997 Tirant	E	92

These are impressive efforts from Rotllan Torra, a winery founded in 1984. The opaque purple 1997 Amadis (2,000 cases from 100-year-old vines and minuscule yields of 10 h/h) was aged 10 months in 100% new French oak before being bottled unfiltered. A blend of 40% Grenache (from 90–100-year-old vines), 25% Cabernet Sauvignon, 20% Carignan (also 90–100-year-old vines), 10% Syrah, and 5% Merlot, it is a blockbuster Priorato with huge, concentrated black raspberry, cassis, and berry fruit mixed with minerals, smoke, licorice, and toasty oak. This intense wine possesses a seamless, sweet, concentrated mid-palate as well as finish. It is a terrific Spanish red to drink over the next 10–12 years.

Even better are the two limited-production offerings of 1997 and 1998 Tirant. This blend of 30% Grenache, 25% Cabernet Sauvignon, 25% Carignan, 10% Syrah, and 10% Merlot (the Carignan and Grenache come from 90–100-year-old vines) spends a full year in new French oak, enjoys malolactic in barrel, and is bottled unfiltered. The superb, opaque purple 1997 Tirant exhibits sweet, concentrated, jammy fruit intertwined with notions of asphalt, pepper, liquid minerals, and subtle spicy wood. A full-bodied, powerful effort, it requires 2–3 years of cellaring but should last 12–15. The 1998 Tirant is richer, with an even more saturated opaque blue/purple color. Extremely full-bodied, dense, powerful, and layered, it has impressive seamlessness, opulence, and thickness. It should drink well for 15+ years.

TRESANTOS (ZAMORA)

2000 Tresantos	B	90

From a viticultural area just north of Toro, this wine is a thermonuclear fruit bomb. Huge levels of hedonistic black currant, cherry, and blackberry fruit are presented in an uncomplicated, fleshy, succulent style that is a total turn-on. This low-acid, beautifully pure 2000 is a treat to drink. Consume it over the next 2–3 years.

BODEGAS VALCONA (RIOJA)

1998 Partal Crianza	C	90

This blend of 60% Mourvèdre and the balance Tempranillo, Cabernet Sauvignon, Merlot, and Syrah, from a vineyard planted 60 miles from the Mediterranean, was aged in 70% French and 30% American oak. It boasts a dense ruby/purple color and a sweet nose of black cherries, vanilla, and spice. This 1998 Crianza is admirably rich and impressively chewy, with a thick mid-palate and a long, spicy, moderately tannic finish. Though it comes close to being rustic, there is a lot of finesse underneath. Drink it over the next 6–7 years.

VALL LLACH (PRIORATO)

1998	E	92+
1998 Embruix	B	90

Proprietor Louis Llach is a well-known Spanish singer who, according to importer Eric Solomon, has produced over 40 albums and has a huge following in his native country. His love of wine has been sanctified by his high-altitude Priorato vineyards. The least expensive offering, the 1998 Embruix, is a blend of 40% Grenache, 40% Cabernet Sauvignon, and 20% Carignan aged in one- and two-year-old French oak barrels. It is a lovely, ripe effort with aromas of plums, black cherries, vanilla, and minerals. Medium- to full-bodied, pure, well balanced, and long, it offers a sweet attack as well as a tannic finish, suggesting another 1–2 years of cellaring is merited. It should keep for 12–15 years. An impressive debut effort.

The 1998 Vall Llach (800 cases produced) is a blend of 50% Carignan (from 80-year-old vines) and 50% Merlot (5–10-year-old vines), aged one year in new French oak. It is an impressive, powerful (15.1% alcohol) wine revealing a deep purple color in addition to a sweet nose of black raspberries, cherry liqueur, and graphite aromas. Full-bodied, thick, and juicy, with moderately high tannin, superb purity, and a Bordeaux-like structure to its flavors and finish, it will benefit from 4–5 years of cellaring, and age well for two decades.

VEGA SAUCO (TORO)

1999 Tinto	B	88

A terrific value, this wine, produced from 70-year-old Tempranillo vines, offers a deep ruby color in addition to explosive, sweet, fragrant aromas of kirsch, smoke, and earth. Powerful, concentrated, and surprisingly rich (particularly for a wine in this price range), it offers more flavor and character than many wines costing 2–3 times as much. Its low acidity and luscious personality suggest consumption over the next 2–3 years.

Past Glories: Unico 1986 (92+), 1985 (93), 1983 (93), 1982 (95), 1980 (90), 1979 (89), 1976 (93), 1975 (95), 1974 (90), 1970 (96), 1968 (99), 1966 (95), 1964 (94), 1962 (93)

VEGA SICILIA (RIBERA DEL DUERO)

NV Reserva Especiale Lot 017/00	EEE	93+
NV Reserva Especial Unico Lot 25	EEE	93
1990 Unico Reserva Especiale	EE	94
1970 Unico Reserva Especiale (Magnum)	EEE	96
1995 Valbuena	D	89

There are 14,000 bottles of the nonvintage Reserva Especial Unico Lot 25, a blend of 1970, 1985, and 1990, all top-quality vintages for Vega Sicilia. This classic boasts a dark ruby color and sweet, creamy, oaky notions intermixed with jammy black raspberry, cassis, and berry aromas. As the wine sits in the glass, roasted herbs, coffee, and floral scents make an appearance. Dense, full-bodied, and superbly concentrated with velvety tannin, low acidity, and nicely integrated wood, this is a complex, delicious effort that can be drunk now as well as over the next 15–20 years. The reasonably priced 1995 Valbuena offers a plum/ruby color followed by aromas of sweet black fruits intermixed with licorice, earth, and spicy oak. Full-bodied, with excellent concentration, a juicy, layered texture, and fine purity, it is forward, plush, and best consumed within its first 10–12 years of life.

The newest Unico Reserva Especiale is the 1990. For a Unico, it exhibits a relatively un-evolved style. A deep opaque plum/garnet color is accompanied by noticeable sweet toasty oak in the nose along with copious quantities of black cherry and cassis fruit. Extremely youthful, vigorous, and full-bodied, with notes of overripeness, low acidity, moderately high tannin, and a layered, concentrated personality, this Unico is less mature upon release than many of its siblings. Give it another 3–4 years of cellaring; it should last for 25 years.

Each year Vega Sicilia releases limited quantities of a nonvintage blend. There are 13,680 bottles of the nonvintage Reserva Especiale Lot 017/00 (this number is on the bottle's label), which is claimed to be a blend of 1985, 1990, and 1994 Unico Reservas. This fabulous, youthful effort exhibits jammy blackberry, cherry, mineral, smoke, cedar, and new-oak aromas as well as flavors. Full-bodied, dense, and concentrated, with great purity in addition to stature, this Reserva Especiale can be drunk now but ideally needs another 2–3 years of cellaring. It should age for 2–3 decades. One of Vega Sicilia's other distinctive practices is to release magnums of great vintages well after the wine's initial release. Magnums of the fabulous 1970 Unico Reserva Especiale (for my taste, 1968 and 1970 are the two finest Vega Sicilias produced in the last 35 years) have just been released. This wine boasts an elegant, complex bouquet of cedarwood, blackberries, cherry liqueur, and vanilla. Opulently textured, with fabulous unctuosity, vivaciousness, and vigor, superb ripeness, a full-bodied, super-concentrated attack as well as a lush mid-palate and finish, this seamless classic can be drunk now or cellared for two decades. This wine was brilliant from the 750-ml format and is equally compelling from magnum.

FINCA VILLA CRECES (RIBERA DEL DUERO)

1999 Crianza	C	90
1998 Crianza	C	89
1999 Nebro	EE	95
1998 Pruno	EE	92

Villa Creces has produced very fine wines over recent vintages. A blend of 75% Tempranillo, 15% Merlot, and 10% Cabernet Sauvignon aged 16 months in French oak, the sexy, deep ruby/purple, Pomerol-like 1999 Crianza exhibits a smoky bouquet with notes of espresso, fudge, and jammy black currants as well as cherries. Supple-textured, medium-bodied, lush, richly fruity, and seamless, it should drink well for a decade. The special *cuvée* of 70-year-old Tempranillo vines located next to one of the oldest Vega Sicilia vineyards, the 1999 Nebro is a spectacular effort. It is a single-vineyard offering aged 16 months in new French oak (Darnajou barrels), and made from yields of 17 h/h. Made in a style reminiscent of Peter Sisseck's 1995 and 1996 Pingus, this glorious wine offers up scents of roasted espresso, vanilla, black cherry liqueur, blackberries, licorice, and spice box. Full-bodied and unctuously textured, with an impressive integration of wood, acidity, and alcohol, it is unformed but accessible. Anticipated maturity: 2003–2025. The bad news . . . only 75 cases were produced.

The 1998 Crianza reveals an impressive dense ruby/purple color as well as a sweet, earthy, blackberry, and charcoal-scented nose with new oak in the background. Medium- to full-bodied, chewy, with low acidity, and abundant fruit, glycerin, and extract, it will drink well for 5–7 years. The super *cuvée* of Villa Creces, the 1998 Pruno (200 bottles produced), is reminiscent of the great Pingus made by Peter Sisseck. The Pruno is powerful, thick, chewy, and unctuously textured, with huge quantities of black cherry, plum, and licorice-infused blackberry fruit. Sadly, because of the limited production, only a handful of readers will ever run across a bottle. Anticipated maturity: now–2020.

VINA ALARBA (CALATAYUD)

2000 Old Vines Grenache	**A**	**89**

Five thousand cases of this *cuvée* have been exported to the U.S. The 2000 Old Vines Grenache (100% Grenache from vines averaging over 50 years of age, and yields of only one ton of fruit per acre) boasts a deeper ruby/purple color and a nose reminiscent of a Châteauneuf-du-Pape or Gigondas. The bouquet offers aromas of kirsch, dried Provençal herbs, licorice, spice box, and underlying pepper. Dense, chewy, and rich, with gobs of fruit, it is best consumed during its first 2–3 years of life. This is an unreal value priced so low most consumers will never believe it is this good.

BODEGAS Y VINEDOS (RIBERA DEL DUERO)

1996 Alion	**D**	**90**

This beautifully made Spanish red represents a more modern approach to winemaking. Sweet toasty oak competes with jammy black cherry and berry fruit in this deep, low-acid offering. This wine possesses excellent to outstanding concentration, topflight purity, and overall equilibrium. Drink this impressively endowed Ribera del Duero over the next 10–12 years.

BODEGAS Y VINEDOS MAURO-TORO (CASTILLA Y LEÓN)

1997 San Romain	**D**	**90**

The former wine-maker from Vega Sicilia is involved with this new project with the Tinta de Toro grape. Five hundred cases have been released for the U.S. Completely aged in 100% new French oak, this wine is a Pomerol-like, lush effort with gobs of black raspberry and cherry fruit meshed with toasty new oak. From its saturated dark ruby/purple color to its gorgeously rich flavors, opulent texture, and low-acid, fleshy finish, this is a pleasure-filled wine to enjoy over the next 5–8 years, although I suspect it will last longer.

BODEGAS Y VINEDOS SOLABAL (RIOJA)

1997 Rioja Crianza	**B**	**88**

A success for this tricky vintage, the 1997 Rioja Crianza (100% Tempranillo) exhibits a ruby/purple color in addition to aromas of melted fudge, vanilla, smoke, and cherry liqueur. Though not complex, it is an impressive, full-bodied, richly fruity, hedonistic offering with copious amounts of accessible fruit. Consume it over the next 3–4 years.

VINICOLA DEL PRIORAT (PRIORATO)

1998 Onix	**A**	**88**
1996 Onix 1163	**C**	**88**

The finest wine I have ever tasted from this producer (selling for one-fifth the price of most Prioratos), the 1998 Onix is made from old-vine Grenache and Carignan. Although monolithic, it is a chewy, boisterous, muscular, full-bodied red. Purely made, with copious quantities of blackberry and cherry fruit in addition to good underlying minerality and spice, it is a substantial, foursquare, but mouth-filling wine to drink over the next 3–4 years.

A blend of 40% Cabernet Sauvignon, 40% Grenache, and 20% Carignan, the 1996 Onix 1163 reveals a deep, opaque purple color in addition to sweet aromas of ripe black raspberry fruit. Full-bodied, with abundant toasty oak, as well as a touch of licorice and prune, this wine, aged in American and French oak casks, is not complex but is chewy, with excellent concentration and purity, and a round, generous, exuberant personality. Drink it over the next 4–5 years.

PORTUGAL

PORT

Americans have finally begun to realize the great pleasures of a mature vintage port after a meal. For years, this sumptuous and mellow fortified red wine was seriously undervalued, as most of it was drunk in the private homes and clubs of the United Kingdom. Prices, which soared in the early and mid-1980s, collapsed in the early 1990s. Although there is not much vintage port produced (there are rarely more than four declared vintages a decade), the international recession and bloated marketplace have resulted in stable prices. Port's richness and sweetness are largely the result of high quality (and high proof) brandy being added as the port wine ferments. This arrests the fermentation process, leaving unfermented sugars in the wine and thus contributing to port's 20% alcohol content.

WHAT TO BUY
It is widely anticipated that 2000 will be considered a great year for vintage port producers. Powerful, thick vines were produced, and, as of this writing, a "vintage year" had been declared by Graham's Dow, Warre, Taylor, Fonseca, Croft, Delaforce, Quinta do Noval, and Symington's Quinta do Vesuvio. Other major houses are also expected to declare 2000 a vintage port year. These wines will be available for sale in 2002–2003. Other outstanding vintage years still available at retail are 1997, 1994, and 1992. As with many fine wines, prices for the newest vintages are higher than older ports that can be purchased through auction houses. Shrewd consumers should consider buying at auction such vintages as 1995 (where it was declared), 1991, 1987, 1983, and 1980. These are very fine rather than great years, but the top houses have turned in impeccable efforts, and the wines are closer to full maturity.

An obvious trend has been the explosion of single-quinta offerings, most of which are very good to excellent, although not as compelling as the greatest vintage ports. Most of the single-quinta ports are offered in years not declared as vintages.

VARIOUS PORT STYLES
Crusted Port   Rarely seen today, crusted port is usually a blend of several vintages that is bottled early and handled in the same manner as a vintage port. Significant sediment will form in the bottle and a crusted port has to be decanted prior to drinking.
Tawny Port   One of the least expensive ways of securing a mature port is to buy the best shippers' tawny ports. Tawny ports are a blend of vintages aged in wood by the top houses for 10, 20, 30, 40, or even 50 years. Tawnys can have exceptional complexity and refinement. I highly recommend some of the best tawnys from firms such as Taylor Fladgate, Fonseca, and Graham's.
Ruby and Branded Ports   Ruby ports are relatively straightforward, deeply colored, young ports that are cherished for their sweet, grapy aromas and supple, exuberant, yet monolithic taste. Most of these are meant to be drunk when released. Each house has its own style. Four of the most popular include Fonseca's Bin No. 27, Taylor's 4XX, Cockburn's Special Reserve, and Graham's Six Grapes. All four of these ruby or branded ports are stylistically different. The richest and fullest is the Fonseca Bin No. 27; the most complex is usu-

ally the Taylor 4XX; the sweetest and fruitiest is the Graham Six Grapes; and the most mature and evolved, as well as least distinguished, is the Cockburn Special Reserve.

White Port   I have never understood the purpose of white port, but the French find it appealing. However, the market for these eccentricities is dead.

Late Bottled Vintage Port (L.B.V.P.)   Certain vintages are held back in cask longer than 2 years (the time required for vintage port) and bottled 5–7 years following the vintage. These ports tend to throw less sediment, as much of it has been already deposited in cask. In general, late bottled ports are ready to drink when released. I often find them less interesting and complex than the best tawnys and vintage ports.

Single-Quinta Vintage Port   This has become an increasingly important area, especially since the late 1980s, when a number of vintages, particularly 1987, 1990, 1991, and 1992, could have been declared vintage years but were not because of the saturated marketplace. Many of the best single-quintas, or vineyards, have been offered as vintage-dated single quinta ports. These are vintage ports from a single vineyard. Most port authorities feel it is the blending from various vineyards that gives vintage port its greatest character. Others will argue that in a top year, the finest single-quinta ports can be as good as a top vintage port. I tend to believe that a great vintage port is superior to a single-quinta port, yet the finest single-quintas from 1987, 1990, 1991, and 1992 are stunning. Star ratings of the different single-quinta port producers are provided where I have had sufficient tasting experience (more than two vintages) to offer a qualitative ranking.

SINGLE-QUINTA VINTAGE PORTS

Quinta Agua Alta (Churchill)

Quinta Boa Vista (Offley)

Quinta do Bomfim (Dow)

Quinta do Cachao (Messias)

Quinta da Cavadinha (Warre)

Quinta do Confradeiro (Sandeman)

Quinta da Corte (Delaforce)

Quinta do Crasto (a consortium)

Quinta da Eira Velha (R. Newan)

Quinta Fojo (Churchill)

Quinta do Forte (Delaforee)

Quinta da Foz (Calem)

Quinta Guimaraens (Fonseca)

Quinta do Infantado (Roseira)

Quinta Malvedossd (Graham's)

Quinta da Roeda (Croft)

Quinta de la Rosa (Bergquist)

Quinta do Seixo (Ferreira)

Quinta do Tua (Cockburn)

Quinta de Val da Figueria (Calem)

Quinta de Vargellas (Taylor Fladgate)

Quinta do Vau (Sandeman)

Quinta do Vesuvio (Symington)

Vintage Port   Potentially the finest and most complex, and the subject of most of this chapter, are the vintage ports. Vintage ports are declared by the port shippers the second spring after the harvest. 1991 was declared a vintage year by most of the top port shippers. For example, Graham's, Dow, Quinta do Noval, and Warre had declared it a vintage, but Fonseca and Taylor did not, preferring to declare 1992 instead. Vintage port, a blend of the very best *cuvées* from various vineyards, is bottled unfiltered two years after the harvest. It can improve and last for 50 or more years. To be a vintage port there must be exceptional ripeness, a great deal of tannin, and plenty of rich fruit and body. In fact, the quality of a shipper's vintage port is the benchmark by which a shipper is evaluated in the international marketplace. Each top house has a distinctive style, which I have tried to capture in the tasting notes.

These ports tend to be blends made from various vineyards rather than products of a single vineyard.

VINTAGE GUIDE

The greatest port vintages in this century have been 1912, 1927, 1931, 1935, 1945, 1948, 1955, 1963, 1970, 1977, 1983, 1985, 1992, 1994, 1997, and 2000.

VINTAGE YEARS FOR MAJOR FIRMS

Cockburn   1947, 1950, 1955, 1960, 1963, 1967, 1970, 1975, 1983, 1985, 1991, 1994, 1997, 2000

Croft   1945, 1950, 1955, 1960, 1963, 1966, 1970, 1975, 1977, 1982, 1985, 1991

Dow   1945, 1947, 1950, 1955, 1960, 1963, 1966, 1970, 1972, 1975, 1977, 1980, 1983, 1985, 1991, 1994, 1997, 2000

Fonseca   1945, 1948, 1955, 1960, 1963, 1966, 1970, 1975, 1977, 1980, 1983, 1985, 1992, 1994, 1997, 2000

Graham's   1945, 1948, 1955, 1960, 1963, 1966, 1970, 1975, 1977, 1980, 1983, 1985, 1991, 1994, 1997, 2000

Quinta do Noval   1945, 1947, 1950, 1955, 1958, 1960, 1963, 1966, 1967, 1970, 1975, 1978, 1982, 1985, 1991, 1994, 1995, 1997, 2000

Quinta do Noval Nacional   1931, 1950, 1960, 1962, 1963, 1964, 1966, 1967, 1970, 1975, 1978, 1980, 1982, 1985, 1987, 1994, 1997, 2000

Sandeman   1945, 1947, 1950, 1955, 1957, 1958, 1960, 1962, 1963, 1966, 1967, 1970, 1975, 1977, 1980, 1982, 1985

Taylor   1945, 1948, 1955, 1960, 1963, 1966, 1970, 1975, 1977, 1980, 1983, 1985, 1992, 1994, 1997, 2000

Warre   1945, 1947, 1950, 1955, 1958, 1960, 1963, 1966, 1970, 1975, 1977, 1980, 1983, 1985, 1991, 1994, 1997, 2000

RATING PORTUGAL'S BEST PRODUCERS OF PORT

* * * * * (OUTSTANDING)

Dow	Quinta do Noval Nacional
Fonseca	Taylor
Graham's	

* * * * (EXCELLENT)

Churchill	Graham's Malvedos
Churchill Quinta Agua Alta	Quinta do Infantado Touriga Nacional
Cockburn	Quinta do Noval
Croft	Symington Quinta do Vesuvio
Dow Quinta do Bomfim	Taylor Quinta de Vargellas
Ferreira Quinta do Seixo	Warre
Fonseca Guimaraens	

* * * (GOOD)

Calem Quinta da Foz	Quarles Harris
Croft Quinta do Roeda	Martinez
Delaforce	Niepoort
Delaforce Quinta do Forte	Offley Forrester
Ferreira	Pocalas Junior
Gould Campbell	Quinta do Crasto

Quinta do Passadouro
Quinta de la Rosa
Quinta do Roriz
Ramos-Pinto

Sandeman
Sandeman Quinta do Vau
Smith-Woodhouse
Warre Quinta da Cavadinha

* * *(AVERAGE)*

Almeida Barros
Borges & Irmao
J. W. Burmester
C. da Silva
Calem
H. & C. J. Feist
Feuerheerd
Hooper
C. N. Kopke

Messias
Osborne
Pintos dos Santos
Quinta do Panascal
Quinta do Romaneira
Vasconcellos
Wiese & Krohn
Van Zellers

COCKBURN

1994 Vintage Port **D 91**

An attractive, smoky, tarry, roasted black fruit character dominates this opaque ruby/purple wine's aromatic profile. Low acidity, sweet, rich fruit, and a forward, expansive feel suggest this full-bodied wine will mature quickly, but it will last for at least two decades. Like a few other 1994s, it seems almost too easy to drink at this stage. Anticipated maturity: 2004–2020.

Past Glories: Quinta do Tua 1987 (94); Vintage Port 1991 (88), 1985 (90), 1983 (95), 1955 (92)

CROFT

1994 Vintage Port **D 90**

The 1994 Croft exhibits an impressive dark ruby/purple color and a developed, forward, more evolved style than expected. It is moderately sweet, full-bodied, expansive, pure, and rich, but made in an up-front, flattering style. Although outstanding, it is not one of the superstars of the vintage. It will keep for 20 years. Anticipated maturity: now–2020.

Past Glories: 1991 (93), 1963 (90)

DOW

1997 Vintage Port **EE 90**

An evolved, less massive than normal port, the 1997 Dow displays a dark ruby/purple color, attractive licorice, chocolate, and roasted coffee aromas, medium to full body, sweet tannin, and a moderately tannic finish. This excellent vintage port should drink well between 2004–2025.

Past Glories: Quinta do Bomfim 1992 (93), 1990 (95); Vintage Port 1994 (96), 1991 (90), 1983 (93), 1977 (95), 1970 (90), 1966 (91), 1963 (93), 1945 (93)

FERREIRA

1997 Vintage Port **E 89**

This dark ruby/purple offering exhibits aromas of animal fur, licorice, blackberries, and earth. Rich and full-bodied, although more monolithic than many of its peers, this excellent 1997 vintage port falls short of being exceptional. Anticipated maturity: now–2020.

FONSECA

1997 Vintage Port	**EE**	**93**

Somewhat lightweight for Fonseca, but undeniably charming, this dark ruby/purple wine offers a floral, exotic, flamboyant bouquet, a sweet, fleshy style, but not a great deal of weight or massiveness. Heady alcohol, sweet tannin, and a velvety texture make for a gorgeous finish. While I would have preferred to have seen more weight, structure, and intensity, this is an outstanding Fonseca. Anticipated maturity: now–2020.

Past Glories: Guimaraens 1991 (93); Late Bottled Vintage Port 1988 (88); Twenty Year Old Tawny Port (86); Thirty Year Old Tawny Port (91); Vintage Port 1994 (97), 1992 (97), 1985 (96), 1983 (92), 1977 (94), 1970 (97), 1966 (92), 1963 (97), 1955 (96), 1948 (100), 1945 (92)

GRAHAM'S

1997 Vintage Port	**EE**	**93**

Blackberries, licorice, and melted asphalt stand out in this full-bodied, beautifully made vintage port's moderately intense bouquet. It is not one of the great Graham's ports and is less sweet than normal, but it is full-bodied, rich, concentrated, and impressive. Anticipated maturity: 2004–2025.

Past Glories: Malvedos Centenary 1990 (92), 1987 (92), 1986 (92), 1976 (90), 1958 (90); Malvedos Vintage Port 1993 (92); Vintage Port 1994 (96), 1991 (94), 1985 (97), 1983 (94), 1980 (90), 1977 (95), 1970 (95), 1966 (92), 1963 (96), 1955 (95), 1948 (99), 1945 (96)

QUINTA DO NOVAL

1997 Vintage Port	**E**	**100**
1997 Vintage Port Nacional	**EEE**	**100**

The 1997 vintage port is the greatest Quinta do Noval I have ever tasted (excluding their Nacional made from prephylloxera vines). The wine of the vintage, this black/purple port boasts fabulous aromatics (espresso, blackberries, licorice, tar, and flowers), followed by massive concentration and levels of depth and richness that surpass every other port of the vintage save for its limited-production sibling, the Nacional. Gorgeously sweet, stunningly concentrated and full-bodied, this profound vintage port should be legendary. Quinta do Noval's production normally approaches 4,000 cases, but in 1997, only 1,200 cases were produced, so availability will be extremely limited. Anticipated maturity: 2005–2035.

The 1997 Nacional is another legend from this prephylloxera vineyard. The color is a saturated black/purple. The nose reveals more floral scents intermixed with coffee, blackberries, tar, cassis, licorice, and chocolate. Extremely full-bodied, but less massive and more seamless than its sibling, this spectacular Nacional will reach its plateau of maturity quickly, where it will remain for 2–3 decades. Anticipated maturity: 2007–2040.

Past Glories: Nacional 1994 (99+), 1987 (92), 1985 (96), 1970 (96), 1966 (92), 1963 (99+), 1962 (98), 1931 (100); Vintage Port 1994 (95), 1991 (89)

QUINTA DO VALE D. MARIA

1997 Vintage Port	**E**	**90**

This elegantly styled, dark ruby/purple 1997 vintage port was produced by Niepoort. Rich and full-bodied, with an evolved style, it does not have the weight of the vintage's blockbusters, but it is well made, pure, rich, and concentrated with copious quantities of blackberry, cassis, and licorice-flavored fruit. The long finish displays sweet tannin.

QUINTA DO VESUVIO

1997 Vintage Port	**E**	**90**

A delicious, forward, dark saturated ruby/purple port, this 1997 reveals copious quantities of jammy, grapy, black fruit flavors intermixed with earth and spice, full body, and silky tannin. Like other 1997s, it should drink well soon, but last 20 years.

ROMARIZ

1997 Vintage Port   **D 92**

An exceptional vintage port, this saturated purple/black-colored effort offers up sweet, jammy notes of blackberries, licorice, and spice. Full-bodied, rich, and moderately sweet, with huge amounts of glycerin, ripeness, and well-integrated tannin, this blockbuster port can be drunk young, but should evolve nicely for 15–20 years. A sleeper as well as an excellent value.

SILVAL

1997 Vintage Port   **D   93**

A small quinta owned by Quinta do Noval, the 1997 Silval is a splendid effort as well as a sleeper of the vintage. This full-bodied, saturated purple-colored wine displays abundant quantities of chocolate, licorice, and coffee bean notes intertwined with blackberry and cassis fruit. Massive in the mouth, with sweet tannin and stunning concentration, this knockout 1997 should drink well in 3–4 years, and last 20 years or more. Very impressive!

TAYLOR FLADGATE

1997 Vintage Port   **EE   96**

Saturated black/purple, with stunning aromatics of blueberries, blackberries, licorice, and iron, this spectacular vintage port is one of the stars of the vintage. Extremely full-bodied, with silky tannin, spectacular concentration and purity, multiple flavor levels, and a more evolved, forward personality than other top vintages, this is an exquisite yet precocious 1997 vintage port. Anticipated maturity: 2004–2030.

Past Glories: Late Bottled Vintage Port 1988 (89); Quinta de Vargellas 1991 (95), 1987 (90); Vintage Ports 1994 (97), 1992 (100), 1985 (90), 1983 (94), 1980 (90), 1977 (96), 1970 (96), 1966 (91), 1963 (96), 1955 (96), 1948 (100), 1945 (96); Ten Year Tawny Port (93); Twenty Year Tawny Port (92); Thirty Year Tawny Port (87)

DON'T FORGET THE MADEIRAS

Sadly, most consumers think of this as a cooking wine. Madeira's glory days were the 19th century. Today, the bulk of Madeira is decidedly unnoble fortified wine sold cheaply throughout the world. However, the "real" Madeira is exceedingly rare and very limited in production. Moreover, 80- to 200-year-old Madeiras from reliable producers are indeed remarkable wines, balancing sweetness against high acidity in a distinctive sweet-sour flavor profile, with explosive aromatics. The finest retail source in the U.S. for authentic Madeira is the Rare Wine Company in Sonoma, CA; telephone (707) 996-4484; fax (707) 996-4491.

STYLES OF VINTAGE MADEIRA

Current laws require that all vintage Madeira be aged at least 20 years in cask prior to being bottled.

Bastardo   Some ancient Muscatels from the firm of d'Oliviras are remarkable, as several bottles of 1900 tasted have shown. Essentially, Bastardos are fortified Muscats made in very limited quantities. For unknown reasons, they have fallen out of favor, but these rare offerings are generally less expensive than similarly aged Madeiras.

Bual   Undeniably richer, fuller, and sweeter than Verdelhos or Sercials, Bual Madeira possesses a deep amber color and, like its siblings, reveals plenty of roasted, smoky, nutty characteristics.

Malmsey   This is the sweetest, most unctuously textured Madeira, with caramel, roasted nut, and espresso notes, thick, succulent flavors, and good acidity. The legal limit of residual sugar is 96–135 grams per liter.

Sercial   Sercial is the Portuguese name for the grape. Madeiras that bear this name tend to be among the lightest, driest, and palest in color. Most Sercials emerge from Madeira's cooler climates. They have high acidity levels, and no more than 18–65 grams of residual sugar per liter. Their alcohol content is around 17%.

Tarrantez   Rarely seen in recent years, the expensive Tarrantezs are 80- to 200-year-old, powerful Madeiras with immortal aging potential. It is more of an historical varietal for Madeira than one of current use, although one would suspect, given the auction value of ancient Tarrantez bottlings, more of it would be planted.

Verdelho   An amber-colored Madeira, Verdelho is made in a moderately sweet style with good balancing acidity. The finish is full and sweet as the legal limit for residual sugar is 49–78 grams per liter.

TABLE WINES

One other decadent, sumptuous Portuguese wine is the Muscatel de Setubal made by the J. M. da Fonseca firm. Quality today is not what it used to be, but some of the ancient bottlings I have tasted, particularly the 1900, have been spectacular.

As for Portugal's dry wines, they have more potential than actual quality. Nearly all are produced from indigenous varietals. While some reveal considerable potential, the whites generally tend to be either oxidized or innocuous, and the reds range from light, fruity wines of little character, to powerful, concentrated efforts possessing various degrees of rustic tannin. The chart below provides a simplistic overview of the finest producers. To date, the two best are Luis Pato, who is accomplishing fine things in Bairrada (a well-known Portuguese viticultural region between Lisbon and Porto), and the dynamic oenologist, João Portugal Ramos, from Alentejo. Ramos is the locomotive for this viticultural region located south of Lisbon.

VINTAGE GUIDE

While vintages have considerable significance with respect to the port trade, for white and red Portuguese table wines, it is more a question of who is making them than the actual vintages.

RATING PORTUGAL'S BEST PRODUCERS OF TABLE WINES

*** *(GOOD)*

Quinta do Carmo (Alentejo)
Quinto do Castro (Douro)
Chryseia (Douro)
Quinta do Cotto (Douro)
Ferreira (Douro)
Quinto do Fojo (Douro)
J. M. da Fonseca (Dao Terras Altas)
J. M. da Fonseca (Garrafeira TE)
J. M. da Fonseca (Morgado do Reguengo-
    Portalegre)
J. M. da Fonseca (Quinta da Camarate)

J. M. da Fonseca (Rosado Fernandes)
Quinta de Foz de Arouce (Beiras)
Quinto da Gaivosa (Douro)
Quinta da Ponte Pedrinha (Dao)
Luis Pato (Bairrada)
João Portugal Ramos Marques de Borba
    (Alentejo)
João Portugal Ramos Trincadeira
    (Alentejo)
Quinta de la Rosa (Douro)
Vimompor Quinta du Pedro (Vinho Verde)

THE WINES OF NORTH AMERICA

California
Oregon
Washington State
The Mid-Atlantic States

5. CALIFORNIA

The Basics

TYPES OF WINE

Virtually every type of wine seen elsewhere in the wine world is made in California. Fortified port-style wines, decadently sweet, late-harvest Rieslings, sparkling wines, and major red and white dry table wines from such super grapes as Chardonnay and Cabernet Sauvignon— all are to be found in California.

GRAPE VARIETIES

The fine wines of California are dominated by Cabernet Sauvignon and Chardonnay, as much of the attention of that state's wine-makers is directed at these two grapes. However, California makes wonderful red Zinfandel and increasing amounts of world-class Merlot and Syrah, plus some Petite Sirah. Despite improved quality, Pinot Noir is still a questionable wine in the hands of all but several dozen or so California wine producers. Two notable trends started in the late 1980s have proven popular with consumers. These include the proliferation of proprietary red wine blends (usually Cabernet Sauvignon–dominated and superexpensive) and the development of authoritatively flavored, robust, supple red wines made from blends of Syrah, Carignan, Grenache, Mourvèdre, and Alicante, collectively referred to as the "Rhône Rangers." As for the white wines, Sauvignon Blanc and Sémillon, and blends thereof, can be complex and fragrant, but the majority remains nondescript. It is a shame that Chenin Blanc has so little sex appeal among consumers, because it can be a very inexpensive, delicious drink. Colombard and Muscat suffer from the same image problems as Chenin Blanc, but shrewd consumers know the good ones and seek them out. Gewürztraminer and dry Rieslings have been dismal wines, although a handful of wineries have broken through the wall of mediocrity. For years California has made it simple for the consumer, naming its wines after the varietal from which it is made. By law a Chardonnay or Cabernet Sauvignon must contain 75% of that grape in the wine. The recent trend, accompanied by very high prices, has been to produce luxury-priced proprietary wines with awe-inspiring, often silly names such as Dominus, Opus, Rubicon, Trilogy, and Insignia. These wines are supposed to be the winery's very best lots of wine blended together for harmony. Some of them are marvelous. But remember: All of them are expensive and most of them are overpriced.

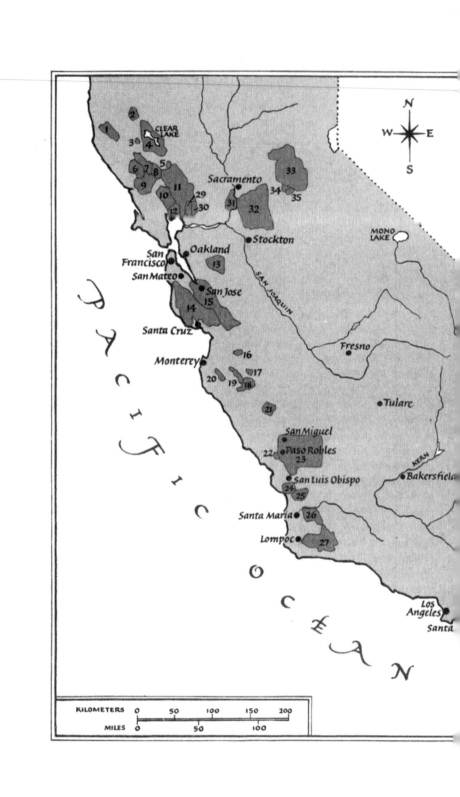

California

NORTH COAST
1. Anderson Valley
2. Potter Valley
3. McDowell Valley
4. Clear Lake
5. Guenoc Valley
6. Dry Creek Valley
7. Alexander Valley
8. Knights Valley
9. Russian River Valley
10. Sonoma Valley
11. Napa Valley
12. Los Carneros

CENTRAL COAST
13. Livermore Valley
14. Santa Cruz Mountains
15. Santa Clara Valley
16. Mount Harlan
17. Chalone
18. Arroyo Seco
19. Santa Lucia Highlands
20. Carmel Valley
21. San Lucas
22. York Mountain
23. Paso Robles
24. Edna Valley
25. Arroyo Grande
26. Santa Maria Valley
27. Santa Ynez Valley
28. Temecula

INTERIOR
29. Solano County Green Valley
30. Suisun Valley
31. Clarksburg
32. Lodi
33. El Dorado
34. Shenandoah Valley
35. Fiddletown

Flavors

RED WINE VARIETALS

Cabernet Franc   Now being used by more and more wineries to give complexity to a wine's bouquet, Cabernet Franc is a cedary, herbaceous-scented wine that is usually lighter in color and body than either Cabernet Sauvignon or Merlot. It rarely can stand by itself, but used judiciously in a blend, it can provide an extra dimension. Reference-point California wines with significant proportions of Cabernet Franc that have stood the test of time include the 1971 Robert Mondavi Reserve Cabernet, 1977 Joseph Phelps Insignia red wine, La Jota's 1986, 1990, 1991, 1992, 1993, 1994, and 1995 Cabernet Franc, Dalla Valle's 1990, 1992, 1993, 1994, 1995, 1996, and 1997 Maya (an exquisite wine with nearly 50% Cabernet Franc in the blend), the Havens Bourriquot (two-thirds Cabernet Franc), 1997, and Pride Mountain 1996, 1997, and 1998.

Cabernet Sauvignon   The king of California's red wine grapes, Cabernet Sauvignon produces densely colored wine with aromas that can include black currants, chocolate, cedar, leather, ground meat, minerals, herbs, tobacco, and tar. Cabernet Sauvignon reaches its pinnacle of success in Napa, Sonoma, and the Santa Cruz Mountains, although a few excellent examples have emanated, infrequently, from Paso Robles, Santa Ynez, and Monterey. The more vegetal side of Cabernet Sauvignon, with intense smells of asparagus and green beans, is found in wines from Monterey or Santa Barbara, two areas that have generally proven too cool for this varietal.

Merlot   If Cabernet Sauvignon provides the power, tannin, and structure, Merlot provides opulence, fatness, higher alcohol, and a lush, chewy texture when crop yields are not too high. It has grown in importance in California. One strong trend is an increased number of wines that are made predominantly from the Merlot grape. Telltale aromas of a top Merlot include scents of plums, black cherries, toffee, tea, herbs, tomatoes sometimes, and a touch of orange. Merlot wines will never have the color density of a Cabernet Sauvignon because the Merlot grape's skin is thinner, but they are lower in acidity and less tannic. The higher alcohol and ripeness result in a fleshy, chewy wine that offers early drinking. Wines made primarily from Merlot are here to stay. The top examples can challenge the best of France, but the vast majority (about 90%) remains hollow and frightfully acidified, as well as too tannic and vegetal.

Petite Sirah   Unfortunately, this varietal has fallen from grace. Petite Sirah, in actuality the Duriff grape, is unrelated to the true Syrah, yet it produces almost purple-colored, very tannic, intense wines with peppery, cassis-scented bouquets. The wines age surprisingly well, as 15- to 20-year-old examples have shown a consistent ability to hold their fruit. The complexity and bouquet will rarely be that of a Cabernet or Merlot, but these are important wines. The Petite Sirah grape has adapted well to the warmer microclimates of California.

Pinot Noir   The thin-skinned, fickle Pinot Noir is a troublesome grape for everybody. While California continues to produce too many mediocre, washed-out, pruny, vegetal wines from this varietal, no region in the New World has demonstrated more progress with Pinot Noir than California. Major breakthroughs have been made. While good Pinot Noirs are increasingly noticeable from the North Coast areas of Mendocino, Napa, and Sonoma, fine Pinot Noirs also emanate from farther south—the Santa Cruz Mountains, the Monterey area, Arroyo Grande, and Santa Barbara. Yet the areas that have shown the greatest potential are the Sonoma Coast and Santa Barbara's Santa Rita Hills, with their cool maritime climate. A good Pinot Noir will exhibit medium to dark ruby color and an intense explosion of aromatics, including red and black fruits, herbs, earth, and floral aromas. Pinot Noir tends to drop what tannin it possesses quickly, so some acidity is important to give it focus and depth. Most

Pinot Noirs are drinkable when released. Few will evolve and improve beyond 7–8 years in the bottle. Consumers should be particularly apprehensive of any Pinot Noir that tastes too tannic or acidic when young.

Sangiovese   The Italian ancestry of many northern California grape growers and producers is increasingly evident with the number of wineries making Sangiovese. There are significant new plantations of this varietal, which is the most important red wine grape in the pastoral countryside of Tuscany, Italy. It is the predominant grape of most Chiantis and Vino da Tavolas. In California's fertile soils it achieves mind-boggling crop levels—8–12 tons of fruit per acre. Without effective pruning practices or severe crop thinnings, the wines produced are diluted, thin, acidic, and of little interest. However, when the vines are crop-thinned by 50% or more, the result can be fruity, strawberry/cherry/leather-scented and -flavored wines with medium body and penetrating acidity that is ideal for cutting through tomato-based sauces and working with the fusion Mediterranean/Pacific Rim cuisines found in California and elsewhere. To date, impressive Sangiovese has emerged from such wineries as Staglin Family Vineyards, Swanson, Shafer, and Ferrari-Carano. The largest plantations are found in the Atlas Peak Vineyard, whose wines have been disappointing to date. Many producers are beginning to add some Cabernet Sauvignon to the blend in order to give the wine more color, body, and depth, as the higher crop yields tend to produce a lighter wine than desired. Overall, Sangiovese is largely a failure.

Syrah   Syrah is the great red grape varietal of France's northern Rhône Valley. An increasing number of California wineries have begun to bottle 100% Syrah wines, and some have been exquisite. The style ranges from light, fruity, almost Beaujolais-like wines to black/purple-colored, thick, rich, ageworthy, highly extracted wines bursting with potential. A great Syrah will possess a hickory, smoky, tar, and cassis/blackberry-scented nose, rich, full-bodied, occasionally massive flavors, and considerable tannin. Like Cabernet Sauvignon, a Syrah-based wine is a thoroughbred when it comes to aging, easily lasting for 10–20 or more years. Neyers, Alban, Edmunds St. John, Dehlinger, Sine Qua Non, Havens, Martinelli, Ojai, Andrew Murray, and Thackrey have made many of the most compelling examples, but there are a bevy of very good Syrahs at reasonable prices.

Zinfandel   Seemingly against all odds, Zinfandel, the red, full-bodied type, has made a fashion comeback. Its accessibility, combined with its gorgeous, peppery, berry (cherries, blackberries, and raspberries) nose, spicy fruit, and lush, supple texture have helped to boost its image. Additionally, Zinfandel's burgeoning popularity might be explained by a growing, and may I say healthy, trend away from excessively priced glamour wines, particularly the chocolate and vanilla flavors of California's Chardonnay and Cabernet Sauvignon. Zinfandel is grown throughout California, but the best clearly comes from relatively old vines grown on hillside vineyards. Selected vineyards (especially head-pruned old vines) from Napa, the Dry Creek Valley, Sonoma, Sierra Foothills, Paso Robles, and Amador have consistently produced the most interesting Zinfandels. While soil certainly plays an important role (gravelly loam is probably the best), low yields, old vines, and harvesting fully mature, physiologically rather than analytically ripe fruit are even more important. Today, most Zinfandels are made in a medium- to full-bodied, spicy, richly fruity style, somewhat in the image of Cabernet Sauvignon. While there is some backbone and structure, it is usually a wine that consumers can take immediate advantage of for its luscious, rich fruit, and can drink during the first decade of its life. While many Zinfandels can last longer, my experience suggests that the wines rarely improve after 4–6 years and are best drunk within that time. One lamentable trend to monitor is the increasingly high prices demanded for Zinfandels. Most good Zinfandels fetch $25–35 a bottle, with some surpassing $50. This is a dangerous direction.

Carignan   A somewhat lowly regarded grape that deserves more attention, some of California's oldest vineyards are planted with Carignan. As wineries such as Trentadue and Cline have proven, where there are old vines, low yields, and full ripeness, the wines can have surprising intensity and richness in a Rhône-like style. There is a dusty earthiness to most Carignan-based wines that goes along with its big, rich, black fruit and spicy flavors.

Alicante Bouchet   Another grape that has fallen out of favor because of its low prestige, it remains revered by those who know it well. It yields a black/purple-colored wine with considerable body and richness. It needs time in the bottle to shed its hardness, but when treated respectfully, as the two Sonoma wineries Trentadue and Topolos do, this can be an overachieving grape that handsomely repays cellaring. When mature, the wine offers an array of spicy, earthy flavors and significant body and alcohol. Coturri has made some monster wines from this grape.

Mourvèdre/Mataro   This variety is making a comeback. Wineries such as Tablas Creek, Edmunds St. John, Cline Cellars, and Sean Thackrey have turned out fascinating wines from this varietal. Mataro produces a moderately dark-colored wine with a mushroomy, earthy, raspberry-scented nose, surprising acidity and tannin, and considerable aging potential.

WHITE WINE VARIETALS

Chardonnay   The great superstar of the white wines, Chardonnay at its best can produce majestically rich, buttery, honeyed wines with seemingly layers of flavors suggesting tropical fruits (pineapples and tangerines), apples, peaches, and even buttered popcorn when the wine has been barrel-fermented. It flourishes in all of California's viticultural districts, with no area having superiority over another. Great examples can be found from Mendocino, Sonoma, Napa, Carneros, Monterey, Santa Cruz, and Santa Barbara. The problem is that of the 600+ California wineries producing Chardonnay, less than 100 make an interesting wine. Crop yields are too high, the wines are manufactured rather than made, they are too frequently over-oaked, and they are excessively acidified, making them technically flawless, but lacking bouquet, flavor intensity, and character, save for their grotesque oakiness. The results are tart, vapid wines of no interest. Moreover, generally the wines have to be drunk within 12 months of the vintage. Another popular trend has been to intentionally leave sizable amounts of residual sugar in the wine while trying to hide part of it with additions of acidity. This cosmetically gives the wine a superficial feel of more richness and roundness, but these wines also crack up within a year of the vintage. Most Chardonnays are mediocre and overpriced, with very dubious aging potentials. Yet they remain the most popular "dry" white wine produced in California.

Chenin Blanc   This maligned, generally misunderstood grape can produce lovely apéritif wines that are both dry and slightly sweet. Most wineries lean toward a fruity, delicate, perfumed, light- to medium-bodied style that pleases increasing numbers of consumers who are looking for delicious wines at reasonable prices. This varietal deserves more attention from consumers.

French Colombard   Like Chenin Blanc, Colombard is a varietal that is rarely accorded much respect. Its charm is its aromatic character and crisp, light-bodied style.

Gewürztraminer   Anyone who has tasted a fine French Gewurztraminer must be appalled by what is sold under this name in California. A handful of wineries, such as Navarro, Martinelli, and Babcock, have produced some attractive although subdued Gewürztraminers. The bald truth remains that most California Gewürztraminers are made in a slightly sweet, watery, shallow, washed-out style.

Muscat   There are several Muscat grapes used in California. This is an underrated and underappreciated varietal that produces remarkably fragrant and perfumed wines that are loaded with tropical fruit flavors. They are ideal as an apéritif wine or with desserts.

Pinot Blanc   This grape, a staple of Alsace, France, where it is used to produce richly fruity but generally straightforward, satisfying wines, has had mixed success in California.

Some producers have barrel-fermented it, attempting to produce a large-scale, Chardonnay-style wine, with little success. Chalone and Arrowood are two of the few wineries to have succeeded with this style. In my opinion, Pinot Blanc is best vinified in a manner that emphasizes its intense fruity characteristics, which range from honeyed tangerines and oranges to a more floral, applelike fruitiness. Pinot Blancs typically do not age well, but they provide immediate appeal and satisfaction in an exuberant yet uncomplicated manner. Other fine Pinot Blancs have emerged from Murphy-Goode. Most Pinot Blancs should be drunk within 2–3 years of the vintage, the only exception being those made in a full-bodied, structured style such as Chalone.

Sauvignon Blanc   California winemaking has failed miserably to take advantage of this grape. Overcropping, excessive acidification, and a philosophy of manufacturing the wines have resulted in hundreds of neutral, bland, empty wines with no bouquet or flavor. This is unfortunate, because Sauvignon is one of the most food-friendly and flexible wines produced in the world. It can also adapt itself to many different styles of fermentation and upbringing. At its best, the nonoaked examples of this wine possess vivid, perfumed noses of figs, melons, herbs, and minerals, crisp fruit, wonderful zesty flavors, and a dry finish. More ambitious, barrel-fermented styles that often have some Sémillon added can have a honeyed, melony character, and rich, medium- to full-bodied, grassy, melon and figlike flavors that offer considerable authority. Unfortunately, too few examples of either type are found in California. No viticultural region can claim a monopoly on either the successes or the failures.

Sémillon   One of the up-and-coming California varietals, on its own Sémillon produces wines with considerable body and creamy richness. It can often be left on the vine and has a tendency to develop botrytis, which lends itself to making sweet, honeyed, dessert wines. But Sémillon's best use is when it is added to Sauvignon, where the two make the perfect marriage, producing wines with considerable richness and complexity.

White Riesling or Johannisberg Riesling   Occasionally some great late-harvest Rieslings have been made in California, but attempts at making a dry Kabinett- or Trocken-style Riesling as produced in Germany most frequently result in dull, lifeless, empty wines with no personality or flavor. Most Riesling is planted in soils that are too rich and in climates that are too hot. This is a shame. Riesling is another varietal that could prove immensely popular to the masses.

AGING POTENTIAL

Cabernet Franc: 5–15 years	Pinot Blanc: 1–3 years
Cabernet Sauvignon: 5–25 years	Pinot Noir: 4–8 years
Chardonnay: 1–6 years	Riesling (dry): 1–2 years
Chenin Blanc: 1–2 years	Riesling (sweet): 2–8 years
Colombard: 1–2 years	Sauvignon Blanc: 1–3 years
Gamay: 2–4 years	Sémillon: 1–4 years
Merlot: 5–12 years	Sparkling Wines: 2–7 years
Muscat: 1–3 years	Syrah: 5–20 years
Petite Sirah: 5–15 years	Zinfandel: 3–10 years

OVERALL QUALITY LEVEL

The top five or six dozen producers of Cabernet Sauvignon, Merlot, or proprietary red wines, as well as the three dozen or so who produce Chardonnay, make wines that are as fine and as multidimensional as anywhere in the world. However, for well over 20 years, my tastings have consistently revealed too many California wines that are not made but manufactured. Excessively acidified by cautious oenologists and sterile-filtered to the point where there is no perceptible aroma, many wines possess little flavor except for the textural abrasiveness caused by shrill levels of acidity and high alcohol, and in the case of the red wines, excessive levels of green, astringent tannins. Producers have tried to hide their excessive crop yields by leaving residual sugar in the finished wine hoping to give the impression of more body. This practice is only a quick fix, as the white wines tend to fall apart 6–9 months after bottling and the red wines taste cloying.

The time-honored philosophy of California winemaking, which includes the obsession with the vineyard as a manufacturing plant, the industrial winemaking in the cellars, and the preoccupation with monolithic, simplistic, squeaky-clean wines that suffer from such strictly controlled technical parameters, is weakening. It is no secret that the principal objective of most California wineries has been to produce sediment-free, spit-polished, stable wines. The means used to attain this goal too frequently eviscerate the wines of their flavor, aromas, personality, and pleasure-giving qualities. But significant changes (especially noticeable in vintages of the nineties) are underfoot.

Only a fool could ignore the fact that California is now producing many of the greatest wines in the world. While most retailers legitimately carp about the microscopic allocations they receive of the limited-production gems from the most fashionable wineries, it is obvious that California wine quality is surging to greater and greater heights.

Why am I so bullish on California wines? Consider the following:

1. California enjoyed a stunning decade of quality in the nineties. Starting with 1990, every vintage has provided that state's growers with enough high-quality fruit to turn out numerous sensational wines. Only 1998, in reality a good year, offers less excitement than the other vintages.

2. Even more important than the eight out of nine outstanding quality vintages is the shift in mind-set of many top wine producers. I have had little help from my colleagues in attempting to change the industrial/food-processor mentality espoused by the University of California at Davis. For as long as I can remember, this school of thought has resulted in sterile, frightfully acidic, nearly undrinkable harsh and hollow wines that, amazingly, garnered raves from segments of the West Coast wine press. Handcrafted wines that reflected the *terroir*, vintage, and varietal, in addition to providing immense pleasure, have had an enormous influence on others. Two decades ago, it was distressing to see the number of wineries that automatically, without any thought whatsoever, compromised and in many cases destroyed a wine by blind faith in the following techniques: (a) by harvesting grapes based on analytical rather than physiological ripeness; (b) by adding frightfully high levels of tartaric acid to the fermenting juice because it was the "risk-free" thing to do; (c) by processing the youthful grape juice utilizing centrifuges and filters that eviscerated and purified the wine before it had a chance to develop any personality; (d) by prefiltering wine intensely before it was allowed to go to barrel; and (e) by fining and sterile-filtering everything as a rule of thumb so that a wine had no aromatics and nothing but a monolithic personality. The adoption of a less-traumatic and less-interventionalistic wine philosophy, emphasizing the importance of the vineyard's fruit and preserving its characteristics, is increasingly widespread. The results are increasing quantities of compellingly rich, natural-tasting, unprocessed wines that should be causing French wine producers to shudder. And while many wineries continue to fight this trend toward higher-quality, more natural wines, often with considerable support from a gullible wine press, the fact is that you, the wine consumer, are the beneficiary!

3. As financially devastating as the phylloxera epidemic has been for California viticulture, the silver lining is that the replanting of vineyards over the last decade has addressed issues that key industry personnel refused to acknowledge as being important prior to this epidemic. Many new vineyards have been planted with tighter spacing, thus making the vines struggle. The result is deeper root systems and vines that produce lower quantities of higher-quality grapes. Additionally, the problem of varietals planted in the wrong soils and/or microclimates can be rectified by these new plantations. Superior rootstocks and less pro-

ductive clones that produce smaller crops with more individual character are other positive results of the phylloxera epidemic. As time passes, it will become evident that the mistakes made in the forties, fifties, and sixties have been largely corrected, ironically because of phylloxera. If the grapes from these new vineyards are markedly superior, as they should be, it takes no genius to realize that wine quality will also improve.

4. The influence of the French, combined with a new generation of well-traveled, open-minded, revisionist California wine-makers, must also be given credit for the remarkable progress in quality. California wines are as rich as they have ever been, but they no longer possess the heaviness of those great vintages of the sixties and seventies. Do readers realize why the finest French cuisine and French wines are cherished throughout the world as standards of reference? Because France, in both her cooking and her wines, achieves, at the highest level of quality, extraordinary intensity of flavor without weight or heaviness. Call this elegance, harmony, finesse, or whatever, but it is what I now detect in increasing numbers of California's finest wines.

BUYING STRATEGY

Except for the so-so 1998 vintage, California experienced a bevy of terrific vintages in the nineties. There was an unprecedented run of eight consecutive years (1990–1997) where most of the state's producers turned out wines that were made from ripe fruit. Only the top producers who keep crop yields to a minimum and refuse to excessively manipulate and process their wines will turn out the best, but it is clearly a good time to be buying California wines. Yet prices are extremely high, especially for the top-rated wines.

RECENT VINTAGES

2001—A fabulous vintage everywhere, but especially in Napa/Sonoma/Mendecino, where it will be one of the all-time greats.

2000—Overall, a challenging vintage in Napa/Sonoma/Mendecino, but very good in the Central Coast and Santa Barbara regions.

1999—Following 1998, this was another cool year with mountain vineyards and cooler *terroirs* challenged to get their fruit fully ripe. It is an excellent year for thin-skinned varietals such as Chardonnay and Pinot Noir. Syrah has also performed well. As in 1998, mountain vineyards had difficulty obtaining fully ripened Cabernet Sauvignon.

1998—This is the first vintage of the nineties to present irregularities and inconsistencies throughout California's viticultural regions. A cool late spring and abnormally cool summer resulted in one of the latest harvests of the decade. Many Cabernet Sauvignon vineyards on the cooler hillsides were not harvested until late October. Some areas, particularly Santa Barbara and to the north, were touched by some rain. The crop size was moderate, and the quality ranged from exceptional to spotty. Overall, 1998 is the least consistent and compelling year of the nineties.

1997—For California's North Coast, this vintage competes with 1994 and 1991 as one of the decade's finest years for Cabernet Sauvignon, Merlot, and Cabernet Franc. The vintage possesses the characteristics that separate great years from merely excellent ones. The finest wines are seamless, with velvety textures, wonderful purity, sweet tannin, and expressive aromatic profiles. Much to the joy of wine-makers, the abundant crop produced ripe wines with surprisingly high extract and alcohol. Pinot Noir looks exceptional throughout the North Coast, and the Chardonnays are very good to excellent. Consumers need to be careful as yields for many producers were entirely too high to produce quality wines. Hence, 1997, which is undeniably great at the top end, has many deceptions and a frustrating irregularity. In the Santa Cruz Mountains, Central Coast, and Santa Barbara, the vintage becomes trickier, but certainly the potential for high quality exists. My visit to these areas left me with the impression that 1997 is a very good vintage as opposed to a potentially great one. One last caveat—Zinfandel is far less successful because of enormous yields.

1996—If this were a vintage from the eighties, it would stand out as one of the greatest years of that decade. However, sandwiched between 1997, 1994, and 1995, 1996, while having no shortcomings, simply does not match up. A hot drought year with a short growing season, the North Coast wines are powerful, concentrated, and weighty, but some lack the sweet tannin and near perfect equilibrium achieved in 1994, 1995, and 1997. Readers will notice more rustic tannin in many Cabernet Sauvignons and certain Pinot Noirs. Brilliant wines were made, but the tannin level is undeniably more aggressive. There are some stellar North Coast Chardonnays, but the year's heat appears to have muted some of that varietal's aromatics. California is a diverse region, and even within such general appellations as Napa and Sonoma, there are infinite microclimates, soil types, and winemaking philosophies. I do not want to give the impression that there is something wrong with the vintage, because it did produce many exceptional wines. If it were not for 1997, 1995, and 1994, this would be considered a topflight year. For now, it is unquestionably an excellent year. The white wines need to be drunk up by the end of 2002. 1996 does appear to be a great year in the Santa Cruz Mountains, where wines of exceptional ripeness, richness, and balance were achieved. In contrast to the North Coast, 1996 appears superior to 1997. Farther south, the vintage is very good, but the Central Coast and Santa Barbara are more difficult regions to handicap.

1995—Like 1994, 1995 enjoyed a long, cool growing season, and while the wines are not as forward, fragrant, and expressive as many 1994s, a bevy of fabulous wines have emerged from Napa and Sonoma's top wineries. 1995 gets my nod as the finest vintage in the nineties for Chardonnay, but most readers buying high-quality California Chardonnay should have consumed them by 2001. For Cabernet Sauvignon and Pinot Noir, 1995 is an outstanding vintage that comes close to rivaling the greatness of 1994. In fact, some producers may have turned out Cabernet Sauvignons, Merlots, and proprietary reds that surpass what they achieved in 1994. In short, 1995 is another phenomenal vintage in a top-notch decade.

1994—In the last six months I have conducted two blind tastings of the 1994 North Coast Cabernet Sauvignons, Merlots, and proprietary reds. In both settings, the tasters were struck by uniformity and prodigious quality. The wines are approachable, exceptionally aromatic, wonderfully sweet, and rich, but neither heavy nor cumbersome. The top producers have made long-lived classics of remarkable symmetry and opulence. It was also a superb year in the Santa Cruz Mountains.

1993—If the 1993s are not as dramatic as the finest 1994s, 1992s, 1991s, and 1990s, they are by no means inferior. This is another rich, velvety-textured vintage for red wines, and a beautifully balanced year for whites. This vintage has been criticized for reasons I am unable to understand, but there are many great red wines.

1992—An abundant crop was harvested that ranged from very good to superb in quality. When Mother Nature is as generous as she was in most viticultural regions in 1992, the potential high quality can be diluted by excessive crop yields and by harvesting grapes that are not physiologically mature. However, the top producers have turned out fat, rich, opulent, low-acid, dramatic wines. The white wines need to be drunk up. The finest reds are flattering and richly fruity, and will keep for 10–20 years.

1991—A cool, surprisingly long growing season resulted in potentially excessive crop yields. However, those producers who had the patience to wait out the cool weather and harvest fully mature fruit, as well as to keep their yields down, made some superb red wines that will compete with the finest 1997s, 1995s, 1994s, 1993s, 1992s, 1990s, 1987s, 1986s, 1985s, and 1984s. For all the red wine varietals it is a splendid year, with many producers expressing a preference for their 1991s because of the incredibly long hang-time on the vine.

The 1991 vintage produced an enormous crop of good white wines that should have been consumed by the end of 1995.

1990—For Cabernet Sauvignon, Zinfandel, and other major red wine varietals, 1990 was a mild growing season. The crop was moderate in size, particularly when compared with 1991 and 1992. The wines are concentrated, rich, and well made. It was a banner year for California's top red wines. For Chardonnay, it was a super year, but most of these wines should have been consumed by mid-1994.

WHERE TO FIND CALIFORNIA'S BEST WINE VALUES
(Wineries That Can Be Counted On for Value)

Alderbrook (Sauvignon Blanc, Chardonnay)

Arrowood Domaine du Grand Archer (Chardonnay, Cabernet Sauvignon)

Belvedere (Chardonnay cuvées)

Beringer (Knights Valley Chardonnay, Sauvignon Blanc, Cabernet Sauvignon)

Bonny Doon (Clos de Gilroy, Ca' Del Solo cuvées, Pacific Rim Riesling)

Buehler (Zinfandel)

Carmenet (Colombard)

Cartridge and Browne (Chardonnay, Zinfandel, Cabernet Sauvignon)

Cline (Côtes d'Oakley)

Duxoup (Gamay, Charbono)

Edmunds St.-John (New World and Port o'Call reds, Pinot Grigio and El Niño whites)

Estancia (Chardonnay cuvées, Meritage red)

Fetzer (Sundial Chardonnay)

Franciscan (Merlot, Chardonnay)

Guenoc (Petite Sirah)

Hess Collection (Hess Select Chardonnay, Cabernet Sauvignon)

Husch Vineyard (Chenin Blanc, Gewürztraminer, La Ribera Red)

Kendall-Jackson (Vintner's Reserve Chardonnay, Fumé Blanc, Vintner's Reserve Zinfandel)

Kenwood (Sauvignon Blanc)

Konocti (Fumé Blanc)

Marietta Cellars (Old Vine Red, Zinfandel, Cabernet Sauvignon)

Mirassou (white burgundy—Pinot Blanc)

Monterey Vineyard (Classic cuvées of Merlot, Cabernet Sauvignon, Chardonnay, Sauvignon Blanc, and Zinfandel, generic Classic White and Classic Red)

Morro Bay Vineyards (Chardonnay)

Mountain View Winery (Sauvignon Blanc, Chardonnay, Pinot Noir, Zinfandel)

Murphy-Goode (Fumé Blanc)

Napa Ridge (Chardonnay, Cabernet Sauvignon, Sauvignon Blanc)

Parducci (Sauvignon Blanc)

J. Pedroncelli (Sauvignon Blanc, Zinfandel, Cabernet Sauvignon)

Joseph Phelps (Vins du Mistral cuvées)

R. H. Phillips (Night Harvest cuvées of Chardonnay and Sauvignon Blanc)

Preston (Cuvée du Fumé)

Ravenswood (Zinfandel and Merlot Vintner's blends)

Château Souverain (Chardonnay, Merlot, Cabernet Sauvignon, Sauvignon Blanc)

Stratford (the Chardonnay and Canterbury line of wines, particularly Chardonnay and Sauvignon Blanc)

Ivan Tamas (Trebbiano, Fumé Blanc, Chardonnay)

Trentadue (Old Patch Red, Zinfandel, Carignan, Sangiovese, Petite Sirah, Merlot, Salute Proprietary Red Wine)

RATING CALIFORNIA'S BEST PRODUCERS OF CABERNET SAUVIGNON, MERLOT, AND BLENDS THEREOF

***** (OUTSTANDING)

Abreu Vineyards Madrona Ranch (Napa)

Araujo Estate Eisele Vineyard (Napa)

Arrowood Reserve Speciale (Sonoma)

Arrowood Reserve Speciale Merlot (Sonoma)

David Arthur Elevation 1147 (Napa)

Behrens and Hitchcock Kenefick Ranch (Napa)
Behrens and Hitchcock Merlot Las Amigas Vineyard (Carneros)
Behrens and Hitchcock TLK Ranch (Napa)
Beringer Chabot Vineyard (Napa)
Beringer Merlot Bancroft Vineyard (Napa)
Beringer Private Reserve (Napa)
Blackjack Ranch Harmonie (Santa Barbara)
Blackjack Ranch Merlot (Santa Barbara)
Blankiet (Napa)
Bryant Family Vineyard (Napa)
Cardinale Proprietary Red Wine (California)
Caymus Special Selection (Napa)
Clark-Claudon (Napa)
Colgin Lamb Vineyard (Napa)
Dalla Valle (Napa)
Dalla Valle Maya Proprietary Red Wine (Napa)
Dominus (Napa)
Dunn (Napa)
Dunn Howell Mountain (Napa)
Fisher Lamb Vineyard (Napa)
Fisher Wedding Vineyard (Sonoma)
Flora Springs Hillside Reserve (Napa)
Grace Family Vineyard (Napa)
Harlan Estate Proprietary Red Wine (Napa)
Hourglass (Napa)

Jones Family Vineyard (Napa)
La Jota Anniversary Cuvée (Napa)
Lokoya Diamond Mountain (Napa)
Lokoya Howell Mountain (Napa)
Lokoya Mount Veeder (Napa)
Lokoya Rutherford (Napa)
Peter Michael Les Pavots Proprietary Red Wine (California)
Robert Mondavi Reserve (Napa)
Robert Mondavi To-Kalon Estate Reserve (Napa)
Château Montelena Estate (Napa)
Pahlmeyer Merlot (Napa)
Pahlmeyer Proprietary Red Wine (Napa)
Joseph Phelps Insignia Proprietary Red Wine (Napa)
Pride Mountain Claret (Napa)
Pride Mountain Reserve (Napa)
Ridge Monte Bello (Santa Cruz Mountain)
Rudd Estate (Napa)
Saddleback Cellars Venge Family Reserve (Napa)
St. Jean Cinq Cépages Proprietary Red Wine (Sonoma)
Screaming Eagle (Napa)
Seavey (Napa)
Shafer Hillside Select (Napa)
Silver Oak (Napa)
Spottswoode (Napa)
Philip Togni (Napa)
Verité (Sonoma/Napa)

* * * * (EXCELLENT)

Anderson's Conn Valley Vineyard (Napa)
Arrowood (Sonoma)
Atalon Beckstoffer Vineyards (Napa)
Atalon Madrona Ranch (Napa)
Atalon Mountain Estates (Napa)
Bacio Divino Proprietary Red Wine (California)
Barnett Spring Mountain Rattlesnake Hill (Napa)
Behrens and Hitchcock Cuvée Lola Proprietary Red Wine (Napa)
Behrens and Hitchcock Merlot (Oakville)
Behrens and Hitchcock Merlot Alder Springs Vineyard (Mendocino)
Beringer St. Helena Vineyard (Napa)
Beringer State Lane Vineyard (Napa)
Beringer Tre Colline Vineyard (Napa)

Cakebread Cellars Benchland Select (Napa)
Cakebread Cellars Three Sisters (Napa)
Carmenet Moon Mountain Estate Reserve Proprietary Red Wine (Sonoma)
Clos Pegase Hommage Proprietary Red Wine (Napa)
Cornerstone Beatty Ranch (Napa)
Cornerstone Black Sears (Napa)
Cornerstone Collage Vineyard (Napa)
Cornerstone Cornerstone Vineyard (Napa)
Robert Craig Affinity Proprietary Red Wine (Napa)
Robert Craig Howell Mountain (Napa)
Robert Craig Mount Veeder (Napa)
Cuvaison ATS Selection (Carneros)
Diamond Creek Gravelly Meadow (Napa)

Diamond Creek Lake (Napa)
Diamond Creek Red Rock Terrace (Napa)
Diamond Creek Volcanic Hill (Napa)
Ferrari-Carano (Sonoma) (since 1991)
Ferrari-Carano Merlot (Sonoma) (since 1991)
Ferrari-Carano Reserve Red Proprietary Wine (Sonoma)
Fisher Coach Insignia (Sonoma) (since 1991)
Flora Springs Cypress Ranch (Pope Valley)
Flora Springs Merlot Windfall Vineyard (Pope Valley)
Robert Foley Claret (Napa)
Forman (Napa)
Forman Merlot (Napa)
Foxen (Santa Barbara)
Franus (Napa)
Frazier (Napa)
Hartwell Stags Leap (Napa)
Havens Bourriquot (Napa)
Havens Merlot Reserve (Napa)
Heitz Martha's Vineyard (Napa) (prior to 1986 a 5-star wine)
Paul Hobbs Black Vineyard Merlot (Napa)
Paul Hobbs Hyde Vineyard (Sonoma)
Judd's Hill (Napa)
Kendall-Jackson Merlot Buckeye Vineyard (Alexander Valley)
Kendall-Jackson Merlot Great Estates (Sonoma)
Kongsgaard Arietta (Napa)
Kunde Drummond Vineyard (Sonoma)
Kunde Estate Reserve (Sonoma)
La Jota (Napa)
La Jota Cabernet Franc (Napa)
Lail Vineyards J. Daniel Cuvée Proprietary Red Wine (Napa)
Lancaster Reserve Proprietary Red Wine (Alexander Valley)
Larkin Cabernet Franc (Napa)
Laurel Glen (Sonoma)
Laurel Glen Terra Rosa (Sonoma)
Lewelling (Napa)
Lewelling Wight Vineyard (Napa)
Marietta (Sonoma)
Matanzas Creek Merlot (Sonoma)
Philip Melka Metisse Proprietary Red Wine (Napa)
Merryvale Profile Proprietary Red Wine (Napa)

Merus (Napa)
Mount Eden Old Vine Reserve (Santa Cruz)
Newton Cabernet Sauvignon (Napa)
Newton Merlot (Napa)
Opus One (Napa)
Paloma Merlot (Spring Mountain)
Paoletti (Napa)
Joseph Phelps Backus Vineyard (Napa)
Plumpjack Reserve (Napa)
Pride Mountain Cabernet Franc (Napa)
Pride Mountain Vineyards (Napa)
Reverie Diamond Mountain (Napa)
Reverie Special Reserve Proprietary Red Wine (Napa)
Saddleback Cellars (Napa)
Saddleback Cellars Venge Family Reserve Merlot (Napa)
St. Francis Reserve (Sonoma)
St. Francis Merlot Reserve (Sonoma)
St. Jean Estate (Sonoma)
St. Jean Merlot Reserve (Sonoma)
Santa Cruz Mountain Merlot (Santa Ynez)
Seavey Merlot (Napa)
Selene Merlot (Napa)
Shafer Merlot (Napa)
Signorello Founder's Reserve (Napa)
Silver Oak (Alexander Valley)
Silverado Limited Reserve (Napa)
Simi Reserve (Sonoma)
Château Souverain Winemaker's Reserve (Sonoma)
Spring Mountain Estate (Napa)
Spring Mountain Mirabelle Alba Chevalier Proprietary Red Wine (Napa)
Spring Mountain La Perla Chevalier Proprietary Red Wine (Napa)
Staglin (Napa)
Stags Leap Cask 23 Proprietary Red Wine (Napa)
Stags Leap Fay Vineyard (Napa)
Stonefly Cabernet Franc (Napa)
Stonestreet Christopher's Vineyard (Sonoma)
Stonestreet Legacy Proprietary Red Wine (Alexander Valley)
Stonestreet Three Block Vineyard (Sonoma)
Viader Proprietary Red Wine (Napa)
Vine Cliff Cellars (Napa)
Vineyard 29 (Napa)

Von Strasser Diamond Mountain (Napa)
Von Strasser Diamond Mountain Reserve
  (Napa)
White Rock Claret Proprietary Red Wine
  (Napa)

Whitehall Lane Leonardi Vineyard
  (Napa)
Whitehall Lane Morisoli (Napa)
Whitehall Lane Reserve (Napa)

* * * (GOOD)

Ahlgren Bates Ranch (Santa Cruz)
Ahlgren Besson Vineyard (Santa Cruz)
Alexander Valley (Sonoma)
Amizetta Vineyards (Napa)
S. Anderson (Napa)
Arrowood Merlot (Sonoma)
Barnett Spring Mountain (Napa)
Beaulieu Cabernet Sauvignon Private
  Reserve (Napa)
Benziger (Glen Ellen)
Benziger Tribute (Glen Ellen)
Beringer Knights Valley (Napa)
Boeger (El Dorado)
Boeger Merlot (El Dorado)
Brutocao Albert Vineyard (Mendocino)
Brutocao Merlot (Mendocino)
Buehler (Napa)***/****
Burgess Cellars Vintage Selection (Napa)
Cain Cellars Cain Five Proprietary Red
  Wine (Napa)
Cain Cellars Merlot (Napa)
Carmenet Proprietary Red Wines (Sonoma)
Caymus (Napa)
Chalk Hill (Sonoma)
Chimney Rock (Napa)
Cinnabar (Santa Cruz)
Clos du Bois (Sonoma)
Clos du Bois Briarcrest (Sonoma)
Clos du Bois Marlstone (Sonoma)
Clos du Bois Merlot (Sonoma)
Clos Pegase (Napa)
Clos Pegase Merlot (Napa)
Clos du Val Merlot (Napa)
Clos du Val Reserve (Napa)
Cloverdale Ranch Estate (Alexander
  Valley)
B. R. Cohn Olive Hill Vineyard (Sonoma)
Corison (Napa)
Cosentino (Napa)
Cuvaison (Napa)
Cuvaison Merlot (Napa)
Dry Creek Meritage (Sonoma)
Duckhorn (Napa)
Duckhorn Merlot (Napa)

Duckhorn Merlot 3 Palms Vineyard (Napa)
Durney Reserve (Monterey)
Eberle (Paso Robles)
Elyse Morisoli Vineyard (Napa)
Estancia (Alexander Valley)
Estancia Meritage Proprietary Red Wine
  (Alexander Valley)
Estancia Merlot (Alexander Valley)
Far Niente (Napa)
Gary Farrell (Sonoma)
Gary Farrell Ladi's Vineyard (Sonoma)
Gary Farrell Merlot Ladi's Vineyard
  (Sonoma)
Franciscan Meritage Oakville Estate
  (Napa)
Franciscan Merlot (Napa)
Franciscan Oakville Estate (Napa)
Frog's Leap (Napa)
Frog's Leap Merlot (Napa)
Gainey Cabernet Franc (Santa Barbara)
Gainey Cabernet Franc Limited Selection
  (Santa Ynez)
Gainey Merlot Limited Selection (Santa
  Barbara)
E. & J. Gallo Estate (Sonoma)
Gallo Frei Ranch (Sonoma)
Geyser Peak Estate Reserve (Sonoma)
Geyser Peak Reserve Alexandre
  Proprietary Red Wine (Sonoma)
Grgich Hills Merlot (Napa)
Groth Merlot (Napa)
Groth Reserve (Napa)
Gundlach-Bundschu Cabernet Franc
  (Sonoma)
Harrison Winery (Napa)
Havens Wine Cellar Merlot (Napa)
Heitz (Napa)
Heitz Bella Oaks (Napa)
Hess Collection (Napa)
Hess Collection Reserve (Napa)
Husch (Mendocino)
Husch Estate La Ribera (Mendocino)
Iron Horse Cabernets Proprietary Red
  Wine (Sonoma)

Johnson-Turnbull (Napa)
Johnson-Turnbull Vineyard Selection 67
  (Napa)
Jordan (Sonoma)
Justin Cabernet Franc (Paso Robles)
Justin Cabernet Sauvignon (Paso Robles)
Justin Isosceles Proprietary Red Wine
  (Paso Robles)
Justin Merlot (Paso Robles)
Kalin Cellars Reserve (Marin)
Robert Keenan (Napa)
Robert Keenan Merlot (Napa)
Kendall-Jackson Grand Reserve
  (California) (since 1991)
Kathryn Kennedy (Santa Clara)
Kenwood (Sonoma)
Kenwood Artists Series (Sonoma)
Kenwood Jack London Vineyard (Sonoma)
Klein Vineyards (Santa Cruz)
Livingston Moffett Vineyard (Napa)
Long (Napa)
Longoria (Santa Ynez)
Longoria Cabernet Franc (Santa Ynez)
Longoria Merlot (Santa Ynez)
Maacama Creek Melim Vineyard (Sonoma)
Madrone (El Dorado)
Madrone Cabernet Franc (El Dorado)
Madrone Quintet Reserve Red Table Wine
  (El Dorado)
Michel-Schlumberger (Dry Creek)
Robert Mondavi Napa (Napa)
Robert Mondavi Oakville Unfiltered (Napa)
Château Montelena Calistoga Cuvée (Napa)
Monticello Cellars Corley Reserve (Napa)
Monticello Cellars Jefferson Cuvée (Napa)
Monticello Cellars Merlot (Napa)
Mount Eden (Santa Clara)
Murphy-Goode Merlot (Sonoma)
Murrieta's Well Vendimia Proprietary Red
  Wine (Livermore)
Napa Ridge (Napa)
Nelson Estate Cabernet Franc (Napa)
Newton Claret (Napa)
Oakville Ranch (Napa)
Page Mill Volker Eisele Vineyard (Napa)
J. Pedroncelli Reserve (Sonoma)
Robert Pepi Vine Hill Ranch (Napa)
Joseph Phelps (Napa)
Joseph Phelps Merlot (Napa)
Pine Ridge Andrus Reserve (Napa)
Pine Ridge Howell Mountain (Napa)

Pine Ridge Merlot (Napa)
Pine Ridge Rutherford Cuvée (Napa)
Pine Ridge Stags Leap District (Napa)
Plumpjack Estate (Napa)
A. Rafanelli (Sonoma)
Rancho Sisquoc Cabernet Franc (Santa
  Barbara)
Rancho Sisquoc Cellar Select Red Estate
  (Santa Maria)
Rancho Sisquoc Estate (Santa Barbara)
Rancho Sisquoc Merlot Estate (Santa
  Barbara)
Ravenswood (Sonoma)
Ravenswood Merlot Sangiacomo (Sonoma)
Ravenswood Merlot Vintner's Blend (North
  Coast)
Ravenswood Pickberry Proprietary Red
  Wine (Sonoma)
Raymond Private Reserve (Napa)
Renaissance (Yuba)
Ridge Santa Cruz (Santa Clara)
Ritchie Creek (Napa)
Rocking Horse (Napa)
Rockland (Napa)
Rubicon Proprietary Red Wine (Napa)
St. Clement (Napa) (since 1991)
St. Clement Oroppas (Napa)
St. Francis Merlot (Sonoma)
Santa Cruz Mountain Bates Ranch (Santa
  Cruz)
Sebastiani single-vineyard *cuvées* (Sonoma)
Signorello Unfined/Unfiltered (Napa)
Silverado (Napa)
Silverado Merlot (Napa)
Simi (Sonoma)
Château Souverain (Sonoma)
Château Souverain Merlot (Sonoma)
Spring Mountain Estate Miravalle Vineyard
  (Napa)
Stags Leap Wine Cellars (Napa)
Stags Leap Wine Cellars Stags Leap
  Vineyard (Napa)
Sterling Diamond Mountain Ranch (Napa)
Stonestreet (Alexander Valley)
Stonestreet Merlot (Alexander Valley)
Swanson (Napa)
Swanson Merlot (Napa)
The Terraces (Napa)
Trefethen Reserve (Napa)
Trentadue (Sonoma)
Trentadue Merlot (Sonoma)

Truchard Merlot (Napa)
Tudal (Napa)
Tulocay Cliff Vineyard (Napa)
Villa Mt. Eden Signature Series
  (Mendocino)

Whitehall Lane (Napa)
Whitehall Lane Merlot Summer's Ranch
  (Alexander Valley)
ZD Estate (Napa)

* * (AVERAGE)

Alexander Valley Vineyard Merlot
  (Sonoma)**/***
Bargetto (Santa Cruz)
Beaulieu Beau Tour (Napa)
Beaulieu Rutherford (Napa)
Del Arbors (California)
Bel Arbors Merlot (California)
Belvedere Wine Co. (Sonoma)
Belvedere Wine Co. Merlot (Sonoma)
Benziger Merlot (Glen Ellen)
Brander Bouchet Proprietary Red Wine
  (Santa Ynez)
Buena Vista Carneros (Sonoma)
Buena Vista Private Reserve (Sonoma)
Buttonwood Farm Merlot (Santa Ynez)
Cafaro (Napa)
Cafaro Merlot (Napa)
Chappellet (Napa)
Chappellet Merlot (Napa)
Clos Pegase Merlot (Napa)
Clos du Val (Napa)
B. R. Cohn Merlot (Sonoma)
Conn Creek (Napa)
Coturri Jessandre Vineyard (Sonoma)
Coturri Merlot Feingold Vineyard (Sonoma)
Coturri Remick Ridge Vineyard (Sonoma)
Coturri View's Land Vineyard (Sonoma)
Creston Manor (San Luis Obispo)
Cronin (Santa Cruz)
Cutler Cellar (Sonoma)
De Loach (Sonoma)
De Moor (Napa)
Dry Creek (Sonoma)
Durney (Monterey)
Fetzer Barrel Select (California)
Field Stone Alexander Valley (Sonoma)
Field Stone Reserve (Sonoma)
Firestone (Santa Ynez)
Firestone Merlot (Santa Barbara)
Firestone Reserve (Santa Ynez)
Firestone Vintage Reserve Proprietary Red
  Wine (Santa Ynez)
Folie à Deux (Napa)
Louis Foppiano (Sonoma)

Louis Foppiano Fox Mountain Reserve
  (Sonoma)
Freemark Abbey Bosché (Napa)
Freemark Abbey Sycamore (Napa)
Gainey Merlot (Santa Ynez)
Glen Ellen (Sonoma)
Grand Cru Vineyards (Sonoma)
Greenwood Ridge (Sonoma)
Groth (Napa)
Guenoc Beckstoffer Vineyard (Carneros)
Gundlach-Bundschu (Sonoma)
Gundlach-Bundschu Rhinefarm Vineyard
  (Sonoma)
Hagafen (Napa)
Hanna (Sonoma)
Hanzell (Sonoma)
Haywood (Sonoma)
William Hill Gold Label Reserve (Napa)
Jekel Home Vineyard (Monterey)
Jekel Symmetry Proprietary Red Wine
  (Monterey)
Château Julien (Monterey)
Château Julien Merlot (Monterey)
Kendall-Jackson Vintner's Reserve
  (California)
Konocti (Lake)
Konocti Merlot (Lake)
Charles Krug Vintage Selection (Napa)
Lakespring (Napa)
Lakespring Reserve (Napa)
Leeward (Ventura)
J. Lohr Reserve (Santa Clara)
Markham (Napa)
Markham Merlot (Napa)
Louis Martini (Sonoma)
Mayacamas (Napa)
McDowell Valley Vineyards (California)
Meridian Vineyards (San Luis Obispo)
Mirassou (Santa Clara)
Montevina (Amador)
Morgan Winery (Monterey)
Mount Veeder (Napa)
Mount Veeder Meritage Proprietary Red
  Wine (Napa)

Mountain View Winery (Santa Clara)
Murphy-Goode (Sonoma)
Nalle (Sonoma)
Domaine Napa (Napa)
Nevada City (Nevada County)
Newlan (Napa)
Parducci (Mendocino)
Parducci Merlot (Mendocino)
Peachy Canyon (Paso Robles)
Peachy Canyon Merlot (Paso Robles)
Robert Pecota (Napa)
J. Pedroncelli (Sonoma)
Peju Province (Napa)
R. H. Phillips (Yolo)
Château Potelle (Napa)
Preston Vineyards (Sonoma)
Raymond Napa (Napa)
Raymond Private Reserve (Napa)
Rocking Horse Claret (Napa)
Rombauer (Napa)
Rombauer Merlot (Napa)
Roudon-Smith (Santa Cruz)
Round Hill (Napa)
Round Hill Reserve (Napa)
Rutherford Hill (Napa)
St. Supery (Napa)
Santa Barbara Winery (Santa Barbara)
Santa Ynez Cabernet Sauvignon Port
   (Santa Ynez)
Sarah's Vineyard Merlot (Santa Clara)
V. Sattui (Napa)
Sebastiani regular *cuvées* (Sonoma)
Seghesio (Sonoma)

Sequoia Grove (Napa)
Sequoia Grove Estate (Napa)
Shenandoah Vineyards Amador (Amador)
Sierra Vista (El Dorado)
Silverado (Napa)
Robert Sinsky Claret (Sonoma)
Smith and Hook Merlot (Santa Lucia)
Stags Leap Winery Napa (Napa)
Steltzner (Napa)
Steltzner Merlot (Napa)
Sterling Merlot (Napa)
Sterling Napa (Napa)
Sterling Reserve Proprietary Red Wine
   (Napa)
Stevenot (Calaveras)
Stone Creek (Napa)
Stonegate (Napa)
Stonegate Merlot (Napa)
Stratford (California)
Rodney Strong Alexander's Crown
   (Sonoma)
Sullivan (Napa)
Sullivan Merlot (Napa)
Sutter Home (Napa)
Ivan Tamas (Livermore)
Tobin James (Paso Robles)
Villa Mt. Eden California (Napa)
Villa Mt. Eden Cellar Select (Napa)
Villa Zapu (Napa)
Weinstock Cellars (Sonoma)
Wellington Vineyards (Sonoma)
Wild Horse (San Luis Obispo)
J. Wile and Sons (California)

RATING CALIFORNIA'S BEST PRODUCERS OF CHARDONNAY

* * * * * *(OUTSTANDING)*

Arrowood Reserve Speciale Michel
   Berthoud (Sonoma)
Beringer Private Reserve (Napa)
Beringer Sbragia Select (Napa)
Brewer-Clifton Katherine's Vineyard (Santa
   Maria)
Brewer-Clifton Marcella's Vineyard (Santa
   Maria)
Brewer-Clifton Sweeney Canyon (Santa
   Maria)
Cuvaison ATS Selection (Carneros)
Ferrari-Carano Reserve (Sonoma)
Fisher Whitney's Vineyard (Sonoma)
Kalin Cellars Cuvée LD (Sonoma)

Kalin Cellars Cuvée W (Livermore)
Kendall-Jackson Clark Vineyard
   (Monterey)
Kendall-Jackson Durell (Sonoma)
Kistler Vineyards Camp Meeting Ridge
   (Sonoma)
Kistler Vineyards Cuvée Cathleen
   (Sonoma)
Kistler Vineyards Durell Vineyard
   (Sonoma)
Kistler Vineyards Dutton Ranch (Sonoma)
Kistler Vineyards Hudson Vineyard
   E-Block (Sonoma)
Kistler Vineyards Kistler Estate (Sonoma)

Kistler Vineyards McCrea Vineyard (Sonoma)
Kistler Vineyards Vine Hill Road (Sonoma)
Kongsgaard (Napa)
Landmark Demaris Reserve (Sonoma)
Landmark Lorenzo Vineyard (Sonoma)
Littorai Mays Canyon (Sonoma)
Littorai Thieriot Vineyard (Sonoma)
Marcassin Marcassin Vineyard (Sonoma)
Marcassin Upper Barn Alexander Valley Estate (Sonoma)
Martinelli Charles Ranch (Sonoma Coast)
Martinelli Martinelli Road (Sonoma Coast)
Martinelli Woolsey Road (Sonoma Coast)
Peter Michael Belle Côte (Sonoma)
Peter Michael Clos du Ciel (Sonoma)
Peter Michael Cuvée Indigene (Sonoma)
Peter Michael Mon Plaisir (Sonoma)
Peter Michael Point Rouge (Sonoma)
Mount Eden Vineyards Santa Cruz Estate (Santa Clara)
Newton Unfiltered (Napa)
Neyers El Novillero (Carneros)

Neyers Thieriot (Sonoma Coast)
Ojai Sanford and Benedict Vineyard (Santa Barbara)
Ojai Talley Reserve (Arroyo Grande)
Pahlmeyer Unfiltered (Napa)
Patz and Hall Alder Springs (Mendocino)
Patz and Hall Carr Vineyard (Napa)
Patz and Hall Hyde Vineyard (Carneros)
Joseph Phelps Ovation (Napa)
Ramey Hudson Vineyard (Carneros)
Ramey Hyde Vineyard (Carneros)
J. Rochioli Allen Vineyard (Sonoma)
J. Rochioli River Block (Sonoma)
J. Rochioli South River (Sonoma)
Shafer Red Shoulder Ranch (Napa)
Silverado Limited Reserve (Napa)
Robert Talbott Estate (Monterey)
Robert Talbott Diamond T Estate (Monterey)
Talley Vineyards Rincon Vineyard (Arroyo Grande)
Talley Vineyards Rosemary Vineyard (Arroyo Grande)

* * * * (EXCELLENT)

Anderson's Conn Valley Fournier Vineyard (Carneros)
Arcadian Bien Nacido (Santa Barbara)
Arcadian Sleepy Hollow (Monterey)
Arrowood (Sonoma)
Artesa (Carneros)
Artesa Reserve (Carneros)
Au Bon Climat Bien Nacido (Santa Barbara)
Au Bon Climat Sanford & Benedict Vineyard (Santa Barbara)
Au Bon Climat Talley Vineyard (Santa Barbara)
Bancroft (Napa)
Bannister Allen Vineyard (Russian River)
Byron Estate (Santa Barbara)
Byron Reserve (Santa Barbara)
Calera Mt. Harlan (San Benito)
Cambria Estate Bench Break (Santa Maria)
Cambria Estate Katherine's Vineyard (Santa Maria)
Cambria Estate Reserve (Santa Maria)
Chalone Estate (Monterey)
Clos Pégase Misuko's Vineyard Hommage Reserve (Carneros)
De Loach O.F.S. (Sonoma)

Dumol (Russian River)
Ferrari-Carano (Sonoma)
Fisher Vineyard Coach Insignia (Sonoma)
Fisher Vineyard Paladini Vineyard (Carneros)
Forman (Napa)
Foxen (Santa Barbara)
Gainey Limited Selection (Santa Ynez)
Walter Hansel (Sonoma)
Walter Hansel Cuvée Alyce (Sonoma)
Hanzell Vineyards (Sonoma)
Paul Hobbs Cuvée Agustina (Sonoma)
Paul Hobbs Dinner Vineyard (Sonoma)
Paul Hobbs Kunde Vineyard (Sonoma)
Kalin Cellars Cuvée CH (Sonoma)
Kalin Cellars Cuvée DD (Marin)
Kendall-Jackson Camelot Vineyard (Lake)
Kunde Estate Kinneybrook Vineyard (Sonoma)
Kunde Estate Reserve (Sonoma)
Kunde Estate Wildwood Vineyard (Sonoma)
Landmark Overlook (California)
Longoria (Santa Barbara)

Peter McCoy Clos des Pierres Vineyard (Sonoma)

Merryvale Silhouette (Napa)

Robert Mondavi Reserve (Napa)

Château Montelena (Napa)

Mount Eden MacGregor Vineyard (Edna Valley)

Murphy-Goode Reserve Island Block (Alexander Valley)

Newton (Napa)

Neyers (Carneros)

Neyers (Napa)

Fess Parker Marcella's Vineyard (Santa Barbara)

Patz and Hall (Napa)

Patz and Hall Dutton Ranch (Sonoma)

Pine Ridge Dijon Clones (Napa)

Château Potelle VGS Mount Veeder (Napa)

Ramey Hyde Vineyard (Carneros)

Rancho Sisquoc Estate (Santa Barbara)

Kent Rasmussen (Carneros)

Château St. Jean Belle Terre Vineyard (Sonoma)

Château St. Jean Robert Young Vineyard (Alexander Valley)

Château St. Jean Reserve (Sonoma)

Saintsbury Reserve (Carneros)

Sanford Barrel Select (Santa Barbara)

Sanford Sanford & Benedict Vineyard (Santa Barbara)

Shafer (Napa)

Signorello Vineyards (Napa)

Signorello Vineyards Founder's Reserve (Napa)

Sonoma-Loeb Private Reserve (Sonoma)

Château Souverain single-vineyard *cuvées* (Sonoma)

Steele Durell Vineyard (Sonoma)

Steele Goodchild Vineyard (Santa Barbara)

Steele Lolonis Vineyard (Mendocino)

Steele Du Pratt Vineyard (Mendocino)

Steele Sangiacomo Vineyard (Carneros)

Stonestreet Block 66 (Alexander Valley)

Stonestreet Upper Barn (Alexander Valley)

Stony Hill (Napa)

Robert Talbott Logan (Monterey)

Talley Vineyards (Arroyo Grande)

Testarossa (Santa Maria)

Testarossa Pisoni Vineyard (Santa Maria)

Thunder Mountain Bald Mountain (Santa Cruz)

Thunder Mountain Beauregard (Santa Cruz)

Varner Amphitheater Block (Santa Cruz)

Varner Bee Block (Santa Cruz)

Williams-Selyem Allen Vineyard (Sonoma)

* * * *(GOOD)*

Acacia (Napa)

Adler Fels (Sonoma)

Alderbrook (Sonoma)

Alderbrook Reserve (Sonoma)

S. Anderson (Napa)

Arrowood Domaine de Grand Archer (Sonoma)

Au Bon Climat (Santa Barbara)

Babcock (Santa Barbara)

Bargetto Cyprus (Central Coast)

Beaulieu Carneros Reserve (Napa)

Belvedere Wine Company (Sonoma)

Benziger (Sonoma)

Beringer (Napa)

Bernardus (Monterey)

Brutocao (Mendocino)

Burgess Cellars Triere Vineyard (Napa)

Cain Cellars (Napa)

Calera Central Coast (California)

Canepa (Alexander Valley)

Chalk Hill (Sonoma)

Chimère (Santa Barbara)

Christophe (Napa)

Cinnabar (Santa Clara)

Clos du Bois Barrel-Fermented (Sonoma)

Clos du Bois Calcaire (Sonoma)

Clos du Bois Flintwood (Sonoma)

Clos Pegase (Napa)

B. R. Cohn Olive Hill Vineyard (Sonoma)

Cooper-Garrod (Santa Cruz)

Crichton Hall (Napa)

Cronin *cuvées* (San Mateo)

Cuvaison (Napa)

De Loach (Sonoma)

Dehlinger (Russian River)

Dehlinger Selection (Russian River)

Durney Estate (Monterey)

Edmeades (Mendocino)

Edna Valley (San Luis Obispo)

El Molino (Napa)

Far Niente (Napa)
Gary Farrell (Sonoma)
Fetzer Barrel Select (Mendocino)
Fetzer Sundial (California)
Thomas Fogarty (Monterey)
Folie à Deux (Napa)
Franciscan (Napa)
Frog's Leap (Napa)
Gainey (Santa Barbara)
Gallo Estate (Sonoma)
Geyser Peak (Sonoma)
Green and Red Catacula Vineyard (Napa)
Grgich Hills (Napa)
Guenoc Estate (Lake County)
Guenoc Genevieve Magoon Vineyard
   (Guenoc Valley)
Hacienda Clair de Lune (Sonoma)
Handley (Dry Creek)
Hanna (Sonoma)
Harrison (Napa)
Hess Collection (Napa)
Hess Collection Hess Select (Napa)
Hidden Cellars (Mendocino)
Husch Vineyards (Mendocino)
Iron Horse Vineyards (Sonoma)
Jekel Vineyard (Monterey)
Kendall-Jackson Proprietor's Grand
   Reserve (California)
Kendall-Jackson Vintner's Reserve
   (California)
Kenwood Vineyards Beltane Ranch
   (Sonoma)
Kistler (Sonoma)
Konocti (Lake)
Charles Krug Carneros Reserve (Napa)
Kunde Estate (Sonoma)
La Crema (California)
J. Lohr Riverstone (Monterey)
Lolonis (Mendocino)
Long Vineyards (Napa)
MacRostie (Carneros)
Matanzas Creek (Sonoma)
Meridian Vineyards (San Luis Obispo)
Merryvale Reserve (Napa)
Michel-Schlumberger (Dry Creek)
Robert Mondavi (Napa)
Monterey Vineyards Classic Chardonnay
   (Monterey)
Monticello Cellars Corley Reserve (Napa)
Monticello Cellars Jefferson Cuvée (Napa)
Morgan (Monterey)

Morro Bay (Central Coast)
Murphy-Goode (Sonoma)
Murphy-Goode Reserve (Sonoma)
Napa Ridge (Napa)
Napa Ridge Frisinger Vineyard (Napa)
Napa Ridge Reserve (North Coast)
Navarro Vineyards (Mendocino)
Fess Parker (Santa Barbara)
R. H. Phillips Vineyard (Yolo)
Pine Ridge Knollside Cuvée (Napa)
Pine Ridge Stags Leap District (Napa)
Ravenswood Sangiacomo (Sonoma)
Ridge Santa Cruz Mountain (Santa Cruz)
Rombauer (Napa)
St. Francis (Sonoma)
St. Francis Reserve (Sonoma)
Saintsbury (Carneros)
Sanford (Santa Barbara)
Santa Barbara (Santa Ynez)
Santa Barbara Winery Lafond Vineyard
   (Santa Ynez)
Sarah's Estate (Santa Clara)
Sarah's Ventana Vineyard (Santa Clara)
Sausal Winery (Sonoma)
Seavey (Napa)
Sebastiani single-vineyard *cuvées*
   (Sonoma)
Silverado Vineyards (Napa)
Simi Winery (Sonoma)
Simi Winery Reserve (Sonoma)
Robert Sinsky (Sonoma)
Sonoma-Cutrer Cutrer (Sonoma)
Sonoma-Cutrer Les Pierres (Sonoma)
Sonoma-Cutrer Russian River Ranches
   (Sonoma)
Sonoma-Loeb (Sonoma)
Château Souverain (Sonoma) (since 1990)
Stags Leap Wine Cellars Reserve (Napa)
Steele California (Sonoma)
Sterling Diamond Mountain Ranch (Napa)
Sterling Winery Lake (Napa)
Stratford (Napa)
Stratford Partner's Reserve (Napa)
Rodney Strong Chalk Hill (Sonoma)
Swanson (Napa)
Ivan Tamas (Livermore)
Thunder Mountain Ciardella (Santa Cruz)
Thunder Mountain DeRose Vineyard
   (Santa Cruz)
Marimar Torres (Sonoma)
Trefethen (Napa)

Truchard (Carneros/Napa)

Vine Cliff Cellars Proprietress Reserve (Napa)

Wente Brothers Reserve (Alameda) (since 1988)

Wente Brothers Wente Vineyard (Alameda) (since 1988)

Whitehall Lane Reserve (Napa)

Wild Horse (Central Coast)

ZD (Napa)

* * *(AVERAGE)*

Alexander Valley (Sonoma)

Beaulieu Napa Beaufort (Napa)

Bel Arbors (California)

Boeger (El Dorado)

Bonny Doon (Santa Cruz)

Bouchaine (Los Carneros)

Bouchaine (Napa)

David Bruce (Santa Cruz)

Buena Vista Carneros (Sonoma)

Buena Vista Private Reserve (Sonoma)

Davis Bynum (Sonoma)

Cakebread Cellars (Napa)

Calloway Calla-Lees (Temecula)

Chamisal (San Luis Obispo)

Chappellet (Napa)

Chimney Rock (Napa)

Clos du Val (Napa)

Congress Springs (Santa Clara)

Conn Creek (Napa)

Cosentino (Napa)

Cottonwood Canyon (San Luis Obispo)

Creston Manor (San Luis Obispo)

De Moor (Napa)

Dry Creek (Sonoma)

Eberle (Paso Robles)

Fetzer Bonterra (North Coast)

Firestone (Santa Barbara)

Louis Foppiano (Sonoma)

Fox Mountain Reserve (Sonoma)

Freemark Abbey (Napa)

Freemont Creek (California)

Glen Ellen (Sonoma)

Groth Vineyards (Napa)

Gundlach-Bundschu (Sonoma)

Hagafen (Napa)

Hagafen Reserve (Napa)

Havens (Napa)

Haywood Winery (Sonoma)

William Hill Gold Label Reserve (Napa)

William Hill Silver Label (Napa)

Indian Springs (Sierra Foothills)

Jordan Vineyard (Sonoma)

Château Julien Barrel Fermented (Monterey)

Robert Keenan (Napa)

Lakespring (Napa)

Leeward (Central Coast)

J. Lohr Cypress (Santa Clara)

Markham Vineyards (Napa)

Louis Martini (Napa)

Mayacamas (Napa)

McDowell Valley Vineyards (Mendocino)

The Meeker Vineyard (Sonoma)

Meridian (San Luis Obispo)

Merryvale Vineyards (Napa)

Mirassou (Monterey)

Morgan Reserve (Monterey)

Mount Veeder (Napa)

Mountain View Winery (Santa Clara)

Napa Creek Winery (Napa)

Newlan (Napa)

Obester Winery Barrel Fermented (Mendocino)

Page Mill (Santa Clara)

Parducci (Mendocino)

J. Pedroncelli (Sonoma)

Robert Pepi (Napa)

Château Potelle (Napa)

Quail Ridge (Napa)

Qupé (Santa Barbara)

Raymond (Napa)

Raymond Private Reserve (Napa)

Richardson (Sonoma)

Round Hill (Napa)

Rutherford Hill Jaeger Vineyard (Napa)

St. Clement (Napa)

St. Supery (Napa)

Santa Barbara Winery Reserve (Santa Ynez)

Schug Cellars Beckstoffer Vineyard (Carneros)

Sea Ridge (Sonoma)

Sebastiani regular *cuvées* (Sonoma)

Seghesio Winery (Sonoma)

Sequoia Grove Carneros (Napa)

Sequoia Grove Estate (Napa)

Sierra Vista (El Dorado)

Stags Leap Wine Cellars (Napa)
Sterling (Napa)
Stevenot (Calaveras)
Stone Creek (all *cuvées*) (Napa)
Taft Street Winery (Sonoma)
Tulocay (Napa)
Villa Mt. Eden Grand Reserve (Napa)
Villa Zapu (Napa)

Weinstock Cellars (Sonoma)
Mark West Vineyards (Sonoma)
William Wheeler (Sonoma)
White Oak (Sonoma)
White Oak Limited Reserve (Sonoma)
Whitehall Lane Le Petit (Napa)
Windemere (Sonoma)
Zaca Mesa (Santa Barbara)

RATING CALIFORNIA'S BEST PRODUCERS OF PINOT NOIR

* * * * * *(OUTSTANDING)*

Brewer-Clifton (Santa Maria Hills)
Brewer-Clifton Clos Pépé (Santa Rita
 Hills)
Brewer-Clifton Julia's (Santa Ynez)
Brewer-Clifton Melville (Santa Rita Hills)
Dehlinger Goldridge Vineyard (Russian
 River)
Dehlinger Octagon Vineyard (Russian
 River)
Dehlinger Reserve (Russian River)
Dumol (Russian River)
Adrian Fog Floodgate Vineyard (Russian
 River)
Hartford Court Arrendel Vineyard (Russian
 River)
Hartford Court Dutton Ranch/Sanchietti
 Vineyard (Russian River)
Hartford Court Marin Vineyard (Marin
 County)
Hartford Court Sevens Bench Vineyard
 (Napa/Carneros)
Hartford Court Velvet Sisters Vineyard
 (Anderson Valley)
Kistler Cuvée Catherine (Sonoma)
Kistler Hirsch Vineyard (Sonoma Coast)
Kistler Kistler Vineyard (Russian River)
Kistler Occidental Vineyard Cuvée
 Elizabeth (Sonoma Coast)

Kistler Vine Hill Vineyard (Sonoma)
Landmark Grand Detour Van der Kamp
 Vineyard (Sonoma Mountain)
Landmark Kastania Vineyard (Sonoma
 Coast)
Marcassin Marcassin Vineyard (Sonoma
 Coast)
Marcassin Three Sisters–Lambing Barn
 Vineyard (Sonoma Coast)
Marcassin Three Sisters–Sea Ridge
 Meadow Vineyard (Sonoma Coast)
Martinelli Blue Slide Ridge (Sonoma
 Coast)
Martinelli Martinelli Vineyard Reserve
 (Russian River)
J. Rochioli Reserve East Block (Russian
 River)
J. Rochioli Reserve Estate West Block
 (Sonoma)
J. Rochioli Reserve Three Corner Vineyard
 (Sonoma)
Saintsbury Reserve (Carneros)
Siduri Pisoni Vineyard (Santa Lucia
 Highlands)
Talley Vineyards Rincon Estate (Arroyo
 Grande)
Talley Vineyards Rosemary's Vineyard
 (Arroyo Grande)

* * * * *(EXCELLENT)*

Ancien Poplar Vineyard (Russian River)
Ancien Steiner Vineyard (Sonoma
 Mountains)
Arcadian Pisoni (Monterey)
Arcardian Sleepy Hollow (Monterey)
Au Bon Climat (Santa Barbara)
David Bruce Reserve (Santa Cruz)
Calera Jensen Vineyard (San Benito)
Calera Mills Vineyard (San Benito)

Calera Reed Vineyard (San Benito)
Calera Selleck Vineyard (San Benito)
Cambria Estate Bench Break (Santa Maria)
Cambria Estate Julia's Vineyard (Santa
 Maria) (since 1991)
Cambria Estate Rae's (Santa Maria)
Carmel Road (Monterey)
Conn Valley Vineyards Valhalla Vineyard
 (Napa)

Davis Bynum Le Pinot Rochioli Vineyard
(Russian River)
L'Ecosse Rochioli Vineyard (Russian
River)
El Molino (Napa)
Etude Winery (Carneros)
Etude Winery Adastre Vineyard (Carneros)
Etude Winery Heirloom (Carneros)
Etude Winery Hudson Vineyard (Carneros)
Etude Winery Hyde Vineyard (Carneros)
Gary Farrell Bien Nacido Vineyard (Santa
Barbara)
Gary Farrell Howard Allen Vineyard
(Sonoma)
Foxen Julia's Vineyard (Santa Maria)
Foxen Sanford & Benedict Vineyard (Santa
Barbara)
Franus-Havens Beau Terroir Vineyard
(Carneros)
Gainey Sanford & Benedict Vineyard
(Santa Barbara)
Handley Reserve (Anderson Valley)
Walter Hansel (Russian River)
Paul Hobbs Cuvée Agustina (Sonoma
Mountain)
Iron Horse (Sonoma)
Kalin Cellars Cuvée DD (Sonoma)
Kalin Cellars Cuvée JL (Sonoma)
Kendall-Jackson Arrendell Vineyard
Stature (Russian River)
Kistler Camp Meeting Ridge (Sonoma)
Littorai One Acre Vineyard (Anderson
Valley)
Littorai Savoy Vineyard (Anderson Valley)
Longoria (Santa Ynez)
Mayo Family Winery Sangiacomo Vineyard
(Carneros)
Peter Michael Le Moulin Rouge (Santa
Lucia Highlands)
Robert Mondavi Reserve (Napa)
Morgan Winery Reserve (Santa Lucia
Highlands)
Mount Eden Vineyards Estate (Santa Cruz)
Mount Eden Vineyards Vieilles Vignes
(Santa Cruz)

Robert Mueller Cellars Emily's Cuvée
(Russian River)
Robert Mueller Cellars Ranch 23 (Russian
River)
Robert Mueller Cellars Summa Vineyard
(Sonoma Coast)
Navarro Methode à l'Ancienne
(Mendocino)
Ojai Bien Nacido Vineyard (Santa Barbara)
Ojai Pisoni Vineyard (Santa Lucia)
Patz and Hall (Sonoma)
Patz and Hall Hyde Vineyard (Carneros)
Patz and Hall Pisoni Vineyard (Santa Lucia
Highlands)
Kent Rasmussen (Carneros)
J. Rochioli Estate (Sonoma)
Château St. Jean Durell Vineyard (Sonoma)
Sanford (Santa Barbara)
Sanford Barrel Select (Santa Barbara)
Sanford Sanford & Benedict Vineyard
(Santa Barbara)
Siduri Christian David (Sonoma Coast)
Siduri Garys' Vineyard (Santa Lucia)
Siduri Hirsch Vineyard (Sonoma Coast)
Siduri Muirfield Vineyard (Oregon)
Signorello (Napa)
Skewis Floodgate Vineyard (Anderson
Valley)
Skewis Montgomery Vineyard (Russian
River)
W. H. Smith Hellenthal Vineyard (Sonoma
Coast)
Solitude Sangiacomo Vineyard (Napa)
Stonestreet (Sonoma)
Talley Vineyards (San Luis Obispo)
Lane Tanner Sanford & Benedict Vineyard
(Santa Barbara)
Williams-Selyem Allen Vineyard
(Sonoma)
Williams-Selyem Cohn Vineyard
(Sonoma)
Williams-Selyem Olivet Lane Vineyard
(Russian River)
Williams-Selyem Rochioli Vineyard
(Sonoma)

* * * *(GOOD)*

Au Bon Climat La Bauge Au Dessus Bien
Nacido Vineyard (Santa Barbara)
Au Bon Climat Sanford & Benedict
Vineyard (Santa Barbara)

Au Bon Climat Talley Vineyard (Arroyo
Grande)
Bernardus (Santa Barbara)
Byron (Santa Barbara)

Byron Reserve (Santa Barbara)
Chalone Estate (Monterey)
Chamisal Vineyards Domaine Alfred Pinot
  Noir (Edna Valley)
Chimère (Santa Maria)
Coturri Horn Vineyard (Sonoma)
Dehlinger (Sonoma)
Edna Valley Vineyards (San Luis Obispo)
Ferrari-Carano (Napa)
Foxen (Santa Maria)
The Hitching Post (Santa Maria)
The Hitching Post Highliner (Santa
  Barbara)
The Hitching Post Sanford & Benedict
  Vineyard (Santa Barbara)
Kendall-Jackson Grand Reserve
  (California)
Meridian Reserve (Santa Barbara)
Robert Mondavi (Napa)

Monticello Estate (Napa)
Morgan (Monterey)
Navarro (Mendocino)
Page Mill Bien Nacido Vineyard (Santa
  Barbara)
Saintsbury Garnet (Napa)
Santa Barbara (Santa Barbara) (since
  1989)
Santa Barbara Reserve (Santa Barbara)
  (since 1989)
Santa Cruz Mountain (Santa Cruz)
Robert Sinsky (Sonoma)
Steele Carneros (Sonoma)
Steele Sangiacomo Vineyard (Sonoma)
Robert Stemmler (Sonoma)
Lane Tanner (Santa Barbara)
Westwood (El Dorado)
Wild Horse Cheval Sauvage (Santa
  Barbara)

* * (AVERAGE)

Adler Fels (Sonoma)
Alexander Valley (Sonoma)
Austin Cellars Reserve (Santa Barbara)
Beaulieu Carneros Reserve (Napa)
Bon Marché (Napa)
Bouchaine (Napa)
David Bruce (Santa Cruz)
Buena Vista (Sonoma)
Davis Bynum (Sonoma)
Calera (Central Coast)
Clos du Val (Napa)
Cottonwood Canyon (Santa Barbara)
Cronin (Santa Cruz)
Thomas Fogarty (Santa Cruz)
Gainey (Santa Barbara)
Gundlach-Bundschu (Sonoma)
Hacienda (Sonoma)
Hanzell Vineyards (Sonoma)
Husch (Mendocino)
Charles Krug Carneros Reserve (Napa)
Meridian (Santa Barbara)
Mountain View Winery (California)
Parducci (Mendocino)

Pepperwood Springs (Mendocino)
Richardson (Sonoma)
Roudon-Smith (Santa Cruz)
Santa Ynez Rancho Vineda Vineyard
  (Santa Maria)
Schug Cellars Beckstoffer Vineyard
  (Carneros)
Schug Cellars Heinemann Vineyard
  (Napa)
Sterling (Napa)
Rodney Strong River East Vineyard
  (Sonoma)
Joseph Swan (Sonoma)
Truchard (Napa)
Tulocay (Napa)
Tulocay Haynes Vineyard (Napa)
Mark West (Sonoma)
Whitcraft Bien Nacido Vineyard (Santa
  Barbara)
Whitcraft Olivet Lane Vineyard (Russian
  River)
Whitehall Lane (Napa)
ZD (Napa)

RATING CALIFORNIA'S RHÔNE RANGERS

* * * * * (OUTSTANDING)

Alban Vineyard Syrah Lorraine
Alban Vineyard Syrah Pandora's
Alban Vineyard Syrah Reserve

Alban Vineyard Syrah Seymour's
  Vineyard
Araujo Estate Syrah Eisele Vineyard

Behrens and Hitchcock Petite Sirah
    Barcini Vineyard
Behrens and Hitchcock Syrah Alder
    Springs
Calera Viognier Mt. Harlan
Carlisle Syrah
Carlisle Two Acres (blend)
Clos Mimi Syrah Shell Creek
Edmunds St. John Syrah Durell Vineyard
Jade Mountain Syrah Paras Vineyard
Kunin Syrah French Camp Vineyard
Kunin Viognier Stolpman
Lewis Syrah
Martinelli Syrah
Andrew Murray Syrah Hillside Reserve
Ojai Vineyard Bien Nacido
Ojai Vineyard Roll Ranch
Ojai Vineyard Stolpman Vineyard
Ojai Vineyard Thompson Vineyard
Paloma Syrah
Fess Parker Syrah Rodney's Vineyard
    Reserve

Pride Mountain Viognier
Ridge York Creek Petite Sirah
Rockland Petite Sirah
Shafer Vineyards Syrah
Sine Qua Non Grenache/Syrah (the name
    changes with each vintage)
Sine Qua Non Roussanne and Chardonnay
    blends (the name changes with each
    vintage)
Sine Qua Non Syrah (the name changes
    with each vintage)
Tablas Creek Grand Cuvée (blend)
Tablas Creek Reserve Cuvée (blend)
Sean Thackrey Orion (Syrah)
Titus Vineyards
Turley Cellars Petite Syrah Aida
    Vineyard
Turley Cellars Petite Syrah Hayne
    Vineyard
Turley Cellars Petite Syrah Rattlesnake
    Acres

* * * * *(EXCELLENT)*

Arrowood Syrah Saralee's Vineyard
Arrowood Viognier Saralee's Vineyard
L'Aventure Optima Syrah/Cabernet Blend
Babcock Vineyards Syrah Black Label
    Cuvée
Beckmen Grenache Purisima Mountain
Blackjack Ranch Le Mas Rouge
Blackjack Ranch Syrah Estate
Bonny Doon Côte de Lune (blend)
Bonny Doon Vin Gris de Cigare Rosé
Linne Caludo Bone Rock
    (Syrah/Mourvèdre blend)
Linne Caludo Cherry Red (blend)
Linne Caludo James Berry Vineyard
    (blend)
Linne Caludo Willow Red (blend)
Cambria Syrah Tepusquet Vineyard
Cline Cellars Côtes d'Oakley (blend)
Cline Cellars Mourvèdre
Robert Craig Syrah
Culler Syrah
Culler Syrah Mt. Veeder
Dehlinger Syrah Estate
Dehlinger Syrah Goldridge Vineyard
Dover Canyon Rhône Reserve
Edmeades Sirah Eaglepoint
Edmunds St. John Les Côtes Sauvage

Edmunds St. John Mourvèdre
Edmunds St. John Syrah Grand Heritage
Familla Jordon Syrah Que Syrah Vineyard
Ferrari-Carano Syrah
Foxen Syrah Carhartt
Foxen Syrah Morehouse
Garretson Wine Co. Syrah Alban Vineyard
    The Finne
Garretson Wine Co. Syrah The Aisling
Havens Syrah Hudson Vineyard
Havens Syrah Napa
Hug Cellars Grenache Alban Vineyard
J. C. Cellars Petite Sirah Frediani Vineyard
J. C. Cellars Syrah Rodney's Vineyard
J. C. Cellars Syrah Ventana Vineyard
Jade Mountain Les Jumeaux (blend)
Jade Mountain Marsanne
Jade Mountain Mourvèdre
Jade Mountain La Provençale (blend)
Jade Mountain Syrah
Jaffurs Syrah Bien Nacido Vineyard
Jaffurs Syrah Melville Vineyard
Jaffurs Syrah Stolpman Vineyard
Jaffurs Syrah Thompson Vineyard
Justin Syrah Halter
Justin Syrah MacGillivray
Kahn Cuvée Jacques (blend)

Kahn Syrah
Kendall-Jackson Syrah Durell Vineyard
Kongsgaard Syrah Hudson Vineyard
Kunin Syrah Santa Rita Hills
La Jota Petite Sirah
Lewis Cellars Alec's Blend (blend)
Loxton Syrah Timberline Ranch
MacRostie Syrah Blue Oaks
MacRostie Syrah Wildcat Mountain
Marietta Old Vine Red
Marietta Petite Sirah
Andrew Murray Les Coteaux
Neyers Syrah Hudson Vineyard
Novy Cellars Alder Springs (blend)
Novy Cellars Syrah
Novy Cellars Syrah Garys' Vineyard
Novy Cellars Syrah Page-Nord Vineyard
Ojai Vin du Soleil (blend)
Ravenswood Icon (blend)
Renard Syrah Timbervine Ranch

Ridge Grenache Lytton Estate
Ridge Mataro Bridgehead
Ridge Mataro Evangelo Vineyard
Ridge Syrah Lytton Estate
Rosenblum Cellars Petite Syrah Rockpile
  Vineyard
Rosenblum Cellars Syrah England-Shaw
  Vineyard
St. Francis Petite Sirah Barlolozzi Ranch
Spring Mountain Syrah Estate
Tablas Creek Petit Cuvée (blend)
Terre Rouge Syrah Ascent
Sean Thackrey Sirius (Petite Sirah)
Sean Thackrey Taurus (Mourvèdre)
Trentadue Petit Sirah
Truchard Syrah
Turnbull Wine Cellars Syrah
Turnbull Wine Cellars Viognier
Unti Syrah Estate
Zaca Mesa Syrah Black Bear Block

* * * *(GOOD)*

Benziger
Beringer Viognier Hudson Ranch
Bonny Doon Le Cigare Volant (blend)
Bonny Doon Clos de Gilroy (Grenache)
Bonny Doon Old Telegram (Mourvèdre)
Bonny Doon Le Sophiste (blend)
Bonny Doon Syrah
David Bruce Petite Sirah
Cambria Viognier
Castle Vineyard Cinsault
Castle Vineyard Syrah
Coturri Alicante Bouchet Ubaldi
  Vineyard
Coturri Petite Sirah Ubaldi Vineyard
Edmunds St. John El Niño
Edmunds St. John Port o'Call (blend)
Edmunds St. John Viognier
Elyse Coeur de Val
Elyse Nero Misto Proprietary Red Wine
Fetzer Petite Sirah Reserve
Field Stone Petite Sirah
Field Stone Viogner Staten Family Reserve
Fife L'Attitude (blend)
Fife Carignan Red Heard
Fife Syrah
Fife Syrah Yokayo Rancho
Folie à Deux Syrah
Frey Syrah

Guenoc Petite Sirah
Hop Kiln Petite Sirah
Jepson Syrah
Marietta Cellars Petite Sirah
McDowell Valley Vineyards Les Vieux
  Cépages
Fess Parker Mélange du Rhône
Fess Parker Syrah
Joseph Phelps Syrah
Joseph Phelps Vin du Mistral *cuvées*
R. H. Phillips Mourvèdre EXP
R. H. Phillips Syrah EXP
R. H. Phillips Viognier EXP
Preston Faux Proprietary Red Wine
Preston Marsanne
Preston Syrah
Qupé Los Olivos Cuvée
Qupé Marsanne
Qupé Syrah Bien Nacido Cuvée
Qupé Viognier Ibarra-Young Vineyard
Ritchie Creek Viognier
Santino Satyricon (blend)
Shenandoah Serene (blend)
Sierra Vista Fleur de Montagne (blend)
Sierra Vista Lynelle (blend)
Stags Leap Winery Petite Sirah
Joseph Swan Côtes du Rosa Unfiltered
Joseph Swan Vin du Mystère

Swanson Syrah
Bedford Thompson Grenache
Bedford Thompson Mourvèdre
Bedford Thompson Syrah
Treanna (white and proprietary blend)
Trentadue Carignan
Trentadue Old Patch Red (blend)

Trentadue Salute
Wellington Vineyards Côtes de Sonoma Old Vines
Wellington Vineyards Syrah Alegrai Vineyards
Zaca Mesa Cuvée Z (blend)
Zaca Mesa Syrah

* * (AVERAGE)

Alderbrook Syrah Shiloh Hill Vineyard
Christopher Creek Petite Sirah
Christopher Creek Syrah
Duxoup Syrah
Louis Foppiano Petite Sirah
Jory (various cuvées)
Karly Petite Sirah
Meridian Syrah
J. W. Morris Petite Sirah Bosun Crest
Parducci Bono Syrah

Parducci Petite Sirah
Preston Viognier
Roudon-Smith Petite Sirah
Sierra-Vista Syrah
Domaine de la Terre Rouge
Topolos Alicante Bouschet
Topolos Grand Noir
Topolos Petite Sirah
William Wheeler Quintet (Blend)

RATING CALIFORNIA'S BEST PRODUCERS OF ITALIAN-INSPIRED VARIETALS—SANGIOVESE, BARBERA, NEBBIOLO

* * * * (EXCELLENT)

Flora Springs Sangiovese
Il Podere Dell'Olivos Barbera
Il Podere Dell'Olivos Teroldego
Jessandre Vineyard (Sangiovese/Cabernet)
Luna Canto
Luna Pinot Grigio
Luna Sangiovese Reserve
Palmina Barbera Bien Nacido Vineyard
Palmina Sangiovese Stolpman Vineyard

La Pantera L'Uvaggio di Giacomo (various cuvées)
Pride Mountain Vineyards
Saddleback Cellars Venge Family Reserve Sangiovese Penny Lane
Shafer Firebreak (Sangiovese/Cabernet)
Staglin Stagliano
Wild Horse Malvasia Bianca Barrel Fermented

* * * (GOOD)

Beringer Sangiovese
Edmunds St. John Pallini Rosso
Edmunds St. John Pinot Grigio
Ferrari-Carano Siena
Robert Pepi Colline di Sassi
Kent Rasmussen Dolcetto

Kent Rasmussen Sangiovese
Staglin Family Vineyard Stagliano Sangiovese
Swanson Sangiovese
Ivan Tamas Trebbiano
Wildhorse Tocai Fruilano

* * (AVERAGE)

Atlas Peak Sangiovese
Bonny Doon Ca do Solo Il Fiasco
Brindiamo Gioveto
Brindiamo Nebbiolo
Brindiamo Rosso Vecchio
Dalla Valle Pietre Rosso
Konrad Barbera

Robert Mondavi Barbera
Robert Mondavi Malvasia
Robert Mondavi Sangiovese
Mosby Brunello di Santa Barbara Carrari Vineyard
Mosby Moscato di Fior
Mosby Primativo

Preston Barbera
Sebastiani Barbera
Sterling Pinot Grigio
Sterling Sangiovese

Sean Thackrey Pleiades
Trentadue Sangiovese
Westwood Barbera

RATING CALIFORNIA'S BEST PRODUCERS OF SAUVIGNON BLANC, SÉMILLON, AND BLENDS THEREOF

* * * * * (OUTSTANDING)

Araujo Estate Eisele Vineyard (Napa)
Ferrari-Carano Fumé Blanc Reserve
  (Sonoma)
Iron Horse Cuvee Reserve (Alexander
  Valley)
Kalin Cellars Sauvignon Blanc Reserve
  (Potter Valley)
Mason Cellars (Napa)

Peter Michael Sauvignon Blanc l'Apres-
  Midi (California)
J. Rochioli Old Vine Block (Russian
  River)
Château St. Jean La Petite Etoile (Sonoma)
Selene Sauvignon Blanc (Napa)
Simi Sendal Proprietary White Wine
  (Sonoma)

* * * * (EXCELLENT)

Babcock Sauvignon Blanc (Santa Barbara)
Babcock Sauvignon Blanc 11 Oaks Ranch
  (Santa Barbara)
Beringer Alluvium (Knights Valley)
Brander Cuvée Nicolas (Santa Ynez)
Byron Sauvignon Blanc (Santa Barbara)
Cain Cellars Sauvignon Musqué (Napa)
Caymus Conundrum Proprietary White
  Wine (Napa)
Chalk Hill Sauvignon Blanc (Sonoma)
Chimney Rock Fumé Blanc (Napa)
Clos du Bois Sauvignon Blanc (Alexander
  Valley)
Dry Creek Fumé Blanc (Sonoma)
Ehler's Grove Sauvignon Blanc Reserve
  (Napa)
Flora Springs Soliloquy (Napa)
Gainey Sauvignon Blanc Limited Selection
  (Santa Ynez)
Gary Farrell Sauvignon Blanc Rochioli
  Vineyard (Russian River)
Handley Cellars Sauvignon Blanc (Dry
  Creek)
Hidden Cellars Alchemy Proprietary White
  Wine (Mendocino)
Hidden Cellars Sauvignon Blanc
  (Mendocino)
Karly Sauvignon Blanc (Amador)
Kendall-Jackson Sauvignon Blanc Grand
  Reserve (California)
Kenwood Vineyards Sauvignon Blanc
  (Sonoma)

Kunde Estate Winery Sauvignon Blanc
  Magnolia Lane (Sonoma)
Matanzas Creek Sauvignon Blanc
  (Sonoma)
Robert Mondavi Fumé Blanc (Napa)
Robert Mondavi Fumé Blanc Reserve
  (Napa)
Robert Mondavi To-Kalon Estate Reserve
  (Napa)
Murphy-Goode Fumé Blanc Reserve
  (Sonoma)
Navarro Sauvignon Blanc (Mendocino)
Ojai Cuvée Speciale Ste. Helene
  (California)
Page Mill Sauvignon Blanc French Camp
  Vineyard (Napa)
Robert Pepi Sauvignon Blanc Reserve
  (Napa)
Preston Cuvée de Fumé (Sonoma)
Rancho Sisquoc Sauvignon Blanc (Santa
  Barbara)
J. Rochioli Sauvignon Blanc (Russian
  River)
Signorello Sauvignon Blanc (Napa)
Signorello Sémillon Barrel Fermented
  (Napa)
Spottswoode Sauvignon Blanc (Napa)
Stonestreet Upper Barn Sauvignon Blanc
  (Alexander Valley)
Rodney Strong Sauvignon Blanc Charlotte's
  Home Vineyard (Sonoma)

* * * (GOOD)

Adler Fels Fumé Blanc (Sonoma)
Ahlgren Sémillon (Santa Cruz)
Alderbrook Sauvignon Blanc (Sonoma)
Babcock Fathom Proprietary White Wine
   (Santa Barbara)
Beaulieu Fumé Blanc (Napa)
Bel Arbors Sauvignon Blanc (California)
Bellerose Sauvignon Blanc (Sonoma)
Benziger Fumé Blanc (Sonoma)
Beringer Sauvignon Blanc (Napa)
Bernadus Sauvignon Blanc (Monterey)
Brutocao Sauvignon Blanc (Mendocino)
Buena Vista Fumé Blanc (Lake)
Buttonwood Farm Sauvignon Blanc (Santa
   Ynez)
Carmenet Meritage Proprietary White
   Wine (Sonoma)
De Loach Fumé Blanc (Sonoma)
De Lorimer Spectrum Estate (Alexander
   Valley)
Duckhorn Sauvignon Blanc (Napa)
Ferrari-Carano Fumé Blanc (Sonoma)
Fetzer Fumé Blanc (Mendocino)
Fetzer Sauvignon Blanc Barrel Select
   (Mendocino)
Field Stone Sauvignon Blanc (Sonoma)

Geyser Peak Sauvignon Blanc (Sonoma)
Geyser Peak Semchard (Sonoma)
Grgich Hills Fumé Blanc (Napa)
Guenoc Winery Langtry Meritage (Lake
   County)
Louis Honig Cellars Sauvignon Blanc
   (Napa)
Husch Vineyards Sauvignon Blanc
   (Mendocino)
Konocti Fumé Blanc (Lake County)
Lolonis Fumé Blanc (Mendocino)
Monterey Vincyards Classic Sauvignon
   Blanc (California)
Morgan Sauvignon Blanc (Monterey)
Murphy-Goode Fumé Blanc (Sonoma)
Napa Ridge Sauvignon Blanc (Napa)
Page Mill Sauvignon Blanc (San Luis
   Obispo)
R. H. Phillips Sauvignon Blanc (Yolo)
Preston Vineyards Cuvée de Fumé (Dry
   Creek)
Sanford Sauvignon Blanc (Santa Barbara)
Stags Leap Sauvignon Blanc Rancho
   Chimiles (Napa)
Ivan Tamas Fumé Blanc (Livermore)
William Wheeler Fumé Blanc (Sonoma)

* * (AVERAGE)

Davis Bynum Fumé Blanc (Sonoma)
Calloway Fumé Blanc/Sauvignon Blanc
   (Temecula)
Christophe Sauvignon Blanc (Napa)
Clos Pegase Sauvignon Blanc (Napa)
Clos du Val Sémillon (Napa)
Louis Foppiano Sauvignon Blanc
   (Sonoma)
E. & J. Gallo Sauvignon Blanc (California)
Glen Ellen Sauvignon Blanc (Sonoma)
Grand Cru Sauvignon Blanc (Sonoma)
Groth Sauvignon Blanc (Napa)
Jekel Scepter Proprietary White Wine
   (Monterey)
Château Julien Sauvignon Blanc
   (Monterey)
Lakespring Sauvignon Blanc (Napa)

Louis Martini Sauvignon Blanc (Napa)
Mayacamas Sauvignon Blanc (Napa)
Obester Sauvignon Blanc (Mendocino)
J. Pedroncelli Primavera Mista Proprietary
   White Wine (California)
Joseph Phelps Sauvignon Blanc (Napa)
Château Potelle Sauvignon Blanc (Napa)
St. Clement Sauvignon Blanc (Napa)
St. Supery Sauvignon Blanc (Napa)
Santa Ynez Sémillon (Santa Ynez)
Seghesio Sauvignon Blanc (Sonoma)
Shenandoah Sauvignon Blanc (Amador)
Silverado Sauvignon Blanc (Napa)
Simi Sémillon (Napa)
Steltzner Sauvignon Blanc (Napa)
Sterling Sauvignon Blanc (Napa)
Weinstock Sauvignon Blanc (Sonoma)

RATING CALIFORNIA'S BEST PRODUCERS OF ZINFANDEL

* * * * * (OUTSTANDING)

Behrens and Hitchcock (Napa)

Hartford Court Fanucchi-Wood Road (Russian River)

Hartford Court Hartford Vineyard (Russian River)

Martinelli Jackass Hill (Russian River)

Martinelli Jackass Vineyard (Russian River)

Ridge Geyserville Proprietary Red Wine (primarily Zinfandel) (Sonoma)

Ridge Lytton Springs (Sonoma)

Storybook Mountain Reserve (Napa)

Turley Cellars Black-Sears Vineyard (Napa)

Turley Cellars Hayne Vineyard (Napa)

Turley Cellars Moore Vineyard (Napa)

Turley Cellars Vineyard 101 (Alexander Valley)

* * * * (EXCELLENT)

Accorn Heritage Alegria Vineyard (Russian River)

Albini Family Vineyards (Sonoma)

L'Aventure Stephan Vineyard (Paso Robles)

Bannister (Dry Creek)

Robert Bialé Aldo's Vineyard (Napa)

Robert Bialé Monte Rosso (Sonoma)

Robert Bialé Old Crane Ranch (Napa)

Blockheadia Ringnosi (Napa)

De Loach O.F.S. (Russian River)

Edmeades Ciapusci (Mendocino)

Edmeades Zeni (Mendocino)

Franus Brandlin Ranch (Napa)

Franus Pianchon (Contra Costa)

Gallo-Sonoma Chiotti Vineyard (Dry Creek)

Gallo-Sonoma Frei Ranch Vineyard (Dry Creek)

Gallo-Sonoma Stefani Vineyard (Dry Creek)

Green and Red Chiles Mill Vineyard (Napa)

Hartford Court Dina's Vineyard (Russian River)

Hartford Court Highwire Vineyard (Russian River)

Hop Kiln Winery Primativo (Sonoma)

Howell Mountain Beatty Ranch (Howell Mountain)

Howell Mountain Black-Sears (Howell Mountain)

Howell Mountain Old Vine (Howell Mountain)

Kunde Estate Robusto (Sonoma)

Limerick Lane Cellars (Sonoma)

Loxton Priest Ranch Orion Vineyard (Napa)

Loxton Stonestreet Vineyard (Sonoma)

Marietta Cellars (Sonoma)

Marietta Cellars Angeli Cuvée (Alexander Valley)

Mayo Family Winery Ricci Vineyard (Russian River)

Neyers Vineyard Pato Ranch (Contra Costa)

Neyers Vineyard Tofanelli Vineyard (Napa)

Château Potelle Mount Veeder (Napa)

A. Rafanelli (Sonoma)

Ravenswood Belloni–Wood Road Vineyard (Sonoma)

Ravenswood Cooke Vineyard (Sonoma)

Ravenswood Monte Rosso Vineyard (Sonoma)

Ravenswood Old Hill Vineyard (Sonoma)

Ravenswood Old Vines (Sonoma)

Ridge Pagani Ranch (Sonoma)

Rosenblum Cellars Brandlin Ranch (Napa)

Rosenblum Cellars George Hendry Vineyard (Napa)

Rosenblum Cellars Marston Vineyard (Napa)

Rosenblum Cellars Samsel Vineyard (Sonoma)

St. Francis Old Vines (Sonoma)

Saddleback Cellar Old Vines (Napa)

Saucelito Canyon Vineyard (Arroyo Grande)

Sausal Winery (Sonoma)

Sausal Winery Private Reserve (Sonoma)

Seghesio Home Ranch (Alexander Valley)

Seghesio Old Vine (Sonoma)

Seghesio San Lorenzo (Alexander Valley)

Sparrow Lane Demostene Vineyard
  (Sonoma)
Sparrow Lane Howell Mountain (Napa)
Storybook Mountain Eastern Exposure
  (Napa)
Storybook Mountain Estate (Napa)
Storybook Mountain Howell Mountain
  (Napa)

Joseph Swan *cuvées* (Sonoma)
The Terraces (Napa)
Turley Cellars Dogtown (California)
Turley Cellars Duerte Vineyard (Contra
  Costa)
Turley Cellars Tofanelli Vineyard (Napa)
Zoom (Contra Costa)

* * * *(GOOD)*

Amador Foothill Grand Père Vineyard
  (Amador)
Benziger (Sonoma)
Beringer (Napa)
David Bruce (Santa Cruz)
Brutocao Cellars (Mendocino)
Buehler (Napa)
Cakebread Cellars (Napa)
Caldwell Aida Vineyard (Napa)
Caymus (Napa)
Cline (Contra Costa)
Cline Reserve (Contra Costa)
Clos du Bois (Sonoma)
De Loach Estate (Sonoma)
De Loach single-vineyard *cuvées*
  (Sonoma)
De Moor (Napa)
Deer Park (Napa)
Deux Amis (Sonoma)
Dry Creek (Sonoma)
Edizione Pennino (Niebaum-Coppola—
  Napa)
Elyse Howell Mountain (Napa)
Elyse Morisoli Vineyard (Napa)
Gary Farrell (Russian River)
Ferrari-Carano (Dry Creek)
Fetzer Barrel Select (Mendocino)
Fetzer Reserve (Mendocino)
Folie à Deux Old Vine Eschen Vineyard
  (Amador)
Franciscan (Napa)
Frey (Mendocino)
Frick (Santa Cruz)
Fritz (Sonoma)
Frog's Leap Winery (Napa)
Greenwood Ridge Vineyards (Sonoma)
Grgich Hills (Sonoma)
Guenoc (Lake County)
Hidden Cellars (Mendocino)
Hop Kiln (Sonoma)
Jacuzzi Family Vineyard (Contra Costa)

Kendall-Jackson Vintner's Reserve
  (California)
Kenwood Jack London Vineyard
  (Sonoma)
Lake Sonoma Old Vine Reserve (Dry
  Creek)
Montevina (Amador)
Nalle (Sonoma)
Norman (Paso Robles)
Peachy Canyon Reserve (Paso Robles)
Peachy Canyon West Side (Paso Robles)
J. Pedroncelli (Sonoma)
Joseph Phelps (Alexander Valley)
Preston (Sonoma)
Quivira (Sonoma)
Ravenswood Dickerson Vineyard (Napa)
Ravenswood Vintner's Blend (Sonoma)
Renwood (Amador)
Ridge (Paso Robles)
Ridge Dusi Ranch (Paso Robles)
Ridge Howell Mountain (Napa)
Ridge Sonoma (Santa Clara)
Rocking Horse Lamborn Vineyard
  (Napa)
Rosenblum Cellars (Contra Costa)
Rosenblum Cellars (Paso Robles)
Rosenblum Cellars (Sonoma)
Rosenblum Cellars Richard Sauret
  Vineyard (Paso Robles)
Eric Ross Occidental Vineyard (Russian
  River)
Scherrer Old Vines (Alexander Valley)
Scherrer Shale Terrace (Alexander
  Valley)
Schuetz-Oles-Korte Ranch (Napa)
Seghesio Winery (Sonoma)
Shenandoah Sobon Estate (Amador)
Sierra Vista (El Dorado)
Sky Vineyards (Napa)
Château Souverain (Dry Creek)
Steele various *cuvées* (California)

Rodney Strong Old Vines River West
  Vineyard (Russian River)
Summit Lake (Napa)
Tobin James (Paso Robles)
Trentadue (Sonoma)

Wellington Vineyards Old Vines (Sonoma)
Whaler Vineyard Estate (Mendocino)
Whaler Vineyard Estate Flagship
  (Mendocino)
Wild Horse (San Luis Obispo)

* * (AVERAGE)

Bel Arbors (California)
Boeger (El Dorado)
Burgess Cellars (Napa)
Clos du Val (Napa)
Cosentino The Zin (Sonoma)
Coturri Chauvet Vineyard (Sonoma)
Coturri Philip Coturri Estate (Sonoma)
Duxoup Wineworks (Sonoma)
Eagle Ridge Fiddletown (Amador)
Eberle (Paso Robles)
Louis Foppiano Reserve (Sonoma)
Gundlach-Bundschu (Sonoma)
Gundlach-Bundschu Rhinefarm Vineyard
  (Sonoma)
Haywood Winery (Sonoma)
Karly (Amador)
Charles Krug (Napa)
Lolonis (Mendocino)
Mariah Vineyards (Mendocino)
Louis Martini (Sonoma)
Mazzocco (Sonoma)
Meeker Vineyard (Sonoma)
Robert Mondavi (Napa)
Obester (San Mateo)

Parducci (Mendocino)
Roudon-Smith (Santa Cruz)
Round Hill (Napa)
St. Supery Vineyards (Napa)
Santa Barbara Beaujour (Santa Ynez)
Santino Wines (Amador)
V. Sattui Suzanne's Vineyard (Napa)
Sebastiani (Sonoma)
Shenandoah Special Reserve (Amador)
Sonora TC Vineyard (Amador)
Sterling (Napa)
Stevenot (Calaveras)
Sutter Home (California)
Sutter Home Reserve (Amador)
Teldeschi (Sonoma)
Topolos Rossi Ranch (Sonoma)
Topolos Russian River Valley (Russian
  River)
Topolos Ultimo (Sonoma)
Twin Hills Ranch (Paso Robles)
Villa Mt. Eden Cellar Select (California)
Mark West Robert Rue Vineyard
  (Sonoma)
White Oak (Sonoma)

RATING CALIFORNIA'S BEST SPARKLING WINES

Where a producer has been assigned a range of stars (***/****), the lower rating has been used for placement in this hierarchy.

* * * * (EXCELLENT)

Domaine Chandon Reserve Brut (Napa)
Congress Springs Equinox (Santa Cruz)
Maison Deutz Blanc de Noir (San Luis
  Obispo)

Iron Horse cuvées (Sonoma)
Mumm Blanc de Noir Rosé (Napa)
Roederer L'Ermitage (Anderson Valley)
Roederer Estate (Anderson Valley)

* * * (GOOD)

Domaine Carneros (Napa)
Domaine Chandon Blanc de Noir (Napa)
Domaine Chandon Brut (Napa)
Domaine Chandon Etoile (Napa)
Maison Deutz (San Luis Obispo)
Handley (Mendocino)

Monticello Domaine Montreaux (Napa)
Domaine Mumm Brut Prestige Cuvée
  (Napa)
Domaine Mumm Brut Winery Lake Cuvée
  (Napa)
Schramsberg Vineyards cuvées (Napa)

* * *(AVERAGE)*

S. Anderson *cuvées* (Napa)**/***   Richard Cuneo (Sonoma)
Beaulieu Brut (Napa)   Gloria Ferrer *cuvées* (Sonoma)**/***
Domaine Carneros (Napa)   Jordan J Cuvée (Sonoma)
Culbertson Blanc de Noir (Riverside)   Mirassou (Monterey)
Culbertson Brut (Riverside)   Piper Sonoma (Sonoma)**/***
Culbertson Brut Rosé (Riverside)   Scharffenberger Cellars *cuvées* (Mendocino)

ABREU VINEYARDS (NAPA)

1999	Cabernet Sauvignon Madrona Ranch	Napa	EEE	(94–96)
1997	Cabernet Sauvignon Madrona Ranch	Napa	EEE	100
1996	Cabernet Sauvignon Madrona Ranch	Napa	E	98
1995	Cabernet Sauvignon Madrona Ranch	Napa	E	95
1994	Cabernet Sauvignon Madrona Ranch	Napa	E	94

David Abreu is a blue-chip vineyard developer and manager whose portfolio of clients includes many of Napa's superstars: Araujo, Bryant Family Vineyards, Colgin, Harlan, Spottswoode, and future superstars such as Sloan and Blankiet. He has also worked closely with Helen Turley and John Wetlaufer in their vineyard development on the Sonoma Coast. Abreu produces 500 cases of spectacular Cabernet Sauvignon from the Madrona vineyard in St. Helena. His wines are made from extremely ripe fruit, picked between 26–28° Brix, given a cold soak, and aged in 100% new French Taransaud oak until they are bottled with neither fining nor filtration. All of this wine is sold through a mailing list, although some of the country's better restaurants seem to get a small allocation. The blend is 90% Cabernet Sauvignon, 5% Cabernet Franc, and 5% Merlot.

The 1999 Cabernet Sauvignon Madrona Ranch reveals all the hallmarks of a David Abreu wine—an opaque black/purple color resembling vintage port, an exquisite bouquet of blackberries, crème de cassis, licorice, and vanilla, immense body, opulent texture, spectacular depth, and a wealth of fruit and extract. This is another profound Cabernet Sauvignon that should drink well young, but last for 20–25 years.

Although I found it to be exceptional, David Abreu decided to declassify his 1998 Madrona Ranch Cabernet as he did not feel it met the standards set by the 1994, 1995, 1996, and 1997.

The 1997 Cabernet Sauvignon Madrona Ranch is a perfect Cabernet Sauvignon. It has been in the bottle for over a year, and this wine, like all the others, has easily soaked up its aging in 100% new Taransaud barrels. It is a sumptuous, unctuously textured, fabulously concentrated Cabernet Sauvignon that hits all the sweet spots on the palate and puts the olfactory senses into overdrive. The wine smells and tastes perfect. It is a compelling effort that one day will be considered part of a small group of elite California Cabernets that may be rewriting the definition of greatness in Cabernet Sauvignon. The 1997 boasts an opaque black/purple color as well as a gorgeous bouquet of roasted meats, scorched earth, blackberry, crème de cassis, minerals, and toast. The soaring aromatics are matched by a phenomenally intense, seamless palate, with full-bodied opulence, exquisite purity and symmetry, and a multidimensional finish that lasts for nearly a minute. This wine will be delicious when released next year, and will last for 25–30 years. It is a tour de force in winemaking.

The 1996 Cabernet Sauvignon Madrona Ranch reveals a blueberry/blackberry, crème de cassis character with smoky oak, new saddle leather, licorice, dried herbs, and mineral scents. Expansive, with terrific intensity, purity, and overall symmetry, it is one of the top half-dozen wines of the 1996 vintage, but with more noticeable tannin in the finish than either the 1997 or 1998. Anticipated maturity: 2003–2030.

The 1995 Cabernet Sauvignon Madrona Ranch is a strikingly superb Cabernet Sauvignon. Although it includes 5% Cabernet Franc and 5% Merlot in the blend, I would never have guessed that. Aged in 100% new Taransaud barrels (as are all his wines), the 1995 boasts an opaque purple color, in addition to a fabulous bouquet of blueberries, blackberries, cassis, licorice, minerals, and smoky, toasty oak. The wine's aromatics soar from the glass, and in the mouth, the bouquet's promise is fulfilled. A thick, juicy, black fruit character comes across in cascades of fruit, glycerin, and extract. All of this has been buttressed by sweet tannin and good acidity. A voluptuously textured, blockbuster, yet remarkably harmonious wine, it is one of the finest efforts of the vintage. Anticipated maturity: now–2025.

The impressively rich, dense purple 1994 Cabernet Sauvignon Madrona Vineyard exhibits a blueberry/blackberry/cassis-scented nose, with a touch of violets and subtle new oak. In the mouth, the wine has disguised its tannic clout with extraordinary extraction of fruit, medium to full body, and a silky yet powerful personality. It, too, is a 20–25 year wine that can be drunk now or cellared.

These are riveting wines produced by a former *Wine Advocate* "Hero of the Year." Once again, readers' only chance of ever sampling one of these sumptuous Cabernet Sauvignons is to get on David Abreu's mailing list.

Past Glories: 1993 Cabernet Sauvignon Madrona Ranch (95)

ACACIA (NAPA)

1998 Pinot Noir Beckstoffer–Las Amigas Vineyard	Carneros	D	88
1998 Pinot Noir Lee Vineyard	Carneros	D	(88–90)

Winemaking at Acacia is in a transitional stage as the tart, high-acid style (historically, their wines had been excessively acidified) is changing in favor of a more natural, open-knit texture with less acid adjustments. This is particularly noticeable with the 1998s, which will introduce a new, seductive, fleshy, friendlier Acacia. The 1998s were completely destemmed, given a pre-fermentation cold soak of several days, and racked less from barrel to barrel. Most important, they possess more natural textures because of less acidification. This is obvious in the single-vineyard 1998 Pinot Noirs, including the 1998 Pinot Noir Beckstoffer–Las Amigas Vineyard. It possesses excellent density and richness in addition to an open-knit texture and fine purity. The outstanding 1998 Pinot Noir Lee Vineyard is the finest Pinot yet produced by Acacia. Plums, sweet black cherries, animal and foresty aromas can be found in this potentially delicious, medium- to full-bodied, concentrated Pinot Noir.

ALBAN VINEYARDS (EDNA VALLEY)

2000 Grenache	Edna Valley	D	(91–93)
1999 Grenache	Edna Valley	D	90
1998 Grenache	Edna Valley	D	89+
1997 Grenache	Edna Valley	D	90
2000 Pandora	Edna Valley	EE	(92–95)
1999 Pandora	Edna Valley	EE	91
1998 Pandora	Edna Valley	EE	90
2000 Roussanne	Edna Valley	D	(90–92)
1999 Roussanne	Edna Valley	D	89
2000 Syrah Lorraine	Edna Valley	E	(92–95)
1999 Syrah Lorraine	Edna Valley	E	90+
1998 Syrah Lorraine	Edna Valley	E	93
1997 Syrah Lorraine	Edna Valley	D	91
1996 Syrah Lorraine	Edna Valley	D	88+
1995 Syrah Lorraine	Edna Valley	D	90
2000 Syrah Reva	Edna Valley	D	(91–94)

1999	Syrah Reva	Edna Valley	D	90
1998	Syrah Reva	Edna Valley	D	90
1997	Syrah Reva	Edna Valley	D	92
2000	Syrah Seymour's Vineyard	Edna Valley	EE	(92–96)
1999	Syrah Seymour's Vineyard	Edna Valley	EE	91+
1998	Syrah Seymour's Vineyard	Edna Valley	EE	90
2000	Viognier Estate	Edna Valley	D	90

One of the pioneers among California's Rhône Valley varietal movement, John Alban settled into a beautiful hillside location in Edna Valley in 1989 and began planting his vineyard the following year. From a family of doctors, Alban broke with tradition by becoming a viticulturist/oenologist. His impressive apprenticeship résumé ranges from Beaujolais to the northern Rhône. His 60-acre vineyard (which could be expanded to 120 acres) is planted with Rhône varietals save for a tiny block of Chardonnay. Production is 5,000 cases as he sells fruit to some of the best Rhône varietal producers (Manfred Krankl of Sine Qua Non is his most prominent client). Alban's wines are aged in small barrels, larger *demi-muids*, and *foudres* or tanks, blended together, and bottled with neither fining nor filtration. This estate is a reference point for what Rhône varietals can achieve in California. In short, Alban not only talks the talk but walks the walk. Low yields, ripe fruit, meticulous handling, and a non-interventionalistic policy result in stunning wines that go from strength to strength.

When I tasted the 2000s, they had not yet been bottled, but they revealed incredible potential. This may be Alban's finest vintage to date, though it is a tough call given the number of profound wines produced at this site. The barrel-fermented 2000 Roussanne is put through full malolactic with a bit of *bâtonnage*. It exhibits wonderful tension between its honeysuckle, thick, juicy fruit, and crisp, citrusy acids. The wine is full-bodied, dense, and chewy, with plenty of upside potential. If it behaves like a French Roussanne, look for it to drink splendidly well for 2–3 years after bottling, close down, then reemerge a decade later.

Alban Vineyards produces California's finest Grenache. According to John Alban, the key is to pick extremely ripe fruit, since Grenache tends to need high sugars to produce its acid and show its full spectrum of flavors. Hence, sugar readings for Grenache can go as high as 27° Brix. The stunningly rich 2000 Grenache (harvested at one-half ton of fruit per acre) boasts amazing color saturation, a boatload of blackberry and kirsch fruit intertwined with licorice and graphite, and a full-bodied, unctuous texture. This stunning effort should turn out to be one of the best Grenaches ever made in California.

The three Syrah *cuvées* emerge from the Reva Vineyard (a relatively cool site with a lot of clay subsoil), Lorraine Vineyard (named after John Alban's elegant wife; planted on stonier soil with terrific drainage), and Seymour's Vineyard (named after his father). The latter vineyard has considerable chalk; perhaps that explains its great complexity. These are all rich, powerful, formidable Syrahs meant for long-term cellaring. The opaque purple-colored 2000 Syrah Reva possesses a superb texture, rich, concentrated, blackberry and cassis flavors, low acidity, and a long finish. Anticipated maturity: 2006–2015. Even sweeter, fleshier, and more flamboyant is the 2000 Syrah Lorraine. It reveals more glycerin, terrific concentration, and an underlying mineral component no doubt attributable to the stony subsoils. This may be the finest Lorraine yet produced. Anticipated maturity: 2005–2015. The outrageously rich 2000 Syrah Seymour's Vineyard boasts an opaque black/purple color as well as aromas and flavors of blackberry liqueur, crème de cassis, licorice, asphalt, and earth. This fabulous 2000 should age gracefully for 15+ years.

The 2000 Pandora blend (usually a Syrah/Grenache blend) had not been assembled when I visited. Normally, it is composed of the finest lots in Alban's cellars and should be profound. The 2000 Viognier Estate is a lovely, peach/apricot-scented and -flavored, honeyed effort with medium to full body, surprising complexity, and a light gold color. It is a muscular, sizeable Viognier to consume over the next 2 years.

In the significantly cooler 1999 vintage, John Alban has succeeded in producing wines which, while not as powerful as his 2000s, are loaded with concentration. His controversial 1999 Roussanne exhibits a pungent, earthy, honeysuckle, and smoky nose with hints of new oak, hazelnuts, and charcoal in the background. This disjointed effort is still seeking its personality. Look for it to evolve for 3–4 years, perhaps longer.

All three Syrahs are extremely successful for such a cool year. The opaque purple-colored 1999 Syrah Reva reveals notes of bacon fat, cassis, spicy oak, and a Hermitage-like character. It comes from the coolest section of the vineyard, and perhaps that's why it seems the most French-like. There are 700 cases of this *cuvée*, which should age well for 10–12 years. With a more saturated color as well as higher extraction, the 1999 Syrah Lorraine (250 cases) offers a combination of structure, elegance, power, and concentration with beautifully integrated wood, tannin, and acidity. This backward effort requires several years of cellaring, but should age for 12–15 years. There are 150 cases of the 1999 Syrah Seymour's Vineyard. It reveals an opaque purple color along with a classic Syrah nose of blackberry and cassis intermixed with smoky oak, bacon fat, and vanilla. Full-bodied, layered, rich, dense, and smoky, this impressively constituted wine will be at its finest between 2004–2014.

The 1999 Grenache (200 cases) exhibits sweet kirsch and raspberry fruit. Although it possesses less color saturation than the Syrahs, it is sexier, more opulent, and hedonistic. My tasting notes said, "a Pinot Noir on steroids." Drink it over the next 5–6 years for its blast of fruit and glycerin. The 1999 Pandora (a 200-case Syrah/Grenache blend) is packaged in a designer bottle with an exquisite label. It boasts a huge, complex bouquet of minerals, black fruits, licorice, earth, and graphite. There is great fruit on the attack, abundant tannin, full body, and a layered, impressive finish. It should drink well for 12–15 years.

The 1998 Grenache's dense ruby/purple color is accompanied by aromas of overripe black cherries, currants, and blackberries, pepper, and spice. Medium- to full-bodied and pure, it plays it tight to the vest, with excellent weight, depth, and a 20-second finish. This youthful 1998 promises to unfold for 4–5 years and drink well for 10–12.

A dynamite effort, the saturated opaque, murky, purple-colored 1998 Syrah Lorraine offers up aromas of bacon fat, mocha, licorice, and crème de cassis. This full-bodied, unctuously textured, stunningly rich, exuberant, robust, super-endowed Syrah is a total turn-on. Still youthful, it promises to evolve gracefully for 10–12 years. The 1998 Syrah Seymour's Vineyard plays it more closely to the vest. Its opaque ruby/purple color is followed by a dense, chewy, tannic, more backward wine revealing more new oak. While loaded with concentrated blackberry and cassis flavors with hints of smoke and underbrush, it requires 1–2 years of cellaring, and should last for 12–18. The 1998 Syrah Reva reveals a dense ruby/purple color as well as a classic nose of bacon fat, smoke, blackberries, and licorice. Full-bodied and rich, with a vanilla note added to the black fruit and smoke characteristics, this lush, full-throttle Syrah is accessible, but should age nicely for a decade. It is the most supple of the three 1998 Syrahs.

The proprietary Rhône varietal blend, the 1998 Pandora, smells like a barrel sample. Its saturated purple color is accompanied by wild (as the French say, *sauvage*) notes of animal fur and black fruits. Slightly rustic, with more noticeable acidity as well as aggressive tannin, this medium-bodied effort reminds me of a coarse, full-throttle, just-bottled Rhône wine. Give it a year or so to settle down and enjoy it over the next 6–15 years.

I adore the 1997 Grenache. It boasts a dense, dark ruby/purple color as well as textbook Grenache aromas of black raspberry liqueur, cherries, and spice. Full-bodied, concentrated, and mouth-filling, this expansive, chewy, gorgeously rich Grenache can be drunk now as well as over the next decade. Impressive! The black/ruby/purple-colored 1997 Syrah Lorraine offers blackberry, tar, and licorice notes in its moderately powerful aromatics. Thick, rich, full-bodied, and concentrated, with excellent purity, this offering exhibits power, richness, symmetry, and the potential to improve for 10–12 years. The 1997 Syrah Reva displays a more saturated purple color along with an element of *sur-maturité*, the telltale blackberry/cassis fruit, and notes of licorice. Full-bodied, superrich, and impeccably pure, this is an exceptional example of Syrah from Edna Valley. Drink it over the next 10–15 years.

The 1996 Syrah Lorraine has bacon fat and blackberry/cassis fruit flavors, medium to full body, and moderately high tannin in the long finish. It is a well-endowed Syrah, with plenty of grip. If the tannin completely melts away, it will merit a higher score. The superb 1995 Syrah Lorraine displays a saturated dark ruby/purple color, and knockout aromatics consisting of hickory smoke, bacon, and cassis fruit. Opulent on the palate, this full-bodied, concentrated, lush, chewy Syrah has low enough acidity and sweet enough fruit to be drunk now, but it promises to develop nicely for 10–15 years. This is an impressive wine from the "first American winery and vineyard established exclusively for Rhône varieties."

ALBINI FAMILY VINEYARDS (RUSSIAN RIVER)

1999 Zinfandel	Russian River	D	90

An outstanding effort, this dark ruby/purple-colored 1999 Zinfandel exhibits impeccable winemaking, a subtle touch of wood, and loads of concentrated black fruits intermixed with spice, pepper, and underbrush. Full-bodied and chewy, it is best consumed over the next 3–4 years. Surprisingly, the alcohol is listed at only 13.8%.

ANDERSON'S CONN VALLEY VINEYARD (NAPA)

1999 Cabernet Sauvignon Reserve	Napa	E	(87–88)
1997 Cabernet Sauvignon Reserve	Napa	E	91+
1996 Cabernet Sauvignon Reserve	Napa	D	90
1995 Cabernet Sauvignon Reserve	Napa	D	91+
1994 Cabernet Sauvignon Reserve	Napa	D	90?
1999 Chardonnay Fournier Vineyard	Carneros	E	(90–92)
1999 Eloge Proprietary Red Wine	Napa	E	(88–90)
1998 Eloge Proprietary Red Wine	Napa	EE	90
1997 Eloge Proprietary Red Wine	Napa	EE	93+
1996 Eloge Proprietary Red Wine	Napa	EE	90
1998 Pinot Noir Dutton Ranch	Russian River	D	88
1996 Pinot Noir Dutton Ranch	Russian River	D	88
1998 Pinot Noir Valhalla Vineyard	Napa	D	90
1997 Pinot Noir Valhalla Vineyard	Napa	D	90

This is an unheralded but interesting as well as excellent source for Pinot Noir and Burgundian-inspired, powerful, non-malolactic, distinctive Chardonnays. Of course, the father-and-son team of Gus and Todd Anderson built their reputation on their long-lived Cabernet Sauvignon Reserve. It is one of the least flamboyant and ostentatious Cabernets from Napa, and thus purchasers need to possess patience, as I have found that most vintages need a good 4–5 years before they begin to strut their stuff. The Andersons also produce a complex Proprietary Red wine called Eloge, a wine with terrific aromatic dimensions as well as elegant, complex flavors. Production has leveled off at 7,000–8,000 cases. Lastly, their Pinot Noirs are sleepers.

At a vertical tasting in October 2000 of all the Conn Valley Cabernet Sauvignons, most of them were rated even higher than their original scores, which is always a good indication of how naturally made wines can improve in the bottle. These are substantially less flamboyant and ostentatious than some of their peers, and perhaps because of that they get the short end of the measuring stick . . . at least out of the starting gate. In any event, readers who have some of the old Conn Valley Cabernet Sauvignons will probably be pleased with the following ratings given at the vertical tasting: 1987 (90, and still youthful), 1988 (85, and fully mature, possibly drying out), 1989 (88, and fully mature), 1990 (94, and absolutely sumptuous), 1991

(93, opulent, sexy, Pomerol-styled), 1992 (90, tight, youthful, structured, tannic, but promising), 1993 (90?, young, tannic, backward, a bit austere), 1994 (90?, gorgeously opulent, sweet, jammy cassis richness), and 1995 (91+, tannic, but complex, with cedar, tobacco, black currants, but tight and needing 3–5 years of cellaring). As for the 1996 Cabernet Sauvignon Reserve, this wine was showing better than it did immediately after bottling. It may not be as concentrated as the 1995 and 1994, but it is a beautifully made Cabernet with a dark ruby/purple color, copious quantities of cassis fruit, and clean, foresty and loamy soil scents. A low-acid, elegant, flavorful, medium- to full-bodied wine, it can be drunk in 1–2 years, yet promises to evolve for 15.

The Cabernet Sauvignon Reserves are challenging to taste. There is no doubt Bordeaux is the inspiration, but the Andersons do not make the mistake of compromising flavor and intensity just for the pursuit of some New World notion of Bordeaux-like elegance. The deep ruby/purple-colored 1999 Cabernet Sauvignon Reserve exhibits excellent ripeness, restrained aromatics, medium body, and a long, austere finish. If past examples are any indication (and I think they are), this wine, which is aged in about 40% new oak, will deepen and put on weight over the next 2–4 years. The outstanding 1997 Cabernet Sauvignon Reserve ranks alongside such top vintages as 1990, 1991, 1994, and 1995. This full-bodied effort exhibits a deep plum/purple color, high tannin, and gorgeously rich, concentrated, floral, and black currant fruit flavors intermixed with mineral, wood smoke, and spice box. It is what the French would call a serious *vin de garde*. Give it 4–5 years of cellaring; it should keep for 30 years, as these wines are built to last. Anticipated maturity: 2005–2030.

Readers looking for more up-front fruit and a more precocious character should seek out Anderson's Eloge. A complex, Cabernet Sauvignon–based effort with Merlot and Cabernet Franc included in the blend, this 100% new oak–aged wine is made in limited quantities (1,000 cases). The 1999 Eloge (a blend of 69% Cabernet Sauvignon, 18% Merlot, and 13% Cabernet Franc) exhibits a dark ruby/purple color in addition to a complex bouquet of dried herbs, blackberries, currants, blueberries, and toasty oak. An outstanding, complete effort, with a sweet attack as well as a rich, medium-bodied, elegant style, a seamless texture, and a long, concentrated finish, it will last for 12–20 years. The 1998 Eloge (65% Cabernet Sauvignon, 25% Cabernet Franc, and 10% Merlot) possesses a more evolved, complex nose offering sweet black cherry and currant fruit intermixed with earth, graphite, tobacco leaf, cedar, and spice. Medium-bodied, velvety-textured, harmonious, and concentrated, it should drink well for 15+ years. The finest Eloge to date is the 1997. This wine has put on weight since last tasted (a tendency of all of the Conn Valley wines). It reveals a complex, Cheval Blanc–like nose of black fruits intermixed with chocolate, cedar, licorice, and Asian spices. A classic, it is deep, opulent, and medium- to full-bodied, with admirable balance between power and elegance. Possessing exceptional purity, an alluring texture, and a long, smooth finish, it can be drunk now or cellared for 15 or more years. In both the 1996 and 1997 vintages, the Eloge is essentially 65% Cabernet Sauvignon, 25% Cabernet Franc, and 10% Merlot. There are 100 cases of the 1996 and 1,000 cases of the 1997. Now that it has had some time in the bottle, the 1996 Eloge reveals more character. Made in an elegant Bordeaux style, it offers tobacco, cedar, and black currant scents and aromas. This medium-bodied, stylish effort is supple enough to be drunk now, yet should age well for 10–12 years.

The 1994 Cabernet Sauvignon Reserve exhibits a dark ruby/purple color and a tight but burgeoning nose of black fruits, white flowers, and earth. On the palate, it reveals a sweet, spicy, black currant–flavored attack, medium to full body, and strong tannin in the finish. The middle needs to fill out a bit more. Drink it over the next two decades. The 1995 Cabernet Sauvignon Reserve may turn out to be the finest Conn Valley Cabernet since 1990. The wine is the sweetest and richest of recent vintages, with nicely integrated tannin, a dense, deep, ruby/purple color, velvety texture, and the seamless quality possessed by many 1994s. It should drink well for 20 years.

One of the sleeper wines in a portfolio justifiably dominated by high-quality Cabernet Sauvignon is Gus and Todd Anderson's Pinot Noir. The 1997 Pinot Noir Valhalla is holding its own, performing better in late 2000 than it did a year earlier. Although the medium ruby color reveals amber at the edge, the bouquet offers up fragrant, spicy, earthy, complex berry scents intermixed with truffle, cherries, and raspberries. There is good underlying acidity as well as a long finish. Drink this 1997 over the next 6 years. In 1998, Pinots were produced from both the Dutton Ranch and Valhalla Vineyard sites. The 1998 Pinot Noir Dutton Ranch offers cherry, root beer, and smoky aromas, followed by a ripe, easygoing, soft, supple texture. It is on a fast evolutionary track, and is best drunk over the next 3–4 years, given its light ruby color and superficial charm and richness. More significant is the 1998 Pinot Noir Valhalla Vineyard. This wine reveals a dark ruby color as well as a sexy, up-front nose of jammy strawberries, cherries, and black raspberries intermixed with toasty new oak. Heady and fleshy, with tangy integrated acidity and tannin, it should drink deliciously for 3–4 years. The 1996 Pinot Noir Dutton Ranch exhibits a light to medium ruby color, a complex nose, and a sweet inner-palate of berry fruit/cherry with a slight notion of chocolate, strawberries, and Asian spices. This attractive Pinot is best consumed over the next 1–3 years.

The impressive, distinctive Chardonnay sees no malolactic fermentation, and thus it must be sterile filtered. However, it is a powerful, concentrated effort from the Fournier Vineyard in Carneros. There are 1,200 cases of this wine, which spends 18 months in French oak, 12 of which are spent on its lees. The wine seems to have all the character of a big Corton-Charlemagne and gives every indication of being relatively long-lived as California Chardonnays go—5–6+ years. The dazzling 1999 Chardonnay Fournier Vineyard may be the finest the Andersons have yet made. Revealing a liquid minerality as well as honey, pineapple, pear, citrus oil, and smoke, it is a full-bodied, intense effort with refreshing, lively acidity.

Past Glories: 1993 Cabernet Sauvignon Reserve (90+), 1993 Eloge Proprietary Red Wine (90), 1992 Cabernet Sauvignon Reserve (92), 1991 Cabernet Sauvignon Reserve (93), 1990 Cabernet Sauvignon Reserve (93)

ARAUJO ESTATE WINES (NAPA)

1999	Cabernet Sauvignon Eisele Vineyard	Napa	EEE	(92–95)
1998	Cabernet Sauvignon Eisele Vineyard	Napa	EEE	92
1997	Cabernet Sauvignon Eisele Vineyard	Napa	EEE	92
1996	Cabernet Sauvignon Eisele Vineyard	Napa	EE	94
1995	Cabernet Sauvignon Eisele Vineyard	Napa	EE	98
1994	Cabernet Sauvignon Eisele Vineyard	Napa	E	95
1999	Sauvignon Blanc	Napa	D	89
1999	Syrah Eisele Vineyard	Napa	E	(92–94)
1998	Syrah Eisele Vineyard	Napa	E	89
1996	Syrah Eisele Vineyard	Napa	E	92
1995	Syrah Eisele Vineyard	Napa	E	97
1994	Syrah Eisele Vineyard	Napa	E	98+

This reference point winery is always one of my favorite stops in northern California. I have been an admirer of the Eisele Vineyard Cabernet Sauvignons since I first tasted the 1974 Conn Creek Eisele. It has been inspiring to see how proprietors Daphne and Bart Araujo have taken this superb *terroir* and built it into a world-class winery and vineyard operation, producing not only spectacular Cabernet Sauvignon but fabulous Syrah and excellent Sauvignon Blanc. One of the more newsworthy stories out of Napa Valley is that famed globe-traveling Pomerol oenologist Michel Rolland was brought in to do consulting work with what is already a talented winemaking team at Araujo. The 1997 Cabernet Sauvignon Eisele Vineyard is a beauty. The healthy ruby/purple color is followed by classic, unevolved but promising aromas of minerals, cedar, smoke, and black currants. The wine is medium- to full-bodied, with admirable purity, a sweet, lush mid-palate, and ripe tannin in the finish. The top-notch 1997 is a more classic, restrained effort than the evolved and flamboyant 1996 as well as the nearly perfect 1995. Anticipated maturity: now–2020. The 1998 Cabernet Sauvignon Eisele Vineyard was bottled earlier than usual as this vintage is not as massive or concentrated as its predecessors. To my palate, the 1998 is as good as the 1997, although I am not convinced it will be as long-lived. There are 2,300 cases of this 90% Cabernet Sauvignon, 7% Petit Verdot, and 3% Cabernet Franc blend. It is supple and elegant, with a complex, evolved bouquet of smoke, black currants, spice box, and cedar. In the mouth, the wine is forward with sweet tannin, gorgeously rich, concentrated fruit, and impressively integrated acidity and tannin. Drink this alluring charmer now and over the next 12–15 years. The 1999 Cabernet Sauvignon Eisele Vineyard appears to be the finest produced by Araujo since their 1995 and 1996. An opaque purple color is accompanied by a sweet nose of crème de cassis intertwined with liquid minerals, flowers, and black fruits. With superb richness, velvety tannin, full body, and a nicely layered, well-textured mid-palate and finish, this is a stupendous effort. The brilliant use of oak adds a subtle toasty note to this impressively endowed Cabernet. It appears to be one of the stars of the vintage. Anticipated maturity: 2003–2025+. The saturated purple-colored 1996 Cabernet Sauvignon Eisele Vineyard offers an attractive nose of black fruits intermixed with toast, minerals, subtle tar, and wood smoke. Full-bodied, with impressive purity, a multilayered mid-palate and finish, it is an expressive, pure, more powerful, and larger-boned wine than either the 1997 or 1998. At this stage, the 1996 would appear to be the slowest to evolve.

I believe the 1995 Cabernet Sauvignon Eisele Vineyard is the finest produced under the Araujo regime. It is close to perfection. The wine combines extraordinary power and richness with remarkable complexity and finesse. The saturated purple/black color is followed by aromas of sweet vanilla intermixed with riveting scents of black currants, minerals, exotic spices, coffee, and toast. There is nothing garish about this subtle yet powerful giant of a wine. A Napa Valley classic, it is full-bodied and extremely rich, yet retains its sense of balance and symmetry. This fabulous Cabernet Sauvignon should age effortlessly for 30 or more years. Anticipated maturity: now–2030. The 1994 Cabernet Sauvignon Eisele Vineyard exhibits an impressively saturated dark purple color. Although slightly less powerful than the 1993 and marginally less concentrated than the 1995, the 1994 is still a profoundly rich, silky-textured wine with an uncanny balance between its smooth tannin and layers of cassis and blackberry/mineral-tinged fruit. This wine is particularly impressive if it is first decanted for 45 or so minutes. It will age well for 15–20 years.

Araujo produces approximately 350 cases of Syrah from their estate vineyards. The 1998 Syrah Eisele Vineyard is a soft, supple-textured, opulent, civilized effort that can be drunk now as well as over the next 8–10 years. Not a blockbuster, it is elegantly rendered, pure, and filled with blackberry/cassis fruit as well as a hint of honeysuckle provided by 8% Viognier in the blend. A potentially superb effort, the 1999 Syrah Eisele Vineyard includes 5% Viognier. It reveals a complex, classic pepper, crème de cassis, blackberry, and bacon fat–scented bouquet. Full-bodied, silky-textured, and crammed with fruit, glycerin, and character, this dazzling Syrah should drink beautifully young, but evolve nicely for at least a decade. Interestingly, the Araujos decided to declassify their 1997 Syrah, which had shown well last year. The 1996 Syrah Eisele Vineyard (350 cases) is a full-bodied, brawny wine revealing the telltale peppery, blackberry, and cassis scents that seem so easy to obtain with this varietal in California. It is rich and pure, with sweet tannin and plenty of power harnessed in a symmetrical, large-scaled effort that is not without considerable elegance for its mass and volume. This wine can be drunk now, but should be even better with 2–3 years of cellaring, and should last for 15 or more years.

The spectacular 1995 Syrah Eisele Vineyard is one of the greatest New World Syrahs I have ever tasted. Approximately 300 cases were made, and it is even better out of bottle than it was in barrel. The color is an opaque purple. The bouquet offers explosive notes of wood fire, licorice, jammy blackberries, and cassis, in addition to the unmistakable scent of black truffles/licorice. Full-bodied and rich, with sensational flavor extraction, remarkable harmony, and a 35+-second finish, this is a profoundly great Syrah. While it is approachable, it will not reach full maturity for another 7–8 years; it will keep for three decades. Wow!

The 1994 Syrah Eisele Vineyard (which is blended with 8% Viognier) may be the single greatest Syrah yet produced in California. The wine exhibits an opaque purple color, followed by a fabulous nose of black fruits, pepper, minerals, and a subtle whiff of Viognier's honeysuckle fruit. It is magnificent on the palate, with massive richness yet, remarkably, no heaviness or coarseness. It is a tour de force in winemaking. Drink it from now–2009.

Lastly, readers should not forget the delicious Sauvignon Blanc produced at Araujo. Some Viognier is included in the blend (10% in 1999) and the wine is partially barrel-fermented (20%). The 1999 Sauvignon Blanc is an elegant, distinctive effort with abundant quantities of mango, passion fruit, grapefruit, and honeysuckle in its complex bouquet. Medium-bodied, dry, crisp, and zesty, it will be a terrific foil for Asian cuisine. Drink this beauty over the next year.

At this high level, it will be interesting to see if Michel Rolland is able to ratchet up the quality. Araujo Estate Wines is another estate where readers should try to get on the mailing list, or at least on the waiting list for the mailing list!

Past Glories: 1993 Cabernet Sauvignon Eisele Vineyard (96), 1992 Cabernet Sauvignon Eisele Vineyard (95), 1991 Cabernet Sauvignon Eisele Vineyard (96)

ARMIDA (DRY CREEK)

1999 Zinfandel Poizin	Dry Creek	E	88

A legitimate debate can be raised concerning whether the lavishly packaged (a designer bottle with a red skull and crossbones packaged in a casket-shaped box) 1999 Poizin is worth $32 more than Armida's regular *cuvée*. It is unquestionably creative, as well as a show-stopping conversation piece. The 1999 Zinfandel Poizin (according to the label, a "wine to die for") offers up aromas of crushed black pepper, soil, berries, and black cherries. Rich and medium- to full-bodied, it reveals underlying Côtes du Rhône–like notes of Provençal herbs and earth. Drink this pure, ripe Zinfandel over the next 3–4 years. In all honesty, the price would appear to be more fatal than the wine.

ARROWOOD (SONOMA)

1999	Cabernet Sauvignon	Sonoma	D	(87–88)
1997	Cabernet Sauvignon	Sonoma	D	90
1996	Cabernet Sauvignon	Sonoma	D	89
1995	Cabernet Sauvignon	Sonoma	D	91
1994	Cabernet Sauvignon	Sonoma	D	91
1997	Cabernet Sauvignon Reserve Speciale	Sonoma	EE	97
1996	Cabernet Sauvignon Reserve Speciale	Sonoma	EEE	90
1995	Cabernet Sauvignon Reserve Speciale	Sonoma	E	94
1994	Cabernet Sauvignon Reserve Speciale	Sonoma	E	95
1999	Chardonnay	Sonoma	D	89
1999	Malbec	Sonoma	D	(89–91)
1997	Malbec	Sonoma	D	89
1996	Malbec	Sonoma	D	89
1995	Malbec	Sonoma	D	90
1994	Malbec	Sonoma	D	92
1999	Merlot	Sonoma	D	(86–88)
1997	Merlot	Sonoma	D	88

1995	Merlot	Sonoma	D	89
1994	Merlot	Sonoma	D	90
1997	Merlot Reserve Speciale	Sonoma	E	90+
1995	Merlot Reserve Speciale	Sonoma	E	90
1994	Merlot Reserve Speciale	Sonoma	E	92
1999	Pinot Blanc Saralee's Vineyard	Russian River	C	91
1999	Syrah	Sonoma	D	(88–90)
1999	Syrah Saralee's Vineyard	Russian River	D	(91–93)
1998	Syrah Saralee's Vineyard	Russian River	D	90
1997	Syrah Saralee's Vineyard	Russian River	D	94
1996	Syrah Saralee's Vineyard	Russian River	D	95
1995	Syrah Saralee's Vineyard	Russian River	D	95
1994	Syrah Saralee's Vineyard	Russian River	D	96+
1999	Viognier Estate	Sonoma	D	88
1999	Viognier Saralee's Vineyard	Russian River	D	90
1999	White Riesling Hoot Owl Vineyard Special Select Late Harvest	Alexander Valley	D	93

Dick Arrowood sold his winery to the Robert Mondavi Corporation in 2000, but he still controls grape acquisition as well as winemaking. His secondary label, Domaine du Grand Archer, gets better and better, and recent vintages of that Chardonnay have been among the best values from California.

Under the Arrowood Winery and Vineyards label, the 1999 Chardonnay may prove to be outstanding. It is a fruit-driven, steely effort with notions of minerals, tropical fruits, and subtle smoky oak. Medium- to full-bodied, with gorgeous purity in addition to an excellent finish, it emphasizes fruit, balance, and flavor intensity. Consume it over the next 2–3 years. Along with Chalone's Pinot Blanc, Arrowood's Pinot Blanc Saralee's Vineyard is one of the finest made in California. The opulent 1999 (14% alcohol, 100% barrel-fermented and put through 100% malolactic) boasts honeyed orange marmalade, buttered apple, and candied citrus aromas and flavors. Sadly, there are only 380 cases. Dick Arrowood told me it is a hard wine to sell, which is puzzling given the fact that no Californian coaxes more character or flavor from this grape than Arrowood. Both the 1999 Viognier Estate (47 cases) and 1999 Viognier Saralee's Vineyard (211 cases) reveal this varietal's ripe honeysuckle, apricot, and peach characteristics. Both are full-bodied, fun whites to enjoy over the next 6–12 months to take advantage of their fragrant aromatics. Both came in with less than 14% alcohol, not easy for Viognier, but still reveal powerful, fruit-bomb personalities. The Saralee's Vineyard reveals more definition as well as a complex underlying mineral component.

This estate rates 1999 alongside 1994 as one of the two finest red wine vintages of the decade. The 1999 Merlot (85% Merlot and 15% Cabernet Franc) exhibits a dense ruby/purple color in addition to big, thick, melted fudge, cocoa, and jammy cherry aromas and flavors. It boasts a high extract level, sweet tannin, medium to full body, and abundant character. This 1999 should easily merit a score in the upper 80s or higher. The 1997 Merlot offers aromas of espresso, mocha, and berry/cherry fruit, a round, medium- to full-bodied texture, and a pure, concentrated finish. Like all of Arrowood's red wines, it was bottled with neither fining nor filtration. The debut vintage of a luxury Merlot *cuvée*, the 1997 Merlot Reserve Speciale (490 cases), is produced from 100% Merlot that was aged for 28 months in predominantly French oak. It possesses super ripeness, beautiful structure, full body, and a dense, thick, chewy personality with exquisite purity, balance, and palate presence. It will be a sumptuous wine after another 1–3 years of cellaring and should keep for two decades, atypically long for a California Merlot.

Each year, Arrowood fashions about 425 cases of one of California's finest Malbecs. This grape tends to fall on its face in most areas of France, but it has done well in selected areas of California. Good Malbecs are produced by Clos du Bois and Pahlmeyer, but the finest is Arrowood's. He obtains a gorgeous blueberry, blackberry, creamy black raspberry character as well as impressive color intensity, intense flavor concentration, and medium body. The wine appears to be weightier than it actually is, with high levels of fruit, extract, and freshness. The 1999 Malbec (100% Malbec) exhibits a sexy, blueberry/blackberry character presented in a medium-bodied, vivacious, exuberant style. The 1999 will spend 26 months in French oak before being bottled without fining or filtration. The 1997 Malbec (250 cases) offers an intriguing perfume of black fruits, gorgeously pure ripe fruit on the palate, decent tannin and acidity, and a lively personality. This wine should drink well during its first 7–8 years.

The dark ruby-colored 1999 Cabernet Sauvignon (9,500 cases) exhibits abundant quantities of black currants, licorice, and tobacco in its unformed aromatics. Ripe and medium- to full-bodied, it represents an excellent blend of 90% Cabernet Sauvignon, 8.5% Merlot, and 1.5% Cabernet Franc. It should drink well for 10–15 years. The outstanding 1997 Cabernet Sauvignon (a blend of 82% Cabernet Sauvignon, 6% Merlot, 5% Malbec, 5% Petit Verdot, and 2% Cabernet Franc) was aged for 23 months in predominantly French oak, and bottled unfined and unfiltered. A classic Cabernet, it is medium- to full-bodied and harmonious, with copious quantities of black currants, black cherries, licorice, and *sous-bois* (underbrush). Pure, fleshy, and multilayered, this moderately tannic, accessible effort will benefit from 2–3 years of cellaring; it should age for 15–16 years.

It sounds preposterous, but when I put my nose in the 1997 Cabernet Sauvignon Reserve Speciale, it reminded me of the 1996 Latour. California Cabernets are bigger, weightier efforts than most Bordeaux, so the comparison ends with the aromatics. There are 1,611 cases of this profound Cabernet Sauvignon, which spent 28 months in primarily French oak (a tiny bit of American oak was utilized), and was bottled with neither fining nor filtration. Its dense black/purple color is accompanied by layers of cassis, cedar-tinged fruit, and abundant spice. Muscular, with remarkable intensity, purity, and overall symmetry, this larger-than-life, full-bodied, profound, 100% Cabernet Sauvignon will be at its best between 2003–2030.

Along with his neighbor Tom Dehlinger, Dick Arrowood was one of the first Sonoma producers to prove how good California Syrah can be. His Saralee's Vineyard Syrah is blended with a touch of Viognier. A big, full-bodied, creamy-textured offering, it can be drunk young but promises to age well for a decade. For 1999, there were two Syrahs. The 1999 Syrah (950 cases) does not contain any Viognier. This fruit bomb exhibits a dense black/purple color, copious quantities of licorice, cassis, and pepper, full body, an unctuous texture, and a long finish. Although still unformed, it is impressive. The 1999 Syrah Saralee's Vineyard (an 825-case *cuvée* with 5% Viognier included) boasts an opaque purple color in addition to a gorgeous bouquet of cassis, bacon fat, black fruits, and licorice. Typically flamboyant, open-knit, expansive, and rich, with low acidity, this hedonistic effort should drink well young, yet keep for a decade. I underrated the superb 1998 Syrah Saralee's Vineyard (575 cases of a 98% Syrah/2% Viognier blend), which has put on considerable weight. This seductive Syrah offers a smoky, charcoal, blackberry, and cassis-scented bouquet with hints of honeysuckle. Full-bodied and long, with fabulous fruit purity, an opulent texture, and sweet tannin, it should drink well for a minimum of 8–10 years. The dazzling 1997 Syrah Saralee's Vineyard, a blend of 97% Syrah and 3% Viognier, boasts wicked aromatics consisting of roasted meats, black fruits, cassis, and bacon. This succulent, fleshy, flamboyantly styled Syrah is more open-knit and accessible than several previous vintages, but it is full-bodied, low in acidity, and loaded with fruit. It is a hedonistic Syrah to drink over the next 8–10 years.

The 1996 Syrah Saralee's Vineyard (made from tiny yields of one ton of fruit per acre) offers up a phenomenal blackberry liqueur–scented bouquet, with a touch of apricot/orange marmalade jam thrown in for additional complexity. Some Viognier was obviously fermented with this offering. Bacon fat, smoky oak, melted road tar, and pepper also emerge in this profoundly complex, super-concentrated, full-bodied classic. This wine is revealing more forwardness than it did previously, but wow, what a stunning Syrah! Anticipated maturity: now–2015. The 1995 Syrah Saralee's Vineyard may be even better. It has the advantage of an extra year of bottle age, so the wine's perfume is more evolved, but both of these *cuvées* are extraordinary. A similar blackberry jam/cassis-scented nose is followed by a sweet, unctuous texture and explosive fruit, glycerin, and extract levels. Soft tannin can be found in the silky 30-second finish. Crammed with fruit, this classic Syrah satisfies both the hedonistic and intellectual senses. It should age effortlessly for 10 or more years.

The excellent 1996 Malbec and Cabernet Sauvignon were bottled with neither fining nor filtration. The 1996 Malbec possesses that varietal's distinctive black raspberry/strawberry liqueur–scented nose with undefined floral aromas (there is nothing quite like it). Spicy and rich, revealing more leanness and austerity than it did last year, it is a delicious Malbec for drinking over the next 5–7 years. The 1996 Cabernet Sauvignon offers spice box, cedar, black currants, and a touch of licorice and toasty wood. Medium- to full-bodied, rich, and moderately tannic, it will age well for 7–8 years.

Arrowood made profoundly rich, complex Cabernet Sauvignon Reserve Speciales in both 1995 and 1994. While the 1996 Cabernet Sauvignon Reserve Speciale is outstanding, it is not up to the quality of the two previous vintages. Aged completely in French oak, this dense, chocolaty, black currant–scented wine possesses abundant spice, richness, power, and intensity. Still youthful, but muscular and impressively endowed, this full-bodied Cabernet requires 2–3 years of cellaring and should keep for two decades or more. The Reserve Speciale wines spend just under two years in oak casks and are bottled unfined and unfiltered. These stunning offerings are among the finest of their type. Production is minuscule for the Reserve Speciale Merlot (108 cases) and modest for the Cabernet Sauvignon Reserve Speciale (1,700 cases for the 1995). The 1995 Merlot Reserve Speciale possesses a dense purple color in addition to a big, smoky, toasty, oaky nose with notes of black currant and cherry fruit. The wine exhibits coffee/chocolate notes in the flavors, an unctuous texture, full body, and outstanding purity and length. Already accessible, this 1995 promises to evolve for 15+ years. The spectacular 1995 Cabernet Sauvignon Reserve Speciale is a worthy rival to the monumental 1994. It offers an opaque purple color and a knockout nose of tobacco, jammy cassis, toast, and floral scents. This wine has superb extract and purity, full body, multiple layers of richness, and a ripe, seamless, palate-staining finish. Although approachable, it is not quite as accessible as the glorious 1994. Anticipated maturity: now–2020.

Arrowood's 1995 Merlot exhibits some of the tannic muscle Dick Arrowood ascribes to this vintage. The wine possesses an opaque purple color, a tight but interesting nose of black cherries and currants intermixed with coffee and smoky notes. Sweet, juicy, intensely ripe fruit hits the palate, yet the wine's tannin gives it definition and a more backward personality than the 1996. While this Merlot can be drunk early, it should keep for 12–15 years. The 1994 Merlot's saturated, inky black color is followed by a sweet, jammy nose of black fruits, licorice, vanilla, and smoke. Full-bodied, with a voluptuous palate, as well as a layered texture, this low-acid, plump, fleshy Merlot should drink well for a decade after its release next year. Yummy!

Arrowood's 1995 Malbec has a slight edge over the 1996, perhaps because it happens to be a year older. It appears to possess more body and intensity. There is no doubting this saturated purple-colored wine's knockout nose of black raspberries, jammy strawberries, and crème fraîche. Extremely opulent and lush, with berry fruit gushing across the palate, this wine possesses a palate feel and texture totally unlike Merlot and Cabernet Sauvignon. It reveals the precision of Cabernet, the body of Merlot, and an indescribable but not unbearable "lightness of being." Pure, with light tannin in the finish, this expressive, personality-filled wine should drink well for 10–12 years. The 1994 Malbec exhibits raspberry jam, vanilla ice cream, and cream puff–scented aromas and flavors. A gush of wild black fruits is allied to a silky texture, medium to full body, and superb purity. Arrowood has been intelligent in not over-oaking these Malbecs, building in just enough new oak to provide delineation. All of these Malbecs can be drunk upon release, yet they promise to last for at least 8–10 years.

There are few Sonoma County Cabernet Sauvignons better than those produced by Dick Arrowood. Arrowood's success with Cabernet Sauvignon, so obvious in the decade of the nineties, continues unabated, with a succession of top-quality wines. The outstanding 1995 Cabernet Sauvignon boasts an opaque purple color, followed by a rich, black currant–dominated bouquet with background aromas of new oak, earth, and spice. Extremely full-bodied with admirable fruit purity and a layered, multidimensional personality, this wine is intensely rich, with formidable levels of glycerin and extract. The wine's tannin is largely concealed by the wealth of fruit. While this Cabernet will be drinkable young, it promises to evolve for 15+ years. Another sensational, opulent, rich, extremely aromatic and concentrated red wine from Arrowood, the 1994 Cabernet Sauvignon possesses stunning concentration and intensity, impressive balance and purity, and copious quantities of sweet tannin in the long finish. It should even eclipse the super 1993.

Arrowood's two 1994 Reserve Speciale wines, a 1994 Merlot and 1994 Cabernet Sauvignon, were made in limited quantities, but, wow, what dazzling wines they are! The 1994 Merlot Reserve Speciale (100 cases) includes about 3.7% Cabernet Franc in the blend. With 13.8% alcohol, it is a sexy, rich, full-bodied Merlot with terrific layers of fruit, glycerin, and extract. The wine spent 22 months in oak casks, but reveals little evidence of new wood given its extraordinary concentration, power, and depth. It possesses a knockout nose of ripe berry fruit intertwined with Asian spices, subtle toast, and a whiff of coffee and chocolate. Powerful, yet round and harmonious, this is a blockbuster Merlot that should drink well for 15+ years. Arrowood's 1994 Cabernet Sauvignon Reserve Speciale is an exquisite wine made from a blend of vineyards (Wildwood, Smothers, Balbi, Belle Terre, and others). The largest percentage of fruit is from Sonoma Valley, although a small quantity comes from Alexander Valley and Dry Creek. The wine exhibits an opaque purple color and a spectacular nose of jammy cassis, lead pencil, vanilla, and spice. Thick, unctuously textured flavors ooze over the palate with extraordinary purity, ripeness, and richness. In spite of its size, the wine somehow manages not to taste heavy or overdone. This sensational Cabernet Sauvignon is one of the finest I have tasted from Sonoma. It is a candidate for 25–30 years of cellaring, although it is soft enough to be drunk young. Production was 1,200 cases.

The 1994 Syrah Saralee's Vineyard, made from yields of one ton per acre, is available in extremely limited quantities. It is one of the most riveting Syrahs I have tasted from California or anywhere for that matter. The color is an opaque inky black, and the nose offers up copious quantities of smoky chocolate, cassis, and bacon fat aromas. The wine is unbelievably rich, yet amazingly well delineated on the palate, with full body, layers of super-concentrated, unctuously textured fruit, and a finish that must be tasted to be believed. It is an exquisite Syrah that even such Rhône Valley icons as Marcel Guigal or Michel Chapoutier would be thrilled to taste. Rhône Ranger fans are advised to get in line for a bottle or two of this Syrah nectar. It should drink well for 15+ years.

Lastly, no one in California has a better track record for producing luxuriously rich, sweet Riesling than Dick Arrowood. His 1999 White Riesling Hoot Owl Vineyard Special Select Late Harvest contains 8.4% alcohol and 25.6% residual sugar. Unctuously textured, with vibrant acidity, and a decadently sweet *trockenbeerenauslese* style, it offers flavors of orange marmalade as well as honeyed tropical fruit. Fresh and lively, without being overbearing, it will be at its best during its first 4–5 years of life.

Past Glories: 1993 Cabernet Sauvignon (90), 1993 Merlot (89+)

DAVID ARTHUR (NAPA)

1996 Cabernet Sauvignon Elevation 1147	Napa	EE	91
1995 Meritaggio	Napa	D	90

David Arthur's Cabernet Sauvignon Elevation 1147 is a beautiful Cabernet Sauvignon, but, sadly, only 100 cases were produced. It is a gloriously fragrant, sweet, dark ruby/purple-colored wine with gorgeously well integrated oak, and ripe black currant fruit intermixed with licorice, toast, and spice. The wine is medium-bodied, with no hard edges, good acidity and tannin, a nicely textured mid-palate, and fine length. This beauty can be drunk now or cellared for 10–15 years. The 1995 Meritaggio, a proprietary blend of 75% Cabernet Sauvignon, 8% Cabernet Franc, 7% Merlot, 5% Petit Verdot, and 5% Sangiovese, displays an opaque purple color and a sweet nose of earth, vanilla, and truffle-scented jammy black fruits. Full-bodied, with low acidity, a viscous texture, and impressive purity and length, this is an exceptionally well endowed, accessible wine that can be drunk now as well as cellared for a decade. Impressive!

ATALON (NAPA)

1997 Cabernet Sauvignon Beckstoffer Vineyard	Oakville	EE	92
1997 Cabernet Sauvignon Mountain Estates	Napa	EE	91+
1998 Merlot	Napa	D	89
1997 Merlot Mountain Estates	Napa	E	91

This is another of the new high-quality wineries that has been set up under the Jackson Family Farms umbrella group of exceptional wine estates. Wine-maker Tom Peffer, who worked at Beringer for many years, is responsible for accessing the fruit that has made the following wines. The 1998 Merlot (2,500 cases) exhibits a dense ruby/purple color as well as a big, thick, chocolaty nose with notes of roasted coffee, black cherry liqueur, and smoke. Full-bodied, dense, with soft tannin, low acidity, and a long, hedonistic, almost succulent finish, it should drink well for at least a decade. The terrific 1997 Merlot Mountain Estates (1,200 cases) is primarily from the Howell Mountain vineyard once owned by Liparita. The wine has a small dosage of Cabernet Sauvignon and Cabernet Franc in the blend, but tastes like pure Merlot, and superb Merlot at that. It is full-bodied with a knockout nose of smoke, coffee, black cherries, plums, and toast. Unctuously textured, very chewy, with fabulous purity and gobs of flavor, this is a hedonistic yet potentially long-lived Merlot that should drink well when released and last for 15 or more years. An exceptional wine, the black/purple-colored 1997 Cabernet Sauvignon Mountain Estates (1,800 cases) has gorgeous blackberry and cassis flavors intermixed with licorice, spice box, Asian spice, and vanilla. It is unctuously textured, full-bodied, with moderate tannin in the finish. Ideally, I would give this wine 2–3 years of cellaring, and drink it over the following two decades. It is a topflight wine and an impressive new entry into the Cabernet sweepstakes. Equally superb (but more expensive) is the 1997 Cabernet Sauvignon Beckstoffer Vineyard. This vineyard, adjacent to Mondavi's To-Kalon Vineyard in Oakville, has been the source of some superb offerings. (Behrens and Hitchcock made a fabulous 1999 from this site.) Black currant liqueur notes intermingled with licorice, chocolate, cedar, and tobacco emerge from this full-bodied, opaque purple-colored wine. Very concentrated, thick, with juicy, very expansive mid-palate and sweet tannin, this is a prodigious Cabernet Sauvignon that can be drunk now or cellared for 15–20+ years. What an impressive set of debut performances.

AU BON CLIMAT (SANTA BARBARA)

1997 Pinot Noir Cuvée Isabelle	California	E	88
1995 Pinot Noir Cuvée Isabelle	California	E	89+
1997 Pinot Noir Rosemary's Vineyard	Santa Barbara	E	88
1997 Pinot Noir Talley Vineyard	Arroyo Grande	E	88
1997 Il Podere dell Olivos Barbera	California	C	88

1995	Il Podere dell Olivos Barbera Riserva			
	Bon Natale	Santa Barbara	C	89
1997	Il Podere dell Olivos Refosco	California	C	88
1996	Il Podere dell Olivos Teroldego	Santa Barbara	C	88

Major changes are planned for Jim Clendenen's Au Bon Climat. Clendenen, one of the most colorful wine-makers in California, has purchased 70 acres and begun to plant a tightly spaced Pinot Noir vineyard from Dijon clones. This will ensure that Clendenen is not dependent on purchased fruit. This winery produces a numbing assortment of offerings, both under the Au Bon Climat label and the funky, quasi-Italian designation, Il Podere dell Olivos label. Given his long-standing image as being in the forefront of Pinot Noir and Chardonnay, I was surprised that Clendenen's efforts with Italian varietals seemed to taste more complete than his recent Chardonnay and Pinot Noir efforts.

Jim Clendenen is successful with Italian varietals. The red wines include a black/purple-colored, licorice, blackberry, melted tar–scented and –flavored, rustic 1997 Refosco and an elegant, rich, strawberry and blackberry-scented and -flavored 1997 Barbera. These are two robustly styled efforts with excellent fruit, an absence of intrusive wood, and lively acids. The Refosco also displays copious tannin. Both should age well, but they are best consumed in their vigorous youth—over the next 3–4 years.

Exuberance, richness, and impressive dimensions are found in the 1995 Barbera and 1996 Teroldego (an unbottled sample of the 1997 Teroldego also looked immensely impressive). The Barbera was opaquely colored and revealed spicy oak, rich, concentrated fruit, and tangy acidity that was balanced by considerable extract and richness. The massive, opaque black-colored 1996 Teroldego boasts an outstanding nose of licorice, tar, prune- and plum-like fruit. Dense, full-bodied, and concentrated, this hulking wine fills the mouth. The 1997 Teroldego should be even bigger if the sample I tasted was an accurate indication. It is hard to predict how long any of these quasi-Italian reds will last, but 4–5 years is a conservative guess, with the Teroldego lasting longer.

The 1997 Pinot Noirs I tasted include a dark plum-colored, excellent 1997 Pinot Noir Cuvée Isabelle. Aromas of damp earth, black cherries, sweet candied plums, and herbs are generous as well as persistent. The wine is medium-bodied, with decent acidity, light to moderate tannin, and a fine finish. It should be consumed over the next 3–4 years. Denser and more concentrated, with black fruit, spicy, leathery, and earthy characteristics, the 1997 Pinot Noir Talley Vineyard reveals excellent ripeness, a fine texture, and a firm, positive finish. It should drink well for 5–6 years. Revealing outstanding potential, Au Bon Climat's 1997 Pinot Noir Rosemary's Vineyard possesses a super ruby/purple color, as well as excellent black raspberry and cherry aromatics intermixed with toast. Medium-bodied, extremely pure, and well knit, this Pinot Noir should reach full maturity in 1–2 years and last for 8–10.

The finest wine among Au Bon Climat's releases is the 1995 Pinot Noir Cuvée Isabelle. It possesses a dark ruby color with purple hues. The nose offers up complex, sweet, black-cherry and raspberry fruit intermixed with toasty, smoky oak. The wine is richer than the 1994, with medium to full body, excellent extract and purity, and a long finish. It is the sweetest, richest, and potentially most complex and long-lived of what is undeniably an irregular showing from one of my favorite Pinot Noir producers.

BABCOCK VINEYARDS (SANTA BARBARA)

1998	Pinot Noir Grand Cuvée	Santa Barbara	E	90
1998	Pinot Noir Mt. Carmel Vineyard	Santa Ynez	E	90
1997	Sangiovese Eleven Oaks	Santa Ynez	D	88
1997	Syrah Black Label Cuvée	Santa Barbara	D	91

This was the strongest group of wines tasted from Bryan Babcock, a longtime member of the Santa Barbara wine community. Although I am not an admirer of most California Sangioveses, Babcock's 1997 Sangiovese Eleven Oaks is a noteworthy effort. It exhibits textbook smoky, ripe cherry jam, saddle leather, and strawberry aromas. Ripe, rich, suave, and medium-bodied, with no hard edges, it should drink well for 2–3 years. Yummy!

Two of the finest Babcock Pinot Noirs produced to date are the 1998 Pinot Noir Mt. Carmel Vineyard and the 1998 Pinot Noir Grand Cuvée. More similar than dissimilar, they both exhibit deep ruby/purple colors, dense, concentrated personalities, ripe, jammy black cherry and raspberry fruit, and a judicious use of toasty new oak. The Mt. Carmel Vineyard may be less intense and powerful in the mouth, but both are topflight. They will offer delicious drinking for 5–7 years. The Grand Cuvée will outlive its sibling. The terrific 1997 Syrah Black Label Cuvée emerges from a cool climate vineyard in Lompoc. This opaque purple-colored Syrah exhibits aromas of melted licorice, blackberries, and cassis. Full-bodied, with great fruit purity and intensity, an alluring texture and superb harmony among its acidity, alcohol, and tannin, this superb Syrah is still an infant in terms of its development. Give it another year of bottle age and drink it over the following 12–15 years.

BACIO DIVINO (NAPA)

1997 Proprietary Red Wine	Napa	EE	90
1996 Proprietary Red Wine	Napa	E	92
1995 Proprietary Red Wine	Napa	E	94

The second awesome release from this tiny winery dedicated to producing intriguing wines, the 1995 Bacio Divino (a blend of 66% Cabernet Sauvignon, 22% Sangiovese, and 12% Petite Sirah) is a formidable wine of exceptional richness, layers of flavor, and a multidimensional personality. The color is a deep saturated ruby/purple. The nose offers up juicy/jammy strawberry, black currant, and blackberry notes wrapped with subtle toasty oak. Full-bodied, with outstanding ripeness and purity, a silky texture, and an explosive finish, this is a sumptuous example of what can be done with three grapes rarely blended together in such proportions. By the way, sentimentalists will be moved by the government warning label that reads "contains sulphites and also some of the wine-maker's heart and soul." This wine should continue to drink well for a decade.

Another terrific offering from this producer, the 1996 Bacio Divino (a blend of 66% Cabernet Sauvignon, 17% Sangiovese, 9% Petite Sirah, and 8% Merlot) offers a spicy, oaky nose with notions of jammy cassis, strawberries, and cherries. Full-bodied and complex, with a dominant black fruit element upstaging the new oak nuances, this fleshy, ostentatious, pure, gorgeously seductive wine will drink well for 7–8 years. Kudos to wine-maker/proprietor Claus Janzen. The 1997 Bacio Divino, an intriguing as well as innovative blend of 63% Cabernet Sauvignon, 20% Sangiovese, 8% Petite Sirah, and 9% Merlot, is again an outstanding effort. Already evolved and delicious, the dark ruby/plum color is followed by aromas of new saddle leather, black raspberries, plum liqueur, cherries, and toasty, smoky new oak. Medium- to full-bodied, with sweet tannin, an open-knit, fleshy texture, and low acidity, this California "super Tuscan look-alike" can be drunk now and over the next decade.

Past Glories: 1993 Proprietary Red Wine (93+)

BALLENTINE VINEYARDS (NAPA)

1999 Zinfandel (Map Label)	Napa	C	90

This offering is differentiated from Ballentine's regular Zinfandel bottling by the fact that this more powerful wine (14.5% alcohol) has an attractive map label. The dark purple-colored, impressively fruity 1999 Zinfandel (Map Label) exhibits Rhône-like characteristics of earth, Provençal herbs, pepper, spice box, licorice, plum, currants, and cherries, a sweet, full-bodied, fruit-driven personality, outstanding ripeness, and superb purity. Drink it over the next 5–6 years.

BANNISTER (SONOMA)

1996 Pinot Noir Floodgate Vineyard	Anderson Valley	D	90
1997 Pinot Noir Seghesio Vineyard–Keyhole Ranch	Russian River	D	88
1996 Zinfandel	Dry Creek	C	89

This excellent producer seems to have a knack for finding terrific sources for high-quality fruit, offering wines that are not only immediately accessible, but already complex, and marked by exceptional fruit quality and purity. The 1997 Pinot Noir Seghesio Vineyard–Keyhole Ranch possesses a dark ruby color, as well as an excellent spicy, toasty, sweet, jammy, red and black fruit–scented nose with a touch of herbaceousness. The wine is round and velvety-textured, with excellent succulence and gobs of fruit. Drink it over the next 2–4 years. The 1996 Pinot Noir Floodgate Vineyard is another example of the high potential for complex Pinot that exists in northern California's Anderson Valley. Other top California Pinot Noir specialists (for example, Siduri, Handley, and Littorai) have also exploited this up-and-coming region. Bannister's 1996 Pinot Noir Floodgate exhibits a dark ruby color, as well as a terrific nose of black fruits, earth, spice, and sweet toast. In the mouth, the wine is ripe, with a nicely layered palate, adequate acidity, exceptional purity and ripeness, and a long, silky-textured, opulent finish. This outstanding Pinot Noir is already delicious, yet promises to last for 4–5 years. The delectable 1996 Zinfandel exhibits a dark ruby color, as well as an elegant, berry-scented nose, and lush, low-acid, medium- to full-bodied flavors with no hard edges. This is a full-flavored yet harmonious and well-balanced wine to consume over the next several years. Kudos to Marty Bannister.

BARBOUR VINEYARDS (NAPA)

1998 Cabernet Sauvignon	Napa	EE	(88–90)
1997 Cabernet Sauvignon	Napa	EE	93

There were about 100 cases produced of this limited production Cabernet. The well-known winemaking consultant, Heidi Barrett, makes the wine, the first vintage being 1997. The dense blue/purple-colored 1997 Cabernet Sauvignon offers a terrific nose of plums, cherry liqueur, cassis, and subtle new oak. It is beautifully pure, with gobs of fruit, low but adequate supporting acidity, and plenty of ripe tannin in the finish. Made from 100% Cabernet Sauvignon and aged for just under two years in French oak, this is a beautifully made wine that can be drunk now or cellared for two decades. The 1998 Cabernet Sauvignon (150 cases) displays good density for the vintage, sweet tannin, and ripe plum and black currant fruit. Slightly less concentrated, with a shorter finish, it is a noteworthy achievement in this difficult vintage. Both of these wines are made from the famed Grace clone of Cabernet Sauvignon (from Grace Family Vineyards).

BARNETT VINEYARDS (NAPA)

1996 Cabernet Sauvignon Rattlesnake Hill	Spring Mountain	E	89+
1994 Cabernet Sauvignon Rattlesnake Hill	Spring Mountain	E	93+

I have superb recollections of Barnett Vineyards' 1991 Cabernet Sauvignon and Cabernet Sauvignon Rattlesnake Hill. The 1996 Cabernet Sauvignon Rattlesnake Hill reveals a saturated ruby/purple color and sweet fruit (rich blueberry, cassis, earth, and wild herbs). Full-bodied, with a nicely layered impact and copious tannin in the long, astringent finish, it requires 2–3 years of cellaring and should keep for 15+ years. The 1994 Cabernet Sauvignon Rattlesnake Hill Estate is undeniably the finest Cabernet Barnett Vineyards has produced since their marvelous 1991. The wine has an opaque purple color, as well as an earthy, raspberry liqueur–scented nose that is vibrant and intense. The wild mountain black fruit quality so common in the top wines of Spring Mountain comes across on the palate of this immensely impressive, explosively rich, super-extracted wine. Patience, however, is required as the tannin is high, and most of the wine's character and richness are in the explosive finish as opposed to its attack. This should turn out to be an exquisite Cabernet Sauvignon, but only for the true connoisseur who is willing to invest in 5–7 years of cellaring. Anticipated maturity: 2003–2030. Wow!

Past Glories: 1991 Cabernet Sauvignon (92), 1991 Cabernet Sauvignon Rattlesnake Hill (96)

BEAULIEU (NAPA)

1995 Cabernet Sauvignon Clone Four	Napa	EE	89?
1994 Cabernet Sauvignon Clone Six Signet Collection	Napa	EE	91
1996 Cabernet Sauvignon Georges de Latour Private Reserve	Napa	EE	88
1994 Cabernet Sauvignon Georges de Latour Private Reserve	Napa	E	91
1995 Zinfandel	Napa	C	88

Beaulieu's flagship, the 1996 Cabernet Sauvignon Georges de Latour Private Reserve, exhibits a deep ruby/purple color as well as aggressive toasty new oak, medium body, and firm tannin. The noticeable acidity exacerbates the firmness and tannic structure. Although very good, possibly excellent, it needs 2–4 years of cellaring. It should keep for 15–20 years. This wine needs more mid-palate as well as additional layers of flavor. Less acidification would open up the wine's texture. Beaulieu's dense, saturated ruby-colored 1995 Zinfandel offers up textbook aromas of jammy black fruits, pepper, and spice. Full-bodied and lush, with loads of glycerin and alcohol (14.5%), this medium- to full-bodied, extremely well made Zin is a treat to drink. The wine's low acidity and luscious abundance of ripe berry fruit suggests near-term drinking (over the next 3–4 years). Kudos to BV for this excellent wine.

The dark ruby-colored, admirably concentrated 1995 Cabernet Sauvignon Clone Four reveals many positive attributes—ripe cassis fruit, loamy soil scents, and toasty notes. It is a rich, medium-bodied, structured, pure wine that needs 4–5 years to settle down. It should last 20–25 years. If the tannin becomes meshed with the wine's other elements, it will be outstanding. If not, the score will fall. Anticipated maturity: 2006–2020. The 1994 Cabernet Sauvignon Clone Six, a limited bottling from BV's Signet Collection series of wines (all expensive and made in small quantities), is an immensely impressive offering. The color is a saturated dark ruby/purple. The wine, from an old clone of Cabernet Sauvignon, is a rich, full-bodied, powerful yet harmonious Cabernet with gobs of black currant fruit, a nice touch of oak, and outstanding ripeness and purity. It is also long in the mouth, with a youthful, unevolved personality. This should prove to be an impressive, long-lived Cabernet Sauvignon. Anticipated maturity: now–2015.

The 1994 Cabernet Sauvignon Georges de Latour Private Reserve is one of the finest efforts from Beaulieu in some time. Not since the mid-1980s has BV made a Private Reserve Cabernet with such richness and potential. The wine boasts a dark ruby/purple color, an attractive nose of sweet, toasty new oak, and ripe red and black fruits. In the mouth, there is a layered texture, full-bodied richness, excellent purity, and sweet tannin in the long finish. This wine can be drunk now as well as over the next 15–20 years.

Past Glories: Cabernet Sauvignon Georges de Latour Private Reserve—1990 (88), 1988 (90), 1985 (89), 1984 (91), 1982 (92), 1980 (93), 1976 (94), 1974 (90), 1970 (94), 1969 (90), 1968 (94), 1958 (95), 1951 (94)

BEDFORD-THOMPSON (SANTA BARBARA)

1997 Cabernet Franc	Santa Barbara	C	88
1997 Syrah	Santa Barbara	C	89

There is no doubting the individuality and artisinal feel to the Bedford-Thompson offerings. Little is held back in the winemaking, and they are to be admired for that. It is hard to find a better Cabernet Franc from southern California than Bedford-Thompson's 1997. Notes of saddle leather, cedar, jammy berries, and spice box offer a fragrant, complex bouquet. The wine is intense, with lovely fruit, not much weight, but medium body, and a long, concentrated finish. Drink it over the next 5–6 years. A more controversial offering is the 1997 Syrah. It has a lot going on, including levels of volatile acidity (VA) that might be off-putting to some technocrats. The wine's dark blue/purple color is followed by jammy, sweet aromas of cherries, black raspberries, smoke, and a bit of VA. Dense and full-bodied, with a luscious texture and outstanding richness, this wine comes close to being over the top, but this could pass for a French Côte Rôtie. Drink it over the next 5–8 years.

BEHRENS AND HITCHCOCK (NAPA)

1998	Cabernet Franc	Oakville	D	(87–89)
1999	Cabernet Sauvignon Beckstoffer Vineyard	Oakville	E	(95–98)
1998	Cabernet Sauvignon Beckstoffer Vineyard	Napa	E	(86–88)
1998	Cabernet Sauvignon Cuvée Juanita	Napa	E	(90–91)
1994	Cabernet Sauvignon Cuvée Lola Unfiltered Reserve	Napa Valley	D	93
1994	Cabernet Sauvignon Hyampom Vineyard Lot 2	Trinity County	C	88
1999	Cabernet Sauvignon Ink Grade	Napa	E	(92–95)
1996	Cabernet Sauvignon Ink Grade	Napa	D	92
1995	Cabernet Sauvignon Ink Grade	Napa	D	92+
1994	Cabernet Sauvignon Ink Grade Vineyard Lot 2	Napa Valley	D	91+
1999	Cabernet Sauvignon Kenefick Ranch	Napa	E	(93–96)
1998	Cabernet Sauvignon Kenefick Ranch	Napa	E	(90–92)
1996	Cabernet Sauvignon Kenefick Ranch	Napa	D	93
1994	Cabernet Sauvignon Staglin Vineyard	Napa Valley	D	90+
1995	Cabernet Sauvignon TLK Ranch	Napa	D	96
1999	Cuvée Lola Proprietary Red Wine	Napa	E	(94–96)
1997	Cuvée Lola Proprietary Red Wine	Napa	D	(90–93)
1996	Cuvée Lola Proprietary Red Wine	Napa	D	92
1999	Merlot	Napa	D	(91–93)
1997	Merlot	Napa	D	(89–92)
1999	Merlot	Oakville	E	(90–92)
1998	Merlot	Oakville	E	(87–88)
1997	Merlot	Oakville	D	(90–93)
1996	Merlot	Oakville	D	94
1995	Merlot	Oakville	D	91
1999	Merlot Alder Springs Vineyard	Mendocino	D	(90–93)
1998	Merlot Alder Springs Vineyard	Mendocino	D	(87–89)
1999	Merlot Las Amigas Vineyard	Carneros	E	(92–94)
1998	Merlot Reserve	Napa	E	(88–90)
1997	Ode to Picasso Proprietary Red Wine	Napa	D	(91–93)
1998	Petite Sirah	Napa	D	(88–90)
1997	Petite Sirah	Napa	D	(91–93)
1995	Petite Sirah	Dry Creek Valley	D	92

1999	Petite Sirah Barcini Vineyard	Napa	D	(89–91)
1999	Syrah Alder Springs Vineyard			
	Hommage to Ed Oliveira	Mendocino	E	(90–92)
1997	Zinfandel	Napa	D	(90–92)
1996	Zinfandel	Dry Creek	D	89
1995	Zinfandel	Napa	D	94

Behrens and Hitchcock and their families represent all that is good about winemaking in the United States. Bob Hitchcock, a former accountant, and Les Behrens, a retired restaurant owner, decided to give up their "real" jobs and begin to acquire fruit to make wines "they liked." Starting first out of a garage in the southern Napa Valley, they have now purchased property on top of Spring Mountain. With a shoestring budget, the Hitchcock/Behrens syndicate has thrown up a functional winery, even going so far as to dig a couple of caves for barrel aging. However, the most important thing is the quality. Neither has an oenological degree, and when you taste these wines, you have to wonder, does anyone need one? The results are spectacular, and the owners are refreshingly candid. The remarkable thing is that these wines embarrass many of the multimillion-dollar corporate wineries on Napa's valley floor that could use a wake-up call from artists/artisans such as Les Behrens and Bob Hitchcock. Readers who are not on their mailing list should sign up immediately.

Behrens and Hitchcock were almost apologetic for what was a good line-up of 1998s. However, their 1999s are the best wines they have yet produced. Made from superripe fruit, they offer bold flavors, high alcohol, and gobs of personality. They are satisfying not only on a hedonistic level, but also intellectually. All of these wines go into the bottle with neither fining nor filtration, and of course, this is another winery that simply refuses to muck around with alcohol levels by reducing them through industrial manipulation or adding water to the fermentation must. For starters, the 1999 Merlot Oakville (500 cases of 100% Merlot) is a dense, very chewy Merlot with oodles of smoky blackberry and cherry fruit. The wine is unctuously textured, with plenty of glycerin, and a heady, concentrated finish. It will be delicious when released and age well for at least 10–12 years. The 1999 Merlot Alder Springs Vineyard (350 cases) is also superb, but shows more of a cooler climate, almost jammy, red berry nose, with notes of graphite, toast, and spice. The wine has gorgeous purity, relatively low acidity, and a thick yet superb finish. Not to be outdone, the 1999 Merlot Napa (700 cases of a blend of three separate vineyards, Kenefick, Jaeger, and Alder Springs) is the most structured of the four Merlots I tasted. It reveals a black/purple color, terrific fruit intensity, a big, weighty, blackberry and cherry-scented nose, and plenty of volume and power in the mouth. The smoky oak is beautifully integrated, as this wine seems to have already sucked up its new oak aging. There is more tannin in the finish, but this is a large-scale, blockbuster Merlot that is probably going to need 2–3 years of cellaring and will last for 15–20 years. Don't be surprised if someone stumbles across a bottle in about two decades and thinks it is one of the finest Merlots ever made in California. If that sounds good, there is an even better Merlot from the Behrens and Hitchcock stable in 1999. Are you ready? The 1999 Merlot Las Amigas Vineyard (350 cases of a thick, 15.6% alcohol, voluptuous Merlot fruit bomb) is full-bodied with remarkable intensity, purity, and equilibrium. This vineyard has been the source of some uninspiring wines from another famed Napa Valley winery, but in the hands of Behrens and Hitchcock, it has turned out a prodigious effort. The wine is opaque black/purple, with plenty of smoke, sweet mulberry, blackberry, and cherry fruit, infused with espresso, cocoa, and toast. This full-bodied, super-extracted, yet velvety-textured wine should drink well for 15 or more years.

The Alder Springs Vineyard Syrah (which is well known for not only Merlot but also Pinot Noir) is the first Syrah from this source. There is a small quantity of the 1999 Syrah Hommage to Ed Oliveira. A 100% Syrah aged in new oak, this wine shows plenty of licorice and cassis notes, gorgeous ripeness, full body, low acidity, but moderate tannin in the finish. It looks to be an outstanding Syrah to drink after several years of bottle age. It should keep for 12–15 years. Another tannic beast is the 1999 Petite Sirah Barcini Vineyard. The wine is a dense purple color, with notes of earth, smoke, licorice, and black fruits. Quite sweet on the attack, full-bodied, with rustic tannin in the finish, this wine will require 5–6 years of cellaring and keep for up to two decades.

The three Cabernet Sauvignons I tasted from Behrens and Hitchcock in 1999 are among the superstars of the vintage. This is a rather remarkable achievement, since these are not from estate grapes but from vineyards they have sourced. The 1999 Cabernet Sauvignon Ink Grade (300 cases of 15.1% alcohol) has an opaque purple color, an intense, very fragrant nose of crème de cassis, smoky new oak, mineral, and almost floral-infused blueberry and blackberry notes. The wine is unctuously textured, with the new wood totally absorbed. Acidity and tannin are also beautifully integrated. This wine should be relatively accessible upon release and last for up to two decades. Another incredible effort is the 1999 Cabernet Sauvignon Kenefick Ranch, located in the northern end of Napa Valley, not far from Araujo's Eisele Vineyard. The 1999 exhibits an opaque purple color and a gorgeous nose of blueberry and cassis fruit, intermixed with melted licorice, mineral, and smoke. Sweet and unctuously textured on the attack, with full-bodied, powerful flavors that are remarkably harmonious, this Cabernet possesses a whopping degree of alcohol (about 15.9%) that is totally integrated and balanced. Look for this wine to evolve for 15 or more years. A potentially prodigious wine is the 1999 Cabernet Sauvignon Beckstoffer Vineyard. From a vineyard located next to the famed To-Kalon Vineyard of Robert Mondavi, it boasts an opaque black/purple color as well as an awesome nose of spice box, black fruits, toast, and mineral. The wine is remarkably rich, full-bodied, and pure, with multiple layers of flavor, sweet tannin, low acidity, and a finish that goes on for a good 45+ seconds. There are 325 cases of this wine that was finished at 15.4% alcohol. Many of the vineyards they draw from are frequently cropped at 5–6 tons, but Les Behrens and Bob Hitchcock reduce yields by 50%.

There was no 1998 Cuvée Lola (named after a deceased cat) but the 1999, a blend dominated by Cabernet Franc (about 75%, with small quantities of Petit Verdot, Merlot, and Cabernet Sauvignon added in), is sensational (375 cases; a "modest" 15.3% alcohol). The wine offers an opaque blue/purple color and an exquisite nose of liquid minerals, black fruits, and spice. Dense, huge, and full-bodied, yet at the same time, remarkably elegant and graceful, it is a tour de force in winemaking, representing a brilliant marriage of power and finesse. Because of the slightly firm tannins in the finish, it will need 2–3 years of cellaring, but should keep 20+ years.

Some potentially outstanding wines were produced in 1998. There is no question that the better 1998s, while lacking power, concentration, and ageability, are ripe, charming, and alluring because of their immediate appeal. Most of the Behrens and Hitchcock 1998s fall within that range. The 1998 Petite Sirah emerges from the same Calistoga vineyard that produces fruit for the Rockland Petite Sirah (a limited production gem I have glowingly reviewed in the past). The Behrens and Hitchcock offering exhibits a dark ruby color with purple nuances. Soft and forward, with supple tannin, good blackberry and peppery-scented fruit, and a pure, lush finish, it will be delicious when released and will last for 7–8 years. The dark ruby-colored 1998 Merlot Oakville displays mineral, smoke, black cherry, and spicy oak aromatics. Medium-bodied, round, and easy to drink, it will be a seductive, delicious Merlot to enjoy during its first 5–6 years of life. Much better is the 1998 Merlot Reserve. Richer and sweeter, with more volume, concentration, and intensity in the mouth, it reveals chocolate, black cherry liqueur, and toasty, smoky oak. Drink this seductive, supple-textured effort during its first 8 years of life. The 1998 Merlot Alder Springs was harvested on November 2 (an indication of just how cold the summer of 1998 proved to be). Dark ruby/purple-colored, with sweet mulberry, blackberry, and cherry fruit, this medium-bodied, dense, attractive Merlot has plenty up-front, but not a great deal of glycerin or intensity once past its superficial appeal. It will be very good, perhaps excellent, but the vintage's lack of generosity and power are clearly evident. Drink it over the next 7–10 years.

I will be anxious to see what Les Behrens and Bob Hitchcock do with Cabernet Franc in a top-notch vintage like 1999. Certainly the 1998 Cabernet Franc Oakville is a complex offering, exhibiting sweet floral, spice, and vanilla aromas as well as black raspberry/blueberry-like fruit. It is medium-bodied, elegant, soft, and seductive. There are about 100 cases of the following new Cabernet Sauvignon from Rutherford. The dense ruby/purple-colored 1998 Cabernet Sauvignon Cuvée Juanita exhibits sweet blackberry and cassis aromas and flavors with spice and toast in the background. A fat, fleshy, low-acid Cabernet Sauvignon, it will be delicious when released and age well for 10–12 years. It is unquestionably a success for the vintage. The 1998 Cabernet Sauvignon Beckstoffer Vineyard reveals excellent purity and ripeness, but not much power and richness. Very good, with sweet black currant and berry fruit intertwined with spice box, vanilla, and cedar, it should drink well for 7–8 years. There are 400 cases of the 1998 Cabernet Sauvignon Kenefick Ranch. This has been a star for Behrens and Hitchcock since they first offered it, and the 1998 appears to be one of the vintage's top efforts. Opaque black/purple-colored, with a knockout bouquet of crème de cassis, blackberry liqueur, and smoky new oak, this intense, full-bodied, surprisingly powerful offering, from a vineyard near the Araujo's Eisele parcel, is long and atypically rich and concentrated for a 1998. Anticipated maturity: now–2015. Bravo!

The dark plum-colored 1997 Merlot Oakville, from a parcel of vines close to Dalla Valle, Screaming Eagle, and the new Rudd Cellars, is a jammy offering with gobs of ostentatiously rich black cherry fruit intermixed with smoke and spicy oak. It hits the palate with generous amounts of glycerin, and thick, juicy fruit. This succulently textured wine is a thrill to drink. It should provide Merlot lovers with plenty of excitement. Moreover, it should continue to drink well for a decade. Named after a long-deceased cat, the 1997 Ode to Picasso (a blend of 80% Syrah and 20% Merlot) is far superior to the very good 1996. It reveals the winery's telltale aromas of blackberries, blueberries, and cassis, as well as terrific fruit intensity, a layered texture, and huge flavors. Although built like a fortress, it possesses glorious levels of fruit and plenty of power. Accessible enough to be drunk young, it will keep for 12–15+ years. The 1997 Cuvée Lola (a blend of 75% Cabernet Franc and 25% Cabernet Sauvignon and Merlot) is one of the finest Cabernet Franc–dominated wines I have tasted from northern California, ranking alongside the superb efforts turned in by Dalla Valle, La Jota, and Pride Mountain. The wine exhibits a cedary, cigar box, black currant, and raspberry-scented nose, superb ripeness, rich, fleshy, low-acid flavors, and a rich but not weighty mid-palate and finish. This wine will be drinkable upon release, and keep for 12+ years.

Readers looking for blockbuster-sized, bigger-than-life wines should check out Behrens and Hitchcock's 1997 Petite Sirah. It boasts a thick, purple color, as well as a huge nose of minerals, Asian spices, smoke, and black fruits. Extremely powerful, full-bodied, and ripe, with a jammy yet well-delineated personality, this monster Petite Sirah will benefit from 4–5 years of cellaring and keep for two decades or more.

I have immensely enjoyed the Zinfandels produced by Behrens and Hitchcock. Their fruit comes from a 30-year-old, head-pruned vineyard. The fine 1997 Zinfandel offers copious quantities of black cherry, briery, raspberry, and peppery fruit. The wine displays loads of glycerin, medium to full body, a lush, round, generous mouth-feel, and heady alcohol in the lusty finish. It is a wine to drink over the next 3–4 years.

My notes also indicate I tasted a 1997 Merlot Napa, which was expected to be bottled separately, rather than blended with Oakville Merlot. This example revealed a more chocolaty, coffee, crème brûlée character than the Oakville cuvée, in addition to full body, outstanding richness of fruit, and a spicy, dense, concentrated finish. More monolithic than the Oakville, but potentially outstanding, it is another superb offering from this small winery.

The 1996 Cabernet Sauvignon Ink Grade exhibits a saturated purple color, followed by a fragrant nose of exotic black fruits (blueberries and cassis). In the mouth, subtle doses of attractive floral notes, spice, and vanilla emerge. This multilayered wine possesses sweet tannin, a voluptuous texture, and superb concentration and purity. It is a sexy, opulently styled Cabernet Sauvignon to drink when released and over the next 15 years. As the wine sat in the glass, the blueberry/blackberry liqueur aspect became even more pronounced, making this wine totally disarming. The 1996 Cabernet Sauvignon Kenefick Ranch, a dense, black/purple-colored wine, is full-bodied and extremely rich, with a sweet, black fruit–scented nose, intertwined with licorice and floral notes. Concentrated, full-bodied, and powerful, yet beautifully balanced, this 1996 has managed to tame the vintage's rustic tannin, resulting in a wine of uncommon silkiness and equilibrium. Anticipated maturity: now–2015.

What a sumptuous, knockout, gloriously rich, layered, and juicy 1996 Merlot Behrens and Hitchcock produced. The 1996 Merlot Oakville possesses a dark ruby/purple color, dazzling, sweet, black cherry liqueur–like notes in its aromatics, and judicious notes of spicy oak. The wine's purity, and multiple layers of texture that combine thrilling levels of fruit, glycerin, and extract into a seamless, voluptuously endowed wine, are to be both enjoyed and admired. Diaphanous, this wine can be peeled one layer at a time given its thick, rich, high-rise effect on the palate. The fruit is superripe and well balanced with copious sweet tannin and low acidity. This is a full-bodied, sensationally endowed Merlot to drink over the next decade. Nearly as impressive is the 1996 Cuvée Lola, a proprietary red wine made from a Bordeaux-like blend of Cabernet Sauvignon, Merlot, and Cabernet Franc. This wine is characterized by a saturated ruby/purple color, layers of flavor, outstanding purity, and black currant, plum, and cassis flavors. The wine is rich, but avoids any sense of heaviness or roughness. The wine's structural components—tannin, acidity, and alcohol—are all meshed together into a silky format. This offering can be drunk now or cellared for 12–15 years.

Made from 85% Zinfandel, 10% Petite Sirah, and 5% Carignan, the dark ruby-colored, medium- to full-bodied 1996 Dry Creek Zinfandel reveals copious quantities of sweet black cherry fruit intermingled with spice, pepper, and dusty notes. The wine is classy and powerful yet elegant, particularly for a Dry Creek Zinfandel. Purely made and stylish, it is ideal for consuming over the next 3–4 years. The fabulously rich 1995 Zinfandel Napa (a blend of 85% Zinfandel, 12% Petite Sirah, and, low and behold, 3% Viognier) is one of the finest I have tasted. The saturated opaque purple color is followed by a knockout nose of blackberry liqueur intermingled with raspberries, pepper, and spice. The wine is explosively rich, with loads of glycerin, layers of concentrated, jammy fruit, full body, and a knockout, heady finish. This is a hedonistic, gloriously perfumed, and decadently concentrated wine to drink over the next 3–4 years.

The opaque black/purple-colored 1995 Merlot Oakville (100 cases) possesses an expressive blueberry-scented nose that is a perfect match for its sumptuous personality. The wine exhibits superb richness, medium to full body, and a natural texture, with sensual levels of fruit and glycerin. It is a full-bodied, seamlessly styled Merlot that should drink well for a decade. This exquisite wine merits the attention of serious wine drinkers.

Lovers of the underrated Petite Sirah varietal will adore Behrens and Hitchcock's 1995, which is close in quality to the extraordinary Petite Sirahs from Ridge's York Creek and Turley's Hayne Vineyard. Boasting 15.2% alcohol, this dense black/purple-colored wine is very full-bodied and extremely powerful, with low acidity, a blackberry, blueberry, cassis character, some pepper, and extraordinary viscosity and intensity. This huge, mouthcoating style of Petite Sirah is not for everybody, but for fans of this wine, it is a knockout. It should drink well for two decades.

The two formidable Cabernet Sauvignons are among the superstars of the 1995 vintage. I do have one reservation with respect to the 1995 Cabernet Sauvignon Ink Grade—some leesy, mercaptan notes in the nose are at first disconcerting. However, they quickly blow off as the wine is exposed to air. Once past that, the wine's opaque purple color and blueberry and exotic floral notes (orchids) are impressive. Ripe and dense, with fabulous flavor concentration, and a long, multilayered, textured personality that caresses and saturates the palate with copious quantities of fruit, glycerin, and richness, this is a large-scaled but beautifully balanced Cabernet Sauvignon that should be at its best with another 2–3 years of cellaring, and last for 15 or more years. The 1995 Cabernet Sauvignon TLK Ranch is a powerhouse, but exhibits remarkable symmetry for its massive size. The color is saturated purple, and the wine possesses fabulously sweet blackberry, blueberry, and cassis aromas nicely dosed with subtle, toasty oak. Thick, juicy, and full-bodied, with outstanding purity and admirably integrated acidity, tannin, and alcohol, this stunningly proportioned Cabernet Sauvignon possesses sweet tannin and low acidity, giving it up-front appeal. However, all the component parts are present for 15–20 years of cellaring.

Except for the Trinity County Cabernet Sauvignon, the differences between the 1994 Cabernet Sauvignon cuvées are negligible. In fact, the wines could be blended together with no loss of character (I actually did such a blending). Nevertheless, I would be happy to own any of these wines. If Behrens and Hitchcock want to continue to offer small quantities of each *cuvée*, so be it . . . they are superb Cabernets. The only non-outstanding example is the excellent 1994 Cabernet Sauvignon Lot 2 Hyampom Vineyard from northern Trinity County, not far from the Oregon border. I do not believe I have ever tasted a Cabernet Sauvignon from this region. The wine possesses a dark purple color, a spicy, sweet, black currant and blueberry-scented nose, medium body, a multiple-layered texture, and a round, generous finish. It should drink well for 12 or more years. The 1994 Cabernet Sauvignon Ink Grade Vineyard Lot 2 offers explosive levels of black fruits. The wine is full-bodied, powerful, and flawlessly made, with sensational concentration and a character not unlike the other Cabernets, but seemingly more evolved aromatically. Anticipated maturity: now–2020. The 1994 Cabernet Sauvignon Cuvée Lola Unfiltered Reserve is singing slightly more loudly than its siblings. The blueberries, cassis, vanilla, toast, high-extract, full body, and silky texture are all present. This *cuvée* possesses even more weight and presence on the palate. If the Cuvée Lola is the most dramatic among this group of impressive wines, the 1994 Cabernet Sauvignon Staglin Vineyard is the most backward. This wine displays all the potential to be superb—natural texture, great ripeness, impeccable purity, full body, and layers of blueberry and cassis fruit. However, the tannin is more pronounced, thus this is a wine to lay away for 5–6 years and drink over the following 10–15.

Did it occur to anyone else that these two seat-of-the-pants wine-makers, along with several dozen other talented producers in California, may well be rewriting the definition of great wine? Think about it. To reiterate, virtually all of these wines are sold by mailing list.

BELLA (SONOMA)

1999 Zinfandel Belle Canyon	Dry Creek	D	91
1999 Zinfandel Big River Ranch	Alexander Valley	D	90
1999 Zinfandel Lilly Hill Estate	Alexander Valley	D	89

This impressive newcomer has fashioned a trio of admirable, well-made Zinfandels that emphasize ripe fruit, a judicious touch of toasty oak, and full-bodied, balanced personalities with high alcohol, but no hotness. The elegant 1999 Zinfandel Lilly Hill Estate exhibits a Burgundy-like character (although it is much fuller-bodied than most Burgundies) in its bouquet of sweet raspberry jam, cherries, and flowers. This full-bodied, firm, pure, powerful offering reveals classy fruit, but delivers plenty of punch on the palate. It should drink well for 5–6 years. The sexy, full-bodied 1999 Zinfandel Big River Ranch boasts an opaque ruby/purple color as well as big, thick aromas of blackberries, cherries, currants, spice box, tobacco, pepper, and smoke. Full-bodied, opulently textured, and succulent, this hedonistic offering will provide outstanding drinking over the next 3–5 years. Lastly, the well-endowed, saturated ruby/purple-colored 1999 Zinfandel Belle Canyon reveals subtle oak notes in its thick, jammy, pure, black cherry fruit, underbrush, and seaweed-scented bouquet. Rich, multidimensional, and layered, with a 20-second finish, it will drink beautifully for 7–8 years. This is a noteworthy newcomer to the Zinfandel sweepstakes.

BELO (NAPA)

1995 Vintage Port Reserve	Napa	D	91

What a surprise! There are 100 cases of this vintage port look-alike produced from the same Portuguese varietals (used for making vintage port) planted in Napa. There is no doubting its complex, licorice, coffee, and sweet jammy blackberry and plum aromas and flavors. Full-bodied, moderately sweet, and a dead-ringer for a top-notch vintage port, this small, artisanal producer has fashioned a gem. Moreover, it is evolved and already drinking beautifully.

BENESSERE (NAPA)

1997 Zinfandel	Napa	C	88
1999 Zinfandel Black Glass Vineyard	Napa	D	90

This winery is dedicated to producing wines from varietals most commonly associated with Italy. Benessere's outstanding, deep ruby/purple-colored 1999 Zinfandel Black Glass Vineyard offers a sweet nose of black fruits intermixed with smoke, dried herbs, and subtle wood. Superrich and explosively ripe with a multilayered texture, this exceptional wine can be drunk now or cellared for 4–5 years. The dark ruby-colored 1997 Zinfandel offers excellent briery fruit woven with pepper and spice. In the mouth, copious quantities of oak make an appearance, but they are nicely complemented by the wine's ripeness, glycerin, and rich, medium-bodied, fruity style. Drink it over the next 1–2 years.

BENZIGER WINERY (SONOMA)

1995 Cabernet Sauvignon Reserve	Sonoma Mountain	D	88+
1995 Imagery Series Cabernet Franc	Alexander Valley	D	90
1994 Imagery Series Cabernet Franc	Alexander Valley	C	88
1995 Imagery Series Malbec Blue Rock Vineyard	Alexander Valley	C	88
1994 Imagery Series Petite Sirah	Paso Robles	C	90
1994 Imagery Series Syrah	Central Coast	C	88
1995 Zinfandel	Sonoma	C	88
1994 Zinfandel	Sonoma	C	88+

This family-owned winery continues to turn out an attractive portfolio of well-made wines. Moreover, given the lofty pricing strategy being employed by many other California wineries, they remain sensibly priced. The 1995 Cabernet Sauvignon Reserve, a blend of 76% Cabernet Sauvignon, 12% Cabernet Franc, and 12% Merlot, is backward, but promising. Rich and fleshy, with copious quantities of black currant and briery fruit, oak, and soil scents, it is medium- to full-bodied and pure, with a textured, layered personality. This large-scaled Cabernet Sauvignon should be at its finest between now–2016.

Produced from grapes grown in the Blue Rock Vineyard in Alexander Valley, Benziger's 1995 Imagery Series Cabernet Franc provides a seductive, silky mouthful of wine. This deep ruby-colored Cabernet Franc offers up an intense, provocative nose of spice, fruitcake, cedar, and black fruits. On the palate, the wine is round, sweet, elegant, and soft. If it's possible for Cabernet Franc to behave as a sumptuous Pinot Noir, this one does. The wine is not likely to make old bones, nor will it please those who like the feel of rough tannin grinding across the palate, but this is a delicious, stylish, complex, silky-smooth Cabernet Franc to drink over the next 3–4 years. The 1995 Imagery Series Malbec, which is also produced from Alexander Valley's Blue Rock Vineyard, will not make California's premier Malbec producer (Dick Arrowood of Arrowood Winery) jealous, but it is a good effort. The nose possesses sweet red currant and raspberry scents, as well as a touch of herbs and earth. This soft, grapy Malbec is a pleasant, plump yet refreshing wine that should drink well for 3–4 years.

An excellent Zinfandel, Benziger's dark ruby/purple-colored 1995 displays textbook aromas of pepper, spice, and black cherries. Deeply etched, full-bodied flavors possess excellent purity and plenty of varietal character. This low-acid, plush, fleshy wine boasts 14.5% alcohol; it can be drunk now and over the next 4–5 years. Benziger's 1994 Zinfandel had not been bottled when I tasted it. It exhibits a dark ruby/purple color, as well as a deep, spicy, lavishly oaked nose. The attack offers gobs of ripe fruit, noticeably American oak notes, and a rich, medium-bodied, spicy style. There is plenty of Zinfandel varietal character displayed in this in-your-face Zin. Drink it over the next 5–6 years.

The 1994 Imagery Series red wine offerings scored well in my peer group tastings. The 1994 Syrah reveals a healthy dark ruby/purple color, plenty of toasty new oak in its peppery nose, and abundant quantities of sweet black currant flavors. This medium- to full-bodied, lush Syrah is ideal for drinking over the next 5–8 years. While I did not detect its presence, the wine includes 4% Viognier in the blend. Benziger's black/purple-colored 1994 Petite Sirah Imagery Series is a monstrous-sized wine displaying huge, roasted herb, smoky black currant fruit with a touch of tar. Full-bodied, moderately tannic, and extremely concentrated, this wine is best aged for 1–3 years and drunk over the subsequent 10–15. Another attractive wine, the 1994 Imagery Series Cabernet Franc, exhibits a dark ruby color, followed by sweet, complex, red and black currant aromas nicely infused with oak and a whiff of menthol. Spicy, medium-bodied, with excellent depth, adequate acidity, but little tannin, this stylish, well-made Cabernet Franc should drink well for the next 5–7 years.

BERINGER (NAPA)

1998 Alluvium Proprietary Red	Knights Valley	D	88
1997 Alluvium Proprietary Red	Knights Valley	D	89
1996 Alluvium Proprietary Red	Knights Valley	D	88+
1995 Alluvium Proprietary Red	Knights Valley	D	89
1994 Alluvium Proprietary Red	Knights Valley	D	89
1999 Alluvium Proprietary White	Knights Valley	C	89
1997 Cabernet Franc	Howell Mountain	C	(87–90)
1996 Cabernet Franc	Howell Mountain	C	89
1995 Cabernet Franc	Howell Mountain	C	90
1995 Cabernet Franc Terre Rouge	Howell Mountain	C	91
1994 Cabernet Franc Terre Rouge	Howell Mountain	C	91
1997 Cabernet Sauvignon	Knights Valley	C	88
1996 Cabernet Sauvignon	Knights Valley	C	88
1994 Cabernet Sauvignon	Knights Valley	C	89
1997 Cabernet Sauvignon Bancroft Ranch	Howell Mountain	E	95
1996 Cabernet Sauvignon Bancroft Ranch	Howell Mountain	E	92+
1995 Cabernet Sauvignon Bancroft Ranch	Howell Mountain	EE	94
1994 Cabernet Sauvignon Bancroft Ranch	Howell Mountain	EE	92
1998 Cabernet Sauvignon Chabot Vineyard	Napa	EE	90
1997 Cabernet Sauvignon Chabot Vineyard	Napa	EE	93
1996 Cabernet Sauvignon Chabot Vineyard	Napa	EE	93+
1995 Cabernet Sauvignon Chabot Vineyard	Napa	E	92+
1994 Cabernet Sauvignon Chabot Vineyard	Napa	E	93+
1997 Cabernet Sauvignon Marston Vineyard	Spring Mountain	E	(89–92)
1996 Cabernet Sauvignon Marston Vineyard	Spring Mountain	E	89
1994 Cabernet Sauvignon Marston Vineyard	Spring Mountain	E	95
1998 Cabernet Sauvignon Private Reserve	Napa	E	89

1997	Cabernet Sauvignon Private Reserve	Napa	E	94
1996	Cabernet Sauvignon Private Reserve	Napa	E	91+
1995	Cabernet Sauvignon Private Reserve	Napa	E	93
1994	Cabernet Sauvignon Private Reserve	Napa	E	94
1998	Cabernet Sauvignon Quarry Vineyard	Napa	E	(86–88)
1997	Cabernet Sauvignon Quarry Vineyard	Napa	E	(86–88)
1998	Cabernet Sauvignon St. Helena Home Vineyard	Napa	E	90
1997	Cabernet Sauvignon St. Helena Home Vineyard	Napa	E	92
1996	Cabernet Sauvignon St. Helena Vineyard	St. Helena	E	88
1995	Cabernet Sauvignon St. Helena Vineyard	St. Helena	E	93
1998	Cabernet Sauvignon State Lane Vineyard	Napa	E	88
1997	Cabernet Sauvignon State Lane Vineyard	Napa	E	90
1996	Cabernet Sauvignon State Lane Vineyard	Napa	E	90
1995	Cabernet Sauvignon State Lane Vineyard	Napa	E	90
1996	Cabernet Sauvignon Terre Rouge	Howell Mountain	E	90
1995	Cabernet Sauvignon Terre Rouge	Howell Mountain	EE	90
1994	Cabernet Sauvignon Terre Rouge	Howell Mountain	EE	88
1997	Cabernet Sauvignon Tre Colline Vineyard	Howell Mountain	EE	93
1996	Cabernet Sauvignon Tre Colline Vineyard	Howell Mountain	EE	88+
1995	Cabernet Sauvignon Tre Colline Vineyard	Howell Mountain	EE	90
1999	Chardonnay Private Reserve	Napa	E	92
1999	Chardonnay Sbragia Limited Release	Napa	E	94
1994	Meritage Red	Knights Valley	D	91
1998	Merlot Bancroft Ranch	Howell Mountain	E	88
1997	Merlot Bancroft Ranch	Howell Mountain	E	92
1996	Merlot Bancroft Ranch	Howell Mountain	E	93
1995	Merlot Bancroft Ranch	Howell Mountain	E	91
1994	Merlot Bancroft Ranch	Howell Mountain	D	92+
1997	Nightingale	Napa	E	91
1998	Petite Sirah Hayne Vineyard	Napa	D	(90–92)
1997	Petite Sirah Hayne Vineyard	Napa	D	91
1996	Petite Sirah Hayne Vineyard	Napa	D	93
1997	Petite Sirah Marston Vineyard	Napa	D	(92–94)
1996	Pinot Noir Stanly Ranch	Napa	D	90+
1995	Pinot Noir Stanly Ranch	Napa	D	90
1998	Syrah Marston Vineyard	Spring Mountain	D	89
1997	Syrah Marston Vineyard	Spring Mountain	D	90+

Beringer's highly respected wine-maker, Ed Sbragia, when asked which he felt were the finest vintages for Cabernet Sauvignon, Merlot, Cabernet Franc, etc., during the decade of the nineties, emphatically stated that 1991, 1997, 1994, and 1990 were the four top years. The largest crops were in 1997 and 1991, and the smallest in 1996 and 1998. The coolest years were 1998 and 1999 (and probably 2000), an interesting succession of three colder than normal years. Beringer has become one of the biggest wine companies in the world, having been acquired by the huge Australian beermeister Foster's. Let's hope they don't change the current formula for success, as Beringer and its sister wineries continue to be staffed by some of the most talented individuals in California winedom.

The 1999 Alluvium Proprietary White is a Bordeaux-inspired blend of 45% Sauvignon Blanc, 45% Sémillon, and the rest Chardonnay and Viognier. It is aged in 50% new oak and put through a complete malolactic fermentation to increase its texture as well as complexity. The result is reminiscent of a white Graves, with notes of passion fruit, a flinty character, spicy oak, and rich, melony, honeysuckle aromas and flavors. This fleshy, potentially outstanding white should age well for 3–4 years. The 1999 Chardonnay Private Reserve (20,000 cases) enjoys about 75% new oak. It is a structured, smoky, buttery, fat effort with oodles of honeyed fruit as well as outstanding ripeness, all wrapped in high-quality wood. Full-bodied and dense, this exceptional wine will drink well for 1–2 years. Beringer has increased the production of their most limited Chardonnay, the Sbragia Limited Release, to 3,500 cases. Made from a selection of the most highly extracted, richest, and densest wines, this Chardonnay can age well for 5–7 years, although it is probably best drunk in its first 3–4. The Sbragia's core component tends to come from Beringer's Gamble Ranch. The 1999 Chardonnay Sbragia Limited Release reveals more structure than previous vintages (due to the cool growing season). Dense and thick, with an unctuous texture as well as fine underlying acidity, smoky oak, rich, leesy, hazelnut married with copious quantities of tropical fruit, and a flamboyant personality, this sensational Chardonnay should drink well for 4–5 years.

Readers should be aware of the serious Petite Sirah and Syrah coming from Beringer. From Spring Mountain, Beringer is producing a Marston Vineyard Syrah. The 1998 exhibits a dense opaque purple color, copious quantities of blackberry, mineral, tar, and licorice aromas and flavors, medium to full body, and sweet tannin in the finish. From this tasting as well as others, it appears Syrah fared better in 1998 than Cabernet Sauvignon. The opaque purple-colored 1997 Syrah Marston Vineyard exhibits a gorgeous nose of blueberry jam, blackberries, minerals, and creosote. Full-bodied, dense, and super-concentrated, this terrific Syrah is backward, and not as open-knit and forward as many California Syrahs. Anticipated maturity: 2003–2020. I thought both the 1997 and 1998 Petite Sirah Hayne Vineyard were exceptional. The black/purple-colored 1997 Petite Sirah Hayne Vineyard reveals a powerful, smoky, black fruit, earth, and mineral-scented bouquet. Closed, but immense in the mouth, with huge tannin as well as gigantic levels of fruit and glycerin, this wine is set for three decades of evolution. It should be cellared for at least 5, possibly 10 years before consumption. Anticipated maturity: 2010–2035. The 1998 Petite Sirah Hayne Vineyard reveals more smoky charcoal notes as well as a more evolved personality. Powerful, dense, and well made, it will age well for 25 years.

The 1998 Cabernet Sauvignon and Merlot-based wines are the lightest produced during the 1990s. They are very good, but readers should not expect wines similar to the blockbuster efforts produced from 1991 through 1996. The 1997s tend to be denser, more concentrated wines. The 1998 Alluvium Proprietary Red is a blend of 75% Merlot, 20% Cabernet Sauvignon, and 5% Petit Verdot, Malbec, and Cabernet Franc from Beringer's holdings in Knights Valley. It offers a classy nose of minerals, lead pencil, plums, raspberries, and cherries. Drink this elegant, medium-bodied offering over the next 5–7 years. From Howell Mountain, an area that produced more compressed, herbaceous 1998s, the 1998 Merlot Bancroft Ranch was performing better with another year of aging. While lighter than most vintages, the 1998 reveals herb-tinged black cherries and plums. Charming, round, and medium-bodied, it is best drunk over the next 5–6 years. A strong effort, the 1998 Cabernet Sauvignon Private Reserve exhibits a dense ruby/purple color as well as a moderately intense bouquet of black currants infused with olive, smoke, licorice, and new oak. Supple, medium-bodied, and surprisingly evolved, with sweet fruit on the mid-palate and in the finish, it is a harmonious, charming offering to enjoy over the next 7–8 years.

Beringer's single-vineyard Cabernet Sauvignons are culled from their top vineyards, many of which are used in the Private Reserve blend. These are usually available in 200-case lots and are largely sold to Beringer's mailing list or directly from the winery. The tasting notes are short because of the wines' limited availability. The 1998 Cabernet Sauvignon State Lane Vineyard (this vineyard was recently sold and will appear in 3–4 years under the name Kapcsandy Estates) exhibits sweet cranberry, tobacco leaf, spice box, and sour cherry notes, medium body, and an elegant, straightforward finish. It should drink well for a decade. One of Beringer's outstanding single-vineyard Cabernets is the 1998 Cabernet Sauvignon Chabot Vineyard. Like all of these single-vineyard wines, it is produced from 100% Cabernet Sauvignon. Aromas of coffee, licorice, plums, blackberries, and currants emerge from the moderately intense bouquet. This opaque ruby-colored, dense, medium-bodied 1998 offers attractive fruit extract as well as concentration. Drink it over the next 10–12 years. The 1998 Cabernet Sauvignon St. Helena Home Vineyard looks to be another successful effort in this challenging year. A dense ruby color is followed by sweet, ripe black currant and cassis fruit. This open-knit, low-acid, evolved, fleshy, opulent Cabernet should drink well for 10–12 years.

As the following notes indicate, all of the 1997s possess denser, more opaque colors, riper fruit, and more body, volume, and expressive personalities than their 1998 counterparts. The 1997 Cabernet Sauvignon Knights Valley is an excellent introduction to Beringer's style. It offers black fruits, a touch of licorice and cedar, a supple texture, medium to full body, and a soft finish. Drink this delicious Cabernet during its first decade of life. There are 15,000 cases of the 1997 Cabernet Sauvignon Private Reserve. Composed of 97% Cabernet Sauvignon and 3% Cabernet Franc, and aged in 100% new French oak for 22–24 months, it is a sensational effort. The opaque plum/purple color is followed by a superb nose of smoked herbs, melted licorice, and black currant jam. Full-bodied, with a silky texture and an opulent personality, this sexy, full-throttle Cabernet Sauvignon will be delicious young, yet last for 18–20 years. The 1997 Cabernet Sauvignon State Lane Vineyard is an elegant, finesse-styled wine with medium to full body, a seamless personality, abundant mineral, red and black currant fruit flavors, as well as a supple texture and finish. Not a big wine (13.8% alcohol), it should drink well for 10–12 years. The 1997 Cabernet Sauvignon St. Helena Home Vineyard offers copious quantities of blackberry/cassis fruit, in addition to more tannin and structure than the Quarry or State Lane offerings. Spicy, with outstanding ripeness, a big, chewy mid-section, and intriguing roasted coffee and black currant flavors, this will be a large-scaled Cabernet to drink during its first 15 years of life. From the cooler climate Spring Mountain vineyard, the 1997 Cabernet Sauvignon Marston Vineyard is a distinctive blackberry and blueberry-scented and -flavored wine, with medium body, moderately high tannin, and a long finish. The provocative 1997 Cabernet Sauvignon Chabot Vineyard is a denser wine with more loamy soil scents intermixed with chocolate, licorice, creosote, and copious blackberry and cassis fruit. Full-bodied and chewy, with superb concentration, symmetry, and purity, as well as moderate tannin in the finish, it will be at its finest between 2004–2022. The beautiful 1997 Cabernet Sauvignon Tre Colline offers sexy, ostentatious notes of licorice, cherry liqueur, black fruits, and spicy oak. On the palate, cigar box flavors add to the mélange of complex characteristics found in the bouquet. Fleshy, juicy, and succulent, with dazzling ripeness, low acidity, and sweet, well-integrated tannin, it will be ready to drink between now–2020. One of the most prodigious 1997 Beringer wines is the 1997 Cabernet Sauvignon Bancroft Ranch. Opaque purple-colored, with an extroverted, floral, blueberry, mineral, and black currant–scented bouquet, this formidably endowed Cabernet possesses dazzling concentration, explosive richness that stains the palate, and finishes with sensational extract and balance. The tannin is high, but sweet and well integrated. This large-scaled, muscular, mountain Cabernet Sauvignon will require 3–5 years of patience. Anticipated maturity: 2005–2025.

The 1997 Merlot Bancroft Ranch (100% new oak) is a dense, full-bodied effort exhibiting black cherry liqueur, chocolate, mineral, and lead pencil aromas and flavors. Fleshy and chewy, it will be undeniably seductive upon release. It should drink well for 15+ years.

To date, Beringer's Alluvium Proprietary Red has been a Merlot-dominated *cuvée*, with small quantities of Cabernet Sauvignon, Cabernet Franc, Petit Verdot, and occasionally Malbec thrown in to provide additional nuances. The 1997 Alluvium Proprietary Red (about 77% Merlot) was showing better in 2000 than it was the previous year. Most of the fruit comes from Beringer's Knights Valley vineyard, and it sees 40% new oak during its upbringing. It is meant to be an elegant wine, and the 1997 offers intense berry and mocha-tinged fruit with background notes of pencil shavings, minerals, and flowers, a lush mid-section, and sweet tannin in the finish. Seamless for such a young wine (a hallmark of the finest 1997s), it should drink well for 10–15 years. A new single-vineyard offering, the medium ruby/purple-colored 1997 Cabernet Sauvignon Quarry Vineyard exhibits a round, supple-textured personality, depth, and, I suspect, early maturity. It should drink well upon release and last for 10–12 years. Lighter and softer, with less persistence and intensity once past the berry/black currant–scented nose, the 1998 Cabernet Sauvignon Quarry Vineyard will be a candidate for early consumption, over the next 7–8 years.

Two wines of compelling concentration and attention-getting power are the 1996 Petite Sirah Hayne Vineyard and 1997 Petite Sirah Marston Vineyard. Both of these wines saw 100% new oak (50% American and 50% French). They are hugely extracted, black/purple-colored, totally unevolved wines. The 1996 Petite Sirah Hayne Vineyard is beginning to reveal secondary aromas of smoke, Asian spices, and cigar box, in addition to classic cassis, blackberry flavors. A monster wine, it needs at least 5–7 years of cellaring; it will keep for 2–3 decades. The 1997 Petite Sirah Marston Vineyard has a small amount of fruit (25%) from the Hayne Vineyard added to the blend. This wine boasts phenomenal intensity, massive body, and a boatload of tannin and glycerin. A huge example, it will not become civilized for another 5–6 years. It should keep for 20–25 years.

The single-vineyard Cabernet Francs from Howell Mountain are aged in 100% new French oak, which has been soaked up nicely. These are charming, softer, less extracted offerings than the single vineyard Merlots or Cabernet Sauvignons. Nevertheless, they are not wimpish wines. The dark ruby/purple-colored 1995 Cabernet Franc Howell Mountain offers a complex nose of herbs, earth, black fruits, and spicy wood. Medium-bodied, round, and velvety-textured, this attractive wine needs to be consumed during its first decade of life. The same finesse, elegance, spice, and fruit character can be found in the medium-bodied 1996 Cabernet Franc Howell Mountain. However, its aromatics include a slight touch of menthol/mint. Drink this stylish wine over the next 7–8 years. The 1997 Cabernet Franc Howell Mountain is cut from the same mold. Spicy, with ripe fruit and intelligently put together, it is not quite as extracted or as flavorful as the 1995 or 1996. However, it should put on more weight after additional cask aging.

I am largely unconvinced by Beringer's Pinot Noirs. Progress has been made, but this is one varietal that appears to be the Achilles' heel in what is otherwise a superb portfolio. There are now two *cuvées*, a Stanly Ranch and a North Coast offering. Beringer occasionally produces merely mortal wines. However, both the 1995 and 1996 Pinot Noir Stanly Ranch are major improvements. The 1995 Pinot Noir Stanly Ranch actually requires a year or two in the bottle. This black/purple-colored wine exhibits a sweet nose of plum and black cherry fruit, followed by subtle spicy, toasty, oaky notes. In the mouth, it is medium-bodied and rich, with plenty of length, and light to moderate tannin. It should age well for 7–8 years. The deep ruby/purple-colored 1996 Pinot Noir Stanly Ranch reveals a blueberry/raspberry-scented nose. The wine is dense and chewy, with excellent purity and light tannin in the finish. Lower in acidity, with softer tannin than the 1995, the 1996 is significantly more concentrated than the 1994 (as is the 1995).

Beringer does a superb job with its production from the Bancroft Ranch on Howell Mountain. About 8,000 cases of their single-vineyard Merlot are produced. This wine spends 20 months in French oak coopered by the well-known house of Seguin-Moreau. The 1995 Merlot Bancroft Ranch exhibits an opaque ruby/purple color, followed by a stunning nose of chocolate, minerals, black cherries, and toast. A serious, mountain-styled Merlot, it displays full body, outstanding concentration and purity, and moderate tannin. It needs to be cellared for another 2–3 years, but will last 15 years. The 1996 Merlot Bancroft Ranch was showing much better when I tasted it in 1998 than it did 11 months earlier. The wine boasts a saturated purple color, as well as an exquisite nose of brandy-infused black cherries intermixed with melted chocolate. Dense and full-bodied, with striking sweetness and purity, this multi-layered Merlot has developed beautifully. Although it will benefit from another 4–5 years of bottle age, it can be drunk now or cellared. It, too, will keep for 15 years. The 1994 Merlot Bancroft Ranch opens quickly in the glass. The dark ruby/purple color is followed by smoky, chocolaty, and black cherry aromas with new oak in the background. In the mouth, this wine is full-bodied, with explosive levels of glycerin and richness on the back of the palate. Dense, concentrated, tannic, and angular, it is capable of lasting 15+ years. In fact, I recommend 3–4 years of cellaring before serious consumption begins.

The following vintages of Beringer's Alluvium Proprietary Red all include a minimum of 75% Merlot, with 10–20% Cabernet Sauvignon. These wines are made in a claret style, with less power and extraction, but more finesse and accessibility. They appear to contain enough tannin for 10–12 years of aging potential. The 1995 Alluvium Proprietary Red reveals a dark ruby color, an elegant, berry, earth, and cherry-scented nose, medium to full body, and admirable complexity and accessibility. When I tasted it in 1997, I thought the wine was outstanding. While I rated it slightly lower after retasting it in 1998, it is nevertheless an excellent offering. I would opt for drinking it over the next 7–10 years. The 1996 Alluvium Proprietary Red is a lusher, riper wine with nicely displayed sweet black currant and cherry fruit. Although there is some tannin at the back of the mouth, the wine's appeal is its savory, fleshy, up-front style and purity of fruit, with an absence of aggressive acidity, tannin, or alcohol. It should drink well for a decade. The 1994 Alluvium is a textbook proprietary wine. It displays a dark ruby color, followed by an attractive black fruit–scented nose with subtle toasty oak intertwined with herbs, earth, and chocolaty notes. In the mouth, black cherry fruit and toast are presented in a medium- to full-bodied, silky-smooth, delicious format. Very accessible, it should continue to drink well for a decade.

Beringer's limited production, single-vineyard Cabernet Sauvignons are part of what Beringer calls their "Vineyard Collection." Produced in 200-case lots, readers expecting to find them sitting on a shelf in their local retail shops will be disappointed, as they are destined to be sold through Beringer's mailing list or directly from the winery. That is not the case with the Knights Valley Cabernet Sauvignon or Private Reserve Cabernet Sauvignon, both of which are made in abundant quantities. One of the safest choices a consumer can make, both have been consistently fine and accurate representations of Cabernet's varietal characteristics. The 1996 Cabernet Sauvignon Knights Valley offers more smokiness intertwined with jammy black currant fruit. The wine's excellent richness, plush, user-friendly style, and fruit-driven personality have resulted in a crowd-pleasing, modestly priced Cabernet Sauvignon that should last for a decade or more. The excellent, nearly outstanding 1994 Cabernet Sauvignon Knights Valley exhibits a dark ruby/purple color and a sweet black currant–scented nose with smoky oak and earthy, chocolaty notes. I thought this medium-bodied, richly fruity, delicious wine was outstanding in 1996, but slightly less prodigious in 1997. It should drink well for a decade, and possibly earn an even higher score.

I cannot recall a disappointing vintage of Beringer's Private Reserve Cabernet Sauvignon.

A production of 10,000–15,000 cases makes the wine's outstanding quality even more enviable. The 1995 Cabernet Sauvignon Private Reserve is a full-bodied, explosively rich, deep purple-colored wine bursting with ripe fruit. It displays smoky oak, gobs of cassis, a touch of cigar box and cedar, and a layered, multidimensional feel. This voluptuous, seductive offering is already drinking well, yet should age effortlessly for 15–20 years. The 1996 Cabernet Sauvignon Private Reserve reveals more concentration as well as higher tannin. I know it is a trade-off, but I suspect this vintage will not be as sexy in its youthfulness as the 1995. The black ruby/purple-colored 1996 offers more licorice, in addition to the obvious levels of toast, jammy black currant fruit, and spice notes. Structured, full-bodied, and powerful, this may be a Private Reserve to cellar for several years and consume over the subsequent 15–18. By the way, statisticians should note that the Private Reserve is always at least 97% Cabernet Sauvignon and aged for 22–24 months in 100% new French oak. One of the common threads I find in the Private Reserve Cabernet Sauvignon is a smoky, chocolaty, licorice character that works well with the lavish quantities of fruit and glycerin these wines possess. The terrific 1994 Cabernet Sauvignon Private Reserve offers an opaque purple color, a gorgeous nose of toasty oak, and a silky, concentrated texture with unobtrusive acidity or tannin. The wine possesses layered richness, remarkable balance, sweet, pure fruit, and a finish that lasts for nearly 30 seconds. These wines are aged in 100% new oak, and tend to possesses at least 97% Cabernet Sauvignon, with the balance Cabernet Franc. Amazingly, the oak is not a pronounced component in the final wine, a testament to excellent winemaking and the concentration these wines possess. Like so many top 1994s from Napa and Sonoma, this wine was accessible when released in early 1998, but will age well for two decades.

The State Lane Vineyard is situated on extremely rocky soil in the Yountville area. Beringer's 1995 Cabernet Sauvignon State Lane Vineyard possess a St.-Emilion-like cherry, tobacco, and sweet currant-scented nose, and soft, round, ripe, berry flavors. A seductively styled, medium- to full-bodied, accessible Cabernet, it is ideal for consuming now and over the next 15 years. The same silky tannins can be found in the 1996 Cabernet Sauvignon State Lane Vineyard. This vintage tended to produce harder, more tannic and rustic wines, but that is not the case with this *cuvée*. The wine possesses plenty of sweet, jammy, plum and black currant fruit, cigar box, and spice aromas, some cedar, and a silky, layered, lush, medium- to full-bodied personality. It can be drunk during its first 15–18 years of life.

The medium- to full-bodied 1996 Cabernet Sauvignon Marston Vineyard reveals more red currant notes than the 1997, but is slightly less concentrated. It is an impressively constructed, rich wine that is not quite as seductive and forward as the State Lane offering. I envision it lasting for two decades. Two hundred cases were produced of the 1994 Cabernet Sauvignon Marston Vineyard. This stunning Cabernet boasts a dense black/purple color, jammy blueberry and cassis aromas, and a fruit-driven style. Despite being aged in 100% new oak, little wood is noticeable in this sexy, voluptuously textured, dazzlingly concentrated, richly fruity wine. Its low acidity and purity make for a compellingly drinkable Cabernet Sauvignon. Anticipated maturity: now–2012.

Beringer's Cabernet Sauvignon Tre Colline from Howell Mountain debuted in 1995. These are tannic, backward, full-bodied wines with considerable punch and depth. The 1995 is a multidimensional, spicy wine with copious quantities of black currant fruit intermixed with cedar and weedy tobacco. Full-bodied, pure, and nicely textured, it should be at its best with another 2–3 years of cellaring, and keep for two decades. The dense purple-colored 1996 Cabernet Sauvignon Tre Colline is backward, tannic, and in need of 5–6 years of bottle age. All the component parts are present, but this wine requires patience.

The St. Helena Vineyard Cabernet Sauvignon series offers another interesting style. The 1995 Cabernet Sauvignon St. Helena Vineyard exhibits a fragrant, smoky nose of loamy soil scents, underbrush, and ripe, brandy-infused black currants and cherries. This rich wine is full-bodied, with superb density and a lush texture. Beautifully made and complex, with a terrific mid-palate and length (always signs of high quality), it can be drunk now or cellared for 15+ years. The 1996 Cabernet Sauvignon St. Helena Vineyard is the antithesis of the 1995—stern, tannic, and backward. While broodingly powerful and brawny, its tannin dominates at present. It was closed when I tasted it, so I am anxious to retaste it prior to release.

Undoubtedly the best-known Beringer single-vineyard Cabernet is from their Chabot Vineyard. Like the other offerings in this series, this is a 100% Cabernet Sauvignon aged in 100% new-oak casks. The accessible 1995 Cabernet Sauvignon Chabot Vineyard reveals medium to full body and a knockout nose of roasted herbs, grilled meats, coffee, cassis, and cherry fruit. In the mouth, it is viscous and full-bodied, with a chewy mid-section and a spicy, long, rich finish. It will last for two decades. The 1996 Cabernet Sauvignon Chabot Vineyard offers aromas and flavors of chocolate liqueur infused with brandy as well as loamy soil intermixed with damp forest, underbrush scents. Full-bodied, with massive power, and chewy, thick, structured, chocolaty fruit flavors, this is a complex yet backward, formidably endowed Cabernet Sauvignon with palate-staining levels of extract and tannin. Give it 3–4 years of bottle age, and consume it over the following two decades. The 1994 Cabernet Sauvignon Chabot Vineyard is a backward, muscular wine that is 5–7 years away from drinkability. With airing, the wine reluctantly gives up scents of pepper, iodine, cassis, mint, and earth. This full-bodied, large-scaled Cabernet begs for more bottle time. This wine should only be purchased by those willing to invest patience, as it will not provide enjoyable drinking when young.

The limited production Cabernet Sauvignon Bancroft Ranch offerings are also outstanding. Previously I had a slight preference for the 1996 over the 1995, but an extra year of bottle age has caused the 1995 to leap-frog over the 1996. For now, the 1995 looks to be slightly more complete and multidimensional than the 1996, but readers should look out for the phenomenal 1997. The 1995 Cabernet Sauvignon Bancroft Ranch exhibits an opaque black/purple color and stunning aromatics consisting of minerals, blueberries, blackberries, and cassis. Terrific in the mouth, it offers full body, a racy, chewy texture, high tannin, but wonderful sweetness and balance. It was impressive and flamboyant when I tasted it in September 1998. Anticipated maturity: now–2025. The 1996 Cabernet Sauvignon Bancroft Ranch may possess an even more saturated, thicker, black/purple color. Some tannin has emerged since I tasted it last year, when it was far more velvety. This is a powerhouse, extremely full-bodied, palate-staining wine. Its enormous extract, richness, and elevated tannin seem to suggest this wine is about ready to settle down for a long period of dormancy. Anticipated maturity: 2005–2025. Also look for the 1994 Cabernet Sauvignon Bancroft Vineyard. This opaque purple-colored wine offers toasty, smoky oak in its nose, as well as the telltale cassis and mineral aromas that emerge from Howell Mountain wines. Rich, powerful, full-bodied flavors, and excellent purity and sweetness of fruit further characterize this broad-shouldered wine. There is also plenty of tannin, suggesting it will require 3–4 years of cellaring after its release. It will keep for two decades.

A Cabernet Sauvignon Terre Rouge was produced in 1994, 1995, and 1996. These are among the more backward, austere, and angular of these single-vineyard wines. The 1994 Cabernet Sauvignon Terre Rouge reveals a dark ruby color, spice, leafy tobacco, and earthy aromas, sweet black cherry and cassis fruit, medium body, and moderate tannin. It will need 2–4 years of cellaring and keep for 15 or more. The 1995 Cabernet Sauvignon Terre Rouge offers a dense, dark purple color, more fatness and fleshiness to its texture, fuller body, and concentrated, rich flavors. More forward than the 1994, with less austerity, it should drink well for 12–15 years. I found the 1996 Cabernet Sauvignon Terre Rouge to be more fruit- than structure-driven. It exhibits copious quantities of red and black fruit in its nose, low acidity, obvious glycerin, a thick, chewy texture, and a spicy, medium- to full-bodied finish. Although the 1996 will not be as backward as the 1994, neither will it be as fleshy as the 1995.

Beringer's 1995 Cabernet Franc Terre Rouge possesses sweet fruit, along with a structured feel. Medium-bodied, with an attractive red and black currant, mineral, spicy-scented nose, this wine displays a moderately intense personality, as well as spice and sweet tannin in the finish. It should drink well young, yet keep for 10–12 years. The 1994 Cabernet Franc Terre Rouge exhibits a dense ruby/purple color, a spicy, fragrant, black fruit, mineral, and chocolaty nose, rich flavors, and a moderately weighty feel on the palate. The wine's tannin and acidity are soft and well integrated. Although it is easy to understand and drink, this Cabernet Franc promises to evolve gracefully for a decade.

Beringer is also turning out some excellent to outstanding Meritage blends, which are mostly Merlot-based wines. The 1994 is composed of 80% Merlot and 20% Cabernet Sauvignon from grapes grown in the Knights Valley. Fat, rich, and ripe, the 1994 Meritage should ensure that Merlot fans have a steady fix of high-quality Merlot for the next several years.

Lastly, there are 400 cases of the 1997 Nightingale, a blend of botrytis-infected Sémillon (70%) and Sauvignon Blanc (30%). A Sauternes look-alike, it boasts a honeyed pineapple, coconut, assorted tropical fruit–scented nose and flavors. Viscous, with good underlying acidity, the wood is subtle, not aggressive. I cannot imagine these wines will age for 30–50 years like a great French Sauternes, but this delicious offering should keep for a decade.

Past Glories: 1993 Alluvium Red (90), 1993 Cabernet Sauvignon (90), 1993 Cabernet Sauvignon Chabot Vineyard (90?), 1993 Meritage Red (90), 1993 Merlot Bancroft Ranch (93+), Cabernet Sauvignon Private Reserve—1994 (95), 1993 (92+), 1991 (95), 1990 (93), 1987 (93), 1986 (91)

ROBERT BIALE VINEYARDS (NAPA)

1999	Zinfandel Aldo's Vineyard	Napa	D	91
1996	Zinfandel Aldo's Vineyard	Napa	D	90
1999	Zinfandel Black Chicken Vineyard	Napa	D	89
1999	Zinfandel Falleri Vineyard	Napa	EE (1.5 ml)	93
1999	Zinfandel Monte Rosso Vineyard	Sonoma	D	91
1996	Zinfandel Monte Rosso Vineyard	Sonoma	D	92
1999	Zinfandel Old Crane Ranch	Napa	D	88
1996	Zinfandel Old Crane Ranch	Napa	D	90
1999	Zinfandel Robert Biale Vineyards	Sonoma	D	90
1999	Zinfandel Spenker Vineyard	Lodi	D	90
1999	Zinfandel Valsecchi Vineyard	Sonoma	D	93

Biale is emerging as one of California's top half-dozen or so Zinfandel producers. His 1999s are consistently brilliant efforts. For starters, the 1999 Zinfandel Spenker Vineyard (14.8% alcohol) is a knockout example of Zinfandel from the unheralded Lodi region. Its dense ruby/purple color is accompanied by copious quantities of sweet, uncomplicated black cherry and berry fruit offered in a spicy, full-bodied, luxuriously rich style. It is delicious to drink now and over the next 3–4 years. Similar in strength (14.9% alcohol), the dense ruby/purple-colored 1999 Zinfandel Old Crane Ranch exhibits a more subdued aromatic profile that, with air, offers up black cherry and berry fruit intertwined with pepper and underbrush scents. More structured and monolithic, with some tannin, it appears to be more ageworthy, but my experience has shown that Zinfandel rarely improves after 5–7 years in the bottle. The 1999 Zinfandel Aldo's Vineyard (14.9% alcohol) reveals a Rhône Valley–like perfume of dried Provençal herbs, pepper, black cherries, and spicy oak. It is voluptuously textured, full-bodied, rich, pure, and harmonious. Consume this sumptuous, large-scaled, dry, friendly Zinfandel over the next 5–6 years. The dark ruby-colored 1999 Zinfandel Robert Biale Vineyards (14.9% alcohol) offers up a sweet, spicy nose of herbs, jammy cherry fruit, pepper, and earth. Medium- to full-bodied, supple, tangy, and spicy, with plenty of flesh and fruit, it will drink well for 2–3 years.

A new vineyard experience for me, the 1999 Zinfandel Valsecchi Vineyard (15.2% alcohol) exhibits an impressively saturated ruby color as well as a sumptuously sweet nose of pure black fruits infused with floral and blueberry characteristics. It possesses a Pomerol-like lushness, berry fruit (cherries, blueberries, and blackberries), full body, and a seamless personality. While it will not make old bones, it will provide compelling drinking over the next 4–6 years. Another Napa offering, the dense ruby-colored 1999 Zinfandel Black Chicken Vineyard (15.3% alcohol) displays a funky bouquet of herbs, oak, and lees, with none of the fruit notes found in its siblings. In the mouth, however, the wine sings. It has a fat, succulent texture, medium to full body, excellent purity, and a long, 20–30-second finish. If the nose develops more nuances, this wine may merit a 90-point score. Consumption over the next 3–4 years is suggested. From a well-known site, the 1999 Zinfandel Monte Rosso Vineyard (15% alcohol) displays strikingly pure aromatics consisting of black fruits, crushed stones, pepper, and earth. Impeccably balanced, full-bodied, with ripe, clean fruit, and a long, thick, rich, smooth finish, it is another terrific effort. The 1999 Zinfandel Falleri Vineyard (15.2% alcohol) is available only in magnums. There were less than 50 cases produced. From a vineyard near Calistoga, it is a dense ruby/purple-colored offering revealing a bouquet reminiscent of a top-class Châteauneuf-du-Pape. Pepper, black cherry jam, and earth aromas are followed by a full-bodied, velvety-textured, ripe, heady Zinfandel with a boatload of fruit, glycerin, and character. It should drink well for 5–7 years. These are all terrific examples of Zinfandel.

Biale's 1996s are all outstanding Zinfandel. The 1996 Zinfandel Aldo's Vineyard (875 cases) is an unfiltered, sexy wine with considerable personality. This dark plum-colored effort offers up earthy, jammy, sweet cranberry and raspberry notes along with pepper, incense, and spice. Generous, with a robust constitution and gobs of glycerin (14.6% alcohol), this supple, full-bodied, concentrated, hedonistic, opulently textured Zinfandel should be consumed over the next 3–4 years. While it is difficult to pick a favorite from this exceptional trio of 1996s, I had a slight preference for the unfiltered 1996 Zinfandel Monte Rosso Vineyard (675 cases produced). It possesses the most saturated plum/purple color and displays its personality in a flamboyant, full-bodied manner. This gorgeous Zin boasts copious quantities of pepper, spice, and rich cherry/black raspberry jam–like notes. The subtle oak influence adds to the creamy texture of this concentrated, dramatically styled wine. Drink this sinfully rich Zinfandel now and over the next 5–6 years. Lastly, the 1996 Zinfandel Old Crane Ranch (800 cases bottled without filtration) is another hedonistic, fat, layered, ostentatious Zinfandel with copious quantities of berry fruit, glycerin, extract, and alcohol (15.4%). The wine's low acidity, lavish richness, and attention-getting style will be immensely pleasing to Zinfandel enthusiasts over the next 4–5 years.

BLACKJACK RANCH (SANTA BARBARA)

1997	Cabernet Sauvignon	Santa Barbara	D	(87–90)
1999	Harmonie Proprietary Red Wine	Santa Barbara	D	92
1997	Harmonie Proprietary Red Wine	Santa Barbara	D	90
1999	Le Mas Rouge	Santa Barbara/		
		San Luis Obispo	C	88
1999	Merlot Billy Goat Hill Estate	Santa Barbara	D	93
1998	Pinot Noir Laetitia Vineyard	San Luis Obispo	D	88
1999	Syrah Estate	Santa Barbara	D	87
1998	Syrah Estate	Santa Barbara	D	89

This promising new performer, situated outside the village of Los Olives, is run by Roger Wisted, who farms approximately 17 acres. Wisted is attempting to capture as much as possible in the wines of Santa Barbara. His first releases were impressive offerings, and in 1999 a Syrah was also produced. Roger Wisted has turned out some very interesting Rhône Ranger *cuvées*. The dark ruby-colored 1998 Syrah Estate reveals a Pinot Noir–like complexity in its smoky, cassis, and camphor-scented bouquet. Flavors of plums, herbs, and pepper are apparent in this medium-bodied, serious, complex Syrah. Its style is a combination of a Côte d'Or red Burgundy and a southern Rhône Crozes-Hermitage. Drink it over the next 6–7 years. From a cooler year, the 1999 Syrah Estate exhibits more herbaceousness as well as a tighter, more restrained and closed style. However, there is plenty of underlying complexity and fruit. The less expensive 1999 Le Mas Rouge, a blend of Santa Barbara and San Luis Obispo fruit, reveals copious notes of cherries, Provençal herbs, crushed pepper, and a hint of *garrigue*. It is a medium-bodied, fun wine to enjoy during its first 3–4 years of life.

Wisted's breakthrough efforts are the Merlot and Cabernet Sauvignon produced in 1999, a cool year that managed to produce wines of exceptional richness and concentration, at least for Blackjack Ranch. The awesome 1999 Merlot Billy Goat Hill Estate (544 cases) is one of the finest produced in California. The fact that it is from Santa Barbara is a revelation. It reminds me of the 1990 Clinet from Pomerol. A saturated purple color is followed by an extraordinary bouquet of espresso, black fruits, cocoa, and vanilla, an explosive attack, an unctuous texture, admirable freshness, and amazing concentration and thickness. It will drink well for 15 years. If this wine were from Napa Valley, it would be selling for three times the price. Readers take note. Another great achievement is the 1999 Harmonie, a blend of 51% Cabernet Sauvignon, 39% Cabernet Franc, 7% Merlot, and 3% Syrah. An opaque black/purple color is accompanied by scents of blackberry liqueur intertwined with cassis, licorice, graphite, and toast. Full-bodied, with a seamless texture, beautifully integrated acidity and tannin, and a long, layered, concentrated finish, it will live for two decades.

The red wine program includes a fine Pinot Noir. The 1998 Laetitia Vineyard could easily pass for a good premier cru from Vosne-Romanée. It exhibits an earthy, spicy, vanilla, floral, and cherry-scented bouquet, an elegant, medium-bodied personality, sweet fruit, and unmistakable Pinot characteristics. This complex effort should continue to develop for 4–5 years. My notes state that this wine had a 91-point bouquet and 87-point flavors. The impressive 1997 Harmonie Proprietary Red Wine (a blend of 86% Cabernet Sauvignon, 6% Petit Verdot, 4% Cabernet Franc, and 4% Merlot) offers a complex nose of black fruits, roasted coffee, dried herbs, and earth. The wine possesses outstanding ripeness, sweet, rich fruit, firm tannin, a nicely delineated personality, as well as vigor and exuberance. Age this wine for another 3–4 years; it should evolve nicely for 15+.

The 1997 Cabernet Sauvignon (under 500 cases) is made from purchased fruit grown in a 17-year-old vineyard in Los Olives. Aged in equal parts American and French oak, it is still grapy, unevolved, and backward, but reveals outstanding potential. The vegetal character often found in Cabernets from this area is not present in this offering. Made from extremely ripe fruit, Blackjack Ranch's 1997 Cabernet Sauvignon is an opaque black/purple-colored wine with moderately intense aromatics consisting of cassis, blackberries, licorice, and cigar box scents. The oak is well integrated and the tannin high, but the wine possesses a sweet, rich mid-palate, excellent to outstanding texture, and fine length. It should be an impressive debut release for Roger Wisted's Blackjack Ranch. Anticipated maturity: now–2020.

BLOCKHEADIA RINGNOSII (NAPA)

1998 Zinfandel	Napa	C	89
1998 Zinfandel	Russian River	C	88
1999 Zinfandel Lorenza Lake Winery	Napa	C	90

Michael Ouellette, the former manager of the popular Napa Valley bistro Mustard's Grill, is now a full-time wine-maker. His Rhône Valley–inspired, full-throttle 1999 Zinfandel Lorenza Lake offers up scents of pepper, kirsch, dried Provençal herbs, spices, and earth. Fleshy, full-bodied, hedonistic, and chewy, with outstanding concentration, excellent purity, and abundant personality, this is a sumptuous Zinfandel to enjoy over the next 3–4 years.

The delicious, full-throttle 1998 Zinfandel Napa exhibits a dense ruby/purple color and a Gigondas-like bouquet and flavors of pepper, smoke, Provençal herbs, black cherries, and blackberries. Full-bodied and chewy, it reveals more of a Rhône-like personality than Zinfandel. Delicious and fleshy, with abundant depth, and a low-acid, plump, chewy finish, it will drink well for 5–7 years. Another Rhône-like offering is the 1998 Zinfandel Russian River. A dark plum/ruby/purple color is accompanied by a moderately intense nose of pepper, spice, plums, dried raspberries, and cherries. Velvety-textured, sexy, and opulent, with abundant quantities of succulent fruit, this is a hedonistic wine to drink over the next 2–3 years. Its medium-bodied fleshiness will offer considerable appeal, but readers looking for a textbook, briery, tangy, cherry, raspberry Zinfandel without a lot of spice will be less impressed with this wine than I was.

BONNY DOON VINEYARD (SANTA CRUZ)

1999 Le Cigare Volant	California	C	87
2000 Old Telegram (Mourvèdre)	California	D	86

The dark ruby/purple-colored 2000 Old Telegram displays an intensely fragrant nose of jammy black raspberries and spice. In the mouth, it is rich and medium- to full-bodied, with admirable layers of flavor and extract. This is a classy, young, expansively flavored, rather elegant Mourvèdre that should age effortlessly for a decade or more.

The 1999 Le Cigare Volant, a Grenache, Mourvèdre, Cinsault, and Syrah blend, is proprietor Randall Grahm's interpretation of a California-styled Châteauneuf-du-Pape. Surprisingly, the best vintage Grahm made was the first one, 1984. The 1999 is a good effort, exhibiting a deep ruby color, plenty of jammy, raspberry, and cherry fruit, medium body, good spice, fine purity, and a long finish. It is ideal for drinking over the next 4–5 years. Think of it as a Côtes du Rhône/St.-Joseph blend, rather than a Châteauneuf-du-Pape.

BREWER-CLIFTON (SANTA BARBARA)

2000 Chardonnay Katherine's Vineyard	Santa Maria	D	92
1999 Chardonnay Katherine's Vineyard	Santa Maria	D	88
2000 Chardonnay Marcella's Vineyard	Santa Maria	D	93+
1999 Chardonnay Marcella's Vineyard	Santa Maria	D	91
2000 Chardonnay Mount Carmel Vineyard	Santa Ynez	D	90
2000 Chardonnay Sweeney Canyon	Santa Ynez	D	94
1999 Chardonnay Sweeney Canyon	Santa Ynez	D	90
1998 Pinot Noir	Santa Maria	D	91
1997 Pinot Noir	Santa Maria	D	90
2000 Pinot Noir Clos Pepé Vineyard	Santa Ynez	D	90
2000 Pinot Noir Julia's Vineyard	Santa Maria	D	94
1997 Pinot Noir Julia's Vineyard	Santa Barbara	D	88
2000 Pinot Noir Melville Vineyard	Santa Ynez	D	96
2000 Pinot Noir Rozak Ranch	Santa Ynez	D	88
2000 Pinot Noir Santa Maria Hills	Santa Maria	D	91
1999 Pinot Noir Santa Maria Hills	Santa Maria	D	92

Greg Brewer and Steve Clifton represent the extraordinary potential that exists in selected microclimates in Santa Barbara County. In a few short years, this young, energetic twosome have astonished this critic with the breadth and complexity of their Chardonnays and Pinot Noirs. Their 2000 Pinot Noirs are among the finest New World Pinots I have ever tasted. Sadly, the production is small, averaging 100–200 cases of each *cuvée*.

The Pinot Noirs are produced from small yields, fermented in one-and-a-half-ton, open-top fermenters, with 100% whole clusters, aged in one-third new French oak, and bottled with neither fining nor filtration. The 2000 Pinot Noir Clos Pepé comes from one of the new vineyards in the cool Santa Rita hills. Exhibiting a premier cru Côtes de Beaune–like style, it offers a dark ruby color along with a sweet perfume of black cherries and apple skins. It is a sexy, charming, full-bodied, lush, generous Pinot Noir to enjoy over the next 6–7 years. The medium ruby-colored 2000 Pinot Noir Rozak Ranch displays a pronounced earthy, peppery, spicy nose, high acidity, a meaty, chewy mid-palate, and a firm finish. It possesses less aromatic and flavor dimension than its siblings, but has plenty of structure. Firm and closed, it is not dissimilar from a structured, moderately tannic Pommard. Anticipated maturity: 2003–2010. There are approximately 200 cases of the stunning 2000 Pinot Noir Santa Maria Hills. This offering reveals a complex nose of earth, figs, black cherries, spice, and apple skin. In the mouth, it is Volnay-like, with sweet red and black fruits, beautifully integrated acidity and tannin, subtle wood, a supple texture, and a 30–35-second finish. This beauty can be drunk now as well as over the next decade. The blockbuster 2000 Pinot Noir Julia's Vineyard is the best effort I have tasted from this well-known site in Santa Maria Valley. Reminiscent of a great vintage of Ponsot's Clos de la Roche Vieilles Vignes, it boasts a dark plum color as well as a broodingly backward but promising nose of flowers, plums, black cherries, flowers, and minerals. It possesses profound concentration, surprisingly high but well-hidden alcohol (15.3%), and a multilayered, sumptuous finish that lasts for nearly 45 seconds. It is a tour de force in New World Pinot Noir. Drink it over the next 7–10 years. Another compelling example is the 2000 Pinot Noir Melville Vineyard, from a new vineyard planted with Dijon clones #114 and #115. This wine gave me a sense of déjà vu (when I first tasted the 1990 Domaine de la Romanée Conti La Tâche). An incredibly complex nose of flowers, red and black fruits, earth, and prunes is followed by a full-bodied, fabulously concentrated wine that is extremely light on its feet. With terrific definition, refreshing underlying acidity, and a staggeringly long finish, this outrageously complex, rich Pinot Noir should drink well for a decade. Remarkably, it is made from young vines.

The evolved, spicy, rich 1999 Pinot Noir Santa Maria Hills is a seductive tease offering plenty of black fruits intermixed with spice, plum, and floral notes. Offering terrific fruit on the attack, mid-palate, and finish, it's the complete package. Drink it over the next 5–7 years.

The 1998 Pinot Noir exhibits a Domaine Dujac–like fragrance and personality. The light to medium ruby color belies the wine's richness and complexity. Notes of kirsch, cherry jam, cinnamon, black tea, and clean foresty aromas (the French say *sous bois*) soar from the glass of this complex Pinot Noir. It is silky-textured, with fine underlying acidity, subtle and nuanced flavors, and a long, medium- to full-bodied finish. Yields were 0.9 tons of fruit per acre, and the production was extremely limited. Hopefully, more wine will be forthcoming in future vintages.

The 1997 Pinot Noir Julia's Vineyard (72 cases) exhibits an attractive, plump, earthy, smoky, Pommard-like nose with notes of apple skins and black cherries. This deep ruby/colored wine displays ripe fruit, medium body, and a friendly, open-knit texture. The outstanding 1997 Pinot Noir (72 cases) offers dried herbs, smoked meats, and black fruits in its complex aromatics. Rich, medium- to full-bodied, long, ripe, and nicely layered, it should drink well for 4–5 years.

Brewer and Clifton don't miss a beat when they turn their enviable talents to Chardonnay. All their Chardonnays are put through full malolactic and lees stirring, and the percentage of new oak is small (about one-third). The 2000 Chardonnay Katherine's Vineyard displays a light green hue to its medium straw color. It tastes like a young, backward Chevalier-Montrachet given its striking notes of honeyed citrus intertwined with liquid minerality. A rich, full-bodied, well-delineated effort, it will benefit from additional cellaring and last for 6–8 years, possibly longer. Readers looking for a blockbuster Chardonnay with plenty of buttery popcorn notions mixed with minerals, orange marmalade, and honeysuckle should check out the 2000 Chardonnay Sweeney Canyon. It's no shy wine at 15% alcohol, but that is incredibly concealed beneath the wealth of fruit and extract. A Bâtard-Montrachet–like offering, it is flamboyant, rich, and sumptuous. The 2000 Chardonnay Marcella's Vineyard is reminiscent of a Louis Latour Bâtard-Montrachet. It, too, manages to hide its 15% alcohol.

Full-bodied, with amazing texture, great ripeness as well as richness, and a distinctive minerality underpinning the fruit and texture, it is a sensational effort. The 2000 Chardonnay Mount Carmel Vineyard exhibits buttery, caramel, and honeysuckle-like fruit intermixed with subtle wood. Although the least complex of Brewer-Clifton's 2000 Chardonnays, it is well formed, full-bodied, and seriously concentrated. It should drink well for 4–5 years.

The 1999s possess higher acidity, without the wealth of fruit and breadth of flavor found in the 2000s. Nevertheless, they are successful wines. The 1999 Chardonnay Katherine's Vineyard will be a keeper given its high levels of acidity as well as liquid minerality and hint of tropical fruit. The 1999 Chardonnay Sweeney Canyon again comes across as a New World version of Chevalier-Montrachet. Plenty of substance, lively acidity, notes of tangerine and oranges mixed with minerals and citrus are presented in a full-bodied, substantial style. It will benefit from cellaring and should keep for 7–8 years. The best of the 1999s is the blockbuster, high-octane 1999 Chardonnay Marcella's Vineyard. Its light gold color is followed by a rich wine with terrific fruit, an unctuous texture, and surprisingly good acidity. It should drink well for 4–5 years.

These are the wines of two up-and-coming California superstars. Don't miss them.

BRYANT FAMILY VINEYARD (NAPA)

1999	Cabernet Sauvignon Pritchard Hill	Napa	EEE	96
1998	Cabernet Sauvignon Pritchard Hill	Napa	EEE	91
1997	Cabernet Sauvignon Pritchard Hill	Napa	EEE	100
1996	Cabernet Sauvignon Pritchard Hill	Napa	EEE	99
1995	Cabernet Sauvignon Pritchard Hill	Napa	EEE	99
1994	Cabernet Sauvignon Pritchard Hill	Napa	EEE	98

This 100% Cabernet Sauvignon, made from the hillsides of eastern Napa Valley, with a gorgeous view of Lake Berryessa, has become one of the world's greatest red wines. Barrel samples of the 2000 appear to be as spectacular as the 1999, 1997, 1996, 1995, and 1994. The 1999 Cabernet Sauvignon Pritchard Hill (800 cases) boasts an opaque black/purple color that resembles vintage port. It reveals tremendously intense blackberry and cassis fruit intermixed with smoke, minerals, and floral (acacia?) scents. The wine possesses awesome intensity, a voluptuous texture, fabulous purity, and sweet tannin. The multidimensions apparent in both the aromatics and flavors are extraordinary. This majestic Cabernet will have 30–40 years of longevity. The 1998 Cabernet Sauvignon Pritchard Hill is one of the finest wines of the vintage. While it does not reveal the weight of previous vintages, it is a dense plum/purple-colored, big, thick, concentrated effort. Evolved aromas of smoke, cedar, tapenade, blackberries, crème de cassis, and creosote are followed by a lush, full-bodied, voluptuously textured 1998 exhibiting superb intensity as well as low-acid, sweet, pure flavors. This is a dazzling example of extremely ripe Cabernet Sauvignon made under less than ideal conditions. It will drink well upon its release and over the following two decades. I have consumed several bottles of the 1997 Cabernet Sauvignon Pritchard Hill. One of the most awesome young reds I have ever tasted, it possesses a black/purple color, a seamless texture, and freakishly high levels of intensity (cassis, blackberries, and blueberries infused with espresso, chocolate, and licorice) that are flawlessly presented in a full-bodied, massive yet elegant wine. Nothing is out of balance in this explosively rich, thick, highly extracted Cabernet. A compelling, historic Cabernet Sauvignon, it will drink well for 30–35 years. It is not too much to suggest that in the future, Bryant's Pritchard Hill might well be one of the wines that redefines greatness in Cabernet Sauvignon. Anticipated maturity: now–2035.

The opaque purple-colored 1996 Cabernet Sauvignon offers a spectacular, exotic bouquet of Peking duck skins, blackberry liqueur and cassis, roasted herbs, and burning charcoal. It is phenomenally intense, with record levels of dry extract and glycerin. This hedonistic blockbuster is crammed with jammy fruits nicely buttressed and framed by adequate acidity and tannin. Drink this marvelous Cabernet Sauvignon now or cellar it for two decades. This is mind-boggling stuff! The 1995 Cabernet Sauvignon is cut from the same mold as the 1996, displaying astonishing levels of black fruits (the usual suspects—blueberries, blackberries, raspberries, and cassis), phenomenal concentration, and virtually perfect balance and equilibrium. Another potentially perfect wine, the 1994 Cabernet Sauvignon boasts a fabulous nose of cassis, cream, blueberries, violets, minerals, and spice. It smells like a hypothetical blend of a great vintage of L'Evangile, Clinet, and Mouton-Rothschild. The opaque purple/black color is followed by a full-bodied wine stacked and packed with fruit, glycerin, and extract. No component part is out of place in this formidably endowed, remarkably well-balanced wine. The purity, richness, sweetness and depth of fruit suggest that the wine's potential is limitless. Much like its cellarmate, the 1994 Colgin Cabernet Sauvignon (also made by Helen Turley), the Bryant Family Vineyard's 1994 should evolve into one of California's legendary Cabernets. It will age effortlessly for 25–30 years.

Don't I wish there were tens of thousands of cases of wine such as this! Believe me, it is frustrating to write about limited production wines with such distinctive characters. I realize that only a handful of readers will be fortunate enough to obtain a bottle. It is also distressing to see these wines fetch museum prices at auctions, bid up to levels that only multimillionaires can afford. Nevertheless, over 20 years of writing has proven time and time again that glowing reviews on these wines motivate other producers to attain a similar level of quality. I wrote an article in *Food & Wine* magazine itemizing the characteristics of a great wine. They are: 1) the ability to please both the palate and the intellect, 2) the ability to hold the taster's interest, 3) the ability to offer intense aromas and flavors without heaviness, 4) the ability to taste better with each sip, 5) the ability to improve with age, and 6) the ability to offer a singular personality. These wines satisfy every one of those requirements. I often wonder if I get too excited about wines such as this. Yet time is on their side. I truly believe that in 20, 40, or 60 years, when the history of what appears to be a golden age for California wines is analyzed, these wines, and the work of their wine-maker, will be even more admired and appreciated by future generations than they are today.

Past Glories: 1993 Cabernet Sauvignon (97)

CAIN CELLARS (NAPA)

1996 Cain Five Proprietary Red Wine	Napa	E	89+
1994 Cain Five Proprietary Red Wine	Napa	E	91

The 1996 proprietary red wine from Cain Cellars is a blend of 63% Cabernet Sauvignon, 18% Merlot, 12% Cabernet Franc, 5% Petit Verdot, and 2% Malbec. A complex nose of cedar, black fruits, tobacco, spice box, and new wood emerges from this dark ruby/purple-colored effort. Rich and moderately tannic, with excellent to outstanding flavor extraction and overall balance, this 1996 should prove to be long-lived and satisfying. The texture is rich, not compressed or clipped, and the acidity, tannin, and alcohol are well integrated. Anticipated maturity: now–2016. The 1994, a blend of 62% Cabernet Sauvignon, 25% Merlot, 6% Cabernet Franc, 4% Malbec, and 3% Petit Verdot, is one of the finest efforts Cain Cellars has yet made. Fortunately, there were 5,500 cases produced. The wine reveals an opaque purple color, followed by a smoky, sweet cassis, subtle vanilla-scented nose, rich, medium- to full-bodied, supple flavors, and beautifully integrated acidity, tannin, alcohol, and wood. This outstanding effort is accessible, but should age effortlessly for 15 years. Shame on me for underrating this wine from cask!

CAKEBREAD CELLARS (NAPA)

1995 Cabernet Sauvignon Benchland Select	Napa	E	89+
1995 Cabernet Sauvignon Three Sisters	Napa	E	90
1994 Zinfandel Howell Mountain	Napa	C	88+

The two 1995 Cabernet Sauvignons are the most impressive I have tasted from Cakebread Cellars. The 1995 Cabernet Sauvignon Three Sisters comes from hillside vineyards planted on the eastern side of Napa Valley. The wine exhibits a saturated dark ruby/purple color, followed by a pure nose of cassis, minerals, and subtle new oak. Rich and expansive in the mouth, with power and concentration nicely allied to finesse and elegance, this wine possesses a soft texture, as well as enough tannin and acidity for delineation. Charming and intense, this is a beautifully rendered Cabernet Sauvignon that can be drunk now or cellared for 10–15 years. Also dark ruby/purple-colored, the 1995 Cabernet Sauvignon Benchland Select offers restrained aromatics, more tannin, and a closed personality. The predominant flavor characteristics are black currants intermixed with tobacco and cedar. The finish is long, with moderate tannin. Anticipated maturity: now–2014.

A tightly knit, more restrained, and firmer-styled Zinfandel, much of the appeal of Cakebread's 1994 Zinfandel Howell Mountain comes at the back of the mouth. There is a mineral and black raspberry–scented nose, rich, dense, black cherry and raspberry flavors, medium to full body, excellent purity, and a spicy, long, structured, stony finish. This classy, potentially complex Zinfandel should be given 6–12 months of bottle age and drunk over the next 7–8 years. Has anyone else noticed that Cakebread is making better and better wines?

OLIVER CALDWELL CELLARS (NAPA)

1997 Zinfandel Aida Vineyard	Napa	D	89

When Zinfandel from this source were made by Turley Cellars, they always possessed a distinctive southern Rhône, Châteauneuf-du-Pape-like character. Now made by Caldwell Cellars, this 1997 Zinfandel Aida Vineyard retains the unmistakable pepper, spice, dried Provençal herb, meaty, *garrigue* (a mélange of earth and herb scents) character that is found in southern Rhône wines. This rich, medium- to full-bodied, spicy, cherry liqueur–flavored offering is hedonistic and luscious. I would opt for drinking it over the next 5–6 years.

CAMBRIA ESTATE (SANTA MARIA)

2000 Chardonnay Bench Break	Santa Maria	D	88
2000 Chardonnay Katherine's Vineyard	Santa Maria	C	90
2000 Chardonnay Rae's	Santa Maria	D	90
1999 Pinot Noir Bench Break	Santa Maria	D	89+
1999 Pinot Noir Julia's Vineyard	Santa Maria	D	89
1999 Pinot Noir Rae's	Santa Maria	E	91

Cambria is now part of Jess Jackson's newly named Jackson Family Farms organization. All of the estates within this organization produce high-quality wines. The following Chardonnays are the best yet from Cambria Estate, and their Pinot Noirs seem to get better with each new vintage. While the Syrah has not yet caught up with the quality of the Pinot Noir and Chardonnay, it shows more and more promise. There are now three *cuvées* of Chardonnay, 1,000 cases of the Bench Break, 500 cases of Rae's, and a whopping 80,000 cases of Katherine's Vineyard. For readers looking for a dazzling, tropical fruit–scented and –flavored Chardonnay that offers tremendous purity, flavor intensity, and character, the 2000 Chardonnay Katherine's Vineyard is one of the best they have made. The vintage's good acidity buttresses the copious quantities of honeyed orange/pineapple fruit infused with citrus oils and gentle, toasty oak. It is a rich, full-bodied, undeniably attractive Chardonnay fruit bomb that should drink well for 2–3 years. The 1,000-case *cuvée* of 2000 Chardonnay Bench Break, which comes from sandy, alluvial soils, reveals considerable mineral characteristics. It is a classic, restrained, yet intensely flavorful Chardonnay that relies on citrus and liquid minerality for much of its character. There is plenty of weight, body, and length as well as a leesy, smoky complexity reminiscent of great white Burgundies. The 2000 Chardonnay Rae's exhibits buttery popcorn notes, rich, full-bodied, powerful flavors, beautiful purity, and the longest finish, with the most intensity and nuances. It is a fabulous Chardonnay capable of lasting 4–5 years. These are all handsomely rendered Chardonnays.

The Pinot Noir program is reaching new heights at Cambria. The current wines are a long way from the old vegetal, tomato (V-8 juice) tasting offerings of the past. The 1999 Pinot Noir Julia's Vineyard sees about 40% new French oak and is made from totally destemmed grapes. It possesses ripe black cherry and cranberry fruit, along with notes of pomegranate, pepper, and spice. Tangy, medium- to full-bodied, and fruit-driven, it should drink nicely for 4–5 years. The dense ruby/plum-colored 1999 Pinot Noir Bench Break exhibits abundant quantities of vibrant berry fruit intermixed with smoke, charcoal, and mineral. The wine was aged in 100% new French oak, and is slightly more structured and denser than the open-knit Julia's Vineyard. This wine will benefit from another 6–8 months of bottle age, and last for up to a decade. My favorite of the three Pinot Noirs is the Volnay-like 1999 Pinot Noir Rae's. It boasts abundant quantities of jammy black cherry fruit, nicely integrated wood smoke, minerals, and vanilla. Its richness of fruit, supple, yet well-delineated personality, beautiful purity, as well as additional layered complexity suggest it will be an impressive Pinot Noir to enjoy over the next decade.

CARDINALE (NAPA)

1999	Proprietary Red Wine	California	EE	93
1998	Proprietary Red Wine	California	EE	90
1997	Proprietary Red Wine	California	EE	95
1996	Proprietary Red Wine	California	EE	94
1995	Proprietary Red Wine	California	EE	91

One of the flagship properties in the Jackson Family Farm empire, Cardinale is made by one of California's most respected young wine-makers, Charles Thomas. The winery seems to go from strength to strength, producing wines of extraordinary power, but also remarkable delineation and elegance. Most of the fruit, which is a blend from Napa as well as Sonoma, tends to come from Jess Jackson's vineyards on Mount Veeder, and the Alexander Valley Mountain Estate, with some additions from the benchlands of Rutherford. There are 3,900 cases of the prodigious 1997 Cardinale, comprised primarily of Cabernet Sauvignon with a tiny dollop of Merlot. The wine has an opaque bluish black/purple color, a knockout nose of black cherry liqueur intermixed with cassis, lead pencil, mineral, and smoky oak. The glorious richness in the mouth is backed up by a full-bodied, opulently textured, super-extracted wine that is neither heavy nor ponderous. Stunning purity, a fabulous multilayered impression, and a finish that goes on for nearly a minute make this the most exciting Cardinale to date. For statisticians, this is a blend of 91% Cabernet Sauvignon and 9% Merlot, of which 79% of the grapes came from Napa and 21% from Sonoma. It spent 22 months in 100% new French oak before being bottled with neither fining nor filtration. It tips the scales at 14.2% alcohol. Anticipated maturity: 2004–2030. The very severe selection because of the difficulties imposed by the 1998 vintage has resulted in only 1,100 cases of the 1998 Cardinale. It has turned out to be a full-bodied, deep, rich wine with plenty of black currant/cherry fruit infused with some cedar, spice box, tobacco, and toasty new oak. While it does not have the depth, volume, and prodigious length of the 1997, it is an outstanding Cabernet Sauvignon–based wine that defies the vintage's so-so reputation for Cabernet and Merlot. Moreover, it should drink well for at least 15+ years. The 1999 Cardinale is 78% Cabernet Sauvignon and 22% Merlot. The wine has an opaque purple color, a huge, broodingly backward personality with fabulous fruit purity, an unctuous texture, sweet tannin, and dazzling length. Already seamless, it may challenge the fabulous 1997 and awesome 1996. Anticipated maturity for the 1999: 2006–2028.

The 1996 Cardinale is a blend of 89% Cabernet Sauvignon and 11% Merlot, of which 62% came from Napa and 38% from Sonoma. Just under 3,000 cases were produced. It is also a top-rank wine and a star of the vintage. A saturated purple color is followed by licorice, cedar, fruitcake, and black currant aromas. Full-bodied, powerful, and concentrated, with low acidity but high tannin, this young, muscular classic should have fabulous aging potential. Anticipated maturity: 2003–2028. The outstanding 1995 (2,800 cases made from a blend of 77% Cabernet Sauvignon and 23% Merlot) is somewhat overwhelmed when tasted next to the extraordinary 1996 and 1997. The wine's opaque purple color is followed by copious quantities of toast, cassis, tobacco, earth, and spice in a full-blown bouquet. Full-bodied, with superb purity and a gorgeous marriage of power and elegance, this classic offering should age effortlessly for 20–25+ years. Kudos to wine-maker Charles Thomas!

CARLISLE WINERY (SONOMA)

1998	Two Acres	Russian River	D	89
1999	Zinfandel	Dry Creek	D	88
1998	Zinfandel	Dry Creek	D	90
1999	Zinfandel	Russian River	D	90
1998	Zinfandel	Russian River	D	88?

This relatively new, impressive estate has fashioned two stylish, yet different 1999 Zinfandel. The elegant, intensely flavored, medium- to full-bodied 1999 Zinfandel Dry Creek is a balanced, harmonious effort with good flesh as well as copious black cherries intermixed with earth and subtle wood. Concentrated and soft, this delicious 1999 can be enjoyed over the next 4–5 years. The sweeter, richer, fuller-bodied, more concentrated, and denser 1999 Zinfandel Russian River displays a deep ruby color with purple nuances, a sweet attack with more glycerin as well as ripeness, and outstanding purity. It is a compelling mouthful.

I believe Carlisle's 1998s were their debut releases. The 1998 Zinfandel Russian River (118 cases; 15.9% alcohol) has a dense ruby/purple color, followed by thick, chocolaty, berry fruit, truffle, licorice, and smoky notes. The dense ruby/purple-colored 1998 Zinfandel Dry Creek (237 cases; 15.8% alcohol) offers terrific aromas of tar, jammy blackberries, cherry liqueur, and smoke. In the mouth, it is rich and full-bodied, with outstanding concentration and depth. Drink this impressive, full tilt Zinfandel over the next 5–7 years. Lastly, the 1998 Two Acres is a limited production (78 cases) proprietary blend of Petite Sirah, Mourvèdre, Refosco, and Alicante as well as other varietals. It reveals abundant quantities of smoky, blackberry, licorice-infused, tarry fruit flavors, full body, admirable muscle and concentration, low acidity, and a sweet mid-palate and finish. Drink it over the next 5–7 years.

CARMENET VINEYARD (SONOMA)

1997	Cabernet Franc	Sonoma	D	89
1997	Dynamite Cabernet Sauvignon	North Coast	C	88
1994	Meritage Moon Mountain Estate	Sonoma	C	90
1996	Merlot Sangiacomo Vineyard	Carneros	D	88
1997	Moon Mountain Cabernet	Sonoma	D	91
1996	Moon Mountain Cabernet	Sonoma	D	89
1995	Moon Mountain Proprietary Red Wine Estate Reserve	Sonoma	D	90
1994	Vin De Garde Moon Mountain Estate	Sonoma	C	91
1999	Zinfandel Evangelo Vineyard	Contra Costa	C	90

A superb offering produced from 109-year-old, head-pruned vineyards planted in the sandy soils of Contra Costa, Carmenet's dense purple-colored 1999 Zinfandel Evangelo Vineyard offers up sweet, fruit-driven aromas of blackberries, cherry liqueur, and underbrush. Dense, full-bodied, and fruity, with an opulent texture as well as a long, lusty finish, this explosively rich Zinfandel will drink beautifully for 3–4 years.

While the Moon Mountain Cabernet has a relatively limited production of 3,000–5,000 cases, there are 45,000 cases of the 1997 Dynamite Cabernet Sauvignon. Given today's ridiculously overpriced wine market, the Dynamite is a terrific bargain. Most of the fruit comes from Pope Valley, a diverse viticultural area that is, inexplicably, part of Napa Valley. However, it has at least one super Cabernet source in the Cypress Vineyard of Flora Springs. Aged in oak barrels (the majority American), the Dynamite's dense ruby/purple color is accompanied by an overripe nose of black currants and jammy cassis. Lush, medium- to full-bodied, and spicy, with low acidity, this is a mouth-filling, pure, textbook Cabernet Sauvignon to drink over the next decade.

Close to outstanding is Carmenet's 1997 Cabernet Franc (600 cases). Made from the estate's vineyards and aged in 100% French oak, of which one-third is new, this 100% Cabernet Franc exhibits a dark ruby/purple color and an attractive nose of black fruits, cedar, spice box, and tobacco. Excellent richness, a lush texture, and real elegance without dilution are the hallmarks of this fine offering crafted by wine-maker Jeff Baker. Drink it over the next 10–12 years. The excellent 1996 Moon Mountain Cabernet (4,815 cases of a blend of Cabernet Sauvignon, Cabernet Franc, and Petit Verdot) was aged in 75% new French oak. Much of the fruit comes from the famed Martini vineyard called Monte Rosso. Dark ruby/purple-colored, with intense aromas of blackberries, minerals, and currants, this elegant, soft, powerful wine is delicious, and promises to evolve nicely for 12–15 years. Even better is the 1997 Moon Mountain Cabernet (4,400 cases made from a blend of 86% Cabernet Sauvignon, 10% Cabernet Franc, and 4% Petit Verdot). A saturated blue/purple color is followed by aromas of minerals, cassis, cigar box, and licorice. Full-bodied, superbly concentrated, pure, and well balanced, this large-scaled, mountain-styled Cabernet Sauvignon–dominated wine will be at its best between now–2020.

The plump, hedonistic 1996 Merlot Sangiacomo Vineyard reveals a dark ruby color and a big, smoky, berry, chocolaty nose. Fleshy and medium-bodied, with excellent richness and depth, it is meant to be drunk over the next 5–7 years.

The substantially endowed 1995 Moon Mountain Estate Reserve reveals a dark ruby/purple color with a textbook cedary, tobacco, weedy, black currant–scented nose. It exhibits good sweetness and ripeness of fruit on the attack, medium body, obvious spicy new oak (almost too much), and a moderately tannic, narrowly focused, spicy finish. This is a very good, potentially excellent wine that should provide restrained yet elegant drinking for 10–14 years.

The 1994 Vin de Garde Moon Mountain Estate exhibits an opaque ruby/purple color, as well as a huge, exotic nose of cassis, herbs, ginger, and coconut. Sweet tannin and an underlying mineral component are present in this fabulously extracted, rich, full-bodied, spicy wine. This large-scaled, structured wine clearly lives up to its name. It will undoubtedly require 5–7 years of cellaring after its release; it displays the potential to last for 20+ years. Lastly, the 1994 Meritage Moon Mountain Estate stood out for its well-focused personality, which exhibited sensational elegance, and, for the vintage, a soft, supple style that came across as less aggressive and extracted than many other 1994s. Deeply colored, with loads of red and black fruits, this will not be one of the biggest wines of the vintage, but it has the potential to be an outstanding effort in a stylish, measured, but authoritatively flavored manner. Because of its softness, it should drink well when released and keep for up to 15 years.

CAYMUS VINEYARD (NAPA)

1994	Cabernet Sauvignon	Napa	E	91
1995	Cabernet Sauvignon Special Selection	Napa	EE	90
1994	Cabernet Sauvignon Special Selection	Napa	EE	95

Caymus is one of a handful of Napa Valley wineries that has enjoyed an enviable success record since the early 1970s. The winery continues to focus on three wines: Sauvignon Blanc, their exotic white proprietary wine called Conundrum (usually a blend of Viognier, Sauvignon Blanc, Chardonnay, and Sémillon), and Cabernet Sauvignon. Chuck Wagner and his father, Charlie, have begun to look south to develop vineyards in Monterey as there is not enough Caymus to fulfill the marketplace's needs. In Monterey, the winery produces a competent but overpriced white and red Rhône varietal blend called Treanna.

Cabernet is king at Caymus. During the nineties, there was a succession of sumptuous, rich, concentrated, lavishly wooded, cassis-flavored Caymus Cabernet Sauvignons. The sumptuous 1994 Cabernet Sauvignon appears to be one of the best Napa Cabernets Caymus has produced. Remarkably, there is plenty to go around—25,000 cases, approximately the same production as Lafite-Rothschild and Margaux. The wine exhibits a dark purple color, and a sweet, jammy black currant–scented nose. The lush, juicy, succulent texture is crammed with glycerin and extract. Surprisingly soft (a hallmark of this vintage), with a smooth texture, this full-bodied, oaky Cabernet should drink well for 10–12+ years. I have followed the Special Selection Cabernet Sauvignon since the debut 1975 vintage, and the 1994 appears to be one of the finest yet made at Caymus. Its saturated purple color is accompanied by an exuberant, sweet, enveloping fragrance of smoky new oak and jammy blackberry and cassis fruit. In the mouth, this lavishly wooded, black fruit–filled Cabernet is extremely full-bodied, with superb levels of fruit, glycerin, and extract. Like many 1994 Cabernet Sauvignons, it possesses extraordinary equilibrium, with the sweet tannin giving the wine considerable accessibility. The finish lasts for nearly 30 seconds. This will be a fun wine to drink young, but do not discount its aging ability as it should last for two decades.

While it is fashionable to criticize this wine because of its price, and the secrecy surrounding the amount produced (who really cares?), the wine is unquestionably outstanding. The 1995 Special Selection boasts a dark ruby/purple color as well as an attractive bouquet with lavish quantities of toasty new oak and black currants. There is moderate tannin, good purity, and an open-knit, sexy style. If the wine had not fallen a bit short on the mid-palate, it would have merited an even higher score. It should drink well for 10–15 years. Based on the fame of this winery and the price of the wine, one would expect this Cabernet to compete with Colgin, Bryant Family Vineyards, Screaming Eagle, Araujo, and Harlan Estate. It does not. Nevertheless, it is an outstanding Cabernet Sauvignon.

Past Glories: Cabernet Sauvignon Special Selection—1992 (91), 1991 (91), 1990 (94), 1986 (94), 1985 (92), 1984 (96), 1980 (91), 1978 (98), 1976 (99), 1975 (98)

CHALONE (GAVILAN)

1999	Chardonnay Estate	Gavilan Mountains	D	90
1999	Chenin Blanc Estate	Gavilan Mountains	C	90
1999	Pinot Blanc Estate	Gavilan Mountains	D	88
1994	Pinot Noir Estate	California	C	88

Chalone's tank-fermented 1999 Chenin Blanc Estate, fashioned from 82-year-old, head-pruned vines, remains one of California's finest expressions of this grape. Fermented dry, it spends 11 months in French oak, of which 20% is new. A wine of extraordinary minerality, intensity, and character, it presents this varietal's fruit cocktail–like characteristic in a steely format. Full-bodied and powerful, as well as a good value, it should drink well for 7–8 years. Chalone also consistently produces one of California's finest Pinot Blancs. Their 1999 Pinot Blanc Estate (4,280 cases) is fermented in both tank and barrel, and aged in French oak, of which 30% is new. About one-half of this *cuvée* comes from 50-year-old vines, and the rest from younger plantings. While tightly knit, it reveals notions of orange blossoms, citrus, and apple skins along with a liquid minerality. This dense, medium- to full-bodied, intense white will age impeccably for a decade or more.

Chalone has dropped its *cuvée* of Reserve Chardonnay, opting to do one master blend. The 1999 Chardonnay Estate (24,300 cases; 14.1% alcohol) represents one of the finest buys for long-lived Chardonnay in the marketplace. About 30% new French oak, with the balance 2–3-year-old barrels, are utilized, and the wine remains on its lees for 12 months. It is not fined, but is filtered. A light gold-colored, intense, full-bodied, muscular effort, it exhibits notes of minerals, pineapples, oranges, and allspice. Chalone's Chardonnays can be extremely long-lived (certain bottles of the 1981, 1980, and 1979 remain extraordinary). While the powerful, structured 1999 may not last that long, it has at least a decade of life ahead of it.

Chalone's 1994 Pinot Noir Estate exhibits a light ruby color, as well as wonderfully sweet, succulent, cherry and berry fruit intermingled with scents of smoke, earth, and wood. Excellent richness, and a long, lush finish make for a glass of sexy Pinot Noir that is far more forward than the old style Chalone Pinots.

In the future, readers can expect some Rhône Ranger blends to emerge from this winery. They have planted 26 acres on a south-facing mountainside consisting of decomposed granite soils. The majority of the plantings are Syrah, but there are small percentages of Viognier, Mourvèdre, and Grenache.

CHAPPELLET (NAPA)

1997 Cabernet Sauvignon	Napa	D	89+

This may be the most impressive Cabernet Sauvignon Chappellet has produced since their great classics in 1969, 1970, and 1973, all made by Philip Togni. The color is a dense ruby purple. The bouquet offers up tight but promising aromas of minerals, smoke, and black currants. A Bordeaux-like austerity greets the taster, but as with Bordeaux, there is plenty of density and concentration in reserve, which is particularly noticeable on the back of the palate. The wine is pure, promising, tannic, medium- to full-bodied, and nicely extracted. Chewy tobacco, spice box, and black fruit characteristics emerge with airing. It is good to see this winery turn out a wine of this quality. It's an ager, however, and patience will be required. Anticipated maturity: 2003–2018.

P.S. By the way, I recently had a bottle of the 1969 Chappellet Cabernet Sauvignon (made by Philip Togni). I would score this wine in the mid-90s. It is a testament to the fact that some California Cabernet Sauvignon can age. The wine reveals a saturated garnet/purple color as well as a striking bouquet of minerals, black fruits, leather, spice box, and cedar. Unbelievably rich, powerful, and muscular, with at least 20 more years of life remaining, it is one of the classics, but many people have probably forgotten how great it was (a friend and I purchased a pristine case of this at auction for $300).

CLARK-CLAUDON VINEYARDS (NAPA)

1997 Cabernet Sauvignon	Napa	EE	92+
1996 Cabernet Sauvignon	Napa	E	93
1995 Cabernet Sauvignon	Napa	D	93+

Another limited production (300 cases) wine made from a vineyard on the eastern side of Howell Mountain, the brilliantly made 1995 Cabernet from Clark-Claudon suggests this winery knows what to do with top-quality fruit. While the 1995 will be hard to find, readers who are interested in profound California Cabernet Sauvignons should seek out future releases. This opaque purple-colored wine boasts knockout aromatics of smoke, charcoal, black currants, lead pencil, minerals, and high-quality French oak. Impressive on the palate, with a classy richness married to well-integrated wood, acidity, and tannin, this is a full-bodied, fabulously rich, expressive, impeccably balanced Cabernet Sauvignon. Anticipated maturity: now–2015.

A brilliant successor to the 1995, Clark Claudon's 1996 Cabernet Sauvignon exhibits a dark purple color, followed by a classic, Bordeaux-like nose of cassis, lead pencil, and smoky new oak. A wine of considerable complexity and elegance, with outstanding purity, richness, and nicely integrated wood and tannin, this is a classic, backward yet promising, symmetrical Cabernet that can be drunk early in life, or cellared for 15+ years. Impressive!

In light of the superb 1996 this winery produced, it is not surprising to see a broodingly backward, promising Cabernet Sauvignon emerge from the 1997 vintage. Neither up-front nor accessible, readers will need a degree of patience, although it would not be infanticide to drink it now. A serious, concentrated, opaque purple-colored effort, it boasts a moderately intense nose of pure cassis, gravel, vanilla, and blackberries. Full-bodied and impressively built, this deep, powerful, concentrated Cabernet begs for cellaring. It is another impressive effort from this newcomer to the high-end Cabernet Sauvignon sweepstakes. Anticipated maturity: 2005–2020. Bravo!

CLOS MIMI (PASO ROBLES)

1997 Syrah Shell Creek Vineyard	Paso Robles	D	90
1996 Syrah Shell Creek Vineyard	Paso Robles	D	92

Produced in minuscule quantities, the immensely impressive, black/purple-colored 1996 Syrah offers a nose of roasted herbs, meat juices, blackberries, cassis, and earth. Peppery, spicy notes emerge from this large-scaled, super-concentrated, impressively endowed, rustic, brilliantly layered, nuanced wine. It will be even better with 3–5 years of cellaring. It should keep for 10–12 years. Brilliant! While not as much of a blockbuster as the phenomenal 1996, Clos Mimi's 1997 is still an outstanding wine. Dense ruby/purple-colored, with the telltale blackberry, peppery aromas, this elegant offering exhibits abundant glycerin, a seductive texture, full body, sweet fruit, and significant length. The 1996 is more powerful and concentrated, but the 1997 is more charming and open-knit. Clos Mimi is an impressive, impeccably made wine. Anticipated maturity: now–2010. These people are serious!

CLOS PEGASE (NAPA)

1997 Cabernet Sauvignon	Carneros/Napa	D	(88–90)
1996 Cabernet Sauvignon	Carneros/Napa	D	88
1998 Cabernet Sauvignon	Napa	D	88
1995 Cabernet Sauvignon	Napa	C	88
1994 Cabernet Sauvignon	Napa	C	91
1998 Cabernet Sauvignon Graveyard Hill	Carneros	E	90
1998 Cabernet Sauvignon Hommage	Napa	EE	(90–91)
1997 Cabernet Sauvignon Hommage Reserve	Napa	E	89
1998 Cabernet Sauvignon Palisades Vineyard	Napa	E	89+
1997 Cabernet Sauvignon Palisades Vineyard	Napa	E	88
1999 Chardonnay Mitsuko's Vineyard Hommage Reserve	Carneros	E	91
1999 Chardonnay Mitsuko's Vineyard Unfiltered	Carneros	C	90
1994 Merlot	Napa	C	90

Under wine-maker Steve Rogstad, the quality at Clos Pegase has gone from appallingly innocuous/mediocre to at least excellent and, in some cases, outstanding. Both *cuvées* of 1999 Chardonnay are the finest Clos Pegase has yet produced. The 1999 Chardonnay Mitsuko's Vineyard Unfiltered is 100% barrel-fermented and most of it was made utilizing indigenous yeasts. It sees about one-third new French oak. The wine exhibits a big, smoky, leesy, roasted hazelnut, buttery, and honeyed pear nose, full body, excellent texture, and fine purity. Drink it over the next 2–3 years. Culled from the same vineyard, the 1999 Chardonnay Mitsuko's Vineyard Hommage Reserve (about 750 cases) is a selection of the finest barrels. Indigenous yeast-fermented and bottled unfiltered, it boasts a terrific nose of honeysuckle, tropical fruit, and smoky, leesy, roasted nut scents. Full-bodied and multilayered, with gorgeous purity and nicely integrated wood, it should drink well for 2–3 years as well.

Quality is clearly on the upswing, as the 1998s, a much more challenging vintage, are better than the 1997s. The 1998 Cabernet Sauvignon exhibits chocolate, cedar, spice box, and black currant characteristics presented in a medium- to full-bodied format. With good depth, ripe tannin, and a long, spicy finish, it can be consumed over the next decade. Clos Pegase produces two single vineyard wines, approximately 100 cases from their Graveyard Hill Vineyard in Carneros and slightly more from their Palisades Vineyard northeast of Calistoga. The 1998 Cabernet Sauvignon Graveyard Hill, which spent 28 months in French oak, was harvested on November 6 (that may give you an idea of just how cool and late the vintage was). It possesses a dark black/purple color, a distinctive nose of scorched earth, and gravell-like notes similar to those found in Bordeaux's famed Haut-Brion. Medium- to full-bodied, with sweet but firm tannin in addition to outstanding concentration, purity, and intensity, it is an impressive 1998 for drinking over the next 10–15 years. The 1998 Cabernet Sauvignon Palisades Vineyard also spent 28 months in French oak. It reveals a dense plum/purple color and an earthy black currant and spice box–scented bouquet with notions of cedar, licorice, and cassis. The wine possesses firm tannin, full body, and a potentially long-lived personal-ity. Cellar it for 3–4 years and consume it over the following 10–15.

The top barrels from the Graveyard Hill and Palisades vineyards are chosen for Hommage. The 1998 (925 cases of 100% Cabernet Sauvignon) came primarily from Graveyard Hill Vineyard with about one-third from the Palisades. A superb 1998, and certainly one of the vintage's most complete wines, it boasts an opaque ruby/purple color in addition to aromas of sweet cherry, cassis, smoke, fudge, and toasty oak. Full-bodied, powerful, and formidably tannic, with excellent balance, it will drink well between 2003–2020.

There are 215 cases of the 1997 Cabernet Sauvignon Palisades Vineyard. Produced from a vineyard near Calistoga, it possesses a black currant, cedar, licorice, and spicy oak–scented nose, low acidity, sweet tannin, and a medium- to full-bodied, nicely concentrated personal-ity. The well-structured 1997 Cabernet Sauvignon Hommage Reserve (mostly Cabernet Sauvi-gnon, with tiny amounts of Petit Verdot and Merlot, of which 65% is from the Graveyard Hill Vineyard and 35% from the Palisades Vineyard) exhibits classy tobacco, cedar, dried herb, licorice, and black currant aromas. Medium- to full-bodied, with moderate tannin and excel-lent purity, this *cuvée* (1,350 cases) needs 1–3 years of cellaring; it should keep for 15 years.

The 1996 Cabernet Sauvignon reveals a complex, spice box, cedar, olive, and black currant–scented bouquet, medium-bodied flavors, and moderate tannin in the finish. A well-made Cabernet that has not been excessively manipulated or acidified, it should drink well for a decade. Even better is the 1997 Cabernet Sauvignon, which possesses a dark ruby/pur-ple color, and a firm underpinning of tannin, sweet, creamy, black currant flavors intertwined with cedar, Provençal herbs, and new oak. Medium- to full-bodied, with a relatively long fin-ish, it should be an excellent, possibly outstanding wine that will be drinkable young, yet keep for 10–12 years. The 1995 Cabernet Sauvignon is a medium-weight, nicely made wine with a dark ruby/purple color, and sweet plum, jammy cassis, and cherry-like aromas with lavish toasty oak in the background. On the palate, the wine reveals adequate acidity, an at-tractive, fleshy, corpulent mouth-feel, good glycerin and extract, and an easy to understand, plump, chewy style. It should drink well for a decade.

The 1994 Merlot offers a dark purple color, and a big, chocolaty, black raspberry/cherry-scented nose bordering on overripeness. Dense and chewy, with surprisingly tough tannin in the finish, this is a fleshy, boldly styled Merlot for drinking during the first dozen years after its release. The 1994 Cabernet Sauvignon exhibits gorgeous ripe blueberry and raspberry fruit in its flamboyant nose. Deep and velvety-textured, with impressive extraction, this full-bodied, sweet-tasting (from ripe fruit, not sugar), sexy Cabernet should drink well now and keep for 12–15 years.

COLGIN CELLARS (NAPA)

1999 Cabernet Sauvignon Herb Lamb Vineyard	Napa	EEE	91
1998 Cabernet Sauvignon Herb Lamb Vineyard	Napa	EEE	90

1997	Cabernet Sauvignon Herb Lamb Vineyard	Napa	EEE	99
1996	Cabernet Sauvignon Herb Lamb Vineyard	Napa	EEE	97
1995	Cabernet Sauvignon Herb Lamb Vineyard	Napa	EE	98
1994	Cabernet Sauvignon Herb Lamb Vineyard	Napa	EE	96
1999	Madrona Ranch (not yet officially named)	Napa	EE	(89–90)

Availability of Colgin will increase as Ann Colgin's new vineyard, Tychson Hill, produced a Cabernet in 2000. Additionally, 23 acres that have been planted in the eastern hills of southern Napa should be fruit-bearing in 3–4 years. From cooler years than 1997, 1996, 1995, and 1994, the three newest offerings possess a more Bordeaux-like weight than previous efforts. Much is expected of new wine-maker Mark Aubert, given his predecessor's (Helen Turley) reputation, but there should be no significant changes in Colgin's harvesting, wine-making, or upbringing. Don't forget, Aubert was responsible for many compelling wines at Peter Michael.

The 1999 Cabernet Sauvignon Herb Lamb Vineyard (300 cases) exhibits a black/purple color along with sumptuously pure aromas of black currants, cassis, charcoal, and toast. Surprisingly medium-bodied as well as lighter than expected, it possesses excellent mineral notes, as well as a Bordeaux-like finesse, austerity, and finish. This beautifully styled Cabernet should be ready to drink in 3–4 years and will keep for 15–18. There are 500 cases of the 1999 Madrona Ranch, a proprietary blend of 55% Cabernet Sauvignon, 35% Merlot, 5% Cabernet Franc, and 5% Petit Verdot. It offers a dense ruby color in addition to an elegant, cedary, and black currant–scented bouquet with smoky oak in the background. There is good ripeness, a soft texture, medium to full body, excellent depth, and sweet tannin in the finish. If this effort puts on a bit more weight it may merit an exceptional rating. Anticipated maturity: 2003–2016. From a tougher vintage, the 1998 Cabernet Sauvignon Herb Lamb Vineyard possesses a dense plum/purple color as well as a sweet perfume of minerals, blackberries, and cassis, medium to full body, an excellent texture, ripe tannin, and a more evolved personality than some of the blockbuster wines that preceded it. An undeniable success for the vintage, it should be consumed over the next 12–15 years.

The nearly perfect 1997 Cabernet Sauvignon Herb Lamb Vineyard was bottled in May 1999 and appears to have recovered beautifully from bottle shock. Saturated black/purple-colored with a knockout nose of blackberries, blueberries, lavender, licorice, and toast, this is a profound, full-bodied Cabernet Sauvignon. It displays a seamless, velvety texture, layers of concentrated fruit, and a 45+-second finish. Am I being too conservative in not giving it a 3-digit score? Anticipated maturity: now–2025. The saturated black/purple-colored 1996 Cabernet Sauvignon Herb Lamb Vineyard displays this winery's hallmark—a provocative nose of blueberry jam, orchid flowers, and smoky new oak intertwined with cassis. Additional aromas of licorice and exotic Asian spices emerge as the wine sits in the glass. Extremely full-bodied and rich, with more noticeable tannin than the 1997, this large-scaled yet extraordinarily rich wine is like drinking cassis/blueberry liqueur. Its sweet tannin and remarkable 40+-second finish are amazing. Anticipated maturity: now–2022.

The 1996 and 1995 could be mistaken for identical twins, although close examination reveals that the 1995 has a slightly firmer tannic edge and the 1996 slightly lower acidity. However, both possess Colgin's telltale opaque black/purple color, phenomenal aromatics consisting of blackberries, raspberries, blueberries, cassis, subtle new oak, and a notion of floral scents (is it acacia or lilac?). In the mouth, both wines are full-bodied, remarkably supple, and opulent, with a purity and presence of fruit that must be tasted to be believed. Their finishes last for 45+ seconds. I suspect each of these wines will get even better over the next 5–10 years before reaching their full plateau of maturity, where they should remain for two decades or more. They are the quintessential examples of Cabernet Sauvignons that marry power with elegance. As a friend said after tasting a Colgin Cabernet Sauvignon, "they float like a butterfly, but sting like a bee." I am not sure Muhammad Ali or Ann Colgin would agree with that, but it paints another picture of these extraordinary wines. These wines were made by Helen Turley, the prodigiously talented wine-maker/consultant.

The potentially perfect 1994 Cabernet Sauvignon Herb Lamb Vineyard is a totally dry wine, but the sweetness and taste of this wine's fruit is akin to a savory blend of a chocolate-covered, blueberry/cassis-filled candy bar, and vanilla ice cream melting in the mouth. This full-bodied wine is silky, seductive, opulent, voluptuously textured, and extraordinarily fragrant, expansive, and rich. In spite of this, the wine remains graceful and well balanced, without any sense of heaviness or obtrusive tannin or acidity. I clearly underrated the 1994 from my earliest barrel tastings, but the last two times I have had it, from barrel immediately prior to bottling and in bottle, have persuaded me that this wine is one of the most exciting and remarkable young Cabernet Sauvignons I have tasted! It should drink well for another 25–30 years. Damn, I adore this wine!

Note: the only way in which to purchase these wines is through the winery's mailing list.
Past Glories: 1993 Cabernet Sauvignon Herb Lamb Vineyard (95)

CONSILIENCE (SANTA BARBARA)

1999 Zinfandel Rhodes Vineyard	Redwood Valley	D	89+?

A serious, internationally styled offering, Consilience's opaque purple-colored 1999 Zinfandel Rhodes Vineyard reveals abundant quantities of new oak along with impressively sweet black currant and blackberry fruit with a hint of cherries. If the oak were not so aggressive, it would be a candidate for an outstanding rating. While it may lack some of Zinfandel's gutsiness, it is a full-bodied effort made in a Bordeaux-like style. It will be interesting to monitor this wine's evolution.

CONSTANT (NAPA)

1995 Diamond Mountain Vineyard Proprietary Red	Napa	EEE	90

This 18-acre vineyard, which sits at a lofty elevation on Diamond Mountain, was replanted in 1984. Proprietors Fred and Mary Constant's objective is to produce complex, elegant, Bordeaux-styled wines from a blend of Cabernet Sauvignon, Merlot, and Cabernet Franc. They obviously believe that no track record is necessary in order to charge high prices. The 1995 Diamond Mountain Vineyard is an outstanding effort. Made with the consultation of Philippe Melka, this blend of 73% Cabernet Sauvignon, 18% Merlot, and 9% Cabernet Franc offers scents of melted tar, loamy soil, black currants, and minerals. Well crafted, with moderate tannin, this austere, medium-bodied effort exhibits a sweet mid-palate, excellent overall harmony, and the telltale lead pencil, toasty oak, and black currant fruit indicative of a high-class Cabernet. Although not weighty, the emphasis is on finesse and complexity. It will benefit from 2–3 years of cellaring, and will last for 15–16 years.

CORNERSTONE (HOWELL MOUNTAIN)

1997 Cabernet Sauvignon Beatty Ranch	Howell Mountain	E	90+
1996 Cabernet Sauvignon Beatty Ranch	Howell Mountain	E	88
1997 Cabernet Sauvignon Black-Sears Vineyard	Howell Mountain	E	93
1996 Cabernet Sauvignon Black-Sears Vineyard	Howell Mountain	E	90
1997 Cabernet Sauvignon Collage Vineyard	Howell Mountain	E	92
1997 Cabernet Sauvignon Cornerstone Vineyard	Howell Mountain	E	94
1996 Zinfandel Beatty Ranch	Howell Mountain	D	88

Cornerstone's 1997s are the most successful efforts yet produced by wine-maker/owner Bruce Scotland. Readers seeking full-throttle Cabernet Sauvignons have plenty to choose from. The opaque purple-colored 1997 Cabernet Sauvignon Black-Sears Vineyard offers a sexy, up-front nose of blackberries, cassis, and smoke. Sweet, succulent, and jammy, with explosive ripeness as well as admirable flavor intensity, this low-acid Cabernet has huge reserves of fruit, glycerin, extract, and tannin that have been melded into a seamless, concentrated wine of exceptional potential. Anticipated maturity: now–2016. The most backward of this quartet is the 1997 Cabernet Sauvignon Beatty Ranch. Notes of new saddle leather, tree bark, and red and black currants emerge from this opaque purple-colored wine. Gritty tannin initially causes concern, but as the wine sits in the glass and on the palate, its substantial richness and powerful, full-bodied, concentrated style becomes apparent. Patience is required. Anticipated maturity: 2004–2018.

Another explosive, succulent, disarmingly thick, opulent effort, the dark purple 1997 Cabernet Sauvignon Cornerstone Vineyard is a hedonist's dream. It offers a combination of powerful black cherry and cassis flavors presented in a flamboyant, full-bodied style with extravagant layers of fruit, glycerin, and extract. New-oak aging is noticeable, but its impact is subtle. The tannin is well concealed by a wealth of fruit. Drink this beauty over the next two decades. Lastly, the 1997 Cabernet Sauvignon Collage Vineyard emphasizes finesse and elegance, although there is no shortage of flavor authority. This beautifully pure, sexy offering boasts abundant quantities of fruit in its intense aromatics as well as medium to full body, low acidity, and sweet tannin. Enjoy it over the next 12–15 years.

The 1996 Cabernet Sauvignon Beatty Ranch is not a typical Howell Mountain Cabernet. Although it possesses plenty of tannin, muscle, and power, it is deep and rich, with more sweetness on the attack than expected considering its origin. It is well balanced, ripe, elegant, and supple for a wine from this area. Drink it over the next 7–8 years. The impressive, opaque ruby/purple-colored 1996 Cabernet Sauvignon Black-Sears Vineyard displays rich blackberry and cassis fruit, excellent purity, a nicely layered mid-palate, and fine sweetness in the intense, glycerin-imbued finish. It should drink well for 12–15 years. Lastly, the 1996 Zinfandel Beatty Ranch (a late release) reveals copious quantities of earthy, smoky, toasty new-oak notes along with saddle leather, and a perfumed, mushroomy, blackberry and cherry-scented nose. Drink this briery, perfumed, concentrated Zin over the next 3–4 years.

ROBERT CRAIG (NAPA)

1997	Affinity Proprietary Red Wine	Napa	D	91
1996	Affinity Proprietary Red Wine	Napa	D	90
1995	Affinity Proprietary Red Wine	Napa	D	90
1997	Cabernet Sauvignon Howell Mountain	Napa	D	92
1996	Cabernet Sauvignon Howell Mountain	Napa	D	91
1995	Cabernet Sauvignon Howell Mountain	Napa	D	91
1994	Cabernet Sauvignon Howell Mountain	Napa	D	90+
1997	Cabernet Sauvignon Mt. Veeder	Napa	D	92+
1996	Cabernet Sauvignon Mt. Veeder	Napa	D	92+
1995	Cabernet Sauvignon Mt. Veeder	Napa	D	90
1994	Cabernet Sauvignon Mt. Veeder	Napa	D	88

Robert Craig's three impressive, concentrated 1997 reds reflect a synthesis between the elegant, austere Bordeaux-styled Cabernet Sauvignon, Merlot, and Cabernet Franc, and the extravagant, ripe, jammy characteristics found in wines fashioned from California's warmer microclimates as well as richer soils. Craig has produced wines with exceptional complexity, gorgeous purity, and 15–20 years of aging potential. The opaque purple-colored 1997 Affinity (primarily Cabernet Sauvignon) possesses exceptional finesse and elegance in addition to authoritative flavors. Highly extracted, medium- to full-bodied, with layers of concentration, it offers notes of lead pencil, well-integrated, subtle, smoky oak, black currants, plums, licorice, and flowers. Everything is well balanced in this classy, gracious Cabernet Sauvignon that combines finesse with intensity. Anticipated maturity: now–2020. The 1997 Cabernet Sauvignon Mt. Veeder exhibits an opaque purple color as well as a gorgeously complex bouquet of cassis, vanilla, minerals, and blueberries. Structured, full-bodied, and opulently textured, this thick, rich, youthful 1997 will be even better with another 2–3 years of cellaring; it will age well for two decades. Readers seeking more earthiness, as well as blackberry, blueberry, and floral characteristics, should check out the saturated ruby/purple-colored 1997 Cabernet Sauvignon Howell Mountain. It is a medium- to full-bodied, tannic, impressively endowed, pure effort that, like its siblings, is gorgeously balanced and intense. Its tannin is more powerful, and thus it requires 2–3 years of cellaring.

Robert Craig's opaque purple-colored 1996 Affinity, a blend of Merlot, Cabernet Sauvignon, and Cabernet Franc, displays a noteworthy blueberry jam–scented nose with aromas of high-quality new oak. The wine is elegant, full-bodied, and complex, with its outstanding aromatics backed up by ripe flavors, and a layered, textured feel with well-integrated oak, acidity, and tannin. Anticipated maturity: now–2012. The powerful, dense, backward, highly extracted, formidable 1996 Cabernet Sauvignon Mt. Veeder boasts a black/purple color. Although impressively endowed and muscular with admirable symmetry, this wine requires 3–5 years of bottle age. Anticipated maturity: 2003–2020. Surprisingly, the 1996 Cabernet Sauvignon Howell Mountain is more supple and velvety-textured than the Mt. Veeder (I would have expected the reverse). This wine exhibits lead pencil, mineral, and black currant notes followed by a structured, concentrated, backward style that, while not impenetrable, certainly requires bottle age. The outstanding purity and sweet fruit suggest cellaring of 2–3 years is prudent. Anticipated maturity: now–2020.

All three of the 1995 offerings from Robert Craig are exceptionally symmetrical, well-balanced wines of elegance, finesse, and purity. They are ideal models of what a Bordeaux-styled red from California should taste like. Although not blockbusters, they offer plenty of flavor depth and complexity. A classic wine, the dark ruby/purple-colored 1995 Affinity reveals a lead pencil, black currant, and vanilla-scented nose that could easily pass for a classy Médoc. It displays good richness and purity on the entry, medium to full body, outstanding concentration, and exceptional harmony. This is a beauty. Anticipated maturity: now–2012. The 1995 Cabernet Sauvignon Mt. Veeder is a fuller-bodied wine more dominated by black currant and cherry fruit. Riper, with more weight, it is still a finesse-styled wine by California standards. Its exceptional purity, subtle oak, complexity, and overall balance suggest it will drink well now, as well as over the next 12–15 years. Not surprisingly, the 1995 Cabernet Sauvignon Howell Mountain possesses the most tannin, but also the richest constitution. The wine exhibits a deep ruby/purple color (similar to its two siblings), a classic, mineral, black currant, and toast-scented nose, deep, rich, powerful flavors with outstanding concentration, considerable finesse, well-integrated tannin, and a structured, well-delineated, austere, but impressively long finish. This wine will benefit from 2–3 years of cellaring, and will keep for 15–20 years.

The 1994 Cabernet Sauvignon Mt. Veeder is a full-bodied, dense, ruby/purple-colored, elegant wine with earthy, cassis fruit. It is a well-structured, medium-weight Cabernet with excellent ripeness, a graceful personality, and attractive layers of fruit. Although tight, it is accessible and should drink well for 10–12+ years. Another enticing offering from Craig is the 1994 Cabernet Sauvignon Howell Mountain. The wine, with a saturated dark purple color, offers up attractive, youthful aromas of lead pencil, vanilla, minerals, spice, and black currant fruit. A typical mountain Cabernet with copious quantities of tannin, this medium- to full-bodied, concentrated, impressively endowed wine is well crafted, yet backward and in need of 4–5 years of cellaring. Anticipated maturity: now–2012.

Past Glories: 1993 Cabernet Sauvignon Howell Mountain (91), 1993 Cabernet Sauvignon Mt. Veeder (90)

DALLA VALLE (NAPA)

1999 Cabernet Sauvignon	Oakville/Napa	E	(92–94)
1998 Cabernet Sauvignon	Oakville/Napa	E	94
1997 Cabernet Sauvignon	Oakville/Napa	E	93
1996 Cabernet Sauvignon	Oakville/Napa	E	93
1995 Cabernet Sauvignon	Oakville/Napa	D	93
1994 Cabernet Sauvignon	Oakville/Napa	D	94
1999 Maya Proprietary Red Wine	Oakville/Napa	EEE	(96–99)
1998 Maya Proprietary Red Wine	Oakville/Napa	EEE	96
1997 Maya Proprietary Red Wine	Oakville/Napa	EEE	99
1996 Maya Proprietary Red Wine	Oakville/Napa	EE	96
1995 Maya Proprietary Red Wine	Oakville/Napa	EE	97+
1994 Maya Proprietary Red Wine	Oakville/Napa	EE	99

These wines, from the property of Naoko Dalla Valle, emerge from the eastern slopes of Oakville. They seem to get better and better. Of course, there is not a lot of room to increase quality, but when readers consider what they achieved in 1998, it is remarkable. Both wines are among the candidates for "Wine of the Vintage."

The 1998 Cabernet Sauvignon (2,400 cases, made from a blend of 88% Cabernet Sauvignon and 12% Cabernet Franc) is even better from bottle than it was from barrel. It is a terrific wine with an opaque blue/purple color and a gorgeously sweet nose of black fruits intermixed with licorice, mineral, and spice. Full-bodied, opulently textured, and drinkable at an earlier age than most vintages, it should keep for at least two decades. The astonishing 1998 Maya (500 cases from a blend of 45% Cabernet Franc and 55% Cabernet Sauvignon) may well *be* the "Wine of the Vintage." This is a staggeringly rich effort that tastes like Cheval Blanc on steroids. It boasts a black/purple color as well as a knockout nose of jammy black fruits, spice, currants, minerals, and spice box, dazzling concentration, multiple layers of flavors, and sweet tannin, giving it that seamless texture that has been so much a characteristic of Maya's greatest vintages. The 1998 should drink well for at least 25 years.

As for the 1999s, they are what one would expect from a vintage that was cool yet less problematic than 1998. There are 2,200 cases of the 1999 Cabernet Sauvignon, which has been blended with 15.5% Cabernet Franc. It offers a beautiful perfume of menthol, black fruits, licorice, mineral, and smoke. Powerful with great purity, full body, and multiple layers, this superrich wine should be even better after bottling. The opaque black/purple-colored 1999 Maya (500 cases of a 45% Cabernet Franc/55% Cabernet Sauvignon blend) offers a superb nose of blueberry, blackberry, cassis, and floral notes intermixed with licorice and mineral. This formidable offering is fabulously intense on the palate with high tannin, full body, and glorious levels of extract and glycerin. It will need 4–5 years of cellaring and keep for at least three decades.

Qualitatively, the 1997s should, based on the vintage, tower over what Dalla Valle's 1998s and 1999s, but that is not the case. Profound they are, but it is a tribute to Naoko Dalla Valle and her winemaking consultant, Mia Klein, that such phenomenal efforts were made in 1998 and 1999. The 1997 Cabernet Sauvignon (2,800 cases from a blend of 85% Cabernet Sauvignon and 15% Cabernet Franc) boasts an opaque purple color as well as a gorgeous nose of mineral-infused black currants and spicy oak. Full-bodied, structured, muscular, and multidimensional, it is approachable, but best cellared for 2–4 years and drunk over the following 20–25 years. Close to perfection, the saturated blue/black-colored 1997 Maya exhibits complex aromatics of crème de cassis, smoke, spice box, iron, and espresso. The wine has a viscous texture, huge, concentrated, ripe fruit, remarkable body, and a seamless, multilayered finish. The tannin, acidity, and alcohol are all beautifully integrated. This is profound stuff! Anticipated maturity: 2005–2030.

The powerful, concentrated, dense ruby/purple-colored 1996 Cabernet Sauvignon, full-bodied and muscular, exhibits copious quantities of black currant fruit mixed with black-berries, minerals, cedar, and Chinese black tea–like notes. The tannin is sweet, in a vintage where this component can be slightly coarse. It can be drunk now or aged for 25 years. The 1996 Maya is another extraordinary example of this sensational blend of Cabernet Sauvignon and Cabernet Franc. Vivid, intense aromas of new saddle leather, plums, black currants, un-derbrush, and licorice are followed by a full-bodied, sensationally concentrated wine with sweet tannin, a deep, exceptionally pure and concentrated mid-palate, and an opulently tex-tured finish. It was surprisingly open-knit and delicious when tasted in October, but there is more tannin lurking beneath the surface. Anticipated maturity: now–2025.

The 1995 Cabernet Sauvignon exhibits an opaque blue/black/purple color, followed by sweet cassis aromas intermingled with scents of earth, spice, smoke, and grilled meats. This dense, powerful, muscular, concentrated wine provides an enormous mouth-feel. Wineries need more than luck to produce multidimensional wines with this concentration, ripeness, sweetness of fruit, and overall intensity and complexity. The terrific 1995 Maya is cut from the same mold as all the great Mayas of this decade. Its tannin may be even riper than in the 1994, but the wine is still an unevolved, massive, and unformed giant, although it is obvious that this will be another legendary effort. Do readers ever wonder why wines such as these are never made in 100,000 case lots? The 1994 Cabernet Sauvignon, which I have drunk with great pleasure despite its backwardness, possesses a full-bodied, multilayered person-ality, with plenty of tannin, but sufficient earthy, black currant/plum-like fruit to balance out the wine's structure. With an opaque purple color, a high tannin level, and gorgeous layers of fruit and intensity, it will be at its peak after 4–6 years of cellaring and will last for 20–25 years. The 1994 Maya is prodigious. The color is saturated opaque purple. The wine offers up restrained but gorgeously sweet earth, oak, mineral, and black fruit aromas. Full-bodied, with substantial quantities of glycerin and extract, this wine's large-scaled tannin seems to be well submerged beneath the wine's fabulous layers of fruit. Although more accessible than I would have thought prior to bottling, it is a candidate for 20–30 years of evolution.

I don't think I need to reinforce the fact that these offerings are extremely difficult to find, but isn't that the way it always is with such extraordinary wines?

Past Glories: Maya—1993 (98), 1992 (100), 1991 (99), 1990 (96)

DASHE CELLARS (SONOMA)

1999 Zinfandel	Dry Creek	C	88
1999 Zinfandel Todd Brothers Ranch	Alexander Valley	C	90

These are both impressive efforts from Dashe Cellars. The 1999 Zinfandel Dry Creek (14.5% alcohol) exhibits copious quantities of deep, rich, earthy, spicy, seaweed, pepper, and black currant/cherry fruit. Medium- to full-bodied, pure, and supple, it should be consumed over the next 3–4 years. The opaque purple-colored 1999 Zinfandel Todd Brothers Ranch boasts a superb bouquet of pure, jammy black raspberries, cherries, minerals, and subtle notions of earth and wood. Full-bodied, powerful, big, and thick, this dense, blockbuster Zinfandel can be drunk now and over the next 7–8 years. Bravo!

DEHLINGER (SONOMA)

1996 Cabernet/Merlot Blend	Russian River	D	91
1995 Cabernet/Merlot Blend	Russian River	D	91
1994 Cabernet/Merlot Blend	Russian River	D	91
1998 Cabernet Sauvignon Estate	Russian River	D	(86–88)
1997 Cabernet Sauvignon Estate	Russian River	D	90
1996 Cabernet Sauvignon Estate	Russian River	D	91
1995 Cabernet Sauvignon	Russian River	D	91
1994 Cabernet Sauvignon	Russian River	D	92

1999	Chardonnay Estate	Russian River	D	(87–89)
1999	Pinot Noir Estate	Russian River	D	(87–88)
1998	Pinot Noir Estate	Russian River	D	91
1997	Pinot Noir Estate	Russian River	D	90
1996	Pinot Noir Estate	Russian River	D	91
1995	Pinot Noir Estate	Russian River	D	89
1994	Pinot Noir Estate	Russian River	C	91
1998	Pinot Noir Goldridge Vineyard	Russian River	D	89
1997	Pinot Noir Goldridge Vineyard	Russian River	D	89
1996	Pinot Noir Goldridge Vineyard	Russian River	D	89
1995	Pinot Noir Goldridge Vineyard	Russian River	C	88
1994	Pinot Noir Goldridge Vineyard	Russian River	C	90
1994	Pinot Noir Goldridge Vineyard 20 Year Old Vines	Russian River	D	91
1999	Pinot Noir Hilltop Vineyard	Russian River	D	(90–92)
1999	Pinot Noir Octagon Vineyard	Russian River	D	(88–89)
1998	Pinot Noir Octagon Vineyard	Russian River	D	92
1997	Pinot Noir Octagon Vineyard	Russian River	D	91
1996	Pinot Noir Octagon Vineyard	Russian River	D	90
1995	Pinot Noir Octagon Vineyard	Russian River	D	90
1994	Pinot Noir Octagon Vineyard	Russian River	D	93
1997	Pinot Noir Reserve Estate	Russian River	D	90+
1994	Pinot Noir Reserve Estate	Russian River	D	92+
1998	Syrah Estate	Russian River	D	(89–90)
1997	Syrah Estate	Russian River	D	90
1996	Syrah Estate	Russian River	D	93
1995	Syrah Estate	Russian River	D	93
1994	Syrah Estate	Russian River	C	91
1998	Syrah Estate East Face	Russian River	D	91
1997	Syrah Goldridge Vineyard	Russian River	D	90
1996	Syrah Goldridge Vineyard	Russian River	D	90
1995	Syrah Goldridge Vineyard	Russian River	C	90
1994	Syrah Goldridge Vineyard	Russian River	C	89

Tom Dehlinger's wines remain among the most reasonably priced in California. It has been a great decade for Dehlinger, who has produced some of California's most hedonistic Pinot Noirs and increasingly tasty Syrahs and Chardonnays. Still in barrel, the 1999 Chardonnay Estate reveals a citrusy, liquid minerality, buttery lemon, pear, honeysuckle, smoke, and steely notes. The wine is full-bodied, clean, and ideal for drinking during its first 3–4 years.

Dehlinger still considers 1994 followed by 1997 to be the two finest vintages for Pinot Noir in the nineties, but his top-notch 1998s are even better this year than they were when tasted a year ago. There are just under 1,200 cases of the 1998 Pinot Noir Goldridge Vineyard. It is a delicious, full-bodied (14.2% alcohol) Pinot Noir with abundant quantities of sweet black cherry fruit, notes of smoke and spicy oak, a velvety texture, and an easy to drink and admire personality. It should be consumed over the next 4–5 years. The outstanding 1998 Pinot Noir Estate (1,050 cases) is a full-bodied, powerful wine with plenty of jammy cherry fruit intermixed with smoke, chocolate, earth, and allspice. Voluptuously textured, chewy, and pure, this is a delectable Pinot Noir that will not make old bones, but for drinking over the next 4–5 years, it is hard to resist. There is a tiny (210 cases) production of the dark plum/purple-colored 1998 Pinot Noir Octagon Vineyard. It exhibits a floral/rose petal note to its sweet black cherry, dried herb, earthy, complex aromatics. Medium- to full-bodied, long, and sumptuous, it is a broad, expansively flavored wine to drink over the next 5–6 years.

The alcohols in Dehlinger's 1999 Pinot Noirs are relatively high (averaging about 14.5%), and, as in all vintages, Dehlinger uses 35–40% new oak. His extensive use of 500-liter oak puncheons works well. The 1999 Pinot Noir Estate offers sweet, smoky, black cherry and strawberry fruit presented in a crisp, elegant, medium-bodied style. It does not have the textural fatness or richness of the 1998, but that may come with further barrel aging. Certainly the 1999 Pinot Noir Octagon Vineyard and 1999 Pinot Noir Hilltop Vineyard (from 25-year-old vines) reveal more impressive richness, texture, and viscosity in their medium- to full-bodied personalities. They have the telltale robust, richly fruity Dehlinger style with explosive mid-palates, and plenty of glycerin, concentration, and alcohol. These should turn out to be his finest Pinot Noirs in 1999, with 5–7 years of ageability. I am still enjoying my 1994s, which give no indication of losing their sumptuous fruit.

There is no doubting that Dehlinger's 1997s are terrific, hedonistically styled Pinot Noirs loaded with fruit and enticing, fleshy textures. The 1997 Pinot Noir Goldridge Vineyard exhibits a dark ruby color and an attractive, sweet, moderately intense nose of cherry jam, plums, spicy oak, and smoke. Its full-bodied, velvety, heady style is already delicious, and the wine is ideal for drinking over the next 3–5 years. The dark ruby/plum-colored 1997 Pinot Noir Estate (1,330 cases) could pass for a top Beaune premier cru. With sweet, chocolaty, smoky, black cherry fruit intermixed with spicy cinnamon and earthy scents, this sexy, hedonistic Pinot Noir fruit bomb is undeniably delicious and compelling. Too good to resist, it will be better with another 6–12 months of bottle age, and last for 5–7 years. It tips the scales at 14.5% alcohol. The Pinot Noir that comes from the vineyard surrounding the spooky-looking house at the top of the knoll overlooking Dehlinger's winery is called Octagon. The big, boldly styled 1997 exhibits a dark ruby/purple color as well as copious quantities of cherry liqueur, roasted meats, dried herbs, spice, and chocolate. Explosive on the palate, with Dehlinger's impressive glycerin, concentration, and fruit extraction, this is another crowd-pleasing, sumptuous Pinot Noir to enjoy now and over the next 7–8 years. Production was 390 cases. The Reserve Pinot Noir is made in only the finest vintages, and the 1997 (450 cases) is the tightest, most backward of these four Pinots. Like its siblings, it possesses low acidity, outstanding concentration and purity, as well as abundant black cherry, plum, and meaty characteristics. There is exciting fruit and overall symmetry, but this effort needs 1–2 years of bottle age because of its more noticeable structure and higher tannin level. It cuts a bold swath across the palate and has the most substance of these Pinot Noirs, but it needs more time. Anticipated maturity: now–2010.

While some of the new Dijon clones have been planted (particularly Clone 777), Dehlinger's Pinots are all from such old California clones (which originally came from Burgundy) as Martini, Swan, and Pommard. There can be as many as four separate Pinot Noirs if Dehlinger decides to produce a Reserve bottling, as he did in 1994 and 1997. In 1996, there were three efforts, Goldridge Vineyard (1,150 cases), Estate (990 cases), and Octagon Vineyard (140 cases). What is so likable about the Dehlinger Pinot Noirs is that they are made in a richly fruity, chocolaty style with plenty of spice, plush textures, and copious quantities of glycerin and alcohol. They are both user-friendly and faithful to the varietal's trademark. For example, the 1996 Pinot Noir Goldridge Vineyard exhibits an impressive dark ruby/purple color and a superb bouquet of jammy plums/cherries intermixed with earthy underbrush and melted chocolate. With airing, Asian spices enter the mélange. This is a chewy, medium- to full-bodied, plump, hedonistic Pinot (14.5% alcohol) that can be drunk now as well as over the next 5–6 years. The outstanding 1996 Pinot Noir Estate is similar, with more glycerin, a sweeter black cherry/kirsch component, roasted herb characteristics, full body, 14.5% alcohol, superb purity, and a nicely layered, chewy texture. This wine should drink well for 5–7 years. The 1996 Pinot Noir Octagon Vineyard is the most limited in availability. It offers up a fabulous nose of jammy strawberries, cherries, a touch of prunes, roasted meat, and spicy oak. Full-bodied, with considerable glycerin and extract, and a dense, lush, voluptuously textured finish, it should drink well for 5–6 years.

The 1995 Pinot Noirs reveal a more meaty, animal, plant material side to their aromatics and flavors than the flamboyantly fruit-driven 1994s. For example, the 1995 Pinot Noir Goldridge Vineyard is a medium ruby-colored wine with a big, spicy, earthy, cinnamon, smoky-scented nose, rich, jammy, silky-textured fruit, medium body, and a lush finish. It should drink well for 1–3 years. The 1995 Pinot Noir Estate exhibits more intensity, a marginally deeper ruby color, and a satiny texture with plenty of ripe black cherry and berry fruit. Medium-bodied and soft, it is ideal for drinking now. The deepest and richest of these Pinots, the 1995 Pinot Noir Octagon Vineyard boasts a ripe strawberry, cherry, chocolaty, earthy character. Medium- to full-bodied, hedonistic, and lush, it possesses savory, expansive flavors, low acidity, and gorgeous ripeness.

The dark ruby-colored 1994 Pinot Noir Goldridge Vineyard offers a spicy, gamey, smoky, complex set of aromatics, outstanding richness, a long, round, full-bodied palate with a silky texture, and plenty of spice, jammy black cherries, and underbrush-like flavors. The gorgeous, flamboyant 1994 Pinot Noir Estate possesses sweet, ripe, layered flavors, and a knockout nose of spices, red and black fruits, earth, and smoke. At 14.5% alcohol, the wine has gobs of glycerin and a sweet mid-palate (from extract and glycerin, not sugar). Full, rich, and loaded with personality and flavor, it is a classic Russian River Pinot Noir. Drink it over the next 5–6 years. The 1994 Pinot Noir Octagon Vineyard (10% stems are retained in this *cuvée* during the fermentation) is slightly more expensive as only 100 cases were produced from Dehlinger's minuscule hilltop vineyard. The wine reveals the telltale Dehlinger intense fragrance of allspice, sweet black fruits, toast, and smoke. On the palate, a cascade of raspberry, cherry flavors are accompanied by power, full body, a silky texture, and ripe tannin in the finish. This bold, lusty Pinot Noir is already difficult to resist. The 1994 Pinot Noir Reserve (500 cases produced), the most structured and closed of these offerings, had only been in bottle for a month when I tasted it. It appears to be another exceptional ripe, rich, concentrated, dense, complex, and expansively flavored Pinot Noir with a 30–35-second finish, as well as exceptional purity and personality.

Cabernet Sauvignon is not one of Tom Dehlinger's favorite wines, yet he makes an excellent Cabernet that somehow gets lost in the excitement of this producer's other efforts. He harvests about 34 tons of Cabernet Sauvignon, of which he retains one-third. The 1997 Cabernet Sauvignon exhibits a dense purple color, as well as abundant chocolate and cassis fruit intermixed with licorice and tobacco. It is a full-bodied, concentrated Cabernet that is likely to surprise consumers who think the Russian River is only a source for fine Chardonnay, Pinot, and Syrah. It should drink well for 10–12 years. The 1998 Cabernet Sauvignon has turned out well for the vintage, but it does not have the lusty richness or intensity of the 1999. Nevertheless, it is elegant and cleanly made, with no herbaceousness or astringency. Drink it over the next 7–8 years. There are only 390 cases of the outstanding 1996 Cabernet Sauvignon. Its dense purple color is accompanied by a sweet nose of chocolate, dried herbs, smoke, licorice, and copious berry and cassis fruit. Full-bodied, dense, and chewy, with moderate tannin in the finish, it needs 2–3 years of cellaring, and should keep for 15–20 years. The 1995 Cabernet Sauvignon (460 cases) is a pure Cabernet with an opaque purple color and telltale aromas of cassis, asphalt, loamy soil notes, and smoky, toasty oak. The wine is full-bodied and layered, with a chewy texture, and impressive purity and length. There is good tannin in the finish, but this remains a grapy, unevolved Cabernet with considerable potential. Anticipated maturity: now–2020. The 1994 Cabernet Sauvignon is another top-notch effort from this classic vintage. This opaque purple-colored, sexy wine reveals the vintage's precocious, flattering style. It offers up plenty of jammy black fruits intermingled with smoke, spice, licorice, and charcoal. Full-bodied, with low acidity, outstanding ripeness, and a fleshy, multilayered feel, this wine can be drunk now or cellared for 15+ years.

1992 was the first vintage for Syrah at Dehlinger, and he continues to show a capable hand with this varietal, which has adapted so well in so many different areas of California. He takes about 50% of the crop off, yet he still gets high yields. Nevertheless, the wine always possesses richness, concentration, and character, and lasts for at least a decade. The 1997 Syrah Estate (550 cases) offers plenty of licorice, blackberry, cassis, pepper, and smoke. Full-bodied and juicy, with excellent purity, it will drink well over the next decade. The 1998 Syrah Estate shows more bacon fat intermingled with cassis and licorice. Although full-bodied, it comes across as more elegant and lighter than the 1997. A successful effort, it should keep for a decade or more. The 1998 Syrah Estate East Face reveals a distinctive blueberry, violet, and blackberry-scented nose, good acidity, plenty of power and richness, no hard edges, and a succulent, nicely textured mid-palate and finish. This wine should drink well for 10–15 years. The 1997 Syrah Goldridge Vineyard (420 cases) seemed slightly better from bottle than it was from barrel. A dark ruby/purple color is accompanied by smoky cassis fruit, full body, outstanding purity and concentration, and a huge, explosively rich finish. Low acidity and a forward, sexy style suggest drinking it over the next decade. The 1996 Syrah Estate (370 cases) exhibits an opaque purple color as well as a gorgeous nose of blackberry liqueur and pepper. Dense and full-bodied, with wonderful sweetness (from high glycerin), this fleshy, multilayered Syrah possesses a succulence and richness that is hard to resist. The wine should age nicely for 10–15 years. The 1996 Syrah Goldridge Vineyard (230 cases) is a hedonistic, fat, succulently textured Syrah with gobs of crème de cassis, a notion of burning wood fires, and pepper, full body, outstanding purity, and no hard edges. Despite its size, it is a Syrah to consume over the next 15 years.

The 1994 Syrah Estate has shut down in the bottle and will require 4–5 years of cellaring, after which it will age well for 5–10 years. The color is an impressive opaque purple, and the wine reluctantly offers up sweet cassis, pepper, tar, and earthy scents. Full-bodied and chewy, with excellent purity, this is a well-endowed yet moderately tannic Syrah for laying down for a few years. The 1994 Syrah Goldridge Vineyard is a richly fruity, medium-weight Syrah with a dark purple color, gobs of sweet black currants in the nose, round, generous flavors, and some tannin in the finish. The wine should drink well for up to a decade. The 1995 Syrah Goldridge Vineyard (aged in 20% new oak) reveals an attractive peppery, bacony, sweet blackberry-scented nose, and ripe, rich, full-bodied flavors with plenty of sweet fruit. With an impressive chewy texture and excellent purity, it is a candidate for 6–12 years of cellaring, although it can be drunk now if matched with rich foods. My notes for the 1995 Syrah Estate said, "amazing Syrah." The wine possesses an opaque black/purple color, outstanding smoky, tar-like, blackberry flavors, immense body, admirable purity, and a long, deep, explosively rich finish with the tannin nearly concealed by the wine's wealth of fruit, glycerin, and extract. This terrific Syrah should age effortlessly for another 8–10 years.

Dehlinger's modesty is best exemplified by the fact that he calls his proprietary red wine a Cabernet/Merlot Blend. Production for this outstanding wine is limited to 400 cases. The 1996 reveals a saturated opaque purple color, followed by a gorgeous nose of blackberries, vanilla, licorice, and floral notes. Chewy and full-bodied, with a viscous texture, low acidity, sensational fruit extraction, and a mouthcoating finish, this is a large-scaled yet sexy wine that can be drunk now or cellared for 10 or more years. It tips the scales at 14.5% alcohol. The 1994 Cabernet/Merlot Blend contains equal proportions of these varietals. The opaque purple/black color is followed by sweet, powerful aromas of black currants, licorice, chocolate, and sweet vanilla. The wine is full-bodied, dense, powerful, yet seamless and silky. The tannin is gorgeously well integrated, a characteristic of the vintage. This wine can be drunk now or cellared for 10–15 years. The opaque purple-colored 1995 Cabernet/Merlot Blend (70% Cabernet Sauvignon / 30% Merlot) displays a sweet, rich nose of melted road tar, black currants, earth, minerals, and toast. Rich, with great fruit and ripeness, this full-bodied wine will be at its best after 2–4 years of cellaring; it will keep for 10 years.

Past Glories: 1993 Bordeaux Blend Proprietary Red Wine (91), 1993 Cabernet/Merlot Blend (91), 1993 Cabernet Sauvignon (90)

DEL DOTTO (NAPA)

1997	Cabernet Franc	Napa	D	90
1997	Cabernet Sauvignon Estate	Napa	D	(90–92)
1996	Cabernet Sauvignon Estate	Napa	D	88
1995	Cabernet Sauvignon	Napa	D	89+
1998	Giovanni's Tuscan Reserve	Napa	E	88
1997	Giovanni's Tuscan Reserve	Napa	E (500 ml)	90
1995	Giovanni's Tuscan Reserve	Napa	D (500 ml)	88
1997	Merlot	Napa	E	(88–90)

This small seven-acre vineyard just north of St. Helena is primarily planted with Cabernet Sauvignon and a tiny amount of Sangiovese. Production has been limited, as part of the crop was sold to Whitehall Lane, but that changed with the 1997 vintage. Consequently, Del Dotto's production has soared from just under 500 to 4,000 cases. The wines are aged in both American and French oak, and the proprietary red, Giovanni's Tuscan Reserve, is available only in 500 ml bottles. My favorite new release from Del Dotto is the 1998 Giovanni's Tuscan Reserve, a 1,000-case blend of 85% Cabernet Sauvignon and 15% Sangiovese, all from the estate vineyards in Rutherford. This wine has a handsome, dark ruby color, a nose of black currants, cherries, leather, spice, and vanilla. The wine cuts a slightly deeper swath on the palate but is still medium-bodied, moderately endowed, and best drunk over the next 5–7 years.

Pride Mountain and La Jota routinely produce California's finest Cabernet Franc, but Del Dotto is not far behind with its lavishly wooded, ostentatious example. The 1997 Cabernet Franc reveals beautiful, sweet, black currant and raspberry fruit, toasty wood, and a sweet mid-palate and finish. It is a seductive, well-layered wine to enjoy over the next 7–10 years. The terrific 1997 Giovanni's Tuscan Reserve (1,199 cases of a blend of 75% Cabernet Sauvignon and 25% Sangiovese) is dominated by its cherry liqueur, strawberry jam, and leathery characteristics. Ripe, with medium to full body, a sweet, concentrated, juicy mid-palate, and outstanding purity, this seductive red is ready to drink. Consume it over the next 7–8 years. The outstanding 1997 Cabernet Sauvignon Estate is produced from a vineyard situated at the corner of Highway 29 and Zinfandel Lane in Rutherford. It exhibits a dense ruby/purple color in addition to a gorgeous nose of blackberry jam intermixed with cedar and spicy new oak. Full-bodied, dense, and pure, with a layered texture and low acidity, this beefy yet voluptuously textured Cabernet Sauvignon should drink well young and evolve nicely for 15 years. The 1997 Merlot (96% Merlot and 4% Cabernet Franc) is limited in production (249 cases). The wine's dark ruby color with purple nuances is followed by lush, mocha-tinged, berry fruit and cherry aromas and flavors. This low-acid, plump, chewy Merlot should drink well young and last for 7–10 years.

The 1996 Cabernet Sauvignon Estate is an elegant, medium-bodied effort with an oaky, black currant, cherry, and loamy soil-scented nose, and moderate tannin. It is more monolithic and less seamless than its 1997 counterpart. Anticipated maturity: now–2012. The Cabernet Sauvignons (500 cases of both the 1995 and 1996) are aged in 100% new oak, of which 50% is American oak coopered by French barrel makers. The exotic, opaque purple-colored 1995 Cabernet Sauvignon offers exceptionally ripe, jammy black cherry and currant flavors intermixed with lavish quantities of toasty new oak. Full-bodied and obvious, but undeniably appealing in an ostentatious manner, this brassy, big, thick, juicy wine is already drinking well, but promises to evolve for 10–12 years. The delicious 1995 Giovanni's Tuscan Reserve, a blend of 70% Cabernet Sauvignon and 30% Sangiovese, displays a dark plum color, full body, gorgeous, jammy strawberry fruit intermixed with raspberries and cassis with a subtle touch of spicy oak and a fleshy, chewy texture. Drink it over the next 3–4 years.

DOMINUS (NAPA)

1999 Dominus	Napa	EE	90
1998 Dominus	Napa	EE	89
1997 Dominus	Napa	EE	94
1996 Dominus	Napa	EE	95
1995 Dominus	Napa	E	93
1994 Dominus	Napa	E	99
1999 Napanook	Napa	D	85
1998 Napanook	Napa	D	87
1997 Napanook	Napa	D	90
1996 Napanook	Napa	D	90

The 1998 Dominus (a 7,000-case blend of 73% Cabernet Sauvignon, 15% Cabernet Franc, 6% Petit Verdot, and 6% Merlot) is very Bordeaux-like in its weight and its aromatic and flavor profile. From this dark garnet/ruby-colored wine emerges a moderately intense, complex nose of herbs, earth, cedar, coffee, and dried cherries and plum-like fruit. It is relatively evolved, with soft tannin, an elegant, medium-bodied style, and some tannin in the finish. While lighter than most recent vintages, that has more to do with the vintage than any change in winemaking. Drink it over the next 10–12 years. Perhaps the surprise was the showing of the 1999 Dominus, a 7,000-case blend of 75% Cabernet Sauvignon, 13% Cabernet Franc, 9% Merlot, and 3% Petit Verdot. The wine seemed to show some green pepper notes in the nose and tasted austere and tannic. It offers an impressive plum color as well as notes of blackberries, coffee, prunes, cedar, and herbs in the moderately intense aromatics. On the palate, this medium-bodied wine effort displays a harder style, with tough tannin and a slightly attenuated finish. If it fleshes out over the next six months, it should prove to be outstanding, but it is not one of the more prodigious offerings from this high-quality estate.

Readers waiting for another 1991 or 1994 Dominus, the two finest wines yet made at this French outpost of Pomerol's famed Christian Moueix, will have to wait for another vintage. Certainly, the 1997 Dominus is exquisite, but not at the level of the virtually perfect 1994 and 1991. The 1997 Dominus, a blend of 86.5% Cabernet Sauvignon, 9% Cabernet Franc, and 4.5% Merlot, is showing fabulously well. With 14.1% alcohol and a pH that would make many New World oenologists shudder (about 3.95), this wine is a fleshy, silky-textured, opulent wine with a gorgeous nose of roasted herbs, coffee, jammy black cherry, and plum-like fruit. Asian spice, licorice, and blackberry and cherry notes with tobacco spice all add to this complex, very involved, yet gorgeously symmetrical Dominus. The wine is medium- to full-bodied, very concentrated, and silky-textured. It is gorgeous to drink now, but should age easily for 10–15 years. The 1996 Dominus, a blend of 82% Cabernet Sauvignon, 10% Cabernet Franc, 4% Merlot, and 4% Petit Verdot, tips the scales at 14.2% alcohol. Although this offering lacks the power, intensity, and compelling characteristics of the 1991 and 1994, it is not far off the pace of those two monumental wines. A super nose of roasted coffee, chocolate, dried herbs, black fruits, and kirsch is both intense and persuasive. The wine displays terrific richness, medium to full body, low acidity, a succulent, opulent texture, and superb purity. This beautifully made 1996 is one of the few wines that has successfully tamed the vintage's elevated tannin level. It should be relatively drinkable upon its release, yet evolve nicely for two decades. Impressive!

The 1995 Dominus (a 6,000-case blend of 80% Cabernet Sauvignon, 10% Cabernet Franc, 6% Petit Verdot, and 4% Merlot) is ripe, plummy, supple, and expansively flavored with copious quantities of black currant fruit. Full-bodied and low in acidity, it possesses exceptional concentration and purity. Qualitatively, it is built along the lines of the 1992 and 1990. While it is not as powerful or intense as the 1996 or 1994, the 1995 is a large-scaled, rich wine that should provide splendid drinking for two decades. I have had a difficult time keeping the corks in my bottles of 1994 Dominus. Eight thousand cases were produced from a blend of 70% Cabernet Sauvignon, 14% Cabernet Franc, 12% Merlot, and 4% Petit Verdot. In this vintage, 174 days passed between bud break and the harvest, a remarkable period of time for any wine region in the world. The 1994 is a strikingly thick, compellingly rich wine with the texture of a great Pomerol, despite being made primarily from Cabernet Sauvignon. The wine exhibits a dense purple color and an incredibly fragrant nose of jammy black fruits, spice, smoke, and loamy, truffle-like scents. In the mouth, it is full-bodied, with thrilling levels of extract and richness, but no sense of heaviness or harshness. This seamless Dominus possesses no hard edges, as its acidity, tannin, and alcohol are beautifully meshed with copious quantities of ripe fruit. This wine offers early drinking, yet has the potential to last for 30+ years.

This estate's second wine, Napanook, is a reasonably good value at about one-third the price of Dominus. The 1999 Napanook (a 3,800-case blend of 70% Cabernet Sauvignon, 14% Cabernet Franc, 3% Merlot, and 3% Petit Verdot) shows some sweet chocolate, along with notes of dried herbs, cedar, spice box, black cherries, and coffee. The wine is medium-bodied, quite spicy, with slightly more structure and tannin than the 1998. It should drink well for 8–10 years upon release. The dark saturated ruby-colored 1998 Napanook (a 4,000-case blend of 94% Cabernet Sauvignon and 6% Petit Verdot) exhibits a Pomerol-like lushness, openness, and delicious black cherry and berry fruit. The wine begins with an excellent attack, then falls off slightly. Medium-bodied and round, it is ideal for restaurants and consumers looking for an immediately drinkable wine. It will last well for 7–8 years.

The 1997 Napanook (a 7,000-case blend of 61% Cabernet Sauvignon, 22% Cabernet Franc, and 17% Merlot) shows even better from bottle than it did from cask. The color is dark ruby with purple nuances. A sweet, open-knit nose offering aromas of tobacco, cedar, blackberry and cherry jam is followed by an opulently textured, succulent, rich, fleshy, user-friendly, delicious wine. Undeniably hedonistic, it caresses the palate. Already delicious, it will age nicely for a decade. There are 2,000 cases of the 1996 Napanook, a blend of 74% Cabernet Sauvignon, 13% Cabernet Franc, and 13% Petit Verdot. Made in a peppery, spicy, herbaceous, earthy style, it exhibits a dark plum color, an intensely aromatic cassis and pepper-scented nose, a lush entry on the palate, and succulent, low-acid, rich, concentrated flavors with more tannin than the 1997. Already drinkable, the 1996 is appealing for its intense fragrance and rich flavors. It should age well for 10–12 years.

Past Glories: Dominus—1992 (94), 1991 (100), 1990 (96), 1987 (92), 1986 (90), 1985 (90), 1984 (92)

DOWNING FAMILY VINEYARDS (NAPA)

1999 Zinfandel Fly by Night	Napa	D	90

This creatively packaged Zinfandel (check out the bottle) boasts an opaque purple color in addition to a sweet nose of black fruits, high-quality new oak, minerals, and flowers, outstanding concentration, impressive purity, medium to full body, and well-integrated acidity as well as tannin. A classy, elegant, complex offering made in the style of a classified growth Bordeaux, it will drink well for 7–8 years.

DRY CREEK VINEYARD (SONOMA)

1999 Zinfandel Heritage Clone	Dry Creek	B	90
1998 Zinfandel Heritage Clone	Dry Creek	C	(86–88)

1999 Zinfandel Old Vines	Sonoma	C	90
1998 Zinfandel Old Vines	Dry Creek	D	89
1997 Zinfandel Old Vines	Sonoma	C	88
1995 Zinfandel Old Vines 25th Anniversary	Dry Creek	D	88
1999 Zinfandel Reserve	Sonoma	D	89+
1998 Zinfandel Reserve	Dry Creek	D	90

A 90-point rating for a $15 bottle of California wine is about as rare as a $15 classified growth 2000 Bordeaux. Dry Creek's 1999 Heritage Clone Zinfandel must be the "value of the vintage," but even the $20 Old Vines is a sensational buy. Ironically, I preferred those two offerings to the more structured, backward 1999 Reserve. As for the 1999 Zinfandel Heritage Clone, it boasts a dense purple color and a sweet nose of blackberries, licorice, pepper, and minerals. There is a terrific mid-palate, beautiful harmony, and well-integrated acidity, tannin, and oak. Drink this opulently styled, pure, classic Zinfandel over the next 4–5 years. The similarly styled, opaque purple-colored 1999 Zinfandel Old Vines offers gorgeously sweet aromas of black cherries, raspberries, and currants. Multilayered, powerful, and rich, with more muscle and structure than the Heritage Clone *cuvée*, it is a topflight, balanced, concentrated yet harmonious wine to enjoy over the next 4–6 years. More backward and less evolved, the 1999 Zinfandel Reserve displays more new oak—not always a welcome characteristic for Zinfandel. Full-bodied and well structured, it exhibits aromas and flavors of red and black fruits intermixed with new saddle leather, vanilla, and earth. Dense and chewy, it needs another 1–2 years of cellaring to round into shape. While it may age longer than the Old Vines and Heritage Clone *cuvées*, it is questionable whether it will ultimately taste better.

All of the 1998 Zinfandels, hopefully, will be bottled without excessive fining or filtration. The well-made, deep ruby-colored 1998 Zinfandel Old Vines offers a heady perfume of blackberry and cherry fruit. Medium- to full-bodied and plush, with low acidity, as well as abundant glycerin and concentration, this opulent wine will have many admirers. Even denser, the opaque ruby/purple-colored 1998 Zinfandel Reserve reveals gorgeously thick, rich, concentrated black cherry and raspberry aromas and flavors infused with pepper, earth, leather, and subtle spicy wood. The vintage's low acidity as well as modest yields have resulted in a wine of considerable richness, extract, and ripeness, but no sense of heaviness. It should drink beautifully for 6–7 years. Interestingly, as it sat in the glass, notes of licorice and melted asphalt emerged. Slightly less impressive, although very good, is the 1998 Zinfandel Heritage Clone. It possesses more tannin in addition to a robust, chunky, rustic personality. There is plenty of density and spice, but the wine tastes slightly disjointed. Anticipated maturity: now–2008.

An elegant, flavorful, medium-bodied Zinfandel, Dry Creek's 1997 Old Vines exhibits a dark ruby color, attractive raspberry and cherry fruit in the spicy bouquet. With a tasty, peppery, open-knit texture, this wine has enough acidity to provide vibrancy and freshness. Drink it over the next 3–4 years. The excellent 1995 Zinfandel Old Vines 25th Anniversary is one of the most noteworthy efforts from this vintage. It possesses a dense ruby/purple color, followed by a big, fragrant, spicy, pungent nose of pepper, jammy red and black fruits, and earth. Rich, medium- to full-bodied, and harmonious, this wine exhibits a pleasing midsection and fine length. It should drink well for 5–6 years.

DUCKHORN (NAPA)

1998 Paraduxx	Napa	D	88

A proprietary blend of 65% Zinfandel, 30% Cabernet Sauvignon, and 5% Merlot, aged in both American and French oak (primarily new), this deep opaque ruby/purple-colored effort offers a sexy bouquet of chocolate, cassis, berries, and melted road tar. Some oak emerges with airing. Medium- to full-bodied and chewy, the Cabernet Sauvignon component presently dominates this excellent wine's personality. Consume it over the next 6–7 years.

DUNN VINEYARDS (NAPA)

1999 Cabernet Sauvignon	Howell Mountain	E	(90–93)
1998 Cabernet Sauvignon	Howell Mountain	E	89
1997 Cabernet Sauvignon	Howell Mountain	E	95
1996 Cabernet Sauvignon	Howell Mountain	E	96+
1995 Cabernet Sauvignon	Howell Mountain	E	96
1994 Cabernet Sauvignon	Howell Mountain	D	96+
1998 Cabernet Sauvignon	Napa	D	87
1997 Cabernet Sauvignon	Napa	D	92+
1996 Cabernet Sauvignon	Napa	D	94
1995 Cabernet Sauvignon	Napa	D	94
1994 Cabernet Sauvignon	Napa	D	94

If Godzilla drank California Cabernet Sauvignon, would there be any doubt as to what choice it would be? Anyone who has regularly tasted Randy Dunn's Cabernet Sauvignons (first produced in 1979) realizes several things. They all possess the following characteristics: 1) remarkable color and richness, 2) massive personalities with huge tannic structures, and 3) gorgeous purity and unreal aging potential. In 1999, I reported on a tasting where all of Dunn's top wines back through the 1982 vintage were served. Remarkably, they had hardly budged in development, yet they were still exceptionally rich in their pure crème de cassis, black raspberry, and blackberry fruit notes. These are obviously more than 20–25 year wines. It is not far-fetched to suggest that Dunn is producing Cabernet Sauvignons that, in top vintages, will be fresh, lively, and rich in fruit at age 50. Unbelievably, Dunn has barely raised his prices in the two decades he has been making wine. For those with patience, these are among the finest values in long-lived, classic Napa Cabernet Sauvignon.

The Howell Mountain 1998 and 1999 Cabernet Sauvignons were produced from very small crops characterized by extremely cool growing seasons and unusually late harvests. Dunn dropped 40% of his crop in 1998 in order to attain ripeness. Consequently, his 1998 Cabernet Sauvignon Howell Mountain does not possess the herbaceousness or weediness found in many 1998 Howell Mountain Cabernets. The wine reveals plenty of sweet black currant fruit infused with minerals. While lighter than his more powerful vintages, it is a successful effort. It may last only 20–25 years, rather than 50! The 1999 Cabernet Sauvignon Howell Mountain experienced a similar growing season. Dunn dropped 30% of the crop in order to guarantee ripeness in his vineyard. The 1999 displays excellent intensity along with pure black currant/cassis notes intermixed with earth, spice, and smoke. Again, there is no astringent tannin or vegetal characteristic to be found in this full-bodied, powerful Cabernet.

The 1998 Cabernet Sauvignon Napa (a composite blend) is highly extracted for the vintage, but lighter than most Dunn Cabernet Sauvignons. It obviously reflects the challenges presented by this vintage. Dry tannin in the finish might turn out to be cause for concern, but there is still plenty of cassis fruit in this medium- to full-bodied Cabernet, though it is more compressed than usual. Dunn will undoubtedly build more flesh and fruit into it before bottling, but we will have to wait another year to find out.

Randy Dunn's 1997s are superb examples of the vintage. But be forewarned, readers planning their purchases should remember that these wines usually require at least a decade of cellaring. Keep in mind that some of Dunn's finest early vintages (1982 and 1984) are still infants! They are crammed with the telltale characteristics of blackberry and crème de cassis fruit tinged with an earthy minerality. The 1997 Cabernet Sauvignon Napa exhibits an opaque purple color as well as a gorgeous nose of pure cassis and blackberries with flinty notions in the background. Full-bodied, powerful, tannic, pure, and backward, it needs another 8–10 years of cellaring. Anticipated maturity: 2010–2035+. The enormous 1997 Cabernet Sauvignon Howell Mountain is a super-powerful, fabulously concentrated, 50-year wine. Aromas and flavors of blackberry/cassis jam, minerals, and subtle oak are found in this extravagantly rich, gargantuan Cabernet Sauvignon that should age effortlessly for half a century. Anticipated maturity: 2015–2050.

The 1996s have turned out to be stunning. The opaque blue/purple-colored 1996 Cabernet Sauvignon Napa boasts an exceptional nose of crème de cassis, minerals, and spice. It takes at least a decade for wines such as this to begin to reveal more identity and vintage character. The cassis/blackberry liqueur–like fruit are present, as are mouth-searing levels of tannin and impressive extract. This blockbuster should be at its peak between 2010–2040. Take all those elements, add a bit more ink to the black/blue/purple color, give the texture slightly more unctuosity and thickness, and readers have a glimpse of Randy Dunn's 1996 Cabernet Sauvignon Howell Mountain. Greatness is suggested by a wonderfully sweet mid-section, gorgeous purity, and this humongous wine's overall symmetry. It also possesses sumptuous layers of concentration, phenomenal richness, remarkably sweet tannin, low acidity, and a 40+ second finish. Anticipated maturity: 2009–2040.

As for the 1995s, this appears to be a fabulous vintage. I doubt there will be much difference in quality between the 1995s and Dunn's spectacular 1994s. The saturated black/purple-colored 1995 Cabernet Sauvignon Napa possesses a promising yet backward nose of minerals, lead pencil, and blackberries/cassis. This mammoth offering displays extraordinary concentration and purity, as well as a thick, unctuous texture with high tannin levels. It will evolve for 30–50 years. When will it reach its plateau of maturity? My best guess is 10–15 years . . . minimum. The 1995 Cabernet Sauvignon Howell Mountain is similar in all respects to the Napa, but somewhat heavier in the mouth, with an aggressive tannic bite and more length. It possesses mineral-tinged blackberry and cassis fruit, massive body, and extraordinary purity and length. It should not be touched for 12–15 years. Again, it will undoubtedly live through the first half of the 21st century.

Randy Dunn is sensitive to the fact that his wines are so remarkably consistent that it is often difficult to tell vintages apart. I think the vintage character will become more apparent when the wines are 15–20 years of age. Even the most professional palate will be inundated with a furious blast of tannin and concentrated cassis and blackberry fruit when these wines are young. With that in mind, the following notes do sound similar, but I feel 1994 may turn out to be one of Dunn's finest vintages. At present, 1995 looks to be the most tannic, and 1996, similar to but softer than 1994. Given the fact that both of Dunn's debut vintages of 1979 and 1980 are still relative infants in terms of development, in all likelihood, the 1994s, 1995s, and 1996s possess a minimum of 25–30 years of aging potential!

The 1994s might be ready to drink within 10–15 years. It is hard to believe these wines spend 30 months in oak casks before bottling as they are incredibly unevolved and backward when released. The 1994 Cabernet Sauvignon Napa reveals an opaque purple color, followed by a sweet, rich, black currant and crème de cassis–scented nose with no evidence of oak. This fruit bomb displays considerable breadth and expansiveness on the palate, in essence revealing only two dimensions—fruit and tannin. It is slightly softer and more precocious than the 1995 and 1996, so perhaps it will only need 10 rather than 15 years of cellaring. This immensely impressive Cabernet is a candidate for 20–30 years of cellaring. Look out for the behemoth 1994 Cabernet Sauvignon Howell Mountain. This black/purple-colored wine adds a few more nuances (minerals, licorice, and floral scents) to the lavish display of crème de cassis. Full-bodied, with a blockbuster level of extract and density, this is an outstanding Cabernet Sauvignon for readers with patience, good genes for longevity, or the foresight to purchase it for their children. Anticipated maturity: 2006–2030.

As a postscript, I have been buying Randy Dunn's wines since he first began producing them in 1979. I have worried about whether they will ever become drinkable given their massive personalities and huge tannic structures. I am not sure I know the answer, but a blind tasting in late September of 1998 was a revelation. What was so striking was that in the first flight, which included vintages from the early eighties, the wines were thought to be from the

early nineties! Undoubtedly, these wines age at a glacial pace. While I have been consistently advising readers that they will last for 25–30 years, they may be 40–50 year wines, possibly needing 25–30 years just to reach their plateau of maturity! No vintage from the eighties or nineties was revealing much age. All the wines were relatively stunning in quality, with some of the lighter years, such as 1983 and 1988, surprisingly impressive, but not as phenomenal as Randy Dunn's greatest vintages (1982, 1984, 1985, 1990, 1991, 1992, 1993, 1994, 1995, and 1996). One of the interesting findings from this vertical tasting is that the fruit levels remain incredibly fresh and concentrated, yet the tannin levels do soften. Because the wines are sterile filtered, I am not sure they will ever develop aromatic complexity, but who really knows? The remarkable aspect is that at 15–18 years of age, Dunn's Cabernet Sauvignons taste as if they are only 3–5 years old. Furthermore, there are no signs of fruit degradation or oxidation, always positive attributes when measuring a wine's ageability.
Past Glories: Dunn Cabernet Sauvignon Howell Mountain—1993 (95), 1992 (97), 1991 (94), 1990 (96), 1987 (94), 1986 (94), 1985 (95), 1984 (95), 1982 (97), 1981 (90), 1979 (90)

EDMEADES ESTATE (MENDOCINO)

1999 Gewürztraminer	Anderson Valley	B	88
1998 Petite Sirah Eaglepoint	Mendocino	D	88
1996 Petite Sirah Eaglepoint	Mendocino	C	89
1998 Pinot Noir	Anderson Valley	C	88
1997 Pinot Noir	Anderson Valley	C	90
1999 Syrah Eaglepoint Vineyard	Mendocino	D	(87–89)
1998 Zinfandel	Mendocino	C	90
1997 Zinfandel	Mendocino	C	88
1998 Zinfandel	Mendocino Ridge	D	89
1997 Zinfandel	Mendocino Ridge	D	89
1997 Zinfandel Ciapusci Vineyard	Mendocino Ridge	C	91
1996 Zinfandel Ciapusci Vineyard	Mendocino	C	88
1998 Zinfandel Eaglepoint Vineyard	Mendocino	D	91
1995 Zinfandel Eaglepoint Vineyard	Mendocino	D	90
1996 Zinfandel Zeni Vineyard	Mendocino	D	90
1998 Zinfandel Zeni Vineyard	Mendocino Ridge	D	88
1997 Zinfandel Zeni Vineyard	Mendocino Ridge	C	88+

An underrated winery for sure, proprietor Jess Jackson and his wine-maker, Van Williamson, are turning out gorgeous wines that seem to go largely unnoticed, probably because they are realistically priced. This is an excellent source of unfined, unfiltered wines, including one of the finest Pinot Noir values in the land. Edmeades also produces a Gewürztraminer and a Chardonnay that sell for a song. The 1999 Gewürztraminer, from a varietal that rarely produces anything of interest, is surprisingly spot-on in terms of its exotic rose petal/lychee nut aromatics. Rich and full-bodied, with some residual sugar, it will drink beautifully over the next year with Asian dishes or sautéed foie gras. There are 2,638 cases of the artisanal 1998 Pinot Noir, a big, rich, earthy, animal-styled Pinot with plenty of black cherry fruit, pepper, and plum aromas as well as flavors. Medium- to full-bodied and fruit-driven, with good glycerin and a silky texture, it requires consumption over the next 2–3 years. The 1998 Petite Sirah Eaglepoint Vineyard is surprisingly soft, round, and forward for a Petite Sirah. The wine has plenty of character, an opaque ruby/purple color, and good peppery, blackberry, and licorice notes. It should drink well for 10–12 years. Another opulently textured wine is the 1999 Syrah Eaglepoint Vineyard. This 100% Syrah aged in both French and American oak exhibits blackberry liqueur aspects along with smoke, creosote, and pepper. It is a full-bodied, luscious Syrah to drink during its first decade of life. A great value when you divide dollars by points is Edmeades' 1997 Pinot Noir. Aged in both American and French oak, this

100% Pinot Noir from an Anderson Valley vineyard called Philo is more limited in availability (just under 2,000 cases). Reminiscent of some of Domaine Parent's old-fashioned Pommards I enjoyed in the early seventies, its medium ruby color is followed by aromas of overripe plums, blackberries, cherries, and toast. Full-bodied (14.5% alcohol), with a nicely layered, plump texture, this low-acid, luxuriously rich, expressive Pinot Noir is one of the sleepers being made in California. Drink it over the next 2–4 years. It is a great value.

Readers looking for muscular, brawny, full-bodied, tannic reds need search no further than Edmeades' 1996 Petite Sirah Eaglepoint. This wine reveals an opaque black/purple color, as well as a boldly styled nose of jammy blackberry fruit intertwined with cassis and earth. It is a broodingly dense, chewy, uncomplex wine with intense flavors, full body, and excellent, nearly outstanding purity and length. Consume it now, or cellar it for 10–15 years.

The bevy of powerful 1998 Zinfandels from Edmeades (ranging from 15.5–17.5% alcohol) includes debut releases from the new Mendocino Ridge appellation, a series of high-altitude, ridge-top vineyards. The dark plum-colored 1998 Zinfandel Mendocino Ridge (15.5% alcohol) offers aromas and flavors of smoke, plums, black raspberries, and black currants. Spicy and round, with a supple texture, and a rich, medium- to full-bodied, luscious texture, this wine can be drunk over the next 4–5 years. The 1998 Zinfandel Mendocino (15.6% alcohol) reveals a slightly more saturated color than its Mendocino Ridge sibling in addition to full, powerful, chewy flavors redolent with blackberries, cherries, incense, spice box, and subtle wood. A heady alcohol content provides glycerin, and the fleshy, full-bodied texture is a hedonist's dream. Enjoy this Zinfandel over the next 6–7 years. Also from the Mendocino Ridge appellation, the 1998 Zinfandel Zeni Vineyard (16.5% alcohol) exhibits a dark ruby color with amber at the edge. The nose is reminiscent of an Asian restaurant, with scents of soy, smoked duck, plums, and assorted black fruits. Ripe and deep, with a slight hotness, this heady wine requires consumption over the next 3–5 years. Again, low acidity gives the wine an extremely forward feel. Lastly, the superb 1998 Zinfandel Eaglepoint Vineyard (16% alcohol) tastes like a fabulous northern Rhône. Blackberry liqueur infused with smoke jumps from the glass of this stupendous Zinfandel. Explosive in the mouth, with huge extract levels, fruit, and glycerin, but no heaviness or heat, this is a full-throttle, opulently textured, hedonistic offering to drink over the next 3-5 years.

All four 1997 Zinfandels are well-made, reasonably priced efforts. My favorite is the 1997 Zinfandel Ciapusci Vineyard. Sadly, there are only 617 cases of this dry, full-bodied, exotic Zinfandel. Fermented with natural yeasts, it achieved 17% alcohol (not to be sipped as a cocktail next to the swimming pool, please). An earthy, gamey, briery, bramble-like perfume jumps from the glass of this medium ruby-colored, luscious, decadently rich effort. Drink it over the next several years. The 1997 Zinfandel Mendocino (10,000 cases; 15.4% alcohol) was aged 10 months in both French and American oak. It is a fat, big, rich, delicious effort bursting with peppery, spicy, cherry fruit with a touch of blackberries. Interestingly, the blend was 78% Zinfandel, 8% Sangiovese, 3% Syrah, and 11% Petite Sirah. Another nearly outstanding effort from wine-maker Van Williamson is the 1997 Zinfandel Mendocino Ridge. Tipping the scales at a whopping 16.3% alcohol, it is a blend from three vineyards—Alden Ranch, Ciapusci, and Zeni. There are just under 600 cases of this big, briery, dense, full-bodied Zinfandel with more noticeable high acidity than some of its siblings. It should drink well for 2–3 years, but it is not quite as lavishly rich and sumptuous as either the Mendocino or Ciapusci Vineyard. The tightest-knit, most backward of this quartet is the 1997 Zinfandel Zeni Vineyard. Also the lowest in alcohol (14.8%), it spent 18 months in both French and American oak. Production for this 100% Zinfandel is 187 cases. It needs another 3–6 months of cellaring, and while it may not improve, it will open up given its fleshy, structured personality. All the Zinfandel varietal characteristics—black cherries, pepper, briery fruit— are present in moderately high levels. This wine should drink well for 4–5 years.

The two fine 1996 Zinfandels include the 1996 Zinfandel Zeni Vineyard, which possesses plenty of this varietal's peppery, briery, raspberry fruit, good freshness, and loads of glycerin and concentration. This lush, supple-textured wine should be consumed over the next several years. The evolved dark plum-colored 1996 Zinfandel Ciapusci Vineyard offers a spicy, peppery, fruity nose, lush, medium-bodied flavors, and good fat and depth. Although not as deep and rich as the Zeni *cuvée*, it is excellent for drinking over the next 1–2 years.

I adored the 1995 Zinfandel Eaglepoint Vineyard. The wine's saturated opaque purple color is accompanied by intense aromas of black raspberries, cherries, minerals, and spice. Opulently textured and rich, with layers of fruit, this wine is atypical of the vintage given its wealth of fruit, surprising level of glycerin, and gorgeously proportioned, layered finish. This is a beautifully made, pure, medium- to full-bodied Zinfandel that has managed to hide its lofty alcohol (15.2%) content. It is fully mature.

Kudos to part hippie, part wild man, wine-maker Van Williamson!

ETUDE (NAPA)

1998	Cabernet Sauvignon	Napa	E	90
1997	Cabernet Sauvignon	Napa	E	96
1996	Cabernet Sauvignon	Napa	E	92
1995	Cabernet Sauvignon	Napa	D	94
1994	Cabernet Sauvignon	Napa	D	95+
1999	Pinot Noir	Carneros	D	90
1998	Pinot Noir	Carneros	D	88
1996	Pinot Noir	Carneros	D	88
1998	Pinot Noir Heirloom	Carneros	D	90
1996	Pinot Noir Heirloom	Carneros	D	91

Wine-maker Tony Soter seems to go from strength to strength, with his 1999s perhaps the most superlative group of wines I have yet tasted from him. There is a bevy of 1999 Pinot Noirs, all of them interesting. Soter's goal is to produce between 6,000–7,000 cases of Pinot Noir under the Etude label, with about 4,000 cases of the core wine from the Carneros blend of Pinot Noir, and the other 2,000–3,000 cases the Heirloom.

The 1998 Pinot Noir (3,400 cases) is an attractive, medium ruby-colored offering with a spicy, cinnamon, root beer, and plum/raspberry-scented nose. This lush, elegant, tasty Pinot offers savory, fleshy flavors exhibiting a judicious touch of oak, and well-integrated soft tannin and acidity. Drink it over the next 3–4 years. The top California *cuvée*, the 1998 Pinot Noir Heirloom Vineyard (380 cases) boasts a dark ruby color as well as a gorgeous bouquet of plums, black cherries, and cola (or is it root beer?), medium to full body, outstanding stuffing and purity, sweet tannin, and integrated acidity. It is a well-delineated, concentrated Pinot for consuming over the next 5–7 years.

Aged in 60% new French oak and bottled without filtration, the deep ruby-colored 1996 Pinot Noir Carneros exhibits a smoky, spicy, intense nose. The wine possesses fine ripeness, plenty of cherry/berry fruit with vague underbrush notes, and silky, round flavors. While this is not a huge Pinot Noir, it is both silky-smooth and complex. The finest Pinot Noir I have yet tasted from Etude is the 1996 Heirloom, a 275-case lot of the best barrels (in this vintage, a selection of 12 separate barrels). Bottled with no fining or filtration, this dark, saturated ruby-colored offering reveals knockout aromatics of smoke, toast, and black fruits. The wine's texture is rich, multilayered, and plush. There is real depth in the mid-palate, and the finish is long, round, and generous. I should note that Tony Soter has a vineyard in Oregon's Willamette Valley, so readers can look forward to what should be some superlative Pinot Noirs starting with the 1998 vintage.

The 1998 Cabernet Sauvignon Napa is one of the most impressive efforts of the vintage. An opaque ruby/purple color is followed by a soft, precocious, evolved, up-front style with gorgeous black fruits, medium to full body, soft tannin, and good fatness allied to elegance and suppleness. While it does not possess the volume or density of the spectacular 1997, or the potential of the 1999, it is a delicious wine to drink over the next decade.

Etude's 1997 Cabernet Sauvignon (1,800 cases) ranks alongside the finest Tony Soter has produced. Don't miss it! Opaque purple-colored, with a gorgeously seamless personality, this unfined/unfiltered wine exhibits classic aromas of cassis, licorice, chocolate, and toast. Rich and full-bodied, with sweet tannin, a multilayered mid-palate, and a terrific finish, it possesses the accessibility and opulence of the finest 1997s, but its balance and overall concentration suggest it will age for two decades or more. Etude's 1996 Cabernet Sauvignon displays an impressively saturated ruby/purple color, and a tight but promising bouquet of licorice, black currants, and toasty oak. There is more tannin than in the 1995 or 1997, but it is not intrusive. Fleshy, with fine purity, medium to full body, and a sweet mid-palate and finish, this wine should be cellared for 3–4 years and consumed over the following 15–20 years. The 1995 Cabernet Sauvignon boasts a saturated black/purple color, as well as a terrific nose of licorice, cassis, and subtle toasty oak. Full-bodied and crammed with extract and rich, ripe black fruits, this dense, symmetrical Cabernet will require several years of cellaring, but it should age effortlessly for 15–20 years. It is every bit as good as the terrific 1994, and may ultimately prove to be better, as well as longer-lived.

The awesomely rich 1994 Cabernet Sauvignon is another spectacular example of this splendid vintage. It possesses an opaque purple color, a wonderful sweetness, full body, and layers of cedary, mineral, and spice-tinged black berry and cassis fruit. Although there is a boatload of tannin, it is sweet and well integrated. The finish lasts for nearly 30 seconds. This dazzling Cabernet Sauvignon is one of the finest Soter has made at Etude.

By the way, I had a chance to do a mini-vertical of the Etude Cabernet Sauvignons, and all of them performed extremely well. Most of them appeared to need additional cellaring, and each of them suggested to me that they have another two decades of life. I rated the 1993, 92+ (needs 2–4 years of cellaring); 1992, 91 (substantial effort, should drink well for 5–7 years), 1991, 95 (an awesome wine); and the 1990, 90 (outstanding, but dwarfed by more recent efforts).

FIFE (NAPA)

1997 Max Cuvée Proprietary Red Wine	Napa	D	88
1995 Max Cuvée Proprietary Red Wine	Napa	C	90
1994 Max Cuvée Proprietary Red Wine	Napa	C	91+
1995 Petite Syrah Redhead Vineyard	Mendocino	C	89
1999 Zinfandel Dalraddy Chiles Valley	Napa	D	90
1997 Zinfandel Redhead Vineyard	Mendocino	C	88
1994 Zinfandel Redhead Vineyard	Mendocino	C	90
1994 Zinfandel Spring Mountain District	Napa	C	90
1998 Zinfandel Uplands	Mendocino	C	88
1994 Zinfandel Les Vieilles Vignes	Napa	C	90
1998 Zinfandel Whaler Vineyard	Mendocino	C	90

A relatively new winery, Fife continues to produce an impressive array of concentrated, well-balanced, ageworthy wines. The 1994 Max Cuvée, a proprietary blend, boasts an inky black/purple color, as well as an exceptionally ripe, pure nose of black fruits, licorice, and spice. Full-bodied, with layers of concentration, a corpulent, thick texture, yet no sense of heaviness, this is an exceptionally rich wine with soft tannin. Although approachable, it will be at its best between now–2015. I am pleased to report that the 1994 Zinfandel Redhead Vineyard (14.6% alcohol) is another textbook Zin from Fife. It offers a dark ruby/purple color, followed by a spicy blast of briery, black raspberry, peppery fruit. This pure, luscious, soft, mouth-filling wine is meant to be drunk over the next 2–3 years. The 1994 Zinfandel Les Vieilles Vignes displays an opulent personality, with a deep ruby/purple color, and a gorgeous display of sweet, toasty, smoky new oak, and jammy, pure, ripe berry fruit. Luscious in the mouth, with low acidity, copious quantities of fruit, chewy glycerin, and heady alcohol, this is a lusty, full-bodied, rich Zin for drinking over the next 5–6 years. The 1994 Spring Mountain District Zinfandel is also a beauty, offering more of a black raspberry–scented nose, exquisite ripeness and purity, and a more elegant, less bulky style than the Vieilles Vignes. The Spring Mountain *cuvée* is all finesse, fruit, and delicacy. These wines are beautifully made Zinfandels.

The 1995 Max Cuvée exhibits an impressively saturated deep purple color and a closed but promising nose of sweet black currant fruit intertwined with high-quality toast and vanilla notes. The wine is dense, closed, tannic, and medium- to full-bodied, as well as impressively pure and rich. Most of the wine's sweetness and intensity are felt at the back of the mouth, indicating this offering needs 4–5 years of cellaring. Anticipated maturity: now–2015. Petite Sirah (at this estate spelled Syrah) lovers will enjoy Fife's 1995 Petite Syrah Redhead Vineyard. The color is a dense ruby/plum. This wine is as ferociously tannic as the Cabernet Sauvignon Reserve, but it manages to integrate the tannin better because of its high extraction of fruit. There is plenty of blackberry, earthy, peppery, sweet fruit in this dense, full-bodied wine. Only masochists will enjoy it at present, but my instincts suggest this wine will be excellent with another 2–5 years of bottle age.

The 1997 Zinfandel Redhead Vineyard possesses the highest alcohol (14.6%) of Fife's 1997 Zinfandels as well as the most saturated dark ruby/purple color. Although less evolved aromatically, it offers aromas of damp forests intermixed with plums and blackberries. Round and rich, with multiple layers in addition to Zinfandel's telltale peppery spice, it should drink well for 4–5 years. The 1997 Max Cuvée exhibits pepper, blackberry, and cassis fruit, along with medium to full body, more structure, and less charm. A denser, ageworthy wine, it will be even better with 1–2 years of cellaring, and should last for a decade.

The 1998 Mendocino offerings from Fife include the 1998 Zinfandel Uplands. The alcohol for these wines ranges between 14.3–14.5%, hardly excessive by Zinfandel standards. This low-acid, plump, opulently textured effort possesses medium body, a sexy, smoky, spicy, blackberry and cherry-scented nose, loads of fruit, good glycerin, and purity, and nicely integrated wood. It is a sexy, up-front style of Zinfandel to enjoy over the next 3–4 years. The gorgeous 1998 Zinfandel Whaler Vineyard (14.5% alcohol) offers classic briery, mineral, spicy Zinfandel aromas. On the palate, the wine is dense, rich, and full-bodied, with copious quantities of glycerin, abundant black cherry/raspberry fruit, low acidity, and a fleshy, succulent finish. It is a gorgeous Zinfandel to drink during its first 5–6 years of life.

Fife's exceptional 1999 Zinfandel Dalraddy Chiles Valley boasts an opaque ruby/purple color as well as powerful, sweet aromas of ripe black cherries, raspberries, and currants, with subtle wood and spice in the background. Layered, full-bodied, dense, and opulent, it is the most concentrated and best balanced of the 1999 Zinfandels released by Fife. Enjoy it over the next 6–7 years.

FISHER VINEYARDS (SONOMA)

1999	Cabernet Sauvignon Coach Insignia	Napa	E	90
1998	Cabernet Sauvignon Coach Insignia	Napa	E	88
1995	Cabernet Sauvignon Coach Insignia	Napa	D	88
1994	Cabernet Sauvignon Coach Insignia	Napa	C	89
1999	Cabernet Sauvignon Lamb Vineyard	Napa	EE	90+

1997 Cabernet Sauvignon Lamb Vineyard	Napa	EE	95
1996 Cabernet Sauvignon Lamb Vineyard	Napa	E	91
1995 Cabernet Sauvignon Lamb Vineyard	Napa	E	88
1994 Cabernet Sauvignon Lamb Vineyard	Napa	D	90
1999 Cabernet Sauvignon Wedding Vineyard	Sonoma	EE	91
1997 Cabernet Sauvignon Wedding Vineyard	Sonoma	EE	99
1996 Cabernet Sauvignon Wedding Vineyard	Sonoma	EE	95
1995 Cabernet Sauvignon Wedding Vineyard	Sonoma	E	92
1994 Cabernet Sauvignon Wedding Vineyard	Sonoma	E	92
1999 Chardonnay Coach Insignia	Sonoma	D	89
1999 Chardonnay Paladini	Carneros/Napa	D	91
1999 Chardonnay Whitney's Vineyard Estate	Sonoma	D	90
1997 Coach Insignia Proprietary Red Wine	Napa	D	90
1996 Coach Insignia Proprietary Red Wine	Napa	D	90
1999 Merlot RCF Vineyard	Napa	D	(88–89)
1998 Merlot RCF Vineyard	Napa	D	88
1997 Merlot RCF Vineyard	Napa	D	89
1996 Merlot RCF Vineyard	Napa	D	88
1994 Merlot RCF Vineyard	Napa	D	89
1997 Unity Proprietary Red Wine	California	EEE (1.5 liter only)	90

Does this winery receive as much praise as it deserves? It is certainly in an obscure location, tucked in the mountains between Santa Rosa on the Sonoma side and Calistoga on the Napa side. Fred Fisher and his wife, Juelle, have added a new Chardonnay to their portfolio of already impressive whites. The 1999 Chardonnay Paladini Vineyard (240 cases) is a fragrant Chardonnay made primarily from one of the old Wente clones of Chardonnay. It sees about 78% new French oak. The wine shows beautiful passion fruit as well as pineapple intermixed with subtle smoke and toast. Full-bodied and rich, it may be Fisher's most impressive 1999 Chardonnay. The 1999 Coach Insignia Chardonnay has more apricot, peach, and tropical fruit notes, full body, excellent purity, and plenty of lively fruit. Lastly, the estate's 1999 Chardonnay Whitney's Vineyard, which is named after the proprietor's daughter, is another full-bodied Chardonnay that has seen full malolactic fermentation, but is different from the others in that it tends to offer more orange/tangerine, citrus oils, and honeysuckle in a full-bodied, concentrated, very graceful style, with good underlying acidity. The 1999 Chardonnays all show beautiful balance and the potential to last for 2–4 years.

Slightly better than I originally thought, the 1998 Merlot RCF Vineyard (a Napa vineyard not far from the famed Araujo Eisele Vineyard) is showing a dark ruby color, plenty of melted fudge, coffee, and berry fruit. The wine is not weighty (very few 1998s are) but shows good harmony and sweet fruit, and is best drunk over the next 5–6 years. The 1999 Merlot RCF

Vineyard is similar to the 1998 (80% Merlot and 20% Cabernet Franc) and has much the same character, but the color seems a bit more saturated purple. There is a bit more depth and fat to the wine, and slightly more weight. It should drink well for at least a decade.

1996 and 1997 were both strong vintages for Fisher Vineyards. The 1997 reds are high in alcohol (most of the wines came in around 14.5%), which is well hidden by the rich fruit and extract. The 1996s are undoubtedly lower in alcoholic power. The Merlot from Fisher's RCF Vineyard in northern Napa Valley is one of California's high-quality Merlots. The 1996 Merlot RCF Vineyard's dark ruby color is followed by a sweet nose of black cherries, cranberries, and a touch of cherry liqueur. There is excellent richness, medium body, tangy acidity, and an elegant, overall impression. This is a flavorful, moderately weighted Merlot to enjoy over the next 10–12 years. The 1997 Merlot RCF Vineyard exhibits abundant black cherry fruit intertwined with minerals, dried herbs, and melted white chocolate. It is a rich, flavorful, fleshy, dense Merlot to consume over the next 10–12 years.

The dark ruby-colored 1994 Merlot RCF offers medium-bodied, elegant, vanilla-tinged, black cherry aromas and flavors. Still tightly knit, this wine will benefit from another year of cellaring; it will drink well for a decade. I initially thought it had the potential to be outstanding, but at present it appears it will fall a point or two short.

The Fishers have gone back to a Cabernet Sauvignon designation for their Coach Insignia. The 1998 Cabernet Sauvignon Coach Insignia benefitted from the fact that both the Lamb and Wedding Vineyard Cabernet Sauvignons were declassified in 1998, and the wine was blended into the Coach Insignia. A blend of 78% Cabernet Sauvignon, 11% Cabernet Franc, and 11% Merlot, aged in 50% new French oak, it possesses a dark ruby color, a big, chocolaty, licorice, and black currant–scented nose, and tannin in the finish. It has certainly sweetened up considerably and is showing better out of bottle than it did from barrel. Look for it to drink well for 10–12 years. The 1999 Cabernet Sauvignon Coach Insignia looks terrific. Thankfully, there are 2,200 cases of this blend of 76% Cabernet Sauvignon, 18% Merlot, and 6% Malbec. It displays impressive extract as well as beautifully pure black currant, mineral, and blackberry flavors nicely dosed with toasty oak. Full-bodied, powerful, rich, and in need of 3–4 years of cellaring, it is a significantly bigger, denser wine than the 1998. Anticipated maturity: 2003–2018. To reiterate, there is no 1998 Lamb Vineyard Cabernet Sauvignon, but the 1999 Cabernet Sauvignon Lamb Vineyard is 100% Cabernet Sauvignon. From a vineyard in the northern part of Napa Valley, it has been aged in 80–90% new Taransaud French oak barrels. Full-bodied, with good underlying acidity, plenty of depth as well as earthy black fruits intermixed with spice box, cedar, and licorice, this impressive effort will be at its best between 2004–2025. From the estate vineyard in the Sonoma hillsides, the 1999 Wedding Vineyard (100% Cabernet Sauvignon) is a wine of great intensity. It has the telltale scorched earth notes, intermixed with blueberry, blackberry, and mineral. The wine is very full-bodied, powerful, dense, and will need a good 4–5 years of cellaring. It should keep for at least two decades or more. The potentially perfect, opaque purple-colored 1997 Cabernet Sauvignon Wedding Vineyard (400 cases of 100% Cabernet Sauvignon) is made from 27-year-old vines and is aged in 100% new French Taransaud barrels. This prodigious Cabernet Sauvignon has only gotten better since my tasting last year. The finest Cabernet I have tasted from Fisher, it represents a California interpretation of La Mission Haut-Brion. The wine offers sweet, tobacco-infused, scorched earth, blackberry, and blueberry notes, with a liquid minerality. The aromatics are matched by the immense, concentrated, seamless, staggeringly rich, powerful palate. This wine will benefit from 4–5 years of cellaring, and keep for 35–40 years. A modern-day California legend, it is one of the most profound California Cabernet Sauvignons ever made on the Sonoma side of California's North Coast viticultural region. Anticipated maturity: 2005–2040.

The 1996 Coach Insignia (1,380 cases) offers classic cassis, coffee, chocolate, and oaky aromas that are followed by deep, concentrated, spicy, rich, berry fruit flavors. A blend of

69% Cabernet Sauvignon, 20% Merlot, and 11% Cabernet Franc, it offers abundant power, purity, and richness. It should drink well for 10–15+ years. The 1997 Coach Insignia (77% Cabernet Sauvignon, with the rest Merlot and Cabernet Franc) is also powerful, with a more seamless personality than the 1996. The wine is moderately tannic and full-bodied, with loads of chocolaty, black cherry, and cassis fruit. Anticipated maturity: now–2014.

The 1994 Cabernet Sauvignon Coach Insignia reveals a medium dark color, a Bordeaux-like, austere, spicy, oaky, earthy, cassis-scented nose, plenty of tannin, medium body, and a firm, closed personality. This wine needs another 1–3 years of cellaring; it will keep for 12–15 years. The 1995 Cabernet Sauvignon Coach Insignia exhibits a deep, rich ruby/purple color, a loamy, red currant–scented, elegant bouquet, medium-bodied, structured, restrained flavors, high acidity, and a grapy, rich finish. This wine continues to close down, and should be cellared for 3–4 years upon its release. It should keep for two decades, but I suspect it will be a more angular, structured, tannic Coach Insignia than other vintages.

The awesome opaque purple-colored 1997 Cabernet Sauvignon Lamb Vineyard exhibits a fabulous nose of lead pencil, coffee, minerals, black currants, and licorice. The wine's massive richness, full body, and super-intense, concentrated fruit make for a spectacular, unctuously textured, backward wine. As it sat in the glass, some of the mountain blueberry notes came forward. This Cabernet requires 4–5 years of cellaring, and should keep for 25–30 years . . . at the minimum. The powerful (14.1% alcohol) 1996 Cabernet Sauvignon Lamb Vineyard has been aged in barrel, of which 50% are new. Like all of Fisher's reds, it is bottled without filtration. The color is an opaque purple, and the wine is closed, offering hints of licorice, blueberries, black currants, and spicy oak. In the mouth, it is long, rich, restrained, with the tannin still making a noticeable impression, with outstanding purity, a full-bodied mouth-feel, and superb potential. This wine requires another 4–5 years of cellaring. Anticipated maturity: 2003–2020.

The 1994 Cabernet Sauvignon Lamb Vineyard exhibits a dark ruby/purple color, and a sweet nose of cassis fruit, lead pencil, and spice. While the wine may have been slightly tired when I saw it a few months after bottling, it still revealed plenty of intensity, sweet berry fruit nicely wrapped in oak, medium to full body, and moderate tannin in the long finish. Sadly, there are only 595 cases of this 100% Cabernet Sauvignon. The 1995 Cabernet Sauvignon Lamb Vineyard is a leaner, tighter, more angular and astringent wine, with a dark purple color, leafy, tobacco, smoky flavors, a backward, unformed personality, and plenty of tannin in the finish. It is certainly excellent, and probably will unfold over the next decade, but the wine still plays it tight to the vest. Anticipated maturity: 2003–2012.

One of California's statuesque Cabernet Sauvignons is from the Wedding Vineyard. The 1995 Cabernet Sauvignon Wedding Vineyard is a massive, full-bodied, black/purple-colored wine with gobs of fruit, as well as high tannin. It offers up mineral, black cherry, spicy, and charcoal-like notes in the nose and flavors. Extremely dense and powerful, yet needing 4–5 years of cellaring, this wine may evolve for two decades or more. Anticipated maturity: 2003–2025. The 1996 Cabernet Sauvignon Wedding Vineyard (produced from one-fourth ton of fruit per acre) continues to remind me of a hypothetical La Mission Haut-Brion made from California's ripe fruit. The roasted tobacco, cedar, scorched earth, and creosote nuances are present, in addition to copious blackberry, blueberry, and cassis flavors. This is a terrific, full-flavored, highly extracted wine with plenty of tannin. However, the tannin is sweet and well integrated, as is the wine's lusty alcohol (14.1%). This is a profound example of Cabernet Sauvignon that should be accessible in 4–5 years and last for 25–30. The 1994 Cabernet Sauvignon Wedding Vineyard (500 cases) displays a knockout Graves-like nose of sweet, medium- to full-bodied, rich, concentrated flavors, good acidity, high tannin, and profound concentration and length. It comes across like a racehorse ready to burst from the starting gate. This wine needs 4–5 years of cellaring and should keep for two or more decades.

The only other wine to note is the 1997 Unity, a proprietary red that is essentially Cabernet Sauvignon (with a tiny bit of Cabernet Franc) made in limited quantities of 250 1.5-liter bottles. It is a dense, classy blend revealing considerable style, as well as intriguing lead pencil, cedary notes, copious black fruits, medium body, and admirable elegance and grace. It should drink well for 15+ years.

Past Glories: 1993 Cabernet Sauvignon Coach Insignia (90+), 1993 Cabernet Sauvignon Lamb Vineyard (95), Cabernet Sauvignon Wedding Vineyard—1993 (93), 1992 (92), 1991 (93+)

FLORA SPRINGS WINE CO. (NAPA)

1995	Cabernet Sauvignon Cypress Ranch	Pope Valley	D	88
1998	Cabernet Sauvignon Eagle Mountain	Pope Valley	D	87
1997	Cabernet Sauvignon Eagle Mountain	Pope Valley	D	90
1994	Cabernet Sauvignon Estate	Napa	C	90
1999	Cabernet Sauvignon Hillside Reserve	Rutherford	EE	91
1997	Cabernet Sauvignon Hillside Reserve	Rutherford	EE	93
1996	Cabernet Sauvignon Hillside Reserve	Rutherford	E	92+
1995	Cabernet Sauvignon Hillside Reserve	Rutherford	E	92
1994	Cabernet Sauvignon Hillside Reserve	Rutherford	E	94+
1996	Cabernet Sauvignon Rutherford Vineyard	Rutherford	D	88
1997	Cabernet Sauvignon 20th Anniversary Reserve	Napa	EEE (magnums only)	96
1999	Cabernet Sauvignon Wild Boar Vineyard	Pope Valley	D	(90–92)
1998	Cabernet Sauvignon Wild Boar Vineyard	Pope Valley	D	(89–91)
1999	Chardonnay Barrel Fermented Reserve	Napa	D	88
1999	Merlot Windfall Vineyard	Napa	E	(90–92)
1998	Merlot Windfall Vineyard	Napa	D	89
1997	Merlot Windfall Vineyard	Napa	D	90
1996	Merlot Windfall Vineyard	Napa	D	91
1995	Merlot Windfall Vineyard	Napa	D	90
1999	Trilogy Proprietary Red	Napa	E	90
1998	Trilogy Proprietary Red	Napa	E	88
1997	Trilogy Proprietary Red	Napa	D	92
1996	Trilogy Proprietary Red	Napa	D	91
1995	Trilogy Proprietary Red	Napa	D	90
1994	Trilogy Proprietary Red	Napa	D	93+

Quietly, confidently, and without a great deal of fanfare or publicity, Flora Springs continues to turn out some of Napa Valley's finest wines that are, for the most part, reasonably priced. Translation: Flora Spring's wines are not priced according to the owner's egos, as so many Napa wines seem to be these days. The 1999 Chardonnay Barrel Fermented Reserve sees some malolactic, but is harvested very late to obtain maximum ripeness. It is a smoky, roasted hazelnut, tropical fruit–scented and –flavored Chardonnay, with medium to full body, and a style not unlike a good premier cru from Chassagne-Montrachet. Fleshy, with good underlying acidity, it should drink well for 2–3 years, if not longer.

The 1998 Trilogy Proprietary Red reveals the vintage's shortcomings. It is a very good, even excellent wine, but the vintage's short, cool growing season has given the wine more austerity than normal. A blend of 45% Cabernet Sauvignon, 43% Merlot, 6% Cabernet Franc, and 6% Malbec, it offers plenty of spicy new oak, mineral, licorice, and damp, foresty aromas and flavors. Elegant and medium-bodied, it is best drunk over the next 10–12 years. The 1999 Trilogy is significantly richer, more textured, and obviously made from riper, more concentrated fruit. A blend of 42% Cabernet Sauvignon, 39% Merlot, and 19% Cabernet Franc that sees about 50% new French oak, it exhibits a dark plum/purple color as well as a sweet nose of minerals, cassis, and smoke. Medium- to full-bodied, moderately tannic, elegant, pure, and well balanced, it should drink well for 15–16 years.

Two impeccably made 100% Merlots emerge from the Windfall Vineyard at the corner of Route 29 and Bella Oaks Lane. Sexy, plump, and fat, they are among the better Merlots being made in Napa. There are about 1,000–1,200 cases produced in each vintage. A success for the vintage, the 1998 Merlot Windfall Vineyard is a seductive red offering aromas of cocoa, melted fudge, and black cherry fruit. This ripe, very silky-textured, plump wine has added weight since I tasted it last year. Anticipated maturity: now–2010. Even better is the dense ruby/purple-colored 1999 Merlot Windfall Vineyard. It displays a big nose of roasted espresso, chocolate, and black cherry scents, low acidity, dense, sexy, opulently textured flavors, and a full-bodied, glycerin-imbued, enticing finish. Drink it over the next 10–12 years.

There was no 1998 Cabernet Sauvignon Hillside Reserve, as the wine was declassified into Trilogy in order to bulk it up. However, the 1999 Cabernet Sauvignon Hillside Reserve offers a dense, opaque purple color, as well as a gorgeous nose of sweet cassis, mixed with leather, vanilla, and spice box. The wine is full-bodied, with moderate tannin, exceptional purity and symmetry, and a layered mid-palate and finish. It should drink well for at least 15 or more years. The sensational 1997 Cabernet Sauvignon Hillside Reserve boasts an opaque ruby/ purple color and a jammy black cherry and cassis nose, intermixed with smoke, toast, cedar, and spice box. Voluptuously textured, concentrated, with hints of smoke, coffee, and toast in its powerful, super-extracted, multilayered flavors, this terrific 1997 should be at its best in 2–3 years and keep for at least 20–25 years. Perhaps the finest Cabernet Sauvignon I have tasted from Flora Springs is their 1997 Cabernet Sauvignon 20th Anniversary Reserve. Bottled only in magnums (250 cases), it is a prodigious Napa Cabernet. Aged in 60% new French oak for 24 months before being bottled without filtration, it reveals an opaque plum/purple color plus an explosive, multidimensional nose of coffee, kirsch, crème de cassis, dried herbs, tobacco, and spice. Full-bodied, with fabulous purity, a seamless texture, and a 40-second finish, it represents Cabernet Sauvignon at its most profound. Remarkably, it is soft enough to be drunk now, but promises to age well for 25 or more years.

More than any other winery, Flora Springs is demonstrating the potential for Cabernet Sauvignon in Napa's Pope Valley. Their only problem is deciding what to name the wine. Formerly called Cypress Vineyard, then Eagle Mountain, they seem to have settled on the name Wild Boar Vineyard. The 1998 Cabernet Sauvignon Wild Boar Vineyard is a big, muscular, back-strapping effort with huge blackberry fruit infused with melted asphalt and earth. Aged in 50% new oak, one-half of which is American wood and the rest French, it is powerful, concentrated, and all-American in its blatant oak and lavish fruit, glycerin, and power. A success for the vintage, it should drink well for another 12–15 years. Even better, the 1999 Cabernet Sauvignon Wild Boar displays more concentrated richness on the palate along with an exuberant, flamboyant nose of black fruits, herbs, leather, tobacco, and licorice. Powerful, gutsy, and chewy, this oversized Cabernet Sauvignon may fall short in terms of elegance and finesse, but it more than compensates for that in its blockbuster display of fruit, glycerin, power, and tannin. It should drink well for 15 or more years.

The 1996 Cabernet Sauvignon Rutherford Vineyard is 100% Cabernet Sauvignon, aged in *barrique*, of which 15% was American. The wine reveals gobs of spicy new oak and tobacco-tinged, weedy, black currant fruit intermixed with cedar, dried herbs, and licorice, high tannin, and medium to full body. This chunky, fleshy, robust Cabernet Sauvignon should be at its best with another 2–3 years of bottle age and keep for 14–15 years.

Flora Springs is making a serious jump into the Merlot sweepstakes, and their effort deserves accolades. The 1995 Merlot Windfall Vineyard (300 cases) possesses a dense ruby/purple color, as well as a gaudy nose of toast, melted chocolate, and jammy cherry flavors. Soft, ripe, medium- to full-bodied, chewy, and fat, this is a delicious, decadent style of Merlot that will drink well for a decade. The outstanding 1996 Merlot Windfall Vineyard possesses a dark purple color, as well as a sweet, expressive, smoky, chocolaty nose with coffee and berry fruit in the background. The wine is succulent, fleshy, full-bodied, and hedonistic. This superb, ripe, mouth-filling Merlot can be drunk over the next 10–12+ years. Bravo! While it is cut from the same mold, the 1997 Merlot Windfall Vineyard displays more tangy acidity, but it shares its predecessor's smoky, roasted coffee, chocolaty, black cherry scents and flavors. There is sweet richness in the mouth, soft tannin, plenty of glycerin, and an evolved style. Once again, the 1997 appears to be on a slightly faster evolutionary track than its older sibling and should drink well during its first decade of life.

The outstanding 1997 Trilogy Proprietary Red Wine offers a dark ruby/purple color and super-expressive aromatics consisting of black fruits, licorice, blueberries, and floral scents. With a fine tannic underpinning, this elegant yet impressively rich, well-endowed, balanced effort is already approachable, and promises to evolve effortlessly for 15–18 years. The 1996 Trilogy, a blend of 44% Cabernet Sauvignon, 40% Merlot, and 16% Cabernet Franc, reveals a saturated dark ruby/purple color and a gorgeous nose of violets, black currants, toast, and minerals. Deep and rich, yet remarkably polished, this medium- to full-bodied, beautifully symmetrical wine has everything in the proper place. Although accessible enough to be drunk early in life, its balance suggests a graceful evolution for 15–20 years. It is a distinctive, beautiful wine! With its curranty, cedary, tobacco-like sweetness and ripeness, Trilogy may be the Napa Valley wine that most recalls certain St.-Emilions. Approximately 3,500–4,000 cases of this wine are made in a top vintage. The 1995 Trilogy (44% Merlot, 39% Cabernet Sauvignon, and 17% Cabernet Franc) is a spicy, Médoc-styled wine with medium to full body, excellent spice and richness, as well as an overall sense of elegance and equilibrium. It is a delicious wine to drink now and over the next 15+ years. The 1994 Trilogy (2,000 cases) exhibits rich, ripe fruit, along with some toasty vanilla and sweet, jammy black fruit scents. Fleshy, harmonious, full-bodied flavors reveal admirable extract and cleanliness. Despite its softness, this impressive wine is unformed, so give it 2–3 years of cellaring; it will age for two decades or more.

The dark ruby/purple-colored, stunningly rich 1996 Cabernet Sauvignon Hillside Reserve is still in need of bottle age. The wine reveals a saturated color, as well as a promising but restrained nose of toasty new oak, jammy blackberries, cassis, licorice, and spice. It is extremely rich and spicy in the mouth, with moderate tannin, full body, superb purity of flavor, and outstanding potential. Anticipated maturity: 2003–2022. The 1995 Cabernet Sauvignon Hillside Reserve is a backward, tannic wine with an opaque purple color and copious quantities of sweet black currant fruit, cedar, and spice. Muscular, rich, and full-bodied, with sweet tannin, this is a layered, concentrated, unevolved, and youthful Cabernet that requires 4–5 years of cellaring. All the necessary "goodies" are present in this formidably endowed wine. While it will not provide seductive drinking at an early age, it will last 20 years. Ken

Deiss thinks that the 1994 and 1995 Cabernet Sauvignon vintages have more similarities than differences. This was borne out in my tastings, as both vintages possess that rare quality of producing very concentrated, ripe Cabernets with sweet, well-integrated tannin. Flora Springs' Hillside Reserve Cabernet Sauvignons have soared in quality in the nineties. This 100% Cabernet Sauvignon is aged in 2–3-year-old barrels, then moved to 1-year-old barrels, and then into 60% new-oak casks for no longer than 8–10 months. The 1994 Cabernet Sauvignon Hillside Reserve exhibits an opaque purple color, a classic, cedar, black currant, and earthy-scented nose, and rich, full-bodied flavors that ooze jammy black currants. The wood influence is subtle, although some spicy vanilla can be detected. This wine possesses terrific fruit purity, an opulent texture, and an impressively long, harmonious finish. The 1994 Reserve should be accessible young, yet long lived (20–30 years).

One of the best bargains in the Flora Springs portfolio is the 1994 Cabernet Sauvignon Estate (unfortunately, only 1,600 cases are available). It is bursting with ripe, jammy black fruits. This full-bodied, fleshy, fat, in your face, 100% Cabernet Sauvignon was bottled unfiltered, revealing a chewy, open-knit texture. It exhibits excellent purity, as well as spicy oak. Drink it over the next 7–10 years.

The 1998 Cabernet Sauvignon Eagle Mountain (harvested during the last week of October) exhibits a jammy cassis-scented nose, full-bodied, pure flavors, and more glycerin, richness, and intensity than many 1998s. It should turn out to be a muscular, surprisingly concentrated 1998 that will drink well for 10–12 years. The outstanding 1997 Cabernet Sauvignon Eagle Mountain is a full-throttle, all-American-styled Cabernet Sauvignon. Aged both in French and American oak, this gutsy, macho, powerful effort is short on finesse, but offers mouth-filling levels of sweet, succulent, jammy black currant fruit combined with toasty oak, cedar, dried herbs, and loamy soil scents. Layered, thick, and juicy, it is fun to drink. Moreover, it will improve over the next 7–8 years, and last for 12–15.

Flora Springs produced a 1995 Cabernet Sauvignon Cypress Ranch. There are only 375 cases of this wine, which is aged in 25% new oak. Like Flora Springs' other wines, with the exception of the barrel-fermented Chardonnay, it was bottled without fining or filtration. A textbook, unformed Cabernet Sauvignon, the Cypress Ranch's pronounced spiciness and weedy, tobacco-tinged black currant fruitiness make for a solid first impression. This lusty, muscular Cabernet possesses aggressive tannin, which should melt away after some time in the bottle. It should age well for 12–15 years.

Past Glories: 1993 Cabernet Sauvignon Hillside Reserve (91+), 1993 Trilogy Proprietary Red Wine (91)

FLOWERS (SONOMA COAST)

1997 Pinot Noir Camp Meeting Ridge	Sonoma Coast	D	90+
1997 Pinot Noir Camp Meeting Ridge Moon Select	Sonoma Coast	E	90+
1997 Pinot Noir Hirsch Vineyard	Sonoma Coast	D	92

This enterprise with well-placed Sonoma Coast vineyards (next to the Marcassin Vineyard and Martinelli's Blue Slide Vineyard) displays considerable promise. The three Pinot Noirs are topflight. The medium ruby-colored 1997 Pinot Noir Hirsch offers a terrific nose of sweet black cherries, cinnamon, earth, and spice, sweet fruit, full body, admirable power and glycerin, and sweet, moderate tannin in the finish. It should drink well for 5–7 years. Equally impressive, the dark ruby-colored 1997 Pinot Noir Camp Meeting Ridge displays a floral and black fruit–scented nose with sweet vanilla in the background. More structured than the Hirsch, with outstanding purity and concentration, this tight but full-bodied Pinot Noir will be even better with another 6–12 months of bottle age. It will last for 7–8 years. The 1997 Pinot Noir Camp Meeting Ridge Moon Select is the most ambitious and concentrated of this Pinot Noir trio. Along with the additional level of extract comes elevated tannin and copious toasty new oak. The wine should settle down, but it does not appear to be the same sure bet as the other two Pinots. Although forceful, rich, and concentrated, it is lavishly wooded and extremely tannic. After 1–2 years of bottle age, it can be drunk over the following decade. Look for a higher score if the tannin and wood become better integrated.

FORMAN VINEYARDS (NAPA)

1999	Cabernet Sauvignon	Napa	E	(90–93)
1998	Cabernet Sauvignon	Napa	E	88
1997	Cabernet Sauvignon	Napa	D	90
1996	Cabernet Sauvignon	Napa	D	92
1995	Cabernet Sauvignon	Napa	D	88+
1994	Cabernet Sauvignon	Napa	D	91
1999	Chardonnay	Napa	D	89
1999	Merlot	Napa	D	(90–92)
1998	Merlot	Napa	D	87
1997	Merlot	Napa	D	88+
1996	Merlot	Napa	D	89
1995	Merlot	Napa	D	88
1994	Merlot	Napa	D	89

Ric Forman, who does not like thick, ripe, or super-concentrated wines, seems to be attempting to build more texture into his wines. His Chardonnays, Merlots, and Cabernet Sauvignons are distinctively elegant, Bordeaux-styled wines, unlike those favored by other cutting-edge California producers. There are 2,000 cases of 1999 Chardonnay, which is to be applauded for its crisp pear, citrus oil, steely style. Medium-bodied, with exceptional purity, it is made in a Chablis-like style and is best drunk during its first 2–3 years of life.

Both 1999 reds have more texture and ripeness, as if Forman is picking at slightly higher Brix than he personally prefers. The 1999 Merlot looks to be terrific. There are 500 cases of this ruby/purple-colored wine that has an opulent texture and plenty of pure, sweet, black cherry and berry fruit. The wine is full-bodied, low in acidity, and intense. The flamboyant 1999 Cabernet Sauvignon reveals a cassis jelly character, medium to full body, excellent mineral-infused, black currant fruit, and superb purity. There are 2,000 cases of this Cabernet, which could turn out to be one of the most hedonistic Forman has made in the nineties.

The 1998s are more austere, without the volume, texture, and overall richness offered by the 1999s. The 1998 Cabernet Sauvignon displays complex, Bordeaux-like aromas that recall a top-notch Médoc. In the mouth, the tannin is dry and angular, but the wine shows plenty of attractive black currant fruit presented in a restrained, understated style. It is medium-bodied, elegant, and best consumed during its first 10–12 years of life. Forman's 1998 Merlot should be appealing upon release. Despite its 14.5% alcohol, it displays good accessibility given its coffee bean, blackberry, and cherry characteristics. Seductive and lush, with low acidity, it should drink well for 7–8 years. It may merit an even higher rating.

The dark ruby/purple-colored 1997 Merlot has closed down since bottling. With coaxing, berry fruit notes intermixed with spice and vanilla emerge. This medium-bodied Merlot possesses a ripe attack, good balance, and moderate tannin. Anticipated maturity: now–2012. The 1997 Cabernet Sauvignon is a beauty. One of Ric Forman's classics, it boasts a dark ruby/purple color as well as a gorgeous bouquet of cassis, dried herbs, cedar, blackberries, and minerals. This medium- to full-bodied Cabernet exhibits firm tannin in the finish, in addition to excellent sweet fruit and a subtle, nuanced personality. Cellar it for 3–4 years and drink it over the following two decades.

The 1996 Merlot (80% Merlot and 20% Cabernet Franc) is made in a Bordeaux-like style. The nose offers up aromas of coffee and berry-tinged fruit intermixed with herbaceous, spicy oak. The wine possesses excellent texture, medium body, and an intriguing black tea flavor in the fruit character. A sexy Merlot made in Ric Forman's telltale polished, refined, and graceful manner, it should drink well for 10–15 years. One of the most impressive recent Cabernet Sauvignons from Forman is their 1996. I was amazed how well it was showing despite having been bottled only a month earlier. The saturated ruby/purple color is followed by gorgeous jammy black currant fruit aromas, along with spicy oak and licorice. There is good acidity, but the wine appears to possess more viscosity than most Forman offerings, as well as a chewy fleshiness, enough acidity for delineation, and moderate tannin in the convincingly long finish. This classic Bordeaux-styled wine should be at its finest between now–2020.

The 1995 red wines were revealing a more closed character than they possessed previously. For example, the 1995 Merlot was softer than the Cabernet Sauvignon, with a deep ruby/purple color, and a cherry and raspberry–scented nose with judicious toasty oak in the background. This is a pretty, elegant, attractive style of Merlot with enough acidity for vibrancy, as well as excellent purity and tasty cherry-like flavors. It should drink well for 10–15 years. The tighter, more tannic 1995 Cabernet Sauvignon exhibits a deep ruby/purple color, followed by an elegant cassis-scented nose with graceful, restrained, and measured fruit flavors. Medium- to full-bodied, with moderate tannin and an overall impression of tightness, this is a harmonious, well-made wine that is not nearly as expressive this year as it was in 1996. Ideally, this Cabernet needs 3–4 years of cellaring and should keep for 20 years.

Forman's 1994 Merlot, the debut vintage for this varietal, is a deep ruby-colored, open, seductive wine with berry/mocha fruit in the nose, medium to full body, and round, generous, nicely oaked flavors. This soft, open-knit, rich, excellent, nearly outstanding Merlot should drink well for 7–8 years. The 1994 Cabernet Sauvignon exhibits a dense, ruby/purple color, an unevolved but promising sweet, cedar, black currant, vanilla-scented nose, medium to full body, fine elegance, underlying acidity, ripe tannin, and a Graves-like tobacco component that provides complexity. This wine should be accessible young, but will not hit its stride for 5–6 years; it will last for two decades.

Past Glories: 1993 Cabernet Sauvignon (92)

FOXEN VINEYARDS (SANTA BARBARA)

1996	Cabernet Sauvignon	Santa Barbara	D	88
1997	Pinot Noir Julia's Vineyard	Santa Maria	D	89
1997	Syrah Morehouse Vineyard	Santa Ynez	D	90
1996	Syrah Morehouse Vineyard	Santa Ynez	D	90

An enviable portfolio of wines has been produced by this high-quality Santa Barbara winery. The red wines are impressive. For example, the 1997 Syrah Morehouse Vineyard offers notes of bacon fat, blackberries, pepper, and vanilla. This large-scaled, full-bodied, dense, powerful Syrah will age well for a decade or more. Another impressive offering is the 1996 Syrah Morehouse Vineyard. This dark ruby/purple-colored wine possesses a textbook bacon fat, fried meat, and smoky-scented nose intermixed with superripe black raspberry and cassis fruit, full body, outstanding concentration and purity, and a luscious, silky finish. Drink this seductive, intensely flavored Syrah now and over the next 7–10 years.

Concentrated, with deep color, the 1997 Pinot Noir Julia's Vineyard's aromas of ripe plums, cherry jam, smoke, and herbs are combined in a medium-bodied, ripe, and dense style of Pinot Noir. It can be drunk now or cellared for 5–7 years. Foxen's dark ruby/purple-colored 1996 Cabernet Sauvignon offers up a dense, black cherry, curranty, weedy, tobacco-tinged nose with plenty of smoke and jammy fruit. This medium- to full-bodied, nicely textured, attractive wine displays better balance between its component parts—alcohol, acidity, tannin, and extract. Although accessible, it promises to age nicely for 10–14 years.

FRANUS (NAPA)

1996 Cabernet Sauvignon	Napa	D	88
1997 Mourvèdre Brandlin Ranch	Mt. Veeder	D	91
1995 Zinfandel	Napa	C	89
1999 Zinfandel Brandlin Ranch	Mt. Veeder	D	90
1998 Zinfandel Brandlin Ranch	Mt. Veeder	D	89
1997 Zinfandel Brandlin Ranch	Mt. Veeder	D	90
1996 Zinfandel Brandlin Ranch	Mt. Veeder	C	90
1995 Zinfandel Brandlin Ranch	Mt. Veeder	C	90
1994 Zinfandel Brandlin Ranch	Mt. Veeder	C	91
1994 Zinfandel Hendry Vineyard	Napa	C	91
1999 Zinfandel Planchon Vineyard	Contra Costa	C	90
1998 Zinfandel Planchon Vineyard	Contra Costa	C	88
1997 Zinfandel Planchon Vineyard	Contra Costa	C	90
1996 Zinfandel Planchon Vineyard	Contra Costa	C	88

For the quality of the wines that consistently emerge from Franus, this winery remains unheralded. The 1999s are typically structured, concentrated, full-bodied Zinfandels with considerable character and aging potential . . . at least for this varietal. The deep ruby/purple-colored, structured, tightly knit 1999 Zinfandel Planchon Vineyard is reminiscent of a Bordeaux in its slightly austere yet deep, dense, intense personality. This full-bodied effort is loaded with dusty, black cherry, currant, and cranberry fruit, but requires another 6–12 months to open. It should age well for 6–8 years. The 1999 Zinfandel Brandlin Vineyard Mt. Veeder boasts a saturated ruby/purple color in addition to a sweet perfume of black fruits, minerals, graphite, and subtle oak. A sweet attack is followed by a closed finish. This big, forceful Zinfandel should be cellared for 1–2 years and enjoyed over the following 7–8. While not the most charming examples, they are loaded with potential.

The 1998 Zinfandel Planchon Vineyard (with vines planted in 1902 in pure sand) exhibits a medium dark ruby color in addition to a spicy, peppery bouquet with scents of resin, balsam wood, and sweet cherry/berry fruit. Medium to full body, low acidity, a ripe, opulent texture, and good fat can be found in this precocious, evolved Zinfandel. It should drink well for 2–3 years. Even more impressive is the dense dark ruby-colored 1998 Zinfandel Brandlin Vineyard. The nose offers up aromas of wild blackberries, minerals, oak, and black currants. Classic, with a nicely structured, medium- to full-bodied, rich entry and mid-palate, this concentrated, pure, well-balanced effort should age nicely for 2–4 years.

Unlike some of his peers, Peter Franus handled the tricky 1997 Zinfandel vintage well. Both are outstanding efforts for this irregular year. The 1997 Zinfandel Planchon Vineyard displays a deep ruby color, and excellent brambleberry, blackberry, and cherry fruit, with none of the earthy, balsam wood notes that often emerge from Contra Costa Zinfandels. Dense and medium- to full-bodied, with lofty alcohol (14.6%), this nicely textured, chewy Zinfandel should drink well for 2–3 years. Also outstanding, the 1997 Zinfandel Brandlin Vineyard is a big, brawny, briery Zin made in a mountain style. Peppery and spicy, with noteworthy licorice, mineral, and blackberry and cherry fruit well displayed in its powerful (14.6% alcohol), full-bodied constitution, it will also drink well for 2–3 years.

With respect to the 1996 Cabernet Sauvignon, this wine reveals a Bordeaux-like, cedary, cigar box, black currant–scented nose. In addition, chocolate notes appear in the mouth. This classic, well-delineated, expansive, medium-bodied wine possesses fine concentration, an attractive perfume, and admirable complexity. Enjoy it over the next 10–15 years. Peter Franus has fashioned a superb 1997 Mourvèdre from the Brandlin Vineyard on Mt. Veeder. It is hard to believe this is a 100% Mourvèdre as this varietal tends to produce frightfully austere, tannic, and backward wines. There is wonderful sweetness to this effort's gorgeous blackberry and black raspberry fruit. Notes of leather, tree bark, and spice are present, but the black fruit characteristics dominate the wine's personality. Even readers who resist Mourvèdre's intensity, ferocity, and tannic clout will find this wine attractive. It should drink well for a decade or longer. The 1996 Zinfandels are all high-quality wines from Peter Franus. Well made with surprising complexity, these Zinfandels will provide lovely drinking for another 1–2 years. The 1996 Zinfandel Planchon Vineyard tips the scales at 14.3% alcohol, yet there is no hint of overripeness or raisiny/pruny notes. The wine offers up a kirsch/plum-scented nose, with pepper and spice. Ripe and medium- to full-bodied, with low acidity, a chewy, fleshy texture, and good glycerin, this plump, hedonistic Zinfandel should drink well for 1–2 years. The intensely spicy, black fruit, and mineral-dominated 1996 Zinfandel Brandlin Ranch emerges from the slopes of Mt. Veeder. It possesses a darker, more saturated ruby color. While medium- to full-bodied, it is structured and possibly more ageworthy (I believe in drinking most Zinfandels during their first 1–7 years of life). This wine reveals some spice, but black fruits and minerals dominate the nose and flavors. It possesses an inner core of rich fruit. Additionally, there is more delineation and structure in the finish, although I would still opt for drinking this wine now.

The 1995 Zinfandel Napa reveals a textbook, briery (the French would call it *sauvage*) nose with aromas of wild berry fruits. The color is an evolved dark garnet, and the wine is dense, medium- to full-bodied, with crisp, tangy acidity, excellent richness, and a spicy, peppery, earthy personality reminiscent of a Rhône. Somewhat tight and structured, it should be consumed over the next 1–2 years. The beautiful, plum-colored 1995 Zinfandel Brandlin Ranch displays a knockout nose of black cherries, raspberries, cola, and peppery fruit. Loads of yummy, glycerin-endowed, chewy fruit hit the palate with medium to full body and excellent purity. Drink this dense, chewy, mouth-filling, savory Zin over the next 1–2 years.

The dark plum/purple-colored 1994 Hendry Vineyard Zinfandel reveals sweet black fruit in the nose. It explodes on the palate, offering full body, layers of rich, creamy fruit, well-hidden, high alcohol (14.2%), and a clean, succulent, fleshy, large-scaled finish. This beautifully made, lush Zinfandel should drink well for 3–4 years. The 1994 Zinfandel Brandlin Ranch displays a similar dark plummy color, a spicy, mineral, peppery nose, sweet, ripe, full-bodied flavors, an inner core of fruit and expansive chewiness, and a long, ripe finish. These wines are pure and rich, with natural, multilayered textures. The Brandlin Ranch will also drink superbly for 3–4 years. This is high-quality winemaking!

FRAZIER (NAPA)

1995 Cabernet Sauvignon	Napa	D	89
1997 Cabernet Sauvignon Lupine Hill Vineyard	Napa	D	88
1995 Merlot Lupine Hill Vineyard	Napa	D	90

Substantial in weight, size, and concentration, the 1997 Cabernet Sauvignon Lupine Hill Vineyard has a dense ruby/purple color followed by aromas of blackberries, cassis, new saddle leather, earth, and spicy oak. A young, unevolved effort with copious tannin in addition to excellent extraction, this dense, medium- to full-bodied Cabernet reveals underlying foresty notes intermixed with black fruits and oak. It will benefit from 2–3 years of cellaring, and will keep for 12–15 years. Frazier's impressive 1995 Merlot Lupine Hill is a textbook, plump, rich Merlot with a dark ruby/purple color, as well as fragrant aromas of white chocolate and cherry jam. Thick, with a soft, unctuously textured, full-bodied personality, this rich, plush, hedonistically satisfying Merlot is a fruit and body-driven wine with a subtle dosage of oak. It should drink well for 7–8 years. The deep, chocolaty, and blackberry-scented, full-bodied, extroverted, fleshy 1995 Cabernet Sauvignon possesses plenty of character. Although it lacks complexity, finesse, and elegance, it offers substantial flavors in a robust, exuberant format. It should drink well for a decade.

GALLO-SONOMA (SONOMA)

1994 Cabernet Sauvignon Frei Ranch	Dry Creek Valley	C	88
1996 Cabernet Sauvignon Stefani Vineyard	Dry Creek Valley	D	88
1997 Zinfandel	Dry Creek	C	87
1997 Zinfandel Barrelli Creek	Alexander Valley	C	90
1995 Zinfandel Barrelli Creek	Alexander Valley	B	89
1997 Zinfandel Chiotti Vineyard	Dry Creek	B	89
1995 Zinfandel Chiotti Vineyard	Dry Creek	C	88
1997 Zinfandel Frei Ranch Vineyard	Dry Creek	C	88
1995 Zinfandel Frei Ranch Vineyard	Dry Creek	B	90
1994 Zinfandel Frei Ranch Vineyard	Dry Creek	C	91
1996 Zinfandel Stefani Vineyard	Dry Creek	C	90
1997 Zinfandel Rancho Zabaco	Dry Creek	C	87

Gallo-Sonoma is a serious producer, a fact that is evidenced by how well all of these wines performed. Readers not yet familiar with the improved quality of the Gallo estate wines should check out these attractive Zinfandels. Unlike many 1997 Zinfandels, there is no shortage of flavor or character in Gallo's 1997s. The 1997 Zinfandel Rancho Zabaco exhibits a dark ruby color as well as sweet black cherry, smoke, licorice, and toasty American oak aromas. Made in a mainstream, soft, plump style, it will drink well for 1–3 years. The 1997 Zinfandel Dry Creek reveals a late harvest character, noticeable tannin, plenty of muscle, and a beefy, robust personality. An exuberant, hefty Zinfandel, it possesses good ripeness, excellent, sweet cherry fruit, and a long finish. It should drink well for 3–4 years. The dark ruby/purple-colored 1997 Zinfandel Frei Ranch displays potentially outstanding raw materials. Notes of chocolate, pepper, dried herbs, and black fruits are followed by a full-bodied, nicely layered, oaky wine with good power. It should drink well for 2–3 years. My favorite of this quartet is the opaque black/purple-colored 1997 Zinfandel Barelli Creek. Super-extracted, intense, and powerful, with good fat, and layers of blackberry and cherry fruit, new oak, dried herbs, and admirable spice and depth, it should drink well for 2–3 years.

The early-released 1997 Zinfandel Chiotti Vineyard possesses explosive fruit, knockout purity, admirable opulence, and a sexy, hedonistic, exotic character. Soft, round, and pure, its gush of black raspberry, smoke-infused, cherry fruit hides the 14.9% alcohol remarkably well. Drink this seductive Zinfandel over the next 1–3 years. As for the 1995s, the saturated ruby/purple-colored 1995 Zinfandel Frei Ranch continues to perform exceptionally well. It is a full-bodied, powerful, concentrated wine with no hard edges, well-integrated acidity, and copious quantities of earthy blackberry and cherry fruit. It is fully mature. Although similar in character, the 1995 Zinfandel Barrelli Creek comes across as more late-harvest in style, with an Amarone/asphalt note in the nose. Also present are aromas and flavors of black cherries, full body, and loads of glycerin. This powerhouse, concentrated, exotic Zinfandel should be consumed over the next 1–2 years.

The 1996 Zinfandel Stefani Vineyard (14.9% alcohol) exhibits a dark ruby/purple color, followed by highly extracted, chewy, viscous, full-bodied flavors, lavish quantities of toasty oak, and a juicy, succulent finish. Along with the other Gallo-Sonoma Zinfandels, this offering reveals a hedonistic, up-front quality. Drink it over the next 2 years. In spite of what appears to be a concentrated, impressively endowed wine, the 1995 Zinfandel Chiotti Vineyard offers leesy, mercaptan aromas that detract from the otherwise impressive components. Two bottles revealed the same defect. In total contrast, the 1994 Zinfandel Frei Ranch Vineyard is a marvelously concentrated, complex, rich, beautifully made wine. Much has been written about Gallo's efforts to compete at the high end of the quality pyramid. This offering is a text-book, full-bodied, gorgeously pure, complex Zinfandel that should drink well for 2–3 years. The big, sweet, smoky nose offers copious quantities of earthy, black cherry fruit with a subtle touch of wood. Rich, full-bodied, and dense, with well-integrated acidity and tannin, this seamlessly styled Zin is sure to please most readers.

The 1996 Cabernet Sauvignon Stefani Vineyard exhibits a dark plum/purple color followed by a jammy, pruny-styled wine with abundant blackberry fruit mixed with licorice, chocolate, and smoky oak. Medium- to full-bodied, moderately tannic, broodingly backward and dense, this well-endowed, chunky Cabernet lacks complexity, but makes up for it in size and richness. Drink it over the next 8–10 years. The saturated dark ruby-colored 1994 Cabernet Sauvignon Frei Ranch displays a moderately intense bouquet of black currants, coffee, crème de cassis, and spice. Pure and rich, this medium- to full-bodied wine possesses well-integrated, unobtrusive acidity and tannin. The finish possesses some dusty tannin, but this spicy, rich Cabernet Sauvignon should continue to evolve and drink well for 7–8 years.

GRACE FAMILY VINEYARD (NAPA)

1995 Cabernet Sauvignon	Napa	EEE	94
1994 Cabernet Sauvignon	Napa	EEE	94+

This wine is only available through the winery's mailing list, and I am sure there are more potential suitors than wine to be sold.

The 1994 Cabernet Sauvignon is the last wine made from the original vineyard plantings. The opaque purple color is accompanied by an explosive bouquet of black currants and cherries, intermingled with toasty, new oak. Full-bodied, with a lead pencil, cedary, cassis-like characteristic not dissimilar from a high-class Pauillac, this tightly knit yet formidably endowed Cabernet should last for 20–25 years. I hope the handful of multimillionaires who latch onto a bottle or two will have enough patience to cellar it for 5–6 years before pulling a cork. The 1995 is a magnificent Cabernet Sauvignon, but, lamentably, only three barrels (425 magnums) were produced as the vineyard is in the process of being replanted. The wine is powerful for a 1995, with an opaque purple color, and intensely ripe black currant aromas intermingled with smoke, toast, licorice, and chocolate. This deep, full-bodied, multilayered wine is the essence of Napa Cabernet Sauvignon. Although it reveals plenty of tannin, it is well meshed in the wine's impressive richness and layered texture. Still youthful and grapy, it will develop well for another 15–20+ years.

Past Glories: 1993 Cabernet Sauvignon (91)

GREEN AND RED VINEYARD (NAPA)

1999 Zinfandel Chiles Mill Vineyard	Napa	C	90
1998 Zinfandel Chiles Mill Vineyard	Napa	C	90
1997 Zinfandel Chiles Mill Vineyard	Napa	C	89
1996 Zinfandel Chiles Mill Vineyard Unfiltered	Napa	C	89
1995 Zinfandel Chiles Mill Vineyard Unfiltered	Napa	C	86
1994 Zinfandel Chiles Mill Vineyard Unfiltered	Napa	C	89
1999 Zinfandel Chiles Valley	Napa	C	89
1997 Zinfandel Chiles Valley	Napa	C	89

One of my favorite Zinfandel producers, Green and Red Vineyard, a model of balance, elegance, and class, has again fashioned elegant, sexy, stylish wines. The 1999 Zinfandel Chiles Valley (14.2% alcohol) is a spicy, medium dark ruby-colored offering with abundant quantities of cherry fruit intermixed with balsam wood and earth. Lush and medium-bodied, it is ideal for drinking over the next 2–3 years. Richer and more textured, the peppery, earthy, spicy, complex 1999 Zinfandel Chiles Mill Vineyard (14.4% alcohol) reveals notes of soy, kirsch, and berry fruit in its aromas as well as flavors. Medium- to full-bodied and pure, with fine underlying acidity, it should be consumed over the next 5–6 years. The outstanding 1998 Zinfandel Chiles Mill Vineyard exhibits a dark ruby/purple color in addition to sweet, pure aromas of pepper, black fruits, kirsch, and vanilla. Measured and elegant, this medium- to full-bodied, restrained yet concentrated wine unfolds on the palate without a hiccup. It is a delicious Zin to enjoy over the next 5–6 years.

The 1997s from Green and Red Vineyard are both Burgundy-styled, elegant, floral and berry-scented, harmonious efforts that offer delicious drinking. The expressive 1997 Zinfandel Chiles Valley (13.9% alcohol) reveals raspberry and black cherry fruit, and soft, medium-bodied, well-knit, elegant flavors. The acidity, tannin, and alcohol are nicely meshed with the fruit. Restrained yet impressive, it will drink well for 3–4 years. The 1997 Zinfandel Chiles Mill Vineyard (13.5% alcohol) exhibits beautiful purity in addition to a fragrant, sweet berry-scented nose with hints of spice and subtle earth. Delicate yet intense, with medium body, impeccable balance, and a long finish, this wine should drink well for 3–4 years.

The most Burgundian of all the 1996 Zinfandels I tasted, the medium ruby-colored 1996 Zinfandel Chiles Mill Vineyard Unfiltered possesses a gorgeously fragrant nose of black cherries, floral scents, minerals, pepper, and spice. It is medium-bodied, lush, and sexy, in the style of a premier cru Beaune or Volnay. There is a nicely textured finish with lively acidity, sweet fruit, and glycerin. This Zin is ready to drink, so readers should take advantage of its considerable charms. The 1995 is a good example of a restrained, subtle Zinfandel that offers enough sweet fruit to give the wine appeal and attractiveness. The medium ruby color is followed by pure, dusty, black cherry aromas that drift from the glass. Dry and elegant, yet concentrated and harmonious, this is a lighter-styled, pretty, delicious Zin that is fully mature. I am not sure I haven't underrated the 1994. It exhibits a dark ruby color, a pure, ripe, cherry/raspberry fruitiness, a seamless, silky texture, medium to full body, and a luscious finish. It is all fruit, beautifully captured without any excesses. Drink this soft, smooth Zinfandel over the next 3–4 years.

HANSEL FAMILY VINEYARD (RUSSIAN RIVER)

1998 Pinot Noir	Russian River	D	89
1996 Pinot Noir	Russian River	D	89

This appears to be a promising newcomer from Russian River. Hansel's wines reveal Burgundy-like personalities with plenty of texture, ripeness, and complexity. Interestingly, the first person to tell me how good these wines were was Tom Rochioli. The 1998 Pinot Noir exhibits an evolved garnet color as well as an attractive bouquet of underbrush, grilled meats, dried herbs, and sweet, cherry, plum, and raspberry-like fruit. Spicy oak complements the ripe, sweet black fruit flavors. This wine cuts a medium- to full-bodied swath across the palate. Good acidity gives uplift and delineation. Drink it over the next 3–4 years.

The 1996 Pinot Noir from this small winery was made with considerable guidance from proprietor Walter Hansel's friend, Tom Rochioli. Readers should note that quantities of the impressive wines from the Hansel Family Vineyard are limited, and the entire production is sold through a mailing list. The complex 1996 Pinot Noir exhibits a Pommard-like earthy/spicy character. Some of Pinot's sweet, apple skin personality comes through in the black cherry flavors. A broad, dense, medium- to full-bodied Pinot Noir with considerable personality and flavor authority, it should drink well for 5–6 years.

HARLAN ESTATE (NAPA)

1999 Proprietary Red Wine	Napa	EEE	92+
1998 Proprietary Red Wine	Napa	EEE	93
1997 Proprietary Red Wine	Napa	EEE	100
1996 Proprietary Red Wine	Napa	EEE	98
1995 Proprietary Red Wine	Napa	EEE	99
1994 Proprietary Red Wine	Napa	EEE	100
1998 The Maiden	Napa	EE	91
1997 The Maiden	Napa	EE	94

1996	The Maiden	Napa	EE	91
1995	The Maiden	Napa	E	90

While Harlan Estate might be the single most distinctive and compelling Cabernet-based wine in northern California, there is more and more competition. It is also becoming increasingly expensive, jumping an average of $25 a year in price. The 1996 came out at $125, the 1997 at $150, and the 1998 at $175. If we run the math, 10 years from now this wine should cost $425 a bottle. Think that is preposterous? Current vintages of Harlan Estate frequently fetch prices in excess of that at wine auctions. Obviously, no expense is spared in producing what might be the most meticulously made wine in the world. The 1998, a candidate for the "Wine of the Vintage," was produced from yields of 0.9 tons per acre. There are only 1,100 cases, and it is the first Harlan Estate to be composed of 100% Cabernet Sauvignon. A spectacular achievement, it boasts an opaque plum/purple color and a sumptuous nose of espresso, mineral, blueberry, blackberry, tobacco, licorice, Asian spice, and roasted meat smells. In the mouth, it is seamless, full-bodied, with an unctuous texture, gorgeously sweet tannin, and layer upon layer of concentration. This is a tour de force in winemaking. It is hard to believe that such a wine has emerged from 1998. Anticipated maturity: 2003–2030. The 1997 Harlan Estate is one of the greatest Cabernet Sauvignon–based wines I have ever tasted. A blend of 80% Cabernet Sauvignon, with the rest Merlot and Cabernet Franc, this enormously endowed, profoundly rich wine must be tasted to be believed. Interestingly, it is the most precocious of the Harlan Estate wines to date, although the 1998 promises to be open-knit, if not as multidimensional. Opaque purple-colored, it boasts spectacular, soaring aromatics of vanilla, minerals, coffee, blackberries, licorice, and cassis. In the mouth, layer after layer unfold powerfully yet gently. Acidity, tannin, and alcohol are well balanced by the wine's unreal richness and singular personality. The finish exceeds one minute. Anticipated maturity: now–2030. Does anyone wonder if wines such as the 1945 Mouton-Rothschild, 1947 Cheval Blanc, and 1961 Latour had similar personalities at two years of age?

Readers should not overlook the dense purple-colored 1997 Maiden, another creamy-textured, full-bodied, unctuously thick, rich wine. Jammy cassis, new oak, smoke, and espresso notes explode from this blockbuster. An amazing effort, it will drink well when released and last for two decades. The 1998 Maiden is also prodigious. I know it is tempting to pooh-pooh second wines, but this is no afterthought from owner Bill Harlan and the winemaking team of American Bob Levy and Frenchman Michel Rolland. The 1998 Maiden (770 cases) possesses a dense purple color and a knockout nose of cocoa, prunes, blackberries, plums, and cassis. Spicy, with moderate tannin, and a viscosity and richness akin to beef blood, it is a gorgeous, concentrated, thick effort. Anticipated maturity: now–2018.

There are only 1,600 cases of the 1996 Harlan Estate and 600 cases of the 1996 Maiden. The opaque purple-colored 1996 Harlan Estate reveals extraordinary intensity, a spicy, black currant, tobacco, cedar, and fruitcake-scented bouquet, full body, a texture oozing with glycerin and concentrated fruit, and moderate tannin in the blockbuster finish. While not as perfect as the 1997 or 1994, it is one of the most concentrated and complete red wines one could hope to taste. Anticipated maturity: 2004–2030. The 1996 Maiden was performing even better this year. The dark saturated plum/purple color is followed by aromas of prunes, coffee, black fruits, and espresso beans. With an opulent personality, low acidity and a plush texture, it is a sexy, well-endowed wine. Anticipated maturity: now–2015.

As for the two *cuvées* of 1995, the Maiden is an outstanding offering (300 cases made from 100% Cabernet Franc). It possesses a dense, murky ruby/purple color and an expressive, cedary, leathery, spicy nose with plenty of black fruits. Some minerality comes through, but this complex, evolved yet structured, full-bodied wine is an amazing second wine. It should drink well for 10–15 years. The 1995 Proprietary Red Wine is almost as perfect as the 1994. It has gotten even better in the bottle, and remains one of the most remarkable young Cabernet Sauvignons I have tasted. The wine, a blend of 85% Cabernet Sauvignon and 15% Merlot, was aged in 100% new oak, which adds subtle toasty scents. This opaque purple-colored Cabernet offers up a nose of smoke, coffee beans, black and blue fruits, minerals, and roasted herbs. It is extremely full-bodied, with spectacular purity, exquisite equilibrium, and a seamless personality with everything in total harmony. The finish lasts for more than 40 seconds. This extravagantly rich, profoundly complex 1995 will give its 1994 sibling a run for its money. Anticipated maturity: now–2027.

What can I say about the 1994? It satisfied all of my requirements for perfection. The opaque purple color is followed by spectacular aromatics that soar from the glass, offering up celestial levels of black currants, minerals, smoked herbs, cedar wood, coffee, and toast. In the mouth, this seamless legend reveals full body and exquisite layers of phenomenally pure and rich fruit, followed by a 40+-second finish. While accessible, the 1994 begs for another 5–7 years of cellaring. It should easily last for 30+ years. Every possible jagged edge—acidity, alcohol, tannin, and wood—is brilliantly intertwined in what seems like a di- aphanous format. What is so extraordinary about this large-scaled wine, with its dazzling dis- play of aromatics and prodigious flavors and depth, is that it offers no hint of heaviness or coarseness. Harlan's 1994 comes close to immortality in the glass.

The 1999 looks to be outstanding, but seemingly not as compellingly rich, textured, and nuanced as previous vintages. For the 1999 vintage, Harlan Estate has converted to wood fermenters, much like their nearby neighbor Robert Mondavi. That decision is interesting in view of the fact that many top Bordeaux châteaux discarded their wood fermenters 10–30 years ago in favor of temperature-controlled stainless steel. More controlled fermentation temperatures and increased sanitation were the obvious reasons for the conversion. Wood fer- menters still exist in Bordeaux, particularly among some of the St. Emilion *gargistes*, but elsewhere they are primarily on display for tourists. In short, most of Bordeaux's wood fer- menters made their way into barbecue pits.

Past Glories: 1993 (95), 1992 (96), 1991 (94), 1990 (90)

HARTFORD COURT (SONOMA)

1999 Pinot Noir Arrendell Vineyard	Russian River	E	92
1997 Pinot Noir Arrendell Vineyard	Green Valley	D	(88–90)
1999 Pinot Noir Dutton Ranch/Sanchietti Vineyard	Russian River	E	89
1999 Pinot Noir Marin Vineyard	Marin County	D	90+
1999 Pinot Noir Sevens Bench Vineyard	Napa/Carneros	D	92
1999 Pinot Noir Velvet Sisters Vineyard	Anderson Valley	D	90
1997 Zinfandel Dina's Vineyard	Russian River	D	90
1997 Zinfandel Hartford Vineyard	Russian River	D	89
1997 Zinfandel High Wire Vineyard	Russian River	D	90
1999 Hartford Zinfandel Dina's Vineyard	Russian River	D	89
1999 Hartford Zinfandel Fanucchi–Wood Road Vineyard	Russian River	D	92
1999 Hartford Zinfandel Hartford Vineyard	Russian River	D	90
1999 Hartford Zinfandel High Wire Vineyard	Russian River	D	92

The 1999 red wine offerings are the finest I have yet tasted from Hartford Court (another of the small, high-quality producers under the umbrella known as the Jackson Family Farms). While Don Hartford sells off some of the production from their 300 acres of vineyards, ap- proximately 9,000 cases are produced under the Hartford Court and Hartford labels. The Hartford Court label includes their Chardonnays and Pinot Noirs, while the Hartford label is used for their Zinfandels. All the 1999s have been bottled, and all represent outstanding ex- amples of their types.

Based on the stunning Pinot Noirs, it appears that Hartford Court has joined the upper echelon of Pinot Noir and Zinfandel producers in northern California. The 1999 Pinot Noir Velvet Sisters Vineyard (175 cases) comes from the cooler northern area of Anderson Valley. Made from such clones as Dijon #115 and Pommard, this dark ruby-colored offering exhibits a sweet, raspberry, brown sugar–like bouquet as well as smoky, attractively integrated toasty scents, medium to full body, decent acidity, and outstanding purity and ripeness. Sixty percent new French oak was utilized during the aging process. While accessible, it promises to drink well for 5–8 years. An outstanding effort, as well as a curiosity, is the 1999 Pinot Noir Marin Vineyard (425 cases). Most Marin County real estate is stratospherically priced, as this county has more than its share of multimillion-dollar homes as well as some of the wealthiest residents of the San Francisco Bay area. Made from a 14-year-old vineyard planted with the Mt. Eden clone, cropped at a meager one ton of fruit per acre, and bottled with no filtration, this earthy, dark ruby-colored Pinot reveals abundant quantities of sweet black fruits, dry tannin, good structure, and notions of melted fudge intermined with black cherries, plums, and raspberries. Dense, deep, youthful, and unevolved, it will age nicely for a decade. Don Hartford's wine-maker, Mike Sullivan, told me that, like all their Pinot Noirs, it enjoyed a six-day cold soak prior to fermentation. About 70% new French oak was utilized. The 1999 Pinot Noir Sevens Bench Vineyard comes from a vineyard planted largely with French Dijon clones. This seven-year-old vineyard, which was cropped at two tons of fruit per acre, has produced an opaque purple-colored, dense, full-bodied, superbly concentrated Pinot with plenty of creamy black fruits intermixed with smoke, toast, and spice. Rich, with moderate tannin, sweet levels of glycerin, and enough acidity to provide delineation, this opulently styled wine can be drunk now or cellared for 6–8 years. Very impressive! More monolithic and less evolved, but potentially outstanding, the 1999 Pinot Noir Dutton Ranch/ Sanchietti Vineyard was muted the day I tasted it. Nevertheless, it is a plump, full-bodied, tannic effort with force and muscle, but not the charm or aromatics of its siblings. Those characteristics may develop over the next year, but this forceful, moderately tannic, dense 1999 does not lack concentration or intensity. Anticipated maturity: now–2009. Hartford Court's 1999 Pinot Noir Arrendell Vineyard is exquisite. Black raspberries intermingled with blueberries and cherry liqueur are wrapped with toasty oak. This rich, full-bodied, expressive Pinot possesses impressive purity, decent acidity, sweet tannin, and layers of concentrated fruit, yet it is neither heavy nor overblown. This superb effort should drink well during its first 7–9 years of life.

Under the new Hartford label are some powerhouse Zinfandels that recall the quality and stylistic approach favored by Ehren Jordan and Larry Turley at Turley Cellars (to my mind, California's preeminent Zinfandel producer). Hartford's 1999 Zinfandel High Wire Vineyard (570 cases produced from 90-year-old vines) contains 15.8% alcohol, but you would never suspect that from tasting it. Bottled without filtration, this wine offers an opaque purple color as well as explosive aromas of blackberries, pepper, and spice. In the mouth, ripe cherries also make an appearance in this unctuously textured, rich, full-bodied, exuberant, superbly concentrated, well-balanced Zinfandel. These wines are best consumed during their robust, powerful youth—over the next 5–6 years. Another outstanding effort is Hartford's 1999 Zinfandel Hartford Vineyard (350 cases). Produced from 80-year-old head-pruned vines, it exhibits boysenberry and blackberry fruit, along with pepper notes. Not as massive as the High Wire, this soft, velvety-textured, elegant (if that word can be attributed to a wine with 15.7% alcohol) offering possesses zesty underlying acidity, ripe tannin, and a big, fleshy mouth-feel with no hard edges. Drink it over the next 4–5 years. The awesome Hartford 1999 Zinfandel Fanucchi–Wood Road (325 cases with 16.1% alcohol) is a powerful, concentrated, intense effort produced from 90-year-old vines. Don Hartford said a touch of Petite Sirah was added, but that was not noticeable. It offers abundant quantities of blackberry and cherry liqueur-like aromas and flavors, along with pepper, minerals, and spice. Voluptuously textured, intense, fragrant, pure, and decadent, this dazzling Zinfandel should drink well for a decade.

Readers looking for a more understated, restrained effort will enjoy Hartford's 1999 Zinfandel Dina's Vineyard (204 cases). This 90-year-old vineyard produced 204 cases of Zinfandel that finished with a mere 14.5% alcohol. Offering up spicy red and black fruit aromas, medium to full body, excellent harmony, good acidity, and impressive balance, it should drink well for 6–7 years. All of these old-vine 1999 Zinfandels are made from yields averaging under two tons of fruit per acre.

The 1997 Pinot Noir Arrendell Vineyard is a beautifully fruity, dark ruby-colored wine with loads of apple skin, cherry jam, and spice in its aromatics and flavors. There is tangy underlying acidity, fine ripeness, and a fleshy mouth-feel with just enough acidity and tannin to buttress the wine and give it delineation. This effort should age nicely for 5–6 years.

Hartford Court produced fine 1997 Zinfandels. All were aged in 100% French oak and achieved natural alcohol levels between 14.7% and 15.2%. Production ranged from 300 cases for Dina's Vineyard to 700 cases for the High Wire Vineyard. Exhibiting a dark ruby/ purple color, the 1997 Zinfandel Hartford Vineyard offers up an attractive nose of jammy, briery, and raspberry fruit, medium to full body, tangy acidity, and a spicy, exuberant personality. This wine should drink well for 4–5 years. The 1997 Zinfandel High Wire Vineyard reveals a saturated dark purple color, as well as more pepper and black raspberries in its moderately intense aromatics. This lovely, rich, medium- to full-bodied wine balances power with finesse. Drink this stylish, flavorful Zinfandel over the next 5–6 years. The outstanding dark ruby/purple-colored 1997 Zinfandel Dina's Vineyard is close in quality to the High Wire. There are abundant quantities of jammy black cherries and raspberries, intermixed with pepper and toasty oak in this medium- to full-bodied yet elegant wine. It should drink well for 5–7 years given its good underlying acidity and extract.

HAVENS WINE CELLARS (NAPA)

1997	Bourriquot Proprietary Red Wine	Napa	D	92
1996	Bourriquot Proprietary Red Wine	Napa	D	91
1995	Bourriquot Proprietary Red Wine	Napa	D	89
1994	Bourriquot Proprietary Red Wine	Napa	D	88+
1997	Merlot	Napa	D	90
1997	Merlot Reserve	Napa	D	91
1996	Merlot Reserve	Napa	D	90
1997	Syrah	Carneros	D	88
1996	Syrah	Carneros	D	89
1994	Syrah	Carneros	D	90

Mike Havens, working out of a warehouse in the city of Napa, appears to have settled into an admirable pattern, producing richer and richer Merlots, complemented by a fine Syrah, and a Cheval Blanc–inspired proprietary red wine called Bourriquot. There is also a small quantity of Sauvignon Blanc. Havens supplements his Carneros vineyard with purchased grapes.

His 1997s make up the strongest quartet of new releases wine-maker Michael Havens has yet produced. The 1997 Merlot (which is nearly as good as the Reserve offering) exhibits a dense ruby/purple color in addition to a superb nose of chocolate, cocoa, cherries, and smoky, earthy notes. The wine is rich and medium- to full-bodied, with low acidity, a sweet, nicely layered palate, and a lush finish. It should drink well for 7–8 years. Slightly more backward and concentrated, the opaque purple-colored 1997 Merlot Reserve possesses fuller body and greater extract and richness, as well as more tannin, volume, and flavor intensity. Although not as beguiling as the regular bottling, it promises to deliver even more goods with another 1–2 years of bottle age. It should keep for 12–15 years. The 1997 Bourriquot (a Cheval Blanc–like blend of approximately two-thirds Cabernet Franc and one-third Merlot) is sensational. My notes start with the words "great stuff." The dark ruby/purple color is accompanied by a sumptuous nose of coconuts, black currants, vanilla, and floral scents.

This medium- to full-bodied wine exhibits exceptional fruit purity and presence, great finesse and elegance, prodigious potential for complexity, and a sexy, opulently textured finish. It can be drunk early, but promises to be even better with 3–4 years of cellaring; it will keep for two decades. The 1997 Syrah displays a crème de cassis–dominated nose intermixed with smoky, earthy scents that emerge with airing. This dark ruby/purple-colored offering possesses full body, low acidity, lush, ripe fruit, a corpulent mouth-feel, and a soft, ripe finish. There is some tannin, but it is mostly buried beneath the cascade of fruit. If additional complexity develops, this Syrah will merit a higher rating. It should drink well for 8–10 years.

The 1996 Merlot Reserve should satisfy Merlot lovers given its deep ruby color, and rich, chocolaty, weedy, intensely smoky and seductive aromatics. Lushly textured, with impressive black cherry, chocolate, and berry flavors, this full-bodied, elegant, stylish Merlot reveals plenty of depth and richness, but no hard edges. Drink it over the next 7–8 years. The 1996 Syrah, while not a blockbuster, is an attractive tar, cassis, bacon, and smoky-scented wine with medium to full body, excellent concentration, soft tannin, and a round, generous, expansive mouth-feel. This delectable, elegantly styled Syrah is ideal for drinking over the next 5–9 years. The 1996 Bourriquot, Napa's answer to Cheval Blanc (each is made from a blend of two-thirds Cabernet Franc and one-third Merlot), offers an exotic, complex, evolved, coffee bean and berry–scented nose. In the mouth, this rich, full-bodied wine exhibits sweet tannin, low acidity, a lush texture, and a moderately long finish. With its gobs of fruit, expansive palate, and distinctive personality, it is more than a good imitation of Cheval Blanc. Drink it over the next 10–15 years.

The 1995 Bourriquot reveals a deep ruby/purple color, followed by big, spicy, mineral, licorice, floral-tinged, black currant aromas, medium body, excellent to outstanding fruit concentration, a soft, layered palate, and a rich, moderately tannic finish. The wine needs 2–3 years of cellaring, but it should keep for 15–18 years, possibly meriting an outstanding rating. The 1994 Bourriquot is also a blend of two-thirds Cabernet Franc and one-third Merlot. It reveals a deep color, some attractive, leafy, curranty-like scents, medium body, plenty of tannin, excellent richness, and a firm, structured finish. Cellar it for 2–3 years and drink it over the subsequent 15 years. The distinctive dark purple-colored 1994 Syrah exhibits an exaggerated, flamboyant set of aromatics (minty, black raspberry, and cassis scents). The wine is soft and medium- to full-bodied, with excellent richness, well-integrated tannin and acidity, and spicy wood. Already delicious, this wine should drink well for another decade. *Past Glories:* 1993 Merlot Reserve (90)

HAYWOOD (SONOMA)

1998 Zinfandel Morning Sun	Sonoma	D	87
1998 Zinfandel Rocky Terrace	Sonoma	D	85

The dense ruby/purple-colored 1998 Zinfandel Rocky Terrace exhibits jammy black cherry/berry flavors intermixed with spice and pepper, low acidity, and toasty new oak, yet the emphasis is on ripe Zin fruit presented in an exuberant, medium- to full-bodied format capable of aging for 5–6 years. Even better is the 1998 Zinfandel Morning Sun. An excellent dark ruby color is followed by aromas of chocolate, smoky barbecue, and briery, black cherry/raspberry fruit. Full-bodied, dense, and chewy, it has low acidity, an excellent texture, and a multilayered finish. This wine has the potential to merit an outstanding score if it is not compromised by too much fining or filtration prior to bottling. Anticipated maturity: now–2008.

HIDDEN CELLARS (MENDOCINO)

1997 Zinfandel Sorcery	Mendocino	C	89
1997 Zinfandel Zaina-Hitzman Vineyard	Mendocino	D	90

These are impressively made, well-constituted Zinfandels. The 1997 Zinfandel Sorcery (75% Zinfandel, 15% Petite Sirah, and 10% Syrah that achieved 15.5% alcohol) is serious stuff. Its opaque ruby/purple color is followed by blackberry, cassis, and spicy aromas. Dense, full-bodied, tannic, and in need of 1–2 years of cellaring, this is a wine to drink between now– 2010. It may develop additional complexity, thus meriting a score close to outstanding. I was thrilled with the 1997 Zinfandel Zaina-Hitzman Vineyard (15.9% alcohol). It is a forceful, full-bodied, fleshy, nicely layered example with tons of ripe blackberry and raspberry fruit, subtle oak, dried herb notes, as well as a monstrous, concentrated, intense finish. With excellent fat, lushness, and equilibrium, it will drink well for 7–8 years.

PAUL HOBBS (SONOMA)

1998	Cabernet Sauvignon	Napa	E	88
1998	Cabernet Sauvignon Hyde Vineyard	Carneros	E	89
1997	Cabernet Sauvignon Hyde Vineyard	Carneros	E	91
1999	Chardonnay	Russian River	D	90
1998	Merlot Black Vineyard	Napa	EE	90
1997	Merlot Black Vineyard	Napa	E	89
1998	Pinot Noir Cuvée Agustina	Sonoma Mountain	E	92
1998	Pinot Noir Hyde Vineyard	Carneros	E	88
1997	Pinot Noir Hyde Vineyard	Carneros	D	88

This is an impressive group of wines from Paul Hobbs, a winery whose production is inching up to 10,000 cases. The 1999 Chardonnay (1,297 cases) sees about 55% new French oak. It enjoys full malolactic, has its lees stirred, and uses indigenous yeasts to ferment the Chardonnay must. Powerful and concentrated, with plenty of fat, leesy, tropical fruit flavors, gorgeous flesh, and notes of honey, toast, smoke, and minerals, it should be consumed over the next 2 years.

Paul Hobbs has displayed a brilliant touch with Pinot Noir. His 1998 Pinot Noir Cuvée Agustina (only 92 cases are made from such Pinot clones as Pommard, Swan, and Calera) is aged in 100% new oak, which has been totally absorbed. This full-bodied Pinot Noir exhibits earthy, black cherry fruit, notes of smoked game and pepper, and meaty, black raspberry flavors. A distinctive, earthy, full-bodied, powerful, accessible Pinot, it should continue to drink well for a decade. There are 630 cases of the 1998 Cabernet Sauvignon, much of which came from the Beckstoffer sector of the To-Kalon Vineyard. Notes of fudge, licorice, earth, and smoke compete with black currants in this medium-bodied wine. The only drawback is some gritty tannin in the finish. Blended with 25% Merlot to give it more texture and plumpness, it is best drunk over the next 7–8 years. The 1998 Cabernet Sauvignon Hyde Vineyard (786 cases) offers an elegant, supple, well-delineated style with notes of vanilla, chocolate, cassis, cedar, and dried Provençal herbs. Medium-bodied and stylish, with a sweet mid-palate, it can be consumed over the next decade. From a three-acre parcel, the 1998 Merlot Black Vineyard (160 cases of 100% Merlot) offers stupendous richness in its cocoa, scorched earth, and black cherry–scented bouquet. Chewy, with earthy, fudge, and berry flavors, it should continue to evolve nicely for a decade.

The dark ruby/purple-colored 1998 Pinot Noir Hyde Vineyard (463 cases) offers sweet plum and black cherry fruit intertwined with underbrush and soil scents. Naturally fermented and bottled without filtration, this medium- to full-bodied Pinot reveals an expansive texture as well as moderate tannin in the finish. The wood is not excessive. The dark ruby-colored 1997 Pinot Noir Hyde Vineyard offers moderately intense aromas of sweet oak intermixed with attractive black raspberry and cherry fruit. Spicy, earthy, underbrush, and foresty flavors are present in this medium-bodied, spicy, soft Pinot. Drink it over the next 2–3 years.

Chocolate, blackberry, mocha, and cherry notes dominate the aromatics and flavors of the impressive 1997 Merlot Black Vineyard (820 cases). Ripe and chewy, with abundant sweet fruit in addition to moderately high tannin, this Merlot can be drunk now, but promises to be even better with another 12 months of aging. It should keep for a decade. Lastly, the classic 1997 Cabernet Sauvignon Hyde Vineyard (1,020 cases) boasts an opaque black/purple color and a gorgeously sweet bouquet of cassis, licorice, and toasty new oak. Full-bodied, with gobs of black fruit, plenty of glycerin, and excellent symmetry, this seamless effort has well-integrated acidity, tannin, and alcohol. It should drink well for 15+ years.

HOWELL MOUNTAIN VINEYARDS (HOWELL MOUNTAIN)

1997	Zinfandel Beatty Ranch	Howell Mountain	D	90+
1996	Zinfandel Beatty Ranch	Howell Mountain	D	90
1997	Zinfandel Black-Sears	Howell Mountain	D	(90–92)
1997	Zinfandel Old Vine	Howell Mountain	D	90
1996	Zinfandel Old Vine	Howell Mountain	C	89+?

Howell Mountain produced three beautiful 1997 Zinfandels, made from extremely old vines. The 1997 Zinfandel Old Vine (from 25- and 80-year-old vines) exhibits a deep ruby/purple color, a fragrant, black cherry, mineral, peppery nose, explosive fruit, low acidity, and a rich, glycerin-endowed, fleshy, hedonistic mouth-feel. It will provide ideal drinking over the next 4–5 years. It tips the scales at 15.5% alcohol, so be forewarned. The 1997 Zinfandel Beatty Ranch (from 80-year-old vines) is more structured and tannic. The nose offers up black raspberry fruit intertwined with dusty soil, pepper, and mineral scents. Medium- to full-bodied, moderately tannic yet gorgeously pure and layered, this Zin may be even better with another 6–12 months of bottle age. It should keep for 7–8 years. Lastly, the 1997 Zinfandel Black-Sears Vineyard (made from 25-year-old vines) is a fat, chewy, full-bodied, beautifully etched offering with gobs of black cherry, raspberry, and blackberry fruit. It reveals more glycerin and a chewier mouth-feel than its two siblings, as well as a plump, hedonistic, opulently textured finish. Consume this brawny (16% alcohol) yet seductive Zin over the next 4–5 years.

These wines are made by Littorai's Ted Lemon. As the numbers attest, they are exceptionally fine Zinfandels. The outstanding 1996 Zinfandel Beatty Ranch received a "wow" in my tasting notes. At 15.5% alcohol, one would expect it to be hot, but this wine is super-concentrated and beautifully balanced. It boasts a deep ruby/purple color, followed by knockout aromatics of black raspberries, minerals, and spice. Deep, full-bodied, and concentrated, with the alcohol well concealed, this large-scaled, intricately detailed, intensely flavored wine can be drunk now or cellared for 7–10 years (atypically long for Zin). Nearly as superb is the 1996 Zinfandel Old Vine. It delivers a similar alcoholic clout (15.5%), but in this case, some heat shows up at the back of the palate. The wine displays a dark plum color, and sweet blackberry, raspberry, and cherry notes dosed with subtle oak and spice. Full-bodied, rich, and slightly hot in the heady, dense finish, it should drink well for 5–6 years.

IRON HORSE (SONOMA)

1997	Benchmark	Alexander Valley	E	90
1997	Cabernet Franc	Alexander Valley	D	89
1999	Cuvée R	Alexander Valley	D	89
1998	Pinot Noir	Sonoma	D	89

The 1999 Cuvée R, an exuberant blend of 80% Sauvignon Blanc and 20% Viognier (an intriguing as well as highly successful idea), offers copious quantities of tropical fruit, honeyed lemons, and spice in a medium- to full-bodied, gorgeously fresh, flavorful, complex format. Loaded with fruit, with good body and a lovely perfume, it should be consumed over the next several years. The 1998 Pinot Noir, which emerges from Sonoma's Green Valley, is an elegant, flavorful, tasty effort to enjoy over the near-term. With 14.6% alcohol, this 1998 is no wimpish wine. In fact, it is the finest Pinot Noir Iron Horse has yet produced. A dark ruby color is accompanied by sweet, jammy plums, black cherries, dried herbs, and meaty animal notes. The wine is plump and medium- to full-bodied, with plenty of glycerin, purity, and ripeness. Flavors of allspice and cinnamon add to the wine's complexity. Firm tannin and good underlying, zesty acidity will provide 7–8 years of drinkability.

The complex 1997 Cabernet Franc (14.6% alcohol) is outstanding for its purity of expression and graceful yet concentrated style. A classic effort, it offers richness as well as finesse, a combination not easily obtained in California, where richness and power are more the norm. A deep ruby color with purple hues is followed by copious black cherry and mulberry fruit nicely dosed with new oak. This medium-bodied wine possesses good sweetness, refreshing acidity, moderate tannin, and excellent depth and richness. It should develop even more perfume over the next 10–12 years. The 1997 Benchmark is a proprietary blend of 76% Cabernet Sauvignon, 12% Merlot, and 12% Cabernet Franc, with 14.6% alcohol. It boasts an opaque saturated ruby/purple color as well as a tight but promising nose of black currants, raspberries, earth, minerals, and tar. Although extremely concentrated, this wine retains its elegance and overall symmetry. As it sits in the mouth, additional layers and nuances develop. Another 1–3 years of cellaring should prove beneficial, and it should age well for 15+ years. For my taste, it is the finest Cabernet-based wine Iron Horse has yet produced. Bravo!

J. C. CELLARS (PASO ROBLES)

1999 Zinfandel Alegria Vineyard	Russian River	D	89
1998 Zinfandel Alegria Vineyard	Russian River	C	88
1999 Zinfandel Bolduc Vineyard	Napa	D	88
1999 Zinfandel Rhodes Vineyard Cuvée Isabel	Redwood Valley	D	89

These wines are made by Jeff Cohen, the wine-maker at Rosenblum Cellars. These three impressive 1999 Zinfandels display plenty of personality as well as considerable fruit. They are big, ruggedly constructed efforts to drink during their first 5–6 years of life. The 1999 Zinfandel Bolduc Vineyard's dense, opaque ruby/purple color is followed by aromas of herbs, leather, blackberries, and spice. While not complex, it offers a big mouthful of spicy, full-bodied Zinfandel. The dark ruby/purple-colored 1999 Zinfandel Alegria Vineyard reveals a more Rhône-like, pepper, earth, garrigue (Provençal herb and soil notes), spicy bouquet, full-bodied, intense black cherry and berry flavors, and a large-framed, muscular finish. The 1999 Zinfandel Rhodes Vineyard Cuvée Isabel exhibits copious quantities of sweet black fruits, medium to full body, currants, blackberries, and a grapier, lustier style with less earth and spice. Unfortunately, there are only 85 cases of the 1998 Zinfandel Alegria Vineyard. This dark ruby/purple-colored effort reveals excellent, briery, sweet black cherry and raspberry fruit infused with spicy, toasty wood. The wine is surprisingly unevolved, robust, slightly foursquare, but deeply concentrated. With a positive upside, this wine will be even better with another year of cellaring. It should drink beautifully for 4–6 years.

JADE MOUNTAIN (NAPA)

1997 Côte du Soleil	California	B	88
1994 Les Jumeaux	California	C	88
1998 Merlot Caldwell Vineyard	Napa	D	90
1997 Merlot Paras Vineyard	Napa	D	90
1997 Mourvèdre	California	C	90
1998 La Provençale	California	C	88
1997 La Provençale	California	C	89
1998 Syrah	Napa	D	90
1997 Syrah	Napa	C	90
1997 Syrah Cask P-10	Napa	D	91
1997 Syrah Hudson Vineyard	Napa	D	91

1995 Syrah Mt. Veeder	Napa	D	88+
1997 Syrah Paras Vineyard	Napa	D	91
1996 Syrah Paras Vineyard	Napa	D	90
1999 Viognier Paras Vineyard	Napa	D	91

Under the helmsmanship of Douglas Danielak, Jade Mountain's promotion of Rhône blends has resulted in a bevy of excellent offerings, all of which are realistically priced. One of the finest Viogniers I have tasted, the 1999 Viognier Paras Vineyard (14.9% alcohol) sees some barrel fermentation. It possesses a superb nose of honeysuckle, peaches, apricots, and tropical fruits. Aged in neutral barrels prior to bottling, the wine exhibits a terrific texture, great fruit purity, and a full-bodied, opulent finish. It requires immediate consumption as these wines do not last. Their least expensive offering, the 1998 La Provençale is a blend of 65% Mourvèdre, 24% Syrah, and 11% Grenache that has been aged 12 months in neutral wood. This medium to dark ruby-colored, Côtes du Rhône-styled effort displays delicious black cherry fruit, smoky notes, and an earthy, middle-weight finish. Drink it over the next 2–3 years as you would an excellent Côtes du Rhône. There are 1,235 cases of the outstanding 1998 Merlot Caldwell Vineyard. A blend of 91% Merlot and 9% Cabernet Sauvignon that achieved 14.5% alcohol, it offers a flamboyant perfume of smoked wood and jammy berry fruit. Seductive, rich, and fruity, it is a treat to drink. This wine will have many admirers for its hedonistic display of fruit and spicy wood presented in a low-acid style. Drink it over the next 5–7 years.

The dark ruby/purple-colored 1998 Syrah (3% Viognier is included in the blend) reveals heady alcohol (14.9%) in its expressive aromas and flavors of camphor, honeysuckle, blackberry, and smoke. Aged 22 months in French oak, this delicious wine exhibits soft tannin as well as plush, fat, round, generous flavors. It is another example of how well Syrah fared in the uneven 1998 vintage. Drink it over the next 5–7 years. The limited production (230 cases) 1997 Syrah Cask P-10 emerges from Mt. Veeder's Paras Vineyard. This 100% Syrah is a dense, powerful, muscular-styled effort that will benefit from another 6–12 months of bottle age. Its opaque black/purple color is accompanied by a dazzling bouquet of chocolate, creosote, cassis, and blackberries. Deep, full-bodied, muscular, and rich, with superb balance between its fruit, tannin, acidity, and alcohol, it will drink well for 10–15 years.

Jade Mountain's 1997s may be their most impressive portfolio of wines to date. Readers looking for immediately appealing, complex, supple reds should check out the 1997 Côte du Soleil and 1997 La Provençale (a blend of Mourvèdre, Syrah, and Grenache). The 1997 Côte du Soleil could be called a California-inspired Côtes du Rhône. The healthy dark ruby color is followed by berry, kirsch, peppery, and sweet fruit aromas, a lush, supple texture, good glycerin, and a heady finish. An attractive, powerful (14.5% alcohol) wine, it is meant for hedonists. Drink it over the next 2–3 years. The 1997 La Provençale (also 14.5% alcohol) reveals blackberry and cassis notes in the nose, as well as a more saturated ruby color. Gorgeously pure black fruits, medium to full body, admirable glycerin, and outstanding purity give this offering tremendous appeal. It should drink well for 4–5 years. The 1997 Mourvèdre (from 100-year-old vines planted in Contra Costa's Evangelho Vineyard) is a successful wine for a varietal that can be difficult to grow and vinify. Moderately intense aromas of blackberries, pepper, loamy soil, leather, and a touch of blueberry are enticing. Expansive, rich, fleshy, and complex, this multidimensional, supple-textured wine can be drunk now and over the next 7–8 years.

The following three 1997 Syrahs all tip the scales at 14.5% alcohol. The 1997 Syrah Napa could have a little Viognier blended in given the honeysuckle, peach/apricot nose intermixed with oodles of blackberry/cassis fruit. Fleshy, succulent, open-knit, and delicious, it may not make old bones, but it will be a velvety-textured, plump, fleshy Syrah to enjoy over the next 5–6 years. From a Mt. Veeder vineyard with a 1,200 foot elevation, the 1997 Syrah Paras Vineyard reveals a murky-looking ruby/purple color in addition to more pepper and intense cassis/blackberry fruit. Thicker, jammier, and fuller-bodied, with additional volume and depth, this superb Syrah has low acidity and sweet tannin, but promises to evolve nicely for a decade. There are a number of Syrahs from the famous Lee Hudson Vineyard in Carneros. Jade Mountain's 1997 Syrah Hudson Vineyard is more structured, closed, and tighter-knit than its two siblings. Nevertheless, it reveals deep, weighty black fruit scents and melted asphalt in the bouquet, along with full-bodied, powerful flavors and a hefty finish. Sweet tannin, low acidity, and superb ripeness characterize this full-throttle Syrah. It will benefit from 6–8 months of bottle age and can be drunk over the following 12+ years.

The 1997 Merlot Paras Vineyard presents an ostentatious, exuberant personality with little in reserve. Dark ruby-colored, this flashy wine offers intense smoky, espresso, sweet cherry/berry aromas, medium to full body, and a low-acid, lush personality. The wine is gorgeous to drink now and over the next 4–5 years, but there is not a great deal of depth behind the sexy display of jammy fruit, oak, and smoke. Seductive! The 1996 Syrah Paras Vineyard reveals smoky bacon fat and cassis aromas. The wine is medium- to full-bodied, lush, nicely textured, expansive, and rich with no hard edges. Drink this seductive Syrah over the next 7–8 years. The 1995 Syrah Mt. Veeder is excellent. It possesses a dense, deep ruby/purple color, followed by a provocative nose of sweet black plums, currants, smoke, and licorice. In the mouth, the wine is ripe, tannic, backward, dense, full-bodied, and pure. This is an excellent, possibly outstanding Syrah that requires 3–4 years of bottle age; it should keep for 15 years.

The 1994 Les Jumeaux (a Cabernet Sauvignon/Mourvèdre/Syrah blend) remains one of my favorite wines from Jade Mountain. It offers an intriguing black cherry, cassis, herb, pepper, spicy component, medium to full body, some tannin, good grip, a savory mouth-feel, and a well-delineated, spicy finish. This wine will continue to improve for another 12–18 months and will keep for 7–8+ years.

JAFFURS (SANTA BARBARA)

1997 Syrah Bien Nacido Vineyard	Santa Barbara	D	89+
1997 Syrah Thompson Vineyard	Santa Barbara	D	90

Stolpman Family Vineyard is one of the large new vineyards coming on line (a percentage of the production will be estate-bottled under its name). This has been a source for high-quality Rhône Ranger grapes such as Roussanne and Syrah, as well as other varietals. The 1997 Syrah Thompson Vineyard (a whopping production of 48 cases) offers a stunning nose of black pepper, blackberries, and floral scents. Dense, rich, and full-bodied, with gorgeously pure fruit, sweet tannin, and unobtrusive acidity, this large but elegant, deep ruby/purple-colored Syrah can be drunk now as well as over the next 10–12 years. What a shame there is not more of it! The 1997 Syrah Bien Nacido Vineyard (49 cases) is more reticent in the nose, but does reveal an impressively saturated dark ruby/purple color, jammy blackberry fruit flavors, more acidity than the Thompson Vineyard, moderate tannin, and a medium- to full-bodied, long finish. It is an excellent, nearly outstanding Syrah to enjoy for 10–12 years.

JONES FAMILY VINEYARD (NAPA)

1998 Cabernet Sauvignon	Napa	EE	90
1997 Cabernet Sauvignon	Napa	EE	94
1996 Cabernet Sauvignon	Napa	D	90+

This wine is the product of a small micro-vinification from a five-acre vineyard on the upper eastern hillsides of Napa Valley. David Abreu, the well-known viticulturist, oversees the vineyard, and acclaimed wine consultant Heidi Barrett makes the wine. The impressive debut release, the 1996 Cabernet Sauvignon, has been followed by two promising efforts. The outstanding 1998 Cabernet Sauvignon (aged in one-third new oak) exhibits a dark ruby/purple color, sweet plum, blackberry, and mineral notes in the moderately intense aromatics, sweet tannin, medium body, and pure fruit. The wine is not massive, but elegant, concentrated, and ideal for drinking over the next 15 years. There were 450 cases produced. The sensational 1997 Cabernet Sauvignon (800 cases produced) is the finest effort yet from the Jones Family. The color is a saturated blue/purple. The nose offers up classic mineral, blueberry, crème de cassis, and subtle toasty oak notes. Full-bodied, with stunning purity, a multilayered palate impression, and an explosive finish, this wine requires 2–3 years of cellaring; it will age nicely for 20–25 years. The first release from this seven-acre vineyard, the 1996 (405 cases) exhibits a dense, dark ruby/purple color, as well as a restrained but promising nose of black currants, blackberries, new oak, and minerals. The wine is sweet, elegant, and medium- to full-bodied, with high tannin and an austere finish. The oak is nicely meshed, and the texture is attractive and chewy. If the tannin softens and its bouquet becomes more forthcoming, this 1996 Cabernet Sauvignon may merit a higher score. Anticipated maturity: now–2014. By the way, this wine improved significantly with exposure to air. The tannin became sweeter and better integrated after 60 minutes of aeration.

The Jones Family is a new star to add to the growing family of impressive Cabernet producers. Because of that, it would be wise for readers to get their names on the winery's mailing list. It may be your only chance to obtain any.

JSJ SIGNATURE SERIES (CALIFORNIA)

1996	Cabernet Sauvignon Buckeye Vineyard	Alexander Valley	D	90
1997	Cabernet Sauvignon Veeder Peak Vineyard	Napa	E	(90–91+)
1996	Cabernet Sauvignon Veeder Peak Vineyard	Napa	E	91+
1996	Merlot Alexander Valley Estate	Alexander Valley	D	89
1996	Merlot Buckeye Vineyard	Alexander Valley	D	88+
1997	Merlot Dry Creek Valley	Dry Creek	D	88
1997	Pinot Noir Arrendell Vineyard	Russian River	E	91

Quantities of these selections personally chosen by Kendall-Jackson's owner, Jess Jackson, range between 250–500 cases. They are packaged in heavy, expensive bottles and are meant to represent the pinnacle of quality that can be obtained from the Kendall-Jackson vineyards.

There are 500 cases of the 1998 Merlot Dry Creek Valley. Produced from a hillside vineyard, this highly extracted, forceful wine was totally closed when I tasted it. It seemed atypically big, full, and rich for a 1998. However, high levels of astringent tannin in the finish raise concerns about the wine's overall balance, but it possesses impressive extract. If the tannin melts away and becomes better integrated, it should merit a score in the upper 80s, possibly 90. However, it will require 2–3 years of cellaring before that question can be resolved. Anticipated maturity: 2004–2016. The 1997 Cabernet Sauvignon Veeder Peak (250 cases) exhibits a terrific nose of scorched earth, minerals, cassis, and blueberries. Full-bodied, powerful, and intensely pure, this brawny, muscular, powerful wine requires 4–5 years of cellaring, but its tannin is sweeter and better integrated than in the 1998 Merlot. Anticipated maturity: 2005–2020. The terrific dark ruby-colored 1997 Pinot Noir Arrendell Vineyard reveals notes of spice, jammy plums, and dried cherry fruit intertwined with toasty oak. A concentrated, medium- to full-bodied, complete, savory, delicious Pinot Noir, it promises to evolve nicely for 5–6 years. There are two single-vineyard Merlots in the JSJ Signature Series. The 1996 Merlot Buckeye Vineyard possesses a dark ruby/purple color, as well as a tightly knit, lavishly oaked nose with black cherry fruit, herbs, white chocolate, and spice scents. Medium- to full-bodied, with good flesh and high tannin, it requires 2–3 more years of cellaring, and should keep for 12–15. The dark ruby/purple-colored 1996 Merlot Alexander Valley Estate offers up a moderately intense, restrained nose of cranberry liqueur intermixed with vanilla and spice. It is a rich, medium- to full-bodied, tannic, backward wine in need of 2–4 years of cellaring. It should age well for 15 years or longer. While it is an impressive offering, it was closed when I tasted it in late September of 1999.

The outstanding 1996 Cabernet Sauvignon Buckeye Vineyard is destined to last for two decades. The wine boasts an opaque purple color and a rich nose of minerals, black currants, and spicy oak. A dense, full-bodied powerhouse, with nicely integrated wood, acidity, and tannin, this firm Cabernet is loaded with extract and richness. The blend contains small quantities of Cabernet Franc and Merlot. Anticipated maturity: now–2020. The opaque purple-colored 1996 Cabernet Sauvignon Veeder Peak offers a Margaux-like nose of spring flower garden scents intermixed with black currants, smoky new oak, and spice. Dense and full-bodied, with outstanding purity and richness, this brawny, muscular, concentrated wine should be at its best between 2003–2022.

JUDD'S HILL (NAPA)

1997 Cabernet Sauvignon Estate	Napa	E	90
1996 Cabernet Sauvignon Estate	Napa	D	88
1994 Cabernet Sauvignon Estate	Napa	C	90

This beautiful estate, tucked high on a hillside overlooking Conn Valley, remains an unheralded as well as underrated source for fine Merlot and Cabernet Sauvignon (the only wines produced). Owners Art and Bunny Finkelstein began Judd's Hill in 1989, after selling their previous winery, Whitehall Lane. Judd's Hill encompasses 14 hillside acres, supplemented by purchases from Knights and Pope Valleys. Their aim is to produce drinkable, supple, yet concentrated wines with both an early appeal and the potential to last for 15 or more years.

The 1997 Cabernet Sauvignon Estate (250-case lot) is a blend of 85% Cabernet Sauvignon and the rest Merlot and Cabernet Franc. It offers a deep purple color, superb concentration and purity, and abundant black currant/cassis fruit intermixed with spice box, cedar, and fruitcake scents. Dried herbs, licorice, and loamy soil notes also make an appearance in this full-bodied, moderately tannic offering. Anticipated maturity: 2004–2017. The dark ruby/purple-colored 1996 Cabernet Sauvignon Estate exhibits a smoky, black currant, dried herb, and licorice-scented nose. Dense, full-bodied, and rich, with excellent concentration and purity, it does not possess the creamy texture and sweet inner mid-palate of the 1997, but it is well made. Anticipated maturity: now–2012. Judd's Hill turned out an outstanding 1994 Cabernet Sauvignon. The wine exhibits a saturated dark ruby/purple color, sweet, ripe, black currant fruit, low acidity, mature tannin, and a well-balanced, flamboyant, succulent, opulent texture with layers of rich fruit nicely married with smoky oak. This hedonistic, forward, Pomerol-styled Cabernet can be drunk now as well as over the next 12–15 years.

ROBERT KEENAN (NAPA)

1998 Cabernet Sauvignon	Napa	D	87
1995 Cabernet Sauvignon Hillside Estate	Napa	D	88
1994 Cabernet Sauvignon Hillside Estate	Napa	D	88
1996 Merlot	Napa	D	88
1997 Merlot Mailbox Vineyard Spring Mountain Reserve	Napa	D	89+
1998 Merlot Reserve	Napa	D	89
1997 Merlot Spring Mountain Estate	Napa	D	86

The Keenan wines are starting to take on more flavor and texture, yet remain fairly priced for their quality level. Saddleback Cellars' renowned wine-maker, Nils Venge, has been brought in to build up the wines. Production remains between 6,000–10,000 cases, although they intend to ultimately produce 14,000 cases. Keenan's 1998 Merlot Reserve (about 35% came from their estate) is excellent and possibly exceptional. A dense plum/cherry color is accompanied by a big, smoky, coffee-scented bouquet revealing abundant berry fruit, low acidity, and a seductive, fleshy, medium- to full-bodied style. This soft, opulent 1998 is already showing exceptionally well. Anticipated maturity: now–2010. The Bordeaux-styled 1998 Cabernet Sauvignon is smooth and round, with aromas and flavors of herbs, earth, and black currants. It has nowhere near the mass and weight of the 1997, but is well balanced and made in a forward, attractive style. Readers should know that 1998 has been deemed by many as a bad vintage for North Coast Cabernet Sauvignon and Merlot, yet many attractive wines have been produced. Anticipated maturity: now–2012.

A wine that may ultimately achieve an outstanding rating is the 1997 Merlot Mailbox Vineyard (430 cases). It exhibits plenty of sweet, toasty oak (much in the Venge style) along with medium- to full-bodied, dense, black cherry/berry flavors, good glycerin, admirable texture, excellent purity, and abundant sweet tannin in the finish. Give it 1–2 years of cellaring, and drink it over the next 15–16 years. Another fine 1997 from Keenan is the 1997 Merlot Spring Mountain Estate. Rich and dense, it exhibits structure, volume, and flavor. While not a superstar, it is a very good effort that should drink nicely for a decade or more. The 1996 Merlot is sweet and rich, with smoky, chocolaty, black cherry fruit, good density, and a clean, long, tannic finish. It should drink well for 10 years.

The 1995 Cabernet Sauvignon Hillside Estate displays the winery's softer, more velvety-textured style of wine without the tough overlay of tannin and compact mid-palate. The 1995 possesses a deep ruby/purple color, spicy, ripe fruit, power and intensity, and moderate tannin in the finish. While it may never merit an exceptional rating, the wine should score in the upper 80s after bottling. The 1994 Cabernet Sauvignon Hillside Estate exhibits a dark ruby/purple color, followed by a sweet, black cherry, earthy, mineral-scented nose, and a fleshy mid-palate with depth and ripe fruit. Some rough tannin springs up in the finish. This wine will benefit from 4–5 years of cellaring and keep for up to 15.

KENDALL-JACKSON (CALIFORNIA)

1997	Cabernet Sauvignon Buckeye Vineyard	Alexander Valley	E	88
1998	Cabernet Sauvignon Buckeye Vineyard Great Estates	Alexander Valley	E	91
1997	Cabernet Sauvignon Great Estates	Alexander Valley	D	90
1998	Cabernet Sauvignon Great Estates	Napa	D	88
1997	Cabernet Sauvignon Great Estates	Napa	D	90
1997	Cabernet Sauvignon Stature	Napa	EE	92
1999	Chardonnay Camelot Vineyard Great Estates	Santa Maria	D	89
1999	Chardonnay Clark Vineyard Great Estates	Monterey	D	90
1999	Chardonnay Durell Vineyard Great Estates	Sonoma	D	91
1999	Chardonnay Grand Reserve	California	C	89
1999	Chardonnay Great Estates	Monterey	D	88
1999	Chardonnay Great Estates	Sonoma Coast	D	88
1999	Chardonnay Stature	Santa Maria	D	89
1998	Merlot Buckeye Vineyard Great Estates	Alexander Valley	D	90
1998	Merlot Great Estates	Sonoma	D	88
1998	Pinot Noir Arrendell Vineyard Stature	Russian River	D	89
1997	Syrah Grand Reserve	California	C	87

There are now five levels to the enormous Kendall-Jackson hierarchy. At the bottom, or least expensive level, are the Collage wines, followed by the Vintner's Reserve offerings. Moving up the ladder in both price and quality are the Grand Reserve wines as well as the two newest levels of the hierarchy, Great Estates and the wines at the pinnacle called Stature. I have reviewed only the wines that merited 88 points or more. Among the single-vineyard offerings, the 1997 Cabernet Sauvignon Buckeye Vineyard (3,410 cases) is excellent. This wine sees 50% new oak and was closed when I tasted it in October 1999. It exhibits a dark ruby/purple color, abundant spicy oak, medium body, and moderate tannin. This Cabernet Sauvignon cuts a structured, rich mouth-feel, with tobacco, cassis, and licorice characteristics. Give it 3–4 years of cellaring; it should last for 15+ years.

At the Grand Reserve level, the 1999 Chardonnay Grand Reserve (62,190 cases) is a substantial wine that is 100% barrel-fermented, mostly in French oak. It possesses good underlying acidity as well as abundant quantities of tangerine, orange marmalade, honeysuckle, and tropical fruit notes. The oak character is more prominent than in the Vintner's Reserve, but this is a medium- to full-bodied, rich Chardonnay to drink over the next several years.

The 1997 Syrah Grand Reserve could turn out to be excellent given its saturated ruby/purple color, attractive, moderately intense crème de cassis and blackberry-scented nose, and fruity, medium-bodied flavors. Soft, with low acidity and spicy, peppery notes in the background, it should age nicely for 4–5 years.

Under the Great Estates moniker, Kendall-Jackson is making appellation-based wines such as the 1999 Chardonnay Great Estates Camelot Vineyard (15,350 cases). It is a fleshy, medium- to full-bodied, well-delineated Chardonnay loaded with tropical fruits infused with subtle, smoky oak. Consume it over the next 2–3 years. The 1999 Chardonnay Great Estates Monterey (4,160 cases aged primarily in French oak) reveals mineral, citrus, and lemon-lime characteristics to its cooler climate fruit profile. Medium-bodied as well as nicely textured, it should drink well for 4–5 years. Even better is the outstanding 1999 Chardonnay Clark Vineyard Great Estates. There are 1,500 cases of this low-acid, fleshy, full-bodied Chardonnay. Offering up notes of passion fruit, apricot, peach, and honeysuckle, it is rich and ostentatious. Drink it over the next 2–3 years. There is also a Sonoma Coast Great Estates Chardonnay, much of which emerges from three sources, Sangiacomo, Three Sisters, and Durell. The 1999 Chardonnay Great Estates Sonoma Coast (3,715 cases) looks to be better. The wine's bouquet exhibits lemon blossom and ripe, tropical fruit scents intermixed with a liquid minerality. It possesses medium to full body, an excellent texture, and a long finish. The superb 1999 Chardonnay Durell Vineyard Great Estates displays more earth and mineral characteristics in its buttered caramel, pineapple, and custard-filled aromas and flavors. Full-bodied and rich, with terrific texture and a long finish, it should drink well for 3–4 years.

Under the Great Estates, there are a Pinot Noir from Monterey, Merlots from Sonoma and Alexander Valley's Buckeye Vineyard, and Cabernet Sauvignons from Napa as well as Alexander Valley's Buckeye Vineyard. All of them are exceptionally well-made wines, with the production ranging from a high of 5,000 cases for the Napa bottling of Cabernet, to a low of 245 cases for the Cabernet Sauvignon Buckeye Vineyard. Potentially outstanding, the dark ruby/purple-colored 1998 Merlot Great Estates Sonoma exhibits abundant quantities of mocha, black cherry, and currant fruit with smoke and fennel in the background. Textured, rich, pure as well as medium- to full-bodied, this wine should drink well for up to a decade. The dense purple-colored 1998 Merlot Great Estates Buckeye Vineyard is superb. From a vineyard planted at 2,500 feet with very poor soils (yields range between 1.5–2.5 tons of fruit per acre), this formidably endowed Merlot possesses aromas and flavors of roasted coffee, black fruits, iron, and smoke. Full-bodied, chewy, and muscular, yet accessible, it should drink well for 10–15 years. Another outstanding effort, the 1997 Cabernet Sauvignon Great Estates Napa (5,000 cases) exhibits copious quantities of pure black currant fruit mixed with cedar, smoke, and spice box. It is full-bodied, opulent, rich, and best drunk over the next 12–15 years. Although made in a lighter, leaner, less concentrated style, the 1998 Cabernet Sauvignon Great Estates Napa offers blueberry, camphor, and black currant fruit, medium body, and Bordeaux-like weight. It should drink well for up to a decade. There are 4,500 cases of the outstanding 1997 Cabernet Sauvignon Great Estates Alexander Valley. With abundant amounts of Asian spices, minerals, black cherries, and cassis as well as admirable structure, this fruit-dominated, full-bodied, large-scaled, opulent wine should drink well for 15+ years. Another superb effort is the 1998 Cabernet Sauvignon Great Estates Buckeye Vineyard. The most tannic and backward of these wines, it exhibits a saturated ruby/purple color as well as tobacco-tinged, cassis fruit mixed with new oak and minerals. It is large-scaled, highly extracted, and while drinkable now, promises to evolve for 12–15 years.

There are currently four wines in the Stature series. Production ranges from a low of 89 cases for the 1998 Pinot Noir Arrendell Vineyard to 3,073 cases for the 1997 Napa Cabernet Sauvignon. The 1999 Chardonnay Stature Santa Maria reveals more acidity and smokiness, without the voluptuous fatness possessed by the 1998. It is certainly fine, with plenty of tropical fruit and nicely integrated wood. Consume it over the next 3–4 years. The dark plum-colored 1998 Pinot Noir Arrendell Vineyard Stature displays smoky tomato and cherry notes in the nose, medium body, tart acidity in mid-palate, but good fruit and depth in the finish. One of the most beautiful wines in the Stature series is the impressive 1997 Cabernet Sauvignon Stature. Sourced from vineyards such as Veeder Peak and Andy Beckstoffer's To-Kalon Vineyard, it offers up crème de cassis aromas intermixed with new saddle leather, vanilla, spice box, and minerals. Full-bodied, rich, and seamless, this voluptuously textured, thick, juicy Cabernet Sauvignon can be drunk now or cellared for up to two decades.

KISTLER VINEYARDS (SONOMA)

1997 Chardonnay Camp Meeting Ridge	Sonoma Coast	E	95
1999 Chardonnay Cuvée Cathleen	Sonoma	E	97
1998 Chardonnay Cuvée Cathleen	Sonoma Coast	E	96
1997 Chardonnay Cuvée Cathleen	Sonoma County	E	(94–96)
1999 Chardonnay Durell Vineyard	Sonoma Valley	E	94
1998 Chardonnay Durell Vineyard	Sonoma Valley	E	91
1997 Chardonnay Durell Vineyard	Sonoma Valley	E	91
1999 Chardonnay Dutton Ranch	Russian River	E	90
1998 Chardonnay Dutton Ranch	Russian River	E	90
1997 Chardonnay Dutton Ranch	Russian River	E	94
1999 Chardonnay Hudson E-Block	Carneros	E	94
1998 Chardonnay Hudson Vineyard	Carneros	E	95
1997 Chardonnay Hudson Vineyard	Carneros	E	95
1999 Chardonnay Hyde Vineyard	Carneros	E	93
1998 Chardonnay Hyde Vineyard	Carneros	E	94
1999 Chardonnay Kistler Vineyard	Sonoma Valley	E	95
1998 Chardonnay Kistler Vineyard	Sonoma Valley	E	95
1997 Chardonnay Kistler Vineyard	Sonoma	E	93
1999 Chardonnay McCrea Vineyard	Sonoma Mountain	E	93
1998 Chardonnay McCrea Vineyard	Sonoma Mountain	E	92
1997 Chardonnay McCrea Vineyard	Sonoma Mountain	E	93
1999 Chardonnay Vine Hill Vineyard	Russian River	E	96
1998 Chardonnay Vine Hill Road Vineyard	Russian River	E	96
1997 Chardonnay Vine Hill Road Vineyard	Russian River	E	91
1998 Pinot Noir Camp Meeting Ridge	Sonoma Coast	E	(92–95)
1997 Pinot Noir Camp Meeting Ridge	Sonoma Coast	E	(91–94)
1996 Pinot Noir Camp Meeting Ridge	Sonoma Coast	E	92
1995 Pinot Noir Camp Meeting Ridge	Sonoma Coast	E	93+
1994 Pinot Noir Camp Meeting Ridge	Sonoma Coast	E	88
1999 Pinot Noir Cuvée Catherine	Russian River	E	(96–98)
1997 Pinot Noir Cuvée Catherine	Russian River	E	(95–97)
1996 Pinot Noir Cuvée Catherine	Russian River	E	96
1995 Pinot Noir Cuvée Catherine	Russian River	E	94
1994 Pinot Noir Cuvée Catherine	Russian River	E	92
1999 Pinot Noir Hirsch Vineyard	Sonoma Coast	E	(94–96)

1998	Pinot Noir Hirsch Vineyard	Sonoma Coast	E	(93–95)
1997	Pinot Noir Hirsch Vineyard	Sonoma Coast	E	(90–93)
1996	Pinot Noir Hirsch Vineyard	Sonoma Coast	E	89
1995	Pinot Noir Hirsch Vineyard	Sonoma Coast	E	92+
1994	Pinot Noir Hirsch Vineyard	Sonoma Coast	E	92
1999	Pinot Noir Kistler Vineyard	Russian River	E	(93–95)
1998	Pinot Noir Kistler Vineyard	Russian River	E	(93–96)
1997	Pinot Noir Kistler Vineyard	Russian River	E	(94–96)
1996	Pinot Noir Kistler Vineyard	Russian River	E	94
1998	Pinot Noir Kistler Cuvée Catherine	Russian River	E	(95–97)
1999	Pinot Noir Occidental Cuvée Elizabeth	Sonoma Coast	E	(98–100)
1998	Pinot Noir Occidental Cuvée Elizabeth	Sonoma Coast	E	(96–98)
1994	Pinot Noir Vine Hill	Sonoma	E	91

I do not know what to add to the accolades I have given over the last decade to Steve Kistler and his assistant, Mark Bixler. Every year the wines are brilliant. Given the breadth of Chardonnays and Pinot Noirs produced by Steve Kistler, he is the undeniable master of these two varietals in California. In short, his Chardonnays and Pinot Noirs are wines of extraordinary intensity, complexity, and richness. Moreover, they should prove to be amazingly age-worthy. I am more and more convinced that Kistler, along with others (notably Helen Turley and her husband, John Wetlaufer, as well as Tom Rochioli), is producing historic Chardonnays and Pinot Noirs that may one day be considered to have rewritten the definition of greatness for these varietals. Steve Kistler believes his 1999s may be the finest wines he has ever made. There have been so many brilliant wines that it is hard to say at this early stage if the 1999s will turn out better. The malolactic fermentations were the slowest he has ever had, and of course the crop was relatively small, much like 1998. Because of the cool growing season, acids were higher than normal, and, combined with the slow malolactics, it does seem the *terroir* characteristics are more vivid in 1999. In any event, these are the wines of a shy genius who obviously prefers to stay out of the limelight. All of the following notes for the 1999s are from tank samples, as the wines have been racked from wood and are in settling tanks prior to being bottled without filtration.

The 1999 Chardonnay McCrea Vineyard (2,000 cases) exhibits an intense liquid minerality, notes of white currants, a full-bodied personality with citrus oils and white flowers, and a remarkably well-delineated finish. Still tightly knit but concentrated and extremely Burgundian, it needs a couple of years of aging and should last for a decade. The softer 1999 Chardonnay Dutton Ranch (2,000 cases) is made in a more typical California style. Orange marmalade, pineapple, and mango aromas and flavors are apparent in this full-bodied, rich, smoky Chardonnay. While exceptional, it lacks the minerality and definition of Kistler's other offerings. It will have 4–6 years of ageability. Perhaps the best Chardonnay I ever tasted from the Durell Vineyard is the 1999. An intensely steely effort, this big, weighty, gorgeously delineated wine displays awesome concentration, fabulous definition, and huge flavors of roasted hazelnuts, lemon blossom, and liquid minerals. As the wine sits in the glass, it comes across as a grand cru Chablis on steroids. Concentrated as well as long, this should be a fascinating Chardonnay to follow as it has the potential to last for up to a decade. Extremely different is the 1999 Chardonnay Hyde Vineyard (1,000 cases). This wine shows the vintage's good, zesty acidity, a white peach, lemon custard, tangerine-flavored palate, full body, and superb purity and length. In a grouping of prodigious Chardonnays, this is exceptional. Look for it to drink well for 5–6 years. Another awesome effort is the 1999 Chardonnay Vine Hill Vineyard. There are 2,000 cases produced from this Russian River vineyard surrounding the Kistler winery. It exhibits telltale minerality as well as a gorgeous nose of white fruits, citrus oils, nuts, minerals, smoke, and butter. With fabulous intensity, purity, and an expansive, multilayered mid-palate, this powerful, impeccably balanced, restrained Chardonnay unfolds on the palate. This will be another 1999 that will have a long and compelling evolution. Back in the big, smoky, tropical fruit, roasted hazelnut, pedal-to-the-metal, in-your-face style is the 1999 Chardonnay Kistler Vineyard (2,000 cases). This wine has terrific tropical fruit flavors infused with smoke and mineral. Again, it is well detailed, pure, concentrated, and long. There are 500 cases of the 1999 Cuvée Cathleen, a selection from the Kistler and Vine Hill Vineyards. It is a prodigious Chardonnay that may merit a perfect rating. The wine has layers of concentrated fruit, but it is neither heavy nor over the top. Aromas and flavors of ripe oranges, passion fruit, and pineapple, infused with hazelnut oil and floral scents (acacia) can be found in this staggering wine; it should evolve effortlessly for 5–10 years. I can't wait to get my hands on (make that my lips around) a bottle of this stuff. The vineyard that Helen Turley made famous, the E-Block of Hudson Vineyard, has produced a flamboyant, ostentatious, full-bodied, dense 1999 Chardonnay (only 250 cases) with exotic notes in its leesy, scorched earth, smoky, tropical fruit characteristics. This 19-year-old vineyard consistently turns out terrific Chardonnay fruit. These Chardonnays justify their differentiation by the winery (something that is often questionable with other wineries that designate the vineyard of many wines). They are fermented with both indigenous and cultured yeasts, given extensive lees stirring and contact, and bottled unfiltered after full malolactic fermentation. The percentage of new French oak varies, usually less than 50%.

The 1998 Chardonnay McCrea Vineyard (made from an old, low-producing Wente clone) exhibits a striking minerality in its lemony, buttery, citrusy style. Full-bodied and complex, it is reminiscent of a grand cru Chassagne-Montrachet. The wine, which becomes more complex in the glass, is powerful, rich, concentrated, and well balanced. It should drink well for 5–7 years. The 1998 Chardonnay Dutton Ranch is smoky, with copious quantities of exotic tropical fruits jumping from the glass. Pineapple, mango, and passion fruits immediately come to mind when tasting this full-bodied, lusty, in-your-face Chardonnay that should drink well for 4–5 years. One of the tightest and most backward offerings in Kistler's portfolio is the 1998 Chardonnay Durell Vineyard. Always the last to be harvested (because of the extremely cool microclimate), the 1998 possesses considerable force and intensity, with a mineral, citrusy, lemon blossom, orange peel component to its full-bodied richness. It reveals good acidity and power, all of which is harnessed and beautifully balanced. Look for this wine to open with another 12 months of cellaring and drink well for 5–7 years. The sensational 1998 Chardonnay Hyde Vineyard emerges from a block of vines that used to be sold to the Mondavis for their reserve Chardonnay. Roasted hazelnut, espresso, zesty tropical fruit, mineral, and buttery aromas and flavors are accompanied by a full-bodied, powerful, gorgeously pure and well-delineated wine. Made from old Chardonnay vines, it should drink well for 5–7 years, possibly longer. Even richer than the wonderful 1997, the 1998 Chardonnay Kistler Vineyard, made from a vineyard planted with the Mt. Eden clone, is extremely full-bodied, with striking purity, and powerful, concentrated, honeyed flavors with nuances of butter, smoke, roasted nuts, and minerals. The creamy texture is buttressed by good acidity. Toast, gravel, and slate-like richness intermixed with fruit make this a compelling, intensely flavored Chardonnay. It should drink well for 5–7 years, perhaps longer. Readers looking for an ostentatious blockbuster should check out Kistler's 1998 Chardonnay Hudson Vineyard. This offering comes from the Hudson E-Block vineyard that was made famous by Helen Turley and John Wetlaufer's Marcassin bottlings. Smoky, roasted hazelnut scents give this a garish, flamboyant, Meursault premier cru–like character. Big and full-bodied, with considerable glycerin, high alcohol, and terrific fruit richness, this thick, juicy, mouth-staining Chardonnay will impress with its power and brash display of fruit, alcohol, and glycerin. It should drink well for 5–6 years.

The last two 1998 Chardonnays represent an evolution in style. They possess all the power and concentration of Steve Kistler's most successful wines, but they also have a certain restraint allied with extraordinary complexity and elegance that a few years ago would have been found only in the finest Burgundy grand crus. The 1998 Chardonnay Cuvée Cathleen is a spectacularly beautiful, well-delineated effort with everything hitting the olfactory senses and palate in measured doses. However, the overall impression is one of stunning concentration, perfect harmony, fabulous density and richness, and that layered, intense mid-palate and length that only great wines possess. It needs a year or more of cellaring and should evolve in an intriguing manner for up to a decade. The 1998 Chardonnay Vine Hill Road Vineyard is profound. While not as boisterous a blockbuster as the Hudson Vineyard or as showy or rich as the Hyde Vineyard, it is a spectacular Chardonnay. Amazingly, a meager 23 tons of fruit emerged from this 15-acre vineyard, and this wine represents the essence of Chardonnay from Vine Hill. The wine has yet to reveal all of its characteristics, but its extraordinary precision, intense mouth-feel, and glorious display of pure fruit that come across in a full-bodied, perfectly balanced fashion make for a riveting drinking experience. It will evolve along the same lines as the Cuvée Cathleen (being tight but obviously loaded with potential) for another year or two, and then explode over the following 2–4 years. It may last for more than a decade, and evolve much like a great grand cru white Burgundy.

The vintage's high yields do not appear to have had an impact on the 1997 Chardonnays' level of concentration and intensity. Moreover, the 1997s possess an atypical level of tangy, underlying acidity, giving the wines a wonderful vibrancy. Additionally, their splendid aromatics are matched only by the 1995's. I tasted eight Chardonnays. While they share a certain similarity, they possess distinctive attributes that justify the winery's decision to differentiate them. All are fermented with both indigenous and commercial yeasts, given extensive stirring during prolonged contact with the lees, and bottled unfiltered after full malolactic fermentation. The percentage of new French oak varies, with higher percentages for the Camp Meeting Ridge, Hudson, and Cuvée Cathleen offerings. The 1997 Chardonnay McCrea Vineyard, made from an old Wente clone, personifies this varietal's lemony, buttery, citrusy, mineral style. It offers medium to full body, splendid concentration, considerable richness and texture on the mid-palate, and gorgeous elegance, purity, and overall balance. Tangy acidity gives the wine admirable freshness. It should age well for 5–7 years. The 1997 Chardonnay Vine Hill Road Vineyard (from both Hyde and Dijon Burgundy clones) is a more restrained wine with noticeably higher acidity. It reveals suggestions of cold steel, wet stones, and that liquid minerality found in certain Chardonnays. Medium- to full-bodied, with excellent depth, and more austerity and backwardness than its siblings, it will benefit from another year of cellaring and keep for 6–7 years. Readers looking for a Chardonnay that offers the tropical fruit spectrum, without completely abandoning the complex mineral character, will be pleased with the 1997 Chardonnay Durell Vineyard. The poor vigor of these rocky soils, combined with such clones as Hyde, has resulted in a wine with zesty acidity, medium to full body, outstanding ripeness and purity, and loads of orange blossom/lemony fruit in addition to hints of peach and pineapple. This 1997 requires 1–2 years of cellaring and should have an unusually long life of 8–10 years. The more flamboyant, Burgundy-styled 1997 Chardonnay Dutton Ranch displays a roasted hazelnut, sweet, rich, tropical fruit–scented nose, full body, and laser-like clarity to its component parts. Rich and intense, it is similar to a tightly knit Burgundian grand cru. With less minerality yet more of the smoky, leesy, roasted nut characteristics, this wine combines abundant tropical fruit and honeyed citrus. It should be delicious upon release, and keep for 5–7 years.

The 1997 Chardonnay Kistler Vineyard (made from the Mt. Eden clone, which is alleged to be a suitcase clone from Burgundy's Corton-Charlemagne vineyard) is a multidimensional wine with a rich, full-bodied, creamy texture, superb buttery, honeyed fruit, subtle toast, gorgeously rich fruit, white flowers, buttered popcorn, and liquid gravel-like notes. Combining power with finesse, it should drink well young and age for 5–7 years. The dazzling 1997

Chardonnay Camp Meeting Ridge Vineyard is the most explosive, viscous, powerful, and mineral-laden of the Kistler Chardonnays. Like its siblings, it surpasses 14% alcohol, but that is well hidden by the wine's outstanding extract and layered personality. A lush, leesy complexity emerges, but this is an extremely rich, highly concentrated, stunning Chardonnay with prodigious fruit extraction in addition to astonishing length. This is the finest Camp Meeting Ridge Chardonnay to date. Another leesy, smoky, Burgundy-styled, exotic offering is the 1997 Chardonnay Hudson Vineyard. Kistler's effort possesses a Meursault-like, buttery character with gobs of tropical fruit and glycerin, yet firm buttressing acidity. My instincts suggest it will be the most forward of these Chardonnays, as well as the shortest-lived (4–5 years). After being blown away by so many sensational Chardonnays, it is difficult to find the adjectives and superlatives to describe the 1997 Chardonnay Cuvée Cathleen. This offering is produced from a selection of barrels that Steve Kistler and Mark Bixler believe to be the richest and most complete. Negligibly better than the other brilliant *cuvées*, it possesses exceptional richness, length, and intensity. Layers of fruit, smoky, buttery popcorn, tropical fruit, and mineral scents soar from the glass, and are exceptionally intense and well balanced. This terrific, full-bodied effort should age for 8–10 years.

Steve Kistler and Mark Bixler are justifiably proud of what they have achieved with Chardonnay, but what really turns them on is their accomplishments with Pinot Noir, which may be the greatest Pinot Noirs being made in the New World. There are 250 cases of the 1999 Pinot Noir Hirsch Vineyard. It possesses a dense ruby/purple color as well as a knockout nose of blackberries infused with smoke, mineral, earth, and floral scents. As the wine sits in the glass, add cherries and pepper to the complex concoction of aromas and flavors. The wine is full-bodied as well as spectacularly concentrated, yet exhibits a youthful vibrancy and good underlying acidity. These wines are all made from destemmed Pinot Noir, and are bottled unfined and unfiltered after 12 months of 100% new-oak aging. Look for the 1999 Hirsch Vineyard to age well for at least a decade. Also profound, the 1999 Pinot Noir Kistler Vineyard exhibits floral, black raspberry, berry, and earth notes. The wine is strikingly rich, with a velvety texture underpinned by good acidity, full body as well as superb density, purity, and equilibrium. This magnificent Pinot Noir should also age for a decade. The 1999 Pinot Noir Cuvée Catherine, a selection of the best barrels from the Kistler Vineyard, displays a bouquet of roasted meats, earth, truffle, blackberry, raspberry, and smoky cherry fruit. Full body, an unctuous texture, and terrific acidity define this large-scaled effort. A monumental Pinot Noir that has to be tasted to be believed, it should hit its prime in about 3–4 years and last for 12–15, if not longer. Lastly, there are 150 cases of the dense purple-colored 1999 Pinot Noir Occidental Vineyard Cuvée Elizabeth. Blueberry and boysenberry liqueur infused with minerals and violets make for dazzling olfactory fireworks. On the palate, the wine is sumptuous yet remarkably fresh and lively. The wine has incredible concentration, purity, and overall equilibrium. Anticipated maturity: now–2012.

The dark ruby/purple-colored 1998 Pinot Noir Hirsch Vineyard (150 cases) has tamed some of the ferocious tannin this offering frequently exhibits. Rich, pure, and deep, with abundant quantities of black cherry fruit, spice, and pepper, this full-bodied Pinot Noir needs 4–5 years of cellaring and should keep for 10–15 years. The dark ruby-colored 1998 Pinot Noir Camp Meeting Ridge Vineyard's (100 cases) smell is akin to a top vintage of Grands-Echezeaux or Richebourg. Notes of black raspberries, blackberries, flowers, and minerals jump from the glass. While it does not have as much power as the Hirsch Vineyard, it reveals a velvety sweetness and unmistakable individuality and distinctiveness. It will be one of Kistler's more showy efforts. Drinkable already, it promises to last for a decade. There are 500 cases of the super-concentrated, full-bodied, fat, luscious, dark purple-colored 1998 Pinot Noir Kistler Vineyard. Made from the Calera clone, it offers a juicy, black cherry, berry, earth, mineral, and spice-scented nose. In the mouth, beef blood and black fruits are present, along with copious fat, glycerin, and moderate tannin. A sumptuous Pinot Noir, it will be fascinating to follow over the next decade or more.

The 250-case lot of 1998 Pinot Noir Kistler Vineyard Cuvée Catherine and 50-case lot of 1998 Pinot Noir Occidental Vineyard Cuvée Elizabeth are, along with the Marcassin Vineyard Pinot Noir, the finest Pinot Noirs I have tasted from California. The dense ruby/purple-colored 1998 Pinot Noir Kistler Vineyard Cuvée Catherine displays a spectacular floral, black raspberry, and cherry-scented nose. Compelling fruit purity offers jammy cherry, strawberry, and smoky aromas with hints of violets (or is it lilacs?). Full body, fine underlying acidity, and sweet tannin make for a sumptuous wine. Anticipated maturity: now–2012. There are only a measly 50 cases of the 1998 Pinot Noir Occidental Vineyard Cuvée Elizabeth, so the tasting notes are brief. It is an exceptional wine that represents the essence of Pinot Noir. If any readers latch onto a bottle or two, let me know.

The opaque black/purple-colored 1997 Pinot Noir Hirsch Vineyard looks more like Syrah than Pinot Noir. However, the nose offers up aromas of blackberries, cherries, and smoke intermixed with toast, roasted herbs, and meat. Medium- to full-bodied, with light to moderate tannin and an exuberant style with firm acidity, this is a classic. Anticipated maturity: now–2014. The 1997 Pinot Noir Camp Meeting Ridge Vineyard exhibits a dark ruby/purple color and a more feminine, less muscular personality with plenty of sweet black raspberry and cherry fruit. A softer, more luscious style of Pinot Noir, it will provide more flattering drinking than the Hirsch. The wine is extremely expansive, with sweet tannin, adequate acidity, and admirable staying power. Anticipated maturity: now–2010.

Two of the most spectacular Pinot Noirs I have ever tasted are Kistler's 1997 Kistler Vineyard and 1997 Cuvée Catherine. The 1997 Pinot Noir Kistler Vineyard (500 cases) is made from the Dijon clone 777 and two California clones, Pommard and Calera. It boasts a dense, saturated dark ruby/purple color, as well as an exceptionally sweet nose of roasted herbs and black cherry jam intermixed with raspberries, truffles, and toasty oak. Sweet and expansive, this full-bodied wine possesses fabulous concentration and purity, a grand cru–like level of potential complexity, and a 30+-second finish. It must be tasted to be believed. Look for this wine to be drinkable upon release, and last for at least a decade. There are approximately 250 cases of the 1997 Pinot Noir Cuvée Catherine. Like its siblings, it has over 14% alcohol, but that is totally obscured by the wine's sensational concentration, extract, and overall equilibrium. A dense ruby/purple-colored, full-bodied Pinot Noir, it offers up aromas of blackberries, raspberries, and cherry liqueur intermixed with licorice, smoke, and meat. Chewy yet not heavy, this wine does reveal some tannin, but it is largely hidden by the wine's fruit, glycerin, and extract. Wow, what an amazing performance!

The two 1996 Pinot Noirs I tasted are remarkable wines. The 1996 Pinot Noir Kistler Vineyard exhibits a Vosne-Romaneé/Richebourg-like violet, black cherry, and smoky-scented nose of considerable intensity. Full-bodied, with superb richness, admirable delineation, a lush, concentrated mid-palate, and black cherry, earthy notes in the spicy finish, this is another impressive, super-concentrated Pinot Noir with both complexity and equilibrium. It should drink well for a decade. The 1996 Pinot Noir Cuvée Catherine, a blend of fruit from the Sonoma Coast and Kistler Vineyard, is another thrilling, sumptuously styled Pinot. The color is a healthy saturated ruby/purple. The wine is spectacularly rich and extremely full-bodied, with floral (violets and lilacs) scents intertwined with cherry jam, over-ripe strawberries, and smoke. With terrific purity and a multilayered texture, this, like the other Kistler Pinot Noirs, is a tour de force! Anticipated maturity: now–2010.

The dense ruby-colored 1996 Pinot Noir Camp Meeting Ridge Vineyard (150 cases) is a fruit bomb, offering copious quantities of lush black fruits intermixed with underbrush, minerals, and spice. Gorgeously proportioned, medium- to full-bodied, with well-integrated tannin and acidity, its vibrancy, purity, and liveliness are commendable. This wine should drink well young and keep for a decade. The 1996 Pinot Noir Hirsch Vineyard (150 cases) requires 3–5 years of cellaring. It is a macho, muscular, tannic wine with meaty, beefy aromas and flavors, and black cherry fruit intertwined with an earthy *terroir* characteristic. However, the tannins are elevated, and the wine in need of cellaring. Because of that, it is more angular and austere than the other *cuvées*.

Kistler's impressive Pinot Noir portfolio was launched with the 1994s. The 1995 Pinot Noirs appear to be as good as the impressive 1994s. The 1995 Pinot Noir Hirsch Vineyard exhibits an opaque ruby color, a beefy, black fruit, spicy, earthy-scented nose, full body, plenty of tannin, and admirable intensity and richness. The wine needs 1–2 years of cellaring, but it promises to keep for a decade. Only 250 cases were produced from this Sonoma Coast vineyard. The 1995 Pinot Noir Camp Meeting Ridge Vineyard (also 250 cases) is a dense, Côte de Nuits–like wine with gobs of sweet black fruits, earth, and underbrush. Full-bodied and powerful, with more tannin and structure than the Hirsch *cuvée*, this is another impressive Sonoma Coast Pinot Noir. The 1995 Pinot Noir Estate Cuvée Catherine is one of the most remarkable Pinot Noirs I have tasted from California. The opaque ruby/purple color and sweet nose of black fruits, smoked meat, and minerals are followed by a wine of exceptional richness, purity, and delineation. It is still backward and closed, but wow, what concentration, intensity, and overall balance.

The 1994 Hirsch Vineyard Pinot Noir boasts a deep ruby/purple color, with a nose of earth, meat, and ripe black fruits. Full-bodied and powerful, this wine could easily be mistaken for a top grand cru from the Côte de Nuits given its richness, aromatic complexity, and flavor dimension. The medium to dark ruby-colored 1994 Camp Meeting Ridge Vineyard Pinot Noir reveals a meaty, cinnamon, cherry-scented bouquet, round, ripe, medium-bodied flavors, and a long, soft, richly fruity finish. The 1994 Pinot Noir Vine Hill Vineyard exhibits a deeper color, a riper, more intense fragrance, superb richness and depth, full body, lovely integrated oak and acidity, and an opulent, silky-textured finish. It could easily pass as a top grand cru from Burgundy's Côte d'Or. It should drink and age well for 5–6 years. The 1994 Pinot Noir Estate Cuvée Catherine exhibits a dense color and gorgeous wild berry aromas ranging from cherries to raspberries. Rich and full-bodied, with layers of creamy fruit and a super texture, this superb Pinot Noir should drink well young yet keep for another 7–8 years.

I am not sure all readers can appreciate it, but these are historic wines, and have been for some time. What is remarkable about Steve Kistler and Mark Bixler is that they just keep pushing the envelope and improving on what is already an enviable record of achievement.

KONGSGAARD (NAPA)

1998	Arietta	Napa	EE	92
1997	Arietta	Napa	EE	91
1999	Arietta Merlot	Napa	EE	92
1998	Arietta Merlot	Napa	EE	90+
1999	Chardonnay	Napa	EE	93
1997	Merlot	Napa	EE	90
1999	Roussanne/Viognier	Napa	EE	93
1999	Syrah Hudson Vineyard	Napa	EE	(92-94+)
1998	Syrah Hudson Vineyard	Napa	EE	92+

John Kongsgaard's philosophy of winemaking is about as natural as practiced anywhere in the world. It involves harvesting fruit from low-yielding vines, picking it ultraripe, and utilizing no yeast, bacteria strain, or enzyme in the winemaking. Obviously everything, both whites and reds, flows into the bottle with neither fining nor filtration. What is a little harder to explain is what Kongsgaard calls his "Death and Resurrection" style of winemaking. In short, he encourages the wines to "die on their lees" before they fight back and resurrect themselves. As he says, there is not much that can be done in the winery, and the last bastion of creativity to produce better wines is "extreme viticulture." Whatever he does, it works, because these are some of the most distinctive and individualistic wines produced in California.

The 1999 Chardonnay, with the core part of the blend coming from his family's Stone Crest Vineyard in Coombsville, is even more intense and concentrated than the 1997. It is obviously made from lower yields, as there are only 600 cases. The wine seems to have everything concentrated, not only fruit and extract but also acidity. It is tightly knit but incredibly intense, and, like a great Montrachet, requires decanting for 30–45 minutes before consuming. A light green-gold color is followed by a huge, intense, liquid minerality intermixed with subtle notes of marmalade, caramel, honeysuckle, citrus oil, and hazelnut. There is remarkable vibrancy to this full-bodied, powerful 1999, and the finish lingers for 40+ seconds. It is an amazing Chardonnay that took more than 12 months to ferment dry. Moreover, it was aged in 100% new oak, yet there is virtually no wood detectable in the wine's aromas or flavors. Don't be surprised to see this wine evolve for at least a decade—it's that special.

A new offering to look for is a remarkable blend of 50% Roussanne and 50% Viognier. Given John Kongsgaard's love of opera, its name undoubtedly will be plucked from the music world. My first descriptor was "explosive." The 1999 was aged in neutral oak and reveals an Alsatian-like, petrol note in the bouquet. Unctuously textured, decadent, and lavishly rich as well as delineated and elegant, it is close to being over the top. Although a contradiction, it is a marvelously complex, intense, dry, full-bodied white that should drink well for 3–4 years.

Readers looking for a California Syrah that has the structure of a Hermitage might do well to consider Kongsgaard's offerings. They are the antithesis of the big, delicious fruit bombs made elsewhere that are best drunk in their first 7–10 years of life. There are about 200 cases of the opaque black/purple-colored 1998 Syrah Hudson Vineyard. As John Kongsgaard said, it was made from "stupidly low yields." The wine is tight in the mouth, but reveals tremendous stuffing along with scents of blackberries, licorice, earth, truffles, pepper, and graphite. Massively tannic, but sweet and rich, this wine should enjoy two decades of life. However, one word of caution—either decant it for 60 or so minutes prior to drinking or wait 2–3 years. The 1999 Syrah Hudson Vineyard is more unctuous, with an opaque black/blue/purple color as well as intensely sweet crème de cassis, blackberry, smoke, and hickory barbecue spice aromas as well as flavors. Huge, rich, full-bodied, and massive, it is on a more rapid evolutionary track than the 1998. Anticipated maturity: 2003-2016.

In partnership with auctioneer Fritz Hatten, Kongsgaard produces about 500 cases of Arietta (a Cabernet Franc/Merlot blend representing this winery's answer to Cheval Blanc). The 1998 is a complete, complex wine that tastes like a synthesis between a top-class St.-Emilion and a Napa Valley red. It possesses the complexity of a top Bordeaux allied to the ripeness and richness of California. Its dense ruby/purple color is accompanied by aromas of black fruits, leather, spice box, and flowers. Medium- to full-bodied and pure, with moderate tannin in the finish, it opens with extended airing. (Blueberries became apparent after about 10 minutes.) This wine should drink well for at least 20 years. In 1997, production of the Arietta was about 450 cases. Beethoven was blaring from speakers situated throughout the winery as I tasted this wine. Kongsgaard says the Arietta may have a Beethoven label, but it is Wagnerian in style. A blend of 85% Cabernet Franc and 15% Merlot, it ranks alongside such famed Cabernet Francs as La Jota, Pride Mountain, and the Maya cuvée from Dalla Valle. Aromatic, with scents of black currants, cherries, flowers, leather, and spice, the stunningly rich, full-bodied wine displays both power and elegance. Its sweet tannin, finesse, and suppleness argue for near-term consumption, but it has the length and inner depth to last for 15+ years.

The 1998 Merlot (400 cases of 95% Merlot and 5% Syrah) makes its debut under the Arietta label. It is a tightly knit, structured Merlot (remember the outstanding Merlots fashioned when John Kongsgaard was the wine-maker at Newton?) revealing expressive aromas and flavors of jammy berry fruit intermixed with chocolate. Full-bodied and rich, yet backward, it requires 2–3 years of cellaring and should keep for 15–18 years. The 1999 Arietta Merlot was blended with 10% Syrah. This bouquet exhibits a blueberry, floral note that quickly transforms to creosote, blackberry, and coffee. Crammed with highly extracted flavors, it is an unevolved, superripe, pure, structured 1999 that will need 2–3 years of cellaring; it should age for two decades.

Kongsgaard's 1997 Merlot includes 25% Syrah in the blend. There are 125 cases of this peppery, leathery, blackberry-flavored Merlot. Medium- to full-bodied, with a fleshy mid-section and an aromatic style, this delicious effort promises to last for a decade.

Everything at Kongsgaard is sold through a mailing list.

CHARLES KRUG (NAPA)

1997 Cabernet Sauvignon Slinsen Vineyard	Napa	D	87
1997 Cabernet Sauvignon Vintage Selection	Napa	D	88
1997 Merlot Reserve	Napa	D	90
1997 Reserve Generations	Napa	D	(87–88)

This large operation (the Mondavi family owns over 800 acres in Napa) has a long history. The original winery was built in 1861, but modern-day history began when Cesare Mondavi purchased the property in 1943. After Robert Mondavi left to start his own winery in 1965, Peter Mondavi took sole control of this estate. Peter was one of the first to utilize cold fermentation for white wines as well as sterile bottling. His two sons, who are now in charge, realized that quality must increase. I was pleasantly surprised by Charles Krug's new vintages. The winemaking is in a transitional period, with wines such as Chenin Blanc, Johannisberg Riesling, Gamay, and white Zinfandel eliminated in favor of the so-called Bordeaux varietals (i.e., Cabernet Sauvignon, Merlot, Sauvignon Blanc). In 1997, wine-maker Jack Cole, formerly of S. Anderson, was brought in to continue the upgrade in quality. Investments have been made, particularly in a bevy of smaller fermentation tanks, a Delta crusher, and new oak barrels to replace the old *foudres* used for aging. Additionally, approximately 200 of the original 800 acres have been replanted with better clonal material. All in all, there is enormous potential at Charles Krug, much of it still unrealized. For bargain hunters, there are some values to be found. Some offerings are still lackluster and unexciting (1997 Merlot, 1997 Cabernet Franc, 1997 Pinot Noir), but quality is on the upswing. Shrewd readers looking for fairly priced Napa Valley wines should put the following information to good use.

Charles Krug's more expensive offerings include their proprietary red wine, the 1997 Generations (a blend of 50% Cabernet Sauvignon, 30% Cabernet Franc, and 20% Merlot). A dark plum color is followed by an elegant, sweet, cranberry, black currant, and spicy-scented nose. Medium-bodied, with fine ripeness and purity, a touch of wood, and an easygoing, fleshy finish, this is a stylish, St.-Emilion look-alike. Drink it over the next 7–10 years. The 1997 Cabernet Sauvignon Slinsen Vineyard (100% Cabernet Sauvignon and made in limited quantities of 250 cases) was tasted from barrel. While the goal at Charles Krug is to cut back on fining and filtration, most of these wines will be bottled with some degree of clarification/processing. The long-range goal is to eliminate filtration for the top *cuvées*. Let's hope wine-maker Jack Cole, with the assistance of Peter and Mark Mondavi, can achieve that. The narrowly constructed 1997 Slinsen Vineyard reveals a bit too much tannin, as well as attractive cedary, spice box, black currant fruit. The tannin may be elevated in the finish, but this is still a work in progress. Anticipated maturity: now–2012. The outstanding 1997 Merlot Reserve (100% Merlot from a Carneros vineyard) is the finest Charles Krug effort I have tasted since some of their single-lot Cabernet Sauvignons from the 1974 vintage. The dark ruby/purple-colored 1997 Merlot Reserve exhibits a textbook nose of roasted coffee, jammy berry fruit, and dried herbs. Medium- to full-bodied, succulent, and rich, this is a noteworthy introduction to the upgrade in quality taking place at Charles Krug. Drink it over the next 7–8 years. The 1997 Cabernet Sauvignon Vintage Selection is meant to be the winery's finest Cabernet. Although I caught it in a relatively closed stage, it exhibits potential. The color is a dark ruby/purple. The bouquet offers cigar box, black currant, cedar, spice, and loamy soil scents. This medium- to full-bodied effort displays excellent concentration and moderately high tannin. It should age well for 15–20 years. Anticipated maturity: 2005–2020.

KUNDE (SONOMA)

1997	Cabernet Sauvignon Drummond Vineyard	Sonoma	C	89+
1997	Cabernet Sauvignon Reserve	Sonoma	D	89
1999	Chardonnay	Sonoma	C	88
1999	Chardonnay C. S. Ridge	Sonoma	C	88
1999	Chardonnay Wildwood Vineyard	Sonoma	C	88
1997	Syrah	Sonoma	C	90
1999	Viognier	Sonoma	C	89
1999	Zinfandel	Sonoma	C	(87-88)
1998	Zinfandel Century Vines-Shaw Vineyard	Sonoma	C	90
1997	Zinfandel Century Vines-Shaw Vineyard	Sonoma	C	88
1998	Zinfandel Robusto	Sonoma	D	90
1997	Zinfandel Robusto	Sonoma	D	90

Shrewd wine consumers seeking both quality and value should check out these offerings from one of Sonoma Valley's oldest farming families. The affable Kundes maintain a down-to-earth attitude that is mirrored by their likeable as well as talented wine-maker, David Noyes. As the prices indicate, egos are kept in check. These very good, unfiltered efforts offer consumers authentic aromatic and fruit profiles that are typical of their varietal composition.

Kunde is an outstanding source for rich, fruit-driven, unfiltered Chardonnays that represent excellent values. The 1999 Chardonnay (30,000 cases) is fermented in 60% barrels and 40% tanks. About 30% new oak is utilized. Pure and clean, it offers a ripe peach, pineapple, and tropical fruit–dominated personality with only a hint of oak. The 1999 Chardonnay C. S. Ridge (standing for "chicken shit" as this site was used in the 19th century for dumping turkey manure) is put through 100% malolactic fermentation. Young and unevolved, it reveals abundant quantities of honeysuckle, white peach, and citrus characteristics in its medium- to full-bodied, concentrated personality. I suspect this wine is even better than it was when tasted given the fact that David Noyes said it had an extremely slow fermentation and had not yet begun to settle down. The 1999 Chardonnay Wildwood Vineyard possesses higher acidity as well as alcohol. A high-toned, austere, mineral-dominated effort, it exhibits a crisp personality, excellent concentration, and notes of lemon, grapefruit, white peaches, and wet stones. It should develop into a complex Chardonnay that will age well for 3–4 years. The 1999 Viognier, one of the finest examples of this varietal being produced in California, is available for a realistic price. The crop was tiny, and the wine shows the extra level of concentration achieved as well as an exuberant personality revealing abundant quantities of orange marmalade, honeysuckle, and peach jam characteristics. This thick, juicy Viognier should drink well until 2003.

The opaque black/purple-colored 1997 Cabernet Sauvignon Drummond Vineyard (100 cases produced from a small 3.5 acre parcel of the Wildwood Vineyard) offers a moderately intense bouquet of cassis, plums, and smoky oak. It spent 20 months in 60% new-oak barrels before being bottled unfiltered. A plump, rich, concentrated effort made from 100% Cabernet Sauvignon, it will drink well for a decade. Also opaque black/purple-colored, the 1997 Cabernet Sauvignon Reserve (450 cases selected from the finest Dummond barrels) exhibits aromas and flavors of prunes, licorice, black currants, and creosote. Rich and seamless, with low acidity, excellent concentration, and fine density, this is a sleeper of the vintage. There was no Reserve bottling produced in 1998.

Kunde produces three Zinfandels, a Sonoma estate offering, the Century Vines *cuvée* from the Shaw Vineyard, and their Zinfandel-dominated, late-harvested Robusto, also made from the Shaw Vineyard. The 1999 Zinfandel Sonoma (Petite Sirah, Grenache, and Mourvèdre represent 22% of the blend) possesses a tangy, berry-scented nose, lively acidity, a briery personality, and a straightforward finish. Drink this medium-weight Zinfandel over the next 3–4 years. More interesting is the exceptional 1998 Zinfandel Century Vines-Shaw Vineyard, which includes a touch of Petite Sirah and Alicante Bouchet in the blend. It boasts a dark plum color, full body, and a soft, peppery, spicy personality with toasty oak in the background. Dense, rich, and chewy, it can be enjoyed over the next 3–4 years. It represents a very good effort from the 1998 vintage, a year that has been largely dismissed by those who tend to view quality in black-and-white terms. Another outstanding effort is the 1998 Zinfandel Robusto (500 cases). It has more in common with a big, chewy Italian Amarone than a California Zinfandel. The dark plum color is followed by aromas and flavors of charcoal, melted asphalt, roasted herbs, dried black cherries, and leather. Thick, powerful, and dry, with abundant fruit as well as a muscular, expansive palate, this mouth-filling wine should be drunk during its first 5–7 years of life. It sports a head-spinning 16.4% alcohol.

The 1997 Zinfandel Robusto (15.8% alcohol) is a 100% late-harvested Zinfandel that tastes totally dry. It reveals a melted asphalt, creosote, charcoal-like personality (similar to that found in certain Rhône Valley and Italian wines), in addition to loads of black fruit, pepper, and berries. The alcohol gives the wine a sweet, glycerin-imbued tactile impression. Drink it over the next several years. In addition to the telltale black cherry note, raspberries, licorice, fennel, and spicy oak make an appearance in the impressively endowed 1997 Zinfandel Century Vines-Shaw Vineyard. It is a fleshy, full-bodied, richly layered Zinfandel that comes close to being outstanding. Drink this beauty over the next 5–6 years.

Two other fine efforts from Kunde are their 1997 Syrah *cuvées*. Hopefully, the 1,200 case production of the 1997 Syrah (which includes 10% Viognier) will increase in future vintages. A fine value, this sexy, dense purple-colored Syrah offers a gorgeous nose of blackberry liqueur, pepper, and licorice. Fat and succulent, with low acidity and explosive fruit, this is a consumer friendly fruit bomb that deserves to be drunk over the next 5–6 years.

During a period where most consumers are turned off by arrogant, elitist prices designed for multimillionaires, Kunde's attitude is a breath of fresh air, producing high-quality wines that are faithful to their respective varietal profiles. Moreover, the wines are made by good people who respect the consumer.

Past Glories: 1993 Cabernet Sauvignon Estate Reserve (90)

KUNIN WINES (PASO ROBLES)

1998 Zinfandel Dante Dusi Vineyards	**Paso Robles**	**D**	**89**

An excellent effort from Paso Robles, the 1998 Zinfandel Dante Dusi Vineyards is a dark ruby-colored wine with lusciously ripe blackberry, cherry, cola, earth, and spice aromas. Full-bodied, with low acidity, outstanding purity, and a husky, layered mouth-feel, this impressive Zinfandel (15.4% alcohol) should be drunk over the next 4–5 years.

LA JOTA VINEYARD (NAPA)

1994 Cabernet Franc	**Napa**	**D**	**93**
1999 Cabernet Franc Howell Mountain	**Napa**	**D**	**87**
1998 Cabernet Franc Howell Mountain	**Napa**	**D**	**90**
1997 Cabernet Franc Howell Mountain	**Napa**	**D**	**94**
1996 Cabernet Franc Howell Mountain	**Napa**	**D**	**93**
1995 Cabernet Franc Howell Mountain	**Napa**	**D**	**93**
1994 Cabernet Sauvignon Howell Mountain	**Napa**	**C**	**92**
1997 Cabernet Sauvignon Howell Mountain Select	**Napa**	**D**	**90**

1996 Cabernet Sauvignon Howell Mountain Select	Napa	D	92
1995 Cabernet Sauvignon Howell Mountain Select	Napa	D	91
1994 Cabernet Sauvignon Howell Mountain Select	Napa	C	93
1999 Cabernet Sauvignon 18th Anniversary Release	Napa	E	88?
1998 Cabernet Sauvignon 17th Anniversary Release	Napa	EE	88?
1997 Cabernet Sauvignon 16th Anniversary Release	Napa	EE	93+
1996 Cabernet Sauvignon 15th Anniversary Release	Napa	E	96
1995 Cabernet Sauvignon 14th Anniversary Release	Napa	D	94
1994 Cabernet Sauvignon 13th Anniversary Release	Napa	D	96
1998 Petite Sirah Howell Mountain	Napa	D	89
1997 Petite Sirah Howell Mountain	Napa	D	92
1996 Petite Sirah Howell Mountain	Napa	D	94
1995 Petite Sirah Howell Mountain	Napa	D	92
1994 Petite Sirah Howell Mountain	Napa	D	97

In the cool, upper elevations of Howell Mountain, former owners (the winery was sold in 2000) Joan and Bill Smith struggled in 1998 and 1999 to get their fruit as ripe as they did during much of the nineties. This is evident when tasting through their 1998s and 1999s, which possess less volume, mass, and sweetness than their spectacular successes in 1997, 1996, 1995, 1994, 1993, and 1992. They have given up making Viognier, but still turn out a fine Petite Sirah as well as one of my favorite California Cabernet Francs. The 1998 Petite Sirah (25% Viognier in the blend) has turned out well in this difficult vintage. Revealing a Rhône Valley–like character, it offers peppery, earthy, honeysuckle mixed with black fruits and smoke. The wine is medium- to full-bodied, engaging, soft, and best drunk over the next 7–8 years.

The finest wine in La Jota's 1998 portfolio is the 1998 Cabernet Franc (250 cases). It displays a complex, luxurious bouquet of plum liqueur, truffles, saddle leather, roasted espresso, cedar, and black fruits. A rich, concentrated attack and mid-palate are accompanied by some jagged tannin in the finish. The 1999 Cabernet Franc may turn out to be outstanding, although it is more herbaceous than previous vintages. Its dense ruby/purple color is followed by aromas of cedar wood, Provençal herbs, bay leaves, and blackberry/plum-like fruit. The wine is medium- to full-bodied, with a creamy entry and mid-palate, but finishes with astringent tannin. We'll see how it evolves in barrel. Anticipated maturity: now–2012.

The dense purple-colored 1999 Cabernet Sauvignon 18th Anniversary Release offers a sweet nose of cassis, earth, herbs, and minerals. In the mouth, it is muscular and austere, with firm, high tannin in addition to a compressed finish. It will need 3–4 years of cellaring when released, and should easily evolve for 15 years. The 1998 Cabernet Sauvignon 17th Anniversary Release offers a dark ruby color as well as a big, peppery, spicy, black currant, plum, mineral, earth, and dried herb–scented bouquet. Medium- to full-bodied, with a fine texture in addition to a medium weight, Bordeaux-like style, it has firmer tannin than the Cabernet Franc, but not the lushness and complexity of that wine. It requires 2–3 years of cellaring, and should keep for 15–16 years.

The 1997s are some of the strongest wines La Jota produced during the successful decade. The prodigious 1997 Cabernet Franc Howell Mountain offers a knockout bouquet of smoky cedar/cigar box, roast beef, and gorgeous blackberry and cassis fruit. Full-bodied and fat, with compelling sweetness, intense new saddle leather notes, and low acidity, this terrific wine can be consumed now as well as over the next 12–15 years. Sadly, there are only 300 cases of this rich, thick, unctuously textured wine. Patience will be required with the 1997 Cabernet Sauvignon Howell Mountain Select, which was closed, but powerful. The saturated ruby/purple color is accompanied by aromas of minerals, toasty oak, and jammy black currants. A tannic, muscular, full-bodied wine, it has outstanding extract and purity. Anticipated maturity: now–2018. The sensational black/purple-colored 1997 Cabernet Sauvignon 16th

Anniversary Release is also closed, but its emerging aromas of charcoal, blackberries, cassis, and minerals are promising. The wine is intense, ripe, with a layered, expansive richness, and exotic notes of Asian spices, beef blood, and assorted black fruits. Anticipated maturity: 2004–2025. Readers should try to latch onto a bottle or two of the 350-case production of the 1997 Petite Sirah Howell Mountain. With 12% Viognier in the blend, it boasts sumptuous, exotic aromas of pepper, blackberries, peaches, and honeysuckle. This wine has been a terrific success for La Jota since their debut 1991, and the 1997 is unquestionably another low-acid, sensationally rich Petite Sirah that should drink well for 15+ years.

The 1996s are impressive. The 1996 Cabernet Sauvignon Howell Mountain Select is a beautifully rendered wine with an opaque plum color and knockout aromatics of cedarwood, cassis, cigar box, and roasted Provençal herbs. With more structure than the 1997, it is a jammy, rich, concentrated, full-bodied wine that can be drunk now or cellared for two decades. This beauty remains one of the better values in great California Cabernet Sauvignon. The 1996 Cabernet Sauvignon 15th Anniversary Release (1,050 cases produced) boasts an opaque purple color as well as beautiful aromas of smoke, blackberries, Asian spices, charcoal, and subtle truffle-like scents. Huge, massive, and full-bodied, with phenomenal flavor extraction and beautifully integrated tannin and acidity, this flamboyant, exceptionally well-endowed Cabernet Sauvignon continues the succession of titanic wines made under this label. Anticipated maturity: now–2027. The unfined and unfiltered 1996 Cabernet Franc reveals a smoky, meaty, beef blood and black fruit–scented nose with loamy soil scents providing additional aromatic dimension. The wine possesses exceptional richness of fruit, thrilling quantities of glycerin, an impressive mid-palate, and an admirably long finish. Fruit ripeness, texture, and richness are important in any wine, but La Jota manages to cram all of these components into the difficult to grow and make Cabernet Franc varietal. This effort is another benchmark Cabernet Franc that should drink well for 12–15+ years. The 1996 Petite Sirah also stands out as a reference point for its type. It offers a saturated black/purple color, followed by a stunning nose of roasted meats, saddle leather, beef juices, and spicy wood. There is compelling richness, super intensity, and gobs of black fruit in this surprisingly supple, chewy, exciting offering. It should drink well for 20 years.

I am convinced La Jota is making one of California's finest Cabernet Francs. I love this wine, and I am consistently reminded of how well it ages whenever I taste the 1986, superb since its birth. This is not one of the more delicate styles of Cabernet Franc, but it does have compelling complexity, as well as a rich, intense, concentrated character. The 1995 Cabernet Franc is another knockout effort that may be even better than the 1996. It boasts a black/ruby/purple color, as well as more structured aromatics with smoke, beef juices, saddle leather, and black fruits soaring out of the glass. On the palate, the wine reveals earthy, roasted meat, blackberry, and cassis flavors, with good glycerin, more noticeable tannin than the 1996, and a well-delineated, spicy, intense finish. The wine may take more time to round out when it is released, but their Cabernet Franc redefines the quality standards for this varietal. The spectacular 1994 Cabernet Franc offers a pronounced sweet, smoky, earthy, roasted meat, black cherry, and cassis-scented nose. Dense, with fabulous concentration, a chewy texture, and a full-bodied, long, layered finish, this wine is already difficult to resist, but it should keep for 12–15 years.

One of the cult wines of La Jota is Petite Sirah. The grapes come from the old Park-Muscatine Vineyard now owned by Randy Dunn (and from which Ridge used to purchase grapes). This vineyard has produced some exceptional Petite Sirahs over the last few years. These wines look like ink, yet possess surprisingly sweet fruit in spite of their massive size. The 1995 Petite Sirah is a huge, monolithic wine with an opaque blue/black color, huge body, copious amounts of thick, juicy fruit, and a lashing of tannin at the back of the palate. It is a touch more angular and backward than either the 1994 is or the 1996 promises to be, but it has exceptional potential. Anticipated maturity: 2005–2020. La Jota's 1994 Petite Sirah

Howell Mountain (aged in 90% new French oak) is an awesome wine. It exhibits one of the most extraordinary jammy blueberry-scented noses I have ever encountered. Unbelievably rich and full-bodied, yet remarkably soft, this multilayered, fabulously concentrated wine will be approachable young (rare for Petite Sirah), yet age for 20 or more years. Petite Sirah can be the most underrated wine made in California. Put this one on your shopping list!

The two Cabernet Sauvignon *cuvées* are similar in quality. The Howell Mountain Select and Anniversary Release share dense, concentrated, full-bodied personalities with superlative levels of fruit and extract. The Anniversary *cuvée* usually has a bit more depth, ripeness, and overall potential, but that is not always easily discernable when they are young. Each wine will last—at the minimum—20 years. Readers can decide whether they prefer the more open-knit opulence of the 1994, the more austere, jagged tannins of the big 1995, or the forceful power of the 1996. As for the 1994 Cabernet Sauvignon Howell Mountain Select, this wine performed exceptionally well in a large tasting of 1994 California Cabernets I conducted. The wine is full-bodied, with an opaque purple color, as well as potentially sweeter, more up-front fruit than the Anniversary Release. It is opulent, aromatic (black fruits, truffles, earth, and spice galore), and fleshy, but it boasts plenty of tannin. Look for it to close down in another year or two, not to reemerge for 7–8 years. It will last two decades. The formidable 1994 Cabernet Sauvignon 13th Anniversary Release may be the finest Cabernet Sauvignon Joan and Bill Smith have yet made. It boasts an opaque purple color, followed by a smoky, toasty, mineral, and cassis-scented nose, great persistence in the mouth, massive body, and an expansive, chewy, blockbuster finish, without coming across as excessively heavy or overweight. Give it 5–6 years of cellaring, and drink it over the following 20–25 years. It is a Cabernet legend in the making!

The 1995 Cabernet Sauvignon Howell Mountain Select revealed some rough tannin when I tasted it in October of 1997. While none of these wines is filtered, the Smiths did do a light egg white fining in an attempt to produce a more civilized style. The 1995 is deep, muscular, rich, and impressive, but it is in need of 5–6 years of cellaring. I suspect this wine will age effortlessly for another two decades. Also a monster, the tannic 1995 Cabernet Sauvignon 14th Anniversary Release is unquestionably a huge, mountain-styled Cabernet. It exhibits a black/purple color and a reticent but promising nose of minerals, smoke, black currants, and underbrush. Although full-bodied and excruciatingly tannic, there is enough fruit to balance out the wine's structure. It may be as backward as the Cabernet Sauvignon made by Dunn on another Howell Mountain slope; this wine needs 5–8 years of cellaring. The stunning 1994 Cabernet Sauvignon Howell Mountain reveals an opaque black color, gobs of sweet cassis and licorice scents, remarkable fat and opulence, and a chewy, long finish.

Past Glories: 1993 Cabernet Sauvignon Howell Mountain 12th Anniversary Release (96), 1992 11th Anniversary Release (98), 1991 10th Anniversary Release (91)

LA SIRENA (NAPA)

1998 Cabernet Sauvignon	Napa	EE	89
1997 Cabernet Sauvignon	Napa	EE	92
1997 Sangiovese Juliana	Napa	D	88

La Sirena is the house label of Napa Valley's highly respected winemaking consultant Heidi Barrett. The 1997 Sangiovese Juliana (640 cases) is her finest Sangiovese to date. It exhibits more intensity than many of the overcropped, diluted, acidic offerings that routinely emerge from this varietal. La Sirena's medium ruby-colored 1997 offers an excellent nose of sweet black cherries, saddle leather, strawberries, and spice. Soft and fruit-driven with low acidity, this round, medium-bodied Sangiovese can be drunk now and over the next 4–5 years.

There are approximately 375 cases of the Cabernet Sauvignon, which emerges from a vineyard in the hotter area of Calistoga. The 1998 Cabernet Sauvignon is undoubtedly a success for the vintage. Harvested in late October, this opaque ruby/purple-colored wine reveals ripe black currants intermixed with cedar and spice box scents. Aged in French oak (of which one-third is new), this medium-bodied effort displays more persistence, depth, and ripeness than many 1998s. Anticipated maturity: now–2015. Even better, the 1997 Cabernet Sauvignon boasts a saturated, opaque blue/purple color in addition to classic crème de cassis aromas meshed with spice, licorice, and tobacco. Dense, powerful, concentrated, and backward, this large-scaled Cabernet requires 3–4 years of cellaring. It should keep for two decades. Given her talent and diverse experience with many different vineyards, what is Heidi Barrett's ranking of the finest Cabernet Sauvignon/Merlot proprietary blend vintages of the nineties? In her opinion, the three top vintages were 1997, 1994, and 1992, followed by 1995 and 1993. For her, 1996 and 1998 were the most challenging.

LAIL VINEYARDS (NAPA)

1998 J. Daniel Cuvée	Howell Mountain	EE	89
1997 J. Daniel Cuvée	Howell Mountain	EE	93
1996 J. Daniel Cuvée	Howell Mountain	E	91
1995 J. Daniel Cuvée	Napa	E	91

Robin Lail is a veteran Napa Valley resident who was raised in a winemaking family (her father was the legendary John Daniel, who fashioned many of Inglenook's greatest Cabernet Sauvignons). A former partner of Christian Moueix in the Dominus operation, Robin Lail has branched out on her own to produce limited quantities (about 450 cases) of a graceful, elegant, proprietary red wine from vineyards in Yountville, Vine Hill Road, and Howell Mountain. The 1995 J. Daniel Cuvée was the debut release from Lail Vineyards. An outstanding effort, it is a blend of 56% Merlot and 44% Cabernet Sauvignon made by Philippe Melka (the wine-maker at Seavey). The wine is a beautifully rendered, Médoc-like California red with a dense, saturated ruby/purple color, and stylish, complex aromatics consisting of tobacco, black currants, crème de cassis, and subtle toasty oak (approximately 33% new-oak casks are utilized). The wine is medium- to full-bodied, with sweet tannin, a graceful, long midpalate and finish, and 15 or more years of potential evolution. From the finesse/elegant school of California proprietary reds, this wine is rich and layered, with everything in impeccable balance. Anticipated maturity: now–2015.

There are 600 cases of the 1996 J. Daniel Cuvée, a blend of 73% Cabernet Sauvignon and 27% Merlot. It exhibits a dense ruby color with a purple hue. The classy nose of chocolate, cassis, black cherries, and toast is followed by a medium- to full-bodied offering with outstanding ripeness, sweet tannin, and a layered, multidimensional personality. Delicious, and already revealing considerable complexity, it can be drunk now and over the next 15 years. The most brilliant wine to date is the 1997 J. Daniel Cuvée, a blend of 64% Cabernet Sauvignon and 36% Merlot (1,200 cases produced). The dense ruby/purple-colored 1997 boasts a lavishly pure nose of blackberries, cassis, minerals, licorice, chocolate, and toast. It is expansive, with the vintage's telltale richness, sweet tannin, and outstanding ripeness and concentration. The persistent finish lasts for nearly 40 seconds. This wine possesses an openness and sweetness that gives it the impression of being ready to drink, but I suspect much more will emerge with aging. Anticipated maturity: now–2020. The softest, most charming and elegant of these wines is the 1998 J. Daniel Cuvée (61% Cabernet Sauvignon and 39% Merlot). It does not possess the power or depth of the 1997, but it may turn out to be outstanding, an enviable achievement in this challenging vintage. There is no herbaceousness (frequently a problem with the 1998 mountain Cabernets) in this black cherry, cassis, and mineral-scented effort. A medium-bodied wine, with excellent sweet fruit on the attack and more persistence than many 1998s, this should turn out to be a Cabernet of considerable charm and seductiveness. Interestingly, the 1998 harvest occurred one month later than it did in 1997.

Kudos to John and Robin Lail for the efforts they have produced to date.

LAMBORN FAMILY VINEYARDS (HOWELL MOUNTAIN)

1999 Zinfandel the Solar Factor	Howell Mountain	D	89
1997 Zinfandel the Team Connection	Howell Mountain	C	88+

The complex, earthy 1999 Zinfandel the Solar Factor offers notes of blueberries, black cherries, currants, and minerals. Beautifully textured, sweet, ripe, and medium- to full-bodied, this dark plum/ruby/purple-colored 1999 will provide delicious drinking over the next 4–5 years. The 1997 Zinfandel the Team Connection is from the first vintage to be produced by well-known wine consultant Heidi Barrett. From a mountain vineyard that has a tendency to turn out rustic, tannic examples, this dense ruby/purple-colored wine possesses fine balance. The bouquet reveals notes of new saddle leather, minerals, and black fruits. The wine is full-bodied and tightly knit, with plenty of muscle and a long, deep, toasty oak-flavored finish. This is one of the few 1997 Zinfandels that will improve for several years and last for 7–8.

LANCASTER RESERVE (ALEXANDER VALLEY)

1995 Proprietary Red Estate	Alexander Valley	E	90

Only 8,600 bottles were produced of this proprietary wine (a blend of 82% Cabernet Sauvignon and 18% Cabernet Franc). It is extremely backward and unevolved, with an opaque purple color and a promising nose of blackberries, raspberries, and copious quantities of toasty new oak. This massive, tightly knit, full-bodied, tannic wine exhibits impressive depth and purity, but it requires 3–4 years of cellaring. Patience will be necessary for those who latch onto this limited production gem. Anticipated maturity: now–2018.

LANDMARK VINEYARDS (SONOMA)

1999 Chardonnay Demaris Reserve	Sonoma	E	91
1999 Chardonnay Lorenzo Vineyard	Russian River	E	91+
1999 Chardonnay Overlook	California	D	90
1999 Pinot Noir Grand Detour Van der Kamp	Sonoma Mountain	D	92
1998 Pinot Noir Grand Detour Van der Kamp	Sonoma Mountain	D	91
1997 Pinot Noir Grand Detour Van der Kamp	Sonoma Mountain	D	90
1996 Pinot Noir Grand Detour Van der Kamp	Sonoma Mountain	D	90
1999 Pinot Noir Kastania Vineyard	Sonoma Coast	D	93
1998 Pinot Noir Kastania Vineyard	Sonoma Coast	D	92
1997 Pinot Noir Kastania Vineyard	Sonoma Coast	D	91

This winery remains one of the best-kept secrets for outstanding Chardonnays as well as increasingly sumptuous Pinot Noirs. Prices are rising, but they remain well behind the stratospheric prices asked for wines of similar quality from other California wineries. Proprietors Mary and Mike Colhoun and their talented wine-maker, Eric Stern, offer consumers a reasonably priced, complex, Burgundy-styled Chardonnay called Overlook. Utilizing indigenous yeasts to ferment the wine, which comes from virtually every region of California (Sonoma Valley and Russian River being the biggest contributors), this wine spends nine months *sur-lie*. It goes through complete malolactic, and is not filtered prior to bottling. The good news is that it sells for a song given its quality. Moreover, there are 18,000 cases available! The 1999 Chardonnay Overlook exhibits a smoky, buttery, leesy nose, a subtle yet delicious display of vanilla and toast, and a layered, concentrated style. Given its purity as well as overall depth, it will drink well for 2–3 years. The 1999 Chardonnay Demaris Reserve (2,500 cases) is a blend of six Chardonnay vineyards averaging 20 years of age. Fermented with indigenous yeasts, aged *sur-lie* for 12 months (with considerable stirring), and bottled unfiltered, it is a bolder, richer effort revealing notes of cloves, honeysuckle, and orange rind, as well as a creamy, full-bodied texture and admirable richness. From the vineyard made famous by Helen Turley (although she no longer purchases grapes from it), the 1999 Chardonnay Lorenzo Vineyard was made from 22-year-old vines cropped at 2.55 tons per acre. There are 400 cases of this stunning, complex Chardonnay that spent 14 months in French oak, of which 60% was new. It boasts a honeyed citrus, tangerine, stony mineral-scented bouquet as well as a full-bodied, concentrated style. More high-toned (because of the mineral character) than its two siblings, with subtle oak, this superb wine will drink well for 4–5 years.

The 1998 Pinot Noir Grand Detour Van der Kamp Vineyard (375 cases) was produced from destemmed grapes fermented with indigenous yeasts in open-top fermenters, transferred to French oak barrels (60% new and 40% one year old) for 12 months, and bottled unfined and unfiltered. It is a complex Pinot that could pass for a top-ranked Burgundy, although it possesses lower acidity. The 1998 has taken on smoky, plum, cherry characteristics infused with violets, roasted herbs, and earthy notes. It tastes like a premier cru Vosne-Romanée from a ripe vintage. Rich, with supple tannin, adequate acidity, and an expansive, rich mouth-feel, it is best drunk over the next 6–7 years. The 1998 Pinot Noir Kastania Vineyard (400 cases) is produced from a combination of old California Pinot Noir clones and new French Dijon clones. Its upbringing is essentially the same as the Grand Detour, but the percentage of new oak is slightly lower. The wine reveals aromas of sweet black cherries mixed with overripe apple skin, earth, clove, spice, and Chinese black tea, plus a ripe pomegranate character. Notes of coffee and smoky new oak add to its tremendous complexity. It should drink well for 6–7 years.

The 1999 Pinot Noirs are also potentially superb. The 1999 Pinot Noir Grand Detour Van der Kamp Vineyard (750 cases) possesses terrific fruit intensity as well as sweet aromas of pepper, cherry syrup, smoke, underbrush, strawberry, and dried tangerines. This full-bodied, sweet (from extract and ripeness, not sugar), long Pinot Noir has completely absorbed its new oak. It has a floral quality reminiscent of certain premier and grand crus from the hillsides of Vosne-Romanée. Drink it over the next 5–7 years. The 1999 Pinot Noir Kastania Vineyard reveals a tighter structure along with its graceful, rich, black cherry, Chinese black tea, floral, pomegranate, smoke, mineral, earth, and new-oak aromas and flavors. This complex Pinot Noir will drink beautifully for 7–8 years. Amazingly, both of these efforts reveal French-like aromatic profiles, but riper, richer fruit as well as plusher textures.

The 1996 Pinot Noir Grand Detour Van der Kamp Vineyard (1,000 cases) offers a big, smoky, complex nose filled with aromas of black cherries, *jus de viande*, clove, and allspice. It is a meaty, full-bodied, richly spicy yet supple-textured, expansive, delicious Pinot Noir. The wine's provocative aromatics and earthy, smoky style will serve it well over the next 5–6 years. Scents of barbecue spice and smoke intermixed with cherry liqueur, sweet foresty smells, and yummy new oak are intense in the full-bodied, hedonistic, nicely textured/layered, and complex 1997 Pinot Noir Grand Detour Van der Kamp Vineyard (950 cases). Already delicious, it promises to drink well for 5–7 years. From a Sonoma Coast hillside vineyard, Landmark has turned out 100 cases of the 1997 Pinot Noir Kastania Vineyard. The dark ruby/purple-colored 1997 is a Burgundy-styled, tannic, complex effort from a cool climate region. It offers a terrific nose of cherry and black raspberry fruit with a touch of cassis. Medium- to full-bodied, the wine boasts a silky attack in addition to good firmness and delineation. This concentrated, powerful, still youthful Pinot Noir will be even better with another 12–18 months of bottle age. It should drink well for a decade.

Kudos for the remarkable improvements evident in all the Landmark offerings over the last 4–5 years. Readers who have not yet tasted Landmark's wines need a wake-up call.

LAUREL GLEN (SONOMA)

1994 Cabernet Sauvignon	Sonoma Mountain	D	92

Laurel Glen is one of California's most admirable operations, and its estate Cabernet Sauvignon is at the top of the qualitative hierarchy. The 1994 reveals an opaque purple color and a tight but promising nose of jammy black fruits, spice, earth, and a whiff of Provençal herbs.

Full-bodied, with layers of chewy, fleshy, ripe fruit, this highly extracted, moderately tannic, blockbuster Cabernet should be cellared for 4–5 years and drunk over the following 15–20. *Past Glories:* 1993 (95), 1992 (94), 1991 (92), 1990 (89), 1987 (91), 1985 (91), 1984 (91)

LEWIS CELLARS (NAPA)

1997 Cabernet Sauvignon Reserve   **Napa   E   90**

Traditionally, this winery has had a tendency to dump entirely too much acidity into the fermentation vats. Consequently, the wines often lacked a mid-palate and possessed chalky, tart, compressed personalities. Winemaking consultant Paul Hobbs was brought in beginning with the 1997 vintage, and he hopes to halt the excessive additions of acidity in favor of more natural, handcrafted wines. Certainly the 1997 Cabernet Sauvignon Reserve (2,400 cases) reveals progress. The wine exhibits toasty sweet oak, jammy black currant fruit, and a touch of licorice, cedar, fruitcake, and cigar box aromas. It is a complex, smoky, ripe, layered wine that can be drunk young or cellared for 15–18 years.

LITTORAI (NAPA)

1999	Chardonnay Charles Heintz Vineyard	Sonoma Coast	E	90
1999	Chardonnay Mays Canyon	Russian River	E	92
1999	Chardonnay Thieriot Vineyard	Sonoma Coast	E	93
1999	Pinot Noir Hirsch Vineyard	Sonoma Coast	E	90
1998	Pinot Noir Hirsch Vineyard	Sonoma Coast	E	(89–90)
1999	Pinot Noir One Acre Vineyard	Anderson Valley	E	90
1998	Pinot Noir One Acre Vineyard	Anderson Valley	E	(87–88)
1997	Pinot Noir One Acre Vineyard	Anderson Valley	D	(90–94)
1999	Pinot Noir Savoy Vineyard	Anderson Valley	E	88
1998	Pinot Noir Savoy Vineyard	Anderson Valley	E	(87–88)
1997	Pinot Noir Savoy Vineyard	Anderson Valley	D	(88–89+)
1999	Pinot Noir Thieriot Vineyard	Sonoma Coast	E	91+
1998	Pinot Noir Thieriot Vineyard	Sonoma Coast	E	90

Burgundy-trained Ted Lemon can usually be counted on to produce some of California's most elegant, restrained, finesse-filled wines. However, in 1999, he has demonstrated that he can also build in a few extra layers of flavor. In short, these look to be Lemon's most impressive wines to date, no small feat given his already impressive track record. The 1999 Chardonnays exhibit the vintage's zesty acidity as well as intense flavor and ripeness. The 1999 Chardonnay Charles Heintz Vineyard offers aromas of citrus oil, orange, pineapple, and minerals. From a vineyard planted in fertile Gold Ridge soils, in a cool coastal area, emerges this rich, creamy-textured, medium- to full-bodied, beautifully pure as well as long wine. It should open slowly and drink well for 4–5 years. The 1999 Chardonnay Mays Canyon offers more smoky oak in the nose, in addition to honeysuckle, tropical fruit, and nutty, leesy notes. Full-bodied, rich, yet at the same time elegant, pure, and well delineated, it is more flamboyant than the Charles Heintz. Drink it over the next 5–6 years. The stunning 1999 Chardonnay Thieriot Vineyard offers a light greenish/gold-tinged straw color in addition to a superb nose of candied citrus, tropical fruit, minerals, and orange marmalade. The oak provides a subtle smoky, almost camphor-like note. The wine is dense, long, and full-bodied, yet exquisitely well balanced with nicely integrated acidity and wood. This terrific, multitextured Chardonnay should drink well for 5–7 years. Lemon feels that the extra layers of texture and complexity might have been the result of the extremely slow malolactic fermentations that characterized 1999.

Littorai's Pinot Noirs are made from completely destemmed fruit. While the 1999s were in bottle, they required opening the night before my tasting, because they needed air to reveal their personalities. None of them showed a trace of oxidation and performed well, as the following notes attest. The 1999 Pinot Noir Hirsch Vineyard (14.4% alcohol) is made from such Pinot Noir clones as Pommard, Dijon #114, and Mt. Eden. The wine exhibits a dark plum/ruby color along with a sweet, moderately intense nose of red/black fruits, apple skins, black cherry fruit, smoke, and earth. Medium-bodied and soft, with firm tannin in the finish, it should evolve nicely for 7–8 years. Although the medium ruby-colored 1999 Pinot Noir Savoy Vineyard does not possess the size and depth of the other offerings, it represents a premier cru Beaune in its aromatics and flavors. Made completely from Dijon clones of Pinot Noir, particularly #114 and #115, it offers finesse, elegance, light to medium body, and sweet plum, cherry, and cranberry fruit. Subtle and restrained, it is best drunk during its first 5–6 years of life. The exceptional, dark ruby-colored 1999 Pinot Noir One Acre Vineyard is another high-toned, textured, delicious Pinot with an intricate perfume of black cherries, minerals, flowers, and a touch of blackberries. Once past the perfumed aromatics, the wine reveals good sweetness on the attack, medium body, and a beautiful pure, delicate, intense personality. It should drink well for 7–8 years. The most backward and possibly the most concentrated offering is the 1999 Pinot Noir Thieriot Vineyard. This wine boasts a dark ruby color as well as scents of root beer, cola, vegetable roots, black fruits, smoke, and mineral. Exhibiting a firm underpinning of tannin, outstanding concentration, overall equilibrium, and a spicy finish, this aggressive/animal-styled Pinot should drink well for 7–8 years.

The medium ruby-colored 1998 Pinot Noir Savoy Vineyard possesses a Beaune premier cru–like style. A sweet nose of black cherries, spice, and mineral scents is followed by a medium-bodied, pure, firmly structured Pinot Noir. It requires 12–18 months of bottle age and should last for 6–7 years. The more meaty, animal-styled, potentially outstanding 1998 Pinot Noir Hirsch Vineyard exhibits a dark ruby color as well as aromas of grilled steak, ripe apples, and black cherries. One of the softest Hirsch Vineyard offerings from Ted Lemon to date, it possesses fine density, medium to full body, and a sweet, lush finish. Readers looking for jammy cherry/strawberry notes infused with fresh damp earth-like smells should check out the 1998 Pinot Noir One Acre Vineyard. Exhibiting more tannin than either the Savoy or Hirsch offering, it requires a year of bottle age, and should evolve nicely for 5–7 years. The most volume and intensity can be found in the 1998 Pinot Noir Thieriot Vineyard. Sadly, only 68 cases were produced. It boasts a dark ruby color in addition to a gorgeous nose of sweet blackberry and cherry fruit meshed with plums, rose petals, and spicy oak. Medium-bodied, with a juicy mid-section and excellent purity and symmetry, it is a complex, elegant Pinot to consume over the next 7–8 years.

Ted Lemon told me that he did a *saignée* of all his 1997 Pinots because of high yields, and that all of these wines were scheduled to be bottled with neither fining nor filtration. The stylish 1997 Pinot Noir Savoy Vineyard, made from the Dijon clone #115 and the Pommard clone, possesses a medium ruby color, attractive, deeper, richer, black cherry and cassis aromas, excellent ripeness on the attack, medium body, firm tannin, and a pure style with a subtle influence of wood. This wine will benefit from 1–2 years of cellaring and keep for nearly a decade. Many of the Pinot Noirs I have tasted from the Sonoma Coast's Hirsch Vineyard tend to be powerhouse Pinots that push tannin levels to the limit—at least for my palate. That seems to be the case even with the subtle touch of Ted Lemon. There are 200 cases of the spectacular 1997 Pinot Noir One Acre Vineyard from Anderson Valley. This wine could easily pass for a top-notch premier cru from the Côte de Nuits. Made from modest yields, it reveals a deep ruby color with purple nuances. The aromatics include black cherries, cassis, spice, herb, and flower blossoms. Medium- to full-bodied, with terrific fruit purity and a lush, open-knit texture, this complex Pinot Noir possesses sensational potential. The wine will be approachable when released, yet should age nicely for 7–8 years.

Virtually the entire production of Littorai is sold through a mailing list . . . readers take note.

LOKOYA (NAPA)

1998 Cabernet Sauvignon Diamond Mountain	Napa	EE	95
1997 Cabernet Sauvignon Diamond Mountain	Napa	EE	95
1995 Cabernet Sauvignon Diamond Mountain	Napa	EE	93
1997 Cabernet Sauvignon Howell Mountain	Napa	EE	93+
1995 Cabernet Sauvignon Howell Mountain	Napa	EE	90
1998 Cabernet Sauvignon Mount Veeder	Napa	EE	93+
1997 Cabernet Sauvignon Mount Veeder	Napa	EE	93+
1995 Cabernet Sauvignon Mount Veeder	Napa	EE	91
1994 Cabernet Sauvignon Mount Veeder	Napa	D	94
1994 Cabernet Sauvignon Oakville District	Napa	D	89
1998 Cabernet Sauvignon Rutherford	Napa	EE	92
1997 Cabernet Sauvignon Rutherford	Napa	EE	94
1995 Cabernet Sauvignon Rutherford	Napa	EE	94

Another flagship estate in the Kendall-Jackson empire (to be precise, part of the Jackson Family Farms), Lokoya is a small, 3,000-case operation dedicated to four limited-production, ageworthy Cabernet Sauvignons. These wines have quickly built a cult following, for which much of the credit must go to the outstanding skills of wine-maker Marco Di Giulio (who also makes the wines at Pepi). They spend 22 months in 100% new French oak and are normally bottled with neither fining nor filtration, although in 1997, the Howell Mountain *cuvée* was given a light filtration. The opaque purple-colored 1997 Cabernet Sauvignon Mount Veeder (220 cases), from an elevation of 1,500 feet, reveals classic crème de cassis/mineral aromas, a superb mid-palate, and a full-bodied personality with impressive length and purity. It is not for readers desiring immediate gratification as it requires 4–5 years of cellaring. Anticipated maturity: 2005–2025. More mineral, blueberry, plum, and earthy characteristics can be found in the dark purple-colored 1997 Cabernet Sauvignon Howell Mountain (700 cases). Softer in the mouth, but full-bodied, dense, and rich, it is an immensely impressive effort. Anticipated maturity: now–2020. The most opulent, sexy, and immediately charming of this admirable quartet of 1997 Lokoya Cabernets is the 1997 Cabernet Sauvignon Diamond Mountain (1,100 cases). It exhibits a saturated purple color in addition to an explosive nose of licorice, cedar, roasted herbs, and black plums and currants. Full-bodied, with a voluptuous texture, low acidity, and heady alcohol, this offering possesses considerable tannin, but it is beautifully submerged by the wine's depth of extract and high glycerin. Impressive, with a flamboyant personality, it should drink well for 18–20 years. There are 1,000 cases of the 1997 Cabernet Sauvignon Rutherford. It offers a distinctive kirsch, black cherry liqueur, and loamy soil-scented character to its full-bodied richness. Along with the Diamond Mountain, it is the most expansive and charming of these blockbuster 1997 Cabernets. Full-bodied, with admirable depth and purity, it can be drunk now as well as over the next 20 years.

In 1998, wine-maker Marco Di Giulio decided to declassify the Howell Mountain because of the cold climate in these upper-elevation vineyards. However, he is still perfecting what he calls "the art of viticulture down to each single berry." In 1998, there are 400 cases of the Rutherford, 750 cases of the Diamond Mountain, and 132 cases of the Mount Veeder. They have all been bottled, and are certainly among the superstar efforts of the vintage. The one difference with the 1998s is they are all relatively drinkable at present, whereas the 1997s generally require 3–5 years of cellaring. The 1998 Cabernet Sauvignon Rutherford is a classic Rutherford Cabernet with about 9% Merlot in the blend. Opaque purple in color, with low acidity and a gorgeously explosive nose of black and red fruits intermixed with cedar wood, this profoundly concentrated wine is dense, opulent, and remarkably voluptuous and concentrated for a 1998. In a blind tasting, readers would certainly think this emanated from a vintage such as 1997 or 1994, given its super-concentrated, gorgeously harmonious personality. Anticipated maturity: now–2015. The flamboyant 1998 Cabernet Sauvignon Diamond Mountain (750 cases of 100% Cabernet made from Lokoya's south-facing vineyard) has fabulous fruit intensity offering notes of jammy black currants mixed with violets and minerals. A potential "Wine of the Vintage" candidate, this wine has immense body, great concentration, and gorgeous plum liqueur, cassis/fruit notes that cascade over the palate with remarkable glycerin and richness. Quite an achievement! Anticipated maturity: now–2015. The tiny *cuvée* of 1998 Cabernet Sauvignon Mount Veeder (132 cases of Cabernet Sauvignon) actually is the only 1998 that needs another 2–3 years of cellaring. It will probably last 20–25 years, but will it achieve the greatness of the Diamond Mountain or the suppleness of the Rutherford? With a dense purple color, notes of scorched earth, liquid minerals, black fruits, cedar, and licorice, this full-bodied, powerful, muscular wine has some tannin to shed, but it is loaded with extract and richness. These are amazing achievements in 1998.

The 1995 Cabernet Sauvignon Mount Veeder (1,600 cases) reveals an opaque purple color and a sumptuous, Médoc-like nose of lead pencil, minerals, black currants, and smoky oak. It is extremely full-bodied and massive in the mouth, with sweet tannin, a layered, plushly textured mid-palate, and a firm, exceptionally long, pure finish. This classic mountain-styled Cabernet Sauvignon can be drunk now, but it will be even better with 5–7 years of cellaring. It will keep for two decades. The limited production 1995 Cabernet Sauvignon Howell Mountain (25 cases) is dominated by minerals and wet stones intertwined with blackberry and cassis flavors. More structured and tannic, as well as less extroverted than the Mount Veeder, the Howell Mountain *cuvée* is not for readers seeking immediate gratification. Anticipated maturity: 2005–2018. The sensational 1995 Cabernet Sauvignon Diamond Mountain (330 cases) boasts an opaque blue/black color, followed by outstanding aromatics of jammy blackberry and currant fruit intertwined with roasted herbs, cold steel, minerals, and spicy new oak. There is fabulous intensity, terrific levels of glycerin and extract, full body, and sweet tannin in the long, low-acid finish. This superb, dazzling Cabernet Sauvignon reveals tremendous up-side potential. Anticipated maturity: now–2020. The 1995 Cabernet Sauvignon Rutherford (300 cases) possesses the most developed aromatics, consisting of black currants, cherries, loamy soil scents, and toast. It is the most expansive and fullest-bodied, with stunningly concentrated flavors that exhibit no angularity or sharpness. The acidity, tannin, alcohol, and wood are all gorgeously integrated into this fleshy, succulent, voluptuously textured wine. The finish lasts for 40+ seconds. Despite its accessibility, this Cabernet will be even better with another 5 years of cellaring and will keep for 20–25 years.

The 1994 Cabernet Sauvignon Oakville District (800 cases) is made from 100% Cabernet Sauvignon, 90% of which came from the Vine Hill Ranch and 10% from Mount Veeder. The wine was aged for 22 months in small barrels, of which 40% were new. It exhibits an opaque purple color, a sweet, ripe, olive, chocolate, smoky, cassis-scented nose, dense, full-bodied flavors, moderate tannin, potentially exceptional extract, fine purity, and a long, spicy finish. The wine admirably combines the purity and ripeness of California fruit with a slight degree of the austerity and restraint exhibited by a top Bordeaux. Even more impressive is the 1994 Cabernet Sauvignon Mount Veeder (700 cases). This wine is an immense, monster-styled, mountain Cabernet that is vaguely reminiscent of the pre-1976 vintages of Mayacamas, but with more complexity and finesse. Its opaque black/purple color is followed by a tight, backward, but promising nose of licorice, minerals, and black fruits. The inky color suggests a formidably endowed wine, and that is just what this huge, super-concentrated, impressively endowed Cabernet Sauvignon represents. The wine is not just a ponderous heavyweight, as anyone who examines its equilibrium, harmony, and potential for 20–30 years of aging should notice. Remarkably, this wine was kept in 60% new French oak barrels, but the oak has been soaked up by the wine's intense fruit level. Patience will be a virtue required by prospective purchasers of this wine. Anticipated maturity: 2003–2020.

LOXTON (PASO ROBLES)

1999 Zinfandel Priest Ranch Orion Vineyard	Napa	C	89

Soft, supple, and concentrated, the peppery, earthy, opulent, dark ruby-colored 1999 Zinfandel Priest Ranch Orion Vineyard tips the scales at just over 14% alcohol. Drink this richly fruity, layered example over the next 2–3 years.

LUNA VINEYARDS (NAPA)

1997 Canto Proprietary Red Wine	Napa	E	89
1997 Merlot	Napa	D	89
1997 Sangiovese	Napa	C	89
1998 Sangiovese Riserva	Napa	E	89

This winery, a partnership of John Kongsgaard and George Vare, specializes in Italian varietals. Kongsgaard makes no compromises, believes in using indigenous yeasts for fermentation, and lets the wine make itself. None of these offerings is filtered. Representing some of the finest California wines being produced from Italian varietals, they are all remarkably intense (unlike many of their insipid, one-dimensional, overcropped, bare-bones peers).

Tired of overpriced, appallingly dull, thin, acidic (and even worse, tannic) California Sangiovese? Check out Luna's 1997 Sangiovese. There are 6,000 cases of this blend of 75% Sangiovese, 20% Merlot, and 5% Syrah. Medium ruby-colored, with an explosive nose of strawberry jam, cherries, new saddle leather, and spice, this is a delicious, pure, medium- to full-bodied, plush, hedonistic Sangiovese fruit cocktail. The 1998 Sangiovese Riserva (which includes 10% Syrah) reveals more concentrated juice. A floral, blackberry-scented nose is attributable to that small dosage of Syrah. Cherry fruit, strawberry jam, spicy saddle leather, and meaty aromas are also present. This is a full-bodied, potentially outstanding wine that should drink nicely for 5–7 years. Luna's entry into the super-Tuscan look-alike contest is their 1997 Canto Proprietary Red, a blend of equal parts Merlot, Sangiovese, and Cabernet Sauvignon, aged in small *barriques*, of which 50% were new. The wine's deep plum/purple color is accompanied by a cedary, fruitcake-scented nose, medium to full body, a sweet attack, and a long, structured, moderately tannic, impressively endowed finish. It needs another year of bottle age, and should keep for a decade. Luna also produces 3,000 cases of Merlot. Obviously John Kongsgaard has the right touch with Merlot, as evidenced by some of the Newton Merlots he fashioned. Luna's 1997 Merlot, which includes 20% Cabernet Franc, exhibits a dark ruby color, big, espresso bean, mocha, chocolate, and berry scents and flavors, good spice, moderate tannin, and a dense, concentrated mid-palate that is just beginning to unfold. I would not be surprised to see this wine merit a 90-point score with another 6–12 months of bottle age. It came in at a hefty 14.1% alcohol.

MARCASSIN VINEYARD (SONOMA)

1997 Chardonnay Gauer Ranch Upper Barn	Sonoma	EE	96
1997 Chardonnay Hudson Vineyard E Block	Carneros	EE	91
1998 Chardonnay Lorenzo Vineyard	Sonoma Coast	EE	93
1997 Chardonnay Lorenzo Vineyard	Sonoma Coast	EE	95+
1999 Chardonnay Marcassin Vineyard	Sonoma Coast	EE	97+
1998 Chardonnay Marcassin Vineyard	Sonoma Coast	EE	99
1997 Chardonnay Marcassin Vineyard	Sonoma Coast	EE	97
1999 Chardonnay Three Sisters–Sea Ridge Meadow	Sonoma Coast	EE	94
1998 Chardonnay Three Sisters–Sea Ridge Meadow	Sonoma Coast	EE	95
1999 Chardonnay Upper Barn–Alexander Mountain Estate	Sonoma	EE	(93–96)

1998 Chardonnay Upper Barn–Alexander Mountain Estate	Sonoma	EE	92
1999 Pinot Noir Blue Slide Ridge	Sonoma Coast	EE	(98–100)
1998 Pinot Noir Blue Slide Ridge	Sonoma Coast	EE	95
1997 Pinot Noir Blue Slide Vineyard	Sonoma Coast	EE	96
1999 Pinot Noir Marcassin Vineyard	Sonoma Coast	EE	(95–96)
1998 Pinot Noir Marcassin Vineyard	Sonoma Coast	EE	98
1997 Pinot Noir Marcassin Vineyard	Sonoma Coast	EE	95+
1996 Pinot Noir Marcassin Vineyard	Sonoma Coast	EE	95
1995 Pinot Noir Marcassin Vineyard	Sonoma Coast	EE	93
1999 Pinot Noir Three Sisters–Lambing Barn	Sonoma Coast	EE	(93–95)
1999 Pinot Noir Three Sisters–Sea Ridge Meadow	Sonoma Coast	EE	(94–96)

The American wine industry's first couple, John Wetlaufer and Helen Turley (by the way, they have been married for 35 years), continue to eschew the spotlight, preferring to let their brilliant viticultural and winemaking skills serve notice that no one does it better. Quantities remain agonizingly small, so in a given vintage, only one or two thousand wine nuts get a chance to taste these elixirs. While I am not against size (obviously such huge qualitative giants as Beringer, Robert Mondavi, and Joseph Phelps can produce 20,000+ cases of high-quality Cabernet Sauvignon or Chardonnay), it is virtually impossible to produce large quantities of wines such as these Marcassins. It is hard to find more complex Chardonnays and Pinot Noirs than those produced by Turley and Wetlaufer from their own Sonoma Coast vineyard. Moreover, their crop-sharing agreement with the Martinelli family for the Three Sisters and Blue Slide Ridge Vineyards also looks set to produce some prodigious wines.

The 1999 Chardonnay Upper Barn–Alexander Mountain Estate *cuvée* (previously named Gauer Ranch Upper Barn, but renamed by its owner, Jess Jackson) comes from a vineyard being replanted with Burgundian Dijon clones. Marcassin shares the fruit from this vineyard with Stonestreet Winery. The fabulous 1999 boasts a smoky, honeyed pineapple, toasty nose with plenty of tropical fruit, butter, and roasted hazelnut scents in addition to gorgeously ripe, layered flavors. This rich, full-throttle Chardonnay is both concentrated and intense. It should drink well for 7–8 years. Readers will find two Chardonnays from the Three Sisters–Sea Ridge Meadow Vineyard. One, produced with the consultation of Helen Turley, will be sold under the Martinelli label, and the other under the Marcassin label. This Sonoma Coast vineyard was severely crop-thinned. Marcassin's 1999 Chardonnay Three Sisters–Sea Ridge Meadow Vineyard is a brilliant effort that was given extensive lees stirring until the spring following the vintage, and then not racked until it was absolutely essential. The result is a wine of extraordinary complexity, texture, and richness with striking buttery citrus and liquid mineral notes as well as a juicy, heady, lemon/pineapple, steely personality. Although extremely full-bodied, it remains exceptionally elegant and stylish. Like all the Marcassin Chardonnays, it will be bottled with neither fining nor filtration. There will be approximately 225 cases of the 1999 Chardonnay Marcassin Vineyard. This wine, from a vineyard planted on a steep, rocky hillside with shallow topsoil and meter-by-meter spacing, comes closest to a magical synthesis of Michel Niellon's Bâtard-Montrachet and Coche-Dury's Corton-Charlemagne blended with California's extraordinary ripeness and richness from low-yielding Chardonnay fruit. It is an unctuous, full-bodied, gorgeously delineated offering with an extraordinary perfume of liquid minerals interspersed with citrus oils, honey, and a steely smokiness. The compelling aromatics are matched by the attack, mid-palate, and finish. This profound Chardonnay is California's most singular expression of this varietal. Moreover, it will have an effortless evolution of 10–12+ years.

There are four 1998 Chardonnays, including the final release from the Sonoma Coast's

Lorenzo Vineyard. The 1998 Chardonnay Gauer Ranch–Upper Barn (now called Upper Barn–Alexander Mountain Estate) exhibits a surprisingly cloudy, evolved medium gold color. With notes of honeysuckle, buttery tropical fruit, minerals, smoke, and hazelnuts, this dense, full-bodied, rich, chewy 1998 seems unusually mature. Drink it over the next 3–5 years. The more mineral-dominated 1998 Chardonnay Three Sisters–Sea Ridge Meadow Vineyard reveals the essence of soil in its flavors. Additionally, it offers creamy custard, citrus, honey, and butternut notes, huge amounts of fruit, phenomenal texture, and a spectacularly long finish. Drink this prodigious Chardonnay over the next 7–8 years. The 1998 Chardonnay Lorenzo Vineyard reveals the smoky, leesy, honeyed complexity characteristic of Helen Turley's Chardonnays. There is good density, ripeness, and richness, fine underlying acidity, and a multinuanced, full-bodied finish. It should drink well for 5–6 years. The 1998 Chardonnay Marcassin Vineyard is a tour de force in Chardonnay winemaking. It has developed gorgeously since last year, and is one of the most compelling Chardonnays produced in either France or California. It reveals the essence of crushed sea shells in its complex, multidimensional bouquet, which also offers up aromas of lemon liqueur, minerals, honeyed citrus, orange marmalade, and smoke. Still tightly knit, it possesses full body, layers of concentration, and a red wine–like structure, power, and finish. The whopping 14.9% alcohol is well-concealed behind the wine's fruit and extract. The overall impression is of an extraordinarily well-delineated, intense, powerful Chardonnay trying to burst loose from its reins. Still backward, it has the potential to develop for at least a decade.

The 1997 Chardonnay Marcassin Vineyard shares some of the same characteristics (as does the 1996) with the 1998 and 1999. Liquid mineral and crushed sea shell aromas and flavors are present in this full-bodied, mineral-laced, lemon, honey, buttery Chardonnay. It boasts layers of flavor (citrus oils, orange marmalade, and hazelnuts), majestic concentration, and an unreal finish that lasts for over 40 seconds. Approachable upon its release in 2001, it should age beautifully for a decade. There are nearly 250 cases of the 1997 Chardonnay Gauer Ranch Upper Barn. This wine offers a compelling waxy, honeyed citrus, subtle toasty, lusty nose, followed by a full-bodied, fabulously concentrated mouthful of leesy, multilayered Chardonnay exhibiting honeyed grapefruit, citrus, and mineral flavors. A powerful, multidimensional, long (nearly a minute) finish adds to this Chardonnay's prodigious characteristics. It should drink well for 7–8 years. The 1997 Chardonnay Lorenzo Vineyard is also compelling, offering the liquid slate/petroleum-like notes found more strongly in the Marcassin Vineyard. Full-bodied, powerful, and expansive, with laser-like focus, the Lorenzo possesses lemony, peach, apricot, steely flavors crammed into an impressively concentrated personality. It is simply sensational, so excuse the verbose wine speak. Anticipated maturity: now–2007. Marcassin's last offering from Lee Hudson's Carneros vineyard, the 1997 Chardonnay Hudson Vineyard E Block, displays an evolved light gold color as well as an exotic nose of smoked tropical fruit intermixed with orange marmalade and roasted coffee scents. Layered, rich, and boisterous, but not nearly as complex or nuanced as the Gauer Ranch Upper Barn or Lorenzo, this is a full-throttle, exuberant, flamboyant Chardonnay. Drink it over the next 3–4 years.

With respect to the Marcassin Pinot Noir program, there is no doubting that, along with several of the Kistler Pinot Noirs as well as those from Brewer-Clifton in Santa Barbara, they are the most remarkable Pinot Noirs being produced in the New World. If only some of the infamous league of apologists for Burgundy would put these wines in a blind tasting against Burgundy's greatest grand crus. Don't expect that to happen anytime soon. A 1999 Pinot Noir Three Sisters–Sea Ridge Meadow Vineyard appears under both the Marcassin and Martinelli label (the Martinellis own this land and farm the vineyard with Turley and Wetlaufer). Marcassin's 1999 offering is an exquisite Pinot Noir revealing a dark ruby/purple color and a sweet nose of cherry jam infused with smoke, minerals, and flowers. The wine's finesse and elegance in addition to glorious levels of black raspberry and cherry fruit, expansiveness, and earthy, rich complexity suggest a grand cru from Morey-St.-Denis. The 1999 Pinot Noir Three Sisters–Lambing Barn Vineyard comes from a small six-acre parcel planted with tightly spaced Burgundy Dijon clones. It offers an exotic, spicy (cinnamon, allspice), new saddle leather, and black cherry/raspberry-scented bouquet. Full-bodied, expansive, dense, and exceptionally complex, it will drink well for 7–8 years. The 1999 Pinot Noir Blue Slide Ridge is awesome! This vineyard, planted with such clones of Pinot Noir as Pommard, #115, #667, and #777, has produced an opaque ruby/purple-colored effort with an exquisite nose of roasted herbs, vanilla, smoke, black fruits, meat, and violets. Aromatically, it is reminiscent of a top vintage of Domaine de la Romanée-Conti's Richebourg or La Tâche. The wine is extraordinarily complex, layered, and rich, with well-integrated acidity and oak, as well as a mind-boggling finish. This exquisite Pinot Noir will be magical to drink over the next 7–10 years. The 1999 Pinot Noir Marcassin Vineyard reveals more of a mineral, soy, Asian plum sauce characteristic, along with notes of black raspberries, scorched earth, steak tartare, and assorted black fruits. Subtle notions of toasty vanilla from new-oak aging also emerge. With full body as well as remarkable concentration, length, and presence, this fabulous Pinot is the youngest, most unevolved of these 1999s. Anticipated maturity: now–2014.

There are only two 1998 Pinot Noirs. The 1998 Pinot Noir Blue Slide Ridge exhibits a sensational nose of plum liqueur intermixed with blueberries, blackberries, smoke, and liquid stones. Displaying good underlying acidity, full body, and superb concentration and purity, it should drink well for a decade. The nearly perfect 1998 Pinot Noir Marcassin Vineyard boasts a deep saturated ruby/purple color in addition to a spectacular bouquet of blackberries, boysenberries, plums, raspberries, and cherries. In the mouth, it represents the essence of black fruits intermingled with aromas of grilled steak and scorched earth. With a thick, rich, full-bodied, meaty chewiness in addition to multiple flavor layers and impressive delineation for a wine of such concentration and size, this is a celestial Pinot Noir. Look for the 1998 Pinot Noir to evolve for 10–15 years.

The 1997 Pinot Noir Marcassin Vineyard has closed down since first tasted. One can sense the enormous weight, fat, ripeness, and richness in both the aromatics and flavors, but the tannin is obvious and the wine tight and structured. While it is undoubtedly a blockbuster, this 1997 Pinot needs 2–3 years of additional bottle age. It should keep for 12–15 years. The mineral characteristics that emerge from both the Marcassin Vineyard Chardonnay and Pinot Noir appear to become more pronounced as the wines age. The spectacularly complex, opulently textured, lavishly rich 1997 Pinot Noir Blue Slide Ridge displays a saturated plum/purple color in addition to gorgeous aromas of blueberries, black cherries, lavender, and smoky oak. Intense and full-bodied, with fabulous concentration, a voluptuous texture, and a long finish, this is a stunning effort. Sadly, production was minuscule—25 cases.

The 1996 Pinot Noir Marcassin Vineyard (275 cases) is also outstanding. In order to get a snapshot of what these wines are really about is to recognize that they are reminiscent of the finest grand crus I have tasted from such sites as Clos de la Roche and Clos St.-Denis. They share an extraordinary minerality with fabulously concentrated plum, black cherry, blueberry/blackberry characteristics. They are fuller-bodied, denser, and more concentrated and alcoholic than any grand cru red Burgundy (although red Burgundies from vintages such as 1997, 1990, and 1989 routinely achieved 14% alcohol). The 1996 Pinot Noir Marcassin Vineyard has not yet begun to reveal additional nuances, but it is the kind of Pinot Noir that suggests that the Sonoma Coast, in 30–50 years, may be one of the world's most fashionable spots for this varietal.

The 1995 Pinot Noir Marcassin Vineyard (only 25 cases for the world) was the debut vintage for this wine. It possesses one of the most enthralling and exquisite Burgundy-like Pinot noses I have ever smelled in a young American Pinot Noir. The color is a healthy medium dark ruby, and the sweet nose of jammy red and black fruits, truffles, smoked duck, and earth reminded this taster of a grand cru from Flagey-Echezeaux or Vosne-Romanée. The wine reveals a delicacy and sweetness on the palate, without the weight one expects from such intense aromas and flavors. A remarkably complex wine, it will be a dazzling, full-bodied, perfumed style of Pinot Noir that should drink well during its first 5–7 years of life. I doubt it will be long-lived, but all the Marcassin wines have held their fruit and character longer than I would have expected.

All these wines are available through the winery's mailing list, although some preferred Napa Valley restaurants, particularly the French Laundry, and a few in New York (Daniel and Le Bernardin) seem to receive noteworthy allocations.

MARIETTA CELLARS (SONOMA)

1996 Cabernet Sauvignon	Sonoma	C	90
1994 Cabernet Sauvignon	Sonoma	C	88
N.V. Old Vine Red Lot 22	California	B	88
N.V. Old Vine Red Lot 15	Sonoma	B	90
N.V. Old Vine Red Lot 18	Sonoma	B	89
1996 Syrah	California	C	88

The 1996 Cabernet Sauvignon and Syrah, and Old Vine Red Lot 22 make up the strongest group of Marietta wines I have tasted in recent vintages. There are some terrific buys, including the 20,000 cases of nonvintage Old Vine Red Lot 22. This wine has become a darling of intelligent consumers, as evidenced by the fact that the entire production is allocated. The Lot 22 offering, primarily from the 1996 and 1997 vintages, is a blend of Zinfandel, Petite Sirah, Carignan, Gamay, and Cabernet Sauvignon, from vineyard sources in Napa, Sonoma, and Mendocino. It is a weighty, seriously endowed wine with a dark purple color, as well as a super nose of cherries, black currants, pepper, spice, and loamy soil notes. Full-bodied and richly extracted, with copious quantities of berry fruit, excellent purity, and an expansive, silky-textured finish, this wine can be drunk now as well as cellared for 2–3 years. Marietta's Old Vine Red is consistently one of the best bargains in exuberant, dry reds.

I suspect one has to go back to the 1990 vintage to find a Marietta Cabernet Sauvignon with as much quality and potential as the 1996. It is a full-bodied, tannic yet promising, opaque purple-colored Cabernet loaded with potential. Some of the rustic tannin should melt away over the next 2–5 years. At present, it is concentrated, with textbook cedary and black currant fruit displayed in a dramatic, rich style. There is good thickness and richness, as well as plenty of lusty alcohol (14.6%) in this large-scaled Cabernet that should age nicely for 10–12 years. In today's inflated marketplace, Cabernet Sauvignons of this quality usually sell for $30+ a bottle. Readers take note. The 1996 Syrah, which emerges from Sonoma and Mendocino vineyards, is a full-bodied, blackberry-scented wine with pepper, sweet licorice, and weedy, underbrush notes. With excellent ripeness, good spice, and a robust, muscular personality, this Syrah offers gutsy, mouth-filling flavors that should continue to develop for 5–7 years.

Proprietor/wine-maker Chris Bilbro should receive an award from consumers for making such tasty wines while maintaining realistic prices. One of the finest values in the wine world is Marietta's Old Vine Red, a recent rendition being Lot 18. This wine, usually a blend of Petite Sirah, Cabernet Sauvignon, Zinfandel, Carignan, and who knows what else, is always a deep ruby/purple-colored wine with copious quantities of peppery black fruits intertwined with scents of earth. A chewy, fleshy, full-bodied, mouth-filling wine, this juicy, burly effort disappears as quickly as Marietta releases the 10,000+ cases produced. While most of the Old Vine Red is consumed within the first 1–2 months of purchase, it gives every indication of lasting for 5 or more years. The Lot 15 is made from 25% Petite Sirah, 20% Cabernet Sauvignon, 5% Carignan, and the rest Zinfandel and other red wine grapes. This opaque purple-colored wine offers up huge quantities of sweet black cherries and cassis, intermixed with scents of pepper, truffles, and spices. Full-bodied, with a kirsch-like flavor, this dense, chewy, fleshy wine is California's answer to a top-notch Châteauneuf-du-Pape. There may be 10,000 cases of this superb wine, but it disappears quickly from the shelves of retailers.

This winery also does a fine job with Cabernet Sauvignon. Although Marietta's 1994 Cabernet Sauvignon is not as brilliant as the 1992, it tastes as good as most Cabernets that cost $10–15 more a bottle. The wine's deep, dense, ruby/purple color is followed by moderately intense aromas of ripe black fruits with toasty wood notes in the background. Full-bodied, tannic, dense, and chewy, this wine will benefit from 1–2 years of cellaring; it should age well for a decade.

MARTINELLI (SONOMA)

1999	Chardonnay Charles Ranch	Sonoma Coast	E	90
1999	Chardonnay Goldridge Vineyard	Russian River	E	90
1999	Chardonnay Martinelli Road	Russian River	D	91
1999	Chardonnay Woolsey Road	Russian River	D	90
1999	Gewurztraminer Martinelli Vineyard	Russian River	E	90
1999	Pinot Noir Blue Slide Ridge	Sonoma Coast	E	91+
1998	Pinot Noir Blue Slide Ridge	Sonoma Coast	E	93
1994	Pinot Noir Estate	Russian River	C	90
1998	Pinot Noir Martinelli Vineyard	Russian River	D	91
1996	Pinot Noir Martinelli Vineyard	Russian River	D	92
1995	Pinot Noir Martinelli Vineyard	Russian River	D	90
1999	Pinot Noir Martinelli Vineyard Reserve	Russian River	D	93
1998	Pinot Noir Martinelli Vineyard Reserve	Russian River	D	93
1997	Pinot Noir Martinelli Vineyard Reserve	Russian River	D	93
1996	Pinot Noir Martinelli Vineyard Reserve	Russian River	D	94
1995	Pinot Noir Martinelli Vineyard Reserve	Russian River	D	92
1999	Pinot Noir Three Colts	Russian River	E	90
1999	Syrah Hop Barn Hill	Russian River	E	97
1999	Zinfandel Guiseppe and Luisa	Russian River	E	95
1998	Zinfandel Guiseppe and Luisa	Russian River	E	94
1999	Zinfandel Jackass Vineyard	Russian River	EE	92
1998	Zinfandel Jackass Vineyard	Russian River	EE	95
1997	Zinfandel Jackass Vineyard	Russian River	EE	95
1996	Zinfandel Jackass Vineyard	Russian River	EE	93
1999	Zinfandel Jackass Hill Vineyard	Russian River	EEE	96
1998	Zinfandel Jackass Hill Vineyard	Russian River	EEE	97
1997	Zinfandel Jackass Hill Vineyard	Russian River	EE	95
1996	Zinfandel Jackass Hill Vineyard	Russian River	EE	96

Readers who have trouble latching onto a bottle of Helen Turley and John Wetlaufer's famed Marcassin Chardonnay or Pinot Noir should try to secure some of the wines from Martinelli. This old Russian River family has seemingly unlimited resources, as well as a bevy of top-notch vineyards. They have also made major investments on the Sonoma Coast. Their vineyard strategist is John Wetlaufer and their consulting wine-maker is his wife, Helen Turley. Since these two people have come aboard, the results have been remarkable, with a bevy of exquisite Chardonnays, Pinot Noirs, and Zinfandels as well as California's finest Gewürztraminer. Their newest offering is microscopic quantities of an unreal Syrah.

The 1999 Chardonnays from Martinelli possess slightly lower alcohol than previous vintages, as well as more steely, mineral-infused characters. The 1999 Chardonnay Woolsey Road (13.4% alcohol) shows attractive, steely, mineral, and orange characteristics, medium to full body, excellent purity, and a Chablis-like character. Elegant and rich, it is destined to last for 4–5 years. The more powerful 1999 Chardonnay Goldridge (14.4% alcohol) displays the most flamboyant character of the 1999s, with notes of honey, butterscotch, mineral, and smoky, leesy characteristics. Freshly baked bread and/or brioche combine with spicy oak and tropical fruit in the most forward of Martinelli's 1999 Chardonnays. Drink it over the next 3–4 years. Honeyed pineapple, orange marmalade, minerals, and butter characterize the full-bodied, surprisingly nuanced, and stylish 1999 Chardonnay Charles Ranch. With only 13.4% alcohol, this wine possesses less power than previous vintages, but there is liquid minerality underneath all the fruit. Citrus oils also make an appearance. This wine should last for 4–5 years. The 1999 Chardonnay Martinelli Road (a Chardonnay vineyard that is essentially the lower slopes of the Jackass and Jackass Hill Zinfandel vineyards) offers steely, waxy, buttery tropical fruits, great ripeness, good underlying acidity, smoky, leesy characteristics, and a full-bodied, fruit-dominated finish. It should drink well for 2–3 years. It offers a slightly more reserved/restrained style than the 1998.

Readers should not overlook Martinelli's limited production, delicious 1999 Gewürztraminer Martinelli Vineyard, the finest Gewürztraminer made in California. Revealing this varietal's classic lychee nut and honeyed grapefruit aromas and flavors, it is a dry, full-bodied, exotic, ostentatious effort that requires consumption over the next 1–2 years in order to take advantage of its intensity and exuberance.

The saturated plum-colored 1999 Pinot Noir Martinelli Vineyard Reserve displays more evolution than found in recent vintages. A black cherry/raspberry-scented nose reveals lavish quantities of toasty oak, sweet black raspberries, *sous bois*, smoke, and soy. Full-bodied and soft, with splendid concentration and enormous depth, it is ideal for drinking over the next 3–4 years. The dense ruby/purple-colored 1999 Pinot Noir Blue Slide Ridge offers gloriously rich blackberry, blueberry, violet, and mineral aromas. Opulently textured, with fabulous fruit, sensational texture, and a full-bodied, long finish, this 1999 California Pinot Noir could easily stand up to many a grand cru from Burgundy's Côte de Nuits. Drink it over the next 7–8 years. Another debut release from the Pinot Noir portfolio is the 1999 Pinot Noir Three Colts. This comes from three young vineyards the Martinellis have planted with 2,000 vines per acre and vertical trellising. It is a powerful Pinot Noir (15.1% alcohol) exhibiting a dark ruby/purple color, sumptuous aromas, and flavors of prunes, plums, root beer, cocoa, and cherry liqueur, and an opulent, lush texture. This is an outstanding, hedonistically styled Pinot Noir to drink over the next 5–6 years.

The three 1998 Pinot Noirs are all exceptional efforts. The 1998 Pinot Noir Martinelli Vineyard (14.5% alcohol) tastes like a premier cru Pommard. It reveals aromas and flavors of pomegranate, apple skins, black cherries, pepper, and earth in addition to a dense, full-bodied, muscular palate, low acidity, copious alcohol, and abundant glycerin. Drink it over the next 5–6 years. The 1998 Pinot Noir Martinelli Vineyard Reserve's bouquet offers scents of earth, seaweed, smoke, black cherry jam, raspberries, and grilled meats. Full-bodied, chewy, and exotic, with an ostentatious/exuberant personality, it possesses adequate acidity, sweet tannin, and subtle notes of new wood. It should drink well for 7–8 years. There are 100 cases of the debut vintage of Martinelli's 1998 Pinot Noir Blue Slide Ridge. An opaque deep ruby/purple color is followed by aromas of sweet plum, black raspberry, and blueberry fruit, fabulous concentration, exquisite purity, medium to full body, and uncanny balance as well as seamlessness. This glorious Pinot Noir can be drunk now and over the next 5–7 years.

The lavishly rich, full-bodied, gloriously perfumed and flavored 1997 Pinot Noir Martinelli Vineyard Reserve is performing terrifically from bottle. In a recent blind tasting with some of America's finest Pinot and three of my favorite Burgundy grand crus from 1990, it was the group's (not my) favorite. It overloads the olfactory senses with kirsch, plum, black cherry fruit, and smoky oak. Heady and lush, it should be drunk over the next 5–8 years.

When I tasted Martinelli's two *cuvées* of 1996 Pinot Noir, they immediately took me back to the late sixties when I was a student living outside Washington, D.C., making frequent buying trips to what was then called plain old Pearson's Liquor Shop. At that time, Pearson's had

an extraordinary collection of 1961, 1962, 1964, and 1966 red Burgundies that could be purchased for a song. I cut my teeth on many a Domaine Parent Pommard Les Grandes
Epenottes and Pommard Les Rugiens from those vintages. They were marvelously full-
bodied, meaty, fragrant Pinots the likes of which I have never tasted again from either Domaine Parent or any other Pommard producer. When I tasted Martinelli's 1996 Pinot Noir
Martinelli Vineyard and 1996 Pinot Noir Martinelli Vineyard Reserve, I was reminded of my
student days of Parent's gloriously decadent, rich Pinots. These are fascinating wines, offering gorgeous levels of smoky, meaty, earthy, black cherry fruit in a full-bodied, glycerin-
imbued, lusty style that is about as hedonistic as Pinot Noir can be. While I was blown away
by the 1996 Pinot Noir Martinelli Vineyard, the Reserve Pinot Noir was even more spectacular and amazingly concentrated. They have it all! Bottled unfined and unfiltered, they represent the essence of the Pinot Noir grape as translated by the Martinellis and their
consultant wine-maker, Helen Turley. Both wines should drink well for 3–4 years, perhaps
longer, but I can't imagine anyone having enough discipline to hold on to these wines as long
as they continue to drink as well as they do today.

Martinelli's 1994 Pinot Noir Estate, also bottled without fining or filtration, is an outstanding example of this varietal. Unfortunately, only 200 cases were produced of this sumptuously styled, meaty, black cherry and smoke-scented wine. It exhibits a dark garnet color,
sweet, chewy, fleshy, Burgundy-like fruit, high alcohol (14.3%), and a soft, gorgeously proportioned, lusty finish. This is what Burgundy should be—pure, expansive, succulent, and
loaded with gobs of fruit—but so rarely is. The 1994 Pinot Noir Estate was the first outstanding Martinelli Pinot Noir. This was followed by two superlative 1995s. The 1995 Pinot Noir
Martinelli Vineyard exhibits a Domaine Dujac–like complexity with its cinnamon, black
cherry, spicy, smoky nose. It offers sweet, gamey, plum and black cherry–like flavors, excellent richness and purity, and a long, lusty finish. Drink this round, generous Pinot Noir over
the next 3–4 years. Remarkably, there is a 1995 Pinot Noir Martinelli Vineyard Reserve, also
a terrific example of this varietal. It possesses a deep ruby color, a big, spicy, smoky, earth,
and black fruit–scented nose, and layers of ripe, jammy flavors buttressed by new oak, acidity, and sweet tannin. The finish is long and authoritative. These Pinot Noirs offer further evidence of just how exciting California Pinot Noir has become. The Reserve was released in
September 1997; it will drink well for 2–4 years, possibly longer.

Martinelli's 1999 Zinfandels are as concentrated and intense as readers might expect from
previous renditions. Production of the 1999 Zinfandel Guiseppe and Luisa (made from the
same clone planted in the Jackass Hill Vineyard) is a whopping 1,600 cases. The dense
plum/purple color is accompanied by a glorious perfume of jammy blackberry and cassis
fruit, an unctuous, opulent texture, high glycerin (17% alcohol), and a dry, long, dense, pure
finish. This is a stunning, flamboyant Zinfandel elixir to drink over the next 6–10 years. The
spectacular 1999 Zinfandel Jackass Vineyard (1,700 cases of 15.9% alcohol) is nearly as
compelling as the Jackass Hill offering. An opaque garnet/purple/plum color is followed by
an exotic bouquet of smoked Peking duck, plum sauce, blackberry and cherry liqueur, and
Asian spices. The wine is exquisitely concentrated, thick, viscous, and rich, but dry and remarkably well balanced, with a blockbuster finish. It should drink well for a decade. Year in
and year out, the following wine gets my nod as one of California's greatest Zinfandels. The
1999 Zinfandel Jackass Hill Vineyard (16.5% alcohol) reveals notes of lavender, jammy
black raspberries and blackberries, smoky oak, soy, *jus de viande*, and a touch of volatile
acidity, all of which explode in the nose and on the palate. Flamboyant, with excellent structure, immense body, and flavors of blackberries and smoky cherries that ooze across the
palate, this is another prodigious wine that should be consumed over the next decade, although its power and force of character will keep it alive for 2–3 decades.

The 1998 Zinfandel Guiseppe and Luisa (15.5% alcohol) is one of the vintage's superstars.

A terrific nose of plum liqueur intermixed with smoke, coffee, Chinese black tea, cherries, plums, raspberries, and spice soars from the glass. Full body, an unctuous texture, and gorgeously pure flavors conceal the wine's high alcohol. With a stupendous texture, finish, and opulence, it can be drunk over the next 4–8 years, although I suspect it will last longer. The murky, plum/purple-colored 1998 Zinfandel Jackass Vineyard is followed by scents of prunes, plum liqueur, licorice, smoke, coffee, and assorted Asian spices. The wine is spectacularly rich, thick, and chewy, with low acidity. Its 16+% alcohol is barely noticeable. The deep purple-colored 1998 Zinfandel Jackass Hill Vineyard (17% alcohol) appears less flamboyant and more tightly knit and structured than the Jackass Vineyard . . . at least initially. After ten minutes of airing, the wine begins to unfold, revealing multiple dimensions in its glorious perfume, richness, and complexity. It is a massive Zinfandel with spectacular aromatics (smoke, prunes, plums, raspberries, coffee, cedar, new saddle leather) as well as viscous, chewy, full-throttle flavors. A wine of enormous force as well as unbelievable symmetry, it should age for a decade. I would not be surprised to see well-stored examples display considerable fruit and complexity at age 20 or 30.

The 1997 Zinfandel Jackass Vineyard may be the finest offering produced under this designation. It tips the scales at over 16% alcohol, but the alcohol is remarkably concealed by the wine's extraordinary wealth of fruit, extract, and layered richness. The dark ruby/purple/garnet color was no doubt intensified by the 3–5 day cold soak the Martinellis and wine-maker Helen Turley give this wine. The nose offers up a plethora of celestial aromas, including plum liqueur, kirsch, spice box, coffee, prunes, and jammy cherries. As the wine sits in the glass, spicy oak, pepper, allspice, and clove scents emerge. Full-bodied, rich, and mouth-filling, this velvety-textured, voluptuous, hedonistic Zinfandel can be drunk now as well as over the next decade. The 1997 Zinfandel Jackass Hill Vineyard is a massive, totally dry wine that came in at 17.5% alcohol and was bottled unfiltered. Dense and full-bodied, it represents Zinfandel in its most concentrated form. Its singular style, unctuous texture, and fabulously concentrated flavors make for an unforgettable tasting experience. While not for everybody, it is the quintessential powerhouse Zinfandel made from tiny yields, a phenomenal vineyard site, and impeccable winemaking. Its characteristics are similar to those of the Jackass Vineyard, only more intense—jammy black cherries, plums, prunes, dried herbs, licorice, chocolate, and coffee. This wine is best drunk in its exuberant youthfulness, but I suspect it will age well beyond a decade.

Martinelli's 1996s are both exceptional Zinfandels. The 1996 Zinfandel Jackass Vineyard (15.6% alcohol) reveals a murky plum/purple color. Outstanding aromatics soar from the glass, offering aromas of licorice, blackberry liqueur, truffles, underbrush, smoke, and meat. The wine's unctuousness, full body, and supple texture result in a decadently rich, lavishly endowed Zinfandel to drink over the next 3–6 years. The 1996 Zinfandel Jackass Hill Vineyard displays a similar plum/purple color. The nose offers a smorgasbord of aromas, including cherry, blackberry, and strawberry liqueur intermingled with smoky, toasty oak, roasted Provençal herbs, Asian spice, and chocolaty, meaty overtones. Exceptionally full-bodied, with gobs of glycerin, remarkable purity, and profound balance for such a large Zinfandel, this is a true work of art. It should drink well for another 7–8+ years. Are the Jackass 1996s better than the 1995s and 1994s? In my estimation, the 1995 and 1994 Jackass and Jackass Hill Zinfandels are among the most amazing wines I have ever tasted. I cannot say the 1996s are superior, but no one who loves Zin should be without them. They are artistic creations.

Lastly, the opaque blue/purple-colored 1999 Syrah Hop Barn Hill is an amazing achievement. Produced from yields of less than one ton of fruit per vine, this wine demonstrates what can be achieved from extremely ripe fruit (picked at 29° Brix) that is fermented dry, and aged in 100% new French oak. A classic Syrah, it possesses aromas and flavors of blackberry liqueur intermixed with cassis, pepper, and bacon fat. With unreal levels of glycerin, richness, and concentration, it is akin to drinking the blood of the grape. There is a viscosity and unctuosity that must be tasted to be believed. It is a thrilling, historic Syrah for California! Sadly, there were less than 50 cases produced. The good news is that the Martinellis have planted several additional acres of Syrah.

More and more wines made from small, high-quality producers such as Martinelli are being sold through a mailing list. Readers wishing to secure a bottle of their most limited production offerings should know what to do. These wines are best drunk young, despite their lofty alcohol levels and extract. I suggest consuming them during their first 5–8 years of life.

THE MAYO FAMILY WINERY (SONOMA)

1999 Zinfandel Ricci Vineyard	Russian River	D	89

This dense plum/purple-colored, blockbuster effort exhibits abundant black cherry, plum, and currant fruit with pepper, incense, and spice notes in the background. Made in a super-concentrated style, with 15.9% alcohol, this blockbuster has layered, viscous, and pure flavors, with copious quantities of glycerin. It will drink well for 4–6 years.

PHILIPPE MELKA (NAPA)

1999 Métisse Proprietary Red Wine	Napa	E	90
1998 Métisse Proprietary Red Wine	Napa	E	91
1997 Métisse Proprietary Red Wine	Napa	E	93
1996 Métisse Proprietary Red Wine	Napa	D	90

Frenchman Philippe Melka is quickly establishing a reputation as one of the finest consultants in Napa Valley. He oversees the winemaking at Lail Vineyards, and has recently added Caldwell Vineyard, Vineyard 29, and Marston Family Vineyard to his portfolio. He is also the person responsible for the fabulous wines emerging from Seavey in Conn Valley. Melka produces approximately 450 cases under his own name.

The 1998 Métisse (a blend of 87% Cabernet Sauvignon, 10% Merlot, and 3% Cabernet Franc) is a gorgeously proportioned, full-bodied, dark purple-colored effort with superb density, soft, sweet tannin, a generous constitution, and copious quantities of blackberry and cassis fruit nicely dosed with subtle new oak. Low in acidity, it is ideal for drinking over the next 12–15 years. It is an exceptional proprietary red from the 1998 vintage. The 1999 Métisse (an assemblage of 80% Cabernet Sauvignon, 17% Merlot, and 3% Cabernet Franc) represents a trial blend, with slightly more Cabernet Sauvignon than the 1998. Approximately 450 cases were produced. Like the 1998, it sees 40–45% new oak, and, if possible, it will be bottled without filtration, although occasionally Melka will fine the wine (as he did in 1998) to soften the tannin. The 1999 exhibits a dense purple color as well as a Pomerol-like bouquet of espresso, blackberries, cherries, and chocolate. Full-bodied and velvety-textured, this promising red should be at its finest between 2004–2020.

The blend of the 1997 Métisse (450 cases made from 53% Cabernet Sauvignon, 27% Merlot, and 20% Cabernet Franc) is similar to that of the famed Château Haut-Brion, but the wine tastes more like a Pomerol. It is deep ruby/purple, with an exuberant, exotic nose of espresso beans lathered in melted chocolate, and jammy cherry/cassis. Full-bodied and velvety-textured, this opulent, hedonistic, gorgeously textured wine is already thrilling to drink. Anticipated maturity: now–2016. The 1996 Métisse (about 240 cases) is a blend of 40% Cabernet Sauvignon, 30% Cabernet Franc, and 30% Merlot. A Bordeaux-styled red (Melka was trained under Christian Moueix), this 1996 is a stylish, complex, elegant wine. It boasts a dark ruby/purple color, followed by attractive aromatics consisting of black currants, lead pencil, cedar, spice box, and toast. Medium-bodied, with graceful, ripe fruit, and nicely integrated tannin and acidity, this is an exceptionally harmonious wine that opens beautifully in the glass. It will not knock tasters over with its power or extract, but there is plenty going on in this stylish, complete wine. Enjoy it now and over the next 12–14 years.

MERRYVALE VINEYARDS (NAPA)

1995 Cabernet Sauvignon Reserve	Napa	D	89
1995 Merlot Beckstoffer IV Vineyard	Napa	D	88
1995 Merlot Reserve	Napa	D	89
1996 Profile Proprietary Red Wine	Napa	E	90
1995 Profile Proprietary Red Wine	Napa	E	90
1994 Profile Proprietary Red Wine	Napa	E	92

Given the quality of Merryvale's wines, I am surprised this winery does not receive more attention. Their Profile Proprietary Red Wine ranks among the top three or four dozen red wines of northern California, and their Silhouette Chardonnay is a brilliant Burgundian-styled wine with extraordinary richness and complexity.

Among the red wines, the 1995 Merlot Reserve may turn out to be an outstanding wine with another 1–2 years of bottle age. The wine reveals a dense purple color and a tight but promising nose of melted chocolate, and jammy blackberry and cherry fruit. It hits the palate with good richness, an attractive spicy, cinnamon component, excellent equilibrium, and a long, lush, concentrated finish. It should drink well over the next 10–12 years. The opaque purple-colored 1995 Merlot Beckstoffer IV Vineyard (250 cases) reveals toasty new oak in the nose, as well as impressive richness, purity, and body, but it was closed and unevolved when I tasted it. My numerical rating may turn out to be somewhat stingy once this wine has a chance to open and expand. This is the type of wine that I wish could have been given 4–5 hours in a decanter to see what is behind its imposing structure. It will last for 12–15+ years.

Another impressive wine that needs time in the cellar is the 1995 Cabernet Sauvignon Reserve. It boasts a dense dark ruby/purple color, as well as a sweet, cedary, vanilla, and black currant–scented nose with hints of weedy tobacco and olives. Full-bodied and highly extracted, but tannic, this wine may merit an outstanding score after 5–6 years of bottle age. It will last for 20+ years.

The exceptional Profile *cuvées* should receive more attention from consumers. The dense plum/purple-colored 1996 Profile Proprietary Red Wine (a blend of Merryvale's finest lots of Cabernet Sauvignon, Merlot, and Cabernet Franc) boasts a persistent sweet, ripe blackberry, prune, and licorice-scented nose. With full body, an opulent texture, a chewy, fleshy personality, and adequate underlying acidity and tannin, it can be drunk now and over the next 12–15 years. The outstanding 1995 Profile (14.5% alcohol) is made from 50% Cabernet Sauvignon, 39% Merlot, and the balance Cabernet Franc. It needs 4–5 years of cellaring, so readers looking for Cabernet-based wines with immediate accessibility should be forewarned. The wine exhibits an opaque purple color, followed by copious amounts of toasty, smoky, high-quality new oak in the nose, along with equally impressive quantities of black currants, plums, and cherries. Deep and full-bodied, with high tannin but outstanding concentration, this is an impressively built, Bordeaux-like wine. Anticipated maturity: now–2020. Even better is the 1994 Profile (a blend of 60% Cabernet Sauvignon, 30% Merlot, and 10% Cabernet Franc). It possesses an opaque purple color, and seems to hit every sweet spot on the palate, offering loads of cassis, roasted herbs, toast, and licorice. This multilayered, rich, concentrated wine also reveals impeccable balance and elegance. There is restraint, power, and concentration—a rare combination in such a big wine. The 1994 is more accessible than the 1995, and thus can be drunk young or cellared for 15–20+ years.

Past Glories: 1993 Profile Proprietary Red Wine (90)

PETER MICHAEL WINERY (SONOMA)

1999 Chardonnay Belle Côte	Knights Valley	EE	90
1998 Chardonnay Belle Côte	Knights Valley	EE	95
1997 Chardonnay Belle Côte	Knights Valley	E	93
1999 Chardonnay La Carrière	Knights Valley	EE	91

1998	Chardonnay La Carrière	Knights Valley	EE	95
1997	Chardonnay La Carrière	Knights Valley	E	94
1999	Chardonnay Crête d'Or	Russian River	EE	93
1999	Chardonnay Cuvée Indigène	Sonoma	EE	93
1998	Chardonnay Cuvée Indigène	Sonoma	EE	96
1997	Chardonnay Cuvée Indigène	Sonoma	EE	95
1999	Chardonnay Mon Plaisir	Sonoma	EE	91
1998	Chardonnay Mon Plaisir	Sonoma	EE	95
1997	Chardonnay Mon Plaisir	Sonoma	EE	94
1999	Chardonnay Point Rouge	Sonoma	EE	94+
1998	Chardonnay Point Rouge	Sonoma	EE	(96–99)
1997	Chardonnay Point Rouge	Sonoma	EE	98
		(750 ml)		
1998	Les Pavots Proprietary	Knights Valley	EE	89+
1997	Les Pavots Proprietary	Knights Valley	EE	96+
1996	Les Pavots Proprietary	Knights Valley	EE	96
		(750 ml)		
1995	Les Pavots Proprietary	Knights Valley	EE	91
1994	Les Pavots Proprietary	Knights Valley	EE	94
1999	Pinot Noir Le Moulin Rouge	Santa Lucia Highlands	EE	92
1997	Pinot Noir Pisoni Ranch	Santa Lucia Highlands	EE	89
1999	Sauvignon Blanc l'Après Midi	Sonoma	E	90
1998	Sauvignon Blanc l'Après Midi	Sonoma	E	88
1997	Sauvignon Blanc l'Après Midi	Sonoma	E	88

As I have written many times in the past, this is one of the world's finest sources of Burgundy-inspired Chardonnay and Pinot Noir, as well as a Bordeaux-styled red, Les Pavots. And don't forget the Sauvignon Blanc called l'Après Midi. Some topflight wine-makers have walked through the doors of Peter Michael, including Helen Turley, Mark Aubert, and Vanessa Wong. The 1999s, from an even colder year than 1998, with an extremely late growing season, possess higher acids, but the small, concentrated crop appears to have compensated for the tendency of the wines to taste too tart. The following offerings continue Peter Michael's amazing progression of brilliant winemaking. Admirers of the crisp, delicious Sauvignon Blanc l'Après Midi will be disappointed that only 214 cases were produced in 1999. The low production was caused by an irregular flowering and poor crop set. This light- to medium-bodied, 100% Sauvignon Blanc reveals notes of grapefruit, melon, tangerine, and assorted citrus. An underlying minerality emerges as the wine sits in the glass. Elegant, with gorgeous levels of fruit as well as a nicely textured mouth-feel, it remains one of California's most nuanced Sauvignon Blancs. Seventy percent of this *cuvée* was fermented with indigenous yeast. Drink it over the next 1–2 years, although I suspect it will last longer.

The fourth vintage for this estate's Belle Côte Chardonnay, the 1999 was produced from three clones of Chardonnay (the Old Wente, Rued, and See). Most of the fermentation was by indigenous yeast, and the wine was aged in 53% new French oak prior to being bottled with neither fining nor filtration. It reveals gorgeous aromas and flavors of tropical fruits, lemon zest, pears, and minerals. This authoritatively rich, complex, elegant Chardonnay is medium-bodied, well delineated, and beautifully concentrated, with exotic floral and spice notes in addition to well-integrated oak. It should drink well for 4–5 years. The 1999 Chardonnay La Carrière emerges from estate vineyards planted at elevations of 1,600–1,800 feet, with a gradient of nearly 40%. This vineyard is planted with both the French Dijon and Californian Hyde clones. The 1999 La Carrière reveals more roasted hazelnut/stony characteristics along with abundant spice, buttered pears, and guava-like fruit. Produced from extremely low yields of 1.7 tons of fruit per acre, it possesses a creamier texture than the Belle Côte, exotic fruit on the mid-palate, and a ripe, rich finish with fine underlying acidity. It is a brilliant Chardonnay that should last for 4–5 years. One of the most flamboyant Peter Michael Chardonnays is their *cuvée* Mon Plaisir. Produced from the Old Wente clone grown in the Alexander Mountain Estate Vineyard owned by Jess Jackson, and aged totally in French oak (50% new), the 1999 Chardonnay Mon Plaisir reveals abundant tropical fruit characteristics in its ostentatious bouquet. Aromas of oranges, ripe honeyed apples, and buttered citrus jump from the glass of this hedonistically styled Chardonnay. The integration of wood provides subtle notes of vanilla and toast, which add to the wine's complex personality. Medium- to full-bodied, pure, long, and concentrated, with enough acidity to provide freshness and focus, it will drink well for 4–5 years. Consistently one of California's finest Chardonnays, the 100% indigenous yeast-fermented Chardonnay Cuvée Indigène also emerges from the Alexander Mountain Estate Vineyard. Typically, the 1999 exhibits distinctive aromas of smoky tropical fruit intermixed with peaches, apricots, and pears. Long, full-bodied, and layered, with terrific texture, gorgeous purity, and loads of fruit, this effort can stand up against the finest Burgundy grand crus (as could its siblings). The Cuvée Indigène possesses more leesy, smoky notes in its rich, concentrated style. It is a young, pure, super-concentrated Chardonnay to enjoy over the next 5–6 years (although it may last nearly a decade). The limited production Chardonnay Point Rouge represents a selection of the finest barrels. In most years, this is essentially the best barrels of Cuvée Indigène, picked for their extra intensity and complex style. This is routinely one of the three or four finest Chardonnays being produced in California, as well as one of the greatest of the world, as tastings against Burgundy's finest Bâtard-Montrachets, Chevalier-Montrachets, and Le Montrachets have consistently proven, much to the chagrin of Burgundians. The 1999 Chardonnay Point Rouge is more steely than previous vintages, as well as more closed and unevolved, but there is no doubting its immense potential. It boasts honeyed citrus, orange, tangerine, liquid mineral, and smoky hazelnut aromas. The liquid minerality evident in the Point Rouge is a prominent characteristic of the better wines from such grand cru Burgundy vineyards as Le Montrachet, Chevalier-Montrachet, and Meursault-Perrières. The finish lasts for more than 40 seconds. This wine is more backward than the other Peter Michael Chardonnays and should have a slow evolution. Anticipated maturity: now–2010. Exquisite!

After working with a Russian River grower for a number of years, overseeing the replanting of a vineyard, the grower sold one crop to Peter Michael, and then signed a long-term contract with another winery. Consequently, the 1999 is the only Chardonnay made by Peter Michael from that vineyard. They have named it Crête d'Or. Made from the Hyde clone, the brilliant 1999 Chardonnay Crête d'Or is a creamy-textured, flamboyant, ostentatiously styled Chardonnay with aromas and flavors of roasted hazelnuts, dried apricots, peaches, and pineapples. A rich, full-bodied effort with good underlying acidity as well as a judicious touch of toasty oak, it should drink well for 5–6 years.

This is one of the world's great sources for Burgundy-styled Chardonnays, and the 1998s are spectacular. All of the following wines are fermented both with commercial and indigenous yeasts, given extensive lees stirring (which promotes complexity and additional textural nuances), and are bottled unfiltered. The 600 cases of 1998 Chardonnay La Carrière, like all these Chardonnays, tip the scales at a hefty 14.1% alcohol. Made from a vineyard planted on a steep, rocky hillside, it exhibits aromas of white peaches, honey, pears, subtle new oak, and citrus. Full-bodied and complex, with good underlying acidity, this wine is reminiscent of a Burgundian Corton-Charlemagne. It should drink well for 5–6 years. The 1998 Chardonnay Belle Côte (1,300 cases) is the finest yet produced from this vineyard situated on the hillsides above La Carrière. Fortunately, the larger production should guarantee some availability. Made from a vineyard planted with the Wente Chardonnay clone, this mouth-filling, full-bodied, impressively pure wine offers a full-throttle bouquet of roasted hazelnuts, honeyed tropical fruits, and exotic passion fruit/mango notes. Rich and full-bodied, with fine underlying acidity, this dazzling Chardonnay is already drinking well, yet promises to last for 5–7 years. There are 1,200 cases of the light gold-colored 1998 Chardonnay Mon Plaisir. This full-bodied, honeyed, heady, powerful, densely concentrated effort includes flamboyant apricot/peach notes in addition to outstanding concentration and more depth and persistence than the superb 1997. It should drink well for 5–6 years. There are 470 cases of the 1998 Chardonnay Cuvée Indigène. The only wine to be completely fermented with 100% indigenous yeast, this Chardonnay is more restrained aromatically than its siblings, but it is terrific on the palate, displaying explosive lemon/butter/honey flavors mixed with tropical fruit, mineral, and smoky, leesy components. Orange/tangerine notes also make an appearance. The aromatics should develop greater dimensions with another 6–12 months of bottle age.

The only 1998 not yet bottled is the Point Rouge. The light gold-colored 1998 Chardonnay Point Rouge displays an emerging nose of honeyed tropical fruits and citrus. It possesses exquisite concentration, admirable singularity, full body, and terrific purity and delineation Only marginally riper than the other Peter Michael offerings, it tastes longer in the mouth. This 1998 is a candidate for a perfect score. The 1997 Chardonnay Point Rouge (140 cases) exhibits a terrific texture and a sensational buttery, leesy nose with subtle toasty oak. Passion fruit, oranges, and honeyed lemons compete with minerals in this exceptionally rich, concentrated Chardonnay. A spectacular, full-throttle effort with impeccable balance, it should drink well for 4–5+ years.

There are 3,000 cases of the exquisite 1997 Chardonnay Belle Côte, which is made primarily from such old California Chardonnay clones as Wente, fermented with indigenous yeasts, aged in French barrels (50% new), and bottled unfiltered. The light straw/gold color is followed by sumptuous leesy, toasty, and honeyed pineapple scents with a touch of mineral. The wine is medium- to full-bodied, with exquisite texture, a sexy, rich aftertaste, and superb purity—a hallmark of every Peter Michael wine. The light gold-colored 1997 Chardonnay La Carrière (only 125 cases produced) comes from a hillside situated below the Belle Côte Vineyard. It is planted with Dijon Burgundy Chardonnay clones, in addition to the Hyde clone. Aged in 30% new oak, this offering reveals a distinctive mineral character not dissimilar from certain Corton-Charlemagnes. Liquid stone-like flavors are pronounced in the mouth, in addition to citrus and subtle oak notes. This distinctive, high-toned, *terroir*-driven, concentrated wine is more subtle than some of Peter Michael's efforts. It should drink well for 3–4 years. The dazzling 1997 Chardonnay Mon Plaisir (1,200 cases) displays a light to medium straw color and expressive aromatics consisting of tangerine/orange and other tropical fruits. In the mouth, notes of lemon butter make an appearance in this full-bodied, expansive, rich, fleshy Chardonnay that tips the scales at 14.1% alcohol. With fabulous fruit, the Mon Plaisir appears to be the qualitative equal of the more expensive Cuvée Indigène and Point Rouge. It should drink well for 3–4 years. The 1997 Chardonnay Cuvée Indigène (named so because it is fermented completely with indigenous vineyard yeasts) exhibits a light gold color, and a complex nose of smoky, leesy Chardonnay fruit intermixed with smoky, roasted hazelnuts, orange blossoms, and citrus. Full-bodied, with excellent underlying acidity, and more minerality to its flavors than Mon Plaisir, this profoundly concentrated, complex Chardonnay is a prodigious offering. Production was 550 cases, with the alcohol a boisterous 14.1%. Look for this wine to drink well for 5–7 years.

The other white wine from Peter Michael is their delicious, vibrant, fragrant Sauvignon Blanc l'Après Midi. In 1998, the source for this fruit changed from the Liparita Vineyard on Howell Mountain to Peter Michael's own estate vineyards. In 1998, there were 480 cases of this powerful (14.1% alcohol) 100% Sauvignon Blanc made from the Musqué clone. The 1998 Sauvignon Blanc l'Après Midi offers honeyed grapefruit, passion fruit, and lemon zest in its aromatic profile. Tart acidity provides good tanginess, and the wine's medium-bodied, fresh, lively personality is enthralling. It will be very flexible with food. The light straw-colored 1997 Sauvignon Blanc l'Après Midi possesses terrific acidity (much more than usual), as well as wonderfully intense, mineral-laden, melony, citrusy fruit. Crisp and medium-bodied, it is ideal for current consumption.

The finest Pinot Noir yet produced by Peter Michael is the 1999 Pinot Noir Le Moulin Rouge. This wine is made from the well-known Pisoni Vineyard in the Santa Lucia Highlands (a source of high-quality grapes sold to a half-dozen or more wineries). According to the grower, the clone was smuggled into this country from one of the two most famous vineyards in Vosne-Romanée. The dense ruby/purple-colored 1999 Le Moulin Rouge offers up a sweet nose of blackberries, pomegranate, vanilla, and Chinese black tea. Gorgeous fruit is found in this full-bodied, concentrated, expansive, potentially profound Pinot. The wood adds nice spice and smoke. Look for this Pinot Noir to drink well in 1–2 years, and last for a decade. Peter Michael's dark ruby-colored 1997 Pinot Noir Pisoni Ranch reveals purple nuances, as well as the telltale black raspberry and cassis notes with spicy oak in the background. Medium- to full-bodied and expansive, with excellent purity, and a lush, seductive palate, this heady (14.1% alcohol) wine should be consumed over the next 5–6 years.

Peter Michael's Les Pavots continue to go from strength to strength, with the 1997 Les Pavots the finest yet produced. This wine originates from a hillside vineyard overlooking the Knights Valley that has 23 acres planted with Bordeaux varietals. The 1997 blend consists of 79% Cabernet Sauvignon, 12% Merlot, and 9% Cabernet Franc. The wine was aged in French oak (50% new) and bottled without filtration. Fortunately, there are 4,351 cases, as well as 330 cases of magnums. A blue/black/purple color is followed by an extraordinary bouquet of toast, blackberries, crème de cassis, licorice, and cedar. Full-bodied, with silky tannin, low acidity, and layers of concentrated, pure black fruits judiciously wrapped in subtle toasty oak, this wine can be drunk early, but promises to hit its peak in 5–7 years, and last for two or more decades. The 1998 Les Pavots (80% Cabernet Sauvignon, 11% Merlot, and 9% Cabernet Franc) was produced from minuscule yields of 1.3 tons of fruit per acre. It exhibits a dense ruby/purple color in addition to aromas of melted fudge, cocoa, tobacco, and black currant fruit. In the mouth, the wine is medium- to full-bodied, with firm tannin, and a compressed, moderately long finish. Not surprisingly, it does not exhibit either the flavor dimension or length of the 1997 or 1996. 1998 was a more difficult vintage, but Les Pavots has turned out well, revealing more of a Bordeaux-like weight profile than the more enormously endowed, concentrated 1997. Nevertheless, it is a successful effort in a challenging year. Anticipated maturity: 2003–2014.

The powerhouse, opaque purple/blue-colored 1996 Les Pavots is a blend of 74% Cabernet Sauvignon, 20% Merlot, and 6% Cabernet Franc. The nose offers up blackberry, licorice, cassis, and toast aromas. The superb extract, well-defined personality, and smoky, licorice, Asian spice, and blackberry flavors provide a thrilling tasting experience. Like its 1997 sibling, it was bottled with neither fining nor filtration. There are approximately 2,800 cases of this fabulous effort. Anticipated maturity: now–2025. The black/ruby/purple-colored 1995 Les Pavots (a 73% Cabernet Sauvignon, 14% Merlot, and 13% Cabernet Franc blend), which achieved 13.9% alcohol naturally, reveals a sweet, tobacco, lavender, and cassis-scented nose, medium-bodied, tannic, elegant flavors, outstanding purity, ripeness, and length, yet a measured, restrained style. Less forthcoming than either the 1996 or 1994, this rich, nicely proportioned proprietary red is California's answer to a graceful Médoc. Anticipated maturity: now–2020. Since the bottling of the superb 1994 Les Pavots, this deep, saturated purple-colored wine has taken on a gorgeous nose of cassis intermixed with violets, licorice, and attractive spicy oak. Sweet, rich, and surprisingly showy for a Les Pavots, this medium- to full-bodied wine possesses a luscious, multilayered texture, outstanding depth, and attractively integrated tannin and acidity. When I tasted it, it was more evolved and delicious than I had anticipated given its recent bottling.

All of Peter Michael's top wines, including the Chardonnays, are bottled without filtration. Readers should make it a point to visit this winery situated in Knights Valley, not far from the

Napa/Sonoma county line. The quality is extraordinary, and the commitment and talent of the winery staff laudatory. Moreover, the winery strives to achieve even greater quality.

Past Glories: 1993 Les Pavots Proprietary Red Wine (92)

ROBERT MONDAVI (NAPA)

1999	Boomerang	Napa	C	(88–90)
1997	Cabernet Sauvignon	Napa	D	90
1996	Cabernet Sauvignon	Napa	D	88
1995	Cabernet Sauvignon	Napa	C	89
1994	Cabernet Sauvignon	Napa	C	88
1998	Cabernet Sauvignon	Oakville	E	88
1997	Cabernet Sauvignon	Oakville	D	91
1996	Cabernet Sauvignon	Oakville District	D	92
1995	Cabernet Sauvignon	Oakville District	D	91
1994	Cabernet Sauvignon	Oakville District	D	90
1997	Cabernet Sauvignon	Stags Leap	D	91
1996	Cabernet Sauvignon	Stags Leap	D	88
1995	Cabernet Sauvignon	Stags Leap	D	89
1999	Cabernet Sauvignon Marjorie's Sunrise	Oakville	E	(86–88)
1999	Cabernet Sauvignon Marjorie's Twilight	Oakville	E	(90–92)
1998	Cabernet Sauvignon Marjorie's Vineyard	Napa	E	(86–88)
1998	Cabernet Sauvignon Old Vine	Napa	E	89
1999	Cabernet Sauvignon Reserve	Napa	EEE	88
1998	Cabernet Sauvignon Reserve	Napa	EEE	87
1997	Cabernet Sauvignon Reserve	Napa	EEE	92
1996	Cabernet Sauvignon Reserve	Napa	EE	92
1995	Cabernet Sauvignon Reserve	Napa	EE	93
1994	Cabernet Sauvignon Reserve	Napa	EE	98
1996	Cabernet Sauvignon 30th Anniversary Reserve	Napa	EE	95
1999	Cabernet Sauvignon To-Kalon	Napa	EEE	90
1998	Cabernet Sauvignon To-Kalon Reserve	Napa	EEE	89
1997	Cabernet Sauvignon To-Kalon Reserve	Napa	EEE	94+
1999	Fumé Blanc I Block	Napa	E	90
1997	Merlot	Carneros	D	88
1996	Merlot	Carneros	D	87
1997	Merlot	Napa	C	88
1996	Merlot	Napa	C	88
1997	Pinot Noir	Napa	C	90
1997	Pinot Noir	Carneros	D	90
1998	Pinot Noir Huichica Hills	Carneros	E	90
1997	Pinot Noir Reserve	Napa	D	92
1996	Pinot Noir Reserve	Napa	D	89

In 22 years, I have never been more distressed as well as perplexed by evaluations of a particular winery than those that follow. No one in the United States has done more to promote the image of fine wine than Robert Mondavi and his family. They have had a profound, positive impact on American culture, and we all have benefitted from it. While it is not too late, I am still hopeful that some president of the United States will give Robert Mondavi our highest civilian honor for what he has accomplished. That being said, Tim Mondavi, who has made many great wines in his winemaking career, is on an almost obsessive mission to produce wines that are "bright, fresh, with a cleansing quality." His use of the word "nerve" and expressions such as "clarity of focus" are to justify what appears to be increasingly light and, to my way of thinking, less interesting wines that err on the side of intellectual vapidness over the pursuit of wines of heart, soul, and pleasure. I believe he is going against what Mother Nature has given California, the ability to produce wines of exceptional ripeness and gorgeously pure, intense flavors. Once past some alluring aromatics, many 1998s and 1999s were, in essence, collectively superficial, with tart, almost stripped-out personalities with little textural interest and short, clipped finishes. Obviously, some of the Cabernet Sauvignons are less at fault than the Sauvignon Blancs, Chardonnays, Pinot Noirs, Merlots, and Zinfandels. Yet the trend toward Euro-styled delicacy started in small increments four or five years ago. Tim Mondavi has produced many profound Cabernet Sauvignons. The pursuit of elegance and finesse is certainly a laudable goal, but many other wineries seem to be accomplishing it without compromising the hedonistic richness and multilayered textures that California can achieve as easily as any viticultural region in the world, assuming yields are kept low and ripe fruit is harvested. Thankfully, barrel samples of the 2000s revealed much greater ripeness and texture than the 1998s and 1999s, so perhaps I'm overreacting.

All the white wines, both Sauvignons and Chardonnays, are given partial malolactic fermentation in order to preserve their vibrant natural acidity. Of course, the Mondavis promote the fact that they are bottled unfiltered, and that is true. However, several former wine-makers have told me they centrifuge many of their whites, and while that is technically not filtration, it is a relatively traumatic process where solids are removed from the wine under extreme force. I will leave it at that, but here are my notes on the best of the 1999s, which all have extremely tart, light-bodied personalities with very little textural pleasure. Of course, 1999 was a very cool year, and the Fumé Blancs largely received no malolactic fermentation, but some received various portions of barrel fermentation. Mondavi's 1999 Fumé Blanc from their famed I Block is 100% barrel-fermented with about 20% new oak. This is a light- to medium-bodied effort with more intense aromatics of lemon zest, grapefruit, mineral, and a touch of honeysuckle. In the mouth, there are several layers of flavor before it takes on the Mondavi signature of light body and an attenuated finish, with mostly acidity and alcohol.

A wine with an interesting bouquet and flavors is the 1999 Boomerang, a blend of 68% Syrah, 26% Cabernet Sauvignon, and 6% Cabernet Franc. The potentially outstanding 1999 Boomerang is full-bodied, with copious quantities of blackberry fruit, adequate acidity, an opulent texture, and clean black cherry and blackberry, peppery flavors that linger in the mouth. Drink it over the next 5–8 years.

The Cabernet Sauvignons, particularly the Napa bottlings, also seem texturally deficient. With clipped, tough finishes, they are relatively weak efforts—at least if pleasure is your goal. The wines that did perform well include the special single-vineyard offerings, as well as the Reserves. There are two *cuvées* of their Oakville, called Marjorie's Sunrise and Marjorie's Twilight. The 1999 Cabernet Sauvignon Marjorie's Sunrise shows a medium/dark ruby color and an elegant, sweet nose of graphite, black currants, and vanilla. The wine has aggressive tannin in the finish and less intrusive, vibrant acidity. This is a medium-bodied, claret-styled Cabernet to drink over the next 10–15 years. Sweeter, riper, richer, and more elegant is the 1999 Cabernet Sauvignon Marjorie's Twilight. It exhibits a saturated ruby/purple color, in addition to pure cassis fruit intermixed with minerals and toasty oak. The wine is riper, yet restrained. It is made from 35–40-year-old Cabernet vines and should turn out to be outstanding. Anticipated maturity: 2003–2020. Readers looking for a St.-Emilion from Oakville might check out the 1998 Cabernet Sauvignon Oakville. Soft herbal notes intermixed with cherries and earth emerge from this garnet/plum-colored wine. It is medium-bodied, round, and best drunk over the next decade. This is a harmonious, complex effort that would be more comfortable in a Bordeaux tasting.

As for the flagship wines, the 1998 Cabernet Sauvignon Reserve is more evolved, a characteristic of this vintage. A plum/ruby color is followed by aromas of toasty oak, tobacco, black currants, smoke, and spice box. In the mouth, it is medium-bodied, with excellent fruit on the attack, some real charm and roundness, but the finish is filled with astringent tannin. If this wine continues to hold its fruit, it is going to be a Bordeaux-styled, medium-weight Cabernet Sauvignon to drink over the next 12–14 years. However, the tannin will need to be monitored because this particular wine could possibly dry out. The 1999 Cabernet Sauvignon Reserve has a deeper ruby/purple color, notes of black currants, minerals, and toasty oak, and an elegant, restrained, aromatic profile. In the mouth, there is high tannin, medium body, and excellent concentration. There are approximately 1,000 cases of Cabernet Sauvignon from the famed Oakville vineyard called To-Kalon. The 1998 Cabernet Sauvignon To-Kalon (virtually 100% Cabernet Sauvignon) displays a dense ruby/purple color, as well as a sweet nose of black currants intermixed with cedar, licorice, toast, and earth. It has lost much of the fat it exhibited last year, and no longer seems as impressive as it once did. A wine of finesse and elegance, it offers much more pleasure than many 1998s. Drink it over the next 14–15 years. As for the 1999 Cabernet Sauvignon To-Kalon Vineyard, this is 100% Cabernet Sauvignon, as opposed to the 1998, which was 97% Cabernet Sauvignon, 2% Cabernet Franc, and 1% Petit Verdot. This wine boasts an excellent texture, although the finish is austere. Sweet black currant and blackberry fruit are wrapped with subtle oak and a weedy, tobacco herbaceousness. It is deep, dense, full-bodied, and impressively textured as well as concentrated. However, the high tannin profile suggests it should be cellared for 4–5 years; it will last 20–25 years.

Mondavi's Pinot Noir vineyards produced approximately 1.5 tons of fruit per acre in 1998. All were fermented with indigenous yeasts and were bottled without filtration. A new offering in the Mondavi portfolio is the 1998 Pinot Noir Huichica Hills, which is reminiscent of a premier cru from the Côte de Beaune. Sweet black cherry, spice, smoke, mineral, and floral aromas give this dark ruby-colored, medium-bodied Pinot plenty of appeal. It is pure as well as exceptionally well delineated and elegant. Drink it over the next 7–8 years.

At Mondavi, no varietal has been studied as intensely as Pinot Noir. Farming has moved toward organic, and the wines are being made as naturally as possible. Mondavi's 1997 Pinot Noirs, which are the finest they have yet produced, are indicative of such qualitative efforts. Much of the new production of California North Coast Pinot Noir is emerging from Dijon plant material (i.e., clones such as #667, #777, and #115). Robert Mondavi also utilizes such old California clones (which were brought from Burgundy years ago) as Calera and Swan. Readers looking for an easy to find, gorgeous Pinot Noir need search no further than Mondavi's 1997 Pinot Noir Napa. A remarkable 33,000 cases were produced, mostly from their Carneros vineyard. An outstanding example, it exhibits a deep ruby color, in addition to superb aromatics of black cherry fruit intertwined with spicy oak, loamy soil scents, and forest aromas. A beautifully textured, medium- to full-bodied palate is soft, pure, and bursting with black cherry fruit. The alcohol is a lofty 13.8%, which gives the wine plenty of glycerin and flesh. This Pinot should drink easily for 4–5 years. The denser, dark ruby-colored 1997 Pinot Noir Carneros reveals more noticeable new oak in the aromatics, as well as high-strung cherry/raspberry aromas and a creamy texture. The fruit is beautifully pure in this medium-bodied, elegant, vibrant wine. It is a more finesse-styled Pinot, and perhaps less obvious than the crowd-pleasing Napa Valley bottling. Like its siblings, the 1997 Pinot Noir Reserve (which sees 70% new oak) is bottled with neither fining nor filtration. It boasts the deepest ruby/purple color, a terrific texture, and copious quantities of sweet cherry/kirsch fruit intermixed with cassis and raspberries. While the oak is noticeable, the wine's greater concentration, body, and power have soaked most of it up. This is an opulently textured Pinot with superb potential. It should be at its best after another 1–2 years of cellaring, and will keep for a decade. Bravo to the Mondavi winery for these efforts. The 1996 Pinot Noir Napa Reserve displays a dark plum color and moderately intense, herbaceous, animal, black plum, and cherry aromas. Restrained but rich, with crisp acidity and clean winemaking, this medium-bodied, tightly knit Pinot will benefit from another 1–2 years of bottle age and last for 4–8 years.

Robert Mondavi has joined the Merlot sweepstakes, producing some excellent wines, but not yet hitting the bull's-eye with this varietal. As Tim Mondavi says, "What is Merlot?" The problem may be that California has fewer clones to choose from, and there is a tendency to give this wine less attention because it seems to be such an easy sell in spite of the ocean of insipid Merlots that inhabit the marketplace. Mondavi's efforts are unquestionably fine, and come close to being outstanding. The excellent, nearly outstanding 1997 Merlot Napa exhibits copious quantities of berry fruit, a touch of mocha, firm tannin, and a medium-bodied, crunchy, deliciously fruity, soft mid-palate and finish. It should drink well for 10–12 years. Even more delectable is the 1997 Merlot Carneros. This dark ruby/purple-colored wine displays espresso bean, mocha, berry fruit flavors in addition to an attractive, multilayered, broad mid-palate and finish. A blend of 94% Merlot, 4% Malbec, and 2% Cabernet Sauvignon, it possesses the seamless texture and sweetness characteristic of this vintage. It should drink well for 10–12 years, if not longer. The 1996 Merlot Napa exhibits a dark ruby/purple color, as well as berry aromas and flavors intermixed with loamy soil, coffee bean, and spicy oak notes. The wine is medium-bodied, with good richness, yet it has a slightly monolithic personality. A very good effort, it should evolve nicely over the next 7–8 years. The 1996 Merlot Carneros is a better effort. There is more clay in Mondavi's Carneros vineyard. This example reveals a deeper, more saturated ruby/purple color, in addition to a more intriguing fragrance of black cherry jam intermixed with loamy soil and new-oak scents. Beautifully rendered in the mouth, with medium body, excellent intensity, and well-integrated tannin and acidity, this impressively endowed Merlot comes close to meriting an outstanding evaluation. It should drink well for a decade or more.

The 1998 Cabernet Sauvignon To-Kalon Reserve exhibits more blackberry characteristics, along with cassis, licorice, and toasty new oak. Medium- to full-bodied, with excellent purity, outstanding concentration, and a surprisingly long finish, this blend of 97% Cabernet Sauvignon, 2% Cabernet Franc, and 1% Petit Verdot is one of the vintage's most impressive efforts. Anticipated maturity: now–2018. The lighter-styled 1998 Cabernet Sauvignon Marjorie's Vineyard aims for flavor and finesse, but it appears to falter slightly because of the winery's stylistic predilection for restraint and politeness. It was out of place alongside the sweeter, richer, more concentrated To-Kalon Reserve, Napa Reserve, and the 1998 Cabernet Sauvignon Old Vine. The latter wine is a seamless, velvety-textured, opulently rich 1998 with gorgeous black fruits, well-integrated oak, acidity, and tannin, and plenty of glycerin and follow-through on the palate. Another 1998 that will be uncommonly delicious when released, look for it to last for 15 or more years.

The five 1997 Cabernet Sauvignons range from outstanding to exhilarating. The 1997 Cabernet Sauvignon Napa is one of the finest regular Cabernet Sauvignons Mondavi has produced. A blend of 89% Cabernet Sauvignon, 7% Merlot, 3% Cabernet Franc, and 1% Syrah (13.9% alcohol), this dark ruby-colored wine with purple nuances has sweet black currant flavors mixed with spice box, licorice, and toast notes. Fleshy and open-knit, it should drink well for 10–14 years. The more powerful (14.1% alcohol), superb 1997 Cabernet Sauvignon Oakville (84% Cabernet Sauvignon, 9% Merlot, and 7% Cabernet Franc) exhibits a complex, Pauillac-like nose of cedar, fruitcake, black currants, and spicy new oak. There is medium to full body, well-integrated sweet tannin and acidity, an opulent texture, and a layered, long finish. Anticipated maturity: now–2025. Completely different, the Château Margaux–inspired 1997 Cabernet Sauvignon Stags Leap District exhibits a dark ruby/purple color as well as a knockout nose of black raspberries, currants, and floral scents. Exotic and open-knit, without the sheer force of the Oakville *cuvée*, with gloriously sweet fruit and impeccable harmony, this terrific 100% Cabernet Sauvignon will benefit from 2–3 years of cellaring, and last for 15–20 years. Very impressive!

The profound 1997 Cabernet Sauvignon Reserve boasts a saturated ruby/purple color. Production (about 20,000 cases) of this sweet, opulently textured, rich, full-bodied wine should guarantee widespread availability. Aged in 100% new French oak, this blend of 91% Cabernet Sauvignon, 8% Cabernet Franc, and 1% Petit Verdot offers a textbook varietal nose of cedar wood, licorice, crème de cassis, and toast. Full-bodied, with explosive sweetness and fruit on the attack, this gloriously pure, superbly well-delineated wine should be drinkable young and last for three decades. Anticipated maturity: now–2025. One of the most extraordinary Cabernet Sauvignons Robert Mondavi has produced is the 1,000 case production of the 1997 Cabernet Sauvignon To-Kalon Reserve. Made from 100% Cabernet Sauvignon, aromas of cedar, licorice, new saddle leather, walnuts, and cassis tumble from the glass. The wine boasts fabulous richness, a silky, sumptuous texture, a deep, chewy mid-palate, and an admirably pure, multilayered finish that exceeds 45 seconds. It will require 3–5 years of cellaring, and will keep for three decades or more. It is a prodigious Cabernet Sauvignon.

The 1996 Cabernet Sauvignon Napa is an elegant, medium-bodied example with more tannin than most regular bottlings (a characteristic of the vintage). This structured wine offers weedy black currant fruit, subtle oak, and a well-built, concentrated finish. About 8% Cabernet Franc was added to the blend. The 1996 is approachable, but it promises to be even better with several more years of bottle age, and will last 12–15+ years. The 1996 Cabernet Sauvignon Stags Leap possesses the crisp, restrained, lighter-bodied style of wines from that region. Sweet black cherries intermixed with floral scents are present in the wine's aromatics. In the mouth, tar and floral characteristics combine with black fruit to give this Cabernet an enthralling, supple, approachable style. There is some tannin in the finish, and the wine is more austere than the Napa bottling, but it should drink well for 12–15 years. The outstanding 1996 Cabernet Sauvignon Oakville offers an opaque purple color and knockout aromas of crème de cassis, vanilla, and weedy tobacco. Full-bodied, rich, and muscular, as well as complex, this fleshy, deep wine is immensely impressive. As it sits in the glass, blueberry/blackberry aromas emerge, adding to its overall appeal. Anticipated maturity: now–2020. The 1996 Cabernet Sauvignon Reserve may be no better than the Oakville, but it is made in a slightly different style. The color is opaque purple, and the wine reveals more vanilla, a touch of mint, and plenty of black currant fruit in its moderately intense aromatics. Some of the vintage's dry tannin (from this year's stressed vineyard conditions) are present in the wine's finish. A more stylish, restrained, less exuberant example than the 1996 Oakville, it is an outstanding offering that should be consumed between now–2025. None of the above 1996 Cabernet Sauvignons matches the majesty, richness, and breadth of the 1996 Cabernet Sauvignon 30th Anniversary Reserve. This special bottling (about 1,000 cases) is a fabulous wine. From its opaque purple color and stunning aromatics of blackberries, cassis, toast, licorice, and Asian spices to its full-bodied, concentrated, superbly extracted style, this wine possesses virtually everything. Layers of fruit, glycerin, extract, and sweet tannin are presented in a flamboyant format. The tannin level is high, but so is the wine's richness and length. It is a sensational effort. Anticipated maturity: 2005–2030.

In 1995, Mondavi added a number of new regionally labeled Cabernet Sauvignons to their portfolio. In addition to their Oakville *cuvée*, they have a Stags Leap District Cabernet and a single-vineyard wine from their famed To-Kalon plantation. The 1995 Cabernet Sauvignon Napa is a beautifully made wine that comes close to being outstanding. It boasts a textbook cassis and eucalyptus-scented nose with oak in the background. On the palate, the wine is medium- to full-bodied, with excellent ripeness, clean fruit, and a long, spicy finish. It avoids some of the vintage's hard tannins. The debut release of the 1995 Cabernet Sauvignon Stags Leap District is an uncommonly elegant, Margaux-styled wine with medium body, and sweet black currants in the nose with a notion of toasty oak. Good acidity and a soft underbelly make for a pleasant, seductive wine that should drink well young, but keep for 15 years. In 1995, the Cabernet Sauvignon Oakville District is again outstanding. The wine reveals textbook cedar, cassis, and toast notes in the nose, terrific fruit intensity and purity, medium to full body, and excellent harmony among its elements. This has resulted in an authoritatively flavored yet graceful Cabernet Sauvignon that will benefit from 2–5 years of cellaring, and keep for two decades. The 1995 Cabernet Sauvignon Reserve is slightly less impressive than when I tasted it last year, although still an outstanding wine. I may have caught it at a closed stage following bottling. There are 15,000–20,000 cases of Reserve Cabernet made, and in 1995, a quintessentially elegant style has been produced. The wine is less weighty than the 1994, 1991, or 1990. It has great promise and raw materials, with superb fruit and richness, medium body, and subtle lead pencil notes to go along with black currant, mineral, and toast scents and flavors. Based on this tasting, I would lower my overall rating, but it is still an exceptional California Cabernet Sauvignon made in a compellingly elegant, graceful style. Anticipated maturity: now–2018.

1994 was unquestionably a great vintage for North Coast Cabernet Sauvignon, standing above 1990, 1991, 1992, and 1993—all outstanding vintages with no shortage of heroic performances. Remarkably, 1995 may turn out to be as profound as 1994, giving California its two greatest back-to-back vintages of Cabernet Sauvignon . . . ever! The quality of the 1994 vintage is well displayed at Mondavi. The 1994 Cabernet Sauvignon Napa (about 80,000 cases produced) is one of the finest regular Cabernets Mondavi has made. It exhibits a deep ruby color and sweet, rich, black currant aromas intertwined with scents of vanilla and spice. Soft, round, medium- to full-bodied, and harmonious, the wine is accessible, yet capable of lasting for 10–15 years. The youthful 1994 Cabernet Sauvignon Oakville District (6,900 cases) could be mistaken for a Mondavi Reserve Cabernet. The color is a saturated ruby/purple, and the nose offers up attractive, complex scents of lead pencil, vanilla, toast, and ripe cassis fruit. Dense, rich, and medium- to full-bodied, with moderate tannin, this young, impressively endowed Cabernet Sauvignon should be at its best between now–2010.

I have drunk some memorable Reserve Cabernet Sauvignons from Robert Mondavi, including the gloriously fragrant, elegant 1971, the powerful, dense 1974, the seductive 1978, the mammothly endowed, tannic blockbuster 1987, the silky, opulent, super-concentrated 1990, and the compellingly rich, layered 1991. However, if I were to select the Reserve Cabernet Sauvignon that may turn out to be the greatest Mondavi has yet made, the 1994 might edge out the 1991 and 1987. It may not appear to be the case, but I am often at a loss for words when it comes to writing about truly profound wines. They seem to have their own stature, presence, and character that transcend the significance of mere words. That being said, Mondavi's 1994 Cabernet Sauvignon Reserve is an exquisite wine, as well as a Cabernet that may turn out to be one of the "wines of the vintage." The deep opaque purple color, and tightly wound nose and flavors still reveal enough profound aromas and flavors to mark this as one of Mondavi's most sensational efforts. The nose possesses a Margaux/Mouton-like cassis, lead pencil, floral aroma, backed up by copious quantities of black currant fruit. In the mouth, my notes said, "great stuff." The wine is full-bodied, layered, multidimensional, and astonishingly well balanced, with an inner depth and core of exceptional richness and intensity. All of this has been accomplished without any notion of obtrusive weight, tannin, or alcohol. The finish lasts for 35+ seconds. Because of its luxurious quantity of fruit, this wine will be accessible young, thus much of it will be drunk long before it ever reaches full maturity. However, for those able to buy more than a bottle or two, and who possess the discipline to wait 10–15 years, this wine should prove to be a formidable California Cabernet with a rare complexity, elegance, and richness. It should be at its best between now–2025.

Past Glories: Cabernet Sauvignon Reserve—1993 (91), 1992 (90), 1991 (96), 1990 (93), 1987 (95), 1978 (90), 1971 (94)

CHÂTEAU MONTELENA (NAPA)

1999	Cabernet Sauvignon Calistoga Cuvée	Napa	D	(87–88)
1998	Cabernet Sauvignon Calistoga Cuvée	Napa	D	89
1997	Cabernet Sauvignon Calistoga Cuvée	Napa	E	(87–88)
1999	Cabernet Sauvignon Estate	Napa	EE	(96–98)
1998	Cabernet Sauvignon Estate	Napa	EE	93
1997	Cabernet Sauvignon Estate	Napa	EE	98
1996	Cabernet Sauvignon Estate	Napa	DD	93
1995	Cabernet Sauvignon Estate	Napa	EE	94
1994	Cabernet Sauvignon Estate	Napa	EE	95
1999	Chardonnay	Napa	D	90
1997	Merlot Estate	Napa	D	88
1999	Riesling Potter Valley	Napa	C	89
1997	St. Vincent (Zinfandel/Primitivo/Sangiovese)	Napa	C	89
1994	Zinfandel Estate	Napa	C	89

There is always something reassuring about visiting Château Montelena. Over the past two decades, wine-maker/owner Bo Barrett and his father, Jim, have never wavered from their goals of producing some of California's finest, longest-lived Cabernet Sauvignon as well as a non-malolactic, flavorful Chardonnay that is high on character and fruit. Château Montelena is also successful with other varietals. For example, one of their best-kept secrets (only sold at the winery) is the excellent Riesling produced from Potter Valley. The 1999 Riesling Potter Valley (13% alcohol) is a dry, Alsatian-styled effort with a touch of honeyed botrytis in the pineapple, orange, and buttery apple-like flavors. Fresh and lively, it will drink brilliantly with an assortment of cuisines. About 10% of Montelena's Chardonnays are now put through malolactic, and, even more revolutionary, about 10% is now being barrel-fermented in new oak. The wine spends six months in neutral, old barrels prior to bottling. While reserved and tight when compared to some of California's more flamboyant Chardonnays, it does merit considerable interest. A virgin expression of Chardonnay, with abundant quantities of crisp, green apple, tangerine, and pear fruit, this wine reveals good acidity, an elegant yet full-bodied personality, surprising depth, and a reserved, austere palate. The 1999 Chardonnay is one of the finest Montelena has made over recent years. Perhaps the introduction of some malolactic as well as barrel fermentation has given the wine more mid-palate and texture, without compromising Montelena's style. The 1999 possesses abundant quantities of lemon, pear, and apple notes, zesty, full-bodied flavors as well as crisp, nicely integrated acidity, 13.8% alcohol, admirable concentration, and more richness and density than the 1998. It should last for 5–6 years.

I do not know of any other California winery that has put together such a blend as Montelena's St. Vincent. This used to be a wine produced to utilize some of their Sangiovese. However, like many wineries, Montelena feels (as do I) that California Sangiovese is generally a failure and cannot compete with Italian Sangiovese. The 1997 St. Vincent (3,000 cases) is an intriguing blend of 60% Zinfandel, 30% Primitivo, and 10% Sangiovese. It reveals a distinctively Italian personality with notes of melted asphalt, new saddle leather, berry fruit, pepper, and spice. With a fat, robust, hearty personality, as well as character and soul, it is meant to be consumed during its first 3–5 years of life.

Quietly and competently (mirroring the proprietors' personalities), Château Montelena's Cabernet Sauvignon Calistoga Cuvée gets better and better. More estate fruit is being added to this blend in order to bulk it up. The 1998 Cabernet Sauvignon Calistoga Cuvée (13.9% alcohol) is better than the 1997, even though I suspect the raw materials were inferior. It exhibits a dark plum/purple color in addition to dense, sweet black currant aromas, soft tannin, and fat, creamy, cassis flavors with hints of tobacco, spice box, and dried herbs. Drink this delicious Cabernet over the next decade. The tighter, more structured 1999 Cabernet Sauvignon Calistoga Cuvée possesses a higher acid profile, but is ripe, rich, and potentially longer-lived than its older sibling. Whether it will be as supple and charming in its youth as the 1998 remains to be seen. Anticipated maturity: now–2012. The 1997 Cabernet Sauvignon Calistoga Cuvée was the first of the "new and improved" Calistoga *cuvées*. It offers a saturated ruby/purple color, and plenty of blackberry and cassis fruit presented in an uncomplicated, medium- to full-bodied, chewy style. Ten percent Cabernet Franc and 10% Merlot have been added to provide softness and aromatic dimension. The wine should drink well for 7–10 years.

There are 10,200 cases of the remarkable 1997 Cabernet Sauvignon Estate. Opaque purple-colored with a dense, chewy, full-bodied personality, it displays abundant cassis, mineral, and earth notes. This brilliantly made, super-concentrated, pure blockbuster possesses sweet tannin as well as a terrific finish. Having added additional weight since last tasted, this sumptuous, multilayered, profoundly concentrated Cabernet contains 14% alcohol. It is a candidate for 25–30 years of longevity. Anticipated maturity: 2003–2030. The decade's most mixed vintage for North Coast Cabernet Sauvignon is 1998. The mountain Cabernets tend to be more herbaceous and compressed than the valley floor offerings, although that is a broad generalization as there are some highly successful mountain Cabernets, as well as some disappointing valley floor efforts (even from some of the more renowned wineries). Montelena's 1998 Cabernet Sauvignon Estate is unquestionably one of the vintage's most successful wines. More evolved than either the 1997 or 1999, it offers an opaque ruby/purple color as well as a fat, complex nose of charcoal, smoke, blackberries, and cassis. Rich, complex, and full-bodied, it is more enjoyable to drink now than the super-sized 1997. Production was significantly less (8,000 cases), and the wine is supple-textured, rich, and better after bottling than it was when tasted from barrel. Bravo to Bo Barrett and his winemaking team for fashioning a wine of such character. While not released until 2002, the 1999 Cabernet Sauvignon Estate appears to be a worthy competitor to the exceptional 1997. It exhibits an opaque, thick black/purple color, spectacular concentration, a multilayered mid-palate, the seamlessness of a great vintage, and a rich, jammy, concentrated finish. The powerful, gorgeously pure black fruits and unctuous texture suggest it will drink well young, yet be capable of 2–3 decades of effortless evolution. It is more of a blockbuster in the style of the 1997 than the more charming, softer 1998. Another behemoth Cabernet is the stern, tannic, concentrated 1996 Cabernet Sauvignon Estate (13.5% alcohol). Full-bodied, but closed, with gorgeously pure black fruits, powerful, loamy, earthy scents along with fruit and extract, this wine also needs 5–6 years of cellaring, and should easily last through the first 2–3 decades of this century. This is another winery where the 1995 Cabernet Sauvignon Estate may be as strong as the 1994. The color is an opaque purple. The wine is full-bodied and powerful, with classic notes of cassis intermixed with loamy soil scents, underbrush, and spice. There is massive body and elevated but sweet tannin that is well integrated with the wine's other components, a blockbuster mid-palate, and a finish that lasts for 30+ seconds. Anticipated maturity: now–2025. The 1994 Cabernet Sauvignon Estate, which has been closed since bottling, has begun to open and display its enormous potential. The saturated black/purple color is followed by aromas of gorgeously pure blackberry and cassis scents. Toasty oak notes are barely discernable given the wine's bombastic display of black fruits, a huge, chewy glycerin level, and sensational finish. It will be exciting to follow the evolution of the 1994 and 1995. Modern-day society seems to always be in search of new stars, but this winery has been a superhero for great California Cabernet Sauvignon for nearly 25 years!

Some Montelena Zinfandels have carried lofty levels of alcohol, but the 1994 Zinfandel Estate possesses a civilized 14%. The wine reveals a medium ruby color, followed by expansive, silky flavors and low acidity. It is fully mature.

The Merlot Estate (500 cases, 100% Merlot) was produced only in 1997. I am generally unimpressed with most California Merlots, but Montelena's 1997 exhibits a deep ruby/garnet color as well as dense, smoky, black cherry flavors, medium to full body, soft tannin, and a plump finish. Although not great, it is unquestionably very good Merlot.

Past Glories: Cabernet Sauvignon Estate—1993 (91+), 1992 (94), 1991 (95), 1990 (96), 1989 (90), 1987 (90), 1986 (94), 1985 (94), 1984 (94), 1982 (93), 1981 (90), 1980 (91), 1979 (90), 1978 (94), 1976 (92), 1975 (90)

MONTEVINA VINEYARDS (AMADOR)

1997	Zinfandel Deaver Old Vines	Amador	C	89
1999	Zinfandel Terra d'Oro	Amador	C	89
1998	Zinfandel Terra d'Oro Deaver Old Vines	Amador	C	(88–90)
1999	Zinfandel Terra d'Oro Home Vineyard	Amador	C	89

Some of the best values in Zinfandel are these 1999s produced by Montevina. The 1999 Zinfandel Terra d'Oro is a superb value. This Zinfandel fruit bomb reveals ripe blackberry and cherry fruit intermixed with smoke, earth, licorice, and tar. Chewy, full-bodied, opulently textured, and pure, with a whopping 15.5% alcohol, this well-balanced effort will drink well for 5–6 years. The similarly styled although more expensive 1999 Zinfandel Terra d'Oro Home Vineyard possesses slightly lower alcohol (15%) as well as oodles of jammy black cherry and currant fruit in its spicy, peppery, full-bodied, opulent style.

The 1998 Zinfandel Terra d'Oro Deaver Old Vines may turn out to be outstanding and one of the finest Montevina Zinfandels produced in nearly two decades. A dark ruby/purple color is accompanied by sweet, jammy blackberry, cherry, briery, pepper, licorice, and incense aromas. Superripe, with terrific fruit, serious richness, full body, and excellent purity and overall harmony, this muscular, large-scaled Zinfandel should be excellent, possibly outstanding. Moreover, it should drink well for 5–6 years. The opaque purple color of the 1997 Zinfandel Deaver Old Vines is followed by aromas of toasty new oak, black cherry liqueur, pepper, and flowers. Velvety-textured, dense, and full-bodied, with rich fruit, this wellendowed Zinfandel can be drunk now or aged for 5–6 years.

MORAGA VINEYARDS (BEL AIR)

1996	Cabernet Sauvignon	Bel Air	E	89
1995	Cabernet Sauvignon	Bel Air	E	89
1994	Cabernet Sauvignon	Bel Air	E	89

One of California's most interesting vineyards, Moraga is a seven-acre parcel located in the wealthy Los Angeles suburb of Bel Air. Think it over—I bet an acre of land in this high-rent district probably sells for as much as an acre of grand cru Chambertin or Montrachet in Burgundy! These wines are intriguing, offering a Bordeaux-like austerity as well as Médoc-like aromatics of weedy tobacco, cedar, and currants. They give every indication of being ageworthy wines with 15–20 years of possible evolution. The vineyard, which I once walked with the proprietor, is made from decomposed fossils, limestone, and sandstone. Recent vintages have been aged in 100% new French oak casks. The 1996 Cabernet Sauvignon displays a dense purple color, a striking toasty, black cherry, and cassis-scented nose, and rich, spicy, medium- to full-bodied flavors with good acidity and moderately high tannin. The wine is tightly knit, and in need of 4–5 years of cellaring. It should keep for 15+ years. The 1995

Cabernet Sauvignon (450 cases produced) is another Bordeaux look-alike, at least aromatically. It exhibits a tobacco leaf, smoky, cedar, and black currant–scented nose, followed by crisp, tart acidity, some austerity, but flavorful, youthful, rich red and black currant fruit. Medium-bodied and spicy, with moderately aggressive tannin in the finish, it needs 4–5 years of cellaring, and should age for two decades. The 1994 Cabernet Sauvignon (545 cases) reveals evolved fruitcake, cedary, tobacco, roasted herb, and cassis aromas, as well as rich, concentrated flavors. It is impressively rich, with an herb-tinged, black currant personality, medium to full body, sweet but noticeable tannin, and excellent purity, all framed by toasty new oak. The wine gives every indication of being ready to drink with another 2–3 years of cellaring. It should last for 15–20 years.

MOUNT EDEN VINEYARDS (SANTA CLARA)

1997	Cabernet Sauvignon Estate	Santa Cruz Mountain	D	88+
1996	Cabernet Sauvignon Estate	Santa Cruz	D	90
1995	Cabernet Sauvignon Estate	Santa Cruz	D	88
1996	Cabernet Sauvignon Old Vine Reserve	Santa Cruz	E	92+
1995	Cabernet Sauvignon Old Vine Reserve	Santa Cruz	E	90+
1997	Pinot Noir Cuvée Vieilles Vignes	Santa Cruz Mountain	E	89
1996	Pinot Noir Estate	Santa Cruz	D	90

Very few vineyard sites can match the extraordinary view from the top of Mount Eden. Overlooking the Santa Clara Valley, this vineyard, at 2,000 feet, was planted by the legendary Martin Ray. In many respects, Mount Eden was the birthplace of the boutique/garage winery. There are five wines produced, two *cuvées* of Cabernet Sauvignon, a Pinot Noir, and two Chardonnays, the estate offering and one from Edna Valley.

Mount Eden's Pinot Noirs are elegant, Côte de Beaune–styled examples, with surprising longevity. I had my last bottle of 1985 this fall and was extremely pleased to see how fresh, lively, and complex it had remained. The 1996 Pinot Noir is reminiscent of a good Beaune or Volnay premier cru. Bright jammy, strawberry, and fruit flavors are intertwined with spicy oak and minerals. Elegant and medium-bodied, with total harmony, this beautifully rendered Pinot Noir should drink well for 5–7 years. The delicious, light ruby-colored 1997 Pinot Noir Cuvée Vieilles Vignes offers aromas of sweet berries/cherries, earth, animal, and spice. Round and generous, with balancing acidity, this complex, evolved Pinot Noir should continue to drink well for 5–7 years. The dark ruby/purple-colored 1997 Cabernet Sauvignon Estate is dense and closed, with abundant black currant fruit, a strong sense of minerality, firm tannin, and earthy notes in the background. Medium-bodied and slightly austere, but well made, it will drink well between 2003–2014.

There have been some legendary Cabernet Sauvignons produced at Mount Eden, with some of the older vintages requiring 2–3 decades of cellaring (i.e., 1974). I asked winemaker/proprietor Jeffrey Patterson what he thought were the top recent vintages of his estate Cabernet Sauvignon. He felt the finest five vintages in the last two decades have been 1994, 1989, 1988, 1987, and 1985. There are two *cuvées* of Cabernet Sauvignon. The 1995 regular *cuvée* of Cabernet Sauvignon, a blend of 75% Cabernet Sauvignon, 22% Merlot, and 3% Cabernet Franc, sees 30% new American oak and 70% used French barrels. The dark ruby/purple-colored 1995 offers a firm, restrained nose of black currants, minerals, earth, and spicy oak. Medium-bodied, moderately tannic, and firmly structured, it requires 2–3 years of cellaring, and should keep for 15+ years. The outstanding 1996 Cabernet Sauvignon possesses greater thickness and richness, medium to full body, fine purity, and a black cherry/cassis component, intermixed with minerals and spice. Although more accessible than the 1995, it promises to be as long-lived.

Mount Eden's flagship Cabernet Sauvignon Old Vine is a 100% Cabernet Sauvignon from two parcels planted in 1955 and 1958. Jeffrey Patterson feels the greatest vintages for this *cuvée* have been 1973, 1974, 1975, 1976, 1986, 1990, 1992, and 1994. I was impressed with both the 1995 and 1996. The 1995 Cabernet Sauvignon Old Vine Reserve was bottled unfiltered, but was given a slight egg white fining. It is a backward, concentrated example in need of a decade of cellaring. Medium- to full-bodied, with a deep ruby/purple color and plenty of ripe cassis in the nose, it displays an unevolved, austere, formidably dense and muscular personality. Anticipated maturity: 2005–2025. The 1996 Cabernet Sauvignon Old Vine Reserve is more highly extracted and full-bodied, with a saturated ruby/purple color, and a restrained but blossoming nose of minerals, licorice, spicy oak, black cherries, and cassis. Pure, rich, dense, and promising, but destined for considerable longevity, this is another wine that should be cellared for 8–10 years. Anticipated maturity: 2007–2035.

MURPHY-GOODE (SONOMA)

1997 Cabernet Sauvignon Reserve Brenda Block	Alexander Valley	D	88
1994 Cabernet Sauvignon Reserve Brenda Block	Alexander Valley	D	09
1997 Cabernet Sauvignon Reserve Sarah Block Swan Song	Alexander Valley	D	89
1994 Merlot Murphy Ranches	Alexander Valley	C	88
1997 Petit Verdot Murphy Ranch	Alexander Valley	D	88
1995 Zinfandel	Sonoma County	C	89
1994 Zinfandel	Sonoma County	C	89
1999 Zinfandel Liar's Dice	Sonoma	C	89
1998 Zinfandel Liar's Dice	Sonoma	C	88

Murphy-Goode's Zinfandels emerge primarily from two vineyard sources, Sonoma's Cuneo and Saini Vineyards. Production is modest, with only 650 cases produced. A large-scaled, succulent fruit bomb, the ripe, jammy, fleshy, medium- to full-bodied 1999 Zinfandel Liar's Dice is a treat to drink. The alcohol came in at 14.5%, and there is a touch of volatile acidity in the complex aromatics. Fleshy and hedonistic, it is best drunk over the next 2–3 years to take advantage of its exuberant youthfulness. The 1998 Zinfandel Liar's Dice is a delicious, opulently textured, sweet, berry, cherry, and strawberry-scented and flavored wine, with medium to full body, low acidity, and good fat and succulence. A hedonistic personality, wonderful purity, and vivid, delicious fruit make for a mainstream, but immensely pleasing Zinfandel that even wine snobs will enjoy. Drink it over the next 2–3 years.

Murphy-Goode's intensely fragrant (jammy blackberries and spices) 1995 Zinfandel offers a deep, saturated ruby/purple color, sweet, spicy oak, plenty of round, soft, rich, berry flavors, admirable opulence, and a lush, silky texture. Drink it up. The fully mature 1994 Zinfandel displays a deep ruby color, followed by Zinfandel's appealing spicy, ripe, pure, peppery, berry fruit character, and a soft, lush, medium- to full-bodied finish.

Petit Verdot can rarely stand on its own, but Murphy-Goode has produced a blend of 78.5% Petit Verdot, 13.5% Cabernet Franc, and 8% Cabernet Sauvignon that is impressive for its ripeness and overall balance and richness. Attractive notes of black fruits (primarily cassis and berries) are intermixed with toasty new oak in the saturated dark ruby/purple-colored 1997 Petit Verdot Murphy Ranch. The wine is rich, medium- to full-bodied, and pure, with attractive spicy oak, low acidity, and sweet tannin. Drink this plush effort over the next 10–12 years. The saturated dense ruby/purple-colored 1997 Cabernet Sauvignon Reserve Brenda Block reveals abundant, toasty vanilla (from 18 months in French oak and 2 months in new American oak) aromas, along with classic tobacco and black currant scents. Moderate tannin, delicious fruit, and nicely integrated acidity as well as new oak frame this medium- to full-bodied, impressively made Cabernet Sauvignon. It will benefit from 1–2 years of bottle age, and will drink well for the following 10–12 years. The 1997 Cabernet Sauvignon Reserve Sarah Block Swan Song exhibits smoky, toasty aromas along with subtle, herb-tinged, ripe, jammy, blackberry and cassis scents. In the mouth, licorice, cedar, and saddle leather flavors add to the wine's complexity. Medium- to full-bodied, and more supple than the oakier, more tannic Brenda Block, with excellent depth, richness, and overall symmetry, it can be drunk now as well as over the next 10–12 years.

The dark ruby-colored 1994 Merlot Murphy Ranches (83% Merlot and 17% Cabernet Sauvignon) offers up a moderately intense nose of coffee beans, smoke, and ripe berry fruit. Although not complicated, it provides plenty of lush, silky, low-acid flavors with good ripeness, fruit, and glycerin. Slightly more complexity and delineation could have elevated this wine to an even higher qualitative category. Drink it over the next 3–5 years. The 1994 Cabernet Sauvignon Reserve Brenda Block (1,700 cases) is a dark garnet/purple-tinged color. The wine exhibits super ripeness, and a jammy, black cherry, cassis character nicely dosed with spicy oak. This vanilla-scented, medium- to full-bodied, dense, layered, low-acid Cabernet Sauvignon possesses plenty of sweet tannin, but the wine's hallmark is its purity and luscious, rich fruit. It should drink well young and age for 10–12 years. It would appear to be one of the finest Cabernet Sauvignons Murphy-Goode has yet produced.

ANDREW MURRAY VINEYARDS (SANTA BARBARA)

2000	Enchanté	Santa Ynez	C	88
1999	Espérance	Santa Barbara	C	87
1998	Espérance	Santa Barbara	C	90
1997	Espérance	Santa Barbara	C	88
1997	Syrah Hillside Reserve	Santa Barbara	D	93+
1996	Syrah Hillside Reserve	Santa Barbara	D	90+
1999	Syrah Les Coteaux	Santa Ynez	C	89
1997	Syrah Les Coteaux	Santa Barbara	C	90
1996	Syrah Les Coteaux	Santa Barbara	C	90
1999	Syrah Roasted Slope Vineyard	Santa Ynez	D	92
1997	Syrah Roasted Slope Vineyard	Santa Barbara	C	92
2000	Syrah Tous les Jours	Central Coast	B	86
2000	Viognier	Santa Ynez	C	90

Andrew Murray Vineyards is one of the shining stars in the Santa Barbara firmament. Extremely low yields (one-half to three-quarters tons of fruit per acre for the Viognier and Roussanne in 1998) and a dedication to hillside vineyards, ripe fruit, and non-interventionalistic winemaking have combined to propel this estate to the top echelon of the Rhône Ranger hierarchy. Production is small (300 cases for the Roussanne, 500 for the Viognier, 600 for Espérance, 600 for Syrah Roasted Slope, and 1000 for the Syrah Les Coteaux), but these wines are well worth seeking out.

Andrew Murray's 2000s and 1999s reveal considerable promise. The 2000 Enchanté, a blend of 80% Viognier, 10% Roussanne, and 10% Marsanne, is a delightful, slightly herbaceous, charming, fruity, medium-bodied, fleshy offering with excellent notes of honeyed citrus intermixed with a floral component. Drink this soft, stylish white Rhône Ranger blend over the next year. The 2000 Viognier is one of the finest produced in California. It exhibits apricot/honeysuckle fruit as well as more definition than most of these fruit-driven wines. Full-bodied, with a serious mid-palate as well as surprising depth, complexity, and underlying minerality, this classy effort should be consumed over the next year. The dark plum/ruby-colored 2000 Syrah Tous les Jours is a peppery, earthy, cherry-scented and flavored Côtes du Rhône–like effort. Drink this medium-bodied, pleasing Syrah during its first several years of life. More serious is the 1999 Espérance, a blend of Syrah, Grenache, and Mourvèdre. It possesses a Crozes-Hermitage–like herbaceous personality with notes of cassis fruit and cigar box. Medium-bodied and moderately weighty, with plenty of spice, fruit, pepper, and herbs, it will drink well for 4–5 years. The 1,000-case *cuvée* of 1999 Syrah Les Coteaux possesses medium body, good bacon-scented and cassis flavors with hints of earth and vanilla. It does not have the depth of some of Murray's finest vintages, but that is probably attributable to 1999's cold growing season. It reveals elegance, sweetness, and a more restrained personality than previous editions. The exceptional 1999 Syrah Roasted Slope (95% Syrah and 5% Viognier) is a top achievement in such a cool year. Its deep ruby/purple color is accompanied by a complex nose of honeysuckle, blackberries, and licorice. Full-bodied, rich, fleshy, well balanced, and pure, it is a super effort for the vintage. Drink it over the next decade.

The 1998 Espérance, a blend of Syrah, Mourvèdre, and Carignan, comes closest in quality to a topflight Crozes-Hermitage. Notes of dried Provençal herbs, leather, licorice, cedar, and cassis intermixed with chocolate and cherries jump from the glass of this open-knit, complex, spicy red wine. Medium-bodied, with excellent concentration, supple tannin, and enough acidity to provide delineation, this is a delicious, complex, Rhône Ranger blend that should drink well for 4–5 years. Andrew Murray's flagship wine is the 1997 Syrah Hillside Reserve, a concentrated, powerful Syrah meant to improve with bottle age. The opaque purple-colored 1997 offers aromas of creosote, licorice, black raspberries, and blackberries. Full-bodied, with explosive fruit, moderately high tannin, low acidity, superb ripeness, and enviable integration of wood, alcohol, and tannin, this powerhouse Syrah will improve for 3–5 years, and last for an additional 10–15. Impressive! According to Andrew Murray, this selection comes from the Durell clone of Syrah grown in Sonoma.

Readers looking for a terrific red wine value should check out Andrew Murray's 1997 Espérance, a blend of Syrah, Grenache, and Mourvèdre. It is a rustic, exuberant, rich, dark ruby/purple-colored wine with full body, plenty of pepper, black fruits, earth, and spice. Although the tannin is slightly elevated, it is well balanced by the gorgeous fruit, mouth-filling texture, and complete personality of this gutsy red wine. Moreover, it will soften and improve over the next 5–8 years. The black/purple-colored 1997 Syrah Les Coteaux is a rich wine with copious extract and tannin, and gorgeously sweet cassis fruit intermixed with pepper, licorice, and floral scents. The tannin level is elevated, but this full-bodied, layered wine will only improve over the next 7–8 years. It should keep for a decade or more. The saturated black/purple-colored 1997 Syrah Roasted Slope Vineyard is a field blend of 95% Syrah and 5% Viognier, both harvested and fermented together. It reveals jammy, syrupy, black raspberry and cherry flavors combined with a floral note and a touch of honey. Full-bodied, expansively textured, and pure, with less aggressive tannin than in Les Coteaux, this sweet (from ripe fruit, not sugar), rich, long wine should drink well for 10–12 years.

The 1996 Syrah Les Coteaux is more rustic, or as the French would say, *sauvage*. Its robust, exuberant, kinky character is hard to ignore. The color is saturated purple. The bouquet offers leesy, peppery, black currant, and berry aromas intermixed with tar and loamy soil scents. This full-bodied wine exhibits explosive fruit, Syrah's telltale smokiness, and a rich, moderately tannic, spicy finish with copious quantities of glycerin. The tannin is not totally integrated, but the wine is impressively large and aromatic. It would provide an ideal accompaniment to grilled steak or game birds. Moreover, it should continue to improve for 5–7 years, and last for 12 or more. The impressive 1996 Syrah Hillside Reserve is more restrained, elegant, tannic, and backward. I admired its saturated purple color, as well as its pure blackberry/cassis aromas intermixed with spicy new oak. There is a touch of minerality and good spice, but it is a more polite, suave, and gracefully constructed wine than its sibling. Nevertheless, it should unleash more of its personality with another 1–2 years of bottle age; it will keep for a decade or more.

At a time when many California wines seem to be priced proportionally to their producers' egos, Andrew Murray's offerings are a breath of fresh air given their exceptionally high quality and realistic prices—readers take note.

P.S. Readers who visit Los Olivos will find the winery has a tasting room in the quaint village center.

NADEAU FAMILY VINTNERS (PASO ROBLES)

1999 Zinfandel Critical Mass	Paso Robles	C	90
1999 Zinfandel Old Vines	Paso Robles	C	88

The star of this attractive duo is the 1999 Zinfandel Critical Mass (15.6% alcohol). While not complex, it is a sexy, explosive Zinfandel fruit bomb offering compelling drinking. Layer upon layer of black cherry, currant, and blackberry fruit tumble over the palate. The oak is kept well in the background. Unctuously textured, fleshy, and fat, it should be drunk over the next 2–3 years. Supple, harmonious, and richly fruity is the 1999 Zinfandel Old Vines. Plenty of black cherry and currant fruit as well as abundant glycerin can be found in this medium- to full-bodied effort. It should drink well for 2–4 years.

NEWLAN VINEYARDS (NAPA)

1999 Zinfandel	Napa	C	88
1998 Zinfandel	Napa	C	88
1997 Zinfandel	Napa	C	88?

The muscular, substantially sized, dark ruby/plum-colored 1999 Zinfandel displays plenty of jammy black cherry and kirsch-like scents in its moderately intense bouquet. Fat and fleshy, with good underlying acidity, it tips the scales at a modest (for Zinfandel) 14.5% alcohol. Consume it over the next 4–5 years. An excellent effort, the full-bodied, deep ruby/purple-colored 1998 Zinfandel exhibits thick, briery flavors in addition to good ripeness, purity, and overall balance. Although not complex, it offers a chunky personality with plenty of flesh and density. Drink it over the next 3–5 years. The 1997 Zinfandel behaved like a barrel sample. An extremely oaky, black/purple-colored effort, it is sure to be controversial because of the lavish display of spicy new wood. Unevolved and full-bodied, with copious quantities of blackberry fruit mixed with vanilla, there is little complexity in this well endowed, pure Zin. It will benefit from 6–8 more months of bottle age and should drink well for 7–8 years.

NEWTON VINEYARDS (NAPA)

1996 Cabernet Sauvignon Unfiltered	Napa	D	93+
1995 Cabernet Sauvignon Unfiltered	Napa	D	92
1997 Merlot Unfiltered	Napa	D	(90–92)
1996 Merlot Unfiltered	Napa	D	90

Newton has one of the most spectacular settings of any winery on California's North Coast. Situated high in the mountains above St. Helena, with gorgeous terraces and flower gardens, this estate has a distinctly French orientation. Much of the winery's staff appears to be French students trying to improve their English skills. Moreover, proprietress Su Hua Newton makes no secret of the fact that she looks for inspiration from France's finest winemakers. Her wines are unquestionably made with this philosophy in place. Not surprisingly, France's talented Michel Rolland is the consulting oenologist. Newton exports 30% of their production, with Switzerland the largest foreign buyer. All of the Newton wines are fermented with natural yeasts in order to obtain more complex aromatics. The malolactic fermentations take place in barrel to promote greater integration of wood and to encourage more textural richness in the wines. All of the wines are bottled without filtration.

Newton was one of the first California wineries to produce high-quality, ageworthy Merlot made in an elegant style, with admirable character, richness, and depth. The 1997 Merlot Unfiltered (produced from a severely thinned crop) possesses a saturated ruby color and a lovely nose of sweet black cherry fruit intermixed with herbs, minerals, and spice. Lush, ripe, and fragrant, this forward Merlot should be accessible when released and last for 12 or more years. The dense ruby/purple-colored 1996 Merlot Unfiltered is a fuller-bodied example, with more of the varietal's chocolate, coffee, roasted herb, and damp foresty characteristics.

The wine is spicy, lightly oaky, tightly knit, rich, pure, and structured. It requires 2–4 more years of cellaring, and should keep for 12–15.

Newton's Cabernet Sauvignons cut a broader, more textured mouth-feel. The 1996 Cabernet Sauvignon Unfiltered exhibits an opaque purple color, as well as a robust, nearly massive constitution, a boatload of tannin, and considerable power, depth, and muscle. Atypically rugged and brawny for a Newton Cabernet Sauvignon, it should age effortlessly for 2–3 decades. Prospective purchasers should be aware that this vintage will require 4–6 years of cellaring for some of the tannin to melt away. Also tannic, but more classically constructed, the 1995 Cabernet Sauvignon Unfiltered offers rich cassis fruit intermixed with loamy soil scents, toast, and floral notes. Long in the mouth, with an expansive texture, impeccable symmetry, and fine overall balance, this wine finishes with a tannic clout, as well as outstanding ripeness and presence in the mouth. Like the 1996, it should be long-lived, but will be ready to drink at an earlier age. Anticipated maturity: now–2020.

Past Glories: Cabernet Sauvignon—1993 (90), 1992 (92), 1991 (94), 1990 (94)

NEYERS VINEYARD (NAPA)

1995	Cabernet Sauvignon	Napa	D	90
1999	Chardonnay	Carneros	D	93
1999	Chardonnay	Napa	D	91
1999	Chardonnay Thieriot Vineyard	Sonoma Coast	E	92+
1999	Merlot Neyers Ranch	Conn Valley	D	89
1997	Merlot Neyers Ranch	Conn Valley	D	89
1999	Syrah Hudson Vineyard	Napa	D	(90–92)
1998	Syrah Hudson Vineyard	Carneros	E	90
1997	Syrah Hudson Vineyard	Napa	D	(91–93)
1996	Syrah Hudson Vineyard	Napa	D	92
1995	Syrah Hudson Vineyard	Napa	D	91
1999	Zinfandel Pato Ranch	Contra Costa	D	90
1999	Zinfandel Tofanelli Vineyard	Napa	D	89

Bruce Neyers, the national sales manager for Kermit Lynch Wine Merchants, has built his portfolio of impressive wines into a 15,000-case operation. The stars have always been his Chardonnays, but some enticing red wines (particularly Syrah and Zinfandel) are also being produced. Hopefully, Neyers will be able to build a bit more flavor into the Grenache, one of my favorite varietals. The 1999 Chardonnays have all been bottled save for the 1999 El Novillero, which was still going through malolactic fermentation when I visited in late October. While promising, it was too unsettled to review. The other Chardonnays appear to be some of the finest Neyers and his talented wine-maker, Ehren Jordan (of Turley Cellars fame), have produced. The full-bodied 1999 Chardonnay Napa exhibits honeyed citrus, tangerine, and other tropical fruit aromas and flavors. Intense and pure, with good underlying acidity as well as a layered, concentrated finish, the 14.5% alcohol is well integrated in this beautifully balanced wine. The 1999 Chardonnay Carneros (14.3% alcohol) reveals a smoky, complex, leesy-scented bouquet with notes of citrus, roasted hazelnuts, and candied apricots. Flavors of brioche, mango, minerals, and clove emerge in the mouth. This full-bodied wine seems fruit-driven, but the longer it sits in the glass, the more nuances become apparent. It is a dazzling Chardonnay to consume over the next 2–3 years. Both of these Chardonnays were aged completely in French oak (one-third was new), enjoyed full malolactic fermentation, and were bottled without filtration. From a cool Sonoma Coast vineyard, the light gold-colored 1999 Chardonnay Thieriot Vineyard displays a deeper color, and is the tightest, most backward of these Chardonnays. With enticing potential, it is loaded with extract and richness, exhibiting notes of ripe oranges, minerals, smoky, overripe lemons, and a clove/hazelnut character in its scents and flavors. Full-bodied, with good underlying acidity, and nicely integrated, toasty oak, it cuts a broad swath across the palate. Young and unevolved, it requires another six months of bottle age, and should drink well for 4–5 years.

The nearly outstanding, dark plum/purple-colored 1999 Merlot Neyers Ranch exhibits scents of toffee, caramel, cherry and berry fruit, and mocha. Soft, fleshy, and plush, it is reminiscent of a chewy, plump, mid-sized Pomerol. Enjoy it during its first 7–8 years of life. The potentially outstanding 1999 Syrah Hudson Vineyard boasts an opaque black/purple color that suggests an unctuous texture. Aromas of pepper, blackberry liqueur, and creosote emerge from this full-bodied, silky-textured, dense, concentrated Syrah. Approximately 40% was aged in new French oak, and the remainder in older wood. While there is firm tannin in the finish, this admirable Syrah possesses a gorgeously viscous texture as well as gobs of fruit and glycerin. Anticipated maturity: now–2014.

Given Ehren Jordan's undeniable skill for turning out lusty Zinfandel at Turley Cellars, it is not surprising that his 1999 Zinfandel Pato Ranch and 1999 Zinfandel Tofanelli Vineyard are potentially top-notch. The 1999 Zinfandel Pato Ranch (produced from a 104-year-old vineyard planted in sandy soils) displays a dense ruby color in addition to a sweet, jammy nose of berries, pepper, and resiny balsam aromas. Full-bodied, exuberant, and robust, with silky tannin as well as low acidity, it is a delicious, hedonistically styled Zinfandel to consume over the next 5–6 years. The dark ruby/purple-colored 1999 Zinfandel Tofanelli Vineyard reveals aromas of English walnuts intermixed with pepper, spice, and cherry liqueur. Long and full-bodied, with superb fruit purity, a viscous texture, and a medium- to full-bodied, heady finish, it is best drunk during its first 5–6 years of life.

The 1997 Merlot Neyers Ranch (from a vineyard in the Conn Valley) exhibits the telltale black chocolate and cherry liqueur fruit components typical of a fine Merlot. The color is a dark plum. In the mouth, this full-bodied, fleshy, seductive Merlot provides gobs of glycerin, a lush texture, and copious fruit. With a bit more complexity, it would have merited an outstanding score. On a purely hedonistic level, this wine may score higher with many readers. Drink it now and over the next 7–8 years.

The Neyers/Jordan team has consistently done stunning work with Syrah from the Hudson Vineyard. The 1997 Syrah, which was bottled without fining or filtration, will benefit from another 1–2 years of bottle age and should keep for 10–15. A knockout Syrah, it offers up huge bacon fat, *jus de viande*, pepper, and smoky notes intermixed with blackberry and cassis fruit. Dense, full-bodied, and powerful, with exceptional richness, outstanding purity, and nicely integrated new oak (50–60% new French oak barrels were utilized), this terrific Syrah is a must purchase for Rhône wine enthusiasts. A sensational Syrah from the Neyers winery, the 1996 Hudson Vineyard has it all. The color is opaque ruby/purple. The nose offers up creamy blackberry and cassis aromas complemented by spicy wood. In the mouth, the wine is full-bodied, tightly knit, and youthful, with expansive, chewy flavors, as well as outstanding purity and length. It will benefit from another 1–2 years of bottle age, and will keep for 10–15 years. Bravo! Neyers' black/purple-colored 1995 Syrah Hudson Vineyard's nose offers up copious quantities of classic pepper and cassis, with a hint of mint in the background. Some attractive new oak frames a well-constituted, full-bodied, rich, pure, smoky, cassis-flavored wine. This wine should drink well through 2010.

I was impressed by the 1995 Cabernet Sauvignon, which combines both power and elegance in a medium- to full-bodied style. The color is a dense, dark ruby/purple. The wine offers up copious quantities of black currant, berry fruit nicely dosed with smoky oak. Purely made, with a flattering texture (a characteristic of the Neyers wines), this luscious, soft, well-endowed Cabernet Sauvignon can be drunk now as well as over the next 7–8 years.

NORMAN VINEYARDS (PASO ROBLES)

1998	Zinfandel Barbara's Vineyard	Paso Robles	C	88
1998	Zinfandel The Monster	Paso Robles	C	88

Some of the finest Zinfandels ever tasted from Norman Vineyards, these are jammy, full-bodied, thick, juicy offerings meant to be consumed for their boisterous, exuberant gutsiness over the next 3–5 years. The intense, full-bodied, heady 1998 Zinfandel The Monster (15.4% alcohol) possesses copious quantities of glycerin, black cherries, and berry fruit. The acidity is low, and some of Paso Robles' loamy soil-like notes make a subtle appearance, but the wine's fruit and glycerin dominate . . . to its credit. The more Amarone-like 1998 Zinfandel Barbara's Vineyard comes close to being too overripe. Jammy, thick, cherry and berry notes are intertwined with soil overtones, dried herbs, and spice. The alcohol is more noticeable, even though it is essentially the same as in The Monster. Drink this big, juicy, in-your-face Zinfandel over the next 3–5 years.

OAKFORD CELLARS (NAPA)

1996 Cabernet Sauvignon	Oakville	E	88+
1995 Cabernet Sauvignon	Oakville	D	90
1994 Cabernet Sauvignon	Oakville	D	91

Oakford Cellars is a tiny Cabernet Sauvignon producer with an eight-acre vineyard strategically located above the Oakville Grade near the Harlan Estate Vineyard and Heitz's Martha's Vineyard. Proprietor Charles Ball first produced a wine in 1987. In 1994 he hired the immensely fashionable, in demand Heidi Barrett, to assist in the winemaking. The wine is aged in 50% French oak casks and 50% American oak casks (one-third of each type is new) for 18–20 months and is bottled with minor clarification. These are tannic, large-scaled, dense, mountain Cabernet Sauvignons that are not flattering in their youth, but possess considerable promise and aging potential. This is another winery where readers are advised to get on the mailing list if they want an opportunity to purchase the wines, as only 1,000 cases are produced. The 1994 Cabernet Sauvignon, somewhat of a sleeper, is a medium- to full-bodied, rich, smoky, mineral, and black currant–laden Cabernet. It reveals a classic structure, but the austerity it once possessed has been shed in favor of a well-structured, undeniably rich, well-delineated, pure Cabernet Sauvignon that should handsomely repay 5–6 years of cellaring; it will keep for 20+ years. Also impressive, the 1995 Cabernet Sauvignon reveals sweeter tannin than the 1994 (an anomaly in comparing these two vintages), rich, ripe, full-bodied fruit, admirable density and extract, fine overall equilibrium, and a long, heady, concentrated finish. Whether it develops as much intensity as the 1994 remains to be seen, but these wines have lived up to, and even surpassed, my earlier reviews.

A brilliant, backward Cabernet Sauvignon, the dark ruby/purple-colored 1996 exhibits blackberry, cassis, and loamy soil scents in the moderately endowed bouquet. The tannin level is high, and the wine slightly austere, but rich, medium- to full-bodied, and concentrated. It will require patience from prospective purchasers. It exhibits good ripeness, admirable purity, and a long finish. Anticipated maturity: 2004–2018.

Past Glories: 1993 Cabernet Sauvignon Estate (91)

OJAI VINEYARD (SANTA BARBARA)

2000 Chardonnay Bien Nacido Vineyard	Santa Barbara	D	89
2000 Chardonnay Clos Pepé Vineyard	Santa Rita Hills	D	91
1999 Chardonnay Clos Pepé Vineyard	Santa Rita Hills	D	89
2000 Chardonnay Talley Vineyard	Arroyo Grande	D	91
1999 Chardonnay Talley Vineyard	Arroyo Grande	D	90
2000 Pinot Noir Bien Nacido Vineyard	Santa Barbara	D	89
1999 Pinot Noir Bien Nacido Vineyard	Santa Barbara	D	93
1998 Pinot Noir Bien Nacido Vineyard	Santa Barbara	D	90
1997 Pinot Noir Bien Nacido Vineyard	Santa Barbara	D	87
1996 Pinot Noir Bien Nacido Vineyard	Santa Barbara	D	90

2000 Pinot Noir Clos Pepé Vineyard	Santa Rita Hills	D	89
2000 Pinot Noir Pisoni Vineyard	Santa Lucia Highlands	D	93
1999 Pinot Noir Pisoni Vineyard	Santa Lucia Highlands	D	93
1998 Pinot Noir Pisoni Vineyard	Santa Lucia Highlands	D	90
1997 Pinot Noir Pisoni Vineyard	Santa Lucia Highlands	D	91
1996 Pinot Noir Pisoni Vineyard	Santa Lucia Highlands	D	93
2000 Sauvignon Blanc	Santa Barbara	C	89
1999 Syrah	California	D	89
1998 Syrah	California	D	88
1997 Syrah	California	C	88
1996 Syrah	California	C	90
1995 Syrah	California	C	88
1994 Syrah	California	C	89
2000 Syrah	Santa Barbara	D	88
1994 Syrah	Santa Barbara	C	93
2000 Syrah Bien Nacido Vineyard	Santa Barbara	D	89
1999 Syrah Bien Nacido Vineyard	Santa Barbara	D	91
1998 Syrah Bien Nacido Vineyard	Santa Barbara	D	91
1997 Syrah Bien Nacido Vineyard	Santa Barbara	D	92
1996 Syrah Bien Nacido Vineyard	Santa Barbara	D	94
1995 Syrah Bien Nacido Vineyard	Santa Barbara	D	92+
1997 Syrah Cuvée Henry Daniel	Santa Barbara	E	95
2000 Syrah Melville Vineyard	Santa Rita Hills	D	92
2000 Syrah Roll Ranch	Santa Ynez	D	92
1999 Syrah Roll Ranch	Santa Ynez	D	92
1998 Syrah Roll Ranch	California	D	92
1997 Syrah Roll Ranch	California	D	92
1996 Syrah Roll Ranch	California	D	95+
1995 Syrah Roll Ranch	Santa Barbara	C	90
1998 Syrah Roll Ranch E.H.	California	E	95
2000 Syrah Stolpman Vineyard	Santa Ynez	D	91
1999 Syrah Stolpman Vineyard	Santa Ynez	D	94
1997 Syrah Stolpman Vineyard	Santa Barbara	D	91
1996 Syrah Stolpman Vineyard	Santa Barbara	D	95
2000 Syrah Thompson Vineyard	Santa Ynez	D	94
1999 Syrah Thompson Vineyard	Santa Ynez	D	96
1998 Syrah Thompson Vineyard	Santa Barbara	D	94
2000 Syrah White Hawk Vineyard	Santa Ynez	D	(90–92)
2000 Vin du Soleil	California	C	90
1999 Vin du Soleil	California	C	90
2000 Vin du Soleil (white)	California	C	90

This winery generally produces 5,000 cases, although production can jump to 7,500 cases in an abundant vintage. As longtime readers know, Ojai, and its owner/wine-maker, Adam Tolmach, get my nod as one of Santa Barbara's great success stories. Almost everything Tolmach touches turns out at least very good. Both the 2000 and 1999 portfolios look extremely strong. The 2000 Chardonnay Bien Nacido Vineyard was produced from a heavy crop and may lack the extra dimension of concentration found in other vintages. It offers notes of minerals and lemony citrus in its smoky, spicy nose, an excellent texture, and medium- to full-bodied flavors. Drink it over the next 2–3 years. The complex 2000 Chardonnay Clos Pepé comes from the cool, sandy soils of the Santa Rita Hills. It offers an intricate, spicy, mineral, and ripe fruit-scented bouquet, underlying minerality, and a structured, complete style reminiscent of a white Burgundy grand cru. Rich yet remarkably restrained, it should drink well for 3–4 years. From the highly regarded Talley Vineyard, the 2000 Chardonnay reveals forward, tropical fruit, a beautiful texture, lower acidity, and abundant quantities of honeysuckle as well as buttery tropical fruits. Enjoy it over the next 1–2 years. The crisp, high-acid, medium- to full-bodied, Chablis-like 1999 Chardonnay Clos Pepé will drink well for 2–3 years. The tropical fruit, buttery-scented and flavored 1999 Chardonnay Talley Vineyard possesses underlying minerality, but not as pronounced as that found in the Clos Pepé. Drink it over the next 1–2 years.

Adam Tolmach continues to produce a tasty, white Graves look-alike Sauvignon Blanc. The 2000, one of the winery's two wines to have its malolactic blocked, comes from a cool, gravelly site. It is crisp, with excellent concentration as well as a striking citrus/mineral character displaying hints of figs and lemon butter. As it sat in the glass, notions of tangerines also emerged. It is an impressive Sauvignon to drink over the next 12–18 months. A new entry in Tolmach's portfolio is the Vin du Soleil, a blend of 75% Roussanne, 20% Viognier, and 5% Chardonnay. The 2000 reveals waxy, mango, and orange marmalade notes in its medium- to full-bodied, ripe, concentrated personality. Like the Sauvignon, it had its malolactic blocked, which is good as it has just enough acidity to balance out its weighty, rich mouth-feel. Made from extremely low yields, this Rhône Ranger blend will prove exciting.

Pinot Noir hits lofty heights at Ojai. Approximately 75% new oak is utilized for these *cuvées*, which are 100% destemmed and aged 12–16 months in French oak before being bottled without fining or filtration. The 2000 Pinot Noir Clos Pepé has a tightly structured, cool-climate feel, medium to full body, deep cherry and currant fruit, and earthy/spicy notes. It is a well-defined, crisp Pinot to enjoy during its first 4–6 years. Displaying more pepper and herbaceousness is the spicy, earthy, dark ruby-colored 2000 Pinot Noir Bien Nacido. Drink this excellent, up-front, precocious 2000 over the next 2–3 years. From a superb vineyard, the 2000 Pinot Noir Pisoni Vineyard exhibits a deep ruby color plus sweet aromas of blackberry and cherry fruit intermixed with licorice, earth, and floral notes. Complex and full-bodied, with a layered texture, this superb Pinot will drink well during its first 7–8 years of life.

The 1999 Pinot Noirs emerged from a colder growing season. The deep ruby/purple-colored 1999 Pinot Noir Bien Nacido Vineyard offers fabulous aromas of smoke, earth, jammy plums, cherries, and dried herbs. With great fruit, medium to full body, and a layered, sweet, rich, mouth-filling personality, it will drink well for 5–6 years. The sensational 1999 Pinot Noir Pisoni Vineyard boasts a saturated ruby/purple color as well as classic Pinot Noir aromatics of smoky black fruits. This *cuvée* always possesses characteristics similar to a grand cru Vosne-Romanée. Floral notes mix with black fruits as well as a distinctive earthiness. This superb, full-bodied Pinot possesses outstanding concentration and a long finish with nicely integrated acidity as well as alcohol. Drink it over the next 7–8 years.

In both 1999 and 2000 Adam Tolmach produced a red Vin du Soleil made from primarily Grenache with some Syrah. Neither *cuvée* saw any new oak. The excellent 2000 Vin du Soleil (80% Grenache and 20% Syrah) possesses abundant quantities of blackberry and cherry fruit presented in a style not unlike a full-bodied, plump, hedonistic Côtes du Rhône. The 1999 Vin du Soleil (90% Grenache and 10% Syrah) is an opulent, hedonistic, decadently rich effort with plenty of body, loads of black fruit, and an easygoing texture. Neither of these wines will make old bones, but for drinking during their first 4–5 years of life, they provide considerable excitement.

Ojai's basic Syrah is a good introduction to this estate's style. It is always approachable, offering plenty of jammy plum, black cherry, and currant fruit. The 2000 Syrah Santa Barbara is a fleshy, medium- to full-bodied, fruit-forward, mainstream, consumer-accessible effort that is ideal for drinking during its first 4–5 years of life. The single-vineyard Syrahs are more serious. For example, the 2000 Syrah Stolpman Vineyard exhibits a saturated black/ruby color as well as crème de cassis and graphite aromas, and elegant, full-bodied, pure flavors that coat the palate. Rich, thick, and low in acidity, it will drink well for 10–12 years. The super-concentrated 2000 Syrah Melville Vineyard offers notes of pepper, crème de cassis, licorice, leather, and earth. With great intensity and full body, it is another example of this promising vineyard in the Santa Rita Hills. Cropped at one ton of fruit per acre, it requires 2–3 years of cellaring and should last for 15 years. Adam Tolmach was not sure if he was going to do a single-vineyard bottling of the 2000 Syrah White Hawk Vineyard. It is a sensationally concentrated effort, but still awkward and disjointed, with earthy, savage characteristics as well as mouth-staining levels of extract and richness. It has enough character to be bottled separately, but it needs to come together and be less disjointed. It is a candidate for 15 or more years of cellaring. The typically elegant, stylish, medium-bodied, dense purple-colored 2000 Syrah Bien Nacido Vineyard possesses rich fruit as well as a peppery characteristic. Reminiscent of a concentrated, top *cuvée* of Crozes-Hermitage, it will drink well for 7–9 years. The most seductive offering is the 2000 Syrah Roll Ranch. This *cuvée* always possesses a voluptuous texture, low acidity, ripe tannin, and undeniable hedonistic appeal. The black/purple-colored 2000 boasts oodles of fruit, glycerin, and extract. This knockout, pure, layered, long Syrah will drink well for a decade. The prodigious 2000 Syrah Thompson Vineyard's stunning aromatics and flavors consist of roasted meats, crème de cassis, new saddle leather, earth, pepper, and asphalt. Fabulously concentrated and extremely rich, with an admirable seamlessness, it will drink well for 12–15 years.

From a cool year, the 1999 Syrah California exhibits aromas and flavors of plums, cassis, figs, smoke, and herbs. Although there is dry tannin in the finish, the wine possesses abundant richness as well as extract in its straightforward, richly fruity personality. The brilliant 1999 Syrah Stolpman Vineyard reveals an opaque purple color along with scents of blackberries, chocolate, espresso, and licorice. Full-bodied, majestically rich and layered, with moderate tannin, this wine requires 2–3 years of cellaring and should drink well for 10–12 years. The blockbuster 1999 Syrah Thompson Vineyard boasts an opaque black/purple color as well as a bouquet that is the essence of smoky Syrah. Frying lard intermixed with cassis, barbecue spice, and blackberry aromas are followed by an unctuously textured, full-bodied, deep, sensationally pure, prodigious Syrah to drink now and over the next 12–15 years. Once again, the 1999 Syrah Roll Ranch proved to be the most flirtatious of the Ojai Syrahs. Displaying a black/purple color and gobs of black fruits intermixed with licorice and a hint of Viognier (2–3% is added to the blend), this voluptuous, seductive offering is a thrill to drink. Low acidity and wealth of fruit make this a compelling Syrah. It should drink well for 10–12 years. The 1999 Syrah Bien Nacido Vineyard comes across as the most French inspired. The complex, nuanced aromatics reveal scents of pepper, dried Provençal herbs, earth, and spice box. Licorice and red as well as black currants make an appearance in the mouth. Although it is less powerful and thick when compared to its siblings, it is a dead ringer for a Rhône Valley Hermitage or topflight Crozes-Hermitage. Consume it over the next 10–12 years.

Lastly, there are 200 cases of the 1998 Syrah Roll Ranch E.H. A special bottling, it tips the scales at a whopping 15% alcohol, and is the only Syrah that Adam Tolmach bottles in a Bordeaux-shaped bottle. This unique offering possesses extraordinary sweetness, an unctuous texture, and high tannin levels. Ripe, with roasted black fruit notes intermixed with asphalt, camphor, meat, and cassis/blackberries, this structured, backward wine requires 2–3 years of cellaring and should last for two decades. Tolmach likes his 1998s even better than his 1997s, saying it was a smaller crop and he was able to wait out the cool weather, so the wines' potential is exciting. Two 1998 Pinot Noirs from Adam Tolmach were outstanding. My favorite is the 1998 Pinot Noir Bien Nacido Vineyard. This dark ruby-colored Pinot offers up copious quantities of pepper, sweet black cherry fruit, smoke, plum jam, and minerals. There is terrific purity, medium to full body, and a vivacious, lively, concentrated feel in the mouth. It should drink well for 4–5 years. It is hard not to be seduced by the Vosne-Romanée-like nose of the 1998 Pinot Noir Pisoni Vineyard. Intertwined with smoke, minerals, and black cherry fruit are notes of allspice, leather, and wood. Pure, soft, and fleshy, with an open-knit, velvety texture, this luscious Pinot Noir should be drunk over the next 3–4 years.

There are five appealing 1998 Syrahs produced at Ojai. The dark ruby/purple-colored 1998 Syrah California (mostly from the Roll Ranch, Stolpman Vineyard, and Bien Nacido Vineyard) exhibits a ripe nose of cassis, licorice, and barbecue spice. A fruit-driven, thick, juicy Syrah, it is ideal for drinking during its first 7–8 years of life. This supple-textured, fleshy effort possesses plenty of stuffing and fruit, but not a great deal of complexity. There are two 1998 Syrahs from the Roll Ranch. One cuvée (225 cases) is designated E.H., which denotes that it was made from a specific clone (Estrella) and bottled separately. It may turn out to be the finest Syrah that Adam Tolmach has yet produced. The 1998 Syrah Roll Ranch, from a warm microclimate, reveals an opaque purple color in addition to a deep, sweet nose of black fruits, low acidity, a muscular, full-bodied personality, and impressive levels of extract and concentration. It is soft and voluptuous enough to be drunk early, but should age nicely for more than a decade. The super-concentrated, essence of Syrah 1998 Syrah Roll Ranch E.H. exhibits a thick, viscous-looking purple color and a bouquet of blackberry liqueur. The wine coats the palate with glorious levels of glycerin, jammy fruit, and sweet tannin. Exceptionally full-bodied, with fabulous intensity and length as well as a blockbuster finish, it is remarkably well balanced and harmonious given its enormous size and inky-colored personality. While it will be fun to drink young, 4–5 years of cellaring will bring multiple secondary nuances and subtleties. Look for this wine to evolve nicely for 10–15 years. The dense black/purple-colored 1998 Syrah Thompson Vineyard (300 cases) displays telltale notes of creosote, cassis, blackberries, scorched earth, and smoke. Although it exhibits more tannin than its siblings, there is more than enough richness to balance it out. Full-bodied, mouth-filling, and impressive, it should drink well for 12–15 years. Although 1998 can be a high-acid year, there is no tartness. The 1998 Syrah Bien Nacido Vineyard was harvested on November 17, 1998, from one of the coolest Syrah vineyards in Santa Barbara. Aromas of fruitcake, licorice, dried herbs, tar, and black currants jump from the glass of this fragrant, elegant, less weighty Syrah. Medium-bodied, with impressive concentration, but nowhere near the size, length, or muscle of its siblings, it will drink well young and last for 5–7 years.

Tasting the 1997 Syrahs from bottle confirms just how successful this vintage was for Tolmach. He rates 1997 below 1998 and 1996, equating it with 1995 as a good vintage for the region, but not as excellent as 1994 or 1998. The deep ruby/purple-colored 1997 Syrah Bien Nacido Vineyard offers a gorgeous nose of incense, spice, pepper, cedar, and black fruits. Silky-textured, lush, and forward, with outstanding richness, this is a beautiful wine to drink over the next decade. Out of bottle, the 1997 Syrah Stolpman Vineyard reveals less aromatics, but more power, richness, and size. Opaque ruby/purple-colored, with sumptuous aromas of blackberry liqueur, smoke, pepper, and earth, this creamy-textured, full-bodied, luscious Syrah has some tannin to shed, but it is hard to resist its ostentatious personality. It should drink well for 12–15 years. More backward and powerful, and the slowest to reveal its personality, is the 1997 Syrah Roll Ranch. There is no doubting either its saturated purple color or subtle yet impressively ripe nose of cassis, smoke, vanilla, and spice. Deep, with exceptional intensity, this wine requires 2–3 years of bottle age and should be consumed over the following 12–15. The 1997 Syrah Cuvée Henry Daniel (named after one of Tolmach's children) is a prodigious Syrah, 75% emerged from the Bedford Thompson Vineyard and the rest from the Bien Nacido. Opaque purple-colored, with a huge, smoky, blackberry liqueur–scented nose, this fabulously concentrated wine exhibits abundant sweet tannin, an unctuous texture, well-integrated new oak (about 50% new wood was utilized), and a layered, deep finish. It should evolve beautifully for 10–15+ years. This wine is only available in six-packs, as production was limited to just over 300 cases. Even though the 1997s were made from higher yields than the 1996s, they are among the most concentrated and finest wines I tasted from Santa Barbara. The deep ruby/purple-colored 1997 Syrah California (10% Grenache and 10% Mourvèdre have been added to the blend) offers a peppery, leathery, mineral, kirsch, and blackberry-scented nose, good depth, not as much complexity (as the other *cuvées*), but full body, and a luscious, accessible, low-acid profile that will give it considerable charm and seductiveness during its first 7–10 years of life.

Pinot Noir yields were higher in 1997 than in 1996. While neither of the 1997s equal their 1996 counterparts, both are well made and merit attention. Ojai's Pinot Noirs are destemmed, fermented at relatively hot temperatures, and kept in barrel, on their lees, until assembled prior to bottling. As with all the winery's reds, there is no fining or filtration. The 1997 Pinot Noir Bien Nacido Vineyard reveals an attractive ruby/purple color and a sweet nose of cherry/plum fruit intermixed with a whiff of green pepper, allspice, and toast notes. The wine is rich and fleshy, with good body and an elegant, Côte de Beaune–like finish, with the cherry fruit component dominating its personality. It should drink well for 3–5 years. The 1997 Pinot Noir Pisoni Vineyard may not be as thick or massively extracted as it was in 1996, but it is a beautifully made Pinot with this varietal's black fruit character offering a complete contrast to the Bien Nacido. The wine's saturated ruby/purple color is followed by a seductive nose of blackberries and raspberries. Full-bodied, with rich fruit, more power, viscosity, and body than Bien Nacido, and a long, silky-textured finish, the Pisoni Vineyard Pinot Noir should drink well for 7–10 years.

Adam Tolmach fashioned two exceptional 1996 Pinot Noirs. The deep ruby/purple-colored 1996 Pinot Noir Bien Nacido Vineyard reveals some of the telltale herb (V-8 vegetable juice) character (a hallmark of Santa Barbara Pinot), combined with copious quantities of full-bodied black cherry and berry fruit. The wine is dense, concentrated, exceptionally pure, and creamy-textured. It is a sumptuous, herb-tinged, full-throttle Pinot Noir with no hard edges. It should drink well for at least 2–4 years. I have been impressed by the quality of Pinot Noirs emerging from the Pisoni Vineyard in the Santa Lucia Highlands (readers may recall that Peter Michael produces a Pinot from this vineyard). Ojai's 1996 Pinot Noir Pisoni Vineyard represents the essence of Pinot Noir. It is one of the most concentrated and well-balanced Pinots I have ever tasted. This wine possesses the extract level one expects from a Domaine Leroy Richebourg or Romanée St.-Vivant. Obviously produced from extremely ripe fruit and low yields, this is a mammoth yet unbelievably harmonious Pinot Noir. The opaque ruby purple color is followed by scents of kirsch, jammy cherries, and spice that are unmistakably Pinot, but leaning toward the black fruit side of this varietal (Côte de Nuits). The wine is full-bodied and saturates the palate with layers of glycerin, ripe fruit, and a sumptuous texture. Beautifully balanced, awesomely rich, and dazzlingly pure, this is one of the most extraordinary expressions of New World Pinot Noir I have ever tasted. I would not be surprised to see this wine evolve magnificently for a decade. Moreover, my score may look stingy with another several years of bottle age.

Ojai turned out four exceptional 1996 Syrahs. If I were to invest in vineyard land in California, I would consider three spots—northern California's Anderson Valley and Sonoma Coast for Pinot Noir and Chardonnay, and Santa Barbara for Syrah. The basic offering, the 1996 Syrah California, is an outstanding wine that could easily pass for a dazzling Rhône. It possesses a beautiful ruby/purple color, as well as a terrific nose of cassis and pepper intermingled with a whiff of tar and herbs. Rich, with luscious smoky fruit, this medium- to full-bodied, ripe, low-acid yet gorgeously knit Syrah can be drunk now and over the next 6–7 years. The 1996 Syrah Bien Nacido is a wine of exceptional extraction, richness, and depth. The color is an opaque black/purple, and the wine offers up classic tar, cassis, and bacon fat aromas. Full-bodied, with no hard edges, this profoundly concentrated, mouth-filling, voluptuously textured Syrah possesses all the necessary components to age beautifully for a decade or more. However, the wine's explosive richness and enticing aromatics will ensure that much of it is drunk within hours of purchase. The 1996 Syrah Stolpman Vineyard comes across as a classic Hermitage with less earth, but with the blackberry liqueur/crème de cassis–like trademarks. It boasts an opaque black/purple color, as well as an extraordinary nose of black fruits, blackberries, and cassis, full-bodied, awesomely concentrated flavors, gobs of glycerin, low acidity, and a 40+ second finish. This is a thrilling, thick, juicy, succulent, formidably endowed Syrah that should age effortlessly for 10–15 years. Lastly, the most backward of this quartet is the 1996 Syrah Roll Ranch Vineyard. Cut from the same mold as its siblings, it is a black/purple-colored, full-bodied blockbuster with gobs of cassis and blackberry liqueur–like flavors, but more tannin and earth in the flavors, as well as a more structured, backward feel in the mouth. The wine has huge extract, fabulous purity, and is another tour de force in Syrah winemaking.

Rhône Ranger enthusiasts will go bonkers over the three splendid Syrahs from the 1995 vintage. The ruby/purple-colored, uncomplicated 1995 Syrah possesses striking levels of sweet cassis fruit in the nose, along with a touch of licorice and pepper. This dense, medium-bodied wine offers delicious levels of jammy fruit and plenty of glycerin and punch. It should drink well for another 5–7 years. The 1995 Syrah Roll Ranch is an explosively rich wine with terrific intensity, a black/purple color, super purity, no hard edges, full body, high glycerin, and moderate tannin, the latter component largely concealed behind the wine's impressive fruit extraction. This is a young, grapy Syrah that should evolve beautifully for 10–12 years. The profound 1995 Syrah Bien Nacido Vineyard makes me think that Syrah may do better than Pinot Noir in selected Santa Barbara microclimates. This killer Syrah boasts an opaque black/purple color and an awesome nose of smoke, licorice, Asian spices, and black fruits. Some toasty notes are present, but they play an accessory role to the wine's cassis-like jamminess. Full-bodied, with superb delineation, this layered, textured, thick yet beautifully balanced, dense Syrah should last for 15 years.

The 1994 Syrah exhibits a deep ruby/purple color, a telltale, smoky, bacon fat, and cassis-scented nose, a succulent, soft, opulent texture, great fruit, and a classic, open-knit Syrah character. The wine almost tastes sweet because of the grape ripeness. This is a hedonistic, lush Syrah to drink over the next 4–5 years. The 1994 Syrah Santa Barbara smells like a terrific Hermitage. A huge, dramatic nose of bacon fat, smoke, and jammy black fruits is followed by a dense, full-bodied, layered wine crammed with ripe fruit. Its creamy texture, sumptuous thickness, lushness, and admirable purity combine to give this full-bodied, flamboyant Syrah a compelling character. I suspect there is more tannin than the wine is currently revealing. This is a mouth-filling, gorgeously proportioned, well-endowed Syrah to drink over the next 10–12 years.

OPUS ONE (NAPA)

1997 Proprietary Red Wine	Napa	EE	88
1996 Proprietary Red Wine	Napa	EE	93
1994 Proprietary Red Wine	Napa	EE	92

Now, don't get me wrong, 88 points signifies a very good to excellent wine. But in the context of the vintage, not to mention the context of what the 1997 should be, this is a disappointment. After a stunningly concentrated, opulent, blockbuster effort in 1996, the 1997 tastes as if it were made from yields that were too high. They may tell you it is elegant and complex, but, truthfully, there is not much depth, and the wine will have a relatively short lifeline of 10–12 years. A dark ruby color is accompanied by a complex nose of plums, black cherries, currants, smoke, and leather. The wine reveals more new oak than normal for Opus, as well as medium body, good depth, dry, hard tannins in the finish, and little weight or length. Drink it over the next 8–10 years. The 1996 is one of the finest Opus Ones to date, offering a dark ruby/purple color, as well as a striking, intense bouquet of sweet licorice intermixed with blackberries, cassis, plums, and saddle leather. This seamless, full-bodied wine is more

velvety-textured, opulent, and succulent than past vintages. The mid-palate is expansive and chewy. The long finish is filled with glycerin, ripe fruit, and sweet tannin. Drink this impressive, user-friendly, yet richly concentrated effort over the next 15 years. The 1994 is another impressive effort from Opus One. The wine, a blend of 95% Cabernet Sauvignon, 2% Cabernet Franc, 2% Merlot, and 1% Malbec, possesses a dark ruby/purple color followed by a generous, complex nose of lead pencil, toasty oak, violets, and black currants. In the mouth, there is a beautiful texture, soft, generous, low-acid, full-bodied richness, and a stunningly proportioned, rich, intense finish. The influence of 18 months in new French oak casks gives the wine a subtle oaky note in addition to giving it excellent delineation. Because of the wine's softness and generosity, it can be drunk now and over the next 18–20 years.
Past Glories: 1992 (90), 1991 (91), 1990 (92), 1987 (92)

· PAHLMEYER (NAPA)

1999 Chardonnay	Napa	E	90
1996 Malbec	Napa	E	91
1999 Merlot	Napa	EE	91
1998 Merlot	Napa	EE	90
1997 Merlot	Napa	EE	96
1996 Merlot	Napa	E	97
1995 Merlot	Napa	E	94
1994 Merlot	Napa	E	95
1999 Proprietary Red Wine	Napa	EE	90+
1998 Proprietary Red Wine	Napa	EE	91
1997 Proprietary Red Wine	Napa	EE	98
1996 Proprietary Red Wine	Napa	EE	95
1995 Proprietary Red Wine	Napa	E	96
1994 Proprietary Red Wine	Napa	D	96

Helen Turley, who made Pahlmeyer famous with her intense style of winemaking, was replaced in 2000 by her former assistant, Erin Green. It should have been a smooth transition as both women appear to share the same winemaking philosophy. The 1999 Chardonnay (which emerges from several areas, the core component being the Berlenbach Vineyard in Coombsville) is a dense, concentrated effort with higher acidity than usual (the result of a cool growing season). This outstanding Chardonnay reveals medium to full body, excellent viscosity, and abundant tangerine, citrus oil, mineral, and buttery tropical fruit aromas and flavors.

Pahlmeyer's 1997 Merlot may be the finest Merlot ever produced in California. A profound blend of 85% Merlot and 15% Cabernet Sauvignon, it offers gorgeous smoky, black cherry liqueur aromas mixed with melted fudge. The wine is unctuously textured, super-concentrated, low in acidity, rich, and multilayered. This is a spectacular, hedonistic effort to drink over the next 15–20 years. Not surprisingly, the 1998 Merlot is lighter, but it is undoubtedly one of the finest Merlots produced in this irregular vintage. A blend of 95% Merlot and 5% Cabernet Franc (1,750 cases), Jayson Pahlmeyer and wine-maker Erin Green decided to eliminate 38% of the wine. Full-bodied, thick, and juicy, with low acidity as well as melted chocolate, cherry, smoke, and toast aromas and flavors, it is best drunk over the next 5–8 years. The 1999 Merlot (100% Merlot; 1,650 cases) is richer and riper than the 1998, but it is doubtful that it will achieve the mind-boggling proportions of the 1997. The dense ruby/purple-colored 1999 offers smoky, licorice, cherry, and chocolaty aromas, medium to full body, better acidity than either the 1997 or 1998, and a thick, full-bodied finish. Anticipated maturity: now–2012. The 1996 Merlot (3,000 cases) is a worthy rival to the 1997. Bottled unfined and unfiltered, this blend of 93% Merlot and 7% Cabernet Franc tips the scales at a heady 14.6% alcohol. The wine is opaque black/purple-colored, with a knockout nose of plums, black cherries, chocolate, raspberries, licorice, and toasty new oak. Viscous in the mouth, with superb purity, this is a riveting, mind-boggling Merlot that sets a new reference point for this varietal in California. It can be drunk now, but has the potential to last for 15 or more years.

I do not believe it is an exaggeration to say that Pahlmeyer's Merlot is now the finest being produced in California. One might quibble over other styles of Merlot, but no producer achieves more complexity, flavor, and thrills per sip than Pahlmeyer. The 1995 Merlot is an awesomely endowed, full-bodied, pedal-to-the-metal style of Merlot with great richness, in addition to a knockout nose of blackberry, raspberry, mocha, and smoky aromas that soar from the glass. The wine has a sweet attack (from its formidable glycerin and extract level, not sugar), full body, extraordinary layers of concentrated fruit, and a blockbuster finish. Amazingly, the wine, like its 1996 counterpart, possesses gorgeously integrated acidity, tannin, and alcohol. Can California Merlot get any better than this? Both Merlots will drink well when released and last for 15–20 years. The 1994 Merlot reveals a dense purple color, followed by a super fragrant nose of chocolate, mocha, toast, and black cherry fruit. Full-bodied, but not heavy, this expansive, chewy, opulently textured wine should drink well for 15+ years.

There are small quantities of 1996 Malbec. Produced from fruit grown in the Napanook Vineyard owned by Christian Moueix, this exotic, wild wine is not for everybody, but it ranks with the finest California Malbecs. The dark saturated ruby/purple color is accompanied by aromas of vanilla ice cream drenched with raspberry jam. Smoky, toasty notes (from aging in new Taransaud barrels) also make an appearance. In the mouth, the wine's display of fruit is so ostentatious as to be gaudy. It does not possess the body or length of Pahlmeyer's Merlots or Proprietary Reds, but it is an enormously fat, fruity, and undeniably sexy and disarming wine that is surprisingly light on its feet. It should drink well for 10–15 years.

The finest proprietary red produced by Pahlmeyer to date is their 1997 (a blend of 72% Cabernet Sauvignon, 17% Merlot, and the rest Petit Verdot, Cabernet Franc, and Malbec). Production is 3,300 cases, and the wine tips the scales at 14.7% alcohol. A superrich, blockbuster effort, it exhibits an opaque purple color in addition to a fabulous bouquet of black fruits, espresso, cocoa, mocha, and flowers. A prodigious red, with low acidity, spectacular concentration, and fabulous purity as well as overall symmetry, it can be drunk now, but promises to last for 20–25 years. The 1998 Proprietary Red is a blend of 75% Cabernet Sauvignon, 15% Merlot, 4% Cabernet Franc, 1% Petit Verdot, and 1% Malbec. A sexy, up-front, plush wine with a deep purple color, medium to full body, and copious quantities of sweet blackberry, crème de cassis, and meaty notes, it is on a fast evolutionary track, and thus should be consumed over the next 10–12 years. The promising, opaque purple-colored 1999 Proprietary Red is a blend of 71.5% Cabernet Sauvignon, 21.5% Merlot, 4% Petit Verdot, 2% Cabernet Franc, and 1% Malbec. It exhibits blueberry liqueur, roasted coffee, spice, and smoky wood aromas. Broad, dense, and full-bodied, with the acidity giving it a firmer edge than the 1997 or 1998, this chewy effort is best consumed during its first 15–18 years of life. The 1996 Proprietary Red (a blend of 73% Cabernet Sauvignon with the balance Malbec, Petit Verdot, Merlot, and Cabernet Franc) is a less weighty (14.3% alcohol) offering. It has become more delineated with a year of bottle age, offering up classic crème de cassis, smoked meat, coffee, prune, and toasty new-oak scents. Concentrated, with fabulously high extract, sweet tannin, and full body, this wine has a more elegant feel on the palate, but is still a blockbuster. Anticipated maturity: now–2025.

The 1995 Proprietary Red Wine boasts an explosive blackberry/blueberry/cassis-scented nose that has completely soaked up all the new oak in which it has been aged for the last 22 months. Purple/black in color, it exhibits fabulously extracted, layered black fruit flavors that coat the palate, offering a seamless texture and voluptuous impression. The 1994 Proprietary

Red Wine exhibits a similar purple/black color, as well as sweet, integrated tannin, a gorgeous black currant, toast, tar, and licorice-scented nose, fabulous texture, and a 35–45 second finish. The 1994 may be slightly sweeter in the mid-palate than the 1995, but the differences are negligible. The abundant tannin is mostly concealed by the wine's wealth of fruit, glycerin, and alcohol. This wine should drink well for the next 20 years.

If great wine satisfies both the palate and the intellect, these Pahlmeyer offerings are prodigious. Despite the forward drinkability of these reds, all of them will last for 20–25 years. These are mind-boggling efforts. This is another winery where getting on the mailing list is essential to securing a few bottles of these liquid gems.

Past Glories: 1993 Merlot (90), 1993 Proprietary Red Wine (96)

PALOMA (NAPA)

1997 Merlot	Napa	D	92
1996 Merlot	Napa	D	94
1995 Merlot	Napa	D	92+
1994 Merlot	Napa	D	91+
1997 Syrah	Napa	D	91

Both the 1997 Merlot and 1997 Syrah are rich, concentrated, multilayered efforts with considerable purity, texture, and intensity. The 1997 Merlot exhibits a dark purple color as well as attractive, spicy, oaky notes intermixed with smoke and black cherry jam. Full-bodied, with low acidity, outstanding concentration and purity, and moderate tannin in the impressively endowed finish, it should be cellared for 2–4 more years and drunk over the following 15. The stunning, black/purple-colored 1997 Syrah offers extraordinary purity of crème de cassis and peppery-like aromas, and powerful, concentrated, full-bodied flavors, with the fruit and glycerin dominating all other components. There is enough acidity to buttress this large wine's considerable power and intensity. Vague notions of licorice, tar, and spice emerge with coaxing. However, this is a giant fruit bomb that should continue to gain complexity, and become more delineated with bottle age. It should drink well for 12–15 years.

Bob Foley, the wine-maker at Pride Mountain, produces Paloma's Merlot from Spring Mountain fruit. The 1996 is about as concentrated, thick, and promising a Merlot as readers are likely to find from either the New or Old World. The color is an impressive opaque purple. The nose merely hints at what should emerge with another 2–3 years of cellaring. At present, readers will have to be content with toasty notes intermingled with plums, prunes, and black cherry liqueur. Full-bodied, deep, and exceptionally well balanced, with beautifully integrated acidity and tannin, this massive, rich, ageworthy Merlot should be at its best between now–2015. The 1995 Merlot is another fine effort from this small winery owned by Barbara and Jim Richards. A blend of 80% Merlot and 20% Cabernet Sauvignon, the wine was fined with egg whites, but not filtered prior to bottling. Its opaque purple color suggests a wine of extraordinary intensity. The nose is subdued, but swirling brings forth scents of jammy cassis, licorice, toast, and sweet cherry fruit. It possesses an inner core of intense fruit, a lush texture, and flavors of fruit and chocolate, with a subtle overlay of smoky oak. Full-bodied, moderately tannic, and exceptionally intense with a lingering finish, this is a Merlot to cellar for 2–3 years and drink over the following two decades. Very impressive!

Only 625 cases were produced of Paloma's 1994 Merlot, a blockbuster, inky/purple-colored wine. It is obviously the result of talented winemaking, given its purity and wonderful integration of toasty French oak with gobs of black cherry and raspberry fruit. The wine reveals full body, marvelous extraction and richness, terrific equilibrium, and a layered, textured, expansively flavored personality. This impressive wine is drinking well, yet should last for another 10–12 years. This is an exceptionally impressive wine made in a large-scaled, boldly styled, massively endowed format!

PARADIGM WINERY (NAPA)

1995 Cabernet Sauvignon Oakville Estate	Napa	D	90
1994 Merlot Oakville Estate	Napa	D	88
1995 Zinfandel Oakville Estate	Napa	C	88

These wines are made by one of Napa's most talented wine consultants, Heidi Barrett (the wife of Bo Barrett of Château Montelena), who is also the consultant to such Napa blue bloods as Grace Family Vineyards, Screaming Eagle, Vineyard 29, Hartwell, and, until 1996, Dalla Valle. Paradigm's offerings are elegant wines that marry Bordeaux-like restraint with California's ripe fruit flavors. The 1995 Zinfandel Oakville Estate offers peppery, briery fruit, along with a classy sweet raspberry richness. The wine is medium-bodied, with more length and flavor dimension than the 1994, a sweet, soft mid-palate and texture, and a succulent, classy, spicy finish. It should drink well for 4–5 years. The 1994 Merlot Oakville Estate is an excellent, medium-bodied, elegant wine offering attractive berry fruit and spice, as well as a subtle dosage of toasty new oak. It is a wine to drink over the next 5–7 years.

With respect to the Cabernet Sauvignons, this is one winery where the 1995 outclasses the 1994. While the 1994 Cabernet Sauvignon Oakville Estate is certainly very good, the 1995 Cabernet Sauvignon Oakville Estate cuts a deeper impression on the palate, offering up copious quantities of black cherry, currant, and herb-tinged flavors in a medium- to full-bodied, plush style. The wine possesses more layers of flavor, excellent purity, and a spicy, long finish. It should drink well for 10 more years.

FESS PARKER (SANTA BARBARA)

2000 Chardonnay	Santa Barbara	C	89
2000 Chardonnay Marcella's Vineyard	Santa Barbara	D	90
1999 Pinot Noir American Tradition Reserve	Santa Barbara	D	89
1999 Syrah American Tradition Release	Santa Barbara	D	88
1998 Syrah American Tradition Release	Santa Barbara	D	88
1999 Syrah Rodney's Vineyard American Tradition Reserve	Santa Barbara	D	90

Like many people my age, Fess Parker remains a favorite childhood hero because of his Hollywood roles as Davy Crockett and later, Daniel Boone. Some of Santa Barbara's cognoscenti obviously find it difficult to detach the Hollywood superstar image from the man as a vineyard developer and moving force in the local county viticultural association. What surprises me on each visit to Santa Barbara is that Fess Parker is controversial. He has developed a splendid hotel, Fess Parker's Doubletree Resort, fronting the Pacific Ocean in the town of Santa Barbara, and also has one of the exceptional venues for food and lodging in the wine country, his Wine Country Inn in Los Olivos. While his critics look at him as a shrewd land developer, what I see is someone committed to producing quality wine and developing some of the finest hillside vineyard sites in the Santa Barbara region. While I am not sure he would like to be called cunning, he has been shrewd enough to purchase some of the finest potential vineyard land in and around Los Olivos, and has been generous enough to share the fruit with the area's most renowned wine-makers. His objective of turning out world-class wines from Rhône varietals is right on target. Moreover, his own wines have improved significantly, and the portfolio tasted in November 1999 shows the winery's finest efforts to date. Fess Parker's son, Eli, is the wine-maker, and there is no doubt that he has learned plenty from working with consulting wine-maker Jed Steele. The bottom line is simple—this looks to be one of the more serious, up-and-coming players in Santa Barbara. This will probably not sit well with some of Parker's critics, who would still like people to believe he is just another Hollywood actor with wine as a hobby. That is a myth. This is a winery with serious aspirations for quality, and, as always, the truth is in the bottle.

One of Fess Parker's impressive new hillside vineyards is Rodney's Vineyard. The 1999

Syrah Rodney's Vineyard reveals the potential of this site. Opaque purple-colored, with a sweet, blackberry and cassis-scented nose intermixed with notes of subtle wood and licorice, it is a full-bodied, spicy, rich, concentrated wine with no hard edges and impressive levels of extract and richness. The tannin, wood, and acidity are nicely meshed with the wine's fruit. Drink it over the next 7–8 years. Earthy, peppery, black currant, and berry aromas emerge from the dark ruby-colored 1998 Syrah American Tradition Release. An accessible style of Syrah with good spice, it is medium-bodied, soft, and plump. Drink this crowd-pleasing Syrah over the next 4–5 years. The 1999 Syrah American Tradition Release is made in a non-aggressive, supple, medium- to full-bodied style that emphasizes plenty of peppery, black currant, and plum fruit. Spicy and rich, with no hard edges, this plump, savory, deliciously fruity Syrah should drink well over the next 7–9 years.

The superb 2000 Chardonnay Marcella's Vineyard (named after Parker's wife) is a structured yet full-bodied wine offering copious mineral and tropical fruit aromas and flavors. It has more volume and definition than the delicious fruit cocktail–styled 2000 Chardonnay Santa Barbara. Another noteworthy effort is the 1999 Pinot Noir American Tradition Reserve. A plush, textured, juicy Pinot with abundant plum, cherry, and earthy fruit, it is seductive as well as medium- to full-bodied. It should drink well for 5–7 years.

While I did not taste it on my recent visit, according to my mother there is not a better Muscat made than Fess Parker's. Readers with a sweet tooth or who have friends and family that like these fragrant, slightly sweet Muscats would be well advised to give them a try. All of Fess Parker's offerings are fairly priced wines for such quality.

PATZ AND HALL WINE CO. (NAPA)

1999 Chardonnay	Napa	D	90
1999 Chardonnay Alder Springs	Mendocino	E	93
1999 Chardonnay Dutton Ranch	Russian River	D	89
1999 Chardonnay Hyde Vineyard	Carneros	D	90
1999 Chardonnay Woolsey Road	Russian River	D	91
1999 Pinot Noir	Sonoma	D	89
1999 Pinot Noir Alder Springs	Mendocino	E	88
1998 Pinot Noir Alder Springs	Mendocino	E	90
1997 Pinot Noir Alder Springs	Mendocino	E	90
1999 Pinot Noir Hyde Vineyard	Carneros	E	90
1998 Pinot Noir Hyde Vineyard	Carneros	E	88
1999 Pinot Noir Pisoni Vineyard	Santa Lucia Highlands	E	90+
1997 Pinot Noir Pisoni Vineyard	Santa Lucia Highlands	D	90

The talented quartet of wine producers—James Hall and his wife, Anne Moses, in addition to Donald and Heather Patz—continues to reveal sure-handed talent with their multiple bottlings of Chardonnay and Pinot Noir. The 1999 vintage produced a slightly bigger crop than 1998 and, because of that, required more crop thinning. Overall, the 1999s look extremely strong from this high-quality source of complex Chardonnays and Pinot Noirs. For those who might think there is no need for so many separate vineyard designations, it is certainly not borne out when tasting their wines.

There are 1,436 cases of the 1999 Chardonnay Woolsey Road. This wine performed beautifully, displaying considerable concentration in its leesy, smoky flavors as well as uncanny elegance for a wine of such richness and beauty. Full-bodied, with subtle oak, and premier cru Chassagne-Montrachet-like characteristics, it should drink well for 2–3 years. The 1999 Chardonnay Dutton Ranch (2,620 cases) is more typically California in style, given its marmalade, pineapple, and tangerine notes. While medium-bodied and elegant, with subtle wood in the background, it does not possess the flavor, depth, or texture of the Woolsey Road. However, that may well emerge with another 6–12 months of bottle age. It should last for 3+

years. A blend of fruit from the Caldwell, Hyde, Carr, and Atlas Peak Vineyards was fashioned into the 1999 Chardonnay Napa. This is a terrific Chardonnay, powerful, with hazelnuts, caramel, citrus oils, and leesy, Burgundian notes. There are 2,178 cases of this richly extracted, multilayered, full-bodied, delineated, impressively endowed Chardonnay; it should last for 4–5 years. From alluvial soils, the 1999 Chardonnay Hyde Vineyard offers flamboyant aromatics of orange marmalade, pineapple, and honeysuckle. In addition to the perfume, the wine offers superb fruit, excellent purity, and a ripe, medium- to full-bodied, long finish. Like most of these wines, it tips the scales between 14–14.2% alcohol. It should also drink well for 3–4 years. Lastly, the 1999 Chardonnay Alder Springs Vineyard exhibits the terrific complexity and richness that this northern Mendocino vineyard (near the Humboldt County line) often displays. Produced from 100% Dijon clones of Chardonnay, the wine possesses a layered personality exhibiting honeyed pear, passion fruit, tangerine, roasted hazelnuts, and a stony minerality. Full-bodied, with abundant texture and glycerin, as well as a clean, rich finish, this bold yet graceful Chardonnay will drink well for 3 years. Unfortunately, there are only 574 cases.

The 1999 Pinot Noir Sonoma (1,400 cases) is a seductive, smoky Pinot offering jammy strawberry and cherry fruit, a velvety texture, and a medium- to full-bodied personality. Drink it over the next 3–4 years. The dark ruby-colored 1999 Pinot Noir Alder Springs Vineyard displays abundant power, but comes across as delicate and restrained with tangy berry fruit interspersed with notes of earth, minerals, and raspberries. Paradoxically, the wine is both soft and structured, which I know does not make much sense. My instincts suggest the wine is probably better than the way it performed the day I tasted it, but it was the least expressive and concentrated of the Patz and Hall 1999 Pinot Noirs. The 1999 Pinot Noir Hyde Vineyard is another impressive Pinot, with silky tannin, an opulent, viscous mid-palate, and a noteworthy sexpot personality (in plain English, a slut). It reveals knockout aromas of black fruits intermixed with smoke and subtle toasty oak. In the mouth, it is plush, succulent, and a total turn-on. This is Pinot at its most hedonistic and exotic best. It should drink well for 5–6 years. I have consistently admired most of the Pinot Noirs that emerge from the Pisoni Vineyard in Monterey's Santa Lucia Highlands. Patz and Hall's outstanding 1999 Pinot Noir Pisoni Vineyard (410 cases) is significantly richer and fuller than their 1998. It reveals the most structure of the 1999s, as well as formidable depth and richness. Aromas of black raspberries, cherry liqueur, flowers, minerals, and spice are followed by a rich, full-bodied, tightly knit, concentrated, impressively pure and long wine. Drink it over the next 8–10 years.

Patz and Hall's 1997 Pinot Noir Pisoni Vineyard exhibits a deep ruby/purple color, as well as sweet black fruits (currants and raspberries), and complex, rich, medium- to full-bodied flavors with surprising fat, glycerin, and lushness. This is an exceptionally pure, lengthy, concentrated, seductive Pinot Noir for drinking now and over the next 5–6 years. Very impressive! Even more exciting is the 1997 Pinot Noir Alder Springs, which is a breakthrough Pinot Noir for Mendocino. Sadly, there are only two barrels (about 46 cases). The wine boasts a saturated dark ruby/purple color, and a knockout nose of smoky, toasty oak intermixed with brandied cherries, mocha, and black raspberries. Rich, concentrated, and full-bodied, this is a hedonistic, decadently rich Pinot Noir to consume over the next 5–6 years. Kudos to Patz and Hall for a brilliant portfolio of wines in 1997.

The 1998 Pinot Noirs are similarly sized, but with more tangy acidity than Patz and Hall's successful 1997s. The 1998 Pinot Noir Hyde Vineyard (250 cases) is made from several clones, including Joseph Swan and a French clone called 113. Sweet black cherry, raspberry, earth, and floral scents are followed by a fresh, zesty, strawberry and floral-flavored wine with elegance, medium body, and crisp acidity. Consume it over the next 5–6 years. Not surprisingly, my favorite of Patz and Hall's 1998 offerings is the 1998 Pinot Noir Alder Springs

Vineyard (295 cases). Dark plum, black raspberry, and cherry flavors are immediately appealing. Spicy, with a black fruit character well displayed in its fleshy, medium- to full-bodied personality, this is the biggest, richest, and potentially most complex of their 1998s.

PEACHY CANYON WINERY (PASO ROBLES)

1997 Zinfandel Benito Dusi Ranch	Paso Robles	D	88
1997 Zinfandel Lakeview Vineyard	Paso Robles	D	88
1997 Zinfandel Snow Vineyard	Russian River	C	88
1997 Zinfandel Westside	Paso Robles	D	90

Peachy Canyon's 1997 Zinfandels are noteworthy efforts in this irregular vintage. For example, the 1997 Zinfandel Lakeview Vineyard offers a dark ruby/garnet color as well as wonderfully jammy strawberry and cherry fruit in the fragrant aromatics. This is a gloriously fruity, decadent, luxuriously rich, fat, medium- to full-bodied, delicious example. Drink it over the next 2–3 years. The saturated dark purple-colored 1997 Zinfandel Snow Vineyard reveals spicy, black currant and cherry notes that are less jammy and more backward than in the Lakeview Vineyard. The wine comes across as less successful, more intellectual, and more structured, with considerable muscle, excellent concentration, and a long, well-delineated finish. It is not as charming and hedonistically appealing as the Lakeview, but it is a serious Zinfandel that will drink well for 5–6 years. The exotic 1997 Zinfandel Benito Dusi Ranch offers up a striking nose of incense, black cherry liqueur, and spicy oak. This dark ruby/purple-colored Zinfandel possesses some brooding backwardness, yet the sweet, rich, glycerin-endowed, chewy, cherry flavors intermixed with earthy, forest-like aromas are an obvious positive. A spicy wine with complexity and character, it should drink well for 5–6 years. My favorite of this generally impressive group is the 1997 Zinfandel Westside (15.8% alcohol). Some new oak makes an appearance in this wickedly aromatic wine. Explosive fruit flavors with gobs of cherry, strawberry, plum, and cassis are complemented by copious fruit and glycerin, and light tannin in the voluptuous finish. Drinking well, it should continue to evolve deliciously for 5–6 years.

J. PEDRONCELLI WINERY (SONOMA)

1999 Zinfandel Mother Clone	Dry Creek	B	86

Earthy, peppery, strawberry and cherry aromas emerge from this attractive, restrained, measured, dark ruby/purple-colored Zinfandel (14.5% alcohol). Drink this mid-weight offering over the next 3–4 years.

PEZZI KING (DRY CREEK)

1998 Zinfandel	Dry Creek	D	89
1999 Zinfandel Estate	Dry Creek	D	89
1999 Zinfandel Maple Vineyard	Dry Creek	C	90
1999 Zinfandel Old Vines	Dry Creek	C	88

I preferred the 1999 Zinfandel Dry Creek Estate *cuvée* to the Dry Creek Old Vines offering. However, both wines are fine efforts. Tipping the scales at 15% alcohol, the 1999 Zinfandel Old Vines exhibits a peppery, earthy style with plenty of structure as well as notes of balsam wood, leather, spice box, cherries, and dried herbs. Drink this medium- to full-bodied Zinfandel over the next 2–4 years. Fatter and more fruit driven, with extra layers of glycerin as well as concentration, the 1999 Zinfandel Estate Dry Creek possesses even higher alcohol than the Old Vines (15.5%). Deep, chewy, well made, and exuberant, it should drink well for 4–5 years. The finest wine of the trio of 1999s is the 1999 Zinfandel Maple Vineyard. It is a thick, juicy, jammy offering revealing copious quantities of black cherry and berry fruit, smoke, oak, and earth. Textured, powerful, yet supple, this juicy, hedonistic Zinfandel should be consumed over the next 4–5 years. The 1998 Zinfandel offers heady alcohol, full body, less delineation, but plenty of sweet and sour cherry fruit intermixed with raspberry, plum, leather, and earth notes. It should be drunk over the next 3–4 years.

JOSEPH PHELPS VINEYARD (NAPA)

1999 Cabernet Sauvignon	Napa	D	89
1997 Cabernet Sauvignon	Napa	D	88
1996 Cabernet Sauvignon	Napa	D	88+
1995 Cabernet Sauvignon	Napa	D	90
1994 Cabernet Sauvignon	Napa	C	89
1999 Cabernet Sauvignon Backus Vineyard	Napa	EE	92
1997 Cabernet Sauvignon Backus Vineyard	Napa	EE	93
1996 Cabernet Sauvignon Backus Vineyard	Napa	EE	92
1995 Cabernet Sauvignon Backus Vineyard	Napa	EE	93
1994 Cabernet Sauvignon Backus Vineyard	Napa	E	94+
1999 Chardonnay Ovation	Napa	D	(88–90)
1999 Insignia Proprietary Red Wine	Napa	EE	94
1998 Insignia Proprietary Red Wine	Napa	EE	91
1997 Insignia Proprietary Red Wine	Napa	EE	96
1996 Insignia Proprietary Red Wine	Napa	EE	92
1995 Insignia Proprietary Red Wine	Napa	EE	97
1994 Insignia Proprietary Red Wine	Napa	EE	96
1999 Merlot	Napa	D	87
1997 Merlot	Napa	D	90
1995 Merlot	Napa	D	88
1994 Merlot	Napa	C	88
1997 Vin du Mistral Le Mistral	California	D	89
1996 Vin de Mistral Le Mistral	Napa	D	88
1999 Vin du Mistral Syrah	Napa	C	87
1997 Vin du Mistral Syrah	Napa	D	89
1996 Vin de Mistral Syrah	Napa	D	90

The venerable Joseph Phelps Winery continues to plant new acreage in California. At present, there are 350 acres under vine in Napa, with another 100 that are plantable. Phelps has also acquired a 100-acre parcel in the Russian River, which will probably be given a separate domaine name. Furthermore, they have 160 acres in Monterey County, 55 acres of which are allocated to the Phelps wines with the balance sold to Meridian. As one would expect, the 1997s are topflight, the 1998s competent, and the 1999s potentially impressive.

The top-of-the-line white, Phelps's Chardonnay Ovation, is a big, leesy, barrel-fermented, Burgundian-styled wine that is frequently exceptional. Almost all of the fruit for this *cuvée* emerges from Napa's cooler areas, particularly Carneros and Yountville. The 1999 Chardonnay Ovation reveals the vintage's coolness in its steely, nicely textured personality. It exhibits honeyed citrus, toasty oak, and puff pastry–like characteristics. Ripe, rich, and medium- to full-bodied, it should drink well for 3–4 years.

Joseph Phelps has consistently done a good job with their Le Mistral offering, which is aged primarily in used oak. It represents an amalgam of many different grapes, predominately Grenache backed up by Syrah, Mourvèdre, Petite Sirah, Alicante Bouchet, and Carignan. The percentages vary from vintage to vintage. The excellent, dense ruby/purple-colored 1997 Vin du Mistral Le Mistral (43% Grenache, 28% Syrah, 12% Mourvèdre, 8% Petite Sirah, 7% Alicante Bouchet, and 2% Carignan) possesses a big, ripe, peppery, spicy, black cherry, and raspberry-scented bouquet. Full-bodied, dense, chewy, and concentrated, with no hard edges, it represents a California imitation of a southern Rhône. Drink it over the next

5–6 years. Phelps's Syrah, which originates from vineyard holdings in Yountville, is aged primarily in French oak, of which 20% is new. The gorgeous, dense ruby/purple-colored 1997 Vin du Mistral Syrah offers sweet blackberry and cassis flavors with a touch of spice and pepper. Full-bodied, deep, lush, voluptuously textured as well as seductive, it should drink well for 7–8 years. The 1999 Vin du Mistral Syrah should turn out to be as impressive as the 1997. A dense saturated ruby/purple color is followed by a blackberry/cassis-scented bouquet, medium to full body, adequate acidity, and soft tannin. It is a wine to drink during its first 6–7 years of life. The dark ruby-colored 1996 Le Mistral is a gutsy, bistro red with an exotic nose of incense, peppers, red and black fruits, and perfume. While it is not complex and is displaying less fat than when I tasted it in 1997, it remains a fun, delicious wine to enjoy over the next 7–8 years. About 700–800 cases of both the 1996 and 1997 Vin de Mistral Syrah were produced. The 1996 Vin de Mistral Syrah is a sexy, lush, opulently styled wine revealing more precociousness and early charm than I predicted a year ago. Aged in both American and French oak, it possesses a dark ruby/purple color, a spicy, bacon fat, cassis, and blackberry-scented nose, soft, lush flavors, and a heady, concentrated finish. It is best drunk during its first 10–12 years of life.

Phelps's Merlot program is coming of age. Approximately 10% Cabernet Sauvignon is included in the blend, and the wine is aged in primarily French oak with a touch of American. About 30% of the barrels are new. The 1999 Merlot exhibits a saturated ruby/purple color in addition to a gorgeous perfume of sweet, jammy black cherries and spice, and a full-bodied mid-palate and finish with well-integrated acidity and tannin. It is a big, fleshy, rich Merlot that should age handsomely for a decade. The beautiful 1997 Merlot boasts a dense ruby color in addition to an attractive bouquet of berry fruit infused with smoke and mocha. This full-bodied, rich Merlot has a fat, succulent, plush texture, and a chewy, heady finish. It will drink well for a decade. In contrast, the 1995 Merlot is not as fat or ripe as the 1997. It exhibits a saturated dark ruby color, followed by a soft, friendly personality with copious quantities of chocolate, licorice, and smoky, berry fruit intermixed with tobacco and dried herbs. Lush, full-bodied, and chewy, this wine should drink well for another decade. An excellent Merlot, the dark ruby/purple-colored 1994 offers plenty of sweet, jammy, chocolaty, black cherry fruit in its moderately intense aromatics. The wine is medium-bodied, soft, and succulent, with low acidity, copious amounts of fruit, and good ripeness. Drink this delicious, lush Merlot over the next 2–4 years.

When I asked wine-maker Craig Williams about his rating of the succession of fine vintages for California Cabernet Sauvignon in the nineties, he felt 1999 would be among the finest, but it was still too early to rate it. His top vintages were 1997, 1995, 1991, 1994, and 1996. He thought the three most challenging vintages were 1998, 1993, and 1992. As for the 20,000+ cases of Joseph Phelps Cabernet Sauvignon, the 1997 is excellent. While not as open-knit and expressive as their Merlot, it is well made, with attractive cedary, tobacco, and black currant fruit, excellent color saturation, a spicy, sweet mid-palate, and soft tannin in its medium- to full-bodied finish. It can be drunk now or cellared for 12–15 years. The 1999 Cabernet Sauvignon reveals a saturated purple color, exceptional ripeness, and sweet black currant aromas and flavors intermixed with licorice, smoke, and minerals. Medium- to full-bodied, dense, and multilayered, this impressive Cabernet should drink well for 10–15 years. Among the Cabernet Sauvignon vintages, I preferred the 1995. Although the 1996 matches the former wine in terms of intensity, it had just been bottled when I tasted it and seemed muted and closed. The 1997 looks very fine, but more forward and round. The 1994 Cabernet Sauvignon Napa (a blend of 95% Cabernet Sauvignon, 4% Cabernet Franc, and 1% Merlot) is a deep ruby/purple-colored wine with a sweet, ripe, black fruit, vanilla, and underbrush-scented nose, medium to full body, a layered texture, adequate acidity, and sweet tannin in the finish. The wine is mouth-filling, pure, and impressive. The 1995 Cabernet Sauvignon spent 16 months in cask (primarily French oak) and was bottled with minimal filtration. It exhibits a dark ruby/purple color as well as an attractive black cherry, cassis, and dried herb–scented nose with spicy oak. Rich, full-bodied, and concentrated, it offers plenty of cassis fruit and a chewy style. It can be drunk or cellared for 15+ years. More structured, tannic, and dense, the 1996 Cabernet Sauvignon requires patience. Most readers will prefer to drink the 1995 or 1997 than the more backward 1996. The 1996 reveals a saturated ruby/ purple color, low acidity, and plenty of tannin and muscle in the brawny finish. Anticipated maturity: now–2015.

From a hillside overlooking the Oakville District, Phelps produces small quantities of their single-vineyard Backus Vineyard Cabernet Sauvignon, which is aged in 100% new French Taransaud oak. The sensational 1997 Cabernet Sauvignon Backus Vineyard is a muscular, highly extracted, full-bodied effort that requires 3–4 years of cellaring. Although less approachable than the 1997 Insignia, it displays great fruit intensity in its huge, thick, viscous flavors redolent with black currants, new saddle leather, spice box and toasty oak. Long, powerful, and intense, it exhibits both sweet tannin and immense concentration. Anticipated maturity: 2004–2025. Because of the difficulties in 1998, no Backus Vineyard was produced. However, the 1999 Cabernet Sauvignon Backus Vineyard may turn out to be as fabulous as both the 1997 and 1994. It is an astonishingly rich, full-bodied, powerful, super-extracted, unctuously textured endeavor with layers of mineral-infused black cherry and cassis fruit wrapped in toasty new oak. Tannin is present, but it is silky and well integrated. Sound acidity provides admirable delineation to the wine's huge framework. Anticipated maturity: 2005–2025. The dense ruby/purple-colored 1996 Cabernet Sauvignon Backus Vineyard reveals a gorgeous nose of sweet cassis fruit, chocolate, iron, and licorice. Full-bodied, powerful, and weighty, with moderately high tannin, it requires 3–4 years of cellaring. It should last 25+ years. Compared to the 1997, the 1996 Backus is more foursquare and monolithic, without the sweetness and precociousness of the 1997.

The 1995 Cabernet Sauvignon Backus Vineyard is a wine of great intensity. A massive, saturated black/purple-colored example, it offers an intriguing bouquet and flavors of prunes, black currants, roasted herbs, chocolate, and coffee, huge amounts of glycerin and body, and a gigantic, oversized finish with considerable tannin. This is one wine where the extract level matches the tannin's ferocity, but readers looking for something to cuddle up with over the near-term should be advised that it needs 5–6 years of cellaring. Anticipated maturity: 2003–2025. I believe the 1994 Cabernet Sauvignon Backus Vineyard is one of the finest wines this vineyard has yet produced. Phelps's 1994 Backus exhibits an opaque black/purple color and huge, sweet aromatics consisting of jammy black cherry and cassis fruit, minerals, smoke, and a hickory-like barbecue spice. The wine is thick and super-extracted, with huge proportions of fruit, extract, and tannin. A gargantuan Cabernet Sauvignon, it demands 5–6 years of cellaring and should last for 20–25 years.

Joseph Phelps's flagship wine is their fabulous Insignia, a wine with a tremendous track record back to the debut vintage of 1974. It is produced in significant quantities (18,000–20,000 cases) for a wine of such quality. The prodigious 1997 Insignia (83% Cabernet Sauvignon, 14% Merlot, and 3% Petit Verdot) lives up to its pre-bottling promise. Tasted on three separate occasions, every bottle has hit the bull's-eye. The color is a saturated, thick-looking blue/purple. The nose offers up explosive aromas of jammy black fruits, licorice, Asian spices, vanilla, and cedar. Full-bodied as well as exceptionally pure and impressively endowed, this blockbuster yet surprisingly elegant wine cuts a brilliant swath across the palate. A seamless effort with beautifully integrated acidity, sweet tannin, and alcohol, it is still an infant, but can be drunk with considerable pleasure. Anticipated maturity: now–2025. Perhaps an even greater achievement, the 1998 Insignia (78% Cabernet Sauvignon and 22% Merlot) is not up to the level of the 1997, but it is a fabulous wine from what was a far more challenging vintage. Approximately 18,000 cases were made, an amazing quantity in a year that produced far less promising raw materials. More evolved than the 1997, with a saturated ruby/purple color, it possesses a sumptuous bouquet of smoke, cedar, licorice, and cassis. This full-bodied, fat, succulent effort reveals admirable purity and symmetry, and a soft finish with remarkably deep flavors that caress the palate. It can be drunk now as well as over the next 15–16 years. Another great Insignia in the making is the 1999. An impressive black/purple color is followed by aromas and flavors of melted licorice and crème de cassis, immense body, a voluptuous texture, and an opulent, multilayered palate. This fabulously concentrated, low-acid yet super-endowed wine should rival the compelling 1997. It is a blend of 80% Cabernet Sauvignon, 17% Merlot, and 1% each of Petit Verdot, Malbec, and Cabernet Franc. After its release in 2002, it should age effortlessly for 2–3 decades. The 1996 Insignia (83% Cabernet Sauvignon and 17% Merlot) is a notch below the 1995, 1994, and 1997. It exhibits a dark purple color in addition to an elegant nose of cedar wood, fruitcake, coffee, and black currants. Medium- to full-bodied, with a firm underpinning of tannin, classic black currant flavors, and a long finish, this effort is impressive, but tighter and more narrowly constructed than the three aforementioned vintages. Anticipated maturity: now–2020.

Perhaps the best back-to-back vintages ever produced of Insignia are the 1994 and 1995, which rival the great Insignias made in 1974 and 1976. The 1994 Insignia (a blend of 88% Cabernet Sauvignon, 10% Merlot, and 2% Cabernet Franc) is spectacular. I have had the wine a half-dozen or more times, and it is unquestionably opulent, sexy, flamboyant, explosively rich, concentrated, and a thrill to drink. Already gorgeous, it promises to evolve gracefully for two decades or more. The color is a healthy saturated dark purple. The spicy nose offers aromas of black currants, allspice, toast, and soy, with scents of a burning wood fire thrown in for additional complexity. This full-bodied, opulent, dazzling wine is exhilarating to drink. Amazingly, the 1995 Insignia may be slightly better—as hard as that is to believe. The final blend is 90% Cabernet Sauvignon, 7% Merlot, and 3% Petit Verdot. The 1995 exhibits a character similar to the 1994—cassis, fruitcake, cedar, herbs, coffee, and black fruits intermixed with smoke—but the 1995 is slightly longer in the mouth. It is a wine of extraordinary extraction, full body, and marvelously pure fruit. Moreover, it has managed to soak up the 100% new-oak aging, leaving only subtle toasty notes. The tannin may be slightly more noticeable in the 1994, but my instincts suggest the 1995 is even richer and longer than the 1994—as amazing as that sounds. This prodigious Insignia should be at its best over the next 20–25 years.

Past Glories: 1993 Cabernet Sauvignon Backus Vineyard (93), 1993 Insignia Proprietary Red Wine (96)

PINE RIDGE WINERY (NAPA)

1995	Andrus Reserve Proprietary Red Wine	Napa	EE	90
1994	Andrus Reserve Proprietary Red Wine	Napa	EE	90+
1996	Cabernet Franc Trois Cuvées	Napa	D	88
1996	Cabernet Sauvignon	Howell Mountain	D	90
1994	Cabernet Sauvignon	Howell Mountain	D	90
1994	Cabernet Sauvignon	Rutherford	C	88
1997	Cabernet Sauvignon	Stags Leap	E	89
1994	Cabernet Sauvignon	Stags Leap	D	89
1996	Epitome Proprietary Red Wine	Stags Leap	EE	90
1996	Merlot	Napa/Carneros	D	88
1994	Merlot	Carneros	D	88

The dense ruby/purple-colored 1997 Cabernet Sauvignon Stags Leap offers red and black currants intertwined with gravelly, vanilla notes. Elegant, sweet cassis, licorice, and earthy flavors are present in this nicely concentrated, medium-bodied, pure, graceful Cabernet. It should drink well for 10–12 years. Only 305 cases were produced of the 1996 Epitome (a Bordeaux-like blend). Dark ruby with purple nuances, the complex aromatics offer scents of black currants, lead pencil, oak, and flowers. The wine displays pure symmetry between its building blocks of tannin, acidity, alcohol, and extract. Sweet ripeness, a velvety texture, medium body, and outstanding purity and concentration result in a brilliant Bordeaux look-alike from Napa's Stags Leap area. Currently, this offering is only being sold at the winery's tasting room. Anticipated maturity: now–2014. The 1996 Cabernet Franc Trois Cuvées (a blend of three clones of Cabernet Franc) was bottled with neither fining nor filtration. The bouquet offers rich, juicy, red currant, and intriguing floral scents. Well-integrated oak complements the elegant, stylish, rich fruitiness. Finesse, fruit, purity, and symmetry are the hallmarks of this delicious Cabernet Franc that is meant to be drunk over the next 7–8 years. Pine Ridge has turned out a very fine 1996 Merlot, with perhaps more structure and grip than many, but with excellent fruit and purity as well as attractive smoky, black cherry, and chocolaty notes. It possesses good oak, medium body, and excellent length. A blend of 89% Merlot, 8% Malbec, and 3% Cabernet Franc, it can be drunk now or cellared for 12 or more years. The most impressive of the 1996 Cabernet Sauvignon offerings from Pine Ridge is the subtly oaked 1996 Cabernet Sauvignon Howell Mountain. Atypically rich and intense for a Pine Ridge wine, this dark purple-colored mountain Cabernet exhibits copious quantities of mineral, blackberry, and cassis aromas. Medium- to full-bodied and powerful, yet elegant, it possesses an impressive mid-palate, structure, richness, and length. Anticipated maturity: now–2018.

A classic Bordeaux (Médoc)-styled wine, the 1995 Andrus Reserve exhibits a dark ruby/purple color, followed by attractive aromas and flavors of lead pencil, spice, cedar, and black currants. While it is moderately tannic, medium-bodied, with outstanding concentration and purity, the wine remains tight and backward. It requires 3–4 years of cellaring and should keep for at least 15. It is an impressively elegant, finesse-styled proprietary red.

All of the following Pine Ridge Cabernets will benefit from 2–3 years of cellaring. They are made in a medium-weight, somewhat austere Bordeaux style. The excellent 1994 Cabernet Sauvignon Rutherford reveals a classic black currant, toasty nose, medium body, high tannin, wonderful elegance, and a measured, rich fruit character that is pronounced, but never excessive. The wine finishes with a bite of tannin. While accessible, 2–4 years of cellaring will be beneficial. This wine should age well for 15 or more years. The refined 1994 Cabernet Sauvignon Stags Leap District boasts a dark ruby/purple color, followed by a spicy, vanilla, herb, mineral, and black currant–scented nose. In the mouth, there are more red than black currants, as well as rich, pure, long, medium-bodied flavors that exhibit exceptional purity and equilibrium. The tannin should gradually fall away to reveal a quintessentially elegant style of Napa Cabernet Sauvignon. Anticipated maturity: now–2016. Pine Ridge's 1994 Cabernet Sauvignon Howell Mountain needs at least 5–6 years of cellaring. It possesses a saturated purple color and a Bordeaux-like nose of black fruits, licorice, minerals, and cedar. Tannic and reserved, with intense richness and concentration, this is a medium- to full-bodied, large-scaled, unevolved 1994 Cabernet that should prove to be outstanding for those with enough discipline to wait it out. Anticipated maturity: 2003–2020. Cut from a similar cloth, the 1994 Andrus Reserve exhibits a dark saturated plum/purple color, followed by a tight nose of cedar, vanilla, and praline-tinged cassis fruit. Extremely dense and rich, with a more backward and tannic personality than even the Howell Mountain cuvée, this well-delineated, full-bodied wine will need—yes—a full decade of cellaring. It is a 25–30-year wine, but patience is essential. Anticipated maturity: 2006–2030.

Pine Ridge's 1994 Merlot exhibits a good dark ruby color, attractive spicy notes, a monolithic aromatic dimension, and admirable weight, brightness, and purity. My instincts suggest the wine is closed, but I liked its purity of fruit, depth, and ripeness. I would not be surprised to see this Merlot merit a higher score after it receives some bottle age. It should drink well for a decade.

Past Glories: 1993 Cabernet Sauvignon Howell Mountain (92), 1993 Cabernet Sauvignon Stags Leap District (90+)

PLUMPJACK (NAPA)

1998 Cabernet Sauvignon Estate	Oakville	D	87
1997 Cabernet Sauvignon Estate	Oakville	D	90
1995 Cabernet Sauvignon Estate	Oakville	D	91
1998 Cabernet Sauvignon Reserve	Oakville	EE	89
1997 Cabernet Sauvignon Reserve	Oakville	EE	90+
1995 Cabernet Sauvignon Reserve	Oakville	E	95+

Plumpjack, which is well situated on what used to be the Cabernet Sauvignon vineyard of Villa Mt. Eden (remember the glorious wines produced there between 1974 and 1978 by Nils Venge?), has increased its production to 7,500 cases from 50 acres of vineyards. The 1998s look to be successful for this difficult vintage. In 1998 many of the finest wines tended to emerge from Napa's Oakville corridor. Plumpjack's 1998 Cabernet Sauvignon Estate (5,000 cases of an 80% Cabernet Sauvignon, 15% Cabernet Franc, and 5% Merlot blend) exhibits copious quantities of black currant fruit, a charming up-front personality, soft tannin, low acidity, and a plump, savory finish. It will be delicious young, yet capable of lasting for a decade. About 500 cases were culled out for the 1998 Cabernet Sauvignon Reserve (100% Cabernet Sauvignon). An impressive wine for the vintage, it is powerful with terrific extraction, an opaque purple color, pure crème de cassis fruit, and a touch of licorice and toast. Surprisingly unevolved for a 1998, with a fine mid-palate and finish, this Cabernet requires 3–4 years of cellaring; it should keep for 15 years. It will be one of the better, longer-lived 1998 Cabernet Sauvignons.

The 1997 Cabernet Sauvignon Estate (5,300 cases) exhibits copious cassis and soil scents as well as a full-bodied, moderately tannic, muscular, big-framed finish. This is no shy wine, but it demands 4–5 years of cellaring, and should keep for 15+. It was forward and precocious last year, but it has firmed up. The 1997 Cabernet Sauvignon Reserve (260 cases) is also backward. Loaded with concentration, it offers up scents of lavender, black currants, minerals, licorice, and smoky oak. Mouth-searing levels of tannin are present in this big, brawny Cabernet. While it will evolve for two decades, it was impossibly closed. All the component parts suggest an exceptional offering, but patience will be required. Anticipated maturity: 2006–2025.

The 1995 Cabernet Sauvignon Estate, made by wine-maker Tuck Beckstoffer with back-up consulting from nearby neighbor Nils Venge of Saddleback Cellars, is a highly extracted, extremely rich Cabernet that will win many fans. Approximately 1,000 cases were produced of this dense purple-colored wine that reveals a ripe prune and cassis-scented nose with lavish smoky oak. Full-bodied, deep, and chewy, with sweet tannin and plenty of extract and glycerin, this is an impressively endowed, supple style of Cabernet Sauvignon that should drink well for 10–15+ years. The 1995 Cabernet Sauvignon Reserve (approximately 500 cases produced) is an awesome wine that tastes like a synthesis in style of some of the richest, most powerful Cabernets from the Oakville district. It may come closest in style to resembling the profound Cabernets of Harlan Estate. This spectacular Cabernet Sauvignon is a worthy candidate for 20–30 years of cellaring. The opaque black/purple color is followed by intense aromatics offering smoke, coffee, roasted meats, and copious quantities of blackberry and cassis fruit. Extremely dense, full-bodied, and crammed with extract, this persuasively rich, authoritative Cabernet Sauvignon is among the most noteworthy wines of the 1995 vintage. While it can be drunk young, this wine begs for 5–6 years of cellaring. It will be a long-distance runner, although I am not sure how many readers will be able to ignore its lavish display of decadent levels of ripe fruit and toasty oak.

PRIDE MOUNTAIN VINEYARD (NAPA)

1998 Cabernet Franc	Sonoma	D	94
1997 Cabernet Franc	Sonoma	D	93+
1996 Cabernet Franc	Sonoma	D	91
1995 Cabernet Franc	Sonoma	C	92
1998 Cabernet Sauvignon	Napa	D	90
1997 Cabernet Sauvignon	Napa	D	92
1997 Cabernet Sauvignon Reserve	Napa	EE	97+
1996 Cabernet Sauvignon Reserve	Napa	EE	99
1995 Cabernet Sauvignon Reserve	Napa	E	98
1994 Cabernet Sauvignon Reserve	Napa	E	95+
1999 Chardonnay	Napa Valley	D	88
1998 Merlot	Napa/Sonoma	D	88
1997 Merlot	Napa	D	93
1996 Merlot	Napa	C	90+
1997 Reserve Claret	Napa	EE	95
1996 Reserve Claret	Napa	EE	95
1995 Reserve Claret	Napa	E	96
1994 Reserve Claret	Napa	E	95
1998 Sangiovese	Sonoma	D	90
1997 Sangiovese	Sonoma	D (500 ml)	94

Owner Jim Pride and wine-maker Robert Foley have quickly pushed Pride Mountain to the top of California's North Coast qualitative hierarchy. The 1999 Chardonnay exhibits a leesy, toasty, ripe tropical fruit complexity, medium to full body, ripe flavors, and an excellent finish. Drink this very good effort over the next 2–3 years.

While the majority of California Sangiovese is mediocre, Pride Mountain manages to cram abundant flavor and intensity into their offering. The dark ruby-colored 1998 Sangiovese exhibits a big, sweet, strawberry jam and cherry-scented bouquet with subtle notes of leather and toast. With expressive fruit, medium body, deep, concentrated flavors, and a tangy edge, this intense yet supple Sangiovese can be drunk over the next 3–4 years.

I am amazed by how spectacular Pride Mountain's Cabernet Franc continues to be. The fabulous 1998 Cabernet Franc is a noteworthy achievement in this difficult vintage. Its deep purple color is accompanied by a gorgeous bouquet of cedar, spice box, black fruits, smoke, and earth. In the mouth, there is a smorgasbord of sweet black fruits with a hint of dried Provençal herbs. Opulent and full-bodied, with marvelous concentration yet an eerie sense of weightlessness, this rich, complex 1998 can be drunk now as well as over the next decade.

The dark ruby/purple-colored 1998 Merlot (a blend of 64% Napa and 36% Sonoma fruit) exhibits copious quantities of toasty new oak in the bouquet in addition to deep, chewy, blackberry and cherry aromas. There is excellent richness, medium to full body, adequate acidity, and a forward appeal. Drink it over the next 7–8 years. The outstanding 1998 Cabernet Sauvignon boasts a dark ruby/purple color as well as surprising opulence for a wine from this vintage, admirable elegance, abundant black currant fruit, a dense, chewy mid-palate, a fleshy texture, low acidity, and a tannic finish. It is a classic Cabernet with medium weight, as well as outstanding ripeness, richness, and balance. Drink it over the next 12 years.

Available only in 500 ml bottles at the winery, the spectacular 1997 Sangiovese is clearly the equal to some of the super Tuscan wines emerging from the 1997 vintage. Pride Mountain's offering is unbelievably concentrated for a Sangiovese. A fabulous wine, its opaque purple color is followed by an extravagant nose of smoke, licorice, cassis, and toast. This intense, full-bodied, mouth-staining effort is gorgeously pure, with multiple layers to its personality and a whoppingly long finish. It should drink well for 10–12 years.

The 1997 Merlot might be called liquefied Viagra. An incredibly sexy nose of smoke, black fruits, cappuccino, and toasty wood is followed by an expansive, terrifically concentrated wine with a sumptuous texture, no hard edges, beautifully integrated acidity and tannin, and a long, 35-second finish. According to the back label, about 5% Cabernet Sauvignon was added in the blend of this stunningly aromatic, multidimensional wine. It should drink well for 12–15 years. Just as impressive is the extraordinary 1997 Cabernet Franc. A massive, mountain-styled offering (unlike other California Cabernet Francs, with the possible exception of La Jota's), it boasts an opaque purple color as well as a fabulously sweet nose of black currants, cranberry liqueur, new oak, and roasted notes. Chewy, full-bodied, and exceptionally huge, this offering should become even more complex with another 5–6 years of cellaring. It should keep for two decades. This is a tour de force, particularly for Cabernet Franc. Anticipated maturity: now–2020.

The accolades don't stop with Pride Mountain's Merlot and Cabernet Franc. While only microscopic quantities were produced of the 1997 Reserve Claret and 1997 Cabernet Sauvignon Reserve, both are immense wines of extraordinary concentration and depth. The compelling 1997 Reserve Claret offers an opaque purple color in addition to a sumptuous bouquet of sweet blackberries, crème de cassis, and minerals, superb richness, exceptional concentration, and huge body. However, it manages to avoid being overbearing or unmanageable. Purity and delineation are also present in this multidimensional, prodigious wine. Although an infant in terms of development, it is accessible because of the ripe tannin and spectacularly concentrated fruit. Anticipated maturity: now–2025. Even more amazing, the 1997 Cabernet Sauvignon Reserve pushes richness to unreal levels. Despite its intense, ultra-concentrated style, it possesses a sense of balance and definition. The color is a saturated inky purple. The aromatics consist of lead pencil shavings, minerals, blackberries, cassis, and flowers. Extremely full-bodied, with amazing purity, mouthcoating richness, sweet tannin, and low acidity, it offers profound drinking even though it has not yet begun to develop secondary nuances. Anticipated maturity: 2003–2025.

The opaque black/purple-colored 1997 Cabernet Sauvignon (3,472 cases) offers sensational notes of black currants, minerals, smoke, licorice, and new oak. Full-bodied, with fabulous extract and power, the acidity, tannin, and potentially harsh components are well meshed with the wine's personality. This is a large, ripe, impeccably balanced Cabernet Sauvignon that achieved 14.1% alcohol naturally. Anticipated maturity: 2003–2020. The virtually perfect 1996 Cabernet Sauvignon Reserve (330 cases) is 100% Cabernet Sauvignon. Opaque purple-colored, with a profound bouquet of minerals, flowers, black fruits, and spice, this awesomely concentrated, multilayered wine represents the essence of Cabernet Sauvignon. Amazingly, it is neither ponderous nor heavy-handed, with the oak, acidity, and tannin woven into the wine's formidable, concentrated personality. The finish lasts for nearly a minute. Sadly, it is extremely limited in availability, but what a compelling wine it is! Anticipated maturity: 2008–2025. Nearly as spectacular as the 1996 Reserve Cabernet Sauvignon is the 1996 Reserve Claret. A blend of 63% Merlot, 32% Cabernet Sauvignon, and 5% Petite Verdot (230 cases), it is a gorgeously balanced, super-concentrated yet hauntingly symmetrical wine with copious quantities of black fruits, spicy new oak, minerals, licorice, and roasted herbs. Full-bodied, with a cherry liqueur–like richness to its fruit, this wine has loads of glycerin, fabulous extract, and no hard edges. The velvety finish lasts for 40+ seconds. These are spectacular wines that must be tasted to be believed.

The 1996 Cabernet Franc (a blend of 75% Cabernet Franc and 25% Cabernet Sauvignon) has filled out considerably, exhibiting a dense ruby/purple color, followed by a knockout nose of black cherries, herbs, and spice. In the mouth, the wine is rich with layers of flavor. This superb, medium- to full-bodied example is the quintessential Cabernet Franc, offering elegance along with plenty of power and richness. It should drink well for 10–15 years. Another wine that tasted better in mid-July of 1998 than it did at the winery nine months earlier is the 1996 Merlot. A blend of 95% Merlot and 5% Cabernet Sauvignon, it boasts a dense purple color as well as a beautiful nose of black fruits, smoke, herbs, and underbrush. Thick and full-bodied, with terrific fruit, purity, and extraction, this is a deeper, richer, more complete wine than I originally predicted. It should age well for 10–12 years.

The two limited-production offerings from Pride Mountain Vineyards are the 1995 Claret Reserve and 1995 Cabernet Sauvignon Reserve. There are 230 cases of the former, and 330 cases of the latter. The fabulous 1995 Claret Reserve (a blend of 64% Cabernet Sauvignon, 33% Merlot, and 3% Petit Verdot) offers an opaque ruby/purple color, and a classic crème de cassis nose intermixed with toasty new oak and minerals. Full-bodied, with superb texture, dense, massively rich flavors, and a 40+-second finish, this is a gorgeously made, Bordeaux-styled wine with dazzling levels of fruit and extract. Anticipated maturity: now–2015. The 1995 Cabernet Sauvignon Reserve has come of age now that it is in the bottle. This is the essence of North Coast Cabernet Sauvignon, offering port-like thickness and richness, a superb black currant, mineral, cedar, and toast-scented nose, full-bodied flavors of extraordinary intensity and overall balance, and a long, moderately tannic, multidimensional finish. Anticipated maturity: 2003–2025. Shame on me for underestimating these beauties!

Pride Mountain's 1995 Cabernet Franc, a blend of 75% Cabernet Franc and 25% Cabernet Sauvignon (400 cases produced), reminded me of the unblended *cuvée* of Cabernet Franc that usually goes into Dalla Valle's extraordinary proprietary red wine Maya. For a Cabernet Franc, it possesses an uncommonly dense black/purple color and a sweet nose of licorice, underbrush, red as well as black currants, and toast. Amazingly extracted, yet somehow retaining its elegance, this wine offers the essence of black fruits in its long, rich, medium- to full-bodied flavors. There is enough acidity and some tannin, but its extraordinary purity and equilibrium are hallmarks of this smashing effort. Anticipated maturity: now–2016.

Pride Mountain's 1994 Reserve Claret (98 cases produced) possesses an opaque purple color, followed by a nose with underbrush, cassis, smoke, and toasty notes. Full-bodied, super-extracted, with layers of ripe fruit, and well-integrated tannin and acidity, this is an enormously endowed, layered wine that unfolds magnificently in the glass and on the palate. Anticipated maturity: now–2020. The 1994 Cabernet Sauvignon Reserve (the first Reserve Cabernet Sauvignon they made) is produced from 100% Cabernet Sauvignon and aged completely in French oak casks. It is another profound Cabernet from the exceptional 1994 vintage. The wine's opaque purple color and huge, massive richness do not come across as heavy, despite the wine's extraordinary intensity and thickness. There is enough acidity for freshness, and plenty of sweet, well-integrated tannin. This large-scaled, magnificently endowed Cabernet Sauvignon needs 5–6 years of cellaring, but it should keep for 25+ years.

QUINTESSA (NAPA)

1994 Proprietary Red Wine	Rutherford	E	89

A blend of 39% Cabernet Sauvignon, 31% Merlot, and 30% Cabernet Franc, this dark ruby/purple-colored 1994 possesses an elegant, graceful bouquet (sweet cherries and kirsch) that has been subtly influenced by toasty new oak. The medium-bodied, subtle yet rich, red currant/black currant flavors unfold nicely in the mouth. This is an understated, measured, impeccably well made, claret-styled Cabernet Sauvignon that offers beautiful richness and layers of harmonious flavors. Impressive. Drink it over the next 10–14 years.

QUIVIRA VINEYARDS (SONOMA)

1998 Zinfandel	Dry Creek	C	88
1994 Zinfandel	Sonoma	C	88

A delicious, elegant, fruit-driven effort, Quivira's medium-bodied 1998 Zinfandel exhibits nicely integrated acidity and subtle wood. The emphasis is on this varietal's berry/briery fruit. With excellent purity and refreshing vibrancy, it can be enjoyed over the next 3–4 years. A classically styled Zin, Quivira's fully mature 1994 is rich and pure, with plenty of the varietal's briery, peppery, black and red fruit character. There is moderate body, plenty of purity, and a clean, crisp, long finish. It is an attractive, medium-weight Zinfandel that requires consumption.

QUPÉ WINE CELLARS (SANTA BARBARA)

1997 Syrah Bien Nacido Vineyard	Santa Barbara	D	89
1997 Syrah Hillside Estate Bien Nacido Vineyard	Santa Barbara	D	(90–92)
1997 Syrah Reserve Bien Nacido Vineyard	Santa Barbara	D	(87–90)

Qupé, one of the original Rhône Rangers, continues to do a fine job with an assortment of varietals. The 1997 Syrahs are serious efforts. Qupé's 1997 Syrah Bien Nacido Vineyard exhibits a deep ruby/purple color with purple nuances. Noteworthy quantities of blackberry fruit, dried herbs, spice, and floral scents jump from the glass. There is terrific fruit, medium to full body, a supple texture with sweet tannin lurking in the background, and a fine finish. Drinkable now, it should continue to evolve for 5–7 years. The 1997 Syrah Reserve Bien Nacido Vineyard possesses a deep ruby/purple color and plenty of smoky, blackberry fruit intermixed with toast, damp foresty scents, and pepper. The wine exhibits excellent richness, sweet tannin, and a medium- to full-bodied, long finish. It should drink well during its first 7–10 years of life. The most concentrated Syrah in this estate's portfolio is the 1997 Syrah Hillside Estate Bien Nacido Vineyard. It boasts an opaque ruby/purple color, as well as thick, juicy fruit, full body, adequate acidity and tannin, and a powerful, gutsy, earthy finish. Unquestionably the most complete wine among these offerings, this impressively endowed Syrah should hit its stride with 2–3 years of bottle age and last for 10–15.

A. RAFANELLI WINERY (SONOMA)

1997 Zinfandel	Dry Creek	C	90
1995 Zinfandel	Dry Creek	C	92
1994 Zinfandel	Dry Creek	C	89

Once again Rafanelli has fashioned one of the vintage's stars. In a year where too many Zinfandels taste as if the grapes were harvested too early from an overly abundant crop, Rafanelli's 1997 Zinfandel exhibits superb purity, wonderful fruit, and the classic black raspberry/cherry, spicy Zin aromatic and flavor profile. The wine's deep ruby/purple color is followed by a sweet attack, dried, full-bodied flavors, copious quantities of black fruits, and a long, lusty finish. This is what Zinfandel should be! Per the label, there is 14.5% alcohol, which is neither wimpish nor excessive. Enjoy this beauty over the next 5–6 years.

Rafanelli has made so many gorgeous Zinfandels it is hard to say the 1995 Zinfandel Unfiltered is one of their finest, but, wow, I was knocked out by the opaque purple color, as well as the gorgeously pure display of blackberry, raspberry, and cherry fruit. Full-bodied, with no hard edges, a voluptuous texture, and layers of fruit, this is a delicious, full-throttle, impeccably well balanced wine that should drink well for another 6–7 years. Kudos to Rafanelli.

Not the super-concentrated heavyweight I would have expected from this vintage, Rafanelli's 1994 is, however, a textbook, richly fruity, peppery, soft, generous, medium-bodied wine with excellent depth and balance. Plenty of sweet black-cherry/raspberry, vanilla-tinged fruit slides over the palate with no bumps or bruises. Drink it up.

RAVENSWOOD WINERY (SONOMA)

1996 Zinfandel	Lodi	B	88
1995 Zinfandel	Sonoma	C	88
1999 Zinfandel Barricia	Sonoma	D	90
1998 Zinfandel Barricia	Sonoma	D	90
1999 Zinfandel Big River	Alexander Valley	D	91
1998 Zinfandel Big River	Alexander Valley	D	90
1997 Zinfandel Cooke Vineyard	Sonoma	D	89
1996 Zinfandel Cooke Vineyard	Sonoma	C	90
1995 Zinfandel Cooke Vineyard	Sonoma	D	92
1999 Zinfandel Dickerson Vineyard	Napa	D	89
1998 Zinfandel Kunde Vineyard	Sonoma	D	89
1997 Zinfandel Monte Rosso Vineyard	Sonoma	D	90
1996 Zinfandel Monte Rosso Vineyard	Sonoma	D	92
1995 Zinfandel Monte Rosso Vineyard	Sonoma	D	92
1999 Zinfandel Old Hill Ranch	Sonoma	D	92
1997 Zinfandel Old Hill Ranch	Sonoma	D	90
1995 Zinfandel Old Hill Ranch	Sonoma	D	91+
1996 Zinfandel Old Hill Ranch Limited Edition	Sonoma	D	90
1999 Zinfandel Teldeschi Vineyard	Dry Creek	D	90
1998 Zinfandel Teldeschi Vineyard	Dry Creek	D	88
1997 Zinfandel Teldeschi Vineyard	Dry Creek	D	90
1996 Zinfandel Wood Road–Belloni Vineyard	Russian River	D	90
1995 Zinfandel Wood Road–Belloni Vineyard	Russian River	D	90

Ravenswood's glories are their single-vineyard Zinfandels, which are consistently among the finest produced in California. The 1999 Zinfandel Dickerson Vineyard is the best example produced from this Napa vineyard in more than a decade. It exhibits copious quantities of sweet black cherry and blackberry fruit as well as a hint of raspberries in its big, spicy, peppery bouquet. Medium- to full-bodied, elegant, concentrated, and powerful, it should drink well for 7–8 years. The nicely textured, deep purple-colored 1999 Zinfandel Barricia offers a sweet perfume of black cherries, berries, smoke, earth, and tar. Full-bodied, chewy, and multilayered, it cuts a big swath across the palate with no hard edges. Drink it over the next 5–7 years. I loved the spectacular Zinfandel Old Hill Ranch (normally a classic as well as a candidate for the Zinfandel of the vintage). The 1999 boasts a dense ruby/purple color in addition to a gorgeous nose of new saddle leather, balsam wood, spice box, black cherry liqueur, and blackberries. The attack is sweet (from glycerin and extract, not sugar), and the finish is full-bodied, rich, and explosive. This 1999 will drink well for a decade or more. Another spectacular offering is the 1999 Zinfandel Big River. Tasting like a confiture of black raspberries and blackberries, this full-bodied, unctuously textured, impressively pure, ripe wine is thrilling to smell and taste. It will drink well for 7–8 years. The opaque purple-colored 1999 Zinfandel Teldeschi Vineyard exhibits complex aromatics consisting of incense, crushed black pepper, and black cherry/berry fruit. Dense, full-bodied, opulently textured, and powerful, with tannin and acidity for structure, it requires another year of cellaring, and should drink well for a decade. There are approximately 1,000 cases each of these.

The 1998 Zinfandel Teldeschi Vineyard is a structured, sinewy, earthy effort with plenty of allspice and pepper infused with scents of saddle leather and berry fruit presented in a medium-bodied, sweet format. It should drink well for 4–5 years. More fruit-driven is the 1998 Zinfandel Kunde Vineyard. A dark ruby color is followed by a tasty, delicious, hedonistically styled, medium- to full-bodied, flavorful wine offering abundant quantities of ripe berry fruit, glycerin, and alcohol. This crowd-pleasing Zin should be consumed over the next 5–6 years. Two outstanding wines include the 1998 Zinfandel Big River Vineyard and 1998

Zinfandel Barricia Vineyard. The 1998 Zinfandel Big River's saturated ruby/purple color is accompanied by ground pepper, briery fruit, underbrush, and sweet red and black currant aromas. In the mouth, notes of lavender and dried herbs give the wine a Mediterranean-like personality. Dense, chewy, and concentrated, this ripe but balanced Zin should drink well for 5–7 years. The opaque purple-colored 1998 Zinfandel Barricia is muscular and full-bodied, with outstanding concentration, extract, and admirable levels of glycerin in the long finish. Youthful and chunky, this wine reveals structure, muscle, and impressive intensity. Give it another 6 months of bottle age and enjoy it over the following 5–7 years.

As might be expected, wine-maker par excellence Joel Peterson has turned out some of the 1997 vintage's finest wines. One of Ravenswood's stars is always the Zinfandel Old Hill Ranch. The 1997 (110-year-old vines and 14.5% alcohol) boasts an opaque purple color, in addition to full-bodied, exuberant, powerful flavors with gritty tannin in the long, impressively endowed finish. This purely made wine provides copious quantities of black fruits along with dusty spice elements. It is one of the few 1997 Zinfandels that warrant 6–12 months of bottle age. It should keep for 7–8 years. The opaque purple-colored 1997 Zinfandel Cooke Vineyard (14.9% alcohol) also displays tangy acidity, but the extra layers of concentrated fruit neutralize the acid. There is a gorgeous nose of roasted meats, new saddle leather, dried herbs, and black fruits. Ripe, deep, medium- to full-bodied, and buttressed by the aforementioned acidity, the finish is slightly compressed, but impressive. It should drink well for 7–8 years. The gorgeous, dark purple-colored 1997 Zinfandel Teldeschi (15.5% alcohol) offers knockout aromas of smoke, licorice, blackberries, and cherries. There is sound acidity, medium to full body, dry tannin, copious fruit and glycerin, and a nicely layered, mouth-filling finish. It should drink well for 7–8 years. Another outstanding effort from Ravenswood is the 1997 Zinfandel Monte Rosso (15.5% alcohol). This effort exhibits an impressively saturated ruby/purple color and sweet mineral and blackberry flavors intermixed with dried herbs, kirsch, and stone-like scents. The vintage's telltale zingy acidity is present, but is more than compensated for by the concentrated, rich fruit. I suspect this will be one of Ravenswood's longest-lived Zinfandels, lasting until 2006+.

Not surprisingly, Ravenswood turned out a portfolio of powerful, full-throttle 1996 Zinfandels that live up to the winery's motto "No Wimpy Wines." The hedonistic 1996 Zinfandel Lodi (14.3% alcohol) reveals a southern Rhône–like, peppery, *herbes de Provence, garrigue*-scented nose intermixed with iodine and cherry liqueur. This is an immensely satisfying, rich, expansively flavored wine for consuming over the next 1–2 years. It should blend beautifully with grilled foods. The 1996 Zinfandel Old Hill Ranch Limited Edition offers a saturated ruby/purple color, followed by a knockout nose of briery fruit, charcoal, chocolate, and peppery spice. In the mouth, there is some rusticity to the wine's structure, but it provides a full-bodied, exciting combination of blackberry and cherry fruit supported by copious quantities of glycerin and decent acidity. It will offer a compelling mouthful over the next 1–2 years. The 1996 Zinfandel Cooke Vineyard (14.8% alcohol) exhibits a dense, dark ruby/purple color, a big, dusty, pepper-tinged, cherry liqueur–scented nose, and full-bodied, multi-layered flavors with plenty of muscle and length. This viscous wine saturates the palate, and finishes with notes of earth and jammy fruit. Drink it over the next 1–2 years for its exuberance and fiery character. (Note that the 1996 Cooke Vineyard is sold only at the winery's tasting room.) The highly extracted, saturated purple-colored 1996 Zinfandel Wood Road–Belloni Vineyard is a macho Zin in every sense of the word. Not only does it boast nearly 15% alcohol, it possesses explosive richness and layers of grilled meat, blackberry and cherry liqueur–like flavors that have been heavily spiced, not to mention crammed with glycerin and extract. This knockout Zinfandel is almost *sauvage* (as the French would say), but it is oh, so rich and gutsy. It should drink well for 1–2 years. My favorite of this noteworthy group is the 1996 Zinfandel Monte Rosso. Another powerhouse with 15% natural alcohol, this exquisite example offers a dark saturated plum/purple color. Sweet cedar, iodine, pepper, fruitcake, Rhône-like notes soar from the glass of this fleshy, massive Zin. Huge and rich in the mouth, yet neither coarse nor ponderous, it boasts layers of flavor, outstanding purity and harmony, and a whoppingly long finish. Already delicious, it should be consumed.

The 1995 Zinfandel Sonoma (14.5% alcohol) is a broadly flavored, mouth-filling, savory wine with Zinfandel's telltale, earthy, peppery, sweet, jammy black cherry–scented aromas, medium to full body, an expansive, chewy texture, and a lusty, high alcohol finish. Already delicious, it should continue to drink well for 1–2 years. Zinfandel lovers will be pleased to know there were 3,045 cases produced of the 1995 Zinfandel Wood Road–Belloni, a wine produced from four separate Russian River vineyards (Arata, Belloni, Chelli, and Rue). This nearly opaque purple-colored wine is a powerful, tight, full-bodied, well-structured Zinfandel that is loaded with earthy, dark fruits. Its broodingly backward, yet formidably endowed personality offers spice, jammy black fruits, and plenty of glycerin and alcohol (14.9%). This is a classic, rich, ageworthy Zinfandel that should provide marvelous drinking over the next decade. The 1995 Zinfandel Cooke Vineyard from Sonoma Valley is made in much more limited quantities (435 cases). It offers an explosive nose of licorice, pepper, allspice, black plum and cherry fruit. A great Zinfandel with fabulous concentration, the wine's wealth of fruit and glycerin conceal the lofty alcohol level of 15.2%. Totally dry, this super-concentrated wine reveals none of the late-harvest characteristics suggested by its high alcohol and huge size. This is a tour de force in Zinfandel winemaking! Drink it over the next 1–2 years. I also thought the 1995 Zinfandel Old Hill Ranch (865 cases produced from 110-year-old vines) to be an outstanding Zinfandel. Although it is the tightest-knit of the Ravenswood offerings, the opaque ruby/purple color, exquisite briery and wild berry–scented nose, full-bodied, powerful flavors, and exceptional purity, texture, and length all point to a lustrous future for this massive Zin. It is fully mature.

The 1995 Zinfandel Monte Rosso Vineyard, an Arnold Schwarzenegger–like Zinfandel (15.4% alcohol; 1,650 cases), screams from the glass with peppery, loamy, black fruit–like scents. On the palate, the wine is huge, with mouthcoating layers of highly extracted fruit allied with chewy glycerin. This opaque purple-colored wine appears to possess another 6–8 years of aging potential. It is one of the great wines of the vintage. Kudos to proprietor Joel Peterson for producing a bevy of Zinfandels that are particularly brilliant in view of the overall quality level that has emerged from this vintage.

Past Glories: 1993 Merlot Sangiacomo (90), 1993 Pickberry Proprietary Red Wine (93)

RENARD (RUSSIAN RIVER)

1997 Syrah Timbervine Ranch Cuvée El Niño	Russian River	D	91

A new producer for me, Bayard Fox ("fox" is *renard* in French) has fashioned a powerful Syrah. The superb 1997 Syrah Timbervine Ranch Cuvée El Niño reveals multiple layers of crème de cassis in addition to a touch of licorice and floral notes. Huge, fat, ripe, and layered, with full body and sensational concentration and purity, this gorgeous Syrah will drink beautifully over the next 12 years.

RENWOOD WINERY (AMADOR)

1997 Zinfandel D'Agostini Brothers	Shenandoah	D	89
1996 Zinfandel D'Agostini Brothers	Shenandoah	D	88

The intense, dark ruby/purple-colored 1997 Zinfandel D'Agostini Brothers (15.6% alcohol) offers copious quantities of rich, chewy, cherry, briery fruit, and spice, as well as a full-bodied, tannic, ruggedly constructed, macho finish. Drink it over the next 1–2 years. The 1996 Zinfandel D'Agostini Brothers displays peppery, plum, black raspberry, and cherry fruit, full body, sweetness and richness on the palate (although it is a dry wine), and none of the coarseness or excessive muscular characteristics of this winery's other 1996 Zinfandels. It should drink well for 1–2 years.

REVERIE (NAPA)

1995	Cabernet Franc Diamond Mountain	Napa	D	89
1996	Cabernet Sauvignon Diamond Mountain	Napa	D	89
1995	Cabernet Sauvignon Diamond Mountain	Napa	D	88
1996	Special Reserve Diamond Mountain	Napa	E	90
1995	Special Reserve Diamond Mountain	Napa	E	90

This winery is experimenting with Tempranillo (the 1995, 1996, and 1997 were all pleasant, but uninspiring efforts), as well as Barbera (the 1997 may turn out to be surprisingly good, but this varietal's naturally high acidity needs to be tamed). So far, Reverie's finest efforts have been with Cabernet Sauvignon. For example, the 1996 Cabernet Sauvignon Diamond Mountain (75% Cabernet Sauvignon and 25% Cabernet Franc) is a complex, Bordeaux-styled offering with tobacco, spice box, cedar, and black currant fruit. This dark ruby-colored wine displays a layered mid-palate and excellent length. While some tannin is noticeable, the wine's overall style is elegant and pure. Reverie's one outstanding offering is the 1996 Special Reserve proprietary red (87% Cabernet Sauvignon and 13% Cabernet Franc). Only 252 cases of this beauty were produced. Bottled unfiltered, this is a Bordeaux-styled wine with a Médoc-like, mineral, lead pencil, and black currant fruitiness intertwined with weedy tobacco and spice-box scents. Dense, with high tannin as well as beautiful rich, ripe fruit, this stylish, graceful, potentially complex wine would be difficult to pick out as a California Cabernet in a blind tasting. Anticipated maturity: now–2020.

The medium dark ruby-colored 1995 Cabernet Franc possesses a 92-point nose and an 88-point palate. It offers a terrific raspberry, floral, and vanilla-scented nose that leaps from the glass. The wine possesses excellent richness, medium body, and fine purity and equilibrium. It should drink well for a decade or more. The classic, elegant, restrained, and closed, medium-bodied 1995 Cabernet Sauvignon displays fine density, but extremely high tannin. Enough black currant fruit emerges for optimism, but patience is required. Give this wine 3–5 years of cellaring, and consume it over the following 15 years. The outstanding 1995 Special Reserve makes me think that its 1996 sibling will certainly come around with more time in barrel. The 1995 Special Reserve, a blend of 90% Cabernet Sauvignon, 5% Cabernet Franc, and 5% Petit Verdot, possesses a deep ruby/purple color, a spicy, ripe, concentrated character, tight aromatics, but enticing quantities of red and black fruits, minerals, and toasty notes. This elegant wine should repay readers willing to cellar it for 5–6 years. It appears to have all the necessary raw materials to last for two decades or more.

RIDGE VINEYARDS (SANTA CLARA)

1997	Cabernet Sauvignon Monte Bello	Santa Cruz	EE	91+
1996	Cabernet Sauvignon Monte Bello	Santa Cruz	EE	95+
1995	Cabernet Sauvignon Monte Bello	Santa Cruz	EE	91+
1998	Dusi Ranch	Paso Robles	D	89
1999	Geyserville Proprietary Red Wine	Sonoma	D	91
1998	Geyserville Proprietary Red Wine	Sonoma	D	90
1997	Geyserville Proprietary Red Wine	Sonoma	D	91
1996	Geyserville Proprietary Red Wine	Sonoma	D	89
1996	Grenache Lytton Estate	Sonoma	C	88
1999	Lytton Estate Late Harvest Proprietary Red Wine	Sonoma	D	92
1999	Lytton Springs Proprietary Red Wine	Sonoma	D	90
1998	Lytton Springs Proprietary Red Wine	Sonoma	D	90
1997	Lytton Springs Proprietary Red Wine	Sonoma	D	92
1996	Lytton Springs Proprietary Red Wine	Sonoma	D	90
1998	Mazzoni Home Ranch Proprietary	Sonoma	D	90

1997 Mazzoni Home Ranch Proprietary (ATP)	Sonoma	D	90
1998 Pagani Ranch	Sonoma	D	88
1998 Sonoma Station	Sonoma	D	89
1996 Syrah Lytton Springs	Sonoma	C	88
1999 Zinfandel	Paso Robles	C	88
1997 Zinfandel	Paso Robles	D	(90–92)
1996 Zinfandel Dusi Ranch	Paso Robles	D	88
1997 Zinfandel Jimsonare	Santa Cruz	D	90+
1999 Zinfandel Late Picked	Sonoma	D	89
1997 Zinfandel Lytton Springs	Sonoma	C	91
1995 Zinfandel Lytton Springs	Sonoma	C	91
1999 Zinfandel Nervo Late Picked (ATP)	California	D	94
1997 Zinfandel Pagani Ranch	Sonoma	D	90
1996 Zinfandel Pagani Ranch	Sonoma	D	88
1997 Zinfandel Sonoma Station	Sonoma	D	89
1996 Zinfandel Sonoma Station	Sonoma	D	89
1997 Zinfandel York Creek–Spring Mountain	Napa	D	88
1996 Zinfandel York Creek–Spring Mountain	Napa	D	89

Note that those wines with the designation ATP (meaning Advance Tasting Program) are sold only through Ridge's mailing list. The other wines are distributed nationally.

Nestled high in the Santa Cruz Mountains, with a precipitous view of the San Andreas fault, Ridge Vineyards has long been one of the classic reference points for high-quality California wines. While the winery now has a Japanese owner, longtime wine-maker Paul Draper continues to have complete control of vineyard management and winemaking. Production has inched up to 60,000 cases, with the potential for 8,000 cases of the famed Monte Bello Cabernet Sauvignon. However, most vintages tend to produce between 3,000–4,000 cases.

A blend of 90% Zinfandel and the rest Petite Sirah and Carignan, the dark ruby/purple-colored 1999 Zinfandel Paso Robles displays aromas of sandalwood, pepper, and black cherries. In the mouth, it is medium- to full-bodied, straightforward, and monolithic, without a great deal of complexity, but with good weight, fruit, and extract. It should drink well for 4–6 years. An exceptional offering from Ridge's portfolio is the 1999 Lytton Springs Proprietary Red Wine. This superb blend of 70% Zinfandel, 17% Petite Sirah, 10% Carignan, and 3% Mataro boasts a deep ruby/purple color in addition to a big, sweet bouquet of jammy berries, and a hint of raspberries as well as strawberries. Elegant and full-bodied, with layers of flavor, superb purity, a subtle dosage of American oak, and a full, long finish, it should drink well for 7–8 years. Also compelling, the 1999 Lytton Estate Late Harvest Proprietary Red Wine is produced from 100-year-old Zinfandel and Petite Sirah vines (50% of each). It tips the scales at a whopping 17.3% alcohol, but the residual sugar is a lowly 1.2%. The wine does not come across as sweet, nor does it reveal any of the pruny, Amarone-like characteristics displayed by many late-harvest Zinfandels. This exceptional, dense purple-colored 1999 exhibits a gorgeous perfume of blackberry jam intermixed with barbecue spice, meat, hickory, and earth. Dry in the mouth, with huge levels of glycerin, extract, and richness, this full-bodied, ripe Zinfandel will drink well for 10–15 years.

The exceptional 1999 Geyserville Proprietary Red Wine (a blend of 68% Zinfandel, 16% Carignan, and 16% Petite Sirah with 14.8% alcohol) offers aromas of black currants, kirsch, minerals, smoky oak, earth, and spice. It possesses superb concentration, excellent definition, tremendous purity, and mouth-staining extract without heaviness. A long finish further enhances this sensational, Zin-dominated offering. Consume it over the next 7–9 years. Late-harvest offerings include the 1999 Zinfandel Late Picked, a blend of primarily Zinfandel with a touch of Petite Sirah that tips the scales at 16% alcohol with 1.2% residual sugar. Neither raisiny nor sweet, it offers abundant amounts of glycerin, ripeness, and pepper in its full-bodied, fleshy, muscular personality. It should drink well for a decade. Readers looking for a Zinfandel made in the style of Henri Bonneau's famed Châteauneuf-du-Pape Réserve des Célestins should check out Ridge's 1999 Zinfandel Nervo Late Picked (ATP). A blend of 92% Zinfandel and 8% Petite Sirah, with only .2% residual sugar, this dry wine is made in an enormously concentrated, full-bodied style. It offers huge layers of blackberry and black cherry fruit intertwined with meat, earth, smoke, and underbrush. Formidably endowed, with enormous amounts of glycerin, this powerful yet supple, accessible 1999 is a tour de force in winemaking. Readers on Ridge's mailing list who enjoy large-scaled wines should be sure to latch onto a few bottles of this gem. It should drink well for 10–15 years.

Readers should note that Ridge dropped the word "Zinfandel" from their 1998s. Of course, all of them are in essence Zinfandels, with various percentages of that varietal included in the blend. None is less than 71% Zinfandel, with the Dusi Ranch made from 100% Zinfandel. The dark ruby/purple-colored 1998 Mazzoni Home Ranch (71% Zinfandel, 21% Carignan, and 8% Petite Sirah) exhibits fat, sweet aromas of melted road tar, black currants, cherry jam, and licorice. Full-bodied, deep, and expansive, this low-acid, plump, fleshy offering is meant to be drunk now and over the next 5–6 years. One of Ridge's classic efforts, the 1998 Geyserville (74% Zinfandel, 15% Petite Sirah, 10% Carignan, and 1% Matero) possesses Bordeaux-like complexity and elegance. The alcohol is listed as 14.1%. The wine was reticent on the day I tasted it, but as it sat in the glass, sweet aromas of minerals, smoky wood, red/black currants, and dried herbs emerged. This classy, elegant, restrained, yet authoritatively rich Zinfandel should be consumed over the next 5–6 years. The 1998 Dusi Ranch (the only 100% Zinfandel offering tasted from Ridge) exhibits aromas of roasted peanuts and smoky, black cherry and currant fruit. There is good structure and delineation, a dense, rich, medium- to full-bodied palate, and a long, concentrated finish. Interestingly, the back label indicated that this was the first time in over 25 years that the Dusi Ranch was harvested in October because of the extremely cold, wet spring. Another Ridge classic, the deep ruby/purple-colored 1998 Lytton Springs (14.3% alcohol; 77% Zinfandel, 16% Petite Sirah, 4% Matero, 2% Carignan, and 1% Alicante) boasts a sweet nose of briery fruit mixed with red and black currants, minerals, pepper, and smoke. Medium- to full-bodied, with dried Provençal herb characteristics that emerge with airing, this fleshy, beautifully pure, and stunningly proportioned Zin can be drunk now as well as over the next 5–6 years. Perhaps the best value in Ridge's Zinfandel portfolio is the 1998 Sonoma Station. A blend of 75% Zinfandel, 11% Carignan, 9% Alicante, and 5% Petite Sirah that achieved 13.7% alcohol, this peppery, dried herb, red and black currant–scented and flavored wine is medium-bodied, with abundant levels of berry fruit, good purity, and a soft, straightforward, fleshy character similar to an impeccably made Côtes du Rhône. Drink it over the next 3–4 years. A more Amarone-like late-harvest character can be found in the 1998 Pagani Ranch (a blend of 88% Zinfandel, 9% Alicante, and 3% Petite Sirah). A dense ruby color is followed by scents of melted road tar, animal fur, sweet, jammy plums, and smoky cherries. Medium- to full-bodied, not terribly complex, but round and chewy, this wine should be consumed over the next 4–5 years.

The 1997 Zinfandels are all high in alcohol, largely because of vintage conditions. All are slightly more successful than Ridge's very fine 1996s. For example, the 1997 Zinfandel Paso Robles offers overripe prunes, plums, and cherries in the nose, explosive fruit, copious glycerin, and a full-bodied, chewy, seductive character. It should be drunk over the next 1–2 years. The 1997 Geyserville Proprietary Red Wine (74% Zinfandel, 15% Carignan, 10% Petite Sirah, and 1% Mourvèdre, with 14.9% alcohol) offers explosive aromas of jammy berry fruit and flavors redolent with notes of plums, cherries, raspberries, and smoky wood. Open-knit and expansive, with low acidity, this evolved, forward, hedonistic wine will drink well for 1–2 years. The opaque purple-colored 1997 Zinfandel Pagani Ranch (88% Zinfandel, 7% Mataro, 3% Petite Sirah, and 2% Alicante Bouchet that achieved 14.6% alcohol) exhibits what the French call *sur-maturité* (overripeness). A monolithic wine with huge, muscular, concentrated flavors, it had not yet begun to reveal much delineation or evolution, despite the fact it is already in bottle. There are layers of concentrated fruit, plenty of blackberry, plum, jammy notes, and enough acidity and tannin to buttress this enormously endowed wine. It will be even better with another six months of bottle age, and will last for 3–4 years. The 1997 Zinfandel Lytton Springs is an effusively fruity, full-bodied wine emphasizing Zinfandel's black cherry/raspberry character. With loads of glycerin, high alcohol, and outstanding purity and finish, this will be a hedonistic, luscious wine to enjoy through 2003. Interestingly, Paul Draper told me the alcohol levels for all these 1997 Zinfandels were well above 15%.

The opaque ruby/purple 1997 Mazzoni Home Ranch Proprietary Red Wine (ATP) (60% Zinfandel, 35% Carignan, and 5% Petite Sirah that achieved 13.8% alcohol) offers a beautiful black raspberry–scented nose with notes of licorice and spicy oak. It is a medium- to full-bodied, smoothly textured, hedonistic wine that will provide luscious drinking over the next 3–4 years. The dark ruby/purple-colored 1997 Zinfandel Sonoma Station (75% Zinfandel, 13% Carignan, 8% Petite Sirah, and 4% Alicante Bouchet) exhibits a big, briery, peppery, spicy nose, dense, rich, cherry and blackberry flavors, a deep, lush texture, and fine purity and intensity. It, too, should be drunk before 2004. Made from a blend of 80% Zinfandel, 15% Petite Sirah, 2% Carignan, 2% Mataro, and 1% Grenache, the 1997 Lytton Springs Proprietary Red Wine (14.9% alcohol) exhibits a saturated purple color in addition to sumptuous aromas of truffles, licorice, loamy soil, blackberry liqueur, and cherries. There are layers of concentration, sweet glycerin in the mid-palate, and a blockbuster, concentrated, opulently textured finish. It should drink well for 6 years.

One of the greatest old Zinfandels I ever tasted was the 1970 Jimsonare. Ridge rarely bottles this as a single-source wine because the vineyard is at such a high elevation that the grapes never fully ripen. That was not the case in 1997. The saturated opaque black/purple-colored 1997 Zinfandel Jimsonare (100% Zinfandel) achieved 14.8% alcohol. It boasts enormously rich, massive, blackberry and cherry flavors, rustic tannin, and a gigantic, monster finish that lasts for over 30 seconds. The wine also exhibits copious quantities of toasty oak. It is by far the most concentrated and immense of the Ridge offerings, as well as the least evolved. This Zinfandel should age well for 5–6 years. In contrast, the 1997 Zinfandel York Creek (95% Zinfandel and 5% Petite Sirah that weighs in at 15.3% alcohol) is a more spice, earth, and licorice-scented wine with plenty of rustic tannin, a gritty texture, medium to full body, and deep, concentrated, muscular flavors. With an uncivilized tannin level and rusticity, it should be consumed over the next 3–4 years.

The 1997 Cabernet Sauvignon Monte Bello exhibits an opaque purple color, as well as a black currant, mineral, and smoky oak-scented nose. The wine is medium- to full-bodied, tannic, and in need of 10 years of cellaring. Not a blockbuster, this offering is more elegant and finesse-styled than usual. However, as with previous Monte Bellos, it will take a long time to come around, yet it will keep for 2–3 decades. The 1996 Cabernet Sauvignon Monte Bello (80% Cabernet Sauvignon, 11% Merlot, and 9% Petit Verdot that reached 13.4% alcohol) represents a severe selection of only 40% of the vineyard's crop. A powerful, concentrated blockbuster, it possesses an opaque purple color, plenty of spicy oak in the nose (100% American oak has always been used for aging Monte Bello), and a deep, layered, concentrated style. There is plenty of tannin, but it is sweeter than that found in the 1997, and the wine is more concentrated and extracted. There is a touch of oak in the flavors, which are otherwise dominated by minerals and jammy black fruits. This is a terrific Monte Bello that will have 30+ years of life. The 1995 Monte Bello is actually a Proprietary Red Wine as the blend is 69% Cabernet Sauvignon, 18% Merlot, 10% Petit Verdot, and 3% Cabernet Franc. It was made from an extremely severe selection of only 25% of the harvest. Draper feels it is the biggest, brawniest, and most muscular Monte Bello of the 1990s and in need of 10–15 more years of cellaring. This saturated ruby/purple-colored effort is still backward, with a closed nose of minerals, oak, and subtle black fruits. In the mouth, it is large-scaled, tannic, rich, and long, but nearly abrasive because of its high tannin level. This youthful, muscular monster will require significant cellaring. Anticipated maturity: 2010–2035.

Ridge owns the Lytton Springs estate, from which it produced two interesting Rhône Ranger wines in 1996. The 1996 Syrah Lytton Springs was blended with 5% Viognier and tips the scales at 14.2% alcohol. The Viognier was vinified with the Syrah, resulting in a richly fruity (blackberries and currants), lush, round, hedonistically styled wine with low acidity, and a plump, savory character. It should drink well until 2004. Also intriguing is the 1996 Grenache Lytton Springs (made from 92% Grenache, 6% Zinfandel, and 2% Petite Sirah). This wine's deep ruby color is followed by a gorgeous nose of jammy strawberries, kirsch, and dried cherries. Fruity, with good glycerin, medium to full body, and loads of fruit, this textbook, very yummy Grenache should be consumed before 2004.

Ridge produced a fine series of 1996 Zinfandels. They reveal the vintage's rich, high-alcohol personality, and forward, immediately drinkable style. I do not believe the 1996 vintage will hold together beyond 2005, despite the high alcohol. The tiny Zinfandel crop resulted in concentrated wines, but they are not as exceptionally deep as one might have expected given the small yields. Ridge's 1996 Zinfandel Sonoma Station (an 80% Zinfandel, 8% Petite Sirah, 8% Alicante, and 4% Carignan blend that achieved 14.4% alcohol) displays a dark ruby color and a rich, briery, raspberry-scented nose with gobs of spice and pepper. Medium-bodied, with excellent concentration and subtle new oak in the background, this delicious, broadly flavored Zinfandel is best drunk over the next 1–3 years. Ridge has consistently done a fine job with their Zinfandel from the Dusi Ranch in Paso Robles. The 1996 (95% Zinfandel and 5% Petite Sirah with 14.6% alcohol) boasts a deep saturated ruby/purple color (among the darkest of the Ridge offerings) and subtle aromatics (primarily earth intermixed with black raspberries, pepper, and licorice). This medium- to full-bodied, spicy Zinfandel appears to possess a firm structure and ageability, but it does not have the underlying depth to warrant cellaring beyond 1–3 years. The 1996 Geyserville Proprietary Red Wine (a blend of 75% Zinfandel, 17% Carignan, 6% Petite Sirah, and 2% Mataro) tips the scales at 14.9% alcohol. In spite of the hefty alcohol content, it is an exceptionally elegant wine, with sweet, black raspberry and cherry fruit, medium body, and a dry, crisp, lightly tannic finish. This wine could easily pass for a high-class, mid-weight 1995 red Burgundy. As the wine sits in the mouth, its glycerin and multilayered texture are very appealing. It should drink well for 1–3 years. The 1996 Zinfandel York Creek–Spring Mountain (91% Zinfandel and 9% Petite Sirah) reveals a Bordeaux-like austerity to its flavor profile. There is plenty of tannin, but that does not mean this offering can be cellared for any length of time. The blackberry/cherry notes combine with spicy oak, pepper, and minerals for a moderately intense, enticing bouquet. In the mouth, the wine exhibits firmness, some American oak, as well as good spice and sweet fruit. Consume this classy, complex Zin over the next 1–2 years. The 1996 Lytton Springs Proprietary Red Wine (78% Zinfandel, 19% Petite Sirah, 2% Carignan, and 1% Grenache) possesses 14.5% alcohol. It boasts the sweetest, jammiest nose, as well as a healthy dark ruby/purple color, full body, robust, chewy flavors, and the best length of these offerings. This expansively flavored wine should drink well for 2–3 years. Lastly, the dark ruby-colored 1996 Zinfandel Pagani Ranch (82% Zinfandel, 11% Mataro, 4% Petite Sirah, and 3% Alicante) offers up aromas of earth, prunes, and ripe black fruits (almost Amarone in style). In the mouth, the wine is dry, medium- to full-bodied, rustic, less concentrated, and more civilized and restrained than several previous Pagani Ranch Zinfandels, which were blockbusters. This cleanly made wine should drink well for 2–3 years. These 1996s are all excellent, nearly outstanding Zinfandels that share a certain firmness and structured feel (particularly when compared to the 1995s, 1994s, and 1993s). Because of the definition and angularity, it would be natural for readers to think these wines require cellaring. My instincts and experience suggest these need to be drunk in their exuberant youth—over the next 2–3 years.

Past Glories: Cabernet Sauvignon Monte Bello—1993 (93+), 1992 (94), 1991 (95), 1990 (91), 1987 (92), 1985 (90), 1984 (92), 1977 (93), 1974 (96), 1971 (94), 1970 (95)

ROCHIOLI VINEYARD (SONOMA)

1997	Cabernet Sauvignon Neoma's Vineyard	Russian River	D	90
1996	Cabernet Sauvignon Neoma's Vineyard	Russian River	D	93
1999	Chardonnay	Russian River	D	90
1999	Chardonnay Allen Vineyard	Russian River	D	93
1999	Chardonnay River Block Vineyard	Russian River	D	92
1999	Chardonnay South River Vineyard	Russian River	D	94
1999	Pinot Noir East Block	Russian River	EE	95
1998	Pinot Noir East Block	Russian River	E	93
1997	Pinot Noir East Block	Russian River	E	92
1995	Pinot Noir East Block	Russian River	E	91
1999	Pinot Noir Estate	Russian River	D	90
1998	Pinot Noir Estate	Russian River	D	89
1997	Pinot Noir Estate	Russian River	D	88
1996	Pinot Noir Estate	Russian River	D	88
1995	Pinot Noir Estate	Russian River	C	89
1999	Pinot Noir Little Hill Block	Russian River	E	92
1998	Pinot Noir Little Hill Block	Russian River	E	91
1997	Pinot Noir Little Hill Block	Russian River	E	94
1996	Pinot Noir Little Hill Block	Russian River	E	91
1995	Pinot Noir Little Hill Block	Russian River	E	90
1999	Pinot Noir River Block	Russian River	EE	92
1998	Pinot Noir Three Corner Vineyard	Russian River	D	90
1997	Pinot Noir Three Corner Vineyard	Russian River	E	91
1996	Pinot Noir Three Corner Vineyard	Russian River	E	93
1995	Pinot Noir Three Corner Vineyard	Russian River	E	90
1999	Pinot Noir West Block	Russian River	E	95
1998	Pinot Noir West Block	Russian River	E	92
1997	Pinot Noir West Block	Russian River	E	88
1996	Pinot Noir West Block	Russian River	E	93
1995	Pinot Noir West Block	Russian River	E	93
1999	Sauvignon Blanc	Russian River	C	88
1999	Zinfandel Rochioli Vineyard	Russian River	D	90
1998	Zinfandel Rochioli Vineyard	Russian River	D	91
1998	Zinfandel Sodini Vineyard	Russian River	D	90
1996	Zinfandel Sodini Vineyard	Russian River	C	93

Virtually all the producers I visit in California are candid and direct about vintage conditions, and how their wines are made. That being said, there is probably no more of a "straight-shooter" in the wine world than Tom Rochioli. His refreshing honesty and self-deprecating style are hard to resist. In fact, I often wonder if he realizes the superb quality of his wines! About the only way readers will be able to obtain the limited-production, single-vineyard Rochioli wines is to get their names on the winery's mailing list, something I highly recommend. The modest Rochioli continues to ratchet up the level of quality, turning out better and better wines. In short, they are among the finest Chardonnays and Pinot Noirs money can buy. His commitment to quality is evident in his basic *cuvée* of Russian River Chardonnay and Pinot Noir. The 1999s are the best he has yet made. There are 2,525 cases of the 1999 Chardonnay Estate, which was bottled without filtration. It is a terrific buy for the quality it possesses. A complex, Burgundian-styled Chardonnay with leesy, orange marmalade, pineapple, mineral, and roasted hazelnut notes, a steely character, fine underlying minerality, full body, and admirable structure, it should drink well for 3–4 years. Seventy percent of the 1999 Sauvignon Blanc comes from a vineyard planted in 1959 and 30% from a vineyard planted in 1985. The wine exhibits flinty, gravelly notes, ripe grapefruit and passion fruit characteristics, light to medium body, and an expressive personality. It is best drunk over the next 2–3 years.

The single-vineyard Chardonnays are made in limited quantities (300 or so cases of each). They are tightly knit, expressive wines bottled without fining or filtration. I have been buying these wines since Tom Rochioli first vineyard-designated them, and they have a good 5–7 years of life. The 1999s reveal the vintage's higher acidity. The superb 1999 Chardonnay River Block (332 cases), made from the sandy, loamy soils, is tightly knit, with great fruit, an underlying liquid minerality, and plenty of leesy, smoky, tropical fruit intermixed with roasted almonds as well as a steely note. This wine is unevolved, but should drink well for 4–6 years. Even more impressive, the 1999 Chardonnay Allen Vineyard displays high-quality French oak intermixed with tropical fruit aromas and scents. This big, thick, super-concentrated wine possesses enough acidity to buttress its powerful and formidable size. Ideally, it needs another 6–12 months of bottle age, and should keep for 5–6 years. The spectacular 1999 Chardonnay South River Vineyard is made from the Hanzell clone of Chardonnay planted in the alluvial soils of an ancient river bed. The wine boasts a multilayered texture, super purity, and notions of minerals, pineapples, peach, smoke, and butter. Like all of these Chardonnays, the oak regime includes 50% new French; it is subtle and unobtrusive. Anticipated maturity: now–2009.

The 1999 Pinot Noir Estate enjoys about one-third new French oak (all François Frères). The finest regular Pinot Rochioli has yet produced, it exhibits a dense ruby color as well as a gorgeous nose of black cherry jam intermixed with earth, smoke, vanilla, and spice. The grapes were picked very ripe, which is reflected in the wine's sweet black fruit character. Drink this impressive Pinot Noir over the next 4–5 years. There are 300–400 cases of the single-vineyard wines except for the River Block (only 150 cases). Tom Rochioli believes in picking extremely high sugars (25–27° Brix), giving the wines a three-to-five-day cold soak, and fermenting them with indigenous yeasts. Virtually no racking is practiced until they are assembled for bottling unfined and unfiltered. His wines rank alongside the top four or five Pinot Noirs produced in California. The 1999 Pinot Noir Little Hill (a rocky hillside vineyard) is a dark ruby/plum-colored wine with medium to full body as well as a gorgeous nose of rose petals, black cherries, raspberries, minerals, and smoke. Rich and well textured, it should hit its prime in about 1–2 years, and keep for 8–9. The opaque ruby/purple-colored 1999 Pinot Noir West Block (a vineyard planted in 1969 and 1970) boasts a sumptuous nose of allspice, blackberries, cherries, and toast. This multilayered Pinot Noir exhibits uncanny balance and purity, an unctuous texture, and a 40-second finish. It is a dazzling effort that looks to be even better than the 1998. Anticipated maturity: now–2009. The awesome, black ruby-colored 1999 Pinot Noir East Block reveals an extravagant bouquet of black raspberries, cherry liqueur, and vanilla. Picked ripe, but with no sense of pruniness or hotness, this massive, full-bodied, unctuously textured Pinot Noir is fabulously concentrated as well as beautifully balanced. The wine is low in acidity, but well delineated and extremely fresh and lively. It should drink well for at least a decade. The 1999 Pinot Noir River Block, picked at 27° Brix, displays no late-harvest characteristics, but abundant glycerin as well as copious quantities of black cherry liqueur intermixed with floral, smoke, and earth characteristics. The texture is terrific, and the wine pure and well balanced. Sadly, there are only 150 cases. Anticipated maturity: now–2014.

Rochioli's 1998 Pinot Noirs are all highly successful for the vintage. It is too early to say they are better than the 1997s and 1996s, but there is no doubt that Tom Rochioli is producing some of California's finest wines from this fickle grape. Sadly, production in 1998 was off by 25%, so there are even fewer cases of these wines than normal. All are made from destemmed Pinot Noir fruit, given up to five days of cold soaking prior to fermentation, and put in French oak, with no settling, in order to obtain as much of the lees in the wine as possible. There are only two rackings, the final one being the assemblage of the wine in tank prior to bottling. The 1998 Pinot Noir Estate is essentially a *cuvée* culled from the single-vineyard wines and from the youngest vines of the Rochioli estate. It is a beautiful, strawberry/cherry-scented wine with a dark ruby color, lively, vibrant fruit, medium to full body, excellent concentration, sweet tannin, and enough acidity to provide delineation. It could easily pass for a premier cru Beaune. Drink it over the next 4–5 years. The 1998 Pinot Noir Three Corner Vineyard (130 cases) offers a vibrant, jammy nose of black cherries, medium to full body, outstanding ripeness, an excellent texture, and fine purity. It should drink well for 5–7 years. The dark ruby-colored 1998 Pinot Noir Little Hill Block (250 cases) reveals richer, deeper, sweeter black cherry and raspberry fruit, medium to full body, and outstanding purity and length. Both the Little Hill Block and Three Corner Vineyard are aged in 50% new French oak and are bottled unfined and unfiltered. Concentration, extract, and perfume increase with the 350-case lot of 1998 Pinot Noir West Block. Also aged in 100% new François Frères oak barrels, it exhibits an alluring bouquet of black raspberries, flowers, and cherry liqueur. Rich and medium- to full-bodied, with gorgeous purity as well as symmetry, this multidimensional Pinot will require 1–2 years of bottle age in order to shed its aggressive tannin. It will last for a decade. Unquestionably, my favorite Rochioli Pinot is the 1998 Pinot Noir East Block. The grapes were harvested at around 26° Brix, hence it tips the scales at nearly 15% alcohol. Aged in 100% new oak, it reveals no pruniness or late-harvest characteristics. Rich, with glorious levels of black cherries, raspberries, cassis, and blackberries, this dense, full-bodied, superbly concentrated Pinot is pure and seductive. Sweet tannin in the finish complements the high level of glycerin and alcohol. This Pinot may turn out to be among the finest produced by Rochioli. It should drink well for a decade.

The dark ruby-colored 1997 Pinot Noir Estate offers an attractive black cherry, earthy, spicy-scented nose, medium to full body, sweet tannin, and excellent cleanliness and overall symmetry. Fleshy, rich, and mouth-filling, this is a robust yet well-balanced Pinot to enjoy over the next 3–4 years. The 1997 Pinot Noir Three Corner Vineyard exhibits a dark ruby/purple color, a sweet plum, black currant, and cherry-scented nose, silky-textured, medium-to full-bodied flavors, and a smoky, toasty finish. The wine presents a seamless style and wonderful sweet fruit, without tasting overbearing or weighty. The alcohol level must be close to 14%, but the taster will never sense that given the wine's concentration and depth. Look for this to evolve nicely for 5–7 years. My favorite 1997 Pinot in the Rochioli stable is the 1997 Pinot Noir Little Hill Block. It boasts a saturated purple color, followed by a spectacular nose that could easily pass for the crème de cassis/black raspberry liqueur found in a top-notch Richebourg. The vineyard, which is planted in extremely rocky soil, achieved sugars that produced a wine with 13.8% alcohol. Aged in 50% new François Frères barrels, with the balance one year old, this wine's silky texture is crammed with glycerin as well as concentrated red and black fruits. Floral scents and smoky, toasty notes add to the wine's appeal and complexity. This full-bodied, gorgeously complete and concentrated Pinot should be drunk over the next 5–6 years. Classic black cherry aromatics intermixed with smoky new oak jump from a glass of the 1997 Pinot Noir West Block. This dark ruby/purple-colored wine, aged in 100% new François Frères oak, is full-bodied and tighter than its predecessors, but nicely layered, with sweet kirsch and black cherry–like flavors, good glycerin, and fine purity. The slightly angular and tannic finish in this compressed example kept my score conservative. Lastly, the 1997 Pinot Noir East Block is made in the mold of the Little Hill *cuvée*. It is a full-throttle effort that, despite its wonderful richness and density, has retained its elegance and lushness. The color is a healthy dark ruby/purple. In the mouth, the wine displays medium to full body, outstanding flavor extraction, and a long, 30-second finish. The wine possesses adequate acidity and moderate tannin, but these components are virtually buried by the precocious fruit and ripeness. This spicy, black fruit–scented and –flavored Pinot should be at its best with another 6–12 months of aging and will evolve nicely for 5–7 years.

The 1996 Pinot Noir Estate exhibits a sweet, smoky, black plum and cherry–scented nose, medium body, excellent ripeness and purity of fruit, enough acidity for definition, and a moderately long, easygoing finish with toasty new-oak notes. It should drink well for 4–5 years. The 1996 Pinot Noir Little Hill Block offers up a knockout nose of raspberries, cherries, smoky, toasty oak, and floral scents. The wine is full-bodied, with intense flavors, a layered, silky texture, and a lush, heady finish. It is a hedonistic and intellectually pleasing Pinot Noir to drink over the next 4–5 years. Remarkably, both the 1996 Pinot Noir Three Corner Vineyard and 1996 Pinot Noir West Block appear to be even more complex and multidimensional. The dense, deep ruby/purple-colored 1996 Pinot Noir Three Corner Vineyard (125 cases) reveals a sweet black raspberry–scented nose with high-quality toasty notes and intriguing Asian spice scents. Sweet and ripe on the attack (from fruit maturity, not sugar), this full-bodied, dense, lushly textured Pinot is an infant in terms of development, but it promises to drink well young and last for 7–8 years. Each year I seem to have a slight preference for the Pinot Noir West Block and the 1996 is again my favorite. Texturally, as well as from a perspective of concentration and length, this wine could easily pass for a great 1990 grand cru red Burgundy. Aromatically, it remains to be seen whether it will offer the same level of complexity, but my instincts suggest this is a profound Pinot that should rival the finest made in America over recent years. The color is a deep ruby/purple. The exotic nose offers a mélange of black fruits intertwined with toast, spice, and meaty nuances. Full-bodied, dense, superbly concentrated, and pure, yet surprisingly fresh and lively, this is a glorious example of the extraordinary progress being made by a handful of U.S. vintners with the fickle Pinot Noir grape. I would not be surprised to see this wine last for a decade.

In 1995 there were five *cuvées* of Pinot Noir. The 1995 Pinot Noir Estate exhibits a deep ruby color, a sweet, blackberry-scented nose, evidence of smoky wood, and round, generous, medium- to full-bodied flavors. This supple Pinot is ideal for drinking over the next 4–5 years. There are four limited-production, single-vineyard 1995 Pinot Noirs. The 1995 Pinot Noir Little Hill Block displays an open-knit, sweet, jammy, black fruit–scented nose, ripe, medium- to full-bodied flavors, and a forward, soft style with excellent purity and plenty of Pinot Noir's unmistakable perfumed silkiness and character. Drink it over the next 4–5 years. The 1995 Pinot Noir Three Corner Vineyard exhibits a deeper color, copious quantities of up-front, sweet, smoky, black-cherry fruit, medium to full body, outstanding purity, and no hard edges. This wine should drink for 5–6 years. The impressive 1995 Pinot Noir West Block offers a nose of raspberries and black cherries, wonderful sweetness and richness, and that layered, soft, opulently textured feel of serious Pinot. Round, concentrated, and full-bodied, this is a lush, silky wine to drink over the next 5–6 years. The 1995 Pinot Noir East Block is cut from the same mold, perhaps more earthy, but opulent and flashy, with gobs of rich fruit. It is hard to imagine many wineries turning out five Pinots of this quality from one vintage.

Do readers realize that the Rochiolis still sell 60% of the production from their vineyards, holding back only the best lots for their own estate bottled program? They still make Zinfandel from extremely old vines. The 1999 Zinfandel Rochioli Vineyard (100 cases) offers gorgeous plum, prune, black cherry, and raspberry fruit notes intermixed with chocolate, smoke, pepper, and earth. Drink this viscous, thick, juicy wine during its first 7–8 years of life. The outstanding 1998 Zinfandel Sodini Vineyard (325 cases) emerges from a hillside vineyard planted in 1905. Plums, prune, cherry liqueur, and pepper aromas jump from a glass of this full-bodied, unctuously textured Zinfandel. Totally dry, with considerable viscosity, it comes closest in style to some of the hedonistic Zinfandel fruit bombs produced by Ehren Jordan and Larry Turley. It should drink well for 5–7 years. Readers looking for more briery Zinfandel fruit, as well as classic blackberry and cassis, should check out the concentrated, thick 1998 Zinfandel Rochioli Vineyard. Full-bodied, intense, and syrupy, it was aged in 50% new-oak casks. Sadly, there are only 100 cases. It should drink well for a decade. Two limited rarities include the superb 1996 Zinfandel Sodoni Vineyard (from vines planted in 1905). There are 400 cases of this fabulously intense, rich, black/purple-colored Zinfandel that must contain 15% alcohol. This full-bodied, voluptuously textured Zin will provide sensational drinking for 5–7 years. Another noteworthy wine is the 1996 Cabernet Sauvignon Neoma's Vineyard (150 cases). Made from 38-year-old vines with yields of under two tons per acre, this wine exhibits a saturated black/purple color, and textbook jammy cassis aromas intermingled with minerals, tobacco, and licorice scents. Extremely full bodied, with phenomenal concentration, this wine reveals the telltale characteristics of the finest 1996s—low acidity, ripe tannin, and drop-dead levels of extract and nearly overripe fruit. Anticipated maturity: now–2025.

I know Tom Rochioli does not get the same thrill from making Cabernet Sauvignon as he does from Pinot Noir, Chardonnay, and Sauvignon Blanc, but that is no reason to ignore his outstanding 1997 Cabernet Sauvignon Neoma's Vineyard, a black/purple-colored wine with superb aromatics of new oak, black raspberries, olives, tar, and smoke. Full-bodied, rich, and chewy, with impressive viscosity and extract, this large-scaled, silky-textured wine should evolve nicely for 15–20 years. Production was approximately 225 cases.

ROCKING HORSE WINERY (NAPA)

1997 Cabernet Sauvignon Garvey Family Vineyard	Rutherford	D	89+
1994 Cabernet Sauvignon Garvey Family Vineyard	Rutherford	D	91

The 1997 Cabernet Sauvignon Garvey Family Vineyard from Rocking Horse has a dense ruby/purple color followed by an earthy, dusty nose with hints of new oak and black currants. On the palate, this wine is long, rich, and full-bodied, with outstanding potential. Pure, with moderate tannin and admirable concentration, it promises to be even better in 3–4 years and keep for 12–15+. Eight hundred and fifty cases of the outstanding 1994 Cabernet Sauvignon Garvey Family Vineyard were produced from 100% Cabernet Sauvignon. The wine boasts an opaque purple color, full body, an explosively rich mid-palate, and a 20–25-second finish. It is loaded with black currant, cedar, chocolate-like fruit, has a glorious texture, superb richness and chewiness, and that telltale, earthy, spicy, "Rutherford dust" characteristic. There are gobs of sweet tannin in the finish, but readers should not conclude that this wine is ready to drink. Purchasers of it should be prepared to give it 3–5 years of cellaring as it is a 20-year wine that could turn out to be even better than my numerical rating suggests.
Past Glories: 1993 Cabernet Sauvignon Garvey Family Vineyard (90)

ROSENBLUM CELLARS (ALAMEDA)

1999 Zinfandel Alegria Vineyard	Sonoma	C	88
1998 Zinfandel Alegria Vineyard	Russian River	D	89
1997 Zinfandel Annette's Reserve Rhodes Vineyard	Redwood Valley	D	88
1999 Zinfandel Carla's Vineyards	San Francisco Bay	C	88
1998 Zinfandel Carla's Vineyards	Contra Costa	C	88
1999 Zinfandel Continente Vineyard	San Francisco Bay	C	90
1998 Zinfandel Continente Vineyard	San Francisco Bay	C	89
1998 Zinfandel Cullinane Vineyard	Sonoma	D	90
1997 Zinfandel Cullinane Vineyard	Sonoma	D	87

1999	Zinfandel Eagle Point Vineyard	Mendocino	C	90
1999	Zinfandel George Hendry Vineyard Reserve	Napa	D	88
1999	Zinfandel Harris Kratka Vineyard	Alexander Valley	C	90
1998	Zinfandel Harris Kratka Vineyard	Alexander Valley	D	89
1999	Zinfandel Lyons Vineyard	Napa	D	91
1998	Zinfandel Lyons Vineyard	Napa	D	90
1997	Zinfandel Lyons Vineyard	Napa	D	89
1999	Zinfandel Monte Rosso Vineyard	Sonoma	D	92
1999	Zinfandel Rhodes Vineyard	Redwood Valley	D	87
1998	Zinfandel Richard Sauret Vineyard	Paso Robles	D	90
1999	Zinfandel Rockpile Road Vineyard	Dry Creek	C	89
1998	Zinfandel Rockpile Road Vineyard	Dry Creek	D	89
1997	Zinfandel Rockpile Road Vineyard	Dry Creek	C	89
1999	Zinfandel Samsel Vineyard Maggie's Reserve	Sonoma	D	92
1998	Zinfandel Samsel Vineyard Maggie's Reserve	Sonoma	D	88
1999	Zinfandel St. Peter's Church Vineyard	Sonoma	D	91
1998	Zinfandel St. Peter's Church Vineyard	Sonoma	D	90

One has to admire the quality Rosenblum is able to achieve given his enormous Zinfandel portfolio, all of which are extremely successful in 1999. The opaque ruby/purple-colored 1999 Zinfandel Lyons Vineyard exhibits a gorgeous perfume of blackberry and raspberry fruit, medium to full body, and a sweet mid-palate with good underlying minerality. There is enough acidity and tannin to provide definition. It should drink well for a decade. Lighter, with higher acidity, the well-made, pure, restrained 1999 Zinfandel George Hendry is a medium-bodied, elegant, mineral, blueberry, raspberry, plum, and currant-scented and -flavored effort to enjoy over the next 7–8 years. The opaque purple-colored 1999 Zinfandel Rhodes Vineyard offers crisp, tangy acidity, an earthy note in its raspberry and cherry fruit, medium to full body, and excellent purity, richness, and overall harmony. It should drink well for 5–6 years. Rosenblum's blockbuster 1999 Zinfandel St. Peter's Church Vineyard boasts a saturated purple color as well as scents of blackberries, blueberries, smoke, minerals, new saddle leather, and earth. Dense, powerful, and muscular, with no hard edges, it exhibits super ripeness, beautifully pure fruit, a multidimensional personality (unusual for Zinfandel), and a long, pure finish. Give it 6–8 more months to round into shape, and consume it over the following decade.

I tasted two offerings from the San Francisco Bay region. The 1999 Zinfandel Carla's Vineyards (14.1% alcohol) is a delicious, open-knit, richly fruity wine exhibiting plum and berry fruit with a touch of pepper and spice. Medium- to full-bodied and soft, it is ideal for drinking over the next 2–3 years. The dark plum/ruby-colored 1999 Zinfandel Continente Vineyard (14.6% alcohol) offers distinctive aromatics of sweet cherry jam and balsam wood. In the mouth, it is fleshy, full-bodied, and unctuous, with good thickness, excellent purity, sweet tannin, and low acidity. Drink it over the next 4–5 years.

The 1999 Zinfandel Alegria Vineyard (14.1% alcohol) is a field blend of 78% Zinfandel, 14% Petite Sirah, and 8% Alicante Bouchet. Some of the vines date back to 1892. Flamboyant aromas of black raspberries, cherries, and currants jump from the glass. There is a subtle oak component, as well as plenty of spice, leather, pepper, and sweet fruit in this medium-bodied, elegant, dark ruby/purple-colored Zinfandel. It is best drunk over the next 4–5 years. The 1999 Zinfandel Eagle Point Vineyard (14.3% alcohol) emerges from a higher-altitude source in the cooler Mendocino region. This superb offering reveals gorgeous blackberry, cherry, and currant aromas. Pure, ripe, and concentrated, with medium- to full-bodied, velvety-textured flavors, and well-concealed wood, this beauty will drink well for 4–5 years. The 1999 Zinfandel Rockpile Road Vineyard (14.6% alcohol) boasts abundant levels of spice, earth, licorice, leather, black cherry, and blackberry characteristics in both its aromas and flavors. Although more subdued than other Rosenblum offerings, it possesses intensity, ripeness, and impressive purity. Fleshy and full-bodied, with good glycerin, purity, texture, and overall balance, this delicious Zinfandel will drink well for 4–5 years.

The powerful (14.8% alcohol) 1999 Zinfandel Harris Kratka Vineyard (a blend of 75% Zinfandel and 25% Carignan) offers a distinctive balsam wood, earthy, crushed sandstone/mineral note in the intriguing nose of black fruits (predominantly cherries). Rich, fleshy, succulent, and hedonistic, with gobs of fruit, abundant glycerin, and a long, seamless, velvety-textured, full-bodied finish, it will drink well for 4–5 years. The dark ruby/purple-colored 1999 Zinfandel Monte Rosso Vineyard (from a vineyard planted 1,400 feet above Sonoma Valley) is a blend of 85% Zinfandel, 8% Petite Sirah, and 7% unidentified field varietals. At 14.6% alcohol, it is no wimpish wine. Provocative notes of road tar, deep, concentrated, ripe black fruits, licorice, and spice are followed by a rich, full-bodied, deep wine with low acidity as well as supple tannin. This multidimensional Zinfandel cascades over the palate with no hard edges. Drink this dazzling 1999 over its first 5–6 years of life, although I suspect it will age well for a decade. The 1999 Zinfandel Samsel Vineyard Maggie's Reserve (a whopping 15.2% alcohol) includes 5% Alicante Bouchet in the blend. Planted in 1901, this vineyard celebrated its 100th birthday in 2001. The dense ruby/purple-colored 1999 offers jammy, sweet kirsch, pepper, spice, and blackberry aromas. The wine's high alcohol provides plenty of glycerin as well as a full-bodied, voluptuous feel in the mouth. There is admirable purity, fine balance, and a multilayered, super-concentrated finish. This is one of the finest Samsel Vineyard Zinfandels Rosenblum has produced. Enjoy it over the next 5–7 years.

An excellent portfolio from the veterinarian turned Zinfandel specialist, Rosenblum's 1998s reveal great color, ripe fruit, thick, juicy textures, and mature flavors. From the San Francisco Bay area, the 1998 Zinfandel Carla's Vineyards reveals the vintage's low acidity as well as attractive, ripe, black cherry and berry fruit, all presented in a medium- to full-bodied, delicious style. It can be drunk over the next 2–3 years. The structured, dark ruby/purple-colored 1998 Zinfandel Alegria Vineyard offers peppery notes in its sweet, herb-tinged, black cherry, and plum-like fruit. Medium- to full-bodied, with a plush texture, low acidity, and fine intensity, it should drink well for 5–6 years. The outstanding, opaque ruby/purple-colored 1998 Zinfandel Lyons Vineyard is an opulent, voluptuously textured offering with copious quantities of superripe blackberry and cherry fruit, spice, a juicy, succulent texture, low acidity, and a terrific, glycerin-imbued, dense finish. It should drink well for 7–8 years. Another winner from Rosenblum, the 1998 Zinfandel Continente Vineyard exhibits a dense, plum/purple color in addition to aromas of jammy black fruits, earth, and pepper. Thick and juicy, with a fleshy, opulent texture, low acidity, and luxurious levels of plum, cherry, and raspberry fruit, this fat Zinfandel has immense appeal. Drink it over the next 2–3 years for its exuberance and vigor. The 1998 Zinfandel Cullinane Vineyard is potentially outstanding. An opaque purple color is accompanied by a medium- to full-bodied wine displaying aromas of melted road tar and leather, heady, high alcohol, and evidence of ripe fruit. This full-throttle, chewy Zinfandel with late-harvest characteristics is reminiscent of an Italian Amarone. Enjoy this dense, mouth-filling Zinfandel over the next 6–8 years. It may be controversial given its Amarone-like personality. Perhaps the finest (for my palate) of this portfolio is the 1998 Zinfandel St. Peter's Church Vineyard. A dazzling fragrance of minerals, black fruits, and smoky oak soars from the glass of this intense, powerful, concentrated yet beautifully balanced wine. Multilayered, with terrific fruit purity and intensity, exceptional opulence, and a long, juicy finish, it can be consumed over the next 5–7 years. From the Alexander Valley, the 1998 Zinfandel Harris Kratka Vineyard exhibits a peppery, Côtes du Rhône–like nose, with scents of dried Provençal herbs, sour black cherries, and earth. Medium- to full-bodied and spicy, with fine ripeness, this chewy Zin can be drunk now as well as over the next 5–6 years. From Paso Robles, the 1998 Zinfandel Richard Sauret Vineyard (14.7% alcohol) reveals low acidity, big, full-bodied, concentrated flavors, abundant quantities of earthy, black cherry, raspberry, and plum-like fruit, admirable purity, and a low-acid, fleshy finish. Drink it over the next 6–7 years. Made in a more elegant style, Rosenblum's 1998 Zinfandel Rockpile Vineyard tips the scales at 14.2% alcohol. It exhibits attractive berry, mineral-like characteristics, excellent purity, fine ripeness, and sweet, medium-bodied, stylish, clean flavors. Drink it over the next 3–4 years. Lastly, the 1998 Zinfandel Samsel Vineyard Maggie's Reserve is even lower in alcohol at 13.9%. The wine's dark ruby color is followed by attractive briery, strawberry, and black cherry fruit, soft, medium-bodied flavors, some pepper and wood notes, but the emphasis is on the fruit as well as overall balance and suppleness. Drink it over the next 4–5 years. All things considered, this is a highly successful group of wines that display more ripeness, fruit, and pleasure than their 1997 counterparts.

The question that comes to my mind is, is it really necessary to vineyard-designate all of these Zinfandels? While there are subtle differences, do such minor variations on a theme justify such an extensive portfolio? More important is the quality of Rosenblum's 1997s. Overall, they seem to be a notch below other recent vintages, with narrower textures and the vintage's screechingly high acidity all too obvious. Moreover, few are as well endowed with fruit and concentration as previous efforts. Nevertheless, these are a few excellent Zinfandels. I enjoyed the 1997 Zinfandel Annette's Reserve Rhodes Vineyard. It displays a Rhône-like, dried herb, peppery, earthy, dark plum character, fleshy, tasty, medium-bodied flavors, a soft mid-palate, and spicy oak in the finish. It is one of Rosenblum's stars of the vintage. It should be drunk over the next 1–2 years. Among the deepest-colored of the 1997 Zinfandels is the 1997 Zinfandel Cullinane Vineyard. It reveals ripe black cherry fruit mixed with obvious toasty new oak. It is among the densest, medium- to full-bodied, powerful wines with very good ripeness and richness, and attractive rather than intrusive acid levels. It should drink well for 2–3 years. The saturated ruby/purple-colored, exotic 1997 Zinfandel Lyons Vineyard possesses layers of glycerin, black cherry and raspberry fruit, new oak, pepper, and spice. This is probably the richest offering in Rosenblum's 1997 portfolio. Drink it over the next 3–4 years. Nearly outstanding is the 1997 Zinfandel Rockpile Road Vineyard. One of the most alcoholic wines in the Rosenblum portfolio (14.9%), it displays excellent purity, loads of blackberry and cherry fruit, a soft, nicely textured, open-knit, expansive texture, medium to full body, and an excellent finish. It is a beautifully made Zinfandel.

ERIC ROSS (RUSSIAN RIVER)

1998 Zinfandel Occidental Vineyard	Sonoma Coast	D	89
1997 Zinfandel Occidental Vineyard Old Vines	Russian River	D	91

Not yet bottled, the dense ruby/purple-colored 1998 Zinfandel Occidental Vineyard reveals abundant quantities of high-quality, spicy new oak, chewy, exotic, allspice, black raspberry, cherry, blackberry aromas and flavors, full body, outstanding density and purity, and a rich, multilayered, concentrated finish. Super-extracted and built for the long haul (as Zinfandels go), it will benefit from 1–2 years of cellaring and keep for 10–12 years. It is a seriously concentrated, impressively endowed Zinfandel. The Bordeaux-styled 1997 Zinfandel Occidental Vineyard Old Vines spent 18 months in American oak casks. It boasts a black/purple color, sumptuous aromas of black fruits, toast, and spice. Built along the lines of a Cabernet Sauvignon, there is superb richness and concentration in this tightly wound Zin. Full-bodied, gloriously pure. and concentrated, this atypical Zinfandel possesses zesty underlying acidity. Surprisingly, it requires 1–2 years of cellaring and should drink well over the following decade. It may even last longer.

RUDD ESTATE (OAKVILLE)

1999 Jericho Canyon Vineyard Proprietary Red Wine	Napa	EE	95
1998 Jericho Canyon Vineyard Proprietary Red Wine	Napa	EE	93
1998 Rudd Estate	Oakville/Napa	E	89
1998 Rudd Estate Rudd Jericho Canyon	Oakville/Napa	E	90

This winery, formerly known as Girard, was purchased in 1996 by Leslie Rudd, current owner of the Dean & DeLuca chain of luxury grocery stores and wine shops. It has become one of Napa's showcase properties. Lamentably, we are still a year away from the release of several sensational red wines that have aged fabulously well since I first tasted them in 1999.

Stunned by the performances of the 1998 and 1999 Jericho Canyon Vineyard proprietary red wines, I obviously underrated them earlier. The unfiltered/unfined 1998 Jericho Canyon Vineyard (2,850 cases) spent 16 months in French oak. A sensational effort, it is one of the stars of this challenging vintage. The opaque black/plum color is accompanied by aromas and flavors reminiscent of a blend of Cheval Blanc and La Mission-Haut-Brion from an overripe vintage. Notes of plums, cassis, blackberries, espresso, Asian spices, licorice, cedar, and tapenade make an appearance in both the aromas and flavors. Extremely full-bodied, with sweet tannin, an opulent/voluptuous texture, brilliant purity, and low acidity, this wine represents a synthesis in style between an exotic Right Bank Bordeaux and a California Cabernet. Having achieved 14.2% alcohol naturally, it is a blend of 79% Cabernet Sauvignon, 11% Merlot, and 10% Cabernet Franc from a vineyard in northern Napa Valley (the Rudd estate vineyards have not yet come into production). Exhibiting a similar opaque black/purple color, the 1999 Jericho Canyon Vineyard boasts a superb perfume of charcoal, creosote, blackberry liqueur, espresso, dried Provençal herbs, licorice, and minerals. Smoke from the toasty new oak also emerges. A superbly dense, full-bodied, exquisite effort, it is a blockbuster, yet incredibly harmonious. Both of these wines are winemaking tour de forces. One can only imagine when the 45 acres of estate vineyards planted with 50% Cabernet Sauvignon, 40% Merlot, 6% Cabernet Franc, and 4% Petit Verdot come into production what might be achieved, since this vineyard's neighbors include such luminary sites as Phelps's Backus Vineyard, Dalla Valle, Screaming Eagle, Venge Family Reserve, Plumpjack, and Opus One. The dark ruby-colored 1998 Rudd Estate Napa Valley (approximately 80% Cabernet Sauvignon, 10% Cabernet Franc, and 10% Merlot) exhibits smoky cassis aromas, an elegant, sweet attack, moderate tannin, and a rich, nicely textured, stylish, graceful finish. Although not a blockbuster, it is a harmonious effort ideal for drinking during its first 12–15 years of life. There are 3,500 cases of the opaque purple-colored, outstanding 1998 Rudd Estate Rudd Jericho Canyon. It displays a sweet blackberry and cassis-scented nose with nicely integrated toasty oak. As the wine sat in the glass, aromas of licorice, dried herbs, and minerals emerged. Deep and classy, with sweet tannin, medium to full body, and excellent harmony, this is an outstanding effort in a difficult vintage.

SADDLEBACK CELLARS (NAPA)

1998 Cabernet Sauvignon	Napa	D	88
1997 Cabernet Sauvignon	Napa	D	90
1996 Cabernet Sauvignon Estate	Napa	C	89
1995 Cabernet Sauvignon Estate	Napa	C	90
1994 Cabernet Sauvignon Estate	Napa	C	90
1998 Venge Family Reserve Cabernet Sauvignon	Oakville	EE	90
1997 Venge Family Reserve Cabernet Sauvignon	Oakville	EE	97
1996 Venge Family Reserve Cabernet Sauvignon	Oakville	EE	96
1995 Venge Family Reserve Cabernet Sauvignon	Oakville	D	95

1994 Venge Family Reserve Cabernet Sauvignon	Oakville	D	95
1997 Venge Family Reserve Merlot	Oakville	D	90
1996 Venge Family Reserve Merlot	Oakville	D	90
1995 Venge Family Reserve Merlot	Oakville	D	91
1994 Venge Family Reserve Merlot	Oakville	D	90
1996 Venge Family Reserve Sangiovese Penny Lane Vineyard	Oakville	C	90
1998 Venge Family Reserve Scout's Honor	Oakville	D	90
1997 Venge Family Reserve Scout's Honor	Oakville	C	90
1996 Venge Family Reserve Scout's Honor	Oakville	C	89
1999 Zinfandel Old Vines	Napa	D	90
1998 Zinfandel Old Vines	Napa	D	89

At this all-American winery for sure, wine-maker/owner Nils Venge makes bold, in-your-face, 100% pure California-styled wines that make no pretension about being French, Italian, or some innocuous international and/or dull Euro blend. In short, these wines are what they are—full-flavored and, in the case of his topflight Cabernet Sauvignons, remarkably long-lived. Venge has an impressive résumé of turning out some of the finest Napa Cabernets of the last three decades (e.g., 1974, 1976, 1978 Villa Mt. Eden Cabernet Sauvignons, and the 1984 and 1985 Groth Reserve Cabernet Sauvignons).

Saddleback Cellars' 1998 Cabernet Sauvignon (40% new American oak was utilized) is a relatively fleshy wine, with deep black cherry and currant flavors intermixed with creosote, toast, and cherries. Chunky and muscular for a 1998, it will drink well for 7–10 years.

The Saddleback Cellars wines are the first tier of Nils Venge's offerings and represent very good values. His top-of-the-line wines are all designated as Venge Family Reserve. Consistently his finest efforts, they are made in relatively limited quantities of 300–500 cases. These wines all possess bold, ripe flavors, and obvious toasty oak. They symbolize a flamboyant, intense style of winemaking. An outstanding effort in nearly every vintage (particularly impressive in 1988) is the Venge Family Reserve Scout's Honor. There are 450 cases of the 1998, a blend of 85% Zinfandel and 15% Charbono aged in American oak. The color is a dense ruby/purple, and the wine brashly displays new oak, along with blackberry, cherry, and raspberry notes. Smoky, toasty, rich, full-bodied, and supple-textured, it will drink well over the next 4–5 years. One of the most compelling Cabernet Sauvignons Venge has produced (and there have been many over the last 30 years) is his 1997 Venge Family Reserve Cabernet Sauvignon. Sadly, there are only 300 cases of this 100% new oak–aged effort. Tipping the scales at 14+% alcohol, it is a super-extracted, black/purple-colored effort displaying a gorgeous nose of crème de cassis intermixed with licorice, spice box, cedar, and smoke. Huge layers of glycerin, fat, and fruit from this formidable effort caress the palate. The wine has marvelous balance for its size as well as a long, impressive finish. While there is tannin to be shed, it is still primary, so 4–6 years of cellaring is suggested. It will keep for 25–30 years! For the first time, Venge has turned out a 1997 Venge Family Reserve Merlot from Oakville. Like the Cabernet Sauvignon, this wine spends 30 months in primarily new oak (75% in the case of the Merlot). There are 300 cases. Big, robust, intense, sweet vanilla, chocolate, and licorice aromas, along with thick, juicy black cherry and currant flavors are apparent in this full-bodied, powerful, supple wine. It should drink well for 15–16 years, atypically long for Merlot. Lastly, the 1998 Venge Family Reserve Cabernet Sauvignon may merit an outstanding score. While it does not possess the stature, mass, volume, and length of the 1997 or 1996, it is a full-bodied, typically Venge offering with copious quantities of toasty new oak, black currant fruit, spice box, licorice, and vanilla. It should drink well when released and last for 12–15 years.

As massive as Saddleback Cellars' red wines can be, they stand the test of time, as evidenced by some of Venge's classics that still remain in my cellar (the 1974 and 1978 Villa

Mt. Eden, and the 1985 Groth Reserve). The thrilling levels of viscously textured fruit in the 1995 Cabernet Sauvignon Estate will impress most Cabernet fans. Still backward and unevolved, it offers juicy, jammy black fruits intermixed with toast. A huge, dense, chewy wine, with a plethora of fruit and glycerin, it should be cellared for 3–4 more years and consumed over the following 10–15. The similarly styled 1996 Cabernet Sauvignon Estate is chewy, full-bodied, and thick. Not yet complex, it is super-concentrated, with gobs of toasty oak (about 40% American oak is utilized in the wine's upbringing), and a low-acid, chunky, heavyweight style. If the 1996 develops more complexity, it will merit a score in the low 90s. Anticipated maturity: now–2015. While the 1998 Cabernet Sauvignon appears to be a good, 88-point effort, it is the 1997 Cabernet Sauvignon that will excite readers. There are 2,000 cases of this potentially outstanding effort. Aged in 60% French and 40% American oak, it is a typical Venge Cabernet Sauvignon, exhibiting an opaque ruby/purple color in addition to almost overripe jammy scents of blackberries, cassis, and prominent wood. Low acidity, in addition to terrific fatness and purity, make this a hedonistically styled Cabernet that will improve for 5–10 years and last for 15 or more.

The 1994 Cabernet Sauvignon Estate is reminiscent of the Groth Cabernets produced in the mid-1980s. The wine exhibits plenty of chocolaty, cassis fruit, a nice touch of toasty oak, a thick, chewy texture, and mouth-filling extract and richness. The tannin is obscured by the wine's ripe fruit. The 1994 should drink well for 12–15 years.

Nils Venge's glories are his red wines, as he has the Midas touch when it comes to turning out full-flavored, gorgeously textured, seductive reds. The outstanding, deep ruby-colored 1997 Venge Family Reserve Scout's Honor (a blend of 85% Zinfandel and 15% Charbono) possesses power (14.5% alcohol) along with gorgeous, sexy, seductive notions of cherries, strawberries, and briery, peppery fruit. Deep, fleshy, and heady, this is a hedonistic fruit bomb to enjoy over the next 2–3 years.

The 1996 Venge Family Reserve Cabernet Sauvignon (only 280 cases) is a dazzling effort. It possesses over 14% alcohol and is highly extracted as well as wooded, as it was aged in 100% new French oak. Exceptionally dense, it offers formidable quantities of black fruits, smoky oak, and licorice, awesome purity, and layers of extract. The finish exceeds 30 seconds. My best guess for this unevolved, backward Cabernet is that it will require 3–5 years of cellaring, but will last for 2–3 decades. It is a remarkably intense, hugely concentrated wine exhibiting the telltale Venge style of viscous cassis/blackberry fruit crammed into a flamboyantly oaked, powerhouse, ageworthy personality. Another fabulous wine I tasted was the 1994 Venge Family Reserve Cabernet Sauvignon. An exquisite Cabernet aged for 18 months in oak casks (about 70% of which were new), it boasts an opaque black/purple color and a nose of cassis, prunes, smoke, licorice, and earth. Exceptionally full-bodied with jammy flavors, low acidity, and awesome levels of glycerin, extract, and fruit, this is a wild, unrestrained, super-concentrated Cabernet that should become increasingly civilized as it ages effortlessly over the next 15–20 years. The superb 1994 Venge Family Reserve Cabernet Sauvignon may well be matched in quality by the spectacular 1995 Venge Family Reserve Cabernet Sauvignon. Its opaque purple color and nose of blackberries, cassis, licorice, coffee, and tar scents are outstanding. Concentrated, thick, and unctuous, with outstanding purity and layers of extract, this large-scaled, beautifully made, all-American-styled Cabernet approaches "bigger than life" status. Anticipated maturity: now–2020.

Nils Venge produces two Sangiovese *cuvées*. The 1996 Venge Family Reserve Sangiovese Penny Lane Vineyard (5% Cabernet Sauvignon is added to the blend) is one of California's finest. The fruit is picked very ripe (14% alcohol), and the wine is aged in Burgundy barrels. There is plenty of sweet, jammy strawberry/cherry/raspberry fruit in the nose, thick, juicy flavors, and soft tannin. Drink this offering over the next 3–4 years for its gutsy, exuberant style. The 1996 Venge Family Reserve Scout's Honor is a blend of 88% Zinfandel and 12% Sangiovese. (Château Montelena produces a similarly styled wine under the St. Vincent label.)

Aged in 100% American oak, this offering is spicy and toasty, with briery, black raspberry, peppery notes in its sweet, jammy fragrance. Full-bodied, hedonistic, and fun to drink, it should continue to offer immense pleasure for 2–4 years.

The outstanding 1996 Venge Family Reserve Merlot is a match for the fabulous 1994. The 1996 was made from Clone 7 and aged in 100% new French oak. By Venge standards the alcohol is relatively modest (13.5%) in this full-bodied, chewy, thick, highly extracted Merlot, which also possesses toasty, chocolaty, cherry-like flavors. Viscous and succulent, it is impossible to resist. This wine should be drinkable upon release and last for 12–15 years. Readers weaned on sterile, insipid, wimpish Merlots will need to have their palates recalibrated after tasting this blockbuster. As a critic of the insipid, vegetal, often appallingly overpriced Merlots that inundate the marketplace, I found it a pleasure to taste the real thing. Venge has produced a number of terrific wines that will please both Merlot and Cabernet Sauvignon lovers. The first Merlot I tasted from Venge was the 1994 Venge Family Reserve Merlot, a wine aged 18 months in 100% new-oak casks. Unfortunately, only 120 cases were made of this lusty, decadent, chewy, intensely flavored Merlot. Gobs of smoke, vanilla-tinged, black cherry, and chocolaty flavors tumble out of a glass of this mouth-filling, creamy-textured wine. Full-bodied, powerful, and dense, it will drink exceptionally well young, but last for 12–15 years. I suspect anyone not on the winery's mailing list will have little chance of tracking down a bottle or two. The 1995 Venge Family Reserve Merlot has also been aged in 100% new oak, but it is so extraordinarily extracted and rich that the oak plays only a minor role in the wine's aromatics and flavors. There are only 200 cases of this thick, black/purple-colored wine. The acidity is low, and the flavor and concentration extraordinarily high. This is a blockbuster, full-bodied, super-concentrated Merlot with a viscous personality and sensational extract. A pure, full-blooded heavyweight, it is even more impressive than the 1994 and will drink well for 15 or more years.

Nils Venge produces Zinfandel with unbridled power and richness. Some critics suggest it is over the top, but I suspect they would have said the same thing about the 1947 Cheval Blanc or 1947 Pétrus if they had tasted those wines at a young age. That being said, readers looking for wimpish, subtle, innocuous wines (this is usually referred to as "elegance") are advised to keep their distance. A classic offering from Venge, Saddleback Cellars' 1999 Zinfandel Old Vines offers explosive aromas of prunes, jammy black fruits, licorice, spice box, and smoky, toasty new oak. Opulent, viscous, and full-bodied, this blockbuster effort is typically over the top, layered, and super-concentrated, but oh so much fun to drink, and isn't that what wine is all about? Anti-elitists should rejoice in this tasty, juicy, succulent, hedonistic Zinfandel. Enjoy it over the next 4–6 years. Venge has fashioned an opaque purple-colored 1998 Zinfandel Old Vines revealing a late-harvest, nearly overripe tar, asphalt, jammy blackberry, prune-like character. Full-bodied, chewy, and viscous, with powerful, concentrated, muscular, black fruit and American oak flavors, this firm yet heavyweight Zin can be drunk now as well as over the next 7–8 years.

Past Glories: 1993 Cabernet Sauvignon Estate (90), 1993 Venge Family Reserve Cabernet Sauvignon (90)

ST. FRANCIS WINERY (SONOMA)

1997	Cabernet Franc Reserve McCoy Vineyard	Sonoma	D	91
1996	Cabernet Franc Reserve McCoy Vineyard	Sonoma	D	89
1998	Cabernet Sauvignon Reserve	Sonoma	E	87
1997	Cabernet Sauvignon Reserve	Sonoma	D	90
1995	Cabernet Sauvignon Reserve	Sonoma	D	89+
1994	Cabernet Sauvignon Reserve	Sonoma	D	91
1998	Cabernet Sauvignon Reserve King's Ridge Vineyard	Sonoma	EE	91

1997 Cabernet Sauvignon Reserve King's Ridge Vineyard	Sonoma	EE	92
1996 Cabernet Sauvignon Reserve King's Ridge Vineyard	Sonoma	EE	91
1994 Cabernet Sauvignon Reserve King's Ridge Vineyard	Sonoma	EE	92
1997 Merlot Reserve	Sonoma	D	89
1994 Merlot Reserve	Sonoma	D	90
1998 Merlot Reserve Nun's Canyon Vineyard	Sonoma	D	88
1997 Merlot Reserve Nun's Canyon Vineyard	Sonoma	D	90
1999 Petite Sirah Bartolozzi Ranch	Sonoma	D	89
1999 Zinfandel Old Vines	Sonoma	D	88
1998 Zinfandel Old Vines	Sonoma	D	88
1994 Zinfandel Old Vines	Sonoma	C	93
1999 Zinfandel Pagani Vineyard	Sonoma	D	89
1998 Zinfandel Pagani Vineyard	Sonoma	D	90
1997 Zinfandel Pagani Vineyard	Sonoma	D	88
1996 Zinfandel Pagani Vineyard	Sonoma	D	89
1995 Zinfandel Pagani Vineyard	Sonoma	C	90
1994 Zinfandel Pagani Vineyard	Sonoma	C	92

St. Francis has grown by five-fold in the last 10 years and is now producing 250,000 cases of wine from their large, high-tech facility south of Santa Rosa. Partially owned by the well-known American importer Kobrand Corporation, it has 550 acres of vineyards. Longtime wine-maker Tom Mackey seems to have everything under control. Five years ago St. Francis served notice to the wine world that they would no longer risk the damaging aromas of moldy corks and began utilizing synthetic corks. The jury is still out on these corks, but they are made with the same material used in artificial heart valves and have proven to be effective in eliminating the moldy aromas that taint approximately 3–5% of bottled wine. How well they will hold up under prolonged cellaring of big, tannic, alcoholic wines remains to be seen.

For the most part, St. Francis's offerings reflect a moderate pricing policy, although they have several *cuvées* priced in triple digits. Most of their wine range from $15–40, which qualifies them as reasonably good values in California's surreal La-La Land of prices. All of St. Francis's red wines are bottled without filtration. They are boldly styled, oaky, rich, concentrated efforts. There are 6,500 cases of the 1997 Merlot Reserve (100% Merlot aged in equal parts French and American oak). It exhibits aromas and flavors of coffee, mocha, cola, black cherry, and currant fruit presented in a sexy, full-bodied, nearly overripe style. This seductive Merlot is best drunk over the next 5–6 years. The Nun's Canyon Vineyard is a steep hillside parcel planted near the Fisher winery. The 1997 Merlot Reserve Nun's Canyon Vineyard is a 100% Merlot aged in French oak. There are only 2,000 cases of this dense, structured, tannic, and more ambitious effort. Full-bodied and rich, with smoky blackberries and cherries intermixed with soil notes, this thick, juicy, well-structured wine will benefit from 2–3 years of cellaring and keep for 12–15. The 1998 Merlot Reserve Nun's Canyon Vineyard displays a Bordeaux-like herbaceousness to its medium-bodied, lightly tannic, modestly endowed flavors. While very good, it is dwarfed by the 1997. Anticipated maturity: now–2009.

There are 400–500 cases of St. Francis's 100% Cabernet Franc, which is picked at high sugars and then fermented in French oak. The dense ruby/purple-colored 1996 Cabernet Franc Reserve McCoy Vineyard offers an excellent bouquet of spice box, cedar, camphor, black cherry, and cassis aromas. While not huge on the palate, it is rich and medium- to full-bodied, with admirable texture as well as sweet, concentrated fruit. Anticipated maturity: now–2012. The superb 1997 Cabernet Franc Reserve McCoy Vineyard was picked extremely ripe (the alcohol level is a well-hidden 15.5%). It reveals aromas and flavors of blueberry liqueur, black currants, smoke, and liquid minerals. Full-bodied, dense, and chewy, as well as elegant and precise, it can be drunk early, but promises to evolve for 15+ years.

With the inflated prices of California wines, readers should be checking out St. Francis's 6,000-case 100% Cabernet Sauvignon aged in equal parts French and American oak. The 1997 Cabernet Sauvignon Reserve (almost totally from the Nun's Canyon Vineyard) is reasonably priced for a wine of such high quality. An opaque purple color is accompanied by a big, bold, spicy, oaky nose infused with licorice, coffee, and abundant quantities of blackberry and cassis fruit. Full-bodied, rich, and impressive, with sweet tannin as well as abundant wood, it will drink well for the next 15 years. The 1998 Cabernet Sauvignon Reserve shows smoky black fruits, less weight and richness, and big tannin, but looks to be successful for the vintage.

St. Francis's most expensive offerings are their King's Ridge Cabernet Sauvignons from the Sonoma Coast. They exploit eight acres of 100% Cabernet Sauvignon usually picked extremely ripe and late, with the harvest sometimes taking place in November. The 1996 Cabernet Sauvignon Reserve King's Ridge Vineyard is aged in 100% new French oak. There are 600 cases of this serious Cabernet. It boasts a dense purple color in addition to aromas and flavors of minerals, crème de cassis, smoke, and toast. Full-bodied and powerful, with moderately high tannin and a long, concentrated finish, it should benefit from 2–3 years of cellaring and last for two decades (assuming the synthetic cork works as well as they say). Even richer, the 1997 Cabernet Sauvignon Reserve King's Ridge Vineyard (900 cases; 14.4% alcohol) boasts a saturated color as well as a gorgeous bouquet of black fruits intermixed with smoke, minerals, licorice, and tobacco. An unctuous texture, huge body, and moderately high tannin suggest this formidably endowed wine has at least 20–25 years of potential cellaring. Because of the sweeter fruit, it is slightly more accessible than the 1996. The 1998 Cabernet Sauvignon Reserve King's Ridge Vineyard is outstanding in this inconsistent vintage. Black/purple-colored, it offers rich, concentrated flavors, full body, a thick texture, and a long, sweet finish. Wine-maker Tom Mackey, who arrived for my tasting on his custom purple Harley-Davidson, said it takes at least a half day, even on his fast bike, to reach the vineyard, which he said might be the westernmost vineyard in the United States.

Warning! The 1995 Cabernet Sauvignon Reserve is exceptionally oaky, so readers who do not want a blatant dosage of toasty smoke in their wines should avoid it. It supports the wood, even though it is lavishly oaked. The color is a dense ruby/purple. In addition to the wood, the wine reveals creamy blackberry and cassis flavors intermixed with smoke and licorice. Thick, rich, and medium- to full-bodied, with low acidity, this garish, ostentatiously styled Cabernet can be drunk now, but promises to be slightly more civilized with more bottle age. Anticipated maturity: now–2014. The 1994 Merlot Estate Reserve exhibits a saturated dark ruby color, followed by intensely smoky, oaky, jammy black cherry and chocolate aromas and flavors. This full-bodied, chewy, fleshy, soft, opulently styled wine should drink well for 7–8 years. Another outstanding effort from St. Francis is the 1994 Cabernet Sauvignon Reserve. It exhibits an opaque purple color, followed by a big, gaudy, ostentatious nose of cedar, Asian spices, jammy black fruits, prunes, and toasty new oak. This intense, ripe, full-bodied wine possesses explosive richness, lavish toasty notes, low acidity, and a heady, lusty, super-long finish. Yes, the new oak is high, but so is the wine's extract and fruit concentration. This is a Cabernet to be drunk with the stereo at high volume. As massive and rich as it is now, it should become more civilized with 3–5 years of cellaring. Anticipated maturity: now–2015. Even more impressive is St. Francis's 1994 Cabernet Sauvignon King's Ridge Vineyard. This wine, with its opaque purple color and strikingly compelling nose of licorice, tobacco leaf, cassis, and smoke, is a full-bodied, heavyweight Cabernet with layers of flavor, a boatload of glycerin and extract, and copious quantities of sweet tannin in the monster finish. It is a dense, super-concentrated wine that should have heads turning in amazement. Anticipated maturity: now–2020.

St. Francis is making monster, pedal-to-the-metal, full-throttle Zinfandels that are likely to score last in terms of subtlety, but who can ignore these opulent, lavishly rich, thrilling wines? I am not sure I could sit down and knock off a bottle of either of these wines, but a glass or two sure is enjoyable. These flamboyant, ostentatious Zinfandels succeed in pushing richness and new oak to the limit. If actors Robin Williams and Jim Carrey were wine-makers, is this the type of Zinfandel they would produce? The 1994 Zinfandel Old Vines screams from the glass, in a reassuring rather than frightening manner. The wine boasts an opaque purple color, followed by a phenomenal nose of overripe black cherries and raspberries doused with high quantities of sweet, toasty, smoky oak, with plenty of licorice and pepper in the background. Superbly rich, smoky, hedonistic, and decadent, this wine is supple and velvety . . . like eating your favorite candy in liquid form (with plenty of alcohol). This spectacular blockbuster will last for 7–8 years, but it is best drunk in its first 4–5 years to take full advantage of its exuberance. The 1994 Zinfandel Pagani Ranch is cut from the same mold, with more structure and alcohol. It, too, is fabulously opulent and rich, with the same unctuous texture, thickness, and density of fruit as the Old Vine cuvée. These are amazing Zinfandels. There are other 1994 Zinfandels that are just as rich and full-bodied, but there are none as ostentatious as this duo. Tipping the scales at 15.1% alcohol, it is amazing how well the strength of the 1995 Zinfandel Reserve Pagani Vineyard is hidden behind its layers of chewy, massively extracted, thick Zinfandel fruit. It boasts a saturated black/purple color, and a big, sweet nose of licorice, earth, vanilla, and raisiny black plums. Lush, full-bodied, and huge, with exceptional concentration, this Zin is sure to turn heads. Readers should not consider buying a bottle unless they enjoy mouth-staining, teeth-coating, full-bodied, behemoth Zinfandels. This wine should age well for at least a decade.

The dark ruby/purple-colored 1996 Zinfandel Reserve Pagani Vineyard (from 100-year-old vines) offers plenty of smoky, toasty new-oak aromas along with jammy blackberry and raspberry, tar, licorice, and pepper notes. Although powerful, rich, and full-bodied, it is not as concentrated as preceding vintages. While it is among the most fruit-driven and glycerin-endowed wines of the vintage, it falls just short of being outstanding. Drink it over the next 3–4 years. The relatively heavy-handed 1997 Zinfandel Pagani Vineyard behaves more like a barrel sample than a finished wine. While it possesses high alcohol, this inky wine also displays viscous, oaky, super-extracted flavors. From its opaque purple color, tasters can glean black raspberries, plums, licorice, Asian spice, and toasty notes. It is whoppingly big, chewy, and powerful. Look for this wine to evolve and continue to drink well (perhaps become even more civilized) over the next 5–7 years. As in the past, St. Francis has produced mammoth, super-concentrated, lavishly wooded 1998s. The deep ruby/purple-colored 1998 Zinfandel Old Vines exhibits a big, sweet, toasty oak-scented nose with abundant quantities of black cherry and berry fruit. Muscular, full-bodied, deep, and low in acidity, it is a plump, mouth-filling, chewy Zinfandel for drinking over the next 3–4 years. The outstanding, opaque purple-colored 1998 Zinfandel Pagani Vineyard is once again luxuriously oaked. This super-extracted, intense, unctuously textured Zin is among the most concentrated wines of the vintage. The high level of wood adds an exotic, almost over-the-top aspect to the wine's style. Thick and jammy, with copious quantities of black raspberry, cherry, and blackberry fruit, this huge effort should drink well for 5–6 years.

The 1999 Old Vines and Pagani Vineyard are typical St. Francis Zinfandels . . . dark ruby/purple-colored with tons of toasty American oak as well as jammy ripe blackberry and cherry flavors infused with licorice, herbs, and smoke. Both are full-bodied, low-acid, decadently fruited and wooded wines with unmistakable "made in California" personalities. Both should be drunk in their exuberant, robust youth . . . over the next 3–4 years.

Readers who enjoy muscular, peppery, earthy, black fruit–filled, excruciatingly tannic Petite Sirah should check out the 1999 Petite Sirah Bartolozzi Ranch (400 cases). Although impressive, it needs 5–10 years of cellaring before it becomes civilized, but it will handsomely repay those who have the discipline and intelligence to hide this beast in the cellar.

CHÂTEAU ST. JEAN (SONOMA)

1997	Cabernet Franc St. Jean Estate	Sonoma	D	90
1996	Cabernet Franc St. Jean Estate	Sonoma	D	91
1997	Cabernet Sauvignon Reserve	Sonoma	E	93
1996	Cabernet Sauvignon Reserve	Sonoma	E	94
1995	Cabernet Sauvignon Reserve	Sonoma	E	90
1994	Cabernet Sauvignon Reserve	Sonoma	E	92
1999	Chardonnay	Sonoma	B	88
1998	Cinq Cépages Proprietary Red Wine	Sonoma	D	89
1997	Cinq Cépages Proprietary Red Wine	Sonoma	D	94
1996	Cinq Cépages Proprietary Red Wine	Sonoma	D	92
1995	Cinq Cépages Proprietary Red Wine	Sonoma	D	92
1999	Fumé Blanc	Sonoma	B	88
1999	Fumé Blanc La Petite Etoile	Russian River	C	90
1997	Malbec St. Jean Estate Vineyard	Sonoma	D	92
1997	Merlot	Sonoma	C	88
1997	Merlot Reserve	Sonoma	E	92
1996	Merlot Reserve	Sonoma	E	90
1995	Merlot Reserve	Sonoma	E	90+
1994	Merlot Reserve	Sonoma	E	91
1997	Merlot St. Jean Estate Vineyard	Sonoma	D	91
1999	Pinot Noir	Sonoma	C	88
1998	Pinot Noir	Sonoma	C	88
1998	Pinot Noir Durell Vineyard	Carneros	D	89
1997	Pinot Noir Durell Vineyard	Carneros	D	88?
1996	Pinot Noir Durell Vineyard	Sonoma	D	88

Château St. Jean, one of the picture-postcard photogenic sites in Sonoma Valley, is making the best wines of its history. This winery has made a 180-degree-turn from the highly sculptured, excessively manipulated, industrial mind-set of the seventies and eighties. Today, St. Jean's winemaking is based on a philosophy of nonmanipulation and natural bottling. The results are obvious, with wines that possess more aromatics and creamier textures. Most important, they provide more pleasure. Wine-maker Steve Reeder continues to fine tune an impressive portfolio of character-filled wines. All of these offerings—from the glorious Fumé Blancs, structured, distinctive Chardonnays, increasingly high-quality Pinot Noirs, to their top-of-the-line Merlots, Cabernet Francs, Cabernet Sauvignon Reserves, and proprietary red called Cinq Cépages—are exciting.

A great value, the 1999 Fumé Blanc includes 11% Sémillon in the blend. Approximately 32% is barrel-fermented and the remainder is fermented in stainless steel. The wine does not see any malolactic, but is picked very ripe, which is obvious from the smoky, honeyed melon, passion fruit, and floral-scented bouquet. Medium-bodied, with gorgeous layers of fruit, it is meant to be consumed over the next 1–2 years. Even better is the exceptional 1999 Fumé Blanc La Petite Etoile. All barrel-fermented (50% new oak is used), it spends 10 months in wood prior to bottling and sees no malolactic. Wine-maker Steve Reeder says it smells like "white Gummi Bears." This powerful (15% alcohol) Fumé reveals a liquid minerality, smoky passion fruit, melon, and citrus in its bouquet and flavors. Structured, rich, and concentrated, this wine should be drunk with full-flavored food. It should last for several years.

Château St. Jean's Chardonnay program is also impressive. All of the wines are barrel-fermented, but there is no lees stirring, and the malolactic fermentation is often blocked. One of the best buys in the Chardonnay world is the 150,000 cases of 1999 Chardonnay. Exhibiting floral, tropical fruit, pear, and peach notes, it is a fruit-driven, beautifully balanced, pure white to enjoy during its first several years.

The Burgundian-styled Pinot Noirs emerging from Château St. Jean are somewhat of a secret, with everyone clamoring over the Chardonnays, Fumé Blancs, Cabernets, and Merlot-based wines. The 1999 Pinot Noir Sonoma exhibits an earthy, smoky, plum, and animal-scented bouquet, and good vegetable root notes in the smoke-infused, cherry flavors. Drink it over the next 3–4 years. The dark plum-colored 1998 Pinot Noir Durell Vineyard possesses more weight and density, in addition to full body, and copious quantities of black cherry fruit endowed with notions of roasted meats, herbs, and flowers. Drink this spicy, rich Pinot over the next 5–7 years. The 1998 Pinot Noir Sonoma was made from 100% destemmed fruit, most of which emerged from the Russian River's Westside Vineyard. A medium ruby color is followed by an attractive sweet, cherry, dried herb, and earthy-scented nose with scents of aged beef, spice, and plums. Complex, supple-textured, and easygoing, this wine should be drunk now and over the next 5–6 years. The 1997 Pinot Noir Durell Vineyard is made in a completely different style. Less charming, more tannic, backward, and restrained, it is a big, oaky, concentrated Pinot with plenty of muscle and structure. I liked it less than its sibling (although it does have more to it). Will it resolve all of its tannin? Give it 1–2 years of cellaring to see what emerges. The 1996 Pinot Noir Durell Vineyard reveals complexity and richness. This dark ruby-colored wine offers meaty, plant, and berry fruit aromas in an exotic, lush, medium- to full-bodied style. It possesses adequate acidity and a supple texture. Drink it over the next 3–4 years.

Château St. Jean's red wine program represents reasonably good value. They are producing attractive Merlots, Cabernet Sauvignons, and proprietary red wines. The 1997 Merlot St. Jean Estate Vineyard, which includes 10% Cabernet Franc in the blend, spent 24 months in new oak before bottling. This sensational, limited-production Merlot boasts a dense ruby/ purple color in addition to blackberry, charcoal, cherry, melted fudge, and new-oak aromas. Exceptionally ripe, full-bodied, and opulently textured, this is a mouth-filling Merlot to enjoy over the next 10–12 years. The dark garnet/plum-colored 1997 Merlot Reserve (87% Merlot, 9% Cabernet Franc, and 4% Malbec that spent three years in 100% new oak) reveals a dense, chewy, thick, viscous personality as well as enormously concentrated, black cherry, chocolate, vanilla, and berry fruit aromas and flavors. This powerful, full-bodied, spectacular Merlot still has some tannin to shed. Anticipated maturity: 2004–2020. The excellent 1997 Merlot Sonoma includes 6% Cabernet Sauvignon and 6% Cabernet Franc in the blend. It reveals copious quantities of berry fruit, roasted coffee, chocolate, and cherries. Open-knit and round, this dark ruby-colored, low-acid wine is ideal for drinking over the next 5–6 years. The 1996 Merlot Reserve is less easy to taste, but potentially a better Merlot. It offers subtle aromas of creosote, black cherries, dried herbs, and vanilla. In the mouth, toffee notes mix with sweet, creamy wood, chocolate, and berries. Medium- to full-bodied, closed, with moderate tannin in the finish, this Merlot requires 2–3 years of cellaring. It should keep for 12–15 years. The 1994 Merlot Reserve reveals copious quantities of chocolate-flavored, jammy black cherry fruit intertwined with lavish quantities of toasty new oak. It cuts a larger, more expansive feel on the palate and displays impressive length and richness. The 1995 Merlot Reserve exhibits less aromatic and flavor dimension when compared to the 1994, but it is still a superbly concentrated, thick, juicy wine that may end up having slightly more tannin. With more of a monolithic personality, it tastes slightly muted and more backward in its development than the other vintages. These Reserve Merlots are all made in limited quantities of about 400 cases.

Since 1995, the Cinq Cépages has been an outstanding effort. The dark ruby/purple-colored 1996 Cinq Cépages (75% Cabernet Sauvignon, and the balance Cabernet Franc,

Merlot, Malbec, and Petit Verdot) exhibits a moderately intense nose of black cherries, chocolate, smoke, dried herbs, and toasty oak. It appears to be California's version of a big, rich St.-Emilion. Offering elegance and finesse along with copious quantities of fruit, glycerin, and flavor, this medium- to full-bodied wine has evolved nicely, and can be drunk now as well as over the next 12–15 years. The 1995 Cinq Cépages is tasting even better than it was prior to bottling. The wine, which spends two years in 50% new-oak barrels, is dominated by Cabernet Sauvignon (77%), with the other four varietals making up this blend. The 1995 offers a combination of finesse, complexity, richness, and accessibility. It possesses a saturated ruby color and a flamboyant nose of cedar, licorice, tobacco-tinged black currant fruit, and sweet vanilla. Concentrated, full-bodied, and loaded with fruit, this high-quality, impressively endowed wine can be drunk now as well as over the next 15–20 years. The 1997 Cinq Cépages is even better than the 1996. A blend of 75% Cabernet Sauvignon and the balance Merlot, Malbec, Cabernet Franc, and Petit Verdot, it boasts a super-complex bouquet of licorice, dried herbs, black currants, spice box, and cherry liqueur. In the mouth, notes of chocolate, new oak, and red and black fruits caress the palate in a medium- to full-bodied, succulent style. Aged in 50% new and 50% one-year-old French barrels, it is also bottled with no fining or filtration. Fleshy and complex, and drinkable now, it promises to last for 12–15 years. Made in a lighter style, the medium-bodied 1998 Cinq Cépages (75% Cabernet Sauvignon, 16% Merlot, 6% Malbec, 2% Cabernet Franc, and 1% Petit Verdot) exhibits a sweet nose of toast, earth, cedar, licorice, black cherries, and chocolate. There is excellent concentration, but because of the vintage conditions, this wine does not possess the volume, breadth of flavor, or intensity of its two predecessors. Drink the 1998 during its first 10–12 years of life.

One of St. Jean's most spectacular offerings is their 1997 Cabernet Sauvignon Reserve. A blend of 90% Cabernet Sauvignon and 10% Cabernet Franc that spends 36 months in barrel prior to being bottled without fining and filtration, it is a beautifully fashioned, smoky, rich, super-concentrated, thick effort loaded with black cherry, cassis, earthy, smoky, toasty oak aromas and flavors as well as a full-bodied, unctuous finish. This Cabernet requires another 3–4 years of cellaring; it should keep for two decades. The 1996 Cabernet Sauvignon Reserve remains one of the finest wines yet produced by Steve Reeder. This offering, which spent 36 months in barrel prior to bottling, is primarily Cabernet Sauvignon, with a dollop of Merlot or Cabernet Franc added. Production is limited to 500 cases. The terrific 1996 boasts a saturated purple color, as well as a stunning bouquet of coconut, vanilla, black currants, plums, and smoke. Full-bodied, thick, yet nicely buttressed by adequate acidity, this juicy, thrillingly proportioned, large-scaled Cabernet Sauvignon will be at its finest after another year of bottle age; it will keep for two decades.

The 1994 Cabernet Sauvignon Reserve possesses an open-knit, complex aromatic profile consisting of black fruits, cedar, tobacco, fruitcake, and new oak. Full-bodied, with sweeter tannin than the 1993, this multidimensional, large-scaled Cabernet Sauvignon has impeccable balance, as well as a finish that lasts for nearly 35 seconds. Although it is already accessible, 3–4 years of cellaring is recommended; it should keep for two decades. The 1995 Cabernet Sauvignon Reserve exhibits less aromatic and flavor dimension, but superb depth, ripeness, and richness. As with many 1995s, there is a muted character to the wine, but my instincts suggest that all the right stuff is present to develop into an outstanding wine. Patience is required, as this wine will need at least 4–5 years of cellaring. It is another 20-year wine. No, I do not believe it will achieve the complexity and richness of the 1994, and perhaps not even the 1993, but it is an exceptional wine that could turn out to be a sleeper in 5–10 years.

Readers should also check out the 1996 Cabernet Franc St. Jean Estate. Only 300 cases were produced of this 90% Cabernet Franc, 5% Merlot, 5% Malbec blend. It reveals explosive aromas of violets, blueberries, leather, and black fruits. Dense and rich, with great finesse and complexity, this wine, aged in 100% new French oak, reveals gorgeous flavor concentration and authority, but no heaviness or thickness. An ethereal effort, it is a breakthrough Cabernet Franc for Château St. Jean. It will drink well young and evolve nicely for 10–12 years. Reeder's fabulous 1996 Cabernet Franc has been followed by another exquisite effort. The beautifully made 1997 Cabernet Franc St. Jean Estate has been blended with 10% Merlot and 5% Malbec. As with all of this estate's red wines, there was neither fining nor filtration prior to bottling. The 100% new-oak aging has been completely absorbed. Cabernet Franc is a more delicate wine than Merlot or Cabernet Sauvignon, and this effort has somehow handled the new wood. It is a complex, full-bodied, beautifully made effort with intense aromas of leather, black fruits, and flowers. Combining power and richness with finesse and complexity, it is an ethereal effort that should drink well for 15–18 years. It is undoubtedly the finest Cabernet Franc I have tasted from Sonoma. Another impressive offering is the 1997 Malbec St. Jean Estate Vineyard (a blend of 75% Malbec and 25% Cabernet Franc). Dick Arrowood has also produced fine Malbec, but this effort is no good. Notes of black raspberry liqueur intertwined with violet/acacia smells jump from the glass of this floral offering. A dark ruby/purple color is followed by a rich attack, although the wine is lighter in the mouth than the aromas suggest. It combines super fruit with elegance and character. It is hard to predict how a wine like this will age, but it should have no problem lasting for 10–15 years.

Kudos to wine-maker Steve Reeder and Beringer for what they have accomplished at Château St. Jean.

Past Glories: 1993 Cabernet Sauvignon Reserve (91), 1993 Merlot Reserve (90)

SCREAMING EAGLE (NAPA)

1999	Cabernet Sauvignon	Napa	EE	94
1998	Cabernet Sauvignon	Napa	EE	92
1997	Cabernet Sauvignon	Napa	EE	100
1996	Cabernet Sauvignon	Napa	EE	98
1995	Cabernet Sauvignon	Napa	EE	99
1994	Cabernet Sauvignon	Napa	EE	94

There are 500 cases of each vintage. As most readers know, this wine has become the ultimate collector's Cabernet Sauvignon, routinely fetching $800 to as much as $2,000 a bottle at wine auctions. Of course, this makes no sense to me or Screaming Eagle's owner, the amiable Jean Phillips, who sells the wine for $125 a bottle. Unquestionably an exquisite wine, it offers remarkably rich crème de cassis aromas and flavors in an unmanipulated, compelling fashion. The winemaking is assisted by well-known consultant Heidi Barrett. From the red, iron-rich soils of the Oakville district, the wines are aged in 65% new French oak for 18–20 months. I bestowed both the 1992 and 1997 Screaming Eagles perfect 100-point scores, but all the vintages have been as prodigious. The 1998 Cabernet Sauvignon, which was bottled in late June of 2000, has turned out even better than I thought when I tasted it from barrel. It boasts a saturated ruby/purple color in addition to an expressive bouquet of cassis, minerals, and smoke. Full-bodied and dense, it is more evolved than other vintages tasted at a similar age, a characteristic of 1998, which has produced less massive Napa Cabernet Sauvignons, with less volume and concentration. The multitextured, round 1998 Screaming Eagle exhibits sweet, well-integrated tannin, a great mid-palate and finish, as well as spectacular purity and palate presence. Consume it now and over the next 15–20 years. It is a candidate for the "wine of the vintage" in 1998. The 1999 Cabernet Sauvignon (a blend of 88% Cabernet Sauvignon, 10% Merlot, and 2% Cabernet Franc) is another exquisite effort that may fall just short of the otherworldly 1997 and 1992. An opaque blue/purple color is followed by a jammy blackberry and crème de cassis–scented bouquet of extraordinary precision and purity. It possesses awesome intensity, but manages not to taste overblown, overweight, or overdone. Thick and unctuously textured, but impeccably balanced, it displays terrific equilibrium as well as depth. With its hallmark silky texture and fabulously concentrated, flawlessly presented style, it is another potential legend from this microsized enterprise. Anticipated maturity: now–2020.

It doesn't get any better than the 1997 Cabernet Sauvignon, another perfect wine. Representing the essence of cassis intermixed with blackberries, minerals, licorice, and toast, this full-bodied, multidimensional classic is fabulous, with extraordinary purity, symmetry, and a finish that lasts for nearly a minute. It has the overall equilibrium to evolve for nearly two decades, but it will be hard to resist upon release. Anticipated maturity: now–2020. The 1996 Cabernet Sauvignon reveals more structure than the 1997, an opaque purple color, and the hallmark blackberry and cassis-like notes. Silky-textured, fabulously concentrated, and gorgeously balanced, it has every component part—acidity, alcohol, tannin, and extract—flawlessly presented. Anticipated maturity: now–2020. The opaque purple-colored 1995 Cabernet Sauvignon exhibits a sensational purity of black currant fruit, intermixed with a notion of raspberries, violets, and well-disguised sweet vanilla. Full-bodied, with remarkable intensity, exquisite symmetry, and a mid-palate and finish to die for, this is a compelling, astonishingly seductive Cabernet that can be drunk now or cellared for 20–25 years. I may have done this wine a disservice by not giving it the big three-digit score.

The opaque purple-colored 1994 Cabernet Sauvignon's forward, gorgeously scented nose offers up a smorgasbord of black fruits, along with a subtle dosage of toasty oak and minerals. Full-bodied, with a seamless, lush texture, this is a profoundly generous wine with everything going for it. The finish lasts for 35 seconds. As gorgeous as it is, this wine can be drunk young or cellared for 20–25 years.

I keep asking Jean Phillips what she does in order to achieve such purity of fruit. There are no secrets—yields are modest, grapes are harvested at 24° Brix (which is normal), the wine is aged in Seguin-Moreau French barrels (about 60–65% are new) for 18–20 months and bottled with no filtration. Considerable punching down is done at Screaming Eagle, and the small, one-half-ton fermenters may hold the secret to the extraordinary fruit quality Phillips achieves. On the other hand, it may simply be the *terroir* combined with the owner's obsession with brilliant wines. And let's not forget the consulting oenologist, Napa Valley's Heidi Barrett. Getting on the winery's mailing list is the only way to latch onto a bottle, unless you get lucky and find a bottle at one of Napa Valley's wine shops or restaurants.

Past Glories: 1993 Cabernet Sauvignon (97), 1992 Cabernet Sauvignon (98)

SEAVEY (NAPA)

1999 Cabernet Sauvignon	Napa	E	92
1998 Cabernet Sauvignon	Napa	E	90
1997 Cabernet Sauvignon	Napa	E	96
1996 Cabernet Sauvignon	Napa	D	92
1995 Cabernet Sauvignon	Napa	D	94
1994 Cabernet Sauvignon	Napa	D	91
1999 Chardonnay	Napa	D	90
1999 Merlot	Napa	D	89
1998 Merlot	Napa	D	90
1997 Merlot	Napa	D	90
1994 Merlot	Napa	C	89

Proprietors Mary and Bill Seavey, along with their talented wine-maker, Philippe Melka, continue to fashion some of Napa Valley's finest wines. Moreover, they are all fairly priced compared to so many Napa wineries that operate in their unreal world. Readers looking for a non-malolactic, powerful Chardonnay that has been gently touched by oak should check out Seavey's refreshing 1999. Indigenous yeasts are used during fermentation, but there is little lees stirring, and only 25% new oak is utilized in the wine's upbringing. Yet this 1999 Chardonnay possesses plenty of power as well as gorgeously ripe pear and honeyed citrus notes, full body, excellent freshness, and impressive extract and richness. Most non-malolactic Chardonnays lack texture and interest, but that is not the case with Seavey's offering. It will drink well for 3–4 years.

The dense garnet/plum/purple-colored 1998 Merlot offers expressive, fragrant aromatics consisting of chocolate soufflé, smoke, coffee, mocha, and berry fruit. Full-bodied, lush, silky-textured, and made in a Pomerol-like, ripe style, it is on a fast evolutionary track, so owners should consume it over the next 5–6 years. The 1999 Merlot is similarly styled, exhibiting a full-bodied, chocolate and berry fruit–scented nose, low acidity, and fleshy, succulent flavors. Both wines are 100% Merlot aged in 40–45% new French oak. The 1999 should have a slightly longer aging curve of 8–10 years.

There are 300 cases of the 1997 Merlot, an intense, full-bodied, gorgeously pure, 100% Merlot that saw 40% new French oak. It reveals the telltale espresso bean, chocolaty, sweet, jammy berry fruit, an unctuous, thick texture, full body, and excellent purity and length. It is a gorgeous Merlot to drink now and over the next 12–15 years. The 1994 Merlot (350 cases) was aged in 35–45% new-oak casks. The opaque purple color is followed by a wine with an impressively rich nose of black currants and spice. This ripe, rich, sweet, medium- to full-bodied 100% Merlot should last longer than I suggested in my first review of it. It now appears it will evolve effortlessly for another 7–8 years and hold at that plateau for 5–6 years.

This estate can be a sensational source of Cabernet Sauvignon that goes largely unnoticed because Seavey is hidden in the backwater Conn Valley, east of St. Helena. Their 1991 Cabernet Sauvignon remains one of the greatest Cabernets of the decade, but it is amazing how many people have never tasted it. The 1997 Cabernet Sauvignon (1,400 cases) is potentially every bit as good. I originally rated this wine 96, but after an additional year of bottle age, it may be even better. It spent 18 months in 40–45% new French oak, and was bottled after a light fining yet no filtration. A monumental, classic California Cabernet Sauvignon, it boasts an opaque plum/purple color as well as an extraordinary bouquet of jammy cassis, plums, toast, and licorice. With its humongous fruit and glycerin, full body, smoky blackberry and coffee flavors on the mid-palate, as well as a silky, moderately tannic finish that lasts for nearly a minute, this seamless effort is a modern-day Cabernet elixir. A blend of 98% Cabernet Sauvignon and 2% Petit Verdot, it should be at its best between 2004–2025. The outstanding 1998 Cabernet Sauvignon, produced from an extremely small crop, is an example of what the Napa Cabernet Sauvignon producers are jokingly saying is "another fine wine from a bad vintage." A rich, full-bodied, dense effort on a faster evolutionary track than the 1997, the 1998 is loaded with chocolaty, black cherry, and cassis fruit, an open-knit, sexy, expansive texture, outstanding concentration and purity, low acidity, and a fat, chewy finish. It will be drinkable upon release, yet promises to age well for 12–15 years. The 1999 Cabernet Sauvignon reveals an opaque purple color in addition to a sweet, highly extracted bouquet of black fruits, coffee, chocolate, cedar, and plum aromas. Silky yet assertive tannin, full body, exceptional concentration and purity, and a dense, layered finish further characterize this wine. Anticipated maturity: 2005–2020.

The 1996 Cabernet Sauvignon is superb. This opaque purple-colored effort reveals aromas of black currants, creosote, smoke, minerals, and plums. It is full-bodied, with exquisite density and terrific fruit purity and intensity, particularly in the mid-palate and length (always good signs for wines that are meant to improve and last). There is plenty of tannin, but this is a generous, impressively endowed wine that should stand the test of several decades of cellaring. Anticipated maturity: 2003–2025. Seavey's opaque 1995 Cabernet Sauvignon (950 cases) displays a fantastic nose of classic black currants intermixed with cigar box and cedar scents. In the mouth, it is full-bodied and backward, but persuasively rich, layered, and marvelously well balanced. There is a deep, sweet mid-palate and explosive ripeness and richness in the long, heady finish. A sleeper pick in this outstanding vintage, it should evolve effortlessly for 20–30 years. Anticipated maturity: now–2028.

Made from low yields of approximately two tons of fruit per acre, from Seavey's east-facing hillside vineyards in the Conn Valley, the 1994 Cabernet Sauvignon exhibits an opaque purple color, and an exuberant yet still young and unformed nose of spice, black fruits, and cedar. Full-bodied, with layers of dense, ripe fruit, this rich, moderately tannic wine should be at its best in 3–5 years. It will keep for two decades or more.

This is another property where getting on the mailing list makes good sense.

Past Glories: Cabernet Sauvignon—1993 (91), 1992 (92), 1991 (99), 1990 (94)

SEGHESIO WINERY (SONOMA)

1999 Zinfandel	Sonoma	C	88
1998 Zinfandel	Sonoma	B	88
1999 Zinfandel Cortina	Alexander Valley	D	89
1999 Zinfandel Home Ranch	Alexander Valley	D	90
1998 Zinfandel Home Ranch	Alexander Valley	D	90
1999 Zinfandel Old Vines	Sonoma	D	90
1998 Zinfandel Old Vines	Sonoma	D	90
1997 Zinfandel Old Vines	Sonoma	D	90
1999 Zinfandel San Lorenzo	Alexander Valley	D	91
1997 Zinfandel San Lorenzo	Alexander Valley	D	88

Seghesio, which possesses well-located vineyards in both Alexander Valley and Sonoma, has become a respectable source for high-quality Zinfandel. Fortunately, prices have not caught up with some of the other outstanding Zinfandel producers who are cashing in on the insatiable thirst for high-quality wine. Consistently fashioning topflight Zinfandels from their old vineyards, Seghesio's 1999s are among the stars of the vintage. One of the best buys is the 1999 Zinfandel Sonoma (14.5% alcohol). An excellent dark ruby/purple color is followed by tangy, classic briery, berry, and cherry fruit mixed with pepper, spice, and earth. It is a polished yet flavorful wine to enjoy over the next 3–4 years. Even more complex, fuller bodied, and layered is the 1999 Zinfandel Old Vines (15.3% alcohol). Exhibiting earthy, Rhône-like characteristics of crushed pepper and black cherries presented in a lusty, full-bodied format, it will drink well for 4–5 years.

All three single-vineyard 1999 offerings are impressive. The deep ruby/purple-colored 1999 Zinfandel Home Ranch reveals some new oak, vanilla, pepper, and sandalwood, but briery, berry, currant, and cherry fruit dominate. Fleshy, full-bodied, powerful, and well balanced, with sweet tannin as well as tangy acidity for definition, this large-scaled Zinfandel should drink well for 6–7 years. The most concentrated and complex effort is the dense ruby/purple-colored 1999 Zinfandel San Lorenzo (15.4% alcohol). Aromas of seaweed, new saddle leather, coffee, tobacco, soy, and black cherries are reminiscent of a top-class Piedmontese Nebbiolo. Full-bodied, with tangy acidity and a complex, multilayered style, it should drink well for 6–7 years. The grapy, unevolved, one-dimensional 1999 Zinfandel Cortina (14.7% alcohol) possesses gobs of fruit and glycerin, but less aromatic and flavor complexity than its siblings. This rich offering should develop well and drink nicely for 5–7 years.

The 1998 Zinfandel Sonoma (14.1% alcohol) is a textbook example of this varietal. Dark ruby-colored with purple nuances, this fruit-driven wine exhibits black cherry and briery characteristics with subtle pepper and oak in the background. Rich, medium- to full-bodied, pure, and low in acidity, it can be enjoyed over the next 3–4 years. The 1998 Zinfandel Old Vines is not dissimilar from the Sonoma *cuvée;* it just has more of everything. The 14.6% alcohol results in a fuller-bodied feel, with more glycerin and concentration. Earthy, peppery, spice, big black raspberry, and cherry notes dominate the wine's aromatics and flavors. Pure, long, and rich, with low acidity, it should be drunk over the next 5–6 years. Another impressive effort is the 1998 Zinfandel Home Ranch, made from a vineyard first planted in 1895. This opaque ruby-colored effort offers sweet berry and cherry fruit on the attack, a touch of toasty new oak, medium to full body, and roasted herb, sweet strawberry and cherry jam–like flavors. Consume it over the next 4–5 years. These are impressive efforts from a winery that deserves more attention.

The 1997 Zinfandel San Lorenzo (14.6% alcohol) possesses a dense, dark ruby/purple color, noticeable new oak, a heady, ripe, structured style with muscle, moderately aggressive acidity, yet admirable ripeness, extract, and length. Drink it over the next 7–8 years. With 14.2% alcohol, the 1997 Zinfandel Old Vines is not a huge wine by modern-day standards. Its saturated ruby/purple color is followed by superb aromas of black raspberries, minerals, and flowers. There is gorgeously integrated acidity and alcohol, a nice structured yet fruit-driven mid-palate and a succulent, concentrated finish. It should drink well for 7–8 years.

SELENE (NAPA)

1998	Merlot	Napa	D	87
1997	Merlot	Napa	D	90
1996	Merlot	Napa	D	91+
1995	Merlot	Napa	D	92
1994	Merlot	Napa	D	90
1998	Merlot Hyde Vineyard	Carneros	D	88
1997	Merlot Hyde Vineyard	Carneros	D	88
1996	Merlot Hyde Vineyard	Carneros	D	90
1995	Merlot Hyde Vineyard	Carneros	D	89

Selene's 1998 Merlots are light but well-made efforts in this difficult vintage. The 1998 Merlot Hyde Vineyard exhibits dried tobacco, Provençal herb, chocolate, and berry fruit aromas. Soft and medium-bodied, it will be delicious upon release. The 1997 Merlot Hyde Vineyard reveals tangier acidity as well as an elegant berry fruit and mocha-scented and -flavored personality. With a fine finish, it should drink well for 5–8 years. The Napa Merlots are always richer and more concentrated. Approximately two-thirds of the fruit comes from the well-known Madrona Ranch, made famous primarily by viticulturist David Abreu. The remainder of the fruit comes from the Caldwell Vineyard, which was formerly used as a source of Merlot fruit by Jayson Pahlmeyer. The excellent, dark ruby/purple-colored 1998 Merlot Napa offers up sweet, chocolaty, coffee-like aromas and flavors that exhibit excellent ripeness, plenty of glycerin, and a medium-bodied, pure finish. It should be delicious during its first 7–8 years of life. The structured 1997 Merlot Napa possesses more noticeable acidity and tannin. Well made, with excellent berry and white chocolate aromas and flavors, it is a bigger, more ageworthy effort than the 1998, but it has less charm and sweetness. Anticipated maturity: now–2008. The 1996 Merlot Hyde Vineyard reveals an attractive purple color, a sweet, licorice, and black cherry–scented nose with medium body, a hint of herbs and coffee, and enough acidity to provide balance. Long, rich, and plump, it will age well for 10 years. Even more impressive is the dense black/purple-colored 1996 Merlot Napa, which is a fatter, richer wine with lower acidity (a higher pH style), an expansive, savory texture, and a long, lush, medium- to full-bodied finish. The wine unfolds beautifully in the glass and will be a hedonistic Merlot to consume over its first decade of life.

The 1995 Merlot Hyde Vineyard offers a dense purple color, followed by a bouquet of black cherries, smoke, and chocolate. Expressive and rich, with abundant black cherry fruit, this tasty, medium-bodied, spicy Merlot should drink well for 5–8 years. The 1995 Merlot Napa is a decadent, luxuriously endowed wine. From its opaque purple color to its knockout nose of roasted coffee, smoky black cherry fruit, and chocolate, this rich, superbly concentrated wine possesses terrific intensity and enough acidity and oak to provide a framework.

The silky finish complements the intensely fragrant personality of this gorgeous Merlot. Drink it over the next 7–8 years. With so many stripped, vegetal, herbal tea–scented Merlots, it is reassuring to taste such yummy stuff as Selene's 1994 Merlot. When it is good, Merlot is a wonderfully soft, silky-textured, medium-weight, aromatically expressive wine with plenty of ripe berry fruit, often intermingled with scents of white chocolate, coffee, and spices. This luscious 1994 possesses plenty of those traits, plus the richness and plumpness to go along with its voluptuous texture. It is already drinking splendidly well—so why wait? I would opt for consuming this beauty over the next 5–6 years.

SEVEN LIONS WINERY (SONOMA)

1999 Zinfandel Martinelli and Duckhorn Vineyard   Russian River   E   89

This opaque purple-colored, medium- to full-bodied Zinfandel is produced from some of the Russian River's finest soils/vineyards. Sweet, ripe black currant and cherry characteristics combine with smoky oak, and tangy acidity provides definition, vibrancy, and freshness in this large-scaled, concentrated, dense effort. This excellent 1999 is sure to please Zinfandel enthusiasts, but the price is hard to swallow.

SHAFER VINEYARDS (NAPA)

1999 Cabernet Sauvignon	Napa	D	90
1998 Cabernet Sauvignon	Napa	D	89
1997 Cabernet Sauvignon	Napa	E	90
1996 Cabernet Sauvignon	Napa	E	89
1995 Cabernet Sauvignon	Napa	E	91
1994 Cabernet Sauvignon	Napa	E	90
1999 Cabernet Sauvignon Hillside Select Stags Leap	Napa	EEE	97
1998 Cabernet Sauvignon Hillside Select Stags Leap	Napa	EEE	92
1997 Cabernet Sauvignon Hillside Select Stags Leap	Napa	EEE	99
1996 Cabernet Sauvignon Hillside Select Stags Leap	Napa	EEE	98
1995 Cabernet Sauvignon Hillside Select Stags Leap	Napa	EE	99
1994 Cabernet Sauvignon Hillside Select Stags Leap	Napa	EE	99
1999 Chardonnay Red Shoulder Ranch	Napa/Carneros	D	(90–92)
1997 Firebreak (Sangiovese/Cabernet Sauvignon)	Napa	C	90
1996 Firebreak (Sangiovese/Cabernet Sauvignon)	Napa	D	88
1999 Merlot	Napa	D	87
1998 Merlot	Napa	D	89
1997 Merlot	Napa	D	90
1996 Merlot	Napa	D	88
1995 Merlot	Stags Leap	D	90
1994 Merlot	Stags Leap	D	89
1999 Syrah	Napa	E	92

Located on the Silverado Trail, in the Stags Leap section of Napa Valley, Shafer Vineyards is the undeniable star of the region. Production is approximately 30,000 cases, with 6,000 cases of Chardonnay Red Shoulder Ranch and 2,000 cases of Cabernet Sauvignon Hillside

Select on strict allocation because of popular demand. The 1999 Chardonnay Red Shoulder Ranch exhibits abundant quantities of rich orange, tangerine, and citrus aromas and flavors, full body, a big, smoky, leesy, barrel-fermented style, good underlying acidity, and tremendous weight and intensity. About 50% new oak (primarily French with a touch of American) is utilized, and the wine is not put through malolactic fermentation. It should age well for 3–4 years.

Shafer's 1998 red wines are successful efforts. The 1998 Merlot (a blend of 76% Merlot, 13% Cabernet Franc, and 11% Cabernet Sauvignon with 14.3% alcohol) offers a blueberry, menthol, and berry-scented nose in addition to crisp but fleshy, pure, long, layered, supple flavors gently touched by spicy oak. This wine has turned out even better than expected. The 1999 Merlot (a blend of 81% Merlot, 10% Cabernet Sauvignon, and 9% Cabernet Franc) reveals a cold-growing-season character, ripe cherry fruit, good acidity, notes of tobacco and spice, medium body, light to moderate tannin, and smoky oak in the background. It will require time to flesh out, but does not appear to be as charming as the 1998.

There is good availability (10,000 cases produced) of the outstanding 1997 Merlot (75% Merlot, 15% Cabernet Franc, and 10% Cabernet Sauvignon). It exhibits copious quantities of cedar, coffee, plum, and black cherry/cassis fruit. The texture is fleshy and open-knit, with gobs of ripeness. Drink this medium-bodied, lush, pure Merlot over the next 10–12 years. The medium- to full-bodied 1996 Merlot (77% Merlot, 16% Cabernet Franc, and 7% Cabernet Sauvignon) is more exotic, with some of Merlot's chocolate overtones emerging in the black cherry fruit. While the 1996 may be fuller and heavier than the 1997, it is also an excellent effort. I would opt for consuming it over the next decade. The 1994 Merlot is one of the best Merlots on the market—soft, velvety-textured, with gobs of ripe cherry/cranberry fruit nicely dosed with smoky oak. The wine is medium- to full-bodied, yet elegant and expansive, with no hard edges. Fully mature, it should drink well and gracefully evolve over the next 3–4 years. The 1995 Merlot appears to be the qualitative equivalent, perhaps slightly superior, to the 1994. Certainly the 1995 is more fragrant and aromatic. Jammy black cherries, toast, and subtle herbaceous notes are followed by a wine with gorgeous layers of rich, glycerin-endowed, creamy-textured fruit. Deeper-colored than the 1994, but as structured, the 1995 possesses more extract and length. It should drink well for 6–8 years.

Shafer's Sangiovese-dominated Firebreak (2,500 cases produced) is to be admired. One of the finest Firebreaks tasted is the 1997. Dark ruby-colored, with sumptuous aromas of black cherries, new saddle leather, dried herbs, licorice, and strawberry jam, this rich, medium-bodied, fruit-driven wine possesses uncanny elegance and complexity for a California Sangiovese (with 15% Cabernet Sauvignon). Displaying beautiful harmony and hitting all the palate's sweet spots, it is fully mature. The 1996 Firebreak (80% Sangiovese and 20% Cabernet Sauvignon) exhibits a dark ruby color as well as a textbook Sangiovese nose of strawberries, leather, cherries, and damp forest scents. The wine possesses excellent richness, medium body, and an elegant, more restrained and subdued style than the richer, more fragrant 1997. It should drink well for another 1–2 years.

A new Shafer project that will tantalize wine consumers is their 17-acre Syrah vineyard planted in southern Napa Valley. While production from the first crop, 1999, will be small, this looks to be a fabulous Syrah. Yields were cut by 50%, producing only 1.5 tons of fruit per acre. The wine is being aged in 75% new French oak casks. The result is a sensational, opaque blue/purple-colored Syrah with a dazzling nose of blackberry liqueur intermixed with barbecue spices and licorice. In the mouth, it is full-bodied, voluptuously textured, super-extracted, and rich, with low acidity. It should provide compelling drinking upon release and keep for 15 years.

The sexy, forward 1998 Cabernet Sauvignon may turn out to be exceptional, particularly for this vintage. A blend of 94% Cabernet Sauvignon and 6% Cabernet Franc, this dense ruby/purple-colored, full-bodied, supple-textured, soft, hedonistic, seductive offering is thick and juicy, with low acidity as well as loads of fruit, glycerin, and appeal. Enjoy it over the next 10–12 years. The 1999 Cabernet Sauvignon (a blend of 97% Cabernet Sauvignon, 2% Cabernet Franc, and 1% Merlot) should be superb. A dense ruby/purple color is accompanied by a full-bodied, concentrated palate, a multilayered mid-palate, and sweet black currant fruit intermixed with minerals, lead pencil, and spice. It should drink well for 10–15+ years. The dark ruby/purple-colored 1997 Cabernet Sauvignon is brilliant. Small quantities (7% of each) of Cabernet Franc and Merlot have been added to the blend, giving the wine more aromatic breadth and flavor dimension. Dense and rich, with high extraction, sweet fruit, full body, outstanding purity, and mineral/spicy aromas, the 1997 should drink well for 10–15 years. The excellent 1996 Cabernet Sauvignon (13.5% alcohol, and made from a blend of 94% Cabernet Sauvignon and 6% Cabernet Franc) is more sternly constructed and possesses rougher tannin than the 1997. The wine's saturated ruby color is followed by a big, spicy, black currant, loamy soil, and smoky-scented bouquet. The mid-palate is rich, pure, and well endowed, and there is noticeable tannin in the moderately long finish (a characteristic of many 1996 North Coast reds). This wine will benefit from 1–3 years of cellaring and will keep for 12–15. The 1995 Cabernet Sauvignon is elegant, yet authoritatively flavored, with copious amounts of cassis fruit, spicy, smoky oak, medium body, and an excellent, restrained but well-balanced personality. It is a nicely extracted, fleshy, complex wine for drinking during its first 10–15 years of life. A gorgeous Cabernet Sauvignon, Shafer's 1994 displays a dark purple color, as well as sweet, floral-scented, cassis fruit mixed with subtle new oak and minerals. Medium- to full-bodied, spicy, and exceptionally pure, with a nicely layered texture and outstanding equilibrium and depth, this is a classic, elegant, authoritatively flavored Cabernet that is impeccably made. It is still youthful, but given the penchant for most Americans (this author included) to enjoy the youthfulness of wines such as this, I would opt for drinking it now and over the next 12–15+ years. Very impressive!

Since 1991, Shafer's Hillside Select Cabernet Sauvignon has unquestionably been one of the top dozen or so California Cabernets. Made from 100% Cabernet Sauvignon and aged 32 months in 100% French oak casks (the majority Taransaud), it possesses the elegance and finesse one would expect from the Stags Leap area, but also monumental power, richness, and intensity. Every Hillside Select *cuvée* produced since 1991 has been spectacular, with the 1994, 1995, 1996, 1997, and 1999 all flirting with perfection. I do not think a blind tasting could establish which is the finest vintage . . . they are all that close in quality. Sadly, there are only about 2,200 cases of this prodigious Cabernet. The 1999 Cabernet Sauvignon Hillside Select exhibits the telltale lead pencil, black currant, and mineral-infused fruit with subtle oak in the aromatics and flavors. Seamless, full-bodied, and fabulously concentrated, with a 45-second finish, it comes closest in style to the 1994. A candidate for Cabernet Sauvignon of the vintage, the 1998 Cabernet Sauvignon Hillside Select is not as massive as the 1996, 1997, or 1999, but it is more concentrated and intense than most top Bordeaux, with beautifully integrated wood. Seemingly on a fast evolutionary track, it offers complex tobacco, mineral, cassis, and vanilla scents in the formidable aromatics. On the palate, the wine is full-bodied and rich, with sweet tannin, perfect balance, and a gentle, layered finish exhibiting no hard edges. The balance, harmony, and complexity suggest this 1998 will be drinkable upon release, and will age well for 15+ years.

Is the prodigious 1997 Cabernet Sauvignon Hillside Select a perfect wine? Bottled in June 2000, this effort is about as spectacular as Cabernet can be. The soaring bouquet of sweet, lavishly rich black currants, plums, cherries, toast, minerals, and smoke cascades from the glass. Opaque purple-colored, extraordinarily intense, and full-bodied, yet amazingly well balanced, this flawless wine will be at its peak between now–2030. One of the greatest young Cabernet Sauvignons I have ever tasted, it represents the quintessential Napa Cabernet, combining both elegance and power. The 1996 Cabernet Sauvignon Hillside Select is one of the vintage's superstars. Its opaque purple color is accompanied by super aromatics, immense body, great fruit extraction, superb purity and overall symmetry, as well as a 40+-second finish. Revealing exceptional intensity (but no heaviness) as well as perfectly integrated acidity, tannin, and alcohol, this fabulous Cabernet will drink wonderfully for three decades. The 1995 Cabernet Sauvignon Hillside Select exhibits the same characteristics as the 1996 and 1997, yet possesses more fatness in the mid-palate. There is plenty of tannin in this full-bodied, rich effort. It is remarkable how the finest California Cabernets combine extraordinary power and richness with balance and elegance. A stupendous wine, it is worth a special effort to obtain. Anticipated maturity: 2003–2030.

The 1994 Cabernet Sauvignon Hillside Select is a prodigious Cabernet. I had it at a tasting in Japan, and the Japanese were as enthusiastic about it as my rating suggested they should be. They were crestfallen when informed they probably would not be able to buy multiple cases of the wine! The 1994 combines the vintage's spectacularly ripe, luscious fruit with a rarely seen degree of elegance and finesse. The wine is extremely rich, as well as gorgeously poised and graceful. The saturated ruby/purple color is accompanied by Médoc-like, lead pencil aromas intermixed with cassis, cedar, minerals, and spice. I wrote the word "great" four different times in my most recent tasting note, which mirrored every other tasting note I have. It is full-bodied and seamless, with a silky texture, voluptuous richness, and fabulous purity. The finish lasts for over 40 seconds. Anticipated maturity: now–2025.

By the way, I asked John and Doug Shafer their ratings of the Hillside Select Cabernet Sauvignon for the vintages of the 1990s. They agreed that the three top vintages were (in no particular order) 1991, 1994, and 1997. Close behind were 1992, 1995, and 1996. They equated 1998 with 1993.

Past Glories: Cabernet Sauvignon Hillside Select Stags Leap—1993 (94), 1992 (96), 1991 (96)

SIDURI (CALIFORNIA)

1998 Novy Cellars Syrah Stage Gulch Vineyard	Petaluma/Sonoma	D	88
1999 Pinot Noir	Santa Lucia Highlands	D	88
1999 Pinot Noir	Sonoma	D	88
1998 Pinot Noir Archery Summit	Oregon	D	93
1997 Pinot Noir Archery Summit	Oregon	D	90
1999 Pinot Noir Christian David	Sonoma Coast	E	90+
1998 Pinot Noir Coastlands Vineyard	Sonoma Coast	D	90+
1999 Pinot Noir Garys' Vineyard	Santa Lucia Highlands	D	89
1999 Pinot Noir Hirsch Vineyard	Sonoma Coast	D	91
1998 Pinot Noir Hirsch Vineyard	Sonoma Coast	D	91
1997 Pinot Noir Hirsch Vineyard	Sonoma Coast	D	88+
1999 Pinot Noir Muirfield Vineyard	Oregon	D	89+
1998 Pinot Noir Muirfield Vineyard	Oregon	D	90
1999 Pinot Noir Pisoni Vineyard	Santa Lucia Highlands	D	92
1998 Pinot Noir Pisoni Vineyard	Santa Lucia Highlands	D	90
1997 Pinot Noir Pisoni Vineyard	Santa Lucia Highlands	D	92
1998 Pinot Noir Van der Kamp Vineyard	Sonoma Mountain	D	(87–88)
1997 Pinot Noir Van der Kamp Vineyard Old Vines	Sonoma Mountain	D	88
1999 Pinot Noir Willamette Valley	Oregon	D	88

I have been a fan of Siduri since their debut offerings. They continue to specialize in high-quality Pinot Noir from choice vineyard sites in both California and Oregon. They have also added a Syrah under the Novy Cellars label. This winery produces numerous Pinot Noirs exhibiting subtle differences, thus the argument supporting separate designations. The 1999 Pinot Noir Willamette Valley, which is a blend of Archery Summit and Muirfield Vineyard fruit, reveals a healthy, dark ruby color, in addition to a sweet nose of black cherries, rich, concentrated fruit, medium body, and excellent purity. It is a delicious wine to drink over the next 5–7 years. The 1999 Pinot Noir Muirfield Vineyard comes from both Dijon clones and the well-known Oregon clone called Wadenswil. Yields were only 1.5 tons per acre. The color is a dense ruby/purple. The wine is thick, quite rich, medium- to full-bodied, and impressively pure, with a thick, black cherry component the distinguishing characteristic. There were 180 cases produced. There are eight offerings of California Pinot Noir from some of the state's most renowned vineyards. For starters, the 1999 Pinot Noir Sonoma has a medium ruby color, a straightforward and sweet nose of jammy cherries, very seductive, medium-bodied, supple flavors, and light tannin. The wine is quite pure and ideal for drinking over the next 2–5 years. There are 226 cases of this Sonoma County Pinot Noir. Siduri has also decided to produce three separate Pinot Noirs from the Santa Lucia Highlands. The 1999 Pinot Noir Santa Lucia (14.4% alcohol) is an open-knit, round, generously endowed wine (214 cases) that shows good, ripe, blackberry and cherry fruit, nicely integrated wood, adequate acidity, and a spicy, clean finish. Drink it over the next 4–5 years. The 1999 Pinot Noir Garys' Vineyard offers overripe jammy strawberry/cherry fruit and a touch of smoky, toasty oak. The wine (542 cases) is relatively fat, fleshy, and pure, with plenty of black fruit and a plump personality. Drink it over the next 4–5 years. Lastly, the superb 1999 Pinot Noir Pisoni Vineyard (576 cases produced) was aged in 60% new French oak and bottled, like all these Pinots, without filtration. The color is a dense ruby/purple. The wine offers up sumptuous quantities of black raspberry, blackberry, and cherry fruit, smoky, toasty oak, and black and Chinese tea in the background. The palate is voluptuous, thick, very pure, rich, and medium- to full-bodied. Even some meatiness is apparent as this wine sits in the glass. This is a terrific Pinot that can be drunk now or aged for 7–8 years.

Siduri produces several Sonoma Coast offerings. The 1999 Pinot Noir Hirsch Vineyard (282 cases made from 1.6 tons per acre of fruit) is a dense, ruby-colored wine with a complex nose of violets, red cherries, and spice. In the mouth, it is voluptuously textured, pure, and ripe, with well-integrated tannin and reasonably low acidity. It is a complex, rich, full, Burgundian-styled Pinot Noir to drink over the next 7–8 years. Named after the proprietor's first child, the 1999 Pinot Noir Christian David (68 cases) was made from 100% Pommard clones from the Hirsch Vineyard. Tight, backward, and tannic, this dense ruby/purple-colored Pinot possesses plenty of structure, but also impressive concentration and overall equilibrium. It needs 1–2 years of cellaring and should keep for 12 or more years. Overall, this is an impressive group of excellent to exceptional Pinot Noirs that merit considerable interest.

1998 can be a terrific vintage for Oregon's top Pinot Noir producers. It is unquestionably the finest vintage since 1994. Siduri's 1998 Pinot Noir Muirfield Vineyard was cropped at only 1.3 tons per acre. Revealing an intriguing Vosne-Romanée style, it possesses a dark ruby color as well as a sweet, toasty nose with aromas of black cherry and raspberry fruit, medium body, sweet tannin, high but well-hidden alcohol (13.9%), and an excellent finish. It should be drinkable upon release next year and evolve nicely for 5–6 years. The superb 1998 Pinot Noir Archery Summit Vineyard was made from Oregon's new Dijon clones for Pinot Noir—#115, #113, and #777. Cropped at an unbelievably low .8 tons of fruit per acre, this wine could easily pass for a grand cru such as Grands-Echezeaux or Richebourg. A dark ruby-colored wine with purple nuances, its soaring aromatics jump from the glass, offering up black raspberries, cherries, plums, toast, and flowers. Medium- to full-bodied, with a terrific mid-palate, a creamy texture, and enough acidity to provide focus and balance, this wine's outstanding purity as well as stunning richness and harmony make for a sumptuous glass of Pinot Noir. It may even improve. Anticipated maturity: now–2007. Bravo! Siduri's persuasive skills convinced the owners of the Coastlands Vineyard to sell them some of their Pinot Noir. (This highly regarded Sonoma Coast vineyard was previously available only as one of the Williams-Selyem offerings.) The dark ruby-colored 1998 Pinot Noir Coastlands Vineyard is one of the firmer, more backward wines of the vintage. It exhibits subtle toasty oak, outstanding concentration, a tight personality, medium body, firm tannin, and a mineral-structured, earthy finish. The 14.1% alcohol is remarkably well hidden. Production was a minuscule half-ton per acre. It should be alluring when released next year. Anticipated maturity: now–2007. Another wine from the Sonoma Coast, the 1998 Pinot Noir Hirsch Vineyard emerges from the Mt. Eden and Pommard clones. A hedonistic Pinot fruit cocktail, it is a gloriously perfumed, exquisitely ripe, rich, lusty, fruit effort. Full-bodied, with well-integrated acidity and tannin, plus copious quantities of black cherries, currants, raspberries, smoke, and toast, this rich, silky textured wine should be drunk during its first 5–6 years of life.

Almost every good Pinot Noir producer who buys grapes in California seems to want to make a wine from the Pisoni Vineyard in Monterey's Santa Lucia Highlands. Siduri's 1998 Pinot Noir Pisoni Vineyard is not quite up to the quality of the stunning 1997, but it is still an outstanding wine. It displays good underlying tangy acidity (more noticeable in this wine than in other offerings), a pronounced sweet Bing cherry fruitiness, medium body, and an emphasis on finesse and elegance. My guess is that the fruit in the 1998 vintage was not nearly as ripe as in 1997 (just the reverse of Oregon). This wine tastes as if it were made from less concentrated juice than the 1997. Drink it over the next 5–6 years. One of the firmer, more angular Pinot Noirs made by Siduri is the 1998 Pinot Noir Van der Kamp Vineyard. Although closed, with coaxing aromas of black raspberries, licorice, pepper, and earth emerge. Dense, with a ruby/purple color and hints that there is more than meets the nose or palate, I would opt for aging this Pinot Noir for a year and drinking it over the following 7–8.

I tasted four impressive 1997 offerings, all of which are bottled with minimal intervention (i.e., no filtration). The medium ruby-colored 1997 Pinot Noir Van der Kamp Vineyard Old Vines offers a moderately intense nose of black raspberries, cherries, and spicy, roasted herbs. The wine is fleshy and open-knit, with nicely integrated toasty new oak, and a lush, heady (14.1% alcohol) finish. This supple, hedonistic example will offer delicious and complex drinking for 3–4 years. The outstanding 1997 Pinot Noir Archery Summit exhibits a darker ruby color and a firmer, more austere personality, but has beautifully pure black raspberry and cassis notes mixed with earthy and vanilla scents. This is a classy, structured, exceptionally pure, backward, medium- to full-bodied Pinot that should be at its best in 12 months and keep for 6–7 years. The 1997 Pinot Noir Hirsch Vineyard is the most Burgundian of this quartet, exhibiting smoky, gamey, meaty notes in the aromatics, as well as sweet black cherry and berry fruit. There is good firmness, a lean, moderately tannic finish, and medium body. Although closed and angular, it is an intriguing Pinot that appears to be more driven by its *terroir* than its siblings. Anticipated maturity: now–2007. It seems like no one can fail with the fruit emerging from the Santa Lucia Highlands' Pisoni Vineyard. Siduri's 1997 Pinot Noir Pisoni Vineyard is a sumptuously rich, dark ruby/purple-colored wine with soaring aromas of blackberry/raspberry and cherry jam. One of the more hedonistic, lushly textured, and sumptuous Pinots I have tasted from Siduri, it will be a huge success with readers lucky enough to latch onto a few bottles. It should drink well for 3–5 years.

Siduri's first Syrah effort appears to be excellent. The dark plum/purple-colored 1998 Novy Cellars Syrah Stage Gulch Vineyard displays a charming nose of blackberries, pepper, cherry liqueur, and spice. It is low in acidity, soft, round, and generous. The spicy richness and evolved, precocious style are typical of the 1998 vintage. This wine should be drunk during its first 6–7 years of life.

SILVER OAK CELLARS (NAPA)

1999 Cabernet Sauvignon	Alexander Valley	E	90
1998 Cabernet Sauvignon	Alexander Valley	E	88
1997 Cabernet Sauvignon	Alexander Valley	E	89
1996 Cabernet Sauvignon	Alexander Valley	E	92
1995 Cabernet Sauvignon	Alexander Valley	E	94
1994 Cabernet Sauvignon	Alexander Valley	E	93
1999 Cabernet Sauvignon	Napa	EE	92
1998 Cabernet Sauvignon	Napa	EE	88
1997 Cabernet Sauvignon	Napa	EE	94
1996 Cabernet Sauvignon	Napa	EE	91
1995 Cabernet Sauvignon	Napa	EE	95
1994 Cabernet Sauvignon	Napa	EE	93

The story of Silver Oak needs little introduction. These highly successful wines are about as California/American as they can be. Aged in 100% new American oak (all from Missouri) for 30 months prior to bottling, they are gaudy, big, spicy oak and fruit bombs that are delicious young, yet seem capable of lasting 12–15 years, and in certain vintages, much longer. Their legion of admirers seems to get larger and larger and, on my tour of Napa and Sonoma, there is rarely a more packed and boisterous tasting room than Silver Oak's, regardless of the time. The 1999 Cabernet Sauvignon Alexander Valley touts an intense olive, smoky, toasty nose intermixed with kirsch and currant fruit. The wine is sweet, dense, with an opaque ruby/purple color, expansive fat mid-palate, and long finish. This certainly should be as good as most of the Alexander Valley Cabernets released this decade. The 1998 Cabernet Sauvignon Alexander Valley is lighter and more overtly herbaceous. The wine is certainly soft and fleshy with good fruit and is undoubtedly very much in the style of the Alexander Valley, but it does not have the weight, density, or thickness of the finest vintages of the nineties. This wine will be ready to drink upon release and is probably best consumed during its first 8–10 years of life. The 1997 Cabernet Sauvignon Alexander Valley is a dense purple color with boisterous, sweet, spicy, new oak, licorice, and olive notes. This flamboyant wine tastes lighter than I would have expected for a 1997. In the mouth, it reveals medium body, sweet jammy cherry fruit, and a soft finish. It needs to be drunk over the next 7–8 years and, frankly, seems no better than the 1998. By the way, the Alexander Valley *cuvées* are always 100% Cabernet Sauvignon. The dark ruby-colored 1996 Cabernet Sauvignon Alexander Valley exhibits a pronounced smoky, espresso bean, and kirsch-scented nose. Round, dense, rich, full-bodied, and open-knit, its low-acid flavors are undeniably appealing. Black olives make an appearance in the wine's aromatics as it sits in the glass. Anticipated maturity: now–2015. The 1995 Cabernet Sauvignon Alexander Valley is performing far better after a year of bottle age. This dark ruby/purple-colored, seductive wine offers blazingly intense aromas of cigar box, smoky oak, and jammy black currants with a hint of Provençal herbs. Ripe and full-bodied, with low acidity and a fleshy, succulent texture, it is a wine to drink over the next 14–15 years. The 1994 Cabernet Sauvignon Alexander Valley reveals a provocative nose of tobacco, black cherries, cloves, fruitcake, and spice. Some plum and raspberry fruit also emerge on the palate. This is a hedonistic, sexy, seductive, full-bodied Cabernet Sauvignon with low acidity and loads of toasty oak. It will be a huge crowd pleaser and should show well for at least 12–15 years.

The Napa offerings from Silver Oak tend to be less herbaceous and more oriented toward Cabernet Sauvignon's black fruit spectrum. They are every bit as exotic and ostentatious as the Alexander Valley *cuvées*, but more classic, tannic, perhaps longer-lived, and slightly less approachable. A blend of 82% Cabernet Sauvignon, 8% Cabernet Franc, 6% Merlot, and the rest Petit Verdot, the terrific 1999 Cabernet Sauvignon Napa boasts a dense ruby/purple color and a concentrated, opulent personality with flashy notes of black currant, kirsch, spice box, cedar, and smoke. Full-bodied, low in acidity, and juicy, this lush, in-your-face Cabernet should be delicious when released and age nicely for 12 or so years. The 1998 Cabernet Sauvignon Napa (93% Cabernet Sauvignon, 4% Cabernet Franc, and 3% Petit Verdot) shows some aggressive, toasty, charred, oaky notes along with melted asphalt. The wine is highly extracted, has plenty of tannin, and notes of smoke, cedar, cherries, and black currants. It is a very good 1998 with moderate tannin. It should drink well for at least 10 years when it is released. The 1997 Cabernet Sauvignon Napa looks to be one of the finest wines made by the winemaking team of proprietor Justin Meyer and wine-maker/viticulturist Daniel Baron. I know Meyer rates 1995 as the top vintage of the nineties for Silver Oak, but the 1997 Napa is an impressive effort. A blend of 93% Cabernet Sauvignon and the rest 5% Cabernet Franc and 2% Petit Verdot, this wine has a flamboyant nose of fruitcake, licorice, Asian spice, black currants, and toasty wood. Deep, opulent, viscous, intense, chewy, and thick it is a classic Napa Cabernet Sauvignon made in an all-American oak lovers' style. It should drink well for 12–15 years. The 1996 Cabernet Sauvignon Napa (91% Cabernet Sauvignon, 7% Cabernet Franc, .5% Merlot, and 1.5% Petit Verdot) has a dark ruby/plum color and a gorgeous, complex nose of cedar, spice box, cherries, jammy plums, and cassis. The wine is fleshy, medium- to full-bodied, seductive, and filled with glycerin. The finish is all silk. This low-acid, big, spicy, lavishly wooded, chewy wine should drink well for another 10–14 years. The 1994 Cabernet Sauvignon Napa (89% Cabernet Sauvignon and 11% Cabernet Franc) reveals toasty sweet oak in the nose, bombastic levels of black currant fruit and spice along with a hint of mint in the background. Supple and full-bodied, with delirious levels of cedar and unctuously textured fruit, this fleshy, gorgeously made wine should drink well for 14–15 years. A blend of 96% Cabernet Sauvignon and 4% Cabernet Franc, the 1995 Cabernet Sauvignon Napa has turned out even better than the 1994. It possesses a more saturated ruby/purple color, as well as a more flamboyant and exotic bouquet. Moreover, it seems less evolved. Full-bodied and pure, with layer upon layer of concentrated black fruits, smoke, cedar, and toast, it should drink well for 16–17 years.

Past Glories: Cabernet Sauvignon Alexander Valley—1993 (90), 1992 (93), 1991 (92), 1990 (89); Cabernet Sauvignon Napa—1993 (90), 1992 (94), 1991 (95), 1990 (93)

SIMI WINERY (SONOMA)

1995 Cabernet Sauvignon Reserve	Sonoma	D	89
1994 Cabernet Sauvignon Reserve	Sonoma	D	89+

In my barrel tastings, the 1995 Simi Cabernet Sauvignon Reserve was among the more forward, opulently styled 1995s. This attractive wine, which has the potential to be outstanding, exhibits a deep ruby/purple color and a friendly, open-knit, spicy, sweet black currant nose that borders on jamminess. Pure, with a multilayered texture, excellent concentration, sweet, plush, fat fruit, decent acidity, and a long, lusty finish, this Cabernet is reminiscent of a deep, rich, right-bank Bordeaux made primarily from Merlot rather than Cabernet Sauvignon. It is capable of lasting for 10–15+ years. Although closed, the 1994 Cabernet Sauvignon Reserve displays plenty of potential and may merit an outstanding score with another 12–18 months of bottle age. The saturated ruby/purple color is accompanied by a tight but promising nose of black fruits, damp earth, wood, and spice. Impressive in the mouth for its purity, elegance, and balance, this well-structured, medium-weight Cabernet has plenty going for it, but patience is required. Anticipated maturity: now–2015.

Past Glories: Cabernet Sauvignon Reserve—1991 (94), 1990 (95)

SINE QUA NON (SANTA BARBARA)

1996 Against the Wall Syrah	Santa Barbara	D	94
2000 Gewürztraminer Eiswein	California	EEE	(94–96+)

2000	The Good Girl	California	E	(92–94)
2000	Grenache (name not determined)	California	E	(95–98)
2000	The Hussy	California	E	93
1999	Icarus (Grenache/Syrah/Viognier)	California	EE	91+
1999	The Marauder (100% Syrah)	California	E	95+
1999	Mr. K. Sémillon Vin de Paille	California	EEE	(98–100)
1998	Mr. K. Sémillon Vin de Paille	California	EEE	99
1999	Mr. K. Viognier Eiswein	California	EEE	(92–94)
1998	Mr. K. Viognier TBA	California	EEE	96
1995	The Other Hand (Syrah)	California	D	92
1999	Ox (Pinot Noir Shea Vineyard)	California	E	92
2000	Pinot Noir Shea Vineyard (name not determined)	California	E	94
1995	Red Handed	California	E	94
2000	Syrah (name not determined)	California	E	(94–96)
1997	Syrah Imposter McCoy	Santa Barbara	E	96
1998	Syrah E-Raised	California	E	96
1999	Tarantella	California	EE	95
1998	Veiled Pinot Noir Shea Vineyard	Oregon	E	90

Most people tend to think of Ojai, several hours north of Los Angeles, as a resort community with the fabulous Ojai Valley Inn. There is no doubting the tourist appeal of this cute town, but down on the valley floor is commercial Ventura. It is here where the garage winery of Elaine and Manfred Krankl can be found . . . but not without considerable difficulty. Since the first releases, the wines of Sine Qua Non have been exciting. They are thrilling to drink given their richness, multiple dimensions, and intensity, but they are also stunning examples of what low-tech winemaking (from two conscientious people who still do not own a vineyard) can do with high-quality fruit. One of the ironies of tasting through Santa Barbara is that many of the region's finest wines emerge from Ojai's two bonded wineries, Sine Qua Non and Ojai Vineyard. Both the Krankls and the owner of Ojai, Adam Tolmach, tend to make better wines from purchased grapes than those who own the vineyards.

The 2000 lineup looks super-impressive, with perhaps the finest Pinot Noir from the Shea Vineyard and the finest Grenache yet made by Manfred Krankl. As for the whites, the 2000 Good Girl (a blend of 49% Chardonnay and 25.5% Viognier from the Alban Vineyard, and 25.5% Roussanne from the Alban and Stolpman Vineyards) is a blockbuster, full-bodied, honeyed, dry white with 15.2% alcohol. It possesses striking aromatics of buttery citrus, oranges, and other tropical fruits. This structured, well-delineated 2000 is a total turn-on. The other white wine offering, the 100% Roussanne that emerged from both the Stolpman and Alban Vineyards, is the 2000 Hussy. The name says it all. Its light gold color is accompanied by fabulously decadent levels of fruit, luxurious glycerin, and a dry, full-bodied, amazingly well-delineated finish. The Hussy or The Good Girl 2000 . . . take your pick. They are both sumptuous, dry whites that are among the most creative produced in California. The spectacular 2000 Pinot Noir Shea Vineyard would make the great Henri Jayer of Vosne-Romanée happy. It boasts a deep ruby/purple color as well as a striking bouquet of black cherries intermixed with subtle oak and floral notes. Ripe, creamy textured, gorgeously pure, and seamless, this spectacular Pinot will drink well for a decade. The unnamed 2000 Syrah (a 725-case blend of 86% Syrah, 10% Grenache, and 4% Viognier) is from an assortment of such vineyard sites as White Hawk, Stolpman, Bien Nacido, and Alban. Its saturated blue/black/purple color is accompanied by a stunning perfume of blackberry liqueur intermixed with camphor, licorice, vanilla, and a hint of bacon. Full-bodied, with great intensity, low acidity, and stupendous ripeness as well as richness, it should drink well for 15+ years. Potentially even better, and possibly the greatest Grenache yet produced in California, is Sine Qua Non's unnamed 2000 Grenache. A blend of 95% Grenache and 5% Syrah that achieved 15.8% natural alcohol, it emerges from the Alban (two-thirds) and Stolpman (one-third) vineyards. A black/ruby/purple-colored, decadently rich effort, it possesses a sweet nose of macerated black fruits, licorice, earth, and spice. It lasts and lasts and lasts in the mouth.

As for the sweet wines, Manfred Krankl, an Austrian by birth, has joined forces with Austria's most famous sweet wine producer, Alois Kracher, to produce limited quantities of stunning Eisweins and Vin de Pailles. My tastings included the unreleased 2000 Gewürztraminer Eiswein, 1999 Mr. K. Viognier Eiswein, and 1999 Mr. K. Sémillon Vin de Paille. The most compelling sweet wines being made in California, they rival the world's finest. Tasting notes do not do them justice. Readers need to taste for themselves to see what the genius of Manfred Krankl and Alois Kracher, along with Krankl's talented wife, Elaine, has concocted. They are all tour de forces in sweet winemaking, with remarkable concentration and intensity as well as striking underlying acidity. The two I tasted that have been released include the 1998 Mr. K. Sémillon Vin de Paille and 1998 Mr. K. Viognier TBA. The 1998 Mr. K. Viognier Trockenbeerenauslese was made from botrytised Viognier from the Alban Vineyard. There are only 1,245 half bottles. Harvested at 37.8% sugar, it retained 14.5% at bottling. The 1998 Mr. K. Sémillon Vin de Paille is a low-alcohol (7.5%) effort whose grapes were pressed when they ranged between 57–59° Brix, almost unheard-of numbers. It was fermented on indigenous yeasts for 15 months, and then bottled. These nectars must be tasted to be believed. Both will last for 100 years.

Krankl's 1999 Tarantella is one of the finest whites he has made. It possesses outstanding underlying acidity, a terrific, citrusy, honeyed perfume that roars from the glass, full body, and brilliant balance. Given past examples of this blend of Roussanne, Viognier, and Chardonnay, the 1999 should age nicely for 7–8 years. The beautiful, dark ruby-colored 1999 Ox (Pinot Noir Shea Vineyard) reveals sweet black cherry fruit intertwined with subtle wood and floral notes. Medium-bodied, with fine underlying acidity, good freshness, and a style not dissimilar from a top-notch premier cru Côte de Beaune, it will drink well for 7–8 years.

The outrageously rich 1999 The Marauder (100% Syrah from the Alban, Stolpman, and Bien Nacido vineyards) is tightly structured but crammed with blackberry and cassis fruit. Full and rich, but not nearly as precocious or seductive in its youth as previous efforts, it is a candidate for 14–15 years of cellaring. Lastly, the 1999 Icarus (a blend of 80% Grenache, 18% Syrah, and 2% Viognier, three-fourths from the Alban Vineyard and one-fourth from the Stolpman) was closed on the two occasions I tasted it. Its deep ruby color is accompanied by sweet black cherry and kirsch-like aromas with an underlying earthiness. Full-bodied and moderately tannic, but more austere and tightly knit than most Sine Qua Non offerings, it, like The Marauder, should be decanted 45 minutes prior to consumption.

Oregon's Shea Vineyard has been the source for many delicious Pinot Noirs from the likes of Ken Wright and others who live and work near the vineyard. One's sense of rational thought might be questioned to think that a winery two hours north of Los Angeles should be leasing a vineyard in Oregon and shipping the fruit to California in refrigerated reefer trucks, but that is just what the Krankls are doing in order to satisfy their masochistic need to produce world-class Pinot Noir from a cool-climate region. While the 1997 (called The Complicator) was a good effort, the 1998 Veiled Pinot Noir Shea Vineyard is outstanding. It reveals the vintage's strengths in its medium ruby color, attractive, sweet, plum, rose petal, black cherry fruit, and smoky-scented nose. Medium-bodied with outstanding concentration and sweetness in the mid-palate, elegance, and balance, this wine should improve nicely over the next 3–4 years and last for 7–8. That being said, the 1999 looked even more impressive in its jammy, sweet, creamy richness, and flamboyant aromatics.

The stars of this minuscule gem of a winery are their Syrah and Grenache. In the near future, a luscious Grenache will be added to the portfolio. The blended Syrah comes from different vineyard sources, primarily the Alban Vineyard in San Luis Obispo, and Bien Nacido and Stolpman Vineyards in Santa Barbara. These wines are always amusingly named (Black and Blue, Against the Wall, Imposter McCoy). The 1998 Syrah E-Raised is great stuff. It is black-colored, jammy, and super-intense with awesome concentration, terrific, chewy, explosive flavors of blackberries, cherries, and cassis interfused with creosote, pepper, and vanilla. As the wine sits in the glass, notes of roasted coffee, licorice, smoke, and barbecue spices emerge, giving it further dimensions of complexity. It is hard to make a prediction at this point, given how sensational previous vintages have been, but it would not surprise me to see the 1998 Syrah turn out to be the finest yet from Sine Qua Non. As for the 1997 Imposter McCoy (529 cases), I have already wolfed down two bottles with equally voracious friends. A thick, juicy, massive Syrah, it gushes copious quantities of licorice-infused blackberry fruit offering smoke, coffee, and meaty notes. The wine is mouth-filling, teeth-staining, and loaded. Its high alcohol (15.3%), glycerin level, and low acidity make it easy to drink, but I suspect it will age easily for 10–20+ years. The 1996 Against the Wall Syrah is cut from the same mold as the 1997. The color is opaque black/purple, and the nose offers a combination of cassis/blackberry jamminess intermixed with tar, pepper, and spice. Thick, massively full, yet wonderfully rich and expansive, with admirable purity and mouth-staining levels of glycerin and extract, this full-bodied, silky-smooth Syrah is deceptively easy to drink, but I suspect it will age effortlessly for 15–20 years. The 1995 The Other Hand is made from 100% Syrah grown in the Alban, Bien Nacido, and Stolpman vineyards, situated respectively in Edna Valley, Santa Maria, and Los Olivos. Aged 18 months in oak, of which 70% is new, this opaque purple-colored blockbuster offers glorious notes of black fruits (primarily blackberry and cassis), subtle smoke, toast, and licorice, and a whiff of plant material and spice. Full-bodied, yet gorgeously layered and nearly seamless in its flamboyant display of fruit, glycerin, and extract, this large-scaled, yet drinkable Syrah will benefit from another 5–6 years in the bottle, but it is already accessible. It is another example of why I think wineries in this region should be ripping out their Pinot Noir vines and re-planting with Syrah! Look for this super Syrah to age effortlessly for another decade.

The limited-production 1995 Red Handed is a blend of 43% Grenache, 40% Syrah, and 17% Mourvèdre blend also aged 18 months in oak, of which 50% was new. This wine wants to be a southern California Châteauneuf-du-Pape, and comes close to duplicating the character of a hedonistic southern Rhône. Sadly, only 80 six-bottle cases were produced. The color is an impressively saturated red/black/purple. The wine offers up aromas of cigar box, fruitcake, cedar, pepper, Provençal herb, and glorious levels of kirsch and other black fruits. The influence of oak frames the wine rather than adding much to the aromas or flavors. Extremely full-bodied, rich, chewy, and loaded with personality (another wine that reflects its makers), with a multidimensional palate, and beautifully integrated alcohol, acidity, and tannin, this wine has a singular personality and stupendous quality. Anticipated maturity: now–2014.

One of the globe's most creative wineries, Sine Qua Non is turning out world-class wines of extraordinary complexity and individuality.

W. H. SMITH WINES (SONOMA COAST)

1997	Pinot Noir	Sonoma Coast	D	88
1998	Pinot Noir Hellenthal Vineyard	Sonoma Coast	D	91
1997	Pinot Noir Hellenthal Vineyard	Sonoma Coast	D	90

Five hundred cases of the saturated dark ruby-colored 1998 Pinot Noir Hellenthal Vineyard have been produced. Enticing notes of smoke, black cherry jam, minerals, and toast emerge from the glass. Full-bodied, with loamy, earthy, soil scents intermixed with gobs of jammy cherry/strawberry fruit, this may be the finest Pinot Noir made by Joan Smith under the W. H. Smith label. It possesses copious glycerin, a full-bodied texture, and heady alcohol. A hedonistic, sumptuous Pinot Noir, it should be consumed over the next 5–7 years.

The 1997 Pinot Noir Sonoma Coast exhibits a distinctive nose of cinnamon, cloves, plums, *garrigue,* and red fruits. In the mouth, it is lush, with cherry/plum fruit notes, medium body, low acidity, and a sweet, ripe, glycerin-endowed finish. Its color is an evolved ruby/garnet, but the wine is tasty and expansive. It should drink well for 2–3 years. The outstanding medium ruby-colored 1997 Pinot Noir Hellenthal Vineyard offers a provocative nose of cherry liqueur intermixed with Asian spices and toast. It has more body, length, and depth, in addition to the rich, velvety-textured palate also shared by its two less expensive siblings. Harmonious and complex, this wine will not make old bones, but will provide considerable silky-textured pleasure if consumed over the next 3–4 years.

CHÂTEAU SOUVERAIN (SONOMA)

1997 Cabernet Sauvignon	Alexander Valley	C	88
1994 Cabernet Sauvignon	Alexander Valley	C	89
1996 Cabernet Sauvignon Library Reserve	Alexander Valley	D	91
1994 Cabernet Sauvignon Library Reserve	Alexander Valley	D	92
1997 Cabernet Sauvignon Stuhmuller	Alexander Valley	E	91
1997 Cabernet Sauvignon Winemaker's Reserve	Alexander Valley	D	91
1996 Cabernet Sauvignon Winemaker's Reserve	Alexander Valley	D	90
1995 Cabernet Sauvignon Winemaker's Reserve	Alexander Valley	D	91
1994 Cabernet Sauvignon Winemaker's Reserve	Alexander Valley	D	90
1997 Merlot	Alexander Valley	C	87
1995 Merlot	Alexander Valley	C	89
1997 Merlot Winemaker's Reserve	Alexander Valley	D	(89–91)
1996 Rhône Blend	Sonoma	C	88
1998 Zinfandel Reserve	Dry Creek Valley	D	(87–88)

Smart buyers in search of wines with an excellent quality/price rapport have been seeking out Château Souverain's offerings for a number of years. The current and upcoming releases continue to offer "real" wine drinkers tasty choices. The deep ruby-colored 1997 Merlot Alexander Valley is dense and fat, with excellent berry fruit, mocha/coffee notes, and a touch of herbaceousness. Made in a rich, evolved style, with plenty of glycerin and fleshiness, this wine should drink well for 5–7 years. The 1997 Merlot Winemaker's Reserve may prove to be outstanding. Approximately 200 cases were produced. The wine boasts an opaque purple color and a knockout nose of black and red fruits, plus spicy oak and coffee. A deep, exotic, expansively flavored Merlot, it will provide hedonistic drinking for 7–8 years. The 1995 Merlot has a deep ruby/purple color plus a raspberry and blueberry-scented nose. Its concentrated, ripe fruit infused with toasty, smoky, new oak nicely complements the wine's black fruit–dominated personality. Supple and expansive, it is a candidate for 5–7 years of delicious drinking.

Consumers are taking a beating on prices for high-quality California Merlot and Cabernet Sauvignon. Château Souverain continues to offer very good, sometimes outstanding quality for realistic prices. The dark ruby/purple-colored 1997 Cabernet Sauvignon displays an excellent black currant, dried Provençal herb, toasty oak, and sweet black fruit–scented nose. The wine possesses tremendous fruit, medium to full body, low acidity, and a soft, succulent texture. It is a delicious Cabernet to drink over the next 7–10 years. Both the 1997 Cabernet Sauvignon Winemaker's Reserve and 1997 Cabernet Sauvignon Stuhmuller Vineyard (formerly known as the Library Reserve) are outstanding efforts that will be delicious young, yet keep for 14–15 years. The 1997 Cabernet Sauvignon Winemaker's Reserve's saturated ruby/purple color is accompanied by a forward, fragrant bouquet consisting of black fruits, toasty oak, licorice, and spice aromas. Dense and medium to full-bodied, with outstanding purity and overall balance, this is a seductive, precocious Cabernet. The 1997 Cabernet Sauvignon Stuhmuller Vineyard is produced from a hillside vineyard in the hot Alexander Valley. Generous quantities of black fruits, cedar, spice box, and toasty oak jump from the glass. Highly extracted and dense, this beauty possesses terrific fruit purity, a sweet, succulent mid-palate, and ripe tannin.

The 1995 Cabernet Sauvignon Winemaker's Reserve offers a knockout nose of smoked herbs, black currants, and toasty oak. It is medium- to full-bodied, with fruit purity, outstanding richness, and a deep, nicely layered texture. The wine's low acidity and plump, fleshy style suggest drinking now and over the next 12 years. The deep ruby/purple-colored 1996 Cabernet Sauvignon Winemaker's Reserve displays plenty of spice box, fruitcake, and black currant fruit intermixed with allspice, toasty oak, and weedy tobacco. Sweet (from extract, not sugar) on the attack, this full-bodied wine reveals copious quantities of glycerin, fruit, and extract. A beauty, it has managed to avoid the hard tannin exhibited by some 1996s. Drink it over the next decade. In 1996 there is also a limited-production Cabernet Sauvignon Library Reserve. While it is no better than the Winemaker's Reserve, the oak is more noticeable and the wine slightly more powerful. The Library Reserve is unquestionably an outstanding Cabernet, with new oak and slightly higher alcohol. It should drink well upon release and last for 10–12 years.

The Cabernet Sauvignons are all best buys, even the more expensive yet still reasonably priced Winemaker's Reserve. These are excellent wines that recall the glory days of Souverain in the late sixties and early seventies. I recently drank the 1974 Souverain Vintage Selection, a Best Buy pick from *The Wine Advocate*, and had suggested drinking it within 5–7 years of release. That wine is still holding on to all of its fruit, an example of how a wine that was never a blockbuster but was concentrated and impeccably well balanced can age so well. The supple and precocious 1994 Cabernet Sauvignon Winemaker's Reserve is already complex and evolved. It can be drunk now or over the next 12–15 years. The 1994 Cabernet Sauvignon Alexander Valley tastes similar to a Cabernet costing $20–30. This beauty offers a deep ruby/purple color, a spicy, black currant, tobacco, cedar, and toasty-scented nose, lush, low-acid, ripe flavors, the silkiness that is a hallmark of the 1994 vintage, and a clean, ripe finish. It should drink well for 5–7 years, perhaps longer. The 1994 Cabernet Sauvignon Library Reserve (only 200 cases, priced in the $30 range) boasts an opaque ruby/purple color, as well as a sweet, jammy nose of blue and blackberry fruit intertwined with subtle herbs, toast, Asian spices, and licorice. Full-bodied, powerful, and rich, this wine, although loaded with extract, is accessible. Sweet tannin gives the wine a precocious, up-front appeal. It should age gracefully for 12–15+ years.

Souverain's 1996 Rhône Blend (60% Syrah, 30% Mourvèdre, 10% Zinfandel) is an impressive debut offering. Blueberry, floral, peppery, and cassis aromas and flavors are packed into a medium- to full-bodied wine with good length and attractive sweet, ripe fruit and spice. It should provide delicious drinking for 7–8+ years. 1998 is a good rather than exciting year for Zinfandel. The 1998s will require consumption within several years of the vintage (except for the most concentrated efforts). Souverain's Zinfandels include a serious, wood-influenced, peppery, medium-bodied, structured 1998 Zinfandel Reserve. Another six months of bottle age will reveal more about this wine's personality.

SPOTTSWOODE WINERY (NAPA)

1998	Cabernet Sauvignon	Napa	EE	88
1997	Cabernet Sauvignon	Napa	EE	91
1996	Cabernet Sauvignon	Napa	E	90
1995	Cabernet Sauvignon	Napa	D	94
1994	Cabernet Sauvignon	Napa	D	93

These are some of the most elegant, harmonious, stylish Cabernets being made in Napa. Might Spottswoode be the Château Margaux of Napa Valley? The 1998 Cabernet Sauvignon exhibits more blueberry fruit than usual, in addition to an attractive, elegant, medium-bodied style. Although lacking the persistence and length found in Napa's finest vintage, it is a successful wine for the vintage. It should be uncommonly precocious, forward, and delicious when released. Anticipated maturity: now–2014. The deep ruby/purple-colored 1997 Cabernet Sauvignon (4,800 cases) reveals a Bordeaux-like, lead pencil and black currant–scented nose with nuances of spice, cedar, and minerals. Medium-bodied and elegant, with graceful flavors and fine balance, this suave wine should age nicely for 15 or more years. The medium-bodied 1996 Cabernet Sauvignon displays some of the attractive gravelly notes often found in this wine, along with black currant fruit, lavender, subtle oak, sweet tannin for the vintage, and a well-balanced, pure finish. Anticipated maturity: now–2016.

Another outstanding example from this consistently high-quality performer, Spottswoode's 1995 Cabernet Sauvignon stood out in my barrel tasting as one of the strongest efforts of the vintage. Although tightly wound, it exhibits an opaque purple color and a tight but gorgeous nose of black currants, vanilla, minerals, and a touch of smoke and blueberries. Medium- to full-bodied and impeccably well balanced, this wine's structural components (acidity, alcohol, and tannin) are beautifully meshed together with the lavishly rich fruit that is presented in a medium- to full-bodied format. This should turn out to be a textbook, classic Napa Cabernet Sauvignon that admirably balances elegance and power. Anticipated maturity: now–2015. With respect to the 1994 Cabernet Sauvignon, a beautifully scented nose of cassis, lead pencil, high-quality new oak, and spice is followed by a striking richness and balance. This dark ruby/purple-colored wine possesses fabulous concentration, yet it never comes across as heavy or out of sync. A gloriously made, elegant yet powerfully flavored wine, it is accessible, yet capable of lasting for another 12–20 years. This sensational Cabernet exhibits the more complex, elegant side of California winemaking. Bravo!

Past Glories: Cabernet Sauvignon—1993 (92), 1992 (92), 1991 (90), 1990 (90)

SPRING MOUNTAIN VINEYARDS (NAPA)

1995 Miravalle Alba Chevalier Proprietary Red Wine	Spring Mountain	D	90
1994 Miravalle Alba Chevalier Proprietary Red Wine	Spring Mountain	D	88
1996 Miravalle La Perla Chevalier Proprietary Red Wine	Spring Mountain	D	90

This operation, headed by veteran wine-maker Tom Farrell (who assisted in the winemaking of the monumental 1968 Heitz Martha's Vineyard), is one of the most extraordinary vineyard developments in northern Napa. Over 240 acres, spread over the Spring Mountain hillsides, are being developed. Amazingly, there are 130 separate vineyard blocks. The origins of this vineyard site can be traced back to 1882. More recently, such estates as Château Chevalier produced fruit from these hillsides. Tom Farrell and his assistant, Bill Wren, sell about 20% of the production each year. Presently, they are making a proprietary red wine (primarily Cabernet Sauvignon) and a proprietary white wine, as well as some experimental wines. They have produced some Syrah (the 1997 is promising) and have planted Mourvèdre, Pinot Gris, and a small amount of Pinot Noir. The ultimate goal is to produce 20,000 cases of luxury-priced wines. The debut and upcoming releases are all impressive, French-styled wines with considerable character.

The red wines, which are given extended macerations of between 14–45 days, tend to be primarily Cabernet Sauvignon–based wines, aged in 100% new oak. The 1994 Miravalle Alba Chevalier Proprietary Red Wine (for Spring Mountain, a large production of 6,250 cases) is a blend of 93% Cabernet Sauvignon, 3% Merlot, and 4% Cabernet Franc. While it is less tannic than the 1993, more elegant and California-like, it retains a certain austerity, but does unfold nicely on the palate to reveal stylish, rich black currant fruit intermixed with subtle herbaceous notes, minerals, and wood spices. It requires 3–4 more years of cellaring and should keep for a minimum of 10–15 years. The 1995 Miravalle Alba Chevalier Proprietary Red Wine (3,044 cases) is made from 100% Cabernet Sauvignon. This wine was performing impressively at a recent tasting, displaying an opaque purple color and sweet black currant/crème de cassis notes intermixed with lead pencil and toast. Margaux-like in its deep, rich, full-bodied, palate-staining personality, it is loaded with black fruits and silky tannin, and possesses the most length and deepest mid-palate of these Cabernet-dominated proprietary reds. Anticipated maturity: now–2020. The 1996 Miravalle La Perla Chevalier Proprietary Red Wine (4,231 cases, made from a blend of 87% Cabernet Sauvignon, 8% Merlot, and 5% Cabernet Franc) is as good as the 1995. It is a medium- to full-bodied, sweet, rich, chocolaty, black currant–scented and –flavored wine with a slight Médoc-like austerity, but sweet fruit and excellent balance, in addition to purity and depth. Although less massive than the 1995, it is as concentrated and long. Anticipated maturity: now–2020.

Past Glories: 1993 Cabernet Sauvignon Estate Chevalier Vineyard (91)

STAGLIN FAMILY VINEYARDS (NAPA)

1999	Cabernet Sauvignon	Rutherford	EE	92
1998	Cabernet Sauvignon	Rutherford	E	91
1997	Cabernet Sauvignon	Rutherford	E	90
1996	Cabernet Sauvignon	Rutherford	E	90
1995	Cabernet Sauvignon	Rutherford	E	90
1994	Cabernet Sauvignon	Rutherford	D	88
1999	Chardonnay	Rutherford	D	92
1998	Stagliano Sangiovese	Rutherford	D	89

One of the Napa Valley's more gorgeous winery and vineyard sites, the Staglin Family Vineyard (the house and vineyard were used by Walt Disney Pictures for the update of the movie *Parent Trap*) consists of 50 acres situated on the Rutherford Bench in western Napa Valley. Staglin Family Vineyard's wines exhibit additional strength with each new vintage. They are one of the few producers making a non-malolactic Chardonnay that competes with some of the most complex malolactic efforts. Staglin's Chardonnay philosophy is to harvest ripe fruit, preserve the acidity, give it 100% barrel fermentation as well as numerous lees stirrings, filter the wine, and bottle it. There are just under 2,000 cases of this pure Chardonnay. The 1999 Chardonnay appears to be the finest that proprietors Shari and Garon Staglin have yet produced. A light green/gold color is followed by a perfume of ripe pears infused with liquid minerality, spice, and subtle wood. Full-bodied and loaded with fruit, this impeccably made wine unfolds beautifully on the palate. Notes of candied apples, white corn, and citrus also make an appearance in this impressively rich, distinctive Chardonnay. Although it is best consumed during its first 2–3 years of life, this offering has the ability to age longer.

The Stagliano Sangiovese is produced from small yields, which is why it often turns out better than most other California Sangiovese. The deep ruby-colored 1998 Stagliano Sangiovese (150 cases) exhibits a sweet nose of strawberry jam intermixed with cherries, foresty scents, leather, and spice. This soft, ripe, medium-bodied red is ideal for drinking over the next 2–3 years.

There are 4,000 cases of Cabernet Sauvignon from Staglin's Rutherford vineyard. (They are in the process of building caves under the hills adjacent to the vineyard.) All of these Cabernets include a touch of Cabernet Franc in their blends, are aged in 100% French oak, and are quickly becoming classic examples of Rutherford Cabernet. The 1997 Cabernet Sauvignon offers ripe cassis, new oak, tobacco, and spice box aromas and flavors. Rich, structured, moderately tannic, and long, it needs 2–3 years of cellaring, but should keep well for two decades. Even better is the 1998 Cabernet Sauvignon. In contrast to the structured 1997, it is all charm and velvety richness, with plenty of succulence in the mid-palate, as well as a gorgeous evolved bouquet of black fruits, cedar wood, spice, and vanilla. There is enough acidity for delineation in this compelling, rich 1998. Drinkable now, it will evolve nicely for 15+ years. The finest Staglin Cabernet Sauvignon to date may be the 1999. It boasts spectacular aromatics (jammy black currants, tobacco, cedar, vanilla) as well as a seamless, concentrated, full-bodied palate with terrific purity, symmetry, and length. The sweet tannin, wood, and alcohol are all beautifully integrated in this flawless Rutherford Cabernet. Anticipated maturity: 2003–2025. The 1996 Cabernet Sauvignon (2% Cabernet Franc is blended in) has filled out nicely since I first tasted it. Aromas of cedar, chocolate, spice box, and black currants are moderately intense. Medium- to full-bodied, with good spice, in addition to excellent richness, symmetry, and harmony, this is an intense yet stylish Cabernet to drink now and over the next 16+ years. The 1995 Cabernet Sauvignon is richer and more intense in the mid-palate, as well as more backward. The wine is high in tannin, extract, and richness, yet the overall elegance, symmetry, and harmony among its elements are present. This pure, black fruit–dominated wine should be at finest between 2003–2020. The 1994 Cabernet Sauvignon is a graceful, vanilla-scented, medium- to full-bodied wine that emphasizes Cabernet's red fruit character. It is pure and well balanced, with moderate tannin in the attractive, Bordeaux-like finish. Anticipated maturity: now–2016.

STAGS LEAP WINE CELLARS (NAPA)

1994 Cabernet Sauvignon Fay Vineyard	Napa	D	89
1994 Cabernet Sauvignon Stags Leap Vineyard	Napa	D	89
1995 Cask 23 Proprietary Red Wine	Napa	EE	89

Surprisingly, the 1995 Cask 23 Proprietary Red Wine is light, acidic, and excessively polite. The tart acid that is so much an annoying component of these 1995s is present in the Cask 23, giving it a lean, clipped and compact feel on the palate. I do not believe this is what fans of Stags Leap Wine Cellars have come to expect. Nevertheless, the spicy, coffee, herb, cedary, red currant nose offers promise. There is good depth, but much of it is shielded by the wine's tart veneer. It should turn out to be graceful and elegant, but I am concerned about the textural deficiencies. The 1994 Cabernet Sauvignon Fay Vineyard offers up a sweet, tobacco, coffee, spicy, herbal nose, followed by elegant, fruitcake, medium-bodied red currant flavors with a subtle hint of black fruits. The wine is round, with tangy acidity, but not the abrasive levels of tartness found in some of the other reds. The finish reveals good structure, purity, and tannin. This wine should drink well for 10–12 years. The 1994 Cabernet Sauvignon Stags Leap Vineyard is a medium-bodied, mid-weight, sweet, ripe, smoky, vanilla, spicy (allspice?) wine with red and black fruits in the nose. On the palate, it is subtle and flavorful, with good acidity, medium body, and firm tannin. This Cabernet will benefit from several years of cellaring and last for 10–12 years.

Past Glories: 1993 Cabernet Sauvignon Napa (90), 1993 Cask 23 Proprietary Red Wine (91)

STONEFLY VINEYARD (NAPA)

1999 Cabernet Franc	Napa	D	90
1997 Cabernet Franc	Napa	D	91
1996 Cabernet Franc	Napa	D	89

Stonefly's 1996 is the first Cabernet Franc I have tasted from California that resembles a high-quality Loire Valley red from a ripe year (thoughts of Joguet's 1990 Chinons came to mind). The wine exhibits a raspberry and red currant–scented bouquet with faint notes of tobacco and cedar. Rich and smoky, this medium-bodied, intense yet elegant wine saw no new oak, and is better because of it. A beautifully crafted, luscious, Loire-styled Cabernet Franc, it is a breakthrough for this varietal in California. It should drink well for 6–7 years.

The limited-production 1997 is spectacular, particularly for readers seeking a Cabernet Franc made in the style of France's Loire Valley. This is a superrich offering, but without the weight one would expect from a wine gushing with fruit. It offers a leafy, cedary, black currant, and raspberry-scented bouquet, lush richness, low acidity, striking purity, and a fabulously textured, explosively fruity finish. This serious, gorgeously proportioned Cabernet Franc is a noteworthy successor to the 1996. Another outstanding effort is the 1999 Cabernet Franc, an exquisite wine of flavor, elegance, and balance. It has many of the characteristics of the other vintages. Drink it over the next 7–8 years.

STONESTREET (SONOMA)

1997	Cabernet Sauvignon	Alexander Valley	D	89
1996	Cabernet Sauvignon	Alexander Valley	D	88
1995	Cabernet Sauvignon	Alexander Valley	D	89
1994	Cabernet Sauvignon	Alexander Valley	D	92
1996	Cabernet Sauvignon Christopher's Vineyard	Alexander Mountain	D	92
1995	Cabernet Sauvignon Three Block Vineyard	Alexander Mountain	E	92
1999	Chardonnay	Sonoma	D	88
1999	Chardonnay Block 66	Alexander Valley	E	91
1999	Chardonnay Upper Barn	Alexander Valley	E	92
1997	Legacy Proprietary Red Wine	Alexander Valley	EE	91
1996	Legacy Proprietary Red Wine	Alexander Valley	EE	91
1995	Legacy Proprietary Red Wine	Alexander Valley	EE	91
1994	Legacy Proprietary Red Wine	Alexander Valley	EE	91
1998	Merlot	Alexander Valley	D	88
1997	Merlot	Alexander Valley	D	88
1996	Merlot	Alexander Valley	D	89
1995	Merlot	Alexander Valley	D	90
1998	Pinot Noir	Russian River	D	88
1994	Pinot Noir	Russian River	D	88
1999	Sauvignon Blanc Upper Barn	Alexander Valley	C	89

The red wines from Stonestreet have always been boldly oaked, fleshy, and chocolaty with robust personalities. They are designed for huge crowd appeal, but even connoisseurs get a charge out of their ostentatious flavors and character. The white wines get better and better at this winery, as the oak appears to be more judiciously used in addition to better fruit sources. For example, the 1999 Sauvignon Blanc Upper Barn, from a vineyard made famous by Helen Turley's exquisite Chardonnays, is a full-bodied, flinty, fresh Sauvignon with plenty of passion fruit, earth, and melony notes offered in a boldly displayed, ripe, concentrated style. Over the next several years, this big Sauvignon should work exquisitely with shellfish. The 1999 Chardonnay (13,000 cases) reveals a big, sexy, smoky nose not unlike some of the Meursaults fashioned by Burgundy's Michelot. Aromas of bacon fat are intermingled with new oak, creamy pineapple, and buttery fruit. Round and full-bodied with decent underlying acidity, this gutsy Chardonnay will drink well for 3–4 years. There are only a measly 250 cases of the potentially dazzling 1999 Chardonnay Block 66, produced from Jess Jackson's Alexander Mountain estate. This light gold-colored effort exhibits a huge, mineral-infused, butter, pear, citrus, and honeyed fruit–scented bouquet as well as flavors. The wine is strikingly deep, well delineated, and super-concentrated. Look for it to drink well for at least 2–3 years. Another fabulous offering, the 1999 Chardonnay Upper Barn, is still in barrel. It reveals a powerful, smoky, leesy bouquet of buttered tangerines, honeysuckle, mineral, and citrus oils. Authoritative but restrained, with admirable length, it has super potential.

The 1998s reflect the strict selection Stonestreet employed. They usually make about 15,000 cases of Merlot, but in 1998, after the selection process, there were only 6,000 cases available. A blend of 82% Merlot, 14% Cabernet Sauvignon, and 4% Cabernet Franc, this wine is showing much better from bottle than it did last year. It reveals smoky, chocolaty, and black cherry notes with well-integrated oak. Full-bodied, powerful, yet slightly angular, it should drink well for a decade. I enjoyed the garish 1998 Pinot Noir. Medium ruby-colored, this seductive, sexy Pinot offers candied cherry/strawberry flavors infused with smoke and toasty oak. Full, fleshy, and heady (14.2% alcohol), this is another crowd pleasing, exceptionally well-made wine. Sadly, production is only 1,000 cases.

The 1997 Cabernet Sauvignon, tasted in 1999 and released in 2000, is powerful, but the tannin is sweet and the wine ripe, rich, and expansive on the mid-palate. It should last for 15–20 years. The dark ruby/purple-colored 1997 Merlot offers an expressive nose of cocoa, fudge, herb-tinged blackberry and berry fruit. The wine has some tannin to shed, but it is a muscular, full-bodied, robust Merlot to drink over the next 10–12 years. The outstanding 1997 Legacy, a proprietary blend of 56% Cabernet Sauvignon, 27% Merlot, and 17% Cabernet Franc, possesses abundant jammy black currant/cherry fruit intermixed with lead pencil, toasty oak, and vanilla. Full-bodied and pure, with moderate tannin, this large-scaled effort (14.2% alcohol) can be drunk early, but promises to evolve for at least two decades.

The 1996 Legacy, a blend of 57% Cabernet Sauvignon, 26% Merlot, and 17% Cabernet Franc, exhibits an opaque ruby/purple color in addition to a toasty nose, chocolate, black currants, lead pencil, and smoke. Full-bodied, with high tannin, this pure, concentrated wine needs another 2–3 years of cellaring. Anticipated maturity: 2003–2020. The 1996 Merlot (a blend of 76% Merlot, 19% Cabernet Sauvignon, and 5% Cabernet Franc) exhibits a deep plum color, followed by knockout aromatics of roasted coffee, chocolate, and berry/cherry liqueur. Rich, smoky, exotic, and hedonistic, it should drink well for a decade. Like the Merlot, the 1996 Cabernet Sauvignon (a blend of 88% Cabernet Sauvignon and 12% Cabernet Franc) is an unfiltered, richly fruity, smoky, oaky, full-bodied wine with fine depth, an easy, open-knit, expansive chewiness, a supple personality, and sweet tannin in the finish. Accessible now, it promises to be even better over the next 4–12 years.

Stonestreet's proprietary red wine called Legacy has proven to be not only a wine of exceptional quality but one of remarkable consistency. The blend can vary (the 1993 is a blend of 70% Cabernet Sauvignon, 20% Merlot, 10% Cabernet Franc) to one less marked by Cabernet Sauvignon (the 1994 is a blend of 51% Cabernet Sauvignon, 39% Merlot, 9% Cabernet Franc, 1% Petit Verdot). The 1995 is composed of 59% Cabernet Sauvignon, 23% Cabernet Franc, 17% Merlot, and 1% Petit Verdot. All of these wines are aged for 20–23 months in 100% new French oak barrels, and are bottled unfined and unfiltered. I found them to be flamboyant, opulently textured, rich, expressive, and dramatic proprietary reds that are loaded with character. Moreover, they possess 10–20 years of aging potential. The 1994 and 1995 may merit higher scores with more aging. These vintages are similar in character, as both were years with exceptionally long hang times for the grapes (always a positive sign). Both wines possess a chocolaty, smoky, cassis, lavishly wooded character, juicy, succulent, full-bodied personalities, and plenty of length, extract, and fruit. Both are also remarkably seamless wines with immense potential. Because of their low acidity and ostentatious personalities, these wines will be flattering to drink young, but will easily last for 12–15 years. The 1995 Legacy, at 14.2% alcohol, is a boldly styled, fleshy, full-bodied wine that can be drunk or cellared for 15 years.

The 1995 Cabernet Sauvignon Three Block Vineyard from the Alexander Valley is made from 96% Cabernet Sauvignon and 4% Cabernet Franc. It is an unfiltered, dense, full-bodied wine with considerable power and richness. Aged in 50% new French oak, with more than 14% alcohol, it exhibits plenty of tannin, as well as impressively endowed flavors of roasted herbs, black currants, chocolate, and blackberries. Anticipated maturity: now–2020. The 1996 Cabernet Sauvignon Christopher's Vineyard (previously called the Three Block Vineyard) is cut from the same mold. It is a hedonistic, opaque purple-colored wine with gobs of toasty new oak, thrilling levels of extract, rich, chewy, black currant and blackberry fruit, impressive glycerin, sweet tannin, and a knockout finish that must contain over 14% alcohol. More than 80% new French oak was utilized in this wine's upbringing. There are 500 cases of this unfiltered beauty. The opaque plum-colored 1995 Merlot is a thick wine with compelling scents of roasted coffee, chocolate cake, smoky oak, and rich, jammy fruit. A blend of 84% Merlot, 15% Cabernet Sauvignon, and 1% Cabernet Franc, this wine is exceptional, seductive, rich, medium- to full-bodied, and ideal for drinking now and over the next dozen years. The 1995 Cabernet Sauvignon is no shy wine, coming in at 14.2% alcohol. The wine reveals the ripe fruit their Alexander Valley vineyard achieves. The use of heavily toasted Demptos barrels and indigenous yeasts for fermentation give these wines provocative aromatics. The Cabernet is built along the line of the Merlot, offering a hedonistic mouthful of fleshy, rich, briery, dense, berry, smoky, and herb-tinged fruit. Full-bodied, with a lashing of sweet tannin, this lusty, decadently rich, flamboyant wine should drink well for 12–15 years.

The 1994 Cabernet Sauvignon is intense and powerful, with an opaque purple color and gobs of lavishly oaked, smoky, cassis fruit intertwined with aromas of roasted herbs and high-quality toasty oak, revealing plenty of tannin, low acidity, and outstanding concentration and purity. This large-scaled, remarkably well balanced wine should drink well young yet last for two decades. The medium ruby-colored, unfined and unfiltered 1994 Pinot Noir exhibits a lusty, smoky, sweet berry-scented nose that reveals copious quantities of both ripe fruit and oak. This medium-bodied, softly textured, delicious wine is not the most concentrated or profoundly complex, but it offers a sexy glass of Pinot for drinking over the next several years. *Past Glories:* 1993 Cabernet Sauvignon (90), 1993 Legacy Proprietary Red Wine (91), 1993 Merlot (90)

STORYBOOK MOUNTAIN VINEYARDS (NAPA)

1999	Zinfandel Eastern Exposure	Napa D	90
1998	Zinfandel Eastern Exposure	Napa D	90
1999	Zinfandel Estate Reserve	Napa D	91
1998	Zinfandel Estate Reserve	Napa D	91+
1999	Zinfandel Mayacamas Range	Napa C	89
1998	Zinfandel Mayacamas Range	Napa C	91

Longtime followers of the classic, built-to-age Storybook Mountain Zinfandels undoubtedly are aware that over the last several years proprietor Jerry Seps has been moving toward an accessible, riper style with more elevated alcohol. However, these are still among the handful of Zinfandels that can age gracefully for a decade. 1999 appears to be another top vintage for this estate. The deep ruby/purple-colored 1999 Zinfandel Mayacamas Range (14.5% alcohol) reveals impressive aromatics of black cherries, currants, minerals, and underbrush. Sweet fruit on the attack is followed by a nicely textured, medium- to full-bodied finish. It should drink well for 7–8 years. Even more impressive is the 1999 Zinfandel Eastern Exposure. The addition of 4% Viognier no doubt accounts for the more perfumed, intense aromatic profile (although I could not detect any Viognier characteristics). Elegant, powerful, rich, and medium- to full-bodied, with stylish black currant, cherry, and blackberry flavors, an excellent texture, sweet tannin, adequate acidity, and a pure, concentrated finish, this beautifully etched Zinfandel can be drunk now and over the next 10–12 years. Storybook's flagship wine is the 600-case *cuvée* of Zinfandel Estate Reserve. The beautiful 1999 is a concentrated, backward, long, multidimensional effort exhibiting notes of earth, spice box, black currants, blackberries, and minerals. This multilayered, concentrated, textured Zinfandel displays great purity, a brilliant marriage of power with finesse, and a long, rich finish. Give it 1–2 years of cellaring, and drink it over the following 12 years.

1998 is another strong vintage for Storybook Mountain Vineyards. Followers of this winery should note a few refinements in style over recent vintages. First, some Viognier has been added to the Eastern Exposure *cuvée* to achieve a more complex bouquet as well as more supple flavors. Second, the harvest dates have been pushed back in order to achieve lower acidity, more color, and an accessible style. Traditionally, Storybook Mountain has produced many of the longest-lived Zinfandels, with some vintages aging easily for a decade or more, particularly the Reserve bottling. The 1998 Zinfandel Mayacamas Range exhibits an opaque dark purple color as well as a gorgeous bouquet of blueberry, black raspberry, liquid mineral, and well-integrated oaky aromas. Beautifully pure, medium-bodied, and ripe, with a sweet fruit character and long finish, this wine possesses more structure than most 1998s, yet also accessibility. It should drink well for 7–10 years. The dark ruby/purple-colored 1998 Zinfandel Eastern Exposure reveals a sweet, blackberry/briery-scented nose with hints of Viognier (4% added to the blend) in its subtle, peach jam–like note. The wine possesses a plush texture, blue and black fruits, a notion of minerals, medium to full body, low acidity, and excellent length. It should drink well for 7–8 years. The backward, dense, classic 1998 Zinfandel Estate Reserve (14.4% alcohol) exhibits a deep ruby/purple color in addition to a tight nose of loamy soil, spice, black fruit, and mineral scents. Rich and full, but structured, backward, and moderately tannic, this impressive wine is one of the most classic statements of the vintage. It is capable of evolving for 10–12+ years. However, it is one of the few 1998 Zinfandels that requires patience. Anticipated maturity: now–2015.

SUMMERS (NAPA)

1999 Zinfandel Howell Mountain	Napa	D	88

A deep ruby/purple color is accompanied by sweet scents of blackberry and currant jam, underbrush, spice, and oak. This medium-bodied, slightly austere Zinfandel is built more along the lines of a Cabernet Sauvignon. It should drink well for 4–5 years.

JOSEPH SWAN VINEYARDS (SONOMA)

1998 Zinfandel Frati Ranch	Russian River	D	88
1998 Zinfandel Mancini Ranch	Russian River	D	88
1998 Zinfandel Stellwagen Vineyard	Sonoma	D	89
1998 Zinfandel Zeigler Vineyard	Russian River	D	87

These wines have more in common with the late-harvest, dry, distinctive, sometimes controversial Italian Amarones than most California Zinfandels. All are forceful and concentrated, but the notes of aged beef, animal fur, and melted asphalt as well as their heavy, ponderous personalities are not for everybody. Most are best drunk with cheese or sipped alone at the end of a meal. My favorite Joseph Swan offerings include the 1998 Zinfandel Mancini Ranch. A dense ruby/purple color is followed by a well-balanced wine exhibiting notes of tar, new saddle leather, and overripe black fruits. Licorice, cinnamon, dried herbs, and earth add to the powerful impression. It is thick, totally dry, and the best balanced of this group of mouth-staining Zinfandels. Drink it over the next 7–8 years. The dark ruby/purple-colored 1998 Zinfandel Zeigler Vineyard exhibits aromas of shoe polish, roasted meats, dried herbs, licorice, and sweet, briery fruit. While rustic, thick, big, and chewy, it is not in total harmony. The super-extracted 1998 Zinfandel Stellwagen Vineyard reveals briery, earthy, herb-tinged fruit, kinky, leather, meaty, licorice, and tar notes, excellent density, and full body. The finish is slightly sweet, but the wine tastes dry. The powerful 1998 Zinfandel Frati Ranch (15.6% alcohol) offers up scents of melted tar, licorice, dried black fruits, loamy soil, and beef blood. Powerful, thick, and huge, but somewhat disjointed, this robust, macho wine will age well for 6–8 years, if not longer.

SWANSON VINEYARDS (NAPA)

1997 Alexis Proprietary Red Wine	Napa	D	90

This Bordeaux-inspired blend is the finest wine I have tasted from Swanson since they let winemaking consultant Helen Turley depart a few years ago. The dense ruby/purple-colored 1997 Alexis (3,400 cases) offers an attractive nose of blackberry, cherry, loamy soil, licorice, and vanilla scents. With medium to full body, a creamy, fleshy texture, sweet tannin, low acidity, and admirable extraction, it is impressive and ageworthy. Moreover, it has not been excessively acidified. Consume it over the next 10–12 years.

TABLAS CREEK (PASO ROBLES)

2000 Antithesis (Chardonnay)	Paso Robles	D	90
2000 Clos Blanc	Paso Robles	D	88
2000 Grand Cuvée	Paso Robles	E	92+
2000 Petit Cuvée	Paso Robles	C	92
1999 Petit Cuvée	Paso Robles	C	87
2000 Reserve Cuvée	Paso Robles	D	93
1999 Reserve Cuvée	Paso Robles	D	90

This promising hillside vineyard west of Highway 101, six miles from the Pacific Ocean, is jointly owned by importer Robert Haas and the Perrin family of Château Beaucastel in Châteauneuf-du-Pape. There is a total of 180 acres, 80 of which are under vine and 30 leased. Except for a small parcel of Chardonnay, only Rhône varietals are planted. The plantings include Mourvèdre (45%), Syrah, (22%), Grenache (22%), and the rest Counoise. The white varietals include Roussanne (50%), Viognier (25%), Marsanne (10%), Grenache Blanc, and the aforementioned Chardonnay. This is still a work in progress, with the winery having only been built in 1997. While the quality was at first uninspiring, it has become exciting over recent vintages, particularly with the 2000s. Planted in 1992, at elevations between 1,400–1,600 feet, the first crop was the 1994. The white wine offerings include the Chablis-like 2000 Antithesis, a 250-case, European-styled Chardonnay. Minimal amounts of new oak are utilized, and the wine reveals plenty of stony, mineral-laced, citrusy fruit presented in a Burgundy-like style. Elegant and restrained, this charming effort seduces by its nuances rather than power. The 2000 Clos Blanc (a blend of 45% Roussanne, 19% Viognier, 19% Marsanne, and 17% Grenache Blanc) exhibits an excellent citrusy nose, no evidence of oak, and hints of orange marmalade intermixed with citrus, candle wax, and spice. It possesses good acidity, freshness, full body, and excellent fruit. Although this 2000 may last for 4–5 years, I recommend drinking it over its first 2–3 years of life.

In most vintages there are two *cuvées* of red wine, although in top years a microscopic quantity of a third *cuvée*, the Grand Cuvée, is produced. These offerings are aged in a combination of small barrels, *demi-muids*, and larger *foudres*. The terrific 2000 Petit Cuvée (600 cases of a blend of 80% Grenache and 20% Syrah) is available at a fair price. It exhibits copious aromas of kirsch, blackberries, and currants. Rich, full-bodied, and loaded with fruit, it is restrained as well as elegant. Already delicious, it will age for a decade or more. The top *cuvée*, the 2000 Reserve Cuvée, is a blend of 35% Mourvèdre, 26% Syrah, 25% Grenache, and 14% Counoise. This 4,800-case offering does an impressive job of emulating a full-throttle southern Rhône red produced in California. A saturated black/purple color is followed by aromas of licorice, roasted herbs, meats, blackberries, and cassis. It is intense and full-bodied, with sweet tannin and impressive concentration. The Mourvèdre component will undoubtedly cause this wine to tighten up after bottling and will provide 10–15 years of aging potential. It is no shy wine at 15% alcohol, but it is well hidden beneath the wealth of fruit and extract. This is the most impressive wine yet made by Tablas Creek, and a clear sign that they are going to be a serious producer among the band of producers dedicated to the grapes from southern France known as the Rhône Rangers. The 75-case 2000 Grand Cuvée

(55% Mourvèdre, 35% Syrah, and 10% Grenache) is a more structured, tightly knit, backward, austere effort. It is an elegant, French-styled, impressive offering.

The 1999s display the cool weather conditions experienced in the Paso Robles region. The 1999 Petit Cuvée (65% Grenache, 25% Syrah, and 10% Mourvèdre) is a sexy, up-front effort. Although not as complex or fleshy and textured as the 2000, it offers a beautifully ripe attack followed by dry, firm tannin in the austere finish. Its 15.2% alcohol is well hidden. The 1999 Reserve Cuvée is a blend of 40% Mourvèdre, 27% Grenache, 23% Syrah, and 10% Counoise. It exhibits a dense purple color as well as a sweet perfume of blackberries, leather, licorice, earth, and pepper. Elegant, rich, medium- to full-bodied, and ripe, with nicely integrated tannin, it will drink well for a decade or more.

An insider tip: Should readers have access to it, they should check out the delightful rosé made at Tablas Creek. Keep in mind, these wines need to be drunk within their first six months of life.

TALLEY VINEYARDS (SAN LUIS OBISPO)

2000	Chardonnay	Arroyo Grande	C	89
1999	Chardonnay	Arroyo Grande	C	89
2000	Chardonnay Oliver's Vineyard	Edna Valley	E	90
2000	Chardonnay Rincon Vineyard	Arroyo Grande	C	92
1999	Chardonnay Rincon Vineyard	Arroyo Grande	C	90+
2000	Chardonnay Rosemary's Vineyard	Arroyo Grande	C	92
1997	Pinot Noir	Arroyo Grande	D	89
2000	Pinot Noir Rincon Vineyard	Arroyo Grande	E	90
1999	Pinot Noir Rincon Vineyard	Arroyo Grande	E	91
1997	Pinot Noir Rincon Vineyard	Arroyo Grande	D	91
1995	Pinot Noir Rincon Vineyard	Arroyo Grande	D	90
2000	Pinot Noir Rosemary's Vineyard	Arroyo Grande	E	92
1999	Pinot Noir Rosemary's Vineyard	Arroyo Grande	E	92+
1997	Pinot Noir Rosemary's Vineyard	Arroyo Grande	D	93

The Talleys are prominent farmers in Edna Valley with over 1,000 acres, primarily planted with peppers, beans, avocados, and cilantro. However, their most profitable crop must be grapes. From their 150 acres of vineyards they produce 16,000 cases of estate-bottled wine. About 25% of the grape production is sold. In the Central Coast, Talley stands out as the one superstar producer of Chardonnay and Pinot Noir, both of which display the Burgundian-like characteristic of elegance allied with considerable flavor authority. All are restrained yet intense. The 2000 Chardonnay Arroyo Grande offers aromas of pears, honey, and citrus in a medium, full-bodied, complex yet elegant personality. It should drink well for 2–3 years. The 2000 Chardonnay Rincon Vineyard possesses more ripeness plus a layered texture and a smoky nose exhibiting scents of hazelnuts, minerals, and buttery fruit. It tastes extremely Burgundian given its restraint and measured yet intense style. The 2000 Chardonnay Rosemary's Vineyard (the coolest of the Talley vineyards) has higher acidity as well as notes of minerals, tangerines, butter, and subtle wood. It is a full-bodied, rich, multilayered effort that should age well for 5–6 years. The 2000 Chardonnay Oliver's Vineyard displays notes of buttered citrus, honeysuckle, candle wax, and subtle toasty oak. Medium- to full-bodied, refreshing, measured, and deep, this intense effort should drink well for 3–4 years.

The light gold-colored 1999 Chardonnay Arroyo Grande offers gorgeous aromas of roasted hazelnuts, honey, and ripe fruit. Textured, with good underlying acidity and delineation, excellent freshness, and a moderately long finish, this medium-bodied, complex, Burgundian-styled Chardonnay will drink well for 2–4 years. The 1999 Chardonnay Rincon Vineyard (4,960 bottles produced) possesses copious quantities of buttery, honeyed toast-like notes in the complex aromatics. Tighter than its siblings, but full-bodied and ripe, with zesty acidity for definition, this large-scaled, impressive yet elegant effort will drink well for 4–6 years, possibly longer.

The 2000 Pinot Noir Rincon Vineyard offers elegant, sweet, plum, and black cherry fruit in a medium- to full-bodied, concentrated, stylish format. It is Volnay-like in its elegance and overall balance and character. Enjoy it over the next 6–7 years. Even better is the 2000 Pinot Noir Rosemary's Vineyard. Dark ruby/purple-colored, rich, intense, and full-bodied, with great purity of black raspberry and cherry fruit, a potent mid-palate, and beautiful ripeness, it should drink well for 8–10 years. By the way, Talley's wines, especially the Pinot Noirs, have an impressive track record of aging well even though their first vintage was as recent as 1986. Recent bottles of the 1995 Pinot Noir Rincon Vineyard and 1994 Pinot Noir Rosemary's Vineyard were sumptuous when drunk in late 2001. The 1999 Pinot Noirs are concentrated, backward offerings that need time in bottle to round out. Both possess high richness as well as tannin. The 1999 Pinot Noir Rosemary's Vineyard (10,115 bottles produced) boasts an impressively saturated ruby/purple color plus a gorgeous perfume of black cherry and raspberry liqueur mixed with mineral, new-oak, and floral scents. The compelling, youthful aromatics are almost primary in their vividness and intensity. The wine is tight, full-bodied, and moderately tannic, with exceptional concentration and depth. This brilliant Pinot needs another 1–2 years of cellaring and should keep for 10–12 years. The 1999 Pinot Noir Rincon Vineyard (6,582 bottles produced) offers aromas of red and black fruits, earth, and herbs. Made in a softer, more accessible style, it possesses copious quantities of rich fruit in addition to plenty of density, purity, and depth. This mouth-filling 1999 is more approachable than the Rosemary's Vineyard and should mature 1–2 years earlier. Anticipated maturity: now–2012.

The dark ruby-colored 1997 Pinot Noir exhibits classic black cherry, floral, and subtle spicy wood aromatics. Medium- to full-bodied, with sweet tannin, tangy acidity, and excellent purity, this is a beautifully knit, black fruit–dominated Pinot with admirable delineation and structure. It should drink well for 5–7 years. The more limited-production 1997 Pinot Noir Rincon Vineyard (4,541 bottles) offers copious quantities of high-quality French oak mixed with blackberry and cherry fruit. Gorgeous aromas reminiscent of a top growth from Vosne-Romanée (violets and raspberries) also make an appearance. Tightly knit and full-bodied, with sweet tannin and a rich, nicely layered mid-section, this impressively endowed Pinot will be better with another 1–2 years of bottle age and will keep for a decade. Another impressive effort, the deep ruby/purple-colored 1997 Pinot Noir Rosemary's Vineyard (3,236 bottles) reveals elements of moderately intense, sweet, forest notes intermixed with black fruits and vanilla. Rich, concentrated, tight, and unevolved, this stunning Pinot is among the finest being produced in California. Delicious and seductive, it will get even better with 1–3 years of cellaring and will keep for a decade. Another exceptional Pinot Noir from Talley Vineyards, the 1995 Rincon Vineyard (3,879 bottles produced) possesses a dark ruby color and sweet black plum and cherry fruit nicely dosed with high-quality spicy new oak. Medium-bodied, flavorful, and intense, yet not heavy, this beautifully made, elegant, and flavorful Pinot should continue to improve for 3–4 years and last for a decade.

P.S. Readers should also check out the exquisite *beerenauslese*-styled white Riesling made at Talley Vineyards.

TITUS (NAPA)

1999 Zinfandel	Napa	C	90
1999 Zinfandel Old Vines Redwood Valley	Mendocino	C	91

To date I have enjoyed everything that has emerged from this high-quality producer. The 1999 Zinfandel Napa (14.5% alcohol) displays Châteauneuf-du-Pape–like aromas of saddle leather, roasted meats, pepper, earth, black raspberries, and kirsch. Ripe, full-bodied, and supple-textured, it provides a big, lusty mouthful of Zinfandel to drink over the next 3–4 years. Even better, the deep ruby/purple-colored 1999 Zinfandel Old Vines Redwood Valley is a pure, harmonious, full-bodied, exuberant offering bursting with black fruits infused with mineral and oak characteristics. Dense, chewy, and unctuously textured, this succulent, fat Zinfandel needs to be consumed over the next 4–5 years.

PHILIP TOGNI VINEYARDS (NAPA)

1999 Cabernet Sauvignon	Spring Mountain	EE	95
1998 Cabernet Sauvignon	Spring Mountain	EE	90
1997 Cabernet Sauvignon	Spring Mountain	E	94+
1996 Cabernet Sauvignon	Spring Mountain	E	96
1995 Cabernet Sauvignon	Spring Mountain	D	95
1994 Cabernet Sauvignon	Spring Mountain	D	96

Spring Mountain, a thriving source of vineyards in the last century, is becoming increasingly congested, with a bevy of vineyards sprouting up across these mountain slopes. Most of the top wine producers, from Jim Pride and Bob Foley at Pride Mountain Vineyard to Les Behrens and Bob Hitchcock at Behrens and Hitchcock, cite the inspiring wines made by Philip Togni as the reason they believe in this high-altitude viticultural region. Feisty Philip Togni continues to turn out spectacular wines that give all indications, even in lighter, more challenging vintages such as 1998, of lasting 20+ years. His great vintages—and there have been quite a few (1984, 1985, 1986, 1987, 1990, 1991, 1994, 1995, 1996, and 1997)—will last 30 or more years considering how slowly these wines evolve. Production has been relatively small with the short crops and cool growing seasons of 1998, 1999, and 2000. There are about 1,200 cases of the 1998, and 1,800 or so cases of the 1999 and 2000. You would think, after a brilliant career of more than 30 years making some of Napa's finest Cabernet Sauvignons, that Togni could rest on his laurels, but he keeps pushing the proverbial envelope. Practicing more intense viticulture, Togni is doing more shoot positioning and leaf pulling in the vineyard, picking in tiny, six-inch-deep bins, and using a sorting table to select out only the ripest and most healthy fruit. His 1998 Cabernet Sauvignon is the smallest-scaled wine of the nineties, but as I told him, "If this is as bad as you can do, bravo!" The 1998 exhibits a dense ruby/purple color. Made from fruit that was harvested between October 30–November 4 (50% of the crop was cut off to guarantee only ripe fruit), it reveals aromas of tapenade, licorice, black currants, smoked herbs, and earth. The wine offers abundant black fruits, outstanding richness and complexity, but is more evolved than most Togni Cabernets at a similar age. It can be drunk early, but will easily age for 15 or more years. Togni's 1999 Cabernet Sauvignon (picked between October 11–15) is a blend of 82% Cabernet Sauvignon, 15% Merlot, and 3% Cabernet Franc. It could easily rival some of Togni's greatest wines of the nineties. This stupendous effort has a saturated, black/purple color and a gorgeously pure nose of licorice, blackberries, cassis, mineral, and smoke. With an unctuous texture, firm but sweet tannin, exquisite purity, and fine overall symmetry, it is one of the vintage's top successes. Anticipated maturity: 2006–2030.

The glorious 1997 Cabernet Sauvignon (a blend of 82% Cabernet Sauvignon, 15% Merlot, and 3% Cabernet Franc) is the most opulently textured Togni offering since his 1992. It possesses a saturated purple color in addition to a thrilling but still reticent nose of blackberries, cassis, minerals, dried herbs, and smoky oak. Full-bodied, pure, thick, and creamy textured, this wine's superb concentration conceals its lofty but sweet tannin. Togni's wines possess exceptional aging potential, but it will be hard to keep your hands off this one after it has had another 2–4 years of bottle age. Anticipated maturity: 2003–2025+.

In contrast, the opaque purple-colored 1996 Cabernet Sauvignon is a blockbuster monster crammed with phenomenal potential. It offers up a sensational nose of licorice, chocolate, cassis, Provençal herbs, and toast. The wine is succulent and full-bodied, as well as extraordinarily powerful and backward. It should be drinkable within 5–7 years, and age beautifully for three decades. All of Togni's wines are bottled with neither fining nor filtration, and, as he likes to say, "made as Bordeaux was . . . a long, long time ago."

The 1995 Cabernet Sauvignon, a vintage that produced a number of top-notch wines (as well as some with rough tannin and muted personalities), is one of the year's bright shining successes. The wine displays an opaque purple color, as well as a lavishly intense nose of blackberry/blueberry/cassis fruit intermingled with chocolate and olive nuances. Dense and fruit-driven, with awesome levels of glycerin and extract, this formidably endowed, moderately tannic wine should be at its best with another 7–8 years of cellaring. Once again, Togni has produced a wine with 25 or more years of aging potential. The 1994 Cabernet Sauvignon is a remarkably rich, multidimensional wine. Extremely full-bodied, with extraordinary fruit purity, this wine is, aromatically and texturally, compelling stuff. Unfortunately, the 1994 is already sold out, but those lucky enough to have purchased a few bottles own a monumental mountainside Cabernet that should age gracefully for 25–30 years. Incredibly, in an open bottle, this wine held up without oxidation an amazing six days!

Part mountain goat, part man, Philip Togni continues to fight vineyard diseases, such as Pierce's, and frightfully low yields from his formidably steep Spring Mountain vineyards to produce some of California's most exciting wines.

Past Glories: Cabernet Sauvignon—1993 (92), 1992 (96), 1991 (95), 1990 (95), 1987 (90), 1986 (92), 1985 (92), 1984 (93)

TRENTADUE (SONOMA)

1999	Old Patch Red	Dry Creek	C	88
1999	Zinfandel	California	C	88
1999	Zinfandel	Dry Creek	C	90

After being absent from these pages for several years, Trentadue has rebounded strongly with its 1999 portfolio. All three wines are good values, but the 1999 Old Patch Red is a terrific bargain for California. The dark ruby-colored 1999 Zinfandel California (15% alcohol) exhibits a sweet nose of jammy black cherry and berry fruit, earth, and pepper. Full-bodied, spicy, supple-textured, and loaded, it will drink well for 3–4 years. More complex, the 1999 Zinfandel Dry Creek reveals a sweeter attack as well as complex but subtle notes of toasty American oak, and dense, full-bodied flavors redolent with raspberries and cherries. It is a thick, juicy, gorgeous Zinfandel to enjoy over the next 5–6 years. Lastly, the 1999 Old Patch Red (a field blend of Zinfandel, Carignan, and Petite Sirah from 100-year-old vines) is a Côtes du Rhône look-alike from California. It offers notes of pepper, leather, animal, blackberry and cherry fruit, full body, an excellent texture, robust, muscular flavors, and a mouthfilling style. Drink it over the next 2–3 years to take advantage of its unabashed exuberance.

TURLEY CELLARS (NAPA)

1999	Charbono Tofanelli Vineyard	Napa	C	91
1998	Charbono Tofanelli Vineyard	Napa	C	90
1997	Petite Syrah Aida Vineyard	Napa	D	90
1999	Petite Syrah Estate	Napa	D	91+
1999	Petite Syrah Hayne Vineyard	Napa	D	96
1998	Petite Syrah Hayne Vineyard	Napa	D	90
1997	Petite Syrah Hayne Vineyard	Napa	D	95
1999	Petite Syrah Rattlesnake Acres	Napa	D	94
1998	Petite Syrah Rattlesnake Acres	Napa	D	89
1997	Petite Syrah Rattlesnake Acres	Napa	D	91
1997	Zinfandel Aida Vineyard	Napa	D	93
1999	Zinfandel Black-Sears Vineyard	Howell Mountain	D	93

1998	Zinfandel Black-Sears Vineyard	Howell Mountain	D	88
1997	Zinfandel Black-Sears Vineyard	Howell Mountain	D	95
1999	Zinfandel Dogtown Vineyard	Lodi	D	92
1998	Zinfandel Dogtown Vineyard	Lodi	D	90
1997	Zinfandel Dogtown Vineyard	Lodi	D	(89–91)
1999	Zinfandel Duarte Vineyard	Contra Costa	D	91
1998	Zinfandel Duarte Vineyard	Contra Costa	D	93
1997	Zinfandel Duarte Vineyard	Contra Costa	D	(90–92)
1999	Zinfandel Grist Vineyard	Bradford Mountain	D	90
1998	Zinfandel Grist Vineyard	Bradford Mountain	D	90
1997	Zinfandel Grist Vineyard	Bradford Mountain	D	93
1999	Zinfandel Hayne Vineyard	Napa	E	96
1998	Zinfandel Hayne Vineyard	Napa	E	94
1997	Zinfandel Hayne Vineyard	Napa	D	95
1999	Zinfandel Juveniles	California	C	92
1999	Zinfandel Moore (Earthquake)	Napa	D	95
1998	Zinfandel Moore (Earthquake)	Napa	D	92
1997	Zinfandel Moore (Earthquake)	Napa	D	94
1999	Zinfandel Old Vines	California	C	93
1998	Zinfandel Old Vines	California	C	90
1997	Zinfandel Old Vines	California	C	92
1999	Zinfandel Pringle Family Vineyard	Howell Mountain	D	96
1998	Zinfandel Pringle Family Vineyard	Howell Mountain	D	90+
1997	Zinfandel Spenker Vineyard	Lodi	D	87
1999	Zinfandel Tofanelli Vineyard	Napa	D	94
1998	Zinfandel Tofanelli Vineyard	Napa	D	91
1997	Zinfandel Tofanelli Vineyard	Napa	D	92
1999	Zinfandel Turley Estate	Napa	D	94
1999	Zinfandel Vineyard 101	Alexander Valley	D	92
1998	Zinfandel Vineyard 101	Alexander Valley	D	91
1997	Zinfandel Vineyard 101	Alexander Valley	D	90

California's preeminent Zinfandel specialists, proprietor Larry Turley and wine-maker Ehren Jordan, may have produced the finest Zinfandels of their relatively short careers. The majority of their 1999s taste even better from bottle than they did from barrel. These wines are hugely popular because they represent the best that Zinfandel can be. This varietal does not produce long-lived wines, and Turley Cellars does not pretend that their offerings will age like a classified-growth Bordeaux or California Cabernet Sauvignon. However, for drinking during their first decade of life, few wines match these for pure opulence, pleasure, concentration, exuberance, and personality. The good news is that their production of 8,200 cases of Zinfandel (there is a tiny amount of Charbono and Roussanne as well) will expand considerably since they have purchased a large Paso Robles vineyard with extremely old, head-pruned vines called Presenti. The first vintage where they controlled the viticulture and winemaking was 2000. Readers can look for that area to become one of the hotbeds for Zinfandel, as well as some Rhône-like blends made from these ancient vines.

The formula espoused by Turley and Jordan is simple: Locate old, head-pruned vineyards, persuade some of the idiosyncratic growers to let them control the viticulture, maintain low crop levels, pick superripe fruit, give the wines a pre-fermentation cold soak to extract color and greater phenolic complexity, do not acidify, fine, or filter, bring the wines up in a mix of 75% French and 25% American oak (only 25% is new), and bottle them after 14–16 months of barrel aging without any clarification. They have followed these rules since their debut vintage in 1993, and the wines have been consistently distinctive, luxuriously rich, and, lest I forget, hedonistic. Year in and year out, they are among the finest Zinfandels money can buy. While some competitors whine that they possess too much alcohol, etc., tasting these offerings reveals the alcohol is remarkably well integrated, as none of them tastes hot. In short, these are thrilling Zinfandels, as I have proven many times by serving them not only to American enthusiasts but to many of my friends in France, who go ga-ga over them.

What sets the 1999s apart is the fact that they are superrich, exceptionally pure, well-balanced, exuberant, mouth-staining, harmonious wines that will provide immense pleasure for a decade. Some of the Zinfandels will last even longer. Turley's Petite Syrahs are 40–50 year wines. Turley and Jordan both said the 1999 malolactic fermentations were extremely slow, which is often a good sign in terms of complexity as well as textural development. The 1999 Zinfandel Juveniles (previous called Young Vines; 450 cases, 15.2% alcohol) was made from tiny parcels of replanted vines in the Hayne, Moore, and Duarte vineyards. Turley Cellars does not want to blend these younger vines with wine from the older vines. A sensational effort, it exhibits a dense ruby/purple color as well as a knockout nose of blackberries and spice, an opulent texture, and a superb finish. It should drink well for a minimum of 5–7 years. The wine with the least color saturation, the 1999 Zinfandel Grist Vineyard (350 cases, 15.3% alcohol), reveals cherry liqueur and sandalwood notes in addition to a voluptuous texture, admirable fat and succulence, exceptionally ripe fruit, low acidity, and excellent length. A compelling wine has been produced from the tiny, two-acre Vineyard 101. The 1999 Zinfandel Vineyard 101 (78 cases, 15.4% alcohol) is akin to drinking blackberry liqueur with subtle pepper and soil notes in the background. Exceptionally full-bodied and lavishly concentrated, it will drink well for a decade. The remarkable 1999 Zinfandel Turley Estate (225 cases, 15.4% alcohol) was made from four-year-old vines (with tight 3 x 6 spacing) planted adjacent to the well-known Aida Vineyard. Drinking this wine is akin to drinking blackberry and strawberry liqueur mixed with smoke, spice, pepper, and truffles. A touch of volatile acidity adds to the aromatic fireworks. Full-bodied, unctuously textured, and exceptionally rich, with enough glycerin and thickness to please the most demanding hedonists, this is Zin on steroids. Drink it over the next decade. I often notice a resiny/balsam wood character in Turley's Contra Costa offering. The 1999 Zinfandel Duarte Vineyard (560 cases, 15.8% natural alcohol) is produced from 104-year-old vines planted in pure sand. A wonderful expression of purity and sweetness, it is not the most concentrated of the 1999 Zinfandels, but it offers sweet black cherry liqueur, strawberry, pepper, kirsch, raspberry, and spice aromas. I also detected a complex note of volatile acidity. Long, deep, intense, and well textured, it will drink well for 7–8 years. The fabulous, saturated dark ruby/purple-colored 1999 Zinfandel Tofanelli Vineyard (450 cases, 16.1% natural alcohol) is reminiscent of a wine from the southern Rhône. It displays a knockout bouquet of black fruits intertwined with licorice, asphalt, pepper, and spice. Exhibiting outstanding fruit richness, great purity, an unctuous texture, and a 45-second finish, this prodigious Zin should drink well for 7–8 years.

Made from a collection of miscellaneous parcels too small to bottle under their vineyard names, the 1999 Zinfandel Old Vines (1,800 cases, 15.8% alcohol) offers aromas and flavors of black fruits, a muscular, briery, peppery, forceful personality, a seamless texture, copious glycerin, amazing concentration, and a smooth finish. The acidity, tannin, and wood are beautifully integrated in this classic, full-throttle Zinfandel. Drink it over the next 7–8 years. It is even better from bottle than from barrel! Another provocative as well as prodigious effort is the opaque purple-colored 1999 Zinfandel Black-Sears Vineyard (640 cases, 16% alcohol). This is the only 1999 that I was unable to retaste from bottle. Produced from an 81-year-old vineyard inhabited by mountain lions, bobcats, and wild pigs, the grapes for this *cuvée* were harvested in November 1999. It boasts a gorgeously pure bouquet of blackberries, raspberries, flowers, and licorice, a remarkably full-bodied, viscous texture, fabulous fruit purity, and a ripe, layered, extravagantly rich finish. This whopper of a Zinfandel is unbelievably well balanced. It should drink well for a decade, but who can wait that long?

Guess who let the dogs out? The finest effort yet produced from the amusingly named Dogtown Vineyard, the 1999 Zinfandel (600 cases, 16% alcohol) is great stuff. Blackberries, kirsch, spice, and pepper are present in this flamboyant, muscular, smooth fruit bomb. With low acidity, ripe tannin, and well-integrated wood, it should drink well for 7–8 years. Readers may remember the tannic and austere Zinfandels produced under the Lamborn Family Vineyard label. This vineyard is now owned by the Pringle family, and Turley Cellars produces a Pringle Family Vineyard Zinfandel. The awesome 1999, which exhibits a Hermitage-like floral, blackberry liqueur, and raspberry-scented bouquet, is as elegant as a wine with 16.1% alcohol can be. Rich and sweet (from extract and glycerin, not sugar), with awesome presence on the palate as well as underlying notes of liquid minerals, jammy black fruit, and pepper, this finesse-styled Zinfandel can be consumed over the next 6–8 years. This is amazing stuff! The prodigious 1999 Zinfandel Moore (Earthquake) Vineyard (490 cases, 16.4% natural alcohol), like its siblings, possesses an opaque dense ruby/purple color. It offers explosive yet elegant aromas of blackberries, pepper, and black cherries as well as full body, low acidity, and magnificent fruit concentration. A long, intense, smooth, peppery personality will be a crowd-pleaser. A remarkable effort, it will develop even more complexity over the next 7–10 years. Year in and year out one of Turley's superstars is the Zinfandel Hayne Vineyard. The 1999 (560 cases, 16.8% alcohol) is a tour de force in Zinfandel winemaking, rivaling the 1999 Pringle *cuvée* as the Turley "Zin of the vintage." Again, the alcohol is totally concealed behind a wealth of glycerin, fruit, layered extraction, and a rich, plush texture. The wine possesses an opaque purple color, marvelous purity, and a minerality that frames its extravagant blackberry, cherry, and currant-dominated richness. The finish lasts for nearly a minute. An astounding effort, it will age well for a decade.

Virtually all of the Turley 1998 Zinfandels were produced from extremely low 1–1.5 tons of fruit per acre. Turley and Jordan bottled all these 1998s without fining or filtration in December 1999. Since their debut releases in 1993, these Zinfandels have been among the most luxuriously rich, complex, and interesting efforts of their respective vintages. The 1998s are more forward and evolved than such vintages as 1997 and are best drunk over the next 5–6 years. As a group, they are impressively endowed and already showing extremely well. In short, I see no reason to defer gratification, even though they are bigger, more concentrated, and alcoholic wines than most 1998s.

The dark ruby/garnet-colored, full-bodied 1998 Zinfandel Tofanelli Vineyard (15.9% alcohol) exhibits spice box and berry fruit aromas and flavors, a sweet, luscious texture, soft, low acidity, and gorgeous voluptuousness. Drink it over the next 5–7 years. Produced from a blend of various small plots, the 1998 Zinfandel Old Vines displays similar opulence, but reveals a more earthy, peppery, dried herb component to its dense black cherry, plum, and raspberry fruit. A delicious, round wine, it is best drunk over the next 4–5 years. One of Turley's great successes is the terrific 1998 Zinfandel Duarte Vineyard. Made from one of their oldest vineyards (a 104-year-old vineyard planted in pure sand), whose grapes achieved 15.8% alcohol naturally, it is the finest Duarte yet produced. An explosive nose of black cherry jam ascends from the glass. In the mouth, cherry liqueur notes continue in this full-bodied, super-endowed, luxuriously rich, opulent, fat, juicy Zinfandel. It is a hedonistic turn-on for sure. Drink it over the next 4–5 years. Less successful than in previous vintages is the 1998 Zinfandel Black-Sears. As Larry Turley acknowledged, their hottest *terroirs* often did the best in the cool 1998 growing season. Consequently, vineyards such as Duarte excelled, whereas the Black-Sears, among the coolest microclimates of Howell Mountain, was not harvested until November. Nevertheless, there is nothing to be upset about. A dense garnet/ruby color is followed by scents of raspberries, underbrush, loamy soil, plum liqueur, and pepper.

Spicy and ripe, but less expressive and thick compared to previous vintages, it is an excellent Zinfandel for consuming over the next 4–5 years. For statisticians, the alcohol level is 16%, so there is no obvious lack of ripeness, even from this cool, high-altitude vineyard. Readers looking for a Zinfandel with a Rhône-like personality should check out the 1998 Zinfandel Vineyard 101. Offering an explosive nose of dried herbs, ground pepper, new saddle leather, rose petals, black raspberries, and cherries, this fat, dense, full-bodied, luscious wine possesses low acidity, but gobs of fruit. Drink it over the next 4–5 years.

It is hard to believe, but the 1998 Zinfandel Grist Vineyard (16.4% alcohol) possesses an undeniable sense of elegance and symmetry. In a blind tasting, it could be mistaken for a premier cru from Volnay by some of those silly *terroirists* who always like to do a lot more postulating than tasting. This medium-bodied Zinfandel reveals a flamboyant side to its elegance and somehow manages to hide its alcohol. It exhibits delicious berry and cherry fruit with a strawberry liqueur–like after-finish. Drink it over the next 5–6 years. One of the new stars in the Turley portfolio is their 1998 Zinfandel Pringle Family Vineyard (16.1% alcohol). This is among the most firmly structured and backward of the Turley Zinfandels. It offers a dense ruby/purple color as well as earthy, foresty, black raspberry, and black cherry liqueur aromas. The wine is deep and full-bodied, with some tannin, excellent purity, and overall symmetry. It will benefit from another 6–12 months of bottle age and will last for 7–8 years or more. Turley and Jordan told me that their 1998 Zinfandel Dogtown Vineyard (16.5% alcohol) produced a mere two-thirds of a ton of fruit per acre. An intriguing wine, it reveals a Provençal-like, black cherry and *garrigue* aroma with scents of the seaweed wrap called nori used in sushi preparations. Deep, opulent, rich, and expansive, with fabulous fruit and low acidity, it is one of the finest efforts from Lodi I have ever tasted. Drink it over the next 4–5 years. Another wine with Provençal dried herb notes as well as abundant kirsch, black raspberries, blackberries, prunes, and plums is the 1998 Zinfandel Moore (Earthquake) Vineyard. A dense, full-bodied, stunningly proportioned, multidimensional Zin, it appears to be the finest wine in this impressive lineup, boasting a dark ruby color, thick, juicy, succulent flavors, and a low-acid, heady, alcoholic (16%) finish. Drink it over the next 5–7 years. Year in and year out, one of the most concentrated and spectacular Zinfandels produced in California emerges from the old vines of St. Helena's Hayne Vineyard. The 1998 Zinfandel Hayne Vineyard (16.4% alcohol) may not be quite as good as the nearly perfect examples from the past, but it is one of the vintage's superstars. Dense ruby/purple-colored, with a flamboyant nose of blackberries, cherries, kirsch, pepper, spice, and earth, this massive, chewy, full-throttle, hedonistic Zin is exceptionally pure, with a finish that lasts for 35–40+ seconds. The emphasis is on superripe fruit, subtle dosages of new oak, and spectacular texture. It should drink well for at least a decade.

As for the 1997 Zinfandels, Larry Turley said at the time, they "are the best wines we have yet made." The wines are amazingly good, and as the following tasting notes suggest, readers could buy blind here and always end up with a juicy, complex, mouth-filling Zinfandel. For starters, the 1997 Zinfandel Spenker Vineyard (from 105-year-old vines, with 15.1% alcohol) is a full-bodied, berry-scented and -flavored, lush wine with intriguing pepper, tar, and spicy notes. With excellent depth and purity, it is a candidate for 7–8 years of drinkability. The 1997 Zinfandel Dogtown (15.3% alcohol) is from a 65-year-old vineyard situated on the border of Amador. Its dark ruby/purple/garnet color is followed by copious quantities of briery, berry fruit intermixed with loamy soil, underbrush, and spicy notes. Full-bodied and chewy, with excellent ripeness, this tasty, fleshy, full-throttle Zinfandel should drink well for 5–7 years. From tiny parcels of 55- to 104-year-old, head-pruned vineyards, the Turley team put together a blend called Zinfandel Old Vines. The dark ruby/purple-colored 1997 (15.3% alcohol) is the finest example of this *cuvée* they have produced. It offers a stunning nose of blackberry, raspberry and cherry fruit intermixed with Asian spices, pepper, and balsam wood. Explosively rich in the mouth, with high glycerin, and a smooth, concentrated finish, this wine should drink well for 7–8 years. The 1997 Zinfandel Duarte Vineyard (from 102-year-old vines; 15.4% alcohol) is the finest wine I have tasted from this source. Duarte is one of the few remaining California vineyards where the vines are planted on their own roots, rather than being grafted, as the region's sandy soils have proved to be resistant to the phylloxera disease. This wine always seems to have a dusty, balsam wood, Provençal herb, peppery note, but the 1997 reveals more cherry liqueur and black raspberries. Additionally, the color is a saturated dark ruby/purple. Full-bodied and concentrated, with deep layers of flavor that inundate the palate, it should drink well for 5–7 years. The 1997 Zinfandel Tofanelli Vineyard (from a 65-year-old vineyard; 15.8% alcohol) is a broodingly backward, expansive yet undeniably hedonistically oriented Zinfandel. The dark ruby/purple color is accompanied by notes of blackberries, *jus de viande*, pepper, roasted herbs, and truffles. Full-bodied, with dazzling fruit extract, a voluptuous texture, and a spectacular finish, this is a superb Zin to enjoy over the next 5–7 years. Slightly superior is the 1997 Zinfandel Grist Vineyard (16.3% alcohol). This is a perfumed, aromatic wine with a glorious display of cherry fruit. Think of a terrific red Burgundy with an element of *sur-maturité* and an unprecedented alcohol level, and readers may get a sense of what this blockbuster tastes like. The wine exhibits a dense ruby/purple color, fabulous purity, copious amounts of glycerin, and layers of kirsch/cherry fruit. This head-turning, knockout Zinfandel will be especially admired by both lovers of Burgundy and those who admire the famed Châteauneuf-du-Pape, Rayas. It should drink well for 7–8 years. The 1997 Zinfandel Vineyard 101 (from 85-year-old vines; 16% alcohol) is another Burgundy-styled wine, but more alcoholic and viscous. Full-bodied, with surprising elegance for its weight and size, it displays a strong sense of minerality intertwined with notes of barbecue spices. With thrilling levels of black cherry and raspberry fruit, it should drink well now and over the next 7 years.

Some of Turley's old standbys are once again compelling wines. The 1997 Zinfandel Aida Vineyard (from 30-year-old vines; 16.8% alcohol) is once again the Châteauneuf-du-Pape of northern California. This wine boasts a *herbes de Provence, garrigue*, peppery, black raspberry-scented, exotic nose that is eerily similar to a top-class Châteauneuf. The color is a saturated dark ruby/purple, and the wine unleashes its full power with layers of roasted meats, pepper, and jammy fruit flavors. This stunning Zinfandel will overload most tasters' olfactory sensors. Moreover, it should drink well for 7–8 years. The 1997 Zinfandel Black-Sears Vineyard (81-year-old vines; 17% alcohol) is the finest Black-Sears Turley has yet produced. Flirting with perfection, it is one of the most extraordinary Zinfandels I have ever tasted. This vineyard, located high on Howell Mountain, in a wilderness area inhabited by mountain lions, bobcats, and wild pigs, has turned out a saturated black/purple-colored wine with fabulous aromas of crème de cassis, minerals, cold steel, Asian spices, violets, and licorice. The wine possesses unbelievable fruit richness, layers of extract and glycerin, phenomenal purity, and a 40+-second finish. Somehow, some way, the 17% alcohol has been concealed beneath the wine's extraordinary richness. Is it any wonder that so many other Zinfandel producers are jealous of Turley Cellars? This offering should drink beautifully for 7–8 years. The 1997 Zinfandel Moore (Earthquake) Vineyard (from 91-year-old vines; 17.1% alcohol) is also spectacular. From its saturated black purple color to its knockout aromatics of framboise, raspberries, and kirsch (essentially the entire spectrum of red and black fruits seems to be present in this wine), this gorgeous, massively endowed, jammy yet structured Zinfandel easily disguises its 17.1% alcohol under its remarkable concentration and intensity. It should drink well for another decade. My favorite Zinfandel in the Turley portfolio is usually the Hayne Vineyard. Along with Martinelli's Jackass Hill Zinfandel, it has tended to represent the be-all and end-all Zinfandel. The 1997 Zinfandel Hayne Vineyard is unquestionably a remarkable wine, but I am not sure it is better than the Black-Sears or Moore Vineyard. However, it will be the most backward and potentially longest-lived of these 1997s. It was the least evolved when I tasted it in September 1998, displaying an opaque saturated, thick-looking purple color, and unevolved but promising notes of black raspberry liqueur intermixed with minerals, spice, and cherry fruit. Massive yet phenomenally rich, admirably pure, and representing the essence of this varietal, this wine requires 12–18 months of bottle age; it should drink well for 10–15 years. An extraordinary Zin, with 17.2% alcohol, it is the most powerful offering in the Turley portfolio. Anticipated maturity: now–2010.

The dynamic duo of Turley and Jordan also produces California's finest Charbono. If more wineries could be as successful with this varietal, we would see an explosion of California Charbono rather than the insufferably innocuous Sangiovese produced throughout the state. Turley's 1999 Charbono Tofanelli Vineyard (109 cases, 13.5% alcohol) is analogous to a full-throttle Dolcetto. An intense black/purple color is accompanied by blueberry, cranberry liqueur, cherry, and chocolate aromas and flavors. It should drink well for 7–8 years. The 1998 Charbono Tofanelli Vineyard (200 cases, 14.8% alcohol) continues the great success Turley and Jordan have had with this lowly esteemed varietal. Dark ruby/purple-colored, with an earthy, spicy, gorgeously pure nose, this wine offers blueberry and blackberry flavors, copious quantities of earthy richness, and a spicy, long, full-bodied, powerful finish. It should drink well for 10–15 years.

One of my best friends has been cellaring Petite Sirah for over 30 years, and we have had some extraordinary tastings of this underrated varietal. Such Petite Sirahs as the 1974 Freemark Abbey, 1971 Ridge York Creek, as well as a bevy of others, remain prodigious wines even as they approach 30 years of age. Turley Cellars' Petite Syrahs are wines for collectors to purchase and then forget for at least a decade. They are enormously concentrated, brutally tannic, awesomely endowed efforts made (like the Zinfandels) with no compromises. The blue/black/purple-colored 1999 Petite Syrah Estate (125 cases, 14.6% alcohol) exhibits thick, concentrated, pure flavors of licorice, minerals, blackberries, and cassis. Monstrous on the palate, this 1999 requires a decade of cellaring. Even more amazing is the 1999 Petite Syrah Rattlesnake Acres (225 cases, 14.8% alcohol). With an appearance reminiscent of vintage Port, it offers notes of blackberries, smoke, and minerals. This blockbuster, gargantuan wine boasts awesome concentration, exquisite purity, and a palate-saturating style. Anticipated maturity: 2010–2050. Potentially perfect, the 1999 Petite Syrah Hayne Vineyard (475 cases, 15.5% alcohol) is a 50-year wine. If it is showing any age after a decade of cellaring, I will be as surprised as its producers. An opaque black/blue color is followed by an extraordinary perfume of blackberry and crème de cassis blended with spices, minerals, and earth. Frightfully tannic, with unreal concentration, texture, and length, this behemoth is one of the most concentrated wines I have ever tasted. Anticipated maturity: 2012–2050+.

There are 275 cases of the dense, tannic, concentrated, outstanding 1998 Petite Syrah Rattlesnake Acres (14.2% alcohol), and 325 cases of the blockbuster, sensationally rich, hyper-concentrated 1998 Petite Syrah Hayne Vineyard (14.5% alcohol). The latter wine exhibits better ripeness, more impressive concentration, and a blockbuster, gargantuan finish that lasts for 40–45 seconds. Like all the Turley wines, these two efforts possess exquisite purity and fabulously ripe, unmanipulated fruit that cuts a creamy, lush texture on the palate. The Rattlesnake Acres will drink well in 3–4 years and keep for 15 or more. The Hayne Vineyard requires 3–4 years of cellaring and will keep for at least two decades.

Turley's 1997 Petite Syrah Aida Vineyard (from 80-year-old vines) assaults the palate with such an overload of fruit, tannin, and extract that the taster's first impression is that this is something more than table wine. It is a massive, almost uncivilized, wildly out of control Petite Syrah that will require 10–15 years of cellaring and last for 30 or more. I have been conservative in my judgment because the tannin nearly melted the fillings in my teeth, but this is an amazing, astonishing wine that will be fascinating to follow over the next 3–4 decades. Lamentably, it will certainly outlive me. Anticipated maturity: 2008–2040. New in 1997, the 1997 Petite Syrah Rattlesnake Acres is from a 50-year-old plantation of Petite Sirah. The wine's notes suggested I needed to return to my hotel to grab my floss after tasting this wine.

The color is a saturated, thick black/purple. The wine reveals surprising amounts of toasty new oak in the nose (Turley only uses 25–30% new oak). In the mouth, it is "beyond immense, massive, and gargantuan," and should be purchased only by those seeking an adventurous wine experience. Anticipated maturity: 2005–2040. I do not believe I have ever tasted a more concentrated, essence-like wine than Turley's 1997 Petite Syrah Hayne Vineyard. Made from 55-year-old vines that yielded only 9.8 tons of fruit for five acres, this opaque black-colored wine is the biggest, richest, most concentrated, tannic wine I have ever tasted. It will need at least a decade to shed some of its ferocious tannin, and will undoubtedly last for 40–50 years. Even more remarkable is its purity and overall equilibrium. Despite its Godzilla-like size, this is an astonishingly concentrated, gorgeously made wine.

VÉRITÉ (SONOMA)

1999 La Joie	Sonoma/Napa	EEE	95
1998 La Joie	Sonoma/Napa	EEE	92
1999 Merlot	Sonoma/Napa	EEE	94
1998 Merlot	Sonoma/Napa	EEE	92

A new boutique producer under the Jackson Family Farms moniker, Vérité and its sister operation, La Joie, are run by a Bordelais, Pierre Seillan, who has done some miracle working with outstanding fruit sources. His first efforts are brilliant, particularly from the challenging vintage of 1998. His 1999s look . . . simply awesome. These wines, which Seillan calls "wines without compromise," are all aged in 100% new French oak for about 13 months. His 1998 Merlot is an inter-appellation blend of 62% Sonoma and 38% Napa. It is a 2,000-case blend of 90% Merlot and 10% Cabernet Sauvignon. Eighty-five percent of the malolactic was done in barrel, and the wine was bottled without any clarification. It is a blockbuster Merlot, and certainly a formidable achievement for 1998. The wine shows a dense black/purple color, an enormous nose of espresso roast, melted chocolate, blackberries, cherries, and sweet truffle/earthy notes. Very full-bodied, astonishingly concentrated, extremely pure, and well balanced, this is a blockbuster effort that can be drunk now (it has relatively high pH and low acidity) or cellared for 15–20 years. The 1999 Merlot (a similar blend of 90% Merlot and 10% Cabernet Sauvignon, with 84% of the wine coming from Sonoma and 16% from Napa) is extravagantly concentrated, with a layered, expansive mid-palate, and a blockbuster finish. The wine is out-and-out massive, with spectacular levels of fruit and glycerin. The basic characteristics are lavish richness (cassis, coffee, chocolate galore) and a low-acid, multitextured, flamboyant finish. In short, this is an amazing wine. It should be drinkable young, but with an uncommon ageability of 20–25 years.

The La Joie wines are dominated by Cabernet Sauvignon with some Merlot in the blend. Again, these 2,000 cases are intercounty blends of Sonoma and Napa fruit. They are both made from 70% Cabernet Sauvignon and 30% Merlot. The 1998 is 85% Sonoma fruit and 15% Napa. The 1999 is virtually identical, with 89% Sonoma and 11% Napa. The 1998 La Joie is a more backward wine than the 1998 Merlot, which is not surprising given the fact that it is dominated by Cabernet Sauvignon. The wine has an opaque purple color, big, powerful, highly extracted flavors, amazing richness for a wine of this vintage, and a long, muscular, dense finish. It needs a good 3–4 years of cellaring, yet should keep for two decades. The 1999 La Joie is super stuff, a prodigious wine of fabulous concentration, with licorice, coffee, black currant, leather, and truffle notes, huge body, sweet tannin, and a big, tannic finish. It is not a wine for those looking for immediate gratification, as this will require 5–6 years of cellaring and keep for 25+ years.

It is obvious that wine-maker Pierre Seillan and proprietor Jess Jackson have a mission to "make a world-class Merlot as good or better than Pétrus." These will no doubt be hot items when released next year.

VIADER VINEYARDS (NAPA)

1998 Proprietary Red Wine	Napa	E	88
1997 Proprietary Red Wine	Napa	E	92
1996 Proprietary Red Wine	Napa	D	88
1995 Proprietary Red Wine	Napa	D	91
1994 Proprietary Red Wine	Napa	C	92

One of the many gorgeous hillside estates in Napa Valley, Viader, whose vineyards are situated on the lower slopes of Howell Mountain, produces about 5,000 cases of a blend composed of almost equal parts Cabernet Sauvignon and Cabernet Franc. The dark ruby/purple-colored 1998 Proprietary Red (a blend of 60% Cabernet Sauvignon and 40% Cabernet Franc) offers a bouquet of subtle herbs, minerals, and red currants. Spicy, elegant, and restrained, this subtle, poised effort should drink well young, yet last for 14–15 years. The terrific 1997 Proprietary Red is the finest Viader I have tasted. It is a wine of exceptional finesse and elegance, yet undeniable richness and intensity. This blend of 59% Cabernet Sauvignon and 41% Cabernet Franc tastes like a top Graves from Bordeaux. Subtle spicy oak emerges from this dark ruby/purple-colored wine, along with scents of black currants, minerals, and lead pencil. In the mouth, earthy, *terroir* characteristics combine with sweet black fruits in this medium-bodied, rich wine. There is a juicy mid-palate as well as considerable grace and harmony in the finish. The tannin is largely obscured by the wine's outstanding concentration. Anticipated maturity: now–2018. A blend of 59% Cabernet Sauvignon and 41% Cabernet Franc, the 1996 is made in a polished, graceful style. Medium-bodied, with lush, herb-tinged, raspberry and black currant fruit intermixed with mineral and lead pencil notes, this lovely, stylish, restrained offering already provides pleasant drinking, yet should keep for 10–12 years. The similarly styled 1995 reveals an opaque purple color, remarkably sweet tannin for a wine from this vintage, and gorgeous levels of black currant fruit nicely complemented by toast, smoke, and floral scents. This rich, medium- to full-bodied wine fills the mouth without any sense of heaviness or harshness. It is a beautifully knit, lush, complex, elegant red wine that should drink well for 12–15 years. Smoky, sweet, black and red currant aromas jump from the glass of the intriguing, saturated purple-colored 1994. Some new oak is noticeable in the background. The wine's attack exhibits terrific purity of fruit, more acidity than many 1994s, and sweet, ripe tannin, all packed into a tightly wound, medium- to full-bodied wine that only hints at its ultimate potential. This is not a large-scaled 1994, but it is a beautifully etched wine with considerable personality. It will benefit from 4–5 years of cellaring and is unquestionably another 20-year effort from this vintage.

Past Glories: 1993 Proprietary Red Wine (90)

VINEYARD 29 (NAPA)

1998 Cabernet Sauvignon	Napa	EE	88
1997 Cabernet Sauvignon	Napa	EE	94

This vineyard's innovative name and beautiful presentation in a heavy, tall Italian bottle make for a grandiose impression. These wines, produced by wine-making consultant Heidi Barrett, are impressive. There are 400 cases of the 1998 and 600 cases of the 1997, all from a 3.5-acre Cabernet Sauvignon parcel planted with the Grace clone. The 1998 Cabernet Sauvignon is a successful effort in this challenging vintage for Cabernet producers. The vintage's charm, softness, ripe fruit, elegance, and fine balance are well displayed. Black currants and cherries compete with cedar, spice, and subtle new oak. It is a medium-bodied, appealing Cabernet Sauvignon that will be drinkable upon release, and will evolve nicely for 7–8 years. Sweeter, richer, fuller, and more concentrated is the 1997 Cabernet Sauvignon. A deep ruby/purple color is followed by pure black currant fruit intertwined with tobacco, vanilla, and spice. This lush, full-bodied effort displays sweet tannin and cuts a powerful swath across the palate. The finish reveals high extraction and harmony. It will be even better in 1–3 years and should last for two decades.

VON STRASSER (NAPA)

1995 Cabernet Sauvignon Diamond Mountain	Napa	D	90
1994 Cabernet Sauvignon Diamond Mountain	Napa	D	91
1995 Cabernet Sauvignon Diamond Mountain Reserve	Napa	D	92+

This winery is doing many things right, as evidenced by these releases. Both 1995 Cabernet Sauvignons are outstanding. The 1995 Cabernet Sauvignon Diamond Mountain possesses a dense ruby/purple color, followed by a promising nose of cassis intertwined with earth, flowers, and spice. In the mouth, there is good grip and tannin, but the overall impression is one of a medium- to full-bodied wine where the fruit characteristics dominate the *terroir* and oak. Subtle vanilla and spice are present in this pure, black currant–flavored, long, impressive wine. Accessible now, it promises to get even better over the next decade, and last for 15+ years. The 1995 Cabernet Sauvignon Diamond Mountain Reserve is prodigious. The color is nearly opaque purple. The nose offers up intense aromas of blackberries and cassis, intermingled with earth and vanilla. On the palate, the wine is formidably endowed, backward and tannic, but exceptionally dense, layered, and extremely rich. Yet there is no sense of heaviness, and the tannin is sweet rather than overbearing or astringent. This superb Cabernet Sauvignon has a long, promising future. Anticipated maturity: now–2020.

The 1994 is a beautifully made Cabernet Sauvignon. The healthy dark purple color is followed by a forward, sexy, up-front nose of jammy plums, black currants, vanilla ice cream, and cassis. On the palate, this full-bodied Cabernet reveals silky tannin, an opulent texture, and a full-bodied, concentrated finish. It manages to offer intensity without heaviness—something that is not easy to obtain. Drink this seductive Cabernet Sauvignon young as well as old, as I suspect it will have a very large window of drinkability—say 15 or more years.
Past Glories: 1993 Cabernet Sauvignon Diamond Mountain (91)

WHITEHALL LANE (NAPA)

1997 Cabernet Sauvignon	Napa	D	88
1995 Cabernet Sauvignon	Napa	C	88
1994 Cabernet Sauvignon	Napa	C	88
1996 Cabernet Sauvignon Leonardini Vineyard	Napa	E	89
1995 Cabernet Sauvignon Leonardini Vineyard	Napa	E	90
1994 Cabernet Sauvignon Morisoli Vineyard	Napa	E	92
1996 Cabernet Sauvignon Reserve	Napa	D	88
1995 Cabernet Sauvignon Reserve	Napa	D	91
1994 Cabernet Sauvignon Reserve Morisoli Vineyard	Napa	D	90
1996 Merlot	Napa	C	88
1994 Merlot Leonardini Vineyard	Napa	D	91
1995 Merlot Reserve Leonardini Vineyard	Napa	D	88
1994 Merlot Reserve Leonardini Vineyard	Napa	D	90

The red wine offerings from this excellent winery are well made, with rich personalities and attractive bouquets. The dark ruby-colored 1997 Cabernet Sauvignon Napa possesses cassis fruit intermixed with spicy wood and earth. Medium- to full-bodied, with some grip but a plush texture, this rich, concentrated Cabernet Sauvignon should drink well for a decade. The 1996 Cabernet Sauvignon Reserve reveals more new oak (in addition to black currant fruit) as well as a tighter framework. More closed and not as supple and evolved as the 1997 Napa, this wine displays more length and intensity at the back of the palate. It is a classy, well-made Napa Cabernet Sauvignon that should be better with 1–2 more years of bottle age and last for 10–15 years. The finest of this trio of Cabernets is the 1996 Cabernet Sauvignon Leonardini Vineyard. Sweet new oak and copious quantities of black currant fruit, cedar, dried herbs, and spice make for a full-bodied impression in the mouth. Expansive and rich, with light to moderate tannin, excellent, possibly outstanding concentration and depth, this beautifully made 1996 should drink well for 12–15 years.

Whitehall Lane's 1995 Cabernet Sauvignon Reserve (2,400 cases) dominated a flight that included 14 of its peers. It exhibits a saturated purple color, as well as a youthful yet promising nose of toasty new oak, briery fruit, cassis, and licorice. The wine is concentrated and pure, with sweet tannin, adequate acidity, and medium to full body. A seamless, beautifully proportioned Cabernet Sauvignon, it should be at its peak with another 2–3 years of bottle age, and keep for 15 or more. The 1996 Merlot is a round, user-friendly, plump wine with significantly more character than most Merlots possess. The color is a dark ruby/purple. The wine offers copious amounts of berry fruit intermixed with smoke, herb, and earthy notes. Fruity and succulent, with medium body and a generous, crowd-pleasing, glycerin-imbued finish, it should be consumed over the next 5–6 years.

The opaque-colored 1995 Cabernet Sauvignon Leonardini Vineyard reveals more new oak, extract, richness, and intensity. There are copious quantities of cassis and vanilla flavors that border on overripeness. Rich, with soft tannin, this larger-scaled, more expansive wine can be drunk now as well as over the next 15 years. The ambitiously styled 1995 Merlot Reserve Leonardini Vineyard reveals an opaque ruby/purple color, less expressiveness aromatically (it's more closed), and more toasty new oak. In the mouth, this wine possesses an extra dimension of richness and concentration. It is not as accessible as the regular Merlot, and over the next several years most readers will probably prefer the latter wine. Nevertheless, the Reserve Merlot is an excellent effort that should age well for 7–8 years. The 1994 Merlot Reserve Leonardini Vineyard is a more extracted, richer, earthier, more aggressively oaked wine with full body, admirable intensity, richness, and length, and a long, spicy finish. Although still youthful and unevolved, it promises to provide considerable enjoyment between now–2010. The blockbuster 1994 Merlot Leonardini Vineyard exhibits a black/purple color, fabulously ripe, rich, concentrated fruit, full body, and a great purity and balance. This is an immensely impressive Merlot that should age well for a decade or more.

An excellent, nearly outstanding Cabernet Sauvignon, Whitehall Lane's 1995 possesses a dark ruby/purple color, as well as sweet, jammy, cassis fruit, an appealingly thick texture, and no hard edges. The acidity, tannin, and alcohol are all well integrated in this seamless, opulently styled Cabernet Sauvignon. It should drink well for a decade or more.

The 1994 Cabernet Sauvignon exhibits a deep ruby/purple color followed by attractive spicy, weedy, cassis aromas, backed up by vanilla and oaky scents. Medium- to full-bodied, with excellent concentration, well-integrated tannin and acidity, and a vibrant, lively feel on the palate, this mid-weight Cabernet should drink well for 7–10 years. The outstanding 1994 Cabernet Sauvignon Reserve Morisoli Vineyard is not quite ready for prime-time drinking. It possesses a healthy dark ruby/purple color, enticing, sweet cassis, cedar, and vanilla components, medium to full body, high tannin, and some of the elusive lead pencil aromas often found in St.-Julien and Pauillac offerings. The wine needs another 2–3 years of cellaring, but it should evolve gracefully for 10–15 years. It is a fine example of this impressive vintage.

The terrific 1994 Cabernet Sauvignon Morisoli Vineyard exhibits a black/purple color, fabulous sweetness and ripeness of fruit, full body, layers of extract and richness, and a stunning finish. The tannin is sweet and long. This gorgeous wine appears to be a terrific effort from what looks to be a sensational vintage for North Coast Cabernet Sauvignon.

Past Glories: 1993 Cabernet Sauvignon Morisoli Vineyard (90), 1993 Merlot Reserve Leonardini Vineyard (90)

WILLIAMS-SELYEM (SONOMA)

1997 Pinot Noir	Sonoma Coastlands	E	90
1997 Pinot Noir Allen Vineyard	Russian River	E	89
1996 Pinot Noir Ferrington Vineyard	Anderson Valley	E	91
1997 Pinot Noir Hirsch Vineyard	Sonoma Coast	E	88
1997 Pinot Noir Precious Mountain	Sonoma Coast	E	89

Williams-Selyem has a near mythical reputation for their wines, which are sold exclusively through a mailing list. This winery was sold in 1997, but Burt Williams has been retained as a consultant to train former Hartford Court wine-maker Bob Cabral. When the history of California wines is written, Williams-Selyem will hold an important place. Not only was it one of the first wineries to exploit the potential of the Sonoma Coast and Russian River, particularly with vineyard-designated Pinot Noir and Chardonnay, but this is the ultimate "garage" winery. It will be interesting to see what direction the new owner follows, as production is scheduled to be increased. Hopefully, the quality can be maintained. All of the following offerings revealed high levels of tangy acidity, a style that allows the winery to utilize extremely low levels of sulphur, a worthy objective.

The 1997 Pinot Noirs possess light ruby colors, aggressive acidity, and copious quantities of the red fruit mélange—kirsch, strawberries, cherries, and red currants. The 1997 Pinot Noir Allen Vineyard (planted in 1972) exhibits a light ruby color, followed by an attractive, jammy strawberry and toasty oak-scented nose. Medium-bodied, with zesty acidity, and a crisp, tart finish, it should drink well for 5–6 years. The 1997 Pinot Noir Sonoma Coastlands exhibits sweeter fruit, intermixed with smoke and toast. This wine possesses a lush, Volnay-like personality with considerable seductiveness and intensity. The acidity is noticeable, but not overbearing. Typical of many wines from this area, the well-made 1997 Pinot Noir Hirsch Vineyard displays a forceful structure, and copious spice, earth, and tannin to go along with its black cherry fruit. It is a candidate for several years of cellaring before consumption. It should keep for 7–8 years, but the tannin may be problematic. The medium ruby-colored 1997 Pinot Noir Precious Mountain reveals a sweet, expansive, black cherry nose intermixed with floral notes, smoky, toasty oak, and herbs. Expansive in the mouth, with fine richness, less intrusive acidity than some *cuvées*, and light tannin in the finish, it should drink well for 5–7 years. I was extremely impressed by the 1996 Pinot Noir Ferrington Vineyard. It boasts the most concentration, richness, and intensity of any Williams-Selyem Pinot Noirs, with enough extract and richness to balance out the tart acidity. The wine's dark ruby/purple color is followed by sweet black cherry and raspberry aromas, with nicely integrated smoky oak. Sweet, floral, and rich, with medium to full body, vibrant acidity, and tannin, this beautifully made, hedonistic, rich, fleshy wine will drink well for 5–6 years.

ZACA MESA WINERY (SANTA BARBARA)

1997 Syrah	Santa Barbara	C	90
1994 Syrah	Santa Barbara	C	92
1996 Syrah Black Bear Block	Santa Barbara	D	88

Zaca Mesa's medium-bodied 1997 Syrah (12% Viognier in the blend) offers a candied blackberry nose with scents of pepper and asphalt. Pure and ripe, with low acidity and sexy, voluptuously textured fruit, this tasty, fleshy, succulent Syrah will have many admirers. According to the winery, the 1996 Syrah Black Bear Block is produced from some of the oldest, most stressed Syrah vineyards. A dark purple color is accompanied by dense, thick, sweet blackberry fruit infused with copious quantities of sweet toasty oak. Fleshy and succulent, with low acidity and excellent concentration, this wine can be drunk over the next decade.

Readers are advised to be on the lookout for the 1994 Syrah from Zaca Mesa. Discounters will probably sell it for $12–13 a bottle, making it unquestionably one of the richest, most hedonistic wines per penny spent that I have tasted and reviewed. This Syrah, blended with

10% Viognier, offers an opaque purple color, an exceptional nose of sweet berry fruit (jammy cassis, tropical fruits, and overripe peaches), a full-bodied, viscous, satiny smooth texture, and outstanding flavor extraction. This is a harmonious, gorgeously rich Syrah that may ultimately turn out to be Santa Barbara's answer to Côte Rôtie. Don't dare miss it!

ZD WINERY (NAPA)

1995 Cabernet Sauvignon	Napa	D	88
1994 Cabernet Sauvignon	Napa	D	90

The opaque purple-colored, exotic 1994 Cabernet Sauvignon is generously wooded, with smoky black raspberry and cassis aromas. Medium- to full-bodied, with copious amounts of fruit and soft tannin, this luscious, youthful, grapy Cabernet can be drunk now, but it promises to be better with 2–3 years of cellaring; it should keep for 12–15 years. The "American-styled" 1995 Cabernet Sauvignon has plenty of macho power, lavish quantities of toasty new oak, and straightforward, pleasing, ripe black currant fruit. Attractive, savory, and mouth-filling, the wine is medium- to full-bodied, monolithic, and cleanly made, with 10–15 years of evolution ahead of it.

ZOOM (PASO ROBLES)

1999 Zinfandel	Napa	C	89
1999 Zinfandel	Paso Robles	C	90
1997 Zinfandel	Paso Robles	C	88
1999 Zinfandel	San Francisco Bay	C	89
1999 Zinfandel Ricetti Vineyard	Redwood Valley	C	90

The four noteworthy 1999 Zinfandels from Zoom offer impressive levels of fruit and ripeness presented in an uncomplicated, full-bodied, user-friendly style with enough complexity and nuances to satisfy both neophytes and connoisseurs. The 1999 Zinfandel Ricetti Vineyard (13.8% alcohol) exhibits a dark ruby/purple color in addition to fat, succulent fruit flavors. Bursting with fruit and glycerin, this full-bodied, layered, hedonistic, sexy Zin should be consumed over the next 3–4 years to take advantage of its exuberance and purity. Made from 31-year-old vines, the dense plum/purple-colored 1999 Zinfandel Paso Robles (14.3% alcohol) reveals loads of kirsch, a layered texture, excellent purity, and a long, spicy, succulent, glycerin-filled finish. Nothing is out of place in this hedonistic, juicy Zinfandel. It, too, should be drunk over the next 3–4 years. Produced from 105-year-old vines, the 1999 Zinfandel San Francisco Bay (14.6% alcohol) is another fruit bomb, but does not express the complexity of the Paso Robles or Ricetti cuvées. Nevertheless, there is a lot to like in its current-laden, cherry fruit–dominated style. With abundant glycerin, a corpulent mouth-feel, purity, and exuberance, it will be fun to drink for 3–4 years. The 1999 Zinfandel Napa (from 33-year-old vines; 14.8% alcohol) is the most powerful and alcoholic of this quartet. Measured and less exuberant with a more structured finish than its three siblings, it offers attractive black cherries and currants in its polished personality. It will drink well for 4–5 years.

Made from 29-year-old vines and possessing 14.6% alcohol, the attractive 1997 Zinfandel Paso Robles' evolved dark plum/garnet color is followed by a delightfully sweet raspberry- and cherry-scented nose. In the mouth, it reveals rich, flavorful, medium- to full-bodied flavors, layers of fruit, and a spicy, peppery, earthy finish. Drink this well-made, mouth-filling Zinfandel over the next 3–4 years. Sadly, only 283 cases were produced.

6. OREGON

The Basics

Oregon makes wine from most of the same grapes used in California, although the cooler, more marginal climate in Oregon's best viticultural area, the Willamette Valley, has meant more success with cool-climate varietals such as Pinot Noir than with hotter-climate varietals such as Cabernet Sauvignon, Merlot, Syrah, and Grenache. Chardonnay and Riesling have done well in Oregon, but the "great white hope" here is Pinot Gris, which has shown fine potential and is the perfect partner for the salmon of the Pacific Northwest. Pinot Blanc has made a significant appearance in recent years, but has not produced wines meriting serious consumer attention, most probably due to severe overcropping. High-quality sparkling wines can be found, particularly under the Argyle label. Oregon's wines are distinctive, with a kinship to European wines. The higher natural acidities, lower alcohol content, and more subtle nature of Oregon's wines bode well for this area's future.

GRAPE VARIETIES
Chardonnay Oregon can make some wonderful Chardonnay, but far too many winemakers let it spend too much time in oak and have not chosen the best clones for their vineyards. The Chardonnay grape in Oregon is naturally high in acidity, and that is the principal difference between California's and Oregon's Chardonnay. In California, most Chardonnays must have tartaric acid added to them for balance. In Oregon, the wines must be put through a secondary or malolactic fermentation, à la Burgundy, in order to lower their perceptible acidity. The high quality of Chardonnays produced from recent plantings of Dijon clones indicates that Oregon may have found the answer to its clonal problems with this varietal.

Pinot Gris This is the hardest wine to find, as virtually all of it is snapped up before it has a chance to leave Oregon. Fruitier and more floral than Chardonnay, Pinot Gris, from the world's most underrated great white wine grape, can be a delicious, opulent, smoky wine with every bit as much character and even more aging potential than Chardonnay. Though a specialty of Oregon, much of it is mediocre and diluted due to overcropping.

Pinot Noir As in Burgundy, the soil, yield per acre, choice of fermentation yeasts, competence of the wine-maker, and type of oak barrel in which this wine is aged profoundly influence its taste, style, and character. The top Oregon Pinot Noirs can have a wonderful purity of cherry, loganberry, and raspberry fruit. Furthermore, they can reveal an expansive, seductive, broad, lush palate, as well as crisp acids for balance. Yet far too many are washed out and hollow because of the tendency to harvest less than fully mature fruit and to permit crop yields to exceed 3 tons per acre.

Other Grape Varieties With respect to white wines, Gewürztraminer has generally proven no more successful in Oregon than in California. However, Oregon can make good Riesling, especially in the drier Alsace style. Recent tastings of delicious sparkling wines from Argyle show promise for this style of wine in Oregon. The Cabernet Sauvignon and Merlot have not been special to date, although some made from vineyards in the southern part of the state have resulted in several good though not exciting wines.

FLAVORS

Chardonnay Compared with California Chardonnay, those of Oregon are noticeably higher in acidity, more oaky, and have less of a processed, manipulated taste than their siblings from California. In many cases the oak is excessive.

Pinot Gris A whiff of smoke, the creamy taste of baked apples and nuts, and gobs of fruit characterize this promising white wine.

Pinot Noir Red berry fruits dominate the taste of Oregon Pinot Noirs. Aromas and flavors of cherries, loganberries, blackberries, cola, and sometimes plums, with a streak of spicy, herbaceous scents characterize these medium ruby-colored wines.

AGING POTENTIAL

Chardonnay: 2–5 years   Pinot Noir: 3–10 years
Dry/Off-Dry Rieslings: 2–4 years   Sparkling Wines: 1–4 years
Pinot Gris: 1–3 years

OVERALL QUALITY LEVEL

Oregon has faced a string of difficult vintages (1995, 1996, and 1997), but these have given the state's wine-makers enormous experience, honing theirs skills and driving them to lower yields. Once a region of underfinanced backyard operations where the owner/wine-makers learned as they went along, Oregon is now stocked with highly skilled and knowledgeable wine-makers. Low-quality grape clones, poorly planted vineyards, and some questionable winemaking decisions can still be found, but the number of high-quality wineries is growing. While they are just beginning to realize the potential for Pinot Noir, Chardonnay, and Pinot Gris, their future is bright. Oregon's wines range in quality from poor to outstanding.

MOST IMPORTANT INFORMATION TO KNOW

To purchase good wine, know the finest vintages, the best wineries, and their best wines. Some additional information worth knowing is that the finest Pinot Noirs generally come from a stretch of vineyards in the Willamette Valley, southwest of Portland.

RECENT VINTAGES

1999—The 1999 vintage in Oregon is outstanding, potentially the finest in this region's short history. With the 1990s, Oregon's top wineries are finally fulfilling their promise to consumers that this state can produce impressively delicious Pinot Noirs with abundant fruit and ageworthy structure. Rains at harvest have been the downfall of numerous Oregon vintages, but 1999 enjoyed an exceptional late season and Indian summer. Sunny days and cool evenings lasted into early October, furthering ripeness while maintaining balanced acidity. In fact, the weather remained excellent through the end of the month, allowing many growers to wait until the third week of October to harvest.

Yields in 1999 were a problem for those wineries that are neither conscientious enough to prune adequately nor unwilling to drop fruit (crop-thin). Wineries that make bad, poor, or

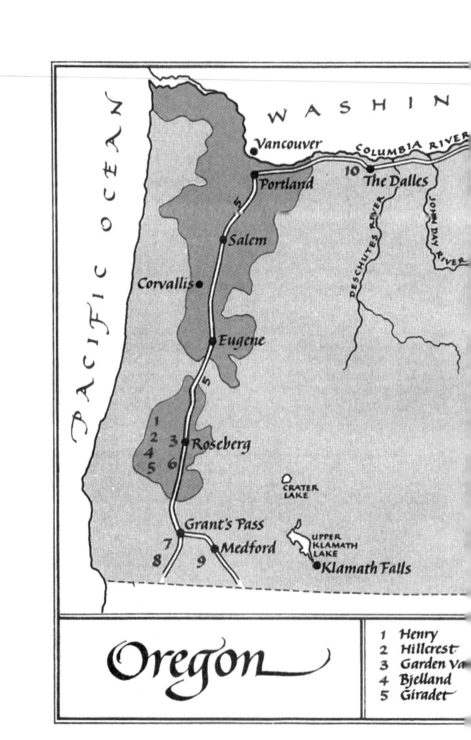

Oregon

1 Henry
2 Hillcrest
3 Garden Va
4 Bjelland
5 Giradet

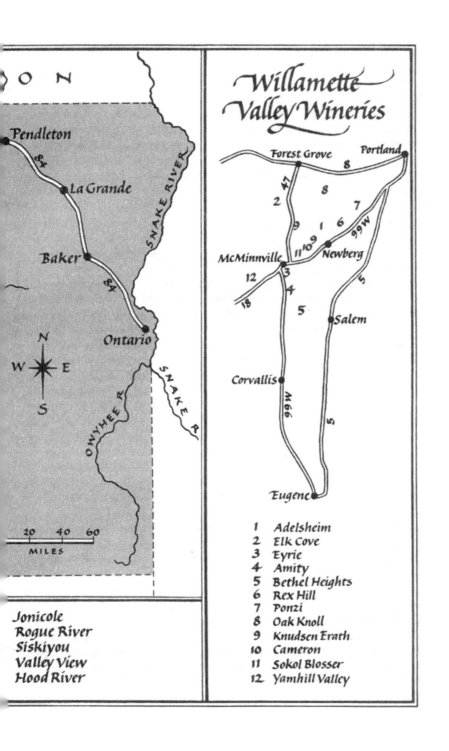

Willamette Valley Wineries

ON N

Pendleton
84
La Grande
SNAKE RIVER
Baker
84
Ontario

N
W E
S

OWYHEE R.
SNAKE R.

20 40 60
MILES

Jonicole
Rogue River
Siskiyou
Valley View
Hood River

Forest Grove   Portland
8
47
2   8
9   7
1   6   99W
11 10 9
McMinnville   Newberg
12   3
18   4   5
5
Salem
Corvallis
99W
5
Eugene

1 Adelsheim
2 Elk Cove
3 Eyrie
4 Amity
5 Bethel Heights
6 Rex Hill
7 Ponzi
8 Oak Knoll
9 Knudsen Erath
10 Cameron
11 Sokol Blosser
12 Yamhill Valley

mediocre wine year in and year out also did so in 1999 because they made no effort to control production. So this is an outstanding vintage for the wineries that care about making top-flight wine, and another failure for those that don't. The finest 1999 Oregon Pinot Noirs have exquisite balance. They are loaded with fruit yet are fresh, juicy, and well structured. Ripeness levels are high, yet the wines are elegant and their alcohol does not show. Unquestionably, most of the vintage's top wines require at least two to three years of patience, as they have high levels of ripe tannin, rendered more noticeable by their acidity levels. Many consumers who prefer Pinots with bottle age will find this a blessing because the 1999 Oregon Pinot Noirs are ageworthy. In short, 1999 appears to be Oregon's finest vintage to date.

1998—The 1998 vintage broke Oregon's recent string of poor vintages. Though not in the same league as the outstanding 1994 and 1999 vintages, 1998 is a very good year for Oregon's Pinot Noirs. Produced from extremely low yields (most growers' averages were below 2 tons per acre, with a few as low as a half ton), the finest 1998 Oregon Pinot Noirs have concentrated fruit, structured backbones, and harmonious personalities. Their flavor profiles tend toward the dark fruits, have good balance, and firm, ripe tannins. Many of them, after airing (even over 48–72 hours, which bodes well for their futures), open their tight, often foursquare personalities to reveal copious amounts of fruit, though others remain firm and, in time, reveal bitter tannins.

1997—Initial reports out of Oregon were guarded but good, but it is now clear that the producers were voicing hopes more than reality. The 1997 vintage is Oregon's third in a string of difficult, rain-plagued harvests. Overall, it is better than the rot-infested 1995 vintage, on a par with 1996. While many 1997 Pinot Noirs have enticing aromatics and pleasant attacks, they are frequently lean, in addition to lacking concentration and length. Moreover, the one trait found in the overwhelming majority of them is astringent tannin, Pinot Noir's nemesis.

1996—Oregon wineries deserved a reprieve from Mother Nature after what she did to them in 1995, but it was not to be. While 1996 is a slightly better vintage than 1995, it is far from good. Rains were again the bane of producers, particularly those with high-yielding vineyards. The 1996s are austere, with firm tannins, and offer darker fruit flavors than are usually found in Oregon Pinots. In time, the tannins in the finest 1996s may melt away, allowing the fruit to blossom. However, this will never be mistaken for a great year. The whites appear to be of good quality, yet their profiles suggest they will need to be drunk in the near term.

1995—After a string of good to outstanding vintages (1988–94), things were bound to change. Overall, 1995 is a poor vintage for Oregon, with only a handful of excellent to outstanding Pinot Noirs. Rain, rot, and poor winemaking were the culprits.

1994—Along with 1999, this is Oregon's best vintage of the 1990s and one of its very best ever. Low yields (the results of poor weather during the flowering season) and a warm summer resulted in the most concentrated and fruit-packed Oregon Pinot Noirs in memory. In fact, as with all great vintages, 1994 was such a wonderful year for Pinot Noir that even some underachieving estates crafted fine wines. Recent tastings indicate that the 1994 Pinot Noirs are quite ageworthy; the finest have the fruit and tannic structure to last another 3–5 years. However, this is an irregular vintage for Pinot Gris and Chardonnay, with quality ranging from excellent to mediocre depending on the harvest date.

1993—A cool summer followed by warm weather in September and October resulted in a vintage that appears to have surpassed 1992. The top Pinot Noirs reveal voluptuous textures, fragrant personalities, and a suppleness and richness that suggest this may be a breakthrough vintage for Oregon Pinot Noir. Limited quantities from the finest producers will make the top wines hard to find.

1992—This could have been the finest vintage for Oregon Pinot Noirs in decades. The weather was almost too hot and dry, though beneficial rains arrived toward the end of the growing season and alleviated the considerable stress in many of the hillside vineyards. Unfortunately, too many producers, worried about low acidity, used a heavy hand when adding acidity, resulting in many wines with incongruous personalities—very ripe flavors and tart, lean-textured personalities. Nevertheless, some terrific Pinot Noirs and big, dramatic, ostentatious Chardonnays have emerged. The Chardonnays must be drunk up, but the finest Pinot Noirs are at their peak of maturity.

1991—This is a very good, potentially excellent vintage of wines that does not have the power or drama of the 1992s or the intensity of the 1990s. Nevertheless, rain at the end of the harvest caught those growers who had excessive crop yields and were waiting for further maturity. For that reason, this is a tricky vintage to handicap, but certainly the Pinot Noirs look richly fruity, although softer and less structured than the 1992s and less tannic than the 1990s. It has good potential for high-quality wine, both red and white.

1990—A top vintage where yields were kept to a minimum. 1990 had plenty of heat and adequate rain, and the harvest occurred under ideal conditions. In fact, if it were not for 1992, this would be the best Oregon vintage in several decades. From the top producers, the Pinot Noirs are rich and full. If there is a disappointment, it is that many of the Pinot Gris wines lack concentration because yields were too high.

1989—A good vintage for Pinot Noir, Chardonnay, and Pinot Gris, the 1989s should have been drunk by 2000. The wines may not have had the intensity of the 1990s, but they were generally rich, soft, elegant wines. In many respects it was a more typical, classic vintage for Oregon's best producers than 1990 or 1992.

1988—The first of an amazing succession of good years for Oregon wines. Fine weather, an abundant crop, and a trouble-free harvest resulted in a number of excellent Pinot Noirs and Chardonnays.

1987—An excessively hot year resulted in most growers' harvesting too soon because they were afraid of losing acidity in their grapes. However, the stress of the summer's heat caused many vineyards not to reach physiological maturity. As a consequence, many 1987s were lean, too acidic, and disappointing. Six years after the vintage the best wines still had a hard edge; all should have been consumed by 1995. If only the growers had waited!

OLDER VINTAGES

As a general rule, most Oregon Pinot Noirs must be consumed within 7–8 years of the vintage. There are always a few exceptions, as anyone who has tasted the 1975 Eyrie or 1975 Knudsen Erath Pinot Noirs can attest. But in general, aging Oregon Pinot Noir for longer than 7–8 years (10–12 for the absolute finest) is a dangerous gamble.

Oregon's white wines should be drunk within several years of the vintage, even though they tend to have better natural acidity than their California counterparts. Yields are frequently too high, and the extract levels questionable, so whether it is Pinot Gris, Chardonnay, or dry Riesling, if you are not drinking these wines within 3–4 years of the vintage you are more likely to be disappointed than pleasantly surprised.

Note: Robert M. Parker, Jr., has a one-third interest in an Oregon vineyard that was commercially bonded in 1992 and began selling wine in 1993. Because of an obvious conflict of interest, this wine has not been reviewed.

RATING OREGON'S BEST PRODUCERS OF PINOT NOIR

Where a producer has been assigned a range of stars (***/****), the lower rating has been used for placement in this hierarchy.

* * * * * *(OUTSTANDING)*

Ken Wright Cellars

* * * * *(EXCELLENT)*

Archery Summit
Bethel Heights
Brick House
Cristom****/*****
Hamacher****/*****

Panther Creek Cellars
Penner-Ash Wine Cellars****/*****
St. Innocent****/*****
Domaine Serene****/*****

* * * *(GOOD)*

Adelsheim***/****
Argyle***/****
Brooks
Cameron***/****
Chehalem***/****
J. Christopher
Domaine Drouhin***/****

Elk Cove Cellars
Evesham Wood
Lemelson
Rex Hill***/****
Shea Wine Cellars
WillaKenzie Estate***/****

* *(AVERAGE)*

ADEA**/***
Abacela**/***
Amity
Château Benoit
Benton Lane
La Bête**/***
Château Bianca
Bridgeview
Broadley**/***
Callahan Ridge
Carabella
Cooper Mountain Vineyards
Domaine Coteau
Duck Pond Cellars
Dundee Springs
Edgefield
Erath Vineyards**/***
Eugene Wine Cellars
Firesteed
Flynn Vineyards
Foris**/***
Girardet Cellars**/***
Golden Valley Vineyards

Granville
Griffin Creek
Hauer of the Dauen
Henry Estate Winery
High Pass Winery
Hinman Vineyards/Sylvan Ridge
King Estate
Lion Valley**/***
Medici Vineyards**/***
Montinore Vineyards
Oak Knoll**/***
Ponzi**/***
Andrew Rich**/***
Sokol Blosser**/***
Starr
Torii Mor
Tualatin Estate Vineyards**/***
Willamette Valley Vineyards
Winter's Hill
Witness Tree
Yamhill Valley Vineyards**/***
Youngberg Hill Vineyards

ADEA

1998 Pinot Noir	D	88
1998 Pinot Noir Reserve	D	89

ADEA, formerly known as Fisher Family Vineyards (renamed to avoid confusion with California's Fisher Winery), was named after the four members of the Fisher family—Anne, Dean, Erica, and Adam. While the 1999 Pinot Noir appeared too rustic and hard to be recommended, both of this winery's 1998s merit consumer attention. The 1998 Pinot Noir is medium to dark ruby-colored and exhibits dark fruit aromas. It is a medium-bodied wine with intense blackberry and cassis-like flavors. This sweet, juicy, fruit-filled wine has some of this vintage's characteristic firmness yet delivers oodles of fruit in its well-structured character. Anticipated maturity: now–2007.

The slightly darker-colored 1998 Pinot Noir Reserve (100 cases produced) has sweet blackberry aromas. It is medium- to full-bodied, concentrated, and highly expressive. Copious quantities of assorted black fruits can be found in this wine's velvety-textured personality, as well as throughout its long, impressive finish. It should be drunk between 2004–2010.

ADELSHEIM

1999 Chardonnay Stoller Vineyard Clone 76	D	89
1999 Chardonnay Stoller Vineyard Clone 96	D	89
1999 Pinot Gris	B	88
1999 Pinot Noir Bryan Creek Vineyard	D	90+
1999 Pinot Noir Elizabeth's Reserve	D	90+
1999 Pinot Noir Goldschmidt Vineyard	D	90

David Adelsheim is justifiably excited about the work being done by his new wine-maker, Bill Musgnung, and the 1999s are the finest Adelsheim wines I have tasted.

The 1999 Pinot Noir Goldschmidt Vineyard (owned by wine enthusiast Neal Goldschmidt, a former governor of Oregon and President Jimmy Carter's secretary of transportation) is an outstanding ruby-colored wine. Bottled unfined and unfiltered, it exhibits spice and black cherry aromas. On the palate, it is medium- to full-bodied, oily-textured, and crammed with wild cherries, black raspberries, and blueberries. This is an opulent, intense, sweet wine with a lush, pure, extensive finish. Anticipated maturity: 2004–2010. The medium to dark ruby 1999 Pinot Noir Bryan Creek Vineyard offers dark cherry aromas and an oily, glycerin-packed character. It is juicy, hugely ripe, yet well structured. Loads of sweet red and black fruits can be found throughout its personality and its long, supple finish. Drink it between 2004–2010. The dark fruit-scented 1999 Pinot Noir Elizabeth's Reserve offers roasted dark fruit aromas. It is medium- to full-bodied, juicy, fresh, and loaded with black and Bing cherries. This satin-textured wine is highly structured and will require cellaring, yet its personality is dominated by its dense, sweet fruit. Anticipated maturity: 2004–2012.

The fresh, honeysuckle-scented 1999 Pinot Gris has a fat, medium-bodied character. Marzipan, spices, and poached white peaches can be found throughout its highly expressive personality as well as throughout its long finish. It is another excellent value. Drink it over the next 2 years. The pear- and spice-scented 1999 Chardonnay Stoller Vineyard Clone 76 has a medium- to full-bodied, expansive, and rich personality. Its pear and clove flavors coat the palate. It is an excellent wine with exquisite balance, purity, and length. The 1999 Chardonnay Stoller Vineyard Clone 96 has less spice than the previous wine in its aromas, yet boasts loads of pear and apple scents. Medium- to full-bodied and oily-textured, it is broad, rich, imbued with glycerin and loads of fat. This is a more detailed and elegant wine than the Clone 76, yet remains its qualitative equivalent. Both these wines should be at their best if consumed over the next 4–5 years.

ARCHERY SUMMIT

1999 Pinot Noir Archery Summit Estate	EE	94
1998 Pinot Noir Archery Summit Estate	EE	92+
1999 Pinot Noir Arcus Estate	E	90+
1998 Pinot Noir Arcus Estate	E	91
1999 Pinot Noir Louise Vineyard	E	89
1999 Pinot Noir Premiere Cuvée	D	87+
1998 Pinot Noir Premiere Cuvée	D	88
1999 Pinot Noir Red Hills Estate	E	93

1998 Pinot Noir Red Hills Estate	E	88+
1999 Pinot Noir Renegade Ridge Estate	E	90+
2000 Vireton	D	88

The expressive aromatics of the medium to dark ruby-colored 1998 Premiere Cuvée Pinot Noir reveal chocolate-infused, plummy black cherries. This firm, medium-bodied wine's flavor profile is composed of roasted black fruits, cocoa, and hints of cinnamon. At least 2 years of cellaring will be required to soften this offering's tannic backbone and finish. Anticipated maturity: 2003–2008. Produced from yields of .77 tons per acre, the medium to dark ruby-colored 1998 Arcus Estate Pinot Noir displays mouthwatering potpourri, red cherry, sweet plum, and spice aromas. This full-bodied, red fruit–packed wine is intense, immensely flavorful, and exceptionally long in the finish. Concentrated layers of cherries, raspberries, touches of strawberries, and hints of blueberries are found in this gorgeously structured yet opulent Pinot Noir. Anticipated maturity: now–2010.

Blackberries and spices can be found in the aromatics of the 1998 Pinot Noir Red Hills Estate. This firm, tight, and tangy medium- to full-bodied wine offers layers of red currants and blackberries. Somewhat foursquare and in need of cellaring, this wine should ultimately deserve an excellent to outstanding rating. Anticipated maturity: 2003–2010. One of Oregon's first "century" wines ($100 a bottle or more) the 1998 Archery Summit Estate is medium to dark ruby-colored and exhibits blackberry, dark cherry, and vanilla-infused oak scents. Medium- to full-bodied, firm, concentrated, and strict, this highly structured, strawberry and black fruit–packed wine is a masculine, intense, and powerful offering. Though at present closed and foursquare, its formidable layers of fruit, outstanding depth, and highly present yet ripe tannins promise a long, successful life. Anticipated maturity: 2005–2012+.

Gary Andrus, the owner and head wine-maker of Archery Summit, describes 1999 as "a vintage of high ripeness. It is more classical Burgundian with persistent fruit depth than what we've seen before or since." He went on to add that it never rained in the late season, and that his vines enjoyed a very long hang time, 120–131 days. "We had a long hang time in 2000 as well," said Andrus, "yet those wines appear to be more tannic than 1997, 1998, or 1999."

Three thousand cases were produced of the 2000 Vireton. Made from a blend of 80% Pinot Gris, 12% Chardonnay, and 8% Pinot Blanc, it boasts white and yellow fruit aromas with an appealing floral element. Medium-bodied and packed with flavors reminiscent of tangy red currants, orange zests, and juicy pears, this is a well-focused, expansive wine. Its silky-textured character leads to a white peach and apricot-flavored finish. It is a delicious wine, loaded with well-ripened fruit. Drink this highly expressive offering over the next 2 years.

The medium to dark ruby-colored 1999 Pinot Noir Louise Vineyard was harvested at two tons per acre. It has a gorgeous nose of sweet black cherries and violets. On the palate, this medium-bodied wine is opulent, with loads of lush black cherries, blackberries, and roses. It is broad yet elegant and harmonious. Anticipated maturity: 2004–2010. Produced entirely from Dijon clones, the medium to dark ruby-colored 1999 Pinot Noir Renegade Ridge Estate has a wild cherry, earth, and Asian spice–scented nose. Loads of juicy, satiny, dark cherry fruits can be found in this seamless, silky-textured offering. It boasts a concentrated, dense nugget of fruit that envelops its superbly ripened tannin. Anticipated maturity: 2004–2011.

The medium to dark ruby-colored 1999 Pinot Noir Arcus Estate (842 cases produced) has a gorgeously pure nose of red cherries, blackberries, and violets. This intense, medium-bodied wine is crammed with cassis, black cherries, blackberries, loads of spices, and dark raspberries. Its attack and mid-palate are focused, juicy, and highly expressive. Its finish is foursquare, yet it possesses the requisite fruit to dominate its tannin. Anticipated maturity: 2005–2012. The outstanding 1999 Pinot Noir Red Hills Estate is medium to dark ruby-colored and has boisterous wild berry and fresh herb aromas. Medium- to full-bodied and hugely concentrated, this elegant wine combines power with harmony, refinement with muscle. It is juicy, deep, and has loads of powerful blackberry and cassis flavors. Drink this marvelous Pinot between 2005–2015. Only 2,604 bottles of the magnificent medium to dark ruby-colored 1999 Pinot Noir Archery Summit Estate were produced. Its spice, rose, and black cherry–scented nose leads to a full-bodied, hugely concentrated personality. This expansive, cherry, chocolate, plum, and licorice-flavored wine is opulent, possesses loads of depth, and yet remains refined, fresh, and exceedingly well balanced. Its sweet, lush fruit carries through its admirably long, impressive finish. Anticipated maturity: 2006–2017.

ARGYLE

1999 Chardonnay Reserve	C	89
1989 Extended Tirage Brut	D	89
1999 Pinot Noir Clubhouse	D	90+
1999 Pinot Noir Nuthouse	D	89
1999 Pinot Noir Reserve	D	88
1999 Pinot Noir Spirithouse	D	90
1999 Riesling Dry Reserve	B	88
1998 Riesling Dry Reserve	B	88

The 1989 Extended Tirage Brut has been recently disgorged. Grilled toast and anise aromas lead to a rich, complex, graham cracker, toast, yeast, and mineral-flavored personality. It is complex, has excellent to outstanding concentration, and a satiny texture rendered lively with present yet unobtrusive bubbles. Drink it over the next 2–3 years.

The 1999 Chardonnay Reserve has a white flower and toasted oak–scented nose. Medium-bodied and possessing excellent focus, it is a delineated spice, honeysuckle, and anise-flavored wine whose flavors last throughout its pure, extensive finish. Anticipated maturity: now–2006. Produced from vines planted in 1975, the 1998 Riesling Dry Reserve has a hugely expressive, Germanic nose of minerals and flowers. Medium-bodied and well focused, it is a boisterous, sweet herbal tea, candied lemon, stone, and white fruit–flavored wine. This excellent Riesling should be consumed over the next 4–5 years. In comparison, the 1999 Riesling Dry Reserve has a demure, somewhat muted nose of stones and earth. However, on the palate, it is rich, opulent, beautifully delineated, and highly expressive. Candied limes, minerals, and spices can be found in this wine's intense personality as well as throughout its long finish. Anticipated maturity: now–2005. These are both excellent values.

Toasted oak and loads of cherries and black raspberries can be found in the aromatics of the 1999 Pinot Noir Reserve. Medium-bodied and extremely spicy, it is packed with Bing cherries and candied raspberries. This is a broad, juicy, fresh wine that possesses a long, pure, tannin-filled (yet ripe) finish. Drink it between 2004–2009. The toasted oak and black fruit–scented 1999 Pinot Noir Nuthouse is medium to dark ruby-colored. Satin-textured and rich, this plump, sweet, candied wine is exceptionally light and loaded with blackberries and cherries. It is pure, well balanced, and long in the finish. Anticipated maturity: 2004–2010.

The medium to dark ruby-colored 1999 Pinot Noir Spirithouse has demure blackberry aromas. On the palate, this medium- to full-bodied, rich, highly concentrated wine is bright, exceedingly well focused, and loaded with layers of cassis, black cherries, and raspberries. It is an outstanding wine, dominated by its luscious fruit and possessing the requisite structure and balance for aging. Anticipated maturity: 2004–2011. The similarly colored 1999 Pinot Noir Clubhouse (only 120 cases produced) has Asian spice and fruitcake aromas. It is a rich, plump, intensely concentrated wine crammed with black cherries, blackberries, red currants, and strawberries. Medium- to full-bodied, delineated, and pure, it is a seamless, fruit-filled wine with an impressively long, fresh finish. Anticipated maturity: 2005–2011.

BETHEL HEIGHTS

1997 Chardonnay Reserve	C	88
1998 Pinot Noir Estate Grown	D	89

1999 Pinot Noir Flat Block Reserve	D	89
1998 Pinot Noir Lewman Vineyard	D	88
1999 Pinot Noir Nysa Vineyard	D	88
1998 Pinot Noir Nysa Vineyard	D	89
1999 Pinot Noir Southeast Block Reserve	D	92+
1998 Pinot Noir Southeast Block Reserve	D	89
1999 Pinot Noir Wädenswil Block Reserve	D	88
1998 Pinot Noir Wädenswil Block Reserve	D	89

Butterscotch and creamed anise aromas are found in the nose of the 1997 Chardonnay Reserve. This silky, flavorful, delicious wine is packed with mouthwatering creamed hazelnut and toasty, sweet oak spices. Extremely well crafted and harmonious, this wine also possesses a long, supple, fruit-filled finish. Drink it over the next 3–4 years.

As with many 1998 Oregon Pinot Noirs, those produced by Bethel Heights evolve and soften considerably after contact with air. The 1998 Pinot Noir Estate Grown offers a host of red cherries and dark berries. Loads of tangy currants can be discerned in its medium-bodied character. This firm yet silky-textured wine will require patience in order for it to blossom. Anticipated maturity: 2003–2009+.

The medium-bodied and ruby-colored 1998 Pinot Noir Lewman Vineyard offers metallic red fruit aromas. This well-made, spicy berry and black cherry–flavored offering is intense, masculine, and in need of 3–4 years of cellaring. Anticipated maturity: 2004–2009.

The medium to dark ruby-colored 1998 Pinot Noir Nysa Vineyard reveals aromas reminiscent of mocha, strawberries, blackberries, and hints of oak. Medium- to full-bodied and chewy-textured, it is packed with cherries and dark raspberries, whose flavors linger throughout its firm yet focused and expressive finish. Anticipated maturity: now–2008.

The similarly colored 1998 Southeast Block Reserve benefited enormously from air. At first it was firm, foursquare, and hard, yet in time revealed tangy red cherry aromas and a medium-bodied, raspberry and assorted red fruit–packed character. Readers with patience will admire this wine's considerable density and structure. Anticipated maturity: 2004–2010.

The medium to dark ruby-colored 1998 Pinot Noir Wädenswil Block Reserve displays blackberry and blueberry aromas. It is broad, ample, and filled with sweet dark fruits whose flavors persist throughout its delightfully long finish. Anticipated maturity: 2003–2009.

The ruby-colored 1999 Pinot Noir Nysa Vineyard has toasted oak and blackberry aromas. On the palate, this wine shows excellent breadth to its blackberry and dark cherry flavors. It is juicy, medium-bodied, firm, and well made. Anticipated maturity: 2003–2009. The slightly darker-colored 1999 Pinot Noir Wädenswil Block Reserve has dark berry and currant aromas. Medium-bodied and filled with plummy blackberries and cherries, this is a well-balanced, lively, expressive, yet firm wine. Its finish is admirably long and reveals loads of ripe tannin. Drink it between 2004–2009.

The medium to dark ruby-colored 1999 Pinot Noir Flat Block Reserve has blackberry and dark cherry aromas. It is juicy, expansive on the palate, and medium-bodied. This mouth-coating blackberry- and brambleberry-flavored wine is masculine, muscular, and possesses a long, pure finish. Anticipated maturity: 2004–2010. The medium to dark ruby-colored 1999 Pinot Noir Southeast Block Reserve is the finest wine I have tasted from this excellent winery. Spicy dark fruits can be discerned in its aromatics. On the palate it is broad, ample, and hugely expansive. Copious quantities of red and black cherries are intermingled with candied raspberries and currants in this dense, satin-textured, and deep wine. Its exceptionally long finish reveals loads of prodigiously ripe tannin. Anticipated maturity: 2005–2014.

BRICK HOUSE

1999 Chardonnay	D	89
1998 Chardonnay Cuvée du Tonnelier	D	88

1999 Gamay Noir	C	90
1998 Gamay Noir	C	88
1999 Pinot Noir Cinquante	D	88
1998 Pinot Noir Cuvée du Tonnelier	D	91+
1997 Pinot Noir Cuvée du Tonnelier	D	88+
1999 Pinot Noir Les Dijonnais	D	89+
1998 Pinot Noir Les Dijonnais	D	90

Proprietor Doug Tunnell's 1997 Pinot Noir Cuvée du Tonnelier is a beauty. Asian spices, violets, and red berries are found in its enthralling aromatics. Medium- to full-bodied, beautifully ripe, and luscious, its character is packed with sweet red and black fruits amid hints of licorice. Like most of Oregon's 1997 Pinot Noirs, this wine's finish reveals copious tannin. However, unlike the majority of its brethren, this offering appears to have the requisite depth of fruit to offset them. Anticipated maturity: now–2006. The anise, gingerbread, and orange rind–scented 1998 Chardonnay Cuvée du Tonnelier has medium body and an oily texture. This broad, well-made wine reveals orange blossom and white fruit flavors. It is lovely, full of character, and flavorful. Drink it over the next 1–2 years.

Tunnell crafted a marvelous, medium to dark ruby-colored 1998 Gamay Noir. Aromatically, it reveals leather, black fruit, and white pepper scents. On the palate, this medium-bodied, velvety-textured wine is packed with juicy blackberries, cracked black pepper, and touches of freshly laid asphalt. This fruit-forward wine should be drunk over the next 2 years. The medium to dark ruby-colored 1998 Pinot Noir Les Dijonnais gets its name from the fact that it is produced entirely from Dijon clones of Pinot Noir. Sweet black cherries, cola, and assorted dark fruits are found in this offering's aromatics. Medium- to full-bodied, well structured, and expressive, it exhibits candied red fruits, cookie dough, and hints of clay in its complex flavor profile. It should be consumed over the next 5–6 years. The slightly darker-colored 1998 Pinot Noir Cuvée du Tonnelier was produced from the Pommard clone of Pinot Noir. Fresh black cherry and pit fruit aromatics lead to a cassis, blueberry, grape, and blackberry-flavored character. Medium- to full-bodied, dense, satiny-textured, and backward, this impressive, long-finishing wine will require cellaring. Anticipated maturity: 2003–2010.

As with all of owner Doug Tunnell's estate-made wines, the 1999 Chardonnay is from organically grown grapes. Its highly expressive aromas reveal loads of spices with anise and an underlying hint of almond paste. Medium-bodied, fresh, and softly textured, this well-delineated wine has flavors reminiscent of a spicy fruitcake, candied apples, and poached pears. It is a juicy, tangy wine for drinking over the next 4 years.

Brick House's 1999 Gamay Noir may be the finest example of this varietal I have tasted from the United States. Harvested on October 19 (as Doug Tunnell said, "We almost forgot it") at 25.2 Brix, or 14.2% natural potential alcohol, this is a medium to dark ruby-colored wine with intense black pepper, spice, and dark berry aromas. Medium- to full-bodied and boasting a fabulously oily texture, this sweet blackberry, jammy, cherry, cassis, and spice-flavored wine is supple, juicy, and intense. Its flavors last throughout its juniper berry, clove, and cracked pepper–laced finish. Drink this outstanding wine over the next 5 years.

The ruby-colored 1999 Pinot Noir Cinquante ("fifty" in French, a reference to the 50% whole clusters used in making this wine) has dark, spicy fruit aromas. It is a firm, blackberry, currant, and fresh herb–flavored, medium-bodied wine, slightly fatter and plumper than the Cuvée du Tonnelier. Anticipated maturity: 2004–2010. The medium to dark ruby-colored 1999 Pinot Noir Les Dijonnais (produced entirely from Dijon clones) has a coffee, caramel, and blackberry-scented nose. Medium-bodied, juicy, and packed with dark fruit flavors, this is an intense, concentrated, and well-extracted wine. The fruit dominates its firm structure, yet it will require patience. Anticipated maturity: 2005–2011.

CAMERON

1997 Chardonnay Reserve Abbey Ridge	D	88
1999 Pinot Noir Abbey Ridge	D	(90–92)
1999 Pinot Noir Clos Electrique	D	(89–91)

The 1997 Chardonnay Reserve Abbey Ridge displays a rich anise- and toast-scented nose. This medium- to full-bodied, thick, oily-textured wine is crammed with spices, touches of vanilla, and jammy white fruits in its full-throttle, plump character. Hints of lemons and baking spices come up in its long, buttery finish. Drink it over the next 4 years.

The medium to dark ruby-colored 1999 Pinot Noir Abbey Ridge (from 25-year-old vines) has boisterous black raspberry, dark cherry, and Asian spice aromas. It is a pure, extremely elegant, medium-bodied wine loaded with cherries, coffee, raspberries, and candied strawberries. This charming, satin-textured wine is complex, intense, yet harmonious and seamless. This exceedingly well made wine will be at its best consumed between 2003–2010.

The 1999 Pinot Noir Clos Electrique is medium to dark ruby-colored and boasts pure dark cherry aromas. Produced from 17-year-old vines, this is a medium-bodied, chewy-textured wine with loads of candied cherries, juicy blackberries, and dark raspberries in its character. It has excellent to outstanding depth, a juicy, lively personality, and hints of rusticity in its flavorful finish. If John Paul is able to civilize this wine prior to bottling, it will certainly merit an outstanding rating.

CHEHALEM

1999 Chardonnay Ian's Reserve	D	89
1998 Chardonnay Ian's Reserve	D	89
1997 Chardonnay Ian's Reserve	D	88
2000 Pinot Gris Reserve	C	89
1998 Pinot Noir 3 Vineyard	D	88
1999 Pinot Noir Ridgecrest Vineyard	D	92+
1999 Pinot Noir Rion Reserve	D	93+
1997 Pinot Noir Stoller Vineyards	D	89
2000 Riesling Dry Reserve	C	88
1999 Riesling Reserve Coral Creek Vineyards	C	88

The 1997 Chardonnay Ian's Reserve displays sweet yellow plum and hints of apricots in its aromas. Medium-bodied, oily-textured, and impressively ripe, this thick, extroverted wine is packed with golden fruit and oak spice flavors. It is certainly one of the finest Chardonnays that has been crafted in Oregon. Anticipated maturity: now–2005.

The admirable 1997 Pinot Noir Stoller Vineyards displays cinnamon-laced, dark cherry aromas. Its silky smooth texture leads to a gorgeously ripe character crammed with blackberries and black cherries. Medium- to full-bodied, sweet, and structured, this wine may be one of the rare Oregon 1997 Pinots to improve with time. Drink it over the next 5 years.

The 1998 Pinot Noir 3 Vineyard is medium to dark ruby-colored and offers delightful aromatics of black cherries, flowers, and dark raspberries. Medium-bodied and redolent, with loads of dark fruits, this tight yet silky-textured wine is intense and full-flavored. Anticipated maturity: now–2008. Certainly one of the finest Oregon Chardonnays I have tasted to date, Chehalem's 1998 Ian's Reserve offers aromas of tropical fruits, loads of spices, and hints of vanilla. This plump yet well-balanced, medium-bodied wine is broad, pure, and has excellent amplitude. Superripe pears and apples can be found in its harmonious, well-crafted character. Drink it over the next 3–4 years.

The flower and Earl Grey tea–scented 1999 Riesling Reserve Coral Creek Vineyards is a highly expressive, concentrated, tangy, focused wine. Spices, minerals, and assorted white fruits can be found in its flavorful and persistent personality. Drink it over the next 3–4 years.

The 2000 Riesling Dry Reserve has intense sweet herbal tea aromas. On the palate, this rich, plump, medium-bodied wine has lovely depth to its boisterous white fruit, mineral, and tea-like flavors. It is highly expressive, well balanced, and a delight. Drink it over the next 4–5 years. The 2000 Pinot Gris Reserve bursts from the glass with white peaches, poached pears, and hints of smoke. On the palate it is fresh, pure, rich, and crammed with white and yellow peach flavors. It is a broad, highly expressive wine for drinking over the next 3 years.

Chehalem's Chardonnay Ian's Reserve is one of Oregon's finest Chardonnays. The 1999 exhibits rich white fruit aromas intermingled with intense spices in its aromatic profile. Medium-bodied, fat, and buttery, it offers layers of superripe pears, white peaches, and candied apples in its intense, lush character. Anticipated maturity: now–2005.

The outstanding 1999 Pinot Noir Ridgecrest Vineyard bursts from the glass with sweet blackberry aromas. This medium-bodied, gorgeously concentrated wine explodes on the palate with dramatically intense sweet cherries, raspberries, strawberries, and candied currants, and sports ripened tannin. It is harmonious, seamless, extremely extroverted, and completely dominated by its lush fruit. Anticipated maturity: 2004–2012. The black cherry, rose, and blackberry-scented 1999 Pinot Noir Rion Reserve is produced from a barrel selection of the Ridgecrest Vineyard. Medium- to full-bodied and layered, with candied berries, compotes of cherries, and jammy strawberries, it is a broad, big, muscular wine with an elegant character and an impressively long, supple, fruit-filled finish. Anticipated maturity: 2005–2012.

J. CHRISTOPHER

1999 Pinot Noir Charlie's Vineyard	D	88

The ruby-colored 1999 Pinot Noir Charlie's Vineyard has blackberry and fresh herb aromas. Medium-bodied and tangy, this wine is filled with sweet red and black cherries as well as cassis and blackberry-like flavors. It has a long yet firmly structured finish. Anticipated maturity: 2003–2008.

CRISTOM

1998 Chardonnay Celilo Vineyard	C	89
1999 Pinot Noir Jessie Vineyard	D	91
1999 Pinot Noir Louise Vineyard	D	90+
1999 Pinot Noir Marjorie Vineyard	D	94
1998 Pinot Noir Marjorie Vineyard	D	92
1999 Pinot Noir Mount Jefferson Cuvée	C	88
1999 Pinot Noir Reserve	D	91
1998 Pinot Noir Reserve	D	89+
1998 Pinot Noir Signature Cuvée	EE	93

Cristom's ability to weave elegance into its fruit-dominated wines has made it one of my favorite estates in Oregon. Owned by Paul Gerrie, this winery's vineyards are the responsibility of Paul Feltz, and its winemaking is in the hands of Steve Doerner.

The white peach, lees, toast, and butter-scented 1998 Chardonnay Celilo Vineyard is another highly successful effort from the Cristom Winery. From the finest *terroir* for this varietal in the Northwest, it exhibits the richness of a Meursault and the beautifully elegant balance of a Puligny-Montrachet. This exuberant, tangy, white fruit, vanilla, and spice-flavored wine is velvety-textured and delightfully rendered. Drink it over the next 4 years.

The medium to dark ruby-colored 1998 Pinot Noir Reserve offers toasted oak and blackberry aromas. Juicy black cherries, cookie dough, and raspberries can be found in its harmonious, well-balanced, and focused personality. This exceptionally long-finishing wine is elegant and medium- to full-bodied. Anticipated maturity: 2003–2008. The similarly colored 1998 Pinot Noir Marjorie Vineyard exhibits roasted fruit and grilled oak aromas. This medium- to full-bodied, concentrated, fat, yet precisely defined and expressive wine is crammed with juicy black cherries. While it has a boisterous personality, it also possesses an outstanding structure, complexity, and a long, detailed finish. Anticipated maturity: now–2010.

Cristom is one of the first two Oregon wineries (Archery Summit is the other) to release $100-a-bottle wines. The medium to dark ruby-colored 1998 Pinot Noir Signature Cuvée (the label bears the signatures of Doerner, Feltz, and Gerrie) reveals delicate cherry and raspberry aromas. On the palate, this medium- to full-bodied wine offers superbly intense red and black fruit, chocolate, roasted cherry and blackberry, as well as fresh black raspberry and spiced flavors. It is well structured, complex, powerful, and elegant. This outstanding offering should be at its best between 2003–2012.

As wine-maker Doerner said, "1999 was a fantastic year, but it will require some cellaring. It is a vintage that can be characterized by its exquisite balance due to extremely high levels of ripeness yet excellent levels of acidity that we retained because the evenings were cool." The medium to dark ruby-colored 1999 Pinot Noir Mount Jefferson Cuvée has expressive black cherry aromas. This is a juicy, medium-bodied wine with loads of lush, sweet, red black cherry cherry fruit flavors. Its supple finish is loaded with exceptionally ripe and round tannin. Drink it between 2003–2009. The similarly colored 1999 Pinot Noir Reserve has a nose of black cherries, cloves, and juniper berries. This wine has outstanding depth to its medium-bodied character. Copious quantities of assorted dark fruit, mostly cherries, are intermingled with spices in its structured core. It will require 5 years of cellaring and last at least through 2013.

The 1999 Pinot Noir Jessie Vineyard is this parcel's third crop. Medium to dark ruby-colored, it has an immensely appealing nose of plums, talcum powder, perfume, roses, and violets. Velvety-textured and seamless, this medium- to full-bodied wine is packed with lush cherries, blackberries, spices, and cloves. Its exceptionally long finish displays beautifully ripened tannin. Anticipated maturity: 2005–2010. The similarly colored 1999 Pinot Noir Louise Vineyard has a brooding, black fruit–scented nose. Medium- to full-bodied, foursquare, and tight, it reluctantly reveals juicy blackberry and currant flavors. This exceedingly youthful wine has outstanding levels of fruit plus loads of ripe tannin. Anticipated maturity: 2006–2014.

The star of the show is Cristom's 1999 Pinot Noir Marjorie Vineyard. Medium to dark ruby-colored and boasting a floral, candied black cherry and spice-scented nose, this is an opulent, silky-textured wine. Its sultry yet complex personality exhibits huge amounts of candied fruits and loads of juicy cherries, as well as a myriad of spices whose flavors linger throughout its admirably long and pure finish. Anticipated maturity: 2005–2014.

DOMAINE DROUHIN

1999 Pinot Noir Laurène	D	89+

The 1999 Pinot Noir Laurène displays spices, cherries, and raspberries in its aromatic profile. It is a structured, tightly wound wine that is concentrated and juicy. Black/red cherries and brambleberries are intermingled with currants and Asian spices in its lively yet foursquare personality. This wine may ultimately merit an outstanding score if it fleshes out with bottle aging. Anticipated maturity: 2005–2011.

ELK COVE

1999 Pinot Noir La Bohème	D	91+
1999 Pinot Noir Estate Reserve	E	90?
1999 Pinot Noir Roosevelt	D	90+
1999 Pinot Noir Windhill	D	88

Elk Cove's winemaking team attributes the success of their 1999 Pinot Noirs to the long hang time in 1999. Harvested at 1.8 tons per acre and produced from 25-year-old vines, the 1999

Pinot Noir Windhill is medium to dark ruby-colored and has gorgeous red cherry aromas. This is a medium-bodied, opulent, juicy wine with attractive black cherry fruit ensconced in a well-structured character. Its texture is soft in the attack and on the mid-palate and leads to a somewhat firm finish that should melt away with 2–3 years of cellaring. Anticipated maturity: 2004–2009. The 1999 Pinot Noir La Bohème is slightly darker-colored and was produced from 16-year-old vines. Plumlike aromas lead to a medium to full-bodied, satin-textured personality. This is a sultry wine crammed with loads of blueberries, blackberries, and cherries. Well focused, concentrated, pure, and admirably long in the finish, this is an outstanding, fruit-packed Pinot for drinking between 2005–2010.

Only 360 cases of the 1999 Pinot Noir Roosevelt were produced. This dark ruby-colored wine has blackberry, cassis, and fresh herb aromas. Loads of dark fruits, licorice, and black currants can be found in its dense, highly structured character. It is intense, powerful, and highly expressive. Anticipated maturity: 2005–2011. One hundred cases of the dark ruby-colored, chocolate, licorice, and black fruit–scented 1999 Pinot Noir Estate Reserve were produced. Medium- to full-bodied, concentrated, backward, and muscular, this is a chewy, tight, dense, and intense wine. It has copious quantities of firm tannin that at present offset its admirable fruit. Only time will tell whether this wine will merit an outstanding rating or remain dominated by its tannin. Anticipated maturity: 2005–2012?

EVESHAM WOOD

1998 Chardonnay Mahonia Vineyard	B	88
1999 Pinot Noir Cuvée J	D	90
1999 Pinot Noir Seven Springs Vineyard	D	89+
1999 Pinot Noir Shea Vineyard	D	89

The 1998 Chardonnay Mahonia Vineyard Unfiltered has a floral nose that also reveals hints of talcum powder and citrus fruits. On the palate this medium-bodied and elegant wine is softly textured, focused, and well balanced. Crisp pears, spices, anise, and loads of minerals can be found in its personality and throughout its impressively fresh finish. Drink this excellent value over the next 4 years.

The ruby-colored 1999 Shea Vineyard Pinot Noir Unfiltered has an appealing spice and sweet cherry–scented nose. Medium-bodied and packed with soft candied cherries, this is a sweet, pure, raspberry, strawberry, and assorted red fruit–flavored wine. It is velvety-textured, has excellent depth, and a long, subtle finish. Drink it between 2003–2009.

The 1999 Seven Springs Vineyard Unfiltered Pinot Noir is medium to dark ruby-colored and has an immensely appealing violet as well as red/black cherry–scented nose. At present it is tight but reveals excellent levels of fruit in its medium-bodied character. This wine has excellent depth, a gorgeously detailed personality, and the potential to ultimately merit an outstanding score. Drink it between 2004–2009. Forty percent of the 1999 Cuvée J Pinot Noir Unfiltered comes from the Temperance Hill Vineyard, 5% from Seven Springs, and 55% from the estate's Le Puits Sec Vineyard. It is medium to dark ruby-colored and has a spicy, black cherry–scented nose. This wine has excellent to outstanding breadth of red and black cherries as well as a distinct new oak signature to its character. It has excellent balance, loads of fruit, and a medium- to full-bodied personality. It is lively, fresh, and has a firm finish that will require 5 years of cellaring and should hold through 2014.

HAMACHER

1999 Chardonnay Cuvée Forêts Diverses	D	89
1998 Chardonnay Cuvée Forêts Diverses	D	89+
1999 Pinot Noir	D	93
1998 Pinot Noir	D	92

1997 Pinot Noir	D	89+
1999 Pinot Noir Mantia	D	90+

The medium to dark ruby-colored 1997 Pinot Noir is one of the vintage's success stories. Gorgeous ripeness can be discerned in its chocolate milk and cherry syrup–scented nose. Blackberries, cherries, and strawberries coat the palate in this thick, medium- to full-bodied, supple-textured wine. Expressive yet well structured, it may very well improve with time. Anticipated maturity: now–2005.

Eric Hamacher, the owner and wine-maker of Hamacher Winery, is one of Oregon's finest makers of white wine. The 1998 Chardonnay Cuvée Forêts Diverses (produced in 100% Taransaud barrels, 50% of which are new, from a blend of different forests) has butterscotch, spice, and anise aromas. Medium-bodied and creamy-textured, this mouthcoating wine expands on the palate with loads of candied lemon, spice, and poached pear flavors. It is seamless, harmonious, and lively. Additionally, its expressive flavors last throughout its pure, fresh, and long finish. Anticipated maturity: now–2005. The 1999 Chardonnay Cuvée Forêts Diverses has a hugely rich nose of anise, almonds, and spices. Medium- to full-bodied, it is fat, plump, and loaded with poached pear and marzipan flavors. At present its oak is in the forefront, but this should be remedied with a few months of bottle age, as its luxuriously textured character displays excellent concentration of fruit. Anticipated maturity: now–2006.

Dick Ponzi, one of Oregon's winemaking pioneers, is Eric Hamacher's father-in-law. He said, "Eric loves Pinots with delicacy and makes absolutely gorgeous ones." Claude Dugat, when served Hamacher's 1999, said, "*la texture et la pureté de fruit de ce vin sont splendides.*" ("The texture and purity of fruit in this wine are splendid"). They are both right.

The 1998 Pinot Noir is an outstanding wine. It exhibits a medium to dark ruby color and cedar, tobacco, and dark fruit aromas. Medium-bodied and gorgeously expansive, this is a satin-textured wine crammed with dark fruits, black cherries, and loads of spices. Hints of chocolate can be discerned in its fruit-dominated yet well-focused and refined personality. It has the firmness characteristic of the 1998 vintage yet possesses the density of fruit to cope with it. Anticipated maturity: 2004–2010.

Hamacher's ruby-colored 1999 Pinot Noir will not win any contests for power or extract, but once again (both his 1997 and 1998 are stars of their respective vintages) it demonstrates that this young wine-maker has grasped two of the hallmarks of Pinot: 1) this varietal can achieve exceptional purity, and 2) its texture is paramount. Hamacher himself stated, "Pinot Noir *must* have great texture, or else it is nothing." This wine exhibits a nose of extraordinary purity, redolent with fresh red cherries, raspberries, and currants. It is sumptuously textured, bringing to mind liquid silk, and coats the mouth with highly detailed sweet red fruit whose flavors linger throughout its admirably long finish. This wine's tannin is well ripened and barely noticeable. If Hamacher can build more depth and concentration into his wines without losing their sublime purity and texture, he will produce some of the most compelling Pinots on earth. Drink this wine over the next 10 years. The medium to dark ruby-colored 1999 Pinot Noir Mantia, named after this vineyard's owner, Joe Mantia, reveals jammy blackberry and licorice aromas. This is a medium- to full-bodied, concentrated, muscular, meaty wine with loads of power and chewy layers of dark fruits. This is a Cabernet lover's Pinot, built for the long haul. Anticipated maturity: 2005–2012.

LEMELSON

1999 Pinot Noir Jerome Reserve	D	90+
1999 Pinot Noir Stermer Vineyard	D	89
1999 Pinot Noir Thea's Selection	D	88

This brand-new winery has already planted 82 acres of vines and plans to have 110 acres planted by next year. Named after owner Eric Lemelson's mother, the 1999 Pinot Noir Thea's Selection is a medium to dark ruby-colored wine with appealing red fruit aromas. This opulent, medium-bodied, velvety-textured wine offers lush cookie dough, candied red fruit, and cherry syrup–like flavors. It is soft, highly expressive, and what it may lack in complexity, it makes up for with loads of delightful fruit flavors. Drink it over the next 4 years.

The 1999 Pinot Noir Stermer Vineyard is dark ruby-colored and has timid, sweet red fruit aromas. On the palate, this medium-bodied wine is firm yet expansive, coating the mouth with blackberry and fresh herb flavors. Its tannin, at first somewhat firm, softens with aeration, promising a good future. Anticipated maturity: 2004–2010. The similarly colored 1999 Pinot Noir Jerome Reserve has mouthwatering licorice and jammy blackberry aromas. Medium-bodied and chewy-textured, this is an intense, muscular wine with dense layers of black fruits, dark cherries, and Asian spices whose flavors last throughout its impressive finish. Anticipated maturity: 2005–2012.

PANTHER CREEK CELLARS

1998 Pinot Noir Bednarik Vineyard	D	91
1999 Pinot Noir Freedom Hill Vineyard	D	91
1998 Pinot Noir Freedom Hill Vineyard	D	92
1999 Pinot Noir Nysa Vineyard	D	91
1998 Pinot Noir Nysa Vineyard	D	88+
1999 Pinot Noir Red Hills Estate Vineyard	E	91
1999 Pinot Noir Reserve	D	93
1998 Pinot Noir Reserve	D	90+
1999 Pinot Noir Shea Vineyard	D	89
1998 Pinot Noir Shea Vineyard	D	89+

The medium to dark ruby-colored 1998 Pinot Noir Shea Vineyard has fresh, sweet, and candied red/black cherry aromas. Tangy currants, juicy berries, stones, and hints of oak can be found in this medium-bodied, well-made, structured offering. It will certainly merit an outstanding score if it is able to integrate its oak and soften with cellaring. Anticipated maturity: now–2007. The firm, medium to dark ruby-colored 1998 Pinot Noir Nysa Vineyard displays dark berry, spice, cookie dough, and red currant aromas. This tight, tangy fruit-flavored wine may develop to earn an excellent, possibly outstanding score. Anticipated maturity: 2003–2008.

The medium to dark ruby-colored 1998 Pinot Noir Bednarik Vineyard has highly expressive pumpkin pie spice and sweet cherry aromas. It is medium- to full-bodied, round, plump, luscious, and sexy, yet has outstanding structure. Lovely cherry, cinnamon, and juniper berry flavors can be discerned in its harmonious, medium- to full-bodied personality. Drink it over the next 8–9 years. The opulent 1998 Pinot Noir Reserve has a gorgeous spice and red fruit–scented nose. This medium-bodied, broad, decadent wine has highly expressive red cherry and pit fruit flavors. It is delicate yet powerful, detailed yet dense. This wine's long and focused finish reveals supple, ripe tannins. Anticipated maturity: now–2010. The explosive dark cherry aromatics of the medium to dark ruby-colored 1998 Pinot Noir Freedom Hill Vineyard lead to a medium- to full-bodied, velvety-textured, and lush personality. This decadent, chewy, and broad wine bursts on the palate with copious quantities of red cherries. It is well balanced, intensely flavored, and harmonious. Anticipated maturity: 2003–2010+.

The medium to dark ruby-colored 1999 Pinot Noir Shea Vineyard has boisterous black fruit aromas. Medium- to full-bodied and deep, this wine is crammed with highly expressive blackberry, black cherry, and cassis flavors. It is beautifully rendered and harmonious. Drink it over the next 7–8 years. The similarly colored 1999 Pinot Noir Nysa Vineyard bursts from the glass with loads of spices, blackberries, and hints of mint. Medium- to full-bodied, big, broad, and supple-textured, this is a prodigiously ripe elderberry, spice, and jammy black raspberry–flavored wine. It is harmonious and possesses a long, fruit-packed, smooth finish. Drink it between 2003–2010.

I had a love affair with the nose of the 1999 Pinot Noir Red Hills Estate Vineyard. This medium to dark ruby-colored wine bursts from the glass with a myriad of spices, flowers, sweet tea, and red cherries. Medium-bodied and intricate, this black cherry–dominated wine is soft, supple, gorgeously balanced, and elegant. Its lush layers of fruit envelop the palate and last throughout its impressively long finish. Anticipated maturity: 2004–2010.

The medium to dark ruby-colored 1999 Pinot Noir Freedom Hill Vineyard has rose, blackberry, and Asian spice aromas. Medium- to full-bodied, muscular, and highly structured, it is packed with road tar, black cherries, and sweet cassis-like flavors. This is a firm, fruit-dominated wine that will require cellaring. Anticipated maturity: 2005–2011. The 1999 Pinot Noir Reserve is my favorite of Panther Creek's recent releases. It has a mouthwatering nose of violets, perfume, potpourri, and cherries. On the palate, this elegant wine is medium-bodied, expansive, and packed with cherries, raspberries, strawberries, and hints of freshly cracked pepper. It is pure, harmonious, has no hard edges, and possesses a long, sweet, fruit-filled finish. Drink this gorgeous Pinot between 2004–2010.

PENNER-ASH WINE CELLARS

1999 Pinot Noir	D	93
1998 Pinot Noir	D	91

The 1998 Pinot Noir is the inaugural wine from Lynn Penner-Ash's (Rex Hill's wine-maker's) winery. It has a medium to dark ruby color and delightful black raspberry, plum, and black cherry aromas. This sweet, voluptuously textured, medium- to full-bodied wine is packed with gorgeously ripe red cherries and touches of strawberry jam. Well structured, bal-anced, and focused, it is a concentrated, powerful, yet elegant wine. Anticipated maturity: 2003–2008+. The 1999 Pinot Noir has a magnificent nose of cookie dough and cherry syrup. Medium- to full-bodied and broad, it is rich, intense, wonderfully concentrated, and highly expressive. Loads of sweet red and black fruits coat the palate and linger for 30–40 seconds. It is a seamless, harmonious wine with gorgeous balance and purity. Anticipated maturity: 2004–2012.

PHANTOM HILL

1998 Pinot Noir Revelation Cuvée	D	88

Located in Idaho, this winery produces Pinot Noir from grapes purchased in Oregon. The medium to dark ruby-colored 1998 Pinot Noir Revelation Cuvée offers black fruit aromas and a forward, medium-bodied character. Plump black raspberries and plums can be found in this wine's flavor profile. It has a somewhat tight finish that will require a year or two of cel-laring. Anticipated maturity: now–2006.

REX HILL

1999 Pinot Gris Reserve	C	89
1999 Pinot Noir Croft Vineyard	E	88
1999 Pinot Noir Jacob-Hart Vineyard	E	91
1998 Pinot Noir Jacob-Hart Vineyard	E	90+
1999 Pinot Noir Maresh Vineyard	E	90
1999 Pinot Noir Reserve	D	89+
1998 Pinot Noir Reserve	D	89
1999 Pinot Noir Seven Springs Vineyard	E	93
1999 Pinot Noir Weber Vineyard	E	89

The medium to dark ruby-colored 1998 Pinot Noir Reserve reveals intense cherry aromas. This potentially outstanding wine has a concentrated, medium- to full-bodied personality. It is velvety-textured and displays loads of dark fruits in its firm and backward flavor profile. Anticipated maturity: 2003–2008. The 1998 Pinot Noir Jacob-Hart Vineyard is aromatically unyielding. This medium to dark ruby-colored wine is, like the previous offering, backward and ungenerous at present, yet it exhibits all of the qualities required for an outstanding rating. Copious quantities of black cherries, blackberries, cola, spices, and hints of mocha can be found in this intensely flavored effort. Firmly structured and somewhat foursquare, it will require cellaring, but should blossom into a powerful, extroverted, and flavorful Pinot. Drink it between 2003–2008+. The darker-colored 1999 Pinot Noir Weber Vineyard has violet, rose, and dark fruit aromas. Medium-bodied, broad, and immensely appealing, it is filled with spices, candied blackberries, and dark cherries. This satin-textured wine should be consumed over the next 5–6 years.

The medium to dark ruby-colored 1999 Pinot Noir Croft Vineyard has an exuberant nose of potpourri, black raspberries, and toasted oak. Medium-bodied and expansive, it is sweet, lush, pure, and loaded with red/black cherries. Some warmth can be discerned in the finish of this otherwise harmonious wine. Drink it over the next 5–6 years.

Loads of spices and black cherries can be discerned in the aromatics of the 1999 Pinot Noir Reserve. Medium-bodied and boasting a fabulously oily texture, this wine is crammed with Asian spices and candied cherries. It is boisterous, opulent, and loaded with fruit. Drink this well-balanced, highly expressive wine over the next 7–8 years.

The beguiling aromatics of the medium to dark ruby-colored 1999 Pinot Noir Jacob-Hart Vineyard reveal dark cherry and hints of chocolate. Medium-bodied and soft, this is a sweet, velvety-textured wine. Its personality is big, broad, and plush. It has a sexy, velvety mouthfeel and loads of candied red fruits whose flavors last throughout its exceedingly long and pure finish. Anticipated maturity: 2003–2011.

Dark spices, cherries, and toast can be discerned in the aromatics of the ruby-colored 1999 Pinot Noir Maresh Vineyard. Medium-bodied, well structured, and spicy, this is a large, muscular wine loaded with sweet blackberry-like flavors. It possesses more tannin than the previous wines, yet they are ripe and supple. Anticipated maturity: 2005–2011.

The outstanding, medium to dark ruby-colored 1999 Pinot Noir Seven Springs Vineyard has intricately detailed violet, blackberry, and cherry aromas. It coats the palate with loads of candied red and black fruits as well as floral flavors. It is gorgeously delineated, powerful, detailed, and exceptionally long. This magnificent wine combines elegance with muscle and subtlety with extravagance. Anticipated maturity: 2004–2012.

The 1999 Pinot Gris Reserve has spicy, smoky, white peach aromas. Medium-bodied and expansive, it is a rich, flavorful wine filled with white peaches, apricots, poached pears, and stones. It is extremely well balanced and has a long, supple, flavor-packed finish. Kudos to Rex Hill's wine-maker, Lynn Penner-Ash, for her gorgeous lineup of 1999s.

ROCKBLOCK CELLARS

1999 Syrah Seven Hills Vineyard	D 89

This winery is owned by Ken and Grace Evenstad, who also own Domaine Serene, and was created to market their non-Burgundian varietal wines. The 1999 Syrah Seven Hills Vineyard (most of this vineyard is located in Oregon, even though it was made famous by Washington State wineries, particularly Leonetti) has sweet blackberry, jammy black raspberry, and Syrah's distinctive sweat aromas. Medium- to full-bodied and loaded with candied blackberries, black cherries, and elderberries, this lush, extremely well made wine also has a touch of fresh herbs that come out in its long, sweet, and supple finish. This highly expressive wine should be consumed over the next four years.

ST. INNOCENT

1999 Chardonnay Seven Springs Vineyard Dijon Clone	C	90
1998 Chardonnay Seven Springs Vineyard Dijon Clone	C	88
1999 Pinot Gris Shea Vineyard Vendange Tardive	C/375ml	89

1999 Pinot Noir Brick House Vineyard	D	89+
1996 Pinot Noir Brick House Vineyard	D	89+
1999 Pinot Noir Freedom Hill Vineyard	D	91
1998 Pinot Noir Freedom Hill Vineyard	C	90+
1996 Pinot Noir Freedom Hill Vineyard	D	90
1998 Pinot Noir O'Connor Vineyard	C	91
1996 Pinot Noir O'Connor Vineyard	D	88
1999 Pinot Noir Seven Springs Vineyard	D	93+
1998 Pinot Noir Seven Springs Vineyard	D	94
1999 Pinot Noir Shea Vineyard	D	92

None of St. Innocent's 1997 Pinot Noirs tasted for this report could be recommended, yet this estate is responsible for some of Oregon's finest 1996s. The 1996 Pinot Noir O'Connor Vineyard is ruby colored and reveals red and black cherry aromas. It is harmonious, beautifully pure, and offers kirsch and blackberry flavors in its well-crafted, medium-bodied character. Its finish displays ripe, supple tannins. Anticipated maturity: now–2006. Similarly colored, the 1996 Pinot Noir Brick House Vineyard offers sweet, creamy red fruit aromatics. Medium- to full-bodied, satin-textured, and powerful, this is a luxurious, cherry-dominated wine. Highly detailed, yet plump and flavorful, it also possesses a long, supple, sweet finish. Anticipated maturity: now–2007.

The 1996 Pinot Noir Freedom Hill Vineyard is medium to dark ruby-colored and reveals black currant and Asian spice aromas. The most powerful of St. Innocent's 1996s, this wine's personality is dense, medium- to full-bodied, chewy-textured, and structured. Road tar, black cherries, and cassis can be found in its intense flavor profile. It is certainly one of the stars of its vintage. Anticipated maturity: now–2006.

As at most of Oregon's quality estates that wish to produce Chardonnay, St. Innocent has adopted the use of Dijon clones, which are earlier-ripening than other clones (in the past, all Oregon Chardonnays were produced from clones originally engineered for California's hot, dry climate). Vlossak's eggnog, spice, and creamy anise–scented 1998 Chardonnay Seven Springs Vineyard Dijon Clone is extremely rich and mouthcoating. Butterscotch, loads of spices, and superripe pears can be found in this medium- to full-bodied, highly expressive wine. Drink it over the next 2–3 years.

While many of Oregon's best-known estates appear to be in a horse race to see who will have the state's most expensive Pinot Noirs, St. Innocent has maintained an intelligent, honorable, and consumer-friendly policy of pricing. The 1998 Pinot Noir O'Connor Vineyard (this is the last vintage St. Innocent will produce from this site) is medium to dark ruby-colored and offers hugely expressive and sweet black cherry and raspberry aromas. This velvety-textured, voluptuous, and supple wine is packed with multitudes of dark fruits, hints of spices, and exhibits first-rate, supple, ripe tannins in its extensive finish. Anticipated maturity: now–2009. In a manner typical of Pinot Noirs from the Freedom Hill Vineyard, St. Innocent's 1998 offers a boisterous, red fruit–packed nose. This big, dense, chewy-textured, medium- to full-bodied wine is well structured and crammed with red and black cherries. While presently firm, this wine has copious quantities of fruit as well as well-ripened tannins. Anticipated maturity: 2004–2010+.

Vlossak believes his 1998 Pinot Noir Seven Springs Vineyard is the finest wine he has fashioned to date (readers should remember he was responsible for making Panther Creek's stellar 1994 Freedom Hill Pinot). I agree. Possessing a nose reminiscent of a Romanée-St.-Vivant, this wine expresses complex aromas of perfume, flowers, red berries, and spices. Medium- to full-bodied, satin-textured, and lush, it possesses great focus, refinement, and complexity. Silky layers of cherries, raspberries, and strawberries can be found in this intricate and exceptionally long-finishing wine. Anticipated maturity: now–2010+. Wow!

Aged in 44% new-oak barrels, the white flower, stone, and pear-scented 1999 Chardonnay

Seven Springs Vineyard Dijon Clone has outstanding focus and delineation to its medium-bodied, broad, and crystalline personality. This pure candied lemon, pear, spice, and mineral-flavored wine is juicy, complex, and expressive. Drink it over the next 5–6 years.

Harvested at 1.6 tons per acre, the 1999 Pinot Gris Shea Vineyard Vendange Tardive has mineral, spice, candied berry, and sweet tea aromas. This rich, opulent, dense, and palate-coating wine was aged 80% in tank and 20% in oak barrels. It boasts white peach and hazel-nut flavors in its deep, medium-bodied personality. Unlike most Oregon whites, this one will require cellaring to fully express itself. Anticipated maturity: 2004–2010.

Save for a strange offering from the Temperance Hill Vineyard, Mark Vlossak has produced a stupendous set of 1999 Oregon Pinot Noirs. He should also be commended for keeping his prices reasonable. Am I the only consumer who is shocked that there are many inferior Oregon wines at two or three times the cost of these? The 1999 Pinot Noir Shea Vineyard is medium to dark ruby-colored and displays a darker fruit as well as a more noticeable structure than is generally associated with this vineyard. It bursts from the glass with loads of blackberries, black cherries, and brambleberries. This is a medium- to full-bodied wine with a gorgeously sappy character, copious quantities of fruitcake, blackberry syrup, dark cherry flavors, and a marvelously long finish. Its tannin is ripe yet present, giving it the backbone that many wines from this vineyard have lacked. Anticipated maturity: 2004–2012.

Produced from fruit acquired from Doug Tunnell's organic vineyard, the medium to dark ruby-colored 1999 Pinot Noir Brick House Vineyard offers massive quantities of spices and violets intermingled with grilled oak in its aromatics. Medium- to full-bodied and possessing outstanding depth, this wine's black fruit is dominated by clovelike flavors. It is firm, yet should soften and ameliorate with cellaring. Anticipated maturity: 2004–2010.

The slightly darker-colored 1999 Pinot Noir Freedom Hill Vineyard is a hugely endowed wine. It bursts from the glass with loads of cherries, red flowers, and sweet, earthy spices (Vlossak compares this last scent to clay). On the palate, it reveals powerful boysenberry, blackberry, and cassis fruit flavors in a more delineated and civilized style than is generally found from wines from this vineyard. It has outstanding focus, copious amounts of ripe tannin, and an impressively long finish. Drink it between 2005–2012.

I am enthralled with the aromatics of Vlossak's Pinots from the Seven Springs Vineyard. A magnum of the 1991 served at this year's International Pinot Noir Celebration was super. A bottle of the 1992, which I served a week before to a chef visiting from Paris, was equally lovely. In its youth, this wine reveals hints of its complex aromatics and tends to be tight and backward (the 1998, tasted three months ago, remains an exception). With cellaring, Vlossak's Pinot Noirs from Seven Springs typically blossom into some of Oregon's real stars. Aromatically, the medium to dark ruby-colored 1999 displays wildflowers, berries, cinnamon, and a myriad of spices. It is rich, juicy, and extremely elegant. Loads of candied red fruits, mostly raspberries and cherries, are found in this ample, structured wine. It is fresh, bright, and beautifully concentrated, and has a long, toasted oak and cherry-flavored finish. Anticipated maturity: 2005–2014.

DOMAINE SERENE

1999	Chardonnay Côte Sud Vineyard Dijon Clones	D	88
1999	Pinot Noir Grace Vineyard	E	90
1998	Pinot Noir Grace Vineyard	E	91+
1998	Pinot Noir Guadalupe Vineyard	E	91
1998	Pinot Noir Mark Bradford Vineyard	E	89
1997	Pinot Noir Reserve	C	88

As would be expected from one of Oregon's premier wineries, Domaine Serene crafted a lovely 1997 Pinot Noir Reserve. Light to medium ruby-colored, it offers demure, spicy red cherry aromas. Its opulent, satin textured character is plush, medium-bodied, and pleasure-inducing. Layers of red and black cherries, intermingled with rosemary and hints of cinnamon, can be found throughout its flavor profile and long, oily finish. Drink it between now–2003.

The luscious 1998 Pinot Noir Grace Vineyard is medium ruby-colored and reveals deep sweet cherry and roasted spice aromas. Medium- to full-bodied, opulent, and hedonistically sweet, this red cherry and candied strawberry–flavored wine is sure to be a crowd pleaser. There are no hard edges or angles in this sexy, pleasure-giving wine. Its finish is long, suave, and silky. Drink it over the next 5 years. The medium to dark ruby-colored 1998 Pinot Noir Mark Bradford Vineyard has loads of blackberry and cassis in its aromatic profile. Medium-bodied and concentrated, this wine has excellent depth to its juicy, blackberry-packed personality. It is backward, tight, and has its vintage's characteristically tough tannin, yet it is an excellent wine, with outstanding density of fruit. Anticipated maturity: 2004–2009. Regrettably, only 100 cases of the dark ruby-colored 1998 Pinot Noir Guadalupe Vineyard were produced. Its gorgeous aromas of blackberries, black cherries, and hints of chocolate lead to a plump, rich, medium- to full-bodied personality. This broad, intense, satin-textured wine possesses copious quantities of assorted dark fruits and Asian spices in its seductive personality. Its impressively long finish reveals ripe tannin. Anticipated maturity: 2004–2010.

Produced from 10-year-old vines, the 1999 Chardonnay Côte Sud Vineyard Dijon Clones has beguiling spice, vanilla, and floral scents. It is silky-textured, expansive, and medium-bodied. This well-focused wine has good to excellent depth of toasty, floral, mineral, and white fruit flavors. It is loaded with white peaches, butter, and hints of hazelnuts. Drink it over the next 2–3 years. The black cherry and fresh herb–scented 1999 Pinot Noir Grace Vineyard has an opulent, lush, medium- to full-bodied character. This feminine, silky-textured, seamless wine is loaded with soft, sweet cherries, raspberries, and strawberries, and has outstanding focus, depth of fruit, and harmony. Anticipated maturity: 2004–2012.

SHEA WINE CELLARS

1999 Pinot Noir Shea Vineyard	D	88

The ruby-colored 1999 Pinot Noir Shea Vineyard has an appealing, if demure, dark cherry and black raspberry–scented nose. Medium- to full-bodied and filled with loads of boisterous red and black cherry fruits, this is a well-made, flavorful Pinot. It displays excellent ripeness, a sound structure, and a long, baked dark fruit–filled finish. Drink it over the next 6 years.

TUALATIN ESTATE VINEYARDS

2000 Semi-Sparkling Muscat	B	89

The 2000 Semi-Sparkling Muscat is a clone of an Italian Moscato d'Asti. Its boisterous orange blossom and raspberry aromas lead to a fresh, zesty, medium-bodied personality. This velvety-textured wine has tangy orange, red berry, and floral flavors in its character. Like the Italian Moscatos, it has low alcohol (6.5%) and an off-dry sweetness. It should be drunk over the next 6–8 months as an apéritif or as I like to drink this style of wine, while watching the first football games of the season on warm Sundays. This is an excellent value that should be consumed soon.

WILLAKENZIE ESTATE

1999 Pinot Noir	C	88
1999 Pinot Noir Aliette	D	91+
1998 Pinot Noir Dijon Clones 777	D	89
1999 Pinot Noir Grande Reserve	E	92
1999 Pinot Noir Pierre Léon	D	89

Regrettably, only 50 cases were produced of the excellent and potentially outstanding medium to dark ruby-colored 1998 Pinot Noir Dijon Clones 777. Candied kumquats and black cherries can be found in its mouthwatering nose. This soft, rich, velvety-textured, medium- to full-bodied wine is packed with plump red and black cherries. Deep, complex, and powerful, this is a firm Pinot to cellar for 2–3 years and drink over the next 7–8 years.

The medium to dark ruby-colored 1999 Pinot Noir has gorgeous blackberry and spice aromas. Dark fruits are intermingled with metallic notes in this medium-bodied, silky-textured wine. Intensely ripe, bordering on overripe, it is supple, soft, and juicy. Anticipated maturity: now–2006. The medium to dark ruby-colored 1999 Pinot Noir Pierre Léon (2,000 cases were produced) bursts from the glass with Asian spices, blackberries, and blueberries. This broad, medium- to full-bodied wine is packed with concentrated layers of black fruits and fresh herbs. It is a masculine, muscular wine with loads of structure, yet remains dominated by its dark fruit flavors. Anticipated maturity: 2004–2010.

The outstanding medium to dark ruby-colored 1999 Pinot Noir Aliette's nose is reminiscent of a compote of red and black cherries intermingled with mocha, thyme, and rosemary. Medium- to full-bodied and expansive, this powerful, concentrated wine is densely packed with blackberries, cassis, black cherries, and a myriad of spices. It is juicy, reveals loads of supple tannin and should do marvelously well with cellaring. Anticipated maturity: 2005–2012. The similarly colored 1999 Pinot Noir Grande Reserve has fresh red and black cherry aromas. Medium- to full-bodied and satin-textured, it is highly concentrated yet elegant. Black cherries, blackberries, and cassis are interspersed with juniper, clove, and cinnamon in this detailed yet boisterous offering. Its flavors last throughout its extensive finish. It is a wine of harmony, power, and seamlessness. Anticipated maturity: 2005–2012.

WILLAMETTE VALLEY VINEYARDS

1998 Pinot Noir Joe Dobbes Signature Cuvée	E	88+

The medium to dark ruby-colored 1998 Pinot Noir Joe Dobbes Signature Cuvée was tasted on three separate occasions, with varying amounts of aeration. It proved to be one of the numerous 1998 Oregon Pinot Noirs that benefited immensely from contact with air. Wildflowers, blackberries, and cherries can be discerned in its aromatics. On the palate, dark fruits, cola, and black raspberries are found in this firm, highly structured, yet densely packed, medium- to full-bodied wine. With proper medium-term cellaring, it should continue to improve and could ultimately merit an outstanding rating. Anticipated maturity: 2003–2008+.

KEN WRIGHT CELLARS

1999 Pinot Noir Abbey Ridge Vineyard	D	90
1998 Pinot Noir Abbey Ridge Vineyard	D	89+
1999 Pinot Noir Canary Hill Vineyard	D	91
1998 Pinot Noir Canary Hill Vineyard	D	92
1997 Pinot Noir Canary Hill Vineyard	D	89
1999 Pinot Noir Carter Vineyard	D	93
1998 Pinot Noir Carter Vineyard	D	90
1997 Pinot Noir Carter Vineyard	D	88+
1999 Pinot Noir Elton Vineyard	D	88
1998 Pinot Noir Elton Vineyard	D	93
1999 Pinot Noir Freedom Hill Vineyard	D	93
1999 Pinot Noir Guadalupe Vineyard	D	92
1998 Pinot Noir Guadalupe Vineyard	D	88+
1997 Pinot Noir Guadalupe Vineyard	D	88+
1999 Pinot Noir McCrone Vineyard	D	92+
1998 Pinot Noir McCrone Vineyard	D	90
1997 Pinot Noir McCrone Vineyard	D	88
1999 Pinot Noir Nysa Vineyard	D	88

1998 Pinot Noir Nysa Vineyard	D	88
1999 Pinot Noir Shea Vineyard	D	92
1997 Pinot Noir Shea Vineyard	D	88
1999 Pinot Noir Wahle Vineyard	D	89+
1998 Pinot Noir Wahle Vineyard	D	90

The bright, medium ruby-colored 1997 Canary Hill Vineyard displays spicy blueberry and black raspberry aromas. This smooth, supple, medium-bodied wine coats the palate, bringing to mind the delightful Burgundies of Claude Dugat. This sultry, hedonistic offering may lack complexity, but it is one of the most successful of the 1997s tasted for this report. Drink it over the next 3–4 years. The slightly lighter-colored 1997 McCrone Vineyard offers sweet, spicy, candied berry aromas. Although tight, structured, and tannic, it regales the palate with blackberry and cassis flavors. Medium-bodied and well balanced, this boisterous Pinot should be consumed over the next 2 years, while the fruit still dominates its tannin.

The ruby-colored 1997 Guadalupe Vineyard offers talcum powder–dusted red fruit aromas. Less structured than the McCrone, the Guadalupe is packed with sexy red cherry fruit that lasts throughout its long finish. This wine may ultimately merit a higher score if, with cellaring, its tannin melts away before its fruit. Anticipated maturity: now–2003+.

The light to medium ruby-colored 1997 Shea Vineyard exhibits blackberry and Asian spice aromas. Medium-bodied, firm, and structured, it is neither as sexy nor as opulent as Ken Wright's previous vintages from this vineyard. Readers will enjoy the blackberries and black cherries that are intermingled with new oak in this wine's composite of flavors. Anticipated maturity: now–2003. The ruby-colored 1997 Carter Vineyard displays baby powder, strawberries, and cherry fruit aromas. Medium-bodied, this wine's character is filled with red/black cherries, tangy blood oranges, and hints of tar, as well as spicy oak. Long, with loads of sweet, ripe tannins, Wright's Carter Vineyard has the potential to improve with age. Anticipated maturity: now–2004.

Once again, in 1998, Ken Wright fashioned an impressive lineup of Oregon Pinot Noirs. Two of his 1998s tasted for this report were perplexing (the Freedom Hill and Shea), and I am reserving judgment on those wines. The medium to dark ruby-colored 1998 McCrone Vineyard reveals deep aromas of spices and sweet red cherries. Medium- to full-bodied, supple-textured, and harmonious, this dark cherry–flavored wine exhibits Wright's characteristic fruit-enveloped tannins. It is extroverted, opulent, and possesses a long, sweet, cherry-filled finish. Drink it over the next 6 years. The similarly colored 1998 Guadalupe Vineyard has aromas reminiscent of red cherries and candy corn. This sweet, sexy, medium-bodied wine has loads of superripe dark cherries in its character and a finish clipped by the presence of copious tannin. If its admirable fruit is capable of outliving the tannin, this wine will merit an even more exalted review. Drink it over the next 5–6 years.

Complex spices and dark fruits are found in the aromas of the ruby-colored 1998 Abbey Ridge Vineyard. Medium-bodied and satin-textured, it has lovely palate presence, exhibited by loads of dark fruit flavors that coat the mouth. It is firmly structured and will require patience. Anticipated maturity: 2003–2009. The aromatically demure 1998 Nysa Vineyard offers candied orange, blackberries, and dark pit fruit flavors. This medium-bodied, foursquare wine has a muscular, masculine personality that will demand cellaring. Anticipated maturity: 2003–2008.

The medium to dark ruby-colored 1998 Canary Hill Vineyard reveals lovely perfumed, dark cherry aromas. This expressive, pure, harmonious, expansive wine is medium- to full-bodied, velvety-textured, and seamless. Sweet red cherries, candied raspberries, and assorted spices can be found throughout its boisterous character and long, supple finish. It has outstanding depth and an intensely flavorful character. Drink it over the next 8–10 years. The ruby-colored 1998 Wahle Vineyard has juicy red cherry and popcorn aromas. This ample, voluptuous, medium- to full-bodied wine is sensual, sexy, and oily-textured. While it is unquestionably outstanding, it lacks the Canary Hill exquisite finish. Drink it over the next 7–8 years.

Complex black raspberry, oak, and spice aromas are found in the nose of the medium to dark ruby-colored 1998 Carter Vineyard. This firmly structured wine is medium- to full-bodied, satin-textured, and loaded with blackberries, cassis, and assorted dark pit fruits. It is a firm, concentrated Pinot that should be at its best between 2003–2009. The superb medium to dark ruby-colored 1998 Elton Vineyard reveals sexy aromas of sweet cherries immersed in vanilla-infused oak. It is luscious, sexy, expansive, and opulent. This medium- to full-bodied wine coats the palate with viscous waves of cherries, blackberries, and spices. It is harmonious, seamless, and immensely gratifying. Anticipated maturity: now–2010.

The ruby-colored 1999 Abbey Ridge Vineyard has black cherry and white pepper aromas. It is light- to medium-bodied, sexy, and gorgeously opulent. Silky-textured layers of black cherries and black raspberries are found in its harmonious personality, as well as throughout its extensive finish. This wine bears Ken Wright's trademark suppleness and candied fruit. Drink it over the next 7–8 years. The slightly darker-colored 1999 Nysa Vineyard has demure dark fruit aromas. It is medium-bodied, plump, soft, and satin-textured. Black cherries are found in the attack and mid-palate, and are intermingled with a metallic, almost copperlike flavor in the finish. This is a broad, sweet, lush wine for drinking between 2003–2009.

The ruby-colored 1999 Canary Hill Vineyard has sweet, jammy cherry aromas. On the palate, this medium-bodied wine is seamless, has outstanding focus, and a delightful red/black cherry and violet-flavored core. It is juicy, has no hard edges, and possesses a pure, long, sweet finish. Drink it over the next 8–9 years. The slightly darker-colored 1999 Carter Vineyard has a mouthwatering nose of jammy black cherries and roses. Medium-bodied and boasting dazzling breadth of fruit, this wine penetrates the palate with its crystalline cherry, strawberry, and violet-like flavors. It is a wine of impressive purity, delineation, and harmony. This outstanding wine should be consumed between 2004–2010.

The ruby-colored 1999 Elton Vineyard has blackberry and cassis aromas. Light- to medium-bodied and spicy, it offers loads of clove and dark fruit flavors in its fresh, zesty character. Drink it over the next 6 years. Awesome candied red fruit aromas burst from the glass of the 1999 Shea Vineyard. Medium- to full-bodied and chewy-textured, this wine is packed with cherries, raspberries, blueberries, and blackberries. It is a boisterous, in-your-face Pinot that will deliver considerable flavor. Anticipated maturity: 2004–2011.

The medium to dark ruby-colored 1999 Wahle Vineyard exhibits graphite, toasted oak, and sweet red cherry aromas. Medium-bodied and intense, it is a masculine wine with a firm backbone. Blackberries, cassis, and oak can be found throughout its personality and its admirably long finish. This is a tightly wound wine that will require patience. Anticipated maturity: 2005–2012. The similarly colored 1999 McCrone Vineyard has sweet black fruit and earth aromas. This gorgeous wine has outstanding depth, concentration, and balance. Its pure, fresh, black cherry and raspberry flavors are intermingled with a distinctive mineral quality throughout this wine's character and superb finish. This opulently layered yet zesty wine will be at its best if consumed between 2004–2010.

The Bing cherry–scented, medium to dark ruby-colored 1999 Guadalupe Vineyard displays abundant juicy red berries and cherries in its impressive flavor profile. This highly expressive, fruit-packed wine has loads of sweet red fruits that burst from the glass. It is pure, sweet, candied, and immensely impressive. This wine should be consumed over the next 8–10 years. The medium to dark ruby-colored 1999 Freedom Hill Vineyard has luscious toasty Bing cherry aromas. Medium- to full-bodied and magnificently delineated, this is a chewy black fruit, mocha, and cherry-packed wine. Broad, fresh, focused, and exceedingly long in the finish, it is a Pinot of compelling fruit and refinement. Drink this outstanding wine between 2004–2012.

7. WASHINGTON STATE

The Basics

Washington State is primed to become an increasingly important factor in the fine-wine marketplace. Presently, with the absurdly high prices charged by the top California wineries and Bordeaux châteaux, Washington's finest offerings (often of equal or better quality) are downright cheap in comparison. In fact, the state's largest wineries, such as Château Ste. Michelle, offer a bevy of reasonably priced wines for budget-conscious consumers. If Washington State's finest producers had resisted the temptation to raise their prices, they would have undoubtedly gained significant market share in the past half-dozen years.

Washington State produces some extraordinary wines and many poor ones. There is no doubt that Washington can produce wines as compelling, intense, flavorful, and elegant as any viticultural region in the world. The fact that the majority of the state's wines are average, or simply bad, should not detract consumers' attention from the glories crafted by those producers who are fulfilling Washington's enormous potential.

Washington's wines are not well known outside the Northwest. As a former retailer, I know how rare it was to hear a customer say, "Tonight I would love to have something from Washington with dinner, what do you recommend?" Bearing this in mind, I am offering some information aimed at providing readers with a basic understanding of the region's geography, climate, wine-makers, and growers, as well as the multitude of wine styles.

A GEOGRAPHY PRIMER

Admittedly, I had misconceptions about Washington State prior to traveling there after joining *The Wine Advocate* a half-dozen years ago. I had tasted numerous wines from there and knew that it was the home of Microsoft and numerous other high-tech companies, and that rain was plentiful. My trips have shown me that my middle school geography teachers were not completely daft (mountains do stop rain, and microclimates really do exist). To begin to understand Washington State wines, I believe it is important to know a little about its geography.

Virtually all the wines described here are from the Columbia Valley appellation (which includes the Yakima and Walla Walla valleys). Primarily a desert, it is located in southeastern Washington and overlaps into Oregon. As Pacific Ocean depressions approach the Washington coastline, they are often trapped by the coastal Olympic Mountains, dropping much of their precipitation on the rain forests located on the range's western slopes. When a weather front is powerful enough to remain intact after traversing the Olympic Mountains, it then faces the even higher elevations of the Cascade Mountains. Very few depressions are capable of clearing both these ranges, and as a consequence, eastern Washington experiences desert-like conditions (as a matter of fact, the U.S. Army stages desert training in Yakima).

As I flew from Seattle to Walla Walla on my first tasting trip, I was amazed to see the contrast between the lush green western slopes of the Cascades and the barren eastern side. From the tips of the Cascades all the way to Walla Walla, the only signs of vegetation were the trees bordering rivers and irrigated farms. One statistic dramatizes this weather pattern—within the town of Walla Walla, on the eastern edge of the Columbia Valley appellation, annual rainfall increases by one inch per mile as one travels eastward. On the parched western edge of Walla Walla, abutting the l'Ecole No. 41 and Woodward Canyon wineries, are dusty asparagus fields. On the eastern edge, where Walla Walla Vintners and Leonetti's new vineyards are located, the rolling hills are lush and green.

Rain, the bane of wine producers the world over, is rarely a nuisance for Washington's main grape-growing region. Because Washington State vineyards are irrigated, viticulturalists can control the quantity of water each row of vines gets.

Readers should not assume that because Washington State borders Canada it has a cold climate. Once spring arrives, the Columbia Valley enjoys a grape-growing season that winemakers the world over would envy. Sun and heat are plentiful, evenings are cool—excellent for maintaining natural acidity levels.

This is not, however, a viticultural paradise. The winters and early springs can be a grape grower's nightmare. Why? The region is prone, on average once every six years, to "killer freezes" (as they are known in these parts), the last of which descended from the Arctic in late January and early February 1996 and devastated the vineyards. Countless vines were destroyed, their trunks exploding because of the Arctic Express's extreme temperatures. Most of the vines that survived produced exceedingly little. Interestingly, Merlot and Sémillon were the most susceptible to the freeze, with Cabernet, Chardonnay, and Rhône varietals faring better. Depending on the varietal, yields in 1996 were down between 25% and 80%.

THE WINE-MAKERS AND GRAPE GROWERS

Unlike those in California, Oregon, Bordeaux, and Burgundy, the majority of Washington State wineries do not own vineyards. With the exception of large producers such as Château Ste. Michelle, Columbia Winery, and some others, wine-makers in this state are dependent upon grapes purchased from growers. For the most part, Washington State's producers are converted home wine-makers. Prior to going into wine full-time, Gary Figgins (Leonetti) was a machinist at the local Walla Walla cannery; Alexander Golitzen (Quilceda Creek) was an engineer for Scott Paper; Chris Camarda (Andrew Will) was a waiter, as was Matthew Loso (Matthews Cellars); and so on. It's the same story—they fell in love with wine, decided to try their hand at it, acquired grapes, and the rest is history.

The grape growers, on the other hand, are farmers. Some are incredibly wealthy, others less so. One grower, whose primary business is producing Washington's famed and delicious Fuji apples, told me that he can earn four times as much money per acre with apple trees than with grapevines. So why the financial sacrifice? I asked. Ego gratification, came the reply. When his apples go to market, they are mixed in with everyone else's. He earns his money by producing the most apples possible per acre, using ingenious systems to ensure that the apples will be evenly colored and unscarred. He has no contact with the people who buy them and laments the fact that there is no market for apples that taste good—only for those that are the most aesthetically pleasing. Growing grapes allows him to compete on a different level. Also, when he drinks wines crafted from his grapes or sees someone order a bottle in a restaurant, he feels he has a strong connection to that wine.

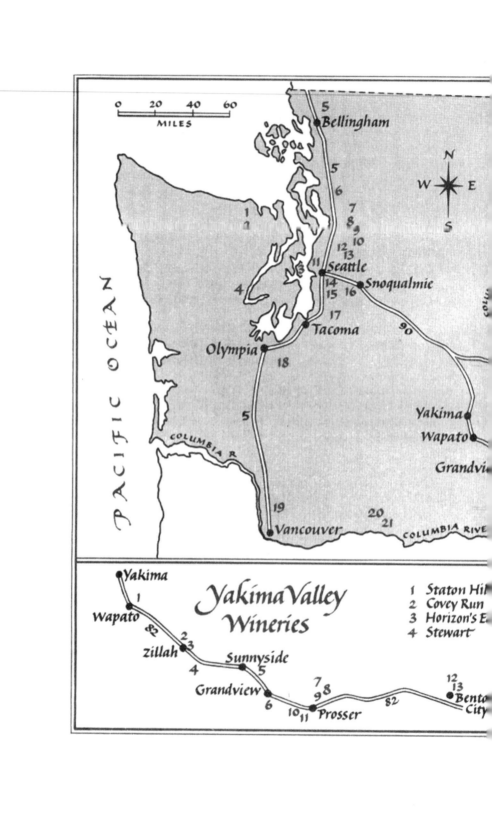

Washington

As a wine lover, I respected the answer to my question. His reason for giving up potential earnings leads him to have moderate yields in order to compete qualitatively, and he is immensely respected by wine-makers. Regrettably, however, few growers are as well off as this gentleman and are not prepared to make the same sacrifice. This leads us to one of Washington wine-makers' biggest problems—yields. Farmers are paid by the ton, regardless of the type of crop they grow, and grapes are no different. The more you produce, the more you earn. Numerous wine-makers in Washington fight constant battles with their grape growers (since very few wineries own their own vineyards) to reduce yields, but the incentives are just not there. In California, Burgundy, Oregon, and elsewhere, quality wineries purchase their fruit by the acre, not the ton. The grower, who is paid the same amount whether 2 tons or 10 tons per acre are produced, has a financial incentive to follow the wine-maker's directives. The "killer freezes" that cause severe damage in the Columbia River appellation every six or so years prevent wineries from instituting this system in Washington. They either do not have or do not wish to risk the financial resources. In a vintage like 1996, a winery with this type of arrangement would have had to pay growers their normal rates for very few grapes.

There is, however, a light at the end of the tunnel. Recently some of the state's top producers, including Golitzen, Camarda, Figgins, and others, have begun purchasing land and planting vineyards. They are reinvesting earnings brought in by their wineries' successes to allow them to control the quality and quantity of the grapes that go into their wines. The results from these new, winery-owned vineyards are just beginning to be reflected in the quality of the wines, but it is clear that the state's five top estates have an exceedingly bright future. Now, if we could just get 20 or 30 other wineries to follow suit . . .

WINE STYLES

We all have notions of what a Bordeaux, Burgundy, California, Tuscan, or Piedmontese wine tastes like. Granted, there are exceptions to every rule, and even the greatest palates in the world can easily be tricked in a blind tasting. However, there are certain basic flavor profiles and styles that characterize all of the great wine-producing regions of the world—except Washington State. Having tasted hundreds of wines from the Columbia, Yakima, and Walla Walla Valleys, I was incapable of finding a regional signature.

The vast majority of the wines produced in Washington State (for which tasting notes do *not* appear in the following pages), are disjointed, fruitless, vegetal, and immensely tannic. Furthermore, a large number of Washington wine-makers have yet to learn what California's top 60–75 producers discovered over the past 15 years—excessive acid adjustments make a wine undrinkable! On my trips to Washington I have conducted large tastings as well as numerous estate visits. The group tastings have the enormous benefit of gathering wines from little-known producers, in addition to saving on travel time (Washington's wineries are spread out over hundreds of miles). The number of appallingly acidified wines I've tasted is mind-boggling. More important, they represent out-and-out bad winemaking. Thankfully, the state's leading producers eschew acidification—wine-makers such as Alexander Golitzen (Quilceda Creek), Chris Camarda (Andrew Will), and Gary Figgins (Leonetti) are crafting wines each year that one hopes will serve as a reference point for others in the industry. Though candied, superripe fruit immersed in loads of oak has brought fame and fortune to such wineries as Leonetti, many other producers craft subtle, elegant, and focused wines (DeLille, for example), and still others have achieved an amazing combination of power and finesse (Quilceda Creek) that is reminiscent of Bordeaux at its very best. Their polar opposites—dense, hyperextracted, alcoholic wines—can also be found in Washington.

Washington State as a wine region is still in its infancy, and that's the beauty of it. These converted home wine-makers are defining the future of Washington wines before our eyes—

and palates. There are no traditions and no parameters. Any style is acceptable. Anything goes. It truly is a frontier.

TYPES OF WINE

Virtually all the varietals seen in California are also grown in Washington. However, Washington has added to this mix Lemberger, a fruity red vinifera grape that is capable of being made into a Beaujolais-style, non-oak-aged wine or, more infrequently, into a serious, cellarworthy wine. A few producers are dabbling with Pinot Noir, and not surprisingly, most have failed. Recently, Rhône Rangers (wines produced from the traditional Rhône varietals) have come into vogue, and a few (particularly those from Glen Fiona and McCrea) show immense promise. However, Washington's wineries are banking on Chardonnay, Cabernet Sauvignon, and especially Merlot to bring them to prominence (Washington is unquestionably one of the three finest regions on earth for Merlot, the other two being Pomerol and Tuscany.) There is also some hope for Sauvignon Blanc and Sémillon. A relatively large percentage of the state's vineyards are planted with Riesling, but this is diminishing as newly planted vineyards rarely include this varietal. Fortunately, Washington's consumers appear to enjoy Riesling, which is usually bargain priced ($8–15), and producers continue to crank it out because it is easy and inexpensive to make—the perfect cash-flow wine. For Riesling aficionados, these wines represent fine values. Washington also produces this country's best Chenin Blancs and Muscats. Their crisp natural acidity, easily obtained due to Washington's northern latitude, makes these wines, finished in an off-dry to slightly sweet style, ideal summer sipping and picnic wines. Sadly, the market for these wines is limited. For better or worse, the state's future rests with the superstar grapes—Cabernet Sauvignon, Merlot, and Chardonnay. The good news is that these are the wines the marketing people claim consumers desire, and Washington State's main rival, California, is pricing itself out of the competition.

RED WINE VARIETALS

Cabernet Sauvignon   This is Washington's most successful grape variety. In capable hands, it renders an almost opaque purple wine. Cabernet Sauvignon usually ripens fully in eastern Washington, resulting in wines with curranty, spicy, plummy, cedary aromas, excellent extract, medium to full body, and good depth and concentration. Overwhelming aromas and flavors of herbs and vegetables are rarely as intrusive in Washington Cabernet Sauvignons as they can be in California.

Merlot   Washington producers are hoping that Merlot will bring the state fame. Some wineries (Leonetti, Andrew Will, Quilceda Creek, and Château Ste. Michelle, for example) are crafting some of the finest Merlots made in the U.S. They have proved that Washington State can compete on the world stage as one of the top three regions for the production of fine wine from this finicky varietal. To no one's surprise, Washington Merlot yields a more supple wine than Cabernet. The acids are lower and the tannins less aggressive. However, due to excessive yields, a number of Merlots continue to exhibit an herbaceous character and frequently lack the depth of flavor and concentration of the state's best Cabernets.

Pinot Noir   Nothing tasted to date remotely resembles what Pinot Noir can achieve in Burgundy or selected California and Oregon vineyards.

Lemberger   Originally grown in Germany, this grape, like Zinfandel, is highly adaptable and can be successfully made in a variety of styles. Only a handful of wineries make Lemberger (vineyard acreage is less than 1% of the total in the state). Sadly, much of the Lemberger produced is dull, hard, and overcropped.

WHITE WINE VARIETALS

Chardonnay Washington Chardonnay occupies more than 15% of vineyard acreage and can ripen fully while retaining excellent natural acidity. This has caused increasing numbers of producers to barrel-ferment it, and to encourage their Chardonnay to complete malolactic fermentation. Extended lees contact, in vogue in California, is also favored by many Washington producers. A number of wineries have invested heavily in new French oak barrels and are trying to make a wine in the Côte de Beaune style. Others are going after a fruitier style (à la Fetzer's Sundial), and still others are aiming for something in between. In short, there is a wide range of styles, but the potential for making outstanding Washington State Chardonnay exists, although much of it remains unrealized. The state's finest Chardonnays are produced by Château Ste. Michelle and Woodward Canyon.

Chenin Blanc Washington is capable of making wonderful Chenin Blanc in a slightly sweet style due to the naturally crisp acidity. Yet most wineries seemed surprised that anyone would be interested in tasting this ignored, often maligned varietal. However, at $9 a bottle, Chenin Blanc can be a true delight, especially on a hot summer day.

Gewürztraminer Fortunately, plantings of this varietal are rapidly decreasing in Washington. It has proven no more successful in Washington than in California.

Sauvignon Blanc When vinified in Washington, the potentially extroverted, herbal, grassy qualities of this grape are held in check. Many wineries also give the wines some exposure to oak barrels. As in California, most wineries strive for a safe, middle-of-the-road style that too often results in bland, insipid wines. Washington State Sauvignons are, however, priced to sell in the $8–15 range, which makes them attractive to consumers.

Sémillon This grape has excellent potential in Washington. It yields a wine with plenty of body and richness combined with the lively acidity typically found in Washington grapes.

White (Johannisberg) Riesling Washington's Rieslings are good but often simple and one-dimensional when compared to the slaty, mineral-scented, aromatic complexity and incredible lightness and zestiness attainable in the best German Rieslings. However, Washington's abundant quantities of Rieslings are practically given away, usually selling for less than $9.

RATING WASHINGTON'S BEST PRODUCERS

Where a producer has been assigned a range of stars (***/****), the lower rating has been used for placement in this hierarchy.

* * * * * (OUTSTANDING)

Andrew Will	Leonetti Cellars
DeLille Cellars	Quilceda Creek

* * * * (EXCELLENT)

Château Ste. Michelle	Northstar****/*****

* * * (GOOD)

Betz***/****	Matthews Cellars
Dunham***/****	McCrea Cellars***/****
l'Ecole No. 41***/****	Reininger***/****
Glen Fiona***/****	Seven Hills
Hedges Cellars	Tamarack
Hightower Cellars	Waterbrook Winery
The Hogue Cellars	Woodward Canyon

* * (AVERAGE)

Apex Cellars**/***	Kiona**/***
Arbor Crest	Latah Creek
Barnard Griffin	Mountain Dome
Blackwood Canyon	Patrick M. Paul
Bookwalter	Preston
W. B. Bridgman	Soos Creek
Canoe Ridge**/***	Stewart
Caterina	Tagaris
Columbia Winery**/***	Teft Cellars
Columbia Crest**/***	Paul Thomas
Covey Run	Tucker
Facelli	Walla Walla Vintners**/***
Gordon Brothers Family Vineyards**/***	Washington Hills
Hyatt	Wilridge Cellars

ANDREW WILL

1999	Cabernet Franc Sheridan	D	90
1999	Cabernet Sauvignon Champoux	D	(93–95+)
1999	Cabernet Sauvignon Ciel du Cheval	D	(92–94)
1998	Cabernet Sauvignon Ciel du Cheval	D	91
1998	Cabernet Sauvignon Klipsun	D	88+
1997	Cabernet Sauvignon Klipsun	D	92
1997	Cabernet Sauvignon Pepper Bridge	D	90+
1997	Cabernet Sauvignon R	D	90+
1996	Cabernet Sauvignon R	D	88+
1998	Cabernet Sauvignon Seven Hills	D	89
1997	Cabernet Sauvignon Seven Hills	D	88
1999	Cabernet Sauvignon Sheridan	D	(90–91)
1999	Merlot Ciel du Cheval	D	90?
1998	Merlot Ciel du Cheval	D	90
1997	Merlot Ciel du Cheval	D	92
1999	Merlot Klipsun	D	88+
1998	Merlot Klipsun	D	91
1997	Merlot Klipsun	D	93
1999	Merlot Pepper Bridge	D	89
1998	Merlot Pepper Bridge	D	91
1997	Merlot Pepper Bridge	D	91
1999	Merlot Seven Hills	D	89+
1998	Merlot Seven Hills	D	89
1997	Merlot Seven Hills	D	89+
1999	Sorella	E	(92–94)
1998	Sorella	E	91+
1997	Sorella	E	92+

Chris Camarda, one of America's finest producers of Merlot, has fashioned an impressive lineup of 1997s. The 1997 Merlot Seven Hills Vineyard is medium to dark ruby-colored and displays an incredibly sweet and spicy, cassis, raspberry, cookie dough, and cherry syrup–scented nose. This beautifully rich, medium-bodied, enticing wine is filled with red cherry and fresh herb flavors. Its slightly warm (alcoholic) finish is long, supple, and sexy. Drink it over the next 5–6 years. The darker-colored 1997 Merlot Pepper Bridge displays candied cherry, cinnamon, and superripe fruit aromas. Complex, oily textured, and structured, this opulent, red and black fruit–crammed wine finishes on loads of firm yet well-ripened tannins. Anticipated maturity: now–2007.

The dark ruby-colored 1997 Merlot Ciel du Cheval exhibits blackberry and candied blood orange aromas. It is explosive, broad, expansive, full-bodied, and intensely ripe. Concentrated layers of jellied red fruits are found in this dense wine and throughout its awesomely long, pure, and soft finish. Anticipated maturity: now–2007+. Camarda's top 1997 Merlot is once again from the Klipsun vineyard (harvested at 3 tons per acre). Its black, saturated color and sweet, jammy, yet fresh red fruit and cookie dough aromas lead to an extravagant, opulent, and elegant character. Coffee ice cream, chocolate-covered cherries, and loads of chewy, intensely ripe red and black fruits are found in this dense, massively intense, full-bodied wine. Its purity of flavors, mind-boggling ripeness, focus, refinement, power, and length improve mightily. Drink it over the next 7–8 years.

Camarda's Cabernet Sauvignons, while not reaching the heights of his Merlots, are certainly some of the finest produced in Washington State. The 1997 Cabernet Sauvignon Seven Hills is medium to dark ruby-colored and reveals oak spice–infused, strawberry aromas. Medium- to full-bodied, it possesses a lovely velvety texture, intense black currant flavors, and a structured, firm character. Anticipated maturity: now–2007. The saturated, medium to dark ruby-colored 1997 Cabernet Sauvignon Pepper Bridge reveals black raspberry and Asian spice aromas. Powerful and medium- to full-bodied, this wine coats the palate with its tarry black fruit flavors. Concentrated, backward, and firm, this wine reveals hints of mint and herbs in its long, tannic finish. Anticipated maturity: now–2008.

The dark ruby-colored 1997 Cabernet Sauvignon Klipsun has candle wax and black fruit aromas. Sweet candied blackberries and cherries are intermingled with vanilla-infused oak flavors in this hugely powerful and concentrated wine. Quite tannic (yet ripe), this muscular, in-your-face Cabernet will require cellaring patience. Anticipated maturity: 2003–2010.

The medium to dark ruby-colored 1996 Cabernet Sauvignon R has ripe Italian tomato and spicy oak aromas. Extracted, firm, tarry black fruits and eucalyptus are found in this tannic, somewhat foursquare Cabernet. If its tannin melts away before its fruit, my score will ultimately appear too conservative. The medium to dark ruby/purple 1997 Cabernet Sauvignon R exhibits blackberry, vanilla, and spice aromatics. Intense, concentrated, and firm, this medium- to full-bodied wine's flavor profile is composed of asphalt, black currants, and notes of toasted oak. It is powerful, muscular, tannic, and firm. Anticipated maturity: now–2008.

The 1997 Sorella (a blend of Cabernet Sauvignon, Cabernet Franc, and Merlot) reveals a saturated medium to dark ruby color. Boisterous aromas of violets and red/blue fruits can be found in this elegant, intense, and harmonious wine's personality. Plums, black currants, chocolate, and spices make up this velvety-textured offering's personality. Camarda's talented hand can be seen in his judicious use of oak; it is present but noticeable only if one searches it out. Anticipated maturity: now–2010+.

The medium to dark ruby-colored 1998 Merlot Ciel du Cheval exhibits sweet Italian tomato and fresh herb aromas, very characteristic of Merlot. This medium- to full-bodied, satin-textured, concentrated, and firmly structured wine will require 2–3 years of cellaring. Anticipated maturity: 2003–2010. The saturated, medium to dark ruby-colored 1998 Merlot Klipsun has overripe dark berry and cherry aromas. On the palate it offers concentrated, powerful layers of beautifully ripened red and black fruits. Velvety-textured and deep, it is muscular, highly concentrated, and well extracted. Anticipated maturity: 2003–2012.

The slightly lighter-colored 1998 Merlot Seven Hills Vineyard reveals rosemary, tomato, and black fruit aromas. This tightly wound, herbal and black fruit–flavored wine is firm, foursquare, and tannic. Anticipated maturity: 2004–2009. The saturated, medium to dark ruby-colored 1998 Merlot Pepper Bridge is full-bodied, thickly textured, and coats the palate with layered black fruit flavors. It is highly extracted, concentrated, and has admirable depth of fruit. This well-structured, powerful, and intense wine should be at its best between 2004–2012.

The dark-colored 1998 Cabernet Sauvignon Ciel du Cheval has a super nose of sweet red fruits, *sur-maturité*-laced blackberries, and copious spices. This medium- to full-bodied wine is crammed with cassis, black cherries, cinnamon, juniper berries, and hints of roasted rosemary. It is powerful, structured, and has a long, ripe tannin-filled finish. Drink it over the next 12–15 years. The medium to dark ruby-colored 1998 Cabernet Sauvignon Seven Hills has a cherry syrup, violet, rose, and perfume-scented nose. Its firm, flavorful character reveals peppery dark berries and tangy black cherries. This well-structured, medium-bodied, ripe wine should be at its peak between now–2008. The medium to dark ruby-colored 1998 Cabernet Sauvignon Klipsun exhibits spicy, sweet cherry aromas. It is medium-bodied, lively, and offers red currants, boysenberries, and brambleberries in its foursquare personality. Anticipated maturity: 2004–2012. The medium to dark ruby-colored 1998 Sorella boasts a sweet, luscious nose of spices, violets, and roses. While it is firmly structured, it is packed with loads of red and black fruits as well as hints of sweet oak spices. This medium- to full-bodied, satin-textured wine should be at its peak between 2004–2015.

The dark ruby-colored 1999 Cabernet Sauvignon Sheridan (it contains 12% Cabernet Franc) bursts from the glass with jammy blackberry, cassis, and Asian spice aromas. It is medium- to full-bodied, silky-textured, and loaded with harmonious layers of blackberries, black cherries, and spices. This seamless, sweet, lush wine is intense, powerful, and harmonious. Anticipated maturity: 2003–2012+. The magnificent dark ruby-colored 1999 Cabernet Sauvignon Champoux contains 20% Cabernet Franc. An extraordinary nose reminiscent of a coulis of cassis leads to a hugely concentrated, broad, candied, medium- to full-bodied personality. It is a satin-textured wine crammed with juicy black fruits whose flavors last 45 seconds or more. An astonishing value given its competition in the $40 range from California, it is exuberant and boisterous, yet deep and refined. A stunning wine loaded with prodigiously ripened tannin. Anticipated maturity: 2004–2015.

Produced entirely from Cabernet Sauvignon, the 1999 Cabernet Sauvignon Ciel du Cheval has a saturated dark ruby color. Its blackberry juice–scented nose leads to a muscular, thick, medium- to full-bodied character. Loads of wild black cherries and blackberries can be found throughout its lively, chewy flavor profile. This superripe, in-your-face Cabernet should be at its best between 2004–2014.

The 1999 Sorella is dark ruby-colored and boasts a floral, black currant, violet-imbued nose. Medium- to full-bodied and refined, it is a wine of gorgeous definition. Silky-textured and crammed with cassis, jammy blackberries, and cherries, this elegant, delineated wine has a magnificently long, pure, flavor-packed finish. Drink it between 2005–2015.

The medium to dark ruby-colored 1999 Cabernet Franc Sheridan reveals violet and sweet red cherry aromas. It is medium-bodied, silky-textured, and loaded with juicy layers of candied red berries, pumpkin, blueberries, and hints of herbs. It is an outstanding, flavorful, and elegant wine for drinking over the next 6–8 years.

The 1999 Merlot Seven Hills Vineyard is medium to dark ruby-colored and offers cherry, blackberry, and vanilla aromas intermingled with hints of candied orange rind. Tangy red and black currants as well as juicy blackberries are found in this medium- to full-bodied wine. It is powerful, concentrated, and has a firm tannic backbone. Anticipated maturity: 2004–2012. The similarly colored 1999 Merlot Pepper Bridge has black fruit and freshly laid asphalt aromas. Its dark, brooding personality reveals loads of blackberries, currants, and hints of grilled herbs. This firm, medium-bodied wine will require cellaring. Drink it between 2005–2012.

The medium-bodied 1999 Merlot Ciel du Cheval has a medium to dark ruby color. It was tasted twice, with vastly different results. The first time it displayed a well-balanced, lively character with cassis, blackberry, black cherry, grilled oak, and tar flavors. It was concentrated, extracted, and had dense layers of fruit as well as a long, highly expressive finish. Additionally, it revealed excellent structure for aging. This bottle earned a 90-point score. The second bottle, tasted two months later with Camarda in Seattle, exhibited aromas of Tallegio, a soft-rind, creamy cheese from Italy, as well as a tight, high-acid personality with an alcoholic streak in the finish. My inclination, given Camarda's outstanding track record, is that the first bottle was the more representative one. However, in the interest of full disclosure, I must report on both. The dark ruby-colored 1999 Merlot Klipsun, often my favorite of Camarda's Merlots, is tightly wound and backward. It offers blackberry jam and hoisin aromas as well as a medium-bodied character. This wine has some rugged tannin, yet it displays impressive amounts of fruit. Blackberries, cassis, charred oak, and hints of Italian tomatoes can be found in its flavor profile. This is a firm wine that has loads of extract and concentration. Its finish reveals abundant quantities of tannin as well as some warmth (from alcohol), which lowered my score. Anticipated maturity: 2005–2012.

BETZ

1998 Cabernet Sauvignon	D	89+
1999 Cabernet Sauvignon Père de Famille	D	(89–91)

The blackberry- and herb-scented, medium to dark ruby-colored 1998 Cabernet Sauvignon is a tight, medium- to full-bodied effort. Delicious layers of intense, powerful blackberries and cassis can be found in its youthfully ungenerous yet muscular personality. This is a bright, well-balanced Cabernet with excellent purity as well as depth. Drink it between 2004–2010. Nine hundred cases of the 1999 Cabernet Sauvignon Père de Famille were produced. It offers sweet black cherry and cassis aromas as well as a broad, medium- to full-bodied character. This intense 1999 is loaded with sweet red and black fruits and a hint of Washington State's trademark fresh herbs. Powerful, highly expressive, and delicious, it will drink well between 2004–2012.

COLUMBIA CREST

1998 Red Wine Reserve	D	88+

The Columbia Crest Winery, part of the larger Stimson Lane corporate structure, which also owns Château Ste. Michelle, produces 1.5 million cases of wine a year, making it all the more remarkable that they are able to achieve the quality of the 1998 Red Wine Reserve (2,000 cases were produced). Medium to dark ruby-colored and boasting a blackberry-scented nose, it is a fat, rich, seamless wine with loads of blackberries and cassis in its juicy character. Its long finish reveals well-ripened tannin and loads of fresh wild herb and black currant flavors. Anticipated maturity: now–2008.

COLUMBIA WINERY

1999 Riesling Cellarmaster's Reserve	A	88

The 1999 Riesling Cellarmaster's Reserve offers delightful candied orange aromas and flavors. This off-dry, medium-bodied wine is silky-textured, well balanced, and immensely flavorful. Drink it over the next 5 years with spicy foods or as an apéritif.

DeLILLE CELLARS

1999 Chaleur Estate (red)	E	(91–92)
1998 Chaleur Estate (red)	D	91+
1997 Chaleur Estate (red)	D	90
1999 Chaleur Estate (white)	D	88
1997 D2	D	88
1998 Doyenne	D	89

1999 Harrison Hill	E	(90–91)
1998 Harrison Hill	D	90
1997 Harrison Hill	D	89

All of DeLille Cellars' wines (including its whites) are aged entirely in new French oak barrels, yet none of their aromas and flavor profiles are dominated by wood influences. In fact, it is difficult to discern the oak in DeLille's reds, a testimony to wine-maker Chris Upchurch's talents. This winery's red wines are crafted from traditional varietals (Cabernet Sauvignon, Merlot, Cabernet Franc) in the style of Bordeaux. Overall, DeLille's 1997s are more backward, less expressive wines than its 1995s and 1996s. The garnet-colored 1997 D2 has a delightful violet, rose, and dark berry–infused nose. This is an elegant, medium-bodied wine with a sultry texture, black cherry, blackberry, and currant fruit. This feminine, well-made wine exhibits exemplary ripeness in its supple, soft, tannin-filled finish. Drink it over the next 6–7 years.

A hint of cedar can be discerned in the floral and dark fruit–scented, garnet-colored 1997 Harrison Hill. Medium- to full-bodied and silky-textured, this spice, exotic wood, cassis, and black cherry–flavored wine is more structured than the forward D2. It reveals excellent concentration and balance in its refined, Bordeaux-like character. Anticipated maturity: now–2008. The 1997 Chaleur Estate is reminiscent of a wine from the Margaux commune in Bordeaux. Dark ruby-colored and boasting a nose of violets, cassis, and blackberries, this is a medium- to full-bodied, powerfully flavored and structured wine. Roses, violets, and assorted other flowers are intermingled with highly expressive cassis, black cherry, and blackberry flavors. Built for the long haul, this is a firmly structured, chewy-textured wine. Anticipated maturity: 2004–2012.

The 1999 Chaleur Estate white, a blend of 70% Sauvignon Blanc and 30% Sémillon from the Red Mountain and Sagemore vineyards, reveals demure aromas of honeydew melon presented in a rich, medium-bodied style. There is excellent fruit depth in its satin-textured, well-balanced personality. Melon and candied citrus flavors last throughout the impressively long finish. This 1999 white should improve with short-term cellaring. Anticipated maturity: now–2007.

The dark-colored 1998 Harrison Hill was produced from vines planted in 1962. Black cherries, blackberries, and spices can be discerned in its aromatic profile. This plump, seamless, refined, light- to medium-bodied, pure 1998 is filled with red and black fruit flavors. There are no hard edges. It is not a powerful wine, but one that delivers oodles of pleasure through its symmetry and detail. Drink it over the next decade.

The medium to dark ruby-colored 1998 Chaleur Estate offers sultry spice, violet, and jammy cherry aromas. This velvety-textured, medium-bodied red reveals loads of muscle to its underlying candied cherry, raspberry, and blueberry character. Another example of Upchurch's elegant, well-detailed offerings, it combines gorgeous layers of sweet, bright, fresh fruit with a delightfully harmonious personality as well as an extensive, pure finish. Enjoy it over the next 10 years. The medium to dark ruby-colored 1998 Doyenne was produced from Syrah acquired from the Boushey and Ciel du Cheval vineyards. It exhibits aromas of smoked bacon, spice, grapes, and blackberries. Medium- to full-bodied and loaded with dark blackberry and black raspberry fruit, this is a silky, deep, pure Syrah with excellent concentration, delineation, and balance. Anticipated maturity: now–2007.

The 1999 Harrison Hill's medium to dark ruby color is followed by aromas of blackberry syrup. On the palate leather, Asian spices, and copious quantities of cherries and blueberries can be found intermingled with prodigiously ripened tannin. Medium- to full-bodied and lush, with an impressively long, pure finish, it will be at its peak between 2004–2012. The similarly colored 1999 Chaleur Estate offers dramatic cassis aromas. It is deep, medium- to full-bodied, and powerful, with outstanding density to its blackberry- and cherry-flavored character. Fresh herbs and black currants can also be discerned throughout this concentrated wine's elegant personality and in its lush finish. Anticipated maturity: 2004–2014.

DUNHAM

1998 Cabernet Sauvignon IV	D	89

The 1998 Cabernet Sauvignon IV is the first wine I have tasted from this Walla Walla–based winery. Dark cherry, herbs, and hints of Scotch whiskey can be found in its aromatics. Velvety-textured and medium- to full-bodied, it is a highly expressive cassis, blackberry, juniper berry, Bing cherry, cigar box, and cedar-flavored wine. This intensely flavored wine has excellent focus and a firm structure. Anticipated maturity: 2003–2010.

L'ECOLE NO. 41

1998 Apogee Pepper Bridge Vineyard	D	89+
1998 Cabernet Sauvignon	D	88
1999 Merlot	D	88
1999 Merlot Seven Hills Vineyard	D	88+
1999 Semillon Fries Vineyard Wahluke Slope	C	88
1998 Semillon Fries Vineyard Wahluke Slope	C	88

The 1998 Semillon Fries Vineyard Wahluke Slope is a fat, rich, ripe wine. Its white peach–laden nose leads to a medium- to full-bodied, ample mouth, crammed with spicy apricots, touches of crème brûlée, and assorted honey-covered berries. This dry, opulent, intense offering should be consumed over the next 3–4 years.

The medium to dark ruby-colored 1999 Merlot displays blackberry aromas and an intense, minty, dark fruit–packed, medium to full body. This is a spicy, licorice-tinged, fruit-filled wine with good structure and loads of ripe tannin. Anticipated maturity: now–2007. The similarly colored 1999 Merlot Seven Hills Vineyard has blackberry and fresh herb aromas. It is medium- to full-bodied and coats the palate with herbal, jammy, dark fruit flavors and highly present yet ripe tannin. This concentrated wine should be at its best between 2003–2008.

The ruby-colored 1998 Cabernet Sauvignon offers minty, dark fruit aromas. It is a juicy, highly structured wine with cassis, fresh earth, mint, and blackberry flavors. This medium-bodied wine is highly expressive, with excellent intensity and loads of firm tannin. Drink it over the next 7–8 years. The 1998 Apogee Pepper Bridge Vineyard is a blend of 60% Merlot, 34% Cabernet Sauvignon, and 6% Cabernet Franc. It is a big, muscular, extracted, and firmly structured wine that offers a rose, violet, and blackberry-scented nose and is crammed with a myriad of black fruits, spices, and touches of red cherries. It has loads of tannins, but they are ripe and should smooth out with aging. Some alcoholic warmth shows through in the finish of this otherwise extremely well crafted Washington State beauty. Anticipated maturity: 2004–2009+.

The 1999 Semillon Fries Vineyard Wahluke Slope is a highly expressive, fascinating wine. Its melon and dried honey aromas lead to a rich, medium-bodied personality filled with yellow fruits and an amazing raspberry bonbon flavor that comes up in the mid-palate and holds throughout its extensive finish. Were it not for the fact that its high alcohol renders the wine somewhat warm, it would have merited even more points. Drink it over the next 3–4 years.

GLEN FIONA

1998 Syrah Basket Press Reserve	E	90
1997 Syrah Basket Press Reserve	D	88+
1999 Syrah Puncheon-Aged	D	88

Berle "Rusty" Figgins, the owner and wine-maker at Glen Fiona (which means "the valley of the vine" in Celtic) is dedicated to making Washington State Syrah. The 1997 Syrah Basket Press Reserve is a blend of 75% Syrah (Morrison Lane Vineyard) and 25% Cinsault (from the

Garton and Coe Farms). Its plum, tar, and black cherry aromas are reminiscent of Syrah-based wines from the Roussillon. Full-bodied and thickly textured, it has American oak spices, dark fruits, and a firm, tight finish. Drink this boisterous wine over the next 5 years.

The 1999 Syrah Puncheon-Aged (1,480 cases were produced) is a blend of 95% Syrah and 5% Viognier. It boasts dark cherry and candied raspberry as well as blackberry aromas. Medium-bodied, fresh, and well made, it is a juicy, black raspberry–dominated, satin-textured wine, full-flavored and harmonious. Drink it over the next 6 years. The 1998 Syrah Basket Press Reserve, a blend of 75% Syrah and 25% Cinsault from 40-year-old vines, has a nose reminiscent of molasses, blackberry, and a silver oak–like spice. Medium-bodied and intense, it is a focused, cassis, juicy blackberry, red cherry, and Asian spice–flavored wine. Additionally, it possesses an immensely impressive, long, delineated finish. This outstanding Washington State Syrah should be consumed over the next 8 years.

HEDGES CELLARS

1997 Three Vineyards	C	88+
2000 Fumé-Chardonnay	A	88

The 2000 Fumé-Chardonnay has apple, grapefruit, and smoke aromas. This expressive, medium-bodied wine reveals crisp pear, lemon, and lime flavors in its zesty, medium-bodied character. A superb value, it is tangy, refreshing, and delicious. Drink this lovely, thirst-quenching wine over the next 2 years. Hedges' ruby-colored 1997 Three Vineyards (a blend of 59% Merlot, 38% Cabernet Sauvignon, and 3% Cabernet Franc) displays lovely red berry and violet-infused aromas. Medium-bodied, this silky-textured offering is packed with cassis and blackberries. Notes of fresh herbs and cedar can be discerned in the well-structured finish. Anticipated maturity: now–2006+.

HIGHTOWER CELLARS

1997 Cabernet Sauvignon	D	89+

The bright ruby-colored 1997 Cabernet Sauvignon is the first wine I have reviewed from Hightower Cellars. A blend of 78% Cabernet Sauvignon, 12% Cabernet Franc, and 10% Merlot from five of the Columbia Valley's better-known vineyards, this is an extremely well made wine with pure red cherry and candied raspberry aromas intermingled with faint touches of vanilla. Medium-bodied and satin-textured, it is refined, red fruit–dominated, and possesses a long, well-furnished finish. Anticipated maturity: now–2006+.

LEONETTI

1999 Cabernet Sauvignon	E	(90–92)
1998 Cabernet Sauvignon	E	93
1996 Cabernet Sauvignon	D	89
1998 Cabernet Sauvignon Reserve	EE	96+
1996 Cabernet Sauvignon Seven Hills Vineyard Reserve	E	90+
1999 Merlot	E	91
1998 Merlot	E	94
1997 Merlot	D	88+
1996 Merlot	D	90
1998 Sangiovese	E	90

No one on earth makes Cabernets and Merlots with quite the same panache as Gary Figgins, Leonetti's owner and wine-maker. In their youth, these are the sweetest, spiciest, most candied wines around. The hedonistic pleasure they dish out is startling. They are sexy, lush, and boisterous. As they age, their opulence wanes and their spiciness/sexiness becomes tamed. This renders them much more civilized yet less distinctive. Do they age? Absolutely, these wines can last for 20–25 years, and maybe longer. However, as they age they seem to lose the characteristics that set them apart from the other thousands of well-made Cabernets and Merlots in the world. My advice is to drink them within their first 5–12 years of life, while they are exotic and totally distinctive. The purple/ruby 1997 Merlot exhibits sweet red cherry and Asian spice aromas. A myriad of wood flavors intermingles with jammy red cherries in this extroverted wine. Figgins's trademark supple personality leads to an atypically firm and structured finish. Anticipated maturity: now–2006.

Because of the killer frost that ravaged Washington State's vineyards, Figgins was compelled to purchase fruit from California's Napa Valley to craft his 1996 Merlot and Cabernet Sauvignon. Sporting the "America" appellation, the 1996 Merlot is medium to dark ruby-colored and reveals a spicy oak and jammy blackberry nose. Medium- to full-bodied, ample, oily-textured, and sexy, this lovely Merlot is crammed with ripe red and black fruits and eucalyptus. This sensual offering's attack and mid-palate lead to a somewhat tannic finish and will be at its peak between now–2006. The medium to dark ruby-colored 1996 Cabernet Sauvignon has a nose composed of blackberries, mint-covered chocolate, and fresh herbs. Intense, mouthcoating layers of red and black fruits are found in this powerful offering. Its sultry personality leads to a tannic, firm finish. Drink this wine between now–2007.

The ruby/purple 1996 Cabernet Sauvignon Seven Hills Vineyard Reserve offers enthralling blackberry, fresh herb, Asian spice, and raspberry aromas. This intense, concentrated, velvety-textured, and medium- to full-bodied wine coats the palate with its blood orange as well as red and black cherry flavors. If its tannic (somewhat bitter) finish softens before the fruit and opulent spices begin to melt away, my score will appear conservative. Anticipated maturity: now–2007+.

Roses, spices, violets, juniper berries, vanilla, candied raspberries, and cherries can be found in the aromatics of the 1999 Merlot. This medium to dark ruby-colored wine has juicy, well-focused layers of spicy cherries, cinnamon, blackberries, and cassis in its well-delineated, concentrated, and long-finishing personality. Anticipated maturity: now–2006.

The 1998 Cabernet Sauvignon's bouquet offers aromas of toasty oak and spice. This mouthcoating, explosive wine is crammed with a myriad of spices, jammy blackberries, sweet cherries, and cherry syrup–drenched fruitcake. This is a hedonist's delight, yet it has loads of tannin that provide a firm, tight, structured finish. Anticipated maturity: now–2011.

I could not help breaking into a smile when I tasted the medium to dark ruby-colored 1998 Cabernet Sauvignon Reserve. Its extraordinarily spicy, cherry syrup–scented nose leads to a flavor profile that explodes on the palate with substantial quantities of cherry syrup, raspberry coulis, and Asian spices. Gary Figgins's Cabernets can be as boisterous as Olivier Humbrecht's Gewurztraminers. The purity and power of the sweet, spicy fruit flavors found in this wine are truly extraordinary. In addition, it possesses an extremely long, candied, sweet tannin–filled finish. This decadent wine should be consumed between 2003–2012.

The outstanding dark ruby-colored 1999 Cabernet Sauvignon exhibits root beer, caramel, black cherry, clove, juniper, and jammy blackberry aromas. This sweet, candied, plump, plush effort is loaded with blackberries, spice, and an assortment of sweet, dark fruits. Sultry, opulent, and highly concentrated, it will drink well for nearly a decade. Potentially the New World's finest Sangiovese producer, Leonetti has fashioned a beautiful 1998 Sangiovese. Its meaty, sweet nose leads to a mouthful of juicy cherries and dark berries. Medium- to full-bodied, spicy, and velvety-textured, this is an in-your-face, fruit-dominated, lush Sangiovese. The dense fruit lingers throughout its long, supple finish. Drink it over the next 5 years.

The medium to dark ruby-colored 1998 Merlot possesses an immensely appealing spice and dark fruit–scented perfume. Though it would be perceived as extroverted, even boisterous from another producer, for Leonetti it is reserved. Medium- to full-bodied and hugely ripe, it is crammed with Asian spices, chocolate, blackberry juice, and a cascade of cherries. This expansive, rich, lively Merlot is unquestionably great stuff! There are no hard edges in its sultry character or exceptionally long, fruit-filled finish. Enjoy it over the next 7–9 years.

McCREA CELLARS

1999 Syrah Boushey Grande Côte Vineyard	D	89
1999 Syrah Ciel du Cheval Vineyard	D	89+
1998 Syrah Ciel du Cheval Vineyard	D	91
1998 Syrah Cuvée Orleans	D	90

The saturated, dark ruby-colored 1998 Syrah Ciel du Cheval Vineyard has a brooding, black cherry, blackberry, and chocolate-scented nose. Medium- to full-bodied and intensely flavored, this is an extremely well made, velvety-textured, highly expressive wine that is sure to please any Syrah lover. Black raspberries, black cherries, cassis, roasted herbs, and touches of leather can be found in its luxuriously layered personality. Drink this winner over the course of the next 6–7 years. The saturated, medium to dark ruby-colored 1998 Syrah Cuvée Orleans displays intense jammy black raspberry aromas. This medium- to full-bodied, velvety-textured wine is plush, lush, sexy, and intense. It coats the palate with oily layers of jammy black raspberries and cassis. Its superripe tannin is barely noticeable in its silky, sweet finish. Drink this immensely appealing fruit bomb over the next 6–7 years.

Dark ruby-colored, the 1999 Syrah Boushey Grande Côte Vineyard is a medium- to full-bodied, highly expressive wine with spicy black cherry scents. On the palate, it is fresh, zesty, and loaded with juicy blackberries, black raspberries, and cherries, with a tight yet ripe finish. Drink this wine over the next 6 years. The black cherry and blackberry syrup–scented 1999 Syrah Ciel du Cheval Vineyard is a tightly wound, medium- to full-bodied wine. It displays loads of sweet, superripe red and black fruit flavors in its velvety-textured personality. A year or two of cellaring will improve its structure. Anticipated maturity: 2003–2008.

NORTHSTAR

1998 Merlot	D	92+

Stimson Lane, which owns Château Ste. Michelle and Columbia Crest as well as a number of other brands, has recently created Northstar Winery, based in Walla Walla, Washington. Northstar's goal is to produce the finest Merlot in Washington State. To reach that end, Northstar's wine-maker has been given the authority to pick and choose among the Merlots from all of the Stimson Lane properties. Just over 1,000 cases were produced of their debut offering, the 1998 Northstar Merlot. Stimson Lane's goal is to raise this figure to 10,000 cases a year. It boasts a saturated dark ruby color and an intense nose of black cherries and cassis. Medium- to full-bodied, broad, big, and juicy, this dense, plump, chewy-textured wine is loaded. Cassis, cherries, blackberries, and hints of licorice can be discerned in this suave, highly concentrated, and expansive wine's character. It is powerful, harmonious, and exhibits an extraordinarily long, fruit-packed, seamless finish. This immensely impressive wine should be at its best between 2003–2012.

QUILCEDA CREEK

2000 Cabernet Sauvignon	E	(93–95)
1999 Cabernet Sauvignon	E	(97–98)
1998 Cabernet Sauvignon	E	95+
1997 Cabernet Sauvignon	E	94+
1996 Cabernet Sauvignon	D	95
1997 Cabernet Sauvignon Champoux Vineyard	E	91
1999 Merlot	E	(91–92)
1998 Merlot	E	(91–93)
1997 Merlot	D	89+

Alexander Golitzen and his son Paul are determined to produce the world's finest Cabernet Sauvignon. Moreover, they are convinced that Washington State is capable of this because of its propitious weather and extensive growing seasons and that it make great wines more regularly than any other Cabernet-producing area in the world. To accomplish this goal, the Golitzens are constantly reinvesting their profits to improve their winery and purchase new equipment. For example, on my last visit to the estate, Alex Golitzen showed me the new system he had designed to punch down the caps (the process of submerging the shell of skins and other solids that rise to the top of vats. "Punching down" increases concentration and structure but can also lead to wines being overextracted if it is done too often or too roughly). An engineer by training, Golitzen uses his inquisitive mind and engineering skills to create new equipment that solves age-old problems.

The Golitzens have also created a second wine (it was not tasted) that is made from the fruit and barrels not deemed good enough for the estate's premiere *cuvées*. Between 36% and 39% of the estate's annual production is relegated to Quilceda Creek's Red Wine.

While Quilceda Creek is dedicated primarily to the production of Cabernet Sauvignon, it also produces small quantities (around 250 cases) of Merlot (which includes 24% Cabernet Sauvignon in the blend). The medium to dark ruby/mahogany 1997 Merlot was made predominantly from fruit purchased from the Klipsun Vineyard. Warm, dark, spicy fruits, fresh herbs, and hints of Italian tomatoes can be discerned in its aromatics. Medium- to full-bodied and velvety-textured, it is an embracing wine, packed with blackberries and cassis. It has excellent concentration, as well as a supple attack in mid-palate. The firm finish suggests cellaring. Anticipated maturity: 2004–2010+. The medium to dark ruby-colored 1998 Merlot boasts a super nose of blackberries, cassis, herbs, and aromatic spices. Medium- to full-bodied and wonderfully elegant, it possesses a flavor profile made up of sweet cassis, lovely black cherries, chocolate, blackberries, and hints of toast. This satin-textured wine is refined and marvelously harmonious. "It's all about pleasure," said Alex Golitzen while serving this beauty. Anticipated maturity: 2003–2012+.

In 1997 the Golitzens purchased a parcel of the Champoux Vineyard. Like the majority of Washington State producers, the Golitzens must purchase fruit from growers, as they have not previously owned any vineyards. The medium to dark ruby-colored 1997 Cabernet Sauvignon Champoux Vineyard displays creamy, sweet, Connecticut white corn and black cherry aromas. Medium- to full-bodied and satin-textured, it is an intense blackberry and dark cherry–flavored wine. This expressive, flavorful offering has outstanding follow-through from its attack to its long, seamless, and focused finish. Anticipated maturity: now–2008. Though it was bottled as a single-vineyard wine to inaugurate the Golitzens' acquisition, they do not plan ever again to produce another single-vineyard bottling.

Strategically placed between Château Margaux and Château Mouton-Rothschild in a blind tasting of the superlative 1996 Bordeaux first growths, the 1996 Cabernet Sauvignon (a blend of 85% Cabernet Sauvignon, 9% Merlot, and 6% Cabernet Franc) not only held its own but was indistinguishable from its Bordeaux brethren. Revealing a saturated dark purple color, its soft, salty, black raspberry jam, licorice, and coconut aromas lead to a medium- to full-bodied character of unbelievable sweetness. Extraordinarily well balanced, this velvety-textured, powerful, elegant wine displays black raspberry flavors that last throughout its exceptionally long, pure finish. Anticipated maturity: 2003–2018. The 1997 Cabernet Sauvignon was fashioned from 89% Cabernet Sauvignon, 9% Merlot, and 2% Cabernet Franc. It offers a boisterous rosemary and black fruit–scented nose. Bigger, broader, and chewier than the 1996, this medium to full bodied wine is packed with black fruits, spices, and hints of tar. It is masculine, concentrated, and in need of cellaring. Anticipated maturity: 2005–2020.

The 1998 Cabernet Sauvignon (2,500 cases produced) is the result of a blend of 98% Cabernet Sauvignon and 2% Cabernet Franc. (Sixty percent of this wine is from the estate-owned Champoux Vineyard and 40% from fruit purchased from the Klipsun Vineyard.) Medium to dark ruby-colored, it boasts a compelling perfume of blackberries, cassis, and cherries. It is a huge, intense, medium- to full-bodied effort. This powerhouse expands on the palate to reveal copious quantities of assorted dark fruits and a profusion of spices. Although immensely concentrated and muscular, it manages to retain Quilceda Creek's trademark harmony and elegance. This exceptional offering's dense layers of fruit last throughout its supple, exceptionally long finish. Drink it between 2006–2018.

The medium- to full-bodied, huge 1999 Merlot exhibits a medium to dark ruby color in addition to intensely sweet blackberry aromas. Loaded with juicy black fruits, tar, licorice, and a myriad of spices, it was fashioned from 75% Merlot (from the Klipsun Vineyard) and 25% Cabernet Sauvignon (from the Ciel du Cheval Vineyard). A Cabernet lover's Merlot, this penetrating offering possesses outstanding depth, concentration, and density of fruit, as well as a structured, fresh, chewy-textured character. Anticipated maturity: 2005–2015.

The magnificent dark ruby-colored 1999 Cabernet Sauvignon is a winemaking tour de force. A blend of 97% Cabernet Sauvignon and 3% Merlot, its bouquet can best be described as syrup of Cabernet Sauvignon. Intensely sweet blackberry, cassis, cherry, and blueberry jam aromas burst from the glass. Produced from the Champoux (70%) and Red Mountain (30%) vineyards, it possesses a medium- to full-bodied character as well as extraordinary breadth to its massive personality. Focused layers of black currant jam and blackberry juice surge across the palate, lasting nearly a minute. A wine of unsurpassed power yet prodigious elegance, it is reminiscent of my first taste of the 1990 Château Margaux. Anticipated maturity: 2006–2020. The awesome dark ruby-colored 2000 Cabernet Sauvignon (100% Cabernet Sauvignon, 92.5% from the Champoux vineyard and the remainder from Red Mountain) reveals blackberry and currant aromas as well as a suave, cassis syrup–laden personality. This classy, medium- to full-bodied, powerful, intense effort displays a seamless, harmonious character. Its concentrated fruit and angle-free structure promise a great future. Anticipated maturity: 2007–2020+.

REININGER

1997 Cabernet Sauvignon	D	88
1998 Merlot	D	88

The medium to dark ruby-colored 1998 Merlot, from the Pepper Bridge and Spring Valley vineyards, was produced from a blend of Merlot (92%), Cabernet Franc (6%), and Cabernet Sauvignon (2%). Only 850 cases were produced. It exhibits sweet cherry, violet, and hints of cookie dough in its spicy aromatics. Medium-bodied and silky-textured, this is a concentrated, firmly structured, blackberry- and cassis-flavored wine. Anticipated maturity: now–2006. The fresh herb and roasted eggplant–scented, medium to dark ruby-colored 1997 Cabernet Sauvignon (only 350 cases produced) is fashioned from 91% Cabernet Sauvignon, 5% Merlot, and 4% Cabernet Franc from grapes purchased from the Seven Hills, Pepper Bridge, and Whitney Vineyards. This well-made, black pit fruit–flavored, medium- to full-bodied wine has a satiny texture and loads of intense black fruit flavors. Anticipated maturity: now–2007+.

CHÂTEAU STE. MICHELLE

1998 Cabernet Sauvignon Canoe Ridge Estate	C	89
1996 Cabernet Sauvignon Canoe Ridge Estate Vineyard	C	91
1998 Cabernet Sauvignon Cold Creek Vineyard	D	89
1996 Cabernet Sauvignon Cold Creek Vineyard	C	89
1998 Cabernet Sauvignon Reserve	D	90
1999 Chardonnay Canoe Ridge Estate Vineyard	D	91
1998 Chardonnay Canoe Ridge Estate Vineyard	D	90
1997 Chardonnay Canoe Ridge Estate Vineyard	D	91
1999 Chardonnay Cold Creek Vineyard	D	89

1998 Chardonnay Cold Creek Vineyard	D	89+
1997 Chardonnay Cold Creek Vineyard	C	90
1999 Chardonnay Indian Wells Vineyard	C	88
1997 Chardonnay Reserve	D	88+
2000 Eroica Riesling Dr. Loosen	C	89
1999 Eroica Riesling Dr. Loosen	C	88
1997 Late Harvest White Riesling Reserve	C/375ml	89
1996 Merlot Canoe Ridge Estate Vineyard	C	89
1999 Single Berry Select	EEE/375ml	94

Château Ste. Michelle, one of the cornerstones of the Stimson Lane wine conglomerate, continues to amaze me with its dedication to quality and its reasonable prices. Château Ste. Michelle's highly talented wine-maker, Mike Januik, resigned his duties to start a winery. This is good news for wine lovers. First, Januik's new venture is sure to quickly join the ranks of Washington State's finest wineries, and second, Allen Shoup, the quality-driven former CEO of Stimson Lane (the corporation that owns Château Ste. Michelle), most certainly replaced him with gifted people (Erik Olsen for whites, Ron Bunnell for reds).

Château Ste. Michelle's 1997s and 1996s are pure Januik—Old World structures and styles with New World fruit. They represent some of the finest wines produced to date by this large winery. The 1997 Chardonnay Cold Creek Vineyard offers lovely aromas of yellow fruits, toast, lees, and a hint of orange marmalade. Medium- to full-bodied and well balanced, this Burgundy-styled wine displays flavors of white peaches and ripe pears in its personality as well as stonelike notes in its long, supple finish. Drink it over the next 5+ years. Even better, the 1997 Chardonnay Canoe Ridge Estate Vineyard has a Chablis-like nose and a flavor character reminiscent of Meursault. It exhibits minerally, smoky, leesy scents intermingled with sweet white fruits. This medium- to full-bodied, oily-textured offering is well structured and filled with almonds, hazelnuts, and pears. Anticipated maturity: now–2005+. While the two preceding wines were highly expressive, the 1997 Chardonnay Reserve was much more structured and reserved. Its muted aromatics and unyielding personality permitted only a glimpse of this wine's harmonious white fruit and floral flavor profile. It is extremely well balanced, medium- to full-bodied, glycerin-packed, and in need of cellaring. Ultimately, if prior vintages are any indication, this wine may develop to outshine its two brethren. Anticipated maturity: now–2006+.

The 1996 Merlot Canoe Ridge Estate Vineyard blows away the overwhelming majority of similarly priced California Merlots. This ruby-colored wine's aromatics are dominated by black cherries and roselike scents. This seamless wine has an appealingly soft texture, medium body, and an elegant, structured character. Red and black fruits are found in its tasty flavor profile and throughout its supple finish. Drink it over the next 4–5 years.

Tasting through Washington State's Cabernet Sauvignons is often difficult due to the high levels of acidity (mostly added) and hard, astringent tannins (from unripe fruit, high yields, and excessive extraction). In contrast, Château Ste. Michelle's 1996s were a joy to encounter. They have plenty of structure, yet their tannins are ripe and enveloped in fruit. The ruby-colored 1996 Cabernet Sauvignon Cold Creek Vineyard offers aromas of perfumed blackberries. Its broad character is penetrating, expressive, and filled with black fruits as well as traces of freshly laid road tar. The similarly colored 1996 Cabernet Sauvignon Canoe Ridge Estate Vineyard is more intense, complex, and powerful. Seemingly sporting more alcohol than the Cold Creek (the label lists them both as being 13.5%), this wine has overt blackberry aromas. Lovely layers of cassis, black cherries, and blackberries are found in its velvety-textured, medium- to full-bodied personality. Both of these offerings will be at their peak between now–2007+.

Each year Château Ste. Michelle fashions a delicious and ageworthy Late Harvest White Riesling Reserve. The 1997 may not be as long-lived as most previous vintages of this wine, yet it is more forward and generous. Raspberry jam, flowers, and candied oranges are discernible in its expressive aromatics. Medium-bodied, rich, and broad, this well-balanced wine is crammed with red and yellow fruits as well as flavors reminiscent of fruit punch. It is thick and possesses a long, sweet (yet not cloying) finish. Anticipated maturity: now–2007.

Château Ste. Michelle continues to impress with its single-vineyard Chardonnays. The 1998 Canoe Ridge Estate offers ripe apple, toast, and mineral aromas. It is luscious, opulent, oily-textured, and medium- to full-bodied. On the palate, pears, apples, and grilled hazelnuts can be discerned in this long and fruit-forward effort. Drink it over the next 4 years. The white fruit, flower, and stone-scented 1998 Chardonnay Cold Creek Vineyard shares the same lush texture as the Canoe Ridge but is tighter and more focused. Its pear, mineral, and spice-laden personality is medium- to full-bodied and persistent in the finish. Anticipated maturity: now–2005.

The apricot-scented 1999 Eroica Riesling Dr. Loosen (made in collaboration with the Mosel's famed Ernst Loosen) has a rich, dense, herbal tea– as well as white and yellow fruit–flavored core. Considerable CO_2 is present, providing good freshness to balance out its rich, opulent fruit. Drink it over the next 4–5 years. Produced from a vineyard planted in 1984, the 1999 Chardonnay Indian Wells Vineyard bursts from the glass with superripe apple and pear aromas and flavors. A broad, anise-spiced Chardonnay, it offers a soft texture in addition to an appealingly long finish. This well-made and balanced 1999 should be consumed over the next 5 years. The outstanding 1999 Chardonnay Canoe Ridge Estate Vineyard displays complex aromatics of candied nuts, white fruits, and distinctive smoky scents. It expands on the palate to reveal mouthcoating spiced pears, candied apples, and a myriad of spices. Rich, gorgeously fashioned, and impressively long in the finish, it will drink well for 5 years. Displaying a more demure, lightly fruity bouquet, the medium-bodied, well-focused 1999 Chardonnay Cold Creek Vineyard offers minerals, pears, and stonelike flavors in its broad, ample personality. Drink it over the next 4–5 years.

The 2000 Eroica Riesling Dr. Loosen offers rich pear and apple aromas in a medium- to full-bodied, fat, plump format. This opulent, plush, mineral, tangerine, and sweet tea–flavored Riesling possesses excellent balance and a long, orange rind–flavored finish. Anticipated maturity: now–2012.

It took 600 man-hours to harvest the 1999 Single Berry Select grape by grape from the end of November through December 4. The wine exhibits candied orange, apricot, and botrytis aromas as well as a flavor profile reminiscent of syrup of apricot blended with nectar of mango. Full-bodied, plump, and intense, with a jellied texture and profound personality, it sports 37 grams of residual sugar. Anticipated maturity: now–2020.

The medium- to full-bodied, cassis-scented, excellent 1998 Cabernet Sauvignon Canoe Ridge Estate Vineyard boasts loads of sweet black currant and blackberry fruit in its focused, deep, lively personality. This structured 1998 also possesses a long, fruit-filled finish. Enjoy it between 2003–2010. The medium to dark ruby-colored 1998 Cabernet Sauvignon Cold Creek Vineyard offers aromas of blackberry juice and smoky bacon. Plump, expansive, and medium-bodied, with abundant quantities of dark fruits as well as an elegant yet powerful core, it will drink well between 2004–2010. The intensely aromatic, medium to dark ruby-colored 1998 Cabernet Sauvignon Reserve reveals scents of blackberry and black cherry jam. Medium- to full-bodied and silky-textured, with loads of depth to its dark fruit and fresh herb–flavored character and an impressively long, supple finish, this well-made effort will drink well for years. Anticipated maturity: now–2012.

SEVEN HILLS WINERY

1997 Cabernet Sauvignon Klipsun Vineyard   **D   88**

The black-colored 1997 Cabernet Sauvignon Klipsun Vineyard has demure rose and black currant aromas. On the palate, this is a powerful, mouthcoating, highly extracted, black tar and blackberry-flavored wine. Intense and firmly structured, it will require cellaring. Antici-pated maturity: 2003–2010+.

TAMARACK CELLARS

1998 Merlot	D	88

The medium ruby-colored 1998 Merlot reveals violet, red cherry, raspberry, and spice aro-mas. Medium-bodied, velvety-textured, and thick, it exhibits loads of red and dark, well-ripened fruit flavors. Hints of vanilla can be discerned in its firmly structured (loads of tannin) finish. Anticipated maturity: 2003–2008.

WOODWARD CANYON

1999 Chardonnay Celilo Vineyard	D	89
1998 Chardonnay Celilo Vineyard	D	88
1998 Merlot	D	89

The 1998 Chardonnay Celilo Vineyard reveals creamed spices and toasty oak aromas. This satin-textured, medium-bodied, supple wine offers buttered minerals, toast, and apples in its long, silky flavor profile. Drink it over the next 3–4 years. Sweet black cherries and black-berries are found in the aromatics of the medium to dark ruby-colored 1998 Merlot. Medium-to full-bodied and well structured, this is an intensely flavorful cassis, cherry syrup, and boysenberry-flavored wine. Extremely well made and seamless, it is reminiscent of an excel-lent Pomerol from a warm, ripe year. Anticipated maturity: now–2008+. The spicy anise and poached pear–scented 1999 Chardonnay Celilo Vineyard has an immensely appealing, oily-textured personality. Spiced apples, cardamom, nutmeg, traces of butterscotch, and anise can be found in its expressive, elegant, and well-balanced character. Drink this delicious wine over the next 4–5 years.

8. THE MID-ATLANTIC STATES

From Long Island's North Fork to the Hudson River valley, and from the hillsides of Pennsylvania, Maryland, and Virginia, a few of the Mid-Atlantic's wineries are producing good, very good, and sometimes excellent wines. Overall, it appears that this region's best potential lies in its Cabernet Franc–based wines, as beauties tasted from Long Island and Virginia have proven. For whites, the Mid-Atlantic is a mixed bag, with the exception of New York's Millbrook Winery, nestled in the Hudson River valley, which has consistently surprised me with excellent to outstanding Chardonnays.

Consumers wishing to taste the best of the Mid-Atlantic's wines should search out those produced by the following wineries:

MARYLAND
Basigniani Winery (the state's finest)   Elk Run
Catoctin Winery

NEW YORK
Bedell   Millbrook Winery
Fox Run   Palmer
Gristina Vineyards   Paumanok
Jamesport   Schneider
Lenz   Wolffer
Macari Vineyards

PENNSYLVANIA
Chaddsford Winery

VIRGINIA
Barboursville Vineyards   White Hall Vineyards
Jefferson Vineyards   Willowcroft Farm Vineyards
Rockbridge Vineyards

THE BEST
OF THE
REST

Australia and New Zealand
Argentina and Chile
South Africa

9. AUSTRALIA AND NEW ZEALAND

AUSTRALIA

TYPES OF WINE

You name it and the Australians no doubt grow it, make it into wine, blend it with something else, and give it an unusual name. The combination of quality and value that many Australian wines offer is the hottest thing in town from London to New York. Australia, like California in America, and Alsace in France, labels its wine after the grape (or grapes) from which it is made. All the major grapes are used here. While great wines are produced from most varietals, Syrah (called Shiraz in Australia) triumphs over all the others. The major viticultural districts (listed alphabetically) are:

Adelaide Hills (South Australia)   Located in southern Australia, this is a high-altitude, cooler-climate region. Petaluma is its most famous winery.

Barossa Valley (South Australia)   In southern Australia, this huge, well-known viticultural area north of Adelaide is the home of some of the quantitative titans of Australia's wine industry (i.e., Penfolds, Henschke, Tollana, Seppelt, Wolf Blass, Orlando, and Yalumba). It is the source for Australia's finest wines, including spectacular old-vine Shiraz *cuvées* produced by Cimicky, Rick Burge, Elderton, Greenock Creek, Rockford, Veritas, Torbreck, and Yalumba. Australia's most renowned wine, Penfold's Grange, is largely a blend from selected Barossa vineyards.

Bendigo (Victoria)   Bendigo is an up-and-coming area, although it has a long history as a wine-producing region. Balgownie, Jasper Hill, and Wild Duck Creek are the finest wineries.

Victoria (Victoria)   The best-known subregions of Victoria are Goulburn Valley, Bendigo, Geelong, Yarra Valley, and Rutherglen, all within a day's drive of Melbourne.

Clare Valley (South Australia)   Located north of Adelaide and the Barossa Valley, this beautiful area is better known for its white than red wines. A number of high-quality wineries call Clare Valley their home, including Clos Clare, Grosset, Pikes, Kilikanoon, Tim Adams, and Knappstein. Some surprisingly fine Riesling emerges from this area.

Coonawarra (South Australia)   Coonawarra is among the most respected red-wine-growing areas of Australia. Situated in South Australia, west of the Goulburn Valley, top wineries such as Penley, Parker, Highbank, Majella, Katnook, and Lindemans (their Limestone Ridge and St. George Vineyards are there) pull their grapes from Coonawarra.

Geelong (Victoria)   Southwest of Melbourne near the coast is the small area of Geelong. The best known wineries are Bannockburn, Clyde Park, and Mount Anakie.

Glenrowan (Victoria)   Located in northeastern Victoria, this hot area is famous for its inky, rich, chewy red wines, especially the full-throttle Shiraz from one of Australia's historic

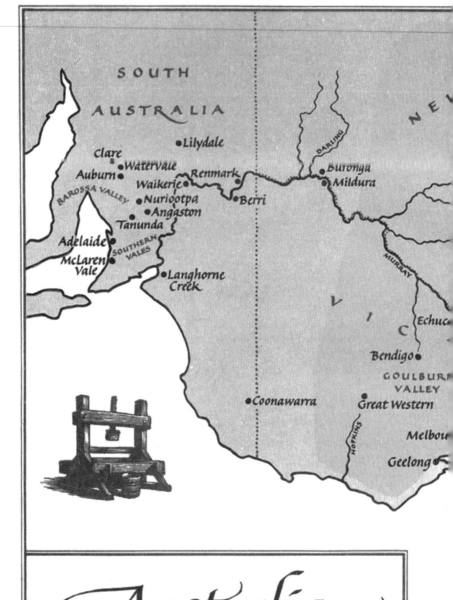

SOUTH

AUSTRALIA

NEW

Clare
●Lilydale
Watervale
Auburn●
Renmark
Waikerie●
●Nuriootpa
●Berri
●Angaston
Tanunda
Adelaide●
SOUTHERN
VALES
McLaren
Vale
●Langhorne
Creek

BAROSSA VALLEY

DARLING
●Buronga
●Mildura

MURRAY

V
I
C
Echuca

Bendigo●

GOULBURN
VALLEY
●Coonawarra
Great Western

HOPKINS

Melbour

Geelong●

Australia

producers, Bailey's. A more commercial Cabernet and Shiraz is made by Wynns. At nearby Milawa, Brown Brothers, one of the most successful high-quality Australian wineries, makes its home.

Gramptans (Victoria)   Situated between Ararat and Stawell, to the northwest of Melbourne and Geelong, is an area known for its sparkling wines (primarily from the huge producer Seppelt), and for its smooth, fat, low-acid but tasty red wines. The top red-wine producers are Mount Langi Ghiran and Cathcart Ridge.

Hunter Valley (New South Wales)   Less than a three-hour drive from Sydney is Australia's famed Hunter Valley. It is to Sydney what the Napa Valley is to San Francisco and the Médoc is to Bordeaux—a major tourist attraction and source for some of Australia's most desired wines. Originally this area was known for its rich, exotic, full-bodied red wines from the Shiraz and Cabernet Sauvignon grapes, but more recently Chardonnay and Sémillon have proven successful as well. No doubt because of their size and the intense competitive spirit here, this area's wineries are well represented in the export market. In spite of this region's renown, considerable quantities of mediocre, industrial swill emerge from both the "lower" and "upper" Hunter Valley. Familiar names from the Hunter Valley include Tyrell, Rothbury Estate, Lindemans, Rosemount, Arrowfield, Hungerford Hill, and Brokenwood.

Great Southern (Western Australia)   In the remote southwestern tip of Australia, approximately 150 miles south of Perth, is a vast, burgeoning viticultural area called Great Southern. Apple orchards thrive more than vineyards, but wineries such as Howard Park, Mount Barker, Frankland Estate, and Alkoomi have well-deserved good reputations.

Margaret River (Western Australia)   In the very southwestern tip of this country is the Margaret River viticultural zone. Australian wine experts claim that Australia's most French-like Cabernet Sauvignons and Chardonnays come from this area, which produces wines with higher natural acidities. There are many fine producers located here, including the likes of Vasse Felix, Moss Wood, Leeuwin Estate, Cullen, Abbey Vale, Devil's Lair, Pierro, and Woody Nook.

McLaren Vale (South Australia)   The traditional fare of this hot area south of Adelaide was high-alcohol, thick, rich Grenache wines. This has all changed in the last 10 years with the advent of cold fermentations and the perception that the public yearns for lighter, fruitier wines. Some of the giants of the Australian wine business are in McLaren Vale, including Hardy's and its higher-quality sibling, Reynella. Smaller wineries, producing some of Australia's most exciting wines, include Kay Brothers, Clarendon Hills, Noon, d'Arenberg, Coriole, Maxwell, and Fox Creek.

Mudgee (New South Wales)   Located in New South Wales west of the famed Hunter Valley, Mudgee (an aboriginal name meaning "nest in the hills") with its cool nights and hot days has proven not only to be a fine red wine area but also a consistent source for tropical fruit–scented, luxuriously rich Chardonnays. For whatever reason, the wines of Mudgee also tend to be less expensive than those from other top areas. Reliable producers include Craigmoor, Montrose, Miramar, and Huntington Estate.

Padthaway (South Australia)   This southern Australian viticultural area has developed a following for its value-priced white wines, especially the Chardonnay and Sauvignon Blanc. Sadly, Padthaway vineyards have proven how easy it is to produce industrial quantities of uninspiring white and red wines. Among the brightest lights are the wines produced by Sparky and Sarah Maguis at Henry's Drive. Their Marguis-Philips wines admirably prove that quality and value can be married.

Pyrenees (Victoria)   The attractive, rolling-hill countryside of the Pyrenees, northwest of Melbourne, forms a triangle between Redbank, Moonambel, and Avoca. The top wines are the reds from the Cabernet Sauvignon and Shiraz grapes. Wineries of note include Redbank, Taltarni, Mount Avoca, and Dalwhinnie.

Riverland (South Australia)   Located in South Australia, Riverland is to Australia what the San Joaquin Valley is to California. This vast source of grapes of mediocre quality is dominated by huge cooperatives and producers who turn out Australia's jug wines and bag-in-the-box generic wines. Some big enterprises have their jug wine business centered here, including Penfolds, Kaiserstuhl, Angove, Berri, and Renmano. While most of the wines from this area are decidedly insipid, some good-value, fresh whites at bargain-basement prices can be found.

Rutherglen (Victoria)   Rutherglen is synonymous with Australia's fortified sweet wines, many of which are extraordinary. The famous sweet, nectarlike, ageless ports and fortified Muscats and Tokays of William Chambers, Campbells, Stanton and Kileen, and Seppelt are made from Rutherglen grapes.

Swan Valley (Western Australia)   This hot, arid area in Western Australia, just northeast of the coastal city of Perth, produces large-framed, muscular red wines and increasingly better white wines. Houghton is the area's most famous winery, but good wines are made by Moondah Brook and Sandalford.

Yarra Valley (Victoria)   This is Australia's most fashionable viticultural area, and its proponents (the provincial Australian wine press) argue that the climate and resulting wines come closest in spirit to those of Bordeaux and Burgundy in France. I am not convinced. Located in Victoria, this is a cool-climate area outside Melbourne, and every major red and white glamour varietal is planted, from Cabernet Sauvignon, Merlot, and Pinot Noir to Chardonnay, Riesling, and Gewurztraminer. The best wineries are Lillydale, Yarra Yering, Coldstream Hills, and St. Huberts, but beware, there is much more "sizzle" than substance for most wines from Yarra Valley.

GRAPE VARIETIES

RED WINES

Cabernet Sauvignon   This varietal can excel in Australia and generally produces a very fruity, often jammy, intensely curranty, fat wine, sometimes low in acidity, but round, generous, and surprisingly ageworthy in spite of an acid deficiency. Sadly, too many wineries continue to go overboard with acid additions, making a soft yet delicious wine into something akin to an underripe lemon!

Pinot Noir   There are those who claim to have made successful wines from this notoriously fickle varietal, but the majority of Australian Pinot Noirs to date have either been raisiny, unusual, and repugnant, or watery, pale, innocuous, and excessively acidified. One prominent exception is Bass Phillip, which produces the country's most profound Pinot Noir from the cool microclimates of South Gippsland in Victoria.

Shiraz   Despite the Aussies' present-day infatuation with such international grapes as Cabernet Sauvignon, Merlot, and Pinot Noir, it is Shiraz that produces their greatest wines. The problem is that there is an enormous amount of it, and only a handful of producers treat Shiraz (Syrah) with the respect and care that is accorded Cabernet. It can produce Australia's greatest red wine when left to stand on its own, as Penfolds Grange has convincingly proven for nearly 50 years! Additionally, it can gain dimension and character when blended with Cabernet Sauvignon, as Penfolds and Petaluma have proven time and time again. The greatest examples emerge from only two regions, Barossa and McLaren Vale. Elsewhere, Shiraz usually produces one-dimensional, heavy wines.

WHITE WINES

Chardonnay   The shrewd Aussies, taking full advantage of the wine consumer's thirst for Chardonnay wines, have consistently offered plump, fat wines filled with the flavors of apples, pears, oranges, and ripe melons. Although the wines still tend to be overoaked, or worse, artificially oaked as well as excessively acidified, more and more Australian Chardonnays are fresh and exuberant, and bottled early to preserve their youthful grapy qualities. With the advent of centrifuges and micropore filters, many Chardonnays have no bouquet or flavor. The one major disappointment is the aging potential of these naturally low-acid wines, but most consumers are drinking them within several months of purchase, so this is probably a moot issue. One positive trend has been the increasing quantities of delicious "non-oaked" or so-called "virgin" Chardonnays.

Gewurztraminer   Contrary to the local salespeople, who hype the quality of Gewurztraminer, this grape produces insipid, pale, watery wines that are a far cry from what Gewurztraminer does in France.

Marsanne   Château Tahbilk and Michelton are proponents of this grape, which tends to turn out one-dimensional, bland wines.

Muscat   This hot-climate grape excels in Australia and is at its best in the decadently rich, sweet, fortified Muscats that can age for decades. It is also made into a medium-sweet table wine with which Brown Brothers does a particularly admirable job.

Riesling   Australia has proven to be the New World's best alternative to German and Alsace, France, Rieslings. This grape has done extremely well with Kabinett and Spatlese-style drier Rieslings in the Barossa Valley, Adelaide Hills, and Clare Valley. Wineries such as Petaluma, Pewsey Vale, Rosemount, Grosset, Leeuwin, and Mount Horrocks have turned out some remarkable wines. Overall, this grape gets good marks.

Sauvignon Blanc   The results have been mixed, as the hot climate causes this grape to overripen and to take on a grotesque, vegetal, oily, thick fruitiness. There are some fresh, tasty, dry Sauvignons coming from Australia, but for now, New Zealand consistently beats Australia when it comes to quality Sauvignon-based wines.

Sémillon   Sémillon can be delicious, whether it is blended with Chardonnay or Sauvignon, or allowed to stand by itself. It produces big, creamy, rich wines loaded with flavor. Wineries such as Rothbury, Rosemount, Montrose, Peter Lehmann, and Henschke have done better with Sémillon than anyone. Some great sweet wines have been made from Sémillon affected by the botrytis fungus. Look for those from Rothbury, Rosemount, and Peter Lehmann, which are world-class.

FLAVORS

RED WINES

Cabernet Sauvignon   These wines can be very ripe, often overripe, with sweet, intense black currant flavors, supple, fat textures, and oodles of fruit. When poorly made or overly acidified, the wines are musty, dirty, and tart.

Pinot Noir   Raisiny, pruny fruit flavors with no finesse or complexity represent appallingly bad examples of Pinot Noir.

Shiraz   Intense aromas of blackberry liqueur, cassis, leather, licorice, cedar, tar, and pepper are found in wines that have a healthy dosage of Shiraz. Quite full-bodied and rich, with softer tannins than Cabernet Sauvignon, these wines are drinkable young, but usually age better than the more glamorous Cabernet Sauvignons. The finest examples almost always emerge from Barossa and McLaren Vale.

WHITE WINES

Chardonnay   Tropical fruit flavors predominate in this creamy-textured, voluptuous wine. Oak is sometimes too noticeable, but better-balanced wines with the fruit in the forefront have been the rule in recent vintages.

Gewurztraminer Where's the spice and exotic lychee nut character found in the great Gewurztraminers of Alsace? These are generally watery, thin, disappointing wines.

Marsanne Marsanne can be described as usually neutral or, as Jancis Robinson says, "reminiscent of glue." It usually tastes much better old than young, but because it tastes so uninteresting young, no one ages it.

Muscat Huge aromas of brown sugar, fruitcake, crème brûlée, buttered and baked apricots, and oranges with honey and nuts give this varietal its appeal.

Riesling The classic Riesling aromas of spring flowers, green apples, and wet stones are present in the drier versions of this wine. As the wines get sweeter, aromas and flavors of oranges, peaches, apricots, butter, baked apples, and honeyed nuts arise.

Sauvignon Blanc Unfortunately, these wines seem to be either feeble, bland, and tasteless, or oily, vegetal, and grotesque.

Sémillon In the drier versions, lemon-lime aromas intertwined with honey and toasty oak are often the most interesting. With the sweet versions, buttery nuts and honey-coated raisin flavors take over.

AGING POTENTIAL

Cabernet Sauvignon:
  5–20 years
Pinot Noir: 4–6 years
Shiraz: 5–30 years
Chardonnay: 1–2 years
Gewurztraminer: 1–2 years
Marsanne: 4–12 years

Muscat (dry): 1–3 years;
  (fortified): 5–50 years
Riesling (dry): 1–4 years;
  (sweet): 4–10 years
Sauvignon Blanc: 1–3 years
Sémillon (dry): 2–8 years;
  (sweet): 4–12 years

OVERALL QUALITY LEVEL

At the top level, wines such as the Penfolds Grange or Bin 707 Cabernet Sauvignon, in addition to some of the old-vine Shiraz *cuvées* from relatively small producers such as Torbreck, Veritas, Greenock Creek, Kay Brothers, and Clarendon Hills, are as fine as any red wine made in the world. Sadly, most of Australia's greatest wines are made in minuscule quantities, but readers lucky enough to latch onto any of the production of my five-star wineries are sure to be impressed. Australia's overall wine quality is average, with oceans of mediocre and poorly made wines. There are, however, plenty of good, agreeable wines at attractive prices, and therein lies the reason for the success of Australia's wines. Australia is the world's leader in offering industrial quantities of tasty, user-friendly wines at low prices. In that area, Australia has little competition.

MOST IMPORTANT INFORMATION TO KNOW

Given the remarkable diversity, the best thing to do is to memorize the names of some of the better producers, and restrict your initial purchases to the surefire successes from that particular winery—usually Chardonnay, Cabernet, and Shiraz. Use the producers' chart for each varietal as a guideline until you have decided which wines and producers you prefer.

BUYING STRATEGY

For 95% of Australia's wines, buy only what you intend to drink over the next 12–16 months. The white wines have a particularly short shelf life, and the great majority of the reds are meant to be consumed within 2–4 years of the vintage. Thus, for dry white wines, only the 2001s, 2000s, and 1999s should be purchased. For inexpensive red wines, readers can safely purchase vintages back to 1996 without worrying about the wine's senility. Australia does produce sensational world-class red wines, but they are often produced in minute quantities, and are just as expensive as a grand cru from France or a California cult wine. Readers should try to buy their Australian wines from some of the most creative American importers, who have done a fabulous job in ferreting out some of the limited-production, spectacularly high-quality estates reviewed on the following pages. In particular, readers should look for Australian wines carrying the import label of Dan Philips, The Grateful Palate, Oxnard, California; John Larchet, The Australian Premium Wine Collection, whose importers at the time of writing were USA Wine West, San Rafael, California, and Chicago Brands, Chicago, Illinois; Peter Weygandt, Weygandt-Metzler, Unionville, Pennsylvania; Ted Schrauth, Old Vines Australia, whose importers are Epic Wines, Santa Cruz, California, and C. Daniele, New York, New York; Benjamin Hammerschlag-Epicurean Wines, Seattle, Washington; and Rob McDonald-Old Bridge Cellars, San Francisco, California. These importers do not have an exclusive on every great wine from Australia, but they are dealing with some of the smaller estates whose approach to winemaking is artisanal and oriented to the true connoisseur. Readers should also remember that Australia produces spectacular late-harvested fortified wines at a fraction of the price one pays for vintage ports and the sweet wines of France and Germany. These decadently rich wines are well worth seeking out.

RECENT VINTAGES

As in California, constant sunny weather virtually guarantees at least good-quality wines in Australia, but each year is different as a result of drought as well as heat or cold waves. However, the extremes in quality that one often sees in Europe do not exist in Australia.

2001—A year of extreme heat as well as drought in southern Australia created problems of dehydration, stress, etc. However, tasting at some of the finest estates in June 2001 revealed that some wines, particularly the old-vine Shiraz and Cabernet Sauvignon *cuvées* from McLaren Vale and Barossa, possess enormous power, concentration, and depth. My instincts suggest it will be an irregular vintage for many varietals, but for the top Shiraz and Cabernet Sauvignons, this is a vintage of extraordinary power, concentration, and longevity.

2000—A light year, the 2000s are good but lack the majesty and multiple dimensions found in southern Australia's finest vintages. In western Australia, quality is more even. Nevertheless, this is not likely to be a top vintage for Australia's most famous regions in Victoria, Hunter Valley, Barossa, and McLaren Vale.

1999—Maligned by the Australian press after the powerful 1998s, 1999 has produced elegant, stylish, well-balanced wines that lack the muscle and power of great vintages. Readers who feel many Australian offerings are over the top in terms of extract, richness, and mouth-staining capacity should check out the 1999s, a more delicate, European-styled vintage.

1998—Most of the top producers claim this may turn out to be the finest vintage in western Australia, South Australia, Victoria, and the Hunter Valley in the 1990s. All the elements came together for a superb year. Full physiological maturity with adequate acidity and an absence of rain has produced potentially great wines in South Australia, Victoria, and possibly Hunter Valley. The only area of concern is Western Australia, where late-summer rains ruined what would have been a great year. Producers who survived the rains and picked later are very pleased with what they have achieved. This is an exciting vintage.

1997—Overall, this vintage does not match the quality of either 1996 or 1998. However, there are pockets of outstanding success. In the Hunter Valley, the red wines should be very good to excellent, but the whites suffered from overripeness. In Victoria, the vintage produced wines of extraordinary ripeness. Producers who kept their yields down made big, forceful, blockbuster wines. The 1997 Victoria offerings could easily rival their 1998 counterparts. In South Australia, rain effected some of the cooler climate areas (i.e., Clare Valley), but producers who waited and harvested ripe grapes in Barossa and McLaren Vale produced excellent, somewhat underrated wines. One varietal that did fantastically well in the cooler

areas is Riesling. In Western Australia, the high heat and rainfall before the harvest produced a good rather than great year.

1996—This has turned out to be a great year in Western Australia, producing fabulously
concentrated, powerful wines, an excellent to great year in South Australia, with abundant
high quality, thick, rich, juicy offerings, and a very good year in Victoria. The latter region
experienced more rain, but the grapes were superripe in every area save the Yarre Valley. In
the Hunter Valley, 1996 is a very good vintage, although irregular.

1995—A very good to excellent vintage in South Australia and Western Australia. While
some of the Coonawarra wines are light, and irregularity surfaced in McLaren Vale, Barossa
Valley and Clare Valley both produced excellent wines. The examples from Western Australia possess extraordinary concentration and power. They may turn out to be as good as
some of the more highly renowned vintages such as 1998. In Victoria, drought conditions
produced tiny berries, as well as stressed fermentations and wines. It is a mixed, irregular
vintage. In the Hunter Valley, 1995 is considered close to a disaster. Some of the white wines
turned out fine, but the red wines are mixed, revealing the effects of the heavy rain that fell
during the harvest.

OLDER VINTAGES

Among the other vintages of the 1990s, 1994 was sensational in South Australia, particularly
in the Barossa and Clare Valleys. It was excellent in Coonawarra, terrific in Victoria, and great
in Western Australia. 1993 was a generally good year throughout Australia, although it never
hit the fabulous peaks of 1994. 1992 was also a sound vintage of very good quality, with the
highlight being the Cabernet Sauvignon produced in Western Australia. Both 1991 and 1990
were top vintages throughout Australia. 1991's top wines emerged from the Hunter Valley,
Barossa Valley, Coonawarra, Victoria, and Western Australia. The one soft spot in the 1991
vintage was Clare Valley. In 1990, the Hunter Valley was a weak link in an otherwise great vintage, particularly in South Australia. 1990 was excellent in Victoria and Western Australia.

RATING AUSTRALIA'S BEST PRODUCERS OF
CABERNET SAUVIGNON, SHIRAZ, MERLOT, AND GRENACHE

*****(OUTSTANDING)*

d'Arenberg Cabernet Sauvignon The
　Coppermine Road (McLaren Vale)
d'Arenberg The Dead-Arm Shiraz
　(McLaren Vale)
d'Arenberg The Laughing Magpie
　(Shiraz/Viognier) (McLaren Vale)
Brokenwood Shiraz Graveyard Vineyard
　(Hunter Valley)
Brokenwood Shiraz Rayner Vineyard
　(McLaren Vale)
Burge Family Grenache Old Vines (Barossa)
Burge Family Shiraz Draycott (Barossa)
Clarendon Hills Astralis (Shiraz)
　(Clarendon)
Clarendon Hills Grenache Old Vine
　Blewitt Springs Vineyard (McLaren Vale)
Clarendon Hills Grenache Old Vine
　Kangarilla Vineyard (McLaren Vale)

Clarendon Hills Grenache Old Vine
　Romas Vineyard (McLaren Vale)
Clarendon Hills Merlot (McLaren
　Vale)
Clarendon Hills Shiraz Brookman
　Vineyard (McLaren Vale)
Clarendon Hills Shiraz Hickinbotham
　Vineyard (McLaren Vale)
Clarendon Hills Shiraz Liandra Vineyard
　(McLaren Vale)
Clarendon Hills Shiraz Piggott Range
　Vineyard (McLaren Vale)
Charles Cimicky Shiraz Signature
　(Barossa)
Coriole Lloyd Shiraz (McLaren Vale)
Elderton Shiraz Command (Barossa)
Greenock Creek Shiraz Apricot Block
　(Barossa)

Greenock Creek Shiraz Creek Block
(Barossa)
Greenock Creek Shiraz Roennfeldt Road
(Barossa)
Greenock Creek Shiraz Seven Acres
(Barossa)
J. J. Hahn Shiraz Block 1914 (Barossa)
Hardy's Shiraz Eileen Hardy (blend of
regions)
Kay Brothers Shiraz Amery Vineyard
Block 6 (McLaren Vale)
Peter Lehmann Shiraz Eight Songs
(Barossa)
The Magpie Estate Shiraz/Mourvèdre
Black Sock (Barossa)
Noon Cabernet Sauvignon Reserve
(Langhorne Creek)
Noon Eclipse Proprietary Red
(Grenache/Shiraz) (McLaren
Vale/Langhorne Creek)
Noon Shiraz Reserve (Langhorne Creek)
Parker Estate Cabernet Sauvignon Terra
Rossa First Growth (Coonawarra)

Penfolds Cabernet Sauvignon Bin 707
(South Australia)
Penfolds Grange (South Australia)
Penley Estate Cabernet Sauvignon
(Coonawarra)
Penley Estate Cabernet Sauvignon Phoenix
(Coonawarra)
Rosabrook Estate Shiraz Abattoir Block
(Margaret River)
Three Rivers Shiraz (Barossa)
Torbreck Run Rig (Shiraz/Viognier)
(Barossa)
Veritas Shiraz Hanisch (Barossa)
Veritas Shiraz Heysen (Barossa)
Wild Duck Creek Estate Cabernet
Sauvignon Reserve (Heathcote)
Yalumba The Octavius (Old Vine Shiraz)
(Barossa)
Yalumba The Reserve (Cabernet/Shiraz)
(Barossa)
Yarra Yering Dry Red #2
(Shiraz/Viognier/Roussanne) (Yarra
Valley)

* * * * (EXCELLENT)

Tim Adams Shiraz (Clare Valley)
Tim Adams Shiraz The Aberfeldy (Clare
Valley)
Australian Domaine Wines Shiraz The
Hattrick (McLaren Vale)
Australian Domaine Wines Shiraz Valley
Floor (Barossa)
d'Arenberg The Custodian (Grenache)
(McLaren Vale)
d'Arenberg Ironstone Pressings
(Grenache/Shiraz) (McLaren Vale)
Berry's Bridge Shiraz (Victoria)
Brokenwood Shiraz (Hunter
Valley/McLaren Vale)
Brothers in Arms Shiraz (Langhorne
Creek)
Burge Family Grenache Old Vines
(Barossa)
Burge Family Grenache/Shiraz/Mourvèdre
(Barossa)
Canonolas Smith Alchemy (Mount
Canobolas)
Cape d'Estaing Shiraz Admiral's Reserve
(Kangaroo Island)
Charles Cimicky Shiraz Signature (Barossa)
Clarendon Shiraz (Clarendon)

Clarendon Hills Shiraz (McLaren Vale)
Clarendon Hills Shiraz Moritz Vineyard
(McLaren Vale)
Clayfield Shiraz Grampians (Victoria)
Coriole Cabernet Sauvignon (McLaren
Vale)
Coriole Mary Kathleen Proprietary Red
Wine (Cabernet Sauvignon/Merlot)
(McLaren Vale)
Coriole Redstone Cabernet Sauvignon
(McLaren Vale)
Coriole Redstone Proprietary Red Wine
(Shiraz/Grenache/Cabernet
Sauvignon/Merlot) (McLaren Vale)
Coriole Shiraz Lloyd Reserve (McLaren
Vale)
Dromana Estate (Cabernet/Merlot)
(Mornington Peninsula)
Dutsche Oscar Seminler Shiraz (Barossa)
Ebenezer Shiraz (Barossa)
Elderton CSM Proprietary Red (Cabernet
Sauvignon/Shiraz/Merlot) (Barossa)
Elderton Shiraz (Barossa)
Fox Creek Shiraz Reserve (McLaren Vale)
Frankland Estate Olmo's Reward (Cabernet
Franc/Merlot) (Western Australia)

Frankland Estate Shiraz Isolation Ridge (Western Australia)
Galah Shiraz (Clare Valley)
Gemtree Vineyards Shiraz (McLaren Vale)
Gnadenfrei Shiraz St. Michael's (Barossa)
Greenock Creek Cabernet Sauvignon (Barossa)
Grosset Gaia Proprietary Red Wine (Clare Valley)
Chris Hackett Shiraz K-1 (Coonawarra)
Chris Hackett Shiraz The Gatekeeper (McLaren Vale)
Richard Hamilton Cabernet Sauvignon Koonawarra Reserve (McLaren Vale)
Richard Hamilton Old Vine Shiraz Reserve (McLaren Vale)
Henry's Drive Cabernet Sauvignon (Padthaway)
Henry's Drive Shiraz (Padthaway)
Henry's Drive Shiraz Reserve (Padthaway)
Henschke Shiraz Hill of Grace (Barossa)
Henschke Shiraz Mount Edelstone (Barossa)
Howard Park Cabernet Sauvignon/Merlot (Western Australia)
Huntington Estate Cabernet Sauvignon Bin FB (Mudgee)
Irvine Grand Merlot (Eden Valley)
Jasper Hill Shiraz Georgia's Paddock (Victoria)
Stephen John Shiraz (Clare Valley)
Trevor Jones Shiraz Wild Witch (Barossa)
Kaesler Stone House Shiraz Old Bastard (Barossa)
Kaesler Stone House Shiraz Old Vine (Barossa)
Katnook Estate Cabernet Sauvignon Odyssey (Coonawarra)
Kay Brothers Cabernet Sauvignon Amery Vineyard (McLaren Vale)
Kay Brothers Shiraz Amery Vineyard (McLaren Vale)
Kay Brothers Shiraz Amery Vineyard Hillside (McLaren Vale)
Kilikanoon Grenache Prodigal (Clare Valley)
Kilikanoon Shiraz Oracle (Clare Valley)
Killibinbin Shiraz (Langhorne Creek)
Château Leamon Shiraz Reserve (Bendigo)
Leeuwin Estate Cabernet Sauvignon Art Series (Margaret River)

Peter Lehmann Cabernet Sauvignon (Barossa)
Peter Lehmann Shiraz Stonewell (Barossa)
Lengs and Cooter Shiraz Old Vines (Clare Valley)
Lengs and Cooter Shiraz Reserve (Clare Valley)
Liebich Vein Shiraz C. W.'s Block (Barossa)
Limelight Syrah (McLaren Vale)
Lost Wolf Cabernet Sauvignon (Barossa)
The Magpie Estate Grenache The Faker (Barossa)
The Magpie Estate Grenache Gomersol (Barossa)
The Magpie Estate Mourvèdre/Grenache (Barossa)
The Magpie Estate Shiraz The Malcolm (Barossa)
Majella Cabernet Sauvignon (Coonawarra)
Majella Cabernet Sauvignon/Shiraz Maleea (Coonawarra)
Majella Shiraz (Coonawarra)
Mak Cabernet Sauvignon (Coonawarra)
Maxwell Wines Cabernet Sauvignon Lime Cave (McLaren Vale)
Maxwell Wines Merlot Reserve (McLaren Vale)
Maxwell Wines Shiraz Ellen Street (McLaren Vale)
Maxwell Wines Shiraz Reserve (McLaren Vale)
Meerea Park Cabernet/Merlot (Hunter Valley)
Meerea Park Shiraz Alexander Munro (Hunter Valley)
Meerea Park Shiraz The Aunts (Hunter Valley)
Charles Melton Cabernet Sauvignon (Barossa)
Charles Melton Nine Popes (Grenache/Shiraz/Mourvèdre) (Barossa)
Charles Melton Shiraz (Barossa)
Moss Wood Cabernet Sauvignon (Margaret River)
Mount Langi Ghiran Cabernet Sauvignon/Merlot (Victoria)
Mount Langi Ghiran Shiraz (Victoria)
Oliver's Shiraz Taranga (McLaren Vale)
Parker Cabernet Sauvignon Coonawarra First Growth (Terra Rosa)
Parson's Flat Cabernet/Shiraz (Padthaway)

Paxton Shiraz (McLaren Vale)
Penfolds Shiraz Bin 128 (South Australia)
Penfolds Shiraz Magill Estate (South
    Australia)
Penfolds Shiraz/Cabernet Koonunga Hill
    (South Australia)
Penley Estate Shiraz Highland
    (Coonawarra)
Petaluma Cabernet/Merlot (Coonawarra)
Petaluma Shiraz (Adelaide Hills)
Pierro Cabernets (Margaret River)
Pikes Cabernet/Merlot (Clare Valley)
Pikes Shiraz (Clare Valley)
Pikes Shiraz Reserve (Clare Valley)
Primo Estate Cabernet Sauvignon/Merlot
    "Joseph" Moda Amarone (Coonawarra)
Primo Estate Shiraz (Adelaide)
The RBJ Mourvèdre/Grenache
    Theologicum (Barossa)
Redbank Cabernet Sauvignon Long
    Paddock (Victoria)
Redbank Sally's Paddock (Victoria)
Rockford Cabernet Sauvignon (Barossa)
Rosemount Cabernet Sauvignon Show
    Reserve (Coonawarra)
Rosemount GSM
    (Grenache/Shiraz/Mourvèdre) (McLaren
    Vale)
Rosemount Mountain Blue
    (Shiraz/Cabernet Sauvignon) (Mudgee)
Rosemount Syrah Balmoral (McLaren Vale)
Rusden Cabernet Sauvignon Boundaries
    (Barossa)
Rusden Grenache (Barossa)
Rusden Grenache Christine's (Barossa)
Rusden Shiraz Black Guts (Barossa)
St. Hubert's Cabernet Sauvignon (Yarra
    Valley)
Scarpantoni School Block Proprietary Red
    (Shiraz, Cabernet Sauvignon, Merlot)
    (McLaren Vale)
Scarpantoni Shiraz Block 3 (McLaren
    Vale)

Summerfield Shiraz (Pyrenees)
Torbreck The Steading
    (Grenache/Shiraz/Mourvèdre)
    (Barossa)
Turkey Flat Shiraz (Barossa)
Veritas Cabernet/Merlot (Barossa)
Veritas Cabernet Sauvignon (Barossa)
Veritas Grenache/Mourvèdre (Barossa)
Veritas Shiraz/Mourvèdre (Barossa)
Viking Wines Cabernet Sauvignon
    (Barossa)
Viking Wines Grand Shiraz (Barossa)
Viking Wines Shiraz (Barossa)
Virgin Hills Cabernet Sauvignon
    (Victoria)
Waninga Shiraz (Clare Valley)
Waninga Shiraz Reserve (Clare Valley)
Warrenmang Grand Pyrenees (Cabernet
    Sauvignon) (Victoria)
Warrenmang Shiraz Moonambel
    (Victoria)
Wild Duck Creek Estate Cabernet
    Sauvignon Alan's (Heathcote)
Wild Duck Creek Estate Cabernets
    Pressings (Heathcote)
Wild Duck Creek Estate Shiraz Springflat
    (Heathcote)
Wild Duck Creek Estate Shiraz Springflat
    Reserve (Heathcote)
Woodstock Winery Grenache (McLaren
    Vale)
Woody Nook Cabernet Sauvignon
    (Margaret River)
Wynns Cabernet Sauvignon John Riddoch
    (Coonawarra)
Yalumba Grenache (Barossa)
Yalumba Grenache Nursery Vineyard
    (Barossa)
Yalumba The Signature (Cabernet
    Sauvignon/Shiraz) (Barossa)
Yarra Yering Cabernet Sauvignon Dry
    Red No. 1 (Yarra Valley)

* * * *(GOOD)*

Abbey Vale Merlot/Shiraz (Margaret
    River)
Tim Adams Cabernet Sauvignon (Clare
    Valley)
Alkoomie Cabernet Sauvignon (Western
    Australia)

Ashbrook Estate Cabernet Sauvignon
    (Western Australia)
Ashton Hills Oblique Proprietary Red
    (Adelaide Hills)
Ashton Hills Oblique Reserve (Adelaide
    Hills)

Bailey's Cabernet Sauvignon (Glenrowan)

Balgownie Cabernet Sauvignon (Bendigo)

Bannockburn Shiraz (Victoria)

Jim Barry Shiraz McCrae Wood (Clare Valley)

Bowen Estate Cabernet Sauvignon (South Australia)

Brand's Laira Cabernet Sauvignon (Coonawarra)

Brokenwood Cabernet Sauvignon (New South Wales)

Brokenwood Shiraz Coach House (Barossa)

Brown Bros. Cabernet Sauvignon (Victoria)

Capel'Vale Cabernet Sauvignon (Western Australia)

Cullen Cabernet Sauvignon (Margaret River)

Cullen Cabernet Sauvignon/Merlot Reserve (Margaret River)

Deakin Estate Shiraz (Victoria)

Fern Hill Cabernet Sauvignon (McLaren Vale)

Richard Hamilton Burton's Vineyard (McLaren Vale)

Richard Hamilton Merlot Reserve (McLaren Vale)

Geoff Hardy Kuitpo Cabernet (Adelaide Hills)

Hewitson Shiraz l'Oizeau (McLaren Vale)

Hickinbotham Cabernet Sauvignon (Geelong)

Highbank Proprietary Red (Cabernet Sauvignon/Merlot/Cabernet Franc) (Coonawarra)

Katherine Hills Cabernet Sauvignon (South Australia)

Hungerford Hill Cabernet Sauvignon (Hunter Valley)

Jindalee Shiraz (Murrays/Darling)

Katnook Estate Cabernet Sauvignon (Coonawarra)

Kilikanoon Cabernet Sauvignon (Clare Valley)

Tim Knappstein Cabernet Sauvignon (Clare Valley)

Lake Breeze Shiraz/Cabernet Bernoota (Langhorne Creek)

Lake Breeze Shiraz Winemaker Selection (Langhorne Creek)

Château Leamon Cabernets/Merlot (Bendigo)

Château Leamon Shiraz (Bendigo)

Peter Lehmann Shiraz (Barossa)

Lillydale Cabernet Sauvignon (Yarra Valley)

Lindemans Cabernet Sauvignon (Coonawarra)

Lindemans Cabernet Sauvignon St. George (New South Wales)

Lindemans Pyrus Proprietary Red (New South Wales)

Lindemans Shiraz/Cabernet Limestone Ridge (New South Wales)

Geoff Merrill Cabernet Sauvignon (South Australia)

Mildara Cabernet Sauvignon (Coonawarra)

Montrose Cabernet Sauvignon (Mudgee)

Oak Ridge Estate Cabernet Sauvignon (Yarra Valley)

Orlando Cabernet Sauvignon Jacaranda Ridge (Coonawarra)

Orlando RF Cabernet Sauvignon (South Australia)

Passing Clouds Cabernet Sauvignon (Bendigo)

Passing Clouds Cabernet/Shiraz (Bendigo)

Passing Clouds Shiraz/Cabernet (Bendigo)

Penfolds Cabernet/Shiraz Bin 389 (South Australia)

Penfolds Shiraz Kalimna Bin 28 (South Australia)

Penfolds Shiraz St. Henri (South Australia)

Petaluma Cabernet Sauvignon (Coonawarra)

Redman Cabernet Sauvignon (Coonawarra)

Riverside Meritage (Barossa)

Robertson's Well Cabernet Sauvignon (Coonawarra)

Rosemount Cabernet Sauvignon Show Reserve (Coonawarra)

Rothbury Estate Shiraz (Hunter Valley)

Rusden Cabernet Sauvignon (Barossa)

Rymill Merlot/Cabernet Franc/Cabernet Sauvignon (Coonawarra)

Rymill Shiraz (Coonawarra)

Saxonvale Cabernet Sauvignon (Hunter Valley)

Seaview Shiraz Edwards and Chaffey (McLaren Vale)

Seppelt Cabernet Sauvignon (Barossa)

Sevenhill Cellars Cabernet Sauvignon
  (Clare Valley)
Seville Estate Cabernet Sauvignon
  (Victoria)
Charles Sturt University Shiraz Reserve
  (New South Wales)
Summerfield Cabernet Reserve (Pyrenees)
Summerfield Shiraz Reserve (Pyrenees)
Château Tahbilk Cabernet Sauvignon
  (Goulburn)
Château Tahbilk Shiraz (Goulburn)
Tait Cabernet Sauvignon (Barossa)
Taltarni Cabernet Sauvignon (Victoria)
Taltarni Shiraz (Victoria)

Vasse Felix Cabernet Sauvignon (Western
  Australia)
Wolf Blass Cabernet Sauvignon President's
  Selection Black Label (Victoria)
Wolf Blass Cabernet Sauvignon Yellow
  Label (Victoria)
Wright's Cabernet Sauvignon (Western
  Australia)
Wyndham Estates Cabernet Sauvignon
  (South Australia)
Wyndham Estates Shiraz (South
  Australia)
Wynns Shiraz (Coonawarra)

RATING AUSTRALIA'S BEST PRODUCERS OF CHARDONNAY

* * * * (EXCELLENT)

Bannockburn (Geelong)
Barratt (Adelaide Hills)
Canobolas Smith (Mount Canobolas)
Clyde Park (Geelong)
Cullen (Margaret River)
Dromana Estate Reserve (Mornington
  Peninsula)
Giaconda (Beechworth)
Grosset Piccadilly (Adelaide Hills)
Howard Park (Western Australia)
Trevor Jones Virgin (South Australia)
Leeuwin Artists Series (Margaret River)
Moorooduc Estate (Mornington Peninsula)
Mountadam (Adelaide Hills)
Nicholson River (Gippsland)

Paringa Estate (Mornington Peninsula)
Petaluma (Piccadilly Valley)
Petaluma Tiers (Piccadilly Valley)
Pierro (Margaret River)
Rosemount Roxburgh (Hunter Valley)
Rosemount Show Reserve (Coonawarra)
Rothbury Estate Broken Back Vineyard
  (Hunter Valley)
Salitage (Pemberton)
Geoff Weaver (Lenswood)
Wise Vineyards Aquercus Unwooded
  (Western Australia)
Wise Vineyards (Western Australia)
Wise Vineyards Coat Door (Western
  Australia)

* * * (GOOD)

Cassegrain (New South Wales)
Cold Stream Hills (Yarra Valley)
Craigmoor (Mudgee)
Dalwhinnie (Victoria)
Katherine Hills (Southeastern Australia)
Hungerford Hill (Hunter Valley)
Jindalee (Murrays/Darling)
Katnook Estate (Coonawarra)
Krondorf (Barossa)
Lake's Folly (New South Wales)
Lindemans Bin 65 (New South Wales)
Maxwell Wines (McLaren Vale)
Michelton (Goulburn)
Miramar (Mudgee)
Moss Wood (Western Australia)

Orlando RF (South Australia)
Penley Estate (Coonawarra)
Petaluma (South Australia)
Reynella (South Australia)
Rothbury Estate Broken Back Vineyard
  Reserve (Hunter Valley)
Seaview Chardonnay Edwards and Chaffey
  (McLaren Vale)
Seppelt (Barossa)
Mark Swann (South Australia)
Tarra Warra (Victoria)
Tyrells Vat 47 (New South Wales)
Wynn's (Coonawarra)
Yarra Yering (Yarra Valley)
Yeringsberg (Yarra Valley)

RATING AUSTRALIA'S BEST PRODUCERS OF RIESLING

* * * * (EXCELLENT)

Tim Adams (Clare Valley)
Ashton Hills (Adelaide Hills)
Clos Clare (Clare Valley)
Grosset Polish Hill (Clare Valley)

Kilikanoon Blocks Road (Clare Valley)
Kilikanoon Morts Block (Clare Valley)
Petaluma (South Australia)
Viking Wines (Barossa)

RATING AUSTRALIA'S BEST PRODUCERS OF DRY SAUVIGNON BLANC AND SEMILLON

* * * * (EXCELLENT)

Branson Wines Semillon (Barossa)
Brokenwood Semillon (Hunter Valley)
Burge Family Semillon Olive Hill (Barossa)
Cullen Sauvignon/Semillon (Margaret
 River)
Fox Creek Semillon/Sauvignon (McLaren
 Vale)
Henschke (Barossa)
Katnook Estate Sauvignon (Coonawarra)
Leeuwin Estate Artists Series (Margaret
 River)
Leland Estate Sauvignon Blanc (Lenswood)
Lenswood Vineyards (Knappstein)
 Sauvignon Blanc (South Australia)

Maxwell Wines Semillon Old Vines
 (McLaren Vale)
Nepenthe Sauvignon (Adelaide Hills)
Nepenthe Semillon (Adelaide Hills)
Nicholson River Semillon (Gippsland)
Pierro Semillon/Sauvignon Blanc
 (Margaret River)
Rothbury Estate (Hunter Valley)
Shaw and Smith Sauvignon Blanc
 (Adelaide Hills)
Stanley Brothers Semillon Full Sister
 (Barossa)
Geoff Weaver Sauvignon Blanc
 (Lenswood)

* * * (GOOD)

Berri Estates (South Australia)
Evans and Tate (Margaret River)
Tim Knappstein (Clare Valley)
Krondorf (Barossa)
Peter Lehmann (Barossa)

Lindemans (Padthaway)
Mildara (Coonawarra)
Rosabrook Estate Sauvignon Blanc
 (Margaret River)
Rosemount (Hunter Valley)

RATING AUSTRALIA'S BEST PRODUCERS OF FORTIFIED WINES

* * * * * (OUTSTANDING)

d'Arenberg Rare Tawny (McLaren
 Vale)
Wm. Chambers Rosewood Tokay and
 Muscat (various *cuvées*) (Rutherglen)
Dutsche Tawny (Barossa)
Ralph Fowler Old and Rare Muscat
 (Limestone Coast)
Trevor Jones (various *cuvées*) (Barossa)

Morris Muscat and Tokay Liquor
 (Rutherglen)
Penfold's Grandfather Port (Barossa)
Seppelt Para Port (Barossa)
Seppelt Show Wines (Barossa)
Veritas Tawny (Barossa)
Yalumba Port (Barossa)
Yarra Yarra Portsorts (Yarra Valley)

AUSTRALIA'S GREATEST WINE BARGAINS FOR LESS THAN $12

d'Arenberg The Stump Jump
 Grenache/Shiraz

Berri Estates Semillon
Brown Brothers Cabernet Sauvignon

Brown Brothers Chardonnay King Valley
Brown Brothers Muscat Lexia
Buckley's Chardonnay
Buckley's Cabernet/Shiraz
Buckley's Chardonnay-Semillon
Hill of Content Benjamin's Blend
Hill of Content Grenache/Shiraz
Peter Lehmann Cabernet Sauvignon
Peter Lehmann Shiraz
Lindemans Chardonnay Bin 65
Mad Fish Chardonnay
Mad Fish Shiraz
Marguls-Phllips (various cuvées)
Michelton Semillon/Chardonnay
Montrose Cabernet Sauvignon
Montrose Chardonnay
Montrose Shiraz
Orlando Cabernet Sauvignon Jacob's Creek
Orlando Chardonnay Jacob's Creek
Orlando Sauvignon Blanc Jacob's Creek
Oxford Landing Cabernet Sauvignon
Oxford Landing Chardonnay
Paringa Cabernet Sauvignon
Paringa Merlot
Paringa Shiraz
Penfolds Cabernet/Shiraz Koonunga Hill
Rosemount Cabernet Sauvignon/Shiraz
  Diamond Reserve

Rosemount Diamond Reserve
  Grenache/Shiraz
Rosemount Diamond Reserve Red
Rosemount Diamond Reserve Sauvignon
  Blanc
Rosemount Diamond Reserve
  Semillon/Chardonnay
Rosemount Diamond Reserve Shiraz
Rosemount Diamond Reserve White
Rothbury Estate Chardonnay Broken Back
  Vineyard
Rothbury Estate Shiraz
Seppelt Cabernet Sauvignon Black Label
Seppelt Cabernet Sauvignon Reserve Bin
Seppelt Chardonnay Black Label
Seppelt Chardonnay Reserve Bin
Seppelt Semillon/Chardonnay
Seppelt Shiraz Black Label
Seppelt Shiraz Reserve Bin
Seppelt Tawny Strafford Port
Tyrells Long Flat Red
Wolf Blass Cabernet Sauvignon Yellow
  Label
Wolf Blass Shiraz President's Selection
Wyndham Estates Cabernet Sauvignon Bin
  444
Wyndham Estates Chardonnay Bin 222
Yalumba Clocktower Port

TIM ADAMS (CLARE VALLEY)

1997	Cabernet Sauvignon	D	91
1998	Fergus	D	89
1997	Shiraz	D	89+
1998	Shiraz The Aberfeldy	D	87
1997	Shiraz The Aberfeldy	D	93

Tim Adams, one of the most reliable names from Australia, produces top-notch wines from all varietals. His reds are lusty, intensely flavored, full-bodied offerings with copious fruit and considerable aging potential. The dark ruby-colored 1998 Fergus (a Grenache-dominated blend with small quantities of Cabernet Sauvignon, Cabernet Franc, Shiraz, and Malbec, which sees no new oak) offers a moderately intense nose of blackberries, cherry liqueur, pepper, dried herbs, and earth. Round and dense, this succulent, exuberantly fruity, full-bodied wine is fun. Drink it over the next 2–3 years.

Tim Adams's Shiraz The Aberfeldy comes from an old head-pruned vineyard planted in 1904. The wine spends 12 months in new American oak and another year in one-year-old American casks. The 1998 Shiraz The Aberfeldy's dense plum/purple color is followed by aggressive oak aromas intermixed with mint, black raspberries, and blackberries. This medium- to full-bodied wine is not the blockbuster I expected given the vintage, but it is nicely concentrated, cleanly made, and spicy/peppery. Revealing some tannin and adequate acidity, it can be drunk now as well as over the next 8 years.

The opaque purple-colored 1997 Shiraz The Aberfeldy is an immense, full-bodied, opaque purple-colored Shiraz with gorgeous aromas of licorice, cassis, black cherries, and tar. Massive, with high levels of glycerin that ooze across the palate, this dense, flavorful wine can be drunk now because of its low acidity and sweet tannin, but should become more civilized as well as complex with further cellaring. Impressive! Anticipated maturity: now–2020.

The 1997 Shiraz plays it closer to the vest, possessing a dense ruby/purple color and plenty of black raspberry, earthy, prunelike fruit. Exhibiting excellent sweetness, ripeness, and a nicely textured palate, it should drink well for 6–7 years. The outstanding 1997 Cabernet Sauvignon's dense ruby/purple color is followed by intense cassis, tobacco, cedar, and spice aromas and flavors. Long, full-bodied, and super-concentrated, this large-framed Cabernet Sauvignon should drink well young, yet age effortlessly for 12–15 years.

ANNVERS (LANGHORNE CREEK)

1999 Cabernet Sauvignon	D	90

Annvers is a new winery that started only in 1998. It produces a 100% Cabernet Sauvignon produced from 40-year-old vines. The wine spends 18 months in both French and American oak, of which 60% is new. Impressively made and California-like, with jammy black cherry and currant fruit, and coffee, chocolate, and toasty American oak in the background, the full-bodied, juicy, ripe 1999 Cabernet Sauvignon has low acidity, plenty of alcohol (15%), and a lusty, hedonistic finish. Drink it over the next 8 years.

D'ARENBERG (McLAREN VALE)

1999 d'Arry's Original (Shiraz/Grenache)	B	89
1998 d'Arry's Original (Shiraz/Grenache)	B	91
1997 d'Arry's Original (Shiraz/Grenache)	B	87
1996 d'Arry's Original (Shiraz/Grenache)	B	88
1995 d'Arry's Original (Shiraz/Grenache)	B	87
1998 Cabernet Sauvignon The Coppermine Road	E	95+
1997 Cabernet Sauvignon The Coppermine Road	E	90+
1996 Cabernet Sauvignon The Coppermine Road	E	90+
1999 The Custodian (Grenache)	C	88
1998 The Custodian (Grenache)	C	91
1997 The Custodian (Grenache)	C	89
1996 The Custodian (Grenache)	C	90
1998 The Dead-Arm (Shiraz)	EE	96
1997 The Dead-Arm (Shiraz)	EE	95
1996 The Dead-Arm (Shiraz)	EE	96
1999 The Footbolt Shiraz	C	89
1998 The Footbolt Shiraz	A	90
1997 The Footbolt Old Vine Shiraz	A	87
1996 The Footbolt Old Vine Shiraz	B	86
1999 Cabernet Sauvignon The High Trellis	B	88
1998 Cabernet Sauvignon The High Trellis	B	89
1996 Cabernet Sauvignon The High Trellis	B	85
1998 Ironstone Pressings	D	92
1997 Ironstone Pressings	D	94
2000 The Laughing Magpie (Shiraz/Viognier)	D	94
1998 The Noble Riesling	C	90
1997 The Noble Riesling	C	91
1999 The Noble Semillon	C	94
1999 The Twenty-Eight Road (Mourvèdre)	C	87
1998 The Twenty-Eight Road (Mourvèdre)	C	86

1996 The Twenty-Eight Road (Mourvèdre)	C	90
NV **Rare Tawny**	D	95

This winery, founded in 1912, continues to amaze me with their enormous portfolio of extremely high-quality wines. Moreover, except for a few fairly high-priced quasi-luxury *cuvées*, they are remarkably fine bargains. The current wine-maker, Chester Osborn, produces superb dry and fortified reds, as well as sweet white wines, and is equally adept at producing dry whites, which, however, are not reviewed here since they have to be consumed within a few years of the vintage. In short, this historic winery from South Australia offers an enviable selection of wines. D'Arenberg's red wines are aged in American oak, except for their new *cuvée*, The Laughing Magpie Shiraz/Viognier, where French wood is utilized. These offerings are classic examples of their varietal composition, and are not burdened by excessive manipulation or blatant new wood.

Readers seeking a natural, pure Cabernet Sauvignon should check out The High Trellis. This wine emerges from a vineyard planted in the 1920s. It is not head-pruned as are so many Australian vineyards, but is trellised much like those in California. As one would expect from vintage conditions, the 1999 Cabernet Sauvignon The High Trellis reveals more vibrancy, elegance, and charm than the 1998. It is a dark ruby/purple-colored effort with medium to full body, sweet cassis fruit, and not much makeup. It should drink well for 7–8 years. The 1998 Cabernet Sauvignon The High Trellis is a thicker, denser, more muscular wine with a broodingly backward personality. The dense plum-colored 1998 displays a big, sweet, cassis nose, medium to full body, and excellent depth as well as chewiness. Anticipated maturity: 2006–2015. The 1996 Cabernet Sauvignon The High Trellis exhibits pruny, raisiny notes in addition to black currant fruit. This straightforward, medium-bodied, overripe wine needs to be drunk over the next several years.

Another fine value is The Footbolt Shiraz. Again, the contrast between the stylish, graceful, medium-weight 1999 vintage and the blockbuster, thicker, more concentrated 1998 vintage is apparent. The deep ruby/purple-colored 1999 The Footbolt Shiraz offers a sweet perfume of new saddle leather intermixed with blackberries, pepper, graphite, and smoke. Medium-bodied, supple, and lively, it will drink well for 4–5 years. The denser, fuller-bodied, more muscular and concentrated 1998 The Footbolt Shiraz has more to it, as well as more tannin and a less evolved personality. It should ultimately prove to be the better wine, but, will it ever be as charming and seductive as the 1999? Drink it before 2012.

The 1997 The Footbolt Old Vine Shiraz's dark ruby/purple color is followed by blackberry/cassis fruit and sweet toasty oak. The well-made 1996 The Footbolt Old Vine Shiraz exhibits peppery, blackberry fruit intermixed with damp foresty aromas, pepper, and tar. With good fruit, spice, and a rustic finish, it should drink well for 4–5 years.

Southern Rhône wine enthusiasts will enjoy d'Arenberg's Châteauneuf-du-Pape look-alike called d'Arry's Original. A Shiraz-Grenache blend aged completely in large oak upright tanks, it is generally made in a style that gives it both immediate appeal and the potential to last for a decade. Five vintages were tasted, all of them robust, gutsy, rustic but subtly endowed wines that would be ideal accompaniments to most bistro-inspired dishes. The 1999 d'Arry's Original (52% Shiraz and 48% Grenache) reveals wonderful scents of blackberries, black cherries, cassis, earth, leather, and spice. Medium- to full-bodied, spicy, and supple-textured, it will provide delicious drinking over the next 5–6 years. The terrific, deep ruby/purple-colored 1998 d'Arry's Original (47% Shiraz and 53% Grenache) offers a gorgeous perfume of jammy black fruits intermixed with earth, charcoal, and leather. Spicy, meaty, fleshy, and full-bodied, this palate-staining 1998 should drink well for 8 years.

The dark ruby-colored 1997 d'Arry's Original (53% Shiraz and 47% Grenache) displays a ripe blackberry, spicy, peppery nose, good underlying acidity, and a rich, lusty finish. Anticipated maturity: now–2007. The 1996 d'Arry's Original (58% Shiraz and 42% Grenache) exhibits a similar blackberry/licorice-scented nose with more smoke and cassis in the picture. Medium- to full-bodied and ripe, with moderate tannin and noticeable acidity, this is a ripe, fleshy, attractive wine to consume in its youth and over the next 7–8 years. The opaque ruby/purple-colored 1995 d'Arry's Original (50% Shiraz and 50% Grenache) offers jammy black cherry fruit infused with earth, pepper, melted asphalt, and dried herbs. Dense, robust, and medium- to full-bodied, this is a gutsy, mouth-filling effort that should drink well for 7–8 years.

D'Arenberg's more tannic, structured, and austere The Twenty-Eight Road (Mourvèdre) emerges from a vineyard planted in the 1920s, and is Australia's version of a French Bandol. The 1999 is sweeter than the more rustic 1998, but both possess considerable tannin levels, earthy, peppery, black cherry and currant notes, and dusty, rustic finishes. They are not for everybody, but they are authentic and well made. Both should drink well for 8 years. In total contrast to the two former vintages, the 1996 The Twenty-Eight Road is outstanding. Dark ruby/purple-colored, with a floral, black raspberry–scented nose, this beautifully ripe, dense, concentrated wine offers up mushroom notes intermixed with tree bark and black fruits. Full-bodied, moderately tannic, and impressively rich, it will keep for 15 years.

I am a sucker for sumptuous Grenache, most of which emerges from the southern Rhône Valley and parts of Spain. Australia has proven that it can also turn out dazzling wines from low-yielding, old, head-pruned Grenache vines. The reference point for Australian Grenache is Clarendon Hills, followed by Greenock Creek. However, d'Arenberg does a noteworthy job with their 100% Grenache cuvée The Custodian. This wine emerges from old head-pruned vineyards and yields of one-third to one ton of fruit per acre. The 1999 The Custodian exhibits copious quantities of kirsch, ripe fruit, medium to full body, excellent purity, and a peppery, spicy, long finish. It is a delicious red to drink over the next 3–4 years. Even more impressive is the exceptional 1998 The Custodian. A larger-scaled effort with more layers and body as well as gobs of black cherry fruit, pepper, and spice, this lusty, multidimensional, impressive 1998 should be consumed over the next 7–8 years. The ruby/purple-colored 1997 The Custodian reveals a sweet, peppery, black raspberry and cherry fruit–dominated personality, medium to full body, and a lusty (14.5% alcohol) finish. Drink it over the next 2–3 years. The 1996 The Custodian is deeper and richer, with more black raspberry fruit, a peppery earthiness, full body, and a head-spinning level of alcohol (14.9%). Long and fat, it is ideal for drinking over the next 4–5 years.

The latest member of d'Arenberg's portfolio, The Laughing Magpie is a blend of 95% Shiraz and 5% Viognier aged completely in French oak. It appears to be an effort to compete with wines such as Torbreck's famed Run Rig. The 2000 is a fabulous debut. I tasted it just after bottling, so it may be even better once it has had a chance to calm down. An opaque purple color is followed by a soaring nose of blackberry and crème de cassis intermixed with honeysuckle, pepper, and high-class French oak. The wine is explosive on the palate, super-rich, full-bodied, voluptuous, and powerful, yet seamless and beautifully balanced with well-integrated tannin, wood, and acidity. It should drink well for 15+ years.

The other d'Arenberg's red wine classics, Ironstone Pressings (a Grenache, Shiraz, and Mourvèdre blend), the renowned Dead-Arm Shiraz (from vines 110+ years old), and their top-of-the-line, staggeringly rich, concentrated Cabernet Sauvignon The Coppermine Road, can rival the luxury-cuvée The Laughing Magpie.

The 1998 Ironstone Pressings (70% Grenache, 20% Shiraz, 10% Mourvèdre) is a powerful, dense, thick, slightly monolithic effort with copious amounts of blackberry fruit, huge body, and the potential to evolve for two decades. Even though it had been in the bottle for some time when I tasted it, it was still unformed. With silky tannin, explosive richness, and potentially top-flight perfume, it should last for 12 years. A killer wine, the sensational 1997 Ironstone Pressings (70% Grenache, 20% Shiraz, and 10% Mourvèdre) boasts an opaque purple color in addition to a spectacular black raspberry, kirsch, and licorice-scented nose, gorgeously full-bodied, super-concentrated flavors with nicely integrated, toasty oak, and fine acidity. Full-bodied, with high alcohol (15%), this is a blockbuster, New World, Rhône look-alike that can be drunk now or cellared for 10–15 years. Impressive!

Year in and year out, d'Arenberg's finest *cuvée* is their spectacular Shiraz made from head-pruned vines more than 100 years old. The 1998, 1997, and 1996 Dead-Arm Shiraz are exquisite, multidimensional wines that are sure to make a formidable impression with readers. This wine is aged in 100% new oak, generally tips the scales at a whopping 14–15% alcohol, yet has glorious levels of fruit and extract. The 1998 Dead-Arm Shiraz is outrageously rich, spectacular stuff, the likes of which only Australia seems capable of making. Whiners may complain that it is too big, too rich, too flavorful, and too damn good, but this opaque purple-colored offering is loaded with blackberry liqueur, smoke, charcoal, pepper, cassis, and licorice. Unctuously textured and full-bodied, but neither heavy nor overbearing, the wine's sweet tannin and low acidity are hidden in the cascade of fruit and glycerin that melt on the palate. This riveting, compelling effort can be drunk now, but promises to age well for two decades or more. The 1997 Dead-Arm Shiraz exhibits an opaque purple color as well as a sweet nose of vanilla, blackberries, and licorice. The wood frames this enormously concentrated, rich, chewy wine. Multilayered, with phenomenal concentration and length as well as moderately high tannin levels, it will be at its finest after 2–3 years of cellaring and will keep for 20 years. Cut from the same cloth, the full-bodied, portlike 1996 Dead-Arm Shiraz displays scents of black fruits, prunes, licorice, and pepper. Thick, rich, and unctuously textured, this is a dazzling old-vine Shiraz that can be drunk now or cellared for 15–20 years.

Readers looking for sensationally concentrated yet well-balanced Cabernet Sauvignon that can be drunk now or cellared for 20 years should check out the 1998 Cabernet Sauvignon The Coppermine Road. It boasts a dense purple color as well as an exquisitely pure nose of cassis, oak, earth, cedar, and spice box. Full-bodied and powerful, with a seamless personality (because of the melted tannin), this large-scaled, classic southern Australian Cabernet Sauvignon can rival the world's finest Cabernets. Anticipated maturity: now–2025. The dense 1997 Cabernet Sauvignon The Coppermine Road exhibits a youthful opaque purple color, high tannin and acidity, and outstanding concentration, richness, and intensity. It develops gorgeous black currant fruit mixed with cedar, tobacco, dried herbs, and earth. This wine should keep for 15+ years. The 1996 Cabernet Sauvignon The Coppermine Road is deep ruby/purple in color and shares the 1997's aromas of cassis, cedar, tobacco, dried herbs, and earth. It also offers additional notes of licorice and prunes in its full-bodied, concentrated, moderately tannic personality. This 1996 should be at its best before 2015.

The botrytised sweeties from d'Arenberg include a captivating 1999 The Noble Sémillon, a wine I would love to put in a blind tasting of the finest Sauternes and Barsacs. Its evolved color is accompanied by an extraordinary bouquet of caramel, orange marmalade, pineapple, honeysuckle, and earth. It reveals astonishing richness, gorgeous sweetness, fine balance, and admirable purity. Whether it will age as well as a Barsac or Sauternes is questionable, but it will impress tasters for at least a decade. Slightly less impressive but still outstanding is the 1998 The Noble Riesling. Honeyed citrus in an Auslese/Beerenauslese style is attractive, but as the wine sat in the glass some of Riesling's less favorable characteristics—paraffin and mothball scents—began to emerge. Drink this 1998 over the next 2–3 years.

The medium amber-colored 1997 The Noble Riesling reveals aromas of peach jam, honeysuckle, and strawberries. Rich and decadent, with enough acidity to provide freshness, this wine should be drunk during its vigorous youthfulness—over the next 5–7 years. Another sensational effort is d'Arenberg's nonvintage Rare Tawny, believed to be 12 years old. The deep amber color is followed by a stunningly rich bouquet offering scents of figs, buttered nuts, smoke, prunes, and sweet dark fruits. It is full-bodied and unctuous, yet remarkably fresh and vibrant. This sensational tawny should continue to drink well for another decade.

ARMSTRONG (VICTORIA)

1998 Shiraz Great Western	EE	89+

From an area renowned as one of the coolest climate regions of this part of Australia, the Médoc-like 1998 Shiraz Great Western exhibits aromas of spice box, mineral, cedar, lead pencil, and black currants. Aged in 100% new French oak, it is a streamlined, linear, interesting product. Tasting more like a stylish Cabernet-based Bordeaux than a Shiraz, it should drink well for 7–10 years given its acid profile.

AUSTRALIAN DOMAINE WINES (BAROSSA)

1998 Cabernet Sauvignon/Merlot Alliance	C	87
1999 Grenache The Alliance	C	85
1999 The Hattrick Proprietary Red	E	89
1998 The Hattrick Proprietary Red	E	95
1999 Shiraz The Alliance	C	88
1998 Shiraz The Alliance	C	91
1999 Shiraz Nova	B	86
1999 Shiraz Sheeraz	C	89+
1998 Shiraz Sheeraz	C	88
1997 Shiraz Valley Floor	E	90

This cooperative alliance among many different wine-makers turns out some tasty offerings. The least expensive wine in the ADW portfolio (around 10 U.S.$) is the Shiraz Nova, which is made from young vines and sees little oak and, in this style, is all the better for it. The 1999 Shiraz Nova shows good briery, spicy, peppery, berry fruit, dark ruby color, supple texture, medium body, and good, clean winemaking. Drink it over the next 2 years.

The Sheeraz is a super value. Annual production is about 2,500 cases. Twenty-five dollars rarely buys such an outstanding wine. The opulently textured 1999 Sheeraz shows a black/purple color, high alcohol, and loads of black fruit in addition to a full-throttle personality with plenty of glycerin, concentration, and power. The wine is ripe, intense, and opulent. It should drink well for 7–8 years. The 1998 Sheeraz is elegant, spicy, straightforward, and French-like in its proportions.

An even better value and slightly superior wine is Shiraz The Alliance. Moreover, there are 4,900 cases of this excellent wine. The 1999 exhibits deep purple color, plenty of spicy, toasty new American oak in the nose, a chewy, fleshy texture, and open-knit, expansive flavors that coat the palate. It is not complex, nor will it be particularly long-lived, but for drinking over the next 7–8 years, there is a lot to like. The dense purple-colored 1998 Shiraz The Alliance reveals a fat, blackberry/cassis-scented and flavored personality, immense body, low acidity, sweet tannin, and subtle integrated wood. This fruit- and glycerin-driven, blockbuster Shiraz should drink well for 10–12 years

The low-key 1999 Grenache The Alliance shows cherry fruit in the nose, some spice, moderate ruby color, medium body, and a straightforward, somewhat one-dimensional character. Nevertheless, there is good fruit. The wine is best drunk over the next 2 years.

The most expensive wine in the portfolio, The Hattrick Proprietary Red, is a 600-case blend of Grenache, Shiraz, and Cabernet Sauvignon. The 1999 shows dense ruby/purple color, excellent, concentrated, smoky black fruits, medium to full body, good sweetness, but then a slight narrowing in the finish that kept it from meriting an outstanding score. Nevertheless, there is a lot to like, and this excellent wine should handsomely repay 5–8 years of cellaring. The blockbuster 1998 The Hattrick is a prodigious effort. Opaque purple-colored, with an explosive nose of melted chocolate, pepper, blackberry jam, and cassis, this chewy, full-throttle, monster red reveals no hard edges. The integration of acidity, alcohol, and tannin have been easily accomplished, but the level of fruit extract is mind-boggling. This wine should drink well for 15–25 years, but who will have the patience to wait?

The Cabernet Sauvignon/Merlot Alliance is a 3,900-case blend of 75% Cabernet Sauvignon and 25% Merlot. It is a reasonably good value given today's excessive prices for Cabernet blends. The 1998 Cabernet Sauvignon/Merlot Alliance is a dark ruby-colored wine with a smoky, sweet, curranty nose, medium body, soft tannin, and a spicy, easygoing finish. Anticipated maturity: now–2008. Another outstanding effort was the 1997 Shiraz Valley Floor. This powerful wine (15% alcohol) has a more earthy, leathery, almost hickory barbecue spice note to the blackberry and cassis fruit. It is sweet, lush, and viscous on the attack, with fine density, full body, and a long finish. Unlike the other wines, where there are reasonable quantities, this is a micro *cuvée* of 70 cases. Anticipated maturity: now–2014.

AUSVETIA (SOUTH AUSTRALIA)

1997 Shiraz	E	87
1996 Shiraz	E	87
1995 Shiraz	E	90+

These wines are a joint venture between Penley Estate and their Swiss importer. They are made in an elegant, European style that avoids the dense, blockbuster style so popular in the States. Made from a blend of 95% Shiraz and 5% Cabernet Sauvignon, they emerge from vineyards in both McLaren and Barossa valleys.

The deep ruby/purple 1997 Shiraz is light-bodied, with excellent fruit, sweet tannin, and admirable purity. It offers an excellent bouquet of sweet blackberries and cassis intermixed with asphalt, licorice, and earth and should be drunk over the next 7–8 years. Similarly styled, the 1996 Shiraz is fuller-bodied, ripe, long, and harmonious. It should drink well for 5–6 years. The 1995 Shiraz is a stunning, flamboyant, black/purple-colored effort with copious quantities of cassis/blackberry fruit and toasty vanilla from new-oak casks. Spicy, dense, rich, full-bodied, and classy, this large-scaled wine will last for 15–17 years.

BALGOWNIE ESTATE (BENDIGO)

1999 Cabernet Sauvignon	C	88
1999 Shiraz	C	90

These are the finest Balgownie offerings I have yet tasted. The deep ruby/purple-colored 1999 Cabernet Sauvignon possesses a smoky, cassis-scented nose, excellent sweet fruit, medium to full body, and an elegant, moderately weighty personality with no hard edges. Drink it over the next 6 years. Even better is the 1999 Shiraz, which includes a touch of Viognier in the blend that gives its aromatics an exotic, decadent note. Aromas and flavors of honeysuckle, blackberries, and cassis are evident in this full-bodied, rich, concentrated wine. Although not a blockbuster, it offers good freshness and delineation, delicious flavors, and plenty of personality. Drink it over the next 5–6 years.

BANNOCKBURN (VICTORIA)

1996 Cabernet Sauvignon/Merlot	D	85
1995 Cabernet Sauvignon/Merlot	D	88
1998 Pinot Noir	E	84
1998 Shiraz	E	89

Bannockburn's 1998 Pinot Noir offers plenty of new oak along with a noteworthy chocolate, burnt cherry character. While not complex, it possesses good fruit, medium to full body, and a soft, ripe style. Drink it over the next 2 years.

My favorite Bannockburn offering is the 1998 Shiraz. It lacks the heft that most Australian Shiraz provide, but this is a cooler-climate wine with a deep ruby/purple color, olive-tinged, black currant flavors, some spice, and wood. It exhibits good sweetness on the attack and a medium-bodied, lightly tannic finish. Drink it over the next 7 years.

The evolved 1996 Cabernet Sauvignon/Merlot reveals a mature, dark garnet color along with cool-climate aromatics of spice box, herbs, violets, and red currants. It is medium-bodied, spicy, but somewhat compressed. It should be drunk over the next 2–3 years.

The tasty 1995 Cabernet Sauvignon/Merlot reveals a herbaceousness and bacon fat/sausage component that is undoubtedly due to the type of wood used for aging the wine, in addition to copious quantities of chocolate and berry fruit. This spicy, woody, obvious but fun blend should be drunk over the next 2–3 years.

BARLETTA BROTHERS (BAROSSA)

1997 Grenache/Shiraz	C	87?
1999 Grenache/Shiraz Barossa Valley	C	89
1999 Grenache/Shiraz Clare Valley	C	88

These wines are all from nonirrigated, old, head-pruned vines in the Barossa, averaging between 30 and 70 years of age. There are 329 cases of the Grenache/Shiraz Barossa Valley and 746 cases of the Grenache/Shiraz Clare Valley. The wines are aged in a combination of both new and old American and French casks. The 1999 Grenache/Shiraz Clare Valley (63% Grenache and 37% Shiraz) shows a smoky, black cherry, and currant nose with some spice and earth. The wine is medium- to full-bodied, supple, and fruit-driven. It is best drunk during its first 4–5 years of life. Somewhat similar in style but a little fuller-bodied, with notes of smoke, wood, earth, and black fruits and a touch of chocolate and animal notes, the fatter, riper, more substantial 1999 Grenache/Shiraz Barossa Valley seems to offer additional volume and length. Drink it during its first 6–8 years of life.

The 1997 Grenache/Shiraz's controversial bouquet of fresh earth, smoke, spice, sweaty saddle leather, and aged beef is followed by a creamy-textured, ripe, delicious wine with copious cherry fruit. The funky bouquet is reminiscent of the old-style Bandols from France's Mediterranean coast. Drink it over the next 2–3 years.

JIM BARRY (CLARE VALLEY)

1997 Cabernet Sauvignon/Malbec McCrae Wood	C	87
1997 Shiraz McCrae Wood	C	87

The 1997 Shiraz McCrae Wood exhibits a big, sweet, woody perfume with scents of jammy blackberry fruit. It is a blatantly fruity/woody effort, with abundant glycerin, low acidity, and a lush, chewy, straightforward appeal. Although not the most complex or ageworthy Shiraz, it will please the masses as well as connoisseurs. Drink it over the next 5 years.

The 1997 Cabernet Sauvignon/Malbec McCrae Wood (60% of the former and 40% of the latter) reveals a more saturated color as well as additional black fruits, earth, licorice, and floral characteristics. Medium-bodied, with sweet fruit, well-integrated wood, and an excellent finish, it should drink well for 5 years.

BASS PHILLIP (WEST GIPPSLAND)

1998 Pinot Noir	E	90
1997 Pinot Noir	E	90
1998 Pinot Noir Premium Vineyard Select	EE	92
1997 Pinot Noir Premium Vineyard Select	EE	91+
1998 Pinot Noir Reserve	EEE	93

Lamentably, Bass Phillip produces only 200 cases of their exquisite Pinot Noirs, among the finest being made in Australia. With a Burgundian character, these wines are made from extremely low yields and are bottled without filtration. They throw a hefty film of sediment at a young age because of their natural winemaking.

All three 1998s exhibit Côte de Nuits–like characteristics in their gorgeously sweet, plum, berry, and cherry fruit flavors infused with cinnamon and allspice. Full-bodied, beautifully concentrated, with superb purity, creamy, big, thick, Burgundian textures (that have not been foolishly acidified), they also develop long, concentrated finishes. Extremely complex, and more forward and evolved than most Burgundies are at a similar age, these are beautifully made wines. There are slight differences (the Premium and Reserve ratchet up the level of concentration), but they are more similar than dissimilar. All three are brilliant efforts. Is the Reserve worth nearly $100 more than the regular bottling? The answer is no, but it is a reference point for what Australian Pinot Noir can achieve in selected microclimates when produced without compromise. Drink all of these 1998s over the next 4–5 years.

The 1997 Pinot Noir's superb aromatic profile consists of black cherries, smoky new oak, and flowers. Lush, with outstanding richness and purity, a multilayered, suave, creamy texture, and terrific fruit, it can be drunk now or cellared for 4–5 years. The opaque ruby-colored 1997 Pinot Noir Premium Vineyard Select offers a huge, concentrated nose of black cherries, bacon fat, dried herbs, and high-quality French oak. Full-bodied, moderately tannic, gorgeously pure and nuanced, this wine will keep for a decade. Impressive!

BERRY'S BRIDGE (PYRENEES, VICTORIA)

1999 Cabernet Sauvignon	D	89
1999 Shiraz	D	93

These top-notch wines are made from ripe fruit and what would appear to be extremely low yields. The blockbuster 1999 Shiraz (14.7% alcohol) has an opaque blue/purple color and an extraordinary nose of blackberries, blueberries, and toast. Full-bodied, ripe, and multilayered with exhilarating levels of glycerin, concentration, and depth, this is a pure, surprisingly supple wine to drink over the next 10 years.

Slightly more structured but not as complex nor as concentrated is the 1999 Cabernet Sauvignon. It has an impressively saturated black/purple color and a sweet nose of blueberry and cassis fruit intermixed with licorice and underbrush. The wine is dense, medium- to full-bodied, and pure, with the fruit holding the upper hand. A bit more complexity and it too would have received an outstanding evaluation. Drink it over the next decade.

BIRCHWOOD (SOUTH AUSTRALIA)

1998 Cabernet Sauvignon Twin Rivers	D	89
1998 Shiraz Decades	D	90

This is a *négociant* operation dedicated to finding good old-vine sources for grapes in South Australia. The 1998 Cabernet Sauvignon Twin Rivers comes from a 40-year-old vineyard. Production is small (250 cases), the wine very good, even excellent, with an elegant black currant, spice box, cedar, and dried herb–scented nose, attractive, medium- to full-bodied flavors, low acidity, sweet tannin, and a clean finish. Drink it over the next 5–6 years.

More interesting is the 1998 Shiraz Decades. Made from vines averaging 30–60 years, this wine was formerly utilized as a component part of the well-known Rosemount Balmoral Shiraz. This dense ruby/purple, full-bodied Shiraz reveals the telltale blackberry liqueur–scented nose with notes of licorice, pepper, and toasty new oak. Dense, powerful, and concentrated, it is a powerhouse to drink over the next 8 years.

BRANSON COACH HOUSE (ASPDEN)

1998 Shiraz Malcolm	EE	97

Limited in availability, this 1998 Shiraz Malcolm entirely made from the "Grange" clone of that varietal, exhibits an opaque black/blue color, a personality similar to a dry vintage port, massive body, phenomenal concentration, and a viscous, huge, juicy, thick underbelly bursting with glycerin, fruit, and extract. The high tannin is nearly concealed by the wine's glycerin and extract level. Tasting more like a barrel sample than a finished wine, this youthful, Goliath-sized Shiraz will handsomely repay 15–20 years of cellaring.

BROKENWOOD (HUNTER VALLEY)

1998 Shiraz	D	86
1998 Shiraz Graveyard Vineyard	EE	90
1997 Shiraz Graveyard Vineyard	EE	92
1998 Shiraz The Mistress Block	E	88+
1997 Shiraz The Mistress Block	E	91
1998 Shiraz Rayner Vineyard	E	90
1997 Shiraz Rayner Vineyard	E	94

Brokenwood has been considered one of the finest practitioners of old-vine Shiraz since their debut vintage in 1970. They are also widely heralded for their interesting whites (Sauvignon Blanc and Sémillon), which are not reviewed here since they have to be consumed within a few years of the vintage. The 1997 Brokenwood Shiraz *cuvées* performed exceptionally well, even though the vintage is considered less successful than the more highly touted 1998. All the impressive, dark ruby/purple 1998s possess admirable levels of fruit and extract and copious quantities of toasty wood. The least expensive wine of the portfolio is the Shiraz, a blend from McLaren Vale, King Valley, and Cowra that is aged in American wood for 20 months prior to bottling. The 1998 is a forward, chocolaty/berry-flavored wine with notes of melted tar and hints of tannin and acidity in the finish. This Shiraz is meant to be drunk over the next 2–3 years for its gutsy richness and uncomplicated style.

The Shiraz The Mistress Block emerges from vines averaging 30 years of age and is aged in American oak. The dense purple-colored 1998 offers generous aromas of pepper, spice, blackberries, chocolate, and vanilla. Full-bodied and moderately tannic, with tart acidity, fine intensity, and a generous, robust constitution, this mouth-filling Shiraz will keep for 8–10 years. The dark ruby/purple 1997 Shiraz The Mistress Block possesses exceptional balance. Sexy and lush, with low acidity, a beautiful, American oak–infused, blackberry-scented nose and flavors, it is creamy-textured and full-bodied, with terrific intensity and purity. This ostentatiously styled Shiraz can be drunk now and over the next decade.

The Shiraz Rayner Vineyard emerges from a dry-farmed Shiraz vineyard. The 1998 is the beefiest, most potent of the 1998 Brokenwood offerings at 14.5% alcohol. Licorice, blackberries, pepper, earth, and sweet oak are abundantly present in this full-bodied, impressively constituted, rich Shiraz. The finish is long and intense. Tight, with noticeable acidity and high tannin, it will keep until 2014. The voluptuous and seamless 1997 Shiraz Rayner Vineyard's beautifully integrated acidity, tannin, and alcohol result in a weighty, full-bodied, explosively rich, monster-sized Shiraz with copious quantities of blackberry and blueberry fruit intertwined with melted tar and pepper. Thick, juicy, and disarming, this lusty effort can be drunk now and over the next 10–12 years.

The 1998 Shiraz Graveyard Vineyard is a seriously structured, dense, impressively constituted effort with well-integrated tannin and oodles of blackberry fruit intermixed with new saddle leather, pepper, and asphalt. Full, lush, and delineated, this big wine is accessible and will last for 15+ years. Less weighty than usual, but clearly the flagship wine of Brokenwood, the 1997 Shiraz Graveyard Vineyard is made in an earthy, perfumed style, without the power, concentration, or palate impact of the Rayner Vineyard. Nevertheless, there is plenty to get excited about in this full-bodied, rich, chewy wine with uncanny balance and beautiful overall purity and equilibrium. Drink it over the next 12 years.

BROTHERS IN ARMS (LANGHORNE CREEK)

1998 Shiraz	D	92

This is a reasonably good value for a full-throttle, massive, super-concentrated Shiraz. There are 570 cases of this wine that "modestly" tips the scales at 16% alcohol. It emerges from a vineyard with many vines over 100 years of age, which is said to have been the source for the top *cuvée* of Shiraz for Mildara Blass before the vineyard owners decided to produce their own wine. The 1998 shows a dense purple color and a gorgeous nose of blue- and black-berries intermixed with some cherry liqueur. Full-bodied, opulent, with plenty of spice, creosote, pepper, and subtle wood, this wine is impressive, concentrated, and already delicious. Anticipated maturity: now–2010. It is undoubtedly a sleeper pick at this price. Look for this winery to attract more and more fans.

BURGE FAMILY (BAROSSA VALLEY)

1998 Grenache Old Vines	D	92
1999 Grenache/Shiraz/Mourvèdre Olive Hill	D	90
1999 Shiraz Draycott	D	88
1998 Shiraz Draycott	D	90
1997 Shiraz Draycott	D	89
1999 Shiraz Grateful Reserve	EE	90
1998 Shiraz Grateful Reserve	EE	98

Burge is another of the exceptional wineries of the Barossa that seems to consistently turn out top-flight wines. The red wines are all noteworthy for their brilliant displays of ripe fruit and consistent purity. The 1999 Grenache/Shiraz/Mourvèdre Olive Hill (43% Shiraz, 34% Grenache, and 23% Mourvèdre) is a strong effort from this vintage. The wine shows a dense ruby/purple color, notes of violets, black fruits, licorice, and a powerful leathery and floral note. The wine is full-bodied with a sweet attack, honeyed black fruits, nicely integrated wood (about one-third new French oak was used), and a layered finish.

The 1999 Shiraz Draycott (86% Shiraz and 14% Grenache from 10- to 40-year-old vines) is lighter than its equivalent in 1998. The wine is still very good, with a peppery cassis nose, sweet jammy fruit on the attack, medium body, and a moderately endowed, clean finish. Drink it over the next 6–7 years. The 1998 Shiraz Draycott shows more fat, a broader, more expansive texture, lower acidity, and a sweet, jammy, blackberry, smoky cassis character. The wine is long, pure, and full-bodied (the alcohol is 14.9%). Drink it over the next decade for its exuberant, powerful, in-your-face style. The 1997 Shiraz Draycott is lighter-styled than the colossal 1998. A blend of 70% Shiraz and 30% Grenache, it exhibits a dark ruby color and a pleasant, sweet, blackberry- and cherry-scented nose with pepper and earth undertones. Lush, fruit-driven, and supple, it will drink well for 5–6 years.

Sadly, there are less than 200 cases annually of the Shiraz Grateful Reserve, which is made from a 40-year-old vineyard. The outstanding 1999 shows a smoky, oaky style with medium body, excellent blackberry/cassis fruit, but not nearly the intensity, texture, and layers of flavor found in Burge's 1998s. Anticipated maturity: now–2015.

It would be difficult to find a better Shiraz than the 1998 Shiraz Grateful Reserve. The color is a saturated blue/purple that looks more like vintage port than dry table wine. A spectacular bouquet of melted chocolate, licorice, blackberry jam, blueberries, and cassis is accompanied by an awesomely concentrated, massively proportioned wine that somehow has just enough acidity and tannin to both pull it together and provide some delineation. The wine is gorgeously pure, with massive power and weight, and a finish that lasts nearly a minute. Low acidity, high glycerin, 14.5% alcohol, and thrilling levels of extract/concentration make for a nearly perfect drinking experience. Anticipated maturity: now–2025+.

The ripeness and concentration, volume, and fuller style from the 1998 vintage is also evident in the 1998 Grenache Old Vines. Made from vines ranging in age from 70 to 80 years old, this 100% Grenache *cuvée* (400 cases) shows serious cherry liqueur in the nose, along with some roasted notes, a full-bodied, lavishly rich palate filled with fruit and glycerin, and a fleshy, rather juicy and succulent finish. It is not meant for long-term aging but for drinking over the next 4–5 years. This will score high on the pleasure meter.

CAMPBELLS (RUTHERGLEN)

NV	Isabella Rare Rutherglen Tokay	E	97
NV	Merchant Prince Rare Muscat	E	95
NV	Muscat	D	90
NV	Tokay	D	90

One of the illustrious names in Australian fortified dessert wines, Campbells has been making these gems since 1870. The rare *cuvées*, Isabella and Merchant Prince (blends that average 70 years in age), are superior fortified wines with extraordinary aromatics, unctuous textures, and luxurious levels of sweetness and concentration. However, there is no question that the nonvintage Muscat and Tokay are terrific buys. They may not possess the intensity of their more powerful siblings, but they are loaded with fruit, unctuous, sweet, and already complex, with stunning aromatics. Moreover, they will keep for decades. These sensational offerings are among the treasures of Australia.

CANOBOLAS SMITH (NEW SOUTH WALES)

1996	Alchemy Proprietary Red Wine	D	94
1998	Cabernet Sauvignon/Merlot Wattleview	C	90

A terrific bargain in New World Cabernet Sauvignon/Merlot, the 1998 Cabernet Sauvignon/Merlot Wattleview, a blend of 60% Cabernet and 40% Merlot aged in French oak, shows plum, cherry, and currants in the expressive nose, and hedonistic, lush, medium- to full-bodied flavors that are seamless, low in acidity, and sexy. This is a seductive, reasonably priced wine to drink now and over the next 7 years. Don't miss it!

The prodigious 1996 Alchemy (predominantly Cabernet Sauvignon, with Shiraz and Cabernet Franc) achieved 15% alcohol naturally. Aged in both French and American oak, and bottled unfiltered, it is a wine of extraordinary purity and multiple dimensions. Knockout aromas of blackberry liqueur, cassis, toasty oak, and spice box are followed by a layered wine with sweet tannin and low acidity. It is full-bodied and massive, yet there is no sense of heaviness or hotness. Pure, thick, and viscous, it should drink well for 12 years. Impressive!

CAPE D'ESTAING (KANGAROO ISLAND)

1999	Cabernet Sauvignon	E	89+
1998	Cabernet Sauvignon	E	92+
1999	Shiraz	E	88
1998	Shiraz	E	94
1998	Shiraz Admiral's Reserve	EEE	91+

From an island off the coast of Adelaide renowned for abundant wildlife, Cape d'Estaing seems to be a high quality producer that offers wine made from a somewhat cooler climate than the Barossa Valley to the north. Yields are generally a lowly 1 ton of fruit per acre. The vineyards are young (five years), but the wines, which are aged in French oak, are of spectacular quality. Fortunately, the annual production averages 1,500 cases for each wine.

The 1999 Cabernet Sauvignon shows a full-bodied style with opaque purple color, sweet, classic black currant fruit mixed with spice box and tobacco. The wine is rich, concentrated, and not dissimilar from a high-class Bordeaux. The alcohol is a modest 13.7% (reasonable by Australian standards). This wine shows excellent purity and fine overall balance. Anticipated maturity: now–2012. The 1998 Cabernet Sauvignon (13.4% alcohol) displays a thick-looking, opaque purple color as well as a terrific nose of black currants, cedar, spice box, and minerals. Medium- to full-bodied, with outstanding purity, remarkable symmetry, and potential complexity for a young wine, this beautifully proportioned, intensely concentrated Cabernet should be at its best after another 2 years of cellaring and should last for two decades.

The 1999 Shiraz (100% Shiraz) is medium- to full-bodied, boasts a dark purple color, somewhat monolithic attack, but then unfolds gracefully on the palate, revealing more finesse and restraint than many of the more humongous offerings of Shiraz from warmer mainland microclimates. This wine is pure, stylish, and best drunk during its first 10–12 years of life.

The flashier 1998 Shiraz exhibits terrific blackberry jam–like aromas intermixed with sweet pepper, espresso, and vanilla scents. Super-concentrated, loaded with ripe fruit, and impressively pure and layered, this is a dazzling Shiraz. Despite the fact that it tasted powerful, the alcohol is only 14.1%. Drink this sumptuous Shiraz over the next 10 years.

The 1998 Shiraz Admiral's Reserve is essentially a 125-case batch selected in the cellar from all the barrels of Shiraz. The wine has an opaque purple color and a sweet nose of blackberry liqueur intermixed with road tar, new saddle leather, pepper, and spice. Full-bodied, rich, structured, and backward, this impressive, large-scaled wine admirably marries a degree of finesse with the boldly flavored, bigger style favored by Australians. Anticipated maturity: now–2010.

SERGIO CARLEI (HEATHCOTE)

1999 Shiraz Green Vineyard Forties Old Block	E	88
1998 Shiraz Green Vineyard Forties Old Block	E	89
1998 Tre Rossi	E	87

The 1998 Tre Rossi's blend of 50% Shiraz and 25% each of Egiodola and Marzemino, two varietals that are alien to my palate, has produced a black/purple wine with high levels of rustic tannin and notes of meat, chocolate, plum liqueur, and earth. Although coarse, it is loaded with character. It is hard to know whether this 1998 will age gracefully or become increasingly attenuated and rustic. For now, it is a substantial wine to enjoy with full-flavored dishes. Both the 1998 and 1999 Shiraz Green Vineyard Forties Old Block are aged completely in French oak. The 1999 displays a blackberry, graphite, charcoal, and smoky-scented nose, medium to full body, good complexity, and a moderately weighty feel in the mouth. It is supple enough to be drunk now and over the next decade. The similarly styled 1998 is richer, with more length, power, and extract. To both wines' credit, the French oak is subtle and nicely integrated. The 1998 should drink well for another 10 years.

CASA FRESCHI (LANGHORNE CREEK)

1999 Profondo	E	92
1999 La Signora	E	90

Based on the first wines I have tasted from proprietor/wine-maker David Freschi, this is an up-and-coming star. Both wines are aged in primarily new French oak, are bottled unfined and unfiltered, and combine a power and uncanny elegance which is unusual in Australia.

The 1999 La Signora could easily pass for a St.-Emilion garage wine. It has a somewhat international style, but the opaque purple color offers up notes of coffee, chocolate, and black currants along with cigar box notes. The wine is rich, dense, and ripe, with beautifully integrated acidity, wood, and alcohol. The finish is long and at the same time elegant. It should drink well for at least 10 years. Even more impressive is the Bordeaux look-alike, the 1999 Profondo. Also a blend of Shiraz, Cabernet Sauvignon, and Malbec, it exhibits an impressive saturated, dark ruby/purple color in addition to a gorgeous nose of blueberry liqueur intermixed with cassis, Chinese black tea, vanilla, and licorice. Stunningly rich on the palate, with multiple layers of concentration, this compelling wine is a dead ringer for a top first or second growth Bordeaux. Anticipated maturity: now–2015.

CASTAGNA (VICTORIA)

1999 Syrah Genesis	EE	86

It seems that Julian Castagna, the proprietor of this winery, is a famous film and television director with a wine bug. However, he needs a reality check with respect to his pricing policy.

The 1999 Syrah Genesis has an uncanny resemblance to a midweight Crozes-Hermitage from France's Rhône Valley. Smoky, olive, black currant notes combine with some new oak and pepper to give this moderately weighted wine plenty of appeal, but there must be five or six dozen offerings from the real Crozes-Hermitage that sell for under $25 a bottle that are as good, if not better.

CHAMBERS ROSEWOOD (RUTHERGLEN)

NV	Muscat	E	95
NV	Rare Muscat	EEE	100
NV	Rare Tokay	EEE	100
NV	Special Muscat	EE	98
NV	Special Tokay	EE	99
NV	Tokay	E	96

I have long believed that Australia remains an unheralded but extraordinary treasure trove for fortified Muscat and Tokay. It is amazing how many sensational efforts emerge from this country. With the exception of William Chambers, they have not received the accolades they deserve. Anyone who has ever tasted his fortified Tokay or Muscat realizes that the world's reference point for these wines begins and ends with Chambers. These luxurious offerings possess such extraordinary unctuosity, thickness, complexity, and richness that they must be tasted to be believed. They are not just big, thick sugar balls, because they have sound underlying acidity as well as remarkable complexity and freshness. A spoonful or two of each wine is enough for most nongluttons to appreciate the riveting heights these *cuvées* represent. Obviously the Rare Muscat and Rare Tokay are surreal, but for the price, the $15 *cuvées* of Muscat and Tokay are sensational bargains. One could even argue that the Rare Muscat and Rare Tokay, believed to be 50–70 years old from the solera system (a blend of vintages with a very old base or dominant portion) that Chambers has long maintained, are even spectacular bargains. What do they taste like? The levels of intensity, perfume, and viscosity rise with each tier, from the regular *cuvées* to the special *cuvées* to the rare *cuvées*. All possess notes of smoke, roasted nuts, coffee, brown sugar, maple syrup, prunes, honey, fruitcake, overripe orange/apricots, and remarkable spicy characters. The Muscats tend to be slightly more fruit-driven, with the Tokays more earthy and raisiny. However, these are all riveting examples of fortified dessert wines that I enthusiastically recommend. I use the Rosewoods for many charitable meals/wine tastings I donate, and guests are always gaga about these rarities. In summary, life is too short not to try one of the Muscats or Tokays from Chambers Rosewood, a true Australian treasure.

CHAPEL HILL (McLAREN VALE)

1998 The Vicar (Shiraz/Cabernet Sauvignon)	D	88

A thick, viscous, dense ruby/purple offering, Chapel Hill's 1998 The Vicar exhibits abundant quantities of new oak (primarily American), loads of blackberry and cassis flavors, and a rich, concentrated, blockbuster finish. A blend of 56% Shiraz and 44% Cabernet Sauvignon, this rich, moderately tannic 1998 is best drunk before 2014.

CHERISE (McLAREN VALE)

1997 Sangiovese	C	91

If only California wineries could make Sangiovese such as this! Wine-maker/owner Stephen Hall (formerly of Coriole) has turned out a terrific 1997 Sangiovese with a deep ruby color and a knockout aromatic profile featuring cherry jam galore intertwined with kirsch and sweet leather. Medium- to full-bodied and muscular, with gorgeous levels of fruit, this soft, opulently styled Sangiovese should be enjoyed over the next 2–3 years.

CHARLES CIMICKY (BAROSSA)

1998	Merlot	D	90
1996	Merlot	D	88
1998	The Red Blend	D	90
1997	The Red Blend	D	90
1998	Shiraz Reserve	D	91+
1998	Shiraz Signature	D	92
1997	Shiraz Signature	D	89

Given the bang for the buck, so to speak, Charles Cimicky's wines are excellent values, consistently full-bodied, concentrated, and well structured. His 1998s seem extremely youthful, and tasted more like barrel samples than finished wines, but there is considerable long-term potential for these *cuvées*. The 1998 Merlot exhibits a deep ruby/purple color and a big, sweet nose of blackberry and cherry fruit intermixed with fudge, coffee, and smoky wood. It is full-bodied, ripe, and sexy. Drink it over the next 8 years. The internationally styled 1996 Merlot exhibits black cherry fruit, lavish, high-quality toasty oak, medium to full body, adequate acidity, and a mouth-filling, plump texture. Aromatic and pure, this fleshy Merlot should drink well for 4–5 years.

The dense purple-colored, full-bodied 1998 The Red Blend, a 58% Cabernet Sauvignon, 22% Merlot, and 20% Cabernet Franc blend, reveals explosive fruit, licorice, tobacco, black cherries, currants, and new oak in the nose, and high levels of tannin. It comes across in the mouth like a St.-Emilion on steroids. The wine seems extremely young, and 1–2 years of cellaring may result in an even more multidimensional effort. It should keep well for 14 years.

The 1997 The Red Blend (58% Cabernet Sauvignon, 22% Merlot, and 20% Cabernet Franc) is a thick, rich, full-bodied, fleshy, dry red with abundant quantities of black fruits intermixed with spicy new oak. Concentrated, with low acidity, sweet tannin, and no hard edges, this mouth-filling big red should drink well for 8 years.

The 1998 Shiraz Reserve is a dense purple-colored effort revealing gorgeously pure, vibrant notes of black raspberries, blackberries, mineral, smoke, and creosote. Full-bodied, dense, tightly knit, and explosive, it requires 1–2 years of cellaring. Consume it over the following 12–15 years, although I suspect it will last longer.

Another wine that seems to be bursting at the seams is the profound, black/purple 1998 Shiraz Signature, a 100% old-vine Shiraz. The exquisite aromatics consist of blueberry/blackberry liqueur followed by a sweet, full-bodied, textured mouth-feel, with superb purity, high tannin, but also superb extract. I would drink it over the following 12–15 years.

The 1997 Shiraz Signature is less powerful than the 1998, but more evolved, with sweet black fruit aromas and flavors, full body, low acidity, and an admirably concentrated, nuanced, and lushly textured style. It should drink well for 6 years.

CLARENDON HILLS (CLARENDON)

1999	Astralis	EEE	91+
1998	Astralis	EEE	95+
1999	Cabernet Sauvignon Brookman Vineyard	D	89
1998	Cabernet Sauvignon Brookman Vineyard	D	87
1999	Cabernet Sauvignon Hickinbotham Vineyard	D	90
1998	Cabernet Sauvignon Hickinbotham Vineyard	D	93+
1999	Cabernet Sauvignon Sandown Vineyard	D	88
1998	Cabernet Sauvignon Sandown Vineyard	D	92+
1999	Grenache Old Vines Blewitt Springs Vineyard	D	92
1998	Grenache Old Vines Blewitt Springs Vineyard	D	92
1999	Grenache Old Vines Clarendon Vineyard	D	87
1998	Grenache Old Vines Clarendon Vineyard	D	93

1999	Grenache Old Vines Hickinbotham Vineyard	D	89
1999	Grenache Old Vines Kangarilla Vineyard	D	91
1998	Grenache Old Vines Kangarilla Vineyard	D	90+
1999	Grenache Old Vines Romas Vineyard	E	92
1999	Merlot Brookman Vineyard	D	90
1998	Merlot Brookman Vineyard	D	88
1999	Merlot Hickinbotham Vineyard	D	91+
1999	Pinot Noir Hickinbotham Vineyard	D	87
1998	Pinot Noir Hickinbotham Vineyard	D	89
1999	Shiraz Brookman Vineyard	E	90
1998	Shiraz Brookman Vineyard	D	94
1999	Shiraz Hickinbotham Vineyard	E	90+
1998	Shiraz Hickinbotham Vineyard	D	92
1999	Shiraz Liandra Vineyard	E	92
1998	Shiraz Liandra Vineyard	D	91
1999	Shiraz Moritz Vineyard	E	92
1999	Shiraz Piggott Range Vineyard	E	91+
1998	Shiraz Piggott Range Vineyard	D	92+

I am an unabashed admirer of proprietor/wine-maker Roman Bratasiuk's super-concentrated, muscular, full-throttle red wines, whether they be Cabernet Sauvignon, Merlot, Shiraz, or his undeniable specialty, Grenache. There is no doubt that the red wines pack all the flavor and concentration one would expect from a no-holds-barred "Aussie" style. Yet his wines, as massive and deep as they are, have impeccable balance and purity. I also applaud his judicious use of French rather than American oak. For my taste, Clarendon Hills is today's undisputed superstar of McLaren Vale.

Reminiscent of a good Pinot made in a dense style, the 1999 Pinot Noir Hickinbotham Vineyard reveals a garnet color and a broodingly backward, smoky, earthy nose of root beer, cola, black cherries, raspberries, and prunes. Spicy, medium- to full-bodied, ripe, and well made, it should drink well for 4–5 years. The dark ruby-colored 1998 Pinot Noir Hickinbotham Vineyard offers an intriguing nose of allspice, black fruits, and earth. Ripe, with plenty of stuffing, good underlying acidity, and a robust, chewy style, this is a flavorful, muscular Pinot to drink over the next decade.

In 1999 (a lighter, more elegant, and often less concentrated vintage than 1998 in South Australia) Clarendon Hills has turned out some stylish, flavorful Cabernet. The 1998s are also superb, with the 1998 Cabernet Sauvignon Sandown Vineyard and 1998 Cabernet Sauvignon Hickinbotham Vineyard being more revealing as well as massive, powerful, highly extracted, and broodingly backward. All of these wines are accessible, but the Hickinbotham *cuvée*, especially the 1998 version, has the best chance of lasting well beyond a decade.

The 1999 Cabernet Sauvignon Brookman Vineyard shows a dark ruby/purple color and a sweet nose of leafy black currants intermixed with earth, spice, and some background wood. The wine is rich, has sweet fruit on the palate, and a supple finish. Drink it over the next 7–8 years. The least impressive and expressive of Cabernet from Clarendon Hills is the 1998 Cabernet Sauvignon Brookman Vineyard. Closed and tannic, with toasty notes in the aromas, it was difficult to penetrate and evaluate. There is size and force to the wine, but it is monolithic. Like its siblings, it is aged in 100% new French oak casks, which is apparent from its toast-scented nose. Anticipated maturity: now–2015. The dark purple-colored 1999 Cabernet Sauvignon Sandown Vineyard possesses chocolate, along with telltale cassis, tobacco, earth, and spice aromas. The wine is very good to excellent, nicely balanced, and best drunk over the first decade of life. The opaque purple-colored 1998 Cabernet Sauvignon Sandown Vineyard displays a dense nose of cassis and jammy cherry fruit intermixed with licorice, tobacco, tar, and dried herbs. Thick, powerful, full-bodied, and moderately tannic, this wine will keep for two decades. The 1999 Cabernet Sauvignon Hickinbotham Vineyard boasts a nice volume and a complex nose of black currants, chocolate, barbecue spice, and toast. The wine is powerful, dense, concentrated, rich, with subtle wood, plenty of fruit, glycerin, and moderate tannin. Anticipated maturity: 2006–2018. The 1998 Cabernet Sauvignon Hickinbotham Vineyard reveals a similar opaque purple color and highly extracted, massive size, with a touch of mint in its black currant/cassis flavors. The acidity is lower as well. This effort possesses a greater degree of ripeness, although all of these wines are ultraripe and concentrated. Huge, chewy, and full-bodied, it should keep for two decades.

The Merlots are outstanding wines. The 1999 Merlot Brookman Vineyard reveals a Starbucks-esque chocolate espresso roasted nose, full body, deep, concentrated flavors, plenty of smokiness, and berry fruit, noteworthy glycerin, low acidity, and a lush, heady texture. This wine will provide hedonistic drinking for at least 8–12 years. The 1998 Merlot Brookman Vineyard is restrained. Its dark ruby color is followed by sweet, ripe aromas of jammy cherries intermixed with herbs and earth. Open-knit and admirably concentrated, with excellent symmetry and purity, this fleshy, fruit/glycerin-dominated Merlot is the finest wine from this varietal being produced in Australia. Drink it over the next 5–7 years. More structured, backward, denser, and delineated is the 1999 Merlot Hickinbotham Vineyard. It reveals similar chocolate, coffee, black cherry, and currant notes, along with more depth, structure, and tannin. Consume it over the following 12–15 years.

I have long been an admirer of the Clarendon Hills Grenaches and have purchased and drunk more than my fair share, always with exceptional pleasure. To my taste, no one makes better old-vine Grenache in Australia than Roman Bratasiuk, and I doubt anyone in California can compete with him. The portfolio comprises five *cuvées*, including the superluxury Grenache called Romas. These are all wines that are gorgeous to drink young, and can probably easily last in a good cellar for 10 years or more. The 1999s are fine efforts that come close to equaling the high-quality *cuvées* of Grenache the proprietor produced in 1998.

The lightest and least impressive of the quintet is the 1999 Grenache Old Vines Clarendon. For a Bratasiuk wine, this has surprisingly modest alcohol (13.5%), an evolved dark garnet color, and notes of Provençal herbs, spice box, cherries, and balsam wood. It tastes like a well-made Côtes du Rhône, with medium to full body and a supple texture. Drink it over the next 3–4 years. More Châteauneuf-du-Pape-like is the 1999 Grenache Old Vines Kangarilla Vineyard (14.5% alcohol). This wine ratchets up the level of volume, depth, and length, offering kirsch, black raspberry, and cherry notes intermixed with roasted herbs and balsam wood notes. The wine is textured, full-bodied, and offers a plum/ruby color. I would opt for drinking this over the next 6–8 years.

Lovers of flamboyant Grenache will get a blast from the exotic, over-the-top 1999 Grenache Old Vines Blewitt Springs Vineyard (14.5% alcohol). This wine has jammy, raspberry notes intermixed with notes of peach/apricot, suggesting ripe fruit. The wine is full-bodied, powerful, super-concentrated, and coats the mouth with enviable levels of glycerin and sweet fruit. It is long, luscious, and a total hedonistic turn-on. Drink it over the next decade. While you are drinking your Blewitt Springs, Clarendon, or Kangarilla, you might still have to wait a few years for the 1999 Grenache Old Vines Hickinbotham to come around (14% alcohol). This is another expression of Grenache, exhibiting more earth, notes of soy sauce, and a sardine-like quality to its herb-tinged, black cherry fruit character. In the mouth, it is tightly structured, with more tannin, mineral, pepper, and spice. The wine is outstanding, but completely different than the other *cuvées*. I would opt for giving it 1–2 years of cellaring and drinking it over the following decade.

The 1999 Grenache Old Vines Romas Vineyard suggests new oak, the only Grenache to exhibit some toasty smells. In addition to that, there is the dense, concentrated, kirsch and raspberry notes intermixed with chewy, ripe, full-bodied, heavy, high alcohol (14.5%) flavors.

Full-bodied, with admirable structure, weight, and volume, it will be even better in another 1–2 years, and last for 10–12 years. The 1998 Grenache Old Vines Clarendon Vineyard reveals characteristics such as kirsch, spicy pepper, a touch of peachlike fruit from its overripeness, and the dried herb, earthy concoction the French call *garrigue*. Full-bodied and ripe, with a fleshy, high-alcohol personality, this voluptuous Châteauneuf-du-Pape look-alike should drink well for 8–10 years.

The 1998 Grenache Old Vines Kangarilla Vineyard exhibits a medium ruby color, a peppery, *garrigue*-scented nose, soft, earthy, medium- to full-bodied flavors, moderate tannin, and a rich, well-concentrated finish. It is not as fleshy, expressive, or explosive as its Clarendon Vineyard sibling. Drink it over the next 10–12 years. The dark ruby-colored 1998 Grenache Old Vines Blewitt Springs Vineyard offers copious quantities of raspberry and cherry jam intermixed with spicy wood, earth, herb, and pepper scents. Heady, high alcohol gives the wine additional levels of glycerin, which coat the palate and teeth. Dense, chewy, and ripe, this large-scaled wine can be drunk now or cellared for 10–12 years.

There are six selections of Shiraz, which are aged in 100% new French oak prior to being bottled with minimum clarification. All of these wines merit outstanding reviews, the 1999s being as superb as the 1998s. The 1999 Shiraz Liandra Vineyard (14.5% alcohol) is a sexy, ripe, multitextured wine with superb fruit, and gorgeous notes of black fruits, saddle leather, and spice. A delicious Shiraz to drink now, it should hold nicely for 10–15 years.

The opaque purple 1999 Shiraz Moritz Vineyard reveals plenty of earth, smoke, and spice in addition to both red and black fruits. The wine is full-bodied, deep, and slightly more fruit-driven, sweeter, with more elevated glycerin than the Liandra. The sweetness (from extract and ripeness, not sugar) is impressive and the wine difficult to resist, even at such a youthful age. Drink it over the next decade.

Readers looking for a more restrained style should check out the lower-key 1999 Shiraz Brookman Vineyard. With 13.5% alcohol, modest for a Clarendon Hills, this dark ruby/purple wine offers a spicy nose of black fruits intermixed with ketchup and vanilla. The wine is excellent, full-bodied, pure, ripe, and impressive. It is more measured and elegant than its two predecessors. Notes of new saddle leather, earth, truffle, smoke, black cherry, and blackberry emerge from the dense purple-colored 1999 Shiraz Hickinbotham Vineyard. It also reveals more new oak in the aromatics. On the palate, it is tannic, closed, and structured. There is a lot going on, but the wine should keep for 12–15 years.

Possibly the most concentrated and unctuously textured of these wines is the 1999 Shiraz Piggott Range Vineyard. A touch of subtle mint emerges along with blackberry liqueur notes intermixed with pepper, melted asphalt, and toast. Viscous, super-concentrated, and moderately tannic, this is a massive Shiraz, particularly in view of the vintage. It came in at 14.5% alcohol and should be cellared for 1–2 years. Anticipated maturity: now–2016.

The dark ruby/purple-colored 1998 Shiraz Liandra Vineyard exhibits beautiful, sweet, blackberry fruit intertwined with pepper, saddle leather, and spice. Rhône-like in its aromatics, this rich, full-bodied, compelling Shiraz displays low acidity as well as a fleshy, succulent mouth-feel. It should drink well for 10–12 years.

The black/purple 1998 Shiraz Hickinbotham Vineyard also reveals extraordinary intensity, but is less precocious and supple than the Liandra. The Hickinbotham exhibits smoky cassis, blackberry, melted asphalt, and toasty oak aromas, purity of fruit, an earthy, peppery character, and massive extract and richness. Drink this blockbuster Shiraz over the next 12 years.

One of the most Hermitage-like wines from Clarendon Hills is the 1998 Shiraz Brookman Vineyard. With a larger-than-life personality, high extraction, opaque purple color, dense, concentrated, peppery, cassis, mineral, and licorice-scented nose, full body, an unctuous texture, and spectacular finish, this superb effort can be drunk now as well as over the next 15–20 years. More closed but exceptionally impressive is the 1998 Shiraz Piggott Range

Vineyard. Exhibiting less revealing aromas than its peers, with coaxing some mint-tinged blackberry fruit emerges. Extremely powerful, with remarkable purity, intensity, and extraction, this Shiraz should keep for 15–20 years.

The limited-production Astralis (450 cases) is entirely made from Shiraz and aged in 100% new French oak. Massive and alcoholic, yet closed, the opaque purple-colored 1999 Astralis reveals abundant quantities of new oak, concentrated blackberry fruit, huge levels of glycerin and concentration, and admirable purity as well as symmetry. It is a gigantic Shiraz that easily competes with the finest wines of Australia. The 1999 requires 3–4 years of patience. Like its predecessors, it should have a prodigious aging potential of 20–30 years.

Closed but enormously constituted, the 1998 Astralis boasts an opaque purple color as well as a sweet mineral, licorice, blackberry- and blueberry-scented nose. This full-bodied, majestic wine is more restrained and subtle than previous efforts. The wine has soaked up the wood beautifully and is dominated by its fruit, glycerin, and high extract. Little complexity has yet emerged, but this is once again a compelling effort that clearly demonstrates what noninterventionalistic winemaking can produce with low-yielding, dry farmed Shiraz vines. Anticipated maturity: 2005–2025.

CLASSIC McLAREN (McLAREN VALE)

1999	Grenache	D	87
1999	Grenache La Testa	E	86?
1998	Grenache La Testa	E	91
1998	Grenache Reserve La Testa	E	85?
1999	La Testa Blend	E	90
1997	Shiraz La Testa	E	98+

The 1999 Grenache, made from 40- to 60-year-old vines, is very good, with plenty of black cherry fruit intermixed with some pepper and roasted notes. The wine shows good texture, purity, and a medium to full body. The Grenache La Testa emerge from 40- to 70-year-old vines that yielded an average of 1.5 tons of fruit per acre. Average production, sadly, is 150 cases annually. The 1999 Grenache La Testa should have been significantly better, but for some reason came across almost too structured and tannic, although there were notes of kirsch along with some pepper and spice. However, the wine's toughness and austerity may be problematic for future aging. Anticipated maturity: now–2010. The dark ruby-colored 1998 Grenache La Testa exhibits a knockout nose of sweet vanilla intermixed with jammy black raspberries and kirsch. Deep, pure, expansive, and fleshy, this is a hedonistic wine to drink over the next decade. The 1998 Grenache Reserve La Testa (only 100 cases produced) tasted tightly knit and muscular, with a dense ruby/purple color, hints of sweet strawberry and kirschlike fruit, but is burdened down by excessive wood and tannin. The 1998 Grenache Reserve and 1999 Grenache La Testa both taste as if they may have spent too long in wood, but perhaps I just caught them in an unflattering period of development.

The one outstanding wine from Classic McLaren is the 1999 La Testa Blend, a typically Australian concoction of 52% Grenache, 41% Shiraz, and 7% Cabernet Sauvignon (70% aged in French oak and the rest in American casks). The wine shows a dense purple color and a big, flamboyant, smoky, black currant, plum, and blackberry-scented nose with noticeable vanilla. Full-bodied, chewy, and full, a multilayered texture, good spice, and an exceptional finish certainly made this the most impressive of the Classic McLaren offerings. Approximately 350 cases were produced. Anticipated maturity: now–2012.

Readers looking for a clone of the famed Clarendon Hills luxury *cuvée* of 100% Shiraz called Astralis can find it in the 1997 Shiraz La Testa. This fabulous effort is one of the great wines from a vintage that has nowhere near the overall quality of 1996 or 1998. Nevertheless, this is a profound, prodigiously rich wine with a saturated black/purple color and knockout aromas of burning charcoal fire, jammy blackberries, cassis, and melted asphalt. Extremely full-bodied, with a viscous texture and high alcohol, this enormously endowed wine will improve for 10–15 years and last three decades.

CLAYFIELD (VICTORIA)

| 1999 Shiraz Grampians | D | 91 |

Aged in 85% new American oak and 15% one-year French oak and bottled unfiltered, the supple, creamy-textured, ripe, dense 1999 Shiraz Grampians shows plenty of layers of fruit, considerable glycerin, a big, peppery, black fruit–scented nose, and a low-acid, plump, lush finish. Drink it now and over the next 12 years.

CLONAKILLA (SOUTH AUSTRALIA)

1998 Shiraz	D	87
1999 Shiraz/Viognier	D	90
1998 Shiraz/Viognier	D	92

Production of the Shiraz/Viognier blend averages 300 cases annually. This wine, made primarily of Shiraz (95%), also contains a small percentage of Viognier (5%), which is discernible in its aromatics. The elegant, complex, and fragrant 1999 Shiraz/Viognier offers up telltale blackberry and cassis, but also a touch of apricot and white flowers due to its Viognier component. The wine is medium- to full-bodied, with supple texture, silky tannin, and a fleshy, moderately weighty feel. Already delicious, it is best drunk over the next 4 years.

The sexy, ostentatious 1998 Shiraz/Viognier exhibits a dark ruby/purple color, full body, and an explosive bouquet of black fruits and Viognier's apricot/peach component, this dense, structured, pure, concentrated wine is reminiscent of a French Côte Rotie as well as the Australian Shiraz/Viognier blend made by the Torbreck winery. Drink it over the next decade.

The pure 1998 Shiraz reveals a deep ruby/purple color, a straightforward, spicy, berry-scented nose, medium to full body, a soft texture, and pleasant, uninspiring, but satisfying levels of fruit, glycerin, and body. Drink it over the next 3–4 years.

CLOS CLARE (CLARE VALLEY)

| 1999 Shiraz | C | 89 |

Two renowned Australian wine-makers, Jeffrey Grosset and David Powell, work at Clos Clare, with Grosset turning out a dry Riesling (not reviewed here because it is meant to be drunk within 1–2 years of the vintage) and Powell the Shiraz. The 1999 Shiraz is something of a fruit bomb, with a deep ruby/purple color, low acidity, supple texture, and copious quantities of blackberry and cassis fruit. The wine would have received an outstanding rating, but it is just not all that complex. However, it is a delicious, opulent Shiraz meant to be drunk over the next 5–6 years.

CORIOLE WINES (McLAREN VALE)

1997 Cabernet Sauvignon	D	87
1999 Lalla Rookh Old Vine Grenache	D	88
1998 Lalla Rookh Old Vine Grenache	D	89
1997 Lalla Rookh Old Vine Grenache	D	89
1998 Mary Kathleen	D	94
1997 Mary Kathleen	D	89
1999 Redstone	C	89
1998 Redstone	C	90
1997 Redstone	C	88
1999 Shiraz	D	87
1998 Shiraz	D	90
1997 Shiraz	D	90

1998 Shiraz Lloyd Reserve	E	92
1997 Shiraz Lloyd Reserve	E	90
1996 Shiraz Lloyd Reserve	E	94

Coriole, founded in 1967, has long been known for its Shiraz, but their entire portfolio is extremely well made. The least expensive red of the series is the Redstone blend of Shiraz, Grenache, Cabernet Sauvignon, and Merlot. Given today's wine market, this is a very good value. The dominant varietals are Shiraz and Grenache.

The opaque purple 1999 Redstone displays a sweet nose of blood, meat, leather, pepper, and black cherry and currant liqueur. The wine is medium- to full-bodied, soft, and best drunk over the next 4–5 years. Also opaque purple, the 1998 Redstone is riper and fuller, with more volume and chewiness. Offering abundant quantities of spicy blackberry and cherry fruit with a touch of oak in the background, it will drink well for 7–8 years. The 1997 Redstone reveals a saturated ruby/purple color in addition to a robust, earthy, meaty, gutsy personality, peppery, leathery black fruits, good density and richness, and a ripe finish. Though a little lacking in complexity and softness, it is well made.

The 1999 and 1998 Lalla Rookh Old Vine Grenache, primarily Grenache with small quantities of Shiraz, are impressive efforts. The 1999 is more elegant, with less power but beautifully balanced fruit (sweet black cherries intermixed with pepper). The 1998 reveals a chewier, fuller-bodied, more muscular style with additional depth and structure. Both wines, which possess copious amounts of pepper and sweet cherry fruit, are best drunk during their first 8–10 years of life. I hope I didn't underrate the 1997 Lalla Rookh Old Vine Grenache. Displaying an unmistakable southern Rhône character, it offers scents of crushed black pepper, kirsch, and cherries. The wine boasts a big, full-bodied, expansive palate with abundant earth, smoke, dried herb, and red fruit flavors. The wood is barely noticeable. Produced largely from 75-year-old Grenache vines, it should drink well for 8–9 years.

Fairly light in style, but still delicious is the 1999 Shiraz, an elegant, richly fruity wine to enjoy over the next 5 years. Readers looking for a textbook McLaren Vale Shiraz should check out Coriole's 1998 Shiraz, an opaque black/purple effort offering aromas of blueberries, blackberry liqueur, pepper, graphite, and licorice. Ripe, full-bodied, and fruit-driven, it should drink well for 10 years. The outstanding, opaque purple 1997 Shiraz offers copious quantities of blackberry, pepper, glycerin, and extract complemented by low acidity and a plush, opulent style. Anticipated maturity: now–2010.

The dark garnet/purple 1997 Cabernet Sauvignon's prune, overripé plum, and cassis aromas are followed by a thick, jammy wine that is close to being over the top. However, its softness and accessible style make for a tasty, though perhaps controversial Cabernet. Anticipated maturity: now–2010.

Coriole's flagship wines are their limited-production Mary Kathleen (80% Cabernet Sauvignon, 20% Merlot) and the Lloyd Reserve Shiraz, made from 60-year-old vines and aged in both American and French oak. The 1998 Mary Kathleen is a spectacular, opaque purple effort with tremendous aging potential. It offers a promising nose of cassis, cedar, blackberries, vanilla, and spice. Full-bodied, with fabulous purity and symmetry, and a mouth-filling, palate-staining style without any heaviness or astringency, it should drink well for two decades. Very impressive! Although tightly knit, the 1997 Mary Kathleen is elegant, with a medium deep red/purple color and a spicy, black currant, berry, and tobacco-scented bouquet. The wine possesses full body and outstanding intensity and richness. Drink it over the following 10–15 years. Another superb effort is the 1998 Shiraz Lloyd Reserve. Although big, fat, brawny, and muscular, it reveals polish and refinement for its size. An opaque purple color is accompanied by telltale blackberry liqueur intermixed with spicy oak, low acidity, abundant glycerin, and a chewy, concentrated, long finish. Anticipated maturity: now–2015. Made in a different style, the 1997 Shiraz Lloyd Reserve exhibits a charred-oak nose, a deep ruby/purple color, and notes of soy, black cherries, black currants, earth, and tar. Lighter than the 1998, more developed and evolved, it is best drunk over the next 10 years. The spectacular 1996 Shiraz Lloyd Reserve boasts a thick-looking, dark purple/garnet color as well as lavish quantities of toasty American oak mixed with blackberry liqueur. The wine possesses fabulous concentration, loads of glycerin, full body, low acidity, and a blockbuster 40+-second finish. A huge, chewy, surprisingly harmonious, mouth-filling Syrah, it should drink well for 15+ years.

CRANEFORD (BAROSSA)

1999 Shiraz	D	88

Aged in a combination of French and American oak, the 200 cases of this unfined, unfiltered 1999 Shiraz exhibit deep ruby/plum color and a sweet, fat nose of jammy black fruits intermixed with smoke and toasty oak. The wine is a hedonistic, glycerin-imbued fruit bomb. Drink it over the next 4 years.

GARRY CRITTENDEN (KING VALLEY, VICTORIA)

1998 "I" Barbera	C	89
1998 "I" Sangiovese	C	89

Some of California's underachievers with Italian-inspired varietal wines should take a page out of Garry Crittenden's book. He is consistently turning out interesting wines from Italian varietals. The smoky, cherry-scented, ripe, medium-bodied, ripe, and fruity 1998 "I" Sangiovese reveals a subtle dosage of wood. Flavorful and cleanly made, it should drink well for 2 years. The exceptional 1998 "I" Barbera could easily pass for a top-notch Piedmontese Barbera, given its strawberry jam, tomato skin, sweet fruit–driven personality, medium to full body, tangy acidity, and nicely layered, pure finish. Drink it over the next 2–3 years.

CULLEN (MARGARET RIVER)

1998 Cabernet Sauvignon/Merlot	D	87
1997 Cabernet Sauvignon/Merlot	D	87
1996 Cabernet Sauvignon/Merlot	D	86
1999 Diana Madeline	E	88

The proprietary red wine blend 1999 Diana Madeline is a blend of 70% Cabernet Sauvignon, 20% Merlot, and 5% Cabernet Franc (95%). Its dark ruby/purple color is followed by sweet aromas of red currants, cedar, plums, earth, and spice. Stylish, elegant, and European in its orientation, it should drink well for a decade. By Australian standards, it is a measured, restrained red wine. The 1998 Cabernet Sauvignon/Merlot (60% Cabernet Sauvignon, 25% Merlot, and 15% Cabernet Franc) is a fatter, fleshier, more tannic, substantial effort. Youthful, with notes of red and black currants, dried herbs, tobacco, and subtle wood, this medium-bodied, elegant 1998 possesses good underlying acidity. It should drink well for 7–8 years.

Both the 1996 and 1997 Cabernet Sauvignon/Merlot blends exhibit elegant, austere personalities, with moderate quantities of black currant fruit. Both are made in a restrained, austere, Bordeaux-like style. Some sweet oak is present (about 80% new oak casks are used), and the wines suggest longevity, although I am not sure the requisite concentration is present for aging beyond 10–12 years. These are well-made, unflashy, polite offerings.

DALWHINNIE (MOONAMBEL)

1997 Shiraz	D	88
1996 Shiraz Eagle Pyrenees	D	90+

Crisp acidity underlies and supports the concentrated cassis and blackberry fruit of the dark ruby/purple 1997 Shiraz. Tightly knit, medium-bodied, dense, and pure, this wine has now emerged from its cloak of tannin and should age nicely for 7–8 years.

Even more impressive is the exquisite 1996 Shiraz Eagle Pyrenees. Aged completely in French oak, this medium- to full-bodied, vibrant, racy Shiraz possesses uncanny elegance and style for this grape, which usually turns out blockbuster heavyweights. Good acidity gives the wine freshness and delineation. Smoky oak is intertwined with blackberry and black currant fruit flavors in this dense, concentrated, backward wine. As it sits in the glass, pepper, cherry liqueur, and roasted herbs emerge. Anticipated maturity: now–2014.

DOG RIDGE (McLAREN VALE)

1999	Shiraz	D	87

There are over 1,000 cases of this 100% Shiraz, aged for 18 months in both new and older French and American wood. The 1999 Shiraz shows a soft yet elegant style with supple black fruits, medium body, good purity, but an ultimately foursquare, somewhat one-dimensional personality. However, the fruit is undeniably charming, making this wine an attractive albeit expensive offering to consume over the next 4–5 years.

DUTSCHKE (BAROSSA)

1998	Shiraz Oscar Semmler	E	90+
1998	Shiraz Saint Jakobi	D	89
NV	The Tawny 25-year-old Port	E	96
1998	Willow Bend	D	87

The Dutschke family is the fifth generation in Barossa. Production of these wines ranges from small lots such as 180 cases of the Tawny 25-year-old Port and 1998 Shiraz Oscar Semmler to nearly 800 cases of the Willow Bend and Saint Jakobi Shiraz.

The 1998 Willow Bend has a dark plum/purple color, loads of fruit, glycerin, and ripeness. Not a great deal of complexity, but this is a lush, consumer-friendly styled wine that is a blend of 47% Merlot, 33% Shiraz, and the rest Cabernet Sauvignon. The focus of the wine is its attractively fruity and pleasant personality. Anticipated maturity: now–2009.

For a slightly more peppery and fleshy, larger-sized wine, the dark ruby/purple-colored 1998 Shiraz Saint Jakobi reveals plenty of smoke, earth, and black fruits. A sweet, earthy entry on the palate is followed by full body and a layered finish with low acidity, ripe tannin, and easy accessibility. It should drink well for 8–10 years. The complex, saturated purple-colored 1998 Shiraz Oscar Semmler emanates from 25-year-old vines. Aged 24 months in new French oak, this opulent, full-bodied wine has a distinctive nose of grilled Italian sausage intermixed with blackberry, pepper, vanilla, and smoke. Chewy, powerful, and rich, with moderate tannin and a youthful exuberance, this large-scaled wine (15% alcohol) will be better with 2–3 years of cellaring. It should drink well for 18–20 years.

Readers looking for a prodigious fortified tawny Port should check out the limited quantities of the The Tawny 25-year-old Port. Made from a mysterious blend of different grapes, this stuff is fabulous. With considerable amber at the edge, a spectacular nose of liquefied caramel intermixed with coffee, kirsch, and even floral notes, this full-bodied, moderately sweet, dense, velvety-styled Tawny is spectacular. It is not going to improve, but will certainly keep for at least another decade.

E AND E (BAROSSA)

1996	Shiraz Black Pepper	D	88

Sweet American oak combined with jammy, peppery, blackberry fruit results in an attractive introduction to this medium- to full-bodied 1996 Shiraz Black Pepper. While not a block-buster, it is a flavorful, concentrated offering to enjoy over the next 4–5 years.

ELDERTON (BAROSSA)

1998	Cabernet Sauvignon	C	90+
1997	Command Shiraz	E	92

1996	Command Shiraz	E	93
1997	CSM Proprietary Red	C	92
1996	CSM Proprietary Red	C	90
1997	Merlot	C	92
1998	Shiraz	C	93
1997	Shiraz	C	93

In the past, Elderton's wines have been love-it-or-leave-it and controversial. Some tasters thought the oak (American and French) was excessive, but an equal number found it compelling. Elderton's latest releases possess far better integrated oak, so some of the complaints leveled by critics may no longer be justified. What these wines have always possessed, and still do, are huge quantities of fruit, glycerin, and personality. With a more subtle integration of the oak, I think Elderton has achieved better wines. The 1998 Cabernet Sauvignon is a super wine that can be drunk now or cellared for 12–15 years. Its saturated black purple color offers up gorgeous notes of sweet, jammy cassis with subtle, smoky wood in the background. The wine exhibits terrific ripeness, an unctuous, full-bodied texture, superb fruit, and a long, lusty finish. This in-your-face, hedonistic, fruit bomb should become more civilized and delineated as it ages. Moreover, the oak is complementary rather than blatant. Bravo!

The superlatives continue with the spectacular 1998 Shiraz. This is another fabulous value. This wine delivers explosive levels of glycerin, and concentrated blackberry and cherry fruit in a sweet, beautifully seamless, ostentatious style of Shiraz, with nicely integrated wood and a huge blockbuster finish. This is teeth-staining, mouthcoating Shiraz, the likes of which can be made nowhere else in the world but from old vines in Barossa. Drink it over the next 10 years. The 1997 Shiraz performed splendidly. This opaque purple wine offers up plenty of sweet blackberry and cassis fruit with a touch of overripe cherries, smoke, and charcoal. This multidimensional, layered, luscious, low-acid, toasty Shiraz is made in an obvious, fat, hedonistic style. Drink it over the next 5–6 years.

The CSMs are blends of 60% Cabernet Sauvignon, 30% Cabernet Franc, and 10% Merlot. My tasting notes for the impressive 1997 CSM started with the words "a whore of a wine." It recalls some of the older Eldertons. While it offers huge amounts of toasty oak in the nose, it is better integrated than young Elderton wines have been in the past. A voluptuous, lusty wine with loads of glycerin, fat, and concentrated fruit as well as decadent levels of pleasure (14.5% alcohol). I doubt there are many Puritans among my readers, but should there be any, they may want to stay clear of this wine. It is so outrageously rich and fruity, it should be a controlled substance. Look for it to drink beautifully young, but age for at least 10–12 years.

Elderton's 1996 CSM Proprietary Red is a glorious, fruit-driven wine with lavish quantities of smoky new oak, dense, thick, juicy, chocolate, blackberry and cherry fruit flavors, low acidity, and a fat, ostentatious, showy midsection and finish. This sumptuous, explosively fruity/oaky wine is not subtle, but it does offer thrilling hedonistic levels of fruit. Drink it over the next 5–6 years. Another blast of fruit, glycerin, smoky oak, though again better integrated and more subtle than in past renditions, is the 1997 Merlot, offering up notes of espresso, coffee, chocolate, and black cherry liqueur in a full-bodied, unctuously textured, lavishly fat, nearly over-the-top style. Its low acidity and sweet tannin suggest it will provide the most pleasure during its first 5–8 years of life.

Elderton's top *cuvée* is their Command Shiraz. These wines see much more French oak and are more structured, with even higher levels of extract as well as tannin. Although not as approachable as the less expensive wines, they are built for 15–20 years of cellaring. The opaque purple 1997 Command Shiraz offers abundant creamy new oak in the nose, gorgeous crème de cassis aromas and flavors, a structured, moderately tannic, full-bodied, powerful, muscular style, and a finish that lasts for 35+ seconds. Anticipated maturity: now–2015. The 1996 Command Shiraz is a bigger, fuller, more powerful offering. While its aromas and flavors are similar to the 1997, there is more to it. A muscular, powerful version of the 1997, it will drink well before 2018.

RALPH FOWLER (LIMESTONE COAST)

NV	Old and Rare Muscat	E	99
1998	Shiraz	E	89
1997	Shiraz	E	89

Ralph Fowler was chosen by Michel Chapoutier to produce that Rhône Valley firm's Australian wines. Fowler has left Chapoutier to start his own label, and these three offerings are the results. Both the 1997 and 1998 Shiraz are mainstream wines with creamy American oak, excellent concentration, and abundant quantities of sweet, peppery, blackberry, and cassis flavors. The textures are supple, and the wines are pure, but both lack complexity and the extra flavor dimensions present in many of the wines from importer Dan Philips. Nevertheless, they are top-notch efforts produced from 30-year-old Shiraz vines cropped at two tons per acre. Anticipated maturity: now–2015. Fowler's nonvintage Old and Rare Muscat is virtually perfect. The material for this wine averages 30 years in age and was kept in small casks until bottling. It exhibits a brown/amber color, the thickness of maple syrup, and unbelievable levels of richness, concentration, and perfume. I cannot imagine any thicker, more concentrated dessert wines than this example except those from William Chambers and Trevor Jones. Fowler's Muscat is almost too rich to drink. A half bottle of this old Muscat will serve 20–30 people! Moreover, it should last for another 40–50 years.

FOX CREEK (McLAREN VALE)

1998	Cabernet Sauvignon Reserve	D	92+
1997	Cabernet Sauvignon Reserve	D	89
1999	Grenache/Shiraz	C	84?
1998	Grenache/Shiraz	D	90
1999	Merlot	D	86
1998	Merlot	D	90
1999	Shiraz Reserve	E	92
1998	Shiraz Reserve	E	98
1999	Shiraz Short Row	D	90
1999	Shiraz/Cabernet JSM	D	89
1998	Shiraz/Cabernet JSM	D	96
NV	Vixen Sparkling Red	C	85?

The largest production of any Fox Creek wine is their 2,500 cases of Shiraz/Cabernet JSM. A blend of Shiraz, Cabernet Franc, and Cabernet Sauvignon, it is aged 12–14 months in one- to three-year-old American oak casks. The 1999 JSM has an opaque ruby/purple color and an intense nose of black cherries and cassis, with noteworthy coffee, vanilla character in the background. In the mouth, this medium- to full-bodied, soft wine introduces some blue- and blackberry fruit to the mix. It is a fruit-driven, up-front style of wine to drink over the next 4–6 years. Readers looking for superintense, ripe wines will be thrilled with the 1998 Shiraz/Cabernet JSM. Opaque purple-colored, with a sumptuous nose of black fruits and spicy new oak, it is explosive on the palate. With an unctuous texture, a full-bodied personality, and intense black cherry/cassis flavors, this is a sensationally layered effort with a 45-second finish. This kind of wine can only be produced in selected areas of California and Australia. It is the antithesis of the polite, restrained, austere style of Bordeaux for which France is so famous. Look for it to drink well young, yet last for 15–20 years.

There are 700 cases of the Merlot, made from young vines, tiny yields of 1.6 tons per acre and aged in new and old French oak. The 1999 Merlot reveals a compact, elegant style typical of the vintage. With pure, ripe, smoky, black cherry fruit, medium body, and an elegant, rather delicate finish, this is a restrained effort for Fox Creek. Drink it over the next 4–5 years. Tannic, but also exhibiting lavish quantities of toasty oak along with equally copious amounts of black cherry and berry fruit, is the 1998 Merlot. This wine is somewhat mono-lithic, but the terrific intensity, rich fruit, and full-bodied generosity are to be admired. It should last 12+ years.

The 1999 Grenache/Shiraz (65%/35%) tasted austere, lean, and narrowly constructed. The color is dark ruby/purple, but the wine was hard and difficult to penetrate. I don't know whether I caught it in an ungenerous stage, but it seemed mediocre. Anticipated maturity: 2003–2010. The 1998 Grenache/Shiraz (70% and 30% respectively) performed better. Once past its black/ruby/purple color, creamy, oaky notes emerge along with ultraripe cherries and assorted black fruits. This hedonistic, voluptuously textured, spicy, fruit-dominated wine has no hard edges, and fills the mouth with terrific intensity yet good balance and freshness. Drink it over the next 4–6 years.

The 1999 Shiraz Short Row (1,500 cases, aged primarily in new American wood) has a dense black/purple color and a sweet nose of blackberry, tar, pepper, and vanilla. The wine is rich, full-bodied, dense, pure, and chewy. It seems tightly knit at present, but one or more years of cellaring should be beneficial, and the wine should last 10–12 years.

The impressive Shiraz Reserve is a 2,000-case *cuvée* aged 14 months in new American oak. The 1999 is a dense purple color, with a sweet, almost blackberry liqueur nose, and smoke, licorice, and oak in the background. Jammy and rich, with huge body, good purity, adequate acidity, and a long finish, this is an impressive, surprisingly large-scaled 1999. It should age well for 10–16 years. Nearly perfect, the opaque black/purple 1998 Shiraz Re-serve plays to the great strength of Australia—powerful, naturally textured, superrich wines that are big and chewy. Exceptionally rich and explosive, with great purity as well as re-markable symmetry and overall balance for such massiveness, this blockbuster can be drunk now or cellared for 12–15 years. Make no doubt about it, this Shiraz will elicit more than a few "wows" in any tasting, blind or otherwise.

Fox Creek produces 1,500 cases of Cabernet Sauvignon Reserve annually. This wine is aged in 100% new French oak. The brilliant 1998 is opaque black/purple-colored, with an explosive nose of licorice, blackberry, cassis, tar, and new oak. This huge, ripe wine is lay-ered, thick, smoky, and concentrated, a true blockbuster from this superb vintage. Antici-pated maturity: now–2018. Remarkably civilized, even restrained by the standards of Fox Creek, the 1997 Cabernet Sauvignon Reserve is clearly the product of a lighter vintage. De-spite its elegant personality, there is nothing wimpy about this wine. A dark ruby/purple color is followed by an attractive smoky, black currant, and toasty-scented nose. Medium-bodied, with excellent balance, and soft tannin, it should be consumed over the next decade.

Finally, the nonvintage Vixen Sparkling Red is a bubbly blend of 52% Shiraz, 34% Caber-net Franc, and 14% Cabernet Sauvignon. Distinctive but eccentric, it has a deep ruby/purple color and a heavy, leaden style, but it is loaded with fruit. Everyone should try one of these sparkling red wines from Australia, though they seem more appropriate for attention-getting party wines than for matching with food. Anticipated maturity: *now*.

FRANKLAND ESTATE (WESTERN AUSTRALIA)

1997	Cabernet Franc/Merlot Olmo's Reward	C	89
1996	Cabernet Franc/Merlot Olmo's Reward	C	90
1998	Shiraz Isolation Ridge	C	90?

Be forewarned: these distinctive wines are totally different from any other Australian wines I have tasted. What sets them apart is an underlying, singular, graphitelike character that gives them an earthy, *terroir*-driven quality in both the aromatics and flavors of these wines. They are well made, but less fruit-driven than many Australian wines.

I loved the 1998 Shiraz Isolation Ridge. However, it is not for everybody. A dense purple color is followed by a distinctive earthiness, a touch of cow manure, and dense peppery, blackberry, cherry fruit. The wine is full-bodied, dense, chewy, and idiosyncratic but fascinating. This wine should drink well for at least 10–12 years.

One of the most intriguing wines from Frankland Estate is their Bordeaux look-alike, the Cabernet Franc/Merlot blend called Olmo's Reward, which also comprises a touch of Petit Verdot, Malbec, and Cabernet Sauvignon. The classy, graceful 1997 exhibits notes of chocolate, cedarwood, menthol, spice box, and red and black fruits. The attack is savory, the mid-palate medium-bodied and moderately tannic, and the finish complex and long. The wine is accessible but made in a restrained, medium-weight style that is totally unusual for Australia. Drink it over the next decade. The 1996 Cabernet Franc/Merlot Olmo's Reward is an intensely aromatic, spicy, Bordeaux-inspired wine with a dusty, new oak, red and black currant–scented nose. As it sits in the glass, berry and cedar aromas emerge, along with some of the telltale earthiness. Medium bodied, with decent acidity, moderate tannin, and a stylish, complex personality, this intriguing wine could easily pass for a top-class Bordeaux in a blind tasting. Anticipated maturity: now–2015.

THE GATEKEEPER (McLAREN VALE)

1998 Cabernet Sauvignon Reserve	D	89+
1998 Shiraz Reserve	D	92

Produced by Simon Hackett, the 1998 Gatekeeper Shiraz Reserve (a selection of his best *cuveés*) is aged in 60% American oak and 40% French oak, half of which is new. The vines are claimed to be 50–75 years old. This is superb, full-blooded, brawny, massive Australian Shiraz at its best. The wine is huge, chewy, deep, and thick. There are notes of black fruits, earth, asphalt, smoke, and pepper. Drink it over the next 12–15 years. More tightly knit as well as restrained and elegant, with considerable tannin, is the 1998 Cabernet Sauvignon Reserve. This wine, which comes from a 76-year-old parcel of Cabernet, exhibits good tobacco-tinged, black currant fruit mixed with some spicy wood. The tannin seems high, which may raise cause for concern if it does not become better integrated. Anticipated maturity: now–2016.

GEMTREE VINEYARDS (McLAREN VALE)

1999 Shiraz	D	90
1998 Shiraz	D	87

This is one of the few wineries where I found the 1999 to be a better wine than the 1998. Both wines come from 30-year-old Shiraz vines that are partially used for the famous Balmoral Shiraz made by Rosemount. There are 500 cases of this wine that is aged in American oak, of which 60% is new. The 1999 Shiraz displays notes of melted tar, coffee, and vanilla, beautiful fruit, sweet tannin, and more density and length than the 1998. The 1998 boasts a dark ruby/purple color, a minty cassis nose, full body, good ripeness and flavor, but a one-dimensional personality. While it possesses fruit, depth, and intensity, there is little complexity. Both wines should be drunk in their exuberant youth—over the next 4–5 years.

GENDERS (McLAREN PARK)

1998 Cabernet Sauvignon	E	87
1976 Port	EE	?
1998 Shiraz	E	86?

The 1998 Cabernet Sauvignon is a very good to excellent wine with textbook weedy, black currant flavors intermixed with some spicy wood. The wine shows good purity and a judicious use of new oak. It can be drunk now or cellared for up to a decade.

The 1998 Shiraz is somewhat monolithic and less expressive, but possesses plenty of weight, ripeness, and blackberry fruit infused with smoke and tar. It should drink well for 7–8 years. It is a shame the wine was not more expressive the day I tasted it.

The 1976 Genders Port, a fortified Shiraz/Cabernet Sauvignon blend, is no doubt a contro-versial wine. The wine has unctuous texture but a pruny, raisiny nose, and somewhat rustic flavors. It is certainly not going to make anyone forget Portuguese vintage ports, nor does it compete with the best from Australia.

GLAETZER (BAROSSA VALLEY)

1997 Cabernet Sauvignon/Malbec	D	89
1997 Shiraz	D	92
1998 Shiraz The Bishop	D	88

A saturated dense ruby/purple color leads to a big, rich, chewy 1998 Shiraz The Bishop with fine balance and overall harmony. It offers abundant quantities of blackberry/cassis flavors, and a touch of pepper and spicy new oak. The wine's texture, purity, and finish are all im-pressive. Already drinking well, it will age nicely for a decade. A blockbuster, massive wine, the dense ruby/purple-colored 1997 Shiraz tips the scales at 14% alcohol. Full-bodied, with low acidity, terrific intensity, and explosive levels of fruit and glycerin, this multilayered, mouth-staining Shiraz can be drunk now and over the next 12 years.

As for the more civilized, restrained, downsized 1997 Cabernet Sauvignon/Malbec, this intriguing blend offers up an open-knit floral, black raspberry, and currant-scented nose, ex-cellent richness, medium to full body, impressive ripeness and purity, and a long, supple-textured finish. If more complexity emerges, this wine could merit an outstanding review. Anticipated maturity: now–2008.

GNADENFREI (BAROSSA)

1999 Shiraz St. Michael's	D	91
1997 Shiraz St. Michael's	D	92

Tiny yields of one ton of fruit per acre, harvested at 14.5% potential alcohol from nonirri-gated old vines, and bottling without filtration after being aged in old wood represents the style of wine-maker Rolf Binder. In 1999, this resulted in a thick, full-bodied, dense, purple-colored Shiraz St. Michael's with notes of Italian sausage, bacon fat, blackberry, and cassis. Full-bodied, unctuously textured, and chewy, it offers a mouthful of blockbuster Australian Shiraz. This is classic Barossa Shiraz at its biggest and boldest. Drink it over the next 10–12 years. I know this does not make any sense, but when smelled and tasted, the 1997 Shiraz St. Michael's brought to mind the 1998 l'Evangile, a wine made from Merlot and Cabernet Franc (Gnadenfrei's 1997 is 100% Shiraz). It is a compelling, lush, Pomerol-styled Shiraz with ter-rific black raspberry fruit, full body, and soaring aromatics. Low acidity and a lush, concen-trated mouth-feel make for a seductive, majestic wine drinking experience. Enjoy this 1997 over the next 10 years. Impressive!

GRALYN (MARGARET RIVER)

1999 Cabernet Sauvignon	E	87+?
1998 Cabernet Sauvignon	E	88

A rustic style of Cabernet Sauvignon, with big, earthy, exuberant tea and currant flavors as well as sharp acidity and tough, nearly uncivilized tannin, the huge, dense, full-bodied 1999 was aged in 100% new French and American oak and bottled unfiltered. The French would call it a *vin de garde*. However, the tannin needs to become better integrated in order for it to merit a higher score. The oak is beautifully absorbed and the wine possesses monstrous lev-els of concentration and depth. If everything comes together, it will merit an outstanding score. If it doesn't, tasters will get an uncivilized mouthful of Cabernet Sauvignon. Antici-pated maturity: 2005–2015. An impressive, dark ruby/purple effort, Gralyn's 1998 Cabernet Sauvignon reveals an earthy, floral, black currant–scented bouquet. Elegant, Bordeaux-like in the mouth, with medium body, sweet fruit, nicely integrated tannin and wood, and a restrained, nicely nuanced personality, it should drink well for a decade.

GREENOCK CREEK (BAROSSA VALLEY)

1998 Cabernet Sauvignon	E	90
1995 Cabernet Sauvignon Roennfeldt Road	EEE	99
1999 Grenache Cornerstone	D	91
1998 Shiraz Apricot Block	E	94+
1998 Shiraz Creek Block	E	98+
1995 Shiraz Roennfeldt Road	EEE	100
1998 Shiraz Seven Acres	E	92

This has quickly become one of my favorite wineries, not only in Australia but in the world. Wine maker Chris Ringland, assisted by Mike Waugh, continues to turn out brilliant, blockbuster wines that demonstrate the quintessential oversized, flamboyant, in-your-face style that makes Australia's top reds so distinctive.

For starters, the 1998 Cabernet Sauvignon (100% Cabernet Sauvignon from 11-year-old vines, aged in a combination of one-year-old and new French oak) is a fruit-dominated wine with the classic cassis intermixed with a touch of herbs, a slight notion of volatile acidity, and a spicy finish. The wine is full-bodied, ripe, but at the same time elegant, particularly for a Greenock Creek wine. Anticipated maturity: 2005–2015.

Among the finest Grenache wines produced in Australia is Greenock Creek's Grenache Cornerstone, a 100% Grenache from 61-year-old vines, of yields of 2 tons of fruit per acre, and aged in one-year-old French barrels. The 1999 is an explosive wine, much like the 1998. Soft, with luxurious levels of kirsch intermixed with some spice, pepper, and berries, this supple, full-bodied wine has high levels of glycerin, gorgeously concentrated fruit, and a layered finish. It is not going to make old bones, but for drinking over the next 5–7 years, this is hedonism at its best.

The three *cuvées* of Shiraz, from the 10-year-old Seven Acres Vineyard, the 61-year-old Creek Block, and the Apricot Block, are fabulous wines. Made from a so-called difficult vintage, the 1997s are simply superb and taste as if they came from a great vintage, and the 1998s are even better. The Shiraz Creek Block is made from 62-year-old vines and aged in a combination of new and French oak. Sadly, there are only 100 cases of it. The 1998 is a near-perfect wine. This opaque, purple-colored classic shows terrific notes of beef blood, new saddle leather, blackberry liqueur, smoke, and earth. Extremely full-bodied yet seamless, with dazzling levels of extract and ripeness, this is a tour de force in winemaking, but there is too little of it. The Creek Block looks to have the potential to go 20–30 years.

The Shiraz Seven Acres is made from 12-year-old vines and aged in American oak (a combination of new and old). Although by no means a wimpish wine, it is lighter-styled than the Creek Block and has greater availability (500 cases). The 1998 is outstanding but tightly knit. An elegant wine in the context of the normally powerful Greenock Creek style, this wine exhibits dark ruby/purple color and a bouquet of black raspberries intermixed with blackberry, currant, pepper, and spicy wood. The wine is deep, full-bodied, and beautifully knit. Some tannin still needs to be resolved in the finish, but this wine should age well for 10–15 years.

A 100% Shiraz *cuvée*, the Apricot Block is made from relatively young vines (10 years). Perhaps the most backward of the 1998s, this wine shows an opaque garnet/purple color and a sweet nose of melted asphalt, smoke, blackberry, and cassis. Extremely full-bodied with great intensity, tremendous purity, and impeccable overall harmony among its rather large-scale elements (14.3% alcohol), this dense, super-extracted wine should be at its best between 2004–2020.

The 1995 Cabernet Sauvignon Roennfeldt Road is 100% Cabernet Sauvignon from 50-year-old vines. The wine was aged three years in new French oak. It has soaked up the wood beautifully. This is an unctuous, blockbuster, opaque, purple-colored wine with a classic nose of charcoal, black currants, cedar, mineral, and licorice. The wine has phenomenal intensity, great purity, a huge, ripe, yet balanced attack, a multilayered mid-palate with no hard edges, and an awesome finish. This is a terrific classic that can be approached now but ideally needs 1–2 years of cellaring. Anticipated maturity: 2004–2025. The prodigious 1995 Shiraz Roennfeldt Road also spent three years in barrel, but in this case, new American wood. Made from 50-year-old vines, it is another Syrup of Shiraz, with compelling blackberry liqueur intermixed with minerals, smoke, and truffles. Huge in the mouth but not overbearing, this wine has a finish that goes on for nearly a minute. With great purity, massive extraction, and a blockbuster, multidimensional personality, this is one of the greatest Shirazes I have ever tasted, rivaling some of the efforts from Three Rivers. Interestingly, both wines were made by the magician himself, Chris Ringland. Anticipated maturity: 2004–2030. How fun it will be to compare this wine with some of the great Penfolds Grange offerings in about 15 years' time.

GROSSET (CLARE VALLEY)

1998 Gaia Proprietary Red Wine	D	91+
1997 Gaia Proprietary Red Wine	D	92+

Wine-maker/proprietor Jeffrey Grosset is one of the Clare Valley's most talented winemakers, as proven by his array of consistently high-quality wines. Established in 1981, his winery is renowned for its Riesling and Chardonnay (not reviewed here since they have to be consumed within a few months of the vintage), and for its high-class blend of 75% Cabernet Sauvignon, 20% Cabernet Franc, and 5% Merlot called Gaia, aged in French oak. The exceptional 1998 Gaia is a full-bodied, classy Australian red that emulates Bordeaux yet possesses Australia's renowned ripeness, as well as terrific purity, sweet black currant, tobacco, spice box, cedar, and vanilla, beautifully integrated acidity, and a long, promising finish. Anticipated maturity: now–2014. The 1997 Gaia displays a Bordeaux-like red and black currant–scented nose with spice box, cedar, and vanilla. This classy effort represents a perfect marriage of traditional European winemaking with Australia's more modern-day approach. Medium-bodied, with moderate tannin, and well-integrated acidity and wood, this elegant wine should drink well for 12 years.

HAAN (BAROSSA VALLEY)

1998 Merlot Prestige	D	88+
1998 Shiraz	D	89

A former pilot of 747s, James Irvine (of Grand Merlot fame) is the wine-maker at Haan. These wines are aged in a combination of one-, two-, and three-year-old French oak. The 1998 Shiraz, is a graceful, elegant effort atypical for Australia. An imitation of Euro-styled wines, it offers elegance, purity, and balance. Revealing fine ripeness, medium to full body, and blackberry fruit nicely dosed with spicy oak, it should be consumed over the next 7–8 years.

The chocolaty, black cherry–scented and –flavored 1998 Merlot Prestige possesses toasty oak, coffee, and berry fruit, but comes across as more internationally styled than most Australian Merlots. Drink it over the next 4–5 years.

CHRIS HACKETT (COONAWARRA)

1998 Shiraz K-1	D	90

The classy 1998 Shiraz K-1 boasts a saturated ruby/purple color, full body, gorgeously ripe, concentrated fruit (primarily cassis and blackberries), a touch of spice, and nicely integrated new oak. Fleshy and rich, this layered, multidimensional wine saturates the palate. Enjoy it over the next 10 years.

SIMON HACKETT (BAROSSA)

1996 Cabernet Sauvignon Foggo's Road	D	91
1997 Shiraz Anthony's Reserve	D	93

A new discovery, both of these wines are impressive, and priced modestly by today's standards.The 1997 Shiraz Anthony's Reserve, from 106-year-old vines, offers explosive peppery, blackberry, and cassis aromas that segue into raspberry ice cream intermixed with pepper and spice. Thick, viscous, and full-bodied, this luxuriously rich Shiraz should be drunk now and over the next 7–10 years. It provides a quintessential hedonistic drinking experience! The 1996 Cabernet Sauvignon Foggo's Road emerges from a parcel of 75-year-old vines and was aged in both French and American oak. The saturated dense purple color is accompanied by aromas of chocolate, hickory, barbecue spices, and sweet toasty oak. Abundant quantities of black currant and plumlike fruit also jump from the glass. Thick, with chocolate/coffee-infused flavors, this naturally textured, full-bodied, supple Cabernet Sauvignon can be drunk now and over the next 10 years.

J. J. HAHN (BAROSSA VALLEY)

1998 Cabernet Sauvignon Block 79	D	88?
1998 Shiraz Block 1914	D	96

It's happening all over the world—growers who once supplied top-quality grapes to the larger wineries are breaking away to start their own labels. The Hahns were grape growers for large wineries such as Mildara Blass, St. Hallets, and Rockford, but have now launched their own label, and, believe me, wine enthusiasts are better off for it. Their vineyard, which includes some incredible old vine blocks of Shiraz dating back to the early 20th century, used to be the source for some of Australia's better Shiraz and Cabernet Sauvignons. Now the finest blocks of old vines are being selected by the proprietor and are estate-bottled. James Hahn has hired Veritas wine-maker supreme Rolf Binder to make these wines.

The Cabernet Sauvignon Block 79 comes from a 26-year-old vineyard. The 1998 is a dark ruby/purple wine with excellent, sweet, earthy, cassis notes with cedar, tobacco, and spice. This somewhat artisanally styled Cabernet has a few jagged edges but a dense, full-bodied, spicy, and loaded personality. It will drink well for 12 years.

The tour de force in the J. J. Hahn portfolio is the Shiraz Block 1914, made from vines that are over 85 years old. Average production is 440 cases. The 1998 is a sumptuous, opulent, individualistic yet sensational Shiraz. The wine has a peppery nose with hints of blackberry, blueberry, volatile acidity, melted asphalt, Band-Aid, and some subtle wood (all American oak was used, of which approximately one-third was new). In the mouth, it is huge, chewy, distinctive, and a true blockbuster in every sense of the word. This rather large-scaled wine should age easily for 15–20 years and become slightly more civilized with cellaring.

R. HAMILTON (ADELAIDE)

1997 Marion (Shiraz/Grenache)	D	92?
1997 Merlot Reserve	D	86
1997 Old Vine Shiraz Reserve	D	86

The star of this attractive trio of wines from R. Hamilton is the 1997 Marion (58% Shiraz and 42% Grenache). Made from 136-year-old Shiraz vines planted within the Adelaide city limits, it is a full-bodied, velvety-textured, saturated purple-colored wine with extraordinary fruit richness. The question mark reflects concern with a pronounced aroma of fresh manure or stinky cheese intermixed with the extravagant levels of blackberry liqueur–like fruit. Low in acidity, full-bodied, but funky, this massive, concentrated wine tips the scales at a realistic 14.3% alcohol. Drink it over the next 5–6 years.

The 1997 Merlot Reserve displays good underlying, tangy acidity, largely because 1997 was a cooler year than normal. It is an elegantly styled effort, with admirable stuffing as well as noteworthy black cherries in the nose, along with spicy oak and cool, leafy herbaceous scents. Black cherry flavors in the mouth are complemented by the wine's medium body and excellent purity. It, too, should be consumed over the next 5–6 years. The compressed style of the Merlot is also evident in the 1997 Old Vine Shiraz Reserve, a compact wine with aromas and flavors of black currant and berries, is medium-bodied and elegant, with good ripeness and a stylish, nicely-textured finish. It will also drink well for 5–6 years.

HAPPS (MARGARET RIVER)

1999 Shiraz	C	90

The first vintage for this producer has turned out a beautiful 1999 Shiraz with dense ruby/purple color, gorgeous aromas of blueberry/blackberry and currant fruit, and only a subtle hint of new oak. The wine is full-bodied, velvety-textured, and layered with plenty of glycerin as well as a pure, harmonious finish with well-integrated acidity, tannin, and wood. The wine comes across as a graceful yet fruit-dominated wine with considerable layers of flavor. I suspect more complexity will emerge as this wine ages gracefully for at least a decade. Impressive and reasonably priced.

HARDYS (McLAREN VALE)

1994 Cabernet Sauvignon Thomas Hardy	D	88
1996 Shiraz Eileen Hardy	D	90

The outstanding 1996 Shiraz Eileen Hardy reveals a saturated ruby/purple color plus a big, sweet nose of American oak, blackberry jam, tar, and spice. Opulent and viscous, with a full-bodied, layered palate, this cleanly made, chewy, rich Shiraz should be drunk over the next 5–7 years. The dark ruby/purple 1994 Cabernet Sauvignon Thomas Hardy exhibits classic aromas of cassis and oak (primarily American) in its moderately intense bouquet. The wine is full-bodied, supple, and cleanly made, with no hard edges. Drink it over the next 4–5 years.

HARE'S CHASE (BAROSSA VALLEY)

1999 Merlot	E	85
1999 Shiraz	E	92

The rather crisp, elegant, narrowly constructed 1999 Merlot is pleasant but uninspiring, and obviously overpriced. The color is a deep ruby, and the flavors evoke some mocha and cherry fruit, with some spicy wood in the background. It is a competently made wine, but it does not take a genius to find more interesting and less expensive Merlots. Anticipated maturity: now–2009. In complete contrast, the 1999 Shiraz looks to be superb. It has a saturated black/purple color with a knockout nose of smoke, blackberry, and cassis mixed with tar, licorice, and spice box. This rich, opulently textured, full-bodied blockbuster should provide dazzling drinking now and over the next 12–15 years. Thankfully, there are 400 cases of this wine that achieved 14.5% alcohol naturally. As a postscript, proprietor/wine-maker Peter Taylor is the chief red wine–maker at Penfolds.

HASTWELL AND LIGHTFOOT (McLAREN VALE)

1998 Cabernet	D	87
1998 Shiraz	D	89

There are two solid efforts at realistic prices. The 1998 Cabernet reveals a deep ruby/purple color, plenty of earthy, spicy, black currant fruit, soft, supple texture, and notes of American oak in the lusty, straightforward finish. Drink it over the next 4 years. The 1998 Shiraz shows an opaque purple color, plenty of sweet, jammy, black pepper–infused berry fruit, full body, some notes of charcoal, earth, and spice. Drink this opulently textured, user-friendly wine over the next 5 years.

HEATHCOTE (SOUTH AUSTRALIA)

1998　Shiraz Curagée	D	91
1999　Shiraz Mail Coach	C	88

Bottled unfined and unfiltered after being aged all in French oak (40% new), the 1998 Shiraz Curagée has tremendous depth, volume, and expansiveness on the palate. It is a strong effort from a superb vintage in South Australia. The color is a dense purple, and the wine is tight but concentrated and powerful, with outstanding purity and overall balance. Give it 2–3 years of cellaring, and drink it over the following 15+ years.

The 1999 Shiraz Mail Coach, which includes 5.5% Viognier in the blend, is a chunky, robust, full-bodied offering revealing aromas and flavors of blackberries, fudge, cassis, and earth. Although not complex, it is a cleanly made Shiraz that coats the palate. It was aged in a combination of French and American oak, but the wood component is subtle compared to the rich, concentrated fruit. Drink it over the next 5–6 years.

HENRY'S DRIVE (PADTHAWAY)

1999　Cabernet Sauvignon	D	90
1998　Cabernet Sauvignon	D	93
1999　Shiraz	D	91
1998　Shiraz	D	93
1999　Shiraz Reserve	E	92+

These wines from a cool climate area north of Coonawarra are made by Sparky and Sarah Marquis, who did such a fantastic job as wine-makers at Fox Creek. The Shiraz and Cabernet vineyards are young (7 years old), but the quality of these efforts is outrageously rich, ultra-ripe, and filled with extract, not dissimilar from the signature style of Fox Creek. The 1999s of this portfolio are among the strongest I have tasted, a vintage clearly inferior to 1998. Both 1998s are superb. For starters, the 1999 Cabernet Sauvignon is a beautifully stylish, almost European Cabernet with sweet, pure black currant fruit, a moderate dosage of oak (80% French and 20% American wood are utilized), excellent texture, and a fresh, well-balanced, harmonious finish. This wine is user-friendly and meant to be drunk during its first decade of life. Blackberry/cassis lovers can get an easy fix with the 1998 Cabernet Sauvignon. This wine is crammed with fruit, has low acidity, full body, and lusty, concentrated flavors that coat the palate. Already delicious, it should get even better over the next 2 years and last 12–15 years. This is an undeniably sexy style of Cabernet.

The two offerings of 1999 Shiraz are certainly among the stars of that particular vintage. The 1999 Shiraz (100% Shiraz that achieved 14.5% alcohol and was aged in 50% new oak, mostly American) is an opaque ruby/purple wine with classic smoky black fruits in the nose, along with some licorice and pepper. The wine is deep, full-bodied, and admirably concentrated, with a plush texture and serious opulence and length. This thick, juicy fruit bomb can be drunk now and over the next decade. One thousand cases were produced. The even more spectacular, beautifully balanced, saturated black purple-colored 1999 Shiraz Reserve offers a terrific nose of floral notes mixed with melted tar, roasted herbs, black fruits, and smoke. The wine has wonderful sweetness because of the high level of glycerin in the attack, a seamless mid-palate and finish, with beautifully integrated alcohol, tannin, and acidity. It is layered, rich, not huge, but gorgeously proportioned and persuasive. Drink it over the following 14–15 years. Revealing toasty American oak and chewy, blackberry and licorice-infused fruit, the 1998 Shiraz possesses multiple layers of concentration. This super-extracted, rich, low-acid wine displays plenty of smoky oak, pepper, and spice, but the fruit dominates in a big way. Drink it over the next 15 years.

HENSCHKE (BAROSSA)

1996	Cabernet Cyril Henschke	E	86?
1998	Grenache/Mourvèdre/Shiraz Johann's Garden	C	88
1997	Merlot/Cabernet Abbotts Prayer	D	86
1997	Pinot Noir Giles	D	87
1997	Shiraz/Cabernet/Malbec Keyneton Estate	D	87
1995	Shiraz Hill of Grace	EEE	92
1997	Shiraz Mount Edelstone	E	87

This famous winery has a good but (with the exception of the 1995 Shiraz Hill of Grace) largely uninspiring portfolio of wines. Certainly they are all competent efforts, but I wonder if quality couldn't be pushed even higher. The red wines, such as the 1997 Merlot/Cabernet Abbotts Prayer, possess tart, acidic profiles, with cranberry, red currant, and cherry aromas. More reminiscent of Pinot Noir than ripe Cabernet and Merlot, this is a tartly styled offering from what tastes like a cool microclimate. Anticipated maturity: now–2008. The same criticism could be made of the 1996 Cabernet Cyril Henschke. Its high, tart acidity suggests to me that much of it was added, and not with a deft touch. There is good red currant, strawberry, and cherry fruit and medium body but a compressed texture and short finish, no doubt because of the high level of acidity. I do not think this wine is going anywhere, although the acidity will ensure a certain degree of longevity. Anticipated maturity: now–2012.

Only a handful of complex Pinot Noirs emerge from Australia. Henschke's medium ruby-colored, elegant 1997 Pinot Noir Giles displays sweet raspberry fruit, notes of vanilla and toast, and a round, supple, medium-bodied style not dissimilar from a Côte de Beaune. Drink it over the next 3–4 years. Another tart red is the 1997 Shiraz/Cabernet/Malbec Keyneton Estate. A blend of 65% Shiraz, 25% Cabernet Sauvignon, and 10% Malbec, its streamlined personality offers graceful blackberry and currant fruit, leathery notes, medium body, and light tannin. Drink it over the next 4–5 years. Similarly styled but exhibiting more mint/eucalyptus is the compressed, medium-bodied 1997 Shiraz Mount Edelstone. This well-made, pure effort possesses red and black fruits, surprising acidity, and a lighter style than I would have expected from such a famous winery and renowned wine. Drink it over the next 5–8 years.

The two finest red wines are the 1998 Grenache/Mourvèdre/Shiraz Johann's Garden and 1995 Shiraz Hill of Grace. The 1998 Johann's Garden offers sweet blueberry and black raspberry fruit, a silky texture, medium to full body, soft, supple tannin, and a long finish. Though not a blockbuster, it is an elegant, finesse-styled wine with flair and character. Drink it over the next 5–6 years. The opaque ruby/purple-colored 1995 Shiraz Hill of Grace (along with Penfolds Grange, one of the most famous Shirazes of Australia) boasts abundant quantities of toasty American oak, fat, blackberry, tar-infused fruit flavors, a deep, unctuous texture, and a powerful, concentrated, long finish. This renowned Shiraz is indeed all it should be for its lofty price tag. It should drink well for 15–20 years.

HERMITAGE ROAD (LIMESTONE COAST)

1998	Shiraz Reserve	C	89

Licorice, blackberry, and spicy wood aromas emerge from the dense ruby/purple-colored 1998 Shiraz Reserve. It possesses abundant fruit, a fleshy texture, full body, and excellent purity. It would have deserved a better rating, had it not been for its slight lack of complexity. Anticipated maturity: now–2010.

HEWITSON (McLAREN VALE)

1999	Mourvèdre Old Garden	D	90
1997	Mourvèdre Old Garden	D	90
1999	Shiraz Barossa	D	87
1998	Shiraz Barossa	D	86
1998	Shiraz l'Oizeau	D	91
1997	Shiraz l'Oizeau	D	86

Produced from a Mourvèdre vineyard first planted in 1853, the impressive Mourvèdre Old Garden also contains 5% Shiraz. The beautiful blackberry, blueberry, raspberry, leathery, spicy, French oak-scented, elegant 1999 possesses excellent delineation, medium body, and moderate tannin. It is a high-quality Mourvèdre made in a modern-day style. Bravo! Anticipated maturity: now–2010. The 1997 Mourvèdre Old Garden was a surprise. Textbook notes of mushrooms, blueberries, earth, tree bark, and saddle leather jump from the glass of this medium-bodied, racy, stylish yet concentrated Mourvèdre. This type of wine is not for everyone, given Mourvèdre's singular personality and dusty tannin. However, this tastes like the real stuff from France's Bandol appellation. This wine was impressively long, well balanced, and loaded with character. Drink it over the next 5–8 years.

The Shiraz l'Oizeau takes its name from some of the oldest Shiraz vines in McLaren Vale. Elegance along with power can be found in the ruby/purple 1998 with notes of crème de cassis, licorice, and new French wood. Long, deep, and beautifully pure, with an unevolved character, this wine is approachable, but promises to be better in 2–3 years and last two decades. Dark ruby-colored, with subtle oak, blackberry, and black cherry fruit aromas and flavors, the 1997 Shiraz l'Oizeau offers a creamy, medium-bodied personality, excellent purity and ripeness, and a sense of delicacy rather than exuberance. It should drink well for 5 years.

Made in a light style, Hewitson's 1999 Shiraz Barossa is stylistically well defined and fresh, offering creamy oak, but more red than black fruits. It should be drunk over the next 4–5 years. The 1998 Shiraz Barossa exhibits moderate quantities of creamy oak and black fruit in the attractive aromatics. Dark ruby-colored with purple nuances, this medium-bodied, fleshy, stylized effort possesses sweet tannin but not a lot of staying power in the mouth. It is an elegant Australian Shiraz to be drunk over the next 5–6 years.

HIGHBANK (COONAWARRA)

1998	Proprietary Red	D	91

The superb, opaque purple-colored, high-class 1998 Proprietary Red (a blend of 68% Cabernet Sauvignon, 20% Merlot, and 12% Cabernet Franc) has brilliantly absorbed its aging in 100% new French oak. The wine is classy, pure, and, according to my tasting notes, "the Léoville-Las Cases of Australia?" With gorgeous black cherry and black currant flavors intermixed with lead pencil, vanilla, and mineral, medium to full body, high tannin, and superb delineation, it will drink well for 15–16 years. This is another candidate for inserting into a blind tasting of top-class Bordeaux to see how it fares.

HILL OF CONTENT (CLARE VALLEY)

1999	Old Vines Grenache/Shiraz	B	86

The Côtes du Rhône–like 1999 Old Vines Grenache/Shiraz possesses an elegant, medium-weight style with notes of cherries and ripe peaches. It is soft, round, and ideal for drinking over the next 2–3 years.

HOLLICK (COONAWARRA)

1998	Cabernet Sauvignon/Merlot	C	87
1999	Shiraz/Cabernet Sauvignon	C	87
1998	Shiraz Wilgha	D	88

The two *cuvées* of Shiraz include the 1999 Shiraz/Cabernet Sauvignon (93% Shiraz and 7% Cabernet Sauvignon). The wine is soft, ripe, straightforward, yet monochromatic. Nevertheless, it is well made, with the telltale pepper and ripe blackberry characteristics. Drink it over the next 3 years. The 1998 Shiraz Wilgha is slightly deeper. This wine, fermented and aged in new American oak, shows predominant levels of toast in its aromatics, which kept my score from going any higher. That is disappointing, given the wine's dense ruby/purple color, jammy, concentrated, full-bodied fruit, real opulence, and a chewy, long finish. If the wood were better integrated, this wine could flirt with an outstanding rating. It should drink well for 8 years, and hopefully the wood will become better integrated with cellaring.

The 1998 Cabernet Sauvignon/Merlot (85%/15%) possesses Bordeaux-like, curranty, coffee, cedary, and tobacco aromatic and flavor profiles. There is good fruit on the attack, medium body, and an austere, lightly tannic finish. It should drink well for 8 years.

HONGELL (BAROSSA VALLEY)

1998 Grenache	C	86
1999 Grenache Old Vine	C	88
1999 Shiraz	C	90

John Hongell has been a supplier to such famous Barossa producers as Charles Melton, Rockford, and Torbreck. He has now decided, like so many growers, to begin estate-bottling his own wines. His first efforts certainly show promise. The regular *cuvée* of 1998 Grenache (from 56-year-old vines) displays a Côtes du Rhône–like, sweet, kirsch note intermixed with balsam wood and earth. Tasty, well made, and medium-bodied, but straightforward and one-dimensional, it requires consumption over the next 3–4 years.

Far more interesting is the complex, supple-textured, dark ruby-colored 1999 Grenache Old Vine. This wine shows notes of bacon fat, sausage, and jammy red and black fruits in its aromatics. It is sweet, dense, full-bodied, and ripe, and if it had additional length and complexity, would have been outstanding. Nevertheless, it is an excellent wine and ideal for drinking over the next 5–6 years. The best of the three wines from Hongell is the 1999 Shiraz, made from low yields of 1.5 tons per acre, all from 8-year-old Shiraz vines. It is a dense ruby/purple-colored, big, sweet, fat fruit bomb with low acidity, abundant quantities of blackberry fruit, barbecue spice, smoke, and earth, plenty of glycerin, and a hedonistic, user-friendly appeal. Drink it over the next 4 years.

HOWARD PARK (WESTERN AUSTRALIA)

1998 Cabernet Sauvignon/Cabernet Franc/Merlot	D	86
1997 Cabernet Sauvignon/Cabernet Franc/Merlot	D	86
1996 Cabernet Sauvignon/Cabernet Franc/Merlot	D	87
1998 Shiraz Leston	D	89

The impressive 1998 Shiraz Leston reveals generous blackberry fruit as well as a dense, concentrated attack and mid-palate, and sweet tannin in the finish. Rich, medium- to full-bodied, and pure, it can be enjoyed over the next 7–8 years. The Cabernet Sauvignon/Cabernet Franc/Merlot blend spends two years in French oak before bottling. The 1998 (75% Cabernet Sauvignon, 13% Cabernet Franc, and 12% Merlot) is a firmly structured, attractive effort offering aromas of cedar, underbrush, black currants, and spice. Medium-bodied and moderately concentrated with firm tannin, it should drink well now and over the next 7–8 years.

As for the 1997 and 1996 Cabernet Sauvignon/Cabernet Franc/Merlots, the 1997 is more compact, exhibiting a dark ruby/purple color, and an attractive ripe black currant and cherry-scented nose with cedar and spice box in the background. Medium-bodied, with very good concentration, this stylish, elegant wine should drink well for 5–7 years. The 1996 is richer, with more complex aromatics, but is not totally dissimilar from its younger sibling.

Dark ruby-colored, with scents of spice box, cedar, tobacco, and black currants, this medium-bodied, nicely packaged wine exhibits good ripeness and purity as well as an over-all sense of grace/balance. Drink it over the next 7 years.

HUTTON VALE (EDEN VALLEY)

1999 Grenache/Mataro	D	91
1998 Grenache/Mataro	D	87+
1995 Shiraz	E	88
1994 Shiraz	E	88?

The Grenache/Mataro blend is a tiny 90-case *cuvée* of old vines. The proportion of the two varietals vary with each vintage. The interesting 1999 Grenache/Mataro (50% of each) is a complex, leathery, spicy, blackberry- and currant-scented and -flavored wine with plenty of depth, good, bright tannin, and a supple, fleshy finish. It should drink well for another 5–7 years. The medium dark ruby-colored, closed, tannic 1998 Grenache/Mataro (60% and 40% respectively) is produced from old vines and tastes as if it came from a cool-climate vineyard. The wine is compressed, but what does pull through the structure is pure cherry and raspberry fruit. The red fruit side of the flavor spectrum dominates this medium-bodied blend. Give it 2 years of cellaring.

I will keep my notes short for both Shirazes, which are only available in small quantities (approximately 30 cases). The 1995 is an earthy, peppery, fully mature wine showing full body, sweet, herb-tinged, cedary, spicy berry fruit. The wine needs to be drunk over the next 4 years. The 1994 reveals intense eucalyptus/minty notes accompanying its blackberry/currant fruit. There is fine density and medium to full body, but it is a wine for those who crave weediness in the aromatic and flavor profiles. It should drink well for 10 years.

IRVINE (EDEN VALLEY)

1997 Grand Merlot	E	92+?
1999 Merlot	C	88

James Irvine is a famous wine consultant, but he also produces what many consider the finest Merlot in Australia, the Grand Merlot. As for the 1999 Merlot, this blend of Eden Valley and Barossa fruit is a very good value. It possesses a chocolate fudge–like character along with mocha and cherry fruit. Seamless, pure, and ripe, it is best drunk over the next 2 years.

The large-scaled 1997 Grand Merlot is a wine of extraordinary extraction. This exotic, full-bodied, powerful Merlot displays lavish quantities of toasty French oak. Aged for 39 months in what appears to be all new barrels prior to bottling, it is a layered, thick, juicy effort with notes of coffee, chocolate, black cherries, liqueur, spice box, and new oak in addition to enormous quantities of extract, glycerin, and richness. The alcohol is a lofty 15.3%, reflecting Irvine's predilection to pick extremely ripe. It gives every indication of aging for a decade or more, but I must say that a minivertical sponsored by the importer suggested this is a wine that really does not benefit from cellaring. Older vintages such as 1987, 1989, 1992, and 1993 were already drying out and extremely attenuated. However, a handful of old vintages, 1991 in particular, had survived cellaring and were in good shape. Nevertheless, I would opt for drinking these wines in their first 3–5 years of life, despite a style that suggests longevity.

JASPER HILL (HEATHCOTE)

1999 Shiraz Georgia's Paddock	E	89
1998 Shiraz Georgia's Paddock	E	91
1997 Shiraz Georgia's Paddock	E	89+

These three red wine offerings are the finest I have tasted from Jasper Hill. From a lighter vintage, the 1999 Shiraz Georgia's Paddock may merit an outstanding rating. The dense purple color is accompanied by abundant quantities of blackberries, pepper, and melted asphalt in its muscular, full-bodied yet supple-textured personality. Remarkably, the lofty alcohol (15.5%) is well concealed in the rich, fruity, glycerin-filled finish. Drink this 1999 over the next decade. More explosive, thicker, and complex is the dense purple-colored 1998 Shiraz Georgia's Paddock. It exhibits a provocative perfume of smoke, barbecue spice, crème de cassis, and blackberries with pepper and vanilla in the background. Full-bodied, opulent, and voluptuous, this sexy, dense, low-acid wine coats the palate with considerable viscosity and purity. It can be drunk now and over the next 12 years. The opaque purple-colored, concentrated 1997 Shiraz Georgia's Paddock boasts crème de cassis aromas. This sweet-smelling, rich, concentrated, full-bodied, dry red wine exhibits plenty of cassis fruit, good spice, and a heady, moderately tannic finish. Still young, it should keep for a decade or more.

STEPHEN JOHN (CLARE VALLEY)

1998	Shiraz	D	87
1997	Shiraz	D	88
1998	Shiraz Reserve	D	90+

The dark ruby/purple, closed, tightly knit, elegant 1998 Shiraz appears to be very good. It should keep for 12 years. The dark plum/purple-colored, unfiltered 1997 Shiraz exhibits a more evolved, peppery, spice box, black currant, and cherry-scented nose, medium- to full-bodied flavors, well-integrated wood and acidity, and a plush, soft finish. It should drink well for the next 8 years. The unfiltered 1998 Shiraz Reserve is quite backward, but very intense. It displays vibrant acidity along with heady quantities of rich, humongous, chewy blackberry and cassis fruit. Pepper, dried cherries, and spice box aromas also appear in this tannic, large-sized Shiraz. Anticipated maturity: now–2020.

JOHN'S BLEND (LANGHORNE CREEK/McLAREN VALE)

1998	Margarete's Shiraz	D	90

Seventy-year-old Shiraz vines have produced a minty, chocolaty, cassis-scented and -flavored 1998 Margarete's Shiraz with plenty of depth, medium to full body, and rustic, old-style tannins in the finish. The wine was aged 26 months in 100% new American oak, as evidenced by the toasty, spicy wood present in both the aromatics and flavor. Drink it over the next 7–8 years for its exuberant, robust style.

ROBERT JOHNSON (EDEN VALLEY)

1997	Merlot	C	88

An impeccably made, symmetrical, unfiltered Merlot that has been aged in French oak, this 1997 reveals dark berry fruit, medium to full body, adequate acidity, attractive sweetness, and a nicely textured, glycerin-imbued finish. Drink it over the next 5–6 years.

TREVOR JONES (BAROSSA VALLEY)

1998	Boots Grenache	C	88
1998	Cabernet Sauvignon/Merlot	D	87
1996	Cabernet Sauvignon/Merlot	D	88
1995	Cabernet Sauvignon/Merlot	D	90+
NV	Old Barossa Muscat	EE	96
NV	Old Barossa Tawny Port	EE	98
1998	Shiraz	D	83
1997	Shiraz	D	86
NV	Shiraz Liqueur	EE	100
1998	Shiraz Reserve Wild Witch	E	85?

1997	Shiraz Reserve Wild Witch	E	90
1996	Shiraz Reserve Wild Witch	E	92+
NV	Tokay Liqueur	EE	100

Trevor Jones's wines are generally impressive. A second label, Boots, a joint project with his American importer, has recently been added to his portfolio, which aims to produce wines of character that are also noteworthy values. The value-priced Boots offerings are in-your-face, fruity wines with surprising character for their modest prices. In addition to his delicious Shiraz and Cabernet/Merlot blends, Jones offers mind-blowing fortified dessert wines. The Muscat and Tawny Port are from base materials at least 30 years old, and the Shiraz and Tokay liqueurs are from base materials at least 50 years old. All four are truly unreal. Coming to the vintages, the three red 1998s are not as good as I hoped, both Shirazes tasting unduly narrow in their textures because of surprisingly high acidity (probably added). However, the 1997s and 1996s are superb. The 1998 Boots Grenache (made from 80-year-old Grenache vines that yielded only 1.5 tons of fruit per acre) is a dead ringer for a top-notch southern Rhône. Medium ruby-colored, with jammy aromas of kirsch, black cherries, and pepper, this spicy, exuberantly fruity, fleshy Grenache tips the scales at 15% alcohol. There is plenty of glycerin as well as a tactile impression of sweetness, even though the wine is totally dry. It is a hedonistic fruit bomb to drink over the next 2–3 years.

The 1998 Shiraz reveals an impressively saturated purple color as well as a sweet perfume of blackberry fruit intermixed with floral and spice notes. In the mouth, it is medium- to full-bodied but becomes compressed because of its copious acidity. Although competent, it lacks excitement and lushness. This wine should last 10–15 years, but how well it will develop remains to be seen. The 1997 Shiraz is a rather elegant, almost claret style of Shiraz with medium body, restrained spice box, red cherry, and currant notes, and a clean, fresh finish. Drink it over the next 5–6 years.

The Shiraz Reserve Wild Witch is produced from extremely old vines (about 40 years of age). Yields are generally a meager one ton of fruit per acre. The 1998 Shiraz Reserve Wild Witch displays generous new oak in its complex bouquet of black fruits, tar, and spice. Rich and full-bodied, with more texture but a narrow finish, it is tightly knit, with surprisingly high acidity. This wine will hold 10–15 years, but how well it will develop remains to be seen.

The 1997 Shiraz Reserve Wild Witch is again an elegant, finesse-style Shiraz with notes of cedar wood, red currants, pepper, and a touch of blackberries. It is well made, surprisingly restrained, and subtle for an Australian Shiraz, but distinctive in its individuality and gracefulness. The 1996 Shiraz Reserve Wild Witch's stunning nose reveals scents of freshly ground pepper intermixed with toast, blackberry, and raspberry fruit. With awesome concentration, medium to full body, and zesty underlying tangy acidity, this complex yet firmly structured, backward Shiraz should unfold nicely for at least 15 years. Impressive!

The Cabernet Sauvignon/Merlot blend is composed of 85% Cabernet and 15% Merlot, and emerges from 36-year-old vines. The 1998 exhibits a saturated ruby/purple color in addition to copious quantities of mint, black fruits, and new oak in the nose. Clean and straightforward but monolithic, it will drink well for 7–8 years. The 1996 Cabernet/Merlot is slightly tough-textured, but almost Bordeaux-like in its earthy, black currant style with nicely balanced wood and tannin. The wine is slightly austere but well made and clean. Enjoy it over the following 7–8 years. It is designed for tasters who prefer their reds on the leaner side of the stylistic spectrum. The 1995 Cabernet Sauvignon/Merlot's deep ruby/purple color is followed by a textbook Bordeaux bouquet of black currants, spicy new oak, and cedar. Rich on the attack, with outstanding ripeness, purity, and overall equilibrium, this is a classic example of power allied to elegance. Anticipated maturity: now–2016.

The point scores say it all when it comes to trying to describe the sumptuous, sublime fortified wines produced by Trevor Jones. They all have approximately 18% alcohol, and levels of concentration and perfume that must be experienced to be believed. The nonvintage Old Barossa Muscat offers a medium amber color, fabulous sweetness, great freshness, and layers of concentration. Amazingly, it gets blown away by the other three offerings. The nonvintage Old Barossa Tawny Port, a blend of Shiraz, Grenache, Muscat, and Tokay, boasts awesome aromatics that could fill a large room. Tremendous richness, refreshing underlying acidity, fabulous fruit, and an unctuous texture result in a profound drinking experience. The Shiraz Liqueur and Tokay Liqueur are off the charts. The only thing to compare them to is some of the rare Muscat or Tokay produced by another Australian, William Chambers. They are phenomenally concentrated, amazingly thick and unctuous, yet multidimensional and totally compelling. Why aren't more of these made? The base material for both liqueurs is 50 or more years of age. Production is limited to 30 cases of 375 ml bottles. These are the kind of spectacular fortifieds that are almost worth killing for to get hold of a half bottle or two.

JOSEPH (McLAREN VALE)

1998 Cabernet/Merlot Moda Amarone	E	91

The distinctive 1998 Cabernet/Merlot Moda Amarone, made from dried Cabernet Sauvignon and Merlot fruit, reveals a dense ruby/purple/garnet color, and a big, sweet, toasty nose filled with aromas of melted asphalt, black currants, damp earth, and plums. Rich, full-bodied, and chewy, this is a singularly styled wine which, to my palate, is successful. It is not for everyone, but for serving with full-flavored dishes, or at the end of a meal, it is an intriguing and commendable effort. Moreover, it should drink well for 10+ years.

KAESSLER'S STONE HORSE (BAROSSA VALLEY)

1998 Shiraz	C	89
1998 Shiraz Old Bastard	E	95
1998 Shiraz Old Vine	C	91

These immensely impressive wines are aged in a combination of both old and new American oak. All three cuvées emerge from a 38-year-old Shiraz vineyard. An excellent value, the 1998 Shiraz is a rich, full-bodied, robust, typically Australian proportioned wine with plenty of glycerin, alcohol, fruit, and body. Although not complex, it is loaded as well as mouth-staining. Drink it over the next 7–8 years. The exceptional 1998 Shiraz Old Vine, reveals greater extraction, a saturated blue/purple color, and an admirably sweet, blackberry, blueberry, smoky bouquet with oak nuances. Flamboyant, full-bodied, and textured, this powerful, hedonistic, soft wine is ideal for drinking over the next 15–16 years.

Sadly, there are less than 50 cases of the 1998 Shiraz Old Bastard. A selection of barrels from the Shiraz Old Vine cuvée, this is a riveting but limited-production offering. It exhibits off-the-chart levels of extract, power, and richness in addition to glorious smoky blackberry and currant fruit. Unctuously textured, enormous, yet symmetrical, this is what Australia does better than anyone. Drink this distinctive/individualistic Shiraz over the next 20 years.

KANGARILLA ROAD (McLAREN VALE)

1999 Cabernet Sauvignon Estate	B	91
1998 Cabernet Sauvignon Estate	B	89
1999 Shiraz Estate	B	90
1997 Shiraz Estate	B	87
1999 Zinfandel	C	86

This relatively new operation has one of the first plantings of Zinfandel in Australia. The wines admirably combine power with a sense of restraint and elegance and possess exuberant personalities and lovely aromatics. Readers looking for exceptional values in outstanding wine should check out Kangarilla Road's Shiraz and Cabernet Sauvignon. The 1999 Zinfandel exhibits briery, cranberry, and peppery notes, medium to full body, and attractive fruit. However, the efforts I have tasted from Australia involving Zinfandel pale in comparison with California's finest, and remain, in large part, uninspiring curiosities. Drink it over the next 2–3 years.

The Shiraz Estate, which was first produced in 1997, is matured in used French and American oak. Availabilities are around 2,000 cases. This one is a great value. The 1999 boasts a dense purple color as well as a gorgeously sweet nose of blackberries, melted licorice, pepper, and caramel. It has admirable purity, layers of fruit and glycerin, full body, a sumptuous mouth-feel, and a long, concentrated finish. It should continue to drink well for another 7–8 years. The 1997 Shiraz Estate, the debut vintage for Kangarilla Road, reveals aromas of pepper, truffle, earth, and black fruits. Medium- to full-bodied, with decent acidity and a forward style, it should be consumed over the next 4–5 years.

Kangarilla's Cabernet Sauvignon is generally impressive, one of the finest Cabernets money can buy for its quality. Composed of 100% Cabernet Sauvignon, it is aged 18 months in American and French oak. The 1999 displays a deep ruby/purple color along with a gorgeous nose of espresso, chocolate fudge, black currants, and cedar. It has sweet tannin, a terrific mouth-feel, medium to full body, and a long, lush finish. Another exceptional value, it will drink well for a decade. The dark ruby/purple-colored 1998 Cabernet Sauvignon Estate offers that varietal's classic hallmarks—cedar, spice box, black currants, and tobacco. This medium-bodied, well-endowed, impressive wine with sweet tannin and adequate acidity should drink well for 10–12 years.

KATNOOK ESTATE (COONAWARRA)

1998 Cabernet Sauvignon	E	87
1996 Cabernet Sauvignon Odyssey	E	89+
1994 Cabernet Sauvignon Odyssey	E	91
1998 Merlot	D	85
1997 Shiraz Jimmy Watson Trophy	E	92

These wines always display a cool-climate character regardless of vintage conditions. Some wines of the portfolio may be disappointing or just pleasant (1998 Shiraz, 1997 Merlot, and 1997 Cabernet Sauvignon), but those reviewed here are very good, if not excellent.

The dense ruby/plum/purple-colored 1998 Cabernet Sauvignon offers aromas of smoke, creosote, cassis, and dried herbs. Medium- to full-bodied, rich, and elegant, this stylish Cabernet can be drunk now and over the next decade. Less saturated in color, the 1998 Merlot offers herb, cedar, black cherry, chocolate, and new oak aromas. It is a medium-weight, moderately endowed offering with a sweet attack, good cleanliness, a distinctive, elegant style, and a narrow finish with tart acidity. Anticipated maturity: 2003–2012.

The nearly opaque purple-colored 1997 Shiraz Jimmy Watson Trophy possesses jammy blackberry and cassis aromas intermixed with scents of melted licorice and pepper. Full-bodied, wild blackberry fruit flavors display abundant glycerin, sweet tannin, and sufficient acidity. As the wine sits in the glass, brandylike, macerated prune aromas and flavors emerge. This superb Shiraz saturates the palate. Drink it over the next 10–12 years.

The luxury *cuvée* Cabernet Sauvignon Odyssey spends 38 months in new French oak barrels before bottling. The 1996's dense plum/purple color is accompanied by distinctive aromas of cedar, spice box, black currants, licorice, and a touch of kirsch and new oak. Full-bodied, highly extracted, and rich, this large-scaled yet balanced wine can be drunk now as well as over the next 15+ years. The black/purple-colored 1994 Cabernet Sauvignon Odyssey offers impressive complexity and richness. The bouquet possesses cedar, black currant, spice box, chocolate, and dried herb scents. Rich, with a thick mid-palate and sweet tannin, it is a powerful yet elegant Cabernet with considerable length and aging potential. Accessible now, it promises to improve over the next 3–4 years and last for 12–15 years.

KAY BROTHERS (McLAREN VALE)

1998 Cabernet Sauvignon Amery Vineyard	D	92?
1998 Merlot Amery Vineyards	D	90
1998 Shiraz Amery Vineyards	D	92
1998 Shiraz Amery Vineyard Hillside	D	94
1996 Shiraz Block 6	D	93
1998 Shiraz Block 6 Amery Vineyards	D	98+

The old-fashioned labels on these wines suggest history, and, in fact, the Kay family's roots in the McLaren Vale go back at least five generations. Their wines are among the most individualistic and impressive wines I have recently tasted from Australia. Possessing undeniable character and individuality, they should be hugely popular in this country. There are just under 850–900 cases of each of these *cuvées*. The 1998 Merlot Amery Vineyards has a dense, opaque purple color, smoky, coffee, black cherry, cough syrup notes, with plenty of toasted new oak. The wine is fat, ripe, pretty, and rather decadent and exotic, with a heavy overlay of new American oak. It is not for everybody, but this is a flamboyant, impressively endowed Merlot from Australia. Drink it over the next 10 years.

The spectacular 1998 Cabernet Sauvignon Amery Vineyard (14.9% alcohol from 25-year-old vines cropped at 2.0–2.5 tons per acre) offers the textbook huge ripeness and burly, muscular style of Australia intertwined with an Italian-like creosote, earthy, rustic, leathery component. The wine has great fruit, a fabulous multilayered texture, massive concentration, and noteworthy levels of glycerin, blackberry, plum, cherry, and cassis fruit. All of this is tied together in a chewy, full-bodied, slightly rustic style. It should continue to evolve for at least two decades. But readers take note—the notions of creosote, bay leaf, anise, and leather are out of the mainstream for Cabernet Sauvignon, and are likely to be controversial.

Shiraz lovers will be electrified by the four offerings from Kay Brothers. The Shiraz Amery Vineyard is made from 15-year-old vines cropped at a meager 1.5–2.5 tons of fruit per acre. It is aged 18 months in American oak barrels, but it is hard to believe there is much new oak based on its aromas and flavors. The 1998, which tips the scales at 14.8% alcohol, is a substantial, full-throttle, somewhat old-style Shiraz with smoky, earthy, leathery, charcoal, and blackberry notes in the nose and flavors. It waddles across the palate with considerable extract, weight, and heaviness. It is deep, chewy, muscular, with the fruit and glycerin largely concealing some tannin. The wood seems to be kept within reason. This wine should evolve for at least another 12–15 years.

The prodigious Shiraz Amery Vineyard Hillside is aged in 100% new American oak from relatively young vines that are the same clone of Shiraz as planted in the Block 6, which still contains 100+-year-old vines. It is vinified in an artisanal way. The 1998 is a full-throttle, powerful, super-concentrated wine with opaque black/purple color, notes of new oak intermixed with licorice, blackberry, cassis, asphalt, and leather. The wine is huge, massive, chewy, and unctuously textured. It is a total turn-on. Drink it over the next 15–20+ years.

Made from 106-year-old head-pruned Shiraz vines, the Shiraz Block 6 is bottled unfiltered after spending 18 months in old American oak upright wood tanks. Annual production averages 900 cases, and the vines are cropped at 1.5–2.0 tons per acre. Both following vintages are nearly perfect. The compelling 1998 is impressively thick-looking, has formidable concentration and gorgeously pure, peppery, crème de cassis notes intermixed with new saddle leather, incense, smoky charcoal, and vanilla. Fabulously concentrated and unctuously textured, with a finish that remained on my palate for 60+ seconds, this large-scaled, classic Australian Shiraz from old, unirrigated, head-pruned vines should age effortlessly for 20–25 years. Anticipated maturity: now–2025.

A sensational blackberry, hickory smoke, and tar-scented and -flavored Shiraz, the 1996 Shiraz Block 6 possesses huge body, fabulous extraction and ripeness, and glorious levels of black fruits, all infused with glycerin and heady alcohol. Fine purity and emerging complexity can be found in this superintense, mouth-filling blockbuster. Anticipated maturity: now–2016. Wow! If you find these wines and can afford them, do not hesitate!

KIES FAMILY WINES (BAROSSA VALLEY)

1999 Shiraz Dedication	D	88

Consulting wine-maker/oenologist James Irvine is the adviser for this wine. The medium- to full-bodied, soft 1999 Dedication Shiraz has more than a passing resemblance to a southern Rhône. Notes of pepper, Provençal herbs, and roasted fruits emerge from the aromatics. Deep, round, and sweet, it is best consumed over the next 5–6 years.

KILIKANOON (CLARE VALLEY)

1999 Cabernet Sauvignon	C	87
1998 Cabernet Sauvignon	D	90
1999 Grenache Prodigal	C	90
1998 Grenache Prodigal	C	88+
1999 Shiraz Oracle	D	94
1998 Shiraz Oracle	D	92

These wines are made at the Torbreck facilities of David Powell. Although I have limited experience with Kilikanoon (I have only tasted three vintages), I have liked everything they have done to date. The Grenache Prodigals are outstanding examples of this varietal, and come close to matching the superb Grenaches made at Clarendon Hills and Greenock Creek. This wine is aged 15 months in old oak prior to being bottled without filtration. The 1999 exhibits a classic Grenache nose of black cherry liqueur mixed with roasted notes and spice. Sweet, exotic, explosive levels of fruit and glycerin cascade seamlessly over the palate. Lush, dense, and impressively hedonistic, it should be drunk over the next 5–6 years. The outstanding 1998 Grenache Prodigal tops the scales at 15% alcohol. Tightly knit for an Australian Grenache, it reveals good structure, tannin, and wood, as well as full-bodied cherry and raspberry flavors. It should drink well for 8 years.

The Cabernet Sauvignons are aged in French oak casks (40% new) and bottled unfiltered. The deep ruby/purple-colored, medium-bodied 1999 is surprisingly graceful. Made in a finesse style that exhibits good, spicy black currant fruit, evidence of new oak, and a round finish, it should drink well for at least a decade. The oustanding 1998 Cabernet Sauvignon boasts a dense purple color, and thick, juicy, cassis, and spicy wood aromas. This wine exhibits good structure and delineation, surprising elegance for an Australian Cabernet, medium to full body, and 12–15 years of aging potential.

The most stunning of this portfolio is the spectacular Shiraz Oracle, made from 40-year-old vines, aged 18 months in 50% new oak, two-thirds American and one-third French, and bottled with no filtration. The 1999 is a serious effort. A dense plum/purple color and stunning aromatics of plum, prune, blackberries, chocolate, and melted road tar are followed by an intense, full-bodied, viscous Shiraz with superb purity, low acidity, and a whoppingly long finish. This mouth-filling wine can be drunk now as well as over the next 10–15 or more years. The 1998 Shiraz Oracle is a full-throttle, opaque purple wine possessing copious quantities of truffle, new saddle leather, pepper, and blackberry fruit aromas. As it sits in the glass, scents of overripe plums, cherries, and spice emerge from this heady, powerful, nicely textured, plush Shiraz. Rich and robust, it should be consumed over the next 8–10 years.

KILLIBINBIN (LANGHORNE CREEK)

1999 Shiraz	D	90
1998 Shiraz	D	96

Killibinbin's amazing 100% Shirazes sell for a song, considering their quality and pleasure-giving characteristics. Annual production averages 500 cases. These wines are unquestionably made from extremely ripe fruit. While the 1999 Shiraz can't measure up to the 1998, it is an outstanding effort. This wine has an opaque purple color and a gorgeous bouquet of sweet cherries, blackberries, and plums mixed with pepper and spice. Fat and fleshy, it offers a chunky mouthful of hedonistic, ripe Shiraz at 14.9% alcohol. The wine shows a subtle influence of wood in its fruit-dominated personality. Drink it over the next 6–8 years.

I was blown away by the 1998 Shiraz. Reminiscent of dry vintage Port, this black/purple behemoth offers aromas of blackberries, cassis, sweet, damp earth, licorice, and chocolate, as well as an explosive, full-bodied entry on the palate. Dry, hugely-concentrated, and clearly a heavyweight, with a whopping 16% alcohol, it is neither hot nor out of balance. An infant in terms of development, this 1998 should continue to evolve for 10–12+ years.

KOPPAMURRA (COONAWARRA)

1998 Cabernet Sauvignon/Merlot/Cabernet Franc	C	89

An excellent value in a high-quality proprietary red (a blend of 46% Cabernet Sauvignon, 27% Merlot, and 27% Cabernet Franc), the 1998 is a smoky, peppery, earthy, black currant–scented effort with good spice, excellent richness, sweet tannin, and a surprisingly well-balanced, long finish. It can be consumed now as well as over the next decade.

LANGMEIL WINERY (BAROSSA VALLEY)

1999 Shiraz	C	86
1998 Shiraz The Freedom	E	88

This winery is reputed to have a plot of the oldest producing Shiraz vines in the world, its vineyards having been planted in 1844. The grapes for The Freedom come from 157-year-old Shiraz vines! Both wines are very good buys. Aged in American oak (50% new), they are bottled with no fining or filtration. The 1998 Shiraz The Freedom exhibits a dark ruby/purple color, a one-dimensional character, but plenty of power, density, richness, and weight. Although foursquare at present, it may develop more nuances/dimensions with another 2–3 years of cellaring. It should age well for 10–12 years. The 1999 Shiraz (2,000 cases) offers a big, peppery, tar, blackberry nose, sweet, ripe, straightforward, fruity flavors, low acidity, and a plump, fleshy finish. Its whopping 16.3% alcohol is surprisingly well concealed beneath the wine's ripe fruit. This is one to drink over the next 2–3 years.

LARRIKIN (SOUTH AUSTRALIA)

1997 Shiraz	D	90

From an 80-year-old Shiraz vineyard, and aged in both French and American oak, the 1997 Shiraz, a "diamond in the rough" (the meaning of the Aboriginal name, Larrikin), is a dense, full-bodied effort offering copious quantities of jammy blackberry fruit and bold, creamy new oak flavors. Spicy, hedonistic, and intense, this low acid, plump, jammy Shiraz will have many fans. Drink it over the next 5–6 years.

LASHMAR (SOUTH AUSTRALIA)

1999 Cabernet	D	87
1999 Shiraz Three Valleys	D	89

The first release from a Cabernet vineyard planted on Kangaroo Island, just off the Adelaide coastline, the 1999 Cabernet (220 cases produced) shows a lighter style than most Australian Cabernets and is a bit narrowly focused, but there is elegance and decent, cool-climate characteristics in its cedary, black and red currant–scented nose. The wine has good density, some sweet tannin, and is well made in a more delicate, restrained style atypical for an Australian wine. Drink it over the next 5–6 years. The 1999 Shiraz Three Valleys shows textbook creosote-infused blackberry liqueur notes. It has medium weight with good ripeness, sweetness, and supple tannin. Drink it over the next 5–6 years.

LEAMON (VICTORIA)

1999 Cabernet Reserve	D	90
1999 Shiraz Reserve	D	88

The 1999 Cabernet Reserve (90% Cabernet Sauvignon and 10% Merlot aged in 100% new French oak and bottled unfiltered) has beautifully absorbed the wood, displaying notes of caramel, black currants, spice box, and earth. It offers an opaque ruby/purple color, deep, full-bodied flavors, good integration of acidity and tannin, and nicely integrated alcohol (listed at 15%). Drink it over the next 10–12 years. The Shiraz Reserve comes from old vines grown in granite soil, is aged in 100% new oak, and is bottled unfiltered. The 1999 is slightly foursquare and monolithic. This wine may be outstanding, but it does not yet exhibit the nuances of the Cabernet. It is full-bodied and loaded with concentrated fruit, spicy new oak, and Syrah's telltale smoky, charred character. Anticipated maturity: 2003–2014.

LEEUWIN ESTATE (MARGARET RIVER)

1995 Cabernet Sauvignon	D	90
1997 Cabernet Sauvignon Art Series	D	91+
1996 Cabernet Sauvignon Art Series	D	91
1998 Cabernet Sauvignon/Merlot Prelude Vineyards	D	88
1997 Cabernet Sauvignon/Merlot Prelude Vineyards	D	90

This estate, better known for its superb whites (not reviewed here since they must be consumed within several months of the vintage), does a great job with respect to the reds. In the past, some of Leeuwin Estate's reds have been slightly herbaceous, but I did not detect that in either their Prelude Vineyards or Art Series offerings.

The 1998 Cabernet Sauvignon/Merlot Prelude Vineyards offers sweet currant, creamy oak, and subtle olive notes in its elegant, medium-bodied, spicy, Provençal-like personality. It is a well-concentrated, excellent Cabernet/Merlot to enjoy over the next 7–8 years. A blend of 83% Cabernet and 17% Merlot, the 1997 Cabernet Sauvignon/Merlot Prelude Vineyards is even better. A Bordeaux-like bouquet of tobacco, cedar, black currants, and new oak is followed by an elegant, austere, but concentrated offering with beautiful purity and flavors, medium to full body, sweet tannin, and a long, nicely textured finish. It should drink well for a decade.

The Art Series Cabernet Sauvignons are powerful efforts (14.5% alcohol) that are meant to evolve for 15+ years. Both the 1996 and 1997 are impressive. Aged in 100% French oak, the dense ruby/plum/purple 1996 offers textbook aromas of tobacco, cedar, cassis, and new oak in addition to deep, full-bodied flavors with good acidity, moderate tannin, and excellent texture. Long, persuasive, rich, and well-balanced, it will be at its finest between now and 2015. The 1997 introduces fudge and cigar smoke to its aromatic combination of cassis, cedar, tobacco, and new oak. It is full-bodied, with super fruit, outstanding purity, and a long, nicely-textured, moderately tannic finish. Anticipated maturity: now–2016.

Another outstanding wine is the 1995 Cabernet Sauvignon. A blend of 75% Cabernet Sauvignon and the rest Merlot and Malbec from their vineyard near the Margaret River, this impressive, highly extracted, dark purple-colored, backward Cabernet requires a little more cellaring. It should keep for two decades. The Bordeaux-like nose of cedarwood, tobacco, red and black currants, and licorice, is followed by a ripe, full-bodied, dense, powerful wine that still plays it close to the vest. Merely hinting at its ultimate potential, this Cabernet Sauvignon should be purchased only by those with the discipline to wait 2–3 years.

PETER LEHMANN (BAROSSA VALLEY)

1999 Cabernet Sauvignon	C	86
1998 Cabernet Sauvignon	C	87
1997 Cabernet Sauvignon	C	89

1999	Clancy's Gold Preference	D	87
1998	Clancy's Gold Preference	D	90
1997	Mentor	E	90
1996	Mentor	E	92
1995	Mentor	E	88
1997	Seven Surveys	C	88
1999	Shiraz	C	87
1998	Shiraz	C	90
1997	Shiraz	C	89
1998	Shiraz Eight Songs	E	93
1997	Shiraz Eight Songs	E	90
1996	Shiraz Eight Songs	E	93
1996	Shiraz Stonewell	E	92+
1994	Shiraz Stonewell	E	95

This is one of the most famous names of Australia's famed Barossa Valley, with a production in excess of 500,000 cases. The consistently reliable wines are made in an exuberant, "Aussie" style. Reasonably good values include the user-friendly, fruit-driven, soft, blackberry- and currant-scented 1999 Shiraz that must be enjoyed over the next 5–6 years. The 1998 Shiraz exhibits a dense ruby/purple color with intense, chocolate-infused, blackberry/cassis aromatics that continue to detonate on the palate with a cascade of jammy, peppery flavors. American oak frames up this full-bodied Shiraz that tips the scales at 14% alcohol. Drink it over the next decade. The deep ruby/purple-colored 1997 Shiraz is a terrific wine value. It offers a big, sweet, peppery, earthy, creosote, blackberry, and cassis-scented bouquet and flavor. Fat and chewy, with low acidity, this plump Shiraz should drink well for a decade.

The Cabernet Sauvignons are also good values. The 1999 is a medium-bodied, spicy offering with plum, cedar, and cherry fruit. This wine requires consumption over the near term. Even better, the 1998 Cabernet Sauvignon is an elegant yet richer version of the 1999, with deep, cedary, currant fruit intermixed with spice box, licorice, and vanilla. It should last 7–8 years. Made in a Pauillac-like style, the dark ruby/purple 1997 Cabernet Sauvignon offers notes of cedar, balsam wood, black currants, fruitcake, and chocolate that emerge from the complex bouquet. On the palate, the wine is full-bodied and concentrated, with low acidity, sweet tannin, and copious glycerin and fat.

A blend of 53% Shiraz, 30% Cabernet Sauvignon, 10% Merlot, and 7% Cabernet Franc, the 1999 Clancy's Gold Preference exhibits an earthy, leathery, meaty bouquet with red and black currants lurking in the background. Some oak is discernible, but this excellent wine is rich, ripe, spicy, and medium- to full-bodied. It should drink well for a decade. The deep ruby/purple-colored 1998 Clancy's Gold Preference, a blend of 54% Shiraz, 22% Cabernet Sauvignon, 12% Merlot, and 12% Cabernet Franc, displays a muted, monolithic nose, but full-bodied, highly concentrated flavors. Another year or two of cellaring will result in more aromatic complexity in this dense, chewy, thick, multilayered wine. It should last for 12+ years.

The 1997 Mentor, a blend of 60% Cabernet Sauvignon, 17% Malbec, 12% Shiraz, and 11% Merlot, is a more tightly knit, less massive effort. It exhibits good aromatics, medium to full body, and pure, sweet red and black currant fruit intermixed with cedarwood and tobacco. Anticipated maturity: now–2015. The seriously endowed 1996 Mentor is a blend of 60% Cabernet Sauvignon, 20% Merlot, 10% Shiraz, and 10% Malbec. An opaque purple color is accompanied by complex aromas of damp earth, cedarwood, mint, plum liqueur, licorice, black currants, and new oak. Full-bodied, deep, and chewy, with moderate tannin and excellent concentration as well as body, it will drink well for 10–15 years. The 1995 Mentor, a blend of 70% Cabernet Sauvignon, 20% Malbec, and 10% Merlot, is rather closed.

It displays few aromas but big, thick, juicy, black raspberry and berry flavors plus weedy tobacco notes. Full-bodied and moderately tannic, it requires some cellaring and should keep for 15+ years.

The excellent 1997 Seven Surveys, a blend of 34% Mourvèdre, 33% Grenache, and 33% Shiraz, offers peppery, cherry jam–like aromas and flavors. Foursquare, spicy, and full-bodied, with austere tannin, it should be drunk in its rustic youth—over the next 4–5 years.

Peter Lehmann's top Shiraz *cuvées* are the Eight Songs and Stonewell. The Shiraz Eight Songs, named for the production of *Eight Songs for a Mad King*, the story of King George III, is aged in 100% French oak and sold only in eight-bottle cases. The Stonewell Shiraz sees 100% American oak. The 1998 Shiraz Eight Songs is a sensational effort. It boasts a black/purple color as well as muscular, full-bodied flavors that make a huge impact on the palate. The abundant black currant and blackberry fruit are intermixed with notes of new oak, minerals, and pepper. Long and layered, with multiple flavor dimensions, it is a powerhouse blockbuster. Anticipated maturity: now–2020. Readers looking for a more laid-back, restrained style that is still robust will enjoy the 1997 Shiraz Eight Songs. It exhibits blackberries, spice box, pepper, and sweet oak in its medium- to full-bodied, more restrained, less massive personality. Deep, harmonious, and concentrated, it will drink well for 10–12 years. The 1996 Shiraz Eight Songs is an exuberant, concentrated effort. A dense opaque purple color is accompanied by flamboyant scents of roasted coffee, cedarwood, cassis, blackberries, and sweet new French oak. In the mouth, flavors of prune liqueur and black currants are backed up by abundant glycerin, extract, and sweet tannin, giving the wine a weighty yet pure, concentrated impression. The French oak provides some restraint in this forward, super-concentrated Shiraz. Consume it now and over the next 10–12 years.

The 1996 Shiraz Stonewell is a big, broodingly backward wine offering aromas and flavors of melted asphalt, black raspberries, smoke, graphite, pepper, and blackberries. Full-bodied and moderately tannic, with good underlying acidity as well as structure, it is still an infant, but should mature over the next two decades, and will be uncommonly long-lived. The thick opaque black/purple-colored 1994 Shiraz Stonewell boasts a sumptuous nose of black raspberries, cassis, toasty American oak, vanilla, spice, and pepper. This monster-sized, chewy, lavishly-endowed Shiraz is soft enough to be drunk now, but promises to age well for 10–15 years.

LENGS AND COOTER (CLARE VALLEY)

1999 Shiraz Old Vines	D	87
1998 Shiraz Old Vines	D	93
1999 Shiraz Reserve	E	89
1998 Shiraz Reserve	E	96
1999 The Victor	B	86

A proprietary blend of 55% Shiraz and 45% Grenache, the 1999 The Victor is a reasonably good value. It is a straightforward, round, ripe, dark ruby/purple-colored wine that is monolithic but pleasant and mouthcoating. Drink it over the next 2–3 years.

Neither the 1999 Shiraz Old Vines nor the 1999 Shiraz Reserve matched the intensity, high volume, and concentration of their 1998 counterparts. Both are more elegant, restrained wines, but are still noteworthy. The Old Vines *cuvée* is made from 25- to 100-year-old vines and aged with 50% new American oak, while the Reserve sees 80% new American oak. There are 450 cases produced of the Old Vines and 140 cases of the Reserve.

The 1999 Shiraz Old Vines is medium weight, has a deep ruby/purple color, a spicy, peppery, black currant nose, and some noticeable American new oak (about 50% is new). Drink it over the next 5–7 years. The opaque purple 1998 Shiraz Old Vines exhibits a stunning, soaring bouquet offering aromas of crème de cassis, smoked herbs, licorice, tar, and creamy new oak. Full-bodied and super-concentrated, with notions of blackberry jam as well as moderate tannin, this dazzling Shiraz can be drunk now or cellared for 10–12 years.

The substantial 1999 Shiraz Reserve shows plenty of toasty notes, but also displays generous licorice, blackberry, and heady fruit. This full-bodied, moderately powerful wine reveals some tannin in the finish and may actually improve with another one to two years of bottle age. However, it seems destined to be best drunk during its first 10–12 years of life.

Even more profound is the 1998 Shiraz Reserve. The telltale bacon fat, pepper, smoke, and blackberry/melted asphalt aromas and flavors can only come from ultraconcentrated, voluptuously textured Shiraz from Australia. Superpowerful, full-bodied, and excitingly pure, this is an unreal wine to drink over the next 15–20 years.

LENSWOOD (ADELAIDE HILLS)

1998 The Palatine   **D 92**

The 1998 The Palatine, a blend of 52% Cabernet Sauvignon, 31% Merlot, and 17% Malbec, is a dense, purple-colored, distinctively styled offering. Twenty percent of the fruit went through the so-called Amarone winemaking technique (an Italian process of running grape must through pomace), and thus there is an earthy, ripe, full-bodied, late-harvest character. The wine shows huge extract, dense, earthy, tar, blackberry, and cassis flavors, superb purity, and good underlying tannin as well as acidity. This rich blend is best drunk with full-flavored meat or earthy dishes. Anticipated maturity: now–2015.

LIEBICH VEIN (BAROSSA VALLEY)

1999 Shiraz C. W.'s Block   **D 93**

With 15% natural alcohol, aging in both older French and American oak and bottled without filtration, this 120-case *cuvée* is sure to sell out quickly. The opaque purple-colored, blockbuster 1999 Shiraz offers notes of melted asphalt, smoke, black fruits, pepper, and animal fur. Full-bodied, thick, and heavy, this massive wine should drink well for 12–15 years.

LIMELIGHT (McLAREN VALE)

1998 Syrah   **D 89**

This is a big, thick, unctuously styled 1998 Syrah with plenty of black fruits intermixed with licorice, tar, pepper, and wood. It spent 18 months in a combination of new and old American oak. Full-bodied, with good structure, plenty of depth, and a chewy mouth-feel, it should be consumed over the next 4–5 years.

LOST WOLF (BAROSSA VALLEY)

1997 Cabernet Sauvignon   **D 88**

1996 Cabernet Sauvignon   **D 91**

I'll keep the tasting notes simple since there are only 50 cases of each of these. The light, graceful 1997 Cabernet Sauvignon offers aromas and flavors of plums, currants, and well-integrated oak, medium body, and sweet tannin. Anticipated maturity: 2004–2015. The 1996 Cabernet Sauvignon is a hedonistic, huge, in-your-face Cabernet with copious quantities of black currant and cherry fruit wrapped in an unctuously textured black fruit and chocolate fruit bomb. Drink this dense, chewy, hedonistic wine over the next decade. A detail worth noting is that these wines were made at David Powell's Torbreck Winery.

MAD FISH (WESTERN AUSTRALIA)

1999 Shiraz   **A 86**

The 1999 Shiraz outperformed many of its peers selling for 3–4 times the price. A healthy dark ruby color is accompanied by peppery, smoky, blackberry, and plum-like fruit. Soft and medium-bodied, it is an ideal choice for uncritical quaffing over the next 2–3 years.

MAGPIE ESTATE (BAROSSA VALLEY)

1999	Grenache Gomersol	E	87?
1999	Mourvèdre/Grenache	C	90
1998	Mourvèdre/Grenache	D	89
1998	Shiraz/Mourvèdre Black Sock	E	95

These wines are made by one of my favorite Australian wine-makers, Rolf Binder. The 1999 Grenache Gomersol (100% Grenache aged in 50% new French and 50% American oak) shows too much creamy wood to merit higher marks. It also has a quasi-international style, moderate tannin, and a structured, almost uncharacteristically tightly knit style for Grenache. The color is a deep ruby/purple, and the wine is cleanly made and pure but lacks the expression and character of other offerings from the Magpie Estate. Drink by 2008.

The Mourvèdre/Grenache blend emerges from 60–80-year-old vines and is composed of equal parts of each varietal. Production is rather small (around 200 cases), but prices remain fair. The outstanding 1999 is a beautiful wine offering a gorgeous nose of pepper, Old Bay spice, black raspberries, and cherries. It is exotic, somewhat kinky, and distinctive, but medium- to full-bodied, with an encroaching note of new saddle leather in the finish. Think of it as an Australian version of Bandol. Anticipated maturity: now–2012. The 1998 Mourvèdre/Grenache's dark plum color is accompanied by a sweet cherry, spice, and dried herb–scented bouquet. It offers lovely, well-balanced, medium-bodied richness, a continuation of the ripe cherry character, low acidity, and a moderately long finish. Drink it over the next 5–6 years.

The Shiraz/Mourvèdre Black Sock emerges from 60–100-year-old vines and is composed of 80% Shiraz and 20% Mourvèdre. It is aged for a whopping 30 months in American wood. Production is small, around 150 cases annually. The prodigious 1998 is a blockbuster. This opaque purple-colored wine offers an almost essence of blackberry and cherry fruit intermixed with earth, leather, charcoal, and new wood. The wine is full-bodied, spectacularly concentrated, with multiple levels to its mid-palate, and a whoppingly powerful, rich finish. I was surprised to learn that the wine has only 13.5% alcohol, given the huge swath it cuts across the palate. Anticipated maturity: now–2018.

MAJELLA (COONAWARRA)

1998	Cabernet Sauvignon	D	91
1997	Cabernet Sauvignon	D	90
1998	Shiraz	D	94
1997	Shiraz	D	88
1998	Shiraz/Cabernet Sauvignon Maleea	E	92
1997	Shiraz/Cabernet Sauvignon Maleea	E	93?

Based on what I have tasted, Majella (owned by Brian and Anthony Lynn) is undoubtedly the finest wine in the Coonawarra. Their current releases all performed admirably and, as readers will note, most of these wines are realistically priced. The most expensive wine of the portfolio, the Shiraz/Cabernet Sauvignon Maleea is worth its price. There are 500 cases of this blend of 55% Cabernet and 45% Shiraz, aged in 100% new French wood. The 1998 is opaque purple in color, with a spectacularly intense and pure nose of melted licorice, cassis, and blackberry. This full-bodied wine is extremely well delineated, has fabulous symmetry and overall harmony, seamless integration of acidity, tannin, and alcohol, and a 35–40-second finish. The wine is still youthful, but promises to evolve nicely for at least 15 or more years. If the lavish quantities of toasty new French oak become better integrated in the 1997 Shiraz/Cabernet Sauvignon Maleea, this wine will easily merit its 93 points. A sensationally rich, impressively structured effort, it possesses a black/purple color, the aforementioned heavy overlay of toasty new oak, gorgeous blueberry, blackberry, and cassis flavors, a ton of toast and vanilla-like scents, full body, and a rich, concentrated finish with impressive levels of sweet fruit. It still tastes like a barrel sample, so give it 1–2 years of cellaring. It should age nicely for two decades.

There are 1,800 cases of the authoritatively flavorful yet stylish 100% Cabernet that is available for a realistic price. The deep ruby/purple-colored 1998 displays notions of American and French oak in its plum, cassis, cedar, and spice box–scented nose. This thick, juicy, full-bodied, opulent, and at the same time well-delineated wine represents a brilliant marriage of power and elegance. Anticipated maturity: now–2015. The 1997 Cabernet Sauvignon exhibits cassis, cedar, smoked herb, prune, and plum liqueur scents. Full-bodied and concentrated, with less noticeable oak, this big Coonawarra Cabernet should be at its finest before 2015.

The 100% Shiraz, which emerges from a cooler climate than the Barossa, is made from 30-year-old vines and aged completely in American oak. There are 1,800 cases of this wine. The 1998 shows dense purple color, a classic cassis, blackberry, leathery, peppery nose, and unctuously textured, full-bodied flavors that are penetrating, brilliantly well defined, and strikingly pure. Again, a long finish, no heaviness, and an almost seamlessness to the wine make it indeed a special offering, and the price makes it a true steal in the marketplace. It can be drunk now and over the next 12–15 years. Abundant quantities of freshly ground pepper and blackberry/cassis fruit jump from the glass of the 1997 Shiraz. It also possesses spicy oak, medium to full body, and a nicely packaged, concentrated style. Although not a blockbuster, it is flavorful, ripe, and well made. Drink it over the next 5–6 years.

MAK (COONAWARRA)

1999 Cabernet Sauvignon/Shiraz Snowy River	B	90
1998 Cabernet Sauvignon/Shiraz Snowy River	B	88

Importer Rob McDonald, of Old Bridge Cellars, has purchased land in Australia and has begun producing his own wine. His first effort, the deep plum/purple 1998 Cabernet Sauvignon/Shiraz Snowy River (which includes tiny dollops of Merlot and Cabernet Franc) is a rustic, tannic, structured effort with plenty of stuffing, muscular, smoky, earthy, blackberry, and cassis flavors offered in a mouth-filling style. It should drink well for 7–8 years.

Even better, the 1999 Cabernet Sauvignon/Shiraz Snowy River (59% Cabernet and 41% Shiraz) is more supple, with a lusher texture. It possesses plenty of power, concentration, and blackberry/cassis fruit intermixed with earth, pepper, smoke, and wood. Consumer-friendly, dense, and chewy, with considerable charm and seductiveness, it will drink well for 5–7 years. Both of these wines are excellent values.

MAXWELL (McLAREN VALE)

1999 Cabernet Sauvignon Lime Cave	D	93
1998 Cabernet Sauvignon Lime Cave	D	94+
1998 Grenache	D	91
1999 Shiraz Ellen Street	D	92
1998 Shiraz Ellen Street	D	91+
1997 Shiraz Ellen Street	D	91

From a winery that consistently turns out fine products, the vines for the Cabernet Sauvignon Lime Cave grow in clay/limestone soils near a cave used for growing mushrooms. This wine is aged in both American and French oak, of which 30% was new, and is bottled unfiltered. The sensational 1999's opaque purple color is followed by an explosive bouquet of black currants, blackberries, and smoke. Full-bodied, with gorgeous density, sweet, concentrated fruit, good purity, and impeccable balance between the tannin, acidity, alcohol, and extract, it will drink well for 12–15 years. The 1998 Cabernet Sauvignon Lime Cave is tightly knit with a beautiful texture. Offering a combination of power and elegance, its Pauillac-like cedary, spice box aromas turn into blackberry liqueur mixed with cassis and other assorted black fruits as it aerates. This spectacular Cabernet requires some cellaring, and should age for 15 years.

The Shiraz Ellen Street is produced from 40-year-old vines. Aged primarily in American oak (and about 20% French oak), it is bottled unfiltered. This wine is consistently an outstanding value in great Australian Shiraz. The 1999 is a dense, fat, thermonuclear Shiraz fruit bomb. Opaque ruby/purple with aromas and flavors of black fruits intermixed with earth, truffles, chocolate, and a hint of coffee, this full-bodied, unctuously textured, pure, large-scaled yet surprisingly well balanced, massive wine can be drunk now and over the next 10–15 years. The promising 1998 Shiraz Ellen Street is quite closed, revealing an opaque black/purple color, sweet, jammy blackberry and cassis fruit, great purity, full body, and multiple layers of fruit. It does not yet display the secondary nuances found in the 1997, but they should emerge after another year of bottle age. It should last 10–15 years. The 1997 Shiraz Ellen Street's black/purple color is followed by an earthy, peppery, spice box, truffle, licorice, and black currant/berry-scented bouquet. Full-bodied and highly extracted, this top-notch, rich, concentrated powerhouse is impressive, even though it has emerged from a less renowned vintage than its younger sibling. Anticipated maturity: now–2016.

The dense purple-colored 1998 Grenache is produced from old vines and bottled unfiltered. This full-bodied Grenache exhibits leathery, earthy, black raspberry, and kirsch flavors, a touch of road tar, and copious glycerin and richness. Drink it over the next 5–6 years.

MEEREA PARK (HUNTER VALLEY)

1999 Cabernet Sauvignon/Merlot	C	88
1998 Shiraz Alexander Munro	D	89
1999 Shiraz The Aunts	C	87

The dark ruby-colored 1999 Cabernet Sauvignon/Merlot reveals aromas of new French oak plus black currants, cherries, and spice box. Although not complex, it is well made, pure, full, deep, ripe, and nicely balanced. As the wine sat in the glass, smoky tobacco characteristics emerged. This Bordeaux-styled good value should drink well for 7–8 years.

The soft, straightforward 1999 Shiraz The Aunts (100% Shiraz) offers chocolaty, blackberry, pepper, earth, and licorice notes. Foursquare but plump and tasty, it will drink well for 4–5 years. The highly extracted, deep purple-colored 1998 Shiraz Alexander Munro was aged in 100% new French and American oak. It is a powerful, moderately tannic, dense wine that remains unevolved and youthful. If it develops more complexity, it will merit an outstanding rating. Large-scaled, muscular, and deep, it offers a classic display of melted tar, blackberries, crème de cassis, and licorice. Drink it over the next 10–12 years.

CHARLES MELTON (BAROSSA VALLEY)

1998 Cabernet Sauvignon	D	86
1998 Grenache	D	90
1998 Nine Popes	D	89
1997 Nine Popes	D	92
1999 Shiraz	D	88
1997 Shiraz	D	88

The Nine Popes, a blend of Grenache, Shiraz, and Mourvèdre, emerges from 80–100-year-old Grenache vines. Beautifully made and fun to drink, this is Australia's version of Châteauneuf-du-Pape. The 1998 Nine Popes boasts a saturated ruby/purple color in addition to abundant quantities of peppery kirsch and earthy notes, and medium to full body, which provide a large, dense, chewy palate impact. Drink it over the next 4–5 years.

The gorgeous 1997 Nine Popes offers aromas of kirsch, cherry jam, raspberries, roasted peanuts, and herbs, terrific fruit intensity, full body, copious glycerin, and a mid-palate that suggests low yields and old vines. Drink it over the next decade.

The big, minty, black currant, and peppery-styled dark ruby/purple 1999 Shiraz offers plenty of spice, excellent concentration plus purity, and a soft finish. Drink it over the next 5–6 years. The 1997 Shiraz seems rather civilized and restrained. It has a dense dark ruby color with purple nuances. Notes of black fruits (particularly berries) emerge from the moderately intense bouquet. Not a blockbuster in the style of many Barossa Valley Shirazes, this is an elegant, well-balanced, concentrated wine exhibiting excellent purity, ripeness, and character. More aromatics will emerge with bottle age. Anticipated maturity: now–2008.

The dense ruby-colored 1998 Grenache exhibits a sweet nose of kirsch, pepper, spice, and earth. Full-bodied, fleshy, and rich, with sweet fruit and copious glycerin, this southern Rhône–like offering can be drunk now and over the next 7–8 years.

The dark ruby/purple 1998 Cabernet Sauvignon offers minty, black currant flavors. Medium- to full-bodied and firm, with moderate tannin, sweet fruit, and a structured, tight finish, it requires 2–3 years of cellaring and should drink well for 10–12 years.

MITCHELL (CLARE VALLEY)

1999 Shiraz Peppertree	C	90

Aged in 100% French oak for 12 months prior to bottling, the impressively endowed 1999 Shiraz Peppertree boasts an opaque ruby/purple color as well as a sweet nose of black fruits, new saddle leather, earth, tar, and licorice—a classic Australian Shiraz aromatic profile. The French oak provides subtlety vis-à-vis some of the more aggressive Shiraz that see American oak. This 1999 possesses supple tannin, full body, outstanding density and purity, and a low-acid, plump finish. It should be drunk over the next decade.

MITCHELTON (VICTORIA)

1997 Cabernet Sauvignon Sidey's	C	87
1999 Shiraz Crescent	C	86
1997 Shiraz Print Label	D	89
1996 Shiraz Print Label	D	88

This Victoria winery offers an array of very good value red and white wines. The whites, which include superb Rieslings, Chardonnays, and a high-quality blend called Airstrip, are not reviewed here since they must be consumed within a few months of the vintage.

The 1999 Shiraz Crescent is a straightforward, ripe, rich, fruity offering with medium to full body, soft tannin, and a peppery, pleasant finish. Anticipated maturity: now–2007.

The 1997 Cabernet Sauvignon Sidey's reveals textbook black currant fruit intermixed with tobacco and coffee. Medium- to full-bodied, with a fruit-driven style, it offers moderate quantities of wood and tannin. It should drink well for 7–8 years. The finest red wine of the portfolio is the dark ruby/purple 1997 Shiraz Print Label. Aromas of plums, blackberries, graphite, smoke, and pepper are followed by a dense, medium- to full-bodied, rich, lightly tannic Shiraz. Anticipated maturity: now–2014.

An opaque ruby/garnet color is followed by heavy, American oak, chocolate, coconut, and black cherry/berry fruit aromas. Full-bodied, soft, obvious, and pleasurable in its blatant combination of fruit and oak, the 1996 Shiraz Print Label should drink well for 5–8 years.

MORAMBRO CREEK (PADTHAWAY)

1999 Cabernet Sauvignon	D	85
1999 Shiraz	D	89

The Bryson family, longtime growers and vineyard owners, is responsible for these wines. Although essentially one-dimensional, the 1999 Cabernet Sauvignon offers a smoky, elegant, black currant nose, medium body, and a cleanly made, pure personality. Anticipated maturity: now–2008. The 1999 Shiraz sports a deep ruby/purple color, a full-bodied, broad, expansive palate, and excellent black fruits intermixed with asphalt, fresh tar, and pepper. There is some oakiness that is not yet integrated. Drink it over the next 10 years.

MOSS WOOD (MARGARET RIVER)

1996 Cabernet Sauvignon	D	93+
1997 Pinot Noir	D	88?

The dark ruby-colored 1997 Pinot Noir does not portray the elegant side of this varietal. It has hefty 14.5% alcohol, and reminds me of well-made Pinot Noirs grown in hot climates. Notes of chocolate, toasty oak, cherry jam, and roasted herbs emerge from this deep, rich, full-bodied offering, which cuts a meaty, earthy profile on the palate. It might be loosely compared to some of the chewier, heavier styles of Pommard from Burgundy's Côte d'Or. In any event, it is a flavorful, intense wine that I enjoyed more because of its flavors and hedonistic qualities than for its depiction of Pinot Noir. Drink it over the next 4–5 years.

Cabernet lovers looking for a compelling example of this varietal should check out the expensive but profound 1996 Cabernet Sauvignon. Opaque purple in color, with a striking bouquet of olives, cassis jam, beef blood, minerals, earth, and new wood, this massive, super-concentrated Cabernet Sauvignon should prove to be a great classic from Down Under. It is oozing with flavor extraction, has high tannin, and cuts a formidable path on the palate. Anticipated maturity: now–2020.

MOUNT HORROCKS (CLARE VALLEY)

1998 Cabernet/Merlot	D	86
1997 Cabernet/Merlot	D	90
2000 Riesling Cordon Cut	D	92
1999 Riesling Cordon Cut	D	92
1998 Shiraz	D	90

The 1998 Cabernet/Merlot is a lean, austere Australian red, with minty, red currant, and cherry characteristics, spice, underlying earthiness, and a moderately long finish. Drink it over the next 5–6 years. The outstanding 1997 Cabernet/Merlot (85% Cabernet and 15% Merlot, aged in 100% French oak) is concentrated, ripe, and backward, exhibiting impressive levels of cassis/blackberry fruit nicely dosed by wood. Deep, classic, and well proportioned, this well-endowed, full-bodied wine will be at its finest until 2015.

The dark ruby/purple 1998 Shiraz is an interesting wine. It offers a sweet, complex, earthy, tar, and jammy red and black fruit–scented bouquet, beautiful purity, medium to full body, and a sense of elegance and overall symmetry. This flavorful, graceful Shiraz can be consumed now and over the next 7–8 years.

The light gold-colored 2000 Riesling Cordon Cut has good acidity, 11% alcohol, and a style somewhere between a sweet Auslese and Beerenauslese from Germany. There are abundant quantities of honeysuckle and jammy tropical fruits in addition to wonderful, refreshing acidity to provide uplift and zest. This pure Riesling is best drunk with fruit desserts over the next 2–4 years. Nectar lovers will be impressed with the Beerenauslese-styled 1999 Riesling Cordon Cut. With 13.5% residual sugar and good underlying acidity, this exceptionally pure wine offers honeyed tropical fruits, an underlying minerality, and a light-bodied, unctuous yet refreshing finish. Drink it over the next 4 years.

MOUNT LANGI GHIRAN (VICTORIA)

1996 Cabernet Sauvignon/Merlot	C	86?
1997 Shiraz	C	91
1997 Shiraz Billi Billi	B	88

Trevor Mast, a longtime proponent of old, head-pruned Shiraz, has produced stunning Shiraz over the last several decades. Readers looking for a reasonably good value in old vine Shiraz should check out the 1997 Shiraz Billi Billi. With its dense ruby/purple color and sweet, jammy, blackberry, pepper, and spicy-scented nose, this full-bodied, supple-textured, luscious, in-your-face wine will have huge commercial appeal. Made from old Shiraz vineyards in both the Barossa and McLaren Vale sectors, it is delicious already, and promises to drink well for 4–5 years. Even more hedonistic and powerful is the black/purple-colored 1997 Shiraz. Exotic, with ripe notes of blackberries, cassis, and spice, this nicely layered wine has considerable tannin, but it is sweet, and hardly noticeable given the wine's low acidity and wealth of rich fruit and copious glycerin. This full-bodied classic should drink well young, yet evolve nicely for 10–12 years.

The 1996 Cabernet Sauvignon/Merlot is less impressive. It has a saturated color, but dry, hard tannin in the finish gives it an attenuated impression. It is medium-bodied, with earthy, black currant fruit and weedy notes on the attack, but then narrows out with severe tannin in the finish. Does it have the requisite depth to balance out the wine's structure?

NEAGLE'S ROCK (CLARE VALLEY)

1998 Cabernet Sauvignon	C	89

A touch more complexity and this 1998 Cabernet Sauvignon would have been outstanding. Nevertheless, it is an excellent value. Boldly styled, with an opaque ruby/purple color and explosive black currant fruit intermixed with smoke and earth, this wine shows wonderful richness, sweet tannin, low acidity in the attack, and a corpulent, chewy mouth-feel. Drink it over the next decade.

NEPENTHE (ADELAIDE HILLS)

1999 Zinfandel	D	86

Nepenthe, a Greek word meaning "elixir that heals all pain and grief," displays a stronger hand with its whites (Sauvignon Blanc, Chardonnay, and Sémillon) than its red wines. For example, a blend of Cabernet Sauvignon, Merlot, and Cabernet Franc, the 1998 Le Fugue was austere and too dependent on Euro-styled elegance for its appeal. Another wine, the 1999 Pinot Noir, revealed a light style without any real center of flavor. However, the 1999 Zinfandel seems to be a good effort. This wine (only 80 cases available) is a soft, briery, tasty, elegant, medium-bodied wine that somehow magically conceals its whopping 16% alcohol. While it will not make anyone forget the finest California Zinfandels, this Adelaide Hills curiosity is well made. Consume it over the next 2–3 years.

NOON (LANGHORN CREEK)

1999 Cabernet Sauvignon Reserve	E	94
1998 Cabernet Sauvignon Reserve	E	98+
1999 Eclipse	D	94
1998 Eclipse	D	96
1999 Noon V.P.	E	90
1998 Noon V.P.	E	94
1999 Shiraz Reserve	E	96
1998 Shiraz Reserve	E	98

This is one of the brilliant wineries of Australia, offering wines of exceptional purity, symmetry, and individuality. Production ranges from minuscule quantities such as the 85 or so cases of the Noon V.P. to 580 cases of the Shiraz Reserve and nearly 1,000 cases of the Eclipse. This winery made fabulous 1998s and has succeeded admirably in 1999, a lighter year.

The 1999 Eclipse is a blend of 66% Grenache and 34% Shiraz aged in American oak and bottled unfiltered. This wine tips the scales at a hefty 14.9% alcohol. The wine has an opaque purple color as well as a fabulously sweet nose of blackberry and cassis interspersed with licorice, truffle, and vanilla. Full-bodied, heady, layered, ripe, pure, and sumptuous, it is a dazzling 1999 to drink over the next 15–16 years. The 1998 Eclipse (from 35- to 65-year-old Shiraz vines cropped at two tons per acre) possesses a whopping 15.7% alcohol, which is totally concealed by the dense, blackberry liqueur–scented and –flavored fruit. Notes of cassis, toast, pepper, and licorice can also be found in this thick, full-bodied effort. It is a phenomenally rich, super-extracted wine of astonishing intensity. The tannin is sweet, the acidity low, and the wine unreal. Drink it over the next 10–15+ years.

It is a shame there is not more of the Noon V.P. This wine is made from 80-year-old Grenache vines and fortified with alcohol, giving it a dry vintage port character. The alcohol levels are 19.6% for the 1999 and 20.1% for the 1998, yet neither comes across as cloying or sweet. They are, however, dense, viscous, full-bodied, after-dinner cheese course wines with extraordinary levels of black fruits, notes of kirsch, pepper, and spice. It is hard to know how they will age, but I would assume 10–15 years is well within conservative estimates. Their flavors and characteristics are unlike anything I have tasted from the Old or New World. They are undeniably singular expressions that are riveting wines in their own right.

For a more conventional dry table wine still made in a large-scaled style, readers should check out the Shiraz Reserve or Cabernet Sauvignon Reserve.

The 100% Cabernet Sauvignon, whch emerges from 35-year-old vines, is, sadly, not widely available, production averaging 300 cases a year. The 1999 Cabernet Sauvignon Reserve could easily be called a Pauillac from Australia. Dense ruby/purple, a classic Cabernet nose of cedar wood, smoke, cassis, mineral, lead pencil, and new oak soars from the glass. In the mouth, it is full-bodied, with fabulous concentration and multilayered texture, high levels of glycerin, and a seamless, concentrated, long finish with well-integrated tannin, acidity, and alcohol. This is no wimpish wine at 14.6% alcohol. Anticipated maturity: now–2020. It would be interesting to insert the 1998 Cabernet Sauvignon Reserve (15.5% alcohol) in a blind tasting with Cabernet fashioned by Bryant Family Vineyard, Harlan Estate, Colgin, Château Montelena, and Screaming Eagle (a salivating proposition). Nearly perfect, this black/purple-colored Cabernet offers extraordinary sweet black cherry/black currant aromas as well as huge, gorgeously proportioned, voluptuously textured flavors that last 50+ seconds. The wine reveals no hotness from the high alcohol, unbelievable purity, symmetry, and the potential to improve for 10–15 years. It should keep for two decades or more.

The Shiraz Reserve emerges from Shiraz vines that average 35–40 years of age, and is aged in a combination of small and large oak barrels. There are 580 cases of this behemoth. The hugely extracted, massive 1999 Shiraz Reserve tips the scales at 15.2% alcohol. An opaque blue/purple color and a knockout nose of blackberry liqueur intermixed with spice box, pepper, asphalt, and licorice soar from the glass. Opulent and viscous, with tremendous palate presence, beautifully integrated acidity, tannin, and alcohol, this superb, larger-than-life wine is a tour de force for a lighter-weight vintage such as 1999. Anticipated maturity: now–2020. The opaque black/blue-colored 1998 Shiraz Reserve displays a fascinating bouquet of violets, black raspberry and blackberry liqueur, cedar, fruitcake, and pepper. Surreal levels of glycerin and richness are present in this full-bodied, surprisingly supple-textured wine. The finish lasts for several minutes. Anticipated maturity: 2005–2020.

NURIOOTPA HIGH SCHOOL (BAROSSA VALLEY)

1999 Class Shiraz	E	90+
1998 Class Shiraz	E	94

This is a winery/school where students get to make wine as part of their education. The expertise and equipment as well as grapes are donated by local wineries. Sadly, the production is extremely small—one barrel, about 30 cases—hence the brief comments. This 100% Shiraz *cuvée*—a limited production blockbuster made from a 31-year-old Koonunga vineyard—is outstanding and certainly a credit to the students of Nuriootpa High School. Neo-prohibitionists and Puritans be warned, high schools in the U.S. may be next in teaching winemaking! Dense, opaque purple-colored with plenty of crème de cassis notes intermixed with some smoke and earth, the full-bodied, slightly rustic, but rich, chewy 1999 Class Shiraz should drink well for at least 10–15 years. The explosive, fabulously concentrated 1998 Class Shiraz is full-bodied and super-concentrated, with abundant quantities of pepper-infused blackberry fruit. Anticipated maturity: now–2017.

ODDFELLOWS (LANGHORNE CREEK)

1998 Shiraz	C	91

A powerful 1998 Shiraz (15.8% alcohol), this chewy, somewhat closed, but dense, muscular Shiraz is crammed with leathery, earthy, blackberry, cassis fruit, has a corpulent personality, sweet tannin, and a lusty, slightly rustic, but powerful finish. I am not sure it is going to gain any finesse, so drink it over the next decade to take full advantage of such exuberance.

OLIVER'S TARANGA (McLAREN VALE)

1999 Shiraz	D	92
1998 Shiraz	D	95
1997 Shiraz	D	90
1996 Shiraz	D	94

For many years, proprietor Don Oliver's family sold fruit to the huge Penfolds operation, where it became one of the primary components of the great Grange. He now produces a 500-case 100% Shiraz from 45-year-old vines cropped at three tons of fruit per acre. These wines appear to be every bit as compelling as recent Granges.

The spectacular 1999 Shiraz (14.5% alcohol) offers a stunning fragrance of black fruits, incense, smoke, pepper, and sausage that soars from the glass in a wickedly exotic yet compelling bouquet. Opaque purple, with full body, awesome concentration, and nicely integrated French and American new wood, this large-scaled, opulent, chewy, super-concentrated wine makes one heck of a hedonistic impression. Anticipated maturity: now–2012.

Potentially the finest effort of this series, the saturated black/purple/blue 1998 Shiraz offers sensational aromas of blueberries, blackberries, and cassis, a huge, super-concentrated palate, fabulous purity, sweet tannin, and well-integrated acidity. While not yet as complex as the 1997 or 1996, the 1998 has more to it, and should prove to be the best wine after some further cellaring. It should age well for two decades.

The lightest wine of this series is the 1997 Shiraz. The most evolved, it provides terrific fruit richness, abundant blackberry, pepper, and sweet earthy notions, an intense, full-bodied palate, low acidity, and a mature, complex finish. The easygoing style and big, rich fruit make it delicious for current consumption. It should continue to drink well for 7–10 years. The 1996 Shiraz reveals mature aromas and flavors of creosote, melted chocolate, and gorgeous blackberry and cassis. Terrific body imbued with lofty glycerin, alcohol, and extract, it is less evolved than the 1997 as well as bigger, richer, and brawnier in the mouth. There is not a hard edge to be found in this accessible Shiraz. It promises to evolve for another 10–15+ years.

PARACOMBE (ADELAIDE HILLS)

1998 Cabernet Franc	C	89
1998 Shiraz	C	88
1997 Shiraz Somerville	E	91

An immensely impressive 100% Cabernet Franc, the 1998, aged 12 months in both American and French oak, exhibits a graceful, stylish, perfumed, raspberry and cherry nose intermixed with flower and subtle wood aromas. Medium-weight, soft, charming, and delicate yet flavorful, it displays hints of underbrush intermixed with floral-infused red and black fruits on the palate. There are no hard edges in this seamless, understated, yet flavorful wine. It is an achievement to produce a wine of such elegance and delicacy that retains plenty of flavor and intensity. Drink it over the next 4–5 years, although it may last longer.

Aged for two years in a combination of French and American barrels, the 1998 Shiraz (14.5% alcohol) possesses a black raspberry, pepper, and earth-scented bouquet, and a soft, layered, fleshy, chunky personality. While it does not have the complexity of the Cabernet Franc, it does offer more depth and fatness. Drink it over the next 4–5 years.

The exceptional 1997 Shiraz Somerville is a limited *cuvée* of 100 cases. I was surprised that the alcohol was listed on the bottle at 15.9%, because it is not apparent in tasting. This full-bodied, ruby/purple Shiraz exhibits a sweet nose of blackberry fruit intermixed with espresso, chocolate, and pepper. Some new wood makes an appearance, but the fruit dominates both the aromas and flavors. Pure, ripe, and long, with plenty of glycerin, it has the potential to drink gorgeously for up to a decade.

PARINGA (SOUTH AUSTRALIA)

2000 Merlot	A	87
2000 Shiraz	A	87
1999 Shiraz	A	88

Importer Dan Philips has hit the jackpot with what looks to be some attractive Australian blends available for a song. The surprises of his portfolio are the Merlot (1,500 cases) and Shiraz (12,000 cases). The 2000 Merlot comes in the door at 14% alcohol. The wine shows jammy, black cherry fruit in a forthright, fat, succulent style. It has deep ruby/purple color and surprising fruit and character. It is ideal to drink over the next 2 years. Plenty of black fruits emerge from the dark ruby color of the full-bodied, dense, chewy, spicy 2000 Shiraz. With undeniable character, this attractive Australian fruit bomb is available for a low price. It should drink well for 2–3 years. The 1999 Shiraz offers a dark purple color, surprising volume and intensity, abundant quantities of cassis fruit, no oak, and plenty of fat and glycerin in its velvety-textured, mouth-filling, friendly style. Drink it over the next 5–6 years.

PARKER COONAWARRA ESTATE (COONAWARRA)

1999 Terra Rosa Cabernet Sauvignon	D	90
1999 Terra Rosa First Growth	E	92+
1998 Terra Rosa First Growth	E	96
1996 Terra Rosa First Growth	E	93

Owner John Parker spares no expense in his attempt to produce Australia's finest Cabernet Sauvignon–based wine. Only 5–10% of any given year's production is used for the Terra Rosa First Growth, and, sadly, there are only 1,500 cases available each year. Parker was not satisfied with the quality of the 1997, 1995, and 1992, so Terra Rosa First Growth was produced, all of it being sold off or bottled under the winery's second label, Terra Rosa Cabernet Sauvignon. Readers weaned on Bordeaux will recognize an affinity to the likes of Mouton-Rothschild or Lynch-Bages, but only in the ripest, most opulently styled vintages. The wines (blends of Cabernet Sauvignon, Merlot, Cabernet Franc, and Petit Verdot) possess tremendous richness and are slightly thicker and juicier than Bordeaux, but they exhibit the telltale lead pencil, chocolate, cedar, spice box, and tobacco characteristics of a terrific Pauillac.

Although outstanding, the 1999 Terra Rosa First Growth is not at the level of the compelling 1998. It offers a ruby/purple color as well as a classic bouquet of black currants, cedar, and high-class French oak. If Jean-Michel Cazes (the proprietor of Lynch-Bages) were making wine in Australia, this is what it would taste like—deep and full-bodied, with attractively integrated acidity, tannin, and alcohol. Anticipated maturity: now–2020.

The second wine, the 1999 Terra Rosa Cabernet Sauvignon, is not to be dismissed. It offers a sweet, cedary, chocolaty, smoky, black currant–scented nose, low acidity, ripe, open-knit flavors, plenty of concentration, and admirable opulence as well as length. Although outstanding, it is not as majestic as its bigger sibling. Drink it over the next 10–15 years.

The 1998 Terra Rosa First Growth's dense purple color is followed by extraordinarily sweet fruit, intense glycerin, and a full-bodied, concentrated mouth-feel. The purity, high extract, and uncanny symmetry are breathtaking. Perhaps the finest Terra Rosa First Growth yet produced, it should drink well for two decades or more. The 1996 Terra Rosa First Growth reveals an opaque purple color, as well as a superb, expressive aromatic profile with the aforementioned scents, huge, fat, full-bodied flavors that coat the palate, low acidity, sweet tannin, and a sensationally long finish. This spectacular offering has few Australian rivals for richness and complexity. It should continue to drink well for 10–15 years.

PARSON'S FLAT (PADTHAWAY)

1999 Cabernet/Shiraz	D	88
1998 Cabernet/Shiraz	D	96

Made by well-known wine-makers Sarah and Sparky Marquis, Parson's Flat Cabernet/Shiraz is a thrilling blend of 65% Shiraz and 35% Cabernet Sauvignon. The elegant, deep ruby-colored 1999 exhibits a claretlike delicacy, medium body, and a stylish, supple-textured finish. Drink it over the next 6–7 years. The opaque purple-colored 1998 Cabernet/Shiraz exhibits layers of concentrated blackberry and cassis fruit intertwined with sausage/charcuterie scents in its intense, full-bodied, super-concentrated style. A gargantuan wine, it is lush enough to be drunk now as well as over the next 10–12 years. Impressive!

PAXTON (McLAREN VALE)

1999 Shiraz	D	87
1998 Shiraz	D	90

Proprietor David Paxton, a viticulturalist responsible for a number of vineyards in McLaren Vale, decided in 1998 to hold back some of the oldest blocks from his own property. The resulting wines were aged in French oak, 60% new. The fairly light and downsized 1999 is elegant, not too alcoholic, and a little lacking in depth and volume. It should drink well for 4–5 years. The 1998 Shiraz (a whopping 14.9% alcohol) has restrained aromatics, but explodes in the mouth to reveal plenty of depth, full body, cassis, blackberry, and peppery fruit, judiciously integrated oak, and a long spicy finish. Drink it over the next 5–7 years.

PENFOLDS (SOUTH AUSTRALIA)

1998 Cabernet Sauvignon Bin 407	C	87
1998 Cabernet Sauvignon Bin 707	E	90
1998 Cabernet Sauvignon/Shiraz Bin 389	C	89
1996 Grange	EEE	92+
1998 Shiraz	E	87

I was disappointed with several of Penfolds' recent releases, which tasted as if they had been excessively acidified. Based on a tasting of the current releases, the following five red wines stood out as the best. The 1998 Cabernet Sauvignon/Shiraz Bin 389's dense saturated purple color is accompanied by an excellent bouquet of blackberries, licorice, and earth. In the mouth, it is a plush, fat, luscious, full-bodied effort with considerable appeal. Loaded with fruit and glycerin, this pure wine should drink well for 7–8 years.

The 1998 Cabernet Sauvignon Bin 407 displays a saturated ruby/purple color as well as classic aromas of cedar and cassis, medium to full body, considerable fruit, sweet tannin, and adequate acidity. Drink it over the next 7–8 years. From a terrific vintage for old-vine Barossa Shiraz, Penfolds' 1998 Shiraz offers gorgeously sweet blackberry fruit intermixed with licorice and pepper. Spicy and medium- to full-bodied, with a velvety texture, this seamless, straightforward, juicy, succulent Shiraz will drink well for 7–8 years.

The outstanding 1998 Cabernet Sauvignon Bin 707 is a thick, rich, full-bodied Cabernet emphasizing copious quantities of cassis fruit. Pure, with nicely integrated oak, acidity, and tannin, it cuts a broad swath across the palate. While still young and grapy, this 1998 is loaded with potential. Anticipated maturity: now–2015. Lastly, the 1996 Grange is not the blockbuster it can be in the greatest vintages. At one time, this was the most renowned wine produced in Australia. While this remains one of Australia's finest wines, it has plenty of competition. The dense ruby/purple-colored 1996 Grange exhibits aromas of sweet blackberry/cassis, tar, licorice, and spice. Medium- to full-bodied, with sweet tannin, a velvety texture, and surprising elegance, it should age effortlessly for 15–20 years.

PENLEY ESTATE (COONAWARRA)

1998 Cabernet Sauvignon Estate	E	95
1997 Cabernet Sauvignon Estate	E	91
1996 Cabernet Sauvignon Estate	E	89+
1999 Cabernet Sauvignon Phoenix	C	89
1998 Cabernet Sauvignon Phoenix	C	90
1997 Cabernet Sauvignon Phoenix	C	85
1999 Merlot	D	87
1996 Merlot	D	88
1998 Shiraz/Cabernet	D	90
1997 Shiraz/Cabernet	D	89
1999 Shiraz Hyland	C	88
1998 Shiraz Hyland	C	86
1997 Shiraz Hyland	C	84

Penley is another Australian winery that appears to be ratcheting up their level of performance. Good values include the fleshy, velvety-textured, elegant 1999 Shiraz Hyland. Its deep ruby/purple color is followed by aromas and flavors of chocolate, blackberries, and pepper presented in a medium-bodied, supple format. Drink it over the next 4–5 years.

The indifferent 1998 Shiraz Hyland is medium-bodied and muted, while the 1997 Shiraz Hyland is good, but tannic and monolithic. Anticipated maturity: 2004–2012.

The Cabernet Sauvignon Phoenixes are attractively priced. The 1999 and 1998 are very good, and clearly surpass the 1997. Fairly light, approachable, and charming is the supple, medium-bodied, deep ruby/plum-colored 1999 Cabernet Sauvignon Phoenix. It offers sweet aromas of cedar, spice box, and currants, and a supple texture. Enjoy it over the next 4–6 years. The dark purple-colored 1998 Cabernet Sauvignon Phoenix is an excellent buy. Broad, backward, and powerful, it offers plum, black currant, licorice, smoke, and earth aromas as well as flavors. This full-bodied, deeply concentrated, dense 1998 can be drunk now and over the next 10–12 years. The 1997 Cabernet Sauvignon Phoenix is a medium-bodied, fresh, and tangy wine that should be consumed over the next several years.

I was unimpressed with the 1997 and 1998 Merlots (truth be known, there are few top-quality Australian Merlots), but the 1999 Merlot exhibits sweet berry flavors intermixed with red currants, olives, and earth. Drink this medium-bodied effort over the next 3–4 years.

The jammy, dark ruby/purple-colored 1996 Merlot exhibits sweet black cherry fruit intermixed with mocha, toasty oak, and dried herbs. Spicy, rich, and medium- to full-bodied, this tasty, fruit-driven Merlot should be consumed over the next 5–6 years.

Two top-flight offerings from Penley are the 1997 and 1998 Shiraz/Cabernet Sauvignon. These *cuvées* tend to be blends of 60% Shiraz and 40% Cabernet Sauvignon, and are aged in both French and American oak. The smokier, richer, dense purple-colored 1998 possesses more fruit and power than its older sibling. This mouth-filling, beefy, smoky, peppery wine will provide delicious drinking over the next decade. The 1997 is a soft, richly fruity blend with excellent texture, medium body, and good, plump flavors. It should drink well for 4–5 years.

The two finest Penley offerings are the 1997 and 1998 Cabernet Sauvignon Estate. Both are sensational wines that represent a synthesis between an elegant Bordeaux and a full-bodied, opulent, powerful Australian red. The fabulous 1998 is initially less charming than its older sibling, but the wine is stacked and packed in the mouth. Its opaque purple color is accompanied by a sweet, smoky, cedary character revealing notes of cassis, licorice, and olives. Voluptuous, with the tannin largely concealed by its wealth of glycerin, fruit, and concentration, this terrific Cabernet will last for 15 years or more. Impressive! The 1997 Cabernet Sauvignon Estate's notes of vanilla, black currants, cedar, cassis, and spicy new oak are presented in a complex format. It should drink well for 10–15 years. The 1996 Cabernet Sauvignon Estate represents a classy combination of weedy black currant fruit and toasty new oak. Pure, ripe, and medium- to full-bodied, with terrific fruit intensity, good spice, moderately sweet tannin, and a long finish, this Cabernet possesses 5–8 years of upside potential.

PENNA LANE (CLARE VALLEY)

1999 Cabernet Sauvignon	C	88?

With a complex nose of chocolate and cedarwood, the only problem with the medium- to full-bodied 1999 Cabernet Sauvignon might be some chalky tannin in the finish. If that does not resolve itself, this rating will look generous. Anticipated maturity: now–2014.

PENNY'S HILL (McLAREN VALE)

1998 Fortified Shiraz	D	90
1998 Merlot/Cabernet/Shiraz Specialized	D	88+?
1998 Shiraz	D	90
1997 Shiraz	D	90

A fine McLaren Vale estate, Penny's Hill has made a tight but promising, deep, full-bodied 1998 Shiraz. It boasts a saturated ruby/purple color, and elegant, ripe notes of blackberries, chocolate, pepper, and vanilla. Initially restrained, it unfolds and becomes increasingly expansive as the wine sits in the glass. It should drink well in 1–2 years and last 12–15.

A big, rich, succulent, peppery, black fruit–scented and –flavored Shiraz, the lush, low-acid, full-bodied 1997 will saturate the palate. There are gobs of fleshy, concentrated fruit in this soft, tasty wine. It promises to drink well for 4–5 years.

The 1998 Merlot/Cabernet/Shiraz Specialized (a blend of equal parts of these three varietals) shows plenty of toasty oak in the nose as well as internationally styled notes of black currants, vanilla, and spice box. Medium- to full-bodied, with good ripeness on the attack, and moderate tannin in the finish, it will be at its peak before 2012.

Port aficionados may get a blast from the 1998 Fortified Shiraz, a wine offering peppery, blackberry liqueur notes, an unctuous texture, and slight sweetness. This interesting Port look-alike should drink well for a decade, and, hopefully, develop even more perfume.

PIERRO (MARGARET RIVER)

1997 Cabernet	E	89
1998 Proprietary Red Wine	E	87

The dark ruby/purple-colored 1998 Proprietary Red Wine, a blend of Cabernet Sauvignon, Merlot, Petit Verdot, and Malbec, possesses a classy perfume of black currants, cherries, mulberries, and smoky oak. It exhibits an elegant, Bordeaux-like austerity and texture, good purity, nicely integrated wood, and a clean finish. Anticipated maturity: 2005–2016.

Do not be surprised by the Bordeaux-like personality of the 1997 Cabernet. A touch of Merlot, Cabernet Franc, and Petit Verdot were added to the blend of this medium-bodied, spicy, plum-colored wine. Stylish, restrained, and elegant, with black currant flavors nicely dosed with oak, this wine would be impossible to pick out as a New World Cabernet in a blind tasting. Anticipated maturity: now–2012.

PIKES (CLARE VALLEY)

1998	Cabernet Sauvignon	C	86
1999	Merlot	C	87
1998	Premio Sangiovese	C	86
1999	Shiraz	C	88
1998	Shiraz	C	87
1999	Shiraz/Grenache/Mourvèdre	C	88

Almost without exception, Pikes' wines tend to possess aggressive acid profiles (more than I generally like to see). That kind of style works better with the whites than with the reds.

As for the red wines, the Premio Sangiovese seems to be good, but no one in the New World is making anything comparable to what exists in central Italy. The 1998 possesses telltale strawberry fruit infused with notes of saddle leather as well as tangy acidity. While well-made, it is essentially one-dimensional and straightforward. Drink it over the next 2–3 years.

Pikes' Bordeaux varietals include the 1999 Merlot. It exhibits a minty, red currant, cassis, and chocolate-scented bouquet, medium body, tart underlying acidity, and a fleshy finish. Acidity is present, but it is not intrusive. The tartness is more problematic in the dense ruby/purple-colored 1998 Cabernet Sauvignon. It exhibits sweet black currants, but crisp acidity gives the wine a lean, compressed palate. In that sense, it had more in common with a Loire Valley red than an Aussie offering. Pikes' Rhône Valley blend, the 1999 Shiraz/ Grenache/Mourvèdre (55% Shiraz, 32% Grenache, and 13% Mourvèdre), reveals telltale eucalyptus notes along with moderate quantities of blackberry and cassis fruit. The wine provides a sweet attack, excellent purity and a bright, well-delineated finish. Interestingly, in 1998 the same *cuvée* tasted muted but also high in acidity, atypical for the vintage.

My favorite of this lean group is the ruby/purple-colored 1999 Shiraz. It exhibits sweet berry fruit, medium body, and well-integrated acidity, tannin, and wood. Consume it over the next 4–6 years. Overall, these wines are cleanly made but generally unexciting. The 1998 Shiraz is well balanced. Attractive aromas of licorice, blackberries, earth, and pepper are present in the moderately endowed bouquet. Acidity is there, but the wine's weight and richness handle it better than its siblings. The finish is short, but the fruit quality is impressive and the wine attractive, medium-bodied, and cleanly made. Drink it over the next 4–5 years.

PUNTERS CORNER SPARTACUS (COONAWARRA)

1998	Shiraz Reserve	D	88

A saturated dark ruby/purple color is followed by scents of smoky wood (both Russian and French casks were utilized), considerable body, a chewy, fleshy texture, and abundant pepper as well as cassis. This 1998 Shiraz Reserve should drink well for a decade.

QUARTETTO (CLARE VALLEY)

1999	Shiraz	D	88

The dark ruby/purple-colored 1999 Shiraz presents a sweet, highly extracted, chewy, cassis fruit mixed with smoke and oak. Ripe and supple-textured, drink it over the next 5–6 years.

RANDALL'S HILL (BAROSSA RANGES)

1995	Shiraz 1910	E	95+

The fruit for this wine comes from the Three Rivers Vineyard owned by Chris Ringland, one of the stars of handcrafted, artisanal, cult, old-vine Shiraz. Made from 90-year-old vines and cropped at two tons of fruit per acre, the 125-case *cuvée* of 1995 Shiraz 1910 exhibits an impressive dark ruby/purple color, and layer upon layer of fruit. Thick, chewy, and full-bodied, this massive Shiraz spent a whopping 32 months in new French oak, but has perfectly absorbed the wood. Majestic flavor breadth, exceptionally pure, and remarkably well balanced, this seamless beauty can be drunk now or cellared for 20–30 years. Bravo!

RBJ (BAROSSA VALLEY)

1998 Theologicum	D	87

Slightly more restrained and less concentrated than several previous vintages, the 1998 Theologicum is still a noteworthy blend of 65% Grenache and 35% Mourvèdre. Aged in old wood, it is reminiscent of an attractive, spicy, cinnamon, cherry, and earthy southern Rhône. The wine is medium-bodied, soft, and best drunk over the next 5–6 years. Approximately 1,000 cases were produced.

RED EDGE (HEATHCOTE)

1998 Cabernet Sauvignon	D	92

This unfined/unfiltered 1998 Cabernet Sauvignon was made from microscopic yields of one ton of fruit per acre. The wine is full-bodied, sensationally concentrated, with fabulous length and purity. Almost over the top, it is beautifully buttressed by decent tannin and low acidity. The purity and density of the cassis fruit is admirable. Anticipated maturity: now–2025.

CHÂTEAU REYNELLA (McLAREN VALE)

1996 Cabernet Sauvignon Basket Press	D	88
1996 Shiraz	C	87
1998 Shiraz Basket Press	D	88

The big, thick, rustic 1998 Shiraz Basket Press exhibits a dense purple color along with scents of smoke, earth, blackberries, asphalt, and pepper. Layered and chewy, with rustic tannin as well as American oak in the background, it should drink well for 10–12 years.

The 1996 Shiraz's deep ruby/purple color is accompanied by smoky, spicy aromas displaying a touch of minerals and pepper. This medium- to full-bodied, well-made Shiraz reveals good purity, noticeable toasty new American oak, and a spicy, supple finish. Drink it over the next 5–6 years. Loads of new oak intermixed with black currants are the hallmarks of the medium- to full-bodied, supple-textured, nicely concentrated, internationally styled 1996 Cabernet Sauvignon Basket Press. The acidity is adequate, and the wine is open-knit, expansive, and ideal for drinking over the next 5–7 years.

ROCKFORD (BAROSSA VALLEY)

NV Black Shiraz	E	?
1997 Cabernet Sauvignon	D	88
1998 Moppa Springs Red	C	87
1998 Shiraz Basket Press	D	90

In spite of Rockford's terrific wine-maker, Chris Ringland, I had a hard time understanding the nonvintage Black Shiraz. For $90, one gets an elegant, tart, fresh but essentially one-dimensional wine with little depth or complexity. I don't know if the bottle I had performed poorly or whether this is typical, but certainly this seems out of character for Rockford and Ringland. The finest offering I tasted was the 1998 Shiraz Basket Press. While not a great value, it is an outstanding effort displaying a dense purple color, a jammy, blackberry fruit bomb character, a supple texture, formidable glycerin, full body, and a lush mid-palate and finish. It should drink well for at least a decade.

The 1998 Moppa Springs Red, a blend of 69% Grenache, 20% Shiraz, and 11% Mataro, aged in larger wood puncheons, reveals a soft, Rhône-ish character with notes of kirsch, pepper, spice, and a sexy, round personality. Drink it over the next 2–4 years.

The 1997 Cabernet Sauvignon is supple-textured, with medium body, excellent cedary, tobacco, and black currant notes, silky tannin, low acidity, and a finish that caresses the palate. It should also be drunk sooner rather than later, over the next 5–6 years.

ROSABROOK (MARGARET RIVER)

1999 Shiraz Abattoir Block	E	92
1998 Shiraz Abattoir Block	E	90+

Two of Australia's most distinctive Shirazes, both the 1998 and 1999 Abattoir Block display Rhône-like, earthy, meaty flavors reminiscent of blood and black fruits. Both are explosive, full-bodied, eccentric efforts made from extremely ripe fruit and aged in 100% French oak before being bottled without filtration. They explode on the palate, offering notes of fruit intermixed with characteristics of meat, sausage, blood, and animal. While not for everybody, they are exquisite expressions of Shiraz made in a different microclimate than those from Barossa or McLaren Vale. The 1998 will keep for 15 or more years, whereas the more seamless, accessible 1999 can be drunk now as well as over the next 12+ years.

ROSEMOUNT (COONAWARRA)

1997 Cabernet Sauvignon Show Reserve	B	89+
2000 Cabernet Sauvignon/Merlot	A	86
1999 Cabernet Sauvignon/Merlot	A	85
1997 GSM	C	89
1996 GSM	C	87
1997 Mountain Blue (Shiraz/Cabernet Sauvignon)	D	87+?
1999 Shiraz	A	86
1999 Shiraz/Cabernet Sauvignon	A	86
1997 Syrah Balmoral	D	89

I tasted nearly three dozen selections from Rosemount, and one-third proved to have considerable merit. The finest Rosemount offerings are terrific values, and some of their upper-end wines are competitive with Australia's finest. Two excellent values are the 1999 and 2000 Cabernet Sauvignon/Merlot. The 2000 is 60% Cabernet Sauvignon and 40% Merlot, and the 1999 is 55% Cabernet Sauvignon and 45% Merlot. Both are fruit-driven efforts revealing the personalities of their blends. The richer, fuller, more forward 2000 reveals no evidence of wood. Soft and lush, with low acidity, it will drink well for 1–2 years. The 1999 is grapy and soft, with plenty of berry fruit, and a silky texture. Anticipated maturity: *now*.

The dark ruby/purple 1999 Shiraz offers copious quantities of black fruits and spice presented in a straightforward, medium-bodied style. Easy to drink as well as understand, it is best consumed over the next 2–3 years to take advantage of its fruit and exuberance.

The dark ruby-colored 1999 Shiraz/Cabernet Sauvignon (65% Shiraz and 35% Cabernet Sauvignon from southeastern Australia) possesses an excellent nose of black fruits and spice. Medium-bodied, soft, silky, and Beaujolais-like, it is a delicious red meant for near-term consumption—over the next 1–2 years.

Among the more prestigious as well as expensive offerings is Rosemount's GSM, a blend of 50% Grenache, 40% Shiraz, and 10% Mourvèdre aged for 18 months in American oak. The 1997's complex bouquet of roasted nuts, flowers, blackberries, smoke, and currants jumps from the glass. This medium- to full-bodied, suave, elegant yet concentrated wine is flavorful. Drink this pure, supple red over the next 5–6 years. The attractive 1996 GSM exhibits a dense, ruby/purple color as well as a big, earthy, leathery, berry-scented nose with abundant oak. Medium- to full-bodied, with sweet fruit on the attack, a good mid-palate, and a compressed finish, this mainstream, attractive blend should be consumed over the next 2–3 years.

The dense ruby/purple-colored 1997 Syrah Balmoral exhibits smoke, blackberry, licorice, and oak aromas, full body, sweet tannin, and a long finish. It is best consumed over the next 7–8 years. The 1997 Cabernet Sauvignon Show Reserve emerges from the red soils of Coonawarra. It was aged for 24 months in a combination of wood barrels. The dense garnet/plum/purple color is accompanied by classic Cabernet aromas of cedar, cassis, and smoky new oak. Thick, rich, and full-bodied, this chewy, structured, well-delineated, still youthful Cabernet will not hit its prime for another 2–3 years and should last 12–15 years.

The 1997 Mountain Blue (a blend of 75% Shiraz and 25% Cabernet Sauvignon aged 24 months in both French and American wood) exhibits a straightforward nose of new oak as well as blueberry and blackberry fruit. Firmly structured, with abundant wood, good tannin, and medium to full body, it is not as expressive as several of its siblings, but it has the potential to age well for 10–12 years.

RUSDEN (BAROSSA VALLEY)

1998	Cabernet Sauvignon Boundary Row	E	92
1997	Cabernet Sauvignon Boundary Row	E	93
1999	Grenache Christine's Vineyard	D	87
1998	Grenache Christine's Vineyard	D	90
1998	Shiraz Black Guts	E	92
1997	Shiraz Black Guts	D	92
1999	Zinfandel Lodestone	E	91

Twenty-two-year-old wine-maker Christian Canute has an impressive résumé, having worked at Rockford and Torbreck. From his family winery, Rusden, he is turning out limited-production gems. Rusden's classic, in a typically Australian oversized sense, is the Cabernet Sauvignon Boundary Row. Sadly, there are only 70 cases of this large, fruit-driven, yet complex effort. Smoky bacon fat, cassis, licorice, and cigar smoke emerge from the dense, plum/purple-colored 1998. In the mouth, it is opulent, full-bodied, and concentrated, with plenty of jammy, low-acid fruit. Drink this between 2005–2014. At first I thought the 1997 Cabernet Sauvignon Boundary Row was controversial, given its pruny, overripe character. However, as the wine sat in the glass, it gathered delineation and its over-the-top personality became more civilized and classic. It is a wine of extreme density, with extraordinary notes of black raspberries, cherries, cassis, prunes, and what the French call *sous-bois* (a clean, foresty/earthy aroma). Low in acidity, thick, and delicious, this Cabernet improved significantly with aeration. Although it will not be long-lived, it will evolve and last for another decade.

The Grenache Christine's Vineyard emerges from 30-year-old Grenache vines. The 1999 is another wine with a barbecue spice, smoky bacon fat–scented, flamboyant nose. Classic Rhône notes of underbrush, pepper, and spice emerge from this medium-bodied, dark plum/ruby-colored wine. Smoky and spicy, it is best drunk over the next 2–3 years.

The 1998 Grenache Christine's Vineyard's dark plum/ruby/garnet color is followed by a sweet nose of kirsch, spice, and earth. Gorgeous fruit and moderately high alcohol (13.7%) provide a sweet, glycerin-dominated impact on the palate. Pure, rich, full-bodied, and delicious, this wine should continue to drink well for 5–6 years. The 1999 Zinfandel Lodestone, a curiosity, is an impressive micro *cuvée* of 56 cases, but only a handful of Americans will ever taste it. Produced from 30-year-old Zinfandel vines and tipping the scales at 15.8% alcohol, it exhibits a Turley Cellars, full-bodied, dry portlike style. Fat, jammy, and full-bodied, with gobs of smoky berry fruit, this is a wine to drink over the next 4–5 years.

Only 115 cases are produced of the Shiraz Black Guts. This wine emerges from 30-year-old vines cropped to two tons per acre. The 1998 is a large-scaled effort. Deep purple in color, with a smoky, creosote/asphalt, blackberry, and cassis-scented bouquet, this ripe, full-bodied Shiraz boasts super fruit, notions of new oak (it was aged for 30 months in a combination of new and old French wood), and plenty of glycerin and length in the long finish. In spite of its size, the wine actually comes across as elegant, particularly for such mass and intensity. It should drink well for up to a decade. The 1997 Shiraz Black Guts tips the scales at a whopping 15.2% alcohol. The high alcohol is barely noticeable, given the wine's wealth of fruit, dense ruby/purple color, and bouquet of rose petals, blackberry liqueur, pepper, and truffles. Deep and full-bodied, with an unctuous texture, superb density, and low acidity, this wine will continue to drink well for 10+ years.

SAINT MICHAEL'S (HEATHCOTE, VICTORIA)

1999 Merlot	E	90

I will keep my notes short since there are only 30 cases of this wine, made at Wild Duck Creek. The dense, textured, opaque purple-colored 1999 Merlot is made in an intense, ripe, over-the-top, full-bodied style with plenty of glycerin, huge amounts of black currant fruit, and a knockout finish. It is hardly subtle, but it is classic, in-your-face Australian Merlot that coats the palate. Drink it over the next 7–8 years.

SCARPANTONI (McLAREN VALE)

1999 Cabernet Sauvignon	C	88
1998 Estate Reserve	C	89
1999 Maslin Beach Blanche Point Proprietary Red	D	87
1999 Merlot	C	85
1999 School Block Proprietary Red	C	88
1999 Shiraz Block 3	C	89
1998 Shiraz Block 3	C	93

One of the more modestly priced wineries in the Grateful Palate portfolio, this family of Italian immigrant origin has produced some interesting wines. One of Scarpantoni's low-keyed efforts, the soft, medium-bodied 1999 Merlot reveals herb-tinged berry fruit. It is acceptable, tasty, soft, and best drunk over the next 3–4 years.

The 1999 School Block Proprietary Red (a blend of 55% Shiraz, 40% Cabernet, and 5% Merlot, 600 cases produced) is a good value. The wine shows excellent blackberry and cassis fruit notes, attractive, supple texture, medium to full body, and gorgeous fruit and length. While it is meant for current drinking, it should hold nicely for another 2–3 years. The 1999 Maslin Beach Blanche Point (named after a nudist beach) reveals abundant spicy American oak in the nose, but pulls back in the mouth to offer concentrated, jammy fruit. With earthiness, spice, and currants plus good overall balance, it will drink well for 4–5 years.

The nearly outstanding 1998 Estate Reserve (a 700-case blend of 75% Shiraz and 25% Cabernet) boasts aggressive sweet oak in addition to jammy black currants, berries, and smoky aromas as well as flavors. With admirable plumpness and fatness, it provides a succulent mouthful of fruit, glycerin, and alcohol (about 14%). Anticipated maturity: now–2011.

Another very good value is the 1999 Cabernet Sauvignon. There are 1,500 cases of this 100% Cabernet Sauvignon made from 28-year-old vines. Offering copious quantities of sweet black currant fruit presented in a fleshy, full-bodied, in-your-face style, this pure, ripe, medium- to full-bodied Cabernet should be consumed over the next 7–8 years. It is hard to find New World Cabernet Sauvignon for under $30 a bottle at this quality level.

The difference between the fabulous 1998 vintage and the good 1999 vintage is sharply displayed in Scarpantoni's two offerings from their 60-year-old Block 3 Shiraz holdings. The 1998 is fabulous, but the restrained 1999, while very good, is no match for its older sibling. The 1998 is a spectacularly full-bodied, black/purple-colored effort with notes of pepper, smoky licorice candy, cassis, blackberries, and earth. It possesses terrific fruit, massive body, sweet tannin, and nicely integrated alcohol as well as wood. At $25, this is one of the great wine bargains in the marketplace today. Moreover, there are 2,500 cases available. This wine can drink well for another 10–15 years. Also a good value, though it does not have the prodigious fat, concentration, and depth of the 1998, the 1999 exhibits a deep ruby/purple color, sweet black currant and berry fruit, an elegant, medium- to full-bodied, spicy personality, and a supple texture. The 1999 is best consumed over the next 6–8 years.

SEVILLE ESTATE (YARRA VALLEY)

1997 Cabernet Sauvignon	C	86

The dark ruby/purple-colored 1997 Cabernet Sauvignon exhibits sweet, ripe black currant fruit infused with subtle French oak. Mint/eucalyptus is also present in this medium-bodied, pure, cassis-flavored, soft, tasty Cabernet. Drink it over the next 3–4 years.

STANTON AND KILLEEN (RUTHERGLEN)

NV	Collector's Muscat	E	90
1997	Durif	C	87
NV	Muscat	D	93
NV	Tokay	D	90

Better known for their fortified dessert wines, Stanton and Killeen's 1997 Durif tips the scales at 14.4% alcohol. Dense ruby/purple, with a peppery, blackberry-scented nose, this full-bodied effort is loaded with fruit. While the finish is rustic, the wine offers plenty of flavor in a straightforward, robust format. Drink it over the next 2–4 years.

The light medium amber-colored nonvintage Tokay is sweet, round, and represents a blend that is approximately 12–15 years of age. Delicious, it is ideal for sipping at the end of a meal. The finest of this trio of fortified dessert wines is the dark amber-colored nonvintage Muscat. It reveals more complexity, richness, and unctuosity than the nonvintage Collector's Muscat. The Muscat is 12–15 years in age, whereas the Collector's Muscat is 25–30 years of age. These powerful, concentrated, impeccably made wines are among Australia's treasures.

THALGARA (HUNTER VALLEY)

1998 Show Shiraz	D	88

In spite of obvious oak, this 1998 Show Shiraz exhibits an opaque ruby/purple color, plenty of fleshy, overripe, blackberry and cassis fruit, a good, chewy, straightforward personality, and a mouth-staining finish. Although not complex, it is an attractive, internationally styled wine for readers looking for immediate gratification. Drink it over the next 2–3 years.

THORN AND CLARKE (BAROSSA VALLEY)

1998 Shiraz	C	86

From a new winery, this dense ruby/purple-colored 1998 Shiraz (300 cases produced) possesses plenty of tannin, an international style, and a foursquare, chunky personality. It is a good wine, but best drunk during its first 3–4 years of life.

THREE RIVERS (BAROSSA VALLEY)

1996 Shiraz	EEE	100
1995 Shiraz	EEE	99

These are colossal efforts and very much in keeping with the style of owner/wine-maker Chris Ringland. The Three Rivers Shiraz (only 100 cases produced) is made from 90-year-old vines. Following malolactic fermentation in cask, it spent 40 months in new oak prior to being bottled unfiltered. This is arguably the greatest Shiraz made in Australia, but, sadly, there is little of it. The viscous, black/purple 1996 Shiraz represents the essence of both wine and Shiraz. With impeccable balance, unreal levels of concentration, yet perfectly integrated tannin, acidity, alcohol, and wood, it is akin to a dry vintage port, but then, so is a 1947 Cheval Blanc, 1947 Pétrus, 1947 Lafleur, and 1947 Latour à Pomerol. Once past the explosive bouquet of crème de cassis, espresso, melted fudge, and graphite, this massive yet seamless wine offers layers of unctuously textured flavors crammed with blackberries, smoke, charcoal, and currants. The finish lasts for 70+ seconds. The wine should prove to be immortal, lasting for 30–50 years, but who is going to wait that long to unleash the magic? This is compelling stuff! Anticipated maturity: 2010–2040. The 1995 Shiraz is a virtually perfect wine of splendid concentration, symmetry, and length (nearly a minute). An opaque black/purple color is followed by staggering aromas of black fruits, truffles, sweet earth, and wood. With amazing viscosity, density, and concentration that transcend any Shiraz I have ever tasted (except for the 1996), this monumental wine represents an extraordinary achievement. Its low acidity and phenomenal richness should offer early accessibility, but it promises to evolve for two decades or more. Kudos to Ringland for these ultimate Australian blockbuster Shirazes. I just wish there were 10 times the quantity produced!

TORBRECK (BAROSSA VALLEY)

1999 Descendent	E	93
1997 Descendent	E	96
1998 The Factor	E	93
2000 Juveniles	D	90
1999 Juveniles	D	94
1998 Run Rig	EEE	99
1997 Run Rig	EEE	98
1999 The Steading	D	91
1998 The Steading	D	96
1999 Woodcutters	C	90

Wine-maker Dave Powell is quickly establishing himself as one of the geniuses of Rhône Valley–influenced, blockbuster red wines from Australia. I have extolled his previous vintages, but the quality (and prices) continues to soar as these are some of the most exciting wines produced not only in Australia but in the world. Production is somewhat limited, ranging from 240 cases of Juveniles to 1,600 cases of The Steading and 400 cases of Run Rig. These are wines of enormous strength but also riveting individuality and extraordinary purity and symmetry. The reds are all spectacular, even some of the less expensive *cuvées*. Of course, the Run Rig has become one of the most fashionable wines in the world, and it deserves its billing as the Guigal Côte Rôtie La Mouline of Australia. I have recently had both the 1996 and 1997 Run Rig, and I am pleased to say that both of these wines still offer extraordinary combinations of power and complexity in an undeniably sumptuous style.

The most expensive red wine of the portfolio is undoubtedly the Run Rig. However, it is not out of line with what wines of similar quality sell for throughout the world, unfortunately a reality. There are nearly 600 cases annually. The wine is made from vines averaging between 50 and 130 years of age, cropped at 1.25 tons of fruit per acre. It is a blend of 97% Shiraz and 3% Viognier, and is aged completely in French oak for approximately 18 months prior to bottling. The 1998 may well be the most concentrated Run Rig to date. The color is an opaque purple, and the bouquet offers an exotic concoction of tropical fruit, blackberry liqueur, crème de cassis, smoke, and honeysuckle notes. Once past the exhilarating fragrance, the wine is sumptuous and full-bodied, with a skyscraper-like profile of fabulous concentration and length that builds in the mouth. A scenario of black fruits galore unfolds to reveal beautifully integrated wood, acidity, tannin, and alcohol (a mere 14.5%). The balance is virtually perfect, and the finish lasts nearly a minute. This luxurious, compelling gem displays a level of complexity and delineation that is rare in a wine of such size. Anticipated maturity: now–2016. Every bit as spectacular is the 1997 Run Rig. I have been blown away by prior efforts, and this huge, exotic wine, which offers up blueberry liqueur, cassis, flowers, a touch of overripe peaches, and sweet vanilla, is a rich, full-bodied, supple-textured wine. I sent a bottle to my French lawyer for a tasting with several top Médoc proprietors after which I received a fax asking how many cases they could purchase! Two or three bottles a year is most people's allocation. The oak is beautifully integrated. The wine is low in acidity, and the impact on the palate is one of awesome levels of fruit, richness, and complexity. This amazing wine may even merit a perfect rating. It should drink well for 10–12 years.

The second most expensive offering in the Torbreck portfolio is the Descendent, a 100% Shiraz fermented on Viognier pomace emerging from a five-year-old vineyard cropped at a minuscule 1.25 tons per acre. There are 220 cases of this *cuvée*, which spends 18 months in used French barrels prior to bottling. No other wine from Australia remotely resembles it. In truth, the closest wine to which it could be compared is Marcel Guigal's single-vineyard Côte Rôtie La Turque. The 1999's dense purple color is followed by blackberry, crème de cassis, and floral aromas, huge body, terrific fat and glycerin, and a seamless, decadently rich finish. While it will not last as long as the Run Rig, it is a tour de force in pleasure for drinking in its first 7–8 years of life. The 1997 Descendent represents Australia's quintessential example of power and elegance. Though not massive, its level of concentration is extraordinary. This black/purple wine offers a feminine, silky voluptuousness allied to fascinating levels of richness, unbelievably sweet tannin, and layers of flavor. In the glass, the wine develops magnificently. A bottle kept open for 48 hours displayed additional nuances and complexity. Full-bodied, but not heavy, this is a tour de force in winemaking, as well as a thrilling Shiraz to drink. Anticipated maturity: now–2010.

Another stunning effort is 1998's The Factor. This 100% Shiraz *cuvée* (240 cases) is made from 50–130-year-old vines. No new oak is used, although some of the press wine does see new American oak. Supple, with a telltale, ostentatious bouquet of black fruits mixed with smoke, licorice, and melted asphalt, this super-extracted, velvety-textured, sumptuous, pure, rich, impeccably well balanced wine is best consumed during its first decade of life.

Continuing to descend in price but not much in quality is The Steading, a southern Rhône blend of 60% Grenache, 20% Shiraz, and 20% Mourvèdre. Two thousand cases are produced annually of this Châteauneuf-du-Pape look-alike from Australia's Barossa Valley. The 1999 is a terrific, deep purple-colored effort offering a sweet nose of pepper, black fruits, earth, tobacco, and cassis. Sweet on the attack (from ripe fruit, not sugar), this full-bodied, concentrated, powerful wine (14.5% alcohol) builds in the mouth to a creamy-textured, blockbuster finish. Though hard to resist, it will drink well for 7–8 years.

The dense ruby/purple 1998 The Steading boasts a creamy texture in addition to a glorious bouquet of black raspberries, kirsch, cassis, minerals, and licorice. Seductive, voluptuously textured flavors unfold on the palate, and the texture is so plush that it feels like the palate is resting on a waterbed of overripe black fruits. Extremely long (45+ seconds), this sensational wine can be drunk now or cellared for 10–12 years.

If readers want to know what the quintessential Australian fruit bomb tastes like, check out the Juveniles, a tank-fermented blend of 60% Grenache, 20% Shiraz, and 20% Mourvèdre made from tiny yields of 1–2 tons of fruit per acre. It is actually the same wine as The Steading, but it is aged in tank rather than spending 18 months in old French and American wood as The Steading does. Bursting at the seams with juicy blackberry, cherry, and currant fruit, the 2000 offers copious quantities of spicy, peppery characteristics, sexy, seductive glycerin levels, and a creamy texture that defines hedonism. It is not going to make old bones, but for drinking over the next 2–3 years, this is a fabulous, fruit-filled effort from Barossa. Anticipated maturity: now–2005. The 1999 Juveniles is an explosive fruit bomb. It almost has a "nouveau" character, but there are such levels of concentration, body, glycerin, and extract that it transcends that category into something unlike anything tasted previously. Opaque purple-colored, with a celestial perfume of jammy black fruit and floral scents, this dense, monstrous, velvety-textured wine is a total hedonistic turn-on. It is impossible to resist and should continue to drink well for 7–8 years.

Finally, the 1999 Woodcutters red (2,300 cases) is essentially declassified juice that did not make it into The Steading. Produced from the same blend, this is an outstanding, reasonably priced effort from David Powell. Sweet, pure, ripe, full-bodied, rich, decadent, chewy, and fat, it is a thrill to drink. Anticipated maturity: now–2008.

These wines not only make for compelling drinking, they are also a huge amount of fun, and isn't that what it's all about? If I had to give an award to Australia's finest wine-maker in 2001, it would be hard not to consider David Powell.

VASSE FELIX (WESTERN AUSTRALIA)

1998 Heytesbury	D	88

The classy, complex 1998 Heytesbury (a blend of Cabernet Sauvignon, Shiraz, and a touch of Malbec, aged in both French and American oak) exhibits a dense ruby/purple color in addition to an elegant, crème de cassis–scented bouquet with notions of blueberries, wood, and earth. It offers excellent concentration and purity, fine integrated acidity, moderate tannin, and a long finish. Enjoy it now and over the next 10–12 years.

VERITAS (BAROSSA VALLEY)

1999	Cabernet/Merlot	C	89
1998	Cabernet/Merlot	C	91
1998	Clement 1309	E	93
1997	Clement 1309	E	93
1990	Fortified Tokay	B	92
1999	Mourvèdre/Grenache	D	91
1998	Mourvèdre/Grenache	D	90
1998	Shiraz Hanisch	E	99
1997	Shiraz Hanisch	E	97
1998	Shiraz Heysen	E	96
1997	Shiraz Heysen	E	96
1998	Shiraz/Mourvèdre Pressings	D	92
1997	Shiraz/Mourvèdre Pressings	D	92
NV	10-year-old Tawny Fortified Dessert	B	90

One of my favorite Australian wineries, Veritas' offerings are never excessively oaked, but possess extraordinarily ripe, concentrated fruit, great individuality, and the potential, in the top examples, to improve for two decades. The wine-maker/proprietor is Rolf Binder, who already has an impressive résumé. A blend of 70% Cabernet Sauvignon and 30% Merlot from 30-year-old vines, the Cabernet/Merlot blend is aged with only 15% new oak. Annual production averages 900 cases. The 1999 exhibits a dark ruby/purple color and a gorgeously sweet nose of jammy black currants mixed with earth and spice box. The wine is excellent, fresh, and juicy, with sweet tannin and plenty of fat. Readers looking for reasonably priced Cabernet to gulp down over the next 5–7 years should check this beauty out. If you are looking for an over-the-top, jammy, superripe Cabernet Sauvignon/Merlot, you need search no further than Veritas' 1998 Cabernet/Merlot. This is a hedonistic Cabernet bomb with full body, low acidity, and gobs of jammy black fruit flavors. It is a thrill to smell, taste, and drink. Moreover, it will last 15 years, given its flamboyant/ostentatious, fruit-driven style. Complexity has yet to emerge, and there is plenty of tannin lurking beneath the fruit, glycerin, and extract.

In ascending order of quality (yet all three of the following wines are exquisite) are the Mourvèdre/Grenache, Shiraz/Mourvèdre Pressings, and Clement 1309. Rhône Valley enthusiasts will get a blast from all of these exceptionally well made efforts. The Mourvèdre/Grenache blends are made of 65% of the former and 35% of the latter varietals, the vines ranging between 30–100 years of age. This wine sees about 10% new American oak. Sadly, the production is only 250 cases. The 1999 Mourvèdre/Grenache is a dazzling, full-bodied 1999. With notes of new saddle leather, blackberry, currant, and raspberry fruit, superb ripeness, a round, generous mid-palate and finish, and excellent balance, this is a wine to drink over the next 5–7 years. The 1998 Mourvèdre/Grenache's dark ruby color is accompanied by a big, spicy, black raspberry and cherry-scented nose, a creamy texture, full body, gorgeous levels of black and red fruits, a silky texture, and abundant glycerin. Drink it over the next 7–8 years.

The Shiraz/Mourvèdre Pressings (55% Shiraz and 45% Mourvèdre) spends about 22 months in French oak prior to being bottled. Interestingly, the Mourvèdre comes from 100-year-old, nonirrigated vines, among the oldest in Barossa. It may be controversial for some readers, given the fact that it is an Australian version of French Bandol. About 500 cases of this exceptional wine are produced annually. Notes of new saddle leather, earth, sweat, and meaty animal-like characteristics compete with black cherry, blackberry, and currant fruit in the 1998 Shiraz/Mourvèdre Pressings. This wine is explosive in the mouth, full-bodied, deep, and concentrated, with layers of flavor as well as a surprisingly supple finish, given that young Mourvèdre can be dry and tannic. Anticipated maturity: now–2012. Another brilliant effort from Binder is his 1997 Shiraz/Mourvèdre Pressings (with a modest 13.5% alcohol). A dense ruby/purple color is followed by intense black cherry, blackberry, and currant flavors intermixed with spice and tar. Full-bodied, with superb concentration, good delineation, and a rich, layered, accessible finish, this youthful offering displays far more accessibility than its predecessor. Anticipated maturity: now–2015.

The Clement 1309 is a blend of Mourvèdre and Grenache from vines averaging 100 years of age. It is aged a whopping 30 months in French and American oak. Production is extremely tiny (less than 70 cases annually), but readers should approach this wine as they would the ferociously tannic, highly extracted 1990 Pradeaux Mourvèdre Vieilles Vignes from Bandol or a backward, concentrated vintage of Beaucastel Châteauneuf-du-Pape. The brilliant, dark, plum/purple-colored 1998 Clement 1309 (a 50% Mourvèdre/50% Grenache blend) offers a flamboyant nose of black fruits, flowers, earth, leather, and pepper. It is ripe and jammy, with superb concentration, great purity, and a finish that goes on for nearly 50 seconds. The exceptional 1997 Clement 1309 is superintense, with huge body, mouth-searing levels of tannin, and extraordinary concentration and potential complexity. It is not close to prime-time drinking, but who can ignore the blackberry, raspberry, melted road tar, licorice, and truffle notes that emerge from the wine's aromatics? Extremely full-bodied and backward, this offering requires 2–3 years of cellaring and will easily last for two decades.

Two of the consistently great Australian Shirazes made over recent vintages have been the Heysen and the Hanisch. The Shiraz Heysen is a dazzling example of what Australia can do so well. A blend of 95% Shiraz and 5% Cabernet Sauvignon from 26-year-old vines and aged in 40% new oak, its production averages 400 cases. The 1998 Shiraz Heysen is off the charts. An opaque black/purple is accompanied by an ostentatious bouquet of raspberries, blackberries, currants, and cherries. With airing, the bouquet also offers up smoke, pepper, licorice, and earth. In the mouth, the wine is unctuously textured and extremely full-bodied, with great purity and layers of flavor. Anticipated maturity: now–2020. The opaque black/purple-colored 1997 Shiraz Heysen reveals aromas of flowers, licorice, blackberries, and new saddle leather. This full-bodied, fat, succulent, low-acid wine is one of the most concentrated and intense Shiraz drinkers will ever taste. Long, powerful, and concentrated, it can be drunk now, but will age effortlessly for 20 years.

The Shiraz Hanisch series are 100% Shiraz blends from 26-year-old vines that age with 40% new oak (300 cases are produced annually). The virtually perfect 1998 (14.7% alcohol) is a huge but impressively balanced effort. Offering up notes of beef blood, blackberries, and jammy cassis, this viscous, massive, full-bodied, fabulously concentrated but not heavy 1998 has a finish that lasts just under a minute. It represents the essence of Shiraz. It can be drunk now because it is so luxuriously rich, but don't expect secondary nuances to develop for at least another 5–8 years. It should keep for 20–25—at the minimum. The 1997 Shiraz

Hanisch tastes like a dry vintage port. Opaque purple-colored, with a knockout bouquet of blackberries, leather, and foresty scents mixed with licorice and pepper, this intense, super-concentrated, phenomenally extracted Shiraz is beyond massive. Amazingly well balanced and delineated for its gargantuan size, it is accessible and soft enough to be drunk now, but it should evolve past two decades.

A superb value in a tawny port look-alike is the 10-year-old Tawny Fortified Dessert wine. A fortified blend of 70% Shiraz and the rest Mourvèdre, Grenache, and Muscat, this wine has plenty of amber at the edge of its light ruby color. Exhibiting jammy red fruits intermixed with roasted nuts, caramel, and spice, this thick, full-bodied, moderately sweet tawny should drink well for another decade. Veritas consistently produces one of Australia's finest fortified Tokays. The 1990 Fortified Tokay's medium amber color is followed by aromas of sweet honeyed nuts, citrus, and orange marmalade. Full-bodied and sweet, with explosive intensity and richness, this is a terrific value. It should drink well for a decade or more.

VIKING WINES (BAROSSA VALLEY)

1998 Asarna Proprietary Red	E	88
1999 Grand Shiraz	E	91+
1998 Grand Shiraz	E	94

These wines are produced by Thord Soderstrom. The Grand Shiraz is aged all in American oak, with a certain percentage of new oak, and bottled without filtration. The full-bodied, super-concentrated, powerful 1999 Grand Shiraz (aged with 75% new oak) is obviously the product of extremely low yields. It exhibits remarkable density, fine chewiness, and pure, black fruit notes, intermixed with smoke, earth, and underbrush. Powerful, long, and youthful, it should only improve over the next decade, and last for almost 20 years. A bottle opened 24 hours displayed no trace of oxidation. The exceptionally concentrated 1998 Grand Shiraz (15% alcohol; 30% new oak) offers a distinctive nose of lavender, roasted herbs, truffles, and gobs of jammy black raspberries, blueberries, and cassis. With tangy acidity, immense body, explosive richness, and a 60-second finish, this is an exciting, distinctive, individualistic Shiraz that should drink well for 10–12 years.

The 1998 Asarna Proprietary Red is an intriguing blend of two-thirds Pinot Noir and one-third Shiraz. Bottled unfiltered, it possesses 90-point aromatics. Dark dense ruby/purple-colored, with a sweet, floral nose of cherry liqueur and raspberries, the Pinot characteristics are well displayed, and the Shiraz gives the wine spice, pepper, and dense body and volume. Excellent, possibly outstanding, it displays a Burgundy-like texture and weight.

WANINGA (CLARE VALLEY)

1998 Shiraz	D	90
1998 Shiraz Reserve	D	89+

The dark purple-colored 1998 Shiraz exhibits creamy vanilla in its user-friendly, black fruit–scented nose. Intense, supple-textured, full-bodied, and rich, with excellent purity and a nicely layered, mouth-filling style, it can be drunk over the next 7 years.

The closed, dense plum/purple-colored 1998 Shiraz Reserve offers scents of underbrush, earth, chocolate, jammy black fruits, and toasty new oak (100% new wood was utilized). Medium- to full-bodied, pure, and deep, with a chewy, layered texture, this tightly knit Shiraz requires additional bottle age. It will evolve for 12–15 years. Although loaded, it is muted at present, and my score may turn out to be conservative.

WARRENMANG (VICTORIA)

1998 Grand Pyrenées	D	91
1997 Grand Pyrenées	D	88+?
1998 Shiraz	D	94+

The dazzling, compelling 1998 Shiraz is easy to figure out. At 15.5% alcohol, this effort, made from superripe fruit, is one of the more backward Shirazes I tasted. It exhibits an opaque purple color as well as fabulous potential with its glorious display of licorice-infused blackberry and cassis fruit. Dense, with low acidity, high tannin, and a whoppingly thick, stacked and packed mid-palate, this enormous monster needs three years of cellaring; it should age well for 20–25 years.

The 1998 Grand Pyrenées is reminiscent of the classic Heitz Martha's Vineyard Cabernet Sauvignons produced from the late 1960s through the early 1980s. A dense ruby/purple color is accompanied by scents of eucalyptus/mint, ripe black currants, tobacco, and licorice. Full-bodied and pure, with only a hint of oak, it has moderate tannin and impressive balance as well as character. It should drink well for 12–15+ years. The 1997 Grand Pyrenées is a tannic, lean wine with notions of eucalyptus, plums, prunes, and black currants. Well made and clean, but backward and hard to evaluate, this medium- to full-bodied blend has a certain affinity to an austere Bordeaux. Anticipated maturity: now–2016.

WATTLE PARK (SOUTH AUSTRALIA)

1998 Cabernet Sauvignon	D	86

The 1998 Cabernet Sauvignon, a juicy fruit concoction, exhibits little complexity, but emerging from the dark ruby/purple color are oodles of jammy blackberry and cherry fruit with a nice touch of pepper. There is no new oak to be found in this explosively ripe, fruity, uncomplicated, pleasurable wine. Drink it over the next 2 years.

GEOFF WEAVER (LENSWOOD)

1997 Cabernet Sauvignon/Merlot	D	86

The 1997 blend of Cabernet Sauvignon (82%) and Merlot (18%) is good but uninspiring. A Bordeaux-styled blend, it exhibits a medium dark ruby color as well as leather, cassis, spicy oak, and dried herbs in the nose. This medium-bodied, austere, cleanly made wine lacks excitement and density. Drink it over the next decade.

WILD DUCK CREEK (HEATHCOTE, VICTORIA)

1998	Cabernet Pressings	E	90
1999	Cabernet Sauvignon Alan's	E	90
1998	Cabernet Sauvignon Reserve	E	93
1997	Shiraz Duck Muck	E	99
1999	Shiraz Springflat	E	92
1998	Shiraz Springflat	E	91+
NV	Sparkling Duck	D	?

These are all interesting, full-throttle wines made by one of Australia's special characters, David Anderson. Yet overpricing seems to be taking on a surreal Hollywood element. For example, the $85 nonvintage Sparkling Duck, a blend of four vintages of Shiraz with some Merlot thrown in that tips the scales at 15.2% alcohol, is an unusual, heavy-handed, dense ruby/purple-colored wine that has plenty of fizz but is bizarre and over the top. A limited production of 65 cases no doubt explains the pricing, but for my palate, this wine is undrinkable.

The dry red wines are all huge, and obviously the lighter style of the 1999 vintage was easily overcome, given what Anderson has done with his 1999 Shiraz Springflat and 1999 Cabernet Sauvignon Alan's. The 1999 Shiraz Springflat has dense, opaque purple color, a real intense, minty, crème de cassis nose, with some spicy new oak. The wine is certainly not shy, at 15.3% alcohol, but the power is well harnessed, and the wine is primarily a big, full-bodied, thick, juicy fruit bomb with plenty of texture, purity, and length. It should drink well for 7–8 years, perhaps longer. With production at 1,200 cases, there is modest availability. A distinctive Shiraz, the black/purple 1998 Springflat's explosive aromatic bouquet is reminiscent of Old Bay spice. The spicy note is accompanied by aromas of blackberries, cassis, licorice, and toasty oak. Rich and backward, with fabulous concentration, it will improve significantly with another 1–2 years of bottle age and should keep for a minimum of 12–15 years. Only 600 cases were produced. The outstanding Cabernet Sauvignon Alan's (100% Cabernet Sauvignon) is aged in French oak, of which 85% is new. Production is 400 cases. The 1999 offers an opaque purple color, and a gorgeously sweet nose of black fruits, licorice, and vanilla. In the mouth, it displays a dry vintage portlike character. It is unctuous, thick, juicy, full-bodied, rich, monolithic, and destined to last for a decade or more.

Two limited-release offerings from Wild Duck include 75 cases of 1998 Cabernet Sauvignon Reserve. Made from 20-year-old 100% Cabernet Sauvignon vines, it exhibits a saturated black purple color plus a gorgeous nose of spice box, licorice, cassis, and classy new French oak. It is deep, full-bodied, and sweet, with supple tannin, and a seamless, concentrated finish that reveals notes of eucalyptus as it cascades over the palate. I was surprised by the sweet tannin as well as overall elegance. Drink this by 2016. Another overpriced offering is the 1998 Cabernet Pressings. Only 150 magnums were produced, and the wine, while not possessing the finish of the Reserve, offers notes of jammy cassis, pepper, creosote, and vanilla. Sweet, rich, and chewy, but rustic, it should drink well for 10–15 years.

Only 70 cases of the terrific 1997 Shiraz Duck Muck (15% alcohol) are available. Made from 1.3 tons of fruit per acre from a relatively young (15 years) vineyard, there is no doubting the extraordinary character and personality Anderson has constructed. My tasting notes begin with the words "great stuff." Opaque black/purple, with a viscosity resembling vintage port, this thick, chewy wine exhibits a panorama of black fruits mixed with licorice, tar, roasted herbs, and sweet oak. The acidity and tannin appear to be missing because of the wine's wealth of fruit, glycerin, and extract. It is a surreal, otherworldly styled Shiraz that needs to be sipped rather than gulped given its power and intensity. Anticipated maturity: now–2025.

WILLOW BEND (BAROSSA VALLEY)

1997 Proprietary Red	D	90?

The intriguing 1997 Proprietary Red (40% Shiraz, 38% Merlot, 19% Cabernet Sauvignon, and 3% Cabernet Franc) reveals a dark ruby/purple color in addition to a big, plummy, fat style with gobs of creamy, oak-infused, black cherry and blackberry fruit. The wood is almost overdone, but there is such a wealth of ripe, chewy fruit that the wine comes across as balanced, if somewhat exotic and aggressive. Drink it over the next 5–6 years.

WIT'S END (McLAREN VALE)

1999 Cabernet Sauvignon	D	90
1998 Shiraz	D	92

The 1999 Cabernet Sauvignon (aged in both French and American oak) offers aromas of toasty sweet vanilla as well as a boatload of crème de cassis–scented and –flavored fruit, full body, a seamless, velvety texture, and a long aftertaste. The 14.5% alcohol is well integrated in this beautifully concentrated, user-friendly, forward 1999. Although hard to ignore, it will drink well for 10–12 years. A stunning 1998 Shiraz, the Wit's End boasts a deep ruby/purple color as well as a sweet nose of blackberry jam intermixed with cassis, blueberries, and flowers. With sweet tannin, subtle vanilla from well-integrated oak, and a full-bodied, layered finish, this seamless effort is best consumed during its first decade of life.

WOODSTOCK (McLAREN VALE)

1998 Grenache	C	89

A blend of 90% Grenache (from 80+-year-old, head-pruned vines) and 10% Shiraz, the dark ruby/purple 1998 Grenache offers scents of kirsch, black pepper, and sweet cassis. A luscious, full-bodied fruit bomb, with low acidity and copious glycerin, it requires consumption over the next 4–5 years. Utterly delicious!

YALUMBA (BAROSSA VALLEY)

1996	Cabernet/Shiraz The Reserve	E	95
1996	Cabernet/Shiraz The Signature	D	91
1995	Cabernet/Shiraz The Signature	D	90
1999	Grenache	B	89
1998	Grenache	B	90
1999	Grenache Nursery Vineyard	D	92
1996	Shiraz Old Vine The Octavius	E	95
1995	Shiraz Old Vine The Octavius	E	90
1998	Shiraz/Viognier	D	90

Yalumba, which traces its origins to 1849, has a strong portfolio of wines, including some sensational values. From their 1,500 acres of vineyards, they produce several levels of quality, starting with their budget-priced Oxford Landing offerings (not reviewed here), and concluding with such flagship efforts as their Signature and Octavius *cuvées*. The estate also produces high-quality whites, which are not reviewed here since they must be consumed within several months of the vintage. Readers looking for fabulous values should check out Yalumba's 1999 and 1998 Grenache *cuvées*. Both wines are made in reasonably large quantities (about 8,000 cases). Neither sees any new oak. They represent Australia's answer to a big, bold, flavorful southern Rhône. The medium- to full-bodied 1999 Grenache reveals pepper and kirsch in its sweet, jammy fruit. Already delicious, it promises to last another 3–4 years.

Even better is the outstanding 1998 Grenache. Like its sibling, it comes from unirrigated, head-pruned vines. A darker ruby-colored effort, it exhibits intense aromas of ground pepper intermixed with strawberry and cherry liqueur, roasted herbs, and spice. Full-bodied, yet silky-textured, and flamboyant, it is a gorgeously fleshy wine to drink over the next 4–5 years.

Readers looking for even more intensity should check out Yalumba's 1999 Grenache Nursery Vineyard. There are 600 cases of this extremely old bush-vine Grenache (some of which date back to 1887). A dense ruby color is accompanied by an explosive nose of black raspberries, intermixed with cherries, pepper, and spice. Full-bodied, unctuous, heady, and a total turn-on to drink, I would love to insert this wine as a ringer in a tasting of sumptuous 1998 Châteauneuf-du-Papes. Drink it over the next 7–10 years.

Yalumba makes 2,000 cases of the 1998 Shiraz/Viognier (15% Viognier, à la Côte Rôtie). The wine sees some American oak, but is characterized by its full-bodied, exotic, jammy, black raspberry and currant fruit. Exotic, complex, fat, low in acidity, and heady, this plush turn-on can be consumed over the next 4–5 years.

One of Yalumba's top *cuvées* is their Cabernet/Shiraz blend called The Signature. Current releases include the 1996 and 1995. Creamy American oak aromas cascade from the dense purple-colored, superb 1996. However, in the mouth, the oak is completely absorbed by the wine's meaty, smoky, blackberry and cassis flavors. As it sits in the glass, notes of melted asphalt, dried Provençal herbs, and additional jammy red and black fruits emerge. Full-bodied and lush, it should drink well for at least 10–12 years. The more austere 1995 The Signature is from a slightly cooler vintage. By the way, for librarians among the readers, the 1990, 1991, and 1992 The Signatures were performing brilliantly, with the 1992 my favorite.

Another premium wine in Yalumba's portfolio is the 600-case *cuvée* of old-vine Shiraz called The Octavius. The current releases are 1995 and 1996. The spectacular 1996 is a basket-pressed Shiraz possessing huge power as well as massive, oozing, cedar- and glycerin-imbued blackberry and cassis aromas and flavors. This superb effort is one of the great old-vine Shiraz *cuvées* available in the marketplace. It should drink well for up to two decades. The similarly styled 1995 Shiraz Old Vine The Octavius, from the same parcel of 70-year-old vines, is aged in American oak. Sweet and oaky, with blackberry/cherry liqueur, high, heady alcohol levels, plenty of glycerin, and a full-bodied, long, spicy finish, it is more evolved than the blockbuster 1996. This is another wine where older vintages have held up gorgeously, including the spectacular 1990 and prodigious 1992. Interestingly, according to the winery, the 1990 and 1992 had 15% Cabernet Sauvignon in the blend. Since 1994, Octavius has been 100% Shiraz.

The other luxury-priced wine from Yalumba is the 300-case *cuvée* of 50% Cabernet Sauvignon and 50% Shiraz called The Reserve. The current release is the 1996. Aged in French oak, it is a compelling, opaque purple-colored wine offering subtle notions of high-class French oak along with enormous quantities of plum liqueur, chocolate fudge, blackberry and cassis fruit, pepper, and smoke. It is enormously concentrated, yet amazingly well balanced and extremely full-bodied, with a seamless personality, and well-integrated acidity, wood, tannin, and alcohol. This classic looks capable of lasting for two decades.

YARRA YERING (YARRA VALLEY)

1998 Dry Red No. 1 (Bordeaux Blend)	E	90
1998 Dry Red No. 2 (Rhône Blend)	E	94
1998 Pinot Noir	E	87
1998 Portsorts	E	92+
1998 Shiraz Underhill	E	91

This historic winery has often left me underwhelmed, but that is not the case with these 1998 efforts, the finest group of Yarra Yering wines I have tasted. They reveal extraordinary authenticity and purity of fruit, giving them each a singular character as well as an unmanipulated, natural style. Packaged in an unconventional light green, Bordeaux-styled bottle, the 1998 Pinot Noir is muted aromatically, but in the mouth textbook flavors of currants, cherries, and cola are present. The texture is supple, the wine builds incrementally, as do all of these dry reds, and follows through with a long, concentrated, noble, elegant finish. It should drink well for 5–7 years. The beautiful texture is also apparent in the 1998 Shiraz Underhill. A dark ruby/purple color is accompanied by a sweet nose of black fruits, minerals, smoke, and spice. This beautifully intense, pure Shiraz displays brilliant flavor definition, medium to full body, and extraordinary intensity without any sense of heaviness or astringent tannin. It is an impressive, stylish, elegant wine to enjoy over the next 10–12 years.

I was blown away by the 1998 Dry Red No. 2. A Rhône blend dominated by Shiraz, with Viognier and Roussanne included, this individualistic, extraordinary effort boasts a dense plum/purple color, as well as a gorgeously complex nose of rose petals, blackberries, cassis, new saddle leather, and truffles. Full-bodied, with a sweet attack, and wonderful harmony among its elements, this exceptionally pure wine can be drunk now, or cellared for 15+ years. It somehow totally conceals its lofty degree of alcohol (14.9%). Sadly, only 50 cases made it to the U.S. The 1998 Dry Red No. 1 is a Bordeaux blend dominated by Cabernet Sauvignon (80–85%) with the rest Merlot, Cabernet Franc, Petit Verdot, and a touch of Malbec. Its finesse, character, complexity, and stature cause it to stand out in a tasting. An individualistic expression of a Cabernet-based wine, it offers notes of red and black currants, minerals, olives, leather, earth, and smoke. This beautifully pure, finely etched, stylish effort requires 2–3 more years of bottle age. It should last nearly two decades.

Made completely from Portuguese varietals used for vintage port (Tourriga Nacional, for example), the 1998 Portsorts is the finest vintage port look-alike I have tasted outside Portugal. It possesses striking complexity, offering notes of licorice, leather, coffee, prunes, blackberries, and cassis. Extremely full-bodied, with beautifully integrated alcohol, this large-scaled, youthful, unevolved wine is a compelling example of what Portuguese varietals can achieve in Australia. This 1998 will drink well for two or more decades.

NEW ZEALAND

An enormous amount of hype is associated with New Zealand's wines. The world's media appears to be enamored of this nation and its vinous products. Having tasted countless wines, it is clear that New Zealand has a number of dedicated producers who craft excellent Sauvignon Blancs and Chardonnays, and a small handful who have made reds capable of competing on the world stage. However, the majority of this nation's wines are overly processed and too expensive for the quality they deliver.

The Sauvignon Blancs elicit the most excitement. They can be surprisingly rich, crammed with juicy gooseberries. However, they can also be mildly herbaceous, or overwhelmingly green. What makes them stand out is that the well-integrated acidity tastes natural, and the best examples possess a stunning mid-palate and length. All you have to do is taste the likes of a Sauvignon Blanc from Cloudy Bay, Goldwater, Grove Mill, Kumeu River, Montana, Morton Estate, Selaks, and Stoneleigh to see that special wines can emerge from this varietal. However, once past these wineries, the Sauvignons are often vegetal and washed out. As for Chardonnay, New Zealanders have learned to handle the cool climate acidity by putting their wines through full malolactic fermentation, giving them less contact, and plenty of exposure to French oak. However, when yields are not kept low, the Chardonnays taste like a two-by-four, with enough oak to turn off a wine-loving lumberjack. The finest Chardonnays, showing balance between oak and fruit, have emerged from Babich's Irongate, Cloudy Bay, Corbins, Delegats, Kumeu River, Matua Valley, Morton Estates Hawke's Bay, Selaks, Te Mata, Vidal Reserve, and the Villa Maria (barrel-fermented).

New Zealand's attempts with Cabernet Sauvignon and Merlot continue to be annoyingly herbaceous and/or atrociously vegetal, with few exceptions. It is unbelievable that anyone can find anything to praise in these offerings. If you like wines that taste like liquefied asparagus, you will find some merit in them. Although recent vintages suggest that New Zealand's wineries are coming closer to purging some of this grotesque character, these wines still possess a nasty vegetal streak. That being said, however, wines produced by Te Mata (Cabernet and Merlot) have demonstrated that New Zealand has potential as a red wine producer if it lowers yields, goes for optimal ripeness, and does not overprocess.

Pinot Noir will most likely prove to be New Zealand's red savior (as Sauvignon Blanc is for its whites). Presently, its vines are too young to predict accurately the potential of the wines, yet it is clear that structurally New Zealand's Pinots are the closest thing to Burgundy any New World region has come. Recently, the high-production, poor-quality clones that made up the vast majority of New Zealand's Pinot vineyards have been replaced with excellent clones from Burgundy. As these vines age, it will be interesting to see if the resulting wines acquire the depth of fruit, complexity, and ageworthiness required to compete with Burgundies. For the other red wines, there are only two words to keep in mind—*caveat emptor*!

Of the vintages currently on the market, 2000 appears better for reds than whites. It was a warm year, optimal for ripening Cabernet and Pinot, yet so hot as to have burned off much of the natural acidity that whites require. In 2001, on the other hand, there was a long, cool season. It fashioned some magnificent Sauvignon Blancs, many of which deliver superb value.

10. ARGENTINA AND CHILE

ARGENTINA

Argentina has broken out of the value category of wines, as has Chile, and now produces wines that can be recommended across the spectrum from below $10 to luxury wines that fetch more than $80. While many wineries have remained faithful to their price points, preferring to fashion large quantities of inexpensive wines, some, like Bodegas Catena Zapata, are presently offering wines that can compete with the finest in the world. Led by Nicolas Catena and others, those wineries wanting to better the quality of their wines have abandoned the Mendoza's highly fertile valley floor for its less productive hillsides.

Delicious and thirst-quenching whites, primarily Chardonnays and Sauvignon Blancs, are produced in Argentina. In recent years, a few outstanding Chardonnays, from the likes of the Catena and Luca wineries, have displayed the depth of fruit, complexity, and concentration found in the world's best examples of this ubiquitous varietal. Malbec, a French varietal that has had limited success in the Old World, can produce magnificent reds in Argentina. Characterized by its spicy dark fruit character, Argentinian Malbecs can be complex, intense, and ageworthy. Cabernet Sauvignon also has the potential to be hugely successful in Argentina, and Merlot can, from time to time, fashion beautiful wines, as well.

Argentina is on the rise. Recent vintages, particularly 1998 and 1999, have been difficult, yet this country's improved viticultural and winemaking practices as well as the arrival on the scene of quality-conscious boutique wineries (such as Luca, Tikal, and Paul Hobbs's Cobos) foreshadow an extremely bright future.

RATING ARGENTINA'S BEST WINES

* * * * * (OUTSTANDING)

Catena Cabernet Sauvignon Agrelo Vineyard
Catena-Alta Cabernet Sauvignon Zapata Vineyard
Catena Chardonnay Agrelo Vineyard
Catena-Alta Chardonnay Adrianna Vineyard
Catena-Alta Malbec Lunlunta Vineyard

* * * * (EXCELLENT)

Alamos
Altos de Madrano Malbec
Luigi Bosca Malbec
Caballero de la Cepa Cabernet Sauvignon
Arnaldo B. Etchart Cafayete
Arnaldo B. Etchart Cabernet Sauvignon
Arnaldo B. Etchart Malbec
Nicolas Fazio Malbec
Fabre Montmayou Grand Vin
Navarro Correas Colección Privada Cabernet Sauvignon
Navarro Correas Malbec

Nieto y Sentiner Cadus Malbec
Norton Privada
San Telmo Malbec
Pascual Toso Cabernet Sauvignon
Bodega Weinert Cabernet Sauvignon

Bodega Weinert Carrascal
Bodega Weinert Cavas de Weinert
Bodega Weinert Malbec
Bodega Weinert Merlot

* * * (GOOD)

Bianchi Cabernet Sauvignon Particular
Bianchi Chenin Blanc
Bianchi Malbec
Humberto Canale Cabernet Sauvignon
  Reserva
Humberto Canale Merlot Reserva
Etchart Torrontes
Flichman Cabernet Sauvignon

Nicolas Fazio Cabernet Sauvignon
Château Mendoza Cabernet Sauvignon
Château Mendoza Merlot
Mendoza Peaks Cabernet Sauvignon
San Telmo Cuesta del Madero (Cabernet
  Sauvignon/Malbec)
Trapiche Cabernet Sauvignon Oak Aged
León Unzue Malbec

* * (AVERAGE)

Andean Cabernet Sauvignon
Clos du Moulin Cabernet Sauvignon

Goyenechea (Aberdeen Angus) Cabernet
  Sauvignon
Comte de Valmont Cabernet Sauvignon

CHILE

Like its Andean neighbor, Chile has made enormous progress in recent years. At present, this South American country produces wines that can satisfy any consumer's desires, from cheap quaffing wines to world-class ageworthy reds.

Although some producers (particularly Casa Lapostolle) have fashioned outstanding Chardonnays in the Casa Blanca valley, the country's strengths are centered around its reds, particularly Cabernet Sauvignon and Merlot. Viña Cousiño Macul, Viña Concha y Toro, Casa Lapostolle, and the newly arrived Yacachuya are among the wineries redefining Chile's future.

Having survived the disastrous "El Niño" 1998 vintage, Chile enjoyed an excellent year in 1999 and a good one in 2000.

RATING CHILE'S BEST WINES

* * * * * (OUTSTANDING)

Almaviva (a Cabernet-based wine made by
  the partnership of Mouton-Rothschild
  and Concha y Toro)
Casa Lapostolle Cuvée Alexandre

Casa Lapostolle Merlot Clos Apalta
Concho y Toro Cabernet Sauvignon Don
  Melchor Private Reserve
Yacachuya

* * * * *(EXCELLENT)*

Casa Lapostolle Cabernet Sauvignon Cuvée
  Alexandre
Casa Lapostolle Chardonnay Cuvée
  Alexandre
Casa Lapostolle Sauvignon Blanc
Concho y Toro Cabernet Sauvignon
  Marques de Casa Concho

Cousiño Macul Cabernet/Merlot Finis
  Terrae
Cousiño Macul Cabernet Sauvignon
  Antiguas Reserva
Santa Rita Cabernet Sauvignon Casa
  Real
Los Vascos Cabernet Sauvignon Reserva

* * * *(GOOD)*

Concho y Toro Cabernet Sauvignon
  Castillero del Diablo
Concho y Toro Chardonnay Castillero del
  Diablo
Cousiño Macul Cabernet Sauvignon
Errazuriz Panquehue Cabernet Sauvignon
  Don Maximiano

Santa Monica Cabernet Sauvignon
Seña
Los Vascos Cabernet Sauvignon
Los Vascos Sauvignon Blanc
Santa Rita Cabernet Sauvignon Medalla
  Real

* *(AVERAGE)*

Caliterra Cabernet Sauvignon
Caliterra Chardonnay
Canepa Sauvignon Blanc
Carta Vieja (all *cuvées*)
Cousiño Macul Chardonnay
Cousiño Macul Sauvignon Blanc
Sage Estate (all *cuvées*)
Saint Morillon Cabernet Sauvignon
Santa Carolina Cabernet Sauvignon
Santa Carolina Chardonnay
Santa Carolina Merlot

Santa Rita Cabernet Sauvignon 120
  Estate
Santa Rita Sauvignon Blanc 120 Estate
Tolva Cabernet Sauvignon
Tolva Sauvignon Blanc
Miguel Torres (all *cuvées*)
Traverso Cabernet Sauvignon
Traverso Merlot
Undurraga Cabernet Sauvignon
Undurraga Sauvignon Blanc
Valdivieso Sparkling NV Brut

11. SOUTH AFRICA

The wines of South Africa deserve more attention from consumers, as they presently offer both value and quality. Shortly after the end of apartheid, numerous South African wines appeared on retailers' shelves throughout the United States, but few merited attention (a lovely 1990 Meerlust Merlot was the exception to the rule). Since then, quality has ameliorated due to both viticultural and vinification improvements.

While the country's Chardonnays tend to be overly wooded or green in character, South African Sauvignon Blancs, Sémillons, and Chenin Blancs can be delightfully balanced, pure, and flavorful. For reds, Cabernet Sauvignon is king in South Africa, with estates such as Boekenhoutskloof, Neil Ellis, and Rustenberg regularly producing outstanding wines with the intensity of the New World yet the charm and complexity of the Old World. Even though Meerlust surprised me with its 1990 Merlot, this varietal appears to be as fickle in South Africa as it is elsewhere. Pinot Noir has yet to be successful in South Africa, and Pinotage remains a wine that I have immense trouble appreciating. It is simply too green, rustic, and leathery. Recent releases of Shiraz/Syrah, particularly those from Boekenhoutskloof, indicate that South Africa has outstanding potential with this grape from the northern Rhône. Other Rhône varietals, such as Grenache, Mourvèdre, and Carignan, have shown some potential, particularly with Fairview's line of Goats do Roam wines.

INDEX

Also by Robert M. Parker, Jr.

BORDEAUX: THE DEFINITIVE GUIDE
FOR THE WINES PRODUCED
SINCE 1961

THE WINES OF THE RHÔNE VALLEY
AND PROVENCE

PARKER'S WINE BUYER'S GUIDE

PARKER'S WINE BUYER'S GUIDE
SECOND EDITION

BURGUNDY: A COMPREHENSIVE GUIDE
TO THE PRODUCERS, APPELLATIONS,
AND WINES

BORDEAUX: A COMPREHENSIVE GUIDE
TO THE WINES PRODUCED
FROM 1961 TO 1990

PARKER'S WINE BUYER'S GUIDE
THIRD EDITION

PARKER'S WINE BUYER'S GUIDE
FOURTH EDITION

THE WINES OF THE RHÔNE VALLEY,
REVISED AND EXPANDED EDITION

BORDEAUX: A COMPREHENSIVE GUIDE
TO THE WINES PRODUCED
FROM 1961 TO 1997

PARKER'S WINE BUYER'S GUIDE
FIFTH EDITION